P9-ARH-226

## GRAPHS OF FUNCTIONS

Linear functions: $f(x) = mx + b$

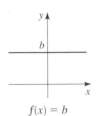

$f(x) = b$

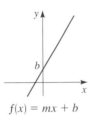

$f(x) = mx + b$

Power functions: $f(x) = x^n$

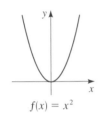

$f(x) = x^2$

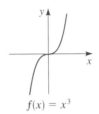

$f(x) = x^3$

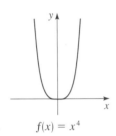

$f(x) = x^4$

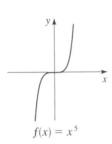

$f(x) = x^5$

Root functions: $f(x) = \sqrt[n]{x}$

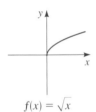

$f(x) = \sqrt{x}$

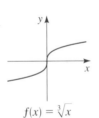

$f(x) = \sqrt[3]{x}$

Reciprocal functions: $f(x) = 1/x^n$

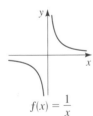

$f(x) = \dfrac{1}{x}$

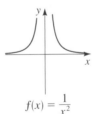

$f(x) = \dfrac{1}{x^2}$

Exponential functions: $f(x) = a^x$

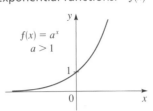
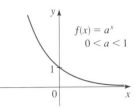

$f(x) = a^x$ $a > 1$

$f(x) = a^x$ $0 < a < 1$

Logarithmic functions: $f(x) = \log_a x$

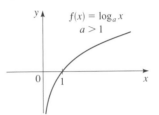
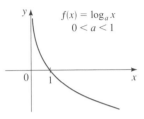

$f(x) = \log_a x$ $a > 1$

$f(x) = \log_a x$ $0 < a < 1$

Absolute value function    Greatest integer function

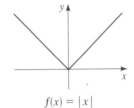
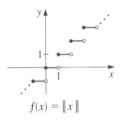

$f(x) = |x|$

$f(x) = \llbracket x \rrbracket$

## SHIFTING OF FUNCTIONS

Vertical shifting

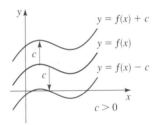

$y = f(x) + c$

$y = f(x)$

$y = f(x) - c$

$c > 0$

Horizontal shifting

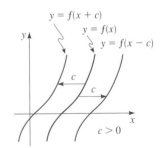

$y = f(x + c)$

$y = f(x)$

$y = f(x - c)$

$c > 0$

# Enhanced WebAssign at a glance . . .

## Content Features

- *Randomized, algorithmic problems based on over 1,500 text exercises* for unlimited practice
- *Interactive examples* from the text
- *Step-by-step tutorials* for specific examples and/or problems
- *Videos* that provide additional instruction on text examples and/or problems
- *Carefully constructed feedback* to help guide students to deeper understanding
- *Relevant eBook pages* from the text
- *Live online tutoring* via whiteboarding, email, and instant messaging

## Program and Technical Features

- Simple, friendly user interface
- Course creation in seven easy steps
- Assignment creation in five minutes
- Instructor gradebook with weighted categories and scores
- Automatic grading of online homework assignments
- Intuitive *Question Editor* that allows questions to be edited or added without learning a programming language
- Proper display of mathematical expressions
- Timed, secure, password- and IP-restricted exercises
- Student forums, bulletin boards, messaging
- Built-in calendar and communication tools
- Compatible with all recent operating systems (Microsoft® Windows®, Apple® Macintosh, Linux®, Sun™ Solaris™)
- Works with most web browsers (e.g., Mozilla Firefox®, Internet Explorer®, Safari™)
- No proprietary plug-ins required

Enhanced WebAssign content is available with these
college algebra and precalculus texts from Brooks/Cole:

Get your free 45-day trial
**academic.cengage.com/math/ewa**

FIFTH EDITION

# College Algebra

# ABOUT THE AUTHORS

JAMES **STEWART** received his MS from Stanford University and his PhD from the University of Toronto. He did research at the University of London and was influenced by the famous mathematician, George Polya, at Stanford University. Stewart is currently a Professor of Mathematics at McMaster University, and his research field is harmonic analysis.

James Stewart is the author of a best-selling calculus textbook series published by Brooks/Cole, Cengage Learning, including *Calculus, Calculus: Early Transcendentals,* and *Calculus: Concepts and Contexts,* a series of precalculus texts, as well as a series of high-school mathematics textbooks.

LOTHAR **REDLIN** grew up on Vancouver Island, received a Bachelor of Science degree from the University of Victoria, and a PhD from McMaster University in 1978. He subsequently did research and taught at the University of Washington, the University of Waterloo, and California State University, Long Beach.

He is currently Professor of Mathematics at The Pennsylvania State University, Abington Campus. His research field is topology.

SALEEM **WATSON** received his Bachelor of Science degree from Andrews University in Michigan. He did graduate studies at Dalhousie University and McMaster University, where he received his PhD in 1978.

He subsequently did research at the Mathematics Institute of the University of Warsaw in Poland. He also taught at The Pennsylvania State University. He is currently Professor of Mathematics at California State University, Long Beach. His research field is functional analysis.

The authors have also published *Precalculus: Mathematics for Calculus, Algebra and Trigonometry,* and *Trigonometry.*

## ABOUT THE COVER

The building portrayed on the cover is 30 St. Mary Axe in London, England. More commonly known as "the Gherkin," it was designed by the renowned architect Sir Norman Foster and completed in 2004. Although the building gives an overall curved appearance, its exterior actually contains only one curved piece of glass—the lens-shaped cap at the very top. In fact, the striking shape of this building hides a complex mathematical structure. Mathematical curves have been used in architecture throughout history, for structural reasons as well as for their intrinsic beauty. In *Focus on Modeling: Conics in Architecture* (pages 595–598) we see how parabolas, ellipses, and hyperbolas are used in architecture.

FIFTH EDITION

# College Algebra

**James Stewart**
McMaster University

**Lothar Redlin**
The Pennsylvania State University, Abington Campus

**Saleem Watson**
California State University, Long Beach

**BROOKS/COLE**
CENGAGE Learning™

Australia • Brazil • Japan • Korea • Mexico • Singapore • Spain • United Kingdom • United States

**BROOKS/COLE**
CENGAGE Learning

*College Algebra,* **Fifth Edition**
**James Stewart, Lothar Redlin, Saleem Watson**

Acquisitions Editor: Gary Whalen
Senior Development Editor: Jay Campbell
Assistant Editor: Natasha Coats
Editorial Assistant: Rebecca Dashiell
Technology Project Manager: Lynh Pham
Marketing Manager: Joe Rogove
Marketing Assistant: Ashley Pickering
Marketing Communications Manager:
Darlene Amidon-Brent
Project Manager, Editorial Production:
Jennifer Risden
Creative Director: Rob Hugel
Art Director: Vernon Boes
Print Buyer: Karen Hunt
Permissions Editor: Roberta Broyer
Production Service: Martha Emry
Text Designer: Lisa Henry
Art Editor: Martha Emry
Photo Researcher: Terri Wright
Copy Editor: Barbara Willette
Illustrator: Precision Graphics; Jade Myers,
Matrix
Cover Designer: Lisa Henry
Cover Image: © Paul Hardy/Corbis
Compositor: Newgen–India

© 2009, 2004 Brooks/Cole, Cengage Learning

ALL RIGHTS RESERVED. No part of this work covered by the copyright herein may be reproduced, transmitted, stored, or used in any form or by any means graphic, electronic, or mechanical, including but not limited to photocopying, recording, scanning, digitizing, taping, Web distribution, information networks, or information storage and retrieval systems, except as permitted under Section 107 or 108 of the 1976 United States Copyright Act, without the prior written permission of the publisher.

For product information and technology assistance, contact us at
**Cengage Learning Customer & Sales Support,**
**1-800-354-9706**

For permission to use material from this text or product, submit all requests online at
**cengage.com/permissions.**
Further permissions questions can be e-mailed to
**permissionrequest@cengage.com.**

Library of Congress Control Number: 2007940271

ISBN-13: 978-0-495-56521-5
ISBN-10: 0-495-56521-0

**Brooks/Cole**
10 Davis Drive
Belmont, CA 94002-3098
USA

Cengage Learning is a leading provider of customized learning solutions with office locations around the globe, including Singapore, the United Kingdom, Australia, Mexico, Brazil, and Japan. Locate your local office at **international.cengage.com/region.**

Cengage Learning products are represented in Canada by Nelson Education, Ltd.

For your course and learning solutions, visit **academic.cengage.com.**

Purchase any of our products at your local college store or at our preferred online store **www.ichapters.com.**

Printed in Canada
1 2 3 4 5 6 7 12 11 10 09 08

# CONTENTS

## 10 **Counting and Probability**                    **657**

# PREFACE

**The art of teaching is the art of assisting discovery.**
MARK VAN DOREN

For many students a College Algebra course represents the first opportunity to discover the beauty and practical power of mathematics. Thus instructors are faced with the challenge of teaching the concepts and skills of algebra while at the same time imparting a sense of its utility in the real world. In this edition, as in the previous four editions, our aim is to provide instructors and students with tools they can use to meet this challenge.

The emphasis is on understanding concepts. Certainly all instructors are committed to encouraging conceptual understanding. For many this is implemented through the *rule of four:* "Topics should be presented geometrically, numerically, algebraically, and verbally." *Technology* facilitates the learning of geometrical and numerical concepts, *extended projects* and *group learning* help students explore their understanding of algebraic concepts, *writing exercises* emphasize the verbal or descriptive point of view, and *modeling* can clarify a concept by connecting it to real life. Underlying all these approaches is an emphasis on algebra as a *problem-solving* endeavor. In this book we have used all these methods of presenting college algebra as enhancements to a central core of fundamental skills. These methods are tools to be used by instructors and students in navigating their own course of action toward the goal of conceptual understanding.

In writing this fifth edition one of our main goals was to encourage students to be active learners. So, for instance, each example in the text is now linked to an exercise that will reinforce the student's understanding of the example. New concept exercises at the beginning of each exercise set encourage students to work with the basic concepts of the section and to use algebra vocabulary appropriately. We have also reorganized and rewritten some chapters (as described below) with the goal of further focusing the exposition on the main concepts. In all these changes and numerous others (small and large) we have retained the main features that have contributed to the success of this book. In particular, our premise continues to be that conceptual understanding, technical skill, and real-world applications all go hand in hand, each reinforcing the others.

## NEW for the Fifth Edition

- New *chapter openers* emphasize how algebra topics in the chapter are used in the real world.

- New study aids include *Learning Objectives* at the beginning of each section and expanded Review sections at the end of each chapter. The review includes a summary of the main *Properties and Formulas* of the chapter and a *Concept Summary* keyed to specific review exercises.

- A new *Practice What You've Learned* feature at the end of each example directs students to a related exercise, allowing them to immediately reinforce the concept in the example.

- Approximately 15% of the exercises are new. New *Concept* exercises at the beginning of each exercise set are designed to encourage students to work with the basic concepts of the section and to use mathematical vocabulary appropriately.

- New *Cumulative Review Tests* appear after Chapters 2, 5, 8, and 10 and help students gauge their progress and gain experience in taking tests that cover a broad range of concepts and skills.

- **Chapter P, Prerequisites**, has been revised to provide a more complete review of the prerequisite basic algebra needed for this course. The properties of real numbers and the real number line now appear in two separate sections (Sections P.2 and P.3).

- **Chapter 3, Functions**, has been rewritten to focus more sharply on the concept of function itself. It now includes a new section entitled "Getting Information from the Graph of a Function." (The material on quadratic functions now appears in the chapter on polynomial functions.)

- **Chapter 4, Polynomial and Rational Functions**, now begins with a section entitled "Quadratic Functions and Models." (This section previously appeared in the chapter on functions.)

- In **Chapter 6, Systems of Equations and Inequalities**, the order of the sections "Partial Fractions" and "Systems of Inequalities" has been switched; the material on systems of inequalities now immediately precedes the section on linear programming.

## Special Features

**Exercise Sets**   The most important way to foster conceptual understanding is through the problems that the instructor assigns. To that end we have provided a wide selection of exercises. Each exercise set is carefully graded, progressing from basic conceptual exercises and skill-development problems to more challenging problems requiring synthesis of previously learned material with new concepts. To help students use the exercise sets effectively, each example in the text is keyed to a specific exercise via the *Practice What You've Learned* feature; this encourages students to "learn by doing" as they read through the text.

**Real-World Applications**   We have included substantial applications of algebra that we believe will capture the interest of students. These are integrated throughout the text in the chapter openers, examples, exercises, *Discovery Projects*, and *Focus on Modeling* sections. In the exercise sets, applied problems are grouped together under the label *Applications*. (See, for example, pages 31, 120, 178, and 234.)

**Discovery, Writing, and Group Learning**   Each exercise set ends with a block of exercises labeled *Discovery • Discussion • Writing*. These exercises are designed to encourage the students to experiment, preferably in groups, with the concepts developed in the section, and then to write out what they have learned, rather than simply look for "the answer." (See, for example, pages 26, 121, 166, and 224.)

**Graphing Calculators and Computers**   Calculator and computer technology extends in a powerful way our ability to calculate and to visualize mathematics. We have integrated the use of the graphing calculator throughout the text—to graph and analyze functions, families of functions, and sequences; to calculate and graph regression curves; to perform matrix algebra; to graph linear inequalities; and other such powerful uses. We also exploit the programming capabilities of the graphing calculator to provide simple programs that model real-life situations (see, for instance, pages 264, 549, and 701). The graphing calculator sections, subsections, examples, and exercises, all marked with the special symbol ▦, are optional and may be omitted without loss of continuity.

**Focus on Modeling**   In addition to many applied problems where students are given a model to analyze, we have included several sections and subsections in which students are required to *construct* models of real-life situations. In addition, we have concluded each chapter with a section entitled *Focus on Modeling*, where we present ways in which algebra is used to model real-life situations. For example, the *Focus on Modeling* after Chapter 2 introduces the basic idea of modeling a real-life situation by fitting lines to data (linear regression). Other *Focus* sections discuss modeling with polynomial, power, and exponential functions, as well as applications of algebra to architecture, computer graphics, optimization, and others. Chapter P concludes with a section entitled *Focus on Problem Solving*.

**Projects**   One way to engage students and make them active learners is to have them work (perhaps in groups) on extended projects that give a feeling of substantial accomplishment when completed. Each chapter contains one or more *Discovery Projects* (listed in the Contents); these provide a challenging but accessible set of activities that enable students to explore in greater depth an interesting aspect of the topic they have just studied.

**Mathematical Vignettes**   Throughout the book we provide short biographies of interesting mathematicians as well as applications of mathematics to the real world. The biographies often include a key insight that the mathematician discovered and which is relevant to algebra. (See, for instance, the vignettes on Viète, page 89; Salt Lake City, page 139; and radiocarbon dating, page 402.) The vignettes serve to enliven the material and show that mathematics is an important, vital activity, and that even at this elementary level it is fundamental to everyday life. A series of vignettes, entitled *Mathematics in the Modern World*, emphasizes the central role of mathematics in current advances in technology and the sciences. (See pages 106, 462, and 554, for example.)

**Check Your Answer**   The *Check Your Answer* feature is used, wherever possible, to emphasize the importance of looking back to check whether an answer is reasonable. (See, for instance, pages 81 and 105.)

**Review Sections and Chapter Tests**   Each chapter ends with an extensive review section, including a *Chapter Test* designed to help students gauge their progress. Brief answers to odd-numbered exercises in each section (including the review exercises), and to all questions in the Chapter Tests, are given in the back of the book. The review material in each chapter begins with a summary of the main *Properties and Formulas* and a *Concept Summary*. These two features provide a concise synopsis of the material in the chapter. *Cumulative Review Tests* follow Chapters 2, 5, 8, and 10.

## Ancillaries

*College Algebra*, Fifth Edition, is supported by a complete set of ancillaries developed under our direction. Each piece has been designed to enhance student understanding and to facilitate creative instruction. New to this edition is **Enhanced WebAssign (EWA)**, our Web-based homework system that allows instructors to assign, collect, grade and record homework assignments online, minimizing workload and streamlining the grading process. EWA also gives students the ability to stay organized with assignments and have up-to-date grade information. For your convenience, the exercises available in EWA are indicated in the instructor's edition by a blue square.

## Acknowledgments

We thank the following reviewers for their thoughtful and constructive comments.

**Reviewers of the First Edition**   Barry W. Brunson, *Western Kentucky University*; Gay Ellis, *Southwest Missouri State University*; Martha Ann Larkin, *Southern Utah University*; Franklin A. Michello, *Middle Tennessee State University*; Kathryn Wetzel, *Amarillo College*.

**Reviewers of the Second Edition**   David Watson, *Rutgers University*; Floyd Downs, *Arizona State University at Tempe*; Muserref Wiggins, *University of Akron*; Marjorie

Kreienbrink, *University of Wisconsin*; Richard Dodge, *Jackson Community College*; Christine Panoff, *University of Michigan at Flint*; Arnold Volbach, *University of Houston, University Park*; Keith Oberlander, *Pasadena City College*; Tom Walsh, *City College of San Francisco*; and George Wang, *Whittier College*.

**Reviewers of the Third Edition**   Christine Oxley, *Indiana University*; Linda B. Hutchison, *Belmont University*; David Rollins, *University of Central Florida*; and Max Warshauer, *Southwest Texas State University*.

**Reviewers of the Fourth Edition**   Mohamed Elhamdadi, *University of South Florida*; Carl L. Hensley, *Indian River Community College*; Scott Lewis, *Utah Valley State College*; Beth-Allyn Osikiewicz, *Kent State University—Tuscarawas Campus*; Stanley Stascinsky, *Tarrant County College*; Fereja Tahir, *Illinois Central College*; and Mary Ann Teel, *University of North Texas*.

**Reviewers of the Fifth Edition**   Faiz Al-Rubaee, *University of North Florida*; Christian Barrientos, *Clayton State University;* Candace Blazek, *Anoka-Ramsey Community College*; Catherine May Bonan-Hamada, *Mesa State College*; José D. Flores, *University of South Dakota*; Christy Leigh Jackson, *University of Arkansas, Little Rock*; George Johnson, *St. Phillips College*; Gene Majors, *Fullerton College*; Theresa McChesney, *Johnson County Community College*; O. Michael Melko, *Northern State University*; Terry Nyman, *University of Wisconsin—Fox Valley*; Randy Scott, *Santiago Canyon College*; George Rust, *West Virginia State University*; Alicia Serfaty de Markus, *Miami Dade College—Kendell Campus*; Vassil Yorgov, *Fayetteville State University*; Naveed Zaman, *West Virginia State University*; Xiaohong Zhang, *West Virginia State University*.

We have benefited greatly from the suggestions and comments of our colleagues who have used our books in previous editions. We extend special thanks in this regard to Larry Brownson, Linda Byun, Bruce Chaderjian, David Gau, Daniel Hernandez, YongHee Kim-Park, Daniel Martinez, David McKay, Robert Mena, Kent Merryfield, Viet Ngo, Marilyn Oba, Alan Safer, Robert Valentini, and Derming Wang, from California State University, Long Beach; to Karen Gold, Betsy Huttenlock, Cecilia McVoy, Mike McVoy, Samir Ouzomgi, and Ralph Rush, of The Pennsylvania State University, Abington College; and to Fred Safier, of the City College of San Francisco. We have learned much from our students; special thanks go to Devaki Shah and Ellen Newman for their helpful suggestions.

Ann Ostberg read the entire manuscript and did a masterful job of checking the correctness of the examples and answers to exercises. We extend our heartfelt thanks for her timely and accurate work. We also thank Phyllis Panman-Watson for solving the exercises and checking the answer manuscript. We thank Andy Bulman-Fleming and Doug Shaw for their inspired work in producing the solutions manuals and the supplemental study guide.

We especially thank Martha Emry, our production service, for her tireless attention to quality and detail. Her energy, devotion, experience, and intelligence were essential components in the creation of this book. We thank Terri Wright for her diligent and beautiful photo research. At Matrix, we thank Jade Myers and his staff for their elegant graphics. We also thank Precision Graphics for bringing many of our illustrations to life. At Brooks/Cole, our thanks go to Senior Developmental Editor Jay Campbell, Assistant Editor Natasha Coats, Editorial Assistant Rebecca Dashiell, Editorial Production Project Manager Jennifer Risden, Executive Marketing Manager Joseph Rogove, and Marketing Coordinator Ashley Pickering. They have all done an outstanding job.

Finally, we thank our editor Gary Whalen for carefully and thoughtfully guiding this book through the writing and production process. His support and editorial insight played a crucial role in completing this edition.

# Ancillaries For College Algebra, Fifth Edition

## INSTRUCTOR RESOURCES

### PRINTED

**Instructor's Solutions Manual**

**ISBN-10: 0-495-56525-3; ISBN-13: 978-0-495-56525-3**

Contains solutions to all even-numbered text exercises.

**Test Bank**

**ISBN-10: 0-495-56526-1; ISBN-13: 978-0-495-56526-0**

The Test Bank includes six tests per chapter as well as three final exams. The tests are made up of a combination of multiple-choice, free-response, true/false, and fill-in-the-blank questions.

**Instructor's Guide**

**ISBN-10: 0-495-56527-X; ISBN-13: 978-0-495-56527-7**

This Instructor's Guide is the ideal course companion. Each section of the main text is discussed from several viewpoints, including suggested time to allot, points to stress, text discussion topics, core materials for lecture, workshop/discussion suggestions, group-work exercises in a form suitable for handout, and suggested homework problems. An electronic version is available on the PowerLecture CD-ROM.

### TESTING SOFTWARE

**ExamView® for Algorithmic Equations (Windows®/Macintosh®)**

Create, deliver, and customize tests and study guides (both print and online) in minutes with this easy-to-use assessment and tutorial software on CD. Includes complete questions from the *College Algebra* Test Bank. Included on the PowerLecture™ CD.

**PowerLecture™ CD**

**ISBN-10: 0-495-56529-6; ISBN-13: 978-0-495-56529-1**

Contains PowerPoint® lecture outlines, a database of all the art in the text, ExamView, and electronic copies of the Instructor's Guide and Instructor's Solution Manual.

### VIDEO

**Text-Specific DVDs**

**ISBN-10: 0-495-56522-9; ISBN-13: 978-0-495-56522-2**

This set of DVDs is available free upon adoption of the text. Each video offers one chapter of the text and is broken down into 10- to 20-minute problem-solving lessons that cover each section of the chapter. These videos can be used as additional explanations for each chapter of the text.

## STUDENT RESOURCES

### PRINTED

**Student Solutions Manual**

**ISBN-10: 0-495-56524-5; ISBN-13: 978-0-495-56524-6**

Contains solutions to all odd-numbered text exercises.

**Study Guide**

**ISBN-10: 0-495-56523-7; ISBN-13: 978-0-495-56523-9**

Reinforces student understanding with detailed explanations, worked-out examples, and practice problems. Lists key ideas to master and builds problem-solving skills. There is a section in the Study Guide corresponding to each section in the text.

# TO THE STUDENT

This textbook was written for you to use as a guide to mastering College Algebra. Here are some suggestions to help you get the most out of your course.

First of all, you should read the appropriate section of text *before* you attempt your homework problems. Reading a mathematics text is quite different from reading a novel, a newspaper, or even another textbook. You may find that you have to reread a passage several times before you understand it. Pay special attention to the examples, and work them out yourself with pencil and paper as you read. Then do the linked exercise(s) referred to in the *Practice What You've Learned* at the end of each example. With this kind of preparation you will be able to do your homework much more quickly and with more understanding.

Don't make the mistake of trying to memorize every single rule or fact you may come across. Mathematics doesn't consist simply of memorization. Mathematics is a *problem-solving art*, not just a collection of facts. To master the subject you must solve problems—lots of problems. Do as many of the exercises as you can. Be sure to write your solutions in a logical, step-by-step fashion. Don't give up on a problem if you can't solve it right away. Try to understand the problem more clearly—reread it thoughtfully and relate it to what you have learned from your teacher and from the examples in the text. Struggle with it until you solve it. Once you have done this a few times you will begin to understand what mathematics is really all about.

Answers to the odd-numbered exercises, as well as all the answers to each chapter test, appear at the back of the book. If your answer differs from the one given, don't immediately assume that you are wrong. There may be a calculation that connects the two answers and makes both correct. For example, if you get $1/(\sqrt{2} - 1)$ but the answer given is $1 + \sqrt{2}$, your answer *is* correct, because you can multiply both numerator and denominator of your answer by $\sqrt{2} + 1$ to change it to the given answer.

The symbol ⊘ is used to warn against committing an error. We have placed this symbol in the margin to point out situations where we have found that many of our students make the same mistake.

# CALCULATORS AND CALCULATIONS

Calculators are essential in most mathematics and science subjects. They free us from performing routine tasks, so we can focus more clearly on the concepts we are studying. Calculators are powerful tools but their results need to be interpreted with care. In what follows, we describe the features that a calculator suitable for a College Algebra course should have, and we give guidelines for interpreting the results of its calculations.

## Scientific and Graphing Calculators

For this course you will need a *scientific* calculator—one that has, as a minimum, the usual arithmetic operations $(+, -, \times, \div)$ as well as exponential and logarithmic functions $(e^x, 10^x, \ln x, \log x)$. In addition, a memory and at least some degree of programmability will be useful.

Your instructor may recommend or require that you purchase a *graphing* calculator. This book has optional subsections and exercises that require the use of a graphing calculator or a computer with graphing software. These special subsections and exercises are indicated by the symbol ▦. Besides graphing functions, graphing calculators can also be used to find functions that model real-life data, solve equations, perform matrix calculations (which are studied in Chapter 7), and help you perform other mathematical operations. All these uses are discussed in this book.

It is important to realize that, because of limited resolution, a graphing calculator gives only an *approximation* to the graph of a function. It plots only a finite number of points and then connects them to form a *representation* of the graph. In Section 2.3, we give guidelines for using a graphing calculator and interpreting the graphs that it produces.

## Calculations and Significant Figures

Most of the applied examples and exercises in this book involve approximate values. For example, one exercise states that the moon has a radius of 1074 miles. This does not mean that the moon's radius is exactly 1074 miles but simply that this is the radius rounded to the nearest mile.

One simple method for specifying the accuracy of a number is to state how many **significant digits** it has. The significant digits in a number are the ones from the first nonzero digit to the last nonzero digit (reading from left to right). Thus, 1074 has four significant digits, 1070 has three, 1100 has two, and 1000 has one significant digit. This rule may sometimes lead to ambiguities. For example, if a distance is 200 km to the nearest kilometer, then the number 200 really has three significant digits, not just one. This ambiguity is avoided if we use scientific notation—that is, if we express the number as a multiple of a power of 10:

$$2.00 \times 10^2$$

When working with approximate values, students often make the mistake of giving a final answer with *more* significant digits than the original data. This is incorrect because you cannot "create" precision by using a calculator. The final result can be no more accurate than the measurements given in the problem. For example, suppose we are told that the two shorter sides of a right triangle are measured to be 1.25 and 2.33 inches long. By the Pythagorean Theorem, we find, using a calculator, that the hypotenuse has length

$$\sqrt{1.25^2 + 2.33^2} \approx 2.644125564 \text{ in.}$$

But since the given lengths were expressed to three significant digits, the answer cannot be any more accurate. We can therefore say only that the hypotenuse is 2.64 in. long, rounding to the nearest hundredth.

In general, the final answer should be expressed with the same accuracy as the *least-accurate* measurement given in the statement of the problem. The following rules make this principle more precise.

### RULES FOR WORKING WITH APPROXIMATE DATA

1. When multiplying or dividing, round off the final result so that it has as many *significant digits* as the given value with the fewest number of significant digits.

2. When adding or subtracting, round off the final result so that it has its last significant digit in the *decimal place* in which the least-accurate given value has its last significant digit.

3. When taking powers or roots, round off the final result so that it has the same number of *significant digits* as the given value.

As an example, suppose that a rectangular table top is measured to be 122.64 in. by 37.3 in. We express its area and perimeter as follows:

Area = length × width = 122.64 × 37.3 ≈ 4570 in²        *Three significant digits*

Perimeter = 2(length + width) = 2(122.64 + 37.3) ≈ 319.9 in.    *Tenths digit*

 Note that in the formula for the perimeter, the value 2 is an exact value, not an approximate measurement. It therefore does not affect the accuracy of the final result. In general, if a problem involves only exact values, we may express the final answer with as many significant digits as we wish.

Note also that to make the final result as accurate as possible, *you should wait until the last step to round off your answer.* If necessary, use the memory feature of your calculator to retain the results of intermediate calculations.

| | | | | |
|---|---|---|---|---|
| **cm** | centimeter | | **mg** | milligram |
| **dB** | decibel | | **MHz** | megahertz |
| **F** | farad | | **mi** | mile |
| **ft** | foot | | **min** | minute |
| **g** | gram | | **mL** | milliliter |
| **gal** | gallon | | **mm** | millimeter |
| **h** | hour | | **N** | Newton |
| **H** | henry | | **qt** | quart |
| **Hz** | Hertz | | **oz** | ounce |
| **in.** | inch | | **s** | second |
| **J** | Joule | | **Ω** | ohm |
| **kcal** | kilocalorie | | **V** | volt |
| **kg** | kilogram | | **W** | watt |
| **km** | kilometer | | **yd** | yard |
| **kPa** | kilopascal | | **yr** | year |
| **L** | liter | | **°C** | degree Celsius |
| **lb** | pound | | **°F** | degree Fahrenheit |
| **lm** | lumen | | **K** | Kelvin |
| **M** | mole of solute per liter of solution | | $\Rightarrow$ | implies |
| | | | $\Leftrightarrow$ | is equivalent to |
| **m** | meter | | | |

# MATHEMATICAL VIGNETTES

FIFTH EDITION

# College Algebra

# Prerequisites

© Daimler AG

**Smart car?** This exciting all-electric concept car, called *smart fortwo EV*, was designed by Daimler Motors, which plans to introduce it in some markets in 2008. Will driving this car help to keep the air we breathe cleaner? What are the cost and environmental impact of producing the electricity where this car is plugged in for recharging? Will driving this car save money? (See Exercise 23, Section P.1.) All these questions involve numbers, and to answer them, we need to know the basic properties of numbers. Algebra is about these properties. The fundamental idea in algebra is to use letters to stand for numbers; this helps us to find patterns in numbers and to answer questions like the ones we asked here. In this chapter we review some of the basic concepts of algebra.

## P.1 | Modeling the Real World with Algebra

**LEARNING OBJECTIVES**
After completing this section, you will be able to:

- Use an algebra model
- Make an algebra model

In algebra we use letters to stand for numbers. This allows us to describe patterns that we see in the real world.

For example, if we let $N$ stand for the number of hours you work and $W$ stand for your hourly wage, then the formula

$$P = NW$$

gives your pay $P$. The formula $P = NW$ is a description or *model* for pay. We can also call this formula an *algebra model*. We summarize the situation as follows:

| **Real World** | **Algebra Model** |
|---|---|
| You work for an hourly *wage*. You would like to know your *pay* for any *number* of hours worked. | $P = NW$ |

The model $P = NW$ gives the pattern for finding the pay for *any* worker, with *any* hourly wage, working *any* number of hours. That's the power of algebra: By using letters to stand for numbers, we can write a single formula that describes many different situations.

We can now use the model $P = NW$ to answer questions such as "I make $10 an hour, and I worked 35 hours; how much do I get paid?" or "I make $8 an hour; how many hours do I need to work to get paid $1000?"

In general, a **model** is a mathematical representation (such as a formula) of a real-world situation. **Modeling** is the process of making mathematical models. Once a model has been made, it can be used to answer questions about the thing being modeled.

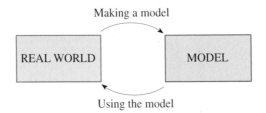

The examples we study in this section are simple, but the methods are far reaching. This will become more apparent as we explore the applications of algebra in the *Focus on Modeling* sections that follow each chapter starting with Chapter 1.

### ■ Using Algebra Models

We begin our study of modeling by using models that are given to us. In the next subsection we learn how to make our own models.

▶ **EXAMPLE 1** | Using a Model for Pay

Use the model $P = NW$ to answer the following question: Aaron makes $10 an hour and worked 35 hours last week. How much did he get paid?

▼ **SOLUTION**   We know that $N = 35$ h and $W = \$10$. We substitute these values into the formula.

$$P = NW \qquad \text{Model}$$
$$= 35 \times 10 \qquad \text{Substitute } N = 35, W = 10$$
$$= 350 \qquad \text{Calculator}$$

So Aaron got paid $350.

✎ **Practice what you've learned: Do Exercise 3.**     ▲

▶ **EXAMPLE 2** | Using a Model for Pay

Use the model $P = NW$ to solve the following problem: Neil makes \$9.00 an hour tutoring mathematics in the Learning Center. He wants to earn enough money to buy a calculus text that costs \$126 (including tax). How many hours does he need to work to earn this amount?

▼ **SOLUTION**   We know that Neil's hourly wage is $W = \$9.00$ and the amount of pay he needs to buy the book is $P = \$126$. To find $N$, we substitute these values into the formula.

$$P = NW \qquad \text{Model}$$
$$126 = 9N \qquad \text{Substitute } P = 126, W = 9.00$$
$$\frac{126}{9} = N \qquad \text{Divide by 9}$$
$$N = 14 \qquad \text{Calculator}$$

So Neil must work 14 hours to buy this book.

✎ **Practice what you've learned: Do Exercise 7.**     ▲

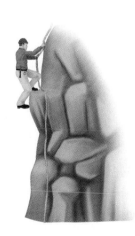

▶ **EXAMPLE 3** | Using an Elevation-Temperature Model

A mountain climber uses the model

$$T = 20 - 10h$$

to estimate the temperature $T$ (in °C) at elevation $h$ (in kilometers, km).

**(a)** Make a table that gives the temperature for each 1-km change in elevation, from elevation 0 km to elevation 5 km. How does temperature change as elevation increases?

**(b)** If the temperature is 5°C, what is the elevation?

▼ **SOLUTION**

**(a)** Let's use the model to find the temperature at elevation $h = 3$ km.

$$T = 20 - 10h \qquad \text{Model}$$
$$= 20 - 10(3) \qquad \text{Substitute } h = 3$$
$$= -10 \qquad \text{Calculator}$$

So at an elevation of 3 km the temperature is $-10$°C. The other entries in the following table are calculated similarly.

| Elevation (km) | Temperature (°C) |
|:---:|:---:|
| 0 | 20° |
| 1 | 10° |
| 2 | 0° |
| 3 | −10° |
| 4 | −20° |
| 5 | −30° |

We see that temperature decreases as elevation increases.

**(b)** We substitute $T = 5°C$ in the model and solve for $h$.

$$T = 20 - 10h \qquad \text{Model}$$

$$5 = 20 - 10h \qquad \text{Substitute } T = 5$$

$$-15 = -10h \qquad \text{Subtract 20}$$

$$\frac{-15}{-10} = h \qquad \text{Divide by −10}$$

$$1.5 = h \qquad \text{Calculator}$$

The elevation is 1.5 km.

✎ **Practice what you've learned: Do Exercise 11.**    ▲

### ■ Making Algebra Models

In the next example we explore the process of making an algebra model for a real-life situation.

▶ **EXAMPLE 4** | Making a Model for Gas Mileage

The gas mileage of a car is the number of miles it can travel on one gallon of gas.

**(a)** Find a formula that models gas mileage in terms of the number of miles driven and the number of gallons of gasoline used.

**(b)** Henry's car used 10.5 gallons to drive 230 miles. Find its gas mileage.

12 mi/gal          40 mi/gal

> **Thinking About the Problem**
>
> Let's try a simple case. If a car uses 2 gallons to drive 100 miles, we easily see that
>
> $$\text{gas mileage} = \frac{100}{2} = 50 \text{ mi/gal}$$
>
> So gas mileage is the number of miles driven divided by the number of gallons used.

▼ **SOLUTION**

**(a)** To find the formula we want, we need to assign symbols to the quantities involved:

| In Words | In Algebra |
|:---|:---:|
| Number of miles driven | $N$ |
| Number of gallons used | $G$ |
| Gas mileage (mi/gal) | $M$ |

We can express the model as follows:

$$\text{gas mileage} = \frac{\text{number of miles driven}}{\text{number of gallons used}}$$

$$M = \frac{N}{G} \qquad \text{Model}$$

**(b)** To get the gas mileage, we substitute $N = 230$ and $G = 10.5$ in the formula.

$$M = \frac{N}{G} \qquad \text{Model}$$

$$= \frac{230}{10.5} \qquad \text{Substitute } N = 230,\ G = 10.5$$

$$\approx 21.9 \qquad \text{Calculator}$$

The gas mileage for Henry's car is 21.9 mi/gal.

✎ **Practice what you've learned: Do Exercise 21.** ▲

# P.1 EXERCISES

## ▼ CONCEPTS

**1.** The model $L = 4S$ gives the total number of legs that $S$ sheep have. Using this model, we find that 12 sheep have

$L =$ _____ legs.

**2.** Suppose gas costs $3 a gallon. We make a model for the cost $C$ of buying $x$ gallons of gas by writing the formula

$C =$ _____ .

## ▼ SKILLS

**3–12** ▪ Use the model given to answer the questions about the object or process being modeled.

✎ **3.** The sales tax $T$ in a certain county is modeled by the formula $T = 0.08x$. Find the sales tax on an item whose price is $120.

**4.** A company finds that the cost $C$ (in dollars) of manufacturing $x$ compact discs is modeled by

$$C = 500 + 0.35x$$

Find the cost of manufacturing 1000 compact discs.

**5.** A company models the profit $P$ (in dollars) on the sale of $x$ CDs by

$$P = 0.8x - 500$$

Find the profit on the sale of 1000 CDs.

**6.** The volume $V$ of a cylindrical can is modeled by the formula

$$V = \pi r^2 h$$

where $r$ is the radius and $h$ is the height of the can. Find the volume of a can with radius 3 in. and height 5 in.

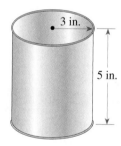

✎ **7.** The gas mileage $M$ (in mi/gal) of a car is modeled by $M = N/G$ where $N$ is the number of miles driven and $G$ is the number of gallons of gas used.
  **(a)** Find the gas mileage $M$ for a car that drove 240 miles on 8 gallons of gas.
  **(b)** A car with a gas mileage $M = 25$ mi/gal is driven 175 miles. How many gallons of gas are used?

**8.** A mountain climber models the temperature $T$ (in °F) at elevation $h$ (in ft) by

$$T = 70 - 0.003h$$

  **(a)** Find the temperature $T$ at an elevation of 1500 ft.
  **(b)** If the temperature is 64°F, what is the elevation?

**9.** The portion of a floating iceberg that is below the water surface is much larger than the portion above the surface. The total volume $V$ of an iceberg is modeled by

$$V = 9.5S$$

where $S$ is the volume showing above the surface.

**(a)** Find the total volume of an iceberg if the volume showing above the surface is 4 km$^3$.

**(b)** Find the volume showing above the surface for an iceberg with total volume 19 km$^3$.

**10.** The power $P$ measured in horsepower (hp) needed to drive a certain ship at a speed of $s$ knots is modeled by

$$P = 0.06s^3$$

**(a)** Find the power needed to drive the ship at 12 knots.

**(b)** At what speed will a 7.5-hp engine drive the ship?

✎ **11.** An ocean diver models the pressure $P$ (in lb/in$^2$) at depth $d$ (in ft) by

$$P = 14.7 + 0.45d$$

**(a)** Make a table that gives the pressure for each 10-ft change in depth, from a depth of 0 ft to 60 ft.

**(b)** If the pressure is 30 lb/in$^2$, what is the depth?

**12.** Arizonans use an average of 40 gallons of water per person each day.

**(a)** Find a model for the number of gallons $W$ of water used by $x$ Arizona residents each day.

**(b)** Make a table that gives the number of gallons of water used for each 1000-person increase in population, from 0 to 5000.

**(c)** Estimate the population of an Arizona town whose water usage is 140,000 gallons per day.

**13–20** ■ Write an algebraic formula that models the given quantity.

**13.** The number $N$ of days in $w$ weeks

**14.** The number $N$ of cents in $q$ quarters

**15.** The average $A$ of two numbers $a$ and $b$

**16.** The average $A$ of three numbers $a$, $b$, and $c$

**17.** The cost $C$ of purchasing $x$ gallons of gas at \$3.50 a gallon

**18.** The amount $T$ of a 15% tip on a restaurant bill of $x$ dollars

**19.** The distance $d$ in miles that a car travels in $t$ hours at 60 mi/h

**20.** The speed $r$ of a boat that travels $d$ miles in 3 hours

▼ **APPLICATIONS**

✎ **21. Cost of a Pizza**  A pizza parlor charges \$12 for a cheese pizza and \$1 for each topping.

**(a)** How much does a 3-topping pizza cost?

**(b)** Find a formula that models the cost $C$ of a pizza with $n$ toppings.

**(c)** If a pizza costs \$16, how many toppings does it have?

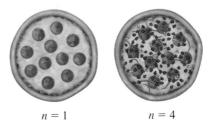

$n = 1$    $n = 4$

**22. Renting a Car**  At a certain car rental agency a compact car rents for \$30 a day and 10¢ a mile.

**(a)** How much does it cost to rent a car for 3 days if the car is driven 280 miles?

**(b)** Find a formula that models the cost $C$ of renting this car for $n$ days if it is driven $m$ miles.

**(c)** If the cost for a 3-day rental was \$140, how many miles was the car driven?

**23. Energy Cost for a Car**  The cost of the electricity needed to drive an all-electric car is about 4 cents per mile. The cost of the gasoline needed to drive the average gasoline-powered car is about 12 cents per mile.

**(a)** Find a formula that models the energy cost $C$ of driving $x$ miles for (i) the all-electric car and (ii) the average gasoline-powered car.

**(b)** Find the cost of driving 10,000 miles with each type of car.

**24. Volume of Fruit Crate**  A fruit crate has square ends and is twice as long as it is wide (see the figure below).

**(a)** Find the volume of the crate if its width is 20 inches.

**(b)** Find a formula for the volume $V$ of the crate in terms of its width $x$.

**25. Cost of a Phone Call**   A phone card company charges a $1 connection fee for each call and 10¢ per minute.
   **(a)** How much does a 10-minute call cost?
   **(b)** Find a formula that models the cost $C$ of a phone call that lasts $t$ minutes.
   **(c)** If a particular call cost $2.20, how many minutes did the call last?
   **(d)** Find a formula that models the cost $C$ (in cents) of a phone call that lasts $t$ minutes if the connection fee is $F$ cents and the rate is $r$ cents per minute.

**26. Grade Point Average**   In many universities students are given grade points for each credit unit according to the following scale:

| | |
|---|---|
| A | 4 points |
| B | 3 points |
| C | 2 points |
| D | 1 point |
| F | 0 point |

For example, a grade of A in a 3-unit course earns $4 \times 3 = 12$ grade points and a grade of B in a 5-unit course earns $3 \times 5 = 15$ grade points. A student's grade point average (GPA) for these two courses is the total number of grade points earned divided by the number of units; in this case the GPA is $(12 + 15)/8 = 3.375$.
   **(a)** Find a formula for the GPA of a student who earns a grade of A in $a$ units of course work, B in $b$ units, C in $c$ units, D in $d$ units, and F in $f$ units.
   **(b)** Find the GPA of a student who has earned a grade of A in two 3-unit courses, B in one 4-unit course, and C in three 3-unit courses.

---

## P.2 | Real Numbers and Their Properties

**LEARNING OBJECTIVES**
After completing this section, you will be able to:
- ■ Classify real numbers
- ■ Use properties of real numbers
- ■ Use properties of negatives
- ■ Add, subtract, multiply, and divide fractions

### ■ Types of Real Numbers

The different types of real numbers were invented to meet specific needs. For example, natural numbers are needed for counting, negative numbers for describing debt or below-zero temperatures, rational numbers for concepts such as "half a gallon of milk," and irrational numbers for measuring certain distances, such as the diagonal of a square.

Let's review the types of numbers that make up the real number system. We start with the **natural numbers**:

$$1, 2, 3, 4, \ldots$$

The **integers** consist of the natural numbers together with their negatives and 0:

$$\ldots, -3, -2, -1, 0, 1, 2, 3, 4, \ldots$$

We construct the **rational numbers** by taking ratios of integers. Thus, any rational number $r$ can be expressed as

$$r = \frac{m}{n}$$

where $m$ and $n$ are integers and $n \neq 0$. Examples are

$$\frac{1}{2} \qquad -\frac{3}{7} \qquad 46 = \frac{46}{1} \qquad 0.17 = \frac{17}{100}$$

(Recall that division by 0 is always ruled out, so expressions such as $\frac{3}{0}$ and $\frac{0}{0}$ are undefined.) There are also real numbers, such as $\sqrt{2}$, that cannot be expressed as a ratio of integers and are therefore called **irrational numbers**. It can be shown, with varying degrees of difficulty, that these numbers are also irrational:

$$\sqrt{3} \qquad \sqrt{5} \qquad \sqrt[3]{2} \qquad \pi \qquad \frac{3}{\pi^2}$$

The set of all real numbers is usually denoted by the symbol $\mathbb{R}$. When we use the word *number* without qualification, we will mean "real number." Figure 1 is a diagram of the types of real numbers that we work with in this book.

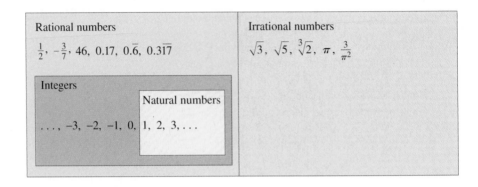

**FIGURE 1** The real number system

Every real number has a decimal representation. If the number is rational, then its corresponding decimal is repeating. For example,

$$\frac{1}{2} = 0.5000\ldots = 0.5\overline{0} \qquad \frac{2}{3} = 0.66666\ldots = 0.\overline{6}$$
$$\frac{157}{495} = 0.3171717\ldots = 0.3\overline{17} \qquad \frac{9}{7} = 1.285714285714\ldots = 1.\overline{285714}$$

A repeating decimal such as
$$x = 3.5474747\ldots$$
is a rational number. To convert it to a ratio of two integers, we write

$$1000x = 3547.47474747\ldots$$
$$\underline{\quad 10x = \quad 35.47474747\ldots}$$
$$990x = 3512.0$$

Thus, $x = \frac{3512}{990}$. (The idea is to multiply $x$ by appropriate powers of 10 and then subtract to eliminate the repeating part.)

(The bar indicates that the sequence of digits repeats forever.) If the number is irrational, the decimal representation is nonrepeating:

$$\sqrt{2} = 1.414213562373095\ldots \qquad \pi = 3.141592653589793\ldots$$

If we stop the decimal expansion of any number at a certain place, we get an approximation to the number. For instance, we can write

$$\pi \approx 3.14159265$$

where the symbol $\approx$ is read "is approximately equal to." The more decimal places we retain, the better our approximation.

▶ **EXAMPLE 1** | Classifying Real Numbers

Determine whether each given real number is a natural number, an integer, a rational number, or an irrational number.

**(a)** 999 **(b)** $-\frac{6}{5}$ **(c)** $-\frac{6}{3}$ **(d)** $\sqrt{25}$ **(e)** $\sqrt{3}$

▼ **SOLUTION**

**(a)** 999 is a positive whole number, so it is a natural number.

**(b)** $-\frac{6}{5}$ is a ratio of two integers, so it is a rational number.

**(c)** $-\frac{6}{3}$ equals $-2$, so it is an integer.

**(d)** $\sqrt{25}$ equals 5, so it is a natural number.

**(e)** $\sqrt{3}$ is a nonrepeating decimal (approximately 1.7320508075689), so it is an irrational number.

✎ **Practice what you've learned: Do Exercise 5.** ▲

### ■ Operations on Real Numbers

Real numbers can be combined using the familiar operations of addition, subtraction, multiplication, and division. When evaluating arithmetic expressions that contain several of these operations, we use the following conventions to determine the order in which the operations are performed:

1. Perform operations inside parentheses first, beginning with the innermost pair. In dividing two expressions, the numerator and denominator of the quotient are treated as if they are within parentheses.
2. Perform all multiplications and divisions, working from left to right.
3. Perform all additions and subtractions, working from left to right.

▶ **EXAMPLE 2** | Evaluating an Arithmetic Expression

Find the value of the expression

$$3\left(\frac{8+10}{2\cdot3}+4\right)-2(5+9)$$

▼ **SOLUTION** First we evaluate the numerator and denominator of the quotient, since these are treated as if they are inside parentheses:

$$3\left(\frac{8+10}{2\cdot3}+4\right)-2(5+9) = 3\left(\frac{18}{6}+4\right)-2(5+9) \qquad \text{Evaluate numerator and denominator}$$

$$= 3(3+4)-2(5+9) \qquad \text{Evaluate quotient}$$

$$= 3\cdot7-2\cdot14 \qquad \text{Evaluate parentheses}$$

$$= 21-28 \qquad \text{Evaluate products}$$

$$= -7 \qquad \text{Evaluate difference}$$

✎ **Practice what you've learned: Do Exercise 7.**                                        ▲

## ■ Properties of Real Numbers

We all know that $2+3=3+2$. We also know that $5+7=7+5$, $513+87=87+513$, and so on. In algebra we express all these (infinitely many) facts by writing

$$a+b=b+a$$

where $a$ and $b$ stand for any two numbers. In other words, "$a+b=b+a$" is a concise way of saying that "when we add two numbers, the order of addition doesn't matter." This fact is called the *Commutative Property of Addition*. From our experience with numbers we know that the properties in the following box are also valid.

---

**PROPERTIES OF REAL NUMBERS**

| Property | Example | Description |
|---|---|---|
| **Commutative Properties** | | |
| $a+b=b+a$ | $7+3=3+7$ | When we add two numbers, order doesn't matter. |
| $ab=ba$ | $3\cdot5=5\cdot3$ | When we multiply two numbers, order doesn't matter. |
| **Associative Properties** | | |
| $(a+b)+c=a+(b+c)$ | $(2+4)+7=2+(4+7)$ | When we add three numbers, it doesn't matter which two we add first. |
| $(ab)c=a(bc)$ | $(3\cdot7)\cdot5=3\cdot(7\cdot5)$ | When we multiply three numbers, it doesn't matter which two we multiply first. |
| **Distributive Property** | | |
| $a(b+c)=ab+ac$ | $2\cdot(3+5)=2\cdot3+2\cdot5$ | When we multiply a number by a sum of two numbers, |
| $(b+c)a=ab+ac$ | $(3+5)\cdot2=2\cdot3+2\cdot5$ | we get the same result as multiplying the number by each of the terms and then adding the results. |

The Distributive Property is crucial because it describes the way addition and multiplication interact with each other.

The Distributive Property applies whenever we multiply a number by a sum. Figure 2 explains why this property works for the case in which all the numbers are positive integers, but the property is true for any real numbers $a$, $b$, and $c$.

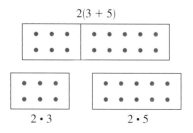

**FIGURE 2** The Distributive Property

▶ **EXAMPLE 3** | Using the Properties of Real Numbers

**(a)** $2 + (3 + 7) = 2 + (7 + 3)$   Commutative Property of Addition
$\qquad\qquad\quad = (2 + 7) + 3$   Associative Property of Addition

**(b)** $2(x + 3) = 2 \cdot x + 2 \cdot 3$   Distributive Property
$\qquad\qquad = 2x + 6$   Simplify

**(c)** $(a + b)(x + y) = (a + b)x + (a + b)y$   Distributive Property
$\qquad\qquad\qquad = (ax + bx) + (ay + by)$   Distributive Property
$\qquad\qquad\qquad = ax + bx + ay + by$   Associative Property of Addition

In the last step we removed the parentheses because, according to the Associative Property, the order of addition doesn't matter.

✎ **Practice what you've learned: Do Exercise 15.**   ▲

### ■ Addition and Subtraction

The number 0 is special for addition; it is called the **additive identity** because $a + 0 = a$ for any real number $a$. Every real number $a$ has a **negative**, $-a$, that satisfies $a + (-a) = 0$. **Subtraction** is the operation that undoes addition; to subtract a number from another, we simply add the negative of that number. By definition

$$a - b = a + (-b)$$

To combine real numbers involving negatives, we use the following properties.

⊘ Don't assume that $-a$ is a negative number. Whether $-a$ is negative or positive depends on the value of $a$. For example, if $a = 5$, then $-a = -5$, a negative number, but if $a = -5$, then $-a = -(-5) = 5$ (Property 2), a positive number.

| PROPERTIES OF NEGATIVES | |
|---|---|
| **Property** | **Example** |
| **1.** $(-1)a = -a$ | $(-1)5 = -5$ |
| **2.** $-(-a) = a$ | $-(-5) = 5$ |
| **3.** $(-a)b = a(-b) = -(ab)$ | $(-5)7 = 5(-7) = -(5 \cdot 7)$ |
| **4.** $(-a)(-b) = ab$ | $(-4)(-3) = 4 \cdot 3$ |
| **5.** $-(a + b) = -a - b$ | $-(3 + 5) = -3 - 5$ |
| **6.** $-(a - b) = b - a$ | $-(5 - 8) = 8 - 5$ |

Property 6 states the intuitive fact that $a - b$ and $b - a$ are negatives of each other. Property 5 is often used with more than two terms:

$$-(a + b + c) = -a - b - c$$

▶ **EXAMPLE 4** | Using Properties of Negatives

Let $x$, $y$, and $z$ be real numbers.

**(a)** $-(3 + 2) = -3 - 2$      Property 5: $-(a + b) = -a - b$

**(b)** $-(x + 2) = -x - 2$      Property 5: $-(a + b) = -a - b$

**(c)** $-(x + y - z) = -x - y - (-z)$      Property 5: $-(a + b) = -a - b$

$\qquad\qquad\quad = -x - y + z$      Property 2: $-(-a) = a$ ▼

> The word **algebra** comes from the ninth-century Arabic book *Hisâb al-Jabr w'al-Muqabala*, written by al-Khowarizmi. The title refers to transposing and combining terms, two processes that are used in solving equations. In Latin translations the title was shortened to *Aljabr*, from which we get the word *algebra*. The author's name itself made its way into the English language in the form of our word *algorithm*.

## ■ Multiplication and Division

The number 1 is special for multiplication; it is called the **multiplicative identity** because $a \cdot 1 = a$ for any real number $a$. Every nonzero real number $a$ has an **inverse**, $1/a$, that satisfies $a \cdot (1/a) = 1$. **Division** is the operation that undoes multiplication; to divide by a number, we multiply by the inverse of that number. If $b \neq 0$, then by definition

$$a \div b = a \cdot \frac{1}{b}$$

We write $a \cdot (1/b)$ as simply $a/b$. We refer to $a/b$ as the **quotient** of $a$ and $b$ or as the **fraction** $a$ over $b$; $a$ is the **numerator**, and $b$ is the **denominator** (or **divisor**). To combine real numbers using the operation of division, we use the following properties.

---

### PROPERTIES OF FRACTIONS

| Property | Example | Description |
|---|---|---|
| 1. $\dfrac{a}{b} \cdot \dfrac{c}{d} = \dfrac{ac}{bd}$ | $\dfrac{2}{3} \cdot \dfrac{5}{7} = \dfrac{2 \cdot 5}{3 \cdot 7} = \dfrac{10}{21}$ | When **multiplying fractions**, multiply numerators and denominators. |
| 2. $\dfrac{a}{b} \div \dfrac{c}{d} = \dfrac{a}{b} \cdot \dfrac{d}{c}$ | $\dfrac{2}{3} \div \dfrac{5}{7} = \dfrac{2}{3} \cdot \dfrac{7}{5} = \dfrac{14}{15}$ | When **dividing fractions**, invert the divisor and multiply. |
| 3. $\dfrac{a}{c} + \dfrac{b}{c} = \dfrac{a + b}{c}$ | $\dfrac{2}{5} + \dfrac{7}{5} = \dfrac{2 + 7}{5} = \dfrac{9}{5}$ | When **adding fractions** with the **same denominator**, add the numerators. |
| 4. $\dfrac{a}{b} + \dfrac{c}{d} = \dfrac{ad + bc}{bd}$ | $\dfrac{2}{5} + \dfrac{3}{7} = \dfrac{2 \cdot 7 + 3 \cdot 5}{35} = \dfrac{29}{35}$ | When **adding fractions** with **different denominators**, find a common denominator. Then add the numerators. |
| 5. $\dfrac{ac}{bc} = \dfrac{a}{b}$ | $\dfrac{2 \cdot 5}{3 \cdot 5} = \dfrac{2}{3}$ | **Cancel** numbers that are **common factors** in the numerator and denominator. |
| 6. If $\dfrac{a}{b} = \dfrac{c}{d}$, then $ad = bc$ | $\dfrac{2}{3} = \dfrac{6}{9}$, so $2 \cdot 9 = 3 \cdot 6$ | **Cross multiply**. |

---

When adding fractions with different denominators, we don't usually use Property 4. Instead, we rewrite the fractions so that they have the smallest possible common denominator (often smaller than the product of the denominators), and then we use Property 3. This denominator is the **L**east **C**ommon **D**enominator (LCD) described in the next example.

▶ **EXAMPLE 5** | Using the LCD to Add Fractions

Evaluate: $\dfrac{5}{36} + \dfrac{7}{120}$

▼ **SOLUTION** Factoring each denominator into prime factors gives

$$36 = 2^2 \cdot 3^2 \qquad \text{and} \qquad 120 = 2^3 \cdot 3 \cdot 5$$

We find the least common denominator (LCD) by forming the product of all the factors that occur in these factorizations, using the highest power of each factor. Thus, the LCD is $2^3 \cdot 3^2 \cdot 5 = 360$. So

$$\frac{5}{36} + \frac{7}{120} = \frac{5 \cdot 10}{36 \cdot 10} + \frac{7 \cdot 3}{120 \cdot 3} \qquad \text{Use common denominator}$$

$$= \frac{50}{360} + \frac{21}{360} = \frac{71}{360} \qquad \text{Property 3: Adding fractions with the same denominator}$$

✎ **Practice what you've learned: Do Exercise 29.** ▲

# P.2 EXERCISES

## ▼ CONCEPTS

**1.** Give an example of each of the following:
(a) A natural number
(b) An integer that is not a natural number
(c) A rational number that is not an integer
(d) An irrational number

**2.** Complete each statement and name the property of real numbers you have used.

(a) $ab =$ _____ ; _____ Property

(b) $a + (b + c) =$ _____ ; _____ Property

(c) $a(b + c) =$ _____ ; _____ Property

**3.** To add two fractions, you must first express them so that they have the same _____.

**4.** To divide two fractions, you _____ the divisor and then multiply.

## ▼ SKILLS

**5–6** ▪ List the elements of the given set that are
(a) natural numbers
(b) integers
(c) rational numbers
(d) irrational numbers

✎ **5.** $\{0, -10, 50, \frac{22}{7}, 0.538, \sqrt{7}, 1.2\overline{3}, -\frac{1}{3}, \sqrt[3]{2}\}$

**6.** $\{1.001, 0.333\ldots, -\pi, -11, 11, \frac{13}{15}, \sqrt{16}, 3.14, \frac{15}{3}\}$

**7–10** ▪ Evaluate the arithmetic expression.

✎ **7.** $-2 + [4 \cdot 7 - 5(9 - \frac{8}{2})]$

**8.** $3(4 \cdot 6 - 2 \cdot 10) + 7(15 - 8 \cdot 2)$

**9.** $\frac{5 + 7}{3} - 6[12 - (17 - 2 \cdot 3)]$

**10.** $1 - 2[3 - 4(5 - 6 \cdot 7)]$

**11–18** ▪ State the property of real numbers being used.

**11.** $7 + 10 = 10 + 7$

**12.** $2(3 + 5) = (3 + 5)2$

**13.** $(x + 2y) + 3z = x + (2y + 3z)$

**14.** $2(A + B) = 2A + 2B$

✎ **15.** $(5x + 1)3 = 15x + 3$

**16.** $(x + a)(x + b) = (x + a)x + (x + a)b$

**17.** $2x(3 + y) = (3 + y)2x$

**18.** $7(a + b + c) = 7(a + b) + 7c$

**19–22** ▪ Rewrite the expression using the given property of real numbers.

**19.** Commutative Property of Addition,   $x + 3 =$

**20.** Associative Property of Multiplication,   $7(3x) =$

**21.** Distributive Property,   $4(A + B) =$

**22.** Distributive Property,   $5x + 5y =$

**23–28** ▪ Use properties of real numbers to write the expression without parentheses.

**23.** $3(x + y)$

**24.** $(a - b)8$

**25.** $4(2m)$

**26.** $\frac{4}{3}(-6y)$

**27.** $-\frac{5}{2}(2x - 4y)$

**28.** $(3a)(b + c - 2d)$

**29–40** ▪ Perform the indicated operations.

✎ **29.** $\frac{3}{10} + \frac{4}{15}$

**30.** $\frac{1}{4} + \frac{1}{5}$

**31.** $\frac{2}{3} - \frac{3}{5}$

**32.** $1 + \frac{5}{8} - \frac{1}{6}$

**33.** $\frac{2}{3}(6 - \frac{3}{2})$

**34.** $0.25(\frac{8}{9} + \frac{1}{2})$

**35.** $(3 + \frac{1}{4})(1 - \frac{4}{5})$

**36.** $(\frac{1}{2} - \frac{1}{3})(\frac{1}{2} + \frac{1}{3})$

**37.** $\dfrac{\frac{2}{3} - \frac{2}{3}}{\frac{2}{3}} \cdot 2$

**38.** $\dfrac{\frac{1}{12}}{\frac{1}{8} - \frac{1}{9}}$

**39.** $\dfrac{2 - \frac{3}{4}}{\frac{1}{2} - \frac{1}{3}}$

**40.** $\dfrac{\frac{2}{5} + \frac{1}{2}}{\frac{1}{10} + \frac{3}{15}}$

**41–42** ▪ Express each repeating decimal as a fraction. (See the margin note on page 8.)

**41.** (a) $0.\overline{7}$   (b) $0.2\overline{8}$   (c) $0.\overline{57}$

**42.** (a) $5.\overline{23}$   (b) $1.3\overline{7}$   (c) $2.1\overline{35}$

## ▼ APPLICATIONS

**43. Area of a Garden**   Mary's backyard vegetable garden measures 20 ft by 30 ft, so its area is $20 \times 30 = 600$ ft². She decides to make it longer, as shown in the figure, so that the area increases to $A = 20(30 + x)$. Which property of real numbers tells us that the new area can also be written $A = 600 + 20x$?

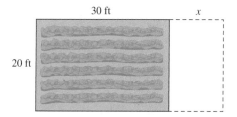

## ▼ DISCOVERY • DISCUSSION • WRITING

**44. Sums and Products of Rational and Irrational Numbers**   Explain why the sum, the difference, and the product of two rational numbers are rational numbers. Is the product of two irrational numbers necessarily irrational? What about the sum?

**45. Combining Rational Numbers with Irrational Numbers**   Is $\frac{1}{2} + \sqrt{2}$ rational or irrational? Is $\frac{1}{2} \cdot \sqrt{2}$ rational or irra-

tional? In general, what can you say about the sum of a rational and an irrational number? What about the product?

**46. Commutative and Noncommutative Operations**   We have seen that addition and multiplication are both commutative operations.
   **(a)** Is subtraction commutative?
   **(b)** Is division of nonzero real numbers commutative?
   **(c)** Are the actions of putting on your socks and putting on your shoes commutative?
   **(d)** Are the actions of putting on your hat and putting on your coat commutative?
   **(e)** Are the actions of washing laundry and drying it commutative?
   **(f)** Give an example of a pair of actions that is commutative.
   **(g)** Give an example of a pair of actions that is not commutative.

---

## P.3 | The Real Number Line and Order

**LEARNING OBJECTIVES**
After completing this section, you will be able to:

- Graph numbers on the real line
- Use the order symbols $<, \leq, >, \geq$
- Work with set and interval notation
- Find and use absolute values of real numbers
- Find distances on the real line

### ■ The Real Line

The real numbers can be represented by points on a line, as shown in Figure 1. The positive direction (toward the right) is indicated by an arrow. We choose an arbitrary reference point $O$, called the **origin**, which corresponds to the real number 0. Given any convenient unit of measurement, each positive number $x$ is represented by the point on the line a distance of $x$ units to the right of the origin, and each negative number $-x$ is represented by the point $x$ units to the left of the origin. Thus, every real number is represented by a point on the line, and every point $P$ on the line corresponds to exactly one real number. The number associated with the point $P$ is called the coordinate of $P$, and the line is then called a **coordinate line**, or a **real number line**, or simply a **real line**. Often we identify the point with its coordinate and think of a number as being a point on the real line.

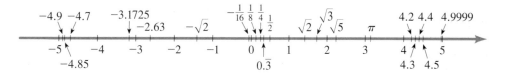

**FIGURE 1**  The real line

### ■ Order on the Real Line

The real numbers are *ordered*. We say that ***a* is less than *b*** and write $a < b$ if $b - a$ is a positive number. Geometrically, this means that $a$ lies to the left of $b$ on the number line. (Equivalently, we can say that ***b* is greater than *a*** and write $b > a$.) The symbol $a \le b$ (or $b \ge a$) means that either $a < b$ or $a = b$ and is read "$a$ is less than or equal to $b$." For instance, the following are true inequalities (see Figure 2):

$$-\pi < -3 \qquad \sqrt{2} < 2 \qquad 2 \le 2 \qquad 7 < 7.4 < 7.5$$

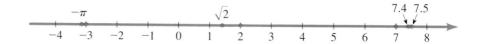

**FIGURE 2**

▶ **EXAMPLE 1** │ Graphing Inequalities

(a) On the real line, graph all the numbers $x$ that satisfy the inequality $x < 3$.

(b) On the real line, graph all the numbers $x$ that satisfy the inequality $x \ge -2$.

▼ **SOLUTION**

(a) We must graph the real numbers that are smaller than 3—those that lie to the left of 3 on the real line. The graph is shown in Figure 3. Note that the number 3 is indicated with an open dot on the real line, since it does not satisfy the inequality.

(b) We must graph the real numbers that are greater than or equal to $-2$: those that lie to the right of $-2$ on the real line, including the number $-2$ itself. The graph is shown in Figure 4. Note that the number $-2$ is indicated with a solid dot on the real line, since it satisfies the inequality.

✎ **Practice what you've learned: Do Exercises 17 and 19.** ▲

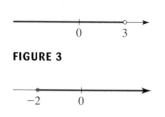

**FIGURE 3**

**FIGURE 4**

### ■ Sets and Intervals

A **set** is a collection of objects, and these objects are called the **elements** of the set. If $S$ is a set, the notation $a \in S$ means that $a$ is an element of $S$, and $b \notin S$ means that $b$ is not an element of $S$. For example, if $Z$ represents the set of integers, then $-3 \in Z$ but $\pi \notin Z$.

Some sets can be described by listing their elements within braces. For instance, the set $A$ that consists of all positive integers less than 7 can be written as

$$A = \{1, 2, 3, 4, 5, 6\}$$

We could also write $A$ in **set-builder notation** as

$$A = \{x \,|\, x \text{ is an integer and } 0 < x < 7\}$$

which is read "$A$ is the set of all $x$ such that $x$ is an integer and $0 < x < 7$."

If $S$ and $T$ are sets, then their **union** $S \cup T$ is the set that consists of all elements that are in $S$ *or* $T$ (or in both). The **intersection** of $S$ and $T$ is the set $S \cap T$ consisting of all elements that are in both $S$ *and* $T$. In other words, $S \cap T$ is the common part of $S$ and $T$. The **empty set**, denoted by $\emptyset$, is the set that contains no element.

▶ **EXAMPLE 2** │ Union and Intersection of Sets

If $S = \{1, 2, 3, 4, 5\}$, $T = \{4, 5, 6, 7\}$, and $V = \{6, 7, 8\}$, find the sets $S \cup T$, $S \cap T$, and $S \cap V$.

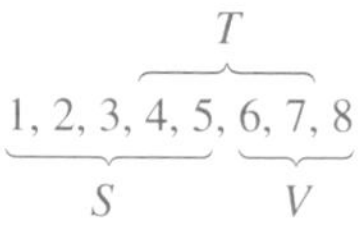

▼ **SOLUTION**

$S \cup T = \{1, 2, 3, 4, 5, 6, 7\}$   All elements in $S$ or $T$

$S \cap T = \{4, 5\}$   Elements common to both $S$ and $T$

$S \cap V = \varnothing$   $S$ and $V$ have no element in common

✎ **Practice what you've learned: Do Exercise 27.** ▲

Certain sets of real numbers, called **intervals**, occur frequently in calculus and correspond geometrically to line segments. For example, if $a < b$, then the **open interval** from $a$ to $b$ consists of all numbers between $a$ and $b$ and is denoted by the symbol $(a, b)$. Using set-builder notation, we can write

$$(a, b) = \{x \mid a < x < b\}$$

Note that the endpoints, $a$ and $b$, are excluded from this interval. This fact is indicated by the parentheses ( ) in the interval notation and the open circles on the graph of the interval in Figure 5.

The **closed interval** from $a$ to $b$ is the set

$$[a, b] = \{x \mid a \leq x \leq b\}$$

Here the endpoints of the interval are included. This is indicated by the square brackets [ ] in the interval notation and the solid circles on the graph of the interval in Figure 6. It is also possible to include only one endpoint in an interval, as shown in the table of intervals below.

We also need to consider infinite intervals, such as

$$(a, \infty) = \{x \mid a < x\}$$

This does not mean that $\infty$ ("infinity") is a number. The notation $(a, \infty)$ stands for the set of all numbers that are greater than $a$, so the symbol $\infty$ simply indicates that the interval extends indefinitely far in the positive direction.

The following table lists the nine possible types of intervals. When these intervals are discussed, we will always assume that $a < b$.

**FIGURE 5** The open interval $(a, b)$

**FIGURE 6** The closed interval $[a, b]$

| Notation | Set description | Graph |
|---|---|---|
| $(a, b)$ | $\{x \mid a < x < b\}$ | $a$    $b$ |
| $[a, b]$ | $\{x \mid a \leq x \leq b\}$ | $a$    $b$ |
| $[a, b)$ | $\{x \mid a \leq x < b\}$ | $a$    $b$ |
| $(a, b]$ | $\{x \mid a < x \leq b\}$ | $a$    $b$ |
| $(a, \infty)$ | $\{x \mid a < x\}$ | $a$ |
| $[a, \infty)$ | $\{x \mid a \leq x\}$ | $a$ |
| $(-\infty, b)$ | $\{x \mid x < b\}$ |  $b$ |
| $(-\infty, b]$ | $\{x \mid x \leq b\}$ |  $b$ |
| $(-\infty, \infty)$ | $\mathbb{R}$ (set of all real numbers) |  |

▶ **EXAMPLE 3** | Graphing Intervals

Express each interval in terms of inequalities, and then graph the interval.

**(a)** $[-1, 2) = \{x \mid -1 \leq x < 2\}$

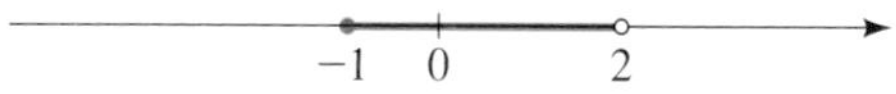

**(b)** $[1.5, 4] = \{x \mid 1.5 \leq x \leq 4\}$

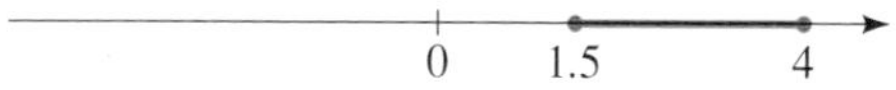

**(c)** $(-3, \infty) = \{x \mid -3 < x\}$

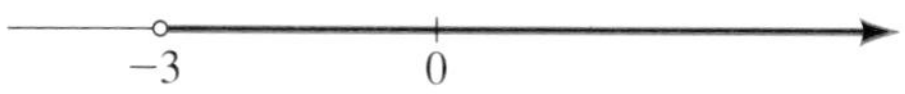

✎ **Practice what you've learned: Do Exercise 33.** ▲

**6.** The absolute value of the difference between $a$ and $b$ is (geometrically) the _____ between them on the real number line.

---

### ▼ SKILLS

**7–8** ■ Place the correct symbol ($<$, $>$, or $=$) in the space.

**7.** (a) $3$ ▢ $\frac{7}{2}$   (b) $-3$ ▢ $-\frac{7}{2}$   (c) $3.5$ ▢ $\frac{7}{2}$

**8.** (a) $\frac{2}{3}$ ▢ $0.67$   (b) $\frac{2}{3}$ ▢ $-0.67$   (c) $|0.67|$ ▢ $|-0.67|$

**9–16** ■ State whether each inequality is true or false.

**9.** $-6 < -10$

**10.** $\sqrt{2} > 1.41$

**11.** $\frac{10}{11} < \frac{12}{13}$

**12.** $-\frac{1}{2} < -1$

**13.** $-\pi > -3$

**14.** $8 \le 9$

**15.** $1.1 > 1.\overline{1}$

**16.** $8 \le 8$

**17–20** ■ On a real number line, graph the numbers that satisfy the inequality.

**17.** $x \ge \dfrac{1}{2}$

**18.** $x > -4$

**19.** $x < -3$

**20.** $x \le 0$

**21–24** ■ Find the inequality whose graph is given.

**21.**

**22.**

**23.**

**24.**

**25–26** ■ Write each statement in terms of inequalities.

**25.** (a) $x$ is positive.
(b) $t$ is less than 4.
(c) $a$ is greater than or equal to $\pi$.
(d) $x$ is less than $\frac{1}{3}$ and is greater than $-5$.
(e) The distance from $p$ to 3 is at most 5.

**26.** (a) $y$ is negative.
(b) $z$ is greater than 1.
(c) $b$ is at most 8.
(d) $w$ is positive and is less than or equal to 17.
(e) $y$ is at least 2 units from $\pi$.

**27–30** ■ Find the indicated set if

$A = \{1, 2, 3, 4, 5, 6, 7\}$   $B = \{2, 4, 6, 8\}$   $C = \{7, 8, 9, 10\}$

**27.** (a) $A \cup B$   (b) $A \cap B$

**28.** (a) $B \cup C$   (b) $B \cap C$

**29.** (a) $A \cup C$   (b) $A \cap C$

**30.** (a) $A \cup B \cup C$   (b) $A \cap B \cap C$

**31–32** ■ Find the indicated set if

$A = \{x \mid x \ge -2\}$   $B = \{x \mid x < 4\}$   $C = \{x \mid -1 < x \le 5\}$

**31.** (a) $B \cup C$   (b) $B \cap C$

**32.** (a) $A \cap C$   (b) $A \cap B$

**33–38** ■ Express the interval in terms of inequalities, and then graph the interval.

**33.** $(-3, 0)$

**34.** $(2, 8]$

**35.** $[2, 8)$

**36.** $\left[-6, -\frac{1}{2}\right]$

**37.** $[2, \infty)$

**38.** $(-\infty, 1)$

**39–44** ■ Express the inequality in interval notation, and then graph the corresponding interval.

**39.** $x \le 1$

**40.** $1 \le x \le 2$

**41.** $-2 < x \le 1$

**42.** $x \ge -5$

**43.** $x > -1$

**44.** $-5 < x < 2$

**45–46** ■ Express each set in interval notation.

**45.** (a)

(b)

**46.** (a)

(b)

**47–52** ■ Graph the set.

**47.** $(-2, 0) \cup (-1, 1)$

**48.** $(-2, 0) \cap (-1, 1)$

**49.** $[-4, 6] \cap [0, 8)$

**50.** $[-4, 6) \cup [0, 8)$

**51.** $(-\infty, -4) \cup (4, \infty)$

**52.** $(-\infty, 6] \cap (2, 10)$

**53–58** ■ Evaluate each expression.

**53.** (a) $|100|$   (b) $|-73|$

**54.** (a) $|\sqrt{5} - 5|$   (b) $|10 - \pi|$

**55.** (a) $\big||-6| - |-4|\big|$   (b) $\dfrac{-1}{|-1|}$

**56.** (a) $\big|2 - |-12|\big|$   (b) $-1 - \big|1 - |-1|\big|$

**57.** (a) $|(-2) \cdot 6|$   (b) $\left|\left(-\frac{1}{3}\right)(-15)\right|$

**58.** (a) $\left|\dfrac{-6}{24}\right|$   (b) $\left|\dfrac{7 - 12}{12 - 7}\right|$

**59–62** ■ Find the distance between the given numbers.

**59.**

**60.**

**61.** (a) 2 and 17   
**62.** (a) $\frac{7}{15}$ and $-\frac{1}{21}$

(b) $-3$ and 21   
(b) $-38$ and $-57$

(c) $\frac{11}{8}$ and $-\frac{3}{10}$   
(c) $-2.6$ and $-1.8$

---

### ▼ APPLICATIONS

**63.** **Temperature Variation**   The bar graph on the next page shows the daily high temperatures for Omak, Washington, and Geneseo, New York, during a certain week in June. Let $T_O$ represent the temperature in Omak and $T_G$ the temperature in Geneseo. Calculate $T_O - T_G$ and $|T_O - T_G|$ for each day shown. Which of these two values gives more information?

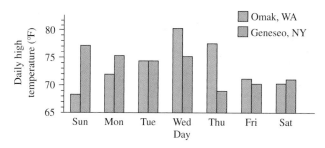

**64. Fuel Consumption**   Suppose an automobile's fuel consumption is 28 mi/gal in city driving and 34 mi/gal in highway driving. If $x$ denotes the number of city miles and $y$ the number of highway miles, then the total miles this car can travel on a 15-gallon tank of fuel must satisfy the inequality

$$\tfrac{1}{28}x + \tfrac{1}{34}y \le 15$$

Use this inequality to answer the following questions. (Assume the car has a full tank of fuel.)
**(a)**  Can the car travel 165 city miles and 230 highway miles before running out of gas?
**(b)**  If the car has been driven 280 miles in the city, how many highway miles can it be driven before running out of fuel?

**65. Mailing a Package**   The post office will accept only packages for which the length plus the "girth" (distance around) is no more than 108 inches. Thus, for the package in the figure, we must have

$$L + 2(x + y) \le 108$$

**(a)**  Will the post office accept a package that is 6 in. wide, 8 in. deep, and 5 ft long? What about a package that measures 2 ft by 2 ft by 4 ft?
**(b)**  What is the greatest acceptable length for a package that has a square base measuring 9 in. by 9 in?

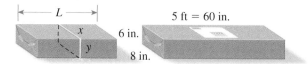

▼ **DISCOVERY • DISCUSSION • WRITING**

**66. Signs of Numbers**   Let $a$, $b$, and $c$ be real numbers such that $a > b > 0$, and $c < 0$. Find the sign of each expression.
**(a)**  $-a$      **(b)**  $-c$      **(c)**  $bc$
**(d)**  $a - b$      **(e)**  $c - a$      **(f)**  $a - bc$
**(g)**  $c^2$      **(h)**  $-abc$

**67. Limiting Behavior of Reciprocals**   Complete the tables. What happens to the size of the fraction $1/x$ as $x$ gets large? As $x$ gets small?

| $x$ | $1/x$ |     | $x$ | $1/x$ |
|-----|-------|-----|-----|-------|
| 1   |       |     | 1.0 |       |
| 2   |       |     | 0.5 |       |
| 10  |       |     | 0.1 |       |
| 100 |       |     | 0.01 |      |
| 1000 |      |     | 0.001 |     |

**68. Irrational Numbers and Geometry**   Using the following figure, explain how to locate the point $\sqrt{2}$ on a number line. Can you locate $\sqrt{5}$ by a similar method? What about $\sqrt{6}$? List some other irrational numbers that can be located this way.

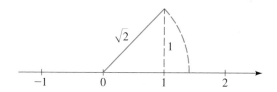

---

| **P.4** | Integer Exponents |
|---------|-------------------|

**LEARNING OBJECTIVES**
After completing this section, you will be able to:

■   Use exponential notation
■   Simplify expressions using the Laws of Exponents
■   Write numbers in scientific notation

In this section we review the rules for working with exponent notation. We also see how exponents can be used to represent very large and very small numbers.

■ **Exponential Notation**

A product of identical numbers is usually written in exponential notation. For example, $5 \cdot 5 \cdot 5$ is written as $5^3$. In general, we have the following definition.

> **EXPONENTIAL NOTATION**
>
> If $a$ is any real number and $n$ is a positive integer, then the **$n$th power** of $a$ is
> $$a^n = \underbrace{a \cdot a \cdots \cdot a}_{n \text{ factors}}$$
>
> The number $a$ is called the **base**, and $n$ is called the **exponent**.

▶ **EXAMPLE 1** | Exponential Notation

**(a)** $\left(\frac{1}{2}\right)^5 = \left(\frac{1}{2}\right)\left(\frac{1}{2}\right)\left(\frac{1}{2}\right)\left(\frac{1}{2}\right)\left(\frac{1}{2}\right) = \frac{1}{32}$

**(b)** $(-3)^4 = (-3) \cdot (-3) \cdot (-3) \cdot (-3) = 81$

**(c)** $-3^4 = -(3 \cdot 3 \cdot 3 \cdot 3) = -81$

⊘ Note the distinction between $(-3)^4$ and $-3^4$. In $(-3)^4$ the exponent applies to $-3$, but in $-3^4$ the exponent applies only to 3.

✎ **Practice what you've learned: Do Exercises 13 and 15.** ▲

We can state several useful rules for working with exponential notation. To discover the rule for multiplication, we multiply $5^4$ by $5^2$:

$$5^4 \cdot 5^2 = \underbrace{(5 \cdot 5 \cdot 5 \cdot 5)}_{4 \text{ factors}}\underbrace{(5 \cdot 5)}_{2 \text{ factors}} = \underbrace{5 \cdot 5 \cdot 5 \cdot 5 \cdot 5 \cdot 5}_{6 \text{ factors}} = 5^6 = 5^{4+2}$$

It appears that *to multiply two powers of the same base, we add their exponents.* In general, for any real number $a$ and any positive integers $m$ and $n$ we have

$$a^m a^n = \underbrace{(a \cdot a \cdots \cdot a)}_{m \text{ factors}}\underbrace{(a \cdot a \cdots \cdot a)}_{n \text{ factors}} = \underbrace{a \cdot a \cdot a \cdots \cdot a}_{m+n \text{ factors}} = a^{m+n}$$

Thus, $a^m a^n = a^{m+n}$.

We would like this rule to be true even when $m$ and $n$ are 0 or negative integers. For instance, we must have

$$2^0 \cdot 2^3 = 2^{0+3} = 2^3$$

But this can happen only if $2^0 = 1$. Likewise, we want to have

$$5^4 \cdot 5^{-4} = 5^{4+(-4)} = 5^{4-4} = 5^0 = 1$$

and this will be true if $5^{-4} = 1/5^4$. These observations lead to the following definition.

> **ZERO AND NEGATIVE EXPONENTS**
>
> If $a \neq 0$ is any real number and $n$ is a positive integer, then
> $$a^0 = 1 \qquad \text{and} \qquad a^{-n} = \frac{1}{a^n}$$

▶ **EXAMPLE 2** | Zero and Negative Exponents

**(a)** $\left(\frac{4}{7}\right)^0 = 1$

**(b)** $x^{-1} = \frac{1}{x^1} = \frac{1}{x}$

**(c)** $(-2)^{-3} = \frac{1}{(-2)^3} = \frac{1}{-8} = -\frac{1}{8}$

✎ **Practice what you've learned: Do Exercise 19.** ▲

## ■ Rules for Working with Exponents

Familiarity with the following rules is essential for our work with exponents and bases. In the table the bases $a$ and $b$ are real numbers, and the exponents $m$ and $n$ are integers.

---

**LAWS OF EXPONENTS**

| Law | Example | Description |
|---|---|---|
| **1.** $a^m a^n = a^{m+n}$ | $3^2 \cdot 3^5 = 3^{2+5} = 3^7$ | To multiply two powers of the same number, add the exponents. |
| **2.** $\dfrac{a^m}{a^n} = a^{m-n}$ | $\dfrac{3^5}{3^2} = 3^{5-2} = 3^3$ | To divide two powers of the same number, subtract the exponents. |
| **3.** $(a^m)^n = a^{mn}$ | $(3^2)^5 = 3^{2 \cdot 5} = 3^{10}$ | To raise a power to a new power, multiply the exponents. |
| **4.** $(ab)^n = a^n b^n$ | $(3 \cdot 4)^2 = 3^2 \cdot 4^2$ | To raise a product to a power, raise each factor to the power. |
| **5.** $\left(\dfrac{a}{b}\right)^n = \dfrac{a^n}{b^n}$ | $\left(\dfrac{3}{4}\right)^2 = \dfrac{3^2}{4^2}$ | To raise a quotient to a power, raise both numerator and denominator to the power. |

---

▼ **PROOF OF LAW 3**  If $m$ and $n$ are positive integers, we have

$$(a^m)^n = (\underbrace{a \cdot a \cdot \cdots \cdot a}_{m \text{ factors}})^n$$

$$= \underbrace{(\underbrace{a \cdot a \cdot \cdots \cdot a}_{m \text{ factors}})(\underbrace{a \cdot a \cdot \cdots \cdot a}_{m \text{ factors}}) \cdots (\underbrace{a \cdot a \cdot \cdots \cdot a}_{m \text{ factors}})}_{n \text{ groups of factors}}$$

$$= \underbrace{a \cdot a \cdot \cdots \cdot a}_{mn \text{ factors}} = a^{mn}$$

The cases for which $m \leq 0$ or $n \leq 0$ can be proved by using the definition of negative exponents. ▲

▼ **PROOF OF LAW 4**  If $n$ is a positive integer, we have

$$(ab)^n = \underbrace{(ab)(ab) \cdots (ab)}_{n \text{ factors}} = (\underbrace{a \cdot a \cdot \cdots \cdot a}_{n \text{ factors}}) \cdot (\underbrace{b \cdot b \cdot \cdots \cdot b}_{n \text{ factors}}) = a^n b^n$$

Here we have used the Commutative and Associative Properties repeatedly. If $n \leq 0$, Law 4 can be proved by using the definition of negative exponents. ▲

You are asked to prove Laws 2 and 5 in Exercise 97.

▶ **EXAMPLE 3** | Using Laws of Exponents

**(a)** $x^4 x^7 = x^{4+7} = x^{11}$        Law 1: $a^m a^n = a^{m+n}$

**(b)** $y^4 y^{-7} = y^{4-7} = y^{-3} = \dfrac{1}{y^3}$     Law 1: $a^m a^n = a^{m+n}$

**(c)** $\dfrac{c^9}{c^5} = c^{9-5} = c^4$         Law 2: $a^m/a^n = a^{m-n}$

**(d)** $(b^4)^5 = b^{4 \cdot 5} = b^{20}$       Law 3: $(a^m)^n = a^{mn}$

**(e)** $(3x)^3 = 3^3 x^3 = 27x^3$      Law 4: $(ab)^n = a^n b^n$

**(f)** $\left(\dfrac{x}{2}\right)^5 = \dfrac{x^5}{2^5} = \dfrac{x^5}{32}$      Law 5: $(a/b)^n = a^n/b^n$

✎ **Practice what you've learned: Do Exercises 37, 41, and 45.**     ▲

▶ **EXAMPLE 4** | Simplifying Expressions with Exponents

Simplify:   (a) $(2a^3b^2)(3ab^4)^3$     (b) $\left(\dfrac{x}{y}\right)^3\left(\dfrac{y^2x}{z}\right)^4$

▼ **SOLUTION**

(a) $(2a^3b^2)(3ab^4)^3 = (2a^3b^2)[3^3a^3(b^4)^3]$     Law 4: $(ab)^n = a^nb^n$

$= (2a^3b^2)(27a^3b^{12})$     Law 3: $(a^m)^n = a^{mn}$

$= (2)(27)a^3a^3b^2b^{12}$     Group factors with the same base

$= 54\, a^6b^{14}$     Law 1: $a^ma^n = a^{m+n}$

(b) $\left(\dfrac{x}{y}\right)^3\left(\dfrac{y^2x}{z}\right)^4 = \dfrac{x^3}{y^3}\dfrac{(y^2)^4x^4}{z^4}$     Laws 5 and 4

$= \dfrac{x^3}{y^3}\dfrac{y^8x^4}{z^4}$     Law 3

$= (x^3x^4)\left(\dfrac{y^8}{y^3}\right)\dfrac{1}{z^4}$     Group factors with the same base

$= \dfrac{x^7y^5}{z^4}$     Laws 1 and 2

✎ **Practice what you've learned: Do Exercises 47 and 61.**     ▲

When simplifying an expression, you will find that many different methods will lead to the same result; you should feel free to use any of the rules of exponents to arrive at your own method. We now give two additional laws that are useful in simplifying expressions with negative exponents.

---

### LAWS OF EXPONENTS

| Law | Example | Description |
|---|---|---|
| **6.** $\left(\dfrac{a}{b}\right)^{-n} = \left(\dfrac{b}{a}\right)^n$ | $\left(\dfrac{3}{4}\right)^{-2} = \left(\dfrac{4}{3}\right)^2$ | To raise a fraction to a negative power, invert the fraction and change the sign of the exponent. |
| **7.** $\dfrac{a^{-n}}{b^{-m}} = \dfrac{b^m}{a^n}$ | $\dfrac{3^{-2}}{4^{-5}} = \dfrac{4^5}{3^2}$ | To move a number raised to a power from numerator to denominator or from denominator to numerator, change the sign of the exponent. |

---

▼ **PROOF OF LAW 7**   Using the definition of negative exponents and then Property 2 of fractions (page 11), we have

$$\frac{a^{-n}}{b^{-m}} = \frac{1/a^n}{1/b^m} = \frac{1}{a^n}\cdot\frac{b^m}{1} = \frac{b^m}{a^n}$$     ▲

You are asked to prove Law 6 in Exercise 98.

▶ **EXAMPLE 5** | Simplifying Expressions with Negative Exponents

Eliminate negative exponents and simplify each expression.

(a) $\dfrac{6st^{-4}}{2s^{-2}t^2}$     (b) $\left(\dfrac{y}{3z^3}\right)^{-2}$

**MATHEMATICS IN THE MODERN WORLD**

Although we are often unaware of its presence, mathematics permeates nearly every aspect of life in the modern world. With the advent of modern technology, mathematics plays an ever greater role in our lives. Today you were probably awakened by a digital alarm clock, made a phone call that used digital transmission, sent an e-mail message over the Internet, drove a car with digitally controlled fuel injection, listened to music on a CD or MP3 player, then fell asleep in a room whose temperature is controlled by a digital thermostat. In each of these activities mathematics is crucially involved. In general, a property such as the intensity or frequency of sound, the oxygen level in a car's exhaust emission, the colors in an image, or the temperature in your bedroom is transformed into sequences of numbers by sophisticated mathematical algorithms. These numerical data, which usually consist of many millions of bits (the digits 0 and 1), are then transmitted and reinterpreted. Dealing with such huge amounts of data was not feasible until the invention of computers, machines whose logical processes were invented by mathematicians.

The contributions of mathematics in the modern world are not limited to technological advances. The logical processes of mathematics are now used to analyze complex problems in the social, political, and life sciences in new and surprising ways. Advances in mathematics continue to be made, some of the most exciting of these just within the past decade.

In other *Mathematics in the Modern World* vignettes, we will describe in more detail how mathematics affects us in our everyday activities.

▼ **SOLUTION**

**(a)** We use Law 7, which allows us to move a number raised to a power from the numerator to the denominator (or vice versa) by changing the sign of the exponent.

$t^{-4}$ moves to denominator and becomes $t^4$.

$s^{-2}$ moves to numerator and becomes $s^2$.

$$\frac{6st^{-4}}{2s^{-2}t^2} = \frac{6s\,s^2}{2t^2\,t^4} \qquad \text{Law 7}$$

$$= \frac{3s^3}{t^6} \qquad \text{Law 1}$$

**(b)** We use Law 6, which allows us to change the sign of the exponent of a fraction by inverting the fraction.

$$\left(\frac{y}{3z^3}\right)^{-2} = \left(\frac{3z^3}{y}\right)^2 \qquad \text{Law 6}$$

$$= \frac{9z^6}{y^2} \qquad \text{Laws 5 and 4}$$

✎ **Practice what you've learned: Do Exercises 63 and 67.**    ▲

## ■ Scientific Notation

Exponential notation is used by scientists as a compact way of writing very large numbers and very small numbers. For example, the nearest star beyond the sun, Proxima Centauri, is approximately 40,000,000,000,000 km away. The mass of a hydrogen atom is about 0.00000000000000000000000166 g. Such numbers are difficult to read and to write, so scientists usually express them in *scientific notation*.

---

**SCIENTIFIC NOTATION**

A positive number $x$ is said to be written in **scientific notation** if it is expressed as follows:

$$x = a \times 10^n \qquad \text{where } 1 \le a < 10 \text{ and } n \text{ is an integer}$$

---

For instance, when we state that the distance to the star Proxima Centauri is $4 \times 10^{13}$ km, the positive exponent 13 indicates that the decimal point should be moved 13 places to the *right*:

$$4 \times 10^{13} = 40,\!000,\!000,\!000,\!000$$

Move decimal point 13 places to the right.

When we state that the mass of a hydrogen atom is $1.66 \times 10^{-24}$ g, the exponent $-24$ indicates that the decimal point should be moved 24 places to the *left*:

$$1.66 \times 10^{-24} = 0.00000000000000000000000166$$

Move decimal point 24 places to the left.

▶ **EXAMPLE 6** | Changing from Decimal to Scientific Notation

Write each number in scientific notation.

**(a)** 56,920          **(b)** 0.000093

▼ **SOLUTION**

**(a)** $56{,}920 = 5.692 \times 10^4$
4 places

**(b)** $0.000093 = 9.3 \times 10^{-5}$
5 places

✎ **Practice what you've learned: Do Exercises 73 and 75.** ▲

▶ **EXAMPLE 7** | Changing from Decimal to Scientific Notation

Write each number in decimal notation.

**(a)** $6.97 \times 10^9$     **(b)** $4.6271 \times 10^{-6}$

▼ **SOLUTION**

**(a)** $6.97 \times 10^9 = 6{,}970{,}000{,}000$       Move decimal 9 places to the right
9 places

**(b)** $4.6271 \times 10^{-6} = 0.0000046271$       Move decimal 6 places to the left
6 places

✎ **Practice what you've learned: Do Exercises 81 and 83.** ▲

To use scientific notation on a calculator, use a key labeled EE or EXP or EEX to enter the exponent. For example, to enter the number $3.629 \times 10^{15}$ on a TI-83 calculator, we enter

3.629 2ND EE 15

and the display reads

3.629ᴇ15

Scientific notation is often used on a calculator to display a very large or very small number. For instance, if we use a calculator to square the number 1,111,111, the display panel may show (depending on the calculator model) the approximation

| 1.234568   12 |   or   | 1.234568   E12 |

Here the final digits indicate the power of 10, and we interpret the result as

$$1.234568 \times 10^{12}$$

▶ **EXAMPLE 8** | Calculating with Scientific Notation

If $a \approx 0.00046$, $b \approx 1.697 \times 10^{22}$, and $c \approx 2.91 \times 10^{-18}$, use a calculator to approximate the quotient $ab/c$.

▼ **SOLUTION**   We could enter the data using scientific notation, or we could use laws of exponents as follows:

$$\frac{ab}{c} \approx \frac{(4.6 \times 10^{-4})(1.697 \times 10^{22})}{2.91 \times 10^{-18}}$$

$$= \frac{(4.6)(1.697)}{2.91} \times 10^{-4+22+18}$$

$$\approx 2.7 \times 10^{36}$$

We state the answer correct to two significant figures because the least accurate of the given numbers is stated to two significant figures.

✎ **Practice what you've learned: Do Exercise 91.** ▲

# P.4 EXERCISES

## ▼ CONCEPTS

**1.** Using exponential notation, we can write the product

$5 \cdot 5 \cdot 5 \cdot 5 \cdot 5 \cdot 5$ as _____ .

**2.** In the expression $3^4$, the number 3 is called the _____ ,

and the number 4 is called the _____ .

**3.** When we multiply two powers with the same base, we

_____ the exponents. So $3^4 \cdot 3^5 =$ _____ .

**4.** When we divide two powers with the same base, we _____

the exponents. So $\dfrac{3^5}{3^2} =$ _____ .

**5.** When we raise a power to a new power, we _____ the exponents. So $(3^4)^2 =$ _____.

**6.** Express the following numbers without using exponents.

   **(a)** $2^{-1} =$ _____      **(b)** $2^{-3} =$ _____

   **(c)** $\left(\frac{1}{2}\right)^{-1} =$ _____

---

## ▼ SKILLS

**7–28** ▪ Evaluate each expression.

**7.** $5^2 \cdot 5$      **8.** $2^3 \cdot 2^2$      **9.** $(2^3)^2$

**10.** $(2^3)^0$      **11.** $(-6)^0$      **12.** $-6^0$

**13.** $-3^2$      **14.** $(-3)^2$      **15.** $\left(\frac{1}{3}\right)^4 (-3)^2$

**16.** $5^4 \cdot 5^{-2}$      **17.** $\dfrac{10^7}{10^4}$      **18.** $\dfrac{3}{3^{-2}}$

**19.** $\left(\frac{5}{3}\right)^0 2^{-1}$      **20.** $\dfrac{2^{-3}}{3^0}$      **21.** $\left(\frac{1}{4}\right)^{-2}$

**22.** $\left(\frac{2}{3}\right)^{-3}$      **23.** $\left(\frac{3}{2}\right)^{-2} \cdot \frac{9}{16}$      **24.** $\left(\frac{1}{2}\right)^4 \left(\frac{5}{2}\right)^{-2}$

**25.** $\left(\frac{1}{13}\right)^0 \left(\frac{2}{3}\right)^6 \left(\frac{4}{9}\right)^{-3}$      **26.** $\dfrac{3^2 \cdot 4^{-2} \cdot 5}{2^{-4} \cdot 3^3 \cdot 25}$

**27.** $2^{-2} + 2^{-3}$      **28.** $3^{-1} - 3^{-3}$

**29–46** ▪ Simplify each expression.

**29.** $x^8 x^2$      **30.** $(3y^2)(4y^5)$      **31.** $x^2 x^{-6}$

**32.** $x^{-5} x^3$      **33.** $w^{-2} w^{-4} w^6$      **34.** $z^5 z^{-3} z^{-4}$

**35.** $\dfrac{y^{10} y^0}{y^7}$      **36.** $\dfrac{x^6}{x^{10}}$      **37.** $\dfrac{a^9 a^{-2}}{a}$

**38.** $\dfrac{z^2 z^4}{z^3 z^{-1}}$      **39.** $(2y^2)^3$      **40.** $(8x)^2$

**41.** $(a^2 a^4)^3$      **42.** $(2a^3 a^2)^4$      **43.** $(3z)^2 (6z^2)^{-3}$

**44.** $(2z^2)^{-5} z^{10}$      **45.** $\left(\dfrac{a^2}{4}\right)^3$      **46.** $\left(\dfrac{3x^4}{4x^2}\right)^2$

**47–72** ▪ Simplify the expression and eliminate any negative exponent(s).

**47.** $(4x^2 y^4)(2x^5 y)$      **48.** $(8a^2 z)(\frac{1}{2} a^3 z^4)$

**49.** $b^4 (3ab^3)(2a^2 b^{-5})$      **50.** $(2s^3 t^{-2})(\frac{1}{4} s^7 t)(16t^4)$

**51.** $(5x^2 y^3)(3x^2 y^5)^4$      **52.** $(2a^3 b^2)^2 (5a^2 b^5)^3$

**53.** $(s^{-2} t^2)^2 (s^2 t)^3$      **54.** $(2u^2 v^3)^3 (3u^{-3} v)^2$

**55.** $(rs)^{-2}(2rs^2)^3$      **56.** $(3x^{-1} y^{-2})^{-2}(x^2 y^5)^{-1}$

**57.** $\dfrac{6y^3 z}{2yz^2}$      **58.** $\dfrac{2x^3 y^4}{x^5 y^3}$

**59.** $\dfrac{(xy^2 z^3)^4}{(x^2 y^2 z)^3}$      **60.** $\dfrac{(2v^3 w)^2}{v^3 w^2}$

**61.** $\left(\dfrac{a^2}{b}\right)^5 \left(\dfrac{a^3 b^2}{c^3}\right)^3$      **62.** $\left(\dfrac{x^4 z^2}{4y^5}\right)\left(\dfrac{2x^3 y^2}{z^3}\right)^2$

**63.** $\dfrac{8a^3 b^{-4}}{2a^{-5} b^5}$      **64.** $\dfrac{5xy^{-2}}{x^{-1} y^{-3}}$

**65.** $\dfrac{(u^{-1} v^2)^2}{(u^3 v^{-2})^3}$      **66.** $\dfrac{(rs^2)^3}{(r^{-3} s^2)^2}$

**67.** $\left(\dfrac{3a}{b^3}\right)^{-1}$      **68.** $\left(\dfrac{x^2 y}{2y^3}\right)^{-2}$

**69.** $\left(\dfrac{y}{5x^{-2}}\right)^{-3}$      **70.** $\left(\dfrac{2a^{-1} b}{a^2 b^{-3}}\right)^{-3}$

**71.** $\left(\dfrac{q^{-1} r^{-1} s^{-2}}{r^{-5} sq^{-8}}\right)^{-1}$      **72.** $\left(\dfrac{xy^{-2} z^{-3}}{x^2 y^3 z^{-4}}\right)^{-3}$

**73–80** ▪ Write each number in scientific notation.

**73.** 69,300,000      **74.** 7,200,000,000,000

**75.** 0.000028536      **76.** 0.0001213

**77.** 129,540,000      **78.** 7,259,000,000

**79.** 0.0000000014      **80.** 0.0007029

**81–88** ▪ Write each number in decimal notation.

**81.** $3.19 \times 10^5$      **82.** $2.721 \times 10^8$

**83.** $2.670 \times 10^{-8}$      **84.** $9.999 \times 10^{-9}$

**85.** $7.1 \times 10^{14}$      **86.** $6 \times 10^{12}$

**87.** $8.55 \times 10^{-3}$      **88.** $6.257 \times 10^{-10}$

**89–90** ▪ Write the number indicated in each statement in scientific notation.

**89.** **(a)** A light-year, the distance that light travels in one year, is about 5,900,000,000,000 mi.

   **(b)** The diameter of an electron is about 0.0000000000004 cm.

   **(c)** A drop of water contains more than 33 billion billion molecules.

**90.** **(a)** The distance from the earth to the sun is about 93 million miles.

   **(b)** The mass of an oxygen molecule is about 0.000000000000000000000053 g.

   **(c)** The mass of the earth is about 5,970,000,000,000,000,000,000,000 kg.

**91–96** ▪ Use scientific notation, the Laws of Exponents, and a calculator to perform the indicated operations. State your answer correct to the number of significant digits indicated by the given data.

**91.** $(7.2 \times 10^{-9})(1.806 \times 10^{-12})$

**92.** $(1.062 \times 10^{24})(8.61 \times 10^{19})$

**93.** $\dfrac{1.295643 \times 10^9}{(3.610 \times 10^{-17})(2.511 \times 10^6)}$

**94.** $\dfrac{(73.1)(1.6341 \times 10^{28})}{0.0000000019}$

**95.** $\dfrac{(0.0000162)(0.01582)}{(594,621,000)(0.0058)}$

**96.** $\dfrac{(3.542 \times 10^{-6})^9}{(5.05 \times 10^4)^{12}}$

**97.** Prove the given Laws of Exponents for the case in which $m$ and $n$ are positive integers and $m > n$.

   **(a)** Law 2      **(b)** Law 5

**98.** Prove Law 6 of Exponents.

## ▼ APPLICATIONS

**99. Distance to the Nearest Star** Proxima Centauri, the star nearest to our solar system, is 4.3 light-years away. Use the information in Exercise 89(a) to express this distance in miles.

**100. Speed of Light** The speed of light is about 186,000 mi/s. Use the information in Exercise 90(a) to find how long it takes for a light ray from the sun to reach the earth.

**101. Volume of the Oceans** The average ocean depth is $3.7 \times 10^3$ m, and the area of the oceans is $3.6 \times 10^{14}$ m². What is the total volume of the ocean in liters? (One cubic meter contains 1000 liters.)

**102. National Debt** As of January 2001, the population of the United States was $2.83 \times 10^8$, and the national debt was $5.736 \times 10^{12}$ dollars. How much was each person's share of the debt?

**103. Number of Molecules** A sealed room in a hospital, measuring 5 m wide, 10 m long, and 3 m high, is filled with pure oxygen. One cubic meter contains 1000 L, and 22.4 L of any gas contains $6.02 \times 10^{23}$ molecules (Avogadro's number). How many molecules of oxygen are there in the room?

**104. Body-Mass Index** The body-mass index is a measure that medical researchers use to determine whether a person is overweight, underweight, or of normal weight. For a person who weighs $W$ pounds and who is $H$ inches tall, the body-mass index $B$ is given by

$$B = 703\frac{W}{H^2}$$

A body-mass index is considered "normal" if it satisfies $18.5 \le B \le 24.9$, while a person with body-mass index $B \ge 30$ is considered obese.

(a) Calculate the body-mass index for each person listed in the table, then determine whether he or she is of normal weight, underweight, overweight, or obese.

| Person | Weight | Height |
|--------|--------|--------|
| Brian | 295 lb | 5 ft 10 in. |
| Linda | 105 lb | 5 ft 6 in. |
| Larry | 220 lb | 6 ft 4 in. |
| Helen | 110 lb | 5 ft 2 in. |

(b) Determine your own body-mass index.

**105. Interest on a CD** A sum of $5000 is invested in a 5-year certificate of deposit paying 3% interest per year, compounded monthly. After $n$ years, the amount of interest $I$ that has accumulated is given by

$$I = 5000[(1.0025)^{12n} - 1]$$

Complete the following table, which gives the amount of interest accumulated after the given number of years.

| Year | Total interest |
|------|----------------|
| 1 | $152.08 |
| 2 | 308.79 |
| 3 | |
| 4 | |
| 5 | |

## ▼ DISCOVERY • DISCUSSION • WRITING

**106. How Big Is a Billion?** If you have a million $(10^6)$ dollars in a suitcase and you spend a thousand $(10^3)$ dollars each day, how many years would it take you to use all the money? If you spent at the same rate, how many years would it take you to empty a suitcase filled with a *billion* $(10^9)$ dollars?

**107. Easy Powers That Look Hard** Calculate these expressions in your head. Use the Laws of Exponents to help you.

(a) $\dfrac{18^5}{9^5}$      (b) $20^6 \cdot (0.5)^6$

**108. Distances between Powers** Which pair of numbers is closer together?

$10^{10}$ and $10^{50}$     or     $10^{100}$ and $10^{101}$

**109. Signs of Numbers** Let $a$, $b$, and $c$ be real numbers with $a > 0$, $b < 0$, and $c < 0$. Determine the sign of each expression.

(a) $b^5$      (b) $b^{10}$      (c) $ab^2c^3$

(d) $(b - a)^3$      (e) $(b - a)^4$      (f) $\dfrac{a^3c^3}{b^6c^6}$

---

# P.5 | Rational Exponents and Radicals

## LEARNING OBJECTIVES:

After completing this section, you will be able to:

■ Simplify expressions involving radicals
■ Simplify expressions involving rational exponents
■ Express radicals using rational exponents
■ Rationalize a denominator

In this section we learn to work with expressions that contain radicals or rational exponents.

## ■ Radicals

We know what $2^n$ means whenever $n$ is an integer. To give meaning to a power, such as $2^{4/5}$, whose exponent is a rational number, we need to discuss radicals.

The symbol $\sqrt{\phantom{a}}$ means "the positive square root of." Thus,

$$\sqrt{a} = b \quad \text{means} \quad b^2 = a \quad \text{and} \quad b \geq 0$$

It is true that the number 9 has two square roots, 3 and $-3$, but the notation $\sqrt{9}$ is reserved for the *positive* square root of 9 (sometimes called the *principal square root* of 9). If we want the negative root, we must write $-\sqrt{9}$, which is $-3$.

Since $a = b^2 \geq 0$, the symbol $\sqrt{a}$ makes sense only when $a \geq 0$. For instance,

$$\sqrt{9} = 3 \quad \text{because} \quad 3^2 = 9 \quad \text{and} \quad 3 \geq 0$$

Square roots are special cases of $n$th roots. The $n$th root of $x$ is the number that, when raised to the $n$th power, gives $x$.

---

**DEFINITION OF $n$th ROOT**

If $n$ is any positive integer, then the **principal $n$th root** of $a$ is defined as follows:

$$\sqrt[n]{a} = b \quad \text{means} \quad b^n = a$$

If $n$ is even, we must have $a \geq 0$ and $b \geq 0$.

---

Thus

$$\sqrt[4]{81} = 3 \quad \text{because} \quad 3^4 = 81 \quad \text{and} \quad 3 \geq 0$$

$$\sqrt[3]{-8} = -2 \quad \text{because} \quad (-2)^3 = -8$$

But $\sqrt{-8}$, $\sqrt[4]{-8}$, and $\sqrt[6]{-8}$ are not defined. (For instance, $\sqrt{-8}$ is not defined because the square of every real number is nonnegative.)

Notice that

$$\sqrt{4^2} = \sqrt{16} = 4 \quad \text{but} \quad \sqrt{(-4)^2} = \sqrt{16} = 4 = |-4|$$

So the equation $\sqrt{a^2} = a$ is not always true; it is true only when $a \geq 0$. However, we can always write $\sqrt{a^2} = |a|$. This last equation is true not only for square roots, but for any even root. This and other rules used in working with $n$th roots are listed in the following box. In each property we assume that all the given roots exist.

---

**PROPERTIES OF $n$th ROOTS**

| Property | Example |
|---|---|
| 1. $\sqrt[n]{ab} = \sqrt[n]{a}\sqrt[n]{b}$ | $\sqrt[3]{-8 \cdot 27} = \sqrt[3]{-8}\sqrt[3]{27} = (-2)(3) = -6$ |
| 2. $\sqrt[n]{\dfrac{a}{b}} = \dfrac{\sqrt[n]{a}}{\sqrt[n]{b}}$ | $\sqrt[4]{\dfrac{16}{81}} = \dfrac{\sqrt[4]{16}}{\sqrt[4]{81}} = \dfrac{2}{3}$ |
| 3. $\sqrt[m]{\sqrt[n]{a}} = \sqrt[mn]{a}$ | $\sqrt{\sqrt[3]{729}} = \sqrt[6]{729} = 3$ |
| 4. $\sqrt[n]{a^n} = a$   if $n$ is odd | $\sqrt[3]{(-5)^3} = -5, \ \sqrt[5]{2^5} = 2$ |
| 5. $\sqrt[n]{a^n} = |a|$   if $n$ is even | $\sqrt[4]{(-3)^4} = |-3| = 3$ |

---

▶ **EXAMPLE 1** | Simplifying Expressions Involving $n$th Roots

(a) $\sqrt[3]{x^4} = \sqrt[3]{x^3 x}$      Factor out the largest cube

$\qquad\quad = \sqrt[3]{x^3}\sqrt[3]{x}$     Property 1: $\sqrt[3]{ab} = \sqrt[3]{a}\sqrt[3]{b}$

$\qquad\quad = x\sqrt[3]{x}$        Property 4: $\sqrt[3]{a^3} = a$

**(b)** $\sqrt[4]{81x^8y^4} = \sqrt[4]{81}\sqrt[4]{x^8}\sqrt[4]{y^4}$     Property 1: $\sqrt[4]{abc} = \sqrt[4]{a}\sqrt[4]{b}\sqrt[4]{c}$

$\qquad\qquad\quad = 3\sqrt[4]{(x^2)^4}|y|$     Property 5: $\sqrt[4]{a^4} = |a|$

$\qquad\qquad\quad = 3x^2|y|$     Property 5: $\sqrt[4]{a^4} = |a|$, $|x^2| = x^2$

✎ **Practice what you've learned: Do Exercises 31 and 33.**   ▲

It is frequently useful to combine like radicals in an expression such as $2\sqrt{3} + 5\sqrt{3}$. This can be done by using the Distributive Property. Thus,

$$2\sqrt{3} + 5\sqrt{3} = (2 + 5)\sqrt{3} = 7\sqrt{3}$$

The next example further illustrates this process.

⊘ Avoid making the following error:

$$\sqrt{a + b} \ \cancel{\times} \ \sqrt{a} + \sqrt{b}$$

For instance, if we let $a = 9$ and $b = 16$, then we see the error:

$$\sqrt{9 + 16} \overset{?}{=} \sqrt{9} + \sqrt{16}$$

$$\sqrt{25} \overset{?}{=} 3 + 4$$

$$5 \overset{?}{=} 7 \quad \text{Wrong!}$$

▶ **EXAMPLE 2** | Combining Radicals

$\sqrt{32} + \sqrt{200} = \sqrt{16 \cdot 2} + \sqrt{100 \cdot 2}$     Factor out the largest squares

$\qquad\qquad\qquad = \sqrt{16}\sqrt{2} + \sqrt{100}\sqrt{2}$     Property 1

$\qquad\qquad\qquad = 4\sqrt{2} + 10\sqrt{2} = 14\sqrt{2}$     Distributive Property

✎ **Practice what you've learned: Do Exercise 39.**   ▲

## ■ Rational Exponents

To define what is meant by a *rational exponent* or, equivalently, a *fractional exponent* such as $a^{1/3}$, we need to use radicals. To give meaning to the symbol $a^{1/n}$ in a way that is consistent with the Laws of Exponents, we would have to have

$$(a^{1/n})^n = a^{(1/n)n} = a^1 = a$$

So by the definition of $n$th root,

$$\boxed{a^{1/n} = \sqrt[n]{a}}$$

In general, we define rational exponents as follows.

**DEFINITION OF RATIONAL EXPONENTS**

For any rational exponent $m/n$ in lowest terms, where $m$ and $n$ are integers and $n > 0$, we define

$$a^{m/n} = (\sqrt[n]{a})^m \quad \text{or, equivalently,} \quad a^{m/n} = \sqrt[n]{a^m}$$

If $n$ is even, then we require that $a \geq 0$.

With this definition it can be proved that *the Laws of Exponents also hold for rational exponents.*

▶ **EXAMPLE 3** | Using the Definition of Rational Exponents

**(a)** $4^{1/2} = \sqrt{4} = 2$

**(b)** $8^{2/3} = (\sqrt[3]{8})^2 = 2^2 = 4$     Alternative solution: $8^{2/3} = \sqrt[3]{8^2} = \sqrt[3]{64} = 4$

**(c)** $(125)^{-1/3} = \dfrac{1}{125^{1/3}} = \dfrac{1}{\sqrt[3]{125}} = \dfrac{1}{5}$

**(d)** $\dfrac{1}{\sqrt[3]{x^4}} = \dfrac{1}{x^{4/3}} = x^{-4/3}$

✎ **Practice what you've learned: Do Exercises 17 and 19.** ▲

▶ **EXAMPLE 4** | Using the Laws of Exponents with Rational Exponents

**(a)** $a^{1/3}a^{7/3} = a^{8/3}$ $\qquad\qquad\qquad\qquad$ Law 1: $a^m a^n = a^{m+n}$

**(b)** $\dfrac{a^{2/5}a^{7/5}}{a^{3/5}} = a^{2/5 + 7/5 - 3/5} = a^{6/5}$ $\qquad$ Law 1, Law 2: $\dfrac{a^m}{a^n} = a^{m-n}$

**(c)** $(2a^3b^4)^{3/2} = 2^{3/2}(a^3)^{3/2}(b^4)^{3/2}$ $\qquad$ Law 4: $(abc)^n = a^n b^n c^n$

$\qquad\qquad = (\sqrt{2})^3 a^{3(3/2)} b^{4(3/2)}$ $\qquad\qquad$ Law 3: $(a^m)^n = a^{mn}$

$\qquad\qquad = 2\sqrt{2}\, a^{9/2} b^6$

**(d)** $\left(\dfrac{2x^{3/4}}{y^{1/3}}\right)^3 \left(\dfrac{y^4}{x^{-1/2}}\right) = \dfrac{2^3(x^{3/4})^3}{(y^{1/3})^3} \cdot (y^4 x^{1/2})$ $\qquad$ Laws 5, 4, and 7

$\qquad\qquad\qquad = \dfrac{8x^{9/4}}{y} \cdot y^4 x^{1/2}$ $\qquad\qquad$ Law 3

$\qquad\qquad\qquad = 8x^{11/4}y^3$ $\qquad\qquad\qquad$ Laws 1 and 2

✎ **Practice what you've learned: Do Exercises 53, 61 and 65.** ▲

▶ **EXAMPLE 5** | Simplifying by Writing Radicals as Rational Exponents

**(a)** $(2\sqrt{x})(3\sqrt[3]{x}) = (2x^{1/2})(3x^{1/3})$ $\qquad$ *Definition of rational exponents*

$\qquad\qquad\quad = 6x^{1/2 + 1/3} = 6x^{5/6}$ $\qquad$ *Law 1*

**(b)** $\sqrt{x\sqrt{x}} = (xx^{1/2})^{1/2}$ $\qquad\qquad\qquad$ *Definition of rational exponents*

$\qquad\quad = (x^{3/2})^{1/2}$ $\qquad\qquad\qquad\qquad$ *Law 1*

$\qquad\quad = x^{3/4}$ $\qquad\qquad\qquad\qquad\qquad$ *Law 3*

✎ **Practice what you've learned: Do Exercises 71 and 81.** ▲

## ■ Rationalizing the Denominator

It is often useful to eliminate the radical in a denominator by multiplying both numerator and denominator by an appropriate expression. This procedure is called **rationalizing the denominator**. If the denominator is of the form $\sqrt{a}$, we multiply numerator and denominator by $\sqrt{a}$. In doing this, we multiply the given quantity by 1, so we do not change its value. For instance,

$$\frac{1}{\sqrt{a}} = \frac{1}{\sqrt{a}} \cdot 1 = \frac{1}{\sqrt{a}} \cdot \frac{\sqrt{a}}{\sqrt{a}} = \frac{\sqrt{a}}{a}$$

Note that the denominator in the last fraction contains no radical. In general, if the denominator is of the form $\sqrt[n]{a^m}$ with $m < n$, then multiplying the numerator and denominator by $\sqrt[n]{a^{n-m}}$ will rationalize the denominator, because (for $a > 0$)

$$\sqrt[n]{a^m}\sqrt[n]{a^{n-m}} = \sqrt[n]{a^{m+n-m}} = \sqrt[n]{a^n} = a$$

▶ **EXAMPLE 6** | Rationalizing Denominators

Rationalize the denominator in each fraction.

(a) $\dfrac{2}{\sqrt{3}}$    (b) $\dfrac{1}{\sqrt[3]{5}}$    (c) $\dfrac{1}{\sqrt[5]{5x^2}}$

▼ **SOLUTION**

This equals 1.

(a) $\dfrac{2}{\sqrt{3}} = \dfrac{2}{\sqrt{3}} \cdot \dfrac{\sqrt{3}}{\sqrt{3}}$     Multiply by $\dfrac{\sqrt{3}}{\sqrt{3}}$

$= \dfrac{2\sqrt{3}}{3}$     $\sqrt{3} \cdot \sqrt{3} = 3$

(b) $\dfrac{1}{\sqrt[3]{5}} = \dfrac{1}{\sqrt[3]{5}} \cdot \dfrac{\sqrt[3]{5^2}}{\sqrt[3]{5^2}}$     Multiply by $\dfrac{\sqrt[3]{5^2}}{\sqrt[3]{5^2}}$

$= \dfrac{\sqrt[3]{25}}{5}$     $\sqrt[3]{5} \cdot \sqrt[3]{5^2} = \sqrt[3]{5^3} = 5$

(c) $\dfrac{1}{\sqrt[5]{x^2}} = \dfrac{1}{\sqrt[5]{x^2}} \cdot \dfrac{\sqrt[5]{x^3}}{\sqrt[5]{x^3}}$     Multiply by $\dfrac{\sqrt[5]{x^3}}{\sqrt[5]{x^3}}$

$= \dfrac{\sqrt[5]{x^3}}{x}$     $\sqrt[5]{x^2} \cdot \sqrt[5]{x^3} = \sqrt[5]{x^5} = x$

✎ **Practice what you've learned: Do Exercises 83 and 87.** ▲

# P.5 EXERCISES

## ▼ CONCEPTS

1. Using exponential notation, we can write $\sqrt[3]{5}$ as _____.

2. Using radicals, we can write $5^{1/2}$ as _____.

3. Is there a difference between $\sqrt{5^2}$ and $(\sqrt{5})^2$? Explain.

4. Explain what $4^{3/2}$ means, then calculate $4^{3/2}$ in two different ways:

$\left(4^{1/2}\right)^{\boxed{\phantom{x}}} = $ _____    or    $\left(4^3\right)^{\boxed{\phantom{x}}} = $ _____

5. Explain how we rationalize a denominator, then complete the following steps to rationalize $\dfrac{1}{\sqrt{3}}$:

$\dfrac{1}{\sqrt{3}} = \dfrac{1}{\sqrt{3}} \cdot \dfrac{\boxed{\phantom{x}}}{\boxed{\phantom{x}}} = \dfrac{\boxed{\phantom{x}}}{\boxed{\phantom{x}}}$

6. Find the missing power in the following calculation:
$5^{1/3} \cdot 5^{\boxed{\phantom{x}}} = 5$.

## ▼ SKILLS

**7–14** ▪ Write each radical expression using exponents, and each exponential expression using radicals.

| | Radical expression | Exponential expression |
|---|---|---|
| 7. | $\dfrac{1}{\sqrt{5}}$ | |
| 8. | $\sqrt[3]{7^2}$ | |
| 9. | | $4^{2/3}$ |
| 10. | | $11^{-3/2}$ |
| 11. | $\sqrt[5]{5^3}$ | |
| 12. | | $2^{-1.5}$ |
| 13. | | $a^{2/5}$ |
| 14. | $\dfrac{1}{\sqrt{x^5}}$ | |

**15–24** ▪ Evaluate each expression.

15. (a) $\sqrt{16}$    (b) $\sqrt[4]{16}$    (c) $\sqrt[4]{\frac{1}{16}}$

16. (a) $\sqrt{64}$    (b) $\sqrt[3]{-64}$    (c) $\sqrt[5]{-32}$

✎ 17. (a) $\sqrt{\frac{4}{9}}$    (b) $\sqrt[4]{256}$    (c) $\sqrt[6]{\frac{1}{64}}$

18. (a) $\sqrt{7}\sqrt{28}$    (b) $\dfrac{\sqrt{48}}{\sqrt{3}}$    (c) $\sqrt[4]{24}\sqrt[4]{54}$

✎ 19. (a) $\left(\frac{4}{9}\right)^{-1/2}$    (b) $(-32)^{2/5}$    (c) $(-125)^{-1/3}$

20. (a) $1024^{-0.1}$    (b) $\left(-\frac{27}{8}\right)^{2/3}$    (c) $\left(\frac{25}{64}\right)^{3/2}$

21. (a) $\left(\frac{1}{32}\right)^{2/5}$    (b) $(27)^{-4/3}$    (c) $\left(\frac{1}{8}\right)^{-2/3}$

22. (a) $(-1000)^{-2/3}$    (b) $10,000^{-3/2}$    (c) $(-8000)^{4/3}$

23. (a) $100^{-1.5}$    (b) $4^{2/3} \cdot 6^{2/3} \cdot 9^{2/3}$    (c) $0.001^{-2/3}$

24. (a) $\left(\frac{1}{16}\right)^{-0.75}$    (b) $0.25^{-0.5}$    (c) $9^{1/3} \cdot 15^{1/3} \cdot 25^{1/3}$

**25–28** ▪ Evaluate the expression using $x = 3$, $y = 4$, and $z = -1$.

25. $\sqrt{x^2 + y^2}$    26. $\sqrt[4]{x^3 + 14y + 2z}$

27. $(9x)^{2/3} + (2y)^{2/3} + z^{2/3}$    28. $(xy)^{2z}$

**29–38** ▪ Simplify the expression. Assume the letters denote any real numbers.

**29.** $\sqrt[4]{x^4}$

**30.** $\sqrt[5]{x^{10}}$

**31.** $\sqrt[4]{16x^8}$

**32.** $\sqrt[3]{x^3y^6}$

**33.** $\sqrt[3]{x^3y}$

**34.** $\sqrt{x^4y^4}$

**35.** $\sqrt[5]{a^6b^7}$

**36.** $\sqrt[3]{a^2b}\,\sqrt[3]{a^4b}$

**37.** $\sqrt[3]{\sqrt{64x^6}}$

**38.** $\sqrt[4]{x^4y^2z^2}$

**39–48** ▪ Simplify the expression.

**39.** $\sqrt{32} + \sqrt{18}$

**40.** $\sqrt{75} + \sqrt{48}$

**41.** $\sqrt{125} - \sqrt{45}$

**42.** $\sqrt[3]{54} - \sqrt[3]{16}$

**43.** $\sqrt[3]{108} - \sqrt[3]{32}$

**44.** $\sqrt{8} + \sqrt{50}$

**45.** $\sqrt{245} - \sqrt{125}$

**46.** $\sqrt[3]{24} - \sqrt[3]{81}$

**47.** $\sqrt[5]{96} + \sqrt[5]{3}$

**48.** $\sqrt[4]{48} - \sqrt[4]{3}$

**49–68** ▪ Simplify the expression and eliminate any negative exponent(s). Assume that all letters denote positive numbers.

**49.** $x^{3/4}x^{5/4}$

**50.** $y^{2/3}y^{4/3}$

**51.** $(4b)^{1/2}(8b^{1/4})$

**52.** $(3a^{3/4})^2(5a^{1/2})$

**53.** $\dfrac{w^{4/3}w^{2/3}}{w^{1/3}}$

**54.** $\dfrac{s^{5/2}(2s^{5/4})^2}{s^{1/2}}$

**55.** $(8a^6b^{3/2})^{2/3}$

**56.** $(4a^6b^8)^{3/2}$

**57.** $(8y^3)^{-2/3}$

**58.** $(u^4v^6)^{-1/3}$

**59.** $(x^{-5}y^{1/3})^{-3/5}$

**60.** $(2x^3y^{-1/4})^2(8y^{-3/2})^{-1/3}$

**61.** $\dfrac{(8s^3t^3)^{2/3}}{(s^4t^{-8})^{1/4}}$

**62.** $\dfrac{(32y^{-5}z^{10})^{1/5}}{(64y^6z^{-12})^{-1/6}}$

**63.** $\left(\dfrac{x^8y^{-4}}{16y^{4/3}}\right)^{-1/4}$

**64.** $\left(\dfrac{-8y^{3/4}}{y^3z^6}\right)^{-1/3}$

**65.** $\left(\dfrac{x^{-2/3}}{y^{1/2}}\right)\left(\dfrac{x^{-2}}{y^{-3}}\right)^{1/6}$

**66.** $\left(\dfrac{4y^3z^{2/3}}{x^{1/2}}\right)^2\left(\dfrac{x^{-3}y^6}{8z^4}\right)^{1/3}$

**67.** $\left(\dfrac{a^{1/6}b^{-3}}{x^{-1}y}\right)^3\left(\dfrac{x^{-2}b^{-1}}{a^{3/2}y^{1/3}}\right)$

**68.** $\dfrac{(9st)^{3/2}}{(27s^3t^{-4})^{2/3}}\left(\dfrac{3s^{-2}}{4t^{1/3}}\right)^{-1}$

**69–82** ▪ Simplify the expression and express the answer using rational exponents. Assume that all letters denote positive numbers.

**69.** $\left(\sqrt[6]{y^5}\right)\left(\sqrt[3]{y^2}\right)$

**70.** $\sqrt[4]{b^3}\sqrt{b}$

**71.** $\left(5\sqrt[3]{x}\right)\left(2\sqrt[4]{x}\right)$

**72.** $\left(2\sqrt{a}\right)\left(\sqrt[3]{a^2}\right)$

**73.** $\sqrt{4st^3}\sqrt[6]{s^3t^2}$

**74.** $\sqrt[5]{x^3y^2}\sqrt[10]{x^4y^{16}}$

**75.** $\dfrac{\sqrt[4]{x^7}}{\sqrt[4]{x^3}}$

**76.** $\dfrac{\sqrt[3]{8x^2}}{\sqrt{x}}$

**77.** $\dfrac{\sqrt{xy}}{\sqrt[3]{16xy}}$

**78.** $\dfrac{\sqrt{a^3b}}{\sqrt[4]{a^3b^2}}$

**79.** $\sqrt{\dfrac{16u^3v}{uv^5}}$

**80.** $\sqrt[3]{\dfrac{54x^2y^4}{2x^5y}}$

**81.** $\sqrt[3]{y\sqrt{y}}$

**82.** $\sqrt{s\sqrt{s^3}}$

**83–88** ▪ Rationalize the denominator.

**83.** (a) $\dfrac{1}{\sqrt{6}}$ (b) $\dfrac{3}{\sqrt{2}}$ (c) $\dfrac{9}{\sqrt{3}}$

**84.** (a) $\dfrac{12}{\sqrt{3}}$ (b) $\dfrac{5}{\sqrt{2}}$ (c) $\dfrac{2}{\sqrt{6}}$

**85.** (a) $\dfrac{1}{\sqrt[3]{4}}$ (b) $\dfrac{1}{\sqrt[4]{3}}$ (c) $\dfrac{8}{\sqrt[5]{2}}$

**86.** (a) $\dfrac{1}{\sqrt[5]{2^3}}$ (b) $\dfrac{2}{\sqrt[4]{3}}$ (c) $\dfrac{3}{\sqrt[4]{2^3}}$

**87.** (a) $\dfrac{1}{\sqrt[3]{x}}$ (b) $\dfrac{1}{\sqrt[5]{x^2}}$ (c) $\dfrac{1}{\sqrt[7]{x^3}}$

**88.** (a) $\dfrac{1}{\sqrt[3]{x^2}}$ (b) $\dfrac{1}{\sqrt[4]{x^3}}$ (c) $\dfrac{1}{\sqrt[3]{x^4}}$

## ▼ APPLICATIONS

**89. How Far Can You See?**    Because of the curvature of the earth, the maximum distance $D$ that you can see from the top of a tall building of height $h$ is estimated by the formula

$$D = \sqrt{2rh + h^2}$$

where $r = 3960$ mi is the radius of the earth and $D$ and $h$ are also measured in miles. How far can you see from the observation deck of the Toronto CN Tower, 1135 ft above the ground?

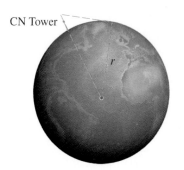

CN Tower

$r$

**90. Speed of a Skidding Car**    Police use the formula $s = \sqrt{30\,fd}$ to estimate the speed $s$ (in mi/h) at which a car is traveling if it skids $d$ feet after the brakes are applied suddenly. The number $f$ is the coefficient of friction of the road, which is a measure of the "slipperiness" of the road. The table gives some typical estimates for $f$.

|      | Tar | Concrete | Gravel |
|------|-----|----------|--------|
| **Dry** | 1.0 | 0.8 | 0.2 |
| **Wet** | 0.5 | 0.4 | 0.1 |

(a) If a car skids 65 ft on wet concrete, how fast was it moving when the brakes were applied?

**(b)** If a car is traveling at 50 mi/h, how far will it skid on wet tar?

**91. Sailboat Races** The speed that a sailboat is capable of sailing is determined by three factors: its total length $L$, the surface area $A$ of its sails, and its displacement $V$ (the volume of water it displaces), as shown in the sketch.

In general, a sailboat is capable of greater speed if it is longer, has a larger sail area, or displaces less water. To make sailing races fair, only boats in the same "class" can qualify to race together. For a certain race, a boat is considered to qualify if

$$0.30L + 0.38A^{1/2} - 3V^{1/3} \le 16$$

where $L$ is measured in feet, $A$ in square feet, and $V$ in cubic feet. Use this inequality to answer the following questions.

**(a)** A sailboat has length 60 ft, sail area 3400 ft$^2$, and displacement 650 ft$^3$. Does this boat qualify for the race?

**(b)** A sailboat has length 65 ft and displaces 600 ft$^3$. What is the largest possible sail area that could be used and still allow the boat to qualify for this race?

**92. Flow Speed in a Channel** The speed of water flowing in a channel, such as a canal or river bed, is governed by the Manning Equation,

$$V = 1.486 \frac{A^{2/3}S^{1/2}}{p^{2/3}n}$$

Here $V$ is the velocity of the flow in ft/s; $A$ is the cross-sectional area of the channel in square feet; $S$ is the downward slope of the channel; $p$ is the wetted perimeter in feet (the distance from the top of one bank, down the side of the channel, across the bottom, and up to the top of the other bank); and $n$ is the roughness coefficient (a measure of the roughness of the channel bottom). This equation is used to predict the capacity of flood channels to handle runoff from heavy rainfalls. For the canal shown in the figure, $A = 75$ ft$^2$, $S = 0.050$, $p = 24.1$ ft, and $n = 0.040$.

**(a)** Find the speed at which water flows through the canal.

**(b)** How many cubic feet of water can the canal discharge per second? [*Hint:* Multiply $V$ by $A$ to get the volume of the flow per second.]

---

▼ **DISCOVERY · DISCUSSION · WRITING**

**93. Limiting Behavior of Powers** Complete the following tables. What happens to the $n$th root of 2 as $n$ gets large? What about the $n$th root of $\frac{1}{2}$?

| $n$ | $2^{1/n}$ |
|---|---|
| 1 | |
| 2 | |
| 5 | |
| 10 | |
| 100 | |

| $n$ | $\left(\frac{1}{2}\right)^{1/n}$ |
|---|---|
| 1 | |
| 2 | |
| 5 | |
| 10 | |
| 100 | |

Construct a similar table for $n^{1/n}$. What happens to the $n$th root of $n$ as $n$ gets large?

**94. Comparing Roots** Without using a calculator, determine which number is larger in each pair.

**(a)** $2^{1/2}$ or $2^{1/3}$      **(b)** $\left(\frac{1}{2}\right)^{1/2}$ or $\left(\frac{1}{2}\right)^{1/3}$

**(c)** $7^{1/4}$ or $4^{1/3}$      **(d)** $\sqrt[3]{5}$ or $\sqrt{3}$

---

## P.6 | Algebraic Expressions

### LEARNING OBJECTIVES

After completing this section, you will be able to:

■ Add and subtract polynomials

■ Multiply algebraic expressions

■ Use the Special Product Formulas

A **variable** is a letter that can represent any number from a given set of numbers. If we start with variables such as $x$, $y$, and $z$ and some real numbers and we combine them using addition, subtraction, multiplication, division, powers, and roots, we obtain an **algebraic expression.** Here are some examples:

$$2x^2 - 3x + 4 \qquad \sqrt{x} + 10 \qquad \frac{y - 2z}{y^2 + 4}$$

A **monomial** is an expression of the form $ax^k$, where $a$ is a real number and $k$ is a nonnegative integer. A **binomial** is a sum of two monomials, and a **trinomial** is a sum of three monomials. In general, a sum of monomials is called a *polynomial*. For example, the first expression listed above is a polynomial, but the other two are not.

---

### POLYNOMIALS

A **polynominal** in the variable $x$ is an expression of the form

$$a_n x^n + a_{n-1}x^{n-1} + \cdots + a_1 x + a_0$$

where $a_0, a_1, \ldots, a_n$ are real numbers and $n$ is a nonnegative integer. If $a_n \neq 0$, then the polynomial has **degree $n$**. The monomials $a_k x^k$ that make up the polynomial are called the **terms** of the polynomial.

---

Note that the degree of a polynomial is the highest power of the variable that appears in the polynomial.

| Polynomial | Type | Terms | Degree |
|---|---|---|---|
| $2x^2 - 3x + 4$ | trinomial | $2x^2, -3x, 4$ | 2 |
| $x^8 + 5x$ | binomial | $x^8, 5x$ | 8 |
| $8 - x + x^2 - \frac{1}{2}x^3$ | four terms | $-\frac{1}{2}x^3, x^2, -x, 8$ | 3 |
| $5x + 1$ | binomial | $5x, 1$ | 1 |
| $9x^5$ | monomial | $9x^5$ | 5 |
| $6$ | monomial | $6$ | 0 |

## ■ Adding and Subtracting Polynomials

We **add** and **subtract** polynomials using the properties of real numbers that were discussed in Section P.2. The idea is to combine **like terms** (that is, terms with the same variables raised to the same powers) using the Distributive Property. For instance,

$$5x^7 + 3x^7 = (5 + 3)x^7 = 8x^7$$

**Distributive Property**
$$ac + bc = (a + b)c$$

In subtracting polynomials, we have to remember that if a minus sign precedes an expression in parentheses, then the sign of every term within the parentheses is changed when we remove the parentheses:

$$-(b + c) = -b - c$$

[This is simply a case of the Distributive Property, $a(b + c) = ab + ac$, with $a = -1$.]

▶ **EXAMPLE 1** | Adding and Subtracting Polynomials

**(a)** Find the sum $(x^3 - 6x^2 + 2x + 4) + (x^3 + 5x^2 - 7x)$.

**(b)** Find the difference $(x^3 - 6x^2 + 2x + 4) - (x^3 + 5x^2 - 7x)$.

▼ **SOLUTION**

**(a)** $(x^3 - 6x^2 + 2x + 4) + (x^3 + 5x^2 - 7x)$

$= (x^3 + x^3) + (-6x^2 + 5x^2) + (2x - 7x) + 4$    Group like terms

$= 2x^3 - x^2 - 5x + 4$    Combine like terms

**(b)** $(x^3 - 6x^2 + 2x + 4) - (x^3 + 5x^2 - 7x)$

$\qquad = x^3 - 6x^2 + 2x + 4 - x^3 - 5x^2 + 7x$      Distributive Property

$\qquad = (x^3 - x^3) + (-6x^2 - 5x^2) + (2x + 7x) + 4$      Group like terms

$\qquad = -11x^2 + 9x + 4$      Combine like terms

✎ **Practice what you've learned: Do Exercise 21.**    ▲

## ■ Multiplying Algebraic Expressions

To find the **product** of polynomials or other algebraic expressions, we need to use the Distributive Property repeatedly. In particular, using it three times on the product of two binomials, we get

$$(a + b)(c + d) = a(c + d) + b(c + d) = ac + ad + bc + bd$$

This says that we multiply the two factors by multiplying each term in one factor by each term in the other factor and adding these products. Schematically, we have

> The acronym **FOIL** helps us to remember that the product of two binomials is the sum of the products of the **F**irst terms, the **O**uter terms, the **I**nner terms, and the **L**ast terms.

$$(a + b)(c + d) = ac + ad + bc + bd$$
$$\phantom{xxxxxxxxxxx}\uparrow\quad\uparrow\quad\uparrow\quad\uparrow$$
$$\phantom{xxxxxxxxxxx}\text{F}\quad\text{O}\quad\text{I}\quad\text{L}$$

In general, we can multiply two algebraic expressions by using the Distributive Property and the Laws of Exponents.

▶ **EXAMPLE 2** | Multiplying Binomials Using FOIL

$$(2x + 1)(3x - 5) = 6x^2 - 10x + 3x - 5 \qquad \text{Distributive Property}$$
$$\phantom{xxxxxxxxxxxxxx}\uparrow\quad\uparrow\quad\uparrow\quad\uparrow$$
$$\phantom{xxxxxxxxxxxxxx}\text{F}\quad\text{O}\quad\text{I}\quad\text{L}$$
$$\phantom{xxxxxxx} = 6x^2 - 7x - 5 \qquad \text{Combine like terms}$$

✎ **Practice what you've learned: Do Exercise 41.**    ▲

When we multiply trinomials or other polynomials with more terms, we use the Distributive Property. It is also helpful to arrange our work in table form. The next example illustrates both methods.

▶ **EXAMPLE 3** | Multiplying Polynomials

Find the product: $(2x + 3)(x^2 - 5x + 4)$

▼ **SOLUTION 1:** Using the Distributive Property

$(2x + 3)(x^2 - 5x + 4) = 2x(x^2 - 5x + 4) + 3(x^2 - 5x + 4)$      Distributive Property

$\qquad = (2x \cdot x^2 - 2x \cdot 5x + 2x \cdot 4) + (3 \cdot x^2 - 3 \cdot 5x + 3 \cdot 4)$      Distributive Property

$\qquad = (2x^3 - 10x^2 + 8x) + (3x^2 - 15x + 12)$      Laws of Exponents

$\qquad = 2x^3 - 7x^2 - 7x + 12$      Combine like terms

▼ **SOLUTION 2:** Using Table Form

| | |
|---|---|
| $x^2 - 5x + 4$ | First factor |
| $2x + 3$ | Second factor |
| $3x^2 - 15x + 12$ | Multiply $x^2 - 5x + 4$ by 3 |
| $2x^3 - 10x^2 + 8x$ | Multiply $x^2 - 5x + 4$ by $2x$ |
| $2x^3 - 7x^2 - 7x + 12$ | Add like terms |

✎ **Practice what you've learned: Do Exercise 71.**    ▲

## P.7 | Factoring

### LEARNING OBJECTIVES

After completing this section, you will be able to:

■ Factor out common factors
■ Factor trinomials by trial and error
■ Use the Special Factoring Formulas
■ Factor algebraic expressions completely
■ Factor by grouping terms

We use the Distributive Property to expand algebraic expressions. We sometimes need to reverse this process (again using the Distributive Property) by **factoring** an expression as a product of simpler ones. For example, we can write

 FACTORING

$$x^2 - 4 = (x - 2)(x + 2)$$

 EXPANDING

We say that $x - 2$ and $x + 2$ are **factors** of $x^2 - 4$.

### ■ Common Factors

The easiest type of factoring occurs when the terms have a common factor.

▶ **EXAMPLE 1** | Factoring Out Common Factors

Factor each expression.

**(a)** $3x^2 - 6x$        **(b)** $8x^4y^2 + 6x^3y^3 - 2xy^4$

▼ **SOLUTION**

**(a)** The greatest common factor of the terms $3x^2$ and $-6x$ is $3x$, so we have

$$3x^2 - 6x = 3x(x - 2)$$

**(b)** We note that

8, 6, and $-2$ have the greatest common factor 2

$x^4$, $x^3$, and $x$ have the greatest common factor $x$

$y^2$, $y^3$, and $y^4$ have the greatest common factor $y^2$

So the greatest common factor of the three terms in the polynomial is $2xy^2$, and we have

$$8x^4y^2 + 6x^3y^3 - 2xy^4 = (2xy^2)(4x^3) + (2xy^2)(3x^2y) + (2xy^2)(-y^2)$$
$$= 2xy^2(4x^3 + 3x^2y - y^2)$$

✎ **Practice what you've learned: Do Exercises 7 and 9.**    ▲

### Check Your Answer

**(a)** Multiplying gives

$3x(x - 2) = 3x^2 - 6x$    ✔

**(b)** Multiplying gives

$2xy^2(4x^3 + 3x^2y - y^2) =$
$\qquad 8x^4y^2 + 6x^3y^3 - 2xy^4$    ✔

▶ **EXAMPLE 2** | Factoring Out a Common Factor

Factor:    $(2x + 4)(x - 3) - 5(x - 3)$

▼ **SOLUTION**    The two terms have the common factor $x - 3$.

$$(2x + 4)(x - 3) - 5(x - 3) = [(2x + 4) - 5](x - 3) \quad \text{Distributive Property}$$
$$= (2x - 1)(x - 3) \quad \text{Simplify}$$

✎ **Practice what you've learned: Do Exercise 11.**                    ▲

## ■ Factoring Trinomials

To factor a trinomial of the form $x^2 + bx + c$, we note that

$$(x + r)(x + s) = x^2 + (r + s)x + rs$$

so we need to choose numbers $r$ and $s$ so that $r + s = b$ and $rs = c$.

▶ **EXAMPLE 3** | Factoring $x^2 + bx + c$ by Trial and Error

Factor:   $x^2 + 7x + 12$

▼ **SOLUTION**    We need to find two integers whose product is 12 and whose sum is 7. By trial and error we find that the two integers are 3 and 4. Thus, the factorization is

$$x^2 + 7x + 12 = (x + 3)(x + 4)$$

factors of 12

**Check Your Answer**

Multiplying gives

$(x + 3)(x + 4) = x^2 + 7x + 12$   ✔

✎ **Practice what you've learned: Do Exercise 13.**                    ▲

To factor a trinomial of the form $ax^2 + bx + c$ with $a \neq 1$, we look for factors of the form $px + r$ and $qx + s$:

$$ax^2 + bx + c = (px + r)(qx + s) = pqx^2 + (ps + qr)x + rs$$

Therefore, we try to find numbers $p$, $q$, $r$, and $s$ such that $pq = a$, $rs = c$, $ps + qr = b$. If these numbers are all integers, then we will have a limited number of possibilities to try for $p$, $q$, $r$, and $s$.

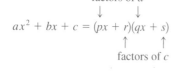

$$ax^2 + bx + c = (px + r)(qx + s)$$

▶ **EXAMPLE 4** | Factoring $ax^2 + bx + c$ by Trial and Error

Factor:   $6x^2 + 7x - 5$

▼ **SOLUTION**    We can factor 6 as $6 \cdot 1$ or $3 \cdot 2$, and $-5$ as $-5 \cdot 1$ or $5 \cdot (-1)$. By trying these possibilities, we arrive at the factorization

$$6x^2 + 7x - 5 = (3x + 5)(2x - 1)$$

factors of 6    factors of −5

**Check Your Answer**

Multiplying gives

$(3x + 5)(2x - 1) = 6x^2 + 7x - 5$   ✔

✎ **Practice what you've learned: Do Exercise 17.**                    ▲

▶ **EXAMPLE 5** | Recognizing the Form of an Expression

Factor each expression.

**(a)** $x^2 - 2x - 3$          **(b)** $(5a + 1)^2 - 2(5a + 1) - 3$

▼ **SOLUTION**

**(a)** $x^2 - 2x - 3 = (x - 3)(x + 1)$      Trial and error

**(b)** This expression is of the form

$$\blacksquare^2 - 2\,\blacksquare - 3$$

where ▮▮ represents $5a + 1$. This is the same form as the expression in part (a), so it will factor as $(▮▮ - 3)(▮▮ + 1)$.

$$(5a + 1)^2 - 2(5a + 1) - 3 = [(5a + 1) - 3][(5a + 1) + 1]$$
$$= (5a - 2)(5a + 2)$$

✏️ **Practice what you've learned: Do Exercise 19.**    ▲

## ■ Special Factoring Formulas

Some special algebraic expressions can be factored by using the following formulas. The first three are simply Special Product Formulas written backward.

**FACTORING FORMULAS**

| Formula | Name |
|---|---|
| **1.** $A^2 - B^2 = (A - B)(A + B)$ | Difference of squares |
| **2.** $A^2 + 2AB + B^2 = (A + B)^2$ | Perfect square |
| **3.** $A^2 - 2AB + B^2 = (A - B)^2$ | Perfect square |
| **4.** $A^3 - B^3 = (A - B)(A^2 + AB + B^2)$ | Difference of cubes |
| **5.** $A^3 + B^3 = (A + B)(A^2 - AB + B^2)$ | Sum of cubes |

▶ **EXAMPLE 6** | Factoring Differences of Squares

Factor each polynomial:    **(a)** $4x^2 - 25$        **(b)** $(x + y)^2 - z^2$

▼ **SOLUTION**

**(a)** Using the Difference of Squares Formula with $A = 2x$ and $B = 5$, we have

$$4x^2 - 25 = (2x)^2 - 5^2 = (2x - 5)(2x + 5)$$

$$A^2 - B^2 = (A - B)(A + B)$$

**(b)** We use the Difference of Squares Formula with $A = x + y$ and $B = z$.

$$(x + y)^2 - z^2 = (x + y - z)(x + y + z)$$

✏️ **Practice what you've learned: Do Exercises 21 and 57.**    ▲

▶ **EXAMPLE 7** | Factoring Differences and Sums of Cubes

Factor each polynomial:    **(a)** $27x^3 - 1$        **(b)** $x^6 + 8$

▼ **SOLUTION**

**(a)** Using the Difference of Cubes Formula with $A = 3x$ and $B = 1$, we get

$$27x^3 - 1 = (3x)^3 - 1^3 = (3x - 1)[(3x)^2 + (3x)(1) + 1^2]$$
$$= (3x - 1)(9x^2 + 3x + 1)$$

**(b)** Using the Sum of Cubes Formula with $A = x^2$ and $B = 2$, we have

$$x^6 + 8 = (x^2)^3 + 2^3 = (x^2 + 2)(x^4 - 2x^2 + 4)$$

✏️ **Practice what you've learned: Do Exercises 23 and 25.**    ▲

A trinomial is a perfect square if it is of the form

$$A^2 + 2AB + B^2 \quad \text{or} \quad A^2 - 2AB + B^2$$

So we **recognize a perfect square** if the middle term $(2AB$ or $-2AB)$ is plus or minus twice the product of the square roots of the outer two terms.

▶ **EXAMPLE 8** | Recognizing Perfect Squares

Factor each trinomial:    **(a)** $x^2 + 6x + 9$        **(b)** $4x^2 - 4xy + y^2$

▼ **SOLUTION**

**(a)** Here $A = x$ and $B = 3$, so $2AB = 2 \cdot x \cdot 3 = 6x$. Since the middle term is $6x$, the trinomial is a perfect square. By the Perfect Square Formula, we have

$$x^2 + 6x + 9 = (x + 3)^2$$

**(b)** Here $A = 2x$ and $B = y$, so $2AB = 2 \cdot 2x \cdot y = 4xy$. Since the middle term is $-4xy$, the trinomial is a perfect square. By the Perfect Square Formula, we have

$$4x^2 - 4xy + y^2 = (2x - y)^2$$

✎ **Practice what you've learned: Do Exercises 53 and 55.**        ▲

## ■ Factoring an Expression Completely

When we factor an expression, the result can sometimes be factored further. In general, we first factor out common factors, then inspect the result to see whether it can be factored by any of the other methods of this section. We repeat this process until we have factored the expression completely.

▶ **EXAMPLE 9** | Factoring an Expression Completely

Factor each expression completely.

**(a)** $2x^4 - 8x^2$        **(b)** $x^5y^2 - xy^6$

▼ **SOLUTION**

**(a)** We first factor out the power of $x$ with the smallest exponent.

$$2x^4 - 8x^2 = 2x^2(x^2 - 4) \qquad \text{Common factor is } 2x^2$$
$$= 2x^2(x - 2)(x + 2) \qquad \text{Factor } x^2 - 4 \text{ as a difference of squares}$$

**(b)** We first factor out the powers of $x$ and $y$ with the smallest exponents.

$$x^5y^2 - xy^6 = xy^2(x^4 - y^4) \qquad \text{Common factor is } xy^2$$
$$= xy^2(x^2 + y^2)(x^2 - y^2) \qquad \text{Factor } x^4 - y^4 \text{ as a difference of squares}$$
$$= xy^2(x^2 + y^2)(x + y)(x - y) \qquad \text{Factor } x^2 - y^2 \text{ as a difference of squares}$$

✎ **Practice what you've learned: Do Exercises 67 and 71.**        ▲

In the next example we factor out variables with fractional exponents. This type of factoring occurs in calculus.

▶ **EXAMPLE 10** | Factoring Expressions with Fractional Exponents

Factor each expression.

**(a)** $3x^{3/2} - 9x^{1/2} + 6x^{-1/2}$        **(b)** $(2 + x)^{-2/3}x + (2 + x)^{1/3}$

▼ **SOLUTION**

**(a)** Factor out the power of $x$ with the *smallest exponent*, that is, $x^{-1/2}$.

$$3x^{3/2} - 9x^{1/2} + 6x^{-1/2} = 3x^{-1/2}(x^2 - 3x + 2) \qquad \text{Factor out } 3x^{-1/2}$$
$$= 3x^{-1/2}(x - 1)(x - 2) \qquad \text{Factor the quadratic } x^2 - 3x + 2$$

**Check Your Answer**

To see that you have factored correctly, multiply using the Laws of Exponents.

**(a)** $3x^{-1/2}(x^2 - 3x + 2)$

$= 3x^{3/2} - 9x^{1/2} + 6x^{-1/2}$  ✔

**(b)** $(2 + x)^{-2/3}[x + (2 + x)]$

$= (2 + x)^{-2/3}x + (2 + x)^{1/3}$  ✔

**(b)** Factor out the power of $2 + x$ with the *smallest exponent*, that is, $(2 + x)^{-2/3}$.

$$(2 + x)^{-2/3}x + (2 + x)^{1/3} = (2 + x)^{-2/3}[x + (2 + x)] \quad \text{Factor out } (2 + x)^{-2/3}$$
$$= (2 + x)^{-2/3}(2 + 2x) \quad \text{Simplify}$$
$$= 2(2 + x)^{-2/3}(1 + x) \quad \text{Factor out 2}$$

✎ **Practice what you've learned: Do Exercises 85 and 87.**  ▲

### ■ Factoring by Grouping Terms

Polynomials with at least four terms can sometimes be factored by grouping terms. The following example illustrates the idea.

▶ **EXAMPLE 11** | Factoring by Grouping

Factor each polynomial.

**(a)** $x^3 + x^2 + 4x + 4$   **(b)** $x^3 - 2x^2 - 3x + 6$

▼ **SOLUTION**

**(a)** $x^3 + x^2 + 4x + 4 = (x^3 + x^2) + (4x + 4)$   Group terms
$= x^2(x + 1) + 4(x + 1)$   Factor out common factors
$= (x^2 + 4)(x + 1)$   Factor out x + 1 from each term

**(b)** $x^3 - 2x^2 - 3x + 6 = (x^3 - 2x^2) - (3x - 6)$   Group terms
$= x^2(x - 2) - 3(x - 2)$   Factor out common factors
$= (x^2 - 3)(x - 2)$   Factor out x − 2 from each term

✎ **Practice what you've learned: Do Exercise 29.**  ▲

## P.7 EXERCISES

▼ **CONCEPTS**

1. Consider the polynomial $2x^5 + 6x^4 + 4x^3$.

   How many terms does this polynomial have? _____

   List the terms: _____

   What factor is common to each term? _____

   Factor the polynomial: $2x^5 + 6x^4 + 4x^3 =$ _____.

2. To factor the trinomial $x^2 + 7x + 10$, we look for two integers whose product is _____ and whose sum is _____.

   These integers are _____ and _____, so the trinomial factors as _____.

3. The Special Factoring Formula for the "difference of squares" is $A^2 - B^2 =$ _____. So $4x^2 - 25$ factors as _____.

4. The Special Factoring Formula for a "perfect square" is $A^2 + 2AB + B^2 =$ _____. So $x^2 + 10x + 25$ factors as _____.

▼ **SKILLS**

**5–12** ■ Factor out the common factor.

**5.** $5a - 20$   **6.** $-3b + 12$

✎ **7.** $-2x^3 + 16x$   **8.** $2x^4 + 4x^3 - 14x^2$

✎ **9.** $2x^2y - 6xy^2 + 3xy$   **10.** $-7x^4y^2 + 14xy^3 + 21xy^4$

✎ **11.** $y(y - 6) + 9(y - 6)$   **12.** $(z + 2)^2 - 5(z + 2)$

**13–20** ■ Factor the trinomial.

✎ **13.** $x^2 + 2x - 3$   **14.** $x^2 - 6x + 5$

**15.** $x^2 + 2x - 15$   **16.** $2x^2 - 5x - 7$

✎ **17.** $3x^2 - 16x + 5$   **18.** $5x^2 - 7x - 6$

✎ **19.** $(3x + 2)^2 + 8(3x + 2) + 12$

**20.** $2(a + b)^2 + 5(a + b) - 3$

**21–28** ■ Use a Factoring Formula to factor the expression.

✎ **21.** $9a^2 - 16$   **22.** $(x + 3)^2 - 4$

✎ **23.** $27x^3 + y^3$   **24.** $a^3 - b^6$

✎ **25.** $8s^3 - 125t^3$   **26.** $1 + 1000y^3$

**27.** $x^2 + 12x + 36$   **28.** $16z^2 - 24z + 9$

**29–34** ▪ Factor the expression by grouping terms.

**29.** $x^3 + 4x^2 + x + 4$

**30.** $3x^3 - x^2 + 6x - 2$

**31.** $2x^3 + x^2 - 6x - 3$

**32.** $-9x^3 - 3x^2 + 3x + 1$

**33.** $x^3 + x^2 + x + 1$

**34.** $x^5 + x^4 + x + 1$

**35–82** ▪ Factor the expression completely.

**35.** $12x^3 + 18x$

**36.** $30x^3 + 15x^4$

**37.** $6y^4 - 15y^3$

**38.** $5ab - 8abc$

**39.** $x^2 - 2x - 8$

**40.** $x^2 - 14x + 48$

**41.** $y^2 - 8y + 15$

**42.** $z^2 + 6z - 16$

**43.** $2x^2 + 5x + 3$

**44.** $2x^2 + 7x - 4$

**45.** $9x^2 - 36x - 45$

**46.** $8x^2 + 10x + 3$

**47.** $6x^2 - 5x - 6$

**48.** $6 + 5t - 6t^2$

**49.** $x^2 - 36$

**50.** $4x^2 - 25$

**51.** $49 - 4y^2$

**52.** $4t^2 - 9s^2$

**53.** $t^2 - 6t + 9$

**54.** $x^2 + 10x + 25$

**55.** $4x^2 + 4xy + y^2$

**56.** $r^2 - 6rs + 9s^2$

**57.** $(a + b)^2 - (a - b)^2$

**58.** $\left(1 + \dfrac{1}{x}\right)^2 - \left(1 - \dfrac{1}{x}\right)^2$

**59.** $x^2(x^2 - 1) - 9(x^2 - 1)$

**60.** $(a^2 - 1)b^2 - 4(a^2 - 1)$

**61.** $t^3 + 1$

**62.** $x^3 - 27$

**63.** $8x^3 - 125$

**64.** $x^6 + 64$

**65.** $x^6 - 8y^3$

**66.** $27a^3 + b^6$

**67.** $x^3 + 2x^2 + x$

**68.** $3x^3 - 27x$

**69.** $x^4 + 2x^3 - 3x^2$

**70.** $x^3 + 3x^2 - x - 3$

**71.** $x^4y^3 - x^2y^5$

**72.** $18y^3x^2 - 2xy^4$

**73.** $y^3 - 3y^2 - 4y + 12$

**74.** $y^3 - y^2 + y - 1$

**75.** $2x^3 + 4x^2 + x + 2$

**76.** $3x^3 + 5x^2 - 6x - 10$

**77.** $(x - 1)(x + 2)^2 - (x - 1)^2(x + 2)$

**78.** $(x + 1)^3x - 2(x + 1)^2x^2 + x^3(x + 1)$

**79.** $y^4(y + 2)^3 + y^5(y + 2)^4$

**80.** $n(x - y) + (n - 1)(y - x)$

**81.** $(a^2 + 1)^2 - 7(a^2 + 1) + 10$

**82.** $(a^2 + 2a)^2 - 2(a^2 + 2a) - 3$

**83–90** ▪ Factor the expression completely. Begin by factoring out the lowest power of each common factor.

**83.** $x^{5/2} - x^{1/2}$

**84.** $3x^{-1/2} + 4x^{1/2} + x^{3/2}$

**85.** $x^{-3/2} + 2x^{-1/2} + x^{1/2}$

**86.** $(x - 1)^{7/2} - (x - 1)^{3/2}$

**87.** $(x^2 + 1)^{1/2} + 2(x^2 + 1)^{-1/2}$

**88.** $x^{-1/2}(x + 1)^{1/2} + x^{1/2}(x + 1)^{-1/2}$

**89.** $2x^{1/3}(x - 2)^{2/3} - 5x^{4/3}(x - 2)^{-1/3}$

**90.** $3x^{-1/2}(x^2 + 1)^{5/4} - x^{3/2}(x^2 + 1)^{1/4}$

**91–96** ▪ Factor the expression completely. (This type of expression arises in calculus in using the "product rule.")

**91.** $3x^2(4x - 12)^2 + x^3(2)(4x - 12)(4)$

**92.** $5(x^2 + 4)^4(2x)(x - 2)^4 + (x^2 + 4)^5(4)(x - 2)^3$

**93.** $3(2x - 1)^2(2)(x + 3)^{1/2} + (2x - 1)^3(\frac{1}{2})(x + 3)^{-1/2}$

**94.** $\frac{1}{3}(x + 6)^{-2/3}(2x - 3)^2 + (x + 6)^{1/3}(2)(2x - 3)(2)$

**95.** $(x^2 + 3)^{-1/3} - \frac{2}{3}x^2(x^2 + 3)^{-4/3}$

**96.** $\frac{1}{2}x^{-1/2}(3x + 4)^{1/2} + \frac{3}{2}x^{1/2}(3x + 4)^{-1/2}$

**97.** (a) Show that $ab = \frac{1}{2}[(a + b)^2 - (a^2 + b^2)]$.

(b) Show that $(a^2 + b^2)^2 - (a^2 - b^2)^2 = 4a^2b^2$.

(c) Show that

$$(a^2 + b^2)(c^2 + d^2) = (ac + bd)^2 + (ad - bc)^2$$

(d) Factor completely: $4a^2c^2 - (a^2 - b^2 + c^2)^2$.

**98.** Verify Factoring Formulas 4 and 5 by expanding their right-hand sides.

---

## ▼ APPLICATIONS

**99. Volume of Concrete** A culvert is constructed out of large cylindrical shells cast in concrete, as shown in the figure. Using the formula for the volume of a cylinder given on the inside back cover of this book, explain why the volume of the cylindrical shell is

$$V = \pi R^2 h - \pi r^2 h$$

Factor to show that

$$V = 2\pi \cdot \text{average radius} \cdot \text{height} \cdot \text{thickness}$$

Use the "unrolled" diagram to explain why this makes sense geometrically.

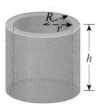

**100. Mowing a Field** A square field in a certain state park is mowed around the edges every week. The rest of the field is kept unmowed to serve as a habitat for birds and small animals (see the figure). The field measures $b$ feet by $b$ feet, and the mowed strip is $x$ feet wide.

(a) Explain why the area of the mowed portion is $b^2 - (b - 2x)^2$.

(b) Factor the expression in (a) to show that the area of the mowed portion is also $4x(b - x)$.

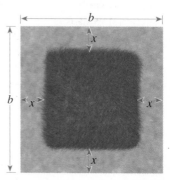

Distance between $a$ and $b$ is

$$d(a, b) = |b - a|$$

## Exponents (p. 21)

$$a^m a^n = a^{m+n}$$

$$\frac{a^m}{a^n} = a^{m-n}$$

$$(a^m)^n = a^{mn}$$

$$(ab)^n = a^n b^n$$

$$\left(\frac{a}{b}\right)^n = \frac{a^n}{b^n}$$

## Radicals (p. 27)

$$\sqrt[n]{a} = b \quad \text{means} \quad b^n = a$$

$$\sqrt[n]{ab} = \sqrt[n]{a}\sqrt[n]{b}$$

$$\sqrt[n]{\frac{a}{b}} = \frac{\sqrt[n]{a}}{\sqrt[n]{b}}$$

$$\sqrt[m]{\sqrt[n]{a}} = \sqrt[mn]{a}$$

If $n$ is odd, then $\sqrt[n]{a^n} = a$

If $n$ is even, then $\sqrt[n]{a^n} = |a|$

$$a^{m/n} = \sqrt[n]{a^m}$$

## Special Product Formulas (p. 35)

Sum and difference of same terms:

$$(A + B)(A - B) = A^2 - B^2$$

Square of a sum or difference:

$$(A + B)^2 = A^2 + 2AB + B^2$$
$$(A - B)^2 = A^2 - 2AB + B^2$$

Cube of a sum or difference:

$$(A + B)^3 = A^3 + 3A^2B + 3AB^2 + B^3$$
$$(A - B)^3 = A^3 - 3A^2B + 3AB^2 - B^3$$

## Factoring Formulas (p. 41)

Difference of squares:

$$A^2 - B^2 = (A + B)(A - B)$$

Perfect squares:

$$A^2 + 2AB + B^2 = (A + B)^2$$
$$A^2 - 2AB + B^2 = (A - B)^2$$

Sum or difference of cubes:

$$A^3 - B^3 = (A - B)(A^2 + AB + B^2)$$
$$A^3 + B^3 = (A + B)(A^2 - AB + B^2)$$

## Rational Expressions (p. 46)

We can cancel common factors:

$$\frac{AC}{BC} = \frac{A}{B}$$

To multiply two fractions, we multiply their numerators together and their denominators together:

$$\frac{A}{B} \times \frac{C}{D} = \frac{AC}{BD}$$

To divide fractions, we invert the divisor and multiply:

$$\frac{A}{B} \div \frac{C}{D} = \frac{A}{B} \times \frac{D}{C}$$

To add fractions, we find a common denominator:

$$\frac{A}{C} + \frac{B}{C} = \frac{A + B}{C}$$

## ▼ CONCEPT SUMMARY

### Section P.1
**Review Exercises**

- Make and use algebra models — 1–2

### Section P.2
**Review Exercises**

- Classify real numbers — 3–4
- Use properties of real numbers — 5–8
- Add, subtract, multiply, and divide fractions — 9–12

### Section P.3
**Review Exercises**

- Graph numbers on the real line — 13–16
- Use the order symbols $<$, $\leq$, $>$, $\geq$ — 13–20
- Work with set and interval notation — 13–24
- Work with absolute values — 25–28
- Find distances on the real line — 37–38

### Section P.4
**Review Exercises**

- Use exponential notation — 29–32, 39–46
- Simplify expressions using the Laws of Exponents — 39–46
- Write numbers in scientific notation — 61–64

### Section P.5
**Review Exercises**

- Simplify expressions involving radicals — 33–36, 40, 93
- Simplify expressions involving rational exponents — 29–32, 59, 77
- Express radicals using rational exponents — 47–50
- Rationalize a denominator — 57–58

### Section P.6
**Review Exercises**

- Add, subtract, and multiply polynomials — 87–92
- Multiply algebraic expressions — 87–95
- Use the Special Product Formulas — 88, 89, 92, 94, 95

## Section P.7

- Factor out common factors
- Factor trinomials by trial and error
- Use the Special Factoring Formulas
- Factor algebraic expressions completely
- Factor by grouping terms

**Review Exercises**

65, 66, 74, 77, 78, 81, 83

67–72, 77, 86

72–75, 78, 80, 85, 123, 124

65–86

76, 82, 84

## Section P.8

- Find the domain of an algebraic expression
- Simplify rational expressions
- Add, subtract, multiply, and divide rational expressions
- Simplify compound fractions
- Rationalize a numerator or a denominator
- Avoid common algebraic errors

**Review Exercises**

111–114

98–101

99–108

107–108

57–58, 110

115–122

## ▼ EXERCISES

**1–2** ■ Make and use an algebra model to solve the problem.

**1.** Elena regularly takes a multivitamin and mineral supplement. She purchases a bottle of 250 tablets and takes two tablets every day.
  **(a)** Find a formula for the number of tablets $T$ that are left in the bottle after she has been taking the tablets for $x$ days.
  **(b)** How many tablets are left after 30 days?
  **(c)** How many days will it take for her to run out of tablets?

**2.** Alonzo's Delivery is having a sale on calzones. Each calzone costs \$2, and there is a \$3 delivery charge for phone-in orders.
  **(a)** Find a formula for the total cost $C$ of ordering $x$ calzones for delivery.
  **(b)** How much would it cost to have 4 calzones delivered?
  **(c)** If you have \$15, how many calzones can you order?

**3–4** ■ Determine whether each number is rational or irrational. If it is rational, determine whether it is a natural number, an integer, or neither.

**3.** **(a)** $16$  **(b)** $-16$  **(c)** $\sqrt{16}$  **(d)** $\sqrt{2}$
  **(e)** $\frac{8}{3}$  **(f)** $-\frac{8}{2}$

**4.** **(a)** $-5$  **(b)** $-\frac{25}{6}$  **(c)** $\sqrt{25}$  **(d)** $3\pi$
  **(e)** $\frac{24}{16}$  **(f)** $10^{20}$

**5–8** ■ State the property of real numbers being used.

**5.** $3 + 2x = 2x + 3$

**6.** $(a + b)(a - b) = (a - b)(a + b)$

**7.** $A(x + y) = Ax + Ay$

**8.** $(A + 1)(x + y) = (A + 1)x + (A + 1)y$

**9–12** ■ Evaluate each expression. Express your answer as a fraction in lowest terms.

**9.** **(a)** $\dfrac{5}{6} + \dfrac{2}{3}$  **(b)** $\dfrac{5}{6} - \dfrac{2}{3}$

**10.** **(a)** $\dfrac{7}{10} - \dfrac{11}{15}$  **(b)** $\dfrac{7}{10} + \dfrac{11}{15}$

**11.** **(a)** $\dfrac{15}{8} \cdot \dfrac{12}{5}$  **(b)** $\dfrac{15}{8} \div \dfrac{12}{5}$

**12.** **(a)** $\dfrac{30}{7} \div \dfrac{12}{35}$  **(b)** $\dfrac{30}{7} \cdot \dfrac{12}{35}$

**13–16** ■ Express the interval in terms of inequalities, and then graph the interval.

**13.** $[-2, 6)$  **14.** $(0, 10]$

**15.** $(-\infty, 4]$  **16.** $[-2, \infty)$

**17–20** ■ Express the inequality in interval notation, and then graph the corresponding interval.

**17.** $x \geq 5$  **18.** $x < -3$

**19.** $-1 < x \leq 5$  **20.** $0 \leq x \leq \frac{1}{2}$

**21–24** ■ The sets $A$, $B$, $C$, and $D$ are defined as follows:

$A = \{-1, 0, 1, 2, 3\}$  $B = \{\frac{1}{2}, 1, 4\}$
$C = \{x \mid 0 < x \leq 2\}$  $D = (-1, 1]$

Find each of the following sets.

**21.** **(a)** $A \cup B$  **(b)** $A \cap B$

**22.** **(a)** $C \cup D$  **(b)** $C \cap D$

**23.** **(a)** $A \cap C$  **(b)** $B \cap D$

**24.** **(a)** $A \cap D$  **(b)** $B \cap C$

**25–36** ■ Evaluate the expression.

**25.** $|7 - 10|$  **26.** $\left|-\frac{3}{2} - 5\right|$

**27.** $\big|3 - |-9|\big|$  **28.** $1 - \big|1 - |-1|\big|$

**29.** $2^{-3} - 3^{-2}$  **30.** $2^{1/2}8^{1/2}$

**31.** $216^{-1/3}$  **32.** $64^{2/3}$

**33.** $\dfrac{\sqrt{242}}{\sqrt{2}}$  **34.** $\sqrt[4]{4}\,\sqrt[4]{324}$

**35.** $\sqrt[3]{-125}$  **36.** $\sqrt{2}\sqrt{50}$

**37–38** ▪ Express the distance between the given numbers on the real line using an absolute value. Then evaluate this distance.

**37. (a)** 3 and 5        **(b)** 3 and $-5$

**38. (a)** 0 and $-4$        **(b)** 4 and $-4$

**39–46** ▪ Write the expression as a power of $x$.

**39.** $\dfrac{1}{x^2}$            **40.** $x\sqrt{x}$

**41.** $x^2 x^m (x^3)^m$      **42.** $((x^m)^2)^n$

**43.** $x^a x^b x^c$        **44.** $((x^a)^b)^c$

**45.** $x^{c+1}(x^{2c-1})^2$     **46.** $\dfrac{(x^2)^n x^5}{x^n}$

**47–50** ▪ Express the radical as a power with a rational exponent.

**47. (a)** $\sqrt[3]{7}$   **(b)** $\sqrt[5]{7^4}$     **48. (a)** $\sqrt[3]{5^7}$   **(b)** $(\sqrt[4]{5})^3$

**49. (a)** $\sqrt[6]{x^5}$   **(b)** $(\sqrt{x})^9$    **50. (a)** $\sqrt{\sqrt{y^3}}$   **(b)** $(\sqrt[8]{y})^2$

**51–60** ▪ Simplify the expression.

**51.** $(2x^3 y)^2 (3x^{-1} y^2)$      **52.** $(a^2)^{-3}(a^3 b)^2 (b^3)^4$

**53.** $\dfrac{x^4 (3x)^2}{x^3}$          **54.** $\left(\dfrac{r^2 s^{4/3}}{r^{1/3} s}\right)^6$

**55.** $\sqrt[3]{(x^3 y)^2 y^4}$       **56.** $\sqrt{x^2 y^4}$

**57.** $\dfrac{x}{2 + \sqrt{x}}$         **58.** $\dfrac{\sqrt{x}+1}{\sqrt{x}-1}$

**59.** $\dfrac{8r^{1/2} s^{-3}}{2r^{-2} s^4}$       **60.** $\left(\dfrac{ab^2 c^{-3}}{2a^2 b^{-4}}\right)^{-2}$

**61.** Write the number 78,250,000,000 in scientific notation.

**62.** Write the number $2.08 \times 10^{-8}$ in decimal notation.

**63.** If $a \approx 0.00000293$, $b \approx 1.582 \times 10^{-14}$, and $c \approx 2.8064 \times 10^{12}$, use a calculator to approximate the number $ab/c$.

**64.** If your heart beats 80 times per minute and you live to be 90 years old, estimate the number of times your heart beats during your lifetime. State your answer in scientific notation.

**65–86** ▪ Factor the expression.

**65.** $2x^2 y - 6xy^2$        **66.** $12x^2 y^4 - 3xy^5 + 9x^3 y^2$

**67.** $x^2 - 9x + 18$       **68.** $x^2 + 3x - 10$

**69.** $3x^2 - 2x - 1$       **70.** $6x^2 + x - 12$

**71.** $4t^2 - 13t - 12$      **72.** $x^4 - 2x^2 + 1$

**73.** $25 - 16t^2$         **74.** $2y^6 - 32y^2$

**75.** $x^6 - 1$           **76.** $y^3 - 2y^2 - y + 2$

**77.** $x^{-1/2} - 2x^{1/2} + x^{3/2}$   **78.** $a^4 b^2 + ab^5$

**79.** $4x^3 - 8x^2 + 3x - 6$    **80.** $8x^3 + y^6$

**81.** $(x^2 + 2)^{5/2} + 2x(x^2 + 2)^{3/2} + x^2\sqrt{x^2 + 2}$

**82.** $3x^3 - 2x^2 + 18x - 12$    **83.** $a^2 y - b^2 y$

**84.** $ax^2 + bx^2 - a - b$    **85.** $(x + 1)^2 - 2(x + 1) + 1$

**86.** $(a + b)^2 + 2(a + b) - 15$

**87–110** ▪ Perform the indicated operations.

**87.** $(2x + 1)(3x - 2) - 5(4x - 1)$

**88.** $(2y - 7)(2y + 7)$

**89.** $(2a^2 - b)^2$

**90.** $(1 + x)(2 - x) - (3 - x)(3 + x)$

**91.** $(x - 1)(x - 2)(x - 3)$      **92.** $(2x + 1)^3$

**93.** $\sqrt{x}(\sqrt{x} + 1)(2\sqrt{x} - 1)$

**94.** $x^3(x - 6)^2 + x^4(x - 6)$    **95.** $x^2(x - 2) + x(x - 2)^2$

**96.** $\dfrac{x^3 + 2x^2 + 3x}{x}$          **97.** $\dfrac{x^2 - 2x - 3}{2x^2 + 5x + 3}$

**98.** $\dfrac{t^3 - 1}{t^2 - 1}$           **99.** $\dfrac{x^2 + 2x - 3}{x^2 + 8x + 16} \cdot \dfrac{3x + 12}{x - 1}$

**100.** $\dfrac{x^3/(x - 1)}{x^2/(x^3 - 1)}$

**101.** $\dfrac{x^2 - 2x - 15}{x^2 - 6x + 5} \div \dfrac{x^2 - x - 12}{x^2 - 1}$

**102.** $x - \dfrac{1}{x + 1}$        **103.** $\dfrac{1}{x - 1} - \dfrac{x}{x^2 + 1}$

**104.** $\dfrac{2}{x} + \dfrac{1}{x - 2} + \dfrac{3}{(x - 2)^2}$   **105.** $\dfrac{1}{x - 1} - \dfrac{2}{x^2 - 1}$

**106.** $\dfrac{1}{x + 2} + \dfrac{1}{x^2 - 4} - \dfrac{2}{x^2 - x - 2}$

**107.** $\dfrac{\dfrac{1}{x} - \dfrac{1}{2}}{x - 2}$       **108.** $\dfrac{\dfrac{1}{x} - \dfrac{1}{x + 1}}{\dfrac{1}{x} + \dfrac{1}{x + 1}}$

**109.** $\dfrac{3(x + h)^2 - 5(x + h) - (3x^2 - 5x)}{h}$

**110.** $\dfrac{\sqrt{x + h} - \sqrt{x}}{h}$    (rationalize the numerator)

**111–114** ▪ Find the domain of the algebraic expression.

**111.** $\dfrac{x + 5}{x + 10}$          **112.** $\dfrac{2x}{x^2 - 9}$

**113.** $\dfrac{\sqrt{x}}{x^2 - 3x - 4}$     **114.** $\dfrac{\sqrt{x - 3}}{x^2 - 4x + 4}$

**115–122** ▪ State whether the given equation is true for all values of the variables. (Disregard any value that makes a denominator 0.)

**115.** $(x + y)^3 = x^3 + y^3$     **116.** $\dfrac{1 + \sqrt{a}}{1 - a} = \dfrac{1}{1 - \sqrt{a}}$

**117.** $\dfrac{12 + y}{y} = \dfrac{12}{y} + 1$    **118.** $\sqrt[3]{a + b} = \sqrt[3]{a} + \sqrt[3]{b}$

**119.** $\sqrt{a^2} = a$         **120.** $\dfrac{1}{x + 4} = \dfrac{1}{x} + \dfrac{1}{4}$

**121.** $x^3 + y^3 = (x + y)(x^2 + xy + y^2)$

**122.** $\dfrac{x^2 + 1}{x^2 + 2x + 1} = \dfrac{1}{2x + 1}$

**123.** If $m > n > 0$ and $a = 2mn$, $b = m^2 - n^2$, $c = m^2 + n^2$, show that $a^2 + b^2 = c^2$.

**124.** If $t = \dfrac{1}{2}\left(x^3 - \dfrac{1}{x^3}\right)$ and $x > 0$, show that

$$\sqrt{1 + t^2} = \dfrac{1}{2}\left(x^3 + \dfrac{1}{x^3}\right)$$

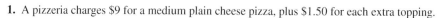

1. A pizzeria charges \$9 for a medium plain cheese pizza, plus \$1.50 for each extra topping.

   **(a)** Find a formula that models the cost $C$ of a medium pizza with $x$ toppings.

   **(b)** Use your model from part (a) to find the cost of a medium pizza with the following extra toppings: anchovies, ham, sausage, and pineapple.

2. Determine whether each number is rational or irrational. If it is rational, determine whether it is a natural number, an integer, or neither.

   **(a)** 5         **(b)** $\sqrt{5}$         **(c)** $-\frac{9}{3}$         **(d)** $-1{,}000{,}000$

3. Let $A = \{-2, 0, 1, 3, 5\}$ and $B = \{0, \frac{1}{2}, 1, 5, 7\}$. Find each of the following sets.

   **(a)** $A \cap B$         **(b)** $A \cup B$

4. **(a)** Graph the intervals $[-4, 2)$ and $[0, 3]$ on a real line.

   **(b)** Find the intersection and the union of the intervals in part (a), and graph each of them on a real line.

   **(c)** Use an absolute value to express the distance between $-4$ and $2$ on the real line, and then evaluate this distance.

5. Evaluate each expression:

   **(a)** $-2^6$         **(b)** $(-2)^6$         **(c)** $2^{-6}$         **(d)** $\dfrac{7^{10}}{7^{12}}$

   **(e)** $\left(\dfrac{3}{2}\right)^{-2}$         **(f)** $\dfrac{\sqrt[5]{32}}{\sqrt{16}}$         **(g)** $\sqrt[4]{\dfrac{3^8}{2^{16}}}$         **(h)** $81^{-3/4}$

6. Write each number in scientific notation.

   **(a)** $186{,}000{,}000{,}000$         **(b)** $0.0000003965$

7. Simplify each expression. Write your final answer without negative exponents.

   **(a)** $\sqrt{200} - \sqrt{32}$         **(b)** $(3a^3b^3)(4ab^2)^2$

   **(c)** $\sqrt[3]{\dfrac{125}{x^{-9}}}$         **(d)** $\left(\dfrac{3x^{3/2}y^3}{x^2y^{-1/2}}\right)^{-2}$

8. Perform the indicated operations and simplify.

   **(a)** $3(x + 6) + 4(2x - 5)$         **(b)** $(x + 3)(4x - 5)$         **(c)** $(\sqrt{a} + \sqrt{b})(\sqrt{a} - \sqrt{b})$

   **(d)** $(2x + 3)^2$         **(e)** $(x + 2)^3$         **(f)** $x^2(x - 3)(x + 3)$

9. Factor each expression completely.

   **(a)** $4x^2 - 25$         **(b)** $2x^2 + 5x - 12$         **(c)** $x^3 - 3x^2 - 4x + 12$

   **(d)** $x^4 + 27x$         **(e)** $3x^{3/2} - 9x^{1/2} + 6x^{-1/2}$         **(f)** $x^3y - 4xy$

10. Simplify the rational expression.

    **(a)** $\dfrac{x^2 + 3x + 2}{x^2 - x - 2}$         **(b)** $\dfrac{2x^2 - x - 1}{x^2 - 9} \cdot \dfrac{x + 3}{2x + 1}$

    **(c)** $\dfrac{x^2}{x^2 - 4} - \dfrac{x + 1}{x + 2}$         **(d)** $\dfrac{\dfrac{y}{x} - \dfrac{x}{y}}{\dfrac{1}{y} - \dfrac{1}{x}}$

11. Rationalize the denominator and simplify.

    **(a)** $\dfrac{6}{\sqrt[3]{4}}$         **(b)** $\dfrac{\sqrt{6}}{2 + \sqrt{3}}$

Stanford University News Service

**George Polya** (1887–1985) is famous among mathematicians for his ideas on problem solving. His lectures on problem solving at Stanford University attracted overflow crowds whom he held on the edges of their seats, leading them to discover solutions for themselves. He was able to do this because of his deep insight into the psychology of problem solving. His well-known book *How To Solve It* has been translated into 15 languages. He said that Euler (see page 100) was unique among great mathematicians because he explained *how* he found his results. Polya often said to his students and colleagues, "Yes, I see that your proof is correct, but how did you discover it?" In the preface to *How To Solve It*, Polya writes, "A great discovery solves a great problem but there is a grain of discovery in the solution of any problem. Your problem may be modest; but if it challenges your curiosity and brings into play your inventive faculties, and if you solve it by your own means, you may experience the tension and enjoy the triumph of discovery."

There are no hard and fast rules that will ensure success in solving problems. However, it is possible to outline some general steps in the problem-solving process and to give principles that are useful in solving certain problems. These steps and principles are just common sense made explicit. They have been adapted from George Polya's insightful book *How To Solve It*.

## 1. Understand the Problem

The first step is to read the problem and make sure that you understand it. Ask yourself the following questions:

> *What is the unknown?*
>
> *What are the given quantities?*
>
> *What are the given conditions?*

For many problems it is useful to

> *draw a diagram*

and identify the given and required quantities on the diagram.

Usually, it is necessary to

> *introduce suitable notation*

In choosing symbols for the unknown quantities, we often use letters such as $a$, $b$, $c$, $m$, $n$, $x$, and $y$, but in some cases it helps to use initials as suggestive symbols, for instance, $V$ for volume or $t$ for time.

## 2. Think of a Plan

Find a connection between the given information and the unknown that enables you to calculate the unknown. It often helps to ask yourself explicitly: "How can I relate the given to the unknown?" If you don't see a connection immediately, the following ideas may be helpful in devising a plan.

### ■ TRY TO RECOGNIZE SOMETHING FAMILIAR

Relate the given situation to previous knowledge. Look at the unknown and try to recall a more familiar problem that has a similar unknown.

### ■ TRY TO RECOGNIZE PATTERNS

Certain problems are solved by recognizing that some kind of pattern is occurring. The pattern could be geometric, numerical, or algebraic. If you can see regularity or repetition in a problem, then you might be able to guess what the pattern is and then prove it.

### ■ USE ANALOGY

Try to think of an analogous problem, that is, a similar or related problem but one that is easier than the original. If you can solve the similar, simpler problem, then it might give you the clues you need to solve the original, more difficult one. For instance, if a problem involves very large numbers, you could first try a similar problem with smaller numbers. Or if the problem is in three-dimensional geometry, you could look for something similar in two-dimensional geometry. Or if the problem you start with is a general one, you could first try a special case.

### ■ INTRODUCE SOMETHING EXTRA

You might sometimes need to introduce something new—an auxiliary aid—to make the connection between the given and the unknown. For instance, in a problem for which a diagram is useful, the auxiliary aid could be a new line drawn in the diagram. In a more algebraic problem the aid could be a new unknown that relates to the original unknown.

### ■ TAKE CASES

You might sometimes have to split a problem into several cases and give a different argument for each case. For instance, we often have to use this strategy in dealing with absolute value.

### ■ WORK BACKWARD

Sometimes it is useful to imagine that your problem is solved and work backward, step by step, until you arrive at the given data. Then you might be able to reverse your steps and thereby construct a solution to the original problem. This procedure is commonly used in solving equations. For instance, in solving the equation $3x - 5 = 7$, we suppose that $x$ is a number that satisfies $3x - 5 = 7$ and work backward. We add 5 to each side of the equation and then divide each side by 3 to get $x = 4$. Since each of these steps can be reversed, we have solved the problem.

### ■ ESTABLISH SUBGOALS

In a complex problem it is often useful to set subgoals (in which the desired situation is only partially fulfilled). If you can attain or accomplish these subgoals, then you might be able to build on them to reach your final goal.

### ■ INDIRECT REASONING

Sometimes it is appropriate to attack a problem indirectly. In using **proof by contradiction** to prove that $P$ implies $Q$, we assume that $P$ is true and $Q$ is false and try to see why this cannot happen. Somehow we have to use this information and arrive at a contradiction to what we absolutely know is true.

### ■ MATHEMATICAL INDUCTION

In proving statements that involve a positive integer $n$, it is frequently helpful to use the Principle of Mathematical Induction, which is discussed in Section 9.4.

## 3. Carry Out the Plan

In Step 2, a plan was devised. In carrying out that plan, you must check each stage of the plan and write the details that prove that each stage is correct.

## 4. Look Back

Having completed your solution, it is wise to look back over it, partly to see whether any errors have been made and partly to see whether you can discover an easier way to solve the problem. Looking back also familiarizes you with the method of solution, which may be useful for solving a future problem. Descartes said, "Every problem that I solved became a rule which served afterwards to solve other problems."

We illustrate some of these principles of problem solving with an example.

▶ **PROBLEM** | Average Speed

A driver sets out on a journey. For the first half of the distance, she drives at the leisurely pace of 30 mi/h; during the second half she drives 60 mi/h. What is her average speed on this trip?

**Thinking About the Problem**

It is tempting to take the average of the speeds and say that the average speed for the entire trip is

$$\frac{30 + 60}{2} = 45 \text{ mi/h}$$

But is this simple-minded approach really correct?

Try a special case ▶   Let's look at an easily calculated special case. Suppose that the total distance traveled is 120 mi. Since the first 60 mi is traveled at 30 mi/h, it takes 2 h. The second 60 mi is traveled at 60 mi/h, so it takes one hour. Thus, the total time is $2 + 1 = 3$ hours and the average speed is

$$\frac{120}{3} = 40 \text{ mi/h}$$

So our guess of 45 mi/h was wrong.

▼ **SOLUTION**

Understand the problem ▶   We need to look more carefully at the meaning of average speed. It is defined as

$$\text{average speed} = \frac{\text{distance traveled}}{\text{time elapsed}}$$

Introduce notation ▶   Let $d$ be the distance traveled on each half of the trip. Let $t_1$ and $t_2$ be the times taken for the first and second halves of the trip. Now we can write down the information we have

State what is given ▶   been given. For the first half of the trip we have

$$30 = \frac{d}{t_1}$$

and for the second half we have

$$60 = \frac{d}{t_2}$$

Identify the unknown ▶   Now we identify the quantity that we are asked to find:

$$\text{average speed for entire trip} = \frac{\text{total distance}}{\text{total time}} = \frac{2d}{t_1 + t_2}$$

Connect the given with the unknown ▶   To calculate this quantity, we need to know $t_1$ and $t_2$, so we solve the above equations for these times:

$$t_1 = \frac{d}{30} \qquad t_2 = \frac{d}{60}$$

Now we have the ingredients needed to calculate the desired quantity:

$$\text{average speed} = \frac{2d}{t_1 + t_1} = \frac{2d}{\dfrac{d}{30} + \dfrac{d}{60}}$$

$$= \frac{60(2d)}{60\left(\dfrac{d}{30} + \dfrac{d}{60}\right)} \qquad \text{Multiply numerator and denominator by 60}$$

$$= \frac{120d}{2d + d} = \frac{120d}{3d} = 40$$

So the average speed for the entire trip is 40 mi/h.

Don't feel bad if you can't solve these problems right away. Problems 2 and 6 were sent to Albert Einstein by his friend Wertheimer. Einstein (and his friend Bucky) enjoyed the problems and wrote back to Wertheimer. Here is part of his reply:

> Your letter gave us a lot of amusement. The first intelligence test fooled both of us (Bucky and me). Only on working it out did I notice that no time is available for the downhill run! Mr. Bucky was also taken in by the second example, but I was not. Such drolleries show us how stupid we are!

(See *Mathematical Intelligencer*, Spring 1990, page 41.)

# Problems

1. **Distance, Time, and Speed**    A man drives from home to work at a speed of 50 mi/h. The return trip from work to home is traveled at the more leisurely pace of 30 mi/h. What is the man's average speed for the round-trip?

2. **Distance, Time, and Speed**    An old car has to travel a 2-mile route, uphill and down. Because it is so old, the car can climb the first mile—the ascent—no faster than an average speed of 15 mi/h. How fast does the car have to travel the second mile—on the descent it can go faster, of course—to achieve an average speed of 30 mi/h for the trip?

3. **A Speeding Fly**    A car and a van are parked 120 mi apart on a straight road. The drivers start driving toward each other at noon, each at a speed of 40 mi/h. A fly starts from the front bumper of the van at noon and flies to the bumper of the car, then immediately back to the bumper of the van, back to the car, and so on, until the car and the van meet. If the fly flies at a speed of 100 mi/h, what is the total distance it travels?

4. **Comparing Discounts**    Which price is better for the buyer, a 40% discount or two successive discounts of 20%?

5. **Cutting up a Wire**    A piece of wire is bent as shown in the figure. You can see that one cut through the wire produces four pieces and two parallel cuts produce seven pieces. How many pieces will be produced by 142 parallel cuts? Write a formula for the number of pieces produced by *n* parallel cuts.

6. **Amoeba Propagation**    An amoeba propagates by simple division; each split takes 3 minutes to complete. When such an amoeba is put into a glass container with a nutrient fluid, the container is full of amoebas in one hour. How long would it take for the container to be filled if we start with not one amoeba, but two?

7. **Running Laps**    Two runners start running laps at the same time, from the same starting position. George runs a lap in 50 s; Sue runs a lap in 30 s. When will the runners next be side by side?

8. **Batting Averages**    Player A has a higher batting average than player B for the first half of the baseball season. Player A also has a higher batting average than player B for the second half of the season. Is it necessarily true that player A has a higher batting average than player B for the entire season?

9. **Coffee and Cream**    A spoonful of cream is taken from a pitcher of cream and put into a cup of coffee. The coffee is stirred. Then a spoonful of this mixture is put into the pitcher of cream. Is there now more cream in the coffee cup or more coffee in the pitcher of cream?

10. **A Melting Ice Cube**    An ice cube is floating in a cup of water, full to the brim, as shown in the sketch. As the ice melts, what happens? Does the cup overflow, or does the water level drop, or does it remain the same? (You need to know Archimedes' Principle: A floating object displaces a volume of water whose weight equals the weight of the object.)

11. **Wrapping the World**    A ribbon is tied tightly around the earth at the equator. How much more ribbon would you need if you raised the ribbon 1 ft above the equator everywhere? (You don't need to know the radius of the earth to solve this problem.)

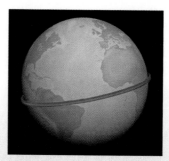

12. **Irrational Powers**  Prove that it's possible to raise an irrational number to an irrational power and get a rational result.  [*Hint:* The number $a = \sqrt{2}^{\sqrt{2}}$ is either rational or irrational. If $a$ is rational, you are done. If $a$ is irrational, consider $a^{\sqrt{2}}$.]

13. **A Perfect Cube**  Show that if you multiply three consecutive integers and then add the middle integer to the result, you get a perfect cube.

14. **Number Patterns**  Find the last digit in the number $3^{459}$.  [*Hint:* Calculate the first few powers of 3, and look for a pattern.]

15. **Number Patterns**  Use the techniques of solving a simpler problem and looking for a pattern to evaluate the number

$$3999999999999^2$$

16. **Ending Up Where You Started**  A woman starts at a point $P$ on the earth's surface and walks 1 mi south, then 1 mi east, then 1 mi north, and finds herself back at $P$, the starting point. Describe all points $P$ for which this is possible (there are infinitely many).

17. **Volume of a Truncated Pyramid**  The ancient Egyptians, as a result of their pyramid building, knew that the volume of a pyramid with height $h$ and square base of side length $a$ is $V = \frac{1}{3}ha^2$. They were able to use this fact to prove that the volume of a truncated pyramid is $V = \frac{1}{3}h(a^2 + ab + b^2)$, where $h$ is the height and $b$ and $a$ are the lengths of the sides of the square top and bottom, as shown in the figure. Prove the truncated pyramid volume formula.

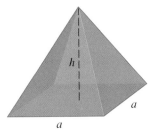
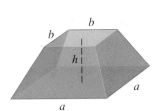

**Bhaskara** (born 1114) was an Indian mathematician, astronomer, and astrologer. Among his many accomplishments was an ingenious proof of the Pythagorean Theorem (see Problem 19). His important mathematical book *Lilavati* [*The Beautiful*] consists of algebra problems posed in the form of stories to his daughter Lilavati. Many of the problems begin "Oh beautiful maiden, suppose . . ." The story is told that using astrology, Bhaskara had determined that great misfortune would befall his daughter if she married at any time other than at a certain hour of a certain day. On her wedding day, as she was anxiously watching the water clock, a pearl fell unnoticed from her headdress. It stopped the flow of water in the clock, causing her to miss the opportune moment for marriage. Bhaskara's *Lilavati* was written to console her.

18. **Area of a Ring**  Find the area of the region between the two concentric circles shown in the figure.

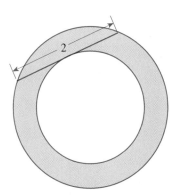

19. **Bhaskara's Proof**  The Indian mathematician Bhaskara sketched the two figures shown here and wrote below them, "Behold!" Explain how his sketches prove the Pythagorean Theorem.

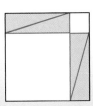

**20. Simple Numbers**

    **(a)** Use a calculator to find the value of the expression

$$\sqrt{3 + 2\sqrt{2}} - \sqrt{3 - 2\sqrt{2}}$$

The number looks very simple. Show that the calculated value is correct.

    **(b)** Use a calculator to evaluate

$$\frac{\sqrt{2} + \sqrt{6}}{\sqrt{2} + \sqrt{3}}$$

Show that the calculated value is correct.

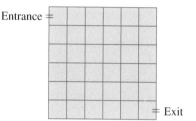

Entrance — Exit

**21. The Impossible Museum Tour**   A museum is in the shape of a square with six rooms to a side; the entrance and exit are at diagonally opposite corners, as shown in the figure. Each pair of adjacent rooms is joined by a door. Some very efficient tourists would like to tour the museum by visiting each room *exactly* once. Can you find a path for such a tour? Here are examples of attempts that failed.

Oops! Missed this room.

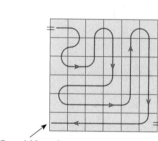 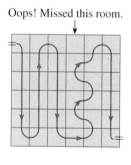

Oops! No exit.

Here is how you can prove that the museum tour is not possible. Imagine that the rooms are colored black and white like a checkerboard.

    **(a)** Show that the room colors alternate between white and black as the tourists walk through the museum.

    **(b)** Use part (a) and the fact that there are an even number of rooms in the museum to conclude that the tour cannot end at the exit.

# CHAPTER 1

# Equations and Inequalities

© Creatas/Photolibrary

**The Age of the Cell Phone?** Cell phones provide us with such an amazing level of communication that some people have labeled our times "the age of the cell phone." With these small hand-held devices we can contact *anyone* from *anywhere* at *any time*! Of course, mathematics is crucially involved in almost every stage of the design and operation of cell phones—from the digital transmission of sound to the complex routing of calls through the network of cell phone towers. Algebra is also involved in answering much more ordinary questions about cell phones, such as these: Am I paying too much for my cell phone plan? Which plan saves me the most money for my level of calling? In this chapter we will see how equations and inequalities can help us to answer such questions. (See Problem 7 in *Focus on Modeling: Making the Best Decisions*, page 135.)

## 1.1 | Basic Equations

**LEARNING OBJECTIVES**

After completing this section, you will be able to:

■  Solve linear equations
■  Solve power equations
■  Solve for one variable in terms of others

Equations are the basic mathematical tool for solving real-world problems. In this chapter we learn how to solve equations, as well as how to construct equations that model real-life situations.

An equation is a statement that two mathematical expressions are equal. For example,

$$3 + 5 = 8$$

is an equation. Most equations that we study in algebra contain variables, which are symbols (usually letters) that stand for numbers. In the equation

$$4x + 7 = 19$$

the letter $x$ is the variable. We think of $x$ as the "unknown" in the equation, and our goal is to find the value of $x$ that makes the equation true. The values of the unknown that make the equation true are called the **solutions** or **roots** of the equation, and the process of finding the solutions is called **solving the equation**.

Two equations with exactly the same solutions are called **equivalent equations**. To solve an equation, we try to find a simpler, equivalent equation in which the variable stands alone on one side of the "equal" sign. Here are the properties that we use to solve an equation. (In these properties, $A$, $B$, and $C$ stand for any algebraic expressions, and the symbol $\Leftrightarrow$ means "is equivalent to.")

$x = 3$ is a solution of the equation $4x + 7 = 19$, because substituting $x = 3$ makes the equation true:

$$x = 3$$

$$4(3) + 7 = 19$$

---

**PROPERTIES OF EQUALITY**

| Property | Description |
|---|---|
| 1. $A = B \quad \Leftrightarrow \quad A + C = B + C$ | Adding the same quantity to both sides of an equation gives an equivalent equation. |
| 2. $A = B \quad \Leftrightarrow \quad CA = CB$    $(C \neq 0)$ | Multiplying both sides of an equation by the same nonzero quantity gives an equivalent equation. |

---

These properties require that you *perform the same operation on both sides of an equation* when solving it. Thus, if we say "*add* −7" when solving an equation, that is just a short way of saying "*add* −7 to each side of the equation."

### ■ Solving Linear Equations

The simplest type of equation is a *linear equation*, or first-degree equation, which is an equation in which each term is either a constant or a nonzero multiple of the variable.

---

**LINEAR EQUATIONS**

A **linear equation** in one variable is an equation that is equivalent to one of the form

$$ax + b = 0$$

where $a$ and $b$ are real numbers and $x$ is the variable.

---

Here are some examples that illustrate the difference between linear and nonlinear equations.

| Linear equations | Nonlinear equations | |
|---|---|---|
| $4x - 5 = 3$ | $x^2 + 2x = 8$ | Not linear; contains the square of the variable |
| $2x = \frac{1}{2}x - 7$ | $\sqrt{x} - 6x = 0$ | Not linear; contains the square root of the variable |
| $x - 6 = \dfrac{x}{3}$ | $\dfrac{3}{x} - 2x = 1$ | Not linear; contains the reciprocal of the variable |

▶ **EXAMPLE 1** | Solving a Linear Equation

Solve the equation $7x - 4 = 3x + 8$.

▼ **SOLUTION**    We solve this by changing it to an equivalent equation with all terms that have the variable $x$ on one side and all constant terms on the other.

$$
\begin{array}{ll}
7x - 4 = 3x + 8 & \text{Given equation} \\
(7x - 4) + 4 = (3x + 8) + 4 & \text{Add 4} \\
7x = 3x + 12 & \text{Simplify} \\
7x - 3x = (3x + 12) - 3x & \text{Subtract } 3x \\
4x = 12 & \text{Simplify} \\
\tfrac{1}{4} \cdot 4x = \tfrac{1}{4} \cdot 12 & \text{Multiply by } \tfrac{1}{4} \\
x = 3 & \text{Simplify}
\end{array}
$$

Because it is important to CHECK YOUR ANSWER, we do this in many of our examples. In these checks, LHS stands for "left-hand side" and RHS stands for "right-hand side" of the original equation.

| **Check Your Answer** | $x = 3$ | $x = 3$ |
|---|---|---|
| $x = 3$: | $\text{LHS} = 7(3) - 4$ | $\text{RHS} = 3(3) + 8$ |
| | $= 17$ | $= 17$ |
| LHS = RHS   ✔ | | |

✎ **Practice what you've learned: Do Exercise 17.**    ▲

When a linear equation involves fractions, solving the equation is usually easier if we first multiply each side by the lowest common denominator (LCD) of the fractions, as we see in the following examples.

▶ **EXAMPLE 2** | Solving an Equation That Involves Fractions

Solve the equation $\dfrac{x}{6} + \dfrac{2}{3} = \dfrac{3}{4}x$.

▼ **SOLUTION**    The LCD of the denominators 6, 3, and 4 is 12, so we first multiply each side of the equation by 12 to clear the denominators.

$$
\begin{array}{ll}
12 \cdot \left( \dfrac{x}{6} + \dfrac{2}{3} \right) = 12 \cdot \dfrac{3}{4}x & \text{Multiply by LCD} \\[2mm]
2x + 8 = 9x & \text{Distributive Property} \\[2mm]
8 = 7x & \text{Subtract } 2x \\[2mm]
\dfrac{8}{7} = x & \text{Divide by 7}
\end{array}
$$

The solution is $x = \frac{8}{7}$.

✎ **Practice what you've learned: Do Exercise 21.**    ▲

In the next example we solve an equation that doesn't look like a linear equation, but it simplifies to one when we multiply by the LCD.

▶ **EXAMPLE 3** | An Equation Involving Fractional Expressions

Solve the equation $\dfrac{1}{x + 1} + \dfrac{1}{x - 2} = \dfrac{x + 3}{x^2 - x - 2}$.

▼ **SOLUTION**    The LCD of the fractional expressions is $(x + 1)(x - 2) = x^2 - x - 2$. So as long as $x \neq -1$ and $x \neq 2$, we can multiply both sides of the equation by the LCD to get

$$(x + 1)(x - 2)\left(\frac{1}{x + 1} + \frac{1}{x - 2}\right) = (x + 1)(x - 2)\left(\frac{x + 3}{x^2 - x - 2}\right) \qquad \text{Mulitiply by LCD}$$

$$(x - 2) + (x + 1) = x + 3 \qquad \text{Expand}$$

$$2x - 1 = x + 3 \qquad \text{Simplify}$$

$$x = 4 \qquad \text{Solve}$$

The solution is $x = 4$.

---

**Check Your Answer**

$x = 4$:

$$\text{LHS} = \frac{1}{4 + 1} + \frac{1}{4 - 2} \qquad \text{RHS} = \frac{4 + 3}{4^2 - 4 - 2} = \frac{7}{10}$$

$$= \frac{1}{5} + \frac{1}{2} = \frac{7}{10}$$

LHS = RHS    ✔

---

✎ **Practice what you've learned: Do Exercise 43.**    ▲

It is always important to check your answer, even if you never make a mistake in your calculations. This is because you sometimes end up with **extraneous solutions**, which are potential solutions that do not satisfy the original equation. The next example shows how this can happen.

▶ **EXAMPLE 4** | An Equation with No Solution

Solve the equation $2 + \dfrac{5}{x - 4} = \dfrac{x + 1}{x - 4}$.

▼ **SOLUTION**    First, we multiply each side by the common denominator, which is $x - 4$.

$$(x - 4)\left(2 + \frac{5}{x - 4}\right) = (x - 4)\left(\frac{x + 1}{x - 4}\right) \qquad \text{Multiply by } x - 4$$

$$2(x - 4) + 5 = x + 1 \qquad \text{Expand}$$

$$2x - 8 + 5 = x + 1 \qquad \text{Distributive Property}$$

$$2x - 3 = x + 1 \qquad \text{Simplify}$$

$$2x = x + 4 \qquad \text{Add 3}$$

$$x = 4 \qquad \text{Subtract } x$$

**Check Your Answer**

$x = 4$:

$$\text{LHS} = 2 + \frac{5}{4 - 4} = 2 + \frac{5}{0}$$

$$\text{RHS} = \frac{4 + 1}{4 - 4} = \frac{5}{0}$$

Impossible—can't divide by 0. LHS and RHS are undefined, so $x = 4$ is not a solution.    ✗

But now if we try to substitute $x = 4$ back into the original equation, we would be dividing by 0, which is impossible. So this equation has *no solution*.

✎ **Practice what you've learned: Do Exercise 47.**    ▲

The first step in the preceding solution, multiplying by $x - 4$, had the effect of multiplying by 0. (Do you see why?) Multiplying each side of an equation by an expression that contains the variable may introduce extraneous solutions. That is why it is important to check every answer.

## ■ Solving Power Equations

Linear equations have variables only to the first power. Now let's consider some equations that involve squares, cubes, and other powers of the variable. Such equations will be studied more extensively in Sections 1.3 and 1.5. Here we just consider basic equations that can be simplified into the form $X^n = a$. Equations of this form are called **power equations** and can be solved by taking radicals of both sides of the equation.

> **SOLVING A POWER EQUATION**
>
> The power equation $X^n = a$ has the solution
>
> $$X = \sqrt[n]{a} \quad \text{if } n \text{ is odd}$$
> $$X = \pm\sqrt[n]{a} \quad \text{if } n \text{ is even and } a \geq 0$$
>
> If $n$ is even and $a < 0$, the equation has no real solution.

"Algebra is a merry science," Uncle Jakob would say. "We go hunting for a little animal whose name we don't know, so we call it $x$. When we bag our game we pounce on it and give it its right name."

ALBERT EINSTEIN

Here are some examples of solving power equations.

The equation $x^5 = 32$ has only one real solution: $x = \sqrt[5]{32} = 2$.

The equation $x^4 = 16$ has two real solutions: $x = \pm\sqrt[4]{16} = \pm 2$.

The equation $x^5 = -32$ has only one real solution: $x = \sqrt[5]{-32} = -2$.

The equation $x^4 = -16$ has no real solutions because $\sqrt[4]{-16}$ does not exist.

▶ **EXAMPLE 5** | Solving Power Equations

Solve each equation.
**(a)** $x^2 - 5 = 0$
**(b)** $(x - 4)^2 = 5$

▼ **SOLUTION**
**(a)** $x^2 - 5 = 0$

$$x^2 = 5 \qquad \text{Add 5}$$
$$x = \pm\sqrt{5} \qquad \text{Take the square root}$$

The solutions are $x = \sqrt{5}$ and $x = -\sqrt{5}$.

**Euclid** (circa 300 B.C.) taught in Alexandria, Egypt. His *Elements* is the most widely influential scientific book in history. For 2000 years it was the standard introduction to geometry in the schools, and for many generations it was considered the best way to develop logical reasoning. Abraham Lincoln, for instance, studied the *Elements* as a way to sharpen his mind. The story is told that King Ptolemy once asked Euclid whether there was a faster way to learn geometry than through the *Elements*. Euclid replied that there is "no royal road to geometry"—meaning by this that mathematics does not respect wealth or social status. Euclid was revered in his own time and was referred to by the title "The Geometer" or "The Writer of the *Elements*." The greatness of the *Elements* stems from its precise, logical, and systematic treatment of geometry. For dealing with equality, Euclid lists the following rules, which he calls "common notions":

**1.** Things that are equal to the same thing are equal to each other.

**2.** If equals are added to equals, the sums are equal.

**3.** If equals are subtracted from equals, the remainders are equal.

**4.** Things that coincide with one another are equal.

**5.** The whole is greater than the part.

© Mary Evans Picture Library/Alamy

**(b)** We can take the square root of each side of this equation as well.

$$(x - 4)^2 = 5$$

$$x - 4 = \pm\sqrt{5} \qquad \text{Take the square root}$$

$$x = 4 \pm \sqrt{5} \qquad \text{Add 4}$$

The solutions are $x = 4 + \sqrt{5}$ and $x = 4 - \sqrt{5}$.

Be sure to check that each answer satisfies the original equation.

✎ **Practice what you've learned: Do Exercises 53 and 59.**  ▲

We will revisit equations like the ones in Example 5 in Section 1.3.

▶ **EXAMPLE 6** | Solving Power Equations

Find all real solutions for each equation.

**(a)** $x^3 = -8$

**(b)** $16x^4 = 81$

▼ **SOLUTION**

**(a)** Since every real number has exactly one real cube root, we can solve this equation by taking the cube root of each side.

$$(x^3)^{1/3} = (-8)^{1/3}$$

$$x = -2$$

**(b)** Here we must remember that if $n$ is even, then every positive real number has *two* real $n$th roots, a positive one and a negative one.

$$x^4 = \tfrac{81}{16} \qquad \text{Divide by 16}$$

$$(x^4)^{1/4} = \pm\left(\tfrac{81}{16}\right)^{1/4} \qquad \text{Take the fourth root}$$

$$x = \pm\tfrac{3}{2}$$

⊘ If $n$ is even, the equation $x^n = c$ ($c > 0$) has two solutions, $x = c^{1/n}$ and $x = -c^{1/n}$.

✎ **Practice what you've learned: Do Exercises 61 and 63.**  ▲

The next example shows how to solve an equation that involves a fractional power of the variable.

▶ **EXAMPLE 7** | Solving an Equation with a Fractional Power

Solve the equation $5x^{2/3} - 2 = 43$.

▼ **SOLUTION**  The idea is to first isolate the term with the fractional exponent, then raise both sides of the equation to the *reciprocal* of that exponent.

⊘ If $n$ is even, the equation $x^{n/m} = c$ has two solutions, $x = c^{m/n}$ and $x = -c^{m/n}$.

$$5x^{2/3} - 2 = 43$$

$$5x^{2/3} = 45 \qquad \text{Add 2}$$

$$x^{2/3} = 9 \qquad \text{Divide by 5}$$

$$x = \pm 9^{3/2} \qquad \text{Raise both sides to } \tfrac{3}{2} \text{ power}$$

$$x = \pm 27 \qquad \text{Simplify}$$

The solutions are $x = 27$ and $x = -27$.

---

**Check Your Answers**

| $x = 27$: | $x = -27$: |
|---|---|
| LHS $= 5(27)^{2/3} - 2$ | LHS $= 5(-27)^{2/3} - 2$ |
| $= 5(9) - 2$ | $= 5(9) - 2$ |
| $= 43$ | $= 43$ |
| RHS $= 43$ | RHS $= 43$ |
| LHS $=$ RHS ✔ | LHS $=$ RHS ✔ |

---

✎ **Practice what you've learned: Do Exercise 73.**    ▲

## ◼ Solving for One Variable in Terms of Others

Many formulas in the sciences involve several variables, and it is often necessary to express one of the variables in terms of the others. In the next example we solve for a variable in Newton's Law of Gravity.

▶ **EXAMPLE 8** | Solving for One Variable in Terms of Others

Solve for the variable $M$ in the equation

$$F = G\frac{mM}{r^2}$$

▼ **SOLUTION**    Although this equation involves more than one variable, we solve it as usual by isolating $M$ on one side and treating the other variables as we would numbers.

$$F = \left(\frac{Gm}{r^2}\right)M \qquad \text{Factor M from RHS}$$

$$\left(\frac{r^2}{Gm}\right)F = \left(\frac{r^2}{Gm}\right)\left(\frac{Gm}{r^2}\right)M \qquad \text{Multiply by reciprocal of } \frac{Gm}{r^2}$$

$$\frac{r^2F}{Gm} = M \qquad \text{Simplify}$$

The solution is $M = \dfrac{r^2F}{Gm}$.

✎ **Practice what you've learned: Do Exercise 83.**    ▲

▶ **EXAMPLE 9** | Solving for One Variable in Terms of Others

The surface area $A$ of the closed rectangular box shown in Figure 1 can be calculated from the length $l$, the width $w$, and the height $h$ according to the formula

$$A = 2lw + 2wh + 2lh$$

Solve for $w$ in terms of the other variables in this equation.

▼ **SOLUTION**    Although this equation involves more than one variable, we solve it as usual by isolating $w$ on one side, treating the other variables as we would numbers.

$$A = (2lw + 2wh) + 2lh \qquad \text{Collect terms involving w}$$

$$A - 2lh = 2lw + 2wh \qquad \text{Subtract 2lh}$$

This is Newton's Law of Gravity. It gives the gravitational force $F$ between two masses $m$ and $M$ that are a distance $r$ apart. The constant $G$ is the universal gravitational constant.

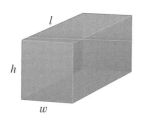

**FIGURE 1** A closed rectangular box

$$A - 2lh = (2l + 2h)w \qquad \text{Factor } w \text{ from RHS}$$

$$\frac{A - 2lh}{2l + 2h} = w \qquad \text{Divide by } 2l + 2h$$

The solution is $w = \dfrac{A - 2lh}{2l + 2h}$.

✎ **Practice what you've learned: Do Exercise 85.**                    ▲

# 1.1 EXERCISES

## ▼ CONCEPTS

**1.** Which of the following equations are linear?

    **(a)** $\dfrac{x}{2} + 2x = 10$    **(b)** $\dfrac{2}{x} - 2x = 1$    **(c)** $x + 7 = 5 - 3x$

**2.** Explain why each of the following equations is not linear.
    **(a)** $x(x + 1) = 6$    **(b)** $\sqrt{x} + 2 = x$    **(c)** $3x^2 - 2x - 1 = 0$

**3.** *True or false?*
    **(a)** Adding the same number to each side of an equation always gives an equivalent equation.
    **(b)** Multiplying each side of an equation by the same number always gives an equivalent equation.
    **(c)** Squaring each side of an equation always gives an equivalent equation.

**4.** To solve the equation $x^3 = 125$, we take the _____ root of each side. So the solution is $x =$ _____.

## ▼ SKILLS

**5–12** ■ Determine whether the given value is a solution of the equation.

**5.** $4x + 7 = 9x - 3$
    **(a)** $x = -2$                 **(b)** $x = 2$

**6.** $2 - 5x = 8 + x$
    **(a)** $x = -1$                 **(b)** $x = 1$

**7.** $1 - [2 - (3 - x)] = 4x - (6 + x)$
    **(a)** $x = 2$                 **(b)** $x = 4$

**8.** $\dfrac{1}{x} - \dfrac{1}{x - 4} = 1$
    **(a)** $x = 2$                 **(b)** $x = 4$

**9.** $2x^{1/3} - 3 = 1$
    **(a)** $x = -1$                 **(b)** $x = 8$

**10.** $\dfrac{x^{3/2}}{x - 6} = x - 8$
    **(a)** $x = 4$                 **(b)** $x = 8$

**11.** $\dfrac{x - a}{x - b} = \dfrac{a}{b}$    $(b \neq 0)$
    **(a)** $x = 0$                 **(b)** $x = b$

**12.** $x^2 - bx + \dfrac{1}{4}b^2 = 0$
    **(a)** $x = \dfrac{b}{2}$                 **(b)** $x = \dfrac{1}{b}$

**13–50** ■ The given equation is either linear or equivalent to a linear equation. Solve the equation.

**13.** $2x + 7 = 31$                 **14.** $5x - 3 = 4$

**15.** $\frac{1}{2}x - 8 = 1$             **16.** $3 + \frac{1}{3}x = 5$

✎ **17.** $x - 3 = 2x + 6$         **18.** $4x + 7 = 9x - 13$

**19.** $-7w = 15 - 2w$         **20.** $5t - 13 = 12 - 5t$

✎ **21.** $\frac{1}{2}y - 2 = \frac{1}{3}y$           **22.** $\dfrac{z}{5} = \dfrac{3}{10}z + 7$

**23.** $2(1 - x) = 3(1 + 2x) + 5$

**24.** $5(x + 3) + 9 = -2(x - 2) - 1$

**25.** $4\left(y - \frac{1}{2}\right) - y = 6(5 - y)$    **26.** $\dfrac{2}{3}y + \dfrac{1}{2}(y - 3) = \dfrac{y + 1}{4}$

**27.** $x - \frac{1}{3}x - \frac{1}{2}x - 5 = 0$    **28.** $2x - \dfrac{x}{2} + \dfrac{x + 1}{4} = 6x$

**29.** $\dfrac{1}{x} = \dfrac{4}{3x} + 1$           **30.** $\dfrac{2x - 1}{x + 2} = \dfrac{4}{5}$

**31.** $\dfrac{2}{t + 6} = \dfrac{3}{t - 1}$         **32.** $\dfrac{1}{t - 1} + \dfrac{t}{3t - 2} = \dfrac{1}{3}$

**33.** $r - 2[1 - 3(2r + 4)] = 61$

**34.** $(t - 4)^2 = (t + 4)^2 + 32$

**35.** $\sqrt{3}x + \sqrt{12} = \dfrac{x + 5}{\sqrt{3}}$    **36.** $\frac{2}{3}x - \frac{1}{4} = \frac{1}{6}x - \frac{1}{9}$

**37.** $\dfrac{2}{x} - 5 = \dfrac{6}{x} + 4$         **38.** $\dfrac{6}{x - 3} = \dfrac{5}{x + 4}$

**39.** $\dfrac{3}{x + 1} - \dfrac{1}{2} = \dfrac{1}{3x + 3}$    **40.** $\dfrac{4}{x - 1} + \dfrac{2}{x + 1} = \dfrac{35}{x^2 - 1}$

**41.** $\dfrac{2x - 7}{2x + 4} = \dfrac{2}{3}$        **42.** $\dfrac{12x - 5}{6x + 3} = 2 - \dfrac{5}{x}$

✎ **43.** $\dfrac{1}{z} - \dfrac{1}{2z} - \dfrac{1}{5z} = \dfrac{10}{z + 1}$    **44.** $\dfrac{1}{1 - \dfrac{3}{2 + w}} = 60$

**45.** $\dfrac{u}{u - \dfrac{u + 1}{2}} = 4$

**46.** $\dfrac{1}{3 - t} + \dfrac{4}{3 + t} + \dfrac{16}{9 - t^2} = 0$

**47.** $\dfrac{x}{2x - 4} - 2 = \dfrac{1}{x - 2}$    **48.** $\dfrac{1}{x + 3} + \dfrac{5}{x^2 - 9} = \dfrac{2}{x - 3}$

**49.** $\dfrac{3}{x + 4} = \dfrac{1}{x} + \dfrac{6x + 12}{x^2 + 4x}$    **50.** $\dfrac{1}{x} - \dfrac{2}{2x + 1} = \dfrac{1}{2x^2 + x}$

**51–74** ▪ The given equation involves a power of the variable. Find all real solutions of the equation.

**51.** $x^2 = 49$                **52.** $x^2 = 18$

**53.** $x^2 - 24 = 0$           **54.** $x^2 - 7 = 0$

**55.** $8x^2 - 64 = 0$          **56.** $5x^2 - 125 = 0$

**57.** $x^2 + 16 = 0$           **58.** $6x^2 + 100 = 0$

**59.** $(x + 2)^2 = 4$          **60.** $3(x - 5)^2 = 15$

**61.** $x^3 = 27$               **62.** $x^5 + 32 = 0$

**63.** $x^4 - 16 = 0$           **64.** $64x^6 = 27$

**65.** $x^4 + 64 = 0$           **66.** $(x - 1)^3 + 8 = 0$

**67.** $(x + 2)^4 - 81 = 0$     **68.** $(x + 1)^4 + 16 = 0$

**69.** $3(x - 3)^3 = 375$       **70.** $4(x + 2)^5 = 1$

**71.** $\sqrt[3]{x} = 5$        **72.** $x^{4/3} - 16 = 0$

**73.** $2x^{5/3} + 64 = 0$      **74.** $6x^{2/3} - 216 = 0$

**75–82** ▪ Find the solution of the equation correct to two decimals.

**75.** $3.02x + 1.48 = 10.92$   **76.** $8.36 - 0.95x = 9.97$

**77.** $2.15x - 4.63 = x + 1.19$    **78.** $3.95 - x = 2.32x + 2.00$

**79.** $3.16(x + 4.63) = 4.19(x - 7.24)$

**80.** $2.14(x - 4.06) = 2.27 - 0.11x$

**81.** $\dfrac{0.26x - 1.94}{3.03 - 2.44x} = 1.76$

**82.** $\dfrac{1.73x}{2.12 + x} = 1.51$

**83–96** ▪ Solve the equation for the indicated variable.

**83.** $PV = nRT$;  for $R$      **84.** $F = G\dfrac{mM}{r^2}$;  for $m$

**85.** $P = 2l + 2w$;  for $w$   **86.** $\dfrac{1}{R} = \dfrac{1}{R_1} + \dfrac{1}{R_2}$;  for $R_1$

**87.** $\dfrac{ax + b}{cx + d} = 2$;  for $x$

**88.** $a - 2[b - 3(c - x)] = 6$;  for $x$

**89.** $a^2x + (a - 1) = (a + 1)x$;  for $x$

**90.** $\dfrac{a + 1}{b} = \dfrac{a - 1}{b} + \dfrac{b + 1}{a}$;  for $a$

**91.** $V = \frac{1}{3}\pi r^2 h$;  for $r$    **92.** $F = G\dfrac{mM}{r^2}$;  for $r$

**93.** $a^2 + b^2 = c^2$;  for $b$

**94.** $A = P\left(1 + \dfrac{i}{100}\right)^2$;  for $i$

**95.** $V = \frac{4}{3}\pi r^3$;  for $r$    **96.** $x^4 + y^4 + z^4 = 100$;  for $x$

▼ **APPLICATIONS**

**97. Shrinkage in Concrete Beams**    As concrete dries, it shrinks; the higher the water content, the greater the shrinkage. If a concrete beam has a water content of $w$ kg/m³, then it will shrink by a factor

$$S = \dfrac{0.032w - 2.5}{10{,}000}$$

where $S$ is the fraction of the original beam length that disappears owing to shrinkage.
 **(a)** A beam 12.025 m long is cast in concrete that contains 250 kg/m³ water. What is the shrinkage factor $S$? How long will the beam be when it has dried?
 **(b)** A beam is 10.014 m long when wet. We want it to shrink to 10.009 m, so the shrinkage factor should be $S = 0.00050$. What water content will provide this amount of shrinkage?

**98. Manufacturing Cost**    A toy maker finds that it costs $C = 450 + 3.75x$ dollars to manufacture $x$ toy trucks. If the budget allows $3600 in costs, how many trucks can be made?

**99. Power Produced by a Windmill**    When the wind blows with speed $v$ km/h, a windmill with blade length 150 cm generates $P$ watts (W) of power according to the formula $P = 15.6\, v^3$.
 **(a)** How fast would the wind have to blow to generate 10,000 W of power?
 **(b)** How fast would the wind have to blow to generate 50,000 W of power?

**100. Food Consumption**    The average daily food consumption $F$ of a herbivorous mammal with body weight $x$, where both $F$ and $x$ are measured in pounds, is given approximately by the equation $F = 0.3x^{3/4}$. Find the weight $x$ of an elephant that consumes 300 lb of food per day.

▼ **DISCOVERY • DISCUSSION • WRITING**

**101. A Family of Equations**    The equation

$$3x + k - 5 = kx - k + 1$$

is really a **family of equations**, because for each value of $k$, we get a different equation with the unknown $x$. The letter $k$ is called a **parameter** for this family. What value should we pick for $k$ to make the given value of $x$ a solution of the resulting equation?

**(a)** $x = 0$      **(b)** $x = 1$      **(c)** $x = 2$

**102. Proof That $0 = 1$?** The following steps appear to give equivalent equations, which seem to prove that $1 = 0$.

Find the error.

| | |
|---|---|
| $x = 1$ | *Given* |
| $x^2 = x$ | *Multiply by x* |
| $x^2 - x = 0$ | *Subtract x* |
| $x(x - 1) = 0$ | *Factor* |
| $x = 0$ | *Divide by x − 1* |
| $1 = 0$ | *Given x = 1* |

---

## 1.2 | Modeling with Equations

### LEARNING OBJECTIVES

After completing this section, you will be able to:

- Make equations that model real-world situations
- Solve problems about interest
- Solve problems about areas and lengths
- Solve problems about mixtures and concentrations
- Solve problems about the time needed to do a job
- Solve problems about distance, speed, and time

Many problems in the sciences, economics, finance, medicine, and numerous other fields can be translated into algebra problems; this is one reason that algebra is so useful. In this section we use equations as mathematical models to solve real-life problems.

### ■ Making and Using Models

We will use the following guidelines to help us set up equations that model situations described in words. To show how the guidelines can help you to set up equations, we note them as we work each example in this section.

---

#### GUIDELINES FOR MODELING WITH EQUATIONS

1. **Identify the Variable.** Identify the quantity that the problem asks you to find. This quantity can usually be determined by a careful reading of the question that is posed at the end of the problem. Then **introduce notation** for the variable (call it $x$ or some other letter).

2. **Translate from Words to Algebra.** Read each sentence in the problem again, and express all the quantities mentioned in the problem in terms of the variable you defined in Step 1. To organize this information, it is sometimes helpful to **draw a diagram** or **make a table**.

3. **Set Up the Model.** Find the crucial fact in the problem that gives a relationship between the expressions you listed in Step 2. **Set up an equation** (or **model**) that expresses this relationship.

4. **Solve the Equation and Check Your Answer.** Solve the equation, check your answer, and express it as a sentence that answers the question posed in the problem.

---

The following example illustrates how these guidelines are used to translate a "word problem" into the language of algebra.

▶ **EXAMPLE 1** | Renting a Car

A car rental company charges $30 a day and 15¢ a mile for renting a car. Helen rents a car for two days, and her bill comes to $108. How many miles did she drive?

▼ **SOLUTION**

**Identify the variable.**    We are asked to find the number of miles Helen has driven. So we let

$$x = \text{number of miles driven}$$

**Translate from words to algebra.**    Now we translate all the information given in the problem into the language of algebra.

| In Words | In Algebra |
|---|---|
| Number of miles driven | $x$ |
| Mileage cost (at $0.15 per mile) | $0.15x$ |
| Daily cost (at $30 per day) | $2(30)$ |

**Set up the model.**    Now we set up the model.

$$\boxed{\text{mileage cost}} \; + \; \boxed{\text{daily cost}} \; = \; \boxed{\text{total cost}}$$

$$0.15x + 2(30) = 108$$

**Solve.**    Now we solve for $x$.

$$0.15x = 48 \qquad \text{Subtract 60}$$

$$x = \frac{48}{0.15} \qquad \text{Divide by 0.15}$$

$$x = 320 \qquad \text{Calculator}$$

Helen drove her rental car 320 miles.

---

**Check Your Answer**

total cost = mileage cost + daily cost

$$= 0.15(320) + 2(30)$$

$$= 108 \qquad ✔$$

---

✎ **Practice what you've learned: Do Exercise 19.**    ▲

In the examples and exercises that follow, we construct equations that model problems in many different real-life situations.

## ▪ Problems About Interest

When you borrow money from a bank or when a bank "borrows" your money by keeping it for you in a savings account, the borrower in each case must pay for the privilege of using the money. The fee that is paid is called **interest**. The most basic type of interest is **simple interest**, which is just an annual percentage of the total amount borrowed or deposited. The amount of a loan or deposit is called the **principal** $P$. The annual percentage paid for the use of this money is the **interest rate** $r$. We will use the variable $t$ to stand for the number of years that the money is on deposit and the variable $I$ to stand for the total interest earned. The following **simple interest formula** gives the amount of interest $I$ earned when a principal $P$ is deposited for $t$ years at an interest rate $r$.

$$\boxed{I = Prt}$$

 When using this formula, remember to convert $r$ from a percentage to a decimal. For example, in decimal form, 5% is 0.05. So at an interest rate of 5%, the interest paid on a $1000 deposit over a 3-year period is $I = Prt = 1000(0.05)(3) = $150$.

▶ **EXAMPLE 2** | Interest on an Investment

Mary inherits $100,000 and invests it in two certificates of deposit. One certificate pays 6% and the other pays $4\frac{1}{2}\%$ simple interest annually. If Mary's total interest is $5025 per year, how much money is invested at each rate?

▼ **SOLUTION**

**Identify the variable.**   The problem asks for the amount she has invested at each rate. So we let

$$x = \text{the amount invested at } 6\%$$

**Translate from words to algebra.**   Since Mary's total inheritance is $100,000, it follows that she invested $100,000 - x$ at $4\frac{1}{2}\%$. We translate all the information given into the language of algebra.

| In Words | In Algebra |
|---|---|
| Amount invested at 6% | $x$ |
| Amount invested at $4\frac{1}{2}\%$ | $100,000 - x$ |
| Interest earned at 6% | $0.06x$ |
| Interest earned at $4\frac{1}{2}\%$ | $0.045(100,000 - x)$ |

**Set up the model.**   We use the fact that Mary's total interest is $5025 to set up the model.

$$\boxed{\text{interest at } 6\%} + \boxed{\text{interest at } 4\tfrac{1}{2}\%} = \boxed{\text{total interest}}$$

$$0.06x + 0.045(100,000 - x) = 5025$$

**Solve.**   Now we solve for $x$.

$$
\begin{aligned}
0.06x + 4500 - 0.045x &= 5025 && \text{Multiply} \\
0.015x + 4500 &= 5025 && \text{Combine the x-terms} \\
0.015x &= 525 && \text{Subtract 4500} \\
x = \frac{525}{0.015} &= 35,000 && \text{Divide by 0.015}
\end{aligned}
$$

So Mary has invested $35,000 at 6% and the remaining $65,000 at $4\frac{1}{2}\%$.

---

**Check Your Answer**

$$
\begin{aligned}
\text{total interest} &= 6\% \text{ of } \$35,000 + 4\tfrac{1}{2}\% \text{ of } \$65,000 \\
&= \$2100 + \$2925 = \$5025 \quad ✔
\end{aligned}
$$

---

✎ **Practice what you've learned: Do Exercise 21.** ▲

## ■ Problems About Area or Length

When we use algebra to model a physical situation, we must sometimes use basic formulas from geometry. For example, we may need a formula for an area or a perimeter, or the formula that relates the sides of similar triangles, or the Pythagorean Theorem. Most of these formulas are listed in the front endpapers of this book. The next two examples use these geometric formulas to solve some real-world problems.

▶ **EXAMPLE 3** | Dimensions of a Garden

A square garden has a walkway 3 ft wide around its outer edge, as shown in Figure 1. If the area of the entire garden, including the walkway, is 18,000 ft², what are the dimensions of the planted area?

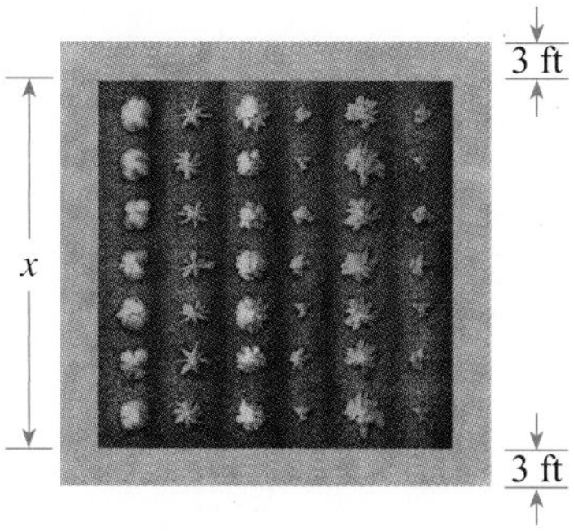

▼ **SOLUTION**

**Identify the variable.**    We are asked to find the length and width of the planted area. So we let

$$x = \text{the length of the planted area}$$

**Translate from words to algebra.**    Next, translate the information from Figure 1 into the language of algebra.

| In Words | In Algebra |
|---|---|
| Length of planted area | $x$ |
| Length of entire garden | $x + 6$ |
| Area of entire garden | $(x + 6)^2$ |

**Set up the model.**    We now set up the model.

$$\text{area of entire garden} = 18{,}000 \text{ ft}^2$$

$$(x + 6)^2 = 18{,}000$$

**Solve.**    Now we solve for $x$.

$$x + 6 = \sqrt{18{,}000} \qquad \text{Take square roots}$$

$$x = \sqrt{18{,}000} - 6 \qquad \text{Subtract 6}$$

$$x \approx 128$$

The planted area of the garden is about 128 ft by 128 ft.

✎ **Practice what you've learned: Do Exercise 41.**  ▲

**FIGURE 1**

▶ **EXAMPLE 4** | Determining the Height of a Building Using Similar Triangles

A man 6 ft tall wishes to find the height of a certain four-story building. He measures its shadow and finds it to be 28 ft long, while his own shadow is $3\frac{1}{2}$ ft long. How tall is the building?

▼ **SOLUTION**

**Identify the variable.**    The problem asks for the height of the building. So let

$$h = \text{the height of the building}$$

**Translate from words to algebra.**    We use the fact that the triangles in Figure 2 on the next page are similar. Recall that for any pair of similar triangles the ratios of corresponding sides are equal. Now we translate these observations into the language of algebra.

| In Words | In Algebra |
|---|---|
| Height of building | $h$ |
| Ratio of height to base in large triangle | $\frac{h}{28}$ |
| Ratio of height to base in small triangle | $\frac{6}{3.5}$ |

**FIGURE 2**

**Set up the model.**   Since the large and small triangles are similar, we get the equation

$$\boxed{\begin{array}{c}\text{ratio of height to}\\\text{base in large triangle}\end{array}} = \boxed{\begin{array}{c}\text{ratio of height to}\\\text{base in small triangle}\end{array}}$$

$$\frac{h}{28} = \frac{6}{3.5}$$

**Solve.**   Now we solve for $h$.

$$h = \frac{6 \cdot 28}{3.5} = 48 \qquad \text{Multiply by 28}$$

So the building is 48 ft tall.

✎ **Practice what you've learned: Do Exercise 43.**                                    ▲

## ■ Problems About Mixtures

Many real-world problems involve mixing different types of substances. For example, construction workers may mix cement, gravel, and sand; fruit juice from concentrate may involve mixing different types of juices. Problems involving mixtures and concentrations make use of the fact that if an amount $x$ of a substance is dissolved in a solution with volume $V$, then the concentration $C$ of the substance is given by

$$C = \frac{x}{V}$$

So if 10 g of sugar is dissolved in 5 L of water, then the sugar concentration is $C = 10/5 = 2$ g/L. Solving a mixture problem usually requires us to analyze the amount $x$ of the substance that is in the solution. When we solve for $x$ in this equation, we see that $x = CV$. Note that in many mixture problems the concentration $C$ is expressed as a percentage, as in the next example.

▶ **EXAMPLE 5** | Mixtures and Concentration

A manufacturer of soft drinks advertises their orange soda as "naturally flavored," although it contains only 5% orange juice. A new federal regulation stipulates that to be called "natural," a drink must contain at least 10% fruit juice. How much pure orange juice must this manufacturer add to 900 gal of orange soda to conform to the new regulation?

▼ **SOLUTION**

**Identify the variable.**   The problem asks for the amount of pure orange juice to be added. So let

$$x = \text{the amount (in gallons) of pure orange juice to be added}$$

Translate from words to algebra.    In any problem of this type—in which two different substances are to be mixed—drawing a diagram helps us to organize the given information (see Figure 3).

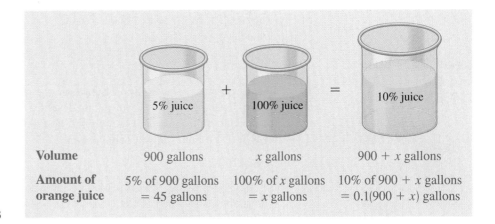

**Volume**

900 gallons     $x$ gallons     $900 + x$ gallons

**Amount of orange juice**

5% of 900 gallons = 45 gallons     100% of $x$ gallons = $x$ gallons     10% of $900 + x$ gallons = $0.1(900 + x)$ gallons

**FIGURE 3**

We now translate the information in the figure into the language of algebra.

| In Words | In Algebra |
|---|---|
| Amount of orange juice to be added | $x$ |
| Amount of the mixture | $900 + x$ |
| Amount of orange juice in the first vat | $0.05(900) = 45$ |
| Amount of orange juice in the second vat | $1 \cdot x = x$ |
| Amount of orange juice in the mixture | $0.10(900 + x)$ |

Set up the model.    To set up the model, we use the fact that the total amount of orange juice in the mixture is equal to the orange juice in the first two vats.

$$\begin{array}{ccc} \text{amount of} & \text{amount of} & \text{amount of} \\ \text{orange juice} & + \;\; \text{orange juice} & = \;\; \text{orange juice} \\ \text{in first vat} & \text{in second vat} & \text{in mixture} \end{array}$$

$$45 + x = 0.1(900 + x) \qquad \text{From Figure 3}$$

Solve.    Now we solve for $x$.

$$45 + x = 90 + 0.1x \qquad \text{Distributive Property}$$

$$0.9x = 45 \qquad \text{Subtract 0.1x and 45}$$

$$x = \frac{45}{0.9} = 50 \qquad \text{Divide by 0.9}$$

The manufacturer should add 50 gal of pure orange juice to the soda.

---

**Check Your Answer**

amount of juice before mixing = 5% of 900 gal + 50 gal pure juice

= 45 gal + 50 gal = 95 gal

amount of juice after mixing = 10% of 950 gal = 95 gal

Amounts are equal.    ✔

---

✏ **Practice what you've learned: Do Exercise 45.**     ▲

### ■ Problems About the Time Needed to Do a Job

When solving a problem that involves determining how long it takes several workers to complete a job, we use the fact that if a person or machine takes $H$ time units to complete the task, then in one time unit the fraction of the task that has been completed is $1/H$. For example, if a worker takes 5 hours to mow a lawn, then in 1 hour the worker will mow $1/5$ of the lawn.

▶ **EXAMPLE 6** | Time Needed to Do a Job

Because of an anticipated heavy rainstorm, the water level in a reservoir must be lowered by 1 ft. Opening spillway A lowers the level by this amount in 4 hours, whereas opening the smaller spillway B does the job in 6 hours. How long will it take to lower the water level by 1 ft if both spillways are opened?

▼ **SOLUTION**

**Identify the variable.**    We are asked to find the time needed to lower the level by 1 ft if both spillways are open. So let

$$x = \text{the time (in hours) it takes to lower the water level}$$
$$\text{by 1 ft if both spillways are open}$$

**Translate from words to algebra.**    Finding an equation relating $x$ to the other quantities in this problem is not easy. Certainly $x$ is not simply $4 + 6$, because that would mean that together the two spillways require longer to lower the water level than either spillway alone. Instead, *we look at the fraction of the job that can be done in 1 hour by each spillway.*

| In Words | In Algebra |
|---|---|
| Time it takes to lower level 1 ft with A and B together | $x$ h |
| Distance A lowers level in 1 h | $\frac{1}{4}$ ft |
| Distance B lowers level in 1 h | $\frac{1}{6}$ ft |
| Distance A and B together lower levels in 1 h | $\frac{1}{x}$ ft |

**Set up the model.**    Now we set up the model.

$$\boxed{\text{fraction done by A}} + \boxed{\text{fraction done by B}} = \boxed{\text{fraction done by both}}$$

$$\frac{1}{4} + \frac{1}{6} = \frac{1}{x}$$

**Solve.**    Now we solve for $x$.

$$3x + 2x = 12 \qquad \text{Multiply by the LCD, } 12x$$
$$5x = 12 \qquad \text{Add}$$
$$x = \frac{12}{5} \qquad \text{Divide by 5}$$

It will take $2\frac{2}{5}$ hours, or 2 h 24 min, to lower the water level by 1 ft if both spillways are open.

✎ **Practice what you've learned: Do Exercise 53.**                          ▲

### ■ Problems About Distance, Rate, and Time

The next example deals with distance, rate (speed), and time. The formula to keep in mind here is

$$\boxed{\text{distance} = \text{rate} \times \text{time}}$$

where the rate is either the constant speed or average speed of a moving object. For example, driving at 60 mi/h for 4 hours takes you a distance of $60 \cdot 4 = 240$ mi.

▶ **EXAMPLE 7** | Distance, Speed, and Time

Bill left his house at 2:00 P.M. and rode his bicycle down Main Street at a speed of 12 mi/h. When his friend Mary arrived at his house at 2:10 P.M., Bill's mother told her the direction in which Bill had gone, and Mary cycled after him at a speed of 16 mi/h. At what time did Mary catch up with Bill?

▼ **SOLUTION**

**Identify the variable.**   We are asked to find the time that it took Mary to catch up with Bill. Let

$$t = \text{the time (in hours) it took Mary to catch up with Bill}$$

**Translate from words to algebra.**   In problems involving motion, it is often helpful to organize the information in a table, using the formula distance = rate × time. First we fill in the "Speed" column in the table, since we are told the speeds at which Mary and Bill cycled. Then we fill in the "Time" column. (Because Bill had a 10-minute, or $\frac{1}{6}$-hour head start, he cycled for $t + \frac{1}{6}$ hours.) Finally, we multiply these columns to calculate the entries in the "Distance" column.

|  | Distance (mi) | Speed (mi/h) | Time (h) |
|---|---|---|---|
| **Mary** | $16t$ | 16 | $t$ |
| **Bill** | $12\left(t + \frac{1}{6}\right)$ | 12 | $t + \frac{1}{6}$ |

**Set up the model.**   At the instant when Mary caught up with Bill, they had both cycled the same distance. We use this fact to set up the model for this problem.

$$\boxed{\text{distance traveled by Mary}} = \boxed{\text{distance traveled by Bill}}$$

$$16t = 12\left(t + \tfrac{1}{6}\right) \qquad \text{From table}$$

**Solve.**   Now we solve for $t$.

$$16t = 12t + 2 \qquad \text{Distributive Property}$$

$$4t = 2 \qquad \text{Subtract } 12t$$

$$t = \tfrac{1}{2} \qquad \text{Divide by 4}$$

Mary caught up with Bill after cycling for half an hour, that is, at 2:40 P.M.

---

**Check Your Answer**

Bill traveled for $\frac{1}{2} + \frac{1}{6} = \frac{2}{3}$ h, so

$$\text{distance Bill traveled} = 12 \text{ mi/h} \times \tfrac{2}{3} \text{ h} = 8 \text{ mi}$$

$$\text{distance Mary traveled} = 16 \text{ mi/h} \times \tfrac{1}{2} \text{ h} = 8 \text{ mi}$$

Distances are equal.   ✔

---

✎ **Practice what you've learned: Do Exercise 57.**   ▲

# 1.2 EXERCISES

## ▼ CONCEPTS

1. Explain in your own words what it means for an equation to model a real-world situation, and give an example.

2. In the formula $I = Prt$ for simple interest, $P$ stands for
_____, $r$ for _____, and $t$ for _____.

3. Give a formula for the area of the geometric figure.

   **(a)** A square of side $x$:    $A =$ _____.

   **(b)** A rectangle of length $l$ and width $w$:    $A =$ _____.

   **(c)** A circle of radius $r$:    $A =$ _____.

4. Balsamic vinegar contains 5% acetic acid, so a 32-oz bottle of balsamic vinegar contains _____ ounces of acetic acid.

5. A painter paints a wall in $x$ hours, so the fraction of the wall that she paints in 1 hour is _____.

6. The formula $d = rt$ models the distance $d$ traveled by an object moving at the constant rate $r$ in time $t$. Find formulas for the following quantities.

   $r =$ _____          $t =$ _____.

## ▼ SKILLS

**7–18** ▪ Express the given quantity in terms of the indicated variable.

7. The sum of three consecutive integers;    $n =$ first integer of the three

8. The sum of three consecutive integers;    $n =$ middle integer of the three

9. The average of three test scores if the first two scores are 78 and 82;    $s =$ third test score

10. The average of four quiz scores if each of the first three scores is 8;    $q =$ fourth quiz score

11. The interest obtained after one year on an investment at $2\frac{1}{2}\%$ simple interest per year;    $x =$ number of dollars invested

12. The total rent paid for an apartment if the rent is $795 a month; $n =$ number of months

13. The area (in ft$^2$) of a rectangle that is three times as long as it is wide;    $w =$ width of the rectangle (in ft)

14. The perimeter (in cm) of a rectangle that is 5 cm longer than it is wide;    $w =$ width of the rectangle (in cm)

15. The distance (in mi) that a car travels in 45 min;    $s =$ speed of the car (in mi/h)

16. The time (in hours) it takes to travel a given distance at 55 mi/h;    $d =$ given distance (in mi)

17. The concentration (in oz/gal) of salt in a mixture of 3 gal of brine containing 25 oz of salt to which some pure water has been added;    $x =$ volume of pure water added (in gal)

18. The value (in cents) of the change in a purse that contains twice as many nickels as pennies, four more dimes than nickels, and as many quarters as dimes and nickels combined; $p =$ number of pennies

## ▼ APPLICATIONS

19. **Renting a Truck**    A rental company charges $65 a day and 20 cents a mile for renting a truck. Michael rents a truck for 3 days, and his bill comes to $275. How many miles did he drive?

20. **Cell Phone Costs**    A cell phone company charges a monthly fee of $10 for the first 1000 text messages and 10 cents for each additional text message. Miriam's bill for text messages for the month of June is $38.50. How many text messages did she send that month?

21. **Investments**    Phyllis invested $12,000, a portion earning a simple interest rate of $4\frac{1}{2}\%$ per year and the rest earning a rate of 4% per year. After 1 year the total interest earned on these investments was $525. How much money did she invest at each rate?

22. **Investments**    If Ben invests $4000 at 4% interest per year, how much additional money must he invest at $5\frac{1}{2}\%$ annual interest to ensure that the interest he receives each year is $4\frac{1}{2}\%$ of the total amount invested?

23. **Investments**    What annual rate of interest would you have to earn on an investment of $3500 to ensure receiving $262.50 interest after 1 year?

24. **Investments**    Jack invests $1000 at a certain annual interest rate, and he invests another $2000 at an annual rate that is one-half percent higher. If he receives a total of $190 interest in 1 year, at what rate is the $1000 invested?

25. **Salaries**    An executive in an engineering firm earns a monthly salary plus a Christmas bonus of $8500. If she earns a total of $97,300 per year, what is her monthly salary?

26. **Salaries**    A woman earns 15% more than her husband. Together they make $69,875 per year. What is the husband's annual salary?

27. **Inheritance**    Craig is saving to buy a vacation home. He inherits some money from a wealthy uncle, then combines this with the $22,000 he has already saved and doubles the total in a lucky investment. He ends up with $134,000—just enough to buy a cabin on the lake. How much did he inherit?

28. **Overtime Pay**    Helen earns $7.50 an hour at her job, but if she works more than 35 hours in a week, she is paid $1\frac{1}{2}$ times her regular salary for the overtime hours worked. One week her gross pay was $352.50. How many overtime hours did she work that week?

29. **Labor Costs**    A plumber and his assistant work together to replace the pipes in an old house. The plumber charges $45 an hour for his own labor and $25 an hour for his assistant's labor. The plumber works twice as long as his assistant on this job, and the labor charge on the final bill is $4025. How long did the plumber and his assistant work on this job?

30. **A Riddle**    A father is four times as old as his daughter. In 6 years, he will be three times as old as she is. How old is the daughter now?

31. **A Riddle**    A movie star, unwilling to give his age, posed the following riddle to a gossip columnist: "Seven years ago, I was eleven times as old as my daughter. Now I am four times as old as she is." How old is the movie star?

**32. Career Home Runs** During his major league career, Hank Aaron hit 41 more home runs than Babe Ruth hit during his career. Together they hit 1469 home runs. How many home runs did Babe Ruth hit?

**33. Value of Coins** A change purse contains an equal number of pennies, nickels, and dimes. The total value of the coins is $1.44. How many coins of each type does the purse contain?

**34. Value of Coins** Mary has $3.00 in nickels, dimes, and quarters. If she has twice as many dimes as quarters and five more nickels than dimes, how many coins of each type does she have?

**35. Length of a Garden** A rectangular garden is 25 ft wide. If its area is 1125 ft$^2$, what is the length of the garden?

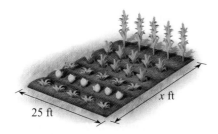

**36. Width of a Pasture** A pasture is twice as long as it is wide. Its area is 115,200 ft$^2$. How wide is the pasture?

**37. Dimensions of a Lot** A square plot of land has a building 60 ft long and 40 ft wide at one corner. The rest of the land outside the building forms a parking lot. If the parking lot has area 12,000 ft$^2$, what are the dimensions of the entire plot of land?

**38. Dimensions of a Lot** A half-acre building lot is five times as long as it is wide. What are its dimensions?
[*Note*: 1 acre = 43,560 ft$^2$.]

**39. Geometry** Find the length $y$ in the figure if the shaded area is 120 in$^2$.

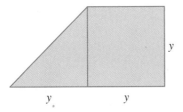

**40. Geometry** Find the length $x$ in the figure if the shaded area is 144 cm$^2$.

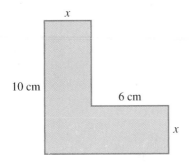

**41. Framing a Painting** Ali paints with watercolors on a sheet of paper 20 in. wide by 15 in. high. He then places this sheet on a mat so that a uniformly wide strip of the mat shows all around the picture. The perimeter of the mat is 102 in. How wide is the strip of the mat showing around the picture?

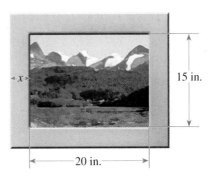

**42. A poster** has a rectangular printed area 100 cm by 140 cm and a blank strip of uniform width around the edges. The perimeter of the poster is $1\frac{1}{2}$ times the perimeter of the printed area. What is the width of the blank strip?

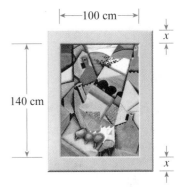

**43. Length of a Shadow** A man is walking away from a lamppost with a light source 6 m above the ground. The man is 2 m tall. How long is the man's shadow when he is 10 m from the lamppost? [*Hint*: Use similar triangles.]

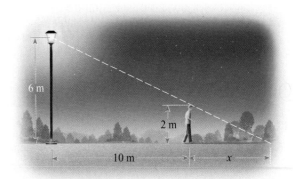

**44. Height of a Tree** A woodcutter determines the height of a tall tree by first measuring a smaller one 125 ft away, then moving so that his eyes are in the line of sight along the tops of the trees and measuring how far he is standing from the small tree (see the figure). Suppose the small tree is 20 ft tall, the man is 25 ft from the small tree, and his eye level is 5 ft above the ground. How tall is the taller tree?

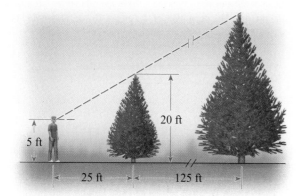

**45. Mixture Problem** What quantity of a 60% acid solution must be mixed with a 30% solution to produce 300 mL of a 50% solution?

**46. Mixture Problem** What quantity of pure acid must be added to 300 mL of a 50% acid solution to produce a 60% acid solution?

**47. Mixture Problem** A jeweler has five rings, each weighing 18 g, made of an alloy of 10% silver and 90% gold. She decides to melt down the rings and add enough silver to reduce the gold content to 75%. How much silver should she add?

**48. Mixture Problem** A pot contains 6 L of brine at a concentration of 120 g/L. How much of the water should be boiled off to increase the concentration to 200 g/L?

**49. Mixture Problem** The radiator in a car is filled with a solution of 60% antifreeze and 40% water. The manufacturer of the antifreeze suggests that for summer driving, optimal cooling of the engine is obtained with only 50% antifreeze. If the capacity of the radiator is 3.6 L, how much coolant should be drained and replaced with water to reduce the antifreeze concentration to the recommended level?

**50. Mixture Problem** A health clinic uses a solution of bleach to sterilize petri dishes in which cultures are grown. The sterilization tank contains 100 gal of a solution of 2% ordinary household bleach mixed with pure distilled water. New research indicates that the concentration of bleach should be 5% for complete sterilization. How much of the solution should be drained and replaced with bleach to increase the bleach content to the recommended level?

**51. Mixture Problem** A bottle contains 750 mL of fruit punch with a concentration of 50% pure fruit juice. Jill drinks 100 mL of the punch and then refills the bottle with an equal amount of a cheaper brand of punch. If the concentration of juice in the bottle is now reduced to 48%, what was the concentration in the punch that Jill added?

**52. Mixture Problem** A merchant blends tea that sells for $3.00 a pound with tea that sells for $2.75 a pound to produce 80 lb of a mixture that sells for $2.90 a pound. How many pounds of each type of tea does the merchant use in the blend?

**53. Sharing a Job** Candy and Tim share a paper route. It takes Candy 70 min to deliver all the papers, and it takes Tim 80 min. How long does it take the two when they work together?

**54. Sharing a Job** Stan and Hilda can mow the lawn in 40 min if they work together. If Hilda works twice as fast as Stan, how long does it take Stan to mow the lawn alone?

**55. Sharing a Job** Betty and Karen have been hired to paint the houses in a new development. Working together, the women can paint a house in two-thirds the time that it takes Karen working alone. Betty takes 6 h to paint a house alone. How long does it take Karen to paint a house working alone?

**56. Sharing a Job** Next-door neighbors Bob and Jim use hoses from both houses to fill Bob's swimming pool. They know that it takes 18 h using both hoses. They also know that Bob's hose, used alone, takes 20% less time than Jim's hose alone. How much time is required to fill the pool by each hose alone?

**57. Distance, Speed, and Time** Wendy took a trip from Davenport to Omaha, a distance of 300 mi. She traveled part of the way by bus, which arrived at the train station just in time for Wendy to complete her journey by train. The bus averaged 40 mi/h, and the train averaged 60 mi/h. The entire trip took $5\frac{1}{2}$ h. How long did Wendy spend on the train?

**58. Distance, Speed, and Time** Two cyclists, 90 mi apart, start riding toward each other at the same time. One cycles twice as fast as the other. If they meet 2 h later, at what average speed is each cyclist traveling?

**59. Distance, Speed, and Time** A pilot flew a jet from Montreal to Los Angeles, a distance of 2500 mi. On the return trip, the average speed was 20% faster than the outbound speed. The round-trip took 9 h 10 min. What was the speed from Montreal to Los Angeles?

**60. Distance, Speed, and Time** A woman driving a car 14 ft long is passing a truck 30 ft long. The truck is traveling at 50 mi/h. How fast must the woman drive her car so that she can pass the truck completely in 6 s, from the position shown in figure (a) to the position shown in figure (b)? [*Hint:* Use feet and seconds instead of miles and hours.]

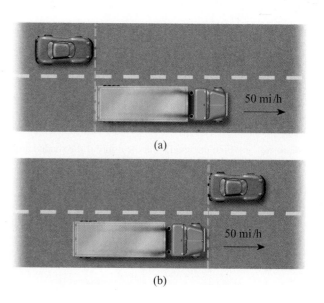

(a)

(b)

**61. Law of the Lever** The figure shows a lever system, similar to a seesaw that you might find in a children's playground. For the system to balance, the product of the weight and its distance from the fulcrum must be the same on each side; that is,

$$w_1 x_1 = w_2 x_2$$

This equation is called the **law of the lever** and was first discovered by Archimedes (see page 557).

A woman and her son are playing on a seesaw. The boy is at one end, 8 ft from the fulcrum. If the son weighs 100 lb and the mother weighs 125 lb, where should the woman sit so that the seesaw is balanced?

62. **Law of the Lever**    A plank 30 ft long rests on top of a flat-roofed building, with 5 ft of the plank projecting over the edge, as shown in the figure. A worker weighing 240 lb sits on one end of the plank. What is the largest weight that can be hung on the projecting end of the plank if it is to remain in balance? (Use the law of the lever stated in Exercise 61.)

63. **Dimensions of a Lot**    A rectangular parcel of land is 50 ft wide. The length of a diagonal between opposite corners is 10 ft more than the length of the parcel. What is the length of the parcel?

64. **Dimensions of a Track**    A running track has the shape shown in the figure, with straight sides and semicircular ends. If the length of the track is 440 yd and the two straight parts are each 110 yd long, what is the radius of the semicircular parts (to the nearest yard)?

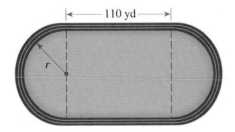

65. **Dimensions of a Structure**    A storage bin for corn consists of a cylindrical section made of wire mesh, surmounted by a conical tin roof, as shown in the figure. The height of the roof is one-third the height of the entire structure. If the total volume of the structure is $1400\pi$ ft$^3$ and its radius is 10 ft, what is its height?    [*Hint:* Use the volume formulas listed on the inside back cover of this book.]

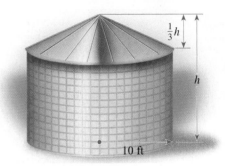

66. **An Ancient Chinese Problem**    This problem is taken from a Chinese mathematics textbook called *Chui-chang suan-shu*, or *Nine Chapters on the Mathematical Art*, which was written about 250 B.C.

A 10-ft-long stem of bamboo is broken in such a way that its tip touches the ground 3 ft from the base of the stem, as shown in the figure. What is the height of the break?

[*Hint:* Use the Pythagorean Theorem.]

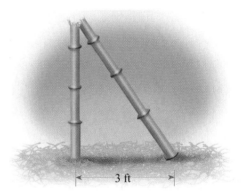

---

## ▼ DISCOVERY • DISCUSSION • WRITING

67. **Historical Research**    Read the biographical notes on Pythagoras (page 284), Euclid (page 69), and Archimedes (page 557). Choose one of these mathematicians and find out more about him from the library or on the Internet. Write a short essay on your findings. Include both biographical information and a description of the mathematics for which he is famous.

# EQUATIONS THROUGH THE AGES

Equations have been used to solve problems throughout recorded history in every civilization. (See, for example, Exercise 66 on page 85.) Here is a problem from ancient Babylon (ca. 2000 B.C.):

> I found a stone but did not weigh it. After I added a seventh, and then added an eleventh of the result, I weighed it and found it weighed 1 mina. What was the original weight of the stone?

The answer given on the cuneiform tablet is $\frac{2}{3}$ mina, 8 sheqel, and $22\frac{1}{2}$ se, where 1 mina = 60 sheqel and 1 sheqel = 180 se.

In ancient Egypt knowing how to solve word problems was a highly prized secret. The Rhind Papyrus (ca. 1850 B.C.) contains many such problems (see page 470). Problem 32 in the Papyrus states:

> A quantity, its third, its quarter, added together become 2. What is the quantity?

The answer in Egyptian notation is $1 + \overline{4} + \overline{76}$, where the bar indicates "reciprocal," much like our notation $4^{-1}$.

The Greek mathematician Diophantus (ca. 250 A.D., see page 49) wrote the book *Arithmetica*, which contains many word problems and equations. The Indian mathematician Bhaskara (12th century A.D., see page 63) and the Chinese mathematician Chang Ch'iu-Chien (6th century A.D.) also studied and wrote about equations. Of course, equations continue to be important today.

1. Solve the Babylonian problem and show that their answer is correct.

2. Solve the Egyptian problem and show that their answer is correct.

3. The ancient Egyptians and Babylonians used equations to solve practical problems. From the examples given here, do you think that they may have enjoyed posing and solving word problems just for fun?

4. Solve this problem from 12th century India:

> A peacock is perched at the top of a 15-cubit pillar, and a snake's hole is at the foot of the pillar. Seeing the snake at a distance of 45 cubits from its hole, the peacock pounces obliquely upon the snake as it slithers home. At how many cubits from the snake's hole do they meet, assuming that each has traveled an equal distance?

5. Consider this problem from 6th century China.

> If a rooster is worth 5 coins, a hen 3 coins, and three chicks together one coin, how many roosters, hens, and chicks, totaling 100, can be bought for 100 coins?

> This problem has several answers. Use trial and error to find at least one answer. Is this a practical problem or more of a riddle? Write a short essay to support your opinion.

6. Write a short essay explaining how equations affect your own life in today's world.

The British Museum

## 1.3 | Quadratic Equations

### LEARNING OBJECTIVES

After completing this section, you will be able to:

- Solve quadratic equations by factoring
- Solve quadratic equations by completing the square
- Solve quadratic equations using the Quadratic Formula
- Model with quadratic equations

**Linear Equations**

$$4x = -7$$

$$6x - 8 = 21$$

$$2 + 3x = \tfrac{1}{2} - \tfrac{3}{4}x$$

**Quadratic Equations**

$$x^2 - 2x - 8 = 0$$

$$3x + 10 = 4x^2$$

$$\tfrac{1}{2}x^2 + \tfrac{1}{3}x - \tfrac{1}{6} = 0$$

In Section 1.1 we learned how to solve linear equations, which are first-degree equations such as $2x + 1 = 5$ or $4 - 3x = 2$. In this section we learn how to solve quadratic equations, which are second-degree equations such as $x^2 + 2x - 3 = 0$ or $2x^2 + 3 = 5x$. We will also see that many real-life problems can be modeled using quadratic equations.

---

**QUADRATIC EQUATIONS**

A **quadratic equation** is an equation of the form

$$ax^2 + bx + c = 0$$

where $a$, $b$, and $c$ are real numbers with $a \neq 0$.

---

### ■ Solving Quadratic Equations by Factoring

Some quadratic equations can be solved by factoring and using the following basic property of real numbers.

---

**ZERO-PRODUCT PROPERTY**

$$AB = 0 \quad \text{if and only if} \quad A = 0 \quad \text{or} \quad B = 0$$

---

This means that if we can factor the left-hand side of a quadratic (or other) equation, then we can solve it by setting each factor equal to 0 in turn. This method works only when the right-hand side of the equation is 0.

▶ **EXAMPLE 1** | Solving a Quadratic Equation by Factoring

Solve the equation $x^2 + 5x = 24$.

▼ **SOLUTION**   We must first rewrite the equation so that the right-hand side is 0.

$$
\begin{array}{ll}
x^2 + 5x = 24 & \text{Given equation} \\
x^2 + 5x - 24 = 0 & \text{Subtract 24} \\
(x - 3)(x + 8) = 0 & \text{Factor} \\
x - 3 = 0 \quad \text{or} \quad x + 8 = 0 & \text{Zero-Product Property} \\
x = 3 \qquad\qquad x = -8 & \text{Solve}
\end{array}
$$

The solutions are $x = 3$ and $x = -8$.

**Check Your Answers**

$x = 3$:

$(3)^2 + 5(3) = 9 + 15 = 24$ ✔

$x = -8$:

$(-8)^2 + 5(-8) = 64 - 40 = 24$ ✔

✎ **Practice what you've learned: Do Exercise 5.**

Do you see why one side of the equation must be 0 in Example 1? Factoring the equation as $x(x + 5) = 24$ does not help us find the solutions, since 24 can be factored in infinitely many ways, such as $6 \cdot 4$, $\frac{1}{2} \cdot 48$, $\left(-\frac{2}{5}\right) \cdot (-60)$, and so on.

### ■ Solving Quadratic Equations by Completing the Square

As we saw in Section 1.1, Example 5(b), if a quadratic equation is of the form $(x \pm a)^2 = c$, then we can solve it by taking the square root of each side. In an equation of this form the left-hand side is a *perfect square*: the square of a linear expression in $x$. So if a quadratic equation does not factor readily, then we can solve it by **completing the square.**

**Completing the Square**
Area of blue region is

$$x^2 + 2\left(\frac{b}{2}\right)x = x^2 + bx$$

Add a small square of area $(b/2)^2$ to "complete" the square.

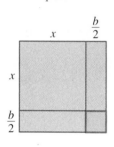

> **COMPLETING THE SQUARE**
>
> To make $x^2 + bx$ a perfect square, add $\left(\dfrac{b}{2}\right)^2$, the square of half the coefficient of $x$. This gives the perfect square
>
> $$x^2 + bx + \left(\frac{b}{2}\right)^2 = \left(x + \frac{b}{2}\right)^2$$

To complete the square, we add a constant to a quadratic expression to make it a perfect square. For example, to make

$$x^2 + 6x$$

a perfect square, we must add $\left(\frac{6}{2}\right)^2 = 9$. Then

$$x^2 + 6x + 9 = (x + 3)^2$$

is a perfect square. The table gives some more examples of completing the square.

| Expression | Add | Complete the square |
|---|---|---|
| $x^2 + 8x$ | $\left(\dfrac{8}{2}\right)^2 = 16$ | $x^2 + 8x + 16 = (x + 4)^2$ |
| $x^2 - 12x$ | $\left(-\dfrac{12}{2}\right)^2 = 36$ | $x^2 - 12x + 36 = (x - 6)^2$ |
| $x^2 + 3x$ | $\left(\dfrac{3}{2}\right)^2 = \dfrac{9}{4}$ | $x^2 + 3x + \dfrac{9}{4} = \left(x + \dfrac{3}{2}\right)^2$ |
| $x^2 - \sqrt{3}x$ | $\left(-\dfrac{\sqrt{3}}{2}\right)^2 = \dfrac{3}{4}$ | $x^2 - \sqrt{3}x + \dfrac{3}{4} = \left(x - \dfrac{\sqrt{3}}{2}\right)^2$ |

▶ **EXAMPLE 2** | Solving Quadratic Equations by Completing the Square

Solve each equation.

**(a)** $x^2 - 8x + 13 = 0$      **(b)** $3x^2 - 12x + 6 = 0$

▼ **SOLUTION**

**(a)**

| | |
|---|---|
| $x^2 - 8x + 13 = 0$ | Given equation |
| $x^2 - 8x = -13$ | Subtract 13 |
| $x^2 - 8x + 16 = -13 + 16$ | Complete the square: add $\left(\dfrac{-8}{2}\right)^2 = 16$ |
| $(x - 4)^2 = 3$ | Perfect square |
| $x - 4 = \pm\sqrt{3}$ | Take square root |
| $x = 4 \pm \sqrt{3}$ | Add 4 |

⊘ When completing the square, make sure the coefficient of $x^2$ is 1. If it isn't, you must factor this coefficient from both terms that contain $x$:

$$ax^2 + bx = a\left(x^2 + \frac{b}{a}x\right)$$

Then complete the square inside the parentheses. Remember that the term added inside the parentheses is multiplied by $a$.

Library of Congress

**François Viète** (1540–1603) had a successful political career before taking up mathematics late in life. He became one of the most famous French mathematicians of the 16th century. Viète introduced a new level of abstraction in algebra by using letters to stand for *known* quantities in an equation. Before Viète's time, each equation had to be solved on its own. For instance, the quadratic equations

$$3x^2 + 2x + 8 = 0$$
$$5x^2 - 6x + 4 = 0$$

had to be solved separately by completing the square. Viète's idea was to consider all quadratic equations at once by writing

$$ax^2 + bx + c = 0$$

where $a$, $b$, and $c$ are known quantities. Thus, he made it possible to write a *formula* (in this case, the Quadratic Formula) involving $a$, $b$, and $c$ that can be used to solve all such equations in one fell swoop.

Viète's mathematical genius proved quite valuable during a war between France and Spain. To communicate with their troops, the Spaniards used a complicated code that Viète managed to decipher. Unaware of Viète's accomplishment, the Spanish king, Philip II, protested to the Pope, claiming that the French were using witchcraft to read his messages.

**(b)** After subtracting 6 from each side of the equation, we must factor the coefficient of $x^2$ (the 3) from the left side to put the equation in the correct form for completing the square.

$$3x^2 - 12x + 6 = 0 \qquad \text{Given equation}$$
$$3x^2 - 12x = -6 \qquad \text{Subtract 6}$$
$$3(x^2 - 4x) = -6 \qquad \text{Factor 3 from LHS}$$

Now we complete the square by adding $(-2)^2 = 4$ *inside* the parentheses. Since everything inside the parentheses is multiplied by 3, this means that we are actually adding $3 \cdot 4 = 12$ to the left side of the equation. Thus, we must add 12 to the right side as well.

$$3(x^2 - 4x + 4) = -6 + 3 \cdot 4 \qquad \text{Complete the square: add 4}$$
$$3(x - 2)^2 = 6 \qquad \text{Perfect square}$$
$$(x - 2)^2 = 2 \qquad \text{Divide by 3}$$
$$x - 2 = \pm\sqrt{2} \qquad \text{Take square root}$$
$$x = 2 \pm \sqrt{2} \qquad \text{Add 2}$$

✎ **Practice what you've learned:** Do Exercises 17 and 25.     ▲

## ■ The Quadratic Formula

We can use the technique of completing the square to derive a formula for the roots of the general quadratic equation $ax^2 + bx + c = 0$.

---

**THE QUADRATIC FORMULA**

The roots of the quadratic equation $ax^2 + bx + c = 0$, where $a \neq 0$, are

$$x = \frac{-b \pm \sqrt{b^2 - 4ac}}{2a}$$

---

▼ **PROOF**    First, we divide each side of the equation by $a$ and move the constant to the right side, giving

$$x^2 + \frac{b}{a}x = -\frac{c}{a} \qquad \text{Divide by } a$$

We now complete the square by adding $(b/2a)^2$ to each side of the equation:

$$x^2 + \frac{b}{a}x + \left(\frac{b}{2a}\right)^2 = -\frac{c}{a} + \left(\frac{b}{2a}\right)^2 \qquad \text{Complete the square: Add } \left(\frac{b}{2a}\right)^2$$

$$\left(x + \frac{b}{2a}\right)^2 = \frac{-4ac + b^2}{4a^2} \qquad \text{Perfect square}$$

$$x + \frac{b}{2a} = \pm\frac{\sqrt{b^2 - 4ac}}{2a} \qquad \text{Take square root}$$

$$x = \frac{-b \pm \sqrt{b^2 - 4ac}}{2a} \qquad \text{Subtract } \frac{b}{2a}$$

▲

The Quadratic Formula could be used to solve the equations in Examples 1 and 2. You should carry out the details of these calculations.

▶ **EXAMPLE 3** | Using the Quadratic Formula

Find all solutions of each equation.

**(a)** $3x^2 - 5x - 1 = 0$ **(b)** $4x^2 + 12x + 9 = 0$ **(c)** $x^2 + 2x + 2 = 0$

▼ **SOLUTION**

**(a)** In this quadratic equation $a = 3$, $b = -5$, and $c = -1$.

$$b = -5$$

$$3x^2 - 5x - 1 = 0$$

$$a = 3 \qquad c = -1$$

By the Quadratic Formula,

$$x = \frac{-(-5) \pm \sqrt{(-5)^2 - 4(3)(-1)}}{2(3)} = \frac{5 \pm \sqrt{37}}{6}$$

If approximations are desired, we can use a calculator to obtain

$$x = \frac{5 + \sqrt{37}}{6} \approx 1.8471 \quad \text{and} \quad x = \frac{5 - \sqrt{37}}{6} \approx -0.1805$$

**Another Method**

$$4x^2 + 12x + 9 = 0$$
$$(2x + 3)^2 = 0$$
$$2x + 3 = 0$$
$$x = -\tfrac{3}{2}$$

**(b)** Using the Quadratic Formula with $a = 4$, $b = 12$, and $c = 9$ gives

$$x = \frac{-12 \pm \sqrt{(12)^2 - 4 \cdot 4 \cdot 9}}{2 \cdot 4} = \frac{-12 \pm 0}{8} = -\frac{3}{2}$$

This equation has only one solution, $x = -\frac{3}{2}$.

**(c)** Using the Quadratic Formula with $a = 1$, $b = 2$, and $c = 2$ gives

$$x = \frac{-2 \pm \sqrt{2^2 - 4 \cdot 2}}{2} = \frac{-2 \pm \sqrt{-4}}{2} = \frac{-2 \pm 2\sqrt{-1}}{2} = -1 \pm \sqrt{-1}$$

Since the square of any real number is nonnegative, $\sqrt{-1}$ is undefined in the real number system. The equation has no real solution.

✎ **Practice what you've learned: Do Exercises 31, 39, and 45.** ▲

In the next section we study the complex number system, in which the square roots of negative numbers do exist. The equation in Example 3(c) does have solutions in the complex number system.

## ■ The Discriminant

The quantity $b^2 - 4ac$ that appears under the square root sign in the Quadratic Formula is called the *discriminant* of the equation $ax^2 + bx + c = 0$ and is given the symbol $D$. If $D < 0$, then $\sqrt{b^2 - 4ac}$ is undefined, and the quadratic equation has no real solution, as in Example 3(c). If $D = 0$, then the equation has only one real solution, as in Example 3(b). Finally, if $D > 0$, then the equation has two distinct real solutions, as in Example 3(a). The following box summarizes these observations.

> **THE DISCRIMINANT**
>
> The **discriminant** of the general quadratic $ax^2 + bx + c = 0$ $(a \neq 0)$ is $D = b^2 - 4ac$.
>
> **1.** If $D > 0$, then the equation has two distinct real solutions.
>
> **2.** If $D = 0$, then the equation has exactly one real solution.
>
> **3.** If $D < 0$, then the equation has no real solution.

▶ **EXAMPLE 4** | Using the Discriminant

Use the discriminant to determine how many real solutions each equation has.

**(a)** $x^2 + 4x - 1 = 0$ **(b)** $4x^2 - 12x + 9 = 0$ **(c)** $\frac{1}{3}x^2 - 2x + 4 = 0$

▼ **SOLUTION**

**(a)** The discriminant is $D = 4^2 - 4(1)(-1) = 20 > 0$, so the equation has two distinct real solutions.

**(b)** The discriminant is $D = (-12)^2 - 4 \cdot 4 \cdot 9 = 0$, so the equation has exactly one real solution.

**(c)** The discriminant is $D = (-2)^2 - 4(\frac{1}{3})4 = -\frac{4}{3} < 0$, so the equation has no real solution.

✎ **Practice what you've learned: Do Exercises 65, 67, and 69.** ▲

## ■ Modeling with Quadratic Equations

Let's look at some real-life problems that can be modeled by quadratic equations. The principles discussed in Section 1.2 for setting up equations as models are useful here as well.

▶ **EXAMPLE 5** | Dimensions of a Building Lot

A rectangular building lot is 8 ft longer than it is wide and has an area of 2900 ft$^2$. Find the dimensions of the lot.

▼ **SOLUTION** We are asked to find the width and length of the lot. So let

Identify the variable ▶

$$w = \text{width of lot}$$

Then we translate the information given in the problem into the language of algebra (see Figure 1).

Translate from words to algebra ▶

| In Words | In Algebra |
|----------|------------|
| Width of lot | $w$ |
| Length of lot | $w + 8$ |

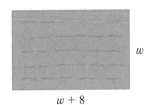

$w + 8$

**FIGURE 1**

Now we set up the model.

**Set up the model** ▶    width of lot $\times$ length of lot $=$ area of lot

**Solve** ▶

$$w(w + 8) = 2900$$
$$w^2 + 8w = 2900 \qquad \text{Expand}$$
$$w^2 + 8w - 2900 = 0 \qquad \text{Subtract 2900}$$
$$(w - 50)(w + 58) = 0 \qquad \text{Factor}$$
$$w = 50 \quad \text{or} \quad w = -58 \qquad \text{Zero-Product Property}$$

Since the width of the lot must be a positive number, we conclude that $w = 50$ ft. The length of the lot is $w + 8 = 50 + 8 = 58$ ft.

✎ **Practice what you've learned: Do Exercise 81.**    ▲

▶ **EXAMPLE 6** | A Distance-Speed-Time Problem

A jet flew from New York to Los Angeles, a distance of 4200 km. The speed for the return trip was 100 km/h faster than the outbound speed. If the total trip took 13 hours, what was the jet's speed from New York to Los Angeles?

▼ **SOLUTION**    We are asked for the speed of the jet from New York to Los Angeles. So let

**Identify the variable** ▶    $s = $ speed from New York to Los Angeles

Then    $s + 100 = $ speed from Los Angeles to New York

Now we organize the information in a table. We fill in the "Distance" column first, since we know that the cities are 4200 km apart. Then we fill in the "Speed" column, since we have expressed both speeds (rates) in terms of the variable $s$. Finally, we calculate the entries for the "Time" column, using

$$\text{time} = \frac{\text{distance}}{\text{rate}}$$

|  | Distance (km) | Speed (km/h) | Time (h) |
|---|---|---|---|
| N.Y. to L.A. | 4200 | $s$ | $\dfrac{4200}{s}$ |
| L.A. to N.Y. | 4200 | $s + 100$ | $\dfrac{4200}{s + 100}$ |

**Translate from words to algebra** ▶

The total trip took 13 hours, so we have the model

**Set up the model** ▶    time from N.Y. to L.A. $+$ time from L.A. to N.Y. $=$ total time

$$\frac{4200}{s} + \frac{4200}{s + 100} = 13$$

Multiplying by the common denominator, $s(s + 100)$, we get

$$4200(s + 100) + 4200s = 13s(s + 100)$$
$$8400s + 420{,}000 = 13s^2 + 1300s$$
$$0 = 13s^2 - 7100s - 420{,}000$$

Although this equation does factor, with numbers this large it is probably quicker to use the Quadratic Formula and a calculator.

Solve ▶

$$s = \frac{7100 \pm \sqrt{(-7100)^2 - 4(13)(-420,000)}}{2(13)}$$

$$= \frac{7100 \pm 8500}{26}$$

$$s = 600 \qquad \text{or} \qquad s = \frac{-1400}{26} \approx -53.8$$

Since $s$ represents speed, we reject the negative answer and conclude that the jet's speed from New York to Los Angeles was 600 km/h.

✎ **Practice what you've learned: Do Exercise 91.**    ▲

▶ **EXAMPLE 7** | The Path of a Projectile

This formula depends on the fact that acceleration due to gravity is constant near the earth's surface. Here, we neglect the effect of air resistance.

An object thrown or fired straight upward at an initial speed of $v_0$ ft/s will reach a height of $h$ feet after $t$ seconds, where $h$ and $t$ are related by the formula

$$h = -16t^2 + v_0 t$$

Suppose that a bullet is shot straight upward with an initial speed of 800 ft/s. Its path is shown in Figure 2.

(a) When does the bullet fall back to ground level?

(b) When does it reach a height of 6400 ft?

(c) When does it reach a height of 2 mi?

(d) How high is the highest point the bullet reaches?

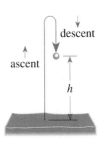

▼ **SOLUTION**    Since the initial speed in this case is $v_0 = 800$ ft/s, the formula is

$$h = -16t^2 + 800t$$

(a) Ground level corresponds to $h = 0$, so we must solve the equation

$$0 = -16t^2 + 800t \qquad \text{Set } h = 0$$

$$0 = -16t(t - 50) \qquad \text{Factor}$$

Thus, $t = 0$ or $t = 50$. This means the bullet starts $(t = 0)$ at ground level and returns to ground level after 50 s.

**FIGURE 2**

(b) Setting $h = 6400$ gives the equation

$$6400 = -16t^2 + 800t \qquad \text{Set } h = 6400$$

$$16t^2 - 800t + 6400 = 0 \qquad \text{All terms to LHS}$$

$$t^2 - 50t + 400 = 0 \qquad \text{Divide by 16}$$

$$(t - 10)(t - 40) = 0 \qquad \text{Factor}$$

$$t = 10 \qquad \text{or} \qquad t = 40 \qquad \text{Solve}$$

The bullet reaches 6400 ft after 10 s (on its ascent) and again after 40 s (on its descent to earth).

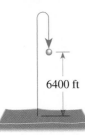

(c) Two miles is $2 \times 5280 = 10{,}560$ ft.

$$10{,}560 = -16t^2 + 800t \qquad \text{Set } h = 10{,}560$$

$$16t^2 - 800t + 10{,}560 = 0 \qquad \text{All terms to LHS}$$

$$t^2 - 50t + 660 = 0 \qquad \text{Divide by 16}$$

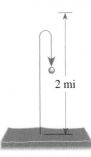

The discriminant of this equation is $D = (-50)^2 - 4(660) = -140$, which is negative. Thus, the equation has no real solution. The bullet never reaches a height of 2 mi.

**(d)** Each height that the bullet reaches is attained twice—once on its ascent and once on its descent. The only exception is the highest point of its path, which is reached only once. This means that for the highest value of $h$, the following equation has only one solution for $t$:

$$h = -16t^2 + 800t$$

$$16t^2 - 800t + h = 0 \qquad \text{All terms to LHS}$$

This in turn means that the discriminant $D$ of the equation is 0, so

$$D = (-800)^2 - 4(16)h = 0$$

$$640,000 - 64h = 0$$

$$h = 10,000$$

The maximum height reached is 10,000 ft.

✎ **Practice what you've learned: Do Exercise 97.** ▲

# 1.3 EXERCISES

## ▼ CONCEPTS

**1.** The Quadratic Formula gives us the solutions of the equation $ax^2 + bx + c = 0$.

 **(a)** State the Quadratic Formula: $x =$ _____.

 **(b)** In the equation $\frac{1}{2}x^2 - x - 4 = 0$, $a =$ _____,

 $b =$ _____, and $c =$ _____. So the solution of the equation is $x =$ _____.

**2.** Explain how you would use each method to solve the equation $x^2 - 4x - 5 = 0$.

 **(a)** By factoring: _____

 **(b)** By completing the square: _____

 **(c)** By using the Quadratic Formula: _____

**3.** For the quadratic equation $ax^2 + bx + c = 0$ the discriminant is $D =$ _____. The discriminant tells us how many solutions a quadratic equation has.

 If $D > 0$, the equation has _____ solution(s).

 If $D = 0$, the equation has _____ solution(s).

 If $D < 0$, the equation has _____ solution(s).

**4.** Make up quadratic equations that have the following number of solutions:

 Two solutions: _____.

 One solution: _____.

 No solution: _____.

## ▼ SKILLS

**5–16** ▪ Solve the equation by factoring.

**5.** $x^2 + x = 12$

**6.** $x^2 + 3x = 4$

**7.** $x^2 - 7x + 12 = 0$

**8.** $x^2 + 8x + 12 = 0$

**9.** $3x^2 - 5x - 2 = 0$

**10.** $4x^2 - 4x - 15 = 0$

**11.** $2y^2 + 7y + 3 = 0$

**12.** $4w^2 = 4w + 3$

**13.** $6x^2 + 5x = 4$

**14.** $3x^2 + 1 = 4x$

**15.** $x^2 = 5(x + 100)$

**16.** $6x(x - 1) = 21 - x$

**17–28** ▪ Solve the equation by completing the square.

**17.** $x^2 + 2x - 5 = 0$

**18.** $x^2 - 4x + 2 = 0$

**19.** $x^2 - 6x - 11 = 0$

**20.** $x^2 + 3x - \frac{7}{4} = 0$

**21.** $x^2 + x - \frac{3}{4} = 0$

**22.** $x^2 - 5x + 1 = 0$

**23.** $x^2 + 22x + 21 = 0$

**24.** $x^2 - 18x = 19$

**25.** $2x^2 + 8x + 1 = 0$

**26.** $3x^2 - 6x - 1 = 0$

**27.** $4x^2 - x = 0$

**28.** $x^2 = \frac{3}{4}x - \frac{1}{8}$

**29–52** ▪ Find all real solutions of the equation.

**29.** $x^2 - 2x - 15 = 0$

**30.** $x^2 + 5x - 6 = 0$

**31.** $x^2 - 7x + 10 = 0$

**32.** $x^2 + 30x + 200 = 0$

**33.** $2x^2 + x - 3 = 0$

**34.** $3x^2 + 7x + 4 = 0$

**35.** $x^2 + 3x + 1 = 0$

**36.** $2x^2 - 8x + 4 = 0$

**37.** $x^2 + 12x - 27 = 0$

**38.** $8x^2 - 6x - 9 = 0$

**39.** $3x^2 + 6x - 5 = 0$

**40.** $x^2 - 6x + 1 = 0$

**41.** $z^2 - \frac{3}{2}z + \frac{9}{16} = 0$

**42.** $2y^2 - y - \frac{1}{2} = 0$

**43.** $4x^2 + 16x - 9 = 0$

**44.** $0 = x^2 - 4x + 1$

**45.** $w^2 = 3(w - 1)$

**46.** $3 + 5z + z^2 = 0$

**47.** $x^2 - \sqrt{5}x + 1 = 0$

**48.** $\sqrt{6}x^2 + 2x - \sqrt{\frac{3}{2}} = 0$

**49.** $10y^2 - 16y + 5 = 0$     **50.** $25x^2 + 70x + 49 = 0$

**51.** $3x^2 + 2x + 2 = 0$     **52.** $5x^2 - 7x + 5 = 0$

**53–58** ▪ Use the quadratic formula and a calculator to find all real solutions, correct to three decimals.

**53.** $x^2 - 0.011x - 0.064 = 0$     **54.** $x^2 - 2.450x + 1.500 = 0$

**55.** $x^2 - 2.450x + 1.501 = 0$     **56.** $x^2 - 1.800x + 0.810 = 0$

**57.** $2.232x^2 - 4.112x = 6.219$     **58.** $12.714x^2 + 7.103x = 0.987$

**59–64** ▪ Solve the equation for the indicated variable.

**59.** $h = \frac{1}{2}gt^2 + v_0t$;   for $t$     **60.** $S = \dfrac{n(n+1)}{2}$;   for $n$

**61.** $A = 2x^2 + 4xh$;   for $x$     **62.** $A = 2\pi r^2 + 2\pi rh$;   for $r$

**63.** $\dfrac{1}{s+a} + \dfrac{1}{s+b} = \dfrac{1}{c}$;   for $s$     **64.** $\dfrac{1}{r} + \dfrac{2}{1-r} = \dfrac{4}{r^2}$;   for $r$

**65–72** ▪ Use the discriminant to determine the number of real solutions of the equation. Do not solve the equation.

**65.** $x^2 - 6x + 1 = 0$     **66.** $x^2 = 6x - 9$

**67.** $x^2 + 2.20x + 1.21 = 0$     **68.** $x^2 + 2.21x + 1.21 = 0$

**69.** $4x^2 + 5x + \frac{13}{8} = 0$     **70.** $9x^2 - 4x + \frac{4}{9} = 0$

**71.** $x^2 + rx - s = 0$   $(s > 0)$

**72.** $x^2 - rx + s = 0$   $(s > 0, r > 2\sqrt{s})$

**73–76** ▪ Solve the equation for $x$.

**73.** $a^2x^2 + 2ax + 1 = 0$   $(a \neq 0)$

**74.** $b^2x^2 - 5bx + 4 = 0$   $(b \neq 0)$

**75.** $ax^2 - (2a + 1)x + (a + 1) = 0$   $(a \neq 0)$

**76.** $bx^2 + 2x + \dfrac{1}{b} = 0$   $(b \neq 0)$

**77–78** ▪ Find all values of $k$ that ensure that the given equation has exactly one solution.

**77.** $4x^2 + kx + 25 = 0$     **78.** $kx^2 + 36x + k = 0$

## ▼ APPLICATIONS

**79. Number Problem**   Find two numbers whose sum is 55 and whose product is 684.

**80. Number Problem**   The sum of the squares of two consecutive even integers is 1252. Find the integers.

**81. Dimensions of a Garden**   A rectangular garden is 10 ft longer than it is wide. Its area is 875 ft$^2$. What are its dimensions?

**82. Dimensions of a Room**   A rectangular bedroom is 7 ft longer than it is wide. Its area is 228 ft$^2$. What is the width of the room?

**83. Dimensions of a Garden**   A farmer has a rectangular garden plot surrounded by 200 ft of fence. Find the length and width of the garden if its area is 2400 ft$^2$.

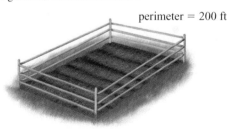

perimeter = 200 ft

**84. Geometry**   Find the length $x$ if the shaded area is 160 in$^2$.

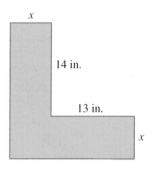

**85. Geometry**   Find the length $x$ if the shaded area is 1200 cm$^2$.

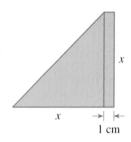

**86. Profit**   A small-appliance manufacturer finds that the profit $P$ (in dollars) generated by producing $x$ microwave ovens per week is given by the formula $P = \frac{1}{10}x(300 - x)$ provided that $0 \le x \le 200$. How many ovens must be manufactured in a given week to generate a profit of \$1250?

**87. Dimensions of a Box**   A box with a square base and no top is to be made from a square piece of cardboard by cutting 4-in. squares from each corner and folding up the sides, as shown in the figure. The box is to hold 100 in$^3$. How big a piece of cardboard is needed?

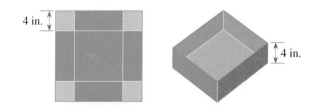

**88. Dimensions of a Can**   A cylindrical can has a volume of $40\pi$ cm$^3$ and is 10 cm tall. What is its diameter? [*Hint:* Use the volume formula listed on the inside back cover of this book.]

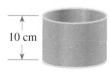

**89. Dimensions of a Lot** A parcel of land is 6 ft longer than it is wide. Each diagonal from one corner to the opposite corner is 174 ft long. What are the dimensions of the parcel?

**90. Height of a Flagpole** A flagpole is secured on opposite sides by two guy wires, each of which is 5 ft longer than the pole. The distance between the points where the wires are fixed to the ground is equal to the length of one guy wire. How tall is the flagpole (to the nearest inch)?

**91. Distance, Speed, and Time** A salesman drives from Ajax to Barrington, a distance of 120 mi, at a steady speed. He then increases his speed by 10 mi/h to drive the 150 mi from Barrington to Collins. If the second leg of his trip took 6 min more time than the first leg, how fast was he driving between Ajax and Barrington?

**92. Distance, Speed, and Time** Kiran drove from Tortula to Cactus, a distance of 250 mi. She increased her speed by 10 mi/h for the 360-mi trip from Cactus to Dry Junction. If the total trip took 11 h, what was her speed from Tortula to Cactus?

**93. Distance, Speed, and Time** It took a crew 2 h 40 min to row 6 km upstream and back again. If the rate of flow of the stream was 3 km/h, what was the rowing speed of the crew in still water?

**94. Speed of a Boat** Two fishing boats depart a harbor at the same time, one traveling east, the other south. The eastbound boat travels at a speed 3 mi/h faster than the southbound boat. After two hours the boats are 30 mi apart. Find the speed of the southbound boat.

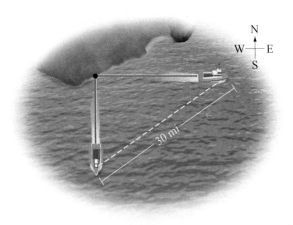

**95–96** ▪ **Falling-Body Problems** Suppose an object is dropped from a height $h_0$ above the ground. Then its height after $t$ seconds is given by $h = -16t^2 + h_0$, where $h$ is measured in feet. Use this information to solve the problem.

**95.** If a ball is dropped from 288 ft above the ground, how long does it take to reach ground level?

**96.** A ball is dropped from the top of a building 96 ft tall.
   **(a)** How long will it take to fall half the distance to ground level?
   **(b)** How long will it take to fall to ground level?

**97–98** ▪ **Falling-Body Problems** Use the formula $h = -16t^2 + v_0 t$ discussed in Example 7.

**97.** A ball is thrown straight upward at an initial speed of $v_0 = 40$ ft/s.
   **(a)** When does the ball reach a height of 24 ft?
   **(b)** When does it reach a height of 48 ft?
   **(c)** What is the greatest height reached by the ball?
   **(d)** When does the ball reach the highest point of its path?
   **(e)** When does the ball hit the ground?

**98.** How fast would a ball have to be thrown upward to reach a maximum height of 100 ft? [*Hint:* Use the discriminant of the equation $16t^2 - v_0 t + h = 0$.]

**99. Fish Population** The fish population in a certain lake rises and falls according to the formula

$$F = 1000(30 + 17t - t^2)$$

Here $F$ is the number of fish at time $t$, where $t$ is measured in years since January 1, 2002, when the fish population was first estimated.
   **(a)** On what date will the fish population again be the same as it was on January 1, 2002?
   **(b)** By what date will all the fish in the lake have died?

**100. Comparing Areas** A wire 360 in. long is cut into two pieces. One piece is formed into a square, and the other is formed into a circle. If the two figures have the same area, what are the lengths of the two pieces of wire (to the nearest tenth of an inch)?

**101. Width of a Lawn** A factory is to be built on a lot measuring 180 ft by 240 ft. A local building code specifies that a lawn of uniform width and equal in area to the factory must surround the factory. What must the width of this lawn be, and what are the dimensions of the factory?

102. **Reach of a Ladder** A $19\frac{1}{2}$-foot ladder leans against a building. The base of the ladder is $7\frac{1}{2}$ ft from the building. How high up the building does the ladder reach?

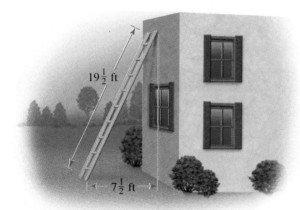

$19\frac{1}{2}$ ft

$7\frac{1}{2}$ ft

103. **Sharing a Job** Henry and Irene working together can wash all the windows of their house in 1 h 48 min. Working alone, it takes Henry $1\frac{1}{2}$ h more than Irene to do the job. How long does it take each person working alone to wash all the windows?

104. **Sharing a Job** Jack, Kay, and Lynn deliver advertising flyers in a small town. If each person works alone, it takes Jack 4 h to deliver all the flyers, and it takes Lynn 1 h longer than it takes Kay. Working together, they can deliver all the flyers in 40% of the time it takes Kay working alone. How long does it take Kay to deliver all the flyers alone?

105. **Gravity** If an imaginary line segment is drawn between the centers of the earth and the moon, then the net gravitational force $F$ acting on an object situated on this line segment is

$$F = \frac{-K}{x^2} + \frac{0.012K}{(239 - x)^2}$$

where $K > 0$ is a constant and $x$ is the distance of the object from the center of the earth, measured in thousands of miles. How far from the center of the earth is the "dead spot" where no net gravitational force acts upon the object? (Express your answer to the nearest thousand miles.)

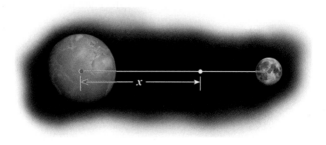

$x$

▼ **DISCOVERY • DISCUSSION • WRITING**

106. **Relationship Between Roots and Coefficients** The Quadratic Formula gives us the roots of a quadratic equation from its coefficients. We can also obtain the coefficients from the roots. For example, find the roots of the equation $x^2 - 9x + 20 = 0$ and show that the product of the roots is the constant term 20 and the sum of the roots is 9, the negative of the coefficient of $x$. Show that the same relationship between roots and coefficients holds for the following equations:

$$x^2 - 2x - 8 = 0$$
$$x^2 + 4x + 2 = 0$$

Use the Quadratic Formula to prove that in general, if the equation $x^2 + bx + c = 0$ has roots $r_1$ and $r_2$, then $c = r_1 r_2$ and $b = -(r_1 + r_2)$.

## 1.4 | Complex Numbers

### LEARNING OBJECTIVES

After completing this section, you will be able to:

- ■ Add and subtract complex numbers
- ■ Multiply and divide complex numbers
- ■ Simplify expressions with roots of negative numbers
- ■ Find complex roots of quadratic equations

See the note on Cardano (page 340) for an example of how complex numbers are used to find real solutions of polynomial equations.

In Section 1.3 we saw that if the discriminant of a quadratic equation is negative, the equation has no real solution. For example, the equation

$$x^2 + 4 = 0$$

has no real solution. If we try to solve this equation, we get $x^2 = -4$, so

$$x = \pm\sqrt{-4}$$

But this is impossible, since the square of any real number is positive. [For example, $(-2)^2 = 4$, a positive number.] Thus, negative numbers don't have real square roots.

To make it possible to solve *all* quadratic equations, mathematicians invented an expanded number system, called the *complex number system*. First they defined the new number

$$i = \sqrt{-1}$$

This means that $i^2 = -1$. A complex number is then a number of the form $a + bi$, where $a$ and $b$ are real numbers.

---

**DEFINITION OF COMPLEX NUMBERS**

A **complex number** is an expression of the form

$$a + bi$$

where $a$ and $b$ are real numbers and $i^2 = -1$. The **real part** of this complex number is $a$ and the **imaginary part** is $b$. Two complex numbers are **equal** if and only if their real parts are equal and their imaginary parts are equal.

---

Note that both the real and imaginary parts of a complex number are real numbers.

▶  **EXAMPLE 1** | Complex Numbers

The following are examples of complex numbers.

$$3 + 4i \qquad \text{Real part 3, imaginary part 4}$$

$$\tfrac{1}{2} - \tfrac{2}{3}i \qquad \text{Real part } \tfrac{1}{2}, \text{ imaginary part } -\tfrac{2}{3}$$

$$6i \qquad \text{Real part 0, imaginary part 6}$$

$$-7 \qquad \text{Real part } -7, \text{ imaginary part 0}$$

✎  **Practice what you've learned: Do Exercises 5 and 9.**                      ▲

A number such as $6i$, which has real part 0, is called a **pure imaginary number**. A real number like $-7$ can be thought of as a complex number with imaginary part 0.

In the complex number system every quadratic equation has solutions. The numbers $2i$ and $-2i$ are solutions of $x^2 = -4$ because

$$(2i)^2 = 2^2 i^2 = 4(-1) = -4 \qquad \text{and} \qquad (-2i)^2 = (-2)^2 i^2 = 4(-1) = -4$$

Although we use the term *imaginary* in this context, imaginary numbers should not be thought of as any less "real" (in the ordinary rather than the mathematical sense of that word) than negative numbers or irrational numbers. All numbers (except possibly the positive integers) are creations of the human mind—the numbers $-1$ and $\sqrt{2}$ as well as the number $i$. We study complex numbers because they complete, in a useful and elegant fashion, our study of the solutions of equations. In fact, imaginary numbers are useful not only in algebra and mathematics, but in the other sciences as well. To give just one example, in electrical theory the *reactance* of a circuit is a quantity whose measure is an imaginary number.

## ■ Arithmetic Operations on Complex Numbers

Complex numbers are added, subtracted, multiplied, and divided just as we would any number of the form $a + b\sqrt{c}$. The only difference that we need to keep in mind is that $i^2 = -1$. Thus, the following calculations are valid.

$$(a + bi)(c + di) = ac + (ad + bc)i + bdi^2 \qquad \text{Multiply and collect like terms}$$

$$= ac + (ad + bc)i + bd(-1) \qquad i^2 = -1$$

$$= (ac - bd) + (ad + bc)i \qquad \text{Combine real and imaginary parts}$$

We therefore define the sum, difference, and product of complex numbers as follows.

---

**ADDING, SUBTRACTING, AND MULTIPLYING COMPLEX NUMBERS**

| Definition | Description |
|---|---|
| **Addition** | |
| $(a + bi) + (c + di) = (a + c) + (b + d)i$ | To add complex numbers, add the real parts and the imaginary parts. |
| **Subtraction** | |
| $(a + bi) - (c + di) = (a - c) + (b - d)i$ | To subtract complex numbers, subtract the real parts and the imaginary parts. |
| **Multiplication** | |
| $(a + bi) \cdot (c + di) = (ac - bd) + (ad + bc)i$ | Multiply complex numbers like binomials, using $i^2 = -1$. |

---

Graphing calculators can perform arithmetic operations on complex numbers.

```
(3+5i)+(4-2i)
                7+3i
(3+5i)*(4-2i)
               22+14i
```

▶ **EXAMPLE 2** | Adding, Subtracting, and Multiplying Complex Numbers

Express the following in the form $a + bi$.

**(a)** $(3 + 5i) + (4 - 2i)$ **(b)** $(3 + 5i) - (4 - 2i)$

**(c)** $(3 + 5i)(4 - 2i)$ **(d)** $i^{23}$

▼ **SOLUTION**

**(a)** According to the definition, we add the real parts and we add the imaginary parts.

$$(3 + 5i) + (4 - 2i) = (3 + 4) + (5 - 2)i = 7 + 3i$$

**(b)** $(3 + 5i) - (4 - 2i) = (3 - 4) + [5 - (-2)]i = -1 + 7i$

**(c)** $(3 + 5i)(4 - 2i) = [3 \cdot 4 - 5(-2)] + [3(-2) + 5 \cdot 4]i = 22 + 14i$

**(d)** $i^{23} = i^{22+1} = (i^2)^{11}i = (-1)^{11}i = (-1)i = -i$

✎ **Practice what you've learned: Do Exercises 15, 19, 25, and 33.** ▲

Division of complex numbers is much like rationalizing the denominator of a radical expression, which we considered in Section P.8. For the complex number $z = a + bi$ we define its **complex conjugate** to be $\bar{z} = a - bi$. Note that

$$z \cdot \bar{z} = (a + bi)(a - bi) = a^2 + b^2$$

So the product of a complex number and its conjugate is always a nonnegative real number. We use this property to divide complex numbers.

Complex Conjugates

| Number | Conjugate |
|---|---|
| $3 + 2i$ | $3 - 2i$ |
| $1 - i$ | $1 + i$ |
| $4i$ | $-4i$ |
| $5$ | $5$ |

---

**DIVIDING COMPLEX NUMBERS**

To simplify the quotient $\dfrac{a + bi}{c + di}$, multiply the numerator and the denominator by the complex conjugate of the denominator:

$$\frac{a + bi}{c + di} = \left(\frac{a + bi}{c + di}\right)\left(\frac{c - di}{c - di}\right) = \frac{(ac + bd) + (bc - ad)i}{c^2 + d^2}$$

Rather than memorizing this entire formula, it is easier to just remember the first step and then multiply out the numerator and the denominator as usual.

▶ **EXAMPLE 3** | Dividing Complex Numbers

Express the following in the form $a + bi$.

**(a)** $\dfrac{3 + 5i}{1 - 2i}$        **(b)** $\dfrac{7 + 3i}{4i}$

▼ **SOLUTION**    We multiply both the numerator and denominator by the complex conjugate of the denominator to make the new denominator a real number.

**(a)** The complex conjugate of $1 - 2i$ is $\overline{1 - 2i} = 1 + 2i$.

$$\frac{3 + 5i}{1 - 2i} = \left(\frac{3 + 5i}{1 - 2i}\right)\left(\frac{1 + 2i}{1 + 2i}\right) = \frac{-7 + 11i}{5} = -\frac{7}{5} + \frac{11}{5}i$$

**(b)** The complex conjugate of $4i$ is $-4i$. Therefore,

$$\frac{7 + 3i}{4i} = \left(\frac{7 + 3i}{4i}\right)\left(\frac{-4i}{-4i}\right) = \frac{12 - 28i}{16} = \frac{3}{4} - \frac{7}{4}i$$

✎ **Practice what you've learned: Do Exercises 37 and 43.**                            ▲

## ■ Square Roots of Negative Numbers

Just as every positive real number $r$ has two square roots ($\sqrt{r}$ and $-\sqrt{r}$), every negative number has two square roots as well. If $-r$ is a negative number, then its square roots are $\pm i\sqrt{r}$, because $(i\sqrt{r})^2 = i^2 r = -r$ and $(-i\sqrt{r})^2 = (-1)^2 i^2 r = -r$.

---

**SQUARE ROOTS OF NEGATIVE NUMBERS**

If $-r$ is negative, then the **principal square root** of $-r$ is

$$\sqrt{-r} = i\sqrt{r}$$

The two square roots of $-r$ are $i\sqrt{r}$ and $-i\sqrt{r}$.

---

We usually write $i\sqrt{b}$ instead of $\sqrt{b}\,i$ to avoid confusion with $\sqrt{bi}$.

Library of Congress

**Leonhard Euler** (1707–1783) was born in Basel, Switzerland, the son of a pastor. When Euler was 13, his father sent him to the University at Basel to study theology, but Euler soon decided to devote himself to the sciences. Besides theology he studied mathematics, medicine, astronomy, physics, and Asian languages. It is said that Euler could calculate as effortlessly as "men breathe or as eagles fly." One hundred years before Euler, Fermat (see page 159) had conjec-

tured that $2^{2^n} + 1$ is a prime number for all $n$. The first five of these numbers are 5, 17, 257, 65537, and 4,294,967,297. It is easy to show that the first four are prime. The fifth was also thought to be prime until Euler, with his phenomenal calculating ability, showed that it is the product $641 \times 6,700,417$ and so is not prime. Euler published more than any other mathematician in history. His collected works comprise 75 large volumes. Although he was blind for the last 17 years of his life, he continued to work and publish. In his writings he popularized the use of the symbols $\pi$, $e$, and $i$, which you will find in this textbook. One of Euler's most lasting contributions is his development of complex numbers.

▶ **EXAMPLE 4** | Square Roots of Negative Numbers

**(a)** $\sqrt{-1} = i\sqrt{1} = i$    **(b)** $\sqrt{-16} = i\sqrt{16} = 4i$    **(c)** $\sqrt{-3} = i\sqrt{3}$

✎ **Practice what you've learned: Do Exercises 47 and 49.**    ▲

Special care must be taken in performing calculations that involve square roots of negative numbers. Although $\sqrt{a} \cdot \sqrt{b} = \sqrt{ab}$ when $a$ and $b$ are positive, this is *not* true when both are negative. For example,

$$\sqrt{-2} \cdot \sqrt{-3} = i\sqrt{2} \cdot i\sqrt{3} = i^2\sqrt{6} = -\sqrt{6}$$

but

$$\sqrt{(-2)(-3)} = \sqrt{6}$$

so

$$\sqrt{-2} \cdot \sqrt{-3} \neq \sqrt{(-2)(-3)}$$

⊘ When multiplying radicals of negative numbers, express them first in the form $i\sqrt{r}$ (where $r > 0$) to avoid possible errors of this type.

▶ **EXAMPLE 5** | Using Square Roots of Negative Numbers

Evaluate $(\sqrt{12} - \sqrt{-3})(3 + \sqrt{-4})$ and express in the form $a + bi$.

▼ **SOLUTION**

$$\begin{aligned}(\sqrt{12} - \sqrt{-3})(3 + \sqrt{-4}) &= (\sqrt{12} - i\sqrt{3})(3 + i\sqrt{4})\\ &= (2\sqrt{3} - i\sqrt{3})(3 + 2i)\\ &= (6\sqrt{3} + 2\sqrt{3}) + i(2\cdot 2\sqrt{3} - 3\sqrt{3})\\ &= 8\sqrt{3} + i\sqrt{3}\end{aligned}$$

✎ **Practice what you've learned: Do Exercise 51.**    ▲

## ■ Complex Solutions of Quadratic Equations

We have already seen that if $a \neq 0$, then the solutions of the quadratic equation $ax^2 + bx + c = 0$ are

$$x = \frac{-b \pm \sqrt{b^2 - 4ac}}{2a}$$

If $b^2 - 4ac < 0$, then the equation has no real solution. But in the complex number system, this equation will always have solutions, because negative numbers have square roots in this expanded setting.

▶ **EXAMPLE 6** | Quadratic Equations with Complex Solutions

Solve each equation.
**(a)** $x^2 + 9 = 0$    **(b)** $x^2 + 4x + 5 = 0$

▼ **SOLUTION**

**(a)** The equation $x^2 + 9 = 0$ means $x^2 = -9$, so

$$x = \pm\sqrt{-9} = \pm i\sqrt{9} = \pm 3i$$

The solutions are therefore $3i$ and $-3i$.

**(b)** By the Quadratic Formula we have

$$x = \frac{-4 \pm \sqrt{4^2 - 4 \cdot 5}}{2}$$

$$= \frac{-4 \pm \sqrt{-4}}{2}$$

$$= \frac{-4 \pm 2i}{2} = \frac{2(-2 \pm i)}{2} = -2 \pm i$$

So the solutions are $-2 + i$ and $-2 - i$.

✎ **Practice what you've learned: Do Exercises 57 and 59.** ▲

We see from Example 6 that if a quadratic equation with real coefficients has complex solutions, then these solutions are complex conjugates of each other. So if $a + bi$ is a solution, then $a - bi$ is also a solution.

▶ **EXAMPLE 7** | Complex Conjugates as Solutions of a Quadratic

Show that the solutions of the equation

$$4x^2 - 24x + 37 = 0$$

are complex conjugates of each other.

▼ **SOLUTION** We use the Quadratic Formula to get

$$x = \frac{24 \pm \sqrt{(24)^2 - 4(4)(37)}}{2(4)}$$

$$= \frac{24 \pm \sqrt{-16}}{8} = \frac{24 \pm 4i}{8} = 3 \pm \frac{1}{2}i$$

So the solutions are $3 + \frac{1}{2}i$ and $3 - \frac{1}{2}i$, and these are complex conjugates.

✎ **Practice what you've learned: Do Exercise 65.** ▲

# 1.4 EXERCISES

## ▼ CONCEPTS

**1.** The imaginary number $i$ has the property that $i^2 =$ _____.

**2.** For the complex number $3 + 4i$ the real part is _____ and the imaginary part is _____.

**3.** (a) The complex conjugate of $3 + 4i$ is $\overline{3 + 4i} =$ _____.

   (b) $(3 + 4i)(\overline{3 + 4i}) =$ _____.

**4.** If $3 + 4i$ is a solution of a quadratic equation with real coefficients, then _____ is also a solution of the equation.

## ▼ SKILLS

**5–14** ▪ Find the real and imaginary parts of the complex number.

**5.** $5 - 7i$

**6.** $-6 + 4i$

**7.** $\dfrac{-2 - 5i}{3}$

**8.** $\dfrac{4 + 7i}{2}$

**9.** $3$

**10.** $-\frac{1}{2}$

**11.** $-\frac{2}{3}i$

**12.** $i\sqrt{3}$

**13.** $\sqrt{3} + \sqrt{-4}$

**14.** $2 - \sqrt{-5}$

**15–46** ▪ Evaluate the expression and write the result in the form $a + bi$.

**15.** $(2 - 5i) + (3 + 4i)$

**16.** $(2 + 5i) + (4 - 6i)$

**17.** $(-6 + 6i) + (9 - i)$

**18.** $(3 - 2i) + \left(-5 - \frac{1}{3}i\right)$

**19.** $\left(7 - \frac{1}{2}i\right) - \left(5 + \frac{3}{2}i\right)$

**20.** $(-4 + i) - (2 - 5i)$

**21.** $(-12 + 8i) - (7 + 4i)$

**22.** $6i - (4 - i)$

**23.** $4(-1 + 2i)$

**24.** $2i\left(\frac{1}{2} - i\right)$

**25.** $(7 - i)(4 + 2i)$

**26.** $(5 - 3i)(1 + i)$

**27.** $(3 - 4i)(5 - 12i)$

**28.** $\left(\frac{2}{3} + 12i\right)\left(\frac{1}{6} + 24i\right)$

**29.** $(6 + 5i)(2 - 3i)$

**30.** $(-2 + i)(3 - 7i)$

**31.** $i^3$

**32.** $(2i)^4$

**33.** $i^{100}$

**34.** $i^{1002}$

**35.** $\dfrac{1}{i}$

**36.** $\dfrac{1}{1+i}$

**37.** $\dfrac{2-3i}{1-2i}$

**38.** $\dfrac{5-i}{3+4i}$

**39.** $\dfrac{26+39i}{2-3i}$

**40.** $\dfrac{25}{4-3i}$

**41.** $\dfrac{10i}{1-2i}$

**42.** $(2-3i)^{-1}$

**43.** $\dfrac{4+6i}{3i}$

**44.** $\dfrac{-3+5i}{15i}$

**45.** $\dfrac{1}{1+i} - \dfrac{1}{1-i}$

**46.** $\dfrac{(1+2i)(3-i)}{2+i}$

**47–56** ▪ Evaluate the radical expression and express the result in the form $a + bi$.

**47.** $\sqrt{-25}$

**48.** $\sqrt{\dfrac{-9}{4}}$

**49.** $\sqrt{-3}\,\sqrt{-12}$

**50.** $\sqrt{\tfrac{1}{3}}\,\sqrt{-27}$

**51.** $(3 - \sqrt{-5})(1 + \sqrt{-1})$

**52.** $(\sqrt{3} - \sqrt{-4})(\sqrt{6} - \sqrt{-8})$

**53.** $\dfrac{2+\sqrt{-8}}{1+\sqrt{-2}}$

**54.** $\dfrac{1-\sqrt{-1}}{1+\sqrt{-1}}$

**55.** $\dfrac{\sqrt{-36}}{\sqrt{-2}\,\sqrt{-9}}$

**56.** $\dfrac{\sqrt{-7}\,\sqrt{-49}}{\sqrt{28}}$

**57–72** ▪ Find all solutions of the equation and express them in the form $a + bi$.

**57.** $x^2 + 49 = 0$

**58.** $9x^2 + 4 = 0$

**59.** $x^2 - 4x + 5 = 0$

**60.** $x^2 + 2x + 2 = 0$

**61.** $x^2 + 2x + 5 = 0$

**62.** $x^2 - 6x + 10 = 0$

**63.** $x^2 + x + 1 = 0$

**64.** $x^2 - 3x + 3 = 0$

**65.** $2x^2 - 2x + 1 = 0$

**66.** $2x^2 + 3 = 2x$

**67.** $t + 3 + \dfrac{3}{t} = 0$

**68.** $z + 4 + \dfrac{12}{z} = 0$

**69.** $6x^2 + 12x + 7 = 0$

**70.** $4x^2 - 16x + 19 = 0$

**71.** $\tfrac{1}{2}x^2 - x + 5 = 0$

**72.** $x^2 + \tfrac{1}{2}x + 1 = 0$

**73–80** ▪ Recall that the symbol $\bar{z}$ represents the complex conjugate of $z$. If $z = a + bi$ and $w = c + di$, prove each statement.

**73.** $\bar{z} + \bar{w} = \overline{z + w}$

**74.** $\overline{zw} = \bar{z} \cdot \bar{w}$

**75.** $(\bar{z})^2 = \overline{z^2}$

**76.** $\bar{\bar{z}} = z$

**77.** $z + \bar{z}$ is a real number

**78.** $z - \bar{z}$ is a pure imaginary number

**79.** $z \cdot \bar{z}$ is a real number

**80.** $z = \bar{z}$ if and only if $z$ is real

▼ **DISCOVERY • DISCUSSION • WRITING**

**81. Complex Conjugate Roots**   Suppose that the equation $ax^2 + bx + c = 0$ has real coefficients and complex roots. Why must the roots be complex conjugates of each other? (Think about how you would find the roots using the Quadratic Formula.)

**82. Powers of $i$**   Calculate the first 12 powers of $i$, that is, $i, i^2, i^3, \ldots, i^{12}$. Do you notice a pattern? Explain how you would calculate any whole number power of $i$, using the pattern that you have discovered. Use this procedure to calculate $i^{4446}$.

---

## 1.5 | Other Types of Equations

### LEARNING OBJECTIVES

After completing this section, you will be able to:

- Solve basic polynomial equations
- Solve equations involving radicals
- Solve equations of quadratic type
- Model with equations

So far, we have learned how to solve linear and quadratic equations. In this section we study other types of equations, including those that involve higher powers, fractional expressions, and radicals.

### ▪ Polynomial Equations

Some equations can be solved by factoring and using the Zero-Product Property, which says that if a product equals 0, then at least one of the factors must equal 0.

▶ **EXAMPLE 1** | Solving an Equation by Factoring

Solve the equation $x^5 = 9x^3$.

▼ **SOLUTION**    We bring all terms to one side and then factor.

$$x^5 - 9x^3 = 0 \qquad \text{Subtract } 9x^3$$

$$x^3(x^2 - 9) = 0 \qquad \text{Factor } x^3$$

$$x^3(x - 3)(x + 3) = 0 \qquad \text{Difference of squares}$$

$$x^3 = 0 \quad \text{or} \quad x - 3 = 0 \quad \text{or} \quad x + 3 = 0 \qquad \text{Zero-Product Property}$$

$$x = 0 \qquad\qquad x = 3 \qquad\qquad x = -3 \qquad \text{Solve}$$

The solutions are $x = 0$, $x = 3$, and $x = -3$. You should check that each of these satisfies the original equation.

✎ **Practice what you've learned: Do Exercise 5.**    ▲

To divide each side of the equation in Example 1 by the common factor $x^3$ would be wrong, because in doing so, we would lose the solution $x = 0$. Never divide both sides of an equation by an expression that contains the variable unless you know that the expression cannot equal 0.

▶ **EXAMPLE 2** | Factoring by Grouping

Solve the equation $x^3 + 3x^2 - 4x - 12 = 0$.

▼ **SOLUTION**    The left-hand side of the equation can be factored by grouping the terms in pairs.

$$(x^3 + 3x^2) - (4x + 12) = 0 \qquad \text{Group terms}$$

$$x^2(x + 3) - 4(x + 3) = 0 \qquad \text{Factor } x^2 \text{ and } 4$$

$$(x^2 - 4)(x + 3) = 0 \qquad \text{Factor } x + 3$$

$$(x - 2)(x + 2)(x + 3) = 0 \qquad \text{Difference of squares}$$

$$x - 2 = 0 \quad \text{or} \quad x + 2 = 0 \quad \text{or} \quad x + 3 = 0 \qquad \text{Zero-Product Property}$$

$$x = 2 \qquad\qquad x = -2 \qquad\qquad x = -3 \qquad \text{Solve}$$

The solutions are $x = 2$, $-2$, and $-3$.

✎ **Practice what you've learned: Do Exercise 15.**    ▲

▶ **EXAMPLE 3** | An Equation Involving Fractional Expressions

Solve the equation $\dfrac{3}{x} + \dfrac{5}{x + 2} = 2$.

▼ **SOLUTION**    To simplify the equation, we multiply each side by the common denominator.

$$\left(\frac{3}{x} + \frac{5}{x + 2}\right)x(x + 2) = 2x(x + 2) \qquad \text{Multiply by LCD } x(x + 2)$$

$$3(x + 2) + 5x = 2x^2 + 4x \qquad \text{Expand}$$

$$8x + 6 = 2x^2 + 4x \qquad \text{Expand LHS}$$

**Check Your Answers**

$x = 3$:

$$\text{LHS} = \frac{3}{3} + \frac{5}{3 + 2} = 2$$

$$\text{RHS} = 2$$

$$\text{LHS} = \text{RHS} \qquad ✔$$

$x = -1$:

$$\text{LHS} = \frac{3}{-1} + \frac{5}{-1 + 2} = 2$$

$$\text{RHS} = 2$$

$$\text{LHS} = \text{RHS} \qquad ✔$$

| | |
|---|---|
| $0 = 2x^2 - 4x - 6$ | Subtract $8x + 6$ |
| $0 = x^2 - 2x - 3$ | Divide both sides by 2 |
| $0 = (x - 3)(x + 1)$ | Factor |
| $x - 3 = 0 \quad$ or $\quad x + 1 = 0$ | Zero-Product Property |
| $x = 3 \qquad\qquad x = -1$ | Solve |

We must check our answers because multiplying by an expression that contains the variable can introduce extraneous solutions (see the *Warning* on pages 68–69). From *Check Your Answers* we see that the solutions are $x = 3$ and $-1$.

✎ **Practice what you've learned: Do Exercise 19.** ▲

## ■ Equations Involving Radicals

When you solve an equation that involves radicals, you must be especially careful to check your final answers. The next example demonstrates why.

▶ **EXAMPLE 4** | An Equation Involving a Radical

Solve the equation $2x = 1 - \sqrt{2 - x}$.

▼ **SOLUTION**    To eliminate the square root, we first isolate it on one side of the equal sign, then square.

| | |
|---|---|
| $2x - 1 = -\sqrt{2 - x}$ | Subtract 1 |
| $(2x - 1)^2 = 2 - x$ | Square each side |
| $4x^2 - 4x + 1 = 2 - x$ | Expand LHS |
| $4x^2 - 3x - 1 = 0$ | Add $-2 + x$ |
| $(4x + 1)(x - 1) = 0$ | Factor |
| $4x + 1 = 0 \quad$ or $\quad x - 1 = 0$ | Zero-Product Property |
| $x = -\frac{1}{4} \qquad\qquad x = 1$ | Solve |

**Check Your Answers**

$x = -\frac{1}{4}$:

$$\text{LHS} = 2\left(-\frac{1}{4}\right) = -\frac{1}{2}$$

$$\text{RHS} = 1 - \sqrt{2 - \left(-\frac{1}{4}\right)}$$

$$= 1 - \sqrt{\frac{9}{4}}$$

$$= 1 - \frac{3}{2} = -\frac{1}{2}$$

$$\text{LHS} = \text{RHS} \qquad ✔$$

$x = 1$:

$$\text{LHS} = 2(1) = 2$$

$$\text{RHS} = 1 - \sqrt{2 - 1}$$

$$= 1 - 1 = 0$$

$$\text{LHS} \neq \text{RHS} \qquad ✗$$

The values $x = -\frac{1}{4}$ and $x = 1$ are only potential solutions. We must check them to see whether they satisfy the original equation. From *Check Your Answers* we see that $x = -\frac{1}{4}$ is a solution but $x = 1$ is not. The only solution is $x = -\frac{1}{4}$.

✎ **Practice what you've learned: Do Exercise 29.** ▲

When we solve an equation, we may end up with one or more **extraneous solutions**, that is, potential solutions that do not satisfy the original equation. In Example 4 the value $x = 1$ is an extraneous solution. Extraneous solutions may be introduced when we square each side of an equation because the operation of squaring can turn a false equation into a true one. For example, $-1 \neq 1$, but $(-1)^2 = 1^2$. Thus, the squared equation may be true for more values of the variable than the original equation. That is why you must always check your answers to make sure that each satisfies the original equation.

## ■ Equations of Quadratic Type

An equation of the form $aW^2 + bW + c = 0$, where $W$ is an algebraic expression, is an equation of **quadratic type**. We solve equations of quadratic type by substituting for the algebraic expression, as we see in the next two examples.

▶ **EXAMPLE 5** | An Equation of Quadratic Type

Solve the equation $\left(1 + \dfrac{1}{x}\right)^2 - 6\left(1 + \dfrac{1}{x}\right) + 8 = 0$.

▼ **SOLUTION**   We could solve this equation by multiplying it out first. But it's easier to think of the expression $1 + \frac{1}{x}$ as the unknown in this equation and give it a new name $W$. This turns the equation into a quadratic equation in the new variable $W$.

$$\left(1 + \frac{1}{x}\right)^2 - 6\left(1 + \frac{1}{x}\right) + 8 = 0 \qquad \text{Given equation}$$

$$W^2 - 6W + 8 = 0 \qquad \text{Let } W = 1 + \frac{1}{x}$$

$$(W - 4)(W - 2) = 0 \qquad \text{Factor}$$

$$W - 4 = 0 \quad \text{or} \quad W - 2 = 0 \qquad \text{Zero-Product Property}$$

$$W = 4 \qquad\qquad W = 2 \qquad \text{Solve}$$

Now we change these values of $W$ back into the corresponding values of $x$.

$$1 + \frac{1}{x} = 4 \qquad 1 + \frac{1}{x} = 2 \qquad W = 1 + \frac{1}{x}$$

$$\frac{1}{x} = 3 \qquad\quad \frac{1}{x} = 1 \qquad \text{Subtract 1}$$

$$x = \frac{1}{3} \qquad\quad x = 1 \qquad \text{Take reciprocals}$$

The solutions are $x = \frac{1}{3}$ and $x = 1$.

✎ **Practice what you've learned: Do Exercise 37.**                    ▲

---

## MATHEMATICS IN THE MODERN WORLD

### Error-Correcting Codes

The pictures sent back by the Pathfinder spacecraft from the surface of Mars on July 4, 1997, were astoundingly clear. But few watching these pictures were aware of the complex mathematics used to accomplish that feat. The distance to Mars is enormous, and the background noise (or static) is many times stronger than the original signal emitted by the spacecraft. So when scientists receive the signal, it is full of errors. To get a clear picture, the errors must be found and corrected. This same problem of errors is routinely encountered in transmitting bank records when you use an ATM or voice when you are talking on the telephone.

To understand how errors are found and corrected, we must first understand that to transmit pictures, sound, or text, we transform them into bits (the digits 0 or 1; see page 175). To help the receiver recognize errors, the message is "coded" by inserting additional bits. For example, suppose you want to transmit the message "10100." A very simple-minded code is as follows: Send each digit a million times. The person receiving the message reads it in blocks of a million digits. If the first block is mostly 1's, the person concludes that you are probably trying to transmit a 1, and so on. To say that this code is not efficient is a bit of an understatement; it requires sending a million times more data than the original message. Another method inserts "check digits." For example, for each block of eight digits insert a ninth digit; the inserted digit is 0 if there is an even number of 1's in the block and 1 if there is an odd number. So if a single digit is wrong (a 0 changed to a 1 or vice versa), the check digits allow us to recognize that an error has occurred. This method does not tell us where the error is, so we can't correct it. Modern error-correcting codes use interesting mathematical algorithms that require inserting relatively few digits but that allow the receiver to not only recognize, but also correct, errors. The first error-correcting code was developed in the 1940s by Richard Hamming at MIT. It is interesting to note that the English language has a built-in error correcting mechanism; to test it, try reading this error-laden sentence: Gve mo libty ox giv ne deth.

▶ **EXAMPLE 6** | A Fourth-Degree Equation of Quadratic Type

Find all solutions of the equation $x^4 - 8x^2 + 8 = 0$.

▼ **SOLUTION**   If we set $W = x^2$, then we get a quadratic equation in the new variable $W$:

$$(x^2)^2 - 8x^2 + 8 = 0 \qquad \text{Write } x^4 \text{ as } (x^2)^2$$

$$W^2 - 8W + 8 = 0 \qquad \text{Let } W = x^2$$

$$W = \frac{-(-8) \pm \sqrt{(-8)^2 - 4 \cdot 8}}{2} = 4 \pm 2\sqrt{2} \qquad \text{Quadratic Formula}$$

$$x^2 = 4 \pm 2\sqrt{2} \qquad\qquad W = x^2$$

$$x = \pm\sqrt{4 \pm 2\sqrt{2}} \qquad\qquad \text{Take square roots}$$

So, there are four solutions:

$$\sqrt{4 + 2\sqrt{2}}, \qquad \sqrt{4 - 2\sqrt{2}}, \qquad -\sqrt{4 + 2\sqrt{2}}, \qquad -\sqrt{4 - 2\sqrt{2}}$$

Using a calculator, we obtain the approximations $x \approx 2.61, 1.08, -2.61, -1.08$.

✎ **Practice what you've learned: Do Exercise 39.**     ▲

▶ **EXAMPLE 7** | An Equation Involving Fractional Powers

Find all solutions of the equation $x^{1/3} + x^{1/6} - 2 = 0$.

▼ **SOLUTION**   This equation is of quadratic type because if we let $W = x^{1/6}$, then $W^2 = (x^{1/6})^2 = x^{1/3}$.

$$x^{1/3} + x^{1/6} - 2 = 0 \qquad \text{Given equation}$$

$$W^2 + W - 2 = 0 \qquad \text{Let } W = x^{1/6}$$

$$(W - 1)(W + 2) = 0 \qquad \text{Factor}$$

$$W - 1 = 0 \quad \text{or} \quad W + 2 = 0 \qquad \text{Zero-Product Property}$$

$$W = 1 \qquad\qquad W = -2 \qquad \text{Solve}$$

$$x^{1/6} = 1 \qquad\qquad x^{1/6} = -2 \qquad W = x^{1/6}$$

$$x = 1^6 = 1 \qquad\qquad x = (-2)^6 = 64 \qquad \text{Take the 6th power}$$

From *Check Your Answers* we see that $x = 1$ is a solution but $x = 64$ is not. The only solution is $x = 1$.

---

**Check Your Answers**

$x = 1$:

$\quad$ LHS $= 1^{1/3} + 1^{1/6} - 2 = 0$

$\quad$ RHS $= 0$

$\quad$ LHS $=$ RHS $\quad$ ✔

$x = 64$:

$\quad$ LHS $= 64^{1/3} + 64^{1/6} - 2$

$\qquad\qquad = 4 + 2 - 2 = 4$

$\quad$ RHS $= 0$

$\quad$ LHS $\neq$ RHS $\quad$ ✗

---

✎ **Practice what you've learned: Do Exercise 45.**     ▲

■ **Applications**

Many real-life problems can be modeled with the types of equations that we have studied in this section.

► **EXAMPLE 8** | Dividing a Lottery Jackpot

A group of people come forward to claim a $1,000,000 lottery jackpot, which the winners are to share equally. Before the jackpot is divided, three more winning ticket holders show up. As a result, each person's share is reduced by $75,000. How many winners were in the original group?

▼ **SOLUTION**   We are asked for the number of people in the original group. So let

Identify the variable ►   $x = $ number of winners in the original group

We translate the information in the problem as follows:

| In Words | In Algebra |
|---|---|
| Number of winners in original group | $x$ |
| Number of winners in final group | $x + 3$ |
| Winnings per person, originally | $\dfrac{1,000,000}{x}$ |
| Winnings per person, finally | $\dfrac{1,000,000}{x + 3}$ |

Translate from words to algebra ►

Now we set up the model.

Set up the model ►

$$\boxed{\begin{array}{c}\text{winnings per}\\\text{person, originally}\end{array}} - \boxed{\$75{,}000} = \boxed{\begin{array}{c}\text{winnings per}\\\text{person, finally}\end{array}}$$

$$\frac{1{,}000{,}000}{x} - 75{,}000 = \frac{1{,}000{,}000}{x + 3}$$

Solve ►

$$1{,}000{,}000(x + 3) - 75{,}000x(x + 3) = 1{,}000{,}000x \qquad \text{Multiply by LCD } x(x + 3)$$

$$40(x + 3) - 3x(x + 3) = 40x \qquad \text{Divide by 25,000}$$

$$x^2 + 3x - 40 = 0 \qquad \begin{array}{l}\text{Expand, simplify, and}\\\text{divide by 3}\end{array}$$

$$(x + 8)(x - 5) = 0 \qquad \text{Factor}$$

$$x + 8 = 0 \quad \text{or} \quad x - 5 = 0 \qquad \text{Zero-Product Property}$$

$$x = -8 \qquad\qquad x = 5 \qquad \text{Solve}$$

Since we can't have a negative number of people, we conclude that there were five winners in the original group.

**Check Your Answer**

$$\text{winnings per person, originally} = \frac{\$1{,}000{,}000}{5} = \$200{,}000$$

$$\text{winnings per person, finally} = \frac{\$1{,}000{,}000}{8} = \$125{,}000$$

$$\$200{,}000 - \$75{,}000 = \$125{,}000 \qquad ✔$$

✎ **Practice what you've learned: Do Exercise 75.**   ▲

► **EXAMPLE 9** | Energy Expended in Bird Flight

Ornithologists have determined that some species of birds tend to avoid flights over large bodies of water during daylight hours, because air generally rises over land and falls over water in the daytime, so flying over water requires more energy. A bird is released from point $A$ on an island, 5 mi from $B$, the nearest point on a straight shoreline. The bird flies to a point $C$ on the shoreline and then flies along the shoreline to its nesting area $D$, as

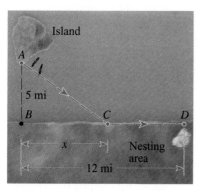

**FIGURE 1**

shown in Figure 1. Suppose the bird has 170 kcal of energy reserves. It uses 10 kcal/mi flying over land and 14 kcal/mi flying over water.

**(a)** Where should the point $C$ be located so that the bird uses exactly 170 kcal of energy during its flight?

**(b)** Does the bird have enough energy reserves to fly directly from $A$ to $D$?

**▼ SOLUTION**

**(a)** We are asked to find the location of $C$. So let

Identify the variable ▶   $x$ = distance from $B$ to $C$

From the figure, and from the fact that

$$\text{energy used} = \text{energy per mile} \times \text{miles flown}$$

we determine the following:

Translate from words to algebra ▶

| In Words | In Algebra | |
|---|---|---|
| Distance from $B$ to $C$ | $x$ | |
| Distance flown over water (from $A$ to $C$) | $\sqrt{x^2 + 25}$ | Pythagorean Theorem |
| Distance flown over land (from $C$ to $D$) | $12 - x$ | |
| Energy used over water | $14\sqrt{x^2 + 25}$ | |
| Energy used over land | $10(12 - x)$ | |

Now we set up the model.

Set up the model ▶

$$\underset{\text{used}}{\text{total energy}} = \underset{\text{over water}}{\text{energy used}} + \underset{\text{over land}}{\text{energy used}}$$

$$170 = 14\sqrt{x^2 + 25} + 10(12 - x)$$

To solve this equation, we eliminate the square root by first bringing all other terms to the left of the equal sign and then squaring each side.

Solve ▶

$$170 - 10(12 - x) = 14\sqrt{x^2 + 25} \qquad \text{Isolate square root term on RHS}$$

$$50 + 10x = 14\sqrt{x^2 + 25} \qquad \text{Simplify LHS}$$

$$(50 + 10x)^2 = (14)^2(x^2 + 25) \qquad \text{Square each side}$$

$$2500 + 1000x + 100x^2 = 196x^2 + 4900 \qquad \text{Expand}$$

$$0 = 96x^2 - 1000x + 2400 \qquad \text{All terms to RHS}$$

This equation could be factored, but because the numbers are so large, it is easier to use the Quadratic Formula and a calculator:

$$x = \frac{1000 \pm \sqrt{(-1000)^2 - 4(96)(2400)}}{2(96)} = \frac{1000 \pm 280}{192}$$

$$x = 6\tfrac{2}{3} \qquad \text{or} \qquad x = 3\tfrac{3}{4}$$

Point $C$ should be either $6\tfrac{2}{3}$ mi or $3\tfrac{3}{4}$ mi from $B$ so that the bird uses exactly 170 kcal of energy during its flight.

**(b)** By the Pythagorean Theorem (see page 284), the length of the route directly from $A$ to $D$ is $\sqrt{5^2 + 12^2} = 13$ mi, so the energy the bird requires for that route is $14 \times 13 = 182$ kcal. This is more energy than the bird has available, so it can't use this route.

✎ **Practice what you've learned: Do Exercise 83.** ▲

# 1.5 EXERCISES

## ▼ CONCEPTS

**1. (a)** The solutions of the equation $x^2(x - 4) = 0$ are _____.

**(b)** To solve the equation $x^3 - 4x^2 = 0$, we _____ the left-hand side.

**2.** Solve the equation $\sqrt{2x} + x = 0$ by doing the following steps.

**(a)** Isolate the radical: _____.

**(b)** Square both sides: _____.

**(c)** The solutions of the resulting quadratic equation are

_____.

**(d)** The solution(s) that satisfy the original equation are

_____.

**3.** The equation $(x + 1)^2 - 5(x + 1) + 6 = 0$ is of _____ type. To solve the equation, we set $W = $ _____. The resulting quadratic equation is _____.

**4.** The equation $x^6 + 7x^3 - 8 = 0$ is of _____ type. To solve the equation, we set $W = $ _____. The resulting quadratic equation is _____.

## ▼ SKILLS

**5–60** ▪ Find all real solutions of the equation.

**5.** $x^3 = 16x$

**6.** $x^5 = 27x^2$

**7.** $x^6 - 81x^2 = 0$

**8.** $x^5 - 16x = 0$

**9.** $x^5 + 8x^2 = 0$

**10.** $x^4 + 64x = 0$

**11.** $x^3 - 5x^2 + 6x = 0$

**12.** $x^4 - x^3 - 6x^2 = 0$

**13.** $x^4 + 4x^3 + 2x^2 = 0$

**14.** $(x - 2)^5 - 9(x - 2)^3 = 0$

**15.** $x^3 - 5x^2 - 2x + 10 = 0$

**16.** $2x^3 + x^2 - 18x - 9 = 0$

**17.** $x^3 - x^2 + x - 1 = x^2 + 1$

**18.** $7x^3 - x + 1 = x^3 + 3x^2 + x$

**19.** $\dfrac{1}{x - 1} + \dfrac{1}{x + 2} = \dfrac{5}{4}$

**20.** $\dfrac{10}{x} - \dfrac{12}{x - 3} + 4 = 0$

**21.** $\dfrac{x^2}{x + 100} = 50$

**22.** $1 + \dfrac{2x}{(x + 3)(x + 4)} = \dfrac{2}{x + 3} + \dfrac{4}{x + 4}$

**23.** $\dfrac{x + 5}{x - 2} = \dfrac{5}{x + 2} + \dfrac{28}{x^2 - 4}$

**24.** $\dfrac{x}{2x + 7} - \dfrac{x + 1}{x + 3} = 1$

**25.** $\dfrac{1}{x - 1} - \dfrac{2}{x^2} = 0$

**26.** $\dfrac{x + \dfrac{2}{x}}{3 + \dfrac{4}{x}} = 5x$

**27.** $\sqrt{x + 2} = x$

**28.** $\sqrt{4 - 6x} = 2x$

**29.** $\sqrt{2x + 1} + 1 = x$

**30.** $x - \sqrt{9 - 3x} = 0$

**31.** $\sqrt{5 - x} + 1 = x - 2$

**32.** $2x + \sqrt{x + 1} = 8$

**33.** $x - \sqrt{x + 3} = \dfrac{x}{2}$

**34.** $x + 2\sqrt{x - 7} = 10$

**35.** $(x + 5)^2 - 3(x + 5) - 10 = 0$

**36.** $\left(\dfrac{x + 1}{x}\right)^2 + 4\left(\dfrac{x + 1}{x}\right) + 3 = 0$

**37.** $\left(\dfrac{1}{x + 1}\right)^2 - 2\left(\dfrac{1}{x + 1}\right) - 8 = 0$

**38.** $\left(\dfrac{x}{x + 2}\right)^2 = \dfrac{4x}{x + 2} - 4$

**39.** $x^4 - 13x^2 + 40 = 0$

**40.** $x^4 - 5x^2 + 4 = 0$

**41.** $2x^4 + 4x^2 + 1 = 0$

**42.** $x^6 - 2x^3 - 3 = 0$

**43.** $x^6 - 26x^3 - 27 = 0$

**44.** $x^8 + 15x^4 = 16$

**45.** $x^{4/3} - 5x^{2/3} + 6 = 0$

**46.** $\sqrt{x} - 3\sqrt[4]{x} - 4 = 0$

**47.** $4(x + 1)^{1/2} - 5(x + 1)^{3/2} + (x + 1)^{5/2} = 0$

**48.** $2(x - 4)^{7/3} - (x - 4)^{4/3} - (x - 4)^{1/3} = 0$

**49.** $x^{3/2} + 8x^{1/2} + 16x^{-1/2} = 0$

**50.** $x^{1/2} + 3x^{-1/2} = 10x^{-3/2}$

**51.** $x^{1/2} - 3x^{1/3} = 3x^{1/6} - 9$

**52.** $x - 5\sqrt{x} + 6 = 0$

**53.** $\dfrac{1}{x^3} + \dfrac{4}{x^2} + \dfrac{4}{x} = 0$

**54.** $4x^{-4} - 16x^{-2} + 4 = 0$

**55.** $\sqrt{\sqrt{x + 5} + x} = 5$

**56.** $\sqrt[3]{4x^2 - 4x} = x$

**57.** $x^2\sqrt{x + 3} = (x + 3)^{3/2}$

**58.** $\sqrt{11 - x^2} - \dfrac{2}{\sqrt{11 - x^2}} = 1$

**59.** $\sqrt{x + \sqrt{x + 2}} = 2$

**60.** $\sqrt{1 + \sqrt{x + \sqrt{2x + 1}}} = \sqrt{5 + \sqrt{x}}$

**61–70** ▪ Find all solutions, real and complex, of the equation.

**61.** $x^3 = 1$

**62.** $x^4 - 16 = 0$

**63.** $x^3 + x^2 + x = 0$

**64.** $x^4 + x^3 + x^2 + x = 0$

**65.** $x^4 - 6x^2 + 8 = 0$

**66.** $x^3 + 3x^2 + 9x + 27 = 0$

**67.** $x^6 - 9x^3 + 8 = 0$

**68.** $x^6 + 9x^4 - 4x^2 - 36 = 0$

**69.** $\sqrt{x^2 + 1} + \dfrac{8}{\sqrt{x^2 + 1}} = \sqrt{x^2 + 9}$

**70.** $1 - \sqrt{x^2 + 7} = 6 - x^2$

**71–74** ▪ Solve the equation for the variable $x$. The constants $a$ and $b$ represent positive real numbers.

**71.** $x^4 + 5ax^2 + 4a^2 = 0$

**72.** $a^3x^3 + b^3 = 0$

**73.** $\sqrt{x + a} + \sqrt{x - a} = \sqrt{2}\sqrt{x + 6}$

**74.** $\sqrt{x} + a\sqrt[3]{x} + b\sqrt[6]{x} + ab = 0$

## ▼ APPLICATIONS

**75. Chartering a Bus** A social club charters a bus at a cost of $900 to take a group of members on an excursion to Atlantic City. At the last minute, five people in the group decide not to go. This raises the transportation cost per person by $2. How many people originally intended to take the trip?

**76. Buying a Cottage**  A group of friends decides to buy a vacation home for $120,000, sharing the cost equally. If they can find one more person to join them, each person's contribution will drop by $6000. How many people are in the group?

**77. Fish Population**  A large pond is stocked with fish. The fish population $P$ is modeled by the formula $P = 3t + 10\sqrt{t} + 140$, where $t$ is the number of days since the fish were first introduced into the pond. How many days will it take for the fish population to reach 500?

**78. The Lens Equation**  If $F$ is the focal length of a convex lens and an object is placed at a distance $x$ from the lens, then its image will be at a distance $y$ from the lens, where $F$, $x$, and $y$ are related by the *lens equation*

$$\frac{1}{F} = \frac{1}{x} + \frac{1}{y}$$

Suppose that a lens has a focal length of 4.8 cm and that the image of an object is 4 cm closer to the lens than the object itself. How far from the lens is the object?

**79. Volume of Grain**  Grain is falling from a chute onto the ground, forming a conical pile whose diameter is always three times its height. How high is the pile (to the nearest hundredth of a foot) when it contains 1000 ft$^3$ of grain?

**80. Radius of a Tank**  A spherical tank has a capacity of 750 gallons. Using the fact that 1 gallon is about 0.1337 ft$^3$, find the radius of the tank (to the nearest hundredth of a foot).

**81. Radius of a Sphere**  A jeweler has three small solid spheres made of gold, of radius 2 mm, 3 mm, and 4 mm. He decides to melt these down and make just one sphere out of them. What will the radius of this larger sphere be?

**82. Dimensions of a Box**  A large plywood box has a volume of 180 ft$^3$. Its length is 9 ft greater than its height, and its width is 4 ft less than its height. What are the dimensions of the box?

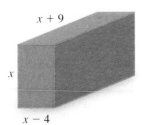

$x + 9$

$x$

$x - 4$

**83. Construction Costs**  The town of Foxton lies 10 mi north of an abandoned east-west road that runs through Grimley, as shown in the figure. The point on the abandoned road closest to Foxton is 40 mi from Grimley. County officials are about to build a new road connecting the two towns. They have determined that restoring the old road would cost $100,000 per mile, while building a new road would cost $200,000 per mile. How much of the abandoned road should be used (as indicated in the figure) if the officials intend to spend exactly $6.8 million? Would it cost less than this amount to build a new road connecting the towns directly?

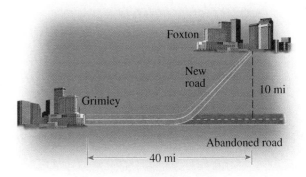

Foxton

New road

Grimley

10 mi

Abandoned road

40 mi

**84. Distance, Speed, and Time**  A boardwalk is parallel to and 210 ft inland from a straight shoreline. A sandy beach lies between the boardwalk and the shoreline. A man is standing on the boardwalk, exactly 750 ft across the sand from his beach umbrella, which is right at the shoreline. The man walks 4 ft/s on the boardwalk and 2 ft/s on the sand. How far should he walk on the boardwalk before veering off onto the sand if he wishes to reach his umbrella in exactly 4 min 45 s?

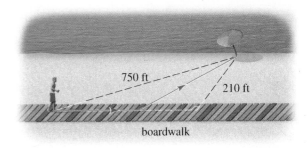

750 ft

210 ft

boardwalk

**85. Dimensions of a Lot**  A city lot has the shape of a right triangle whose hypotenuse is 7 ft longer than one of the other sides. The perimeter of the lot is 392 ft. How long is each side of the lot?

**86. TV Monitors**  Two television monitors sitting beside each other on a shelf in an appliance store have the same screen height. One has a conventional screen, which is 5 in. wider than it is high. The other has a wider, high-definition screen, which is 1.8 times as wide as it is high. The diagonal measure of the wider screen is 14 in. more than the diagonal measure of the smaller. What is the height of the screens, correct to the nearest 0.1 in.?

**87. Depth of a Well**  One method for determining the depth of a well is to drop a stone into it and then measure the time it takes until the splash is heard. If $d$ is the depth of the well (in feet)

and $t_1$ the time (in seconds) it takes for the stone to fall, then $d = 16t_1^2$, so $t_1 = \sqrt{d}/4$. Now if $t_2$ is the time it takes for the sound to travel back up, then $d = 1090t_2$ because the speed of sound is 1090 ft/s. So $t_2 = d/1090$. Thus, the total time elapsed between dropping the stone and hearing the splash is

$$t_1 + t_2 = \sqrt{d}/4 + d/1090$$

How deep is the well if this total time is 3 s?

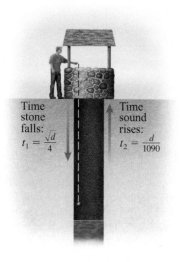

Time stone falls: $t_1 = \dfrac{\sqrt{d}}{4}$

Time sound rises: $t_2 = \dfrac{d}{1090}$

## ▼ DISCOVERY • DISCUSSION • WRITING

**88. Solving an Equation in Different Ways** We have learned several different ways to solve an equation in this section. Some equations can be tackled by more than one method. For example, the equation $x - \sqrt{x} - 2 = 0$ is of quadratic type: We can solve it by letting $\sqrt{x} = u$ and $x = u^2$ and factoring. Or we could solve for $\sqrt{x}$, square each side, and then solve the resulting quadratic equation. Solve the following equations using both methods indicated, and show that you get the same final answers.

**(a)** $x - \sqrt{x} - 2 = 0$    quadratic type; solve for the radical, and square

**(b)** $\dfrac{12}{(x-3)^2} + \dfrac{10}{x-3} + 1 = 0$    quadratic type; multiply by LCD

---

## 1.6 | Inequalities

### LEARNING OBJECTIVES

After completing this section, you will be able to:

- Solve linear inequalities
- Solve nonlinear inequalities
- Model with inequalities

Some problems in algebra lead to **inequalities** instead of equations. An inequality looks just like an equation, except that in the place of the equal sign is one of the symbols $<$, $>$, $\leq$, or $\geq$. Here is an example of an inequality:

$$4x + 7 \leq 19$$

| $x$ | $4x + 7 \leq 19$ |
|-----|------------------|
| 1 | $11 \leq 19$ ✔ |
| 2 | $15 \leq 19$ ✔ |
| 3 | $19 \leq 19$ ✔ |
| 4 | $23 \leq 19$ ✘ |
| 5 | $27 \leq 19$ ✘ |

The table in the margin shows that some numbers satisfy the inequality and some numbers do not.

To **solve** an inequality that contains a variable means to find all values of the variable that make the inequality true. Unlike an equation, an inequality generally has infinitely many solutions, which form an interval or a union of intervals on the real line. The following illustration shows how an inequality differs from its corresponding equation:

|  | | Solution | Graph |
|--|--|----------|-------|
| Equation: | $4x + 7 = 19$ | $x = 3$ | 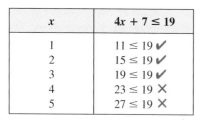 |
| Inequality: | $4x + 7 \leq 19$ | $x \leq 3$ |  |

To solve inequalities, we use the following rules to isolate the variable on one side of the inequality sign. These rules tell us when two inequalities are *equivalent* (the symbol $\Leftrightarrow$ means "is equivalent to"). In these rules the symbols $A$, $B$, and $C$ stand for real numbers or

## ▼ APPLICATIONS

✎ **57. Thickness of a Laminate**   A company manufactures industrial laminates (thin nylon-based sheets) of thickness 0.020 in., with a tolerance of 0.003 in.

  **(a)** Find an inequality involving absolute values that describes the range of possible thickness for the laminate.

  **(b)** Solve the inequality that you found in part (a).

0.020 in.

**58. Range of Height**   The average height of adult males is 68.2 in., and 95% of adult males have height $h$ that satisfies the inequality

$$\left| \frac{h - 68.2}{2.9} \right| \le 2$$

Solve the inequality to find the range of heights.

## ▼ DISCOVERY • DISCUSSION • WRITING

**59. Using Distances to Solve Absolute Value Inequalities**   Recall that $|a - b|$ is the distance between $a$ and $b$ on the number line. For any number $x$, what do $|x - 1|$ and $|x - 3|$ represent? Use this interpretation to solve the inequality $|x - 1| < |x - 3|$ geometrically. In general, if $a < b$, what is the solution of the inequality $|x - a| < |x - b|$?

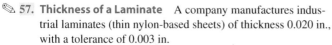

# ▶ CHAPTER 1 | REVIEW

## ▼ PROPERTIES AND FORMULAS

### Properties of Equality (p. 66)

$A = B \iff A + C = B + C$

$A = B \iff CA = CB \quad (C \neq 0)$

### Linear Equations (p. 66)

A **linear equation** is an equation of the form $ax + b = 0$

### Power Equations (p. 69)

A **power equation** is an equation of the form $X^n = a$. Its solutions are

$$X = \sqrt[n]{a} \quad \text{if } n \text{ is odd}$$
$$X = \pm\sqrt[n]{a} \quad \text{if } n \text{ is even}$$

If $n$ is even and $a < 0$, the equation has no real solution.

### Simple Interest (p. 75)

If a principal $P$ is invested at simple annual interest rate $r$ for $t$ years, then the interest $I$ is given by

$$I = Prt$$

### Zero-Product Property (p. 87)

If $AB = 0$ then $A = 0$ or $B = 0$.

### Completing the Square (p. 88)

To make $x^2 + bx$ a perfect square, add $\left(\dfrac{b}{2}\right)^2$. This gives the perfect square

$$x^2 + bx + \left(\frac{b}{2}\right)^2 = \left(x + \frac{b}{2}\right)^2$$

### Quadratic Formula (pp. 89–91)

A **quadratic equation** is an equation of the form

$$ax^2 + bx + c = 0$$

Its solutions are given by the **Quadratic Formula**:

$$x = \frac{-b \pm \sqrt{b^2 - 4ac}}{2a}$$

The **discriminant** is $D = b^2 - 4ac$.

If $D > 0$, the equation has two real solutions.

If $D = 0$, the equation has one solution.

If $D < 0$, the equation has two complex solutions.

### Complex Numbers (pp. 98–101)

A **complex number** is a number of the form $a + bi$, where $i = \sqrt{-1}$.

The **complex conjugate** of $a + bi$ is

$$\overline{a + bi} = a - bi$$

To **multiply** complex numbers, treat them as binomials and use $i^2 = -1$ to simplify the result.

To **divide** complex numbers, multiply numerator and denominator by the complex conjugate of the denominator:

$$\frac{a + bi}{c + di} = \left(\frac{a + bi}{c + di}\right) \cdot \left(\frac{c - di}{c - di}\right) = \frac{(a + bi)(c - di)}{c^2 + d^2}$$

### Inequalities (p. 113)

**Adding** the same quantity to each side of an inequality gives an equivalent inequality:

$$A < B \iff A + C < B + C$$

**Multiplying** each side of an inequality by the same *positive* quantity gives an equivalent inequality. Multiplying each side by the same *negative* quantity reverses the direction of the inequality:

$$A < B \iff CA < CB \quad \text{if } C > 0$$
$$A < B \iff CA > CB \quad \text{if } C < 0$$

### Absolute Value Equations (p. 122)

To solve an absolute value equation, we use

$$|x| = C \iff x = C \quad \text{or} \quad x = -C$$

### Absolute Value Inequalities (p. 123)

To solve an absolute value inequality, we use

$$|x| < C \iff -C < x < C$$
$$|x| > C \iff x < -C \quad \text{or} \quad x > C$$

## ▼ CONCEPT SUMMARY

| | Review Exercises |
|---|---|
| **Section 1.1** | |
| ▪ Solve linear equations | 1–12 |
| ▪ Solve power equations | 13–18, 23–28 |
| ▪ Solve for one variable in terms of another | 19–22 |
| **Section 1.2** | **Review Exercises** |
| ▪ Make equations that model real-world situations | 49–56 |
| ▪ Use equations to answer questions about real-world situations | 49–56 |
| **Section 1.3** | **Review Exercises** |
| ▪ Solve quadratic equations by factoring, completing the square, or using the quadratic formula | 31–38 |
| ▪ Model with quadratic equations | 52, 53, 55, 56 |
| **Section 1.4** | **Review Exercises** |
| ▪ Add and subtract complex numbers | 57–58 |
| ▪ Multiply and divide complex numbers | 59–64 |
| ▪ Simplify expressions with roots of negative numbers | 65–66 |
| ▪ Find complex roots of quadratic equations | 67–70 |
| **Section 1.5** | **Review Exercises** |
| ▪ Solve basic polynomial equations | 69–74 |
| ▪ Solve equations involving radicals or fractional powers | 25–28, 42–44 |
| ▪ Solve equations of quadratic type | 41–44 |
| ▪ Model with equations | 51, 53, 54 |
| **Section 1.6** | **Review Exercises** |
| ▪ Solve linear inequalities | 75–78 |
| ▪ Solve nonlinear inequalities | 79–84, 89 |
| ▪ Model with inequalities | 90 |
| **Section 1.7** | **Review Exercises** |
| ▪ Solve absolute value equations | 45–48 |
| ▪ Solve absolute value inequalities | 85–88 |

## ▼ EXERCISES

**1–18** ▪ Find all real solutions of the equation.

**1.** $5x + 11 = 36$

**2.** $3 - x = 5 + 3x$

**3.** $3x + 12 = 24$

**4.** $5x - 7 = 42$

**5.** $7x - 6 = 4x + 9$

**6.** $8 - 2x = 14 + x$

**7.** $\frac{1}{3}x - \frac{1}{2} = 2$

**8.** $\frac{2}{3}x + \frac{3}{5} = \frac{1}{5} - 2x$

**9.** $2(x + 3) - 4(x - 5) = 8 - 5x$

**10.** $\dfrac{x-5}{2} - \dfrac{2x+5}{3} = \dfrac{5}{6}$

**11.** $\dfrac{x+1}{x-1} = \dfrac{2x-1}{2x+1}$

**12.** $\dfrac{x}{x+2} - 3 = \dfrac{1}{x+2}$

**13.** $x^2 = 144$

**14.** $4x^2 = 49$

**15.** $5x^4 - 16 = 0$

**16.** $x^3 - 27 = 0$

**17.** $5x^3 - 15 = 0$

**18.** $6x^4 + 15 = 0$

**19–22** ▪ Solve the equation for the indicated variable.

**19.** $A = \dfrac{x+y}{2}$;  solve for $x$

**20.** $V = xy + yz + xz$;  solve for $y$

**21.** $J = \dfrac{1}{t} + \dfrac{1}{2t} + \dfrac{1}{3t}$;  solve for $t$

**22.** $F = k\dfrac{q_1 q_2}{r^2}$;  solve for $r$

**23–48** ▪ Find all real solutions of the equation.

**23.** $(x+1)^3 = -64$

**24.** $(x+2)^2 - 2 = 0$

**25.** $\sqrt[3]{x} = -3$

**26.** $x^{2/3} - 4 = 0$

**27.** $4x^{3/4} - 500 = 0$

**28.** $(x-2)^{1/5} = 2$

**29.** $\dfrac{x+1}{x-1} = \dfrac{3x}{3x-6}$

**30.** $(x+2)^2 = (x-4)^2$

**31.** $x^2 - 9x + 14 = 0$

**32.** $x^2 + 24x + 144 = 0$

**33.** $2x^2 + x = 1$

**34.** $3x^2 + 5x - 2 = 0$

**35.** $4x^3 - 25x = 0$

**36.** $x^3 - 2x^2 - 5x + 10 = 0$

**37.** $3x^2 + 4x - 1 = 0$

**38.** $x^2 - 3x + 9 = 0$

**39.** $\dfrac{1}{x} + \dfrac{2}{x-1} = 3$

**40.** $\dfrac{x}{x-2} + \dfrac{1}{x+2} = \dfrac{8}{x^2-4}$

**41.** $x^4 - 8x^2 - 9 = 0$

**42.** $x - 4\sqrt{x} = 32$

**43.** $x^{-1/2} - 2x^{1/2} + x^{3/2} = 0$

**44.** $(1 + \sqrt{x})^2 - 2(1 + \sqrt{x}) - 15 = 0$

**45.** $|x - 7| = 4$

**46.** $|3x| = 18$

**47.** $|2x - 5| = 9$

**48.** $4|3 - x| + 3 = 15$

**49.** A shopkeeper sells raisins for $3.20 per pound and nuts for $2.40 per pound. She decides to mix the raisins and nuts and sell 50 lb of the mixture for $2.72 per pound. What quantities of raisins and nuts should she use?

**50.** Anthony leaves Kingstown at 2:00 P.M. and drives to Queensville, 160 mi distant, at 45 mi/h. At 2:15 P.M. Helen leaves Queensville and drives to Kingstown at 40 mi/h. At what time do they pass each other on the road?

**51.** A woman cycles 8 mi/h faster than she runs. Every morning she cycles 4 mi and runs $2\frac{1}{2}$ mi, for a total of 1 hour of exercise. How fast does she run?

**52.** The approximate distance $d$ (in feet) that drivers travel after noticing that they must come to a sudden stop is given by the following formula, where $x$ is the speed of the car (in mi/h):

$$d = x + \dfrac{x^2}{20}$$

If a car travels 75 ft before stopping, what was its speed before the brakes were applied?

**53.** The hypotenuse of a right triangle has length 20 cm. The sum of the lengths of the other two sides is 28 cm. Find the lengths of the other two sides of the triangle.

**54.** Abbie paints twice as fast as Beth and three times as fast as Cathie. If it takes them 60 min to paint a living room with all three working together, how long would it take Abbie if she works alone?

**55.** A rectangular swimming pool is 8 ft deep everywhere and twice as long as it is wide. If the pool holds 8464 ft$^3$ of water, what are its dimensions?

**56.** A gardening enthusiast wishes to fence in three adjoining garden plots, one for each of his children, as shown in the figure. If each plot is to be 80 ft$^2$ in area and he has 88 ft of fencing material at hand, what dimensions should each plot have?

**57–66** ▪ Evaluate the expression and write the result in the form $a + bi$.

**57.** $(3 - 5i) - (6 + 4i)$

**58.** $(-2 + 3i) + (\tfrac{1}{2} - i)$

**59.** $(2 + 7i)(6 - i)$

**60.** $3(5 - 2i)\dfrac{i}{5}$

**61.** $\dfrac{2 - 3i}{2 + 3i}$

**62.** $\dfrac{2 + i}{4 - 3i}$

**63.** $i^{45}$

**64.** $(3 - i)^3$

**65.** $(1 - \sqrt{-3})(2 + \sqrt{-4})$

**66.** $\sqrt{-5} \cdot \sqrt{-20}$

**67–74** ▪ Find all real and imaginary solutions of the equation.

**67.** $x^2 + 16 = 0$

**68.** $x^2 = -12$

**69.** $x^2 + 6x + 10 = 0$

**70.** $2x^2 - 3x + 2 = 0$

**71.** $x^4 - 256 = 0$

**72.** $x^3 - 2x^2 + 4x - 8 = 0$

**73.** $x^2 + 4x = (2x + 1)^2$

**74.** $x^3 = 125$

**75–88** ▪ Solve the inequality. Express the solution using interval notation, and graph the solution set on the real number line.

**75.** $3x - 2 > -11$

**76.** $12 - x \geq 7x$

**77.** $-1 < 2x + 5 \leq 3$

**78.** $3 - x \leq 2x - 7$

**79.** $x^2 + 4x - 12 > 0$

**80.** $x^2 \le 1$

**81.** $\dfrac{2x + 5}{x + 1} \le 1$

**82.** $2x^2 \ge x + 3$

**83.** $\dfrac{x - 4}{x^2 - 4} \le 0$

**84.** $\dfrac{5}{x^3 - x^2 - 4x + 4} < 0$

**85.** $|x - 5| \le 3$

**86.** $|x - 4| < 0.02$

**87.** $|2x + 1| \ge 1$

**88.** $|x - 1| < |x - 3|$

[*Hint*: Interpret the quantities as distances.]

**89.** For what values of $x$ is the algebraic expression defined as a real number?

(a) $\sqrt{24 - x - 3x^2}$

(b) $\dfrac{1}{\sqrt[4]{x - x^4}}$

**90.** The volume of a sphere is given by $V = \frac{4}{3}\pi r^3$, where $r$ is the radius. Find the interval of values of the radius so that the volume is between 8 ft$^3$ and 12 ft$^3$, inclusive.

1. Find all real solutions of each equation.

   (a) $4x - 3 = 2x + 7$

   (b) $8x^3 = -125$

   (c) $x^{2/3} - 64 = 0$

   (d) $\dfrac{x}{2x - 5} = \dfrac{x + 3}{2x - 1}$

2. Einstein's famous equation $E = mc^2$ gives the relationship between energy $E$ and mass $m$. In this equation $c$ represents the speed of light. Solve the equation to express $c$ in terms of $E$ and $m$.

3. Natasha drove from Bedingfield to Portsmouth at an average speed of 100 km/h to attend a job interview. On the way back she decided to slow down to enjoy the scenery, so she drove at just 75 km/h. Her trip involved a total of 3.5 hours of driving time. What is the distance between Bedingfield and Portsmouth?

4. Calculate, and write the result in the standard form for complex numbers: $a + bi$.

   (a) $(3 - 5i) + (2 + i)$

   (b) $(3 - 5i) - (2 + i)$

   (c) $(1 + i)(5 - 2i)$

   (d) $\dfrac{1 + 2i}{3 - 4i}$

   (e) $i^{25}$

   (f) $(2 - \sqrt{-2})(\sqrt{8} - \sqrt{-4})$

5. Find all solutions, real and complex, of each equation.

   (a) $x^2 - x - 12 = 0$

   (b) $2x^2 + 4x + 3 = 0$

   (c) $\sqrt{3 - \sqrt{x + 5}} = 2$

   (d) $x^{1/2} - 3x^{1/4} + 2 = 0$

   (e) $x^4 - 16x^2 = 0$

   (f) $3\,|x - 4| - 10 = 0$

6. A rectangular parcel of land is 70 ft longer than it is wide. Each diagonal between opposite corners is 130 ft. What are the dimensions of the parcel?

7. Solve each inequality. Sketch the solution on a real number line, and write the answer using interval notation.

   (a) $-1 \le 5 - 2x < 10$

   (b) $x(x - 1)(x - 2) > 0$

   (c) $|x - 3| < 2$

   (d) $\dfrac{2x + 5}{x + 1} \le 1$

8. A bottle of medicine must be stored at a temperature between 5°C and 10°C. What range does this correspond to on the Fahrenheit scale? [*Note:* The Fahrenheit ($F$) and Celsius ($C$) scales satisfy the relation $C = \frac{5}{9}(F - 32)$.]

9. For what values of $x$ is the expression $\sqrt{4x - x^2}$ defined as a real number?

# MAKING THE BEST DECISIONS

When you buy a car, subscribe to a cell phone plan, or put an addition on your house, you need to make decisions. Such decisions are usually difficult because they require you to choose between several good alternatives. For example, there are many good car models, but which one has the optimal combination of features for the amount of money you want to spend? In this *Focus* we explore how to construct and use algebraic models of real-life situations to help make the best (or optimal) decisions.

▶ **EXAMPLE 1** │ Buying a Car

Ben wants to buy a new car, and he has narrowed his choices to two models.

  Model A sells for $12,500, gets 25 mi/gal, and costs $350 a year for insurance.

  Model B sells for $16,100, gets 48 mi/gal, and costs $425 a year for insurance.

Ben drives about 36,000 miles a year, and gas costs about $1.50 a gallon.

**(a)** Find a formula for the total cost of owning model A for any number of years.

**(b)** Find a formula for the total cost of owning model B for any number of years.

**(c)** Make a table of the total cost of owning each model from 1 year to 6 years, in 1-year increments.

**(d)** If Ben expects to keep the car for 3 years, which model is more economical? What if he expects to keep it for 5 years?

---

**Thinking About the Problem**

Model A has a smaller initial price and costs less in insurance per year but is more costly to operate (uses more gas) than model B. Model B has a larger initial price and costs more to insure but is cheaper to operate (uses less gas) than model A. If Ben drives a lot, then what he will save in gas with model B could make up for the initial cost of buying the car and the higher yearly insurance premiums. So how many years of driving does it take before the gas savings make up for the initial higher price? To find out, we must write formulas for the total cost for each car:

$$\text{cost} = \text{price} + \text{insurance cost} + \text{gas cost}$$

The insurance costs and gas costs depend on the number of years Ben drives the car.

---

▼ **SOLUTION** The cost of operating each model depends on the number of years of ownership. So let

$$n = \text{number of years Ben expects to own the car}$$

**(a)** For model A we have the following.

| In Words | In Algebra |
|---|---|
| Price of car | 12,500 |
| Insurance cost for $n$ years | $350n$ |
| Cost of gas per year | $(36{,}000/25) \times \$1.50 = \$2160$ |
| Cost of gas for $n$ years | $2160n$ |

# Coordinates and Graphs

Pal Hermansen /Getty Images

**Global Warming?** Is the world getting hotter or are we just having a temporary warm spell? To answer this question, scientists collect huge amounts of data on global temperature. A graph of the data can help to reveal long-term changes in temperature, but more precise algebra methods are used to detect any trend that is different from the normal temperature fluctuations. Significant global warming could have drastic consequences for the survival of many species. For example, melting polar ice eliminates the ice paths that polar bears need to reach their feeding grounds, resulting in the bears' drowning. (See *Focus on Modeling: Fitting Lines to Data*, Problem 6, page 199.) Of course, any changes in the global ecology also have implications for our own well-being.

## 2.1 | The Coordinate Plane

### LEARNING OBJECTIVES

After completing this section, you will be able to:

- Graph points and regions in the coordinate plane
- Use the Distance Formula
- Use the Midpoint Formula

The *coordinate plane* is the link between algebra and geometry. In the coordinate plane we can draw graphs of algebraic equations. The graphs, in turn, allow us to "see" the relationship between the variables in the equation.

Just as points on a line can be identified with real numbers to form the coordinate line, points in a plane can be identified with ordered pairs of numbers to form the **coordinate plane** or **Cartesian plane**. To do this, we draw two perpendicular real lines that intersect at 0 on each line. Usually, one line is horizontal with positive direction to the right and is called the **x-axis**; the other line is vertical with positive direction upward and is called the **y-axis**. The point of intersection of the x-axis and the y-axis is the **origin O**, and the two axes divide the plane into four **quadrants**, labeled I, II, III, and IV in Figure 1. (The points *on* the coordinate axes are not assigned to any quadrant.)

The Cartesian plane is named in honor of the French mathematician René Descartes (1596–1650), although another Frenchman, Pierre Fermat (1601–1665), also invented the principles of coordinate geometry at the same time. (See their biographies on pages 245 and 159.)

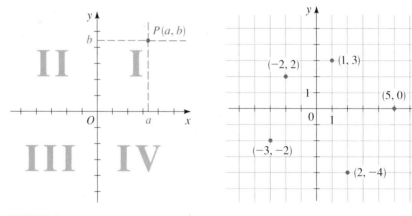

**FIGURE 1**          **FIGURE 2**

Although the notation for a point $(a, b)$ is the same as the notation for an open interval $(a, b)$, the context should make clear which meaning is intended.

Any point $P$ in the coordinate plane can be located by a unique **ordered pair** of numbers $(a, b)$, as shown in Figure 1. The first number $a$ is called the **x-coordinate** of $P$; the second number $b$ is called the **y-coordinate** of $P$. We can think of the coordinates of $P$ as its "address," because they specify its location in the plane. Several points are labeled with their coordinates in Figure 2.

▶ **EXAMPLE 1** | Graphing Regions in the Coordinate Plane

Describe and sketch the regions given by each set.

**(a)** $\{(x, y) \mid x \geq 0\}$     **(b)** $\{(x, y) \mid y = 1\}$     **(c)** $\{(x, y) \mid |y| < 1\}$

▼ **SOLUTION**

**(a)** The points whose x-coordinates are 0 or positive lie on the y-axis or to the right of it, as shown in Figure 3(a).

**(b)** The set of all points with y-coordinate 1 is a horizontal line one unit above the x-axis, as in Figure 3(b).

### Coordinates as Addresses

The coordinates of a point in the *xy*-plane uniquely determine its location. We can think of the coordinates as the "address" of the point. In Salt Lake City, Utah, the addresses of most buildings are in fact expressed as coordinates. The city is divided into quadrants with Main Street as the vertical (North-South) axis and S. Temple Street as the horizontal (East-West) axis. An address such as

1760 W     2100 S

indicates a location 17.6 blocks west of Main Street and 21 blocks south of S. Temple Street. (This is the address of the main post office in Salt Lake City.) With this logical system it is possible for someone who is unfamiliar with the city to locate any address immediately, as easily as one locates a point in the coordinate plane.

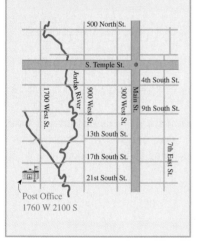

**(c)** Recall from Section 1.7 that

$$|y| < 1 \qquad \text{if and only if} \qquad -1 < y < 1$$

So the given region consists of those points in the plane whose *y*-coordinates lie between $-1$ and $1$. Thus, the region consists of all points that lie between (but not on) the horizontal lines $y = 1$ and $y = -1$. These lines are shown as broken lines in Figure 3(c) to indicate that the points on these lines do not lie in the set.

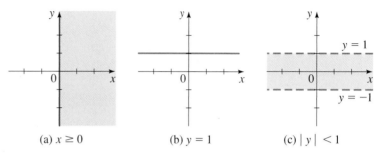

(a) $x \geq 0$          (b) $y = 1$          (c) $|y| < 1$

**FIGURE 3**

✎ **Practice what you've learned: Do Exercises 7 and 9.**          ▲

## ■ The Distance Formula

We now find a formula for the distance $d(A, B)$ between two points $A(x_1, y_1)$ and $B(x_2, y_2)$ in the plane. Recall from Section P.3 that the distance between points $a$ and $b$ on a number line is $d(a, b) = |b - a|$. So from Figure 4 we see that the distance between the points $A(x_1, y_1)$ and $C(x_2, y_1)$ on a horizontal line must be $|x_2 - x_1|$ and the distance between $B(x_2, y_2)$ and $C(x_2, y_1)$ on a vertical line must be $|y_2 - y_1|$.

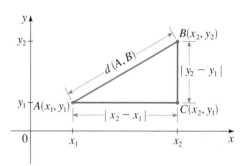

**FIGURE 4**

Since triangle $ABC$ is a right triangle, the Pythagorean Theorem gives

$$d(A, B) = \sqrt{|x_2 - x_1|^2 + |y_2 - y_1|^2} = \sqrt{(x_2 - x_1)^2 + (y_2 - y_1)^2}$$

**DISTANCE FORMULA**

The distance between the points $A(x_1, y_1)$ and $B(x_2, y_2)$ in the plane is

$$d(A, B) = \sqrt{(x_2 - x_1)^2 + (y_2 - y_1)^2}$$

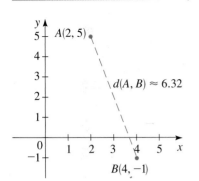

**FIGURE 5**

▶ **EXAMPLE 2** | Finding the Distance Between Two Points

Find the distance between the points $A(2, 5)$ and $B(4, -1)$.

▼ **SOLUTION** Using the Distance Formula, we have

$$d(A, B) = \sqrt{(4-2)^2 + (-1-5)^2}$$
$$= \sqrt{2^2 + (-6)^2}$$
$$= \sqrt{4 + 36} = \sqrt{40} \approx 6.32$$

See Figure 5.

✎ **Practice what you've learned: Do Exercise 25(b).** ▲

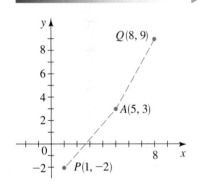

**FIGURE 6**

▶ **EXAMPLE 3** | Applying the Distance Formula

Which of the points $P(1, -2)$ or $Q(8, 9)$ is closer to the point $A(5, 3)$?

▼ **SOLUTION** By the Distance Formula we have

$$d(P, A) = \sqrt{(5-1)^2 + [3-(-2)]^2} = \sqrt{4^2 + 5^2} = \sqrt{41}$$
$$d(Q, A) = \sqrt{(5-8)^2 + (3-9)^2} = \sqrt{(-3)^2 + (-6)^2} = \sqrt{45}$$

This shows that $d(P, A) < d(Q, A)$, so $P$ is closer to $A$ (see Figure 6).

✎ **Practice what you've learned: Do Exercise 39.** ▲

## ■ The Midpoint Formula

Now let's find the coordinates $(x, y)$ of the midpoint $M$ of the line segment that joins the point $A(x_1, y_1)$ to the point $B(x_2, y_2)$. In Figure 7, notice that triangles $APM$ and $MQB$ are congruent because $d(A, M) = d(M, B)$ and the corresponding angles are equal.

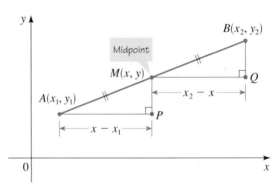

**FIGURE 7**

It follows that $d(A, P) = d(M, Q)$, so

$$x - x_1 = x_2 - x$$

Solving for $x$, we get $2x = x_1 + x_2$, so $x = \dfrac{x_1 + x_2}{2}$. Similarly, $y = \dfrac{y_1 + y_2}{2}$.

---

**MIDPOINT FORMULA**

The midpoint of the line segment from $A(x_1, y_1)$ to $B(x_2, y_2)$ is

$$\left( \frac{x_1 + x_2}{2}, \frac{y_1 + y_2}{2} \right)$$

---

▶ **EXAMPLE 4** | Finding the Midpoint

The midpoint of the line segment that joins the points $(-2, 5)$ and $(4, 9)$ is

$$\left( \frac{-2 + 4}{2}, \frac{5 + 9}{2} \right) = (1, 7)$$

See Figure 8.

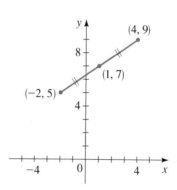

**FIGURE 8**

✎ **Practice what you've learned: Do Exercise 25(c).**    ▲

---

▶ **EXAMPLE 5** | Applying the Midpoint Formula

Show that the quadrilateral with vertices $P(1, 2)$, $Q(4, 4)$, $R(5, 9)$, and $S(2, 7)$ is a parallelogram by proving that its two diagonals bisect each other.

▼ **SOLUTION**    If the two diagonals have the same midpoint, then they must bisect each other. The midpoint of the diagonal $PR$ is

$$\left( \frac{1 + 5}{2}, \frac{2 + 9}{2} \right) = \left( 3, \frac{11}{2} \right)$$

and the midpoint of the diagonal $QS$ is

$$\left( \frac{4 + 2}{2}, \frac{4 + 7}{2} \right) = \left( 3, \frac{11}{2} \right)$$

so each diagonal bisects the other, as shown in Figure 9. (A theorem from elementary geometry states that the quadrilateral is therefore a parallelogram.)

✎ **Practice what you've learned: Do Exercise 43.**    ▲

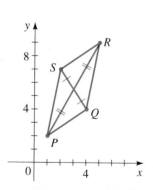

**FIGURE 9**

# 2.1 EXERCISES

## ▼ CONCEPTS

**1.** The point that is 3 units to the right of the $y$-axis and 5 units below the $x$-axis has coordinates (_____, _____).

**2.** If $x$ is negative and $y$ is positive, then the point $(x, y)$ is in Quadrant _____.

**3.** The distance between the points $(a, b)$ and $(c, d)$ is _____. So the distance between $(1, 2)$ and $(7, 10)$ is _____.

**4.** The point midway between $(a, b)$ and $(c, d)$ is _____. So the point midway between $(1, 2)$ and $(7, 10)$ is _____.

## ▼ SKILLS

**5.** Plot the given points in a coordinate plane:

$(2, 3), (-2, 3), (4, 5), (4, -5), (-4, 5), (-4, -5)$

**6.** Find the coordinates of the points shown in the figure.

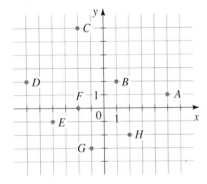

**7–20** ▪ Sketch the region given by the set.

**7.** $\{(x, y) \mid x \le 0\}$

**8.** $\{(x, y) \mid y \ge 0\}$

**9.** $\{(x, y) \mid x = 3\}$

**10.** $\{(x, y) \mid y = -2\}$

**11.** $\{(x, y) \mid 1 < x < 2\}$

**12.** $\{(x, y) \mid 0 \le y \le 4\}$

**13.** $\{(x, y) \mid xy < 0\}$

**14.** $\{(x, y) \mid xy > 0\}$

**15.** $\{(x, y) \mid x \ge 1 \text{ and } y < 3\}$

**16.** $\{(x, y) \mid -2 < x < 2 \text{ and } y \ge 3\}$

**17.** $\{(x, y) \mid |x| > 4\}$

**18.** $\{(x, y) \mid |y| \le 2\}$

**19.** $\{(x, y) \mid |x| \le 2 \text{ and } |y| \le 3\}$

**20.** $\{(x, y) \mid |x| > 2 \text{ and } |y| > 3\}$

**21–24** ▪ A pair of points is graphed. **(a)** Find the distance between them. **(b)** Find the midpoint of the segment that joins them.

**21.**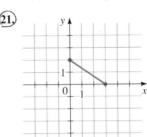

**22.**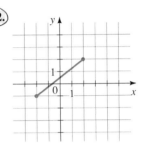

**23.**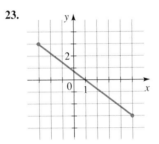

**24.**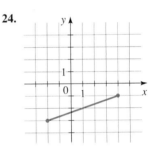

**25–34** ▪ A pair of points is graphed. **(a)** Plot the points in a coordinate plane. **(b)** Find the distance between them. **(c)** Find the midpoint of the segment that joins them.

**25.** $(0, 8), (6, 16)$      **26.** $(-2, 5), (10, 0)$

**27.** $(-3, -6), (4, 18)$      **28.** $(-1, -1), (9, 9)$

**29.** $(6, -2), (-1, 3)$      **30.** $(-1, 6), (-1, -3)$

**31.** $(7, 3), (11, 6)$      **32.** $(2, 13), (7, 1)$

**33.** $(3, 4), (-3, -4)$      **34.** $(5, 0), (0, 6)$

**35.** Draw the rectangle with vertices $A(1, 3)$, $B(5, 3)$, $C(1, -3)$, and $D(5, -3)$ on a coordinate plane. Find the area of the rectangle.

**36.** Draw the parallelogram with vertices $A(1, 2)$, $B(5, 2)$, $C(3, 6)$, and $D(7, 6)$ on a coordinate plane. Find the area of the parallelogram.

**37.** Plot the points $A(1, 0)$, $B(5, 0)$, $C(4, 3)$, and $D(2, 3)$ on a coordinate plane. Draw the segments $AB$, $BC$, $CD$, and $DA$. What kind of quadrilateral is $ABCD$, and what is its area?

**38.** Plot the points $P(5, 1)$, $Q(0, 6)$, and $R(-5, 1)$ on a coordinate plane. Where must the point $S$ be located so that the quadrilateral $PQRS$ is a square? Find the area of this square.

**39.** Which of the points $A(6, 7)$ or $B(-5, 8)$ is closer to the origin?

**40.** Which of the points $C(-6, 3)$ or $D(3, 0)$ is closer to the point $E(-2, 1)$?

**41.** Which of the points $P(3, 1)$ or $Q(-1, 3)$ is closer to the point $R(-1, -1)$?

**42.** **(a)** Show that the points $(7, 3)$ and $(3, 7)$ are the same distance from the origin.
**(b)** Show that the points $(a, b)$ and $(b, a)$ are the same distance from the origin.

**43.** Show that the triangle with vertices $A(0, 2)$, $B(-3, -1)$, and $C(-4, 3)$ is isosceles.

**44.** Find the area of the triangle shown in the figure.

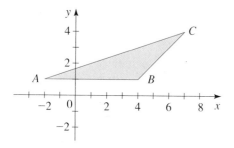

**45.** Refer to triangle $ABC$ in the figure.
**(a)** Show that triangle $ABC$ is a right triangle by using the converse of the Pythagorean Theorem (see page 284).
**(b)** Find the area of triangle $ABC$.

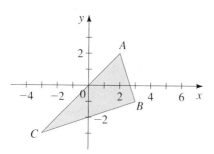

**46.** Show that the triangle with vertices $A(6, -7)$, $B(11, -3)$, and $C(2, -2)$ is a right triangle by using the converse of the Pythagorean Theorem. Find the area of the triangle.

**47.** Show that the points $A(-2, 9)$, $B(4, 6)$, $C(1, 0)$, and $D(-5, 3)$ are the vertices of a square.

**48.** Show that the points $A(-1, 3)$, $B(3, 11)$, and $C(5, 15)$ are collinear by showing that $d(A, B) + d(B, C) = d(A, C)$.

**49.** Find a point on the $y$-axis that is equidistant from the points $(5, -5)$ and $(1, 1)$.

**50.** Find the lengths of the medians of the triangle with vertices $A(1, 0)$, $B(3, 6)$, and $C(8, 2)$. (A *median* is a line segment from a vertex to the midpoint of the opposite side.)

**51.** Find the point that is one-fourth of the distance from the point $P(-1, 3)$ to the point $Q(7, 5)$ along the segment $PQ$.

**52.** Plot the points $P(-2, 1)$ and $Q(12, -1)$ on a coordinate plane. Which (if either) of the points $A(5, -7)$ and $B(6, 7)$ lies on the perpendicular bisector of the segment $PQ$?

**53.** Plot the points $P(-1, -4)$, $Q(1, 1)$, and $R(4, 2)$ on a coordinate plane. Where should the point $S$ be located so that the figure $PQRS$ is a parallelogram?

**54.** If $M(6, 8)$ is the midpoint of the line segment $AB$, and if $A$ has coordinates $(2, 3)$, find the coordinates of $B$.

**55.** **(a)** Sketch the parallelogram with vertices $A(-2, -1)$, $B(4, 2)$, $C(7, 7)$, and $D(1, 4)$.
**(b)** Find the midpoints of the diagonals of this parallelogram.
**(c)** From part (b), show that the diagonals bisect each other.

**56.** The point $M$ in the figure is the midpoint of the line segment $AB$. Show that $M$ is equidistant from the vertices of triangle $ABC$.

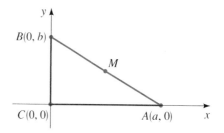

## ▼ APPLICATIONS

**57. Distances in a City**  A city has streets that run north and south and avenues that run east and west, all equally spaced. Streets and avenues are numbered sequentially, as shown in the figure. The *walking* distance between points $A$ and $B$ is 7 blocks—that is, 3 blocks east and 4 blocks north. To find the *straight-line* distances $d$, we must use the Distance Formula.
**(a)** Find the straight-line distance (in blocks) between $A$ and $B$.
**(b)** Find the walking distance and the straight-line distance between the corner of 4th St. and 2nd Ave. and the corner of 11th St. and 26th Ave.
**(c)** What must be true about the points $P$ and $Q$ if the walking distance between $P$ and $Q$ equals the straight-line distance between $P$ and $Q$?

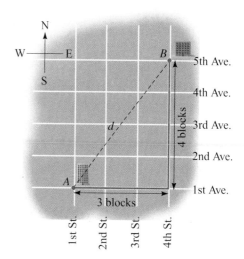

**58. Halfway Point** Two friends live in the city described in Exercise 57, one at the corner of 3rd St. and 7th Ave. and the other at the corner of 27th St. and 17th Ave. They frequently meet a coffee shop halfway between their homes.
   **(a)** At what intersection is the coffee shop located?
   **(b)** How far must each of them walk to get to the coffee shop?

**59. Pressure and Depth** The graph shows the pressure experienced by an ocean diver at two different depths. Find and interpret the midpoint of the line segment shown in the graph.

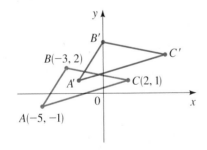

**61. Reflecting in the Coordinate Plane** Suppose that the $y$-axis acts as a mirror that reflects each point to the right of it into a point to the left of it.
   **(a)** The point $(3, 7)$ is reflected to what point?
   **(b)** The point $(a, b)$ is reflected to what point?
   **(c)** What point is reflected to $(-4, -1)$?
   **(d)** Triangle $ABC$ in the figure is reflected to triangle $A'B'C'$. Find the coordinates of the points $A'$, $B'$, and $C'$.

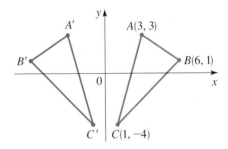

**62. Completing a Line Segment** Plot the points $M(6, 8)$ and $A(2, 3)$ on a coordinate plane. If $M$ is the midpoint of the line segment $AB$, find the coordinates of $B$. Write a brief description of the steps you took to find $B$ and your reasons for taking them.

**63. Completing a Parallelogram** Plot the points $P(0, 3)$, $Q(2, 2)$, and $R(5, 3)$ on a coordinate plane. Where should the point $S$ be located so that the figure $PQRS$ is a parallelogram? Write a brief description of the steps you took and your reasons for taking them.

▼ **DISCOVERY • DISCUSSION • WRITING**

**60. Shifting the Coordinate Plane** Suppose that each point in the coordinate plane is shifted 3 units to the right and 2 units upward.
   **(a)** The point $(5, 3)$ is shifted to what new point?
   **(b)** The point $(a, b)$ is shifted to what new point?
   **(c)** What point is shifted to $(3, 4)$?
   **(d)** Triangle $ABC$ in the figure has been shifted to triangle $A'B'C'$. Find the coordinates of the points $A'$, $B'$, and $C'$.

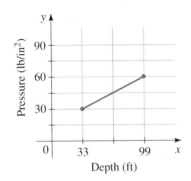

## VISUALIZING DATA

When scientists analyze data, they look for a trend or pattern from which they can draw a conclusion about the process they are studying. It is often hard to look at lists of numbers and see any kind of pattern. One of the best ways to reveal a hidden pattern in data is to draw a graph. For instance, a biologist measures the levels of three different enzymes (call them A, B, and C) in 20 blood samples taken from expectant mothers, yielding the data shown in the table (enzyme levels in milligrams per deciliter).

| Sample | A | B | C | Sample | A | B | C |
|--------|-----|-----|-----|--------|-----|-----|-----|
| 1 | 1.3 | 1.7 | 49 | 11 | 2.2 | 0.6 | 25 |
| 2 | 2.6 | 6.8 | 22 | 12 | 1.5 | 4.8 | 32 |
| 3 | 0.9 | 0.6 | 53 | 13 | 3.1 | 1.9 | 20 |
| 4 | 3.5 | 2.4 | 15 | 14 | 4.1 | 3.1 | 10 |
| 5 | 2.4 | 3.8 | 25 | 15 | 1.8 | 7.5 | 31 |
| 6 | 1.7 | 3.3 | 30 | 16 | 2.9 | 5.8 | 18 |
| 7 | 4.0 | 6.7 | 12 | 17 | 2.1 | 5.1 | 30 |
| 8 | 3.2 | 4.3 | 17 | 18 | 2.7 | 2.5 | 20 |
| 9 | 1.3 | 8.4 | 45 | 19 | 1.4 | 2.0 | 39 |
| 10 | 1.4 | 5.8 | 47 | 20 | 0.8 | 2.3 | 56 |

The biologist wishes to determine whether there is a relationship between the serum levels of these enzymes, so she makes some **scatter plots** of the data. The scatter plot in Figure 1 shows the levels of enzymes A and B. Each point represents the results for one sample—for instance, sample 1 had 1.3 mg/dL of enzyme A and 1.7 mg/dL of enzyme B, so we plot the point (1.3, 1.7) to represent this pair of data. Similarly, Figure 2 shows the levels of enzymes A and C. From Figure 1 the biologist sees that there is no obvious relationship between enzymes A and B, but from Figure 2 it appears that when the level of enzyme A goes up, the level of enzyme C goes down.

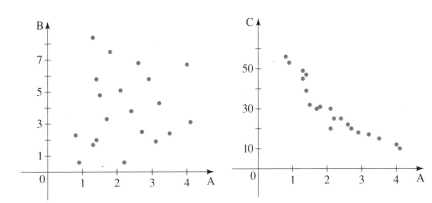

**FIGURE 1** Enzymes A and B are not related.

**FIGURE 2** Enzymes A and C are strongly related.

(CONTINUES)

1. Make a scatter plot of the levels of enzymes B and C in the blood samples. Do you detect any relationship from your graph?
2. For each scatter plot, determine whether there is a relationship between the two variables in the graphs. If there is, describe the relationship; that is, explain what happens to *y* as *x* increases.

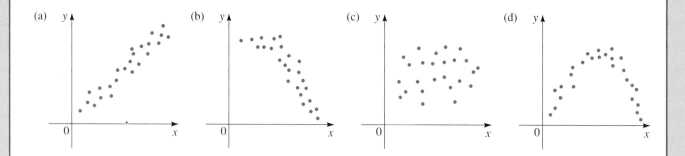

3. In each scatter plot below, the value of *y* increases as *x* increases. Explain how the relationship between *x* and *y* differs in the two cases.

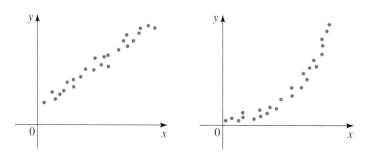

4. For the data given in the following table, make three scatter plots: one for enzymes A and B, one for B and C, and one for A and C. Determine whether any of these pairs of variables are related. If so, describe the relationship.

| Sample | A | B | C |
|--------|-----|-----|------|
| 1 | 58 | 4.1 | 51.7 |
| 2 | 39 | 5.2 | 15.4 |
| 3 | 15 | 7.6 | 2.0 |
| 4 | 30 | 6.0 | 7.3 |
| 5 | 46 | 4.3 | 34.2 |
| 6 | 59 | 3.9 | 72.4 |
| 7 | 22 | 6.3 | 4.1 |
| 8 | 7 | 8.1 | 0.5 |
| 9 | 41 | 4.7 | 22.6 |
| 10 | 62 | 3.7 | 96.3 |
| 11 | 10 | 7.9 | 1.3 |
| 12 | 6 | 8.3 | 0.2 |

## 2.2 | Graphs of Equations in Two Variables

### LEARNING OBJECTIVES

After completing this section, you will be able to:

- Graph equations by plotting points
- Find intercepts of the graph of an equation
- Identify the equation of a circle
- Graph circles in a coordinate plane
- Determine symmetry properties of an equation

**Fundamental Principle of Analytic Geometry**

A point $(x, y)$ lies on the graph of an equation if and only if its coordinates satisfy the equation.

An **equation in two variables**, such as $y = x^2 + 1$, expresses a relationship between two quantities. A point $(x, y)$ **satisfies** the equation if it makes the equation true when the values for $x$ and $y$ are substituted into the equation. For example, the point $(3, 10)$ satisfies the equation $y = x^2 + 1$ because $10 = 3^2 + 1$, but the point $(1, 3)$ does not, because $3 \neq 1^2 + 1$.

#### THE GRAPH OF AN EQUATION

The **graph** of an equation in $x$ and $y$ is the set of all points $(x, y)$ in the coordinate plane that satisfy the equation.

### ■ Graphing Equations by Plotting Points

The graph of an equation is a curve, so to graph an equation, we plot as many points as we can, then connect them by a smooth curve.

▶ **EXAMPLE 1** | Sketching a Graph by Plotting Points

Sketch the graph of the equation $2x - y = 3$.

▼ **SOLUTION**    We first solve the given equation for $y$ to get

$$y = 2x - 3$$

This helps us to calculate the $y$-coordinates in the following table.

| $x$ | $y = 2x - 3$ | $(x, y)$ |
|-----|--------------|----------|
| $-1$ | $-5$ | $(-1, -5)$ |
| $0$ | $-3$ | $(0, -3)$ |
| $1$ | $-1$ | $(1, -1)$ |
| $2$ | $1$ | $(2, 1)$ |
| $3$ | $3$ | $(3, 3)$ |
| $4$ | $5$ | $(4, 5)$ |

Of course, there are infinitely many points on the graph, and it is impossible to plot all of them. But the more points we plot, the better we can imagine what the graph represented by the equation looks like. We plot the points that we found in Figure 1; they appear to lie on a line. So we complete the graph by joining the points by a line. (In Section 2.4 we verify that the graph of this equation is indeed a line.)

✎ **Practice what you've learned: Do Exercise 15.**    ▲

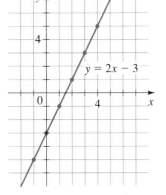

**FIGURE 1**

▶ **EXAMPLE 2** | Sketching a Graph by Plotting Points

Sketch the graph of the equation $y = x^2 - 2$.

A detailed discussion of parabolas and their geometric properties is presented in Chapter 8.

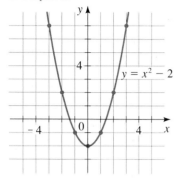

**FIGURE 2**

**▼ SOLUTION**    We find some of the points that satisfy the equation in the table below. In Figure 2 we plot these points and then connect them by a smooth curve. A curve with this shape is called a *parabola*.

| $x$ | $y = x^2 - 2$ | $(x, y)$ |
|---|---|---|
| $-3$ | $7$ | $(-3, 7)$ |
| $-2$ | $2$ | $(-2, 2)$ |
| $-1$ | $-1$ | $(-1, -1)$ |
| $0$ | $-2$ | $(0, -2)$ |
| $1$ | $-1$ | $(1, -1)$ |
| $2$ | $2$ | $(2, 2)$ |
| $3$ | $7$ | $(3, 7)$ |

✎ **Practice what you've learned: Do Exercise 19.**    ▲

▶ **EXAMPLE 3** | Graphing an Absolute Value Equation

Sketch the graph of the equation $y = |x|$.

**▼ SOLUTION**    We make a table of values:

| $x$ | $y = |x|$ | $(x, y)$ |
|---|---|---|
| $-3$ | $3$ | $(-3, 3)$ |
| $-2$ | $2$ | $(-2, 2)$ |
| $-1$ | $1$ | $(-1, 1)$ |
| $0$ | $0$ | $(0, 0)$ |
| $1$ | $1$ | $(1, 1)$ |
| $2$ | $2$ | $(2, 2)$ |
| $3$ | $3$ | $(3, 3)$ |

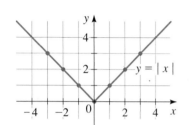

**FIGURE 3**

In Figure 3 we plot these points and use them to sketch the graph of the equation.

✎ **Practice what you've learned: Do Exercise 31.**    ▲

## ■ Intercepts

The $x$-coordinates of the points where a graph intersects the $x$-axis are called the **$x$-intercepts** of the graph and are obtained by setting $y = 0$ in the equation of the graph. The $y$-coordinates of the points where a graph intersects the $y$-axis are called the **$y$-intercepts** of the graph and are obtained by setting $x = 0$ in the equation of the graph.

**DEFINITION OF INTERCEPTS**

| Intercepts | How to find them | Where they are on the graph |
|---|---|---|
| **$x$-intercepts:** The $x$-coordinates of points where the graph of an equation intersects the $x$-axis | Set $y = 0$ and solve for $x$ | |
| **$y$-intercepts:** The $y$-coordinates of points where the graph of an equation intersects the $y$-axis | Set $x = 0$ and solve for $y$ | |

▶  **EXAMPLE 4** | Finding Intercepts

Find the $x$- and $y$-intercepts of the graph of the equation $y = x^2 - 2$.

▼ **SOLUTION**    To find the $x$-intercepts, we set $y = 0$ and solve for $x$. Thus,

$$0 = x^2 - 2 \qquad \text{Set } y = 0$$
$$x^2 = 2 \qquad \text{Add 2 to each side}$$
$$x = \pm\sqrt{2} \qquad \text{Take the square root}$$

The $x$-intercepts are $\sqrt{2}$ and $-\sqrt{2}$.

To find the $y$-intercepts, we set $x = 0$ and solve for $y$. Thus,

$$y = 0^2 - 2 \qquad \text{Set } x = 0$$
$$y = -2$$

The $y$-intercept is $-2$.

The graph of this equation was sketched in Example 2. It is repeated in Figure 4 with the $x$- and $y$-intercepts labeled.

✎ **Practice what you've learned: Do Exercise 43.**    ▲

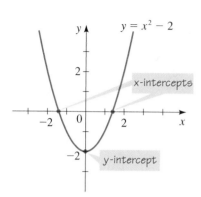

**FIGURE 4**

## ■ Circles

So far, we have discussed how to find the graph of an equation in $x$ and $y$. The converse problem is to find an equation of a graph, that is, an equation that represents a given curve in the $xy$-plane. Such an equation is satisfied by the coordinates of the points on the curve and by no other point. This is the other half of the fundamental principle of analytic geometry as formulated by Descartes and Fermat. The idea is that if a geometric curve can be represented by an algebraic equation, then the rules of algebra can be used to analyze the curve.

As an example of this type of problem, let's find the equation of a circle with radius $r$ and center $(h, k)$. By definition, the circle is the set of all points $P(x, y)$ whose distance from the center $C(h, k)$ is $r$ (see Figure 5). Thus, $P$ is on the circle if and only if $d(P, C) = r$. From the Distance Formula we have

$$\sqrt{(x - h)^2 + (y - k)^2} = r$$
$$(x - h)^2 + (y - k)^2 = r^2 \qquad \text{Square each side}$$

This is the desired equation.

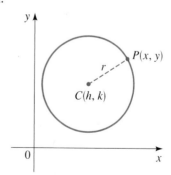

**FIGURE 5**

---

**EQUATION OF A CIRCLE**

An equation of the circle with center $(h, k)$ and radius $r$ is

$$(x - h)^2 + (y - k)^2 = r^2$$

This is called the **standard form** for the equation of the circle. If the center of the circle is the origin $(0, 0)$, then the equation is

$$x^2 + y^2 = r^2$$

▶ **EXAMPLE 5** | Graphing a Circle

Graph each equation.

**(a)** $x^2 + y^2 = 25$          **(b)** $(x - 2)^2 + (y + 1)^2 = 25$

▼ **SOLUTION**

**(a)** Rewriting the equation as $x^2 + y^2 = 5^2$, we see that this is an equation of the circle of radius 5 centered at the origin. Its graph is shown in Figure 6.

**(b)** Rewriting the equation as $(x - 2)^2 + (y + 1)^2 = 5^2$, we see that this is an equation of the circle of radius 5 centered at $(2, -1)$. Its graph is shown in Figure 7.

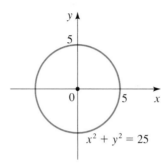

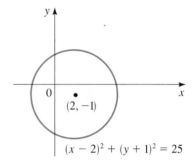

**FIGURE 6**                    **FIGURE 7**

✎ **Practice what you've learned: Do Exercises 49 and 51.**          ▲

▶ **EXAMPLE 6** | Finding an Equation of a Circle

**(a)** Find an equation of the circle with radius 3 and center $(2, -5)$.

**(b)** Find an equation of the circle that has the points $P(1, 8)$ and $Q(5, -6)$ as the endpoints of a diameter.

▼ **SOLUTION**

**(a)** Using the equation of a circle with $r = 3$, $h = 2$, and $k = -5$, we obtain

$$(x - 2)^2 + (y + 5)^2 = 9$$

The graph is shown in Figure 8.

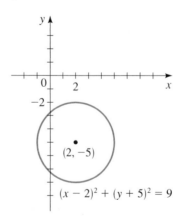

**FIGURE 8**

**(b)** We first observe that the center is the midpoint of the diameter $PQ$, so by the Midpoint Formula the center is

$$\left( \frac{1 + 5}{2}, \frac{8 - 6}{2} \right) = (3, 1)$$

The radius $r$ is the distance from $P$ to the center, so by the Distance Formula

$$r^2 = (3 - 1)^2 + (1 - 8)^2 = 2^2 + (-7)^2 = 53$$

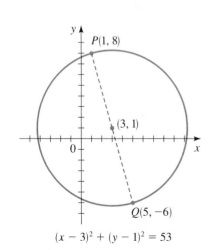

$(x - 3)^2 + (y - 1)^2 = 53$

**FIGURE 9**

Therefore, the equation of the circle is

$$(x - 3)^2 + (y - 1)^2 = 53$$

The graph is shown in Figure 9.

✎ **Practice what you've learned: Do Exercises 55 and 59.** ▲

Completing the square is used in many contexts in algebra. In Section 1.3 we used completing the square to solve quadratic equations.

Let's expand the equation of the circle in the preceding example.

$$(x - 3)^2 + (y - 1)^2 = 53 \qquad \text{Standard form}$$

$$x^2 - 6x + 9 + y^2 - 2y + 1 = 53 \qquad \text{Expand the squares}$$

$$x^2 - 6x + y^2 - 2y = 43 \qquad \text{Subtract 10 to get expanded form}$$

Suppose we are given the equation of a circle in expanded form. Then to find its center and radius, we must put the equation back in standard form. That means that we must reverse the steps in the preceding calculation, and to do that, we need to know what to add to an expression such as $x^2 - 6x$ to make it a perfect square—that is, we need to complete the square, as in the next example.

▶ **EXAMPLE 7** | Identifying an Equation of a Circle

Show that the equation $x^2 + y^2 + 2x - 6y + 7 = 0$ represents a circle, and find the center and radius of the circle.

▼ **SOLUTION** We first group the $x$-terms and $y$-terms. Then we complete the square within each grouping. That is, we complete the square for $x^2 + 2x$ by adding $\left(\frac{1}{2} \cdot 2\right)^2 = 1$, and we complete the square for $y^2 - 6y$ by adding $\left[\frac{1}{2} \cdot (-6)\right]^2 = 9$.

$$(x^2 + 2x \quad) + (y^2 - 6y \quad) = -7 \qquad \text{Group terms}$$

$$(x^2 + 2x + 1) + (y^2 - 6y + 9) = -7 + 1 + 9 \qquad \text{Complete the square by adding 1 and 9 to each side}$$

$$(x + 1)^2 + (y - 3)^2 = 3 \qquad \text{Factor and simplify}$$

⊘ We must add the same numbers to *each side* to maintain equality.

Comparing this equation with the standard equation of a circle, we see that $h = -1$, $k = 3$, and $r = \sqrt{3}$, so the given equation represents a circle with center $(-1, 3)$ and radius $\sqrt{3}$.

✎ **Practice what you've learned: Do Exercise 65.** ▲

■ **Symmetry**

Figure 10 shows the graph of $y = x^2$. Notice that the part of the graph to the left of the $y$-axis is the mirror image of the part to the right of the $y$-axis. The reason is that if the point $(x, y)$ is on the graph, then so is $(-x, y)$, and these points are reflections of each other about the $y$-axis. In this situation we say that the graph is **symmetric with respect to the $y$-axis**. Similarly, we say that a graph is **symmetric with respect to the $x$-axis** if whenever the point $(x, y)$ is on the graph, then so is $(x, -y)$. A graph is **symmetric with respect to the origin** if whenever $(x, y)$ is on the graph, so is $(-x, -y)$.

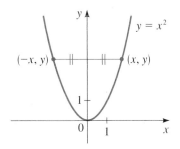

**FIGURE 10**

**DEFINITION OF SYMMETRY**

| Type of symmetry | How to test for symmetry | What the graph looks like (figures in this section) | Geometric meaning |
|---|---|---|---|
| **Symmetry with respect to the *x*-axis** | The equation is unchanged when *y* is replaced by −*y* |  (Figures 6, 11, 12) | Graph is unchanged when reflected in the *x*-axis |
| **Symmetry with respect to the *y*-axis** | The equation is unchanged when *x* is replaced by −*x* |  (Figures 2, 3, 4, 6, 10, 12) | Graph is unchanged when reflected in the *y*-axis |
| **Symmetry with respect to the origin** | The equation is unchanged when *x* is replaced by −*x* and *y* by −*y* |  (Figures 6, 12) | Graph is unchanged when rotated 180° about the origin |

The remaining examples in this section show how symmetry helps us to sketch the graphs of equations.

▶ **EXAMPLE 8** | Using Symmetry to Sketch a Graph

Test the equation $x = y^2$ for symmetry, and sketch the graph.

▼ **SOLUTION**   If *y* is replaced by −*y* in the equation $x = y^2$, we get

$$x = (-y)^2 \qquad \text{Replace } y \text{ by } -y$$

$$x = y^2 \qquad \text{Simplify}$$

so the equation is unchanged. Therefore, the graph is symmetric about the *x*-axis. But changing *x* to −*x* gives the equation $-x = y^2$, which is not the same as the original equation, so the graph is not symmetric about the *y*-axis.

We use the symmetry about the *x*-axis to sketch the graph by first plotting points just for $y > 0$ and then reflecting the graph in the *x*-axis, as shown in Figure 11 on the next page.

| $y$ | $x = y^2$ | $(x, y)$ |
|-----|-----------|----------|
| 0 | 0 | $(0, 0)$ |
| 1 | 1 | $(1, 1)$ |
| 2 | 4 | $(4, 2)$ |
| 3 | 9 | $(9, 3)$ |

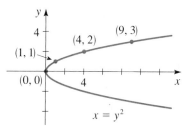

**FIGURE 11**

✏ **Practice what you've learned: Do Exercises 77 and 83.**    ▲

▶ **EXAMPLE 9** | Testing an Equation for Symmetry

Test the equation $y = x^3 - 9x$ for symmetry.

▼ **SOLUTION**    If we replace $x$ by $-x$ and $y$ by $-y$ in the equation, we get

$$-y = (-x)^3 - 9(-x) \qquad \text{Replace } x \text{ by } -x \text{ and } y \text{ by } -y$$

$$-y = -x^3 + 9x \qquad \text{Simplify}$$

$$y = x^3 - 9x \qquad \text{Multiply by } -1$$

so the equation is unchanged. This means that the graph is symmetric with respect to the origin.

✏ **Practice what you've learned: Do Exercise 79.**    ▲

▶ **EXAMPLE 10** | A Circle That Has All Three Types of Symmetry

Test the equation of the circle $x^2 + y^2 = 4$ for symmetry.

▼ **SOLUTION**    The equation $x^2 + y^2 = 4$ remains unchanged when $x$ is replaced by $-x$ and $y$ is replaced by $-y$, since $(-x)^2 = x^2$ and $(-y)^2 = y^2$, so the circle exhibits all three types of symmetry. It is symmetric with respect to the $x$-axis, the $y$-axis, and the origin, as shown in Figure 12.

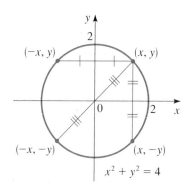

**FIGURE 12**

✏ **Practice what you've learned: Do Exercise 81.**    ▲

# 2.2 EXERCISES

## ▼ CONCEPTS

**1.** If the point $(2, 3)$ is on the graph of an equation in $x$ and $y$, then the equation is satisfied when we replace $x$ by

_____ and $y$ by _____. Is the point $(2, 3)$ on the graph of the equation $2y = x + 1$?

**2.** **(a)** To find the $x$-intercept(s) of the graph of an equation, we set _____ equal to 0 and solve for _____. So the $x$-intercept of $2y = x + 1$ is _____.

**(b)** To find the $y$-intercept(s) of the graph of an equation, we set _____ equal to 0 and solve for _____. So the $y$-intercept of $2y = x + 1$ is _____.

**3.** The graph of the equation $(x - 1)^2 + (y - 2)^2 = 9$ is a circle with center $(\_\_\_, \_\_\_)$ and radius _____.

**4. (a)** If a graph is symmetric with respect to the $x$-axis and $(a, b)$ is on the graph, then $(\_\_\_, \_\_\_)$ is also on the graph.

**(b)** If a graph is symmetric with respect to the $y$-axis and $(a, b)$ is on the graph, then $(\_\_\_, \_\_\_)$ is also on the graph.

**(c)** If a graph is symmetric about the origin and $(a, b)$ is on the graph, then $(\_\_\_, \_\_\_)$ is also on the graph.

## ▼ SKILLS

**5–10** ■ Determine whether the given points are on the graph of the equation.

**5.** $y = 3x - 2$;  $(0, 2), \left(\frac{1}{3}, 1\right), (1, 1)$

**6.** $y = \sqrt{x + 1}$;  $(1, 0), (0, 1), (3, 2)$

**7.** $x - 2y - 1 = 0$;  $(0, 0), (1, 0), (-1, -1)$

**8.** $y(x^2 + 1) = 1$;  $(1, 1), \left(1, \frac{1}{2}\right), \left(-1, \frac{1}{2}\right)$

**9.** $x^2 + xy + y^2 = 4$;  $(0, -2), (1, -2), (2, -2)$

**10.** $x^2 + y^2 = 1$;  $(0, 1), \left(\frac{1}{\sqrt{2}}, \frac{1}{\sqrt{2}}\right), \left(\frac{\sqrt{3}}{2}, \frac{1}{2}\right)$

**11–36** ■ Make a table of values and sketch the graph of the equation. Find the $x$- and $y$-intercepts.

**11.** $y = -x$

**12.** $y = 2x$

**13.** $y = -x + 4$

**14.** $y = 3x + 3$

**15.** $2x - y = 6$

**16.** $x + y = 3$

**17.** $y = 1 - x^2$

**18.** $y = x^2 + 2$

**19.** $4y = x^2$

**20.** $8y = x^3$

**21.** $y = x^2 - 9$

**22.** $y = 9 - x^2$

**23.** $xy = 2$

**24.** $x + y^2 = 4$

**25.** $y = \sqrt{x}$

**26.** $x^2 + y^2 = 9$

**27.** $y = \sqrt{4 - x^2}$

**28.** $y = -\sqrt{4 - x^2}$

**29.** $y = |x|$

**30.** $x = |y|$

**31.** $y = 4 - |x|$

**32.** $y = |4 - x|$

**33.** $x = y^3$

**34.** $y = x^3 - 1$

**35.** $y = x^4$

**36.** $y = 16 - x^4$

**37–40** ■ An equation and its graph are given. Find the $x$- and $y$-intercepts.

**37.** $y = 4x - x^2$

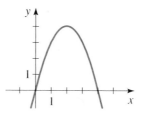

**38.** $\dfrac{x^2}{9} + \dfrac{y^2}{4} = 1$

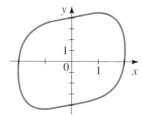

**39.** $x^4 + y^2 - xy = 16$

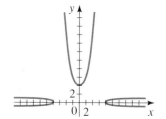

**40.** $x^2 + y^3 - x^2y^2 = 64$

**41–48** ■ Find the $x$- and $y$-intercepts of the graph of the equation.

**41.** $y = x - 3$

**42.** $y = x^2 - 5x + 6$

**43.** $y = x^2 - 9$

**44.** $y - 2xy + 2x = 1$

**45.** $x^2 + y^2 = 4$

**46.** $y = \sqrt{x + 1}$

**47.** $xy = 5$

**48.** $x^2 - xy + y = 1$

**49–54** ■ Find the center and radius of the circle, and sketch its graph.

**49.** $x^2 + y^2 = 9$

**50.** $x^2 + y^2 = 5$

**51.** $(x - 3)^2 + y^2 = 16$

**52.** $x^2 + (y - 2)^2 = 4$

**53.** $(x + 3)^2 + (y - 4)^2 = 25$

**54.** $(x + 1)^2 + (y + 2)^2 = 36$

**55–62** ■ Find an equation of the circle that satisfies the given conditions.

**55.** Center $(2, -1)$;  radius 3

**56.** Center $(-1, -4)$;  radius 8

**57.** Center at the origin;  passes through $(4, 7)$

**58.** Center $(-1, 5)$;  passes through $(-4, -6)$

**59.** Endpoints of a diameter are $P(-1, 1)$ and $Q(5, 9)$

**60.** Endpoints of a diameter are $P(-1, 3)$ and $Q(7, -5)$

**61.** Center $(7, -3)$;  tangent to the $x$-axis

**62.** Circle lies in the first quadrant, tangent to both $x$-and $y$-axes; radius 5

**63–64** ▪ Find the equation of the circle shown in the figure.

**63.**

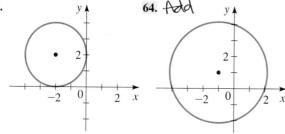

**64.** Add

**65–72** ▪ Show that the equation represents a circle, and find the center and radius of the circle.

**65.** $x^2 + y^2 - 2x + 4y + 1 = 0$

**66.** $x^2 + y^2 - 2x - 2y = 2$

**67.** $x^2 + y^2 - 4x + 10y + 13 = 0$

**68.** $x^2 + y^2 + 6y + 2 = 0$

**69.** $x^2 + y^2 + x = 0$

**70.** $x^2 + y^2 + 2x + y + 1 = 0$

**71.** $x^2 + y^2 - \frac{1}{2}x + \frac{1}{2}y = \frac{1}{8}$

**72.** $x^2 + y^2 + \frac{1}{2}x + 2y + \frac{1}{16} = 0$

**73–76** ▪ Sketch the graph of the equation.

**73.** $x^2 + y^2 + 4x - 10y = 21$

**74.** $4x^2 + 4y^2 + 2x = 0$

**75.** $x^2 + y^2 + 6x - 12y + 45 = 0$

**76.** $x^2 + y^2 - 16x + 12y + 200 = 0$

**77–82** ▪ Test the equation for symmetry.

**77.** $y = x^4 + x^2$          **78.** $x = y^4 - y^2$

**79.** $y = x^3 + 10x$          **80.** $y = x^2 + |x|$

**81.** $x^4y^4 + x^2y^2 = 1$          **82.** $x^2y^2 + xy = 1$

**83–86** ▪ Complete the graph using the given symmetry property.

**83.** Symmetric with respect to the $y$-axis

**84.** Symmetric with respect to the $x$-axis

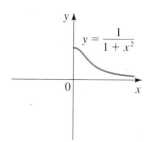

**85.** Symmetric with respect to the origin

**86.** Symmetric with respect to the origin

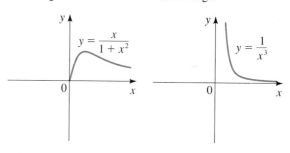

**87–90** ▪ Sketch the region given by the set.

**87.** $\{(x, y) \mid x^2 + y^2 \le 1\}$

**88.** $\{(x, y) \mid x^2 + y^2 > 4\}$

**89.** $\{(x, y) \mid 1 \le x^2 + y^2 < 9\}$

**90.** $\{(x, y) \mid 2x < x^2 + y^2 \le 4\}$

**91.** Find the area of the region that lies outside the circle $x^2 + y^2 = 4$ but inside the circle

$$x^2 + y^2 - 4y - 12 = 0$$

**92.** Sketch the region in the coordinate plane that satisfies both the inequalities $x^2 + y^2 \le 9$ and $y \ge |x|$. What is the area of this region?

▼ **APPLICATIONS**

**93. U.S. Inflation Rates**   The graph shows the annual inflation rate in the United States from 1975 to 2003.
   **(a)** Estimate the inflation rates in 1980, 1991, and 1999 to the nearest percent.
   **(b)** For which years in this period did the inflation rate exceed 6%?
   **(c)** Did the inflation rate generally increase or decrease in the years from 1980 to 1985? What about from 1987 to 1992?
   **(d)** Estimate the highest and lowest inflation rates in this time period to the nearest percent.

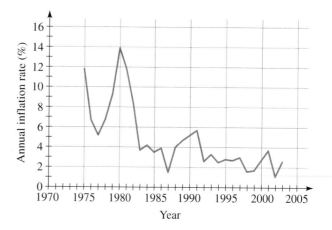

**94. Orbit of a Satellite**   A satellite is in orbit around the moon. A coordinate plane containing the orbit is set up with the center of the moon at the origin, as shown in the graph on the next page, with distances measured in megameters (Mm). The equation of the satellite's orbit is

$$\frac{(x-3)^2}{25} + \frac{y^2}{16} = 1$$

(a) From the graph, determine the closest and the farthest that the satellite gets to the center of the moon.

(b) There are two points in the orbit with $y$-coordinates 2. Find the $x$-coordinates of these points, and determine their distances to the center of the moon.

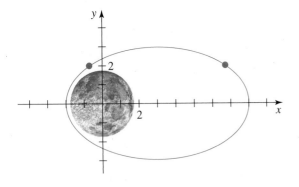

## ▼ DISCOVERY • DISCUSSION • WRITING

**95.** **Circle, Point, or Empty Set?** Complete the squares in the general equation $x^2 + ax + y^2 + by + c = 0$ and simplify the result as much as possible. Under what conditions on the coefficients $a$, $b$, and $c$ does this equation represent a circle? A single point? The empty set? In the case in which the equation does represent a circle, find its center and radius.

**96.** **Do the Circles Intersect?**

(a) Find the radius of each circle in the pair and the distance between their centers; then use this information to determine whether the circles intersect.

(i) $(x-2)^2 + (y-1)^2 = 9$;
$(x-6)^2 + (y-4)^2 = 16$

(ii) $x^2 + (y-2)^2 = 4$;
$(x-5)^2 + (y-14)^2 = 9$

(iii) $(x-3)^2 + (y+1)^2 = 1$;
$(x-2)^2 + (y-2)^2 = 25$

(b) How can you tell, just by knowing the radii of two circles and the distance between their centers, whether the circles intersect? Write a short paragraph describing how you would decide this, and draw graphs to illustrate your answer.

**97.** **Making a Graph Symmetric** The graph shown in the figure is not symmetric about the $x$-axis, the $y$-axis, or the origin. Add more line segments to the graph so that it exhibits the indicated symmetry. In each case, add as little as possible.

(a) Symmetry about the $x$-axis

(b) Symmetry about the $y$-axis

(c) Symmetry about the origin

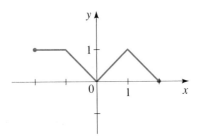

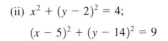

# Graphing Calculators: Solving Equations and Inequalities Graphically

**2.3**

## LEARNING OBJECTIVES

After completing this section, you will be able to:

■ Use a graphing calculator to graph equations
■ Solve equations graphically
■ Solve inequalities graphically

In Chapter 1 we solved equations and inequalities algebraically. In the preceding section we learned how to sketch the graph of an equation in a coordinate plane. In this section we use graphs to solve equations and inequalities. To do this, we must first draw a graph using a graphing device. So we begin by giving a few guidelines to help us use graphing devices effectively.

## ■ Using a Graphing Calculator

A graphing calculator or computer displays a rectangular portion of the graph of an equation in a display window or viewing screen, which we call a **viewing rectangle**. The default screen often gives an incomplete or misleading picture, so it is important to choose the viewing rectangle with care. If we choose the $x$-values to range from a minimum value of $\text{Xmin} = a$ to a maximum value of $\text{Xmax} = b$ and the $y$-values to range from a minimum value of $\text{Ymin} = c$ to a maximum value of $\text{Ymax} = d$, then the displayed portion of the graph lies in the rectangle

$$[a, b] \times [c, d] = \{(x, y) \mid a \le x \le b, c \le y \le d\}$$

as shown in Figure 1. We refer to this as the $[a, b]$ by $[c, d]$ viewing rectangle.

The graphing device draws the graph of an equation much as you would. It plots points of the form $(x, y)$ for a certain number of values of $x$, equally spaced between $a$ and $b$. If the equation is not defined for an $x$-value or if the corresponding $y$-value lies outside the viewing rectangle, the device ignores this value and moves on to the next $x$-value. The machine connects each point to the preceding plotted point to form a representation of the graph of the equation.

**FIGURE 1** The viewing rectangle $[a, b]$ by $[c, d]$

▶ **EXAMPLE 1** | Choosing an Appropriate Viewing Rectangle

Graph the equation $y = x^2 + 3$ in an appropriate viewing rectangle.

▼ **SOLUTION**   Let's experiment with different viewing rectangles. We start with the viewing rectangle $[-2, 2]$ by $[-2, 2]$, so we set

$$\text{Xmin} = -2 \qquad \text{Ymin} = -2$$
$$\text{Xmax} = 2 \qquad \text{Ymax} = 2$$

The resulting graph in Figure 2(a) is blank! This is because $x^2 \ge 0$, so $x^2 + 3 \ge 3$ for all $x$. Thus, the graph lies entirely above the viewing rectangle, so this viewing rectangle is not appropriate. If we enlarge the viewing rectangle to $[-4, 4]$ by $[-4, 4]$, as in Figure 2(b), we begin to see a portion of the graph.

Now let's try the viewing rectangle $[-10, 10]$ by $[-5, 30]$. The graph in Figure 2(c) seems to give a more complete view of the graph. If we enlarge the viewing rectangle even further, as in Figure 2(d), the graph doesn't show clearly that the $y$-intercept is 3.

So the viewing rectangle $[-10, 10]$ by $[-5, 30]$ gives an appropriate representation of the graph.

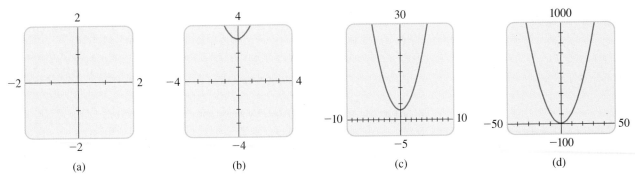

(a)          (b)          (c)          (d)

**FIGURE 2** Graphs of $y = x^2 + 3$

✎ **Practice what you've learned: Do Exercise 5.**

▶ **EXAMPLE 2** | Two Graphs on the Same Screen

Graph the equations $y = 3x^2 - 6x + 1$ and $y = 0.23x - 2.25$ together in the viewing rectangle $[-1, 3]$ by $[-2.5, 1.5]$. Do the graphs intersect in this viewing rectangle?

▼ **SOLUTION**    Figure 3(a) shows the essential features of both graphs. One is a parabola, and the other is a line. It looks as if the graphs intersect near the point $(1, -2)$. However, if we zoom in on the area around this point as shown in Figure 3(b), we see that although the graphs almost touch, they do not actually intersect.

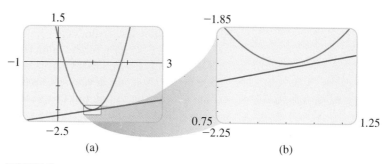

(a)                                    (b)

**FIGURE 3**

✎ **Practice what you've learned: Do Exercise 23.**                          ▲

You can see from Examples 1 and 2 that the choice of a viewing rectangle makes a big difference in the appearance of a graph. If you want an overview of the essential features of a graph, you must choose a relatively large viewing rectangle to obtain a global view of the graph. If you want to investigate the details of a graph, you must zoom in to a small viewing rectangle that shows just the feature of interest.

Most graphing calculators can only graph equations in which $y$ is isolated on one side of the equal sign. The next example shows how to graph equations that don't have this property.

▶ **EXAMPLE 3** | Graphing a Circle

Graph the circle $x^2 + y^2 = 1$.

▼ **SOLUTION**    We first solve for $y$, to isolate it on one side of the equal sign.

$$y^2 = 1 - x^2 \qquad \text{Subtract } x^2$$

$$y = \pm\sqrt{1 - x^2} \qquad \text{Take square roots}$$

The graph in Figure 4(c) looks somewhat flattened. Most graphing calculators allow you to set the scales on the axes so that circles really look like circles. On the TI-82 and TI-83, from the  ZOO  menu, choose ZSquare to set the scales appropriately. (On the TI-86 the command is Zsq.)

Therefore, the circle is described by the graphs of *two* equations:

$$y = \sqrt{1 - x^2} \qquad \text{and} \qquad y = -\sqrt{1 - x^2}$$

The first equation represents the top half of the circle (because $y \geq 0$), and the second represents the bottom half of the circle (because $y \leq 0$). If we graph the first equation in the viewing rectangle $[-2, 2]$ by $[-2, 2]$, we get the semicircle shown in Figure 4(a). The graph of the second equation is the semicircle in Figure 4(b). Graphing these semicircles together on the same viewing screen, we get the full circle in Figure 4(c).

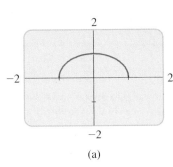

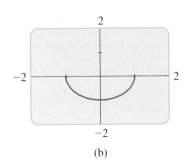

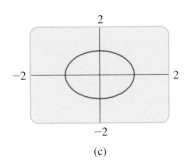

(a)                                   (b)                                   (c)

**FIGURE 4**  Graphing the equation $x^2 + y^2 = 1$

✎ **Practice what you've learned: Do Exercise 27.**    ▲

## ■ Solving Equations Graphically

In Chapter 1 we learned how to solve equations. To solve an equation such as

$$3x - 5 = 0$$

we used the **algebraic method**. This means that we used the rules of algebra to isolate $x$ on one side of the equation. We view $x$ as an *unknown,* and we use the rules of algebra to hunt it down. Here are the steps in the solution:

$$3x - 5 = 0$$
$$3x = 5 \qquad \text{Add 5}$$
$$x = \tfrac{5}{3} \qquad \text{Divide by 3}$$

So the solution is $x = \tfrac{5}{3}$.

We can also solve this equation by the **graphical method**. In this method we view $x$ as a *variable* and sketch the graph of the equation

$$y = 3x - 5$$

Different values for $x$ give different values for $y$. Our goal is to find the value of $x$ for which $y = 0$. From the graph in Figure 5 we see that $y = 0$ when $x \approx 1.7$. Thus, the solution is $x \approx 1.7$. Note that from the graph we obtain an approximate solution. We summarize these methods in the box on the following page.

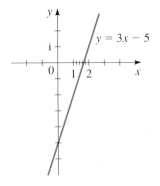

$y = 3x - 5$

**FIGURE 5**

Bettmann /CORBIS

**Pierre de Fermat** (1601–1665) was a French lawyer who became interested in mathematics at the age of 30. Because of his job as a magistrate, Fermat had little time to write complete proofs of his discoveries and often wrote them in the margin of whatever book he was reading at the time. After his death, his copy of Diophantus' *Arithmetica* (see page 49) was found to contain a particularly tantalizing comment. Where Diophantus discusses the solutions of $x^2 + y^2 = z^2$ (for example, $x = 3$, $y = 4$, and $z = 5$), Fermat states in the margin that for $n \geq 3$ there are no natural number solutions to the equation $x^n + y^n = z^n$. In other words, it's impossible for a cube to equal the sum of two cubes, a fourth power to equal the sum of two fourth powers, and so on. Fermat writes "I have discovered a truly wonderful proof for this but the margin is too small to contain it." All the other margin comments in Fermat's copy of *Arithmetica* have been proved. This one, however, remained unproved, and it came to be known as "Fermat's Last Theorem."

In 1994, Andrew Wiles of Princeton University announced a proof of Fermat's Last Theorem, an astounding 350 years after it was conjectured. His proof is one of the most widely reported mathematical results in the popular press.

**SOLVING AN EQUATION**

**Algebraic method**

Use the rules of algebra to isolate the unknown $x$ on one side of the equation.

**Example:** $2x = 6 - x$

$\qquad 3x = 6 \qquad$ Add $x$

$\qquad\quad x = 2 \qquad$ Divide by 3

The solution is $x = 2$.

**Graphical method**

Move all terms to one side and set equal to $y$. Sketch the graph to find the value of $x$ where $y = 0$.

**Example:** $2x = 6 - x$

$\qquad\quad 0 = 6 - 3x$

Set $y = 6 - 3x$ and graph.

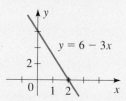

From the graph the solution is $x \approx 2$.

The advantage of the algebraic method is that it gives exact answers. Also, the process of unraveling the equation to arrive at the answer helps us to understand the algebraic structure of the equation. On the other hand, for many equations it is difficult or impossible to isolate $x$.

The graphical method gives a numerical approximation to the answer. This is an advantage when a numerical answer is desired. (For example, an engineer might find an answer expressed as $x \approx 2.6$ more immediately useful than $x = \sqrt{7}$.) Also, graphing an equation helps us to visualize how the solution is related to other values of the variable.

The *Discovery Project* on page 333 describes a numerical method for solving equations.

▶ **EXAMPLE 4** | Solving a Quadratic Equation Algebraically and Graphically

Solve the quadratic equations algebraically and graphically.

**(a)** $x^2 - 4x + 2 = 0$      **(b)** $x^2 - 4x + 4 = 0$      **(c)** $x^2 - 4x + 6 = 0$

▼ **SOLUTION 1:** Algebraic

We use the Quadratic Formula to solve each equation.

National Portrait Gallery

**Alan Turing** (1912–1954) was at the center of two pivotal events of the 20th century: World War II and the invention of computers. At the age of 23 Turing made his mark on mathematics by solving an important problem in the foundations of mathematics that had been posed by David Hilbert at the 1928 International Congress of Mathematicians (see page 531). In this research he invented a theoretical machine, now called a Turing machine, which was the inspiration for modern digital computers. During World War II Turing was in charge of the British effort to decipher secret German codes. His complete success in this endeavor played a decisive role in the Allies' victory. To carry out the numerous logical steps that are required to break a coded message, Turing developed decision procedures similar to modern computer programs. After the war he helped to develop the first electronic computers in Britain. He also did pioneering work on artificial intelligence and computer models of biological processes. At the age of 42 Turing died of poisoning after eating an apple that had mysteriously been laced with cyanide.

The Quadratic Formula is discussed on page 89.

**(a)** $x = \dfrac{-(-4) \pm \sqrt{(-4)^2 - 4 \cdot 1 \cdot 2}}{2} = \dfrac{4 \pm \sqrt{8}}{2} = 2 \pm \sqrt{2}$

There are two solutions, $x = 2 + \sqrt{2}$ and $x = 2 - \sqrt{2}$.

**(b)** $x = \dfrac{-(-4) \pm \sqrt{(-4)^2 - 4 \cdot 1 \cdot 4}}{2} = \dfrac{4 \pm \sqrt{0}}{2} = 2$

There is just one solution, $x = 2$.

**(c)** $x = \dfrac{-(-4) \pm \sqrt{(-4)^2 - 4 \cdot 1 \cdot 6}}{2} = \dfrac{4 \pm \sqrt{-8}}{2}$

There is no real solution.

▼ **SOLUTION 2:** Graphical

We graph the equations $y = x^2 - 4x + 2$, $y = x^2 - 4x + 4$, and $y = x^2 - 4x + 6$ in Figure 6. By determining the $x$-intercepts of the graphs, we find the following solutions.

**(a)** $x \approx 0.6$ and $x \approx 3.4$

**(b)** $x = 2$

**(c)** There is no $x$-intercept, so the equation has no solution.

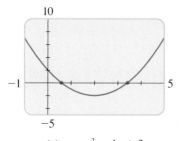
(a) $y = x^2 - 4x + 2$

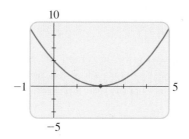
(b) $y = x^2 - 4x + 4$

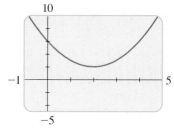
(c) $y = x^2 - 4x + 6$

**FIGURE 6**

✎ **Practice what you've learned: Do Exercise 35.**     ▲

The graphs in Figure 6 show visually why a quadratic equation may have two solutions, one solution, or no real solution. We proved this fact algebraically in Section 1.3 when we studied the discriminant.

▶ **EXAMPLE 5** | Another Graphical Method

Solve the equation algebraically and graphically:   $5 - 3x = 8x - 20$

▼ **SOLUTION 1:** Algebraic

$$5 - 3x = 8x - 20$$
$$-3x = 8x - 25 \qquad \text{Subtract 5}$$
$$-11x = -25 \qquad \text{Subtract 8x}$$
$$x = \frac{-25}{-11} = 2\tfrac{3}{11} \qquad \text{Divide by } -11 \text{ and simplify}$$

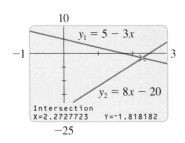

**FIGURE 7**

▼ **SOLUTION 2:** Graphical

We could move all terms to one side of the equal sign, set the result equal to $y$, and graph the resulting equation. But to avoid all this algebra, we graph two equations instead:

$$y_1 = 5 - 3x \qquad \text{and} \qquad y_2 = 8x - 20$$

The solution of the original equation will be the value of $x$ that makes $y_1$ equal to $y_2$; that is, the solution is the $x$-coordinate of the intersection point of the two graphs. Using the [TRACE] feature or the `intersect` command on a graphing calculator, we see from Figure 7 that the solution is $x \approx 2.27$.

✎ **Practice what you've learned: Do Exercise 31.**   ▲

In the next example we use the graphical method to solve an equation that is extremely difficult to solve algebraically.

▶ **EXAMPLE 6** | Solving an Equation in an Interval

Solve the equation

$$x^3 - 6x^2 + 9x = \sqrt{x}$$

in the interval $[1, 6]$.

▼ **SOLUTION**   We are asked to find all solutions $x$ that satisfy $1 \le x \le 6$, so we will graph the equation in a viewing rectangle for which the $x$-values are restricted to this interval.

$$x^3 - 6x^2 + 9x = \sqrt{x}$$

$$x^3 - 6x^2 + 9x - \sqrt{x} = 0 \qquad \text{Subtract } \sqrt{x}$$

We can also use the `zero` command to find the solutions, as shown in Figures 8(a) and 8(b).

Figure 8 shows the graph of the equation $y = x^3 - 6x^2 + 9x - \sqrt{x}$ in the viewing rectangle $[1, 6]$ by $[-5, 5]$. There are two $x$-intercepts in this viewing rectangle; zooming in, we see that the solutions are $x \approx 2.18$ and $x \approx 3.72$.

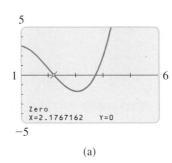

(a)

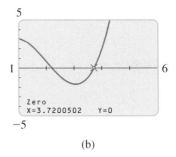

(b)

**FIGURE 8**

✎ **Practice what you've learned: Do Exercise 43.**   ▲

The equation in Example 6 actually has four solutions. You are asked to find the other two in Exercise 71.

▶ **EXAMPLE 7** | Intensity of Light

Two light sources are 10 m apart. One is three times as intense as the other. The light intensity $L$ (in lux) at a point $x$ meters from the weaker source is given by

$$L = \frac{10}{x^2} + \frac{30}{(10 - x)^2}$$

(See Figure 9.) Find the points at which the light intensity is 4 lux.

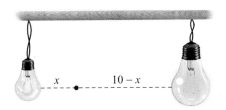

**FIGURE 9**

▼ **SOLUTION**    We need to solve the equation

$$4 = \frac{10}{x^2} + \frac{30}{(10-x)^2}$$

The graphs of

$$y_1 = 4 \quad \text{and} \quad y_2 = \frac{10}{x^2} + \frac{30}{(10-x)^2}$$

are shown in Figure 10. Zooming in (or using the `intersect` command) we find two solutions, $x \approx 1.67431$ and $x \approx 7.1927193$. So the light intensity is 4 lux at the points that are 1.67 m and 7.19 m from the weaker source.

✎ **Practice what you've learned:** Do Exercise 73.    ▲

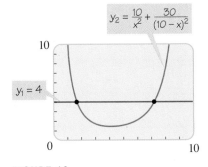

**FIGURE 10**

### ■ Solving Inequalities Graphically

Inequalities can be solved graphically. To describe the method, we solve

$$x^2 - 5x + 6 \le 0$$

This inequality was solved algebraically in Section 1.6, Example 3. To solve the inequality graphically, we draw the graph of

$$y = x^2 - 5x + 6$$

Our goal is to find those values of $x$ for which $y \le 0$. These are simply the $x$-values for which the graph lies below the $x$-axis. From Figure 11 we see that the solution of the inequality is the interval $[2, 3]$.

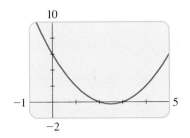

**FIGURE 11**
$x^2 - 5x + 6 \le 0$

▶ **EXAMPLE 8** | Solving an Inequality Graphically

Solve the inequality $3.7x^2 + 1.3x - 1.9 \le 2.0 - 1.4x$.

▼ **SOLUTION**    We graph the equations

$$y_1 = 3.7x^2 + 1.3x - 1.9 \quad \text{and} \quad y_2 = 2.0 - 1.4x$$

in the same viewing rectangle in Figure 12. We are interested in those values of $x$ for which $y_1 \le y_2$; these are points for which the graph of $y_2$ lies on or above the graph of $y_1$. To determine the appropriate interval, we look for the $x$-coordinates of points where the graphs intersect. We conclude that the solution is (approximately) the interval $[-1.45, 0.72]$.

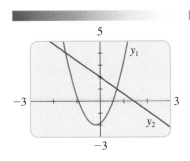

**FIGURE 12**
$y_1 = 3.7x^2 + 1.3x - 1.9$
$y_2 = 2.0 - 1.4x$

✎ **Practice what you've learned:** Do Exercise 59.    ▲

▶ **EXAMPLE 9** | Solving an Inequality Graphically

Solve the inequality $x^3 - 5x^2 \geq -8$.

▼ **SOLUTION**    We write the inequality as

$$x^3 - 5x^2 + 8 \geq 0$$

and then graph the equation

$$y = x^3 - 5x^2 + 8$$

in the viewing rectangle $[-6, 6]$ by $[-15, 15]$, as shown in Figure 13. The solution of the inequality consists of those intervals on which the graph lies on or above the $x$-axis. By moving the cursor to the $x$-intercepts, we find that, correct to one decimal place, the solution is $[-1.1, 1.5] \cup [4.6, \infty)$.

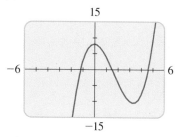

**FIGURE 13** $x^3 - 5x^2 + 8 \geq 0$

✎ **Practice what you've learned: Do Exercise 61.**

▲

# 2.3 EXERCISES

▼ **CONCEPTS**

1. The solutions of the equation $x^2 - 2x - 3 = 0$ are the

   _____-intercepts of the graph of $y = x^2 - 2x - 3$.

2. The solutions of the inequality $x^2 - 2x - 3 > 0$ are the $x$-coordinates of the points on the graph of $y = x^2 - 2x - 3$

   that lie _____ the $x$-axis.

3. The figure shows a graph of $y = x^4 - 3x^3 - x^2 + 3x$.
   Use the graph to do the following.
   **(a)** Find the solutions of the equation $x^4 - 3x^3 - x^2 + 3x = 0$.
   **(b)** Find the solutions of the inequality $x^4 - 3x^3 - x^2 + 3x \leq 0$.

$$y = x^4 - 3x^3 - x^2 + 3x$$

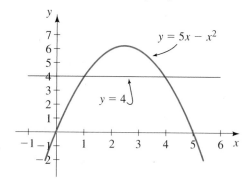

4. The figure shows the graphs of $y = 5x - x^2$ and $y = 4$. Use the graphs to do the following.

**(a)** Find the solutions of the equation $5x - x^2 = 4$.
**(b)** Find the solutions of the inequality $5x - x^2 > 4$.

▼ **SKILLS**

**5–10** ■ Use a graphing calculator or computer to decide which viewing rectangle (a)–(d) produces the most appropriate graph of the equation.

✎ **5.** $y = x^4 + 2$
   **(a)** $[-2, 2]$ by $[-2, 2]$
   **(b)** $[0, 4]$ by $[0, 4]$
   **(c)** $[-8, 8]$ by $[-4, 40]$
   **(d)** $[-40, 40]$ by $[-80, 800]$

**6.** $y = x^2 + 7x + 6$
   **(a)** $[-5, 5]$ by $[-5, 5]$
   **(b)** $[0, 10]$ by $[-20, 100]$
   **(c)** $[-15, 8]$ by $[-20, 100]$
   **(d)** $[-10, 3]$ by $[-100, 20]$

**7.** $y = 100 - x^2$
   **(a)** $[-4, 4]$ by $[-4, 4]$
   **(b)** $[-10, 10]$ by $[-10, 10]$
   **(c)** $[-15, 15]$ by $[-30, 110]$
   **(d)** $[-4, 4]$ by $[-30, 110]$

**8.** $y = 2x^2 - 1000$
   **(a)** $[-10, 10]$ by $[-10, 10]$
   **(b)** $[-10, 10]$ by $[-100, 100]$
   **(c)** $[-10, 10]$ by $[-1000, 1000]$
   **(d)** $[-25, 25]$ by $[-1200, 200]$

**9.** $y = 10 + 25x - x^3$
   **(a)** $[-4, 4]$ by $[-4, 4]$
   **(b)** $[-10, 10]$ by $[-10, 10]$
   **(c)** $[-20, 20]$ by $[-100, 100]$
   **(d)** $[-100, 100]$ by $[-200, 200]$

**10.** $y = \sqrt{8x - x^2}$
   **(a)** $[-4, 4]$ by $[-4, 4]$
   **(b)** $[-5, 5]$ by $[0, 100]$
   **(c)** $[-10, 10]$ by $[-10, 40]$
   **(d)** $[-2, 10]$ by $[-2, 6]$

**11–22** ▪ Determine an appropriate viewing rectangle for the equation, and use it to draw the graph.

**11.** $y = 100x^2$        **12.** $y = -100x^2$

**13.** $y = 4 + 6x - x^2$     **14.** $y = 0.3x^2 + 1.7x - 3$

**15.** $y = \sqrt[4]{256 - x^2}$     **16.** $y = \sqrt{12x - 17}$

**17.** $y = 0.01x^3 - x^2 + 5$     **18.** $y = x(x + 6)(x - 9)$

**19.** $y = x^4 - 4x^3$     **20.** $y = \dfrac{x}{x^2 + 25}$

**21.** $y = 1 + |x - 1|$     **22.** $y = 2x - |x^2 - 5|$

**23–26** ▪ Do the graphs intersect in the given viewing rectangle? If they do, how many points of intersection are there?

**23.** $y = -3x^2 + 6x - \frac{1}{2}$, $y = \sqrt{7 - \frac{7}{12}x^2}$;   $[-4, 4]$ by $[-1, 3]$

**24.** $y = \sqrt{49 - x^2}$, $y = \frac{1}{5}(41 - 3x)$;   $[-8, 8]$ by $[-1, 8]$

**25.** $y = 6 - 4x - x^2$, $y = 3x + 18$;   $[-6, 2]$ by $[-5, 20]$

**26.** $y = x^3 - 4x$, $y = x + 5$;   $[-4, 4]$ by $[-15, 15]$

**27.** Graph the circle $x^2 + y^2 = 9$ by solving for $y$ and graphing two equations as in Example 3.

**28.** Graph the circle $(y - 1)^2 + x^2 = 1$ by solving for $y$ and graphing two equations as in Example 3.

**29.** Graph the equation $4x^2 + 2y^2 = 1$ by solving for $y$ and graphing two equations corresponding to the negative and positive square roots. (This graph is called an *ellipse*.)

**30.** Graph the equation $y^2 - 9x^2 = 1$ by solving for $y$ and graphing the two equations corresponding to the positive and negative square roots. (This graph is called a *hyperbola*.)

**31–40** ▪ Solve the equation both algebraically and graphically.

**31.** $x - 4 = 5x + 12$     **32.** $\frac{1}{2}x - 3 = 6 + 2x$

**33.** $\dfrac{2}{x} + \dfrac{1}{2x} = 7$     **34.** $\dfrac{4}{x + 2} - \dfrac{6}{2x} = \dfrac{5}{2x + 4}$

**35.** $x^2 - 32 = 0$     **36.** $x^3 + 16 = 0$

**37.** $x^2 + 9 = 0$     **38.** $x^2 + 3 = 2x$

**39.** $16x^4 = 625$     **40.** $2x^5 - 243 = 0$

**41.** $(x - 5)^4 - 80 = 0$     **42.** $6(x + 2)^5 = 64$

**43–50** ▪ Solve the equation graphically in the given interval. State each answer correct to two decimals.

**43.** $x^2 - 7x + 12 = 0$;   $[0, 6]$

**44.** $x^2 - 0.75x + 0.125 = 0$;   $[-2, 2]$

**45.** $x^3 - 6x^2 + 11x - 6 = 0$;   $[-1, 4]$

**46.** $16x^3 + 16x^2 = x + 1$;   $[-2, 2]$

**47.** $x - \sqrt{x + 1} = 0$;   $[-1, 5]$

**48.** $1 + \sqrt{x} = \sqrt{1 + x^2}$;   $[-1, 5]$

**49.** $x^{1/3} - x = 0$;   $[-3, 3]$

**50.** $x^{1/2} + x^{1/3} - x = 0$;   $[-1, 5]$

**51–54** ▪ Use the graphical method to solve the equation in the indicated exercise from Section 1.5.

**51.** Exercise 11       **52.** Exercise 12

**53.** Exercise 31       **54.** Exercise 32

**55–58** ▪ Find all real solutions of the equation, correct to two decimals.

**55.** $x^3 - 2x^2 - x - 1 = 0$     **56.** $x^4 - 8x^2 + 2 = 0$

**57.** $x(x - 1)(x + 2) = \frac{1}{6}x$     **58.** $x^4 = 16 - x^3$

**59–66** ▪ Find the solutions of the inequality by drawing appropriate graphs. State each answer correct to two decimals.

**59.** $x^2 \le 3x + 10$     **60.** $0.5x^2 + 0.875x \le 0.25$

**61.** $x^3 + 11x \le 6x^2 + 6$     **62.** $16x^3 + 24x^2 > -9x - 1$

**63.** $x^{1/3} < x$     **64.** $\sqrt{0.5x^2 + 1} \le 2|x|$

**65.** $(x + 1)^2 < (x - 1)^2$     **66.** $(x + 1)^2 \le x^3$

**67–70** ▪ Use the graphical method to solve the inequality in the indicated exercise from Section 1.6.

**67.** Exercise 43       **68.** Exercise 44

**69.** Exercise 53       **70.** Exercise 54

**71.** In Example 6 we found two solutions of the equation $x^3 - 6x^2 + 9x = \sqrt{x}$, the solutions that lie between 1 and 6. Find two more solutions, correct to two decimals.

## ▼ APPLICATIONS

**72. Estimating Profit** An appliance manufacturer estimates that the profit $y$ (in dollars) generated by producing $x$ cooktops per month is given by the equation

$$y = 10x + 0.5x^2 - 0.001x^3 - 5000$$

where $0 \le x \le 450$.
(a) Graph the equation.
(b) How many cooktops must be produced to begin generating a profit?
(c) For what range of values of $x$ is the company's profit greater than $15,000?

**73. How Far Can You See?** If you stand on a ship in a calm sea, then your height $x$ (in ft) above sea level is related to the farthest distance $y$ (in mi) that you can see by the equation

$$y = \sqrt{1.5x + \left(\frac{x}{5280}\right)^2}$$

(a) Graph the equation for $0 \le x \le 100$.
(b) How high up do you have to be to be able to see 10 mi?

## ▼ DISCOVERY • DISCUSSION • WRITING

**74. Misleading Graphs** Write a short essay describing different ways in which a graphing calculator might give a misleading graph of an equation.

**75. Algebraic and Graphical Solution Methods** Write a short essay comparing the algebraic and graphical methods for solving equations. Make up your own examples to illustrate the advantages and disadvantages of each method.

**76. Equation Notation on Graphing Calculators** When you enter the following equations into your calculator, how does what you see on the screen differ from the usual way of writing the equations? (Check your user's manual if you're not sure.)

(a) $y = |x|$
(b) $y = \sqrt[5]{x}$
(c) $y = \dfrac{x}{x-1}$
(d) $y = x^3 + \sqrt[3]{x+2}$

**77. Enter Equations Carefully** A student wishes to graph the equations

$$y = x^{1/3} \qquad \text{and} \qquad y = \frac{x}{x+4}$$

on the same screen, so he enters the following information into his calculator:

$$Y_1 = X \wedge 1/3 \qquad Y_2 = X/X + 4$$

The calculator graphs two lines instead of the equations he wanted. What went wrong?

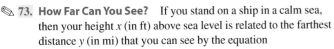

| 2.4 | Lines |

### LEARNING OBJECTIVES

After completing this section, you will be able to:

- Find the slope of a line
- Find the point-slope form of the equation of a line
- Find the slope-intercept form of the equation of a line
- Find equations of horizontal and vertical lines
- Find the general equation of a line
- Find equations for parallel and perpendicular lines
- Model with linear equations: interpret slope as rate of change

In this section we find equations for straight lines lying in a coordinate plane. The equations will depend on how the line is inclined, so we begin by discussing the concept of slope.

## ■ The Slope of a Line

We first need a way to measure the "steepness" of a line, or how quickly it rises (or falls) as we move from left to right. We define *run* to be the distance we move to the right and *rise* to be the corresponding distance that the line rises (or falls). The *slope* of a line is the ratio of rise to run:

$$\text{slope} = \frac{\text{rise}}{\text{run}}$$

Figure 1 shows situations in which slope is important. Carpenters use the term *pitch* for the slope of a roof or a staircase; the term *grade* is used for the slope of a road.

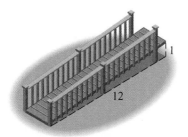

Slope of a ramp

Slope $= \frac{1}{12}$

Pitch of a roof

Slope $= \frac{1}{3}$

Grade of a road

Slope $= \frac{8}{100}$

**FIGURE 1**

If a line lies in a coordinate plane, then the **run** is the change in the *x*-coordinate and the **rise** is the corresponding change in the *y*-coordinate between any two points on the line (see Figure 2). This gives us the following definition of slope.

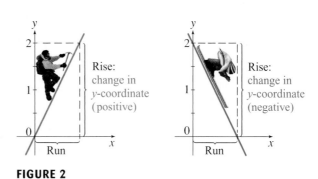

**FIGURE 2**

---

**SLOPE OF A LINE**

The **slope** $m$ of a nonvertical line that passes through the points $A(x_1, y_1)$ and $B(x_2, y_2)$ is

$$m = \frac{\text{rise}}{\text{run}} = \frac{y_2 - y_1}{x_2 - x_1}$$

The slope of a vertical line is not defined.

The slope is independent of which two points are chosen on the line. We can see that this is true from the similar triangles in Figure 3:

$$\frac{y_2 - y_1}{x_2 - x_1} = \frac{y_2' - y_1'}{x_2' - x_1'}$$

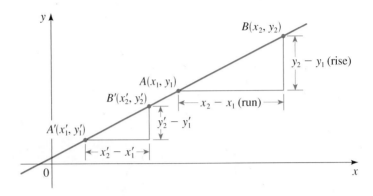

**FIGURE 3**

Figure 4 shows several lines labeled with their slopes. Notice that lines with positive slope slant upward to the right, whereas lines with negative slope slant downward to the right. The steepest lines are those for which the absolute value of the slope is the largest; a horizontal line has slope zero.

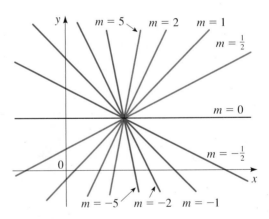

**FIGURE 4**  Lines with various slopes

▶ **EXAMPLE 1** | Finding the Slope of a Line Through Two Points

Find the slope of the line that passes through the points $P(2, 1)$ and $Q(8, 5)$.

▼ **SOLUTION**    Since any two different points determine a line, only one line passes through these two points. From the definition the slope is

$$m = \frac{y_2 - y_1}{x_2 - x_1} = \frac{5 - 1}{8 - 2} = \frac{4}{6} = \frac{2}{3}$$

This says that for every 3 units we move to the right, the line rises 2 units. The line is drawn in Figure 5.

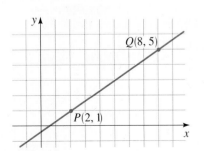

**FIGURE 5**

✎ **Practice what you've learned: Do Exercise 5.**

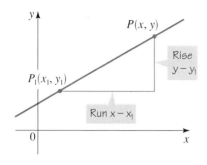

**FIGURE 6**

## Point-Slope Form of the Equation of a Line

Now let's find the equation of the line that passes through a given point $P(x_1, y_1)$ and has slope $m$. A point $P(x, y)$ with $x \neq x_1$ lies on this line if and only if the slope of the line through $P_1$ and $P$ is equal to $m$ (see Figure 6), that is,

$$\frac{y - y_1}{x - x_1} = m$$

This equation can be rewritten in the form $y - y_1 = m(x - x_1)$; note that the equation is also satisfied when $x = x_1$ and $y = y_1$. Therefore, it is an equation of the given line.

> **POINT-SLOPE FORM OF THE EQUATION OF A LINE**
>
> An equation of the line that passes through the point $(x_1, y_1)$ and has slope $m$ is
>
> $$y - y_1 = m(x - x_1)$$

▶ **EXAMPLE 2** | Finding the Equation of a Line with Given Point and Slope

(a) Find an equation of the line through $(1, -3)$ with slope $-\frac{1}{2}$.

(b) Sketch the line.

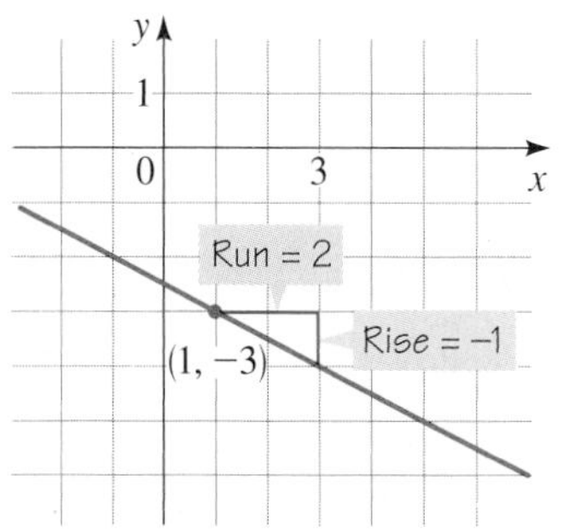

▼ **SOLUTION**

(a) Using the point-slope form with $m = -\frac{1}{2}$, $x_1 = 1$, and $y_1 = -3$, we obtain an equation of the line as

$$y + 3 = -\tfrac{1}{2}(x - 1) \qquad \text{From point-slope equation}$$

$$2y + 6 = -x + 1 \qquad \text{Multiply by 2}$$

$$x + 2y + 5 = 0 \qquad \text{Rearrange}$$

(b) The fact that the slope is $-\frac{1}{2}$ tells us that when we move to the right 2 units, the line drops 1 unit. This enables us to sketch the line in Figure 7.

✎ **Practice what you've learned: Do Exercise 19.**  ▲

**FIGURE 7**

▶ **EXAMPLE 3** | Finding the Equation of a Line Through Two Given Points

Find an equation of the line through the points $(-1, 2)$ and $(3, -4)$.

▼ **SOLUTION**    The slope of the line is

$$m = \frac{-4 - 2}{3 - (-1)} = -\frac{6}{4} = -\frac{3}{2}$$

We can use *either* point, $(-1, 2)$ *or* $(3, -4)$, in the point-slope equation. We will end up with the same final answer.

Using the point-slope form with $x_1 = -1$ and $y_1 = 2$, we obtain

$$y - 2 = -\tfrac{3}{2}(x + 1) \qquad \text{From point-slope equation}$$

$$2y - 4 = -3x - 3 \qquad \text{Multiply by 2}$$

$$3x + 2y - 1 = 0 \qquad \text{Rearrange}$$

✎ **Practice what you've learned: Do Exercise 23.**  ▲

## Slope-Intercept Form of the Equation of a Line

Suppose a nonvertical line has slope $m$ and $y$-intercept $b$ (see Figure 8). This means that the line intersects the $y$-axis at the point $(0, b)$, so the point-slope form of the equation of

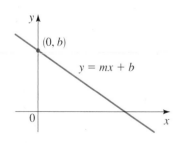

**FIGURE 8**

the line, with $x = 0$ and $y = b$, becomes

$$y - b = m(x - 0)$$

This simplifies to $y = mx + b$, which is called the **slope-intercept form** of the equation of a line.

---

### SLOPE-INTERCEPT FORM OF THE EQUATION OF A LINE

An equation of the line that has slope $m$ and $y$-intercept $b$ is

$$y = mx + b$$

---

▶ **EXAMPLE 4** | Lines in Slope-Intercept Form

**(a)** Find the equation of the line with slope 3 and $y$-intercept $-2$.

**(b)** Find the slope and $y$-intercept of the line $3y - 2x = 1$.

▼ **SOLUTION**

**(a)** Since $m = 3$ and $b = -2$, from the slope-intercept form of the equation of a line we get

$$y = 3x - 2$$

**(b)** We first write the equation in the form $y = mx + b$:

$$3y - 2x = 1$$
$$3y = 2x + 1 \qquad \text{Add } 2x$$
$$y = \tfrac{2}{3}x + \tfrac{1}{3} \qquad \text{Divide by 3}$$

From the slope-intercept form of the equation of a line, we see that the slope is $m = \frac{2}{3}$ and the $y$-intercept is $b = \frac{1}{3}$.

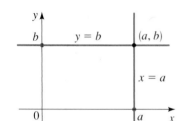

Slope   y-intercept

$y = \frac{2}{3}x + \frac{1}{3}$

✎ **Practice what you've learned: Do Exercises 25 and 47.** ▲

### ■ Vertical and Horizontal Lines

If a line is horizontal, its slope is $m = 0$, so its equation is $y = b$, where $b$ is the $y$-intercept (see Figure 9). A vertical line does not have a slope, but we can write its equation as $x = a$, where $a$ is the $x$-intercept, because the $x$-coordinate of every point on the line is $a$.

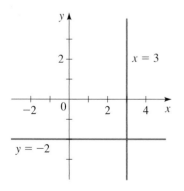

**FIGURE 9**

---

### VERTICAL AND HORIZONTAL LINES

An equation of the vertical line through $(a, b)$ is $x = a$.

An equation of the horizontal line through $(a, b)$ is $y = b$.

---

**EXAMPLE 5** | Vertical and Horizontal Lines

**(a)** An equation for the vertical line through $(3, 5)$ is $x = 3$.

**(b)** The graph of the equation $x = 3$ is a vertical line with $x$-intercept 3.

**(c)** An equation for the horizontal line through $(8, -2)$ is $y = -2$.

**(d)** The graph of the equation $y = -2$ is a horizontal line with $y$-intercept $-2$.

The lines are graphed in Figure 10.

**FIGURE 10**

✎ **Practice what you've learned: Do Exercises 29 and 33.** ▲

## ■ General Equation of a Line

A **linear equation** is an equation of the form

$$Ax + By + C = 0$$

where $A$, $B$, and $C$ are constants and $A$ and $B$ are not both 0. The equation of a line is a linear equation:

- A nonvertical line has the equation $y = mx + b$ or $-mx + y - b = 0$, which is a linear equation with $A = -m$, $B = 1$, and $C = -b$.
- A vertical line has the equation $x = a$ or $x - a = 0$, which is a linear equation with $A = 1$, $B = 0$, and $C = -a$.

Conversely, the graph of a linear equation is a line:

- If $B \neq 0$, the equation becomes

$$y = -\frac{A}{B}x - \frac{C}{B} \qquad \text{Divide by } B$$

and this is the slope-intercept form of the equation of a line (with $m = -A/B$ and $b = -C/B$).
- If $B = 0$, the equation becomes

$$Ax + C = 0 \qquad \text{Set } B = 0$$

or $x = -C/A$, which represents a vertical line.

We have proved the following.

---

### GENERAL EQUATION OF A LINE

The graph of every **linear equation**

$$Ax + By + C = 0 \qquad (A, B \text{ not both zero})$$

is a line. Conversely, every line is the graph of a linear equation.

---

▶ **EXAMPLE 6** | Graphing a Linear Equation

Sketch the graph of the equation $2x - 3y - 12 = 0$.

▼ **SOLUTION 1**  Since the equation is linear, its graph is a line. To draw the graph, it is enough to find any two points on the line. The intercepts are the easiest points to find.

$x$-intercept:  Substitute $y = 0$, to get $2x - 12 = 0$, so $x = 6$

$y$-intercept:  Substitute $x = 0$, to get $-3y - 12 = 0$, so $y = -4$

With these points we can sketch the graph in Figure 11.

▼ **SOLUTION 2**  We write the equation in slope-intercept form:

$$2x - 3y - 12 = 0$$
$$2x - 3y = 12 \qquad \text{Add 12}$$
$$-3y = -2x + 12 \qquad \text{Subtract } 2x$$
$$y = \tfrac{2}{3}x - 4 \qquad \text{Divide by } -3$$

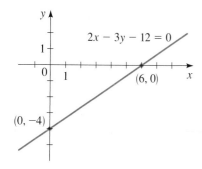

**FIGURE 11**

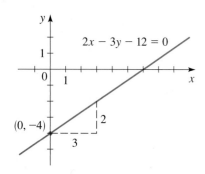

**FIGURE 12**

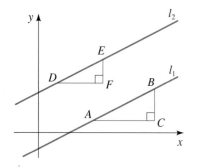

**FIGURE 13**

This equation is in the form $y = mx + b$, so the slope is $m = \frac{2}{3}$ and the $y$-intercept is $b = -4$. To sketch the graph, we plot the $y$-intercept and then move 3 units to the right and 2 units up as shown in Figure 12.

✎ **Practice what you've learned: Do Exercise 53.**    ▲

## ■ Parallel and Perpendicular Lines

Since slope measures the steepness of a line, it seems reasonable that parallel lines should have the same slope. In fact, we can prove this.

| **PARALLEL LINES** |
| --- |
| Two nonvertical lines are parallel if and only if they have the same slope. |

▼ **PROOF**    Let the lines $l_1$ and $l_2$ in Figure 13 have slopes $m_1$ and $m_2$. If the lines are parallel, then the right triangles $ABC$ and $DEF$ are similar, so

$$m_1 = \frac{d(B, C)}{d(A, C)} = \frac{d(E, F)}{d(D, F)} = m_2$$

Conversely, if the slopes are equal, then the triangles will be similar, so $\angle BAC = \angle EDF$ and the lines are parallel.    ▲

▶ **EXAMPLE 7** | Finding the Equation of a Line Parallel to a Given Line

Find an equation of the line through the point $(5, 2)$ that is parallel to the line $4x + 6y + 5 = 0$.

▼ **SOLUTION**    First we write the equation of the given line in slope-intercept form.

$$4x + 6y + 5 = 0$$

$$6y = -4x - 5 \qquad \text{Subtract } 4x + 5$$

$$y = -\tfrac{2}{3}x - \tfrac{5}{6} \qquad \text{Divide by 6}$$

So the line has slope $m = -\frac{2}{3}$. Since the required line is parallel to the given line, it also has slope $m = -\frac{2}{3}$. From the point-slope form of the equation of a line, we get

$$y - 2 = -\tfrac{2}{3}(x - 5) \qquad \text{Slope } m = -\tfrac{2}{3} \text{, point } (5, 2)$$

$$3y - 6 = -2x + 10 \qquad \text{Multiply by 3}$$

$$2x + 3y - 16 = 0 \qquad \text{Rearrange}$$

Thus, the equation of the required line is $2x + 3y - 16 = 0$.

✎ **Practice what you've learned: Do Exercise 31.**    ▲

The condition for perpendicular lines is not as obvious as that for parallel lines.

| **PERPENDICULAR LINES** |
| --- |
| Two lines with slopes $m_1$ and $m_2$ are perpendicular if and only if $m_1 m_2 = -1$, that is, their slopes are negative reciprocals: $$m_2 = -\frac{1}{m_1}$$ Also, a horizontal line (slope 0) is perpendicular to a vertical line (no slope). |

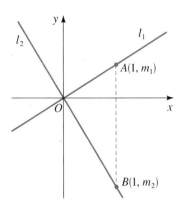

**FIGURE 14**

▼ **PROOF**    In Figure 14 we show two lines intersecting at the origin. (If the lines intersect at some other point, we consider lines parallel to these that intersect at the origin. These lines have the same slopes as the original lines.)

If the lines $l_1$ and $l_2$ have slopes $m_1$ and $m_2$, then their equations are $y = m_1 x$ and $y = m_2 x$. Notice that $A(1, m_1)$ lies on $l_1$ and $B(1, m_2)$ lies on $l_2$. By the Pythagorean Theorem and its converse (see page 284), $OA \perp OB$ if and only if

$$[d(O, A)]^2 + [d(O, B)]^2 = [d(A, B)]^2$$

By the Distance Formula this becomes

$$(1^2 + m_1^2) + (1^2 + m_2^2) = (1 - 1)^2 + (m_2 - m_1)^2$$

$$2 + m_1^2 + m_2^2 = m_2^2 - 2m_1 m_2 + m_1^2$$

$$2 = -2m_1 m_2$$

$$m_1 m_2 = -1$$    ▲

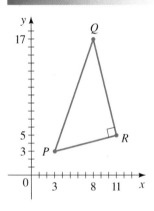

**FIGURE 15**

▶ **EXAMPLE 8** | Perpendicular Lines

Show that the points $P(3, 3)$, $Q(8, 17)$, and $R(11, 5)$ are the vertices of a right triangle.

▼ **SOLUTION**    The slopes of the lines containing $PR$ and $QR$ are, respectively,

$$m_1 = \frac{5 - 3}{11 - 3} = \frac{1}{4} \quad \text{and} \quad m_2 = \frac{5 - 17}{11 - 8} = -4$$

Since $m_1 m_2 = -1$, these lines are perpendicular, so $PQR$ is a right triangle. It is sketched in Figure 15.

✎ **Practice what you've learned: Do Exercise 57.**    ▲

▶ **EXAMPLE 9** | Finding an Equation of a Line Perpendicular to a Given Line

Find an equation of the line that is perpendicular to the line $4x + 6y + 5 = 0$ and passes through the origin.

▼ **SOLUTION**    In Example 7 we found that the slope of the line $4x + 6y + 5 = 0$ is $-\frac{2}{3}$. Thus, the slope of a perpendicular line is the negative reciprocal, that is, $\frac{3}{2}$. Since the required line passes through $(0, 0)$, the point-slope form gives

$$y - 0 = \tfrac{3}{2}(x - 0)$$

$$y = \tfrac{3}{2}x$$

✎ **Practice what you've learned: Do Exercise 35.**    ▲

▶ **EXAMPLE 10** | Graphing a Family of Lines

Use a graphing calculator to graph the family of lines

$$y = 0.5x + b$$

for $b = -2, -1, 0, 1, 2$. What property do the lines share?

▼ **SOLUTION**   The lines are graphed in Figure 16 in the viewing rectangle $[-6, 6]$ by $[-6, 6]$. The lines all have the same slope, so they are parallel.

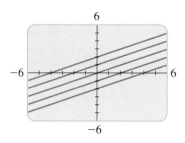

**FIGURE 16** $y = 0.5x + b$

✎ **Practice what you've learned: Do Exercise 41.**                                              ▲

## ■ Modeling with Linear Equations: Slope as Rate of Change

When a line is used to model the relationship between two quantities, the slope of the line is the **rate of change** of one quantity with respect to the other. For example, the graph in Figure 17(a) gives the amount of gas in a tank that is being filled. The slope between the indicated points is

$$m = \frac{6 \text{ gallons}}{3 \text{ minutes}} = 2 \text{ gal/min}$$

The slope is the *rate* at which the tank is being filled, 2 gallons per minute. In Figure 17(b) the tank is being drained at the *rate* of 0.03 gallon per minute, and the slope is $-0.03$.

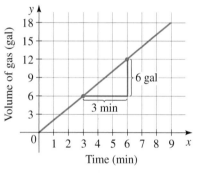          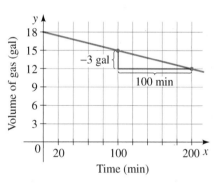

(a) Tank filled at 2 gal/min          (b) Tank drained at 0.03 gal/min
    Slope of line is 2                     Slope of line is –0.03

**FIGURE 17**

The next two examples give other situations in which the slope of a line is a rate of change.

▶ **EXAMPLE 11** | Slope as Rate of Change

A dam is built on a river to create a reservoir. The water level $w$ in the reservoir is given by the equation

$$w = 4.5t + 28$$

where $t$ is the number of years since the dam was constructed and $w$ is measured in feet.

**(a)** Sketch a graph of this equation.

**(b)** What do the slope and $w$-intercept of this graph represent?

**45. Growing Cabbages** In the short growing season of the Canadian arctic territory of Nunavut, some gardeners find it possible to grow gigantic cabbages in the midnight sun. Assume that the final size of a cabbage is proportional to the amount of nutrients it receives and inversely proportional to the number of other cabbages surrounding it. A cabbage that received 20 oz of nutrients and had 12 other cabbages around it grew to 30 lb. What size would it grow to if it received 10 oz of nutrients and had only 5 cabbage "neighbors"?

**46. Heat of a Campfire** The heat experienced by a hiker at a campfire is proportional to the amount of wood on the fire and inversely proportional to the cube of his distance from the fire. If he is 20 ft from the fire and someone doubles the amount of wood burning, how far from the fire would he have to be so that he feels the same heat as before?

$x$

**47. Frequency of Vibration** The frequency $f$ of vibration of a violin string is inversely proportional to its length $L$. The constant of proportionality $k$ is positive and depends on the tension and density of the string.
(a) Write an equation that represents this variation.
(b) What effect does doubling the length of the string have on the frequency of its vibration?

**48. Spread of a Disease** The rate $r$ at which a disease spreads in a population of size $P$ is jointly proportional to the number $x$ of infected people and the number $P - x$ who are not infected. An infection erupts in a small town that has population $P = 5000$.
(a) Write an equation that expresses $r$ as a function of $x$.
(b) Compare the rate of spread of this infection when 10 people are infected to the rate of spread when 1000 people are infected. Which rate is larger? By what factor?
(c) Calculate the rate of spread when the entire population is infected. Why does this answer make intuitive sense?

---

## ▼ DISCOVERY • DISCUSSION • WRITING

**49. Is Proportionality Everything?** A great many laws of physics and chemistry are expressible as proportionalities. Give at least one example of a function that occurs in the sciences that is *not* a proportionality.

---

## ▶ CHAPTER 2 | REVIEW

## ▼ PROPERTIES AND FORMULAS

### The Distance Formula (p. 139)

The distance between the points $A(x_1, y_1)$ and $B(x_2, y_2)$ is
$$d(A, B) = \sqrt{(x_1 - x_2)^2 + (y_1 - y_2)^2}$$

### The Midpoint Formula (p. 141)

The midpoint of the line segment from $A(x_1, y_1)$ to $B(x_2, y_2)$ is
$$\left( \frac{x_1 + x_2}{2}, \frac{y_1 + y_2}{2} \right)$$

### Intercepts (p. 148)

To find the **x-intercepts** of the graph of an equation, set $y = 0$ and solve for $x$.

To find the **y-intercepts** of the graph of an equation, set $x = 0$ and solve for $y$.

### Circles (p. 149)

The circle with center $(0, 0)$ and radius $r$ has equation
$$x^2 + y^2 = r^2$$

The circle with center $(h, k)$ and radius $r$ has equation
$$(x - h)^2 + (y - k)^2 = r^2$$

### Symmetry (p. 152)

The graph of an equation is **symmetric with respect to the x-axis** if the equation remains unchanged when you replace $y$ by $-y$.

The graph of an equation is **symmetric with respect to the y-axis** if the equation remains unchanged when you replace $x$ by $-x$.

The graph of an equation is **symmetric with respect to the origin** if the equation remains unchanged when you replace $x$ by $-x$ and $y$ by $-y$.

### Slope of a Line (p. 167)

The slope of the nonvertical line that contains the points $A(x_1, y_1)$ and $B(x_2, y_2)$ is
$$m = \frac{\text{rise}}{\text{run}} = \frac{y_2 - y_1}{x_2 - x_1}$$

## Equations of Lines (pp. 169–171)

If a line has slope $m$, has $y$-intercept $b$, and contains the point $(x_1, y_1)$, then:

the **point-slope form** of its equation is

$$y - y_1 = m(x - x_1)$$

the **slope-intercept form** of its equation is

$$y = mx + b$$

The equation of any line can be expressed in the **general form**

$$Ax + By + C = 0$$

(where $A$ and $B$ can't both be 0).

## Vertical and Horizontal Lines (p. 170)

The **vertical** line containing the point $(a, b)$ has the equation $x = a$.

The **horizontal** line containing the point $(a, b)$ has the equation $y = b$.

## Parallel and Perpendicular Lines (p. 172)

Two lines with slopes $m_1$ and $m_2$ are

**parallel** if and only if $m_1 = m_2$

**perpendicular** if and only if $m_1 m_2 = -1$

## Variation (p. 179)

If $y$ is **directly proportional** to $x$, then

$$y = kx$$

If $y$ is **inversely proportional** to $x$, then

$$y = \frac{k}{x}$$

If $z$ is **jointly proportional** to $x$ and $y$, then

$$z = kxy$$

In each case, $k$ is the **constant of proportionality**.

## ▼ CONCEPT SUMMARY

| Section 2.1 | Review Exercises |
|---|---|
| ▪ Graph points and regions in the coordinate plane | 1(a)–4(a), 5, 6 |
| ▪ Use the Distance Formula | 1(b)–4(b), 7 |
| ▪ Use the Midpoint Formula | 1(c)–4(c) |

| Section 2.2 | Review Exercises |
|---|---|
| ▪ Graph equations by plotting points | 15–24 |
| ▪ Find intercepts of the graph of an equation | 25–30 |
| ▪ Identify the equation of a circle | 1(e)–4(e), 8–14, 63, 64 |
| ▪ Graph circles in a coordinate plane | 1(e)–4(e), 11–14 |
| ▪ Determine symmetry properties of an equation | 25–30 |

| Section 2.3 | Review Exercises |
|---|---|
| ▪ Use a graphing calculator to graph equations | 31–34 |
| ▪ Solve equations graphically | 35–38 |
| ▪ Solve inequalities graphically | 39–42 |

| Section 2.4 | Review Exercises |
|---|---|
| ▪ Find the slope of a line | 1(d)–4(d) |
| ▪ Find the point-slope form of the equation of a line | 1(d)–4(d) |
| ▪ Find the slope-intercept form of the equation of a line | 1(d)–4(d), 43–52, 63, 64 |
| ▪ Find equations for horizontal and vertical lines | 47–48 |
| ▪ Find the general form for the equation of a line | 43–52 |
| ▪ Find equations for parallel or perpendicular lines | 49–52 |
| ▪ Model with linear equations: interpret slope as rate of change | 53–54 |

| Section 2.5 | Review Exercises |
|---|---|
| ▪ Find equations for direct variation | 55, 59, 60 |
| ▪ Find equations for inverse variation | 56–58 |
| ▪ Find equations for joint variation | 61–62 |

# ▼ EXERCISES

**1–4** ▪ Two points $P$ and $Q$ are given.
**(a)** Plot $P$ and $Q$ on a coordinate plane.
**(b)** Find the distance from $P$ to $Q$.
**(c)** Find the midpoint of the segment $PQ$.
**(d)** Find the slope of the line determined by $P$ and $Q$, and find equations for the line in point-slope form and in slope-intercept form. Then sketch a graph of the line.
**(e)** Sketch the circle that passes through $Q$ and has center $P$, and find the equation of this circle.

**1.** $P(0, 3)$,   $Q(3, 7)$
**2.** $P(2, 0)$,   $Q(-4, 8)$
**3.** $P(-6, 2)$,   $Q(4, -14)$
**4.** $P(5, -2)$,   $Q(-3, -6)$

**5–6** ▪ Sketch the region given by the set.

**5.** $\{(x, y) \mid -4 < x < 4 \ \ \text{and} \ \ -2 < y < 2\}$

**6.** $\{(x, y) \mid x \geq 4 \ \ \text{or} \ \ y \geq 2\}$

**7.** Which of the points $A(4, 4)$ or $B(5, 3)$ is closer to the point $C(-1, -3)$?

**8.** Find an equation of the circle that has center $(2, -5)$ and radius $\sqrt{2}$.

**9.** Find an equation of the circle that has center $(-5, -1)$ and passes through the origin.

**10.** Find an equation of the circle that contains the points $P(2, 3)$ and $Q(-1, 8)$ and has the midpoint of the segment $PQ$ as its center.

**11–14** ▪ **(a)** Complete the square to determine whether the equation represents a circle or a point or has no graph. **(b)** If the equation is that of a circle, find its center and radius, and sketch its graph.

**11.** $x^2 + y^2 + 2x - 6y + 9 = 0$
**12.** $2x^2 + 2y^2 - 2x + 8y = \frac{1}{2}$
**13.** $x^2 + y^2 + 72 = 12x$
**14.** $x^2 + y^2 - 6x - 10y + 34 = 0$

**15–24** ▪ Sketch the graph of the equation by making a table and plotting points.

**15.** $y = 2 - 3x$
**16.** $2x - y + 1 = 0$
**17.** $x + 3y = 21$
**18.** $x = 2y + 12$
**19.** $\dfrac{x}{2} - \dfrac{y}{7} = 1$
**20.** $\dfrac{x}{4} + \dfrac{y}{5} = 0$
**21.** $y = 16 - x^2$
**22.** $8x + y^2 = 0$
**23.** $x = \sqrt{y}$
**24.** $y = -\sqrt{1 - x^2}$

**25–30** ▪ **(a)** Test the equation for symmetry with respect to the $x$-axis, the $y$-axis, and the origin. **(b)** Find the $x$- and $y$-intercepts of the graph of the equation.

**25.** $y = 9 - x^2$
**26.** $6x + y^2 = 36$
**27.** $x^2 + (y - 1)^2 = 1$
**28.** $x^4 = 16 + y$
**29.** $9x^2 - 16y^2 = 144$
**30.** $y = \dfrac{4}{x}$

**31–34** ▪ Use a graphing device to graph the equation in an appropriate viewing rectangle.

**31.** $y = x^2 - 6x$
**32.** $y = \sqrt{5 - x}$
**33.** $y = x^3 - 4x^2 - 5x$
**34.** $\dfrac{x^2}{4} + y^2 = 1$

**35–38** ▪ Solve the equation graphically.

**35.** $x^2 - 4x = 2x + 7$
**36.** $\sqrt{x + 4} = x^2 - 5$
**37.** $x^4 - 9x^2 = x - 9$
**38.** $\big| |x + 3| - 5 \big| = 2$

**39–42** ▪ Solve the inequality graphically.

**39.** $4x - 3 \geq x^2$
**40.** $x^3 - 4x^2 - 5x > 2$
**41.** $x^4 - 4x^2 < \frac{1}{2}x - 1$
**42.** $|x^2 - 16| - 10 \geq 0$

**43–52** ▪ A description of a line is given. Find an equation for the line in **(a)** slope-intercept form and **(b)** general form.

**43.** The line that has slope 2 and $y$-intercept 6

**44.** The line that has slope $-\frac{1}{2}$ and passes through the point $(6, -3)$

**45.** The line that passes through the points $(-1, -6)$ and $(2, -4)$

**46.** The line that has $x$-intercept 4 and $y$-intercept 12

**47.** The vertical line that passes through the point $(3, -2)$

**48.** The horizontal line with $y$-intercept 5

**49.** The line that passes through the point $(1, 1)$ and is parallel to the line $2x - 5y = 10$

**50.** The line that passes through the origin and is parallel to the line containing $(2, 4)$ and $(4, -4)$

**51.** The line that passes through the origin and is perpendicular to the line $y = \frac{1}{2}x - 10$

**52.** The line that passes through the point $(1, 7)$ and is perpendicular to the line $x - 3y + 16 = 0$

**53.** Hooke's Law states that if a weight $w$ is attached to a hanging spring, then the stretched length $s$ of the spring is linearly related to $w$. For a particular spring we have

$$s = 0.3w + 2.5$$

where $s$ is measured in inches and $w$ in pounds.
**(a)** What do the slope and $s$-intercept in this equation represent?
**(b)** How long is the spring when a 5-lb weight is attached?

**54.** Margarita is hired by an accounting firm at a salary of \$60,000 per year. Three years later her annual salary has increased to \$70,500. Assume that her salary increases linearly.
**(a)** Find an equation that relates her annual salary $S$ and the number of years $t$ that she has worked for the firm.
**(b)** What do the slope and $S$-intercept of her salary equation represent?
**(c)** What will her salary be after 12 years with the firm?

**55.** Suppose that $M$ varies directly as $z$ and that $M = 120$ when $z = 15$. Write an equation that expresses this variation.

**56.** Suppose that $z$ is inversely proportional to $y$ and that
$z = 12$ when $y = 16$. Write an equation that expresses
$z$ in terms of $y$.

**57.** The intensity of illumination $I$ from a light varies inversely as
the square of the distance $d$ from the light.
  **(a)** Write this statement as an equation.
  **(b)** Determine the constant of proportionality if it is known
    that a lamp has an intensity of 1000 candles at a distance
    of 8 m.
  **(c)** What is the intensity of this lamp at a distance of 20 m?

**58.** The frequency of a vibrating string under constant tension is
inversely proportional to its length. If a violin string 12 inches
long vibrates 440 times per second, to what length must it be
shortened to vibrate 660 times per second?

**59.** The terminal velocity of a parachutist is directly proportional
to the square root of his weight. A 160-lb parachutist attains a
terminal velocity of 9 mi/h. What is the terminal velocity for a
parachutist who weighs 240 lb?

**60.** The maximum range of a projectile is directly proportional
to the square of its velocity. A baseball pitcher throws a ball
at 60 mi/h, with a maximum range of 242 ft. What is his
maximum range if he throws the ball at 70 mi/h?

**61.** Suppose that $F$ is jointly proportional to $q_1$ and $q_2$ and that
$F = 0.006$ when $q_1 = 4$ and $q_2 = 12$. Find an equation that
expresses $F$ in terms of $q_1$ and $q_2$.

**62.** The kinetic energy $E$ of a moving object is jointly proportional
to the object's mass $m$ and the square of its speed $v$. A rock
with mass 10 kg that is moving at 6 m/s has a kinetic energy of
180 J (joules). What is the kinetic energy of a car with mass
1700 kg that is moving at 30 m/s?

**63–64** ▪ Find equations for the circle and the line in the figure.

**63.**

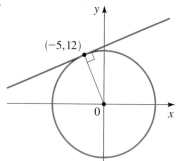

**64.**

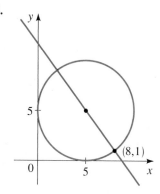

1. Let $P(1, -3)$ and $Q(7, 5)$ be two points in the coordinate plane.
   (a) Plot $P$ and $Q$ in the coordinate plane.
   (b) Find the distance between $P$ and $Q$.
   (c) Find the midpoint of the segment $PQ$.
   (d) Find the slope of the line that contains $P$ and $Q$.
   (e) Find the perpendicular bisector of the line that contains $P$ and $Q$.
   (f) Find an equation for the circle for which the segment $PQ$ is a diameter.

2. Find the center and radius of each circle, and sketch its graph.
   (a) $x^2 + y^2 = \frac{25}{4}$    (b) $(x - 3)^2 + y^2 = 9$    (c) $x^2 + 6x + y^2 - 2y + 6 = 0$

3. Test each equation for symmetry. Find the $x$- and $y$-intercepts, and sketch a graph of the equation.
   (a) $x = 4 - y^2$    (b) $y = |x - 2|$

4. A line has the general linear equation $3x - 5y = 15$.
   (a) Find the $x$- and $y$-intercepts of the graph of this line.
   (b) Graph the line. Use the intercepts that you found in part (a) to help you.
   (c) Write the equation of the line in slope-intercept form.
   (d) What is the slope of the line?
   (e) What is the slope of any line perpendicular to the given line?

5. Find an equation for the line with the given property.
   (a) It passes through the point $(3, -6)$ and is parallel to the line $3x + y - 10 = 0$.
   (b) It has $x$-intercept 6 and $y$-intercept 4.

6. A geologist uses a probe to measure the temperature $T$ (in °C) of the soil at various depths below the surface, and finds that at a depth of $x$ cm, the temperature is given by the linear equation $T = 0.08x - 4$.
   (a) What is the temperature at a depth of one meter (100 cm)?
   (b) Sketch a graph of the linear equation.
   (c) What do the slope, the $x$-intercept, and the $T$-intercept of the graph of this equation represent?

7. Solve the equation or inequality graphically, correct to two decimals.
   (a) $x^3 - 9x - 1 = 0$
   (b) $\frac{1}{2}x + 2 \geq \sqrt{x^2 + 1}$

8. The maximum weight $M$ that can be supported by a beam is jointly proportional to its width $w$ and the square of its height $h$ and inversely proportional to its length $L$.
   (a) Write an equation that expresses this proportionality.
   (b) Determine the constant of proportionality if a beam 4 in. wide, 6 in. high, and 12 ft long can support a weight of 4800 lb.
   (c) If a 10-ft beam made of the same material is 3 in. wide and 10 in. high, what is the maximum weight it can support?

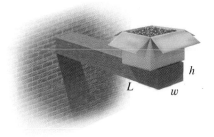

1. Johanna earns 4.75% simple interest on her bank account annually. If she earns $380 interest in a given year, what amount of money did she have in her account at the beginning of the year?

2. Calculate each complex number and write the result in the form $a + bi$.

   (a) $\left(3 + \frac{5}{2}i\right) - \left(\frac{10}{3} - \frac{1}{2}i\right)$

   (b) $(\sqrt{3} + \sqrt{-2})(\sqrt{12} - \sqrt{-8})$

   (c) $\dfrac{-15i}{4 + 3i}$

   (d) The complex conjugate of $\dfrac{4 - \sqrt{-3}}{2}$

3. Find all solutions, real and complex, of each equation.

   (a) $x + 7 = 2 - \frac{3}{2}x$

   (b) $\dfrac{4x - 1}{2x + 6} = \dfrac{2x - 3}{x + 2}$

   (c) $x^2 - 5x = 6$

   (d) $3x^2 - 4x + 2 = 0$

   (e) $x^4 = 16$

   (f) $|x - 0.5| = 2.25$

4. Solve each inequality. Graph the solution on a real number line, and express the solution in interval notation.

   (a) $x - 5 \geq 4 - 2x$

   (b) $7 - 2|x + 1| < 1$

   (c) $2x^2 - x - 1 \leq 0$

   (d) $\dfrac{x}{x - 3} > 1$

5. (a) Use a graphing calculator to graph the equation $y = x^4 - 2x^3 - 7x^2 + 8x + 12$.

   (b) Use your graph to solve the equation $x^4 - 2x^3 - 7x^2 + 8x + 12 = 0$.

   (c) Use your graph to solve the inequality $x^4 - 2x^3 - 7x^2 + 8x + 12 \leq 0$.

6. Let $P(-3, 6)$ and $Q(10, 1)$ be two points in the coordinate plane.

   (a) Find the distance between $P$ and $Q$.

   (b) Find the slope-intercept form of the equation of the line that contains $P$ and $Q$.

   (c) Find an equation of the circle that contains $P$ and $Q$ and whose center is the midpoint of the segment $PQ$.

   (d) Find an equation for the line that contains $P$ and that is perpendicular to the segment $PQ$.

   (e) Find an equation for the line that passes through the origin and that is parallel to the segment $PQ$.

7. Sketch a graph of each equation. Label all $x$- and $y$-intercepts. If the graph is a circle, find its center and radius.

   (a) $2x - 5y = 20$

   (b) $x^2 - 6x + y^2 = 0$

8. Find an equation for each graph.

   (a)

   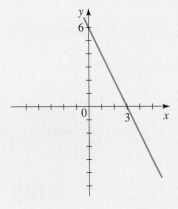

   (b)

   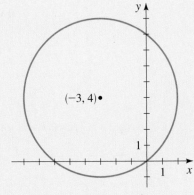

**9.** A sailboat departed from an island and traveled north for 2 hours, then east for $1\frac{1}{2}$ hours, all at the same speed. At the end of the trip it was 20 miles from where it started. At what speed did the boat travel?

**10.** A survey finds that the average starting salary for young people in their first full-time job is proportional to the square of the number of years of education they have completed. College graduates with 16 years of education have an average starting salary of $48,000.

   **(a)** Write an equation that expresses the relationship between years of education $x$ and average starting salary $S$.

   **(b)** What is the average starting salary of a person who drops out of high school after completing the tenth grade?

   **(c)** A person with a master's degree has an average starting salary of $60,750. How many years of education does this represent?

# FITTING LINES TO DATA

In Section 2.4 we used linear equations to model relationships between varying quantities. In practice, such relationships are discovered by collecting data about the quantities being studied. But data seldom fall into a precise line. Because of measurement errors or other random factors, a scatter plot of real-world data may appear to lie more or less on a line but not exactly. For example, the scatter plot in Figure 1(a) shows the results of a study on childhood obesity; the graph plots the body mass index (BMI) versus the number of hours of television watched per day for 25 adolescent subjects. Of course, we would not expect an *exact* relationship between these variables as in Figure 1(b), but clearly, the scatter plot in Figure 1(a) indicates a linear *trend*: The more hours a subject spends watching TV, the higher the BMI. So although we cannot fit a line exactly through the data points, a line like the one in Figure 1(a) shows the general trend of the data.

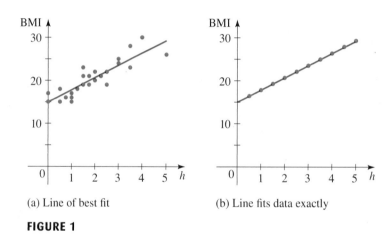

(a) Line of best fit          (b) Line fits data exactly

**FIGURE 1**

Fitting lines to data is one of the most important tools available to researchers who need to analyze numerical data. In this section we learn how to find and use lines that best fit data that exhibits a linear trend.

## ■ The Line That Best Fits the Data

Until recently, infant mortality in the United States was declining steadily. Table 1 gives the nationwide infant mortality rate for the period from 1950 to 2000; the *rate* is the number of infants who died before reaching their first birthday, out of every 1000 live births. Over this half century the mortality rate was reduced by over 75%, a remarkable achievement in neonatal care.

**TABLE 1**
U.S. Infant Mortality

| Year | Rate |
|------|------|
| 1950 | 29.2 |
| 1960 | 26.0 |
| 1970 | 20.0 |
| 1980 | 12.6 |
| 1990 | 9.2 |
| 2000 | 6.9 |

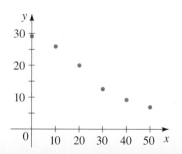

**FIGURE 2** U.S. infant mortality rate

The scatter plot in Figure 2 shows that the data lie roughly on a straight line. We can try to fit a line visually to approximate the data points, but since the data aren't *exactly* linear, there are many lines that might seem to work. Figure 3 shows two attempts at "eyeballing" a line to fit the data.

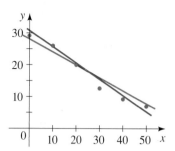

**FIGURE 3** Visual attempts to fit line to data

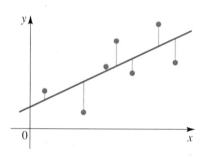

**FIGURE 4** Distance from the data points to the line

Of all the lines that run through these data points, there is one that "best" fits the data, in the sense that it provides the most accurate linear model for the data. We now describe how to find this line.

It seems reasonable that the line of best fit is the line that is as close as possible to all the data points. This is the line for which the sum of the vertical distances from the data points to the line is as small as possible (see Figure 4). For technical reasons it is better to use the line where the sum of the squares of these distances is smallest. This is called the **regression line**. The formula for the regression line is found by using calculus, but fortunately, the formula is programmed into most graphing calculators. In Example 1 we see how to use a TI-83 calculator to find the regression line for the infant mortality data described above. (The process for other calculators is similar.)

▶ **EXAMPLE 1** | Regression Line for U.S. Infant Mortality Rates

(a) Find the regression line for the infant mortality data in Table 1.

(b) Graph the regression line on a scatter plot of the data.

(c) Use the regression line to estimate the infant mortality rates in 1995 and 2006.

▼ **SOLUTION**

(a) To find the regression line using a TI-83 calculator, we must first enter the data into the lists $L_1$ and $L_2$, which are accessed by pressing the [STAT] key and selecting [EDIT]. Figure 5 shows the calculator screen after the data have been entered. (Note that we are letting $x = 0$ correspond to the year 1950, so that $x = 50$ corresponds to 2000. This makes the equations easier to work with.)

| L1 | L2 | L3 | 1 |
|----|------|---------|---|
| 0 | 29.2 | ------- | |
| 10 | 26 | | |
| 20 | 20 | | |
| 30 | 12.6 | | |
| 40 | 9.2 | | |
| 50 | 6.9 | | |
| ------- | | | |

L2(7)=

**FIGURE 5** Entering the data

We then press the $\boxed{\text{STAT}}$ key again and select $\boxed{\text{CALC}}$, then 4:LinReg(ax+b), which provides the output shown in Figure 6(a). This tells us that the regression line is

$$y = -0.48x + 29.4$$

Here $x$ represents the number of years since 1950, and $y$ represents the corresponding infant mortality rate.

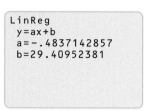

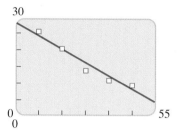

(a) Output of the LinReg command

(b) Scatter plot and regression line

**FIGURE 6**

**(b)** The scatter plot and the regression line have been plotted on a graphing calculator screen in Figure 6(b).

**(c)** The year 1995 is 45 years after 1950, so substituting 45 for $x$, we find that $y = -0.48(45) + 29.4 = 7.8$. So the infant mortality rate in 1995 was about 7.8. Similarly, substituting 56 for $x$, we find that the infant mortality rate predicted for 2006 was about $-0.48(56) + 29.4 \approx 2.5$. ▲

An Internet search shows that the actual infant mortality rate was 7.6 in 1995 and 6.4 in 2006. So the regression line is fairly accurate for 1995 (the actual rate was slightly lower than the predicted rate), but it is considerably off for 2006 (the actual rate was more than twice the predicted rate). The reason is that infant mortality in the United States stopped declining and actually started rising in 2002, for the first time in more than a century. This shows that we have to be very careful about extrapolating linear models outside the domain over which the data are spread.

## Examples of Regression Analysis

Since the modern Olympic Games began in 1896, achievements in track and field events have been improving steadily. One example in which the winning records have shown an upward linear trend is the pole vault. Pole vaulting began in the northern Netherlands as a practical activity: When traveling from village to village, people would vault across the many canals that crisscrossed the area to avoid having to go out of their way to find a bridge. Households maintained a supply of wooden poles of lengths appropriate for each member of the family. Pole vaulting for height rather than distance became a collegiate track and field event in the mid-1800s and was one of the events in the first modern Olympics. In the next example we find a linear model for the gold-medal-winning records in the men's Olympic pole vault.

AP/Wide World Photos

Tim Mack, 2004 Olympic Gold Medal Winner

**4. Carbon Dioxide Levels**   The Mauna Loa Observatory, located on the island of Hawaii, has been monitoring carbon dioxide ($CO_2$) levels in the atmosphere since 1958. The table lists the average annual $CO_2$ levels measured in parts per million (ppm) from 1984 to 2006.

(a)  Make a scatter plot of the data.

(b)  Find and graph the regression line.

(c)  Use the linear model in part (b) to estimate the $CO_2$ level in the atmosphere in 2005. Compare your answer with the actual $CO_2$ level of 379.7 that was measured in 2005.

| Year | $CO_2$ level (ppm) |
|------|--------------------|
| 1984 | 344.3 |
| 1986 | 347.0 |
| 1988 | 351.3 |
| 1990 | 354.0 |
| 1992 | 356.3 |
| 1994 | 358.9 |
| 1996 | 362.7 |
| 1998 | 366.5 |
| 2000 | 369.4 |
| 2002 | 372.0 |
| 2004 | 377.5 |
| 2006 | 380.9 |

**5. Temperature and Chirping Crickets**   Biologists have observed that the chirping rate of crickets of a certain species appears to be related to temperature. The table shows the chirping rates for various temperatures.

(a)  Make a scatter plot of the data.

(b)  Find and graph the regression line.

(c)  Use the linear model in part (b) to estimate the chirping rate at 100°F.

| Temperature (°F) | Chirping rate (chirps/min) |
|------------------|----------------------------|
| 50 | 20 |
| 55 | 46 |
| 60 | 79 |
| 65 | 91 |
| 70 | 113 |
| 75 | 140 |
| 80 | 173 |
| 85 | 198 |
| 90 | 211 |

**6. Extent of Arctic Sea Ice**   The National Snow and Ice Data Center monitors the amount of ice in the Arctic year round. The table gives approximate values for the sea ice extent in millions of square kilometers from 1980 to 2006, in two-year intervals.

(a)  Make a scatter plot of the data.

(b)  Find and graph the regression line.

(c)  Use the linear model in part (b) to estimate the ice extent in the year 2010.

| Year | Ice extent (million km²) | Year | Ice extent (million km²) |
|------|--------------------------|------|--------------------------|
| 1980 | 7.9 | 1994 | 7.1 |
| 1982 | 7.4 | 1996 | 7.9 |
| 1984 | 7.2 | 1998 | 6.6 |
| 1986 | 7.6 | 2000 | 6.3 |
| 1988 | 7.5 | 2002 | 6.0 |
| 1990 | 6.2 | 2004 | 6.1 |
| 1992 | 7.6 | 2006 | 5.7 |

**7. Mosquito Prevalence**   The table lists the relative abundance of mosquitoes (as measured by the mosquito positive rate) versus the flow rate (measured as a percentage of maximum flow) of canal networks in Saga City, Japan.

(a)  Make a scatter plot of the data.

(b)  Find and graph the regression line.

(c)  Use the linear model in part (b) to estimate the mosquito positive rate if the canal flow is 70% of maximum.

| Flow rate (%) | Mosquito positive rate (%) |
|---------------|-----------------------------|
| 0 | 22 |
| 10 | 16 |
| 40 | 12 |
| 60 | 11 |
| 90 | 6 |
| 100 | 2 |

8. **Noise and Intelligibility**   Audiologists study the intelligibility of spoken sentences under different noise levels. Intelligibility, the MRT score, is measured as the percent of a spoken sentence that the listener can decipher at a certain noise level in decibels (dB). The table shows the results of one such test.

(a) Make a scatter plot of the data.

(b) Find and graph the regression line.

(c) Find the correlation coefficient. Is a linear model appropriate?

(d) Use the linear model in part (b) to estimate the intelligibility of a sentence at a 94-dB noise level.

| Noise level (dB) | MRT score (%) |
|:---:|:---:|
| 80 | 99 |
| 84 | 91 |
| 88 | 84 |
| 92 | 70 |
| 96 | 47 |
| 100 | 23 |
| 104 | 11 |

9. **Life Expectancy**   The average life expectancy in the United States has been rising steadily over the past few decades, as shown in the table.

(a) Make a scatter plot of the data.

(b) Find and graph the regression line.

(c) Use the linear model you found in part (b) to predict the life expectancy in the year 2006.

(d) Search the Internet or your campus library to find the actual 2006 average life expectancy. Compare to your answer in part (c).

| Year | Life expectancy |
|:---:|:---:|
| 1920 | 54.1 |
| 1930 | 59.7 |
| 1940 | 62.9 |
| 1950 | 68.2 |
| 1960 | 69.7 |
| 1970 | 70.8 |
| 1980 | 73.7 |
| 1990 | 75.4 |
| 2000 | 76.9 |

10. **Olympic Pole Vault**   The graph in Figure 7 indicates that in recent years the winning Olympic men's pole vault height has fallen below the value predicted by the regression line in Example 2. This might have occurred because when the pole vault was a new event, there was much room for improvement in vaulters' performances, whereas now even the best training can produce only incremental advances. Let's see whether concentrating on more recent results gives a better predictor of future records.

(a) Use the data in Table 2 to complete the table on the next page of winning pole vault heights. (Note that we are using $x = 0$ to correspond to the year 1972, where this restricted data set begins.)

(b) Find the regression line for the data in part (a).

(c) Plot the data and the regression line on the same axes. Does the regression line seem to provide a good model for the data?

(d) What does the regression line predict as the winning pole vault height for the 2008 Olympics? Research the Internet or other sources to find the actual winning height for 2008, and compare it to this predicted value. Has this new regression line provided a better prediction than the line in Example 2?

| Year | $x$ | Height (m) |
|------|-----|------------|
| 1972 | 0 | 5.64 |
| 1976 | 4 | |
| 1980 | 8 | |
| 1984 | | |
| 1988 | | |
| 1992 | | |
| 1996 | | |
| 2000 | | |
| 2004 | | |

11. **Olympic Swimming Records**  The tables give the gold medal times in the men's and women's 100-m freestyle Olympic swimming event.

(a) Find the regression lines for the men's data and the women's data.

(b) Sketch both regression lines on the same graph. When do these lines predict that the women will overtake the men in the event? Does this conclusion seem reasonable?

### MEN

| Year | Gold medalist | Time (s) |
|------|---------------|----------|
| 1908 | C. Daniels, USA | 65.6 |
| 1912 | D. Kahanamoku, USA | 63.4 |
| 1920 | D. Kahanamoku, USA | 61.4 |
| 1924 | J. Weissmuller, USA | 59.0 |
| 1928 | J. Weissmuller, USA | 58.6 |
| 1932 | Y. Miyazaki, Japan | 58.2 |
| 1936 | F. Csik, Hungary | 57.6 |
| 1948 | W. Ris, USA | 57.3 |
| 1952 | C. Scholes, USA | 57.4 |
| 1956 | J. Henricks, Australia | 55.4 |
| 1960 | J. Devitt, Australia | 55.2 |
| 1964 | D. Schollander, USA | 53.4 |
| 1968 | M. Wenden, Australia | 52.2 |
| 1972 | M. Spitz, USA | 51.22 |
| 1976 | J. Montgomery, USA | 49.99 |
| 1980 | J. Woithe, E. Germany | 50.40 |
| 1984 | R. Gaines, USA | 49.80 |
| 1988 | M. Biondi, USA | 48.63 |
| 1992 | A. Popov, Russia | 49.02 |
| 1996 | A. Popov, Russia | 48.74 |
| 2000 | P. van den Hoogenband, Netherlands | 48.30 |
| 2004 | P. van den Hoogenband, Netherlands | 48.17 |

### WOMEN

| Year | Gold medalist | Time (s) |
|------|---------------|----------|
| 1912 | F. Durack, Australia | 82.2 |
| 1920 | E. Bleibtrey, USA | 73.6 |
| 1924 | E. Lackie, USA | 72.4 |
| 1928 | A. Osipowich, USA | 71.0 |
| 1932 | H. Madison, USA | 66.8 |
| 1936 | H. Mastenbroek, Holland | 65.9 |
| 1948 | G. Andersen, Denmark | 66.3 |
| 1952 | K. Szoke, Hungary | 66.8 |
| 1956 | D. Fraser, Australia | 62.0 |
| 1960 | D. Fraser, Australia | 61.2 |
| 1964 | D. Fraser, Australia | 59.5 |
| 1968 | J. Henne, USA | 60.0 |
| 1972 | S. Nielson, USA | 58.59 |
| 1976 | K. Ender, E. Germany | 55.65 |
| 1980 | B. Krause, E. Germany | 54.79 |
| 1984 | (Tie) C. Steinseifer, USA | 55.92 |
| | N. Hogshead, USA | 55.92 |
| 1988 | K. Otto, E. Germany | 54.93 |
| 1992 | Z. Yong, China | 54.64 |
| 1996 | L. Jingyi, China | 54.50 |
| 2000 | I. DeBruijn, Netherlands | 53.83 |
| 2004 | J. Henry, Australia | 53.84 |

12. **Shoe Size and Height**   Do you think that shoe size and height are correlated? Find out by surveying the shoe sizes and heights of people in your class. (Of course, the data for men and women should be separate.) Find the correlation coefficient.

13. **Demand for Candy Bars**   In this problem you will determine a linear demand equation that describes the demand for candy bars in your class. Survey your classmates to determine what price they would be willing to pay for a candy bar. Your survey form might look like the sample to the left.

    **(a)** Make a table of the number of respondents who answered "yes" at each price level.

    **(b)** Make a scatter plot of your data.

    **(c)** Find and graph the regression line $y = mp + b$, which gives the number of responents $y$ who would buy a candy bar if the price were $p$ cents. This is the *demand equation*. Why is the slope $m$ negative?

    **(d)** What is the $p$-intercept of the demand equation? What does this intercept tell you about pricing candy bars?

---

*Would you buy a candy bar from the vending machine in the hallway if the price is as indicated?*

| Price | Yes or No |
|-------|-----------|
| 30¢ | |
| 40¢ | |
| 50¢ | |
| 60¢ | |
| 70¢ | |
| 80¢ | |
| 90¢ | |
| $1.00 | |
| $1.10 | |
| $1.20 | |

# Functions

Courtesy Blue Skies Skydiving Adventures, Inc., www.blueskies-skydiving.com

**Do you know the rule?** We need to know a lot of rules for our everyday living—such as the rule that relates the amount of gas left in the gas tank to the distance we have driven or the rule that relates the grade we get in our algebra course to our exam scores. If we're more adventuresome, like these sky divers, we may also need to know the rule that relates the distance fallen to the time we've been falling. Rules like these are modeled in algebra by using functions. In fact, a function is simply a rule that relates two quantities. One of the most famous such rules says that the distance $d$ that an object falls in $t$ seconds is $16t^2$ ft (see Example 2 in Section 3.4). This rule works in a vacuum, where there is no air resistance. But for these sky divers it's air resistance that makes the experience so much fun! (We'll study the rule that takes air resistance into account in Chapter 5.)

| 3.1 | What Is a Function? |

**LEARNING OBJECTIVES**
After completing this section, you will be able to:

- Recognize functions in the real world
- Work with function notation
- Find domains of functions
- Represent functions verbally, algebraically, graphically, and numerically

Perhaps the most useful mathematical idea for modeling the real world is the concept of function, which we study in this chapter. In this section we explore the idea of a function and then give the mathematical definition of function.

## Functions All Around Us

In nearly every physical phenomenon we observe that one quantity depends on another. For example, your height depends on your age, the temperature depends on the date, the cost of mailing a package depends on its weight (see Figure 1). We use the term *function* to describe this dependence of one quantity on another. That is, we say the following:

- Height is a function of age.
- Temperature is a function of date.
- Cost of mailing a package is a function of weight.

The U.S. Post Office uses a simple rule to determine the cost of mailing a first-class parcel on the basis of its weight. But it's not so easy to describe the rule that relates height to age or the rule that relates temperature to date.

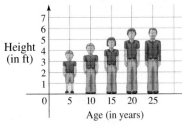

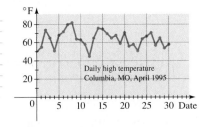

| $w$ (ounces) | Postage (dollars) |
|---|---|
| $0 < w \leq 1$ | 1.13 |
| $1 < w \leq 2$ | 1.30 |
| $2 < w \leq 3$ | 1.47 |
| $3 < w \leq 4$ | 1.64 |
| $4 < w \leq 5$ | 1.81 |
| $5 < w \leq 6$ | 1.98 |

**FIGURE 1**        Height is a function of age.        Temperature is a function of date.        Postage is a function of weight.

Can you think of other functions? Here are some more examples:

- The area of a circle is a function of its radius.
- The number of bacteria in a culture is a function of time.
- The weight of an astronaut is a function of her elevation.
- The price of a commodity is a function of the demand for that commodity.

The rule that describes how the area $A$ of a circle depends on its radius $r$ is given by the formula $A = \pi r^2$. Even when a precise rule or formula describing a function is not available, we can still describe the function by a graph. For example, when you turn on a hot water faucet, the temperature of the water depends on how long the water has been running. So we can say

- Temperature of water from the faucet is a function of time.

Figure 2 shows a rough graph of the temperature $T$ of the water as a function of the time $t$ that has elapsed since the faucet was turned on. The graph shows that the initial temperature of the water is close to room temperature. When the water from the hot water tank reaches the faucet, the water's temperature $T$ increases quickly. In the next phase, $T$ is constant at the temperature of the water in the tank. When the tank is drained, $T$ decreases to the temperature of the cold water supply.

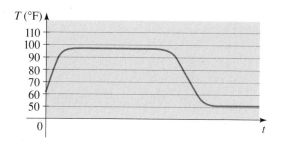

**FIGURE 2** Graph of water temperature $T$ as a function of time $t$

## Definition of Function

*We have previously used letters to stand for numbers. Here we do something quite different. We use letters to represent rules.*

A function is a rule. To talk about a function, we need to give it a name. We will use letters such as $f, g, h, \ldots$ to represent functions. For example, we can use the letter $f$ to represent a rule as follows:

"$f$"   is the rule   "square the number"

When we write $f(2)$, we mean "apply the rule $f$ to the number 2." Applying the rule gives $f(2) = 2^2 = 4$. Similarly, $f(3) = 3^2 = 9$, $f(4) = 4^2 = 16$, and in general $f(x) = x^2$.

---

### DEFINITION OF A FUNCTION

A **function** $f$ is a rule that assigns to each element $x$ in a set $A$ exactly one element, called $f(x)$, in a set $B$.

---

We usually consider functions for which the sets $A$ and $B$ are sets of real numbers. The symbol $f(x)$ is read "$f$ of $x$" or "$f$ at $x$" and is called the **value of $f$ at $x$**, or the **image of $x$ under $f$**. The set $A$ is called the **domain** of the function. The **range** of $f$ is the set of all possible values of $f(x)$ as $x$ varies throughout the domain, that is,

$$\text{range of } f = \{f(x) \mid x \in A\}$$

The symbol that represents an arbitrary number in the domain of a function $f$ is called an **independent variable**. The symbol that represents a number in the range of $f$ is called a **dependent variable**. So if we write $y = f(x)$, then $x$ is the independent variable and $y$ is the dependent variable.

It is helpful to think of a function as a **machine** (see Figure 3). If $x$ is in the domain of the function $f$, then when $x$ enters the machine, it is accepted as an **input** and the machine produces an **output** $f(x)$ according to the rule of the function. Thus, we can think of the domain as the set of all possible inputs and the range as the set of all possible outputs.

The $\boxed{\sqrt{\phantom{x}}}$ key on your calculator is a good example of a function as a machine. First you input $x$ into the display. Then you press the key labeled $\boxed{\sqrt{\phantom{x}}}$. (On most *graphing* calculators the order of these operations is reversed.) If $x < 0$, then $x$ is not in the domain of this function; that is, $x$ is not an acceptable input, and the calculator will indicate an error. If $x \geq 0$, then an approximation to $\sqrt{x}$ appears in the display, correct to a certain number of decimal places. (Thus, the $\boxed{\sqrt{\phantom{x}}}$ key on your calculator is not quite the same as the exact mathematical function $f$ defined by $f(x) = \sqrt{x}$.)

**FIGURE 3** Machine diagram of $f$

Another way to picture a function is by an **arrow diagram** as in Figure 4 on the next page. Each arrow connects an element of $A$ to an element of $B$. The arrow indicates that $f(x)$ is associated with $x$, $f(a)$ is associated with $a$, and so on.

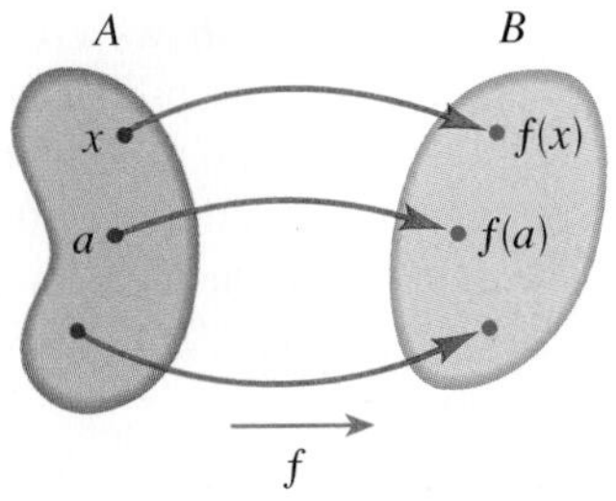

**A**      **B**

**FIGURE 4** Arrow diagram of $f$

▶ **EXAMPLE 1 |** Analyzing a Function

A function $f$ is defined by the formula

$$f(x) = x^2 + 4$$

**(a)** Express in words how $f$ acts on the input $x$ to produce the output $f(x)$.

**(b)** Evaluate $f(3)$, $f(-2)$, and $f(\sqrt{5})$.

**(c)** Find the domain and range of $f$.

**(d)** Draw a machine diagram for $f$.

▼ **SOLUTION**

**(a)** The formula tells us that $f$ first squares the input $x$ and then adds 4 to the result. So $f$ is the function

"square, then add 4"

**(b)** The values of $f$ are found by substituting for $x$ in the formula $f(x) = x^2 + 4$.

$$f(3) = 3^2 + 4 = 13 \qquad \text{Replace } x \text{ by } 3$$

$$f(-2) = (-2)^2 + 4 = 8 \qquad \text{Replace } x \text{ by } -2$$

$$f(\sqrt{5}) = (\sqrt{5})^2 + 4 = 9 \qquad \text{Replace } x \text{ by } \sqrt{5}$$

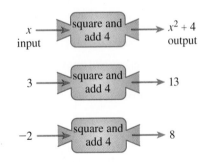

**(c)** The domain of $f$ consists of all possible inputs for $f$. Since we can evaluate the formula $f(x) = x^2 + 4$ for every real number $x$, the domain of $f$ is the set $\mathbb{R}$ of all real numbers.

The range of $f$ consists of all possible outputs of $f$. Because $x^2 \geq 0$ for all real numbers $x$, we have $x^2 + 4 \geq 4$, so for every output of $f$ we have $f(x) \geq 4$. Thus, the range of $f$ is $\{y \mid y \geq 4\} = [4, \infty)$.

**(d)** A machine diagram for $f$ is shown in Figure 5.

**FIGURE 5** Machine diagram

✎ **Practice what you've learned: Do Exercises 9, 13, 17, and 43.**      ▲

## ■ Evaluating a Function

In the definition of a function the independent variable $x$ plays the role of a "placeholder." For example, the function $f(x) = 3x^2 + x - 5$ can be thought of as

$$f(\blacksquare) = 3 \cdot \blacksquare^2 + \blacksquare - 5$$

To evaluate $f$ at a number, we substitute the number for the placeholder.

▶ **EXAMPLE 2 |** Evaluating a Function

Let $f(x) = 3x^2 + x - 5$. Evaluate each function value.

**(a)** $f(-2)$      **(b)** $f(0)$      **(c)** $f(4)$      **(d)** $f(\tfrac{1}{2})$

(c) We use the points tabulated in part (b) to help us draw the graph of this function in Figure 6.

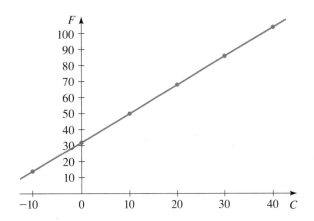

**FIGURE 6** Celsius and Fahrenheit

✎ **Practice what you've learned: Do Exercise 65.** ▲

# 3.1 EXERCISES

## ▼ CONCEPTS

**1.** If a function $f$ is given by the formula $y = f(x)$, then $f(a)$ is the _____ of $f$ at $x = a$.

**2.** For a function $f$, the set of all possible inputs is called the _____ of $f$, and the set of all possible outputs is called the _____ of $f$.

**3.** (a) Which of the following functions have 5 in their domain?

$$f(x) = x^2 - 3x \qquad g(x) = \frac{x - 5}{x} \qquad h(x) = \sqrt{x - 10}$$

(b) For the functions from part (a) that *do* have 5 in their domain, find the value of the function at 5.

**4.** A function is given algebraically by the formula $f(x) = (x - 4)^2 + 3$. Complete these other ways to represent $f$:

(a) *Verbal:* "Subtract 4, then _____ and _____.
(b) *Numerical:*

| $x$ | $f(x)$ |
|-----|--------|
| 0   | 19     |
| 2   |        |
| 4   |        |
| 6   |        |

## ▼ SKILLS

**5–8** ■ Express the rule in function notation. (For example, the rule "square, then subtract 5" is expressed as the function $f(x) = x^2 - 5$.)

**5.** Add 3, then multiply by 2    **6.** Divide by 7, then subtract 4

**7.** Subtract 5, then square

**8.** Take the square root, add 8, then multiply by $\frac{1}{3}$

**9–12** ■ Express the function (or rule) in words.

✎ **9.** $h(x) = x^2 + 2$      **10.** $k(x) = \sqrt{x + 2}$

**11.** $f(x) = \dfrac{x - 4}{3}$      **12.** $g(x) = \dfrac{x}{3} - 4$

**13–14** ■ Draw a machine diagram for the function.

✎ **13.** $f(x) = \sqrt{x - 1}$      **14.** $f(x) = \dfrac{3}{x - 2}$

**15–16** ■ Complete the table.

**15.** $f(x) = 2(x - 1)^2$      **16.** $g(x) = |2x + 3|$

| $x$ | $f(x)$ |
|-----|--------|
| −1  |        |
| 0   |        |
| 1   |        |
| 2   |        |
| 3   |        |

| $x$ | $g(x)$ |
|-----|--------|
| −3  |        |
| −2  |        |
| 0   |        |
| 1   |        |
| 3   |        |

**17–26** ■ Evaluate the function at the indicated values.

✎ **17.** $f(x) = x^2 - 6$;   $f(-3), f(3), f(0), f(\frac{1}{2}), f(10)$

**18.** $f(x) = x^3 + 2x$;   $f(-2), f(1), f(0), f(\frac{1}{3}), f(0.2)$

✎ **19.** $f(x) = 2x + 1$;

$f(1), f(-2), f(\frac{1}{2}), f(a), f(-a), f(a + b)$

**20.** $f(x) = x^2 + 2x$;

$f(0), f(3), f(-3), f(a), f(-x), f\left(\dfrac{1}{a}\right)$

**21.** $g(x) = \dfrac{1-x}{1+x}$;

$g(2), g(-2), g(\tfrac{1}{2}), g(a), g(a-1), g(-1)$

**22.** $h(t) = t + \dfrac{1}{t}$;

$h(1), h(-1), h(2), h(\tfrac{1}{2}), h(x), h\left(\dfrac{1}{x}\right)$

**23.** $f(x) = 2x^2 + 3x - 4$;

$f(0), f(2), f(-2), f(\sqrt{2}), f(x+1), f(-x)$

**24.** $f(x) = x^3 - 4x^2$;

$f(0), f(1), f(-1), f(\tfrac{3}{2}), f\left(\dfrac{x}{2}\right), f(x^2)$

**25.** $f(x) = 2|x-1|$;

$f(-2), f(0), f(\tfrac{1}{2}), f(2), f(x+1), f(x^2+2)$

**26.** $f(x) = \dfrac{|x|}{x}$;

$f(-2), f(-1), f(0), f(5), f(x^2), f\left(\dfrac{1}{x}\right)$

**27–30** ▪ Evaluate the piecewise defined function at the indicated values.

**27.** $f(x) = \begin{cases} x^2 & \text{if } x < 0 \\ x+1 & \text{if } x \geq 0 \end{cases}$

$f(-2), f(-1), f(0), f(1), f(2)$

**28.** $f(x) = \begin{cases} 5 & \text{if } x \leq 2 \\ 2x-3 & \text{if } x > 2 \end{cases}$

$f(-3), f(0), f(2), f(3), f(5)$

**29.** $f(x) = \begin{cases} x^2 + 2x & \text{if } x \leq -1 \\ x & \text{if } -1 < x \leq 1 \\ -1 & \text{if } x > 1 \end{cases}$

$f(-4), f(-\tfrac{3}{2}), f(-1), f(0), f(25)$

**30.** $f(x) = \begin{cases} 3x & \text{if } x < 0 \\ x+1 & \text{if } 0 \leq x \leq 2 \\ (x-2)^2 & \text{if } x > 2 \end{cases}$

$f(-5), f(0), f(1), f(2), f(5)$

**31–34** ▪ Use the function to evaluate the indicated expressions and simplify.

**31.** $f(x) = x^2 + 1$;   $f(x+2), f(x) + f(2)$

**32.** $f(x) = 3x - 1$;   $f(2x), 2f(x)$

**33.** $f(x) = x + 4$;   $f(x^2), (f(x))^2$

**34.** $f(x) = 6x - 18$;   $f\left(\dfrac{x}{3}\right), \dfrac{f(x)}{3}$

**35–42** ▪ Find $f(a)$, $f(a+h)$, and the difference quotient $\dfrac{f(a+h) - f(a)}{h}$, where $h \neq 0$.

**35.** $f(x) = 3x + 2$

**36.** $f(x) = x^2 + 1$

**37.** $f(x) = 5$

**38.** $f(x) = \dfrac{1}{x+1}$

**39.** $f(x) = \dfrac{x}{x+1}$

**40.** $f(x) = \dfrac{2x}{x-1}$

**41.** $f(x) = 3 - 5x + 4x^2$

**42.** $f(x) = x^3$

**43–64** ▪ Find the domain of the function.

**43.** $f(x) = 2x$

**44.** $f(x) = x^2 + 1$

**45.** $f(x) = 2x, \quad -1 \leq x \leq 5$

**46.** $f(x) = x^2 + 1, \quad 0 \leq x \leq 5$

**47.** $f(x) = \dfrac{1}{x-3}$

**48.** $f(x) = \dfrac{1}{3x-6}$

**49.** $f(x) = \dfrac{x+2}{x^2-1}$

**50.** $f(x) = \dfrac{x^4}{x^2+x-6}$

**51.** $f(x) = \sqrt{x-5}$

**52.** $f(x) = \sqrt[4]{x+9}$

**53.** $f(t) = \sqrt[3]{t-1}$

**54.** $g(x) = \sqrt{7-3x}$

**55.** $h(x) = \sqrt{2x-5}$

**56.** $G(x) = \sqrt{x^2-9}$

**57.** $g(x) = \dfrac{\sqrt{2+x}}{3-x}$

**58.** $g(x) = \dfrac{\sqrt{x}}{2x^2+x-1}$

**59.** $g(x) = \sqrt[4]{x^2-6x}$

**60.** $g(x) = \sqrt{x^2-2x-8}$

**61.** $f(x) = \dfrac{3}{\sqrt{x-4}}$

**62.** $f(x) = \dfrac{x^2}{\sqrt{6-x}}$

**63.** $f(x) = \dfrac{(x+1)^2}{\sqrt{2x-1}}$

**64.** $f(x) = \dfrac{x}{\sqrt[4]{9-x^2}}$

**65–68** ▪ A verbal description of a function is given. Find **(a)** algebraic, **(b)** numerical, and **(c)** graphical representations for the function.

**65.** To evaluate $f(x)$, divide the input by 3 and add $\tfrac{2}{3}$ to the result.

**66.** To evaluate $g(x)$, subtract 4 from the input and multiply the result by $\tfrac{3}{4}$.

**67.** Let $T(x)$ be the amount of sales tax charged in Lemon County on a purchase of $x$ dollars. To find the tax, take 8% of the purchase price.

**68.** Let $V(d)$ be the volume of a sphere of diameter $d$. To find the volume, take the cube of the diameter, then multiply by $\pi$ and divide by 6.

## ▼ APPLICATIONS

**69. Production Cost**   The cost $C$ in dollars of producing $x$ yards of a certain fabric is given by the function

$$C(x) = 1500 + 3x + 0.02x^2 + 0.0001x^3$$

**(a)** Find $C(10)$ and $C(100)$.
**(b)** What do your answers in part (a) represent?
**(c)** Find $C(0)$. (This number represents the *fixed costs*.)

**70. Area of a Sphere**   The surface area $S$ of a sphere is a function of its radius $r$ given by

$$S(r) = 4\pi r^2$$

**(a)** Find $S(2)$ and $S(3)$.
**(b)** What do your answers in part (a) represent?

**71. Torricelli's Law**   A tank holds 50 gallons of water, which drains from a leak at the bottom, causing the tank to empty in 20 minutes. The tank drains faster when it is nearly full because the pressure on the leak is greater. **Torricelli's Law** gives the volume of water remaining in the tank after $t$ minutes as

$$V(t) = 50\left(1 - \frac{t}{20}\right)^2 \qquad 0 \le t \le 20$$

(a) Find $V(0)$ and $V(20)$.
(b) What do your answers to part (a) represent?
(c) Make a table of values of $V(t)$ for $t = 0, 5, 10, 15, 20$.

**72. How Far Can You See?**   Because of the curvature of the earth, the maximum distance $D$ that you can see from the top of a tall building or from an airplane at height $h$ is given by the function

$$D(h) = \sqrt{2rh + h^2}$$

where $r = 3960$ mi is the radius of the earth and $D$ and $h$ are measured in miles.
(a) Find $D(0.1)$ and $D(0.2)$.
(b) How far can you see from the observation deck of Toronto's CN Tower, 1135 ft above the ground?
(c) Commercial aircraft fly at an altitude of about 7 mi. How far can the pilot see?

**73. Blood Flow**   As blood moves through a vein or an artery, its velocity $v$ is greatest along the central axis and decreases as the distance $r$ from the central axis increases (see the figure). The formula that gives $v$ as a function of $r$ is called the **law of laminar flow**. For an artery with radius 0.5 cm, we have

$$v(r) = 18{,}500(0.25 - r^2) \qquad 0 \le r \le 0.5$$

(a) Find $v(0.1)$ and $v(0.4)$.
(b) What do your answers to part (a) tell you about the flow of blood in this artery?
(c) Make a table of values of $v(r)$ for $r = 0, 0.1, 0.2, 0.3, 0.4, 0.5$.

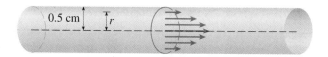

**74. Pupil Size**   When the brightness $x$ of a light source is increased, the eye reacts by decreasing the radius $R$ of the pupil. The dependence of $R$ on $x$ is given by the function

$$R(x) = \sqrt{\frac{13 + 7x^{0.4}}{1 + 4x^{0.4}}}$$

(a) Find $R(1)$, $R(10)$, and $R(100)$.
(b) Make a table of values of $R(x)$.

**75. Relativity**   According to the Theory of Relativity, the length $L$ of an object is a function of its velocity $v$ with respect to an observer. For an object whose length at rest is 10 m, the function is given by

$$L(v) = 10\sqrt{1 - \frac{v^2}{c^2}}$$

where $c$ is the speed of light.
(a) Find $L(0.5c)$, $L(0.75c)$, and $L(0.9c)$.
(b) How does the length of an object change as its velocity increases?

**76. Income Tax**   In a certain country, income tax $T$ is assessed according to the following function of income $x$:

$$T(x) = \begin{cases} 0 & \text{if } 0 \le x \le 10{,}000 \\ 0.08x & \text{if } 10{,}000 < x \le 20{,}000 \\ 1600 + 0.15x & \text{if } 20{,}000 < x \end{cases}$$

(a) Find $T(5{,}000)$, $T(12{,}000)$, and $T(25{,}000)$.
(b) What do your answers in part (a) represent?

**77. Internet Purchases**   An Internet bookstore charges $15 shipping for orders under $100 but provides free shipping for orders of $100 or more. The cost $C$ of an order is a function of the total price $x$ of the books purchased, given by

$$C(x) = \begin{cases} x + 15 & \text{if } x < 100 \\ x & \text{if } x \ge 100 \end{cases}$$

(a) Find $C(75)$, $C(90)$, $C(100)$, and $C(105)$.
(b) What do your answers in part (a) represent?

**78. Cost of a Hotel Stay**   A hotel chain charges $75 each night for the first two nights and $50 for each additional night's stay. The total cost $T$ is a function of the number of nights $x$ that a guest stays.
(a) Complete the expressions in the following piecewise defined function.

$$T(x) = \begin{cases} \rule{1.5cm}{0.3cm} & \text{if } 0 \le x \le 2 \\ \rule{1.5cm}{0.3cm} & \text{if } x > 2 \end{cases}$$

(b) Find $T(2)$, $T(3)$, and $T(5)$.
(c) What do your answers in part (b) represent?

**79. Speeding Tickets**   In a certain state the maximum speed permitted on freeways is 65 mi/h and the minimum is 40. The fine $F$ for violating these limits is $15 for every mile above the maximum or below the minimum.

(a) Complete the expressions in the following piecewise defined function, where $x$ is the speed at which you are driving.

$$F(x) = \begin{cases} \rule{1.5em}{0.6em} & \text{if } 0 < x < 40 \\ \rule{1.5em}{0.6em} & \text{if } 40 \le x \le 65 \\ \rule{1.5em}{0.6em} & \text{if } x > 65 \end{cases}$$

(b) Find $F(30)$, $F(50)$, and $F(75)$.

(c) What do your answers in part (b) represent?

80. **Height of Grass** A home owner mows the lawn every Wednesday afternoon. Sketch a rough graph of the height of the grass as a function of time over the course of a four-week period beginning on a Sunday.

81. **Temperature Change** You place a frozen pie in an oven and bake it for an hour. Then you take it out and let it cool before eating it. Sketch a rough graph of the temperature of the pie as a function of time.

82. **Daily Temperature Change** Temperature readings $T$ (in °F) were recorded every 2 hours from midnight to noon in Atlanta, Georgia, on March 18, 1996. The time $t$ was measured in hours from midnight. Sketch a rough graph of $T$ as a function of $t$.

| $t$ | $T$ |
|-----|-----|
| 0 | 58 |
| 2 | 57 |
| 4 | 53 |
| 6 | 50 |
| 8 | 51 |
| 10 | 57 |
| 12 | 61 |

83. **Population Growth** The population $P$ (in thousands) of San Jose, California, from 1988 to 2000 is shown in the table. (Midyear estimates are given.) Draw a rough graph of $P$ as a function of time $t$.

| $t$ | $P$ |
|------|-----|
| 1988 | 733 |
| 1990 | 782 |
| 1992 | 800 |
| 1994 | 817 |
| 1996 | 838 |
| 1998 | 861 |
| 2000 | 895 |

### ▼ DISCOVERY • DISCUSSION • WRITING

84. **Examples of Functions** At the beginning of this section we discussed three examples of everyday, ordinary functions: Height is a function of age, temperature is a function of date, and postage cost is a function of weight. Give three other examples of functions from everyday life.

85. **Four Ways to Represent a Function** In the box on page 210 we represented four different functions verbally, algebraically, visually, and numerically. Think of a function that can be represented in all four ways, and write the four representations.

---

| 3.2 | Graphs of Functions |
|-----|---------------------|

### LEARNING OBJECTIVES

After completing this section, you will be able to:

■ Graph a function by plotting points
■ Graph a function using a graphing calculator
■ Graph piecewise defined functions
■ Use the Vertical Line Test
■ Determine whether an equation defines a function

The most important way to visualize a function is through its graph. In this section we investigate in more detail the concept of graphing functions.

## ■ Graphing Functions by Plotting Points

To graph a function $f$, we plot the points $(x, f(x))$ in a coordinate plane. In other words, we plot the points $(x, y)$ whose $x$-coordinate is an input and whose $y$-coordinate is the corresponding output of the function.

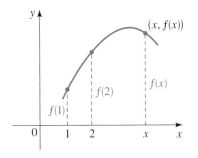

**FIGURE 1** The height of the graph above the point $x$ is the value of $f(x)$.

---

**THE GRAPH OF A FUNCTION**

If $f$ is a function with domain $A$, then the **graph** of $f$ is the set of ordered pairs

$$\{(x, f(x)) \mid x \in A\}$$

In other words, the graph of $f$ is the set of all points $(x, y)$ such that $y = f(x)$; that is, the graph of $f$ is the graph of the equation $y = f(x)$.

---

The graph of a function $f$ gives a picture of the behavior or "life history" of the function. We can read the value of $f(x)$ from the graph as being the height of the graph above the point $x$ (see Figure 1).

A function $f$ of the form $f(x) = mx + b$ is called a **linear function** because its graph is the graph of the equation $y = mx + b$, which represents a line with slope $m$ and $y$-intercept $b$. A special case of a linear function occurs when the slope is $m = 0$. The function $f(x) = b$, where $b$ is a given number, is called a **constant function** because all its values are the same number, namely, $b$. Its graph is the horizontal line $y = b$. Figure 2 shows the graphs of the constant function $f(x) = 3$ and the linear function $f(x) = 2x + 1$.

**FIGURE 2**

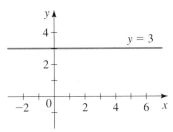

The constant function $f(x) = 3$

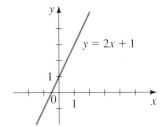

The linear function $f(x) = 2x + 1$

▶ **EXAMPLE 1** | Graphing Functions by Plotting Points

Sketch the graphs of the following functions.

**(a)** $f(x) = x^2$    **(b)** $g(x) = x^3$    **(c)** $h(x) = \sqrt{x}$

▼ **SOLUTION**    We first make a table of values. Then we plot the points given by the table and join them by a smooth curve to obtain the graph. The graphs are sketched in Figure 3 on the next page.

| $x$ | $f(x) = x^2$ |
|---|---|
| 0 | 0 |
| $\pm\frac{1}{2}$ | $\frac{1}{4}$ |
| $\pm 1$ | 1 |
| $\pm 2$ | 4 |
| $\pm 3$ | 9 |

| $x$ | $g(x) = x^3$ |
|---|---|
| 0 | 0 |
| $\frac{1}{2}$ | $\frac{1}{8}$ |
| 1 | 1 |
| 2 | 8 |
| $-\frac{1}{2}$ | $-\frac{1}{8}$ |
| $-1$ | $-1$ |
| $-2$ | $-8$ |

| $x$ | $h(x) = \sqrt{x}$ |
|---|---|
| 0 | 0 |
| 1 | 1 |
| 2 | $\sqrt{2}$ |
| 3 | $\sqrt{3}$ |
| 4 | 2 |
| 5 | $\sqrt{5}$ |

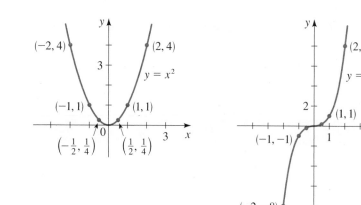
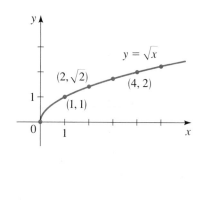

**FIGURE 3**          (a)  $f(x) = x^2$          (b)  $g(x) = x^3$          (c)  $h(x) = \sqrt{x}$

✎ **Practice what you've learned: Do Exercises 11, 15, and 19.**          ▲

## ■ Graphing Functions with a Graphing Calculator

A convenient way to graph a function is to use a graphing calculator. Because the graph of a function $f$ is the graph of the equation $y = f(x)$, we can use the methods of Section 2.3 to graph functions on a graphing calculator.

▶ **EXAMPLE 2** | Graphing a Function with a Graphing Calculator

Use a graphing calculator to graph the function $f(x) = x^3 - 8x^2$ in an appropriate viewing rectangle.

▼ **SOLUTION**     To graph the function $f(x) = x^3 - 8x^2$, we graph the equation $y = x^3 - 8x^2$. On the TI-83 graphing calculator the default viewing rectangle gives the graph in Figure 4(a). But this graph appears to spill over the top and bottom of the screen. We need to expand the vertical axis to get a better representation of the graph. The viewing rectangle $[-4, 10]$ by $[-100, 100]$ gives a more complete picture of the graph, as shown in Figure 4(b).

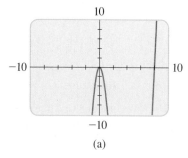
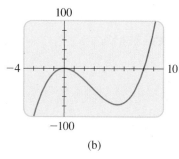

**FIGURE 4** Graphing the function $f(x) = x^3 - 8x^2$

(a)          (b)

✎ **Practice what you've learned: Do Exercise 29.**          ▲

▶ **EXAMPLE 3** | A Family of Power Functions

**(a)** Graph the functions $f(x) = x^n$ for $n = 2$, 4, and 6 in the viewing rectangle $[-2, 2]$ by $[-1, 3]$.

**(b)** Graph the functions $f(x) = x^n$ for $n = 1$, 3, and 5 in the viewing rectangle $[-2, 2]$ by $[-2, 2]$.

**(c)** What conclusions can you draw from these graphs?

▼ **SOLUTION**   To graph the function $f(x) = x^n$, we graph the equation $y = x^n$. The graphs for parts (a) and (b) are shown in Figure 5.

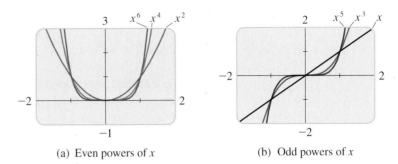

**FIGURE 5**  A family of power functions $f(x) = x^n$

(a) Even powers of $x$                    (b) Odd powers of $x$

**(c)** We see that the general shape of the graph of $f(x) = x^n$ depends on whether $n$ is even or odd.

If $n$ is even, the graph of $f(x) = x^n$ is similar to the parabola $y = x^2$.

If $n$ is odd, the graph of $f(x) = x^n$ is similar to that of $y = x^3$.

✎ **Practice what you've learned: Do Exercise 69.**   ▲

Notice from Figure 5 that as $n$ increases, the graph of $y = x^n$ becomes flatter near 0 and steeper when $x > 1$. When $0 < x < 1$, the lower powers of $x$ are the "bigger" functions. But when $x > 1$, the higher powers of $x$ are the dominant functions.

## ■ Graphing Piecewise Defined Functions

A piecewise defined function is defined by different formulas on different parts of its domain. As you might expect, the graph of such a function consists of separate pieces.

▶  **EXAMPLE 4** | Graph of a Piecewise Defined Function

Sketch the graph of the function.

$$f(x) = \begin{cases} x^2 & \text{if } x \le 1 \\ 2x + 1 & \text{if } x > 1 \end{cases}$$

On many graphing calculators the graph in Figure 6 can be produced by using the logical functions in the calculator. For example, on the TI-83 the following equation gives the required graph:

$Y_1 = (X \le 1)X^2 + (X > 1)(2X + 1)$

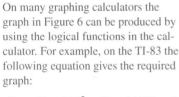

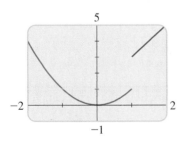

(To avoid the extraneous vertical line between the two parts of the graph, put the calculator in D o t mode.)

▼ **SOLUTION**   If $x \le 1$, then $f(x) = x^2$, so the part of the graph to the left of $x = 1$ coincides with the graph of $y = x^2$, which we sketched in Figure 3. If $x > 1$, then $f(x) = 2x + 1$, so the part of the graph to the right of $x = 1$ coincides with the line $y = 2x + 1$, which we graphed in Figure 2. This enables us to sketch the graph in Figure 6.

The solid dot at $(1, 1)$ indicates that this point is included in the graph; the open dot at $(1, 3)$ indicates that this point is excluded from the graph.

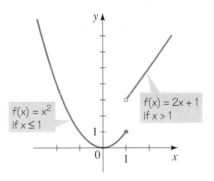

$f(x) = x^2$
if $x \le 1$

$f(x) = 2x + 1$
if $x > 1$

**FIGURE 6**

$$f(x) = \begin{cases} x^2 & \text{if } x \le 1 \\ 2x + 1 & \text{if } x > 1 \end{cases}$$

✎ **Practice what you've learned: Do Exercise 35.**   ▲

▶ **EXAMPLE 5** | Graph of the Absolute Value Function

Sketch the graph of the absolute value function $f(x) = |x|$.

▼ **SOLUTION**    Recall that

$$|x| = \begin{cases} x & \text{if } x \geq 0 \\ -x & \text{if } x < 0 \end{cases}$$

Using the same method as in Example 4, we note that the graph of $f$ coincides with the line $y = x$ to the right of the $y$-axis and coincides with the line $y = -x$ to the left of the $y$-axis (see Figure 7).

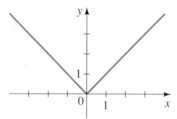

**FIGURE 7** Graph of $f(x) = |x|$

✎ **Practice what you've learned: Do Exercise 23.**                                    ▲

The **greatest integer function** is defined by

$$[\![x]\!] = \text{greatest integer less than or equal to } x$$

For example, $[\![2]\!] = 2$, $[\![2.3]\!] = 2$, $[\![1.999]\!] = 1$, $[\![0.002]\!] = 0$, $[\![-3.5]\!] = -4$, and $[\![-0.5]\!] = -1$.

▶ **EXAMPLE 6** | Graph of the Greatest Integer Function

Sketch the graph of $f(x) = [\![x]\!]$.

▼ **SOLUTION**    The table shows the values of $f$ for some values of $x$. Note that $f(x)$ is constant between consecutive integers, so the graph between integers is a horizontal line segment, as shown in Figure 8.

| $x$ | $[\![x]\!]$ |
|---|---|
| ⋮ | ⋮ |
| $-2 \leq x < -1$ | $-2$ |
| $-1 \leq x < 0$ | $-1$ |
| $0 \leq x < 1$ | $0$ |
| $1 \leq x < 2$ | $1$ |
| $2 \leq x < 3$ | $2$ |
| ⋮ | ⋮ |

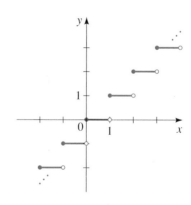

**FIGURE 8**  The greatest integer function, $y = [\![x]\!]$   ▲

The greatest integer function is an example of a **step function**. The next example gives a real-world example of a step function.

▶ **EXAMPLE 7** | The Cost Function for Long-Distance Phone Calls

The cost of a long-distance daytime phone call from Toronto to Mumbai, India, is 69 cents for the first minute and 58 cents for each additional minute (or part of a minute). Draw the graph of the cost $C$ (in dollars) of the phone call as a function of time $t$ (in minutes).

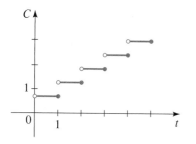

**FIGURE 9** Cost of a long-distance call

▼ **SOLUTION**    Let $C(t)$ be the cost for $t$ minutes. Since $t > 0$, the domain of the function is $(0, \infty)$. From the given information we have

$$
\begin{aligned}
C(t) &= 0.69 & &\text{if } 0 < t \le 1 \\
C(t) &= 0.69 + 0.58 = 1.27 & &\text{if } 1 < t \le 2 \\
C(t) &= 0.69 + 2(0.58) = 1.85 & &\text{if } 2 < t \le 3 \\
C(t) &= 0.69 + 3(0.58) = 2.43 & &\text{if } 3 < t \le 4
\end{aligned}
$$

and so on. The graph is shown in Figure 9.

✎ **Practice what you've learned: Do Exercise 81.**     ▲

## ■ The Vertical Line Test

The graph of a function is a curve in the $xy$-plane. But the question arises: Which curves in the $xy$-plane are graphs of functions? This is answered by the following test.

> **THE VERTICAL LINE TEST**
>
> A curve in the coordinate plane is the graph of a function if and only if no vertical line intersects the curve more than once.

We can see from Figure 10 why the Vertical Line Test is true. If each vertical line $x = a$ intersects a curve only once at $(a, b)$, then exactly one functional value is defined by $f(a) = b$. But if a line $x = a$ intersects the curve twice, at $(a, b)$ and at $(a, c)$, then the curve cannot represent a function because a function cannot assign two different values to $a$.

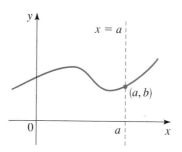
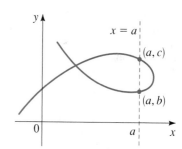

**FIGURE 10** Vertical Line Test

Graph of a function          Not a graph of a function

▶ **EXAMPLE 8** | Using the Vertical Line Test

Using the Vertical Line Test, we see that the curves in parts (b) and (c) of Figure 11 represent functions, whereas those in parts (a) and (d) do not.

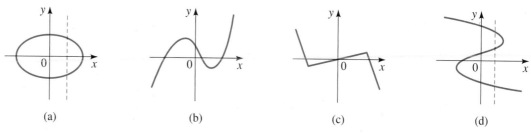

(a)        (b)        (c)        (d)

**FIGURE 11**

✎ **Practice what you've learned: Do Exercise 51.**     ▲

## ■ Equations That Define Functions

Any equation in the variables $x$ and $y$ defines a relationship between these variables. For example, the equation

$$y - x^2 = 0$$

defines a relationship between $y$ and $x$. Does this equation define $y$ as a *function* of $x$? To find out, we solve for $y$ and get

$$y = x^2$$

We see that the equation defines a rule, or function, that gives one value of $y$ for each value of $x$. We can express this rule in function notation as

$$f(x) = x^2$$

But not every equation defines $y$ as a function of $x$, as the following example shows.

▶ **EXAMPLE 9** | Equations That Define Functions

Does the equation define $y$ as a function of $x$?
**(a)** $y - x^2 = 2$          **(b)** $x^2 + y^2 = 4$

▼ **SOLUTION**

**(a)** Solving for $y$ in terms of $x$ gives

$$y - x^2 = 2$$
$$y = x^2 + 2 \qquad \text{Add } x^2$$

The last equation is a rule that gives one value of $y$ for each value of $x$, so it defines $y$ as a function of $x$. We can write the function as $f(x) = x^2 + 2$.

**(b)** We try to solve for $y$ in terms of $x$:

$$x^2 + y^2 = 4$$
$$y^2 = 4 - x^2 \qquad \text{Subtract } x^2$$
$$y = \pm\sqrt{4 - x^2} \qquad \text{Take square roots}$$

The last equation gives two values of $y$ for a given value of $x$. Thus, the equation does not define $y$ as a function of $x$.

✎ **Practice what you've learned: Do Exercises 57 and 61.**          ▲

The graphs of the equations in Example 9 are shown in Figure 12. The Vertical Line Test shows graphically that the equation in Example 9(a) defines a function but the equation in Example 9(b) does not.

Stanford University News Service

**Donald Knuth** was born in Milwaukee in 1938 and is Professor Emeritus of Computer Science at Stanford University. While still a graduate student at Caltech, he started writing a monumental series of books entitled *The Art of Computer Programming*. President Carter awarded him the National Medal of Science in 1979. When Knuth was a high school student, he became fascinated with graphs of functions and laboriously drew many hundreds of them because he wanted to see the behavior of a great variety of functions. (Today, of course, it is far easier to use computers and graphing calculators to do this.) Knuth is famous for his invention of TEX, a system of computer-assisted typesetting. This system was used in the preparation of the manuscript for this textbook.

Dr. Knuth has received numerous honors, among them election as an associate of the French Academy of Sciences, and as a Fellow of the Royal Society.

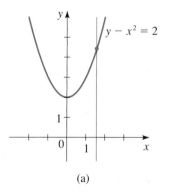

(a)

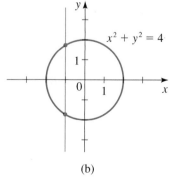

(b)

**FIGURE 12**

**50. Gravity Near the Moon** We can use Newton's Law of Gravitation to measure the gravitational attraction between the moon and an algebra student in a space ship located a distance $x$ above the moon's surface:

$$F(x) = \frac{350}{x^2}$$

Here $F$ is measured in newtons (N), and $x$ is measured in millions of meters.

(a) Graph the function $F$ for values of $x$ between 0 and 10.

(b) Use the graph to describe the behavior of the gravitational attraction $F$ as the distance $x$ increases.

**51. Radii of Stars** Astronomers infer the radii of stars using the Stefan Boltzmann Law:

$$E(T) = (5.67 \times 10^{-8})T^4$$

where $E$ is the energy radiated per unit of surface area measured in watts (W) and $T$ is the absolute temperature measured in kelvins (K).

(a) Graph the function $E$ for temperatures $T$ between 100 K and 300 K.

(b) Use the graph to describe the change in energy $E$ as the temperature $T$ increases.

**52. Migrating Fish** A fish swims at a speed $v$ relative to the water, against a current of 5 mi/h. Using a mathematical model of energy expenditure, it can be shown that the total energy $E$ required to swim a distance of 10 mi is given by

$$E(v) = 2.73v^3 \frac{10}{v - 5}$$

Biologists believe that migrating fish try to minimize the total energy required to swim a fixed distance. Find the value of $v$ that minimizes energy required.

NOTE This result has been verified; migrating fish swim against a current at a speed 50% greater than the speed of the current.

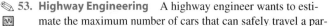

**53. Highway Engineering** A highway engineer wants to estimate the maximum number of cars that can safely travel a particular highway at a given speed. She assumes that each car is 17 ft long, travels at a speed $s$, and follows the car in front of it at the "safe following distance" for that speed. She finds that the number $N$ of cars that can pass a given point per minute is modeled by the function

$$N(s) = \frac{88s}{17 + 17\left(\dfrac{s}{20}\right)^2}$$

At what speed can the greatest number of cars travel the highway safely?

**54. Volume of Water** Between 0°C and 30°C, the volume $V$ (in cubic centimeters) of 1 kg of water at a temperature $T$ is given by the formula

$$V = 999.87 - 0.06426T + 0.0085043T^2 - 0.0000679T^3$$

Find the temperature at which the volume of 1 kg of water is a minimum.

**55. Coughing** When a foreign object that is lodged in the trachea (windpipe) forces a person to cough, the diaphragm thrusts upward, causing an increase in pressure in the lungs. At the same time, the trachea contracts, causing the expelled air to move faster and increasing the pressure on the foreign object. According to a mathematical model of coughing, the velocity $v$ of the airstream through an average-sized person's trachea is related to the radius $r$ of the trachea (in centimeters) by the function

$$v(r) = 3.2(1 - r)r^2 \qquad \tfrac{1}{2} \le r \le 1$$

Determine the value of $r$ for which $v$ is a maximum.

---

## ▼ DISCOVERY • DISCUSSION • WRITING

**56. Functions That Are Always Increasing or Decreasing** Sketch rough graphs of functions that are defined for all real numbers and that exhibit the indicated behavior (or explain why the behavior is impossible).

(a) $f$ is always increasing, and $f(x) > 0$ for all $x$

(b) $f$ is always decreasing, and $f(x) > 0$ for all $x$

(c) $f$ is always increasing, and $f(x) < 0$ for all $x$

(d) $f$ is always decreasing, and $f(x) < 0$ for all $x$

**57. Maxima and Minima** In Example 7 we saw a real-world situation in which the maximum value of a function is important. Name several other everyday situations in which a maximum or minimum value is important.

**58. Minimizing a Distance** When we seek a minimum or maximum value of a function, it is sometimes easier to work with a simpler function instead.

(a) Suppose $g(x) = \sqrt{f(x)}$, where $f(x) \ge 0$ for all $x$. Explain why the local minima and maxima of $f$ and $g$ occur at the same values of $x$.

(b) Let $g(x)$ be the distance between the point $(3, 0)$ and the point $(x, x^2)$ on the graph of the parabola $y = x^2$. Express $g$ as a function of $x$.

(c) Find the minimum value of the function $g$ that you found in part (b). Use the principle described in part (a) to simplify your work.

## 3.4 | Average Rate of Change of a Function

### LEARNING OBJECTIVES

After completing this section, you will be able to:

■ Find the average rate of change of a function
■ Interpret average rate of change in real-world situations
■ Recognize that a function with constant average rate of change is linear

Functions are often used to model changing quantities. In this section we learn how to find the rate at which the values of a function change as the input variable changes.

### ■ Average Rate of Change

We are all familiar with the concept of speed: If you drive a distance of 120 miles in 2 hours, then your average speed, or rate of travel, is $\frac{120 \text{ mi}}{2 \text{ h}} = 60$ mi/h.

Now suppose you take a car trip and record the distance that you travel every few minutes. The distance $s$ you have traveled is a function of the time $t$:

$$s(t) = \text{total distance traveled at time } t$$

We graph the function $s$ as shown in Figure 1. The graph shows that you have traveled a total of 50 miles after 1 hour, 75 miles after 2 hours, 140 miles after 3 hours, and so on. To find your *average* speed between any two points on the trip, we divide the distance traveled by the time elapsed.

Let's calculate your average speed between 1:00 P.M. and 4:00 P.M. The time elapsed is $4 - 1 = 3$ hours. To find the distance you traveled, we subtract the distance at 1:00 P.M. from the distance at 4:00 P.M., that is, $200 - 50 = 150$ mi. Thus, your average speed is

$$\text{average speed} = \frac{\text{distance traveled}}{\text{time elapsed}} = \frac{150 \text{ mi}}{3 \text{ h}} = 50 \text{ mi/h}$$

The average speed that we have just calculated can be expressed by using function notation:

$$\text{average speed} = \frac{s(4) - s(1)}{4 - 1} = \frac{200 - 50}{3} = 50 \text{ mi/h}$$

Note that the average speed is different over different time intervals. For example, between 2:00 P.M. and 3:00 P.M. we find that

$$\text{average speed} = \frac{s(3) - s(2)}{3 - 2} = \frac{140 - 75}{1} = 65 \text{ mi/h}$$

Finding average rates of change is important in many contexts. For instance, we might be interested in knowing how quickly the air temperature is dropping as a storm approaches or how fast revenues are increasing from the sale of a new product. So we need to know how to determine the average rate of change of the functions that model these quantities. In fact, the concept of average rate of change can be defined for any function.

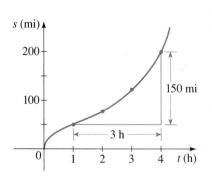

**FIGURE 1** Average speed

**AVERAGE RATE OF CHANGE**

The **average rate of change** of the function $y = f(x)$ between $x = a$ and $x = b$ is

$$\text{average rate of change} = \frac{\text{change in } y}{\text{change in } x} = \frac{f(b) - f(a)}{b - a}$$

The average rate of change is the slope of the **secant line** between $x = a$ and $x = b$ on the graph of $f$, that is, the line that passes through $(a, f(a))$ and $(b, f(b))$.

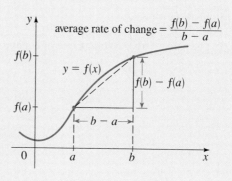

▶ **EXAMPLE 1** | Calculating the Average Rate of Change

For the function $f(x) = (x - 3)^2$, whose graph is shown in Figure 2, find the average rate of change between the following points:

**(a)** $x = 1$ and $x = 3$        **(b)** $x = 4$ and $x = 7$

▼ **SOLUTION**

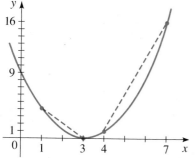

**FIGURE 2** $f(x) = (x - 3)^2$

**(a)** Average rate of change $= \dfrac{f(3) - f(1)}{3 - 1}$     Definition

$= \dfrac{(3 - 3)^2 - (1 - 3)^2}{3 - 1}$     Use $f(x) = (x - 3)^2$

$= \dfrac{0 - 4}{2} = -2$

**(b)** Average rate of change $= \dfrac{f(7) - f(4)}{7 - 4}$     Definition

$= \dfrac{(7 - 3)^2 - (4 - 3)^2}{7 - 4}$     Use $f(x) = (x - 3)^2$

$= \dfrac{16 - 1}{3} = 5$

✎ **Practice what you've learned: Do Exercise 11.**     ▲

▶ **EXAMPLE 2** | Average Speed of a Falling Object

If an object is dropped from a high cliff or a tall building, then the distance it has fallen after $t$ seconds is given by the function $d(t) = 16t^2$. Find its average speed (average rate of change) over the following intervals:

**(a)** Between 1 s and 5 s        **(b)** Between $t = a$ and $t = a + h$

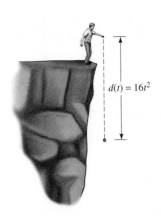

**Function:** In $t$ seconds the stone falls $16t^2$ ft.

$d(t) = 16t^2$

▼ **SOLUTION**

**(a)** Average rate of change $= \dfrac{d(5) - d(1)}{5 - 1}$    Definition

$= \dfrac{16(5)^2 - 16(1)^2}{5 - 1}$    Use $d(t) = 16t^2$

$= \dfrac{400 - 16}{4}$

$= 96$ ft/s

**(b)** Average rate of change $= \dfrac{d(a + h) - d(a)}{(a + h) - a}$    Definition

$= \dfrac{16(a + h)^2 - 16(a)^2}{(a + h) - a}$    Use $d(t) = 16t^2$

$= \dfrac{16(a^2 + 2ah + h^2 - a^2)}{h}$    Expand and factor 16

$= \dfrac{16(2ah + h^2)}{h}$    Simplify numerator

$= \dfrac{16h(2a + h)}{h}$    Factor $h$

$= 16(2a + h)$    Simplify

✎ **Practice what you've learned: Do Exercise 15.**    ▲

The average rate of change calculated in Example 2(b) is known as a *difference quotient*. In calculus we use difference quotients to calculate *instantaneous* rates of change. An example of an instantaneous rate of change is the speed shown on the speedometer of your car. This changes from one instant to the next as your car's speed changes.

The graphs in Figure 3 show that if a function is increasing on an interval, then the average rate of change between any two points is positive, whereas if a function is decreasing on an interval, then the average rate of change between any two points is negative.

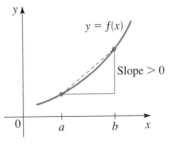

$f$ increasing
Average rate of change positive

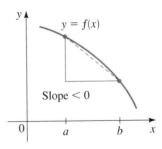

$f$ decreasing
Average rate of change negative

**FIGURE 3**

| Time | Temperature (°F) |
|------|------------------|
| 8:00 A.M. | 38 |
| 9:00 A.M. | 40 |
| 10:00 A.M. | 44 |
| 11:00 A.M. | 50 |
| 12:00 NOON | 56 |
| 1:00 P.M. | 62 |
| 2:00 P.M. | 66 |
| 3:00 P.M. | 67 |
| 4:00 P.M. | 64 |
| 5:00 P.M. | 58 |
| 6:00 P.M. | 55 |
| 7:00 P.M. | 51 |

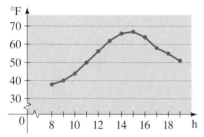

**FIGURE 4**

▶ **EXAMPLE 3** | Average Rate of Temperature Change

The table gives the outdoor temperatures observed by a science student on a spring day. Draw a graph of the data, and find the average rate of change of temperature between the following times:

**(a)** 8:00 A.M. and 9:00 A.M.

**(b)** 1:00 P.M. and 3:00 P.M.

**(c)** 4:00 P.M. and 7:00 P.M.

▼ **SOLUTION**     A graph of the temperature data is shown in Figure 4. Let $t$ represent time, measured in hours since midnight (so, for example, 2:00 P.M. corresponds to $t = 14$). Define the function $F$ by

$$F(t) = \text{temperature at time } t$$

**(a)** Average rate of change $= \dfrac{\text{temperature at 9 A.M.} - \text{temperature at 8 A.M.}}{9 - 8}$

$$= \frac{F(9) - F(8)}{9 - 8} = \frac{40 - 38}{9 - 8} = 2$$

The average rate of change was 2°F per hour.

**(b)** Average rate of change $= \dfrac{\text{temperature at 3 P.M.} - \text{temperature at 1 P.M.}}{15 - 13}$

$$= \frac{F(15) - F(13)}{15 - 13} = \frac{67 - 62}{2} = 2.5$$

The average rate of change was 2.5°F per hour.

**(c)** Average rate of change $= \dfrac{\text{temperature at 7 P.M.} - \text{temperature at 4 P.M.}}{19 - 16}$

$$= \frac{F(19) - F(16)}{19 - 16} = \frac{51 - 64}{3} \approx -4.3$$

The average rate of change was about −4.3°F per hour during this time interval. The negative sign indicates that the temperature was dropping.

✎ **Practice what you've learned: Do Exercise 25.**     ▲

## ■ Linear Functions Have Constant Rate of Change

For a linear function $f(x) = mx + b$ the average rate of change between any two points is the same constant $m$. This agrees with what we learned in Section 2.4: that the slope of a line $y = mx + b$ is the average rate of change of $y$ with respect to $x$. On the other hand, if a function $f$ has constant average rate of change, then it must be a linear function. You are asked to prove this fact in Exercise 34. In the next example we find the average rate of change for a particular linear function.

▶ **EXAMPLE 4** | Linear Functions Have Constant Rate of Change

Let $f(x) = 3x - 5$. Find the average rate of change of $f$ between the following points.

**(a)** $x = 0$ and $x = 1$

**(b)** $x = 3$ and $x = 7$

**(c)** $x = a$ and $x = a + h$

What conclusion can you draw from your answers?

▼ **SOLUTION**

**(a)** Average rate of change $= \dfrac{f(1) - f(0)}{1 - 0} = \dfrac{(3 \cdot 1 - 5) - (3 \cdot 0 - 5)}{1}$

$= \dfrac{(-2) - (-5)}{1} = 3$

**(b)** Average rate of change $= \dfrac{f(7) - f(3)}{7 - 3} = \dfrac{(3 \cdot 7 - 5) - (3 \cdot 3 - 5)}{4}$

$= \dfrac{16 - 4}{4} = 3$

**(c)** Average rate of change $= \dfrac{f(a + h) - f(a)}{(a + h) - a} = \dfrac{[3(a + h) - 5] - [3a - 5]}{h}$

$= \dfrac{3a + 3h - 5 - 3a + 5}{h} = \dfrac{3h}{h} = 3$

It appears that the average rate of change is always 3 for this function. In fact, part (c) proves that the rate of change between any two arbitrary points $x = a$ and $x = a + h$ is 3.

✎ **Practice what you've learned: Do Exercise 21.**                                     ▲

# 3.4 EXERCISES

▼ **CONCEPTS**

**1.** If you travel 100 miles in two hours, then your average speed for the trip is

$$\text{average speed} = \dfrac{\phantom{xxx}}{\phantom{xxx}} = \underline{\hspace{2cm}}$$

**2.** The average rate of change of a function $f$ between $x = a$ and $x = b$ is

$$\text{average rate of change} = \dfrac{\phantom{xxx}}{\phantom{xxx}}$$

**3.** The average rate of change of the function $f(x) = x^2$ between $x = 1$ and $x = 5$ is

$$\text{average rate of change} = \dfrac{\phantom{xxx}}{\phantom{xxx}} = \underline{\hspace{2cm}}$$

**4.** **(a)** The average rate of change of a function $f$ between $x = a$ and $x = b$ is the slope of the _____ line between $(a, f(a))$ and $(b, f(b))$.

**(b)** The average rate of change of the linear function $f(x) = 3x + 5$ between any two points is _____.

▼ **SKILLS**

**5–8** ▪ The graph of a function is given. Determine the average rate of change of the function between the indicated points on the graph.

**5.**

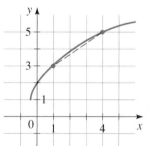

**6.**

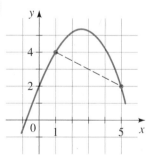

**7.**

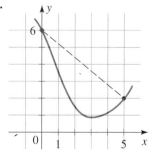

**8.**

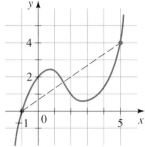

**9–20** ■ A function is given. Determine the average rate of change of the function between the given values of the variable.

**9.** $f(x) = 3x - 2$;  $x = 2, x = 3$

**10.** $g(x) = 5 + \frac{1}{2}x$;  $x = 1, x = 5$

**11.** $h(t) = t^2 + 2t$;  $t = -1, t = 4$

**12.** $f(z) = 1 - 3z^2$;  $z = -2, z = 0$

**13.** $f(x) = x^3 - 4x^2$;  $x = 0, x = 10$

**14.** $f(x) = x + x^4$;  $x = -1, x = 3$

**15.** $f(x) = 3x^2$;  $x = 2, x = 2 + h$

**16.** $f(x) = 4 - x^2$;  $x = 1, x = 1 + h$

**17.** $g(x) = \dfrac{1}{x}$;  $x = 1, x = a$

**18.** $g(x) = \dfrac{2}{x + 1}$;  $x = 0, x = h$

**19.** $f(t) = \dfrac{2}{t}$;  $t = a, t = a + h$

**20.** $f(t) = \sqrt{t}$;  $t = a, t = a + h$

**21–22** ■ A linear function is given. **(a)** Find the average rate of change of the function between $x = a$ and $x = a + h$. **(b)** Show that the average rate of change is the same as the slope of the line.

**21.** $f(x) = \frac{1}{2}x + 3$         **22.** $g(x) = -4x + 2$

---

## ▼ APPLICATIONS

**23. Changing Water Levels**   The graph shows the depth of water $W$ in a reservoir over a one-year period as a function of the number of days $x$ since the beginning of the year. What was the average rate of change of $W$ between $x = 100$ and $x = 200$?

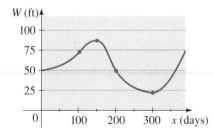

**24. Population Growth and Decline**   The graph shows the population $P$ in a small industrial city from 1950 to 2000. The variable $x$ represents the number of years since 1950.

**(a)** What was the average rate of change of $P$ between $x = 20$ and $x = 40$?

**(b)** Interpret the value of the average rate of change that you found in part (a).

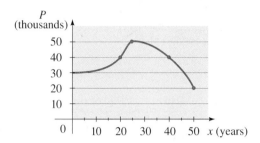

**25. Population Growth and Decline**   The table gives the population in a small coastal community for the period 1997–2006. Figures shown are for January 1 in each year.

**(a)** What was the average rate of change of population between 1998 and 2001?

**(b)** What was the average rate of change of population between 2002 and 2004?

**(c)** For what period of time was the population increasing?

**(d)** For what period of time was the population decreasing?

| Year | Population |
|------|------------|
| 1997 | 624 |
| 1998 | 856 |
| 1999 | 1,336 |
| 2000 | 1,578 |
| 2001 | 1,591 |
| 2002 | 1,483 |
| 2003 | 994 |
| 2004 | 826 |
| 2005 | 801 |
| 2006 | 745 |

**26. Running Speed**   A man is running around a circular track that is 200 m in circumference. An observer uses a stopwatch to record the runner's time at the end of each lap, obtaining the data in the following table.

**(a)** What was the man's average speed (rate) between 68 s and 152 s?

**(b)** What was the man's average speed between 263 s and 412 s?

**(c)** Calculate the man's speed for each lap. Is he slowing down, speeding up, or neither?

| Time (s) | Distance (m) |
|----------|--------------|
| 32 | 200 |
| 68 | 400 |
| 108 | 600 |
| 152 | 800 |
| 203 | 1000 |
| 263 | 1200 |
| 335 | 1400 |
| 412 | 1600 |

**27. CD Player Sales** The table shows the number of CD players sold in a small electronics store in the years 1993–2003.
(a) What was the average rate of change of sales between 1993 and 2003?
(b) What was the average rate of change of sales between 1993 and 1994?
(c) What was the average rate of change of sales between 1994 and 1996?
(d) Between which two successive years did CD player sales *increase* most quickly? *Decrease* most quickly?

| Year | CD players sold |
|------|----------------|
| 1993 | 512 |
| 1994 | 520 |
| 1995 | 413 |
| 1996 | 410 |
| 1997 | 468 |
| 1998 | 510 |
| 1999 | 590 |
| 2000 | 607 |
| 2001 | 732 |
| 2002 | 612 |
| 2003 | 584 |

**28. Book Collection** Between 1980 and 2000, a rare book collector purchased books for his collection at the rate of 40 books per year. Use this information to complete the following table. (Note that not every year is given in the table.)

| Year | Number of books |
|------|-----------------|
| 1980 | 420 |
| 1981 | 460 |
| 1982 | |
| 1985 | |
| 1990 | |
| 1992 | |
| 1995 | |
| 1997 | |
| 1998 | |
| 1999 | |
| 2000 | 1220 |

**29. Cooling Soup** When a bowl of hot soup is left in a room, the soup eventually cools down to room temperature. The temperature $T$ of the soup is a function of time $t$. The table below gives the temperature (in °F) of a bowl of soup $t$ minutes after it was set on the table. Find the average rate of change of the temperature of the soup over the first 20 minutes and over the next 20 minutes. Which interval had the higher average rate of change?

| $t$ (min) | $T$ (°F) | $t$ (min) | $T$ (°F) |
|-----------|----------|-----------|----------|
| 0 | 200 | 35 | 94 |
| 5 | 172 | 40 | 89 |
| 10 | 150 | 50 | 81 |
| 15 | 133 | 60 | 77 |
| 20 | 119 | 90 | 72 |
| 25 | 108 | 120 | 70 |
| 30 | 100 | 150 | 70 |

**30. Farms in the United States** The graph gives the number of farms in the United States from 1850 to 2000.
(a) Estimate the average rate of change in the number of farms between (i) 1860 and 1890 and (ii) 1950 and 1970.
(b) In which decade did the number of farms experience the greatest average rate of decline?

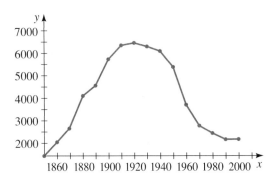

---

▼ **DISCOVERY • DISCUSSION • WRITING**

**31. 100-Meter Race** A 100-m race ends in a three-way tie for first place. The graph shows distance as a function of time for each of the three winners.
(a) Find the average speed for each winner.
(b) Describe the differences between the ways in which the three runners ran the race.

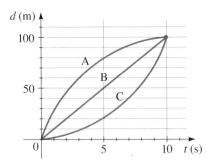

**32. Changing Rates of Change: Concavity** The two tables and graphs on the next page give the distances traveled by a racing car during two different 10-s portions of a race. In each case, calculate the average speed at which the car is traveling between the observed data points. Is the speed increasing or decreasing? In other words, is the car *accelerating* or *decelerating* on each of these intervals? How does the shape of the graph tell you whether the car is accelerating or decelerating? (The first graph is said to be *concave up*, and the second graph is said to be *concave down*.)

**(a)**

| Time (s) | Distance (ft) |
|----------|---------------|
| 0 | 0 |
| 2 | 34 |
| 4 | 70 |
| 6 | 196 |
| 8 | 490 |
| 10 | 964 |

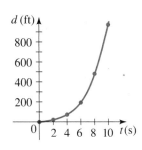

**(b)**

| Time (s) | Distance (ft) |
|----------|---------------|
| 30 | 5208 |
| 32 | 5734 |
| 34 | 6022 |
| 36 | 6204 |
| 38 | 6352 |
| 40 | 6448 |

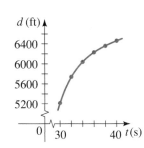

**33. Linear Functions Have Constant Rate of Change**    If $f(x) = mx + b$ is a linear function, then the average rate of change of $f$ between any two real numbers $x_1$ and $x_2$ is

$$\text{average rate of change} = \frac{f(x_2) - f(x_1)}{x_2 - x_1}$$

Calculate this average rate of change to show that it is the same as the slope $m$.

**34. Functions with Constant Rate of Change Are Linear**    If the function $f$ has the same average rate of change $c$ between any two points, then for the points $a$ and $x$ we have

$$c = \frac{f(x) - f(a)}{x - a}$$

Rearrange this expression to show that

$$f(x) = cx + (f(a) - ca)$$

and conclude that $f$ is a linear function.

---

**3.5** | Transformations of Functions

**LEARNING OBJECTIVES**

After completing this section, you will be able to:

- Shift graphs vertically
- Shift graphs horizontally
- Stretch or shrink graphs vertically
- Stretch or shrink graphs horizontally
- Determine whether a function is odd or even

In this section we study how certain transformations of a function affect its graph. This will give us a better understanding of how to graph functions. The transformations that we study are shifting, reflecting, and stretching.

■ **Vertical Shifting**

Adding a constant to a function shifts its graph vertically: upward if the constant is positive and downward if it is negative.

In general, suppose we know the graph of $y = f(x)$. How do we obtain from it the graphs of

$$y = f(x) + c \qquad \text{and} \qquad y = f(x) - c \qquad (c > 0)$$

Recall that the graph of the function $f$ is the same as the graph of the equation $y = f(x)$.

The $y$-coordinate of each point on the graph of $y = f(x) + c$ is $c$ units above the $y$-coordinate of the corresponding point on the graph of $y = f(x)$. So we obtain the graph of $y = f(x) + c$ simply by shifting the graph of $y = f(x)$ upward $c$ units. Similarly, we obtain the graph of $y = f(x) - c$ by shifting the graph of $y = f(x)$ downward $c$ units.

## VERTICAL SHIFTS OF GRAPHS

Suppose $c > 0$.

To graph $y = f(x) + c$, shift the graph of $y = f(x)$ upward $c$ units.

To graph $y = f(x) - c$, shift the graph of $y = f(x)$ downward $c$ units.

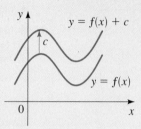 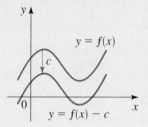

▶ **EXAMPLE 1** | Vertical Shifts of Graphs

Use the graph of $f(x) = x^2$ to sketch the graph of each function.

**(a)** $g(x) = x^2 + 3$          **(b)** $h(x) = x^2 - 2$

▼ **SOLUTION**    The function $f(x) = x^2$ was graphed in Example 1(a), Section 3.2. It is sketched again in Figure 1.

**(a)** Observe that

$$g(x) = x^2 + 3 = f(x) + 3$$

So the $y$-coordinate of each point on the graph of $g$ is 3 units above the corresponding point on the graph of $f$. This means that to graph $g$ we shift the graph of $f$ upward 3 units, as in Figure 1.

**(b)** Similarly, to graph $h$, we shift the graph of $f$ downward 2 units, as shown.

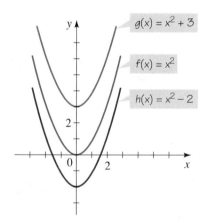

**FIGURE 1**

✎ **Practice what you've learned: Do Exercises 11 and 13.**                    ▲

## ■ Horizontal Shifting

Suppose that we know the graph of $y = f(x)$. How do we use it to obtain the graphs of

$$y = f(x + c) \qquad \text{and} \qquad y = f(x - c) \qquad (c > 0)$$

The value of $f(x - c)$ at $x$ is the same as the value of $f(x)$ at $x - c$. Since $x - c$ is $c$ units to the left of $x$, it follows that the graph of $y = f(x - c)$ is just the graph of $y = f(x)$

shifted to the right $c$ units. Similar reasoning shows that the graph of $y = f(x + c)$ is the graph of $y = f(x)$ shifted to the left $c$ units. The following box summarizes these facts.

---

**HORIZONTAL SHIFTS OF GRAPHS**

Suppose $c > 0$.

To graph $y = f(x - c)$, shift the graph of $y = f(x)$ to the right $c$ units.

To graph $y = f(x + c)$, shift the graph of $y = f(x)$ to the left $c$ units.

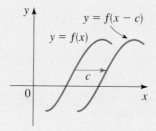 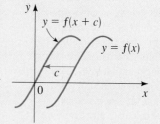

---

▶ **EXAMPLE 2** | Horizontal Shifts of Graphs

Use the graph of $f(x) = x^2$ to sketch the graph of each function.

**(a)** $g(x) = (x + 4)^2$    **(b)** $h(x) = (x - 2)^2$

▼ **SOLUTION**

**(a)** To graph $g$, we shift the graph of $f$ to the left 4 units.

**(b)** To graph $h$, we shift the graph of $f$ to the right 2 units.

The graphs of $g$ and $h$ are sketched in Figure 2.

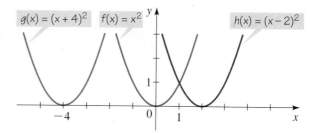

**FIGURE 2**

✐ **Practice what you've learned: Do Exercises 15 and 17.**                                          ▲

---

Library of Congress

**René Descartes** (1596–1650) was born in the town of La Haye in southern France. From an early age Descartes liked mathematics because of "the certainty of its results and the clarity of its reasoning." He believed that to arrive at truth, one must begin by doubting everything, including one's own existence; this led him to formulate perhaps the best-known sentence in all of philosophy: "I think, therefore I am." In his book *Discourse on Method* he described what is now called the Cartesian plane. This idea of combining algebra and geometry enabled mathematicians for the first time to "see" the equations they were studying. The philosopher John Stuart Mill called this invention "the greatest single step ever made in the progress of the exact sciences." Descartes liked to get up late and spend the morning in bed thinking and writing. He invented the coordinate plane while lying in bed watching a fly crawl on the ceiling, reasoning that he could describe the exact location of the fly by knowing its distance from two perpendicular walls. In 1649 Descartes became the tutor of Queen Christina of Sweden. She liked her lessons at 5 o'clock in the morning, when, she said, her mind was sharpest. However, the change from his usual habits and the ice-cold library where they studied proved too much for Descartes. In February 1650, after just two months of this, he caught pneumonia and died.

**MATHEMATICS IN THE MODERN WORLD**

**Computers**

For centuries machines have been designed to perform specific tasks. For example, a washing machine washes clothes, a weaving machine weaves cloth, an adding machine adds numbers, and so on. The computer has changed all that.

The computer is a machine that does nothing—until it is given instructions on what to do. So your computer can play games, draw pictures, or calculate $\pi$ to a million decimal places; it all depends on what program (or instructions) you give the computer. The computer can do all this because it is able to accept instructions and logically change those instructions based on incoming data. This versatility makes computers useful in nearly every aspect of human endeavor.

The idea of a computer was described theoretically in the 1940s by the mathematician Allan Turing (see page 160) in what he called a *universal machine.* In 1945 the mathematician John Von Neumann, extending Turing's ideas, built one of the first electronic computers.

Mathematicians continue to develop new theoretical bases for the design of computers. The heart of the computer is the "chip," which is capable of processing logical instructions. To get an idea of the chip's complexity, consider that the Pentium chip has over 3.5 million logic circuits!

▶ **EXAMPLE 3** | Combining Horizontal and Vertical Shifts

Sketch the graph of $f(x) = \sqrt{x - 3} + 4$.

▼ **SOLUTION**    We start with the graph of $y = \sqrt{x}$ (Example 1(c), Section 3.2) and shift it to the right 3 units to obtain the graph of $y = \sqrt{x - 3}$. Then we shift the resulting graph upward 4 units to obtain the graph of $f(x) = \sqrt{x - 3} + 4$ shown in Figure 3.

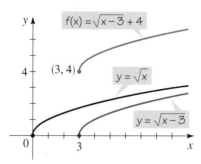

**FIGURE 3**

✎ **Practice what you've learned: Do Exercise 27.**    ▲

## ■ Reflecting Graphs

Suppose we know the graph of $y = f(x)$. How do we use it to obtain the graphs of $y = -f(x)$ and $y = f(-x)$? The $y$-coordinate of each point on the graph of $y = -f(x)$ is simply the negative of the $y$-coordinate of the corresponding point on the graph of $y = f(x)$. So the desired graph is the reflection of the graph of $y = f(x)$ in the $x$-axis. On the other hand, the value of $y = f(-x)$ at $x$ is the same as the value of $y = f(x)$ at $-x$, so the desired graph here is the reflection of the graph of $y = f(x)$ in the $y$-axis. The following box summarizes these observations.

---

**REFLECTING GRAPHS**

To graph $y = -f(x)$, reflect the graph of $y = f(x)$ in the $x$-axis.

To graph $y = f(-x)$, reflect the graph of $y = f(x)$ in the $y$-axis.

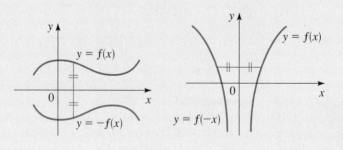

---

▶ **EXAMPLE 4** | Reflecting Graphs

Sketch the graph of each function.

**(a)** $f(x) = -x^2$    **(b)** $g(x) = \sqrt{-x}$

▼ **SOLUTION**

**(a)** We start with the graph of $y = x^2$. The graph of $f(x) = -x^2$ is the graph of $y = x^2$ reflected in the $x$-axis (see Figure 4).

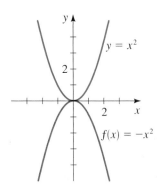

**FIGURE 4**

**(b)** We start with the graph of $y = \sqrt{x}$ (Example 1(c) in Section 3.2). The graph of $g(x) = \sqrt{-x}$ is the graph of $y = \sqrt{x}$ reflected in the $y$-axis (see Figure 5). Note that the domain of the function $g(x) = \sqrt{-x}$ is $\{x \mid x \leq 0\}$.

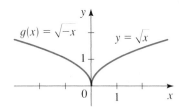

**FIGURE 5**

✎ **Practice what you've learned: Do Exercises 19 and 21.** ▲

## ■ Vertical Stretching and Shrinking

Suppose we know the graph of $y = f(x)$. How do we use it to obtain the graph of $y = cf(x)$? The $y$-coordinate of $y = cf(x)$ at $x$ is the same as the corresponding $y$-coordinate of $y = f(x)$ multiplied by $c$. Multiplying the $y$-coordinates by $c$ has the effect of vertically stretching or shrinking the graph by a factor of $c$.

### VERTICAL STRETCHING AND SHRINKING OF GRAPHS

To graph $y = cf(x)$:

If $c > 1$, stretch the graph of $y = f(x)$ vertically by a factor of $c$.

If $0 < c < 1$, shrink the graph of $y = f(x)$ vertically by a factor of $c$.

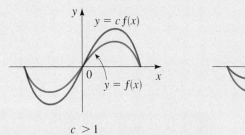 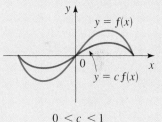

$c > 1$ $\qquad\qquad\qquad\qquad$ $0 < c < 1$

▶ **EXAMPLE 5** | Vertical Stretching and Shrinking of Graphs

Use the graph of $f(x) = x^2$ to sketch the graph of each function.

**(a)** $g(x) = 3x^2$ $\qquad\qquad$ **(b)** $h(x) = \frac{1}{3}x^2$

▼ **SOLUTION**

**(a)** The graph of $g$ is obtained by multiplying the $y$-coordinate of each point on the graph of $f$ by 3. That is, to obtain the graph of $g$, we stretch the graph of $f$ vertically by a factor of 3. The result is the narrower parabola in Figure 6.

**(b)** The graph of $h$ is obtained by multiplying the $y$-coordinate of each point on the graph of $f$ by $\frac{1}{3}$. That is, to obtain the graph of $h$, we shrink the graph of $f$ vertically by a factor of $\frac{1}{3}$. The result is the wider parabola in Figure 6.

✎ **Practice what you've learned: Do Exercises 23 and 25.** ▲

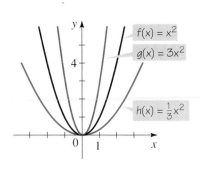

**FIGURE 6**

We illustrate the effect of combining shifts, reflections, and stretching in the following example.

▶ **EXAMPLE 6** | Combining Shifting, Stretching, and Reflecting

Sketch the graph of the function $f(x) = 1 - 2(x - 3)^2$.

▼ **SOLUTION**    Starting with the graph of $y = x^2$, we first shift to the right 3 units to get the graph of $y = (x - 3)^2$. Then we reflect in the $x$-axis and stretch by a factor of 2 to get the graph of $y = -2(x - 3)^2$. Finally, we shift upward 1 unit to get the graph of $f(x) = 1 - 2(x - 3)^2$ shown in Figure 7.

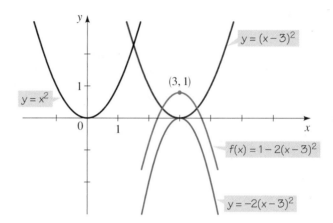

**FIGURE 7**

✎ **Practice what you've learned:** Do Exercise 29.                                  ▲

## ■ Horizontal Stretching and Shrinking

Now we consider horizontal shrinking and stretching of graphs. If we know the graph of $y = f(x)$, then how is the graph of $y = f(cx)$ related to it? The $y$-coordinate of $y = f(cx)$ at $x$ is the same as the $y$-coordinate of $y = f(x)$ at $cx$. Thus, the $x$-coordinates in the graph of $y = f(x)$ correspond to the $x$-coordinates in the graph of $y = f(cx)$ multiplied by $c$. Looking at this the other way around, we see that the $x$-coordinates in the graph of $y = f(cx)$ are the $x$-coordinates in the graph of $y = f(x)$ multiplied by $1/c$. In other words, to change the graph of $y = f(x)$ to the graph of $y = f(cx)$, we must shrink (or stretch) the graph horizontally by a factor of $1/c$, as summarized in the following box.

---

**HORIZONTAL SHRINKING AND STRETCHING OF GRAPHS**

To graph $y = f(cx)$:

  If $c > 1$, shrink the graph of $y = f(x)$ horizontally by a factor of $1/c$.

  If $0 < c < 1$, stretch the graph of $y = f(x)$ horizontally by a factor of $1/c$.

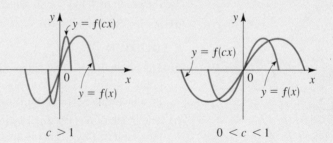

---

▶ **EXAMPLE 7** | Horizontal Stretching and Shrinking of Graphs

The graph of $y = f(x)$ is shown in Figure 8 on the next page. Sketch the graph of each function.

**(a)** $y = f(2x)$          **(b)** $y = f\left(\tfrac{1}{2}x\right)$

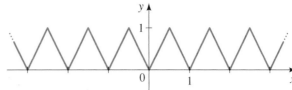

**FIGURE 8**
$y = f(x)$

▼ **SOLUTION**   Using the principles described in the preceding box, we obtain the graphs shown in Figures 9 and 10.

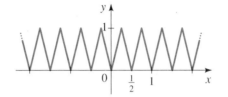

**FIGURE 9**  $y = f(2x)$

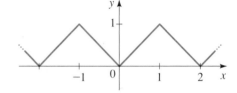

**FIGURE 10**  $y = f\left(\frac{1}{2}x\right)$

✎ **Practice what you've learned: Do Exercise 53.**                                ▲

## ■ Even and Odd Functions

If a function $f$ satisfies $f(-x) = f(x)$ for every number $x$ in its domain, then $f$ is called an **even function**. For instance, the function $f(x) = x^2$ is even because

$$f(-x) = (-x)^2 = (-1)^2 x^2 = x^2 = f(x)$$

The graph of an even function is symmetric with respect to the $y$-axis (see Figure 11). This means that if we have plotted the graph of $f$ for $x \geq 0$, then we can obtain the entire graph simply by reflecting this portion in the $y$-axis.

If $f$ satisfies $f(-x) = -f(x)$ for every number $x$ in its domain, then $f$ is called an **odd function**. For example, the function $f(x) = x^3$ is odd because

$$f(-x) = (-x)^3 = (-1)^3 x^3 = -x^3 = -f(x)$$

The graph of an odd function is symmetric about the origin (see Figure 12). If we have plotted the graph of $f$ for $x \geq 0$, then we can obtain the entire graph by rotating this portion through $180°$ about the origin. (This is equivalent to reflecting first in the $x$-axis and then in the $y$-axis.)

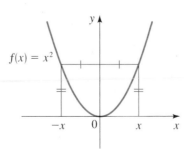

**FIGURE 11**  $f(x) = x^2$ is an even function.

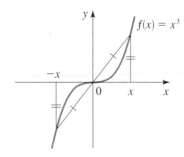

**FIGURE 12**  $f(x) = x^3$ is an odd function.

The Granger Collection, New York

**Sonya Kovalevsky** (1850–1891) is considered the most important woman mathematician of the 19th century. She was born in Moscow to an aristocratic family. While a child, she was exposed to the principles of calculus in a very unusual fashion: Her bedroom was temporarily wallpapered with the pages of a calculus book. She later wrote that she "spent many hours in front of that wall, trying to understand it." Since Russian law forbade women from studying in universities, she entered a marriage of convenience, which allowed her to travel to Germany and obtain a doctorate in mathematics from the University of Göttingen. She eventually was awarded a full professorship at the University of Stockholm, where she taught for eight years before dying in an influenza epidemic at the age of 41. Her research was instrumental in helping to put the ideas and applications of functions and calculus on a sound and logical foundation. She received many accolades and prizes for her research work.

### EVEN AND ODD FUNCTIONS

Let $f$ be a function.

$f$ is **even** if $f(-x) = f(x)$ for all $x$ in the domain of $f$.

$f$ is **odd** if $f(-x) = -f(x)$ for all $x$ in the domain of $f$.

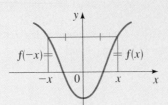

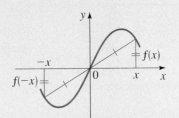

The graph of an even function is symmetric with respect to the $y$-axis.

The graph of an odd function is symmetric with respect to the origin.

▶ **EXAMPLE 8** | Even and Odd Functions

Determine whether the functions are even, odd, or neither even nor odd.

**(a)** $f(x) = x^5 + x$

**(b)** $g(x) = 1 - x^4$

**(c)** $h(x) = 2x - x^2$

▼ **SOLUTION**

**(a)** $f(-x) = (-x)^5 + (-x)$

$\qquad = -x^5 - x = -(x^5 + x)$

$\qquad = -f(x)$

Therefore, $f$ is an odd function.

**(b)** $g(-x) = 1 - (-x)^4 = 1 - x^4 = g(x)$

So $g$ is even.

**(c)** $h(-x) = 2(-x) - (-x)^2 = -2x - x^2$

Since $h(-x) \neq h(x)$ and $h(-x) \neq -h(x)$, we conclude that $h$ is neither even nor odd.

✎ **Practice what you've learned: Do Exercises 65, 67, and 69.**    ▲

The graphs of the functions in Example 8 are shown in Figure 13. The graph of $f$ is symmetric about the origin, and the graph of $g$ is symmetric about the $y$-axis. The graph of $h$ is not symmetric either about the $y$-axis or the origin.

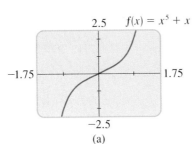

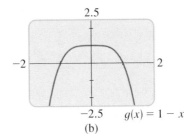

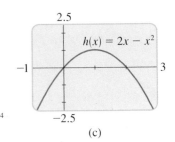

**FIGURE 13**

# 3.5 EXERCISES

## ▼ CONCEPTS

1. Fill in the blank with the appropriate direction (left, right, up, or down).
   (a) The graph of $y = f(x) + 3$ is obtained from the graph of
   $y = f(x)$ by shifting _____ 3 units.
   (b) The graph of $y = f(x + 3)$ is obtained from the graph of
   $y = f(x)$ by shifting _____ 3 units.

2. Fill in the blank with the appropriate direction (left, right, up, or down).
   (a) The graph of $y = f(x) - 3$ is obtained from the graph of
   $y = f(x)$ by shifting _____ 3 units.
   (b) The graph of $y = f(x - 3)$ is obtained from the graph of
   $y = f(x)$ by shifting _____ 3 units.

3. Fill in the blank with the appropriate axis ($x$-axis or $y$-axis).
   (a) The graph of $y = -f(x)$ is obtained from the graph of
   $y = f(x)$ by reflecting in the _____.
   (b) The graph of $y = f(-x)$ is obtained from the graph of
   $y = f(x)$ by reflecting in the _____.

4. Match the graph with the function.
   (a) $y = |x + 1|$      (b) $y = |x - 1|$
   (c) $y = |x| - 1$      (d) $y = -|x|$

I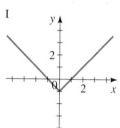

II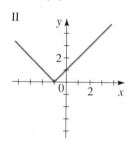

III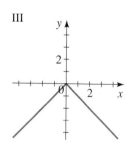

IV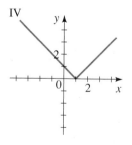

## ▼ SKILLS

5–8 ▪ Explain how the graph of $g$ is obtained from the graph of $f$.

5. (a) $f(x) = x^2$,  $g(x) = (x + 2)^2$
   (b) $f(x) = x^2$,  $g(x) = x^2 + 2$

6. (a) $f(x) = x^3$,  $g(x) = (x - 4)^3$
   (b) $f(x) = x^3$,  $g(x) = x^3 - 4$

7. (a) $f(x) = |x|$,  $g(x) = |x + 2| - 2$
   (b) $f(x) = |x|$,  $g(x) = |x - 2| + 2$

8. (a) $f(x) = \sqrt{x}$,  $g(x) = -\sqrt{x} + 1$
   (b) $f(x) = \sqrt{x}$,  $g(x) = \sqrt{-x} + 1$

9. Use the graph of $f(x) = x^2$ in Example 3 to graph the following.
   (a) $g(x) = x^2 + 1$
   (b) $g(x) = (x - 1)^2$
   (c) $g(x) = -x^2$
   (d) $g(x) = (x - 1)^2 + 3$

10. Use the graph of $f(x) = \sqrt{x}$ in Example 4 to graph the following.
    (a) $g(x) = \sqrt{x - 2}$
    (b) $g(x) = \sqrt{x} + 1$
    (c) $g(x) = \sqrt{x + 2} + 2$
    (d) $g(x) = -\sqrt{x} + 1$

11–34 ▪ Sketch the graph of the function, not by plotting points, but by starting with the graph of a standard function and applying transformations.

11. $f(x) = x^2 - 1$ 　　　　 12. $f(x) = x^2 + 5$

13. $f(x) = \sqrt{x} + 1$ 　　　 14. $f(x) = |x| - 1$

15. $f(x) = (x - 5)^2$ 　　　 16. $f(x) = (x + 1)^2$

17. $f(x) = \sqrt{x + 4}$ 　　　 18. $f(x) = |x - 3|$

19. $f(x) = -x^3$ 　　　　　 20. $f(x) = -|x|$

21. $y = \sqrt[4]{-x}$ 　　　　　 22. $y = \sqrt[3]{-x}$

23. $y = \frac{1}{4}x^2$ 　　　　　 24. $y = -5\sqrt{x}$

25. $y = 3|x|$ 　　　　　　 26. $y = \frac{1}{2}|x|$

27. $y = (x - 3)^2 + 5$ 　　 28. $y = \sqrt{x + 4} - 3$

29. $y = 3 - \frac{1}{2}(x - 1)^2$ 　 30. $y = 2 - \sqrt{x + 1}$

31. $y = |x + 2| + 2$ 　　　 32. $y = 2 - |x|$

33. $y = \frac{1}{2}\sqrt{x + 4} - 3$ 　 34. $y = 3 - 2(x - 1)^2$

35–44 ▪ A function $f$ is given, and the indicated transformations are applied to its graph (in the given order). Write the equation for the final transformed graph.

35. $f(x) = x^2$; shift upward 3 units

36. $f(x) = x^3$; shift downward 1 unit

37. $f(x) = \sqrt{x}$; shift 2 units to the left

38. $f(x) = \sqrt[3]{x}$; shift 1 unit to the right

39. $f(x) = |x|$; shift 3 units to the right and shift upward 1 unit

40. $f(x) = |x|$; shift 4 units to the left and shift downward 2 units

41. $f(x) = \sqrt[4]{x}$; reflect in the $y$-axis and shift upward 1 unit

42. $f(x) = x^2$; shift 2 units to the left and reflect in the $x$-axis

43. $f(x) = x^2$; stretch vertically by a factor of 2, shift downward 2 units, and shift 3 units to the right

44. $f(x) = |x|$; shrink vertically by a factor of $\frac{1}{2}$, shift to the left 1 unit, and shift upward 3 units

**45–50** ■ The graphs of $f$ and $g$ are given. Find a formula for the function $g$.

**45.**

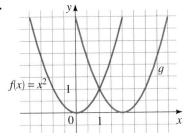

$f(x) = x^2$

**46.**

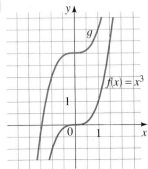

$f(x) = x^3$

**47.**

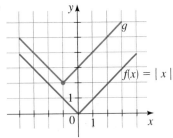

$f(x) = |x|$

**48.**

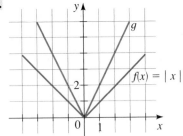

$f(x) = |x|$

**49.**

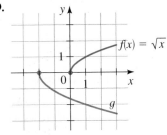

$f(x) = \sqrt{x}$

**50.**

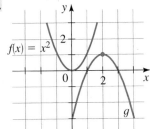

$f(x) = x^2$

**51–52** ■ The graph of $y = f(x)$ is given. Match each equation with its graph.

**51. (a)** $y = f(x - 4)$      **(b)** $y = f(x) + 3$
    **(c)** $y = 2f(x + 6)$      **(d)** $y = -f(2x)$

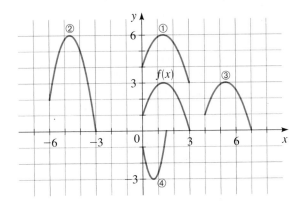

**52. (a)** $y = \frac{1}{3}f(x)$      **(b)** $y = -f(x + 4)$
    **(c)** $y = f(x - 4) + 3$      **(d)** $y = f(-x)$

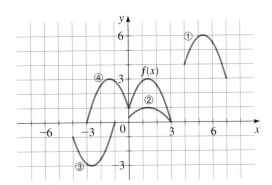

**53.** The graph of $f$ is given. Sketch the graphs of the following functions.
    **(a)** $y = f(x - 2)$      **(b)** $y = f(x) - 2$
    **(c)** $y = 2f(x)$      **(d)** $y = -f(x) + 3$
    **(e)** $y = f(-x)$      **(f)** $y = \frac{1}{2}f(x - 1)$

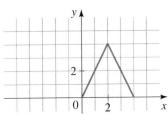

the domain of $f$ is $A$ and the domain of $g$ is $B$, then the domain of $f + g$ is the intersection of these domains, that is, $A \cap B$. Similarly, we can define the **difference** $f - g$, the **product** $fg$, and the **quotient** $f/g$ of the functions $f$ and $g$. Their domains are $A \cap B$, but in the case of the quotient we must remember not to divide by 0.

---

**ALGEBRA OF FUNCTIONS**

Let $f$ and $g$ be functions with domains $A$ and $B$. Then the functions $f + g$, $f - g$, $fg$, and $f/g$ are defined as follows.

$$(f + g)(x) = f(x) + g(x) \qquad \text{Domain } A \cap B$$

$$(f - g)(x) = f(x) - g(x) \qquad \text{Domain } A \cap B$$

$$(fg)(x) = f(x)g(x) \qquad \text{Domain } A \cap B$$

$$\left(\frac{f}{g}\right)(x) = \frac{f(x)}{g(x)} \qquad \text{Domain } \{x \in A \cap B \,|\, g(x) \neq 0\}$$

---

▶ **EXAMPLE 1** | Combinations of Functions and Their Domains

Let $f(x) = \dfrac{1}{x - 2}$ and $g(x) = \sqrt{x}$.

**(a)** Find the functions $f + g$, $f - g$, $fg$, and $f/g$ and their domains.

**(b)** Find $(f + g)(4)$, $(f - g)(4)$, $(fg)(4)$, and $(f/g)(4)$.

▼ **SOLUTION**

**(a)** The domain of $f$ is $\{x \,|\, x \neq 2\}$, and the domain of $g$ is $\{x \,|\, x \geq 0\}$. The intersection of the domains of $f$ and $g$ is

$$\{x \,|\, x \geq 0 \text{ and } x \neq 2\} = [0, 2) \cup (2, \infty)$$

Thus, we have

To divide fractions, invert the denominator and multiply:

$$\frac{1/(x - 2)}{\sqrt{x}} = \frac{1/(x - 2)}{\sqrt{x}/1}$$

$$= \frac{1}{x - 2} \cdot \frac{1}{\sqrt{x}}$$

$$= \frac{1}{(x - 2)\sqrt{x}}$$

$$(f + g)(x) = f(x) + g(x) = \frac{1}{x - 2} + \sqrt{x} \qquad \text{Domain } \{x \,|\, x \geq 0 \text{ and } x \neq 2\}$$

$$(f - g)(x) = f(x) - g(x) = \frac{1}{x - 2} - \sqrt{x} \qquad \text{Domain } \{x \,|\, x \geq 0 \text{ and } x \neq 2\}$$

$$(fg)(x) = f(x)g(x) = \frac{\sqrt{x}}{x - 2} \qquad \text{Domain } \{x \,|\, x \geq 0 \text{ and } x \neq 2\}$$

$$\left(\frac{f}{g}\right)(x) = \frac{f(x)}{g(x)} = \frac{1}{(x - 2)\sqrt{x}} \qquad \text{Domain } \{x \,|\, x > 0 \text{ and } x \neq 2\}$$

Note that in the domain of $f/g$ we exclude 0 because $g(0) = 0$.

**(b)** Each of these values exist because $x = 4$ is in the domain of each function.

$$(f + g)(4) = f(4) + g(4) = \frac{1}{4 - 2} + \sqrt{4} = \frac{5}{2}$$

$$(f - g)(4) = f(4) - g(4) = \frac{1}{4 - 2} - \sqrt{4} = -\frac{3}{2}$$

$$(fg)(4) = f(4)g(4) = \left(\frac{1}{4 - 2}\right)\sqrt{4} = 1$$

$$\left(\frac{f}{g}\right)(4) = \frac{f(4)}{g(4)} = \frac{1}{(4 - 2)\sqrt{4}} = \frac{1}{4}$$

✎ **Practice what you've learned: Do Exercise 5.**  ▲

The graph of the function $f + g$ can be obtained from the graphs of $f$ and $g$ by **graphical addition**. This means that we add corresponding $y$-coordinates, as illustrated in the next example.

▶ **EXAMPLE 2** | Using Graphical Addition

The graphs of $f$ and $g$ are shown in Figure 1. Use graphical addition to graph the function $f + g$.

▼ **SOLUTION**   We obtain the graph of $f + g$ by "graphically adding" the value of $f(x)$ to $g(x)$ as shown in Figure 2. This is implemented by copying the line segment $PQ$ on top of $PR$ to obtain the point $S$ on the graph of $f + g$.

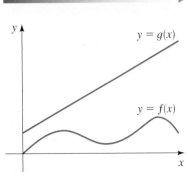

**FIGURE 1**

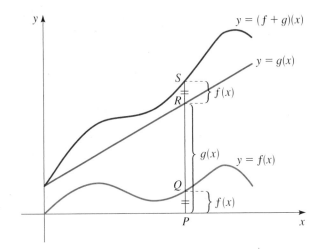

**FIGURE 2**  Graphical addition

✎ **Practice what you've learned: Do Exercise 15.**                         ▲

## ■ Composition of Functions

Now let's consider a very important way of combining two functions to get a new function. Suppose $f(x) = \sqrt{x}$ and $g(x) = x^2 + 1$. We may define a function $h$ as

$$h(x) = f(g(x)) = f(x^2 + 1) = \sqrt{x^2 + 1}$$

The function $h$ is made up of the functions $f$ and $g$ in an interesting way: Given a number $x$, we first apply to it the function $g$, then apply $f$ to the result. In this case, $f$ is the rule "take the square root," $g$ is the rule "square, then add 1," and $h$ is the rule "square, then add 1, then take the square root." In other words, we get the rule $h$ by applying the rule $g$ and then the rule $f$. Figure 3 shows a machine diagram for $h$.

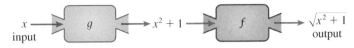

**FIGURE 3**  The $h$ machine is composed of the $g$ machine (first) and then the $f$ machine.

In general, given any two functions $f$ and $g$, we start with a number $x$ in the domain of $g$ and find its image $g(x)$. If this number $g(x)$ is in the domain of $f$, we can then calculate the value of $f(g(x))$. The result is a new function $h(x) = f(g(x))$ that is obtained by substituting $g$ into $f$. It is called the *composition* (or *composite*) of $f$ and $g$ and is denoted by $f \circ g$ ("$f$ composed with $g$").

**COMPOSITION OF FUNCTIONS**

Given two functions $f$ and $g$, the **composite function** $f \circ g$ (also called the **composition** of $f$ and $g$) is defined by

$$(f \circ g)(x) = f(g(x))$$

The domain of $f \circ g$ is the set of all $x$ in the domain of $g$ such that $g(x)$ is in the domain of $f$. In other words, $(f \circ g)(x)$ is defined whenever both $g(x)$ and $f(g(x))$ are defined. We can picture $f \circ g$ using an arrow diagram (Figure 4).

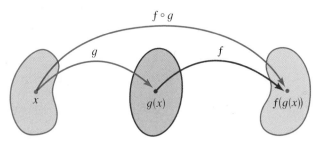

**FIGURE 4** Arrow diagram for $f \circ g$

▶ **EXAMPLE 3** | Finding the Composition of Functions

Let $f(x) = x^2$ and $g(x) = x - 3$.

**(a)** Find the functions $f \circ g$ and $g \circ f$ and their domains.

**(b)** Find $(f \circ g)(5)$ and $(g \circ f)(7)$.

▼ **SOLUTION**

In Example 3, $f$ is the rule "square" and $g$ is the rule "subtract 3." The function $f \circ g$ *first* subtracts 3 and *then* squares; the function $g \circ f$ *first* squares and *then* subtracts 3.

**(a)** We have

$$\begin{aligned}
(f \circ g)(x) &= f(g(x)) && \text{Definition of } f \circ g \\
&= f(x - 3) && \text{Definition of } g \\
&= (x - 3)^2 && \text{Definition of } f
\end{aligned}$$

and

$$\begin{aligned}
(g \circ f)(x) &= g(f(x)) && \text{Definition of } g \circ f \\
&= g(x^2) && \text{Definition of } f \\
&= x^2 - 3 && \text{Definition of } g
\end{aligned}$$

The domains of both $f \circ g$ and $g \circ f$ are $\mathbb{R}$.

**(b)** We have

$$(f \circ g)(5) = f(g(5)) = f(2) = 2^2 = 4$$
$$(g \circ f)(7) = g(f(7)) = g(49) = 49 - 3 = 46$$

✎ **Practice what you've learned: Do Exercises 21 and 35.**    ▲

You can see from Example 3 that, in general, $f \circ g \neq g \circ f$. Remember that the notation $f \circ g$ means that the function $g$ is applied first and then $f$ is applied second.

The graphs of $f$ and $g$ of Example 4, as well as $f \circ g$, $g \circ f$, $f \circ f$, and $g \circ g$, are shown below. These graphs indicate that the operation of composition can produce functions that are quite different from the original functions.

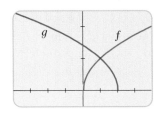

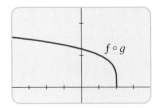

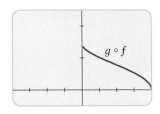

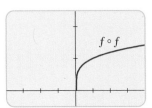

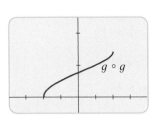

▶ **EXAMPLE 4** | Finding the Composition of Functions

If $f(x) = \sqrt{x}$ and $g(x) = \sqrt{2 - x}$, find the following functions and their domains.

**(a)** $f \circ g$       **(b)** $g \circ f$       **(c)** $f \circ f$       **(d)** $g \circ g$

▼ **SOLUTION**

**(a)**
$$\begin{aligned}
(f \circ g)(x) &= f(g(x)) && \text{Definition of } f \circ g \\
&= f(\sqrt{2 - x}) && \text{Definition of } g \\
&= \sqrt{\sqrt{2 - x}} && \text{Definition of } f \\
&= \sqrt[4]{2 - x}
\end{aligned}$$

The domain of $f \circ g$ is $\{x \mid 2 - x \geq 0\} = \{x \mid x \leq 2\} = (-\infty, 2]$.

**(b)**
$$\begin{aligned}
(g \circ f)(x) &= g(f(x)) && \text{Definition of } g \circ f \\
&= g(\sqrt{x}) && \text{Definition of } f \\
&= \sqrt{2 - \sqrt{x}} && \text{Definition of } g
\end{aligned}$$

For $\sqrt{x}$ to be defined, we must have $x \geq 0$. For $\sqrt{2 - \sqrt{x}}$ to be defined, we must have $2 - \sqrt{x} \geq 0$, that is, $\sqrt{x} \leq 2$, or $x \leq 4$. Thus, we have $0 \leq x \leq 4$, so the domain of $g \circ f$ is the closed interval $[0, 4]$.

**(c)**
$$\begin{aligned}
(f \circ f)(x) &= f(f(x)) && \text{Definition of } f \circ f \\
&= f(\sqrt{x}) && \text{Definition of } f \\
&= \sqrt{\sqrt{x}} && \text{Definition of } f \\
&= \sqrt[4]{x}
\end{aligned}$$

The domain of $f \circ f$ is $[0, \infty)$.

**(d)**
$$\begin{aligned}
(g \circ g)(x) &= g(g(x)) && \text{Definition of } g \circ g \\
&= g(\sqrt{2 - x}) && \text{Definition of } g \\
&= \sqrt{2 - \sqrt{2 - x}} && \text{Definition of } g
\end{aligned}$$

This expression is defined when both $2 - x \geq 0$ and $2 - \sqrt{2 - x} \geq 0$. The first inequality means $x \leq 2$, and the second is equivalent to $\sqrt{2 - x} \leq 2$, or $2 - x \leq 4$, or $x \geq -2$. Thus, $-2 \leq x \leq 2$, so the domain of $g \circ g$ is $[-2, 2]$.

✎ **Practice what you've learned: Do Exercise 41.**                          ▲

It is possible to take the composition of three or more functions. For instance, the composite function $f \circ g \circ h$ is found by first applying $h$, then $g$, and then $f$ as follows:

$$(f \circ g \circ h)(x) = f(g(h(x)))$$

▶ **EXAMPLE 5** | A Composition of Three Functions

Find $f \circ g \circ h$ if $f(x) = x/(x + 1)$, $g(x) = x^{10}$, and $h(x) = x + 3$.

▼ **SOLUTION**

$$\begin{aligned}
(f \circ g \circ h)(x) &= f(g(h(x))) && \text{Definition of } f \circ g \circ h \\
&= f(g(x + 3)) && \text{Definition of } h \\
&= f((x + 3)^{10}) && \text{Definition of } g \\
&= \frac{(x + 3)^{10}}{(x + 3)^{10} + 1} && \text{Definition of } f
\end{aligned}$$

✎ **Practice what you've learned: Do Exercise 45.**                          ▲

So far, we have used composition to build complicated functions from simpler ones. But in calculus it is useful to be able to "decompose" a complicated function into simpler ones, as shown in the following example.

▶ **EXAMPLE 6** | Recognizing a Composition of Functions

Given $F(x) = \sqrt[4]{x + 9}$, find functions $f$ and $g$ such that $F = f \circ g$.

▼ **SOLUTION**    Since the formula for $F$ says to first add 9 and then take the fourth root, we let

$$g(x) = x + 9 \quad \text{and} \quad f(x) = \sqrt[4]{x}$$

Then

$$
\begin{aligned}
(f \circ g)(x) &= f(g(x)) && \text{Definition of } f \circ g \\
&= f(x + 9) && \text{Definition of } g \\
&= \sqrt[4]{x + 9} && \text{Definition of } f \\
&= F(x)
\end{aligned}
$$

✎ **Practice what you've learned: Do Exercise 49.**    ▲

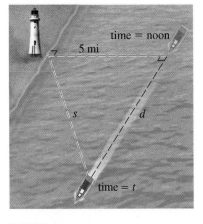

**FIGURE 5**

distance $=$ rate $\times$ time

▶ **EXAMPLE 7** | An Application of Composition of Functions

A ship is traveling at 20 mi/h parallel to a straight shoreline. The ship is 5 mi from shore. It passes a lighthouse at noon.

**(a)** Express the distance $s$ between the lighthouse and the ship as a function of $d$, the distance the ship has traveled since noon; that is, find $f$ so that $s = f(d)$.

**(b)** Express $d$ as a function of $t$, the time elapsed since noon; that is, find $g$ so that $d = g(t)$.

**(c)** Find $f \circ g$. What does this function represent?

▼ **SOLUTION**    We first draw a diagram as in Figure 5.

**(a)** We can relate the distances $s$ and $d$ by the Pythagorean Theorem. Thus, $s$ can be expressed as a function of $d$ by

$$s = f(d) = \sqrt{25 + d^2}$$

**(b)** Since the ship is traveling at 20 mi/h, the distance $d$ it has traveled is a function of $t$ as follows:

$$d = g(t) = 20t$$

**(c)** We have

$$
\begin{aligned}
(f \circ g)(t) &= f(g(t)) && \text{Definition of } f \circ g \\
&= f(20t) && \text{Definition of } g \\
&= \sqrt{25 + (20t)^2} && \text{Definition of } f
\end{aligned}
$$

The function $f \circ g$ gives the distance of the ship from the lighthouse as a function of time.

✎ **Practice what you've learned: Do Exercise 63.**    ▲

# 3.6 EXERCISES

## ▼ CONCEPTS

**1.** From the graphs of $f$ and $g$ in the figure, we find

$(f + g)(2) = $ _____    $(f - g)(2) = $ _____

$(fg)(2) = $ _____    $\left(\dfrac{f}{g}\right)(2) = $ _____

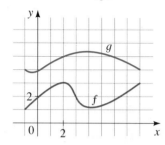

**2.** By definition, $f \circ g(x) = $ _____. So if $g(2) = 5$ and

$f(5) = 12$, then $f \circ g(2)$ _____.

**3.** If the rule of the function $f$ is "add one" and the rule of the function $g$ is "multiply by 2," then the rule of $f \circ g$ is

"_____," and the rule of $g \circ f$ is "_____."

**4.** We can express the functions in Exercise 3 algebraically as

$f(x) = $ _____    $g(x) = $ _____

$f \circ g(x) = $ _____    $g \circ f(x) = $ _____

## ▼ SKILLS

**5–10** ▪ Find $f + g$, $f - g$, $fg$, and $f/g$ and their domains.

**5.** $f(x) = x - 3$,   $g(x) = x^2$

**6.** $f(x) = x^2 + 2x$,   $g(x) = 3x^2 - 1$

**7.** $f(x) = \sqrt{4 - x^2}$,   $g(x) = \sqrt{1 + x}$

**8.** $f(x) = \sqrt{9 - x^2}$,   $g(x) = \sqrt{x^2 - 4}$

**9.** $f(x) = \dfrac{2}{x}$,   $g(x) = \dfrac{4}{x + 4}$

**10.** $f(x) = \dfrac{2}{x + 1}$,   $g(x) = \dfrac{x}{x + 1}$

**11–14** ▪ Find the domain of the function.

**11.** $f(x) = \sqrt{x} + \sqrt{1 - x}$   **12.** $g(x) = \sqrt{x + 1} - \dfrac{1}{x}$

**13.** $h(x) = (x - 3)^{-1/4}$   **14.** $k(x) = \dfrac{\sqrt{x + 3}}{x - 1}$

**15–16** ▪ Use graphical addition to sketch the graph of $f + g$.

**15.**

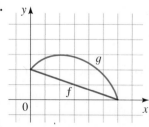

**16.**

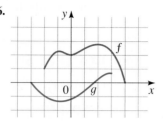

**17–20** ▪ Draw the graphs of $f$, $g$, and $f + g$ on a common screen to illustrate graphical addition.

**17.** $f(x) = \sqrt{1 + x}$,   $g(x) = \sqrt{1 - x}$

**18.** $f(x) = x^2$,   $g(x) = \sqrt{x}$

**19.** $f(x) = x^2$,   $g(x) = \frac{1}{3}x^3$

**20.** $f(x) = \sqrt[4]{1 - x}$,   $g(x) = \sqrt{1 - \dfrac{x^2}{9}}$

**21–26** ▪ Use $f(x) = 3x - 5$ and $g(x) = 2 - x^2$ to evaluate the expression.

**21. (a)** $f(g(0))$    **(b)** $g(f(0))$

**22. (a)** $f(f(4))$    **(b)** $g(g(3))$

**23. (a)** $(f \circ g)(-2)$    **(b)** $(g \circ f)(-2)$

**24. (a)** $(f \circ f)(-1)$    **(b)** $(g \circ g)(2)$

**25. (a)** $(f \circ g)(x)$    **(b)** $(g \circ f)(x)$

**26. (a)** $(f \circ f)(x)$    **(b)** $(g \circ g)(x)$

**27–32** ▪ Use the given graphs of $f$ and $g$ to evaluate the expression.

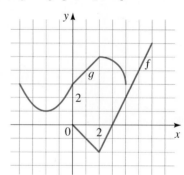

**27.** $f(g(2))$

**28.** $g(f(0))$

**29.** $(g \circ f)(4)$

**30.** $(f \circ g)(0)$

**31.** $(g \circ g)(-2)$

**32.** $(f \circ f)(4)$

**33–44** ▪ Find the functions $f \circ g$, $g \circ f$, $f \circ f$, and $g \circ g$ and their domains.

**33.** $f(x) = 2x + 3$,   $g(x) = 4x - 1$

**34.** $f(x) = 6x - 5$,   $g(x) = \dfrac{x}{2}$

**35.** $f(x) = x^2$, $g(x) = x + 1$

**36.** $f(x) = x^3 + 2$, $g(x) = \sqrt[3]{x}$

**37.** $f(x) = \dfrac{1}{x}$, $g(x) = 2x + 4$

**38.** $f(x) = x^2$, $g(x) = \sqrt{x - 3}$

**39.** $f(x) = |x|$, $g(x) = 2x + 3$

**40.** $f(x) = x - 4$, $g(x) = |x + 4|$

**41.** $f(x) = \dfrac{x}{x + 1}$, $g(x) = 2x - 1$

**42.** $f(x) = \dfrac{1}{\sqrt{x}}$, $g(x) = x^2 - 4x$

**43.** $f(x) = \sqrt[3]{x}$, $g(x) = \sqrt[4]{x}$

**44.** $f(x) = \dfrac{2}{x}$, $g(x) = \dfrac{x}{x + 2}$

**45–48** ▪ Find $f \circ g \circ h$.

**45.** $f(x) = x - 1$, $g(x) = \sqrt{x}$, $h(x) = x - 1$

**46.** $f(x) = \dfrac{1}{x}$, $g(x) = x^3$, $h(x) = x^2 + 2$

**47.** $f(x) = x^4 + 1$, $g(x) = x - 5$, $h(x) = \sqrt{x}$

**48.** $f(x) = \sqrt{x}$, $g(x) = \dfrac{x}{x - 1}$, $h(x) = \sqrt[3]{x}$

**49–54** ▪ Express the function in the form $f \circ g$.

**49.** $F(x) = (x - 9)^5$

**50.** $F(x) = \sqrt{x} + 1$

**51.** $G(x) = \dfrac{x^2}{x^2 + 4}$

**52.** $G(x) = \dfrac{1}{x + 3}$

**53.** $H(x) = |1 - x^3|$

**54.** $H(x) = \sqrt{1 + \sqrt{x}}$

**55–58** ▪ Express the function in the form $f \circ g \circ h$.

**55.** $F(x) = \dfrac{1}{x^2 + 1}$

**56.** $F(x) = \sqrt[3]{\sqrt{x} - 1}$

**57.** $G(x) = (4 + \sqrt[3]{x})^9$

**58.** $G(x) = \dfrac{2}{(3 + \sqrt{x})^2}$

---

### ▼ APPLICATIONS

**59–60** ▪ **Revenue, Cost, and Profit**    A print shop makes bumper stickers for election campaigns. If $x$ stickers are ordered (where $x < 10{,}000$), then the price per sticker is $0.15 - 0.000002x$ dollars, and the total cost of producing the order is $0.095x - 0.0000005x^2$ dollars.

**59.** Use the fact that

$$\boxed{\text{revenue} \;=\; \text{price per item} \;\times\; \text{number of items sold}}$$

to express $R(x)$, the revenue from an order of $x$ stickers, as a product of two functions of $x$.

**60.** Use the fact that

$$\boxed{\text{profit} \;=\; \text{revenue} \;-\; \text{cost}}$$

to express $P(x)$, the profit on an order of $x$ stickers, as a difference of two functions of $x$.

**61.** **Area of a Ripple**    A stone is dropped in a lake, creating a circular ripple that travels outward at a speed of 60 cm/s.
(a) Find a function $g$ that models the radius as a function of time.
(b) Find a function $f$ that models the area of the circle as a function of the radius.
(c) Find $f \circ g$. What does this function represent?

**62.** **Inflating a Balloon**    A spherical balloon is being inflated. The radius of the balloon is increasing at the rate of 1 cm/s.
(a) Find a function $f$ that models the radius as a function of time.
(b) Find a function $g$ that models the volume as a function of the radius.
(c) Find $g \circ f$. What does this function represent?

**63.** **Area of a Balloon**    A spherical weather balloon is being inflated. The radius of the balloon is increasing at the rate of 2 cm/s. Express the surface area of the balloon as a function of time $t$ (in seconds).

**64. Multiple Discounts** You have a $50 coupon from the manufacturer good for the purchase of a cell phone. The store where you are purchasing your cell phone is offering a 20% discount on all cell phones. Let $x$ represent the regular price of the cell phone.

(a) Suppose only the 20% discount applies. Find a function $f$ that models the purchase price of the cell phone as a function of the regular price $x$.

(b) Suppose only the $50 coupon applies. Find a function $g$ that models the purchase price of the cell phone as a function of the sticker price $x$.

(c) If you can use the coupon and the discount, then the purchase price is either $f \circ g(x)$ or $g \circ f(x)$, depending on the order in which they are applied to the price. Find both $f \circ g(x)$ and $g \circ f(x)$. Which composition gives the lower price?

**65. Multiple Discounts** An appliance dealer advertises a 10% discount on all his washing machines. In addition, the manufacturer offers a $100 rebate on the purchase of a washing machine. Let $x$ represent the sticker price of the washing machine.

(a) Suppose only the 10% discount applies. Find a function $f$ that models the purchase price of the washer as a function of the sticker price $x$.

(b) Suppose only the $100 rebate applies. Find a function $g$ that models the purchase price of the washer as a function of the sticker price $x$.

(c) Find $f \circ g$ and $g \circ f$. What do these functions represent? Which is the better deal?

**66. Airplane Trajectory** An airplane is flying at a speed of 350 mi/h at an altitude of one mile. The plane passes directly above a radar station at time $t = 0$.

(a) Express the distance $s$ (in miles) between the plane and the radar station as a function of the horizontal distance $d$ (in miles) that the plane has flown.

(b) Express $d$ as a function of the time $t$ (in hours) that the plane has flown.

(c) Use composition to express $s$ as a function of $t$.

**▼ DISCOVERY • DISCUSSION • WRITING**

**67. Compound Interest** A savings account earns 5% interest compounded annually. If you invest $x$ dollars in such an account, then the amount $A(x)$ of the investment after one year is the initial investment plus 5%; that is, $A(x) = x + 0.05x = 1.05x$. Find

$$A \circ A$$

$$A \circ A \circ A$$

$$A \circ A \circ A \circ A$$

What do these compositions represent? Find a formula for what you get when you compose $n$ copies of $A$.

**68. Composing Linear Functions** The graphs of the functions

$$f(x) = m_1 x + b_1$$

$$g(x) = m_2 x + b_2$$

are lines with slopes $m_1$ and $m_2$, respectively. Is the graph of $f \circ g$ a line? If so, what is its slope?

**69. Solving an Equation for an Unknown Function** Suppose that

$$g(x) = 2x + 1$$

$$h(x) = 4x^2 + 4x + 7$$

Find a function $f$ such that $f \circ g = h$. (Think about what operations you would have to perform on the formula for $g$ to end up with the formula for $h$.) Now suppose that

$$f(x) = 3x + 5$$

$$h(x) = 3x^2 + 3x + 2$$

Use the same sort of reasoning to find a function $g$ such that $f \circ g = h$.

**70. Compositions of Odd and Even Functions** Suppose that

$$h = f \circ g$$

If $g$ is an even function, is $h$ necessarily even? If $g$ is odd, is $h$ odd? What if $g$ is odd and $f$ is odd? What if $g$ is odd and $f$ is even?

# ITERATION AND CHAOS

The **iterates** of a function $f$ at a point $x_0$ are $f(x_0)$, $f(f(x_0))$, $f(f(f(x_0)))$, and so on. We write

$$x_1 = f(x_0) \qquad \text{The first iterate}$$

$$x_2 = f(f(x_0)) \qquad \text{The second iterate}$$

$$x_3 = f(f(f(x_0))) \qquad \text{The third iterate}$$

$$\vdots \quad \vdots \qquad \vdots$$

For example, if $f(x) = x^2$, then the iterates of $f$ at 2 are $x_1 = 4$, $x_2 = 16$, $x_3 = 256$, and so on. (Check this.) Iterates can be described graphically as in Figure 1. Start with $x_0$ on the $x$-axis, move vertically to the graph of $f$, then horizontally to the line $y = x$, then vertically to the graph of $f$, and so on. The $x$-coordinates of the points on the graph of $f$ are the iterates of $f$ at $x_0$.

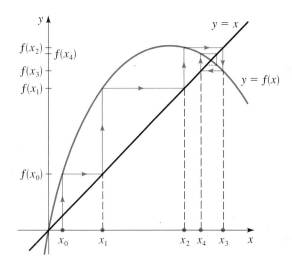

**FIGURE 1**

Iterates are important in studying the **logistic function**

$$f(x) = kx(1 - x)$$

which models the population of a species with limited potential for growth (such as rabbits on an island or fish in a pond). In this model, the maximum population that the environment can support is 1 (that is, 100%). If we start with a fraction of that population, say, 0.1 (10%), then the iterates of $f$ at 0.1 give the population after each time interval (days, months, or years, depending on the species). The constant $k$ depends on the rate of growth of the species being modeled; it is called the **growth constant**. For example, for $k = 2.6$ and $x_0 = 0.1$ the iterates shown in the table to the left give the population of the species for the first 12 time intervals. The population seems to be stabilizing around 0.615 (that is, 61.5% of maximum).

| $n$ | $x_n$ |
|-----|-------|
| 0 | 0.1 |
| 1 | 0.234 |
| 2 | 0.46603 |
| 3 | 0.64700 |
| 4 | 0.59382 |
| 5 | 0.62712 |
| 6 | 0.60799 |
| 7 | 0.61968 |
| 8 | 0.61276 |
| 9 | 0.61694 |
| 10 | 0.61444 |
| 11 | 0.61595 |
| 12 | 0.61505 |

(CONTINUES)

In the three graphs in Figure 2, we plot the iterates of $f$ at 0.1 for different values of the growth constant $k$. For $k = 2.6$ the population appears to stabilize at a value 0.615 of maximum, for $k = 3.1$ the population appears to oscillate between two values, and for $k = 3.8$ no obvious pattern emerges. This latter situation is described mathematically by the word **chaos**.

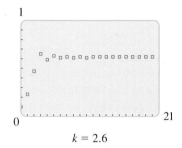

$k = 2.6$

$k = 3.1$

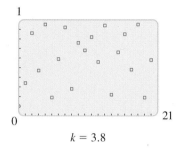

$k = 3.8$

**FIGURE 2**

The following TI-83 program draws the first graph in Figure 2. The other graphs are obtained by choosing the appropriate value for K in the program.

```
PROGRAM:ITERATE
:ClrDraw
:2.6→K
:0.1→X
:For(N,1,20)
:K*X*(1-X)→Z
:Pt-On(N,Z,2)
:Z→X
:End
```

1. Use the graphical procedure illustrated in Figure 1 to find the first five iterates of $f(x) = 2x(1 - x)$ at $x = 0.1$.

2. Find the iterates of $f(x) = x^2$ at $x = 1$.

3. Find the iterates of $f(x) = \dfrac{1}{x}$ at $x = 2$.

4. Find the first six iterates of $f(x) = 1/(1 - x)$ at $x = 2$. What is the 1000th iterate of $f$ at 2?

5. Find the first 10 iterates of the logistic function at $x = 0.1$ for the given value of $k$. Does the population appear to stabilize, oscillate, or is it chaotic?

   (a) $k = 2.1$      (b) $k = 3.2$      (c) $k = 3.9$

6. It's easy to find iterates using a graphing calculator. The following steps show how to find the iterates of $f(x) = kx(1 - x)$ at 0.1 for $k = 3$ on a TI-83 calculator. (The procedure can be adapted for any graphing calculator.)

| | |
|---|---|
| $Y_1 = K * X * (1 - X)$ | Enter $f$ as $Y_1$ on the graph list |
| $3 → K$ | Store 3 in the variable K |
| $0.1 → X$ | Store 0.1 in the variable X |
| $Y_1 → X$ | Evaluate $f$ at X and store result back in X |
| $\quad\quad 0.27$ | Press ENTER and obtain first iterate |
| $\quad\quad 0.5913$ | Keep pressing ENTER to re-execute the |
| $\quad\quad 0.72499293$ | command and obtain successive iterates |
| $\quad\quad 0.59813454435$ | |

You can also use the program in the margin to graph the iterates and study them visually.

Use a graphing calculator to experiment with how the value of $k$ affects the iterates of $f(x) = kx(1 - x)$ at 0.1. Find several different values of $k$ that make the iterates stabilize at one value, oscillate between two values, and exhibit chaos. (Use values of $k$ between 1 and 4.) Can you find a value of $k$ that makes the iterates oscillate between *four* values?

**3.7** | One-to-One Functions and Their Inverses

### LEARNING OBJECTIVES

After completing this section, you will be able to:

- Determine whether a function is one-to-one
- Find the inverse function of a one-to-one function
- Draw the graph of an inverse function

The *inverse* of a function is a rule that acts on the output of the function and produces the corresponding input. So the inverse "undoes" or reverses what the function has done. Not all functions have inverses; those that do are called *one-to-one*.

### ■ One-to-One Functions

Let's compare the functions $f$ and $g$ whose arrow diagrams are shown in Figure 1. Note that $f$ never takes on the same value twice (any two numbers in $A$ have different images), whereas $g$ does take on the same value twice (both 2 and 3 have the same image, 4). In symbols, $g(2) = g(3)$ but $f(x_1) \neq f(x_2)$ whenever $x_1 \neq x_2$. Functions that have this latter property are called *one-to-one*.

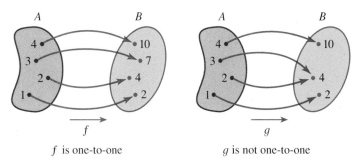

*f* is one-to-one                     *g* is not one-to-one

**FIGURE 1**

---

#### DEFINITION OF A ONE-TO-ONE FUNCTION

A function with domain $A$ is called a **one-to-one function** if no two elements of $A$ have the same image, that is,

$$f(x_1) \neq f(x_2) \quad \text{whenever } x_1 \neq x_2$$

---

An equivalent way of writing the condition for a one-to-one function is this:

$$\text{If } f(x_1) = f(x_2), \text{ then } x_1 = x_2.$$

If a horizontal line intersects the graph of $f$ at more than one point, then we see from Figure 2 that there are numbers $x_1 \neq x_2$ such that $f(x_1) = f(x_2)$. This means that $f$ is not one-to-one. Therefore, we have the following geometric method for determining whether a function is one-to-one.

---

#### HORIZONTAL LINE TEST

A function is one-to-one if and only if no horizontal line intersects its graph more than once.

---

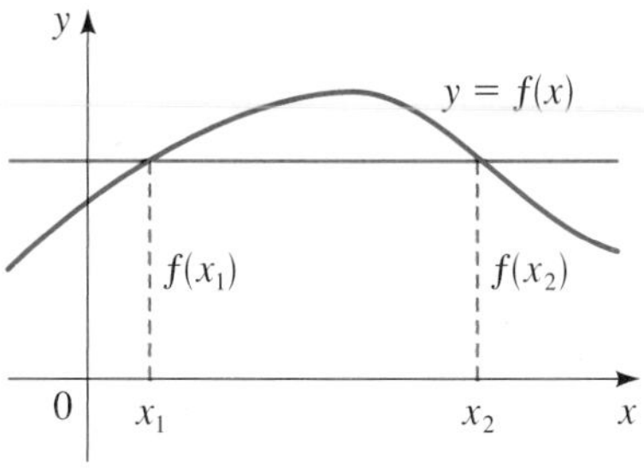

**FIGURE 2** This function is not one-to-one because $f(x_1) = f(x_2)$.

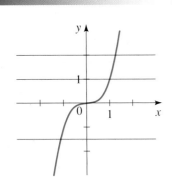

**FIGURE 3** $f(x) = x^3$ is one-to-one.

▶ **EXAMPLE 1** | Deciding Whether a Function Is One-to-One

Is the function $f(x) = x^3$ one-to-one?

▼ **SOLUTION 1**    If $x_1 \neq x_2$, then $x_1^3 \neq x_2^3$ (two different numbers cannot have the same cube). Therefore, $f(x) = x^3$ is one-to-one.

▼ **SOLUTION 2**    From Figure 3 we see that no horizontal line intersects the graph of $f(x) = x^3$ more than once. Therefore, by the Horizontal Line Test, $f$ is one-to-one.

✎ **Practice what you've learned: Do Exercise 13.**    ▲

Notice that the function $f$ of Example 1 is increasing and is also one-to-one. In fact, it can be proved that *every increasing function and every decreasing function is one-to-one*.

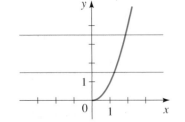

**FIGURE 4** $f(x) = x^2$ is not one-to-one.

▶ **EXAMPLE 2** | Deciding Whether a Function Is One-to-One

Is the function $g(x) = x^2$ one-to-one?

▼ **SOLUTION 1**    This function is not one-to-one because, for instance,

$$g(1) = 1 \qquad \text{and} \qquad g(-1) = 1$$

so 1 and $-1$ have the same image.

▼ **SOLUTION 2**    From Figure 4 we see that there are horizontal lines that intersect the graph of $g$ more than once. Therefore, by the Horizontal Line Test, $g$ is not one-to-one.

✎ **Practice what you've learned: Do Exercise 15.**    ▲

Although the function $g$ in Example 2 is not one-to-one, it is possible to restrict its domain so that the resulting function is one-to-one. In fact, if we define

$$h(x) = x^2 \qquad x \geq 0$$

then $h$ is one-to-one, as you can see from Figure 5 and the Horizontal Line Test.

**FIGURE 5** $f(x) = x^2 \, (x \geq 0)$ is one-to-one.

▶ **EXAMPLE 3** | Showing That a Function Is One-to-One

Show that the function $f(x) = 3x + 4$ is one-to-one.

▼ **SOLUTION**    Suppose there are numbers $x_1$ and $x_2$ such that $f(x_1) = f(x_2)$. Then

$$3x_1 + 4 = 3x_2 + 4 \qquad \text{Suppose } f(x_1) = f(x_2)$$
$$3x_1 = 3x_2 \qquad \text{Subtract 4}$$
$$x_1 = x_2 \qquad \text{Divide by 3}$$

Therefore, $f$ is one-to-one.

✎ **Practice what you've learned: Do Exercise 11.**    ▲

■ **The Inverse of a Function**

One-to-one functions are important because they are precisely the functions that possess inverse functions according to the following definition.

### DEFINITION OF THE INVERSE OF A FUNCTION

Let $f$ be a one-to-one function with domain $A$ and range $B$. Then its **inverse function** $f^{-1}$ has domain $B$ and range $A$ and is defined by

$$f^{-1}(y) = x \iff f(x) = y$$

for any $y$ in $B$.

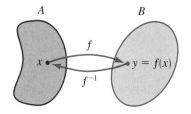

**FIGURE 6**

This definition says that if $f$ takes $x$ to $y$, then $f^{-1}$ takes $y$ back to $x$. (If $f$ were not one-to-one, then $f^{-1}$ would not be defined uniquely.) The arrow diagram in Figure 6 indicates that $f^{-1}$ reverses the effect of $f$. From the definition we have

$$\text{domain of } f^{-1} = \text{range of } f$$
$$\text{range of } f^{-1} = \text{domain of } f$$

⊘ Don't mistake the $-1$ in $f^{-1}$ for an exponent.

$$f^{-1} \quad does\ not\ mean \quad \frac{1}{f(x)}$$

The reciprocal $1/f(x)$ is written as $(f(x))^{-1}$.

▶ **EXAMPLE 4** | Finding $f^{-1}$ for Specific Values

If $f(1) = 5$, $f(3) = 7$, and $f(8) = -10$, find $f^{-1}(5)$, $f^{-1}(7)$, and $f^{-1}(-10)$.

▼ **SOLUTION**   From the definition of $f^{-1}$ we have

$$f^{-1}(5) = 1 \quad \text{because} \quad f(1) = 5$$
$$f^{-1}(7) = 3 \quad \text{because} \quad f(3) = 7$$
$$f^{-1}(-10) = 8 \quad \text{because} \quad f(8) = -10$$

Figure 7 shows how $f^{-1}$ reverses the effect of $f$ in this case.

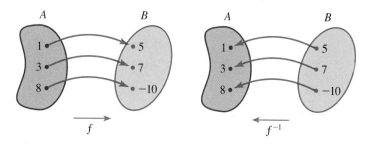

**FIGURE 7**

✎ **Practice what you've learned: Do Exercise 21.**   ▲

By definition the inverse function $f^{-1}$ undoes what $f$ does: If we start with $x$, apply $f$, and then apply $f^{-1}$, we arrive back at $x$, where we started. Similarly, $f$ undoes what $f^{-1}$ does. In general, any function that reverses the effect of $f$ in this way must be the inverse of $f$. These observations are expressed precisely as follows.

### INVERSE FUNCTION PROPERTY

Let $f$ be a one-to-one function with domain $A$ and range $B$. The inverse function $f^{-1}$ satisfies the following cancellation properties.

$$f^{-1}(f(x)) = x \quad \text{for every } x \text{ in } A$$
$$f(f^{-1}(x)) = x \quad \text{for every } x \text{ in } B$$

Conversely, any function $f^{-1}$ satisfying these equations is the inverse of $f$.

These properties indicate that $f$ is the inverse function of $f^{-1}$, so we say that $f$ and $f^{-1}$ are *inverses of each other*.

▶ **EXAMPLE 5** | Verifying That Two Functions Are Inverses

Show that $f(x) = x^3$ and $g(x) = x^{1/3}$ are inverses of each other.

▼ **SOLUTION**   Note that the domain and range of both $f$ and $g$ is $\mathbb{R}$. We have

$$g(f(x)) = g(x^3) = (x^3)^{1/3} = x$$
$$f(g(x)) = f(x^{1/3}) = (x^{1/3})^3 = x$$

So by the Property of Inverse Functions, $f$ and $g$ are inverses of each other. These equations simply say that the cube function and the cube root function, when composed, cancel each other.

✎ **Practice what you've learned: Do Exercise 27.**   ▲

Now let's examine how we compute inverse functions. We first observe from the definition of $f^{-1}$ that

$$y = f(x) \quad \Leftrightarrow \quad f^{-1}(y) = x$$

So if $y = f(x)$ and if we are able to solve this equation for $x$ in terms of $y$, then we must have $x = f^{-1}(y)$. If we then interchange $x$ and $y$, we have $y = f^{-1}(x)$, which is the desired equation.

> **HOW TO FIND THE INVERSE OF A ONE-TO-ONE FUNCTION**
>
> **1.** Write $y = f(x)$.
> **2.** Solve this equation for $x$ in terms of $y$ (if possible).
> **3.** Interchange $x$ and $y$. The resulting equation is $y = f^{-1}(x)$.

In Example 6 note how $f^{-1}$ reverses the effect of $f$. The function $f$ is the rule "multiply by 3, then subtract 2," whereas $f^{-1}$ is the rule "add 2, then divide by 3."

Note that Steps 2 and 3 can be reversed. In other words, we can interchange $x$ and $y$ first and then solve for $y$ in terms of $x$.

▶ **EXAMPLE 6** | Finding the Inverse of a Function

Find the inverse of the function $f(x) = 3x - 2$.

▼ **SOLUTION**   First we write $y = f(x)$.

$$y = 3x - 2$$

Then we solve this equation for $x$.

$$3x = y + 2 \qquad \text{Add 2}$$
$$x = \frac{y + 2}{3} \qquad \text{Divide by 3}$$

Finally, we interchange $x$ and $y$.

$$y = \frac{x + 2}{3}$$

Therefore, the inverse function is $f^{-1}(x) = \dfrac{x + 2}{3}$.

**Check Your Answer**

We use the Inverse Function Property.

$$f^{-1}(f(x)) = f^{-1}(3x - 2)$$
$$= \frac{(3x - 2) + 2}{3}$$
$$= \frac{3x}{3} = x$$

$$f(f^{-1}(x)) = f\left(\frac{x + 2}{3}\right)$$
$$= 3\left(\frac{x + 2}{3}\right) - 2$$
$$= x + 2 - 2 = x \quad ✔$$

✎ **Practice what you've learned: Do Exercise 35.**   ▲

In Example 7 note how $f^{-1}$ reverses the effect of $f$. The function $f$ is the rule "Take the fifth power, subtract 3, then divide by 2," whereas $f^{-1}$ is the rule "Multiply by 2, add 3, then take the fifth root."

---

**Check Your Answer**

We use the Inverse Function Property.

$$f^{-1}(f(x)) = f^{-1}\left(\frac{x^5 - 3}{2}\right)$$

$$= \left[2\left(\frac{x^5 - 3}{2}\right) + 3\right]^{1/5}$$

$$= (x^5 - 3 + 3)^{1/5}$$

$$= (x^5)^{1/5} = x$$

$$f(f^{-1}(x)) = f((2x + 3)^{1/5})$$

$$= \frac{[(2x + 3)^{1/5}]^5 - 3}{2}$$

$$= \frac{2x + 3 - 3}{2}$$

$$= \frac{2x}{2} = x \quad ✔$$

---

▶ **EXAMPLE 7** | Finding the Inverse of a Function

Find the inverse of the function $f(x) = \dfrac{x^5 - 3}{2}$.

▼ **SOLUTION**   We first write $y = (x^5 - 3)/2$ and solve for $x$.

$$y = \frac{x^5 - 3}{2} \qquad \text{Equation defining function}$$

$$2y = x^5 - 3 \qquad \text{Multiply by 2}$$

$$x^5 = 2y + 3 \qquad \text{Add 3 (and switch sides)}$$

$$x = (2y + 3)^{1/5} \qquad \text{Take fifth root of each side}$$

Then we interchange $x$ and $y$ to get $y = (2x + 3)^{1/5}$. Therefore, the inverse function is $f^{-1}(x) = (2x + 3)^{1/5}$.

✎ **Practice what you've learned: Do Exercise 47.**    ▲

## ■ Graphing the Inverse of a Function

The principle of interchanging $x$ and $y$ to find the inverse function also gives us a method for obtaining the graph of $f^{-1}$ from the graph of $f$. If $f(a) = b$, then $f^{-1}(b) = a$. Thus, the point $(a, b)$ is on the graph of $f$ if and only if the point $(b, a)$ is on the graph of $f^{-1}$. But we get the point $(b, a)$ from the point $(a, b)$ by reflecting in the line $y = x$ (see Figure 8). Therefore, as Figure 9 illustrates, the following is true.

> The graph of $f^{-1}$ is obtained by reflecting the graph of $f$ in the line $y = x$.

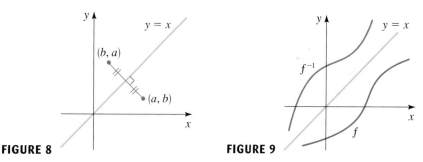

**FIGURE 8**          **FIGURE 9**

▶ **EXAMPLE 8** | Graphing the Inverse of a Function

**(a)** Sketch the graph of $f(x) = \sqrt{x - 2}$.

**(b)** Use the graph of $f$ to sketch the graph of $f^{-1}$.

**(c)** Find an equation for $f^{-1}$.

▼ **SOLUTION**

**(a)** Using the transformations from Section 3.5, we sketch the graph of $y = \sqrt{x - 2}$ by plotting the graph of the function $y = \sqrt{x}$ (Example 1(c) in Section 3.2) and moving it to the right 2 units.

**(b)** The graph of $f^{-1}$ is obtained from the graph of $f$ in part (a) by reflecting it in the line $y = x$, as shown in Figure 10.

**(c)** Solve $y = \sqrt{x - 2}$ for $x$, noting that $y \geq 0$.

$$\sqrt{x - 2} = y$$

$$x - 2 = y^2 \qquad \text{Square each side}$$

$$x = y^2 + 2 \qquad y \geq 0 \quad \text{Add 2}$$

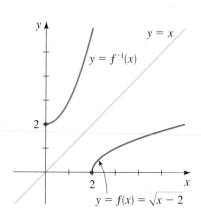

**FIGURE 10**

In Example 8 note how $f^{-1}$ reverses the effect of $f$. The function $f$ is the rule "Subtract 2, then take the square root," whereas $f^{-1}$ is the rule "Square, then add 2."

Interchange $x$ and $y$:

$$y = x^2 + 2 \qquad x \geq 0$$

Thus,

$$f^{-1}(x) = x^2 + 2 \qquad x \geq 0$$

This expression shows that the graph of $f^{-1}$ is the right half of the parabola $y = x^2 + 2$, and from the graph shown in Figure 10, this seems reasonable.

✎ **Practice what you've learned: Do Exercise 57.** ▲

# 3.7 EXERCISES

## ▼ CONCEPTS

1. A function $f$ is one-to-one if different inputs produce _____ outputs. You can tell from the graph that a function is one-to-one by using the _____ Test.

2. (a) For a function to have an inverse, it must be _____. So which one of the following functions has an inverse?

    $$f(x) = x^2 \qquad g(x) = x^3$$

    (b) What is the inverse of the function that you chose in part (a)?

3. A function $f$ has the following verbal description: "Multiply by 3, add 5, and then take the third power of the result."
    (a) Write a verbal description for $f^{-1}$.
    (b) Find algebraic formulas that express $f$ and $f^{-1}$ in terms of the input $x$.

4. *True or false?*

    (a) If $f$ has an inverse, then $f^{-1}(x)$ is the same as $\dfrac{1}{f(x)}$.

    (b) If $f$ has an inverse, then $f^{-1}(f(x)) = x$.

## ▼ SKILLS

**5–10** ▪ The graph of a function $f$ is given. Determine whether $f$ is one-to-one.

5.

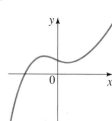

6.

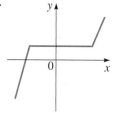

7.

8.

9.

10.

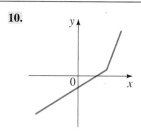

**11–20** ▪ Determine whether the function is one-to-one.

✎ 11. $f(x) = -2x + 4$       12. $f(x) = 3x - 2$

✎ 13. $g(x) = \sqrt{x}$       14. $g(x) = |x|$

✎ 15. $h(x) = x^2 - 2x$       16. $h(x) = x^3 + 8$

17. $f(x) = x^4 + 5$

18. $f(x) = x^4 + 5, \quad 0 \leq x \leq 2$

19. $f(x) = \dfrac{1}{x^2}$       20. $f(x) = \dfrac{1}{x}$

**21–22** ▪ Assume that $f$ is a one-to-one function.

✎ 21. (a) If $f(2) = 7$, find $f^{-1}(7)$.
    (b) If $f^{-1}(3) = -1$, find $f(-1)$.

22. (a) If $f(5) = 18$, find $f^{-1}(18)$.
    (b) If $f^{-1}(4) = 2$, find $f(2)$.

23. If $f(x) = 5 - 2x$, find $f^{-1}(3)$.

24. If $g(x) = x^2 + 4x$ with $x \geq -2$, find $g^{-1}(5)$.

**25–34** ▪ Use the Inverse Function Property to show that $f$ and $g$ are inverses of each other.

25. $f(x) = x - 6; \quad g(x) = x + 6$

26. $f(x) = 3x; \quad g(x) = \dfrac{x}{3}$

✎ 27. $f(x) = 2x - 5; \quad g(x) = \dfrac{x + 5}{2}$

28. $f(x) = \dfrac{3 - x}{4}; \quad g(x) = 3 - 4x$

29. $f(x) = \dfrac{1}{x}; \quad g(x) = \dfrac{1}{x}$

30. $f(x) = x^5; \quad g(x) = \sqrt[5]{x}$

**31.** $f(x) = x^2 - 4, \quad x \geq 0;$
$g(x) = \sqrt{x + 4}, \quad x \geq -4$

**32.** $f(x) = x^3 + 1; \quad g(x) = (x - 1)^{1/3}$

**33.** $f(x) = \dfrac{1}{x - 1}, \quad x \neq 1; \quad g(x) = \dfrac{1}{x} + 1, \quad x \neq 0$

**34.** $f(x) = \sqrt{4 - x^2}, \quad 0 \leq x \leq 2;$
$g(x) = \sqrt{4 - x^2}, \quad 0 \leq x \leq 2$

**35–54** ▪ Find the inverse function of $f$.

**35.** $f(x) = 2x + 1$          **36.** $f(x) = 6 - x$

**37.** $f(x) = 4x + 7$          **38.** $f(x) = 3 - 5x$

**39.** $f(x) = \dfrac{x}{2}$          **40.** $f(x) = \dfrac{1}{x^2}, \quad x > 0$

**41.** $f(x) = \dfrac{1}{x + 2}$          **42.** $f(x) = \dfrac{x - 2}{x + 2}$

**43.** $f(x) = \dfrac{1 + 3x}{5 - 2x}$          **44.** $f(x) = 5 - 4x^3$

**45.** $f(x) = \sqrt{2 + 5x}$          **46.** $f(x) = x^2 + x, \quad x \geq -\frac{1}{2}$

**47.** $f(x) = 4 - x^2, \quad x \geq 0$          **48.** $f(x) = \sqrt{2x - 1}$

**49.** $f(x) = 4 + \sqrt[3]{x}$          **50.** $f(x) = (2 - x^3)^5$

**51.** $f(x) = 1 + \sqrt{1 + x}$

**52.** $f(x) = \sqrt{9 - x^2}, \quad 0 \leq x \leq 3$

**53.** $f(x) = x^4, \quad x \geq 0$          **54.** $f(x) = 1 - x^3$

**55–58** ▪ A function $f$ is given. **(a)** Sketch the graph of $f$. **(b)** Use the graph of $f$ to sketch the graph of $f^{-1}$. **(c)** Find $f^{-1}$.

**55.** $f(x) = 3x - 6$          **56.** $f(x) = 16 - x^2, \quad x \geq 0$

**57.** $f(x) = \sqrt{x + 1}$          **58.** $f(x) = x^3 - 1$

**59–64** ▪ Draw the graph of $f$ and use it to determine whether the function is one-to-one.

**59.** $f(x) = x^3 - x$          **60.** $f(x) = x^3 + x$

**61.** $f(x) = \dfrac{x + 12}{x - 6}$          **62.** $f(x) = \sqrt{x^3 - 4x + 1}$

**63.** $f(x) = |x| - |x - 6|$          **64.** $f(x) = x \cdot |x|$

**65–68** ▪ A one-to-one function is given. **(a)** Find the inverse of the function. **(b)** Graph both the function and its inverse on the same screen to verify that the graphs are reflections of each other in the line $y = x$.

**65.** $f(x) = 2 + x$          **66.** $f(x) = 2 - \frac{1}{2}x$

**67.** $g(x) = \sqrt{x + 3}$          **68.** $g(x) = x^2 + 1, \quad x \geq 0$

**69–72** ▪ The given function is not one-to-one. Restrict its domain so that the resulting function *is* one-to-one. Find the inverse of the function with the restricted domain. (There is more than one correct answer.)

**69.** $f(x) = 4 - x^2$          **70.** $g(x) = (x - 1)^2$

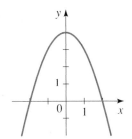
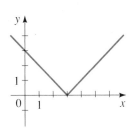

**71.** $h(x) = (x + 2)^2$          **72.** $k(x) = |x - 3|$

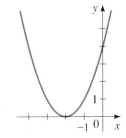
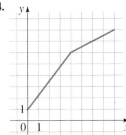

**73–74** ▪ Use the graph of $f$ to sketch the graph of $f^{-1}$.

**73.**          **74.**

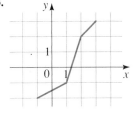

▼ **APPLICATIONS**

**75. Fee for Service** For his services, a private investigator requires a \$500 retention fee plus \$80 per hour. Let $x$ represent the number of hours the investigator spends working on a case.
**(a)** Find a function $f$ that models the investigator's fee as a function of $x$.
**(b)** Find $f^{-1}$. What does $f^{-1}$ represent?
**(c)** Find $f^{-1}(1220)$. What does your answer represent?

**76. Toricelli's Law** A tank holds 100 gallons of water, which drains from a leak at the bottom, causing the tank to empty in 40 minutes. Toricelli's Law gives the volume of water remaining in the tank after $t$ minutes as

$$V(t) = 100 \left( 1 - \frac{t}{40} \right)^2$$

**(a)** Find $V^{-1}$. What does $V^{-1}$ represent?
**(b)** Find $V^{-1}(15)$. What does your answer represent?

**77. Blood Flow** As blood moves through a vein or artery, its velocity $v$ is greatest along the central axis and decreases as the distance $r$ from the central axis increases (see the figure below). For an artery with radius 0.5 cm, $v$ is given as a function of $r$ by

$$v(r) = 18{,}500(0.25 - r^2)$$

**(a)** Find $v^{-1}$. What does $v^{-1}$ represent?

**(b)** Find $v^{-1}(30)$. What does your answer represent?

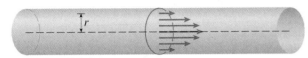

**78. Demand Function** The amount of a commodity that is sold is called the *demand* for the commodity. The demand $D$ for a certain commodity is a function of the price given by

$$D(p) = -3p + 150$$

**(a)** Find $D^{-1}$. What does $D^{-1}$ represent?

**(b)** Find $D^{-1}(30)$. What does your answer represent?

**79. Temperature Scales** The relationship between the Fahrenheit ($F$) and Celsius ($C$) scales is given by

$$F(C) = \tfrac{9}{5}C + 32$$

**(a)** Find $F^{-1}$. What does $F^{-1}$ represent?

**(b)** Find $F^{-1}(86)$. What does your answer represent?

**80. Exchange Rates** The relative value of currencies fluctuates every day. When this problem was written, one Canadian dollar was worth 1.0573 U.S. dollar.

**(a)** Find a function $f$ that gives the U.S. dollar value $f(x)$ of $x$ Canadian dollars.

**(b)** Find $f^{-1}$. What does $f^{-1}$ represent?

**(c)** How much Canadian money would $12,250 in U.S. currency be worth?

**81. Income Tax** In a certain country, the tax on incomes less than or equal to €20,000 is 10%. For incomes that are more than €20,000, the tax is €2000 plus 20% of the amount over €20,000.

**(a)** Find a function $f$ that gives the income tax on an income $x$. Express $f$ as a piecewise defined function.

**(b)** Find $f^{-1}$. What does $f^{-1}$ represent?

**(c)** How much income would require paying a tax of €10,000?

**82. Multiple Discounts** A car dealership advertises a 15% discount on all its new cars. In addition, the manufacturer offers a $1000 rebate on the purchase of a new car. Let $x$ represent the sticker price of the car.

**(a)** Suppose only the 15% discount applies. Find a function $f$ that models the purchase price of the car as a function of the sticker price $x$.

**(b)** Suppose only the $1000 rebate applies. Find a function $g$ that models the purchase price of the car as a function of the sticker price $x$.

**(c)** Find a formula for $H = f \circ g$.

**(d)** Find $H^{-1}$. What does $H^{-1}$ represent?

**(e)** Find $H^{-1}(13{,}000)$. What does your answer represent?

**83. Pizza Cost** Marcello's Pizza charges a base price of $7 for a large pizza plus $2 for each topping. Thus, if you order a large pizza with $x$ toppings, the price of your pizza is given by the

function $f(x) = 7 + 2x$. Find $f^{-1}$. What does the function $f^{-1}$ represent?

---

## ▼DISCOVERY • DISCUSSION • WRITING

**84. Determining When a Linear Function Has an Inverse** For the linear function $f(x) = mx + b$ to be one-to-one, what must be true about its slope? If it is one-to-one, find its inverse. Is the inverse linear? If so, what is its slope?

**85. Finding an Inverse "in Your Head"** In the margin notes in this section we pointed out that the inverse of a function can be found by simply reversing the operations that make up the function. For instance, in Example 6 we saw that the inverse of

$$f(x) = 3x - 2 \quad \text{is} \quad f^{-1}(x) = \frac{x + 2}{3}$$

because the "reverse" of "Multiply by 3 and subtract 2" is "Add 2 and divide by 3." Use the same procedure to find the inverse of the following functions.

**(a)** $f(x) = \dfrac{2x + 1}{5}$      **(b)** $f(x) = 3 - \dfrac{1}{x}$

**(c)** $f(x) = \sqrt{x^3 + 2}$      **(d)** $f(x) = (2x - 5)^3$

Now consider another function:

$$f(x) = x^3 + 2x + 6$$

Is it possible to use the same sort of simple reversal of operations to find the inverse of this function? If so, do it. If not, explain what is different about this function that makes this task difficult.

**86. The Identity Function** The function $I(x) = x$ is called the **identity function**. Show that for any function $f$ we have $f \circ I = f$, $I \circ f = f$, and $f \circ f^{-1} = f^{-1} \circ f = I$. (This means that the identity function $I$ behaves for functions and composition just the way the number 1 behaves for real numbers and multiplication.)

**87. Solving an Equation for an Unknown Function** In Exercise 69 of Section 3.6 you were asked to solve equations in which the unknowns were functions. Now that we know about inverses and the identity function (see Exercise 86), we can use algebra to solve such equations. For instance, to solve $f \circ g = h$ for the unknown function $f$, we perform the following steps:

| | |
|---|---|
| $f \circ g = h$ | Problem: Solve for $f$ |
| $f \circ g \circ g^{-1} = h \circ g^{-1}$ | Compose with $g^{-1}$ on the right |
| $f \circ I = h \circ g^{-1}$ | $g \circ g^{-1} = I$ |
| $f = h \circ g^{-1}$ | $f \circ I = f$ |

So the solution is $f = h \circ g^{-1}$. Use this technique to solve the equation $f \circ g = h$ for the indicated unknown function.

**(a)** Solve for $f$, where $g(x) = 2x + 1$ and $h(x) = 4x^2 + 4x + 7$

**(b)** Solve for $g$, where $f(x) = 3x + 5$ and $h(x) = 3x^2 + 3x + 2$

**10. (a)** If $f(x) = \sqrt{3 - x}$, find the inverse function $f^{-1}$.

**(b)** Sketch the graphs of $f$ and $f^{-1}$ on the same coordinate axes.

**11.** The graph of a function $f$ is given.

**(a)** Find the domain and range of $f$.

**(b)** Sketch the graph of $f^{-1}$.

**(c)** Find the average rate of change of $f$ between $x = 2$ and $x = 6$.

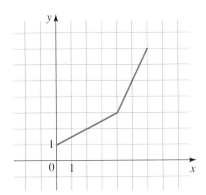

**12.** Let $f(x) = 3x^4 - 14x^2 + 5x - 3$.

**(a)** Draw the graph of $f$ in an appropriate viewing rectangle.

**(b)** Is $f$ one-to-one?

**(c)** Find the local maximum and minimum values of $f$ and the values of $x$ at which they occur. State each answer correct to two decimal places.

**(d)** Use the graph to determine the range of $f$.

**(e)** Find the intervals on which $f$ is increasing and on which $f$ is decreasing.

# MODELING WITH FUNCTIONS

Many of the processes that are studied in the physical and social sciences involve understanding how one quantity varies with respect to another. Finding a function that describes the dependence of one quantity on another is called *modeling*. For example, a biologist observes that the number of bacteria in a certain culture increases with time. He tries to model this phenomenon by finding the precise function (or rule) that relates the bacteria population to the elapsed time.

In this *Focus* we will learn how to find models that can be constructed using geometric or algebraic properties of the object under study. Once the model is found, we use it to analyze and predict properties of the object or process being studied.

## Modeling with Functions

We begin with a simple real-life situation that illustrates the modeling process.

▶ **EXAMPLE 1** | Modeling the Volume of a Box

A breakfast cereal company manufactures boxes to package their product. For aesthetic reasons, the box must have the following proportions: Its width is 3 times its depth, and its height is 5 times its depth.

**(a)** Find a function that models the volume of the box in terms of its depth.

**(b)** Find the volume of the box if the depth is 1.5 in.

**(c)** For what depth is the volume 90 in$^3$?

**(d)** For what depth is the volume greater than 60 in$^3$?

---

### Thinking About the Problem

Let's experiment with the problem. If the depth is 1 in., then the width is 3 in. and the height is 5 in. So in this case, the volume is $V = 1 \times 3 \times 5 = 15$ in$^3$. The table gives other values. Notice that all the boxes have the same shape, and the greater the depth the greater the volume.

| Depth | Volume |
|-------|--------|
| 1 | $1 \times 3 \times 5 = 15$ |
| 2 | $2 \times 6 \times 10 = 120$ |
| 3 | $3 \times 9 \times 15 = 405$ |
| 4 | $4 \times 12 \times 20 = 960$ |

---

▼ **SOLUTION**

**(a)** To find the function that models the volume of the box, we use the following steps.

| First number | Second number | Product |
|:---:|:---:|:---:|
| 1 | 18 | 18 |
| 2 | 17 | 34 |
| 3 | 16 | 48 |
| ⋮ | ⋮ | ⋮ |

(b) Find a function that models the product in terms of one of the two numbers.

(c) Use your model to solve the problem, and compare with your answer to part (a).

**20. Minimizing a Sum**    Find two positive numbers whose sum is 100 and the sum of whose squares is a minimum.

**21. Fencing a Field**    Consider the following problem: A farmer has 2400 ft of fencing and wants to fence off a rectangular field that borders a straight river. He does not need a fence along the river (see the figure). What are the dimensions of the field of largest area that he can fence?

(a) Experiment with the problem by drawing several diagrams illustrating the situation. Calculate the area of each configuration, and use your results to estimate the dimensions of the largest possible field.

(b) Find a function that models the area of the field in terms of one of its sides.

(c) Use your model to solve the problem, and compare with your answer to part (a).

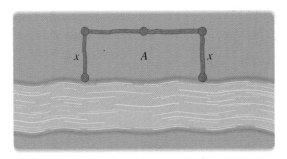

**22. Dividing a Pen**    A rancher with 750 ft of fencing wants to enclose a rectangular area and then divide it into four pens with fencing parallel to one side of the rectangle (see the figure).

(a) Find a function that models the total area of the four pens.

(b) Find the largest possible total area of the four pens.

**23. Fencing a Garden Plot**    A property owner wants to fence a garden plot adjacent to a road, as shown in the figure. The fencing next to the road must be sturdier and costs $5 per foot, but the other fencing costs just $3 per foot. The garden is to have an area of 1200 ft$^2$.

(a) Find a function that models the cost of fencing the garden.

(b) Find the garden dimensions that minimize the cost of fencing.

(c) If the owner has at most $600 to spend on fencing, find the range of lengths he can fence along the road.

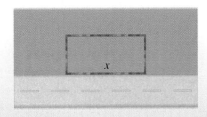

**24. Maximizing Area**    A wire 10 cm long is cut into two pieces, one of length $x$ and the other of length $10 - x$, as shown in the figure. Each piece is bent into the shape of a square.

(a) Find a function that models the total area enclosed by the two squares.

(b) Find the value of $x$ that minimizes the total area of the two squares.

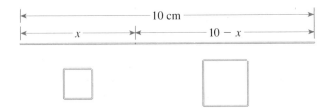

**25. Light from a Window**    A Norman window has the shape of a rectangle surmounted by a semicircle, as shown in the figure to the left. A Norman window with perimeter 30 ft is to be constructed.

(a) Find a function that models the area of the window.

(b) Find the dimensions of the window that admits the greatest amount of light.

**26. Volume of a Box**    A box with an open top is to be constructed from a rectangular piece of cardboard with dimensions 12 in. by 20 in. by cutting out equal squares of side $x$ at each corner and then folding up the sides (see the figure).

(a) Find a function that models the volume of the box.

(b) Find the values of $x$ for which the volume is greater than 200 in$^3$.

(c) Find the largest volume that such a box can have.

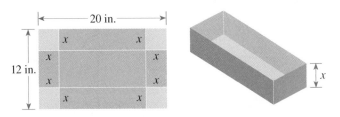

**27. Area of a Box**    An open box with a square base is to have a volume of 12 ft$^3$.

(a) Find a function that models the surface area of the box.

(b) Find the box dimensions that minimize the amount of material used.

**28. Inscribed Rectangle**    Find the dimensions that give the largest area for the rectangle shown in the figure. Its base is on the $x$-axis and its other two vertices are above the $x$-axis, lying on the parabola $y = 8 - x^2$.

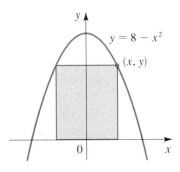

**29. Minimizing Costs**    A rancher wants to build a rectangular pen with an area of 100 m$^2$.

(a) Find a function that models the length of fencing required.

(b) Find the pen dimensions that require the minimum amount of fencing.

**30. Minimizing Time**   A man stands at a point $A$ on the bank of a straight river, 2 mi wide. To reach point $B$, 7 mi downstream on the opposite bank, he first rows his boat to point $P$ on the opposite bank and then walks the remaining distance $x$ to $B$, as shown in the figure. He can row at a speed of 2 mi/h and walk at a speed of 5 mi/h.

(a) Find a function that models the time needed for the trip.

(b) Where should he land so that he reaches $B$ as soon as possible?

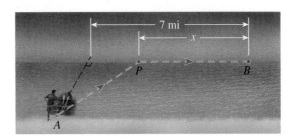

**31. Bird Flight**   A bird is released from point $A$ on an island, 5 mi from the nearest point $B$ on a straight shoreline. The bird flies to a point $C$ on the shoreline and then flies along the shoreline to its nesting area $D$ (see the figure). Suppose the bird requires 10 kcal/mi of energy to fly over land and 14 kcal/mi to fly over water.

(a) Use the fact that

$$\text{energy used} = \text{energy per mile} \times \text{miles flown}$$

to show that the total energy used by the bird is modeled by the function

$$E(x) = 14\sqrt{x^2 + 25} + 10(12 - x)$$

(b) If the bird instinctively chooses a path that minimizes its energy expenditure, to what point does it fly?

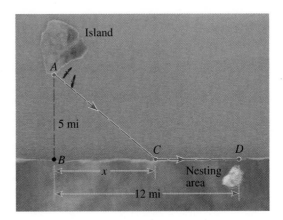

**32. Area of a Kite**   A kite frame is to be made from six pieces of wood. The four pieces that form its border have been cut to the lengths indicated in the figure. Let $x$ be as shown in the figure.

(a) Show that the area of the kite is given by the function

$$A(x) = x\left(\sqrt{25 - x^2} + \sqrt{144 - x^2}\right)$$

(b) How long should each of the two crosspieces be to maximize the area of the kite?

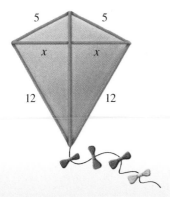

CHAPTER 4
# Polynomial and Rational Functions

© Tom Mackie /Alamy

**Beautiful curves?** An artist can draw a beautiful curve with a graceful sweep of pencil on paper. But to construct such a curve in steel and concrete, on the grand scale of the famous Disney Center, an architect needs a more precise description of the curve. In this chapter we will see that graphs of polynomial functions have gentle curves that are more varied the higher the degree of the polynomial. Such graphs can be pieced together to precisely reproduce any artist's curve to any scale! We will also see how polynomial graphs, with their many peaks and valleys, are used to model real-world quantities that vary in more intricate ways than we've studied so far—from the seasonal demand for different types of clothing to the uneven growth of living things over their lifetime (see *Focus on Modeling: Fitting Polynomial Curves to Data*, pages 364–368).

| # Quadratic Functions and Models

## LEARNING OBJECTIVES

After completing this section, you will be able to:

◼ Express a quadratic function in standard form
◼ Graph a quadratic function using its standard form
◼ Find maximum and minimum values of quadratic functions
◼ Model with quadratic functions

A polynomial function is a function that is defined by a polynomial expression. So a **polynomial function of degree $n$** is a function of the form

$$P(x) = a_n x^n + a_{n-1} x^{n-1} + \cdots + a_1 x + a_0$$

Polynomial expressions are defined in Section P.5.

We have already studied polynomial functions of degree 0 and 1. These are functions of the form $P(x) = a_0$ and $P(x) = a_1 x + a_0$, respectively, whose graphs are lines. In this section we study polynomial functions of degree 2. These are called quadratic functions.

### QUADRATIC FUNCTIONS

A **quadratic function** is a polynomial function of degree 2. So a quadratic function is a function of the form

$$f(x) = ax^2 + bx + c \qquad (a \neq 0)$$

We see in this section how quadratic functions model many real-world phenomena. We begin by analyzing the graphs of quadratic functions.

## ◼ Graphing Quadratic Functions Using the Standard Form

If we take $a = 1$ and $b = c = 0$ in the quadratic function

$$f(x) = ax^2 + bx + c$$

we get the quadratic function

$$f(x) = x^2$$

whose graph is the parabola graphed in Example 1 of Section 3.2. In fact, the graph of any quadratic function is a **parabola**; it can be obtained from the graph of $f(x) = x^2$ by the transformations given in Section 3.5.

### STANDARD FORM OF A QUADRATIC FUNCTION

A quadratic function $f(x) = ax^2 + bx + c$ can be expressed in the **standard form**

$$f(x) = a(x - h)^2 + k$$

by completing the square. The graph of $f$ is a parabola with **vertex** $(h, k)$; the parabola opens upward if $a > 0$ or downward if $a < 0$.

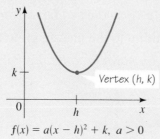

$f(x) = a(x - h)^2 + k, \ a > 0$

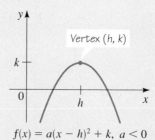

$f(x) = a(x - h)^2 + k, \ a < 0$

▶ **EXAMPLE 1** | Standard Form of a Quadratic Function

Let $f(x) = 2x^2 - 12x + 23$.

**(a)** Express $f$ in standard form.    **(b)** Sketch the graph of $f$.

▼ **SOLUTION**

**(a)** Since the coefficient of $x^2$ is not 1, we must factor this coefficient from the terms involving $x$ before we complete the square.

Completing the square is discussed in Section 1.3.

$$f(x) = 2(x - 3)^2 + 5$$

Vertex is $(3, 5)$

$$\begin{aligned}
f(x) &= 2x^2 - 12x + 23 \\
&= 2(x^2 - 6x) + 23 & \text{Factor 2 from the x-terms} \\
&= 2(x^2 - 6x + 9) + 23 - 2 \cdot 9 & \text{Complete the square: Add 9 inside} \\
& & \text{parentheses, subtract } 2 \cdot 9 \text{ outside} \\
&= 2(x - 3)^2 + 5 & \text{Factor and simplify}
\end{aligned}$$

The standard form is $f(x) = 2(x - 3)^2 + 5$.

**(b)** The standard form tells us that we get the graph of $f$ by taking the parabola $y = x^2$, shifting it to the right 3 units, stretching it by a factor of 2, and moving it upward 5 units. The vertex of the parabola is at $(3, 5)$, and the parabola opens upward. We sketch the graph in Figure 1 after noting that the $y$-intercept is $f(0) = 23$.

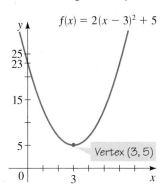

$f(x) = 2(x - 3)^2 + 5$

Vertex $(3, 5)$

**FIGURE 1**

✎ **Practice what you've learned: Do Exercise 13.**    ▲

**Galileo Galilei** (1564–1642) was born in Pisa, Italy. He studied medicine, but later abandoned this in favor of science and mathematics. At the age of 25 he demonstrated that light objects fall at the same rate as heavier ones, by dropping cannonballs of various sizes from the Leaning Tower of Pisa. This contradicted the then-accepted view of Aristotle that heavier objects fall more quickly. He also showed that the distance an object falls is proportional to the square of the time it has been falling, and from this was able to prove that the path of a projectile is a parabola.

Galileo constructed the first telescope, and using it, discovered the moons of Jupiter. His advocacy of the Copernican view that the earth revolves around the sun (rather than being stationary) led to his being called before the Inquisition. By then an old man, he was forced to recant his views, but he is said to have muttered under his breath "the earth nevertheless does move." Galileo revolutionized science by expressing scientific principles in the language of mathematics. He said, "The great book of nature is written in mathematical symbols."

The Granger Collection, New York

## ■ Maximum and Minimum Values of Quadratic Functions

If a quadratic function has vertex $(h, k)$, then the function has a minimum value at the vertex if its graph opens upward and a maximum value at the vertex if its graph opens downward. For example, the function graphed in Figure 1 has minimum value 5 when $x = 3$, since the vertex $(3, 5)$ is the lowest point on the graph.

**MAXIMUM OR MINIMUM VALUE OF A QUADRATIC FUNCTION**

Let $f$ be a quadratic function with standard form $f(x) = a(x - h)^2 + k$. The maximum or minimum value of $f$ occurs at $x = h$.

If $a > 0$, then the **minimum value** of $f$ is $f(h) = k$.

If $a < 0$, then the **maximum value** of $f$ is $f(h) = k$.

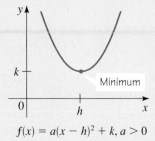

Minimum

$f(x) = a(x - h)^2 + k, a > 0$

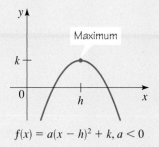

Maximum

$f(x) = a(x - h)^2 + k, a < 0$

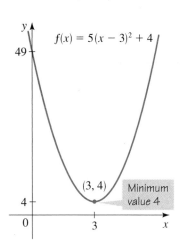

$f(x) = 5(x - 3)^2 + 4$

(3, 4)   Minimum value 4

**FIGURE 2**

▶ **EXAMPLE 2** | Minimum Value of a Quadratic Function

Consider the quadratic function $f(x) = 5x^2 - 30x + 49$.

**(a)** Express $f$ in standard form.

**(b)** Sketch the graph of $f$.

**(c)** Find the minimum value of $f$.

▼ **SOLUTION**

**(a)** To express this quadratic function in standard form, we complete the square.

$$f(x) = 5x^2 - 30x + 49$$

$$= 5(x^2 - 6x) + 49 \qquad \text{Factor 5 from the x-terms}$$

$$= 5(x^2 - 6x + 9) + 49 - 5 \cdot 9 \qquad \begin{array}{l}\text{Complete the square: Add 9 inside}\\ \text{parentheses, subtract } 5 \cdot 9 \text{ outside}\end{array}$$

$$= 5(x - 3)^2 + 4 \qquad \text{Factor and simplify}$$

**(b)** The graph is a parabola that has its vertex at $(3, 4)$ and opens upward, as sketched in Figure 2.

**(c)** Since the coefficient of $x^2$ is positive, $f$ has a minimum value. The minimum value is $f(3) = 4$.

✎ **Practice what you've learned: Do Exercise 25.** ▲

▶ **EXAMPLE 3** | Maximum Value of a Quadratic Function

Consider the quadratic function $f(x) = -x^2 + x + 2$.

**(a)** Express $f$ in standard form.

**(b)** Sketch the graph of $f$.

**(c)** Find the maximum value of $f$.

▼ **SOLUTION**

**(a)** To express this quadratic function in standard form, we complete the square.

$$y = -x^2 + x + 2$$

$$= -(x^2 - x) + 2 \qquad \text{Factor } -1 \text{ from the x-terms}$$

$$= -\left(x^2 - x + \tfrac{1}{4}\right) + 2 - (-1)\tfrac{1}{4} \qquad \begin{array}{l}\text{Complete the square: Add } \tfrac{1}{4} \text{ inside}\\ \text{parentheses, subtract } (-1)\tfrac{1}{4} \text{ outside}\end{array}$$

$$= -\left(x - \tfrac{1}{2}\right)^2 + \tfrac{9}{4} \qquad \text{Factor and simplify}$$

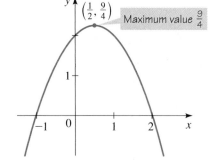

$\left(\tfrac{1}{2}, \tfrac{9}{4}\right)$   Maximum value $\tfrac{9}{4}$

**FIGURE 3** Graph of $f(x) = -x^2 + x + 2$

**(b)** From the standard form we see that the graph is a parabola that opens downward and has vertex $\left(\tfrac{1}{2}, \tfrac{9}{4}\right)$. As an aid to sketching the graph, we find the intercepts. The $y$-intercept is $f(0) = 2$. To find the $x$-intercepts, we set $f(x) = 0$ and factor the resulting equation.

$$-x^2 + x + 2 = 0 \qquad \text{Set } y = 0$$

$$x^2 - x - 2 = 0 \qquad \text{Multiply by } -1$$

$$(x - 2)(x + 1) = 0 \qquad \text{Factor}$$

Thus, the $x$-intercepts are $x = 2$ and $x = -1$. The graph of $f$ is sketched in Figure 3.

**(c)** Since the coefficient of $x^2$ is negative, $f$ has a maximum value, which is $f\left(\tfrac{1}{2}\right) = \tfrac{9}{4}$.

✎ **Practice what you've learned: Do Exercise 27.** ▲

Expressing a quadratic function in standard form helps us to sketch its graph as well as find its maximum or minimum value. If we are interested only in finding the maximum or minimum value, then a formula is available for doing so. This formula is obtained by completing the square for the general quadratic function as follows:

$$f(x) = ax^2 + bx + c$$

$$= a\left(x^2 + \frac{b}{a}x\right) + c \qquad \text{Factor } a \text{ from the x-terms}$$

$$= a\left(x^2 + \frac{b}{a}x + \frac{b^2}{4a^2}\right) + c - a\left(\frac{b^2}{4a^2}\right) \qquad \begin{array}{l}\text{Complete the square:}\\ \text{Add } \frac{b^2}{4a^2} \text{ inside parentheses,}\\ \text{subtract } a\left(\frac{b^2}{4a^2}\right) \text{ outside}\end{array}$$

$$= a\left(x + \frac{b}{2a}\right)^2 + c - \frac{b^2}{4a} \qquad \text{Factor}$$

This equation is in standard form with $h = -b/(2a)$ and $k = c - b^2/(4a)$. Since the maximum or minimum value occurs at $x = h$, we have the following result.

---

**MAXIMUM OR MINIMUM VALUE OF A QUADRATIC FUNCTION**

The maximum or minimum value of a quadratic function $f(x) = ax^2 + bx + c$ occurs at

$$x = -\frac{b}{2a}$$

If $a > 0$, then the **minimum value** is $f\left(-\dfrac{b}{2a}\right)$.

If $a < 0$, then the **maximum value** is $f\left(-\dfrac{b}{2a}\right)$.

---

▶ **EXAMPLE 4** | Finding Maximum and Minimum Values of Quadratic Functions

Find the maximum or minimum value of each quadratic function.

**(a)** $f(x) = x^2 + 4x$ **(b)** $g(x) = -2x^2 + 4x - 5$

▼ **SOLUTION**

**(a)** This is a quadratic function with $a = 1$ and $b = 4$. Thus, the maximum or minimum value occurs at

$$x = -\frac{b}{2a} = -\frac{4}{2 \cdot 1} = -2$$

Since $a > 0$, the function has the *minimum* value

$$f(-2) = (-2)^2 + 4(-2) = -4$$

**(b)** This is a quadratic function with $a = -2$ and $b = 4$. Thus, the maximum or minimum value occurs at

$$x = -\frac{b}{2a} = -\frac{4}{2 \cdot (-2)} = 1$$

Since $a < 0$, the function has the *maximum* value

$$f(1) = -2(1)^2 + 4(1) - 5 = -3$$

✎ **Practice what you've learned: Do Exercises 33 and 35.** ▲

The minimum value occurs at $x = -2$.

The maximum value occurs at $x = 1$.

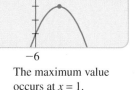

## ■ Modeling with Quadratic Functions

We study some examples of real-world phenomena that are modeled by quadratic functions. These examples and the *Application* exercises for this section show some of the variety of situations that are naturally modeled by quadratic functions.

▶ **EXAMPLE 5** | Maximum Gas Mileage for a Car

Most cars get their best gas mileage when traveling at a relatively modest speed. The gas mileage $M$ for a certain new car is modeled by the function

$$M(s) = -\frac{1}{28}s^2 + 3s - 31, \qquad 15 \le s \le 70$$

where $s$ is the speed in mi/h and $M$ is measured in mi/gal. What is the car's best gas mileage, and at what speed is it attained?

▼ **SOLUTION**    The function $M$ is a quadratic function with $a = -\frac{1}{28}$ and $b = 3$. Thus, its maximum value occurs when

$$s = -\frac{b}{2a} = -\frac{3}{2\left(-\frac{1}{28}\right)} = 42$$

The maximum is $M(42) = -\frac{1}{28}(42)^2 + 3(42) - 31 = 32$. So the car's best gas mileage is 32 mi/gal, when it is traveling at 42 mi/h.

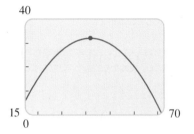

The maximum gas mileage occurs at 42 mi/h.

✎ **Practice what you've learned: Do Exercise 67.**    ▲

▶ **EXAMPLE 6** | Maximizing Revenue from Ticket Sales

A hockey team plays in an arena that has a seating capacity of 15,000 spectators. With the ticket price set at $14, average attendance at recent games has been 9500. A market survey indicates that for each dollar the ticket price is lowered, the average attendance increases by 1000.

**(a)** Find a function that models the revenue in terms of ticket price.

**(b)** Find the price that maximizes revenue from ticket sales.

**(c)** What ticket price is so high that no one attends and so no revenue is generated?

▼ **SOLUTION**

**(a)** The model that we want is a function that gives the revenue for any ticket price.

Express the model in words ▶    |    revenue = ticket price × attendance

There are two varying quantities: ticket price and attendance. Since the function we want depends on price, we let

Choose the variable ▶    |    $x$ = ticket price

Next, we express attendance in terms of $x$.

| In Words | In Algebra |
|---|---|
| Ticket price | $x$ |
| Amount ticket price is lowered | $14 - x$ |
| Increase in attendance | $1000(14 - x)$ |
| Attendance | $9500 + 1000(14 - x)$ |

The model that we want is the function $R$ that gives the revenue for a given ticket price $x$.

Set up the model ▶

$$\text{revenue} = \text{ticket price} \times \text{attendance}$$

$$R(x) = x \times [9500 + 1000(14 - x)]$$

$$R(x) = x(23{,}500 - 1000x)$$

$$R(x) = 23{,}500x - 1000x^2$$

Use the model ▶  **(b)** Since $R$ is a quadratic function with $a = -1000$ and $b = 23{,}500$, the maximum occurs at

$$x = -\frac{b}{2a} = -\frac{23{,}500}{2(-1000)} = 11.75$$

So a ticket price of $11.75 gives the maximum revenue.

Use the model ▶  **(c)** We want to find the ticket price for which $R(x) = 0$:

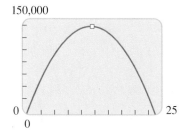

150,000

0             25
 0

Maximum attendance occurs
when ticket price is $11.75.

| | |
|---|---|
| $23{,}500x - 1000x^2 = 0$ | Set $R(x) = 0$ |
| $23.5x - x^2 = 0$ | Divide by 1000 |
| $x(23.5 - x) = 0$ | Factor |
| $x = 0 \quad \text{or} \quad x = 23.5$ | Solve for $x$ |

So according to this model, a ticket price of $23.50 is just too high; at that price, no one attends to watch this team play. (Of course, revenue is also zero if the ticket price is zero.)

✎ **Practice what you've learned. Do Exercises 75 and 77.**   ▲

# 4.1 EXERCISES

## ▼ CONCEPTS

**1.** To put the quadratic function $f(x) = ax^2 + bx + c$ in standard

form, we complete the _____.

**2.** The quadratic function $f(x) = a(x - h)^2 + k$ is in standard form.
 **(a)** The graph of $f$ is a parabola with vertex (____, ____).

 **(b)** If $a > 0$, the graph of $f$ opens _____. In this case

  $f(h) = k$ is the _____ value of $f$.

 **(c)** If $a < 0$, the graph of $f$ opens _____. In this case

  $f(h) = k$ is the _____ value of $f$.

**3.** The graph of $f(x) = 2(x - 3)^2 + 5$ is a parabola that opens

 _____, with its vertex at (____, ____), and

 $f(3) = $ _____ is the (minimum/maximum) _____
 value of $f$.

**4.** The graph of $f(x) = -2(x - 3)^2 + 5$ is a parabola that

 opens _____, with its vertex at (____, ____), and

$f(3) = $ _____ is the (minimum/maximum) _____ value
of $f$.

## ▼ SKILLS

**5–8** ▪ The graph of a quadratic function $f$ is given. **(a)** Find the coordinates of the vertex. **(b)** Find the maximum or minimum value of $f$. **(c)** Find the domain and range of $f$.

**5.** $f(x) = -x^2 + 6x - 5$    **6.** $f(x) = -\frac{1}{2}x^2 - 2x + 6$

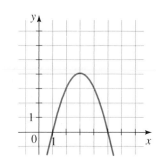

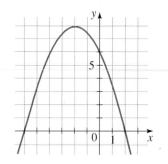

**7.** $f(x) = 2x^2 - 4x - 1$   **8.** $f(x) = 3x^2 + 6x - 1$

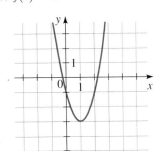   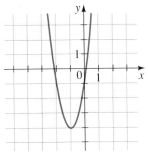

**9–22** ■ A quadratic function is given. **(a)** Express the quadratic function in standard form. **(b)** Find its vertex and its $x$- and $y$-intercept(s). **(c)** Sketch its graph.

**9.** $f(x) = x^2 - 6x$   **10.** $f(x) = x^2 + 8x$

**11.** $f(x) = 2x^2 + 6x$   **12.** $f(x) = -x^2 + 10x$

**13.** $f(x) = x^2 + 4x + 3$   **14.** $f(x) = x^2 - 2x + 2$

**15.** $f(x) = -x^2 + 6x + 4$   **16.** $f(x) = -x^2 - 4x + 4$

**17.** $f(x) = 2x^2 + 4x + 3$   **18.** $f(x) = -3x^2 + 6x - 2$

**19.** $f(x) = 2x^2 - 20x + 57$   **20.** $f(x) = 2x^2 + x - 6$

**21.** $f(x) = -4x^2 - 16x + 3$   **22.** $f(x) = 6x^2 + 12x - 5$

**23–32** ■ A quadratic function is given. **(a)** Express the quadratic function in standard form. **(b)** Sketch its graph. **(c)** Find its maximum or minimum value.

**23.** $f(x) = x^2 + 2x - 1$   **24.** $f(x) = x^2 - 8x + 8$

**25.** $f(x) = 3x^2 - 6x + 1$   **26.** $f(x) = 5x^2 + 30x + 4$

**27.** $f(x) = -x^2 - 3x + 3$   **28.** $f(x) = 1 - 6x - x^2$

**29.** $g(x) = 3x^2 - 12x + 13$   **30.** $g(x) = 2x^2 + 8x + 11$

**31.** $h(x) = 1 - x - x^2$   **32.** $h(x) = 3 - 4x - 4x^2$

**33–42** ■ Find the maximum or minimum value of the function.

**33.** $f(x) = x^2 + x + 1$   **34.** $f(x) = 1 + 3x - x^2$

**35.** $f(t) = 100 - 49t - 7t^2$   **36.** $f(t) = 10t^2 + 40t + 113$

**37.** $f(s) = s^2 - 1.2s + 16$   **38.** $g(x) = 100x^2 - 1500x$

**39.** $h(x) = \frac{1}{2}x^2 + 2x - 6$   **40.** $f(x) = -\frac{x^2}{3} + 2x + 7$

**41.** $f(x) = 3 - x - \frac{1}{2}x^2$   **42.** $g(x) = 2x(x - 4) + 7$

**43.** Find a function whose graph is a parabola with vertex $(1, -2)$ and that passes through the point $(4, 16)$.

**44.** Find a function whose graph is a parabola with vertex $(3, 4)$ and that passes through the point $(1, -8)$.

**45–48** ■ Find the domain and range of the function.

**45.** $f(x) = -x^2 + 4x - 3$   **46.** $f(x) = x^2 - 2x - 3$

**47.** $f(x) = 2x^2 + 6x - 7$   **48.** $f(x) = -3x^2 + 6x + 4$

**49–50** ■ A quadratic function is given. **(a)** Use a graphing device to find the maximum or minimum value of the quadratic function $f$,

correct to two decimal places. **(b)** Find the exact maximum or minimum value of $f$, and compare it with your answer to part (a).

**49.** $f(x) = x^2 + 1.79x - 3.21$

**50.** $f(x) = 1 + x - \sqrt{2}x^2$

**51–54** ■ Find all local maximum and minimum values of the function whose graph is shown.

**51.**    **52.**

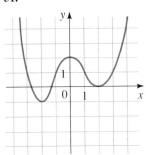   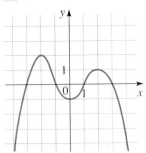

**53.**    **54.**

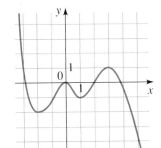   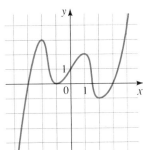

**55–62** ■ Find the local maximum and minimum values of the function and the value of $x$ at which each occurs. State each answer correct to two decimal places.

**55.** $f(x) = x^3 - x$   **56.** $f(x) = 3 + x + x^2 - x^3$

**57.** $g(x) = x^4 - 2x^3 - 11x^2$   **58.** $g(x) = x^5 - 8x^3 + 20x$

**59.** $U(x) = x\sqrt{6 - x}$   **60.** $U(x) = x\sqrt{x - x^2}$

**61.** $V(x) = \frac{1 - x^2}{x^3}$   **62.** $V(x) = \frac{1}{x^2 + x + 1}$

## ▼ APPLICATIONS

**63. Height of a Ball**   If a ball is thrown directly upward with a velocity of 40 ft/s, its height (in feet) after $t$ seconds is given by $y = 40t - 16t^2$. What is the maximum height attained by the ball?

**64. Path of a Ball**   A ball is thrown across a playing field from a height of 5 ft above the ground at an angle of 45° to the horizontal at a speed of 20 ft/s. It can be deduced from physical principles that the path of the ball is modeled by the function

$$y = -\frac{32}{(20)^2}x^2 + x + 5$$

where $x$ is the distance in feet that the ball has traveled horizontally.

**(a)** Find the maximum height attained by the ball.

**(b)** Find the horizontal distance the ball has traveled when it hits the ground.

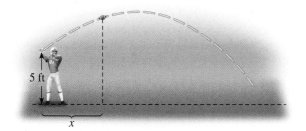

5 ft

*x*

**65. Revenue**   A manufacturer finds that the revenue generated by selling *x* units of a certain commodity is given by the function $R(x) = 80x - 0.4x^2$, where the revenue $R(x)$ is measured in dollars. What is the maximum revenue, and how many units should be manufactured to obtain this maximum?

**66. Sales**   A soft-drink vendor at a popular beach analyzes his sales records and finds that if he sells *x* cans of soda pop in one day, his profit (in dollars) is given by

$$P(x) = -0.001x^2 + 3x - 1800$$

What is his maximum profit per day, and how many cans must he sell for maximum profit?

**67. Advertising**   The effectiveness of a television commercial depends on how many times a viewer watches it. After some experiments an advertising agency found that if the effectiveness *E* is measured on a scale of 0 to 10, then

$$E(n) = \tfrac{2}{3}n - \tfrac{1}{90}n^2$$

where *n* is the number of times a viewer watches a given commercial. For a commercial to have maximum effectiveness, how many times should a viewer watch it?

**68. Pharmaceuticals**   When a certain drug is taken orally, the concentration of the drug in the patient's bloodstream after *t* minutes is given by $C(t) = 0.06t - 0.0002t^2$, where $0 \le t \le 240$ and the concentration is measured in mg/L. When is the maximum serum concentration reached, and what is that maximum concentration?

**69. Agriculture**   The number of apples produced by each tree in an apple orchard depends on how densely the trees are planted. If *n* trees are planted on an acre of land, then each tree produces $900 - 9n$ apples. So the number of apples produced per acre is

$$A(n) = n(900 - 9n)$$

How many trees should be planted per acre to obtain the maximum yield of apples?

**70. Agriculture**   At a certain vineyard it is found that each grape vine produces about 10 pounds of grapes in a season when about 700 vines are planted per acre. For each additional vine that is planted, the production of each vine decreases by about 1 percent. So the number of pounds of grapes produced per acre is modeled by

$$A(n) = (700 + n)(10 - 0.01n)$$

where *n* is the number of additional vines planted. Find the number of vines that should be planted to maximize grape production.

**71–74** ■ Use the formulas of this section to give an alternative solution to the indicated problem in *Focus on Modeling: Modeling with Functions* on pages 287–288.

**71.** Problem 21            **72.** Problem 22

**73.** Problem 25            **74.** Problem 24

**75. Fencing a Horse Corral**   Carol has 1200 ft of fencing to fence in a rectangular horse corral.

**(a)** Find a function that models the area of the corral in terms of the width *x* of the corral.

**(b)** Find the dimensions of the rectangle that maximize the area of the corral.

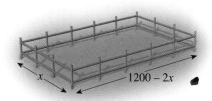

*x*            $1200 - 2x$

**76. Making a Rain Gutter**   A rain gutter is formed by bending up the sides of a 30-inch-wide rectangular metal sheet as shown in the figure.

**(a)** Find a function that models the cross-sectional area of the gutter in terms of *x*.

**(b)** Find the value of *x* that maximizes the cross-sectional area of the gutter.

**(c)** What is the maximum cross-sectional area for the gutter?

*x*            30 in.

**77. Stadium Revenue**   A baseball team plays in a stadium that holds 55,000 spectators. With the ticket price at $10, the average attendance at recent games has been 27,000. A market survey indicates that for every dollar the ticket price is lowered, attendance increases by 3000.

**(a)** Find a function that models the revenue in terms of ticket price.

**(b)** Find the price that maximizes revenue from ticket sales.

**(c)** What ticket price is so high that no revenue is generated?

**78. Maximizing Profit** A community bird-watching society makes and sells simple bird feeders to raise money for its conservation activities. The materials for each feeder cost $6, and the society sells an average of 20 per week at a price of $10 each. The society has been considering raising the price, so it conducts a survey and finds that for every dollar increase, it loses 2 sales per week.

**(a)** Find a function that models weekly profit in terms of price per feeder.

**(b)** What price should the society charge for each feeder to maximize profits? What is the maximum weekly profit?

**▼ DISCOVERY • DISCUSSION • WRITING**

**79. Vertex and $x$-Intercepts** We know that the graph of the quadratic function $f(x) = (x - m)(x - n)$ is a parabola. Sketch a rough graph of what such a parabola would look like. What are the $x$-intercepts of the graph of $f$? Can you tell from your graph the $x$-coordinate of the vertex in terms of $m$ and $n$? (Use the symmetry of the parabola.) Confirm your answer by expanding and using the formulas of this section.

**80. Maximum of a Fourth-Degree Polynomial** Find the maximum value of the function

$$f(x) = 3 + 4x^2 - x^4$$

[*Hint:* Let $t = x^2$.]

---

## 4.2 | Polynomial Functions and Their Graphs

### LEARNING OBJECTIVES

After completing this section, you will be able to:

▦ Graph basic polynomial functions
▦ Use end behavior of a polynomial function to help sketch its graph
▦ Use the zeros of a polynomial function to sketch its graph
▦ Use the multiplicity of a zero to help sketch the graph of a polynomial function
▦ Find local maxima and minima of polynomial functions

In this section we study polynomial functions of any degree. But before we work with polynomial functions, we must agree on some terminology.

**POLYNOMIAL FUNCTIONS**

A **polynomial function of degree $n$** is a function of the form

$$P(x) = a_n x^n + a_{n-1} x^{n-1} + \cdots + a_1 x + a_0$$

where $n$ is a nonnegative integer and $a_n \neq 0$.

The numbers $a_0, a_1, a_2, \ldots, a_n$ are called the **coefficients** of the polynomial.

The number $a_0$ is the **constant coefficient** or **constant term**.

The number $a_n$, the coefficient of the highest power, is the **leading coefficient**, and the term $a_n x^n$ is the **leading term**.

We often refer to polynomial functions simply as *polynomials*. The following polynomial has degree 5, leading coefficient 3, and constant term $-6$.

Leading coefficient 3    Degree 5    Constant term $-6$

$$3x^5 + 6x^4 - 2x^3 + x^2 + 7x - 6$$

Leading term $3x^5$

Coefficients 3, 6, $-2$, 1, 7, and $-6$

Here are some more examples of polynomials.

$$P(x) = 3 \qquad \text{Degree 0}$$
$$Q(x) = 4x - 7 \qquad \text{Degree 1}$$
$$R(x) = x^2 + x \qquad \text{Degree 2}$$
$$S(x) = 2x^3 - 6x^2 - 10 \qquad \text{Degree 3}$$

If a polynomial consists of just a single term, then it is called a **monomial**. For example, $P(x) = x^3$ and $Q(x) = -6x^5$ are monomials.

## ■ Graphing Basic Polynomial Functions

The graphs of polynomials of degree 0 or 1 are lines (Section 2.4), and the graphs of polynomials of degree 2 are parabolas (Section 4.1). The greater the degree of the polynomial, the more complicated its graph can be. However, the graph of a polynomial function is always a smooth curve; that is, it has no breaks or corners (see Figure 1). The proof of this fact requires calculus.

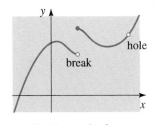

Not the graph of a polynomial function

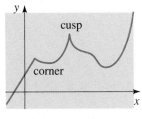

Not the graph of a polynomial function

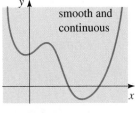

Graph of a polynomial function

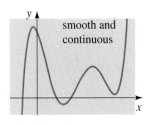

Graph of a polynomial function

**FIGURE 1**

The simplest polynomial functions are the monomials $P(x) = x^n$, whose graphs are shown in Figure 2. As the figure suggests, the graph of $P(x) = x^n$ has the same general shape as $y = x^2$ when $n$ is even and the same general shape as $y = x^3$ when $n$ is odd. However, as the degree $n$ becomes larger, the graphs become flatter around the origin and steeper elsewhere.

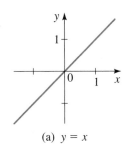

(a) $y = x$

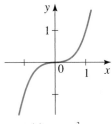

(b) $y = x^2$

(c) $y = x^3$

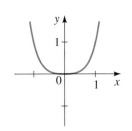

(d) $y = x^4$

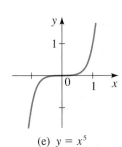

(e) $y = x^5$

**FIGURE 2** Graphs of monomials

▶ **EXAMPLE 1** | Transformations of Monomials

Sketch the graphs of the following functions.

**(a)** $P(x) = -x^3$      **(b)** $Q(x) = (x - 2)^4$

**(c)** $R(x) = -2x^5 + 4$

▼ **SOLUTION** We use the graphs in Figure 2 and transform them using the techniques of Section 3.5.

(a) The graph of $P(x) = -x^3$ is the reflection of the graph of $y = x^3$ in the $x$-axis, as shown in Figure 3(a) below.

(b) The graph of $Q(x) = (x - 2)^4$ is the graph of $y = x^4$ shifted to the right 2 units, as shown in Figure 3(b).

(c) We begin with the graph of $y = x^5$. The graph of $y = -2x^5$ is obtained by stretching the graph vertically and reflecting it in the $x$-axis (see the dashed blue graph in Figure 3(c)). Finally, the graph of $R(x) = -2x^5 + 4$ is obtained by shifting upward 4 units (see the red graph in Figure 3(c)).

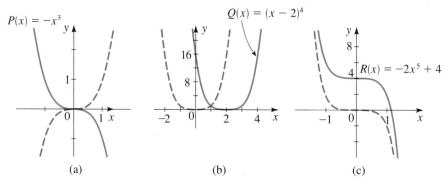

(a)          (b)          (c)

**FIGURE 3**

✎ **Practice what you've learned: Do Exercise 5.**    ▲

## End Behavior and the Leading Term

The **end behavior** of a polynomial is a description of what happens as $x$ becomes large in the positive or negative direction. To describe end behavior, we use the following notation:

$x \to \infty$     means     "$x$ becomes large in the positive direction"

$x \to -\infty$     means     "$x$ becomes large in the negative direction"

## MATHEMATICS IN THE MODERN WORLD

### Splines

A spline is a long strip of wood that is curved while held fixed at certain points. In the old days shipbuilders used splines to create the curved shape of a boat's hull. Splines are also used to make the curves of a piano, a violin, or the spout of a teapot.

Mathematicians discovered that the shapes of splines can be obtained by piecing together parts of polynomials. For example, the graph of a cubic polynomial can be made to fit specified points by adjusting the coefficients of the polynomial (see Example 10, page 311).

Curves obtained in this way are called cubic splines. In modern computer design programs, such as Adobe Illustrator or Microsoft Paint, a curve can be drawn by fixing two points, then using the mouse to drag one or more anchor points. Moving the anchor points amounts to adjusting the coefficients of a cubic polynomial.

For example, the monomial $y = x^2$ in Figure 2(b) has the following end behavior:

$$y \to \infty \quad \text{as} \quad x \to \infty \qquad \text{and} \qquad y \to \infty \quad \text{as} \quad x \to -\infty$$

The monomial $y = x^3$ in Figure 2(c) has the following end behavior:

$$y \to \infty \quad \text{as} \quad x \to \infty \qquad \text{and} \qquad y \to -\infty \quad \text{as} \quad x \to -\infty$$

For any polynomial, *the end behavior is determined by the term that contains the highest power of x*, because when x is large, the other terms are relatively insignificant in size. The following box shows the four possible types of end behavior, based on the highest power and the sign of its coefficient.

---

**END BEHAVIOR OF POLYNOMIALS**

The end behavior of the polynomial $P(x) = a_n x^n + a_{n-1} x^{n-1} + \cdots + a_1 x + a_0$ is determined by the degree $n$ and the sign of the leading coefficient $a_n$, as indicated in the following graphs.

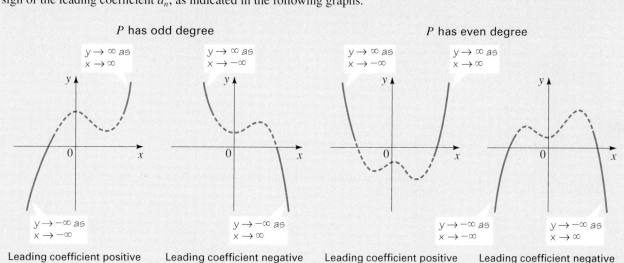

---

▶ **EXAMPLE 2** | End Behavior of a Polynomial

Determine the end behavior of the polynomial

$$P(x) = -2x^4 + 5x^3 + 4x - 7$$

▼ **SOLUTION**    The polynomial $P$ has degree 4 and leading coefficient $-2$. Thus, $P$ has *even* degree and *negative* leading coefficient, so it has the following end behavior:

$$y \to -\infty \quad \text{as} \quad x \to \infty \qquad \text{and} \qquad y \to -\infty \quad \text{as} \quad x \to -\infty$$

The graph in Figure 4 illustrates the end behavior of $P$.

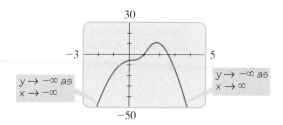

**FIGURE 4**
$P(x) = -2x^4 + 5x^3 + 4x - 7$

✎ **Practice what you've learned: Do Exercise 11.**     ▲

▶ **EXAMPLE 3** | End Behavior of a Polynomial

(a) Determine the end behavior of the polynomial $P(x) = 3x^5 - 5x^3 + 2x$.

(b) Confirm that $P$ and its leading term $Q(x) = 3x^5$ have the same end behavior by graphing them together.

▼ **SOLUTION**

(a) Since $P$ has odd degree and positive leading coefficient, it has the following end behavior:

$$y \to \infty \quad \text{as} \quad x \to \infty \quad \text{and} \quad y \to -\infty \quad \text{as} \quad x \to -\infty$$

(b) Figure 5 shows the graphs of $P$ and $Q$ in progressively larger viewing rectangles. The larger the viewing rectangle, the more the graphs look alike. This confirms that they have the same end behavior.

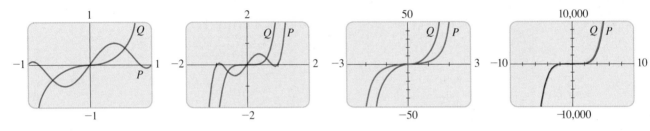

**FIGURE 5**

$P(x) = 3x^5 - 5x^3 + 2x$

$Q(x) = 3x^5$

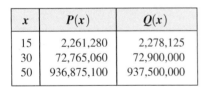 **Practice what you've learned: Do Exercise 41.** ▲

To see algebraically why $P$ and $Q$ in Example 3 have the same end behavior, factor $P$ as follows and compare with $Q$.

$$P(x) = 3x^5 \left( 1 - \frac{5}{3x^2} + \frac{2}{3x^4} \right) \qquad Q(x) = 3x^5$$

| $x$ | $P(x)$ | $Q(x)$ |
|-----|--------|--------|
| 15 | 2,261,280 | 2,278,125 |
| 30 | 72,765,060 | 72,900,000 |
| 50 | 936,875,100 | 937,500,000 |

When $x$ is large, the terms $5/3x^2$ and $2/3x^4$ are close to 0 (see Exercise 67 on page 19). So for large $x$, we have

$$P(x) \approx 3x^5(1 - 0 - 0) = 3x^5 = Q(x)$$

So when $x$ is large, $P$ and $Q$ have approximately the same values. We can also see this numerically by making a table like the one in the margin.

By the same reasoning we can show that the end behavior of *any* polynomial is determined by its leading term.

## ■ Using Zeros to Graph Polynomials

If $P$ is a polynomial function, then $c$ is called a **zero** of $P$ if $P(c) = 0$. In other words, the zeros of $P$ are the solutions of the polynomial equation $P(x) = 0$. Note that if $P(c) = 0$, then the graph of $P$ has an $x$-intercept at $x = c$, so the $x$-intercepts of the graph are the zeros of the function.

---

**REAL ZEROS OF POLYNOMIALS**

If $P$ is a polynomial and $c$ is a real number, then the following are equivalent:

**1.** $c$ is a zero of $P$.

**2.** $x = c$ is a solution of the equation $P(x) = 0$.

**3.** $x - c$ is a factor of $P(x)$.

**4.** $c$ is an $x$-intercept of the graph of $P$.

**86. Maximum Number of Local Extrema**   What is the smallest possible degree that the polynomial whose graph is shown can have? Explain.

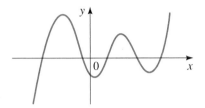

**87. Possible Number of Local Extrema**   Is it possible for a third-degree polynomial to have exactly one local extremum? Can a fourth-degree polynomial have exactly two local extrema? How many local extrema can polynomials of third, fourth, fifth, and sixth degree have? (Think about the end behavior of such polynomials.) Now give an example of a polynomial that has six local extrema.

**88. Impossible Situation?**   Is it possible for a polynomial to have two local maxima and no local minimum? Explain.

---

## 4.3 | Dividing Polynomials

### LEARNING OBJECTIVES

After completing this section, you will be able to:

- Use long division to divide polynomials
- Use synthetic division to divide polynomials
- Use the Remainder Theorem to find values of a polynomial
- Use the Factor Theorem to factor a polynomial
- Find a polynomial with specified zeros

So far in this chapter we have been studying polynomial functions *graphically*. In this section we begin to study polynomials *algebraically*. Most of our work will be concerned with factoring polynomials, and to factor, we need to know how to divide polynomials.

### ■ Long Division of Polynomials

Dividing polynomials is much like the familiar process of dividing numbers. When we divide 38 by 7, the quotient is 5 and the remainder is 3. We write

$$\underset{\text{Divisor}}{\underset{\big\uparrow}{\phantom{x}}}\ \frac{\overset{\text{Dividend}}{\overset{\big\downarrow}{38}}}{7} = \underset{\text{Quotient}}{\underset{\big\uparrow}{5}} + \frac{3}{7}\ \overset{\text{Remainder}}{}$$

To divide polynomials, we use long division, as follows.

> To write the division algorithm another way, divide through by $D(x)$:
>
> $$\frac{P(x)}{D(x)} = Q(x) + \frac{R(x)}{D(x)}$$

### DIVISION ALGORITHM

If $P(x)$ and $D(x)$ are polynomials, with $D(x) \neq 0$, then there exist unique polynomials $Q(x)$ and $R(x)$, where $R(x)$ is either 0 or of degree less than the degree of $D(x)$, such that

$$\underset{\text{Dividend}}{P(x)} = \underset{\text{Divisor}}{D(x)} \cdot \underset{\text{Quotient}}{Q(x)} + \underset{\text{Remainder}}{R(x)}$$

The polynomials $P(x)$ and $D(x)$ are called the **dividend** and **divisor**, respectively, $Q(x)$ is the **quotient**, and $R(x)$ is the **remainder**.

▶ **EXAMPLE 1** | Long Division of Polynomials

Divide $6x^2 - 26x + 12$ by $x - 4$.

▼ **SOLUTION** The *dividend* is $6x^2 - 26x + 12$ and the *divisor* is $x - 4$. We begin by arranging them as follows:

$$x - 4 \overline{)\, 6x^2 - 26x + 12}$$

Next we divide the leading term in the dividend by the leading term in the divisor to get the first term of the quotient: $6x^2/x = 6x$. Then we multiply the divisor by $6x$ and subtract the result from the dividend.

$$
\begin{array}{r}
6x \phantom{xxxxxxxxxx} \\
x - 4 \overline{)\, 6x^2 - 26x + 12} \\
6x^2 - 24x \phantom{xxxx} \\
\hline
-2x + 12
\end{array}
$$

Divide leading terms: $\dfrac{6x^2}{x} = 6x$

Multiply: $6x(x - 4) = 6x^2 - 24x$

Subtract and "bring down" 12

We repeat the process using the last line $-2x + 12$ as the dividend.

$$
\begin{array}{r}
6x^2 - 2 \phantom{xxxx} \\
x - 4 \overline{)\, 6x^2 - 26x + 12} \\
6x^2 - 24x \phantom{xxxx} \\
\hline
-2x + 12 \\
-2x + 8 \\
\hline
4
\end{array}
$$

Divide leading terms: $\dfrac{-2x}{x} = -2$

Multiply: $-2(x - 4) = -2x + 8$

Subtract

The division process ends when the last line is of lesser degree than the divisor. The last line then contains the *remainder*, and the top line contains the *quotient*. The result of the division can be interpreted in either of two ways.

Dividend

Quotient

$$\frac{6x^2 - 26x + 12}{x - 4} = 6x - 2 + \frac{4}{x - 4}$$

Remainder

Divisor

or

$$6x^2 - 26x + 12 = (x - 4)(6x - 2) + 4$$

Remainder

Dividend    Divisor    Quotient

✎ **Practice what you've learned: Do Exercise 3.** ▲

▶ **EXAMPLE 2** | Long Division of Polynomials

Let $P(x) = 8x^4 + 6x^2 - 3x + 1$ and $D(x) = 2x^2 - x + 2$. Find polynomials $Q(x)$ and $R(x)$ such that $P(x) = D(x) \cdot Q(x) + R(x)$.

▼ **SOLUTION** We use long division after first inserting the term $0x^3$ into the dividend to ensure that the columns line up correctly.

$$
\begin{array}{r}
4x^2 + 2x \phantom{xxxxxxx} \\
2x^2 - x + 2 \overline{)\, 8x^4 + 0x^3 + 6x^2 - 3x + 1} \\
8x^4 - 4x^3 + 8x^2 \phantom{xxxxxxx} \\
\hline
4x^3 - 2x^2 - 3x \phantom{xxx} \\
4x^3 - 2x^2 + 4x \phantom{xxx} \\
\hline
-7x + 1
\end{array}
$$

Multiply divisor by $4x^2$

Subtract

Multiply divisor by $2x$

Subtract

The process is complete at this point because $-7x + 1$ is of lesser degree than the divisor $2x^2 - x + 2$. From the above long division we see that $Q(x) = 4x^2 + 2x$ and $R(x) = -7x + 1$, so

$$8x^4 + 6x^2 - 3x + 1 = (2x^2 - x + 2)(4x^2 + 2x) + (-7x + 1)$$

✎ **Practice what you've learned: Do Exercise 19.** ▲

## ■ Synthetic Division

**Synthetic division** is a quick method of dividing polynomials; it can be used when the divisor is of the form $x - c$. In synthetic division we write only the essential parts of the long division. Compare the following long and synthetic divisions, in which we divide $2x^3 - 7x^2 + 5$ by $x - 3$. (We'll explain how to perform the synthetic division in Example 3.)

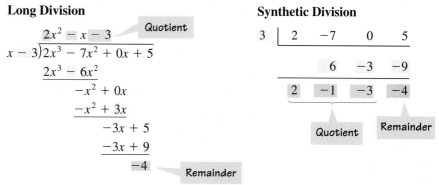

**Long Division**

$$
\begin{array}{r}
2x^2 - x - 3 \\
x - 3 \overline{)\ 2x^3 - 7x^2 + 0x + 5} \\
\underline{2x^3 - 6x^2} \\
-x^2 + 0x \\
\underline{-x^2 + 3x} \\
-3x + 5 \\
\underline{-3x + 9} \\
-4
\end{array}
$$

Quotient

Remainder

**Synthetic Division**

$$
\begin{array}{c|cccc}
3 & 2 & -7 & 0 & 5 \\
  &   & 6 & -3 & -9 \\
\hline
  & 2 & -1 & -3 & -4
\end{array}
$$

Quotient    Remainder

Note that in synthetic division we abbreviate $2x^3 - 7x^2 + 5$ by writing only the coefficients: 2  −7  0  5, and instead of $x - 3$, we simply write 3. (Writing 3 instead of −3 allows us to add instead of subtract, but this changes the sign of all the numbers that appear in the gold boxes.)

The next example shows how synthetic division is performed.

▶ **EXAMPLE 3** | Synthetic Division

Use synthetic division to divide $2x^3 - 7x^2 + 5$ by $x - 3$.

▼ **SOLUTION**    We begin by writing the appropriate coefficients to represent the divisor and the dividend.

Divisor $x - 3$

$$
\begin{array}{c|cccc}
3 & 2 & -7 & 0 & 5
\end{array}
$$

Dividend $2x^3 - 7x^2 + 0x + 5$

We bring down the 2, multiply $3 \cdot 2 = 6$, and write the result in the middle row. Then we add.

$$
\begin{array}{c|cccc}
3 & 2 & -7 & 0 & 5 \\
  &   & 6 &   &   \\
\hline
  & 2 & -1 &   &
\end{array}
$$

Multiply: $3 \cdot 2 = 6$

Add: $-7 + 6 = -1$

We repeat this process of multiplying and then adding until the table is complete.

$$
\begin{array}{c|cccc}
3 & 2 & -7 & 0 & 5 \\
  &   & 6 & -3 &   \\
\hline
  & 2 & -1 & -3 &
\end{array}
$$

Multiply: $3(-1) = -3$

Add: $0 + (-3) = -3$

$$
\begin{array}{r|rrrr}
3 & 2 & -7 & 0 & 5 \\
  &   & 6 & -3 & -9 \\
\hline
  & 2 & -1 & -3 & -4
\end{array}
$$

Multiply: $3(-3) = -9$

Add: $5 + (-9) = -4$

Quotient
$2x^2 - x - 3$

Remainder
$-4$

From the last line of the synthetic division we see that the quotient is $2x^2 - x - 3$ and the remainder is $-4$. Thus

$$2x^3 - 7x^2 + 5 = (x - 3)(2x^2 - x - 3) - 4$$

✎ **Practice what you've learned: Do Exercise 31.**  ▲

## ■ The Remainder and Factor Theorems

The next theorem shows how synthetic division can be used to evaluate polynomials easily.

---

**REMAINDER THEOREM**

If the polynomial $P(x)$ is divided by $x - c$, then the remainder is the value $P(c)$.

---

▼ **PROOF**  If the divisor in the Division Algorithm is of the form $x - c$ for some real number $c$, then the remainder must be a constant (since the degree of the remainder is less than the degree of the divisor). If we call this constant $r$, then

$$P(x) = (x - c) \cdot Q(x) + r$$

Replacing $x$ by $c$ in this equation, we get $P(c) = (c - c) \cdot Q(x) + r = 0 + r = r$, that is, $P(c)$ is the remainder $r$.  ▲

▶ **EXAMPLE 4** | Using the Remainder Theorem to Find the Value of a Polynomial

Let $P(x) = 3x^5 + 5x^4 - 4x^3 + 7x + 3$.

**(a)** Find the quotient and remainder when $P(x)$ is divided by $x + 2$.

**(b)** Use the Remainder Theorem to find $P(-2)$.

▼ **SOLUTION**

**(a)** Since $x + 2 = x - (-2)$, the synthetic division for this problem takes the following form.

$$
\begin{array}{r|rrrrrr}
-2 & 3 & 5 & -4 & 0 & 7 & 3 \\
   &   & -6 & 2 & 4 & -8 & 2 \\
\hline
   & 3 & -1 & -2 & 4 & -1 & 5
\end{array}
$$

Remainder is 5,
so $P(-2) = 5$.

The quotient is $3x^4 - x^3 - 2x^2 + 4x - 1$, and the remainder is 5.

**(b)** By the Remainder Theorem, $P(-2)$ is the remainder when $P(x)$ is divided by $x - (-2) = x + 2$. From part (a) the remainder is 5, so $P(-2) = 5$.

✎ **Practice what you've learned: Do Exercise 39.**  ▲

The next theorem says that *zeros* of polynomials correspond to *factors*; we used this fact in Section 4.2 to graph polynomials.

---

**FACTOR THEOREM**

$c$ is a zero of $P$ if and only if $x - c$ is a factor of $P(x)$.

---

▼ **PROOF**    If $P(x)$ factors as $P(x) = (x - c) \cdot Q(x)$, then

$$P(c) = (c - c) \cdot Q(c) = 0 \cdot Q(c) = 0$$

Conversely, if $P(c) = 0$, then by the Remainder Theorem

$$P(x) = (x - c) \cdot Q(x) + 0 = (x - c) \cdot Q(x)$$

so $x - c$ is a factor of $P(x)$.    ▲

▶ **EXAMPLE 5** | Factoring a Polynomial Using the Factor Theorem

Let $P(x) = x^3 - 7x + 6$. Show that $P(1) = 0$, and use this fact to factor $P(x)$ completely.

▼ **SOLUTION**    Substituting, we see that $P(1) = 1^3 - 7 \cdot 1 + 6 = 0$. By the Factor Theorem this means that $x - 1$ is a factor of $P(x)$. Using synthetic or long division (shown in the margin), we see that

$$
\begin{aligned}
P(x) &= x^3 - 7x + 6 \\
&= (x - 1)(x^2 + x - 6) & \text{See margin} \\
&= (x - 1)(x - 2)(x + 3) & \text{Factor quadratic } x^2 + x - 6
\end{aligned}
$$

✎ **Practice what you've learned: Do Exercises 53 and 57.**    ▲

$$
\begin{array}{r|rrrr}
1 & 1 & 0 & -7 & 6 \\
  &   & 1 & 1 & -6 \\
\hline
  & 1 & 1 & -6 & 0
\end{array}
$$

$$
\require{enclose}
\begin{array}{r}
x^2 + x - 6 \\[-3pt]
x - 1 \enclose{longdiv}{x^3 + 0x^2 - 7x + 6} \\
\underline{x^3 - x^2}\phantom{xxxxxxxx} \\
x^2 - 7x\phantom{xxx} \\
\underline{x^2 - x}\phantom{xxx} \\
-6x + 6 \\
\underline{-6x + 6} \\
0
\end{array}
$$

▶ **EXAMPLE 6** | Finding a Polynomial with Specified Zeros

Find a polynomial of degree 4 that has zeros $-3, 0, 1,$ and $5$.

▼ **SOLUTION**    By the Factor Theorem $x - (-3)$, $x - 0$, $x - 1$, and $x - 5$ must all be factors of the desired polynomial, so let

$$
\begin{aligned}
P(x) &= (x + 3)(x - 0)(x - 1)(x - 5) \\
&= x^4 - 3x^3 - 13x^2 + 15x
\end{aligned}
$$

Since $P(x)$ is of degree 4, it is a solution of the problem. Any other solution of the problem must be a constant multiple of $P(x)$, since only multiplication by a constant does not change the degree.

✎ **Practice what you've learned: Do Exercise 59.**    ▲

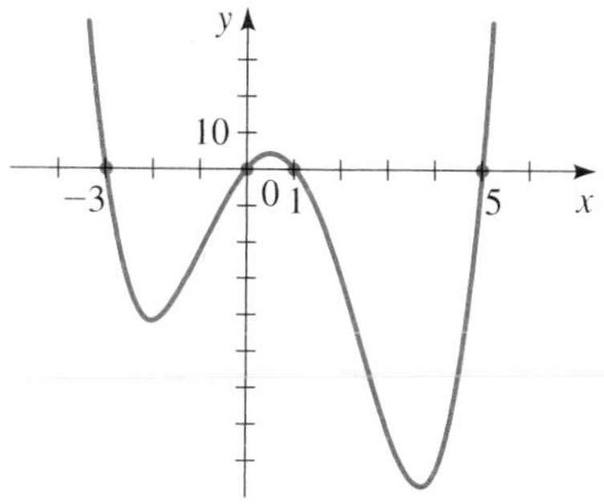

**FIGURE 1**

$P(x) = (x + 3)x(x - 1)(x - 5)$ has zeros $-3, 0, 1,$ and $5$.

The polynomial $P$ of Example 6 is graphed in Figure 1. Note that the zeros of $P$ correspond to the $x$-intercepts of the graph.

# 4.3 EXERCISES

## ▼ CONCEPTS

**1.** If we divide the polynomial $P$ by the factor $x - c$ and we obtain the equation $P(x) = (x - c)Q(x) + R(x)$, then we say that $x - c$ is the divisor, $Q(x)$ is the _____, and $R(x)$ is the _____.

**2.** **(a)** If we divide the polynomial $P(x)$ by the factor $x - c$ and we obtain a remainder of 0, then we know that $c$ is a

_____ of $P$.

**(b)** If we divide the polynomial $P(x)$ by the factor $x - c$ and we obtain a remainder of $k$, then we know that

$P(c) = $ _____.

## ▼ SKILLS

**3–8** ▪ Two polynomials $P$ and $D$ are given. Use either synthetic or long division to divide $P(x)$ by $D(x)$, and express $P$ in the form $P(x) = D(x) \cdot Q(x) + R(x)$.

**3.** $P(x) = 3x^2 + 5x - 4$, $D(x) = x + 3$

**4.** $P(x) = x^3 + 4x^2 - 6x + 1$, $D(x) = x - 1$

**5.** $P(x) = 2x^3 - 3x^2 - 2x$, $D(x) = 2x - 3$

**6.** $P(x) = 4x^3 + 7x + 9$, $D(x) = 2x + 1$

**7.** $P(x) = x^4 - x^3 + 4x + 2$, $D(x) = x^2 + 3$

**8.** $P(x) = 2x^5 + 4x^4 - 4x^3 - x - 3$, $D(x) = x^2 - 2$

**9–14** ▪ Two polynomials $P$ and $D$ are given. Use either synthetic or long division to divide $P(x)$ by $D(x)$, and express the quotient $P(x)/D(x)$ in the form

$$\frac{P(x)}{D(x)} = Q(x) + \frac{R(x)}{D(x)}$$

**9.** $P(x) = x^2 + 4x - 8$, $D(x) = x + 3$

**10.** $P(x) = x^3 + 6x + 5$, $D(x) = x - 4$

**11.** $P(x) = 4x^2 - 3x - 7$, $D(x) = 2x - 1$

**12.** $P(x) = 6x^3 + x^2 - 12x + 5$, $D(x) = 3x - 4$

**13.** $P(x) = 2x^4 - x^3 + 9x^2$, $D(x) = x^2 + 4$

**14.** $P(x) = x^5 + x^4 - 2x^3 + x + 1$, $D(x) = x^2 + x - 1$

**15–24** ▪ Find the quotient and remainder using long division.

**15.** $\dfrac{x^2 - 6x - 8}{x - 4}$

**16.** $\dfrac{x^3 - x^2 - 2x + 6}{x - 2}$

**17.** $\dfrac{4x^3 + 2x^2 - 2x - 3}{2x + 1}$

**18.** $\dfrac{x^3 + 3x^2 + 4x + 3}{3x + 6}$

**19.** $\dfrac{x^3 + 6x + 3}{x^2 - 2x + 2}$

**20.** $\dfrac{3x^4 - 5x^3 - 20x - 5}{x^2 + x + 3}$

**21.** $\dfrac{6x^3 + 2x^2 + 22x}{2x^2 + 5}$

**22.** $\dfrac{9x^2 - x + 5}{3x^2 - 7x}$

**23.** $\dfrac{x^6 + x^4 + x^2 + 1}{x^2 + 1}$

**24.** $\dfrac{2x^5 - 7x^4 - 13}{4x^2 - 6x + 8}$

**25–38** ▪ Find the quotient and remainder using synthetic division.

**25.** $\dfrac{x^2 - 5x + 4}{x - 3}$

**26.** $\dfrac{x^2 - 5x + 4}{x - 1}$

**27.** $\dfrac{3x^2 + 5x}{x - 6}$

**28.** $\dfrac{4x^2 - 3}{x + 5}$

**29.** $\dfrac{x^3 + 2x^2 + 2x + 1}{x + 2}$

**30.** $\dfrac{3x^3 - 12x^2 - 9x + 1}{x - 5}$

**31.** $\dfrac{x^3 - 8x + 2}{x + 3}$

**32.** $\dfrac{x^4 - x^3 + x^2 - x + 2}{x - 2}$

**33.** $\dfrac{x^5 + 3x^3 - 6}{x - 1}$

**34.** $\dfrac{x^3 - 9x^2 + 27x - 27}{x - 3}$

**35.** $\dfrac{2x^3 + 3x^2 - 2x + 1}{x - \frac{1}{2}}$

**36.** $\dfrac{6x^4 + 10x^3 + 5x^2 + x + 1}{x + \frac{2}{3}}$

**37.** $\dfrac{x^3 - 27}{x - 3}$

**38.** $\dfrac{x^4 - 16}{x + 2}$

**39–51** ▪ Use synthetic division and the Remainder Theorem to evaluate $P(c)$.

**39.** $P(x) = 4x^2 + 12x + 5$, $c = -1$

**40.** $P(x) = 2x^2 + 9x + 1$, $c = \frac{1}{2}$

**41.** $P(x) = x^3 + 3x^2 - 7x + 6$, $c = 2$

**42.** $P(x) = x^3 - x^2 + x + 5$, $c = -1$

**43.** $P(x) = x^3 + 2x^2 - 7$, $c = -2$

**44.** $P(x) = 2x^3 - 21x^2 + 9x - 200$, $c = 11$

**45.** $P(x) = 5x^4 + 30x^3 - 40x^2 + 36x + 14$, $c = -7$

**46.** $P(x) = 6x^5 + 10x^3 + x + 1$, $c = -2$

**47.** $P(x) = x^7 - 3x^2 - 1$, $c = 3$

**48.** $P(x) = -2x^6 + 7x^5 + 40x^4 - 7x^2 + 10x + 112$, $c = -3$

**49.** $P(x) = 3x^3 + 4x^2 - 2x + 1$, $c = \frac{2}{3}$

**50.** $P(x) = x^3 - x + 1$, $c = \frac{1}{4}$

**51.** $P(x) = x^3 + 2x^2 - 3x - 8$, $c = 0.1$

**52.** Let

$$P(x) = 6x^7 - 40x^6 + 16x^5 - 200x^4$$
$$- 60x^3 - 69x^2 + 13x - 139$$

Calculate $P(7)$ by **(a)** using synthetic division and **(b)** substituting $x = 7$ into the polynomial and evaluating directly.

**53–56** ▪ Use the Factor Theorem to show that $x - c$ is a factor of $P(x)$ for the given value(s) of $c$.

**53.** $P(x) = x^3 - 3x^2 + 3x - 1$, $c = 1$

**54.** $P(x) = x^3 + 2x^2 - 3x - 10, \quad c = 2$

**55.** $P(x) = 2x^3 + 7x^2 + 6x - 5, \quad c = \frac{1}{2}$

**56.** $P(x) = x^4 + 3x^3 - 16x^2 - 27x + 63, \quad c = 3, -3$

**57–58** ▪ Show that the given value(s) of $c$ are zeros of $P(x)$, and find all other zeros of $P(x)$.

**57.** $P(x) = x^3 - x^2 - 11x + 15, \quad c = 3$

**58.** $P(x) = 3x^4 - x^3 - 21x^2 - 11x + 6, \quad c = \frac{1}{3}, -2$

**59–62** ▪ Find a polynomial of the specified degree that has the given zeros.

**59.** Degree 3;  zeros $-1, 1, 3$

**60.** Degree 4;  zeros $-2, 0, 2, 4$

**61.** Degree 4;  zeros $-1, 1, 3, 5$

**62.** Degree 5;  zeros $-2, -1, 0, 1, 2$

**63.** Find a polynomial of degree 3 that has zeros 1, $-2$, and 3 and in which the coefficient of $x^2$ is 3.

**64.** Find a polynomial of degree 4 that has integer coefficients and zeros 1, $-1$, 2, and $\frac{1}{2}$.

**65–68** ▪ Find the polynomial of the specified degree whose graph is shown.

**65.** Degree 3

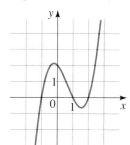

**66.** Degree 3

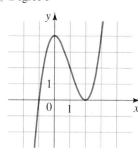

**67.** Degree 4

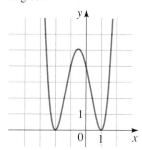

**68.** Degree 4

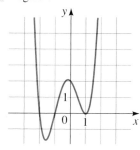

▼ **DISCOVERY • DISCUSSION • WRITING**

**69. Impossible Division?**  Suppose you were asked to solve the following two problems on a test:
  **A.** Find the remainder when $6x^{1000} - 17x^{562} + 12x + 26$ is divided by $x + 1$.
  **B.** Is $x - 1$ a factor of $x^{567} - 3x^{400} + x^9 + 2$?

Obviously, it's impossible to solve these problems by dividing, because the polynomials are of such large degree. Use one or more of the theorems in this section to solve these problems *without* actually dividing.

**70. Nested Form of a Polynomial**  Expand $Q$ to prove that the polynomials $P$ and $Q$ are the same.

$$P(x) = 3x^4 - 5x^3 + x^2 - 3x + 5$$
$$Q(x) = (((3x - 5)x + 1)x - 3)x + 5$$

Try to evaluate $P(2)$ and $Q(2)$ in your head, using the forms given. Which is easier? Now write the polynomial $R(x) = x^5 - 2x^4 + 3x^3 - 2x^2 + 3x + 4$ in "nested" form, like the polynomial $Q$. Use the nested form to find $R(3)$ in your head.

  Do you see how calculating with the nested form follows the same arithmetic steps as calculating the value of a polynomial using synthetic division?

---

| **4.4** | Real Zeros of Polynomials |

**LEARNING OBJECTIVES**

After completing this section, you will be able to:

- ▪ Use the Rational Zeros Theorem to find the rational zeros of a polynomial
- ▪ Use Descartes' Rule of Signs to determine the number of positive and negative zeros of a polynomial
- ▪ Use the Upper and Lower Bounds Theorem to find upper and lower bounds for the zeros of a polynomial
- ▪ Use algebra and graphing devices to solve polynomial equations

The Factor Theorem tells us that finding the zeros of a polynomial is really the same thing as factoring it into linear factors. In this section we study some algebraic methods that help us to find the real zeros of a polynomial and thereby factor the polynomial. We begin with the *rational* zeros of a polynomial.

### ■ Rational Zeros of Polynomials

To help us understand the next theorem, let's consider the polynomial

$$P(x) = (x - 2)(x - 3)(x + 4) \qquad \text{Factored form}$$
$$= x^3 - x^2 - 14x + 24 \qquad \text{Expanded form}$$

From the factored form we see that the zeros of $P$ are 2, 3, and $-4$. When the polynomial is expanded, the constant 24 is obtained by multiplying $(-2) \times (-3) \times 4$. This means that the zeros of the polynomial are all factors of the constant term. The following generalizes this observation.

---

**RATIONAL ZEROS THEOREM**

If the polynomial $P(x) = a_n x^n + a_{n-1} x^{n-1} + \cdots + a_1 x + a_0$ has integer coefficients, then every rational zero of $P$ is of the form

$$\frac{p}{q}$$

where   $p$ is a factor of the constant coefficient $a_0$
and      $q$ is a factor of the leading coefficient $a_n$.

---

▼ **PROOF**   If $p/q$ is a rational zero, in lowest terms, of the polynomial $P$, then we have

$$a_n\left(\frac{p}{q}\right)^n + a_{n-1}\left(\frac{p}{q}\right)^{n-1} + \cdots + a_1\left(\frac{p}{q}\right) + a_0 = 0$$

$$a_n p^n + a_{n-1} p^{n-1} q + \cdots + a_1 p q^{n-1} + a_0 q^n = 0 \qquad \text{Multiply by } q^n$$

$$p(a_n p^{n-1} + a_{n-1} p^{n-2} q + \cdots + a_1 q^{n-1}) = -a_0 q^n \qquad \begin{array}{l}\text{Subtract } a_0 q^n \\ \text{and factor LHS}\end{array}$$

Now $p$ is a factor of the left side, so it must be a factor of the right side as well. Since $p/q$ is in lowest terms, $p$ and $q$ have no factor in common, and so $p$ must be a factor of $a_0$. A similar proof shows that $q$ is a factor of $a_n$.   ▲

We see from the Rational Zeros Theorem that if the leading coefficient is 1 or $-1$, then the rational zeros must be factors of the constant term.

▶ **EXAMPLE 1** | Using the Rational Zeros Theorem

Find the rational zeros of $P(x) = x^3 - 3x + 2$.

▼ **SOLUTION**   Since the leading coefficient is 1, any rational zero must be a divisor of the constant term 2. So the possible rational zeros are $\pm 1$ and $\pm 2$. We test each of these possibilities.

$$P(1) = (1)^3 - 3(1) + 2 = 0$$
$$P(-1) = (-1)^3 - 3(-1) + 2 = 4$$
$$P(2) = (2)^3 - 3(2) + 2 = 4$$
$$P(-2) = (-2)^3 - 3(-2) + 2 = 0$$

The rational zeros of $P$ are 1 and $-2$.

✎ **Practice what you've learned: Do Exercise 15.**   ▲

The following box explains how we use the Rational Zeros Theorem with synthetic division to factor a polynomial.

---

**FINDING THE RATIONAL ZEROS OF A POLYNOMIAL**

1. **List Possible Zeros.**   List all possible rational zeros, using the Rational Zeros Theorem.
2. **Divide.**   Use synthetic division to evaluate the polynomial at each of the candidates for the rational zeros that you found in Step 1. When the remainder is 0, note the quotient you have obtained.
3. **Repeat.**   Repeat Steps 1 and 2 for the quotient. Stop when you reach a quotient that is quadratic or factors easily, and use the quadratic formula or factor to find the remaining zeros.

---

▶ **EXAMPLE 2** | Finding Rational Zeros

Factor the polynomial $P(x) = 2x^3 + x^2 - 13x + 6$, and find all its zeros.

▼ **SOLUTION**   By the Rational Zeros Theorem the rational zeros of $P$ are of the form

$$\text{possible rational zero of } P = \frac{\text{factor of constant term}}{\text{factor of leading coefficient}}$$

The constant term is 6 and the leading coefficient is 2, so

$$\text{possible rational zero of } P = \frac{\text{factor of 6}}{\text{factor of 2}}$$

The factors of 6 are $\pm 1$, $\pm 2$, $\pm 3$, $\pm 6$ and the factors of 2 are $\pm 1$, $\pm 2$. Thus, the possible rational zeros of $P$ are

$$\pm\frac{1}{1}, \quad \pm\frac{2}{1}, \quad \pm\frac{3}{1}, \quad \pm\frac{6}{1}, \quad \pm\frac{1}{2}, \quad \pm\frac{2}{2}, \quad \pm\frac{3}{2}, \quad \pm\frac{6}{2}$$

Simplifying the fractions and eliminating duplicates, we get the following list of possible rational zeros:

$$\pm 1, \quad \pm 2, \quad \pm 3, \quad \pm 6, \quad \pm\frac{1}{2}, \quad \pm\frac{3}{2}$$

**Evariste Galois** (1811–1832) is one of the very few mathematicians to have an entire theory named in his honor. Not yet 21 when he died, he completely settled the central problem in the theory of equations by describing a criterion that reveals whether a polynomial equation can be solved by algebraic operations. Galois was one of the greatest mathematicians in the world at that time, although no one knew it but him. He repeatedly sent his work to the eminent mathematicians Cauchy and Poisson, who either lost his letters or did not understand his ideas. Galois wrote in a terse style and included few details, which probably played a role in his failure to pass the entrance exams at the Ecole Polytechnique in Paris. A political radical, Galois spent several months in prison for his revolutionary activities. His brief life came to a tragic end when he was killed in a duel over a love affair. The night before his duel, fearing that he would die, Galois wrote down the essence of his ideas and entrusted them to his friend Auguste Chevalier. He concluded by writing "there will, I hope, be people who will find it to their advantage to decipher all this mess." The mathematician Camille Jordan did just that, 14 years later.

Library of Congress

To check which of these *possible* zeros actually *are* zeros, we need to evaluate $P$ at each of these numbers. An efficient way to do this is to use synthetic division.

**Test whether 1 is a zero**

$$
\begin{array}{r|rrrr}
1 & 2 & 1 & -13 & 6 \\
  &   & 2 & 3 & -10 \\
\hline
  & 2 & 3 & -10 & -4
\end{array}
$$

Remainder is *not 0*, so 1 is *not a zero.*

**Test whether 2 is a zero**

$$
\begin{array}{r|rrrr}
2 & 2 & 1 & -13 & 6 \\
  &   & 4 & 10 & -6 \\
\hline
  & 2 & 5 & -3 & 0
\end{array}
$$

Remainder is *0*, so 2 is a zero.

From the last synthetic division we see that 2 is a zero of $P$ and that $P$ factors as

$$
\begin{aligned}
P(x) &= 2x^3 + x^2 - 13x + 6 \\
&= (x - 2)(2x^2 + 5x - 3) \qquad \text{From synthetic division} \\
&= (x - 2)(2x - 1)(x + 3) \qquad \text{Factor } 2x^2 + 5x - 3
\end{aligned}
$$

From the factored form we see that the zeros of $P$ are 2, $\frac{1}{2}$, and $-3$.

✎ **Practice what you've learned: Do Exercise 27.**            ▲

▶ **EXAMPLE 3** | Using the Rational Zeros Theorem and the Quadratic Formula

Let $P(x) = x^4 - 5x^3 - 5x^2 + 23x + 10$.

**(a)** Find the zeros of $P$.

**(b)** Sketch the graph of $P$.

▼ **SOLUTION**

**(a)** The leading coefficient of $P$ is 1, so all the rational zeros are integers: They are divisors of the constant term 10. Thus, the possible candidates are

$$\pm 1, \quad \pm 2, \quad \pm 5, \quad \pm 10$$

$$
\begin{array}{r|rrrrr}
1 & 1 & -5 & -5 & 23 & 10 \\
  &   & 1 & -4 & -9 & 14 \\
\hline
  & 1 & -4 & -9 & 14 & \boxed{24}
\end{array}
$$

$$
\begin{array}{r|rrrrr}
2 & 1 & -5 & -5 & 23 & 10 \\
  &   & 2 & -6 & -22 & 2 \\
\hline
  & 1 & -3 & -11 & 1 & \boxed{12}
\end{array}
$$

$$
\begin{array}{r|rrrrr}
5 & 1 & -5 & -5 & 23 & 10 \\
  &   & 5 & 0 & -25 & -10 \\
\hline
  & 1 & 0 & -5 & -2 & \boxed{0}
\end{array}
$$

Using synthetic division (see the margin), we find that 1 and 2 are not zeros but that 5 is a zero and that $P$ factors as

$$x^4 - 5x^3 - 5x^2 + 23x + 10 = (x - 5)(x^3 - 5x - 2)$$

We now try to factor the quotient $x^3 - 5x - 2$. Its possible zeros are the divisors of $-2$, namely,

$$\pm 1, \quad \pm 2$$

Since we already know that 1 and 2 are not zeros of the original polynomial $P$, we don't need to try them again. Checking the remaining candidates $-1$ and $-2$, we see that $-2$ is a zero (see the margin), and $P$ factors as

$$
\begin{array}{r|rrrr}
-2 & 1 & 0 & -5 & -2 \\
   &   & -2 & 4 & 2 \\
\hline
   & 1 & -2 & -1 & \boxed{0}
\end{array}
$$

$$
\begin{aligned}
x^4 - 5x^3 - 5x^2 + 23x + 10 &= (x - 5)(x^3 - 5x - 2) \\
&= (x - 5)(x + 2)(x^2 - 2x - 1)
\end{aligned}
$$

Now we use the quadratic formula to obtain the two remaining zeros of $P$:

$$x = \frac{2 \pm \sqrt{(-2)^2 - 4(1)(-1)}}{2} = 1 \pm \sqrt{2}$$

The zeros of $P$ are 5, $-2$, $1 + \sqrt{2}$, and $1 - \sqrt{2}$.

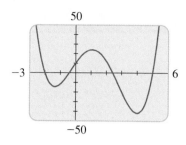

**FIGURE 1**
$P(x) = x^4 - 5x^3 - 5x^2 + 23x + 10$

| Polynomial | Variations in sign |
|---|---|
| $x^2 + 4x + 1$ | 0 |
| $2x^3 + x - 6$ | 1 |
| $x^4 - 3x^2 - x + 4$ | 2 |

**(b)** Now that we know the zeros of $P$, we can use the methods of Section 4.2 to sketch the graph. If we want to use a graphing calculator instead, knowing the zeros allows us to choose an appropriate viewing rectangle—one that is wide enough to contain all the $x$-intercepts of $P$. Numerical approximations to the zeros of $P$ are

$$5, \quad -2, \quad 2.4, \quad \text{and} \quad -0.4$$

So in this case we choose the rectangle $[-3, 6]$ by $[-50, 50]$ and draw the graph shown in Figure 1.

✎ **Practice what you've learned: Do Exercises 45 and 55.** ▲

## ■ Descartes' Rule of Signs and Upper and Lower Bounds for Roots

In some cases, the following rule—discovered by the French philosopher and mathematician René Descartes around 1637 (see page 245)—is helpful in eliminating candidates from lengthy lists of possible rational roots. To describe this rule, we need the concept of *variation in sign*. If $P(x)$ is a polynomial with real coefficients, written with descending powers of $x$ (and omitting powers with coefficient 0), then a **variation in sign** occurs whenever adjacent coefficients have opposite signs. For example,

$$P(x) = 5x^7 - 3x^5 - x^4 + 2x^2 + x - 3$$

has three variations in sign.

---

**DESCARTES' RULE OF SIGNS**

Let $P$ be a polynomial with real coefficients.

**1.** The number of positive real zeros of $P(x)$ either is equal to the number of variations in sign in $P(x)$ or is less than that by an even whole number.

**2.** The number of negative real zeros of $P(x)$ either is equal to the number of variations in sign in $P(-x)$ or is less than that by an even whole number.

---

▶ **EXAMPLE 4** | Using Descartes' Rule

Use Descartes' Rule of Signs to determine the possible number of positive and negative real zeros of the polynomial

$$P(x) = 3x^6 + 4x^5 + 3x^3 - x - 3$$

▼ **SOLUTION** The polynomial has one variation in sign, so it has one positive zero. Now

$$P(-x) = 3(-x)^6 + 4(-x)^5 + 3(-x)^3 - (-x) - 3$$
$$= 3x^6 - 4x^5 - 3x^3 + x - 3$$

So $P(-x)$ has three variations in sign. Thus, $P(x)$ has either three or one negative zero(s), making a total of either two or four real zeros.

✎ **Practice what you've learned: Do Exercise 65.** ▲

We say that $a$ is a **lower bound** and $b$ is an **upper bound** for the zeros of a polynomial if every real zero $c$ of the polynomial satisfies $a \le c \le b$. The next theorem helps us to find such bounds for the zeros of a polynomial.

### THE UPPER AND LOWER BOUNDS THEOREM

Let $P$ be a polynomial with real coefficients.

**1.** If we divide $P(x)$ by $x - b$ (with $b > 0$) using synthetic division and if the row that contains the quotient and remainder has no negative entry, then $b$ is an upper bound for the real zeros of $P$.

**2.** If we divide $P(x)$ by $x - a$ (with $a < 0$) using synthetic division and if the row that contains the quotient and remainder has entries that are alternately nonpositive and nonnegative, then $a$ is a lower bound for the real zeros of $P$.

A proof of this theorem is suggested in Exercise 95. The phrase "alternately nonpositive and nonnegative" simply means that the signs of the numbers alternate, with 0 considered to be positive or negative as required.

▶ **EXAMPLE 5** | Upper and Lower Bounds for Zeros of a Polynomial

Show that all the real zeros of the polynomial $P(x) = x^4 - 3x^2 + 2x - 5$ lie between $-3$ and $2$.

▼ **SOLUTION** We divide $P(x)$ by $x - 2$ and $x + 3$ using synthetic division.

$$
\begin{array}{r|rrrrr}
2 & 1 & 0 & -3 & 2 & -5 \\
  &   & 2 & 4  & 2 & 8 \\
\hline
  & 1 & 2 & 1  & 4 & 3
\end{array}
\qquad
\begin{array}{r|rrrrr}
-3 & 1 & 0 & -3 & 2 & -5 \\
   &   & -3 & 9 & -18 & 48 \\
\hline
   & 1 & -3 & 6 & -16 & 43
\end{array}
$$

All entries positive

Entries alternate in sign.

By the Upper and Lower Bounds Theorem, $-3$ is a lower bound and 2 is an upper bound for the zeros. Since neither $-3$ nor 2 is a zero (the remainders are not 0 in the division table), all the real zeros lie between these numbers.

✎ **Practice what you've learned: Do Exercise 69.** ▲

▶ **EXAMPLE 6** | Factoring a Fifth-Degree Polynomial

Factor completely the polynomial

$$P(x) = 2x^5 + 5x^4 - 8x^3 - 14x^2 + 6x + 9$$

▼ **SOLUTION** The possible rational zeros of $P$ are $\pm\frac{1}{2}$, $\pm 1$, $\pm\frac{3}{2}$, $\pm 3$, $\pm\frac{9}{2}$, and $\pm 9$. We check the positive candidates first, beginning with the smallest.

$$
\begin{array}{r|rrrrrr}
\frac{1}{2} & 2 & 5 & -8 & -14 & 6 & 9 \\
 &  & 1 & 3 & -\frac{5}{2} & -\frac{33}{4} & -\frac{9}{8} \\
\hline
 & 2 & 6 & -5 & -\frac{33}{2} & -\frac{9}{4} & \frac{63}{8}
\end{array}
\qquad
\begin{array}{r|rrrrrr}
1 & 2 & 5 & -8 & -14 & 6 & 9 \\
 &  & 2 & 7 & -1 & -15 & -9 \\
\hline
 & 2 & 7 & -1 & -15 & -9 & 0
\end{array}
$$

$\frac{1}{2}$ is not a zero

$P(1) = 0$

So 1 is a zero, and $P(x) = (x - 1)(2x^4 + 7x^3 - x^2 - 15x - 9)$. We continue by factoring the quotient. We still have the same list of possible zeros except that $\frac{1}{2}$ has been eliminated.

$$
\begin{array}{r|rrrrr}
1 & 2 & 7 & -1 & -15 & -9 \\
 &  & 2 & 9 & 8 & -7 \\
\hline
 & 2 & 9 & 8 & -7 & -16
\end{array}
$$

1 is not a zero.

$$
\begin{array}{r|rrrrr}
\frac{3}{2} & 2 & 7 & -1 & -15 & -9 \\
 &  & 3 & 15 & 21 & 9 \\
\hline
 & 2 & 10 & 14 & 6 & 0
\end{array}
$$

$P(\frac{3}{2}) = 0$, all entries nonnegative

We see that $\frac{3}{2}$ is both a zero and an upper bound for the zeros of $P(x)$, so we do not need to check any further for positive zeros, because all the remaining candidates are greater than $\frac{3}{2}$.

$$P(x) = (x - 1)(x - \tfrac{3}{2})(2x^3 + 10x^2 + 14x + 6)$$   From synthetic division

$$= (x - 1)(2x - 3)(x^3 + 5x^2 + 7x + 3)$$   Factor 2 from last factor, multiply into second factor

By Descartes' Rule of Signs, $x^3 + 5x^2 + 7x + 3$ has no positive zero, so its only possible rational zeros are $-1$ and $-3$.

$$
\begin{array}{r|rrrr}
-1 & 1 & 5 & 7 & 3 \\
 &  & -1 & -4 & -3 \\
\hline
 & 1 & 4 & 3 & 0
\end{array}
$$

$P(-1) = 0$

Therefore

$$P(x) = (x - 1)(2x - 3)(x + 1)(x^2 + 4x + 3)$$   From synthetic division

$$= (x - 1)(2x - 3)(x + 1)^2(x + 3)$$   Factor quadratic

This means that the zeros of $P$ are $1, \frac{3}{2}, -1$, and $-3$. The graph of the polynomial is shown in Figure 2.

✎ **Practice what you've learned: Do Exercise 77.** ▲

**FIGURE 2**

$P(x) = 2x^5 + 5x^4 - 8x^3 - 14x^2 + 6x + 9$

$= (x - 1)(2x - 3)(x + 1)^2(x + 3)$

### ■ Using Algebra and Graphing Devices to Solve Polynomial Equations

In Section 2.3 we used graphing devices to solve equations graphically. We can now use the algebraic techniques that we've learned to select an appropriate viewing rectangle when solving a polynomial equation graphically.

▶ **EXAMPLE 7** | Solving a Fourth-Degree Equation Graphically

Find all real solutions of the following equation, correct to the nearest tenth.

$$3x^4 + 4x^3 - 7x^2 - 2x - 3 = 0$$

▼ **SOLUTION**   To solve the equation graphically, we graph

$$P(x) = 3x^4 + 4x^3 - 7x^2 - 2x - 3$$

We use the Upper and Lower Bounds Theorem to see where the solutions can be found.

First we use the Upper and Lower Bounds Theorem to find two numbers between which all the solutions must lie. This allows us to choose a viewing rectangle that is certain to contain all the $x$-intercepts of $P$. We use synthetic division and proceed by trial and error.

To find an upper bound, we try the whole numbers, 1, 2, 3, . . . , as potential candidates. We see that 2 is an upper bound for the solutions.

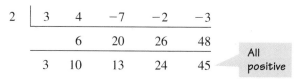

$$
\begin{array}{r|rrrrr}
2 & 3 & 4 & -7 & -2 & -3 \\
  &   & 6 & 20 & 26 & 48 \\
\hline
  & 3 & 10 & 13 & 24 & 45 \\
\end{array}
$$

All positive

Now we look for a lower bound, trying the numbers −1, −2, and −3 as potential candidates. We see that −3 is a lower bound for the solutions.

$$
\begin{array}{r|rrrrr}
-3 & 3 & 4 & -7 & -2 & -3 \\
   &   & -9 & 15 & -24 & 78 \\
\hline
   & 3 & -5 & 8 & -26 & 75 \\
\end{array}
$$

Entries alternate in sign.

Thus, all the solutions lie between −3 and 2. So the viewing rectangle $[-3, 2]$ by $[-20, 20]$ contains all the $x$-intercepts of $P$. The graph in Figure 3 has two $x$-intercepts, one between −3 and −2 and the other between 1 and 2. Zooming in, we find that the solutions of the equation, to the nearest tenth, are −2.3 and 1.3.

✎ **Practice what you've learned: Do Exercise 91.**                              ▲

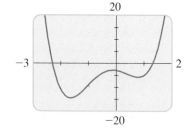

**FIGURE 3**
$y = 3x^4 + 4x^3 - 7x^2 - 2x - 3$

▶ **EXAMPLE 8** | Determining the Size of a Fuel Tank

A fuel tank consists of a cylindrical center section that is 4 ft long and two hemispherical end sections, as shown in Figure 4. If the tank has a volume of 100 ft$^3$, what is the radius $r$ shown in the figure, correct to the nearest hundredth of a foot?

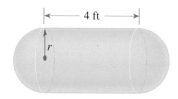

**FIGURE 4**

▼ **SOLUTION**   Using the volume formula listed on the inside back cover of this book, we see that the volume of the cylindrical section of the tank is

$$\pi \cdot r^2 \cdot 4$$

Volume of a cylinder: $V = \pi r^2 h$

The two hemispherical parts together form a complete sphere whose volume is

$$\tfrac{4}{3}\pi r^3$$

Volume of a sphere: $V = \tfrac{4}{3}\pi r^3$

Because the total volume of the tank is 100 ft$^3$, we get the following equation:

$$\tfrac{4}{3}\pi r^3 + 4\pi r^2 = 100$$

A negative solution for $r$ would be meaningless in this physical situation, and by substitution we can verify that $r = 3$ leads to a tank that is over 226 ft$^3$ in volume, much larger than the required 100 ft$^3$. Thus, we know the correct radius lies somewhere between 0 and 3 ft, so we use a viewing rectangle of $[0, 3]$ by $[50, 150]$ to graph the function $y = \tfrac{4}{3}\pi x^3 + 4\pi x^2$, as shown in Figure 5. Since we want the value of this function to be 100, we also graph the horizontal line $y = 100$ in the same viewing rectangle. The correct radius will be the $x$-coordinate of the point of intersection of the curve and the line. Using the cursor and zooming in, we see that at the point of intersection $x \approx 2.15$, correct to two decimal places. Thus, the tank has a radius of about 2.15 ft.

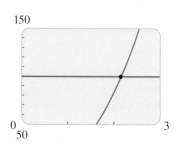

**FIGURE 5**
$y = \tfrac{4}{3}\pi x^3 + 4\pi x^2$ and $y = 100$

✎ **Practice what you've learned: Do Exercise 97.**                              ▲

Note that we also could have solved the equation in Example 8 by first writing it as

$$\tfrac{4}{3}\pi r^3 + 4\pi r^2 - 100 = 0$$

and then finding the $x$-intercept of the function $y = \tfrac{4}{3}\pi x^3 + 4\pi x^2 - 100$.

# 4.4 EXERCISES

## ▼ CONCEPTS

**1.** If the polynomial function

$$P(x) = a_n x^n + a_{n-1} x^{n-1} + \cdots + a_1 x + a_0$$

has integer coefficients, then the only numbers that could possibly be rational zeros of $P$ are all of the

form $\dfrac{p}{q}$, where $p$ is a factor of _____ and $q$ is a

factor of _____. The possible rational zeros of

$P(x) = 6x^3 + 5x^2 - 19x - 10$ are _____.

**2.** Using Descartes' Rule of Signs, we can tell that the polynomial

$P(x) = x^5 - 3x^4 + 2x^3 - x^2 + 8x - 8$ has _____,

_____, or _____ positive real zeros and _____ negative real zeros.

**3.** *True or false?* If $c$ is a real zero of the polynomial $P$, then all the other zeros of $P$ are zeros of $P(x)/(x - c)$.

**4.** *True or false?* If $a$ is an upper bound for the real zeros of the polynomial $P$, then $-a$ is necessarily a lower bound for the real zeros of $P$.

## ▼ SKILLS

**5–10** ▪ List all possible rational zeros given by the Rational Zeros Theorem (but don't check to see which actually are zeros).

**5.** $P(x) = x^3 - 4x^2 + 3$

**6.** $Q(x) = x^4 - 3x^3 - 6x + 8$

**7.** $R(x) = 2x^5 + 3x^3 + 4x^2 - 8$

**8.** $S(x) = 6x^4 - x^2 + 2x + 12$

**9.** $T(x) = 4x^4 - 2x^2 - 7$

**10.** $U(x) = 12x^5 + 6x^3 - 2x - 8$

**11–14** ▪ A polynomial function $P$ and its graph are given. **(a)** List all possible rational zeros of $P$ given by the Rational Zeros Theorem. **(b)** From the graph, determine which of the possible rational zeros actually turn out to be zeros.

**11.** $P(x) = 5x^3 - x^2 - 5x + 1$

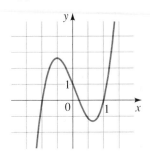

**12.** $P(x) = 3x^3 + 4x^2 - x - 2$

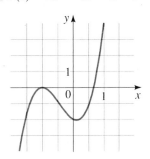

**13.** $P(x) = 2x^4 - 9x^3 + 9x^2 + x - 3$

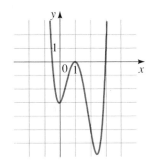

**14.** $P(x) = 4x^4 - x^3 - 4x + 1$

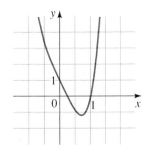

**15–44** ▪ Find all rational zeros of the polynomial, and write the polynomial in factored form.

**15.** $P(x) = x^3 + 3x^2 - 4$

**16.** $P(x) = x^3 - 7x^2 + 14x - 8$

**17.** $P(x) = x^3 - 3x - 2$

**18.** $P(x) = x^3 + 4x^2 - 3x - 18$

**19.** $P(x) = x^3 - 6x^2 + 12x - 8$

**20.** $P(x) = x^3 - x^2 - 8x + 12$

**21.** $P(x) = x^3 - 4x^2 + x + 6$

**22.** $P(x) = x^3 - 4x^2 - 7x + 10$

**23.** $P(x) = x^3 + 3x^2 - x - 3$

**24.** $P(x) = x^3 - 4x^2 - 11x + 30$

**25.** $P(x) = x^4 - 5x^2 + 4$

**26.** $P(x) = x^4 - 2x^3 - 3x^2 + 8x - 4$

**27.** $P(x) = x^4 + 6x^3 + 7x^2 - 6x - 8$

**28.** $P(x) = x^4 - x^3 - 23x^2 - 3x + 90$

**29.** $P(x) = 4x^4 - 25x^2 + 36$

**30.** $P(x) = 2x^4 - x^3 - 19x^2 + 9x + 9$

**31.** $P(x) = 3x^4 - 10x^3 - 9x^2 + 40x - 12$

**32.** $P(x) = 2x^3 + 7x^2 + 4x - 4$

**33.** $P(x) = 4x^3 + 4x^2 - x - 1$

**34.** $P(x) = 2x^3 - 3x^2 - 2x + 3$

**35.** $P(x) = 4x^3 - 7x + 3$

**36.** $P(x) = 8x^3 + 10x^2 - x - 3$

**37.** $P(x) = 4x^3 + 8x^2 - 11x - 15$

**38.** $P(x) = 6x^3 + 11x^2 - 3x - 2$

**39.** $P(x) = 2x^4 - 7x^3 + 3x^2 + 8x - 4$

**40.** $P(x) = 6x^4 - 7x^3 - 12x^2 + 3x + 2$

**41.** $P(x) = x^5 + 3x^4 - 9x^3 - 31x^2 + 36$

**42.** $P(x) = x^5 - 4x^4 - 3x^3 + 22x^2 - 4x - 24$

**43.** $P(x) = 3x^5 - 14x^4 - 14x^3 + 36x^2 + 43x + 10$

**44.** $P(x) = 2x^6 - 3x^5 - 13x^4 + 29x^3 - 27x^2 + 32x - 12$

**45–54** ▪ Find all the real zeros of the polynomial. Use the quadratic formula if necessary, as in Example 3(a).

**45.** $P(x) = x^3 + 4x^2 + 3x - 2$

**46.** $P(x) = x^3 - 5x^2 + 2x + 12$

**47.** $P(x) = x^4 - 6x^3 + 4x^2 + 15x + 4$

**48.** $P(x) = x^4 + 2x^3 - 2x^2 - 3x + 2$

**49.** $P(x) = x^4 - 7x^3 + 14x^2 - 3x - 9$

**50.** $P(x) = x^5 - 4x^4 - x^3 + 10x^2 + 2x - 4$

**51.** $P(x) = 4x^3 - 6x^2 + 1$

**52.** $P(x) = 3x^3 - 5x^2 - 8x - 2$

**53.** $P(x) = 2x^4 + 15x^3 + 17x^2 + 3x - 1$

**54.** $P(x) = 4x^5 - 18x^4 - 6x^3 + 91x^2 - 60x + 9$

**55–62** ▪ A polynomial $P$ is given. **(a)** Find all the real zeros of $P$. **(b)** Sketch the graph of $P$.

**55.** $P(x) = x^3 - 3x^2 - 4x + 12$

**56.** $P(x) = -x^3 - 2x^2 + 5x + 6$

**57.** $P(x) = 2x^3 - 7x^2 + 4x + 4$

**58.** $P(x) = 3x^3 + 17x^2 + 21x - 9$

**59.** $P(x) = x^4 - 5x^3 + 6x^2 + 4x - 8$

**60.** $P(x) = -x^4 + 10x^2 + 8x - 8$

**61.** $P(x) = x^5 - x^4 - 5x^3 + x^2 + 8x + 4$

**62.** $P(x) = x^5 - x^4 - 6x^3 + 14x^2 - 11x + 3$

**63–68** ▪ Use Descartes' Rule of Signs to determine how many positive and how many negative real zeros the polynomial can have. Then determine the possible total number of real zeros.

**63.** $P(x) = x^3 - x^2 - x - 3$

**64.** $P(x) = 2x^3 - x^2 + 4x - 7$

**65.** $P(x) = 2x^6 + 5x^4 - x^3 - 5x - 1$

**66.** $P(x) = x^4 + x^3 + x^2 + x + 12$

**67.** $P(x) = x^5 + 4x^3 - x^2 + 6x$

**68.** $P(x) = x^8 - x^5 + x^4 - x^3 + x^2 - x + 1$

**69–72** ▪ Show that the given values for $a$ and $b$ are lower and upper bounds for the real zeros of the polynomial.

**69.** $P(x) = 2x^3 + 5x^2 + x - 2;\quad a = -3, b = 1$

**70.** $P(x) = x^4 - 2x^3 - 9x^2 + 2x + 8;\quad a = -3, b = 5$

**71.** $P(x) = 8x^3 + 10x^2 - 39x + 9;\quad a = -3, b = 2$

**72.** $P(x) = 3x^4 - 17x^3 + 24x^2 - 9x + 1;\quad a = 0, b = 6$

**73–76** ▪ Find integers that are upper and lower bounds for the real zeros of the polynomial.

**73.** $P(x) = x^3 - 3x^2 + 4$

**74.** $P(x) = 2x^3 - 3x^2 - 8x + 12$

**75.** $P(x) = x^4 - 2x^3 + x^2 - 9x + 2$

**76.** $P(x) = x^5 - x^4 + 1$

**77–82** ▪ Find all rational zeros of the polynomial, and then find the irrational zeros, if any. Whenever appropriate, use the Rational Zeros Theorem, the Upper and Lower Bounds Theorem, Descartes' Rule of Signs, the quadratic formula, or other factoring techniques.

**77.** $P(x) = 2x^4 + 3x^3 - 4x^2 - 3x + 2$

**78.** $P(x) = 2x^4 + 15x^3 + 31x^2 + 20x + 4$ ▪

**79.** $P(x) = 4x^4 - 21x^2 + 5$

**80.** $P(x) = 6x^4 - 7x^3 - 8x^2 + 5x$

**81.** $P(x) = x^5 - 7x^4 + 9x^3 + 23x^2 - 50x + 24$

**82.** $P(x) = 8x^5 - 14x^4 - 22x^3 + 57x^2 - 35x + 6$

**83–86** ▪ Show that the polynomial does not have any rational zeros.

**83.** $P(x) = x^3 - x - 2$

**84.** $P(x) = 2x^4 - x^3 + x + 2$

**85.** $P(x) = 3x^3 - x^2 - 6x + 12$

**86.** $P(x) = x^{50} - 5x^{25} + x^2 - 1$

**87–90** ▪ The real solutions of the given equation are rational. List all possible rational roots using the Rational Zeros Theorem, and then graph the polynomial in the given viewing rectangle to determine which values are actually solutions. (All solutions can be seen in the given viewing rectangle.)

**87.** $x^3 - 3x^2 - 4x + 12 = 0;\quad [-4, 4]$ by $[-15, 15]$

**88.** $x^4 - 5x^2 + 4 = 0;\quad [-4, 4]$ by $[-30, 30]$

**89.** $2x^4 - 5x^3 - 14x^2 + 5x + 12 = 0;\quad [-2, 5]$ by $[-40, 40]$

**90.** $3x^3 + 8x^2 + 5x + 2 = 0;\quad [-3, 3]$ by $[-10, 10]$

**91–94** ▪ Use a graphing device to find all real solutions of the equation, correct to two decimal places.

**91.** $x^4 - x - 4 = 0$

**92.** $2x^3 - 8x^2 + 9x - 9 = 0$

**93.** $4.00x^4 + 4.00x^3 - 10.96x^2 - 5.88x + 9.09 = 0$

**94.** $x^5 + 2.00x^4 + 0.96x^3 + 5.00x^2 + 10.00x + 4.80 = 0$

**95.** Let $P(x)$ be a polynomial with real coefficients and let $b > 0$. Use the Division Algorithm to write

$$P(x) = (x - b) \cdot Q(x) + r$$

Suppose that $r \geq 0$ and that all the coefficients in $Q(x)$ are nonnegative. Let $z > b$.
**(a)** Show that $P(z) > 0$.
**(b)** Prove the first part of the Upper and Lower Bounds Theorem.
**(c)** Use the first part of the Upper and Lower Bounds Theorem to prove the second part. [*Hint:* Show that if $P(x)$ satisfies the second part of the theorem, then $P(-x)$ satisfies the first part.]

**96.** Show that the equation

$$x^5 - x^4 - x^3 - 5x^2 - 12x - 6 = 0$$

has exactly one rational root, and then prove that it must have either two or four irrational roots.

---

## ▼ APPLICATIONS

**97. Volume of a Silo** A grain silo consists of a cylindrical main section and a hemispherical roof. If the total volume of the silo (including the part inside the roof section) is 15,000 ft$^3$ and the cylindrical part is 30 ft tall, what is the radius of the silo, correct to the nearest tenth of a foot?

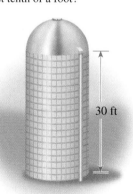

30 ft

**98. Dimensions of a Lot** A rectangular parcel of land has an area of 5000 ft$^2$. A diagonal between opposite corners is measured to be 10 ft longer than one side of the parcel. What are the dimensions of the land, correct to the nearest foot?

$x$

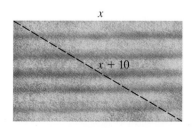

$x + 10$

**99. Depth of Snowfall** Snow began falling at noon on Sunday. The amount of snow on the ground at a certain location at time $t$ was given by the function

$$h(t) = 11.60t - 12.41t^2 + 6.20t^3$$
$$- 1.58t^4 + 0.20t^5 - 0.01t^6$$

where $t$ is measured in days from the start of the snowfall and $h(t)$ is the depth of snow in inches. Draw a graph of this function, and use your graph to answer the following questions.
**(a)** What happened shortly after noon on Tuesday?
**(b)** Was there ever more than 5 in. of snow on the ground? If so, on what day(s)?
**(c)** On what day and at what time (to the nearest hour) did the snow disappear completely?

**100. Volume of a Box** An open box with a volume of 1500 cm$^3$ is to be constructed by taking a piece of cardboard 20 cm by 40 cm, cutting squares of side length $x$ cm from each corner, and folding up the sides. Show that this can be done in two different ways, and find the exact dimensions of the box in each case.

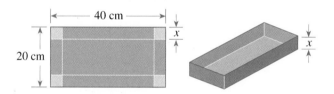

**101. Volume of a Rocket** A rocket consists of a right circular cylinder of height 20 m surmounted by a cone whose height and diameter are equal and whose radius is the same as that of the cylindrical section. What should this radius be (correct to two decimal places) if the total volume is to be $500\pi/3$ m$^3$?

20 m

**102. Volume of a Box** A rectangular box with a volume of $2\sqrt{2}$ ft$^3$ has a square base as shown below. The diagonal of the box (between a pair of opposite corners) is 1 ft longer than each side of the base.
**(a)** If the base has sides of length $x$ feet, show that

$$x^6 - 2x^5 - x^4 + 8 = 0$$

**(b)** Show that two different boxes satisfy the given conditions. Find the dimensions in each case, correct to the nearest hundredth of a foot.

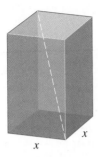

**103. Girth of a Box** A box with a square base has length plus girth of 108 in. (Girth is the distance "around" the box.) What is the length of the box if its volume is 2200 in³?

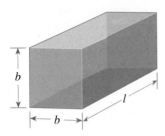

---

## ▼ DISCOVERY · DISCUSSION · WRITING

**104. How Many Real Zeros Can a Polynomial Have?** Give examples of polynomials that have the following properties, or explain why it is impossible to find such a polynomial.
**(a)** A polynomial of degree 3 that has no real zeros
**(b)** A polynomial of degree 4 that has no real zeros
**(c)** A polynomial of degree 3 that has three real zeros, only one of which is rational
**(d)** A polynomial of degree 4 that has four real zeros, none of which is rational

What must be true about the degree of a polynomial with integer coefficients if it has no real zeros?

**105. The Depressed Cubic** The most general cubic (third-degree) equation with rational coefficients can be written as

$$x^3 + ax^2 + bx + c = 0$$

**(a)** Show that if we replace $x$ by $X - a/3$ and simplify, we end up with an equation that doesn't have an $X^2$ term, that is, an equation of the form

$$X^3 + pX + q = 0$$

This is called a *depressed cubic*, because we have "depressed" the quadratic term.

**(b)** Use the procedure described in part (a) to depress the equation $x^3 + 6x^2 + 9x + 4 = 0$.

**106. The Cubic Formula** The quadratic formula can be used to solve any quadratic (or second-degree) equation. You might have wondered whether similar formulas exist for cubic (third-degree), quartic (fourth-degree), and higher-degree equations. For the depressed cubic $x^3 + px + q = 0$, Cardano (page 340) found the following formula for one solution:

$$x = \sqrt[3]{\frac{-q}{2} + \sqrt{\frac{q^2}{4} + \frac{p^3}{27}}} + \sqrt[3]{\frac{-q}{2} - \sqrt{\frac{q^2}{4} + \frac{p^3}{27}}}$$

A formula for quartic equations was discovered by the Italian mathematician Ferrari in 1540. In 1824 the Norwegian mathematician Niels Henrik Abel proved that it is impossible to write a quintic formula, that is, a formula for fifth-degree equations. Finally, Galois (page 323) gave a criterion for determining which equations can be solved by a formula involving radicals.

Use the cubic formula to find a solution for the following equations. Then solve the equations using the methods you learned in this section. Which method is easier?

**(a)** $x^3 - 3x + 2 = 0$
**(b)** $x^3 - 27x - 54 = 0$
**(c)** $x^3 + 3x + 4 = 0$

# ZEROING IN ON A ZERO

We have seen how to find the zeros of a polynomial algebraically and graphically. Let's work through a **numerical method** for finding the zeros. With this method we can find the value of any real zero to as many decimal places as we wish.

The Intermediate Value Theorem states: If $P$ is a polynomial and if $P(a)$ and $P(b)$ are of opposite sign, then $P$ has a zero between $a$ and $b$. (See page 305.) The Intermediate Value Theorem is an example of an **existence theorem**—it tells us that a zero exists but doesn't tell us exactly where it is. Nevertheless, we can use the theorem to zero in on the zero.

For example, consider the polynomial $P(x) = x^3 + 8x - 30$. Notice that $P(2) < 0$ and $P(3) > 0$. By the Intermediate Value Theorem $P$ must have a zero between 2 and 3. To "trap" the zero in a smaller interval, we evaluate $P$ at successive tenths between 2 and 3 until we find where $P$ changes sign, as in Table 1. From the table we see that the zero we are looking for lies between 2.2 and 2.3, as shown in Figure 1.

**TABLE 1**

| $x$ | $P(x)$ |
|-----|--------|
| 2.1 | $-3.94$ |
| 2.2 | $-1.75$ |
| 2.3 | $0.57$ |

}change of sign

**TABLE 2**

| $x$ | $P(x)$ |
|-----|--------|
| 2.26 | $-0.38$ |
| 2.27 | $-0.14$ |
| 2.28 | $0.09$ |

}change of sign

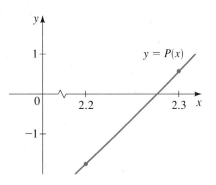

**FIGURE 1**

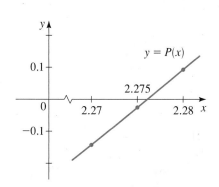

**FIGURE 2**

We can repeat this process by evaluating $P$ at successive 100ths between 2.2 and 2.3, as in Table 2. By repeating this process over and over again, we can get a numerical value for the zero as accurately as we want. From Table 2 we see that the zero is between 2.27 and 2.28. To see whether it is closer to 2.27 or 2.28, we check the value of $P$ halfway between these two numbers: $P(2.275) \approx -0.03$. Since this value is negative, the zero we are looking for lies between 2.275 and 2.28, as illustrated in Figure 2. Correct to the nearest 100th, the zero is 2.28.

1. **(a)** Show that $P(x) = x^2 - 2$ has a zero between 1 and 2.

   **(b)** Find the zero of $P$ to the nearest tenth.

   **(c)** Find the zero of $P$ to the nearest 100th.

   **(d)** Explain why the zero you found is an approximation to $\sqrt{2}$. Repeat the process several times to obtain $\sqrt{2}$ correct to three decimal places. Compare your results to $\sqrt{2}$ obtained by a calculator.

2. Find a polynomial that has $\sqrt[3]{5}$ as a zero. Use the process described here to zero in on $\sqrt[3]{5}$ to four decimal places.

(CONTINUES)

3. Show that the polynomial has a zero between the given integers, and then zero in on that zero, correct to two decimals.

(a) $P(x) = x^3 + x - 7$; between 1 and 2

(b) $P(x) = x^3 - x^2 - 5$; between 2 and 3

(c) $P(x) = 2x^4 - 4x^2 + 1$; between 1 and 2

(d) $P(x) = 2x^4 - 4x^2 + 1$; between $-1$ and 0

4. Find the indicated irrational zero, correct to two decimals.

(a) The positive zero of $P(x) = x^4 + 2x^3 + x^2 - 1$

(b) The negative zero of $P(x) = x^4 + 2x^3 + x^2 - 1$

5. In a passageway between two buildings, two ladders are propped up from the base of each building to the wall of the other so that they cross, as shown in the figure.

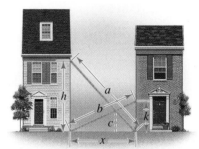

If the ladders have lengths $a = 3$ m and $b = 2$ m and the crossing point is at height $c = 1$ m, then it can be shown that the distance $x$ between the buildings is a solution of the equation

$$x^8 - 22x^6 + 163x^4 - 454x^2 + 385 = 0$$

(a) This equation has two positive solutions, which lie between 1 and 2. Use the technique of "zeroing in" to find both of these correct to the nearest tenth.

(b) Draw two scale diagrams, like the figure, one for each of the two values of $x$ that you found in part (a). Measure the height of the crossing point on each. Which value of $x$ seems to be the correct one?

(c) Here is how to get the above equation. First, use similar triangles to show that

$$\frac{1}{c} = \frac{1}{h} + \frac{1}{k}$$

Then use the Pythagorean Theorem to rewrite this as

$$\frac{1}{c} = \frac{1}{\sqrt{a^2 - x^2}} + \frac{1}{\sqrt{b^2 - x^2}}$$

Substitute $a = 3$, $b = 2$, and $c = 1$, then simplify to obtain the desired equation. [Note that you must square twice in this process to eliminate both square roots. This is why you obtain an extraneous solution in part (a). (See the *Warning* on page 105.)]

▶ **EXAMPLE 4** | Finding Polynomials with Specified Zeros

(a) Find a polynomial $P(x)$ of degree 4, with zeros $i$, $-i$, 2, and $-2$, and with $P(3) = 25$.

(b) Find a polynomial $Q(x)$ of degree 4, with zeros $-2$ and 0, where $-2$ is a zero of multiplicity 3.

▼ **SOLUTION**

(a) The required polynomial has the form

$$P(x) = a(x - i)(x - (-i))(x - 2)(x - (-2))$$

$$= a(x^2 + 1)(x^2 - 4) \qquad \text{Difference of squares}$$

$$= a(x^4 - 3x^2 - 4) \qquad \text{Multiply}$$

We know that $P(3) = a(3^4 - 3 \cdot 3^2 - 4) = 50a = 25$, so $a = \frac{1}{2}$. Thus,

$$P(x) = \tfrac{1}{2}x^4 - \tfrac{3}{2}x^2 - 2$$

(b) We require

$$Q(x) = a[x - (-2)]^3(x - 0)$$

$$= a(x + 2)^3 x$$

$$= a(x^3 + 6x^2 + 12x + 8)x \qquad \text{Special Product Formula 4 (Section P.5)}$$

$$= a(x^4 + 6x^3 + 12x^2 + 8x)$$

Since we are given no information about $Q$ other than its zeros and their multiplicity, we can choose any number for $a$. If we use $a = 1$, we get

$$Q(x) = x^4 + 6x^3 + 12x^2 + 8x$$

✎ **Practice what you've learned: Do Exercise 35.** ▲

▶ **EXAMPLE 5** | Finding All the Zeros of a Polynomial

Find all four zeros of $P(x) = 3x^4 - 2x^3 - x^2 - 12x - 4$.

▼ **SOLUTION** Using the Rational Zeros Theorem from Section 4.4, we obtain the following list of possible rational zeros: $\pm1$, $\pm2$, $\pm4$, $\pm\frac{1}{3}$, $\pm\frac{2}{3}$, $\pm\frac{4}{3}$. Checking these using synthetic division, we find that 2 and $-\frac{1}{3}$ are zeros, and we get the following factorization.

$$P(x) = 3x^4 - 2x^3 - x^2 - 12x - 4$$

$$= (x - 2)(3x^3 + 4x^2 + 7x + 2) \qquad \text{Factor } x - 2$$

$$= (x - 2)\left(x + \tfrac{1}{3}\right)(3x^2 + 3x + 6) \qquad \text{Factor } x + \tfrac{1}{3}$$

$$= 3(x - 2)\left(x + \tfrac{1}{3}\right)(x^2 + x + 2) \qquad \text{Factor 3}$$

The zeros of the quadratic factor are

$$x = \frac{-1 \pm \sqrt{1 - 8}}{2} = -\frac{1}{2} \pm i\frac{\sqrt{7}}{2} \qquad \text{Quadratic formula}$$

so the zeros of $P(x)$ are

$$2, \quad -\frac{1}{3}, \quad -\frac{1}{2} + i\frac{\sqrt{7}}{2}, \quad \text{and} \quad -\frac{1}{2} - i\frac{\sqrt{7}}{2}$$

✎ **Practice what you've learned: Do Exercise 45.** ▲

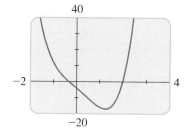

**FIGURE 1**
$P(x) = 3x^4 - 2x^3 - x^2 - 12x - 4$

Figure 1 shows the graph of the polynomial $P$ in Example 5. The $x$-intercepts correspond to the real zeros of $P$. The imaginary zeros cannot be determined from the graph.

## ■ Complex Zeros Come in Conjugate Pairs

As you might have noticed from the examples so far, the complex zeros of polynomials with real coefficients come in pairs. Whenever $a + bi$ is a zero, its complex conjugate $a - bi$ is also a zero.

### CONJUGATE ZEROS THEOREM

If the polynomial $P$ has real coefficients and if the complex number $z$ is a zero of $P$, then its complex conjugate $\bar{z}$ is also a zero of $P$.

▼ **PROOF**    Let

$$P(x) = a_n x^n + a_{n-1} x^{n-1} + \cdots + a_1 x + a_0$$

where each coefficient is real. Suppose that $P(z) = 0$. We must prove that $P(\bar{z}) = 0$. We use the facts that the complex conjugate of a sum of two complex numbers is the sum of the conjugates and that the conjugate of a product is the product of the conjugates.

$$
\begin{aligned}
P(\bar{z}) &= a_n(\bar{z})^n + a_{n-1}(\bar{z})^{n-1} + \cdots + a_1\bar{z} + a_0 \\
&= \overline{a_n}\,\overline{z^n} + \overline{a_{n-1}}\,\overline{z^{n-1}} + \cdots + \overline{a_1}\,\overline{z} + \overline{a_0} \qquad \text{Because the coefficients are real} \\
&= \overline{a_n z^n} + \overline{a_{n-1} z^{n-1}} + \cdots + \overline{a_1 z} + \overline{a_0} \\
&= \overline{a_n z^n + a_{n-1} z^{n-1} + \cdots + a_1 z + a_0} \\
&= \overline{P(z)} = \overline{0} = 0
\end{aligned}
$$

This shows that $\bar{z}$ is also a zero of $P(x)$, which proves the theorem.    ▲

▶ **EXAMPLE 6** | A Polynomial with a Specified Complex Zero

Find a polynomial $P(x)$ of degree 3 that has integer coefficients and zeros $\frac{1}{2}$ and $3 - i$.

▼ **SOLUTION**    Since $3 - i$ is a zero, then so is $3 + i$ by the Conjugate Zeros Theorem. This means that $P(x)$ must have the following form.

Copyright © North Wind/North Wind Picture Archives. All rights reserved.

**Gerolamo Cardano** (1501–1576) is certainly one of the most colorful figures in the history of mathematics. He was the best-known physician in Europe in his day, yet throughout his life he was plagued by numerous maladies, including ruptures, hemorrhoids, and an irrational fear of encountering rabid dogs. He was a doting father, but his beloved sons broke his heart—his favorite was eventually beheaded for murdering his own wife. Cardano was also a compulsive gambler; indeed, this vice might have driven him to write the *Book on Games of Chance*, the first study of probability from a mathematical point of view.

In Cardano's major mathematical work, the *Ars Magna*, he detailed the solution of the general third- and fourth-degree polynomial equations. At the time of its publication, mathematicians were uncomfortable even with negative numbers, but Cardano's formulas paved the way for the acceptance not just of negative numbers, but also of imaginary numbers, because they occurred naturally in solving polynomial equations. For example, for the cubic equation

$$x^3 - 15x - 4 = 0$$

one of his formulas gives the solution

$$x = \sqrt[3]{2 + \sqrt{-121}} + \sqrt[3]{2 - \sqrt{-121}}$$

(See page 332, Exercise 106). This value for $x$ actually turns out to be the *integer* 4, yet to find it, Cardano had to use the imaginary number $\sqrt{-121} = 11i$.

$$P(x) = a\left(x - \tfrac{1}{2}\right)[x - (3 - i)][x - (3 + i)]$$

$$= a\left(x - \tfrac{1}{2}\right)[(x - 3) + i][(x - 3) - i] \qquad \text{Regroup}$$

$$= a\left(x - \tfrac{1}{2}\right)[(x - 3)^2 - i^2] \qquad \text{Difference of Squares Formula}$$

$$= a\left(x - \tfrac{1}{2}\right)(x^2 - 6x + 10) \qquad \text{Expand}$$

$$= a\left(x^3 - \tfrac{13}{2}x^2 + 13x - 5\right) \qquad \text{Expand}$$

To make all coefficients integers, we set $a = 2$ and get

$$P(x) = 2x^3 - 13x^2 + 26x - 10$$

Any other polynomial that satisfies the given requirements must be an integer multiple of this one.

✎ **Practice what you've learned: Do Exercise 39.**    ▲

## ■ Linear and Quadratic Factors

We have seen that a polynomial factors completely into linear factors if we use complex numbers. If we don't use complex numbers, then a polynomial with real coefficients can always be factored into linear and quadratic factors. We use this property in Section 6.4 when we study partial fractions. A quadratic polynomial with no real zeros is called **irreducible** over the real numbers. Such a polynomial cannot be factored without using complex numbers.

> **LINEAR AND QUADRATIC FACTORS THEOREM**
>
> Every polynomial with real coefficients can be factored into a product of linear and irreducible quadratic factors with real coefficients.

▼ **PROOF**    We first observe that if $c = a + bi$ is a complex number, then

$$(x - c)(x - \bar{c}) = [x - (a + bi)][x - (a - bi)]$$

$$= [(x - a) - bi][(x - a) + bi]$$

$$= (x - a)^2 - (bi)^2$$

$$= x^2 - 2ax + (a^2 + b^2)$$

The last expression is a quadratic with *real* coefficients.

Now, if $P$ is a polynomial with real coefficients, then by the Complete Factorization Theorem

$$P(x) = a(x - c_1)(x - c_2) \cdots (x - c_n)$$

Since the complex roots occur in conjugate pairs, we can multiply the factors corresponding to each such pair to get a quadratic factor with real coefficients. This results in $P$ being factored into linear and irreducible quadratic factors.    ▲

▶ **EXAMPLE 7** | Factoring a Polynomial into Linear and Quadratic Factors

Let $P(x) = x^4 + 2x^2 - 8$.

**(a)** Factor $P$ into linear and irreducible quadratic factors with real coefficients.

**(b)** Factor $P$ completely into linear factors with complex coefficients.

▼ **SOLUTION**

**(a)**
$$P(x) = x^4 + 2x^2 - 8$$
$$= (x^2 - 2)(x^2 + 4)$$
$$= (x - \sqrt{2})(x + \sqrt{2})(x^2 + 4)$$

The factor $x^2 + 4$ is irreducible, since it has no real zeros.

**(b)** To get the complete factorization, we factor the remaining quadratic factor.

$$P(x) = (x - \sqrt{2})(x + \sqrt{2})(x^2 + 4)$$
$$= (x - \sqrt{2})(x + \sqrt{2})(x - 2i)(x + 2i)$$

✎ **Practice what you've learned: Do Exercise 65.**                               ▲

# 4.5 EXERCISES

## ▼ CONCEPTS

**1.** The polynomial $P(x) = 3(x - 5)^3(x - 3)(x + 2)$ has degree

_____. It has zeros 5, 3, and _____. The zero 5 has mul-

tiplicity _____, and the zero 3 has multiplicity _____.

**2. (a)** If $a$ is a zero of the polynomial $P$, then _____ must be
a factor of $P(x)$.
  **(b)** If $a$ is a zero of multiplicity $m$ of the polynomial $P$, then

  _____ must be a factor of $P(x)$ when we factor $P$
  completely.

**3.** A polynomial of degree $n \geq 1$ has exactly _____ zeros if a
zero of multiplicity $m$ is counted $m$ times.

**4.** If the polynomial function $P$ has real coefficients and if $a + bi$

is a zero of $P$, then _____ is also a zero of $P$.

## ▼ SKILLS

**5–16** ▪ A polynomial $P$ is given. **(a)** Find all zeros of $P$, real and
complex. **(b)** Factor $P$ completely.

✎ **5.** $P(x) = x^4 + 4x^2$                     **6.** $P(x) = x^5 + 9x^3$

**7.** $P(x) = x^3 - 2x^2 + 2x$              **8.** $P(x) = x^3 + x^2 + x$

**9.** $P(x) = x^4 + 2x^2 + 1$             **10.** $P(x) = x^4 - x^2 - 2$

**11.** $P(x) = x^4 - 16$                      **12.** $P(x) = x^4 + 6x^2 + 9$

**13.** $P(x) = x^3 + 8$                        **14.** $P(x) = x^3 - 8$

**15.** $P(x) = x^6 - 1$                        **16.** $P(x) = x^6 - 7x^3 - 8$

**17–34** ▪ Factor the polynomial completely, and find all its zeros.
State the multiplicity of each zero.

**17.** $P(x) = x^2 + 25$                      **18.** $P(x) = 4x^2 + 9$

✎ **19.** $Q(x) = x^2 + 2x + 2$            **20.** $Q(x) = x^2 - 8x + 17$

**21.** $P(x) = x^3 + 4x$                       **22.** $P(x) = x^3 - x^2 + x$

**23.** $Q(x) = x^4 - 1$                        **24.** $Q(x) = x^4 - 625$

**25.** $P(x) = 16x^4 - 81$                   **26.** $P(x) = x^3 - 64$

**27.** $P(x) = x^3 + x^2 + 9x + 9$       **28.** $P(x) = x^6 - 729$

✎ **29.** $Q(x) = x^4 + 2x^2 + 1$         **30.** $Q(x) = x^4 + 10x^2 + 25$

**31.** $P(x) = x^4 + 3x^2 - 4$            **32.** $P(x) = x^5 + 7x^3$

**33.** $P(x) = x^5 + 6x^3 + 9x$          **34.** $P(x) = x^6 + 16x^3 + 64$

**35–44** ▪ Find a polynomial with integer coefficients that satisfies
the given conditions.

✎ **35.** $P$ has degree 2 and zeros $1 + i$ and $1 - i$.

**36.** $P$ has degree 2 and zeros $1 + i\sqrt{2}$ and $1 - i\sqrt{2}$.

**37.** $Q$ has degree 3 and zeros 3, $2i$, and $-2i$.

**38.** $Q$ has degree 3 and zeros 0 and $i$.

✎ **39.** $P$ has degree 3 and zeros 2 and $i$.

**40.** $Q$ has degree 3 and zeros $-3$ and $1 + i$.

**41.** $R$ has degree 4 and zeros $1 - 2i$ and 1, with 1 a zero of multiplicity 2.

**42.** $S$ has degree 4 and zeros $2i$ and $3i$.

**43.** $T$ has degree 4, zeros $i$ and $1 + i$, and constant term 12.

**44.** $U$ has degree 5, zeros $\frac{1}{2}$, $-1$, and $-i$, and leading coefficient 4;
the zero $-1$ has multiplicity 2.

**45–62** ▪ Find all zeros of the polynomial.

✎ **45.** $P(x) = x^3 + 2x^2 + 4x + 8$

**46.** $P(x) = x^3 - 7x^2 + 17x - 15$

**47.** $P(x) = x^3 - 2x^2 + 2x - 1$

**48.** $P(x) = x^3 + 7x^2 + 18x + 18$

**49.** $P(x) = x^3 - 3x^2 + 3x - 2$

**50.** $P(x) = x^3 - x - 6$

**51.** $P(x) = 2x^3 + 7x^2 + 12x + 9$

**52.** $P(x) = 2x^3 - 8x^2 + 9x - 9$

**53.** $P(x) = x^4 + x^3 + 7x^2 + 9x - 18$

**54.** $P(x) = x^4 - 2x^3 - 2x^2 - 2x - 3$

**55.** $P(x) = x^5 - x^4 + 7x^3 - 7x^2 + 12x - 12$

**56.** $P(x) = x^5 + x^3 + 8x^2 + 8$   [*Hint:* Factor by grouping.]

**57.** $P(x) = x^4 - 6x^3 + 13x^2 - 24x + 36$

**58.** $P(x) = x^4 - x^2 + 2x + 2$

**59.** $P(x) = 4x^4 + 4x^3 + 5x^2 + 4x + 1$

**60.** $P(x) = 4x^4 + 2x^3 - 2x^2 - 3x - 1$

**61.** $P(x) = x^5 - 3x^4 + 12x^3 - 28x^2 + 27x - 9$

**62.** $P(x) = x^5 - 2x^4 + 2x^3 - 4x^2 + x - 2$

**63–68** ▪ A polynomial $P$ is given. **(a)** Factor $P$ into linear and irreducible quadratic factors with real coefficients. **(b)** Factor $P$ completely into linear factors with complex coefficients.

**63.** $P(x) = x^3 - 5x^2 + 4x - 20$

**64.** $P(x) = x^3 - 2x - 4$

**65.** $P(x) = x^4 + 8x^2 - 9$      **66.** $P(x) = x^4 + 8x^2 + 16$

**67.** $P(x) = x^6 - 64$      **68.** $P(x) = x^5 - 16x$

**69.** By the Zeros Theorem, every $n$th-degree polynomial equation has exactly $n$ solutions (including possibly some that are repeated). Some of these may be real, and some may be imaginary. Use a graphing device to determine how many real and imaginary solutions each equation has.
**(a)** $x^4 - 2x^3 - 11x^2 + 12x = 0$
**(b)** $x^4 - 2x^3 - 11x^2 + 12x - 5 = 0$
**(c)** $x^4 - 2x^3 - 11x^2 + 12x + 40 = 0$

**70–72** ▪ So far, we have worked only with polynomials that have real coefficients. These exercises involve polynomials with real and imaginary coefficients.

**70.** Find all solutions of the equation.
**(a)** $2x + 4i = 1$      **(b)** $x^2 - ix = 0$
**(c)** $x^2 + 2ix - 1 = 0$      **(d)** $ix^2 - 2x + i = 0$

**71. (a)** Show that $2i$ and $1 - i$ are both solutions of the equation

$$x^2 - (1 + i)x + (2 + 2i) = 0$$

but that their complex conjugates $-2i$ and $1 + i$ are not.
**(b)** Explain why the result of part (a) does not violate the Conjugate Zeros Theorem.

**72. (a)** Find the polynomial with *real* coefficients of the smallest possible degree for which $i$ and $1 + i$ are zeros and in which the coefficient of the highest power is 1.
**(b)** Find the polynomial with *complex* coefficients of the smallest possible degree for which $i$ and $1 + i$ are zeros and in which the coefficient of the highest power is 1.

▼ **DISCOVERY • DISCUSSION • WRITING**

**73. Polynomials of Odd Degree**   The Conjugate Zeros Theorem says that the complex zeros of a polynomial with real coefficients occur in complex conjugate pairs. Explain how this fact proves that a polynomial with real coefficients and odd degree has at least one real zero.

**74. Roots of Unity**   There are two square roots of 1, namely, 1 and $-1$. These are the solutions of $x^2 = 1$. The fourth roots of 1 are the solutions of the equation $x^4 = 1$ or $x^4 - 1 = 0$. How many fourth roots of 1 are there? Find them. The cube roots of 1 are the solutions of the equation $x^3 = 1$ or $x^3 - 1 = 0$. How many cube roots of 1 are there? Find them. How would you find the sixth roots of 1? How many are there? Make a conjecture about the number of $n$th roots of 1.

---

## 4.6 | Rational Functions

### LEARNING OBJECTIVES

After completing this section, you will be able to:

▪ Find the vertical asymptotes of a rational function
▪ Find the horizontal asymptote of a rational function
▪ Use asymptotes to graph a rational function
▪ Find the slant asymptote of a rational function

A rational function is a function of the form

$$r(x) = \frac{P(x)}{Q(x)}$$

where $P$ and $Q$ are polynomials. We assume that $P(x)$ and $Q(x)$ have no factor in common. Even though rational functions are constructed from polynomials, their graphs look quite different than the graphs of polynomial functions.

## ■ Rational Functions and Asymptotes

Domains of rational expressions are discussed in Section P.7.

The *domain* of a rational function consists of all real numbers $x$ except those for which the denominator is zero. When graphing a rational function, we must pay special attention to the behavior of the graph near those $x$-values. We begin by graphing a very simple rational function.

▶ **EXAMPLE 1** | A Simple Rational Function

Sketch a graph of the rational function $f(x) = \dfrac{1}{x}$.

▼ **SOLUTION** The function $f$ is not defined for $x = 0$. The following tables show that when $x$ is close to zero, the value of $|f(x)|$ is large, and the closer $x$ gets to zero, the larger $|f(x)|$ gets.

For positive real numbers,

$$\frac{1}{\text{BIG NUMBER}} = \text{small number}$$

$$\frac{1}{\text{small number}} = \text{BIG NUMBER}$$

| $x$ | $f(x)$ |
|---|---|
| $-0.1$ | $-10$ |
| $-0.01$ | $-100$ |
| $-0.00001$ | $-100{,}000$ |

Approaching $0^-$    Approaching $-\infty$

| $x$ | $f(x)$ |
|---|---|
| $0.1$ | $10$ |
| $0.01$ | $100$ |
| $0.00001$ | $100{,}000$ |

Approaching $0^+$    Approaching $\infty$

We describe this behavior in words and in symbols as follows. The first table shows that as $x$ approaches 0 from the left, the values of $y = f(x)$ decrease without bound. In symbols,

$$f(x) \to -\infty \quad \text{as} \quad x \to 0^-$$

"$y$ approaches negative infinity as $x$ approaches 0 from the left"

The second table shows that as $x$ approaches 0 from the right, the values of $f(x)$ increase without bound. In symbols,

$$f(x) \to \infty \quad \text{as} \quad x \to 0^+$$

"$y$ approaches infinity as $x$ approaches 0 from the right"

The next two tables show how $f(x)$ changes as $|x|$ becomes large.

| $x$ | $f(x)$ |
|---|---|
| $-10$ | $-0.1$ |
| $-100$ | $-0.01$ |
| $-100{,}000$ | $-0.00001$ |

Approaching $-\infty$    Approaching $0$

| $x$ | $f(x)$ |
|---|---|
| $10$ | $0.1$ |
| $100$ | $0.01$ |
| $100{,}000$ | $0.00001$ |

Approaching $\infty$    Approaching $0$

These tables show that as $|x|$ becomes large, the value of $f(x)$ gets closer and closer to zero. We describe this situation in symbols by writing

$$f(x) \to 0 \quad \text{as} \quad x \to -\infty \quad \text{and} \quad f(x) \to 0 \quad \text{as} \quad x \to \infty$$

Using the information in these tables and plotting a few additional points, we obtain the graph shown in Figure 1.

| $x$ | $f(x) = \frac{1}{x}$ |
|---|---|
| $-2$ | $-\frac{1}{2}$ |
| $-1$ | $-1$ |
| $-\frac{1}{2}$ | $-2$ |
| $\frac{1}{2}$ | $2$ |
| $1$ | $1$ |
| $2$ | $\frac{1}{2}$ |

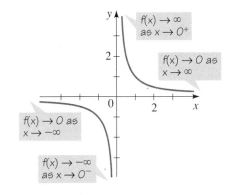

**FIGURE 1**
$f(x) = \frac{1}{x}$

✎ **Practice what you've learned: Do Exercise 7.**  ▲

In Example 1 we used the following arrow notation.

| Symbol | Meaning |
|---|---|
| $x \to a^-$ | $x$ approaches $a$ from the left |
| $x \to a^+$ | $x$ approaches $a$ from the right |
| $x \to -\infty$ | $x$ goes to negative infinity; that is, $x$ decreases without bound |
| $x \to \infty$ | $x$ goes to infinity; that is, $x$ increases without bound |

The line $x = 0$ is called a *vertical asymptote* of the graph in Figure 1, and the line $y = 0$ is a *horizontal asymptote*. Informally speaking, an asymptote of a function is a line to which the graph of the function gets closer and closer as one travels along that line.

---

**DEFINITION OF VERTICAL AND HORIZONTAL ASYMPTOTES**

**1.** The line $x = a$ is a **vertical asymptote** of the function $y = f(x)$ if $y$ approaches $\pm\infty$ as $x$ approaches $a$ from the right or left.

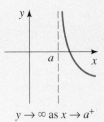

$y \to \infty$ as $x \to a^+$

$y \to \infty$ as $x \to a^-$

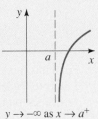

$y \to -\infty$ as $x \to a^+$

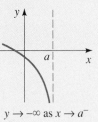

$y \to -\infty$ as $x \to a^-$

**2.** The line $y = b$ is a **horizontal asymptote** of the function $y = f(x)$ if $y$ approaches $b$ as $x$ approaches $\pm\infty$.

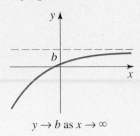

$y \to b$ as $x \to \infty$

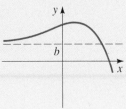

$y \to b$ as $x \to -\infty$

---

A rational function has vertical asymptotes where the function is undefined, that is, where the denominator is zero.

## ■ Transformations of $y = \dfrac{1}{x}$

A rational function of the form

$$r(x) = \frac{ax + b}{cx + d}$$

can be graphed by shifting, stretching, and/or reflecting the graph of $f(x) = \frac{1}{x}$ shown in Figure 1, using the transformations studied in Section 3.5. (Such functions are called *linear fractional transformations*.)

▶ **EXAMPLE 2** | Using Transformations to Graph Rational Functions

Sketch a graph of each rational function.

**(a)** $r(x) = \dfrac{2}{x - 3}$      **(b)** $s(x) = \dfrac{3x + 5}{x + 2}$

▼ **SOLUTION**

**(a)** Let $f(x) = \frac{1}{x}$. Then we can express $r$ in terms of $f$ as follows:

$$r(x) = \frac{2}{x - 3}$$

$$= 2\left(\frac{1}{x - 3}\right) \qquad \text{Factor 2}$$

$$= 2(f(x - 3)) \qquad \text{Since } f(x) = \frac{1}{x}$$

From this form we see that the graph of $r$ is obtained from the graph of $f$ by shifting 3 units to the right and stretching vertically by a factor of 2. Thus, $r$ has vertical asymptote $x = 3$ and horizontal asymptote $y = 0$. The graph of $r$ is shown in Figure 2.

**(b)** Using long division (see the margin), we get $s(x) = 3 - \frac{1}{x + 2}$. Thus, we can express $s$ in terms of $f$ as follows:

$$s(x) = 3 - \frac{1}{x + 2}$$

$$= -\frac{1}{x + 2} + 3 \qquad \text{Rearrange terms}$$

$$= -f(x + 2) + 3 \qquad \text{Since } f(x) = \frac{1}{x}$$

From this form we see that the graph of $s$ is obtained from the graph of $f$ by shifting 2 units to the left, reflecting in the *x*-axis, and shifting upward 3 units. Thus, $s$ has vertical asymptote $x = -2$ and horizontal asymptote $y = 3$. The graph of $s$ is shown in Figure 3.

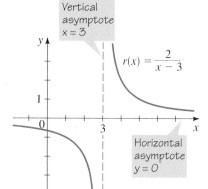

**FIGURE 2**

$$\begin{array}{r} 3 \phantom{x + 5} \\ x + 2 \overline{)\, 3x + 5} \\ \underline{3x + 6} \\ -1 \end{array}$$

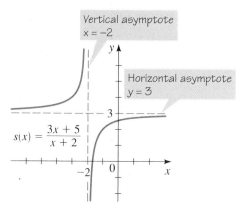

**FIGURE 3**

✎ **Practice what you've learned: Do Exercises 35 and 37.**

### ■ Asymptotes of Rational Functions

The methods of Example 2 work only for simple rational functions. To graph more complicated ones, we need to take a closer look at the behavior of a rational function near its vertical and horizontal asymptotes.

▶  **EXAMPLE 3** | Asymptotes of a Rational Function

Graph the rational function $r(x) = \dfrac{2x^2 - 4x + 5}{x^2 - 2x + 1}$.

▼ **SOLUTION**

**Vertical asymptote:**   We first factor the denominator

$$r(x) = \frac{2x^2 - 4x + 5}{(x - 1)^2}$$

The line $x = 1$ is a vertical asymptote because the denominator of $r$ is zero when $x = 1$.

To see what the graph of $r$ looks like near the vertical asymptote, we make tables of values for $x$-values to the left and to the right of 1. From the tables shown below we see that

$$y \to \infty \quad \text{as} \quad x \to 1^- \qquad \text{and} \qquad y \to \infty \quad \text{as} \quad x \to 1^+$$

$x \to 1^-$

| $x$ | $y$ |
|-----|-----|
| 0 | 5 |
| 0.5 | 14 |
| 0.9 | 302 |
| 0.99 | 30,002 |

Approaching 1⁻    Approaching ∞

$x \to 1^+$

| $x$ | $y$ |
|-----|-----|
| 2 | 5 |
| 1.5 | 14 |
| 1.1 | 302 |
| 1.01 | 30,002 |

Approaching 1⁺    Approaching ∞

Thus, near the vertical asymptote $x = 1$, the graph of $r$ has the shape shown in Figure 4.

**Horizontal asymptote:**   The horizontal asymptote is the value $y$ approaches as $x \to \pm\infty$. To help us find this value, we divide both numerator and denominator by $x^2$, the highest power of $x$ that appears in the expression:

$$y = \frac{2x^2 - 4x + 5}{x^2 - 2x + 1} \cdot \frac{\dfrac{1}{x^2}}{\dfrac{1}{x^2}} = \frac{2 - \dfrac{4}{x} + \dfrac{5}{x^2}}{1 - \dfrac{2}{x} + \dfrac{1}{x^2}}$$

The fractional expressions $\frac{4}{x}$, $\frac{5}{x^2}$, $\frac{2}{x}$, and $\frac{1}{x^2}$ all approach 0 as $x \to \pm\infty$ (see Exercise 67, page 19). So as $x \to \pm\infty$, we have

These terms approach 0.

$$y = \frac{2 - \dfrac{4}{x} + \dfrac{5}{x^2}}{1 - \dfrac{2}{x} + \dfrac{1}{x^2}} \quad \to \quad \frac{2 - 0 + 0}{1 - 0 + 0} = 2$$

These terms approach 0.

Thus, the horizontal asymptote is the line $y = 2$.

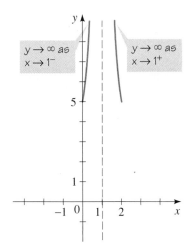

$y \to \infty$ as $x \to 1^-$

$y \to \infty$ as $x \to 1^+$

**FIGURE 4**

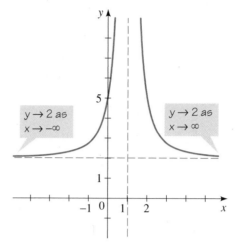

**FIGURE 5**

$$r(x) = \frac{2x^2 - 4x + 5}{x^2 - 2x + 1}$$

Since the graph must approach the horizontal asymptote, we can complete it as in Figure 5.

✎ **Practice what you've learned: Do Exercise 45.**   ▲

From Example 3 we see that the horizontal asymptote is determined by the leading coefficients of the numerator and denominator, since after dividing through by $x^2$ (the highest power of $x$) all other terms approach zero. In general, if $r(x) = P(x)/Q(x)$ and the degrees of $P$ and $Q$ are the same (both $n$, say), then dividing both numerator and denominator by $x^n$ shows that the horizontal asymptote is

$$y = \frac{\text{leading coefficient of } P}{\text{leading coefficient of } Q}$$

The following box summarizes the procedure for finding asymptotes.

---

**FINDING ASYMPTOTES OF RATIONAL FUNCTIONS**

Let $r$ be the rational function

$$r(x) = \frac{a_n x^n + a_{n-1}x^{n-1} + \cdots + a_1 x + a_0}{b_m x^m + b_{m-1}x^{m-1} + \cdots + b_1 x + b_0}$$

1. The vertical asymptotes of $r$ are the lines $x = a$, where $a$ is a zero of the denominator.

2. (a) If $n < m$, then $r$ has horizontal asymptote $y = 0$.

   (b) If $n = m$, then $r$ has horizontal asymptote $y = \dfrac{a_n}{b_m}$.

   (c) If $n > m$, then $r$ has no horizontal asymptote.

---

▶ **EXAMPLE 4** | Asymptotes of a Rational Function

Find the vertical and horizontal asymptotes of $r(x) = \dfrac{3x^2 - 2x - 1}{2x^2 + 3x - 2}$.

▼ **SOLUTION**

**Vertical asymptotes:**    We first factor

$$r(x) = \frac{3x^2 - 2x - 1}{(2x - 1)(x + 2)}$$

> This factor is 0 when $x = \frac{1}{2}$.

> This factor is 0 when $x = -2$.

The vertical asymptotes are the lines $x = \frac{1}{2}$ and $x = -2$.

**Horizontal asymptote:**    The degrees of the numerator and denominator are the same, and

$$\frac{\text{leading coefficient of numerator}}{\text{leading coefficient of denominator}} = \frac{3}{2}$$

Thus, the horizontal asymptote is the line $y = \frac{3}{2}$.

To confirm our results, we graph $r$ using a graphing calculator (see Figure 6).

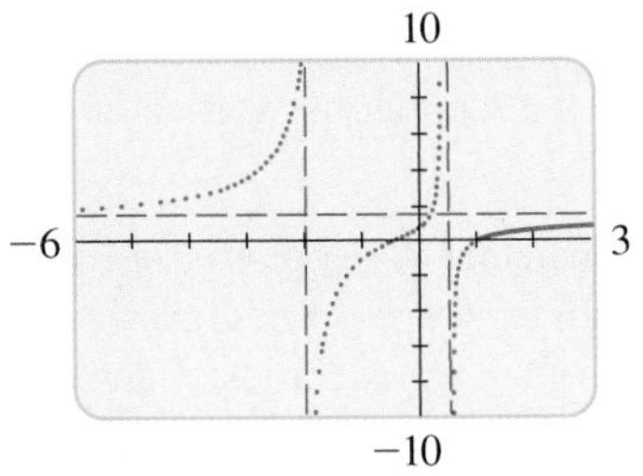

✎ **Practice what you've learned: Do Exercises 23 and 25.**    ▲

**FIGURE 6**
$r(x) = \dfrac{3x^2 - 2x - 1}{2x^2 + 3x - 2}$
Graph is drawn using dot mode to avoid extraneous lines.

## Graphing Rational Functions

We have seen that asymptotes are important when graphing rational functions. In general, we use the following guidelines to graph rational functions.

A fraction is 0 if and only if its numerator is 0.

---

### SKETCHING GRAPHS OF RATIONAL FUNCTIONS

1. **Factor.**    Factor the numerator and denominator.

2. **Intercepts.**    Find the $x$-intercepts by determining the zeros of the numerator and the $y$-intercept from the value of the function at $x = 0$.

3. **Vertical Asymptotes.**    Find the vertical asymptotes by determining the zeros of the denominator, and then see whether $y \to \infty$ or $y \to -\infty$ on each side of each vertical asymptote by using test values.

4. **Horizontal Asymptote.**    Find the horizontal asymptote (if any), using the procedure described in the box on page 348.

5. **Sketch the Graph.**    Graph the information provided by the first four steps. Then plot as many additional points as needed to fill in the rest of the graph of the function.

---

▶ **EXAMPLE 5** | Graphing a Rational Function

Graph the rational function $r(x) = \dfrac{2x^2 + 7x - 4}{x^2 + x - 2}$.

▼ **SOLUTION**    We factor the numerator and denominator, find the intercepts and asymptotes, and sketch the graph.

**Factor:**    $y = \dfrac{(2x - 1)(x + 4)}{(x - 1)(x + 2)}$

*x*-Intercepts: The *x*-intercepts are the zeros of the numerator, $x = \frac{1}{2}$ and $x = -4$.

*y*-Intercept: To find the *y*-intercept, we substitute $x = 0$ into the original form of the function.

$$r(0) = \frac{2(0)^2 + 7(0) - 4}{(0)2 + (0) - 2} = \frac{-4}{-2} = 2$$

The *y*-intercept is 2.

Vertical asymptotes: The vertical asymptotes occur where the denominator is 0, that is, where the function is undefined. From the factored form we see that the vertical asymptotes are the lines $x = 1$ and $x = -2$.

Behavior near vertical asymptotes: We need to know whether $y \to \infty$ or $y \to -\infty$ on each side of each vertical asymptote. To determine the sign of *y* for *x*-values near the vertical asymptotes, we use test values. For instance, as $x \to 1^-$, we use a test value close to and to the left of 1 ($x = 0.9$, say) to check whether *y* is positive or negative to the left of $x = 1$.

> When choosing test values, we must make sure that there is no *x*-intercept between the test point and the vertical asymptote.

$$y = \frac{(2(0.9) - 1)((0.9) + 4)}{((0.9) - 1)((0.9) + 2)} \qquad \text{whose sign is} \qquad \frac{(+)(+)}{(-)(+)} \quad \text{(negative)}$$

So $y \to -\infty$ as $x \to 1^-$. On the other hand, as $x \to 1^+$, we use a test value close to and to the right of 1 ($x = 1.1$, say), to get

$$y = \frac{(2(1.1) - 1)((1.1) + 4)}{((1.1) - 1)((1.1) + 2)} \qquad \text{whose sign is} \qquad \frac{(+)(+)}{(+)(+)} \quad \text{(positive)}$$

So $y \to \infty$ as $x \to 1^+$. The other entries in the following table are calculated similarly.

| As $x \to$ | $-2^-$ | $-2^+$ | $1^-$ | $1^+$ |
|---|---|---|---|---|
| the sign of $y = \dfrac{(2x - 1)(x + 4)}{(x - 1)(x + 2)}$ is | $\dfrac{(-)(+)}{(-)(-)}$ | $\dfrac{(-)(+)}{(-)(+)}$ | $\dfrac{(+)(+)}{(-)(+)}$ | $\dfrac{(+)(+)}{(+)(+)}$ |
| so $y \to$ | $-\infty$ | $\infty$ | $-\infty$ | $\infty$ |

Horizontal asymptote: The degrees of the numerator and denominator are the same, and

$$\frac{\text{leading coefficient of numerator}}{\text{leading coefficient of denominator}} = \frac{2}{1} = 2$$

Thus, the horizontal asymptote is the line $y = 2$.

Graph: We use the information we have found, together with some additional values, to sketch the graph in Figure 7.

| $x$ | $y$ |
|---|---|
| $-6$ | 0.93 |
| $-3$ | $-1.75$ |
| $-1$ | 4.50 |
| 1.5 | 6.29 |
| 2 | 4.50 |
| 3 | 3.50 |

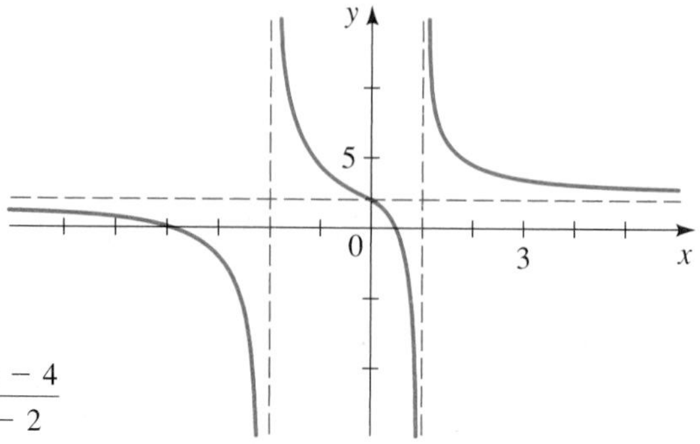

**FIGURE 7**

$$r(x) = \frac{2x^2 + 7x - 4}{x^2 + x - 2}$$

✎ **Practice what you've learned: Do Exercise 53.**

▶ **EXAMPLE 6** | Graphing a Rational Function

Graph the rational function $r(x) = \dfrac{5x + 21}{x^2 + 10x + 25}$.

▼ **SOLUTION**

**Factor:** $\quad y = \dfrac{5x + 21}{(x + 5)^2}$

**x-Intercept:** $\quad -\dfrac{21}{5}$, from $5x + 21 = 0$

**y-Intercept:** $\quad \dfrac{21}{25}$, because $r(0) = \dfrac{5 \cdot 0 + 21}{0^2 + 10 \cdot 0 + 25}$

$$= \dfrac{21}{25}$$

**Vertical asymptote:** $\quad x = -5$, from the zeros of the denominator

**Behavior near vertical asymptote:**

| As $x \to$ | $-5^-$ | $-5^+$ |
|---|---|---|
| the sign of $y = \dfrac{5x + 21}{(x + 5)^2}$ is | $\dfrac{(-)}{(-)(-)}$ | $\dfrac{(-)}{(+)(+)}$ |
| so $y \to$ | $-\infty$ | $-\infty$ |

**Horizontal asymptote:** $\quad y = 0$, because the degree of the numerator is less than the degree of the denominator

---

## MATH IN THE MODERN WORLD

### Unbreakable Codes

If you read spy novels, you know about secret codes and how the hero "breaks" the code. Today secret codes have a much more common use. Most of the information that is stored on computers is coded to prevent unauthorized use. For example, your banking records, medical records, and school records are coded. Many cellular and cordless phones code the signal carrying your voice so that no one can listen in. Fortunately, because of recent advances in mathematics, today's codes are "unbreakable."

Modern codes are based on a simple principle: Factoring is much harder than multiplying. For example, try multiplying 78 and 93; now try factoring 9991. It takes a long time to factor 9991 because it is a product of two primes $97 \times 103$, so to factor it, we have to find one of these primes. Now imagine trying to factor a number $N$ that is the product of two primes $p$ and $q$, each about 200 digits long. Even the fastest computers would take

many millions of years to factor such a number! But the same computer would take less than a second to multiply two such numbers. This fact was used by Ron Rivest, Adi Shamir, and Leonard Adleman in the 1970s to devise the RSA code. Their code uses an extremely large number to encode a message but requires us to know its factors to decode it. As you can see, such a code is practically unbreakable.

The RSA code is an example of a "public key encryption" code. In such codes, anyone can code a message using a publicly known procedure based on $N$, but to decode the message, they must know $p$ and $q$, the factors of $N$. When the RSA code was developed, it was thought that a carefully selected 80-digit number would provide an unbreakable code. But interestingly, recent advances in the study of factoring have made much larger numbers necessary.

**Graph:**   We use the information we have found, together with some additional values, to sketch the graph in Figure 8.

| $x$ | $y$ |
|-----|-----|
| $-15$ | $-0.5$ |
| $-10$ | $-1.2$ |
| $-3$ | $1.5$ |
| $-1$ | $1.0$ |
| $3$ | $0.6$ |
| $5$ | $0.5$ |
| $10$ | $0.3$ |

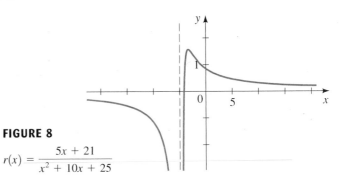

**FIGURE 8**

$$r(x) = \frac{5x + 21}{x^2 + 10x + 25}$$

✎ **Practice what you've learned: Do Exercise 55.**    ▲

⊘   From the graph in Figure 8 we see that, contrary to the common misconception, a graph may cross a horizontal asymptote. The graph in Figure 8 crosses the $x$-axis (the horizontal asymptote) from below, reaches a maximum value near $x = -3$, and then approaches the $x$-axis from above as $x \to \infty$.

▶ **EXAMPLE 7** | Graphing a Rational Function

Graph the rational function $r(x) = \dfrac{x^2 - 3x - 4}{2x^2 + 4x}$.

▼ **SOLUTION**

**Factor:**   $y = \dfrac{(x + 1)(x - 4)}{2x(x + 2)}$

**$x$-Intercepts:**   $-1$ and $4$, from $x + 1 = 0$ and $x - 4 = 0$

**$y$-Intercept:**   None, because $r(0)$ is undefined

**Vertical asymptotes:**   $x = 0$ and $x = -2$, from the zeros of the denominator

**Behavior near vertical asymptotes:**

| As $x \to$ | $-2^-$ | $-2^+$ | $0^-$ | $0^+$ |
|---|---|---|---|---|
| the sign of $y = \dfrac{(x + 1)(x - 4)}{2x(x + 2)}$ is | $\dfrac{(-)(-)}{(-)(-)}$ | $\dfrac{(-)(-)}{(-)(+)}$ | $\dfrac{(+)(-)}{(-)(+)}$ | $\dfrac{(+)(-)}{(+)(+)}$ |
| so $y \to$ | $\infty$ | $-\infty$ | $\infty$ | $-\infty$ |

**Horizontal asymptote:**   $y = \frac{1}{2}$, because the degree of the numerator and the degree of the denominator are the same and

$$\frac{\text{leading coefficient of numerator}}{\text{leading coefficient of denominator}} = \frac{1}{2}$$

**Graph:**   We use the information we have found, together with some additional values, to sketch the graph in Figure 9.

| $x$ | $y$ |
|------|-------|
| $-3$ | $2.33$ |
| $-2.5$ | $3.90$ |
| $-0.5$ | $1.50$ |
| $1$ | $-1.00$ |
| $3$ | $-0.13$ |
| $5$ | $0.09$ |

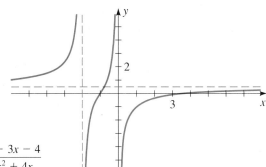

**FIGURE 9**

$$r(x) = \frac{x^2 - 3x - 4}{2x^2 + 4x}$$

✎ **Practice what you've learned: Do Exercise 57.**                                                    ▲

## ■ Slant Asymptotes and End Behavior

If $r(x) = P(x)/Q(x)$ is a rational function in which the degree of the numerator is one more than the degree of the denominator, we can use the Division Algorithm to express the function in the form

$$r(x) = ax + b + \frac{R(x)}{Q(x)}$$

where the degree of $R$ is less than the degree of $Q$ and $a \neq 0$. This means that as $x \to \pm\infty$, $R(x)/Q(x) \to 0$, so for large values of $|x|$ the graph of $y = r(x)$ approaches the graph of the line $y = ax + b$. In this situation we say that $y = ax + b$ is a **slant asymptote**, or an **oblique asymptote**.

▶ **EXAMPLE 8** | A Rational Function with a Slant Asymptote

Graph the rational function $r(x) = \dfrac{x^2 - 4x - 5}{x - 3}$.

▼ **SOLUTION**

**Factor:**   $y = \dfrac{(x + 1)(x - 5)}{x - 3}$

**x-Intercepts:**   $-1$ and $5$, from $x + 1 = 0$ and $x - 5 = 0$

**y-Intercepts:**   $\dfrac{5}{3}$, because $r(0) = \dfrac{0^2 - 4 \cdot 0 - 5}{0 - 3} = \dfrac{5}{3}$

**Horizontal asymptote:**   None, because the degree of the numerator is greater than the degree of the denominator

**Vertical asymptote:**   $x = 3$, from the zero of the denominator

**Behavior near vertical asymptote:**   $y \to \infty$ as $x \to 3^-$ and $y \to -\infty$ as $x \to 3^+$

**Slant asymptote:**   Since the degree of the numerator is one more than the degree of the denominator, the function has a slant asymptote. Dividing (see the margin), we obtain

$$r(x) = x - 1 - \frac{8}{x - 3}$$

Thus, $y = x - 1$ is the slant asymptote.

$$\begin{array}{r}
x - 1 \phantom{00000} \\
x - 3 \overline{\smash{)}x^2 - 4x - 5} \\
\underline{x^2 - 3x \phantom{0000}} \\
-x - 5 \\
\underline{-x + 3} \\
-8
\end{array}$$

**Graph:**   We use the information we have found, together with some additional values, to sketch the graph in Figure 10.

| $x$ | $y$ |
|-----|-----|
| $-2$ | $-1.4$ |
| $1$ | $4$ |
| $2$ | $9$ |
| $4$ | $-5$ |
| $6$ | $2.33$ |

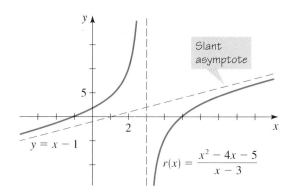

**FIGURE 10**

✎ **Practice what you've learned: Do Exercise 65.**    ▲

So far, we have considered only horizontal and slant asymptotes as end behaviors for rational functions. In the next example we graph a function whose end behavior is like that of a parabola.

▶ **EXAMPLE 9** | End Behavior of a Rational Function

Graph the rational function

$$r(x) = \frac{x^3 - 2x^2 + 3}{x - 2}$$

and describe its end behavior.

▼ **SOLUTION**

**Factor:**   $y = \dfrac{(x + 1)(x^2 - 3x + 3)}{x - 2}$

**$x$-Intercepts:**   $-1$, from $x + 1 = 0$ (The other factor in the numerator has no real zeros.)

**$y$-Intercepts:**   $-\dfrac{3}{2}$, because $r(0) = \dfrac{0^3 - 2 \cdot 0^2 + 3}{0 - 2} = -\dfrac{3}{2}$

**Vertical asymptote:**   $x = 2$, from the zero of the denominator

**Behavior near vertical asymptote:**   $y \to -\infty$ as $x \to 2^-$ and $y \to \infty$ as $x \to 2^+$

**Horizontal asymptote:**   None, because the degree of the numerator is greater than the degree of the denominator

**End behavior:**   Dividing (see the margin), we get

$$r(x) = x^2 + \frac{3}{x - 2}$$

This shows that the end behavior of $r$ is like that of the parabola $y = x^2$ because $3/(x - 2)$ is small when $|x|$ is large. That is, $3/(x - 2) \to 0$ as $x \to \pm\infty$. This means that the graph of $r$ will be close to the graph of $y = x^2$ for large $|x|$.

**Graph:**   In Figure 11(a) we graph $r$ in a small viewing rectangle; we can see the intercepts, the vertical asymptotes, and the local minimum. In Figure 11(b) we graph $r$ in a larger viewing rectangle; here the graph looks almost like the graph of a parabola. In Figure 11(c) we graph both $y = r(x)$ and $y = x^2$; these graphs are very close to each other except near the vertical asymptote.

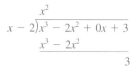

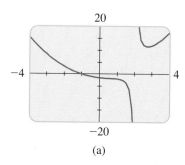
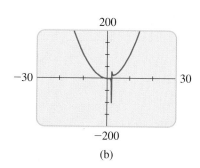
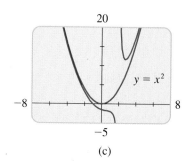

(a)                          (b)                          (c)

**FIGURE 11**

$$r(x) = \frac{x^3 - 2x^2 + 3}{x - 2}$$

✎ **Practice what you've learned: Do Exercise 73.**    ▲

## ■ Applications

Rational functions occur frequently in scientific applications of algebra. In the next example we analyze the graph of a function from the theory of electricity.

▶ **EXAMPLE 10** | Electrical Resistance

When two resistors with resistances $R_1$ and $R_2$ are connected in parallel, their combined resistance $R$ is given by the formula

$$R = \frac{R_1 R_2}{R_1 + R_2}$$

Suppose that a fixed 8-ohm resistor is connected in parallel with a variable resistor, as shown in Figure 12. If the resistance of the variable resistor is denoted by $x$, then the combined resistance $R$ is a function of $x$. Graph $R$, and give a physical interpretation of the graph.

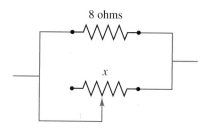

**FIGURE 12**

▼ **SOLUTION**    Substituting $R_1 = 8$ and $R_2 = x$ into the formula gives the function

$$R(x) = \frac{8x}{8 + x}$$

Since resistance cannot be negative, this function has physical meaning only when $x > 0$. The function is graphed in Figure 13(a) using the viewing rectangle $[0, 20]$ by $[0, 10]$. The function has no vertical asymptote when $x$ is restricted to positive values. The combined resistance $R$ increases as the variable resistance $x$ increases. If we widen the viewing rectangle to $[0, 100]$ by $[0, 10]$, we obtain the graph in Figure 13(b). For large $x$ the combined resistance $R$ levels off, getting closer and closer to the horizontal asymptote $R = 8$. No matter how large the variable resistance $x$, the combined resistance is never greater than 8 ohms.

**FIGURE 13**

$$R(x) = \frac{8x}{8 + x}$$

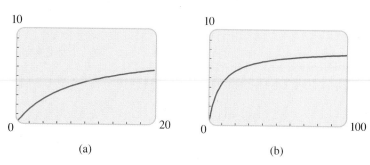

(a)                          (b)

✎ **Practice what you've learned: Do Exercise 83.**    ▲

# 4.6 EXERCISES

## ▼ CONCEPTS

**1.** If the rational function $y = r(x)$ has the vertical asymptote $x = 2$, then as $x \to 2^+$, either $y \to$ _____ or $y \to$ _____.

**2.** If the rational function $y = r(x)$ has the horizontal asymptote $y = 2$, then $y \to$ _____ as $x \to \pm\infty$.

**3–6** ▪ The following questions are about the rational function

$$r(x) = \frac{(x + 1)(x - 2)}{(x + 2)(x - 3)}$$

**3.** The function $r$ has $x$-intercepts _____ and _____.

**4.** The function $r$ has $y$-intercept _____.

**5.** The function $r$ has vertical asymptotes $x =$ _____ and $x =$ _____.

**6.** The function $r$ has horizontal asymptote $y =$ _____.

## ▼ SKILLS

**7–10** ▪ A rational function is given. **(a)** Complete each table for the function. **(b)** Describe the behavior of the function near its vertical asymptote, based on Tables 1 and 2. **(c)** Determine the horizontal asymptote, based on Tables 3 and 4.

**TABLE 1**

| $x$ | $r(x)$ |
|-----|--------|
| 1.5 | |
| 1.9 | |
| 1.99 | |
| 1.999 | |

**TABLE 2**

| $x$ | $r(x)$ |
|-----|--------|
| 2.5 | |
| 2.1 | |
| 2.01 | |
| 2.001 | |

**TABLE 3**

| $x$ | $r(x)$ |
|-----|--------|
| 10 | |
| 50 | |
| 100 | |
| 1000 | |

**TABLE 4**

| $x$ | $r(x)$ |
|-----|--------|
| −10 | |
| −50 | |
| −100 | |
| −1000 | |

**7.** $r(x) = \dfrac{x}{x - 2}$

**8.** $r(x) = \dfrac{4x + 1}{x - 2}$

**9.** $r(x) = \dfrac{3x - 10}{(x - 2)^2}$

**10.** $r(x) = \dfrac{3x^2 + 1}{(x - 2)^2}$

**11–16** ▪ Find the $x$- and $y$-intercepts of the rational function.

**11.** $r(x) = \dfrac{x - 1}{x + 4}$

**12.** $s(x) = \dfrac{3x}{x - 5}$

**13.** $t(x) = \dfrac{x^2 - x - 2}{x - 6}$

**14.** $r(x) = \dfrac{2}{x^2 + 3x - 4}$

**15.** $r(x) = \dfrac{x^2 - 9}{x^2}$

**16.** $r(x) = \dfrac{x^3 + 8}{x^2 + 4}$

**17–20** ▪ From the graph, determine the $x$- and $y$-intercepts and the vertical and horizontal asymptotes.

**17.**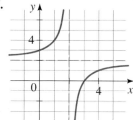

**18.**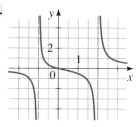

**19.**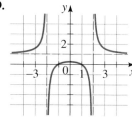

**20.**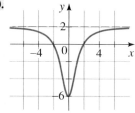

**21–32** ▪ Find all horizontal and vertical asymptotes (if any).

**21.** $r(x) = \dfrac{5}{x - 2}$

**22.** $r(x) = \dfrac{2x - 3}{x^2 - 1}$

**23.** $r(x) = \dfrac{6x}{x^2 + 2}$

**24.** $r(x) = \dfrac{2x - 4}{x^2 + x + 1}$

**25.** $s(x) = \dfrac{6x^2 + 1}{2x^2 + x - 1}$

**26.** $s(x) = \dfrac{8x^2 + 1}{4x^2 + 2x - 6}$

**27.** $s(x) = \dfrac{(5x - 1)(x + 1)}{(3x - 1)(x + 2)}$

**28.** $s(x) = \dfrac{(2x - 1)(x + 3)}{(3x - 1)(x - 4)}$

**29.** $r(x) = \dfrac{6x^3 - 2}{2x^3 + 5x^2 + 6x}$

**30.** $r(x) = \dfrac{5x^3}{x^3 + 2x^2 + 5x}$

**31.** $t(x) = \dfrac{x^2 + 2}{x - 1}$

**32.** $r(x) = \dfrac{x^3 + 3x^2}{x^2 - 4}$

**33–40** ▪ Use transformations of the graph of $y = \frac{1}{x}$ to graph the rational function, as in Example 2.

**33.** $r(x) = \dfrac{1}{x - 1}$

**34.** $r(x) = \dfrac{1}{x + 4}$

**35.** $s(x) = \dfrac{3}{x + 1}$

**36.** $s(x) = \dfrac{-2}{x - 2}$

**37.** $t(x) = \dfrac{2x - 3}{x - 2}$

**38.** $t(x) = \dfrac{3x - 3}{x + 2}$

**39.** $r(x) = \dfrac{x + 2}{x + 3}$

**40.** $r(x) = \dfrac{2x - 9}{x - 4}$

**41–64** ▪ Find the intercepts and asymptotes, and then sketch a graph of the rational function. Use a graphing device to confirm your answer.

**41.** $r(x) = \dfrac{4x - 4}{x + 2}$

**42.** $r(x) = \dfrac{2x + 6}{-6x + 3}$

**43.** $s(x) = \dfrac{4 - 3x}{x + 7}$

**44.** $s(x) = \dfrac{1 - 2x}{2x + 3}$

**45.** $r(x) = \dfrac{18}{(x - 3)^2}$

**46.** $r(x) = \dfrac{x - 2}{(x + 1)^2}$

**47.** $s(x) = \dfrac{4x - 8}{(x - 4)(x + 1)}$

**48.** $s(x) = \dfrac{x + 2}{(x + 3)(x - 1)}$

**49.** $s(x) = \dfrac{6}{x^2 - 5x - 6}$

**50.** $s(x) = \dfrac{2x - 4}{x^2 + x - 2}$

**51.** $t(x) = \dfrac{3x + 6}{x^2 + 2x - 8}$

**52.** $t(x) = \dfrac{x - 2}{x^2 - 4x}$

**53.** $r(x) = \dfrac{(x - 1)(x + 2)}{(x + 1)(x - 3)}$

**54.** $r(x) = \dfrac{2x(x + 2)}{(x - 1)(x - 4)}$

**55.** $r(x) = \dfrac{x^2 - 2x + 1}{x^2 + 2x + 1}$

**56.** $r(x) = \dfrac{4x^2}{x^2 - 2x - 3}$

**57.** $r(x) = \dfrac{2x^2 + 10x - 12}{x^2 + x - 6}$

**58.** $r(x) = \dfrac{2x^2 + 2x - 4}{x^2 + x}$

**59.** $r(x) = \dfrac{x^2 - x - 6}{x^2 + 3x}$

**60.** $r(x) = \dfrac{x^2 + 3x}{x^2 - x - 6}$

**61.** $r(x) = \dfrac{3x^2 + 6}{x^2 - 2x - 3}$

**62.** $r(x) = \dfrac{5x^2 + 5}{x^2 + 4x + 4}$

**63.** $s(x) = \dfrac{x^2 - 2x + 1}{x^3 - 3x^2}$

**64.** $t(x) = \dfrac{x^3 - x^2}{x^3 - 3x - 2}$

**65–72** ▪ Find the slant asymptote, the vertical asymptotes, and sketch a graph of the function.

**65.** $r(x) = \dfrac{x^2}{x - 2}$

**66.** $r(x) = \dfrac{x^2 + 2x}{x - 1}$

**67.** $r(x) = \dfrac{x^2 - 2x - 8}{x}$

**68.** $r(x) = \dfrac{3x - x^2}{2x - 2}$

**69.** $r(x) = \dfrac{x^2 + 5x + 4}{x - 3}$

**70.** $r(x) = \dfrac{x^3 + 4}{2x^2 + x - 1}$

**71.** $r(x) = \dfrac{x^3 + x^2}{x^2 - 4}$

**72.** $r(x) = \dfrac{2x^3 + 2x}{x^2 - 1}$

**73–76** ▪ Graph the rational function $f$, and determine all vertical asymptotes from your graph. Then graph $f$ and $g$ in a sufficiently large viewing rectangle to show that they have the same end behavior.

**73.** $f(x) = \dfrac{2x^2 + 6x + 6}{x + 3}$,   $g(x) = 2x$

**74.** $f(x) = \dfrac{-x^3 + 6x^2 - 5}{x^2 - 2x}$,   $g(x) = -x + 4$

**75.** $f(x) = \dfrac{x^3 - 2x^2 + 16}{x - 2}$,   $g(x) = x^2$

**76.** $f(x) = \dfrac{-x^4 + 2x^3 - 2x}{(x - 1)^2}$,   $g(x) = 1 - x^2$

**77–82** ▪ Graph the rational function, and find all vertical asymptotes, $x$- and $y$-intercepts, and local extrema, correct to the nearest decimal. Then use long division to find a polynomial that has the same end behavior as the rational function, and graph both functions in a sufficiently large viewing rectangle to verify that the end behaviors of the polynomial and the rational function are the same.

**77.** $y = \dfrac{2x^2 - 5x}{2x + 3}$

**78.** $y = \dfrac{x^4 - 3x^3 + x^2 - 3x + 3}{x^2 - 3x}$

**79.** $y = \dfrac{x^5}{x^3 - 1}$

**80.** $y = \dfrac{x^4}{x^2 - 2}$

**81.** $r(x) = \dfrac{x^4 - 3x^3 + 6}{x - 3}$

**82.** $r(x) = \dfrac{4 + x^2 - x^4}{x^2 - 1}$

---

## ▼ APPLICATIONS

**83. Population Growth**   Suppose that the rabbit population on Mr. Jenkins' farm follows the formula

$$p(t) = \frac{3000t}{t + 1}$$

where $t \geq 0$ is the time (in months) since the beginning of the year.

(a) Draw a graph of the rabbit population.

(b) What eventually happens to the rabbit population?

**84. Drug Concentration**   After a certain drug is injected into a patient, the concentration $c$ of the drug in the bloodstream is monitored. At time $t \geq 0$ (in minutes since the injection), the concentration (in mg/L) is given by

$$c(t) = \frac{30t}{t^2 + 2}$$

(a) Draw a graph of the drug concentration.

(b) What eventually happens to the concentration of drug in the bloodstream?

**85. Drug Concentration**   A drug is administered to a patient, and the concentration of the drug in the bloodstream is monitored. At time $t \geq 0$ (in hours since giving the drug), the concentration (in mg/L) is given by

$$c(t) = \frac{5t}{t^2 + 1}$$

Graph the function $c$ with a graphing device.

(a) What is the highest concentration of drug that is reached in the patient's bloodstream?

(b) What happens to the drug concentration after a long period of time?

(c) How long does it take for the concentration to drop below 0.3 mg/L?

**86. Flight of a Rocket**   Suppose a rocket is fired upward from the surface of the earth with an initial velocity $v$ (measured in m/s). Then the maximum height $h$ (in meters) reached by the rocket is given by the function

$$h(v) = \frac{Rv^2}{2gR - v^2}$$

where $R = 6.4 \times 10^6$ m is the radius of the earth and $g = 9.8$ m/s$^2$ is the acceleration due to gravity. Use a graphing device to draw a graph of the function $h$. (Note that $h$ and $v$ must both be positive, so the viewing rectangle need not contain negative values.) What does the vertical asymptote represent physically?

**87. The Doppler Effect**   As a train moves toward an observer (see the figure), the pitch of its whistle sounds higher to the observer than it would if the train were at rest, because the crests of the sound waves are compressed closer together. This phenomenon is called the *Doppler effect*. The observed pitch $P$ is a function of the speed $v$ of the train and is given by

$$P(v) = P_0 \left( \frac{s_0}{s_0 - v} \right)$$

where $P_0$ is the actual pitch of the whistle at the source and $s_0 = 332$ m/s is the speed of sound in air. Suppose that a train has a whistle pitched at $P_0 = 440$ Hz. Graph the function $y = P(v)$ using a graphing device. How can the vertical asymptote of this function be interpreted physically?

**88. Focusing Distance**   For a camera with a lens of fixed focal length $F$ to focus on an object located a distance $x$ from the lens, the film must be placed a distance $y$ behind the lens, where $F$, $x$, and $y$ are related by

$$\frac{1}{x} + \frac{1}{y} = \frac{1}{F}$$

(See the figure.) Suppose the camera has a 55-mm lens ($F = 55$).
**(a)** Express $y$ as a function of $x$ and graph the function.
**(b)** What happens to the focusing distance $y$ as the object moves far away from the lens?

**(c)** What happens to the focusing distance $y$ as the object moves close to the lens?

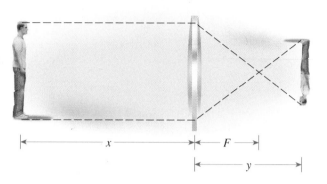

---

▼ **DISCOVERY • DISCUSSION • WRITING**

**89. Constructing a Rational Function from Its Asymptotes**
Give an example of a rational function that has vertical asymptote $x = 3$. Now give an example of one that has vertical asymptote $x = 3$ *and* horizontal asymptote $y = 2$. Now give an example of a rational function with vertical asymptotes $x = 1$ and $x = -1$, horizontal asymptote $y = 0$, and $x$-intercept 4.

**90. A Rational Function with No Asymptote**   Explain how you can tell (without graphing it) that the function

$$r(x) = \frac{x^6 + 10}{x^4 + 8x^2 + 15}$$

has no $x$-intercept and no horizontal, vertical, or slant asymptote. What is its end behavior?'

**91. Graphs with Holes**   In this chapter we adopted the convention that in rational functions, the numerator and denominator don't share a common factor. In this exercise we consider the graph of a rational function that does not satisfy this rule.
**(a)** Show that the graph of

$$r(x) = \frac{3x^2 - 3x - 6}{x - 2}$$

is the line $y = 3x + 3$ with the point $(2, 9)$ removed. [*Hint:* Factor. What is the domain of $r$?]
**(b)** Graph the rational functions:

$$s(x) = \frac{x^2 + x - 20}{x + 5}$$

$$t(x) = \frac{2x^2 - x - 1}{x - 1}$$

$$u(x) = \frac{x - .2}{x^2 - 2x}$$

**92. Transformations of $y = 1/x^2$**   In Example 2 we saw that some simple rational functions can be graphed by shifting, stretching, or reflecting the graph of $y = 1/x$. In this exercise we consider rational functions that can be graphed by transforming the graph of $y = 1/x^2$, shown on the following page.
**(a)** Graph the function

$$r(x) = \frac{1}{(x - 2)^2}$$

by transforming the graph of $y = 1/x^2$.

**(b)** Use long division and factoring to show that the function

$$s(x) = \frac{2x^2 + 4x + 5}{x^2 + 2x + 1}$$

can be written as

$$s(x) = 2 + \frac{3}{(x+1)^2}$$

Then graph $s$ by transforming the graph of $y = 1/x^2$.

**(c)** One of the following functions can be graphed by transforming the graph of $y = 1/x^2$; the other cannot. Use transformations to graph the one that can be, and explain why this method doesn't work for the other one.

$$p(x) = \frac{2 - 3x^2}{x^2 - 4x + 4} \qquad q(x) = \frac{12x - 3x^2}{x^2 - 4x + 4}$$

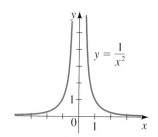

---

# ▶ CHAPTER 4 | REVIEW

## ▼ PROPERTIES AND FORMULAS

### Quadratic Functions (pp. 292–295)

A **quadratic function** is a function of the form

$$f(x) = ax^2 + bx + c$$

It can be expressed in the **standard form**

$$f(x) = a(x - h)^2 + k$$

by completing the square.

The graph of a quadratic function in standard form is a **parabola** with **vertex** $(h, k)$.

If $a > 0$, then the quadratic function $f$ has the **minimum value** $k$ at $x = h$.

If $a < 0$, then the quadratic function $f$ has the **maximum value** $k$ at $x = h$.

### Polynomial Functions (p. 300)

A **polynomial function** of **degree** $n$ is a function $P$ of the form

$$P(x) = a_n x^n + a_{n-1} x^{n-1} + \cdots + a_1 x + a_0$$

The numbers $a_i$ are the **coefficients** of the polynomial; $a_n$ is the **leading coefficient**, and $a_0$ is the **constant coefficient** (or **constant term**).

The graph of a polynomial function is a smooth, continuous curve.

### Real Zeros of Polynomials (p. 304)

A **zero** of a polynomial $P$ is a number $c$ for which $P(c) = 0$. The following are equivalent ways of describing real zeros of polynomials:

**1.** $c$ is a real zero of $P$.

**2.** $x = c$ is a solution of the equation $P(x) = 0$.

**3.** $x - c$ is a factor of $P(x)$.

**4.** $c$ is an $x$-intercept of the graph of $P$.

### Multiplicity of a Zero (p. 309)

A zero $c$ of a polynomial $P$ has multiplicity $m$ if $m$ is the highest power for which $(x - c)^m$ is a factor of $P(x)$.

### Local Maxima and Minima (p. 310)

A polynomial function $P$ of degree $n$ has $n - 1$ or fewer **local extrema** (i.e., local maxima and minima).

### Division of Polynomials (p. 315)

If $P$ and $D$ are any polynomials (with $D(x) \neq 0$), then we can divide $P$ by $D$ using either **long division** or (if $D$ is linear) **synthetic division**. The result of the division can be expressed in one of the following equivalent forms:

$$P(x) = D(x) \cdot Q(x) + R(x)$$

$$\frac{P(x)}{D(x)} = Q(x) + \frac{R(x)}{D(x)}$$

In this division, $P$ is the **dividend**, $D$ is the **divisor**, $Q$ is the **quotient**, and $R$ is the **remainder**. When the division is continued to its completion, the degree of $R$ will be less than the degree of $D$ (or $R(x) = 0$).

### Remainder Theorem (p. 318)

When $P(x)$ is divided by the linear divisor $D(x) = x - c$, the **remainder** is the constant $P(c)$. So one way to **evaluate** a polynomial function $P$ at $c$ is to use synthetic division to divide $P(x)$ by $x - c$ and observe the value of the remainder.

### Rational Zeros of Polynomials (pp. 322–323)

If the polynomial $P$ given by

$$P(x) = a_n x^n + a_{n-1} x^{n-1} + \cdots + a_1 x + a_0$$

has integer coefficients, then all the **rational zeros** of $P$ have the form

$$x = \pm \frac{p}{q}$$

where $p$ is a divisor of the constant term $a_0$ and $q$ is a divisor of the leading coefficient $a_n$.

So to find all the rational zeros of a polynomial, we list all the *possible* rational zeros given by this principle and then check to see which *actually* are zeros by using synthetic division.

## Descartes' Rule of Signs (p. 325)

Let $P$ be a polynomial with real coefficients. Then:

The number of positive real zeros of $P$ either is the number of **changes of sign** in the coefficients of $P(x)$ or is less than that by an even number.

The number of negative real zeros of $P$ either is the number of **changes of sign** in the coefficients of $P(-x)$ or is less than that by an even number.

## Upper and Lower Bounds Theorem (p. 326)

Suppose we divide the polynomial $P$ by the linear expression $x - c$ and arrive at the result

$$P(x) = (x - c) \cdot Q(x) + r$$

If $c > 0$ and the coefficients of $Q$, followed by $r$, are all nonnegative, then $c$ is an **upper bound** for the zeros of $P$.

If $c < 0$ and the coefficients of $Q$, followed by $r$ (including zero coefficients), are alternately nonnegative and nonpositive, then $c$ is a **lower bound** for the zeros of $P$.

## The Fundamental Theorem of Algebra, Complete Factorization, and the Zeros Theorem (pp. 335–337)

Every polynomial $P$ of degree $n$ with complex coefficients has exactly $n$ complex zeros, provided that each zero of multiplicity $m$ is counted $m$ times. $P$ factors into $n$ linear factors as follows:

$$P(x) = a(x - c_1)(x - c_2) \cdots (x - c_n)$$

where $a$ is the leading coefficient of $P$ and $c_1, c_1, \ldots, c_n$ are the zeros of $P$.

## Conjugate Zeros Theorem (p. 340)

If the polynomial $P$ has real coefficients and if $a + bi$ is a zero of $P$, then its complex conjugate $a - bi$ is also a zero of $P$.

## Linear and Quadratic Factors Theorem (p. 341)

Every polynomial with real coefficients can be factored into linear and irreducible quadratic factors with real coefficients.

## Rational Functions (p. 344)

A **rational function** $r$ is a quotient of polynomial functions:

$$r(x) = \frac{P(x)}{Q(x)}$$

We generally assume that the polynomials $P$ and $Q$ have no factors in common.

## Asymptotes (pp. 344–345)

The line $x = a$ is a **vertical asymptote** of the function $y = f(x)$ if

$$y \to \infty \quad \text{or} \quad y \to -\infty \quad \text{as} \quad x \to a^+ \quad \text{or} \quad x \to a^-$$

The line $y = b$ is a **horizontal asymptote** of the function $y = f(x)$ if

$$y \to b \quad \text{as} \quad x \to \infty \quad \text{or} \quad x \to -\infty$$

## Asymptotes of Rational Functions (pp. 345–348)

Let $r(x) = \dfrac{P(x)}{Q(x)}$ be a rational function.

The vertical asymptotes of $r$ are the lines $x = a$ where $a$ is a zero of $Q$.

If the degree of $P$ is less than the degree of $Q$, then the horizontal asymptote of $r$ is the line $y = 0$.

If the degrees of $P$ and $Q$ are the same, then the horizontal asymptote of $r$ is the line $y = b$, where

$$b = \frac{\text{leading coefficient of } P}{\text{leading coefficient of } Q}$$

If the degree of $P$ is greater than the degree of $Q$, then $r$ has no horizontal asymptote.

## ▼ CONCEPT SUMMARY

### Section 4.1 — Review Exercises

- Express a quadratic function in standard form — 1(a)–4(a)
- Graph a quadratic function using its standard form — 1(b)–4(b)
- Find maximum and minimum values of quadratic functions — 5–6
- Model with quadratic functions — 7–8

### Section 4.2 — Review Exercises

- Graph basic polynomial functions — 9–14
- Use end behavior of a polynomial function to help sketch its graph — 15–20, 39–46
- Use the zeros of a polynomial function to sketch its graph — 15–20, 39–46
- Use the multiplicity of a zero to help sketch the graph of a polynomial function — 15–16, 39–46
- Find local maxima and minima of polynomial functions — 17–20

### Section 4.3 — Review Exercises

- Use long division to divide polynomials — 29–30
- Use synthetic division to divide polynomials — 23–28
- Use the remainder theorem to find values of a polynomial — 31–32, 35–36
- Use the Factor Theorem to factor a polynomial — 33–34
- Find a polynomial with specified zeros — 47–50

**Section 4.4**

**Section 4.5**

**Section 4.6**

## ▼ EXERCISES

**1–4** ▪ A quadratic function is given. **(a)** Express the function in standard form. **(b)** Graph the function.

**1.** $f(x) = x^2 + 4x + 1$

**2.** $f(x) = -2x^2 + 12x + 12$

**3.** $g(x) = 1 + 8x - x^2$

**4.** $g(x) = 6x - 3x^2$

**5–6** ▪ Find the maximum or minimum value of the quadratic function.

**5.** $f(x) = 2x^2 + 4x - 5$

**6.** $g(x) = 1 - x - x^2$

**7.** A stone is thrown upward from the top of a building. Its height (in feet) above the ground after $t$ seconds is given by the function $h(t) = -16t^2 + 48t + 32$. What maximum height does the stone reach?

**8.** The profit $P$ (in dollars) generated by selling $x$ units of a certain commodity is given by the function

$$P(x) = -1500 + 12x - 0.004x^2$$

What is the maximum profit, and how many units must be sold to generate it?

**9–14** ▪ Graph the polynomial by transforming an appropriate graph of the form $y = x^n$. Show clearly all $x$- and $y$-intercepts.

**9.** $P(x) = -x^3 + 64$

**10.** $P(x) = 2x^3 - 16$

**11.** $P(x) = 2(x + 1)^4 - 32$

**12.** $P(x) = 81 - (x - 3)^4$

**13.** $P(x) = 32 + (x - 1)^5$

**14.** $P(x) = -3(x + 2)^5 + 96$

**15–16** ▪ A polynomial function $P$ is given. **(a)** Determine the multiplicity of each zero of $P$. **(b)** Sketch a graph of $P$.

**15.** $P(x) = x^3(x - 2)^2$

**16.** $P(x) = x(x + 1)^3(x - 1)^2$

**17–20** ▪ Use a graphing device to graph the polynomial. Find the $x$- and $y$-intercepts and the coordinates of all local extrema, correct to the nearest decimal. Describe the end behavior of the polynomial.

**17.** $P(x) = x^3 - 4x + 1$

**18.** $P(x) = -2x^3 + 6x^2 - 2$

**19.** $P(x) = 3x^4 - 4x^3 - 10x - 1$

**20.** $P(x) = x^5 + x^4 - 7x^3 - x^2 + 6x + 3$

**21.** The strength $S$ of a wooden beam of width $x$ and depth $y$ is given by the formula $S = 13.8xy^2$. A beam is to be cut from a log of diameter 10 in., as shown in the figure.
   **(a)** Express the strength $S$ of this beam as a function of $x$ only.
   **(b)** What is the domain of the function $S$?
   **(c)** Draw a graph of $S$.
   **(d)** What width will make the beam the strongest?

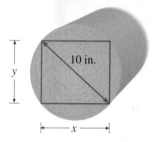

**22.** A small shelter for delicate plants is to be constructed of thin plastic material. It will have square ends and a rectangular top and back, with an open bottom and front, as shown in the figure. The total area of the four plastic sides is to be 1200 in².
   **(a)** Express the volume $V$ of the shelter as a function of the depth $x$.
   **(b)** Draw a graph of $V$.
   **(c)** What dimensions will maximize the volume of the shelter?

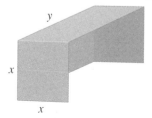

**23–30** ■ Find the quotient and remainder.

**23.** $\dfrac{x^2 - 3x + 5}{x - 2}$

**24.** $\dfrac{x^2 + x - 12}{x - 3}$

**25.** $\dfrac{x^3 - x^2 + 11x + 2}{x - 4}$

**26.** $\dfrac{x^3 + 2x^2 - 10}{x + 3}$

**27.** $\dfrac{x^4 - 8x^2 + 2x + 7}{x + 5}$

**28.** $\dfrac{2x^4 + 3x^3 - 12}{x + 4}$

**29.** $\dfrac{2x^3 + x^2 - 8x + 15}{x^2 + 2x - 1}$

**30.** $\dfrac{x^4 - 2x^2 + 7x}{x^2 - x + 3}$

**31–32** ■ Find the indicated value of the polynomial using the Remainder Theorem.

**31.** $P(x) = 2x^3 - 9x^2 - 7x + 13$; find $P(5)$

**32.** $Q(x) = x^4 + 4x^3 + 7x^2 + 10x + 15$; find $Q(-3)$

**33.** Show that $\frac{1}{2}$ is a zero of the polynomial

$$P(x) = 2x^4 + x^3 - 5x^2 + 10x - 4$$

**34.** Use the Factor Theorem to show that $x + 4$ is a factor of the polynomial

$$P(x) = x^5 + 4x^4 - 7x^3 - 23x^2 + 23x + 12$$

**35.** What is the remainder when the polynomial

$$P(x) = x^{500} + 6x^{201} - x^2 - 2x + 4$$

is divided by $x - 1$?

**36.** What is the remainder when $x^{101} - x^4 + 2$ is divided by $x + 1$?

**37–38** ■ A polynomial $P$ is given.

**(a)** List all possible rational zeros (without testing to see whether they actually are zeros).

**(b)** Determine the possible number of positive and negative real zeros using Descartes' Rule of Signs.

**37.** $P(x) = x^5 - 6x^3 - x^2 + 2x + 18$

**38.** $P(x) = 6x^4 + 3x^3 + x^2 + 3x + 4$

**39–46** ■ A polynomial $P$ is given.

**(a)** Find all real zeros of $P$, and state their multiplicities.

**(b)** Sketch the graph of $P$.

**39.** $P(x) = x^3 - 16x$

**40.** $P(x) = x^3 - 3x^2 - 4x$

**41.** $P(x) = x^4 + x^3 - 2x^2$

**42.** $P(x) = x^4 - 5x^2 + 4$

**43.** $P(x) = x^4 - 2x^3 - 7x^2 + 8x + 12$

**44.** $P(x) = x^4 - 2x^3 - 2x^2 + 8x - 8$

**45.** $P(x) = 2x^4 + x^3 + 2x^2 - 3x - 2$

**46.** $P(x) = 9x^5 - 21x^4 + 10x^3 + 6x^2 - 3x - 1$

**47.** Find a polynomial of degree 3 with constant coefficient 12 and zeros $-\frac{1}{2}$, 2, and 3.

**48.** Find a polynomial of degree 4 that has integer coefficients and zeros $3i$ and 4, with 4 a double zero.

**49.** Does there exist a polynomial of degree 4 with integer coefficients that has zeros $i$, $2i$, $3i$, and $4i$? If so, find it. If not, explain why.

**50.** Prove that the equation $3x^4 + 5x^2 + 2 = 0$ has no real root.

**51–60** ■ Find all rational, irrational, and complex zeros (and state their multiplicities). Use Descartes' Rule of Signs, the Upper and Lower Bounds Theorem, the Quadratic Formula, or other factoring techniques to help you whenever possible.

**51.** $P(x) = x^3 - 3x^2 - 13x + 15$

**52.** $P(x) = 2x^3 + 5x^2 - 6x - 9$

**53.** $P(x) = x^4 + 6x^3 + 17x^2 + 28x + 20$

**54.** $P(x) = x^4 + 7x^3 + 9x^2 - 17x - 20$

**55.** $P(x) = x^5 - 3x^4 - x^3 + 11x^2 - 12x + 4$

**56.** $P(x) = x^4 - 81$

**57.** $P(x) = x^6 - 64$

**58.** $P(x) = 18x^3 + 3x^2 - 4x - 1$

**59.** $P(x) = 6x^4 - 18x^3 + 6x^2 - 30x + 36$

**60.** $P(x) = x^4 + 15x^2 + 54$

**61–64** ■ Use a graphing device to find all real solutions of the equation.

**61.** $2x^2 = 5x + 3$

**62.** $x^3 + x^2 - 14x - 24 = 0$

**63.** $x^4 - 3x^3 - 3x^2 - 9x - 2 = 0$

**64.** $x^5 = x + 3$

**65–66** ■ A polynomial function $P$ is given. Find all the real zeros of $P$, and factor $P$ completely into linear and irreducible quadratic factors with real coefficients.

**65.** $P(x) = x^3 - 2x - 4$  **66.** $P(x) = x^4 + 3x^2 - 4$

**67–72** ■ Graph the rational function. Show clearly all $x$- and $y$-intercepts and asymptotes.

**67.** $r(x) = \dfrac{3x - 12}{x + 1}$

**68.** $r(x) = \dfrac{1}{(x + 2)^2}$

**69.** $r(x) = \dfrac{x - 2}{x^2 - 2x - 8}$

**70.** $r(x) = \dfrac{2x^2 - 6x - 7}{x - 4}$

**71.** $r(x) = \dfrac{x^2 - 9}{2x^2 + 1}$

**72.** $r(x) = \dfrac{x^3 + 27}{x + 4}$

**73–76** ■ Use a graphing device to analyze the graph of the rational function. Find all $x$- and $y$-intercepts and all vertical, horizontal, and slant asymptotes. If the function has no horizontal or slant asymptote, find a polynomial that has the same end behavior as the rational function.

**73.** $r(x) = \dfrac{x - 3}{2x + 6}$

**74.** $r(x) = \dfrac{2x - 7}{x^2 + 9}$

**75.** $r(x) = \dfrac{x^3 + 8}{x^2 - x - 2}$

**76.** $r(x) = \dfrac{2x^3 - x^2}{x + 1}$

**77.** Find the coordinates of all points of intersection of the graphs of

$$y = x^4 + x^2 + 24x \qquad \text{and} \qquad y = 6x^3 + 20$$

1. Express the quadratic function $f(x) = x^2 - x - 6$ in standard form, and sketch its graph.

2. Find the maximum or minimum value of the quadratic function $g(x) = 2x^2 + 6x + 3$.

3. A cannonball fired out to sea from a shore battery follows a parabolic trajectory given by the graph of the equation

$$h(x) = 10x - 0.01x^2$$

where $h(x)$ is the height of the cannonball above the water when it has traveled a horizontal distance of $x$ feet.

   (a) What is the maximum height that the cannonball reaches?

   (b) How far does the cannonball travel horizontally before splashing into the water?

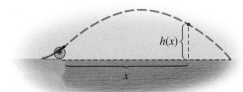

4. Graph the polynomial $P(x) = -(x + 2)^3 + 27$, showing clearly all $x$- and $y$-intercepts.

5. (a) Use synthetic division to find the quotient and remainder when $x^4 - 4x^2 + 2x + 5$ is divided by $x - 2$.

   (b) Use long division to find the quotient and remainder when $2x^5 + 4x^4 - x^3 - x^2 + 7$ is divided by $2x^2 - 1$.

6. Let $P(x) = 2x^3 - 5x^2 - 4x + 3$.

   (a) List all possible rational zeros of $P$.

   (b) Find the complete factorization of $P$.

   (c) Find the zeros of $P$.

   (d) Sketch the graph of $P$.

7. Find all real and complex zeros of $P(x) = x^3 - x^2 - 4x - 6$.

8. Find the complete factorization of $P(x) = x^4 - 2x^3 + 5x^2 - 8x + 4$.

9. Find a fourth-degree polynomial with integer coefficients that has zeros $3i$ and $-1$, with $-1$ a zero of multiplicity 2.

10. Let $P(x) = 2x^4 - 7x^3 + x^2 - 18x + 3$.

   (a) Use Descartes' Rule of Signs to determine how many positive and how many negative real zeros $P$ can have.

   (b) Show that 4 is an upper bound and $-1$ is a lower bound for the real zeros of $P$.

   (c) Draw a graph of $P$, and use it to estimate the real zeros of $P$, correct to two decimal places.

   (d) Find the coordinates of all local extrema of $P$, correct to two decimals.

11. Consider the following rational functions:

$$r(x) = \frac{2x - 1}{x^2 - x - 2} \qquad s(x) = \frac{x^3 + 27}{x^2 + 4}$$

$$t(x) = \frac{x^3 - 9x}{x + 2} \qquad u(x) = \frac{x^2 + x - 6}{x^2 - 25}$$

   (a) Which of these rational functions has a horizontal asymptote?

   (b) Which of these functions has a slant asymptote?

   (c) Which of these functions has no vertical asymptote?

   (d) Graph $y = u(x)$, showing clearly any asymptotes and $x$- and $y$-intercepts the function may have.

   (e) Use long division to find a polynomial $P$ that has the same end behavior as $t$. Graph both $P$ and $t$ on the same screen to verify that they have the same end behavior.

We have learned how to fit a line to data (see *Focus on Modeling*, page 192). The line models the increasing or decreasing trend in the data. If the data exhibit more variability, such as an increase followed by a decrease, then to model the data, we need to use a curve rather than a line. Figure 1 shows a scatter plot with three possible models that appear to fit the data. Which model fits the data best?

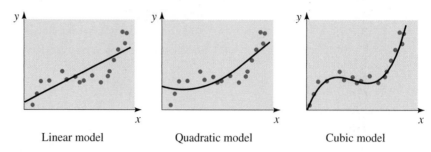

Linear model    Quadratic model    Cubic model

**FIGURE 1**

## Polynomial Functions as Models

Polynomial functions are ideal for modeling data where the scatter plot has peaks or valleys (that is, local maxima or minima). For example, if the data have a single peak as in Figure 2(a), then it may be appropriate to use a quadratic polynomial to model the data. The more peaks or valleys the data exhibit, the higher the degree of the polynomial needed to model the data (see Figure 2).

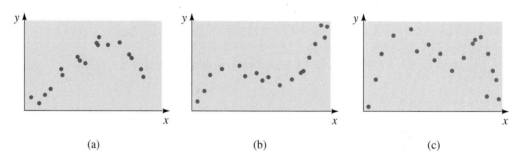

(a)    (b)    (c)

**FIGURE 2**

Graphing calculators are programmed to find the **polynomial of best fit** of a specified degree. As is the case for lines (see page 193), a polynomial of a given degree fits the data *best* if the sum of the squares of the distances between the graph of the polynomial and the data points is minimized.

▶ **EXAMPLE 1** | Rainfall and Crop Yield

Rain is essential for crops to grow, but too much rain can diminish crop yields. The data give rainfall and cotton yield per acre for several seasons in a certain county.

**(a)** Make a scatter plot of the data. What degree polynomial seems appropriate for modeling the data?

**(b)** Use a graphing calculator to find the polynomial of best fit. Graph the polynomial on the scatter plot.

© Ted Wood / The Image Bank / Getty Images

**(c)** Use the model that you found to estimate the yield if there are 25 in. of rainfall.

| Season | Rainfall (in.) | Yield (kg/acre) |
|--------|----------------|-----------------|
| 1 | 23.3 | 5311 |
| 2 | 20.1 | 4382 |
| 3 | 18.1 | 3950 |
| 4 | 12.5 | 3137 |
| 5 | 30.9 | 5113 |
| 6 | 33.6 | 4814 |
| 7 | 35.8 | 3540 |
| 8 | 15.5 | 3850 |
| 9 | 27.6 | 5071 |
| 10 | 34.5 | 3881 |

▼ **SOLUTION**

**(a)** The scatter plot is shown in Figure 3. The data appear to have a peak, so it is appropriate to model the data by a quadratic polynomial (degree 2).

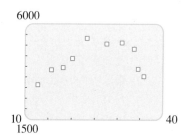

**FIGURE 3**  Scatter plot of yield vs. rainfall data

**(b)** Using a graphing calculator, we find that the quadratic polynomial of best fit is

$$y = -12.6x^2 + 651.5x - 3283.2$$

The calculator output and the scatter plot, together with the graph of the quadratic model, are shown in Figure 4.

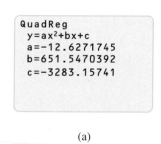

(a)                    (b)

**FIGURE 4**

**(c)** Using the model with $x = 25$, we get

$$y = -12.6(25)^2 + 651.5(25) - 3283.2 \approx 5129.3$$

We estimate the yield to be about 5130 kg per acre.    ▲

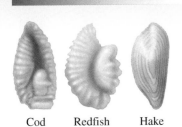

Cod      Redfish      Hake

Otoliths for several fish species.

▶ **EXAMPLE 2** │ Length-at-Age Data for Fish

Otoliths ("earstones") are tiny structures that are found in the heads of fish. Microscopic growth rings on the otoliths, not unlike growth rings on a tree, record the age of a fish. The table gives the lengths of rock bass caught at different ages, as determined by the otoliths. Scientists have proposed a cubic polynomial to model this data.

**(a)** Use a graphing calculator to find the cubic polynomial of best fit for the data.

**(b)** Make a scatter plot of the data and graph the polynomial from part (a).

**(c)** A fisherman catches a rock bass 20 in. long. Use the model to estimate its age.

| Age (yr) | Length (in.) | Age (yr) | Length (in.) |
|---|---|---|---|
| 1 | 4.8 | 9 | 18.2 |
| 2 | 8.8 | 9 | 17.1 |
| 2 | 8.0 | 10 | 18.8 |
| 3 | 7.9 | 10 | 19.5 |
| 4 | 11.9 | 11 | 18.9 |
| 5 | 14.4 | 12 | 21.7 |
| 6 | 14.1 | 12 | 21.9 |
| 6 | 15.8 | 13 | 23.8 |
| 7 | 15.6 | 14 | 26.9 |
| 8 | 17.8 | 14 | 25.1 |

▼ **SOLUTION**

**(a)** Using a graphing calculator (see Figure 5(a)), we find the cubic polynomial of best fit:

$$y = 0.0155x^3 - 0.372x^2 + 3.95x + 1.21$$

**(b)** The scatter plot of the data and the cubic polynomial are graphed in Figure 5(b).

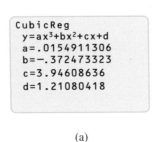

(a)

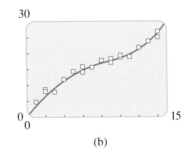

(b)

**FIGURE 5**

**(c)** Moving the cursor along the graph of the polynomial, we find that $y = 20$ when $x \approx 10.8$. Thus, the fish is about 11 years old.   ▲

## Problems

**1. Tire Inflation and Treadwear**   Car tires need to be inflated properly. Overinflation or underinflation can cause premature treadwear. The data and scatter plot on the next page show tire life for different inflation values for a certain type of tire.

**(a)** Find the quadratic polynomial that best fits the data.

**(b)** Draw a graph of the polynomial from part (a) together with a scatter plot of the data.

**(c)** Use your result from part (b) to estimate the pressure that gives the longest tire life.

| Pressure (lb/in²) | Tire life (mi) |
|---|---|
| 26 | 50,000 |
| 28 | 66,000 |
| 31 | 78,000 |
| 35 | 81,000 |
| 38 | 74,000 |
| 42 | 70,000 |
| 45 | 59,000 |

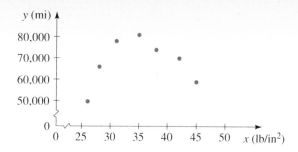

**2. Too Many Corn Plants per Acre?**    The more corn a farmer plants per acre, the greater is the yield the farmer can expect, but only up to a point. Too many plants per acre can cause over-crowding and decrease yields. The data give crop yields per acre for various densities of corn plantings, as found by researchers at a university test farm.

(a) Find the quadratic polynomial that best fits the data.

(b) Draw a graph of the polynomial from part (a) together with a scatter plot of the data.

(c) Use your result from part (b) to estimate the yield for 37,000 plants per acre.

| Density (plants/acre) | Crop yield (bushels/acre) |
|---|---|
| 15,000 | 43 |
| 20,000 | 98 |
| 25,000 | 118 |
| 30,000 | 140 |
| 35,000 | 142 |
| 40,000 | 122 |
| 45,000 | 93 |
| 50,000 | 67 |

**3. How Fast Can You List Your Favorite Things?**    If you are asked to make a list of objects in a certain category, how fast you can list them follows a predictable pattern. For example, if you try to name as many vegetables as you can, you'll probably think of several right away—for example, carrots, peas, beans, corn, and so on. Then after a pause you might think of ones you eat less frequently—perhaps zucchini, eggplant, and asparagus. Finally, a few more exotic vegetables might come to mind—artichokes, jicama, bok choy, and the like. A psychologist performs this experiment on a number of subjects. The table below gives the average number of vegetables that the subjects named by a given number of seconds.

(a) Find the cubic polynomial that best fits the data.

(b) Draw a graph of the polynomial from part (a) together with a scatter plot of the data.

(c) Use your result from part (b) to estimate the number of vegetables that subjects would be able to name in 40 seconds.

(d) According to the model, how long (to the nearest 0.1 s) would it take a person to name five vegetables?

| Seconds | Number of Vegetables |
|---|---|
| 1 | 2 |
| 2 | 6 |
| 5 | 10 |
| 10 | 12 |
| 15 | 14 |
| 20 | 15 |
| 25 | 18 |
| 30 | 21 |

**4. Clothing Sales Are Seasonal**   Clothing sales tend to vary by season, with more clothes sold in spring and fall. The table gives sales figures for each month at a certain clothing store.

**(a)** Find the quartic (fourth-degree) polynomial that best fits the data.

**(b)** Draw a graph of the polynomial from part (a) together with a scatter plot of the data.

**(c)** Do you think that a quartic polynomial is a good model for these data? Explain.

| Month | Sales ($) |
|---|---|
| January | 8,000 |
| February | 18,000 |
| March | 22,000 |
| April | 31,000 |
| May | 29,000 |
| June | 21,000 |
| July | 22,000 |
| August | 26,000 |
| September | 38,000 |
| October | 40,000 |
| November | 27,000 |
| December | 15,000 |

**5. Height of a Baseball**   A baseball is thrown upward, and its height measured at 0.5-second intervals using a strobe light. The resulting data are given in the table.

**(a)** Draw a scatter plot of the data. What degree polynomial is appropriate for modeling the data?

**(b)** Find a polynomial model that best fits the data, and graph it on the scatter plot.

**(c)** Find the times when the ball is 20 ft above the ground.

**(d)** What is the maximum height attained by the ball?

| Time (s) | Height (ft) |
|---|---|
| 0 | 4.2 |
| 0.5 | 26.1 |
| 1.0 | 40.1 |
| 1.5 | 46.0 |
| 2.0 | 43.9 |
| 2.5 | 33.7 |
| 3.0 | 15.8 |

**6. Torricelli's Law**   Water in a tank will flow out of a small hole in the bottom faster when the tank is nearly full than when it is nearly empty. According to Torricelli's Law, the height $h(t)$ of water remaining at time $t$ is a quadratic function of $t$.

A certain tank is filled with water and allowed to drain. The height of the water is measured at different times as shown in the table.

**(a)** Find the quadratic polynomial that best fits the data.

**(b)** Draw a graph of the polynomial from part (a) together with a scatter plot of the data.

**(c)** Use your graph from part (b) to estimate how long it takes for the tank to drain completely.

| Time (min) | Height (ft) |
|---|---|
| 0 | 5.0 |
| 4 | 3.1 |
| 8 | 1.9 |
| 12 | 0.8 |
| 16 | 0.2 |

# CHAPTER 5
# Exponential and Logarithmic Functions

© David Iliff

**Population explosion?** Cities and towns all over the world have experienced huge increases in population over the past century. The above photos of Hollywood in the 1920s and in 2000 tell the population story quite dramatically. But to find out where population is really headed, we need a mathematical model. Population grows in much the same way as money grows in a bank account: the more money in the account, the more interest is paid. In the same way, the more people there are in the world, the more babies are born. This type of growth is modeled by exponential functions. According to some exponential models, world population will double in successive forty-year periods, resulting in a population explosion. However, different exponential models, which take into account the limited resources available for growth, predict that world population will eventually stabilize at a level that our planet can support (see Exercise 65, Section 5.1, and *Focus on Modeling: Fitting Exponential and Power Curves to Data*, page 431).

## 5.1 │ Exponential Functions

**LEARNING OBJECTIVES**

After completing this section, you will be able to:

▪ Evaluate exponential functions
▪ Graph exponential functions
▪ Evaluate and graph the natural exponential function
▪ Find compound interest
▪ Find continuously compounded interest

In this chapter we study a new class of functions called *exponential functions*. For example,

$$f(x) = 2^x$$

is an exponential function (with base 2). Notice how quickly the values of this function increase:

$$f(3) = 2^3 = 8$$

$$f(10) = 2^{10} = 1024$$

$$f(30) = 2^{30} = 1,073,741,824$$

Compare this with the function $g(x) = x^2$, where $g(30) = 30^2 = 900$. The point is that when the variable is in the exponent, even a small change in the variable can cause a dramatic change in the value of the function.

In spite of this incomprehensibly huge growth, exponential functions are appropriate for modeling population growth for all living things, from bacteria to elephants. To understand how a population grows, consider the case of a single bacterium, which divides every hour. After one hour we would have 2 bacteria, after two hours $2^2$ or 4 bacteria, after three hours $2^3$ or 8 bacteria, and so on. After $x$ hours we would have $2^x$ bacteria. This leads us to model the bacteria population by the function $f(x) = 2^x$.

|  |  |  |  |  |  |  |
|---|---|---|---|---|---|---|
| 0 | 1 | 2 | 3 | 4 | 5 | 6 |

The principle governing population growth is the following: The larger the population, the greater the number of offspring. This same principle is present in many other real-life situations. For example, the larger your bank account, the more interest you get. So we also use exponential functions to find compound interest.

To study exponential functions, we must first define what we mean by the exponential expression $a^x$ when $x$ is any real number.

### ▪ Exponential Functions

In Section P.5 we defined $a^x$ for $a > 0$ and $x$ a rational number, but we have not yet defined irrational powers. So what is meant by $5^{\sqrt{3}}$ or $2^\pi$? To define $a^x$ when $x$ is irrational, we approximate $x$ by rational numbers.

For example, since

$$\sqrt{3} \approx 1.73205\ldots$$

is an irrational number, we successively approximate $a^{\sqrt{3}}$ by the following rational powers:

$$a^{1.7}, a^{1.73}, a^{1.732}, a^{1.7320}, a^{1.73205}, \ldots$$

Intuitively, we can see that these rational powers of $a$ are getting closer and closer to $a^{\sqrt{3}}$. It can be shown by using advanced mathematics that there is exactly one number that these powers approach. We define $a^{\sqrt{3}}$ to be this number.

For example, using a calculator, we find

$$5^{\sqrt{3}} \approx 5^{1.732}$$

$$\approx 16.2411\ldots$$

The more decimal places of $\sqrt{3}$ we use in our calculation, the better our approximation of $5^{\sqrt{3}}$.

It can be proved that the *Laws of Exponents are still true when the exponents are real numbers.*

The Laws of Exponents are listed on page 21.

---

### EXPONENTIAL FUNCTIONS

The **exponential function with base $a$** is defined for all real numbers $x$ by

$$f(x) = a^x$$

where $a > 0$ and $a \neq 1$.

---

We assume that $a \neq 1$ because the function $f(x) = 1^x = 1$ is just a constant function. Here are some examples of exponential functions:

$$f(x) = 2^x \qquad g(x) = 3^x \qquad h(x) = 10^x$$

Base 2          Base 3          Base 10

▶ **EXAMPLE 1** | Evaluating Exponential Functions

Let $f(x) = 3^x$, and evaluate the following:

**(a)** $f(2)$    **(b)** $f\left(-\frac{2}{3}\right)$    **(c)** $f(\pi)$    **(d)** $f(\sqrt{2})$

▼ **SOLUTION**    We use a calculator to obtain the values of $f$.

| | Calculator keystrokes | Output |
|---|---|---|
| **(a)** $f(2) = 3^2 = 9$ | 3 ^ 2 ENTER | 9 |
| **(b)** $f\left(-\frac{2}{3}\right) = 3^{-2/3} \approx 0.4807$ | 3 ^ ( (−) 2 ÷ 3 ) ENTER | 0.4807498 |
| **(c)** $f(\pi) = 3^\pi \approx 31.544$ | 3 ^ π ENTER | 31.5442807 |
| **(d)** $f(\sqrt{2}) = 3^{\sqrt{2}} \approx 4.7288$ | 3 ^ √ 2 ENTER | 4.7288043 |

✎ **Practice what you've learned: Do Exercise 5.**    ▲

---

### ■ Graphs of Exponential Functions

We first graph exponential functions by plotting points. We will see that the graphs of such functions have an easily recognizable shape.

▶ **EXAMPLE 2** | Graphing Exponential Functions by Plotting Points

Draw the graph of each function.

**(a)** $f(x) = 3^x$          **(b)** $g(x) = \left(\dfrac{1}{3}\right)^x$

▼ **SOLUTION**   We calculate values of $f(x)$ and $g(x)$ and plot points to sketch the graphs in Figure 1.

| $x$ | $f(x) = 3^x$ | $g(x) = \left(\frac{1}{3}\right)^x$ |
|:---:|:---:|:---:|
| $-3$ | $\frac{1}{27}$ | $27$ |
| $-2$ | $\frac{1}{9}$ | $9$ |
| $-1$ | $\frac{1}{3}$ | $3$ |
| $0$ | $1$ | $1$ |
| $1$ | $3$ | $\frac{1}{3}$ |
| $2$ | $9$ | $\frac{1}{9}$ |
| $3$ | $27$ | $\frac{1}{27}$ |

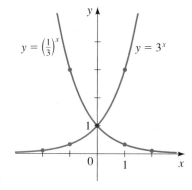

**FIGURE 1**

Notice that

$$g(x) = \left(\frac{1}{3}\right)^x = \frac{1}{3^x} = 3^{-x} = f(-x)$$

Reflecting graphs is explained in Section 3.5.

so we could have obtained the graph of $g$ from the graph of $f$ by reflecting in the $y$-axis.

✎ **Practice what you've learned: Do Exercise 17.**                          ▲

Figure 2 shows the graphs of the family of exponential functions $f(x) = a^x$ for various values of the base $a$. All of these graphs pass through the point $(0, 1)$ because $a^0 = 1$ for $a \neq 0$. You can see from Figure 2 that there are two kinds of exponential functions: If $0 < a < 1$, the exponential function decreases rapidly. If $a > 1$, the function increases rapidly (see the margin note).

To see just how quickly $f(x) = 2^x$ increases, let's perform the following thought experiment. Suppose we start with a piece of paper that is a thousandth of an inch thick, and we fold it in half 50 times. Each time we fold the paper, the thickness of the paper stack doubles, so the thickness of the resulting stack would be $2^{50}/1000$ inches. How thick do you think that is? It works out to be more than 17 million miles!

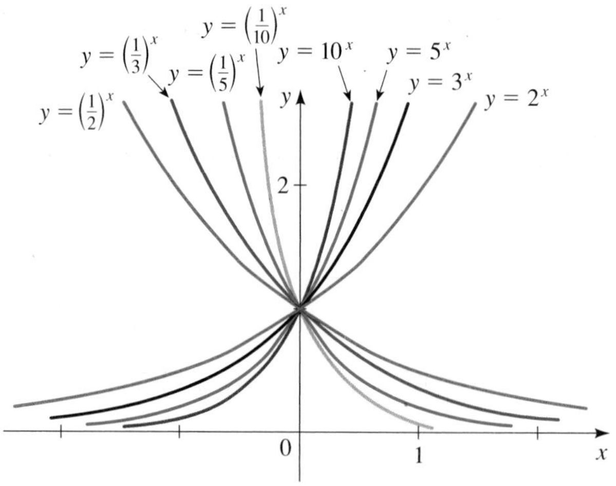

$y = \left(\frac{1}{2}\right)^x$   $y = \left(\frac{1}{3}\right)^x$   $y = \left(\frac{1}{5}\right)^x$   $y = \left(\frac{1}{10}\right)^x$   $y = 10^x$   $y = 5^x$   $y = 3^x$   $y = 2^x$

**FIGURE 2**  A family of exponential functions

The $x$-axis is a horizontal asymptote for the exponential function $f(x) = a^x$. This is because when $a > 1$, we have $a^x \to 0$ as $x \to -\infty$, and when $0 < a < 1$, we have $a^x \to 0$ as

See Section 4.6, page 345, where the "arrow notation" used here is explained.

$x \to \infty$ (see Figure 2). Also, $a^x > 0$ for all $x \in \mathbb{R}$, so the function $f(x) = a^x$ has domain $\mathbb{R}$ and range $(0, \infty)$. These observations are summarized in the following box.

---

**GRAPHS OF EXPONENTIAL FUNCTIONS**

The exponential function

$$f(x) = a^x \qquad (a > 0, a \neq 1)$$

has domain $\mathbb{R}$ and range $(0, \infty)$. The line $y = 0$ (the $x$-axis) is a horizontal asymptote of $f$. The graph of $f$ has one of the following shapes.

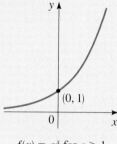

$f(x) = a^x$ for $a > 1$

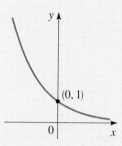

$f(x) = a^x$ for $0 < a < 1$

---

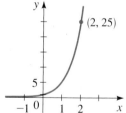

The **Gateway Arch** in St. Louis, Missouri, is shaped in the form of the graph of a combination of exponential functions (*not* a parabola, as it might first appear). Specifically, it is a **catenary**, which is the graph of an equation of the form

$$y = a(e^{bx} + e^{-bx})$$

(see Exercise 53). This shape was chosen because it is optimal for distributing the internal structural forces of the arch. Chains and cables suspended between two points (for example, the stretches of cable between pairs of telephone poles) hang in the shape of a catenary.

© Garry McMichael/Photo Researchers, Inc.

▶ **EXAMPLE 3** | Identifying Graphs of Exponential Functions

Find the exponential function $f(x) = a^x$ whose graph is given.

**(a)**

**(b)**

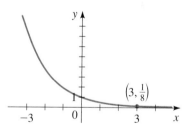

▼ **SOLUTION**

**(a)** Since $f(2) = a^2 = 25$, we see that the base is $a = 5$. So $f(x) = 5^x$.

**(b)** Since $f(3) = a^3 = \frac{1}{8}$, we see that the base is $a = \frac{1}{2}$. So $f(x) = \left(\frac{1}{2}\right)^x$.

✎ **Practice what you've learned: Do Exercise 21.**    ▲

In the next example we see how to graph certain functions, not by plotting points, but by taking the basic graphs of the exponential functions in Figure 2 and applying the shifting and reflecting transformations of Section 3.5.

▶ **EXAMPLE 4** | Transformations of Exponential Functions

Use the graph of $f(x) = 2^x$ to sketch the graph of each function.

**(a)** $g(x) = 1 + 2^x$

**(b)** $h(x) = -2^x$

**(c)** $k(x) = 2^{x-1}$

▼ **SOLUTION**

**(a)** To obtain the graph of $g(x) = 1 + 2^x$, we start with the graph of $f(x) = 2^x$ and shift it upward 1 unit. Notice from Figure 3(a) that the line $y = 1$ is now a horizontal asymptote.

Shifting and reflecting of graphs is explained in Section 3.5.

**(b)** Again we start with the graph of $f(x) = 2^x$, but here we reflect in the $x$-axis to get the graph of $h(x) = -2^x$ shown in Figure 3(b).

**(c)** This time we start with the graph of $f(x) = 2^x$ and shift it to the right by 1 unit to get the graph of $k(x) = 2^{x-1}$ shown in Figure 3(c).

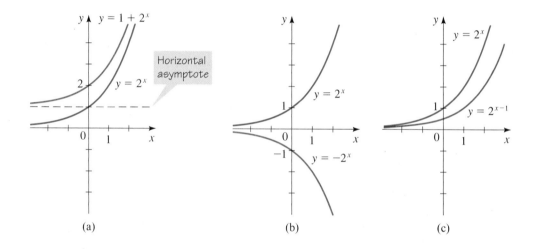

**FIGURE 3**

(a)          (b)          (c)

✎ **Practice what you've learned: Do Exercises 27, 29, and 33.**          ▲

▶ **EXAMPLE 5** | Comparing Exponential and Power Functions

Compare the rates of growth of the exponential function $f(x) = 2^x$ and the power function $g(x) = x^2$ by drawing the graphs of both functions in the following viewing rectangles.

**(a)** $[0, 3]$ by $[0, 8]$

**(b)** $[0, 6]$ by $[0, 25]$

**(c)** $[0, 20]$ by $[0, 1000]$

▼ **SOLUTION**

**(a)** Figure 4(a) shows that the graph of $g(x) = x^2$ catches up with, and becomes higher than, the graph of $f(x) = 2^x$ at $x = 2$.

**(b)** The larger viewing rectangle in Figure 4(b) shows that the graph of $f(x) = 2^x$ overtakes that of $g(x) = x^2$ when $x = 4$.

**(c)** Figure 4(c) gives a more global view and shows that when $x$ is large, $f(x) = 2^x$ is much larger than $g(x) = x^2$.

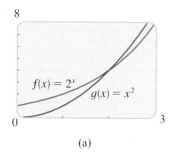

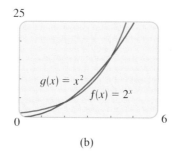

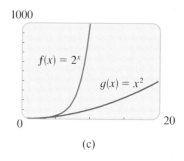

(a)                              (b)                              (c)

**FIGURE 4**

✎ **Practice what you've learned: Do Exercise 47.**   ▲

## ■ The Natural Exponential Function

Any positive number can be used as the base for an exponential function, but some bases are used more frequently than others. We will see in the remaining sections of this chapter that the bases 2 and 10 are convenient for certain applications, but the most important base is the number denoted by the letter $e$.

The number $e$ is defined as the value that $(1 + 1/n)^n$ approaches as $n$ becomes large. (In calculus this idea is made more precise through the concept of a limit. See Exercise 51.) The table in the margin shows the values of the expression $(1 + 1/n)^n$ for increasingly large values of $n$. It appears that, correct to five decimal places, $e \approx 2.71828$; in fact, the approximate value to 20 decimal places is

$$e \approx 2.71828182845904523536$$

It can be shown that $e$ is an irrational number, so we cannot write its exact value in decimal form.

Why use such a strange base for an exponential function? It might seem at first that a base such as 10 is easier to work with. We will see, however, that in certain applications the number $e$ is the best possible base. In this section we study how $e$ occurs in the description of compound interest.

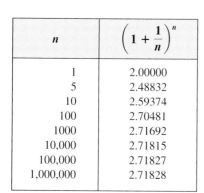

| $n$ | $\left(1 + \dfrac{1}{n}\right)^n$ |
|---|---|
| 1 | 2.00000 |
| 5 | 2.48832 |
| 10 | 2.59374 |
| 100 | 2.70481 |
| 1000 | 2.71692 |
| 10,000 | 2.71815 |
| 100,000 | 2.71827 |
| 1,000,000 | 2.71828 |

The notation $e$ was chosen by Leonhard Euler (see page 100), probably because it is the first letter of the word *exponential*.

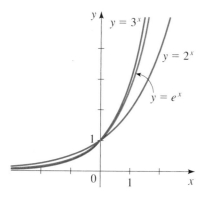

**FIGURE 5** Graph of the natural exponential function

---

**THE NATURAL EXPONENTIAL FUNCTION**

The **natural exponential function** is the exponential function

$$f(x) = e^x$$

with base $e$. It is often referred to as *the* exponential function.

---

Since $2 < e < 3$, the graph of the natural exponential function lies between the graphs of $y = 2^x$ and $y = 3^x$, as shown in Figure 5.

Scientific calculators have a special key for the function $f(x) = e^x$. We use this key in the next example.

▶ **EXAMPLE 6** | Evaluating the Exponential Function

Evaluate each expression correct to five decimal places.

**(a)** $e^3$    **(b)** $2e^{-0.53}$    **(c)** $e^{4.8}$

▼ **SOLUTION**   We use the $\boxed{e^x}$ key on a calculator to evaluate the exponential function.

**(a)** $e^3 \approx 20.08554$    **(b)** $2e^{-0.53} \approx 1.17721$    **(c)** $e^{4.8} \approx 121.51042$

✎ **Practice what you've learned: Do Exercise 9.**   ▲

▶ **EXAMPLE 7** | Transformations of the Exponential Function

Sketch the graph of each function.

**(a)** $f(x) = e^{-x}$      **(b)** $g(x) = 3e^{0.5x}$

▼ **SOLUTION**

**(a)** We start with the graph of $y = e^x$ and reflect in the $y$-axis to obtain the graph of $y = e^{-x}$ as in Figure 6.

**(b)** We calculate several values, plot the resulting points, then connect the points with a smooth curve. The graph is shown in Figure 7.

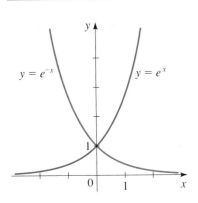

**FIGURE 6**

| $x$ | $f(x) = 3e^{0.5x}$ |
|-----|--------------------|
| $-3$ | 0.67 |
| $-2$ | 1.10 |
| $-1$ | 1.82 |
| 0 | 3.00 |
| 1 | 4.95 |
| 2 | 8.15 |
| 3 | 13.45 |

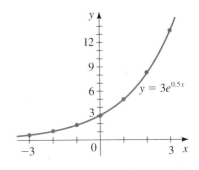

**FIGURE 7**

✎ **Practice what you've learned: Do Exercise 15.** ▲

▶ **EXAMPLE 8** | An Exponential Model for the Spread of a Virus

An infectious disease begins to spread in a small city of population 10,000. After $t$ days, the number of people who have succumbed to the virus is modeled by the function

$$v(t) = \frac{10{,}000}{5 + 1245e^{-0.97t}}$$

**(a)** How many infected people are there initially (at time $t = 0$)?

**(b)** Find the number of infected people after one day, two days, and five days.

**(c)** Graph the function $v$, and describe its behavior.

▼ **SOLUTION**

**(a)** Since $v(0) = 10{,}000/(5 + 1245e^0) = 10{,}000/1250 = 8$, we conclude that 8 people initially have the disease.

**(b)** Using a calculator, we evaluate $v(1)$, $v(2)$, and $v(5)$ and then round off to obtain the following values.

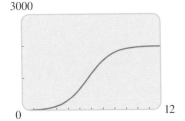

**FIGURE 8**

$$v(t) = \frac{10{,}000}{5 + 1245e^{-0.97t}}$$

| Days | Infected people |
|------|-----------------|
| 1 | 21 |
| 2 | 54 |
| 5 | 678 |

**(c)** From the graph in Figure 8 we see that the number of infected people first rises slowly, then rises quickly between day 3 and day 8, and then levels off when about 2000 people are infected.

✎ **Practice what you've learned: Do Exercise 63.** ▲

The graph in Figure 8 is called a *logistic curve* or a *logistic growth model*. Curves like it occur frequently in the study of population growth. (See Exercises 63–66.)

## ■ Compound Interest

Exponential functions occur in calculating compound interest. If an amount of money $P$, called the **principal**, is invested at an interest rate $i$ per time period, then after one time period the interest is $Pi$, and the amount $A$ of money is

$$A = P + Pi = P(1 + i)$$

If the interest is reinvested, then the new principal is $P(1 + i)$, and the amount after another time period is $A = P(1 + i)(1 + i) = P(1 + i)^2$. Similarly, after a third time period the amount is $A = P(1 + i)^3$. In general, after $k$ periods the amount is

$$A = P(1 + i)^k$$

Notice that this is an exponential function with base $1 + i$.

If the annual interest rate is $r$ and if interest is compounded $n$ times per year, then in each time period the interest rate is $i = r/n$, and there are $nt$ time periods in $t$ years. This leads to the following formula for the amount after $t$ years.

---

**COMPOUND INTEREST**

**Compound interest** is calculated by the formula

$$A(t) = P\left(1 + \frac{r}{n}\right)^{nt}$$

where

$A(t)$ = amount after $t$ years

$P$ = principal

$r$ = interest rate per year

$n$ = number of times interest is compounded per year

$t$ = number of years

---

*r is often referred to as the nominal annual interest rate.*

▶ **EXAMPLE 9** | Calculating Compound Interest

A sum of $1000 is invested at an interest rate of 12% per year. Find the amounts in the account after 3 years if interest is compounded annually, semiannually, quarterly, monthly, and daily.

▼ **SOLUTION**   We use the compound interest formula with $P = \$1000$, $r = 0.12$, and $t = 3$.

| Compounding | $n$ | Amount after 3 years | |
|---|---|---|---|
| Annual | 1 | $1000\left(1 + \dfrac{0.12}{1}\right)^{1(3)}$ | = $1404.93 |
| Semiannual | 2 | $1000\left(1 + \dfrac{0.12}{2}\right)^{2(3)}$ | = $1418.52 |
| Quarterly | 4 | $1000\left(1 + \dfrac{0.12}{4}\right)^{4(3)}$ | = $1425.76 |
| Monthly | 12 | $1000\left(1 + \dfrac{0.12}{12}\right)^{12(3)}$ | = $1430.77 |
| Daily | 365 | $1000\left(1 + \dfrac{0.12}{365}\right)^{365(3)}$ | = $1433.24 |

✎ **Practice what you've learned: Do Exercise 69.**                    ▲

We see from Example 9 that the interest paid increases as the number of compounding periods $n$ increases. Let's see what happens as $n$ increases indefinitely. If we let $m = n/r$, then

$$A(t) = P\left(1 + \frac{r}{n}\right)^{nt} = P\left[\left(1 + \frac{r}{n}\right)^{n/r}\right]^{rt} = P\left[\left(1 + \frac{1}{m}\right)^{m}\right]^{rt}$$

Recall that as $m$ becomes large, the quantity $(1 + 1/m)^m$ approaches the number $e$. Thus, the amount approaches $A = Pe^{rt}$. This expression gives the amount when the interest is compounded at "every instant."

---

**CONTINUOUSLY COMPOUNDED INTEREST**

**Continuously compounded interest** is calculated by the formula

$$A(t) = Pe^{rt}$$

where    $A(t)$ = amount after $t$ years

   $P$ = principal

   $r$ = interest rate per year

   $t$ = number of years

---

▶ **EXAMPLE 10** | Calculating Continuously Compounded Interest

Find the amount after 3 years if $1000 is invested at an interest rate of 12% per year, compounded continuously.

▼ **SOLUTION**  We use the formula for continuously compounded interest with $P = $1000$, $r = 0.12$, and $t = 3$ to get

$$A(3) = 1000e^{(0.12)3} = 1000e^{0.36} = \$1433.33$$

Compare this amount with the amounts in Example 9.

✎ **Practice what you've learned: Do Exercise 71.** ▲

# 5.1 EXERCISES

▼ **CONCEPTS**

**1.** The function $f(x) = 5^x$ is an exponential function with base

_____ ; $f(-2) = $ _____ , $f(0) = $ _____ ,

$f(2) = $ _____ , and $f(6) = $ _____ .

**2.** Match the exponential function with its graph.

(a) $f(x) = 2^x$   (b) $f(x) = 2^{-x}$   (c) $f(x) = -2^x$

**3.** The function $f(x) = e^x$ is called the _____ exponential function. The number $e$ is approximately equal to _____ .

**4.** In the formula $A(t) = Pe^{rt}$ for continuously compound interest, the letters $P$, $r$, and $t$ stand for _____ , _____ , and _____ , respectively, and $A(t)$ stands for _____ . So if $100 is invested at an interest rate of 6% compounded continuously, then the amount after 2 years is _____ .

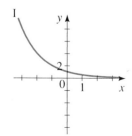

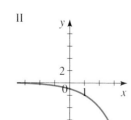

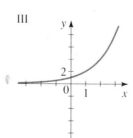

## ▼ SKILLS

**5–10** ▪ Use a calculator to evaluate the function at the indicated values. Round your answers to three decimals.

**5.** $f(x) = 4^x$;  $f(0.5), f(\sqrt{2}), f(\pi), f(\frac{1}{3})$

**6.** $f(x) = 3^{x+1}$;  $f(-1.5), f(\sqrt{3}), f(e), f(-\frac{5}{4})$

**7.** $g(x) = (\frac{2}{3})^{x-1}$;  $g(1.3), g(\sqrt{5}), g(2\pi), g(-\frac{1}{2})$

**8.** $g(x) = (\frac{3}{4})^{2x}$;  $g(0.7), g(\sqrt{7}/2), g(1/\pi), g(\frac{2}{3})$

**9.** $h(x) = e^x$;  $h(3), h(0.23), h(1), h(-2)$

**10.** $h(x) = e^{-2x}$;  $h(1), h(\sqrt{2}), h(-3), h(\frac{1}{2})$

**11–16** ▪ Sketch the graph of the function by making a table of values. Use a calculator if necessary.

**11.** $f(x) = 2^x$

**12.** $g(x) = 8^x$

**13.** $f(x) = (\frac{1}{3})^x$

**14.** $h(x) = (1.1)^x$

**15.** $g(x) = 3e^x$

**16.** $h(x) = 2e^{-0.5x}$

**17–20** ▪ Graph both functions on one set of axes.

**17.** $f(x) = 2^x$  and  $g(x) = 2^{-x}$

**18.** $f(x) = 3^{-x}$  and  $g(x) = (\frac{1}{3})^x$

**19.** $f(x) = 4^x$  and  $g(x) = 7^x$

**20.** $f(x) = (\frac{2}{3})^x$  and  $g(x) = (\frac{4}{3})^x$

**21–24** ▪ Find the exponential function $f(x) = a^x$ whose graph is given.

**21.**

**22.**

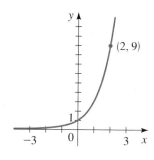

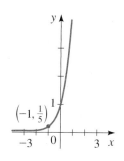

**23.**

**24.**

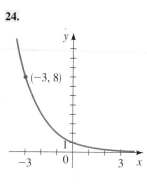

**25–26** ▪ Match the exponential function with one of the graphs labeled I or II.

**25.** $f(x) = 5^{x+1}$

**26.** $f(x) = 5^x + 1$

I

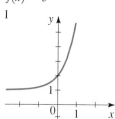

II

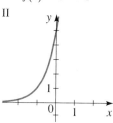

**27–40** ▪ Graph the function, not by plotting points, but by starting from the graphs in Figures 2 and 5. State the domain, range, and asymptote.

**27.** $f(x) = -3^x$

**28.** $f(x) = 10^{-x}$

**29.** $g(x) = 2^x - 3$

**30.** $g(x) = 2^{x-3}$

**31.** $h(x) = 4 + (\frac{1}{2})^x$

**32.** $h(x) = 6 - 3^x$

**33.** $f(x) = 10^{x+3}$

**34.** $f(x) = -(\frac{1}{5})^x$

**35.** $f(x) = -e^x$

**36.** $y = 1 - e^x$

**37.** $y = e^{-x} - 1$

**38.** $f(x) = -e^{-x}$

**39.** $f(x) = e^{x-2}$

**40.** $y = e^{x-3} + 4$

**41. (a)** Sketch the graphs of $f(x) = 2^x$ and $g(x) = 3(2^x)$.
   **(b)** How are the graphs related?

**42. (a)** Sketch the graphs of $f(x) = 9^{x/2}$ and $g(x) = 3^x$.
   **(b)** Use the Laws of Exponents to explain the relationship between these graphs.

**43.** Compare the functions $f(x) = x^3$ and $g(x) = 3^x$ by evaluating both of them for $x = 0, 1, 2, 3, 4, 5, 6, 7, 8, 9, 10, 15,$ and $20$. Then draw the graphs of $f$ and $g$ on the same set of axes.

**44.** If $f(x) = 10^x$, show that $\dfrac{f(x + h) - f(x)}{h} = 10^x\left(\dfrac{10^h - 1}{h}\right)$.

**45.** The *hyperbolic cosine function* is defined by
$$\cosh(x) = \frac{e^x + e^{-x}}{2}$$
   **(a)** Sketch the graphs of the functions $y = \frac{1}{2}e^x$ and $y = \frac{1}{2}e^{-x}$ on the same axes, and use graphical addition (see Section 3.6) to sketch the graph of $y = \cosh(x)$.
   **(b)** Use the definition to show that $\cosh(-x) = \cosh(x)$.

**46.** The *hyperbolic sine function* is defined by
$$\sinh(x) = \frac{e^x - e^{-x}}{2}$$
   **(a)** Sketch the graph of this function using graphical addition as in Exercise 45.
   **(b)** Use the definition to show that $\sinh(-x) = -\sinh(x)$

**47. (a)** Compare the rates of growth of the functions $f(x) = 2^x$ and $g(x) = x^5$ by drawing the graphs of both functions in the following viewing rectangles.
     (i) $[0, 5]$ by $[0, 20]$
     (ii) $[0, 25]$ by $[0, 10^7]$
     (iii) $[0, 50]$ by $[0, 10^8]$
   **(b)** Find the solutions of the equation $2^x = x^5$, correct to one decimal place.

**48.** (a) Compare the rates of growth of the functions $f(x) = 3^x$ and $g(x) = x^4$ by drawing the graphs of both functions in the following viewing rectangles:

(i) $[-4, 4]$ by $[0, 20]$  (ii) $[0, 10]$ by $[0, 5000]$
(iii) $[0, 20]$ by $[0, 10^5]$

(b) Find the solutions of the equation $3^x = x^4$, correct to two decimal places.

**49–50** ▪ Draw graphs of the given family of functions for $c = 0.25, 0.5, 1, 2, 4$. How are the graphs related?

**49.** $f(x) = c2^x$

**50.** $f(x) = 2^{cx}$

**51.** Illustrate the definition of the number $e$ by graphing the curve $y = (1 + 1/x)^x$ and the line $y = e$ on the same screen, using the viewing rectangle $[0, 40]$ by $[0, 4]$.

**52.** Investigate the behavior of the function

$$f(x) = \left(1 - \frac{1}{x}\right)^x$$

as $x \to \infty$ by graphing $f$ and the line $y = 1/e$ on the same screen, using the viewing rectangle $[0, 20]$ by $[0, 1]$.

**53.** (a) Draw the graphs of the family of functions

$$f(x) = \frac{a}{2}(e^{x/a} + e^{-x/a})$$

for $a = 0.5, 1, 1.5,$ and $2$.

(b) How does a larger value of $a$ affect the graph?

**54–55** ▪ Find the local maximum and minimum values of the function and the value of $x$ at which each occurs. State each answer correct to two decimal places.

**54.** $g(x) = x^x$ $(x > 0)$

**55.** $g(x) = e^x + e^{-3x}$

**56–57** ▪ Find, correct to two decimal places, **(a)** the intervals on which the function is increasing or decreasing and **(b)** the range of the function.

**56.** $y = 10^{x-x^2}$

**57.** $y = xe^{-x}$

---

## ▼ APPLICATIONS

**58. Medical Drugs** When a certain medical drug is administered to a patient, the number of milligrams remaining in the patient's bloodstream after $t$ hours is modeled by

$$D(t) = 50e^{-0.2t}$$

How many milligrams of the drug remain in the patient's bloodstream after 3 hours?

**59. Radioactive Decay** A radioactive substance decays in such a way that the amount of mass remaining after $t$ days is given by the function

$$m(t) = 13e^{-0.015t}$$

where $m(t)$ is measured in kilograms.
(a) Find the mass at time $t = 0$.
(b) How much of the mass remains after 45 days?

**60. Radioactive Decay** Doctors use radioactive iodine as a tracer in diagnosing certain thyroid gland disorders. This type of iodine decays in such a way that the mass remaining after $t$ days is given by the function

$$m(t) = 6e^{-0.087t}$$

where $m(t)$ is measured in grams.
(a) Find the mass at time $t = 0$.
(b) How much of the mass remains after 20 days?

**61. Sky Diving** A sky diver jumps from a reasonable height above the ground. The air resistance she experiences is proportional to her velocity, and the constant of proportionality is 0.2. It can be shown that the downward velocity of the sky diver at time $t$ is given by

$$v(t) = 80(1 - e^{-0.2t})$$

where $t$ is measured in seconds and $v(t)$ is measured in feet per second (ft/s).
(a) Find the initial velocity of the sky diver.
(b) Find the velocity after 5 s and after 10 s.
(c) Draw a graph of the velocity function $v(t)$.
(d) The maximum velocity of a falling object with wind resistance is called its *terminal velocity*. From the graph in part (c) find the terminal velocity of this sky diver.

$$v(t) = 80(1 - e^{-0.2t})$$

**62. Mixtures and Concentrations** A 50-gallon barrel is filled completely with pure water. Salt water with a concentration of 0.3 lb/gal is then pumped into the barrel, and the resulting mixture overflows at the same rate. The amount of salt in the barrel at time $t$ is given by

$$Q(t) = 15(1 - e^{-0.04t})$$

where $t$ is measured in minutes and $Q(t)$ is measured in pounds.
(a) How much salt is in the barrel after 5 min?
(b) How much salt is in the barrel after 10 min?
(c) Draw a graph of the function $Q(t)$.
(d) Use the graph in part (c) to determine the value that the amount of salt in the barrel approaches as $t$ becomes large. Is this what you would expect?

$$Q(t) = 15(1 - e^{-0.04t})$$

✎ **63. Logistic Growth**    Animal populations are not capable of un-restricted growth because of limited habitat and food supplies. Under such conditions the population follows a *logistic growth model*:

$$P(t) = \frac{d}{1 + ke^{-ct}}$$

where $c$, $d$, and $k$ are positive constants. For a certain fish popu-lation in a small pond $d = 1200$, $k = 11$, $c = 0.2$, and $t$ is measured in years. The fish were introduced into the pond at time $t = 0$.

(a) How many fish were originally put in the pond?
(b) Find the population after 10, 20, and 30 years.
(c) Evaluate $P(t)$ for large values of $t$. What value does the population approach as $t \rightarrow \infty$? Does the graph shown confirm your calculations?

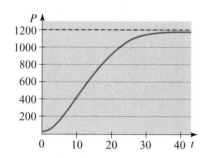

**64. Bird Population**    The population of a certain species of bird is limited by the type of habitat required for nesting. The popu-lation behaves according to the logistic growth model

$$n(t) = \frac{5600}{0.5 + 27.5e^{-0.044t}}$$

where $t$ is measured in years.

(a) Find the initial bird population.
(b) Draw a graph of the function $n(t)$.
(c) What size does the population approach as time goes on?

**65. World Population**    The relative growth rate of world popula-tion has been decreasing steadily in recent years. On the basis of this, some population models predict that world population will eventually stabilize at a level that the planet can support. One such logistic model is

$$P(t) = \frac{73.2}{6.1 + 5.9e^{-0.02t}}$$

where $t = 0$ is the year 2000 and population is measured in billions.

(a) What world population does this model predict for the year 2200? For 2300?
(b) Sketch a graph of the function $P$ for the years 2000 to 2500.
(c) According to this model, what size does the world popula-tion seem to approach as time goes on?

**66. Tree Diameter**    For a certain type of tree the diameter $D$ (in feet) depends on the tree's age $t$ (in years) according to the logistic growth model

$$D(t) = \frac{5.4}{1 + 2.9e^{-0.01t}}$$

Find the diameter of a 20-year-old tree.

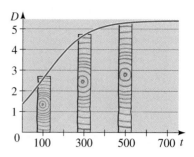

**67–68** ▪ **Compound Interest**    An investment of $5000 is depos-ited into an account in which interest is compounded monthly. Complete the table by filling in the amounts to which the invest-ment grows at the indicated times or interest rates.

**67.** $r = 4\%$

| Time (years) | Amount |
| --- | --- |
| 1 | |
| 2 | |
| 3 | |
| 4 | |
| 5 | |
| 6 | |

**68.** $t = 5$ years

| Rate per year | Amount |
| --- | --- |
| 1% | |
| 2% | |
| 3% | |
| 4% | |
| 5% | |
| 6% | |

✎ **69. Compound Interest**    If $10,000 is invested at an interest rate of 10% per year, compounded semiannually, find the value of the investment after the given number of years.

(a) 5 years
(b) 10 years
(c) 15 years

**70. Compound Interest**    If $4000 is borrowed at a rate of 16% interest per year, compounded quarterly, find the amount due at the end of the given number of years.

(a) 4 years
(b) 6 years
(c) 8 years

✎ **71. Compound Interest**    If $3000 is invested at an interest rate of 9% per year, find the amount of the investment at the end of 5 years for the following compounding methods.

(a) Annual          (b) Semiannual          (c) Monthly
(d) Weekly          (e) Daily               (f) Hourly
(g) Continuously

**72. Compound Interest** If $4000 is invested in an account for which interest is compounded quarterly, find the amount of the investment at the end of 5 years for the following interest rates.
(a) 6%                    (b) $6\frac{1}{2}$%
(c) 7%                    (d) 8%

**73. Compound Interest** Which of the given interest rates and compounding periods would provide the best investment?
(i) $8\frac{1}{2}$% per year, compounded semiannually
(ii) $8\frac{1}{4}$% per year, compounded quarterly
(iii) 8% per year, compounded continuously

**74. Compound Interest** Which of the given interest rates and compounding periods would provide the better investment?
(i) $9\frac{1}{4}$% per year, compounded semiannually
(ii) 9% per year, compounded continuously

**75. Present Value** The **present value** of a sum of money is the amount that must be invested now, at a given rate of interest, to produce the desired sum at a later date.
(a) Find the present value of $10,000 if interest is paid at a rate of 9% per year, compounded semiannually, for 3 years.
(b) Find the present value of $100,000 if interest is paid at a rate of 8% per year, compounded monthly, for 5 years.

**76. Investment** A sum of $5000 is invested at an interest rate of 9% per year, compounded semiannually.
(a) Find the value $A(t)$ of the investment after $t$ years.
(b) Draw a graph of $A(t)$.

(c) Use the graph of $A(t)$ to determine when this investment will amount to $25,000.

## ▼ DISCOVERY • DISCUSSION • WRITING

**77. Growth of an Exponential Function** Suppose you are offered a job that lasts one month, and you are to be very well paid. Which of the following methods of payment is more profitable for you?
(a) One million dollars at the end of the month
(b) Two cents on the first day of the month, 4 cents on the second day, 8 cents on the third day, and, in general, $2^n$ cents on the $n$th day

**78. The Height of the Graph of an Exponential Function** Your mathematics instructor asks you to sketch a graph of the exponential function

$$f(x) = 2^x$$

for $x$ between 0 and 40, using a scale of 10 units to one inch. What are the dimensions of the sheet of paper you will need to sketch this graph?

# EXPONENTIAL EXPLOSION

To help us grasp just how explosive exponential growth is, let's try a thought experiment.

Suppose you put a penny in your piggy bank today, two pennies tomorrow, four pennies the next day, and so on, doubling the number of pennies you add to the bank each day (see the table). How many pennies will you put in your piggy bank on day 30? The answer is $2^{30}$ pennies. That's simple, but can you guess how many dollars that is? $2^{30}$ pennies is more than 10 million dollars!

$10,000,000 in pennies!

| Day | Pennies |
|-----|---------|
| 0 | 1 |
| 1 | 2 |
| 2 | 4 |
| 3 | 8 |
| 4 | 16 |
| ⋮ | ⋮ |
| $n$ | $2^n$ |
| ⋮ | ⋮ |

As you can see, the exponential function

$$f(x) = 2^x$$

grows extremely fast. This is the principle behind atomic explosions. An atom splits releasing two neutrons, which cause two atoms to split, each releasing two neutrons, causing four atoms to split, and so on. At the $n$th stage $2^n$ atoms split—an exponential explosion!

Populations also grow exponentially. Let's see what this means for a type of bacteria that splits every minute. Suppose that at 12:00 noon a single bacterium colonizes a discarded food can. The bacterium and his descendants are all happy, but they fear the time when the can is completely full of bacteria—doomsday.

1. How many bacteria are in the can at 12:05? At 12:10?

2. The can is completely full of bacteria at 1:00 P.M. At what time was the can only half full of bacteria?

3. When the can is exactly half full, the president of the bacteria colony reassures his constituents that doomsday is far away—after all, there is as much room left in the can as has been used in the entire previous history of the colony. Is the president correct? How much time is left before doomsday?

4. When the can is one-quarter full, how much time remains till doomsday?

5. A wise bacterium decides to start a new colony in another can and slow down splitting time to 2 minutes. How much time does this new colony have?

## 5.2 | Logarithmic Functions

**LEARNING OBJECTIVES**

After completing this section, you will be able to:

- Evaluate logarithmic functions
- Change between logarithmic and exponential forms of an expression
- Use basic properties of logarithms
- Graph logarithmic functions
- Use common and natural logarithms

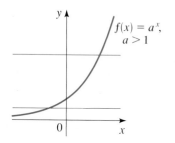

**FIGURE 1** $f(x) = a^x$ is one-to-one

In this section we study the inverses of exponential functions.

### ■ Logarithmic Functions

Every exponential function $f(x) = a^x$, with $a > 0$ and $a \neq 1$, is a one-to-one function by the Horizontal Line Test (see Figure 1 for the case $a > 1$) and therefore has an inverse function. The inverse function $f^{-1}$ is called the *logarithmic function with base a* and is denoted by $\log_a$. Recall from Section 3.7 that $f^{-1}$ is defined by

$$f^{-1}(x) = y \quad \Leftrightarrow \quad f(y) = x$$

This leads to the following definition of the logarithmic function.

---

**DEFINITION OF THE LOGARITHMIC FUNCTION**

Let $a$ be a positive number with $a \neq 1$. The **logarithmic function with base $a$**, denoted by $\log_a$, is defined by

$$\log_a x = y \quad \Leftrightarrow \quad a^y = x$$

So $\log_a x$ is the *exponent* to which the base $a$ must be raised to give $x$.

---

We read $\log_a x = y$ as "log base $a$ of $x$ is $y$."

By tradition the name of the logarithmic function is $\log_a$, not just a single letter. Also, we usually omit the parentheses in the function notation and write

$$\log_a(x) = \log_a x$$

When we use the definition of logarithms to switch back and forth between the **logarithmic form** $\log_a x = y$ and the **exponential form** $a^y = x$, it is helpful to notice that, in both forms, the base is the same:

**Logarithmic form**

Exponent

$$\log_a x = y$$

Base

**Exponential form**

Exponent

$$a^y = x$$

Base

▶ **EXAMPLE 1** | Logarithmic and Exponential Forms

The logarithmic and exponential forms are equivalent equations: If one is true, then so is the other. So we can switch from one form to the other as in the following illustrations.

| $x$ | $\log_{10} x$ |
|---|---|
| $10^4$ | 4 |
| $10^3$ | 3 |
| $10^2$ | 2 |
| 10 | 1 |
| 1 | 0 |
| $10^{-1}$ | $-1$ |
| $10^{-2}$ | $-2$ |
| $10^{-3}$ | $-3$ |
| $10^{-4}$ | $-4$ |

| Logarithmic form | Exponential form |
|---|---|
| $\log_{10} 100{,}000 = 5$ | $10^5 = 100{,}000$ |
| $\log_2 8 = 3$ | $2^3 = 8$ |
| $\log_2\left(\frac{1}{8}\right) = -3$ | $2^{-3} = \frac{1}{8}$ |
| $\log_5 s = r$ | $5^r = s$ |

✎ **Practice what you've learned: Do Exercise 5.**  ▲

It is important to understand that $\log_a x$ is an *exponent*. For example, the numbers in the right column of the table in the margin are the logarithms (base 10) of the numbers in the left column. This is the case for all bases, as the following example illustrates.

▶ **EXAMPLE 2** | Evaluating Logarithms

**(a)** $\log_{10} 1000 = 3$    because    $10^3 = 1000$

**(b)** $\log_2 32 = 5$    because    $2^5 = 32$

**(c)** $\log_{10} 0.1 = -1$    because    $10^{-1} = 0.1$

**(d)** $\log_{16} 4 = \frac{1}{2}$    because    $16^{1/2} = 4$

✎ **Practice what you've learned: Do Exercises 7 and 9.**  ▲

Inverse Function Property:
$$f^{-1}(f(x)) = x$$
$$f(f^{-1}(x)) = x$$

When we apply the Inverse Function Property described on page 267 to $f(x) = a^x$ and $f^{-1}(x) = \log_a x$, we get

$$\log_a(a^x) = x \qquad x \in \mathbb{R}$$
$$a^{\log_a x} = x \qquad x > 0$$

We list these and other properties of logarithms discussed in this section.

**PROPERTIES OF LOGARITHMS**

| Property | Reason |
|---|---|
| **1.** $\log_a 1 = 0$ | We must raise $a$ to the power 0 to get 1. |
| **2.** $\log_a a = 1$ | We must raise $a$ to the power 1 to get $a$. |
| **3.** $\log_a a^x = x$ | We must raise $a$ to the power $x$ to get $a^x$. |
| **4.** $a^{\log_a x} = x$ | $\log_a x$ is the power to which $a$ must be raised to get $x$. |

▶ **EXAMPLE 3** | Applying Properties of Logarithms

We illustrate the properties of logarithms when the base is 5.

$$\log_5 1 = 0 \quad \text{Property 1} \qquad\qquad \log_5 5 = 1 \quad \text{Property 2}$$
$$\log_5 5^8 = 8 \quad \text{Property 3} \qquad\qquad 5^{\log_5 12} = 12 \quad \text{Property 4}$$

✎ **Practice what you've learned: Do Exercises 19 and 25.**  ▲

## ■ Graphs of Logarithmic Functions

Recall that if a one-to-one function $f$ has domain $A$ and range $B$, then its inverse function $f^{-1}$ has domain $B$ and range $A$. Since the exponential function $f(x) = a^x$ with $a \neq 1$ has domain $\mathbb{R}$ and range $(0, \infty)$, we conclude that its inverse function, $f^{-1}(x) = \log_a x$, has domain $(0, \infty)$ and range $\mathbb{R}$.

The graph of $f^{-1}(x) = \log_a x$ is obtained by reflecting the graph of $f(x) = a^x$ in the line $y = x$. Figure 2 shows the case $a > 1$. The fact that $y = a^x$ (for $a > 1$) is a very rapidly

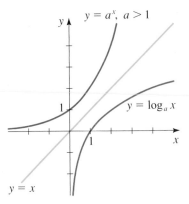

**FIGURE 2** Graph of the logarithmic function $f(x) = \log_a x$

Arrow notation is explained on page 345.

increasing function for $x > 0$ implies that $y = \log_a x$ is a very slowly increasing function for $x > 1$ (see Exercise 88).

Since $\log_a 1 = 0$, the $x$-intercept of the function $y = \log_a x$ is 1. The $y$-axis is a vertical asymptote of $y = \log_a x$ because $\log_a x \to -\infty$ as $x \to 0^+$.

▶ **EXAMPLE 4** | Graphing a Logarithmic Function by Plotting Points

Sketch the graph of $f(x) = \log_2 x$.

▼ **SOLUTION**    To make a table of values, we choose the $x$-values to be powers of 2 so that we can easily find their logarithms. We plot these points and connect them with a smooth curve as in Figure 3.

| $x$ | $\log_2 x$ |
|:---:|:---:|
| $2^3$ | 3 |
| $2^2$ | 2 |
| 2 | 1 |
| 1 | 0 |
| $2^{-1}$ | $-1$ |
| $2^{-2}$ | $-2$ |
| $2^{-3}$ | $-3$ |
| $2^{-4}$ | $-4$ |

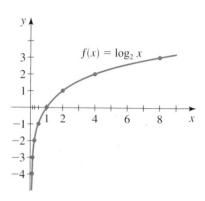

**FIGURE 3**

✎ **Practice what you've learned: Do Exercise 41.**                                    ▲

Figure 4 shows the graphs of the family of logarithmic functions with bases 2, 3, 5, and 10. These graphs are drawn by reflecting the graphs of $y = 2^x$, $y = 3^x$, $y = 5^x$, and $y = 10^x$ (see Figure 2 in Section 5.1) in the line $y = x$. We can also plot points as an aid to sketching these graphs, as illustrated in Example 4.

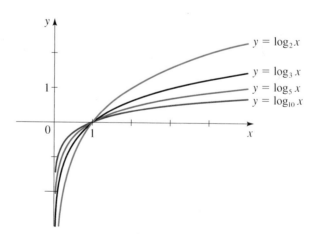

**FIGURE 4**  A family of logarithmic functions

In the next two examples we graph logarithmic functions by starting with the basic graphs in Figure 4 and using the transformations of Section 3.5.

▶ **EXAMPLE 5** | Reflecting Graphs of Logarithmic Functions

Sketch the graph of each function.

**(a)** $g(x) = -\log_2 x$

**(b)** $h(x) = \log_2(-x)$

▼ **SOLUTION**

**(a)** We start with the graph of $f(x) = \log_2 x$ and reflect in the $x$-axis to get the graph of $g(x) = -\log_2 x$ in Figure 5(a).

**(b)** We start with the graph of $f(x) = \log_2 x$ and reflect in the $y$-axis to get the graph of $h(x) = \log_2(-x)$ in Figure 5(b).

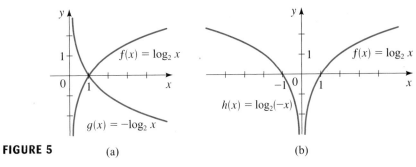

**FIGURE 5**     (a)                              (b)

✎ **Practice what you've learned: Do Exercise 55.**

▶ **EXAMPLE 6** | Shifting Graphs of Logarithmic Functions

Find the domain of each function, and sketch the graph.

**(a)** $g(x) = 2 + \log_5 x$

**(b)** $h(x) = \log_{10}(x - 3)$

▼ **SOLUTION**

**(a)** The graph of $g$ is obtained from the graph of $f(x) = \log_5 x$ (Figure 4) by shifting upward 2 units (see Figure 6 on the next page). The domain of $f$ is $(0, \infty)$.

---

## MATHEMATICS IN THE MODERN WORLD

### Law Enforcement

© Bettmann/CORBIS    © Hulton-Deutsch
                      Collection/CORBIS

Mathematics aids law enforcement in numerous and surprising ways, from the reconstruction of bullet trajectories to determining the time of death to calculating the probability that a DNA sample is from a particular person. One interesting use is in the search for missing persons. If a person has been missing for several years, that person might look quite different from his or her most recent available photograph. This is particularly true if the missing person is a child. Have you ever wondered what you will look like 5, 10, or 15 years from now?

Researchers have found that different parts of the body grow at different rates. For example, you have no doubt noticed that a baby's head is much larger relative to its body than an adult's. As another example, the ratio of arm length to height is $\frac{1}{3}$ in a child but about $\frac{2}{5}$ in an adult. By collecting data and analyzing the graphs, researchers are able to determine the functions that model growth. As in all growth phenomena, exponential and logarithmic functions play a crucial role. For instance, the formula that relates arm length $l$ to height $h$ is $l = ae^{kh}$ where $a$ and $k$ are constants. By studying various physical characteristics of a person, mathematical biologists model each characteristic by a function that describes how it changes over time. Models of facial characteristics can be programmed into a computer to give a picture of how a person's appearance changes over time. These pictures aid law enforcement agencies in locating missing persons.

Library of Congress

**John Napier** (1550–1617) was a Scottish landowner for whom mathematics was a hobby. We know him today because of his key invention: logarithms, which he published in 1614 under the title *A Description of the Marvelous Rule of Logarithms*. In Napier's time, logarithms were used exclusively for simplifying complicated calculations. For example, to multiply two large numbers, we would write them as powers of 10. The exponents are simply the logarithms of the numbers. For instance,

$$4532 \times 57783$$
$$\approx 10^{3.65629} \times 10^{4.76180}$$
$$= 10^{8.41809}$$
$$\approx 261{,}872{,}564$$

The idea is that multiplying powers of 10 is easy (we simply add their exponents). Napier produced extensive tables giving the logarithms (or exponents) of numbers. Since the advent of calculators and computers, logarithms are no longer used for this purpose. The logarithmic functions, however, have found many applications, some of which are described in this chapter.

Napier wrote on many topics. One of his most colorful works is a book entitled *A Plaine Discovery of the Whole Revelation of Saint John*, in which he predicted that the world would end in the year 1700.

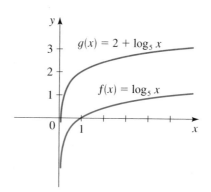

**FIGURE 6**

**(b)** The graph of $h$ is obtained from the graph of $f(x) = \log_{10} x$ (Figure 4) by shifting to the right 3 units (see Figure 7 below). The line $x = 3$ is a vertical asymptote. Since $\log_{10} x$ is defined only when $x > 0$, the domain of $h(x) = \log_{10}(x - 3)$ is

$$\{x \mid x - 3 > 0\} = \{x \mid x > 3\} = (3, \infty)$$

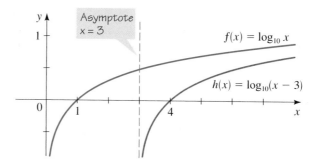

**FIGURE 7**

✏️ **Practice what you've learned: Do Exercises 53 and 57.** ▲

## ■ Common Logarithms

We now study logarithms with base 10.

---

**COMMON LOGARITHM**

The logarithm with base 10 is called the **common logarithm** and is denoted by omitting the base:

$$\log x = \log_{10} x$$

---

From the definition of logarithms we can easily find that

$$\log 10 = 1 \quad \text{and} \quad \log 100 = 2$$

But how do we find log 50? We need to find the exponent $y$ such that $10^y = 50$. Clearly, 1 is too small and 2 is too large. So

$$1 < \log 50 < 2$$

To get a better approximation, we can experiment to find a power of 10 closer to 50. Fortunately, scientific calculators are equipped with a $\boxed{\text{LOG}}$ key that directly gives values of common logarithms.

▶ **EXAMPLE 7** | Evaluating Common Logarithms

Use a calculator to find appropriate values of $f(x) = \log x$ and use the values to sketch the graph.

▼ **SOLUTION**   We make a table of values, using a calculator to evaluate the function at those values of $x$ that are not powers of 10. We plot those points and connect them by a smooth curve as in Figure 8.

| $x$ | $\log x$ |
|------|----------|
| 0.01 | $-2$ |
| 0.1 | $-1$ |
| 0.5 | $-0.301$ |
| 1 | 0 |
| 4 | 0.602 |
| 5 | 0.699 |
| 10 | 1 |

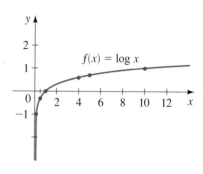

**FIGURE 8**

✎ **Practice what you've learned: Do Exercise 43.**

Scientists model human response to stimuli (such as sound, light, or pressure) using logarithmic functions. For example, the intensity of a sound must be increased manyfold before we "feel" that the loudness has simply doubled. The psychologist Gustav Fechner formulated the law as

$$S = k \log\left(\frac{I}{I_0}\right)$$

where $S$ is the subjective intensity of the stimulus, $I$ is the physical intensity of the stimulus, $I_0$ stands for the threshold physical intensity, and $k$ is a constant that is different for each sensory stimulus.

Human response to sound and light intensity is logarithmic.

We study the decibel scale in more detail in Section 5.5.

▶ **EXAMPLE 8** | Common Logarithms and Sound

The perception of the loudness $B$ (in decibels, dB) of a sound with physical intensity $I$ (in W/m²) is given by

$$B = 10 \log\left(\frac{I}{I_0}\right)$$

where $I_0$ is the physical intensity of a barely audible sound. Find the decibel level (loudness) of a sound whose physical intensity $I$ is 100 times that of $I_0$.

▼ **SOLUTION**   We find the decibel level $B$ by using the fact that $I = 100I_0$.

$$B = 10 \log\left(\frac{I}{I_0}\right) \qquad \text{Definition of } B$$

$$= 10 \log\left(\frac{100I_0}{I_0}\right) \qquad I = 100I_0$$

$$= 10 \log 100 \qquad \text{Cancel } I_0$$

$$= 10 \cdot 2 = 20 \qquad \text{Definition of log}$$

The loudness of the sound is 20 dB.

✎ **Practice what you've learned: Do Exercise 83.**

### ■ Natural Logarithms

Of all possible bases $a$ for logarithms, it turns out that the most convenient choice for the purposes of calculus is the number $e$, which we defined in Section 5.1.

The notation ln is an abbreviation for the Latin name *logarithmus naturalis*.

---

**NATURAL LOGARITHM**

The logarithm with base $e$ is called the **natural logarithm** and is denoted by **ln**:

$$\ln x = \log_e x$$

---

The natural logarithmic function $y = \ln x$ is the inverse function of the exponential function $y = e^x$. Both functions are graphed in Figure 9. By the definition of inverse functions we have

$$\ln x = y \iff e^y = x$$

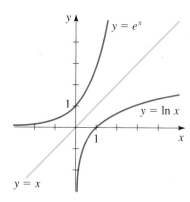

**FIGURE 9** Graph of the natural logarithmic function

If we substitute $a = e$ and write "ln" for "$\log_e$" in the properties of logarithms mentioned earlier, we obtain the following properties of natural logarithms.

---

**PROPERTIES OF NATURAL LOGARITHMS**

| Property | Reason |
|---|---|
| **1.** $\ln 1 = 0$ | We must raise $e$ to the power 0 to get 1. |
| **2.** $\ln e = 1$ | We must raise $e$ to the power 1 to get $e$. |
| **3.** $\ln e^x = x$ | We must raise $e$ to the power $x$ to get $e^x$. |
| **4.** $e^{\ln x} = x$ | $\ln x$ is the power to which $e$ must be raised to get $x$. |

---

Calculators are equipped with an ⌴LN⌴ key that directly gives the values of natural logarithms.

▶ **EXAMPLE 9** | Evaluating the Natural Logarithm Function

**(a)** $\ln e^8 = 8$             Definition of natural logarithm

**(b)** $\ln\left(\dfrac{1}{e^2}\right) = \ln e^{-2} = -2$     Definition of natural logarithm

**(c)** $\ln 5 \approx 1.609$           Use ⌴LN⌴ key on calculator

✎ **Practice what you've learned: Do Exercise 39.**      ▲

▶ **EXAMPLE 10** | Finding the Domain of a Logarithmic Function

Find the domain of the function $f(x) = \ln(4 - x^2)$.

▼ **SOLUTION**   As with any logarithmic function, $\ln x$ is defined when $x > 0$. Thus, the domain of $f$ is

$$\{x \mid 4 - x^2 > 0\} = \{x \mid x^2 < 4\} = \{x \mid |x| < 2\}$$
$$= \{x \mid -2 < x < 2\} = (-2, 2)$$

✎ **Practice what you've learned: Do Exercise 63.**                                    ▲

▶ **EXAMPLE 11** | Drawing the Graph of a Logarithmic Function

Draw the graph of the function $y = x \ln(4 - x^2)$, and use it to find the asymptotes and local maximum and minimum values.

▼ **SOLUTION**   As in Example 10 the domain of this function is the interval $(-2, 2)$, so we choose the viewing rectangle $[-3, 3]$ by $[-3, 3]$. The graph is shown in Figure 10, and from it we see that the lines $x = -2$ and $x = 2$ are vertical asymptotes.

The function has a local maximum point to the right of $x = 1$ and a local minimum point to the left of $x = -1$. By zooming in and tracing along the graph with the cursor, we find that the local maximum value is approximately 1.13 and this occurs when $x \approx 1.15$. Similarly (or by noticing that the function is odd), we find that the local minimum value is about $-1.13$, and it occurs when $x \approx -1.15$.

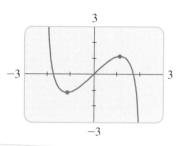

**FIGURE 10**
$y = x \ln(4 - x^2)$

✎ **Practice what you've learned: Do Exercise 69.**                                    ▲

# 5.2 EXERCISES

▼ **CONCEPTS**

**1.** $\log x$ is the exponent to which the base 10 must be raised to get

_____. So we can complete the following table for $\log x$.

| $x$ | $10^3$ | $10^2$ | $10^1$ | $10^0$ | $10^{-1}$ | $10^{-2}$ | $10^{-3}$ | $10^{1/2}$ |
|-----|--------|--------|--------|--------|-----------|-----------|-----------|------------|
| $\log x$ | | | | | | | | |

**2.** The function $f(x) = \log_9 x$ is the logarithm function with

base _____. So $f(9) =$ _____, $f(1) =$ _____,

$f(\frac{1}{9}) =$ _____, $f(81) =$ _____, and $f(3) =$ _____.

**3. (a)** $5^3 = 125$, so $\log_{\blacksquare} \blacksquare = \blacksquare$

   **(b)** $\log_5 25 = 2$, so $\blacksquare^{\blacksquare} = \blacksquare$

**4.** Match the logarithmic function with its graph.
   **(a)** $f(x) = \log_2 x$   **(b)** $f(x) = \log_2(-x)$   **(c)** $f(x) = -\log_2 x$

▼ **SKILLS**

**5–6** ■ Complete the table by finding the appropriate logarithmic or exponential form of the equation, as in Example 1.

✎ **5.**

| Logarithmic form | Exponential form |
|------------------|------------------|
| $\log_8 8 = 1$ | |
| $\log_8 64 = 2$ | |
| | $8^{2/3} = 4$ |
| | $8^3 = 512$ |
| $\log_8\left(\frac{1}{8}\right) = -1$ | |
| | $8^{-2} = \frac{1}{64}$ |

I 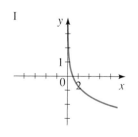   II 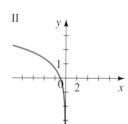   III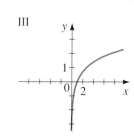

**6.**

| Logarithmic form | Exponential form |
|---|---|
| | $4^3 = 64$ |
| $\log_4 2 = \frac{1}{2}$ | |
| | $4^{3/2} = 8$ |
| $\log_4\left(\frac{1}{16}\right) = -2$ | |
| $\log_4\left(\frac{1}{2}\right) = -\frac{1}{2}$ | |
| | $4^{-5/2} = \frac{1}{32}$ |

**7–12** ▪ Express the equation in exponential form.

**7.** (a) $\log_5 25 = 2$ (b) $\log_5 1 = 0$

**8.** (a) $\log_{10} 0.1 = -1$ (b) $\log_8 512 = 3$

**9.** (a) $\log_8 2 = \frac{1}{3}$ (b) $\log_2\left(\frac{1}{8}\right) = -3$

**10.** (a) $\log_3 81 = 4$ (b) $\log_8 4 = \frac{2}{3}$

**11.** (a) $\ln 5 = x$ (b) $\ln y = 5$

**12.** (a) $\ln(x + 1) = 2$ (b) $\ln(x - 1) = 4$

**13–18** ▪ Express the equation in logarithmic form.

**13.** (a) $5^3 = 125$ (b) $10^{-4} = 0.0001$

**14.** (a) $10^3 = 1000$ (b) $81^{1/2} = 9$

**15.** (a) $8^{-1} = \frac{1}{8}$ (b) $2^{-3} = \frac{1}{8}$

**16.** (a) $4^{-3/2} = 0.125$ (b) $7^3 = 343$

**17.** (a) $e^x = 2$ (b) $e^3 = y$

**18.** (a) $e^{x+1} = 0.5$ (b) $e^{0.5x} = t$

**19–28** ▪ Evaluate the expression.

**19.** (a) $\log_3 3$ (b) $\log_3 1$ (c) $\log_3 3^2$

**20.** (a) $\log_5 5^4$ (b) $\log_4 64$ (c) $\log_3 9$

**21.** (a) $\log_6 36$ (b) $\log_9 81$ (c) $\log_7 7^{10}$

**22.** (a) $\log_2 32$ (b) $\log_8 8^{17}$ (c) $\log_6 1$

**23.** (a) $\log_3\left(\frac{1}{27}\right)$ (b) $\log_{10} \sqrt{10}$ (c) $\log_5 0.2$

**24.** (a) $\log_5 125$ (b) $\log_{49} 7$ (c) $\log_9 \sqrt{3}$

**25.** (a) $2^{\log_2 37}$ (b) $3^{\log_3 8}$ (c) $e^{\ln\sqrt{5}}$

**26.** (a) $e^{\ln \pi}$ (b) $10^{\log 5}$ (c) $10^{\log 87}$

**27.** (a) $\log_8 0.25$ (b) $\ln e^4$ (c) $\ln(1/e)$

**28.** (a) $\log_4 \sqrt{2}$ (b) $\log_4\left(\frac{1}{2}\right)$ (c) $\log_4 8$

**29–36** ▪ Use the definition of the logarithmic function to find $x$.

**29.** (a) $\log_2 x = 5$ (b) $\log_2 16 = x$

**30.** (a) $\log_5 x = 4$ (b) $\log_{10} 0.1 = x$

**31.** (a) $\log_3 243 = x$ (b) $\log_3 x = 3$

**32.** (a) $\log_4 2 = x$ (b) $\log_4 x = 2$

**33.** (a) $\log_{10} x = 2$ (b) $\log_5 x = 2$

**34.** (a) $\log_x 1000 = 3$ (b) $\log_x 25 = 2$

**35.** (a) $\log_x 16 = 4$ (b) $\log_x 8 = \frac{3}{2}$

**36.** (a) $\log_x 6 = \frac{1}{2}$ (b) $\log_x 3 = \frac{1}{3}$

**37–40** ▪ Use a calculator to evaluate the expression, correct to four decimal places.

**37.** (a) $\log 2$ (b) $\log 35.2$ (c) $\log\left(\frac{2}{3}\right)$

**38.** (a) $\log 50$ (b) $\log \sqrt{2}$ (c) $\log(3\sqrt{2})$

**39.** (a) $\ln 5$ (b) $\ln 25.3$ (c) $\ln(1 + \sqrt{3})$

**40.** (a) $\ln 27$ (b) $\ln 7.39$ (c) $\ln 54.6$

**41–44** ▪ Sketch the graph of the function by plotting points.

**41.** $f(x) = \log_3 x$ **42.** $g(x) = \log_4 x$

**43.** $f(x) = 2 \log x$ **44.** $g(x) = 1 + \log x$

**45–48** ▪ Find the function of the form $y = \log_a x$ whose graph is given.

**45.**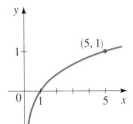

**46.**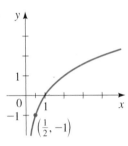

**47.**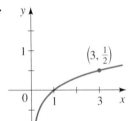

**48.**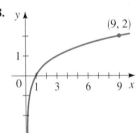

**49–50** ▪ Match the logarithmic function with one of the graphs labeled I or II.

**49.** $f(x) = 2 + \ln x$ **50.** $f(x) = \ln(x - 2)$

I
(1, 2)

II
$x = 2$
(3, 0)

**51.** Draw the graph of $y = 4^x$, then use it to draw the graph of $y = \log_4 x$.

**52.** Draw the graph of $y = 3^x$, then use it to draw the graph of $y = \log_3 x$.

**53–62** ▪ Graph the function, not by plotting points, but by starting from the graphs in Figures 4 and 9. State the domain, range, and asymptote.

**53.** $f(x) = \log_2(x - 4)$ **54.** $f(x) = -\log_{10} x$

**55.** $g(x) = \log_5(-x)$ **56.** $g(x) = \ln(x + 2)$

**57.** $y = 2 + \log_3 x$

**58.** $y = \log_3(x - 1) - 2$

**59.** $y = 1 - \log_{10} x$

**60.** $y = 1 + \ln(-x)$

**61.** $y = |\ln x|$

**62.** $y = \ln |x|$

**63–68** ▪ Find the domain of the function.

 **63.** $f(x) = \log_{10}(x + 3)$

**64.** $f(x) = \log_5(8 - 2x)$

**65.** $g(x) = \log_3(x^2 - 1)$

**66.** $g(x) = \ln(x - x^2)$

**67.** $h(x) = \ln x + \ln(2 - x)$

**68.** $h(x) = \sqrt{x - 2} - \log_5(10 - x)$

**69–74** ▪ Draw the graph of the function in a suitable viewing rectangle, and use it to find the domain, the asymptotes, and the local maximum and minimum values.

**69.** $y = \log_{10}(1 - x^2)$

**70.** $y = \ln(x^2 - x)$

**71.** $y = x + \ln x$

**72.** $y = x(\ln x)^2$

**73.** $y = \dfrac{\ln x}{x}$

**74.** $y = x \log_{10}(x + 10)$

**75.** Compare the rates of growth of the functions $f(x) = \ln x$ and $g(x) = \sqrt{x}$ by drawing their graphs on a common screen using the viewing rectangle $[-1, 30]$ by $[-1, 6]$.

**76.** **(a)** By drawing the graphs of the functions

$$f(x) = 1 + \ln(1 + x) \qquad \text{and} \qquad g(x) = \sqrt{x}$$

in a suitable viewing rectangle, show that even when a logarithmic function starts out higher than a root function, it is ultimately overtaken by the root function.

**(b)** Find, correct to two decimal places, the solutions of the equation $\sqrt{x} = 1 + \ln(1 + x)$.

**77–78** ▪ A family of functions is given. **(a)** Draw graphs of the family for $c = 1, 2, 3$, and 4. **(b)** How are the graphs in part (a) related?

**77.** $f(x) = \log(cx)$

**78.** $f(x) = c \log x$

**79–80** ▪ A function $f(x)$ is given. **(a)** Find the domain of the function $f$. **(b)** Find the inverse function of $f$.

**79.** $f(x) = \log_2(\log_{10} x)$

**80.** $f(x) = \ln(\ln(\ln x))$

**81.** **(a)** Find the inverse of the function $f(x) = \dfrac{2^x}{1 + 2^x}$.

**(b)** What is the domain of the inverse function?

## ▼ APPLICATIONS

**82.** **Absorption of Light**   A spectrophotometer measures the concentration of a sample dissolved in water by shining a light through it and recording the amount of light that emerges. In other words, if we know the amount of light that is absorbed, we can calculate the concentration of the sample. For a certain substance the concentration (in moles/liter) is found by using the formula

$$C = -2500 \ln\left(\frac{I}{I_0}\right)$$

where $I_0$ is the intensity of the incident light and $I$ is the intensity of light that emerges. Find the concentration of the substance if the intensity $I$ is 70% of $I_0$.

**83.** **Carbon Dating**   The age of an ancient artifact can be determined by the amount of radioactive carbon-14 remaining in it. If $D_0$ is the original amount of carbon-14 and $D$ is the amount remaining, then the artifact's age $A$ (in years) is given by

$$A = -8267 \ln\left(\frac{D}{D_0}\right)$$

Find the age of an object if the amount $D$ of carbon-14 that remains in the object is 73% of the original amount $D_0$.

**84.** **Bacteria Colony**   A certain strain of bacteria divides every three hours. If a colony is started with 50 bacteria, then the time $t$ (in hours) required for the colony to grow to $N$ bacteria is given by

$$t = 3\frac{\log(N/50)}{\log 2}$$

Find the time required for the colony to grow to a million bacteria.

**85.** **Investment**   The time required to double the amount of an investment at an interest rate $r$ compounded continuously is given by

$$t = \frac{\ln 2}{r}$$

Find the time required to double an investment at 6%, 7%, and 8%.

**86.** **Charging a Battery**   The rate at which a battery charges is slower the closer the battery is to its maximum charge $C_0$. The time (in hours) required to charge a fully discharged battery to a charge $C$ is given by

$$t = -k \ln\left(1 - \frac{C}{C_0}\right)$$

where $k$ is a positive constant that depends on the battery. For a certain battery, $k = 0.25$. If this battery is fully discharged, how long will it take to charge to 90% of its maximum charge $C_0$?

**87.** **Difficulty of a Task**   The difficulty in "acquiring a target" (such as using your mouse to click on an icon on your computer screen) depends on the distance to the target and the size of the target. According to Fitts's Law, the index of difficulty (ID) is given by

$$ID = \frac{\log(2A/W)}{\log 2}$$

where $W$ is the width of the target and $A$ is the distance to the center of the target. Compare the difficulty of clicking on an icon that is 5 mm wide to clicking on one that is 10 mm wide. In each case, assume that the mouse is 100 mm from the icon.

▼ **DISCOVERY • DISCUSSION • WRITING**

**88. The Height of the Graph of a Logarithmic Function**
Suppose that the graph of $y = 2^x$ is drawn on a coordinate plane where the unit of measurement is an inch.
   **(a)** Show that at a distance 2 ft to the right of the origin the height of the graph is about 265 mi.
   **(b)** If the graph of $y = \log_2 x$ is drawn on the same set of axes, how far to the right of the origin do we have to go before the height of the curve reaches 2 ft?

**89. The Googolplex** A **googol** is $10^{100}$, and a **googolplex** is $10^{\text{googol}}$. Find

$$\log(\log(\text{googol})) \quad \text{and} \quad \log(\log(\log(\text{googolplex})))$$

**90. Comparing Logarithms** Which is larger, $\log_4 17$ or $\log_5 24$? Explain your reasoning.

**91. The Number of Digits in an Integer** Compare log 1000 to the number of digits in 1000. Do the same for 10,000. How many digits does any number between 1000 and 10,000 have? Between what two values must the common logarithm of such a number lie? Use your observations to explain why the number of digits in any positive integer $x$ is $[\![\log x]\!] + 1$. (The symbol $[\![n]\!]$ is the greatest integer function defined in Section 3.2.) How many digits does the number $2^{100}$ have?

---

## 5.3 | Laws of Logarithms

### LEARNING OBJECTIVES

After completing this section, you will be able to:

- Use the Laws of Logarithms to evaluate logarithmic expressions
- Use the Laws of Logarithms to expand logarithmic expressions
- Use the Laws of Logarithms to combine logarithmic expressions
- Use the Change of Base Formula

In this section we study properties of logarithms. These properties give logarithmic functions a wide range of applications, as we will see in Section 5.5.

### ■ Laws of Logarithms

Since logarithms are exponents, the Laws of Exponents give rise to the Laws of Logarithms.

**LAWS OF LOGARITHMS**

Let $a$ be a positive number, with $a \neq 1$. Let $A$, $B$, and $C$ be any real numbers with $A > 0$ and $B > 0$.

| Law | Description |
|---|---|
| **1.** $\log_a(AB) = \log_a A + \log_a B$ | The logarithm of a product of numbers is the sum of the logarithms of the numbers. |
| **2.** $\log_a\left(\dfrac{A}{B}\right) = \log_a A - \log_a B$ | The logarithm of a quotient of numbers is the difference of the logarithms of the numbers. |
| **3.** $\log_a(A^C) = C \log_a A$ | The logarithm of a power of a number is the exponent times the logarithm of the number. |

▼ **PROOF**    We make use of the property $\log_a a^x = x$ from Section 5.2.

**Law 1**    Let $\log_a A = u$ and $\log_a B = v$. When written in exponential form, these equations become

$$a^u = A \quad\text{and}\quad a^v = B$$

Thus

$$\log_a(AB) = \log_a(a^u a^v) = \log_a(a^{u+v})$$

$$= u + v = \log_a A + \log_a B$$

**Law 2**    Using Law 1, we have

$$\log_a A = \log_a\left[\left(\frac{A}{B}\right)B\right] = \log_a\left(\frac{A}{B}\right) + \log_a B$$

so

$$\log_a\left(\frac{A}{B}\right) = \log_a A - \log_a B$$

**Law 3**    Let $\log_a A = u$. Then $a^u = A$, so

$$\log_a(A^C) = \log_a(a^u)^C = \log_a(a^{uC}) = uC = C\log_a A \qquad ▲$$

▶ **EXAMPLE 1** | Using the Laws of Logarithms to Evaluate Expressions

Evaluate each expression.

(a) $\log_4 2 + \log_4 32$

(b) $\log_2 80 - \log_2 5$

(c) $-\frac{1}{3}\log 8$

▼ **SOLUTION**

(a) $\log_4 2 + \log_4 32 = \log_4(2 \cdot 32)$     Law 1

                  $= \log_4 64 = 3$     Because $64 = 4^3$

(b) $\log_2 80 - \log_2 5 = \log_2\left(\frac{80}{5}\right)$     Law 2

                  $= \log_2 16 = 4$     Because $16 = 2^4$

(c) $-\frac{1}{3}\log 8 = \log 8^{-1/3}$     Law 3

             $= \log\left(\frac{1}{2}\right)$     Property of negative exponents

             $\approx -0.301$     Calculator

✎ **Practice what you've learned: Do Exercises 7, 9, and 11.**     ▲

## ■ Expanding and Combining Logarithmic Expressions

The Laws of Logarithms allow us to write the logarithm of a product or a quotient as the sum or difference of logarithms. This process, called *expanding* a logarithmic expression, is illustrated in the next example.

▶ **EXAMPLE 2** | Expanding Logarithmic Expressions

Use the Laws of Logarithms to expand each expression.

(a) $\log_2(6x)$      (b) $\log_5(x^3 y^6)$      (c) $\ln\left(\dfrac{ab}{\sqrt[3]{c}}\right)$

▼ **SOLUTION**

(a) $\log_2(6x) = \log_2 6 + \log_2 x$     Law 1

**(b)** $\log_5(x^3 y^6) = \log_5 x^3 + \log_5 y^6$     Law 1

$$= 3 \log_5 x + 6 \log_5 y \qquad \text{Law 3}$$

**(c)** $\ln\left(\dfrac{ab}{\sqrt[3]{c}}\right) = \ln(ab) - \ln \sqrt[3]{c}$     Law 2

$$= \ln a + \ln b - \ln c^{1/3} \qquad \text{Law 1}$$

$$= \ln a + \ln b - \tfrac{1}{3} \ln c \qquad \text{Law 3}$$

✎ **Practice what you've learned: Do Exercises 19, 21, and 33.** ▲

The Laws of Logarithms also allow us to reverse the process of expanding that was done in Example 2. That is, we can write sums and differences of logarithms as a single logarithm. This process, called *combining* logarithmic expressions, is illustrated in the next example.

▶ **EXAMPLE 3** | Combining Logarithmic Expressions

Combine $3 \log x + \tfrac{1}{2} \log(x + 1)$ into a single logarithm.

▼ **SOLUTION**

$$3 \log x + \tfrac{1}{2} \log(x + 1) = \log x^3 + \log(x + 1)^{1/2} \qquad \text{Law 3}$$

$$= \log(x^3 (x + 1)^{1/2}) \qquad \text{Law 1}$$

✎ **Practice what you've learned: Do Exercise 47.** ▲

▶ **EXAMPLE 4** | Combining Logarithmic Expressions

Combine $3 \ln s + \tfrac{1}{2} \ln t - 4 \ln(t^2 + 1)$ into a single logarithm.

▼ **SOLUTION**

$$3 \ln s + \tfrac{1}{2} \ln t - 4 \ln(t^2 + 1) = \ln s^3 + \ln t^{1/2} - \ln(t^2 + 1)^4 \qquad \text{Law 3}$$

$$= \ln(s^3 t^{1/2}) - \ln(t^2 + 1)^4 \qquad \text{Law 1}$$

$$= \ln\left(\frac{s^3 \sqrt{t}}{(t^2 + 1)^4}\right) \qquad \text{Law 2}$$

✎ **Practice what you've learned: Do Exercise 49.** ▲

**WARNING** Although the Laws of Logarithms tell us how to compute the logarithm of a product or a quotient, *there is no corresponding rule for the logarithm of a sum or a difference.* For instance,

$$\log_a(x + y) \neq \log_a x + \log_a y$$

In fact, we know that the right side is equal to $\log_a(xy)$. Also, don't improperly simplify quotients or powers of logarithms. For instance,

$$\frac{\log 6}{\log 2} \neq \log\left(\frac{6}{2}\right) \qquad \text{and} \qquad (\log_2 x)^3 \neq 3 \log_2 x$$

Logarithmic functions are used to model a variety of situations involving human behavior. One such behavior is how quickly we forget things we have learned. For example, if you learn algebra at a certain performance level (say, 90% on a test) and then don't use algebra for a while, how much will you retain after a week, a month, or a year? Hermann Ebbinghaus (1850–1909) studied this phenomenon and formulated the law described in the next example.

▶ **EXAMPLE 5** | The Law of Forgetting

Ebbinghaus' Law of Forgetting states that if a task is learned at a performance level $P_0$, then after a time interval $t$ the performance level $P$ satisfies

$$\log P = \log P_0 - c \log(t + 1)$$

where $c$ is a constant that depends on the type of task and $t$ is measured in months.

**(a)** Solve for $P$.

**(b)** If your score on a history test is 90, what score would you expect to get on a similar test after two months? After a year? (Assume that $c = 0.2$.)

▼ **SOLUTION**

**(a)** We first combine the right-hand side.

Forgetting what we've learned depends logarithmically on how long ago we learned it.

| | |
|---|---|
| $\log P = \log P_0 - c \log(t + 1)$ | Given equation |
| $\log P = \log P_0 - \log(t + 1)^c$ | Law 3 |
| $\log P = \log \dfrac{P_0}{(t + 1)^c}$ | Law 2 |
| $P = \dfrac{P_0}{(t + 1)^c}$ | Because log is one-to-one |

**(b)** Here $P_0 = 90$, $c = 0.2$, and $t$ is measured in months.

In two months:    $t = 2$    and    $P = \dfrac{90}{(2 + 1)^{0.2}} \approx 72$

In one year:    $t = 12$    and    $P = \dfrac{90}{(12 + 1)^{0.2}} \approx 54$

Your expected scores after two months and one year are 72 and 54, respectively.

✎ **Practice what you've learned: Do Exercise 69.**    ▲

## Change of Base

For some purposes, we find it useful to change from logarithms in one base to logarithms in another base. Suppose we are given $\log_a x$ and want to find $\log_b x$. Let

$$y = \log_b x$$

We write this in exponential form and take the logarithm, with base $a$, of each side.

| | |
|---|---|
| $b^y = x$ | Exponential form |
| $\log_a(b^y) = \log_a x$ | Take $\log_a$ of each side |
| $y \log_a b = \log_a x$ | Law 3 |
| $y = \dfrac{\log_a x}{\log_a b}$ | Divide by $\log_a b$ |

This proves the following formula.

We may write the Change of Base Formula as

$$\log_b x = \left(\frac{1}{\log_a b}\right)\log_a x$$

So $\log_b x$ is just a constant multiple of $\log_a x$; the constant is $\dfrac{1}{\log_a b}$.

**CHANGE OF BASE FORMULA**

$$\log_b x = \frac{\log_a x}{\log_a b}$$

In particular, if we put $x = a$, then $\log_a a = 1$, and this formula becomes

$$\log_b a = \frac{1}{\log_a b}$$

We can now evaluate a logarithm to *any* base by using the Change of Base Formula to express the logarithm in terms of common logarithms or natural logarithms and then using a calculator.

▶ **EXAMPLE 6** | Evaluating Logarithms with the Change of Base Formula

Use the Change of Base Formula and common or natural logarithms to evaluate each logarithm, correct to five decimal places.

**(a)** $\log_8 5$ **(b)** $\log_9 20$

▼ **SOLUTION**

We get the same answer whether we use $\log_{10}$ or ln:

$$\log_8 5 = \frac{\ln 5}{\ln 8} \approx 0.77398$$

**(a)** We use the Change of Base Formula with $b = 8$ and $a = 10$:

$$\log_8 5 = \frac{\log_{10} 5}{\log_{10} 8} \approx 0.77398$$

**(b)** We use the Change of Base Formula with $b = 9$ and $a = e$:

$$\log_9 20 = \frac{\ln 20}{\ln 9} \approx 1.36342$$

✎ **Practice what you've learned: Do Exercises 55 and 57.** ▲

▶ **EXAMPLE 7** | Using the Change of Base Formula to Graph a Logarithmic Function

Use a graphing calculator to graph $f(x) = \log_6 x$.

▼ **SOLUTION**   Calculators don't have a key for $\log_6$, so we use the Change of Base Formula to write

$$f(x) = \log_6 x = \frac{\ln x}{\ln 6}$$

Since calculators do have an ⎣LN⎦ key, we can enter this new form of the function and graph it. The graph is shown in Figure 1.

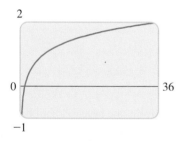

**FIGURE 1** $f(x) = \log_6 x = \dfrac{\ln x}{\ln 6}$

✎ **Practice what you've learned: Do Exercise 63.** ▲

# 5.3 EXERCISES

## ▼ CONCEPTS

**1.** The logarithm of a product of two numbers is the same as the _____ of the logarithms of these numbers. So

$$\log_5(25 \cdot 125) = \underline{\hspace{1cm}} + \underline{\hspace{1cm}}.$$

**2.** The logarithm of a quotient of two numbers is the same as the _____ of the logarithms of these numbers. So

$$\log_5\left(\tfrac{25}{125}\right) = \underline{\hspace{1cm}} - \underline{\hspace{1cm}}.$$

**3.** The logarithm of a number raised to a power is the same as the power _____ the logarithm of the number. So

$$\log_5(25^{10}) = \underline{\hspace{1cm}} \cdot \underline{\hspace{1cm}}.$$

**4. (a)** We can expand $\log\left(\dfrac{x^2 y}{z}\right)$ to get _____.

 **(b)** We can combine $2\log x + \log y - \log z$ to get

 _____.

**5.** Most calculators can find logarithms with base _____ and base _____. To find logarithms with different bases, we use the _____ Formula. To find $\log_7 12$, we write

$$\log_7 12 = \frac{\log \quad}{\log \quad} = \underline{\hspace{1cm}}$$

**6.** *True or false?* We get the same answer if we do the calculation in Exercise 5 using ln in place of log.

## ▼ SKILLS

**7–18** ▪ Evaluate the expression.

**7.** $\log_3 \sqrt{27}$

**8.** $\log_2 160 - \log_2 5$

**9.** $\log 4 + \log 25$

**10.** $\log \dfrac{1}{\sqrt{1000}}$

**11.** $\log_4 192 - \log_4 3$

**12.** $\log_{12} 9 + \log_{12} 16$

**13.** $\log_2 6 - \log_2 15 + \log_2 20$

**14.** $\log_3 100 - \log_3 18 - \log_3 50$

**15.** $\log_4 16^{100}$

**16.** $\log_2 8^{33}$

**17.** $\log(\log 10^{10,000})$

**18.** $\ln(\ln e^{e^{200}})$

**19–44** ▪ Use the Laws of Logarithms to expand the expression.

**19.** $\log_2(2x)$

**20.** $\log_3(5y)$

**21.** $\log_2(x(x-1))$

**22.** $\log_5 \dfrac{x}{2}$

**23.** $\log 6^{10}$

**24.** $\ln \sqrt{z}$

**25.** $\log_2(AB^2)$

**26.** $\log_6 \sqrt[4]{17}$

**27.** $\log_3(x\sqrt{y})$

**28.** $\log_2(xy)^{10}$

**29.** $\log_5 \sqrt[3]{x^2 + 1}$

**30.** $\log_a\left(\dfrac{x^2}{yz^3}\right)$

**31.** $\ln \sqrt{ab}$

**32.** $\ln \sqrt[3]{3r^2 s}$

**33.** $\log\left(\dfrac{x^3 y^4}{z^6}\right)$

**34.** $\log\left(\dfrac{a^2}{b^4 \sqrt{c}}\right)$

**35.** $\log_2\left(\dfrac{x(x^2+1)}{\sqrt{x^2-1}}\right)$

**36.** $\log_5 \sqrt{\dfrac{x-1}{x+1}}$

**37.** $\ln\left(x\sqrt{\dfrac{y}{z}}\right)$

**38.** $\ln \dfrac{3x^2}{(x+1)^{10}}$

**39.** $\log \sqrt[4]{x^2 + y^2}$

**40.** $\log\left(\dfrac{x}{\sqrt[3]{1-x}}\right)$

**41.** $\log \sqrt{\dfrac{x^2+4}{(x^2+1)(x^3-7)^2}}$

**42.** $\log \sqrt{x\sqrt{y\sqrt{z}}}$

**43.** $\ln\left(\dfrac{x^3 \sqrt{x-1}}{3x+4}\right)$

**44.** $\log\left(\dfrac{10^x}{x(x^2+1)(x^4+2)}\right)$

**45–54** ▪ Use the Laws of Logarithms to combine the expression.

**45.** $\log_3 5 + 5\log_3 2$

**46.** $\log 12 + \tfrac{1}{2}\log 7 - \log 2$

**47.** $\log_2 A + \log_2 B - 2\log_2 C$

**48.** $\log_5(x^2 - 1) - \log_5(x - 1)$

**49.** $4\log x - \tfrac{1}{3}\log(x^2+1) + 2\log(x-1)$

**50.** $\ln(a+b) + \ln(a-b) - 2\ln c$

**51.** $\ln 5 + 2\ln x + 3\ln(x^2+5)$

**52.** $2(\log_5 x + 2\log_5 y - 3\log_5 z)$

**53.** $\tfrac{1}{3}\log(x+2)^3 + \tfrac{1}{2}[\log x^4 - \log(x^2 - x - 6)^2]$

**54.** $\log_a b + c\log_a d - r\log_a s$

**55–62** ▪ Use the Change of Base Formula and a calculator to evaluate the logarithm, correct to six decimal places. Use either natural or common logarithms.

**55.** $\log_2 5$

**56.** $\log_5 2$

**57.** $\log_3 16$

**58.** $\log_6 92$

**59.** $\log_7 2.61$

**60.** $\log_6 532$

**61.** $\log_4 125$

**62.** $\log_{12} 2.5$

**63.** Use the Change of Base Formula to show that

$$\log_3 x = \dfrac{\ln x}{\ln 3}$$

Then use this fact to draw the graph of the function $f(x) = \log_3 x$.

**64.** Draw graphs of the family of functions $y = \log_a x$ for $a = 2$, $e$, 5, and 10 on the same screen, using the viewing rectangle $[0, 5]$ by $[-3, 3]$. How are these graphs related?

**65.** Use the Change of Base Formula to show that

$$\log e = \dfrac{1}{\ln 10}$$

**66.** Simplify: $(\log_2 5)(\log_5 7)$

**67.** Show that $-\ln(x - \sqrt{x^2 - 1}) = \ln(x + \sqrt{x^2 - 1})$.

## ▼ APPLICATIONS

**68. Forgetting** Use Ebbinghaus' Law of Forgetting (Example 5) to estimate a student's score on a biology test two years after he got a score of 80 on a test covering the same material. Assume that $c = 0.3$ and $t$ is measured in months.

**69. Wealth Distribution** Vilfredo Pareto (1848–1923) observed that most of the wealth of a country is owned by a few members of the population. **Pareto's Principle** is

$$\log P = \log c - k\log W$$

where $W$ is the wealth level (how much money a person has) and $P$ is the number of people in the population having that much money.
**(a)** Solve the equation for $P$.
**(b)** Assume that $k = 2.1$, $c = 8000$, and $W$ is measured in millions of dollars. Use part (a) to find the number of people who have \$2 million or more. How many people have \$10 million or more?

**70. Biodiversity** Some biologists model the number of species $S$ in a fixed area $A$ (such as an island) by the species-area relationship

$$\log S = \log c + k\log A$$

where $c$ and $k$ are positive constants that depend on the type of species and habitat.
**(a)** Solve the equation for $S$.

**(b)** Use part (a) to show that if $k = 3$, then doubling the area increases the number of species eightfold.

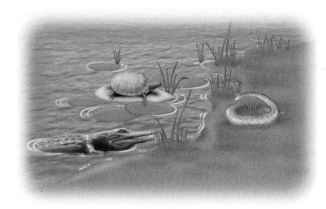

**71. Magnitude of Stars**   The magnitude $M$ of a star is a measure of how bright a star appears to the human eye. It is defined by

$$M = -2.5 \log\left(\frac{B}{B_0}\right)$$

where $B$ is the actual brightness of the star and $B_0$ is a constant.
**(a)** Expand the right-hand side of the equation.
**(b)** Use part (a) to show that the brighter a star, the less its magnitude.
**(c)** Betelgeuse is about 100 times brighter than Albiero. Use part (a) to show that Betelgeuse is 5 magnitudes less bright than Albiero.

---

▼ **DISCOVERY • DISCUSSION • WRITING**

**72. True or False?**   Discuss each equation and determine whether it is true for all possible values of the variables. (Ignore values of the variables for which any term is undefined.)

**(a)** $\log\left(\dfrac{x}{y}\right) = \dfrac{\log x}{\log y}$

**(b)** $\log_2(x - y) = \log_2 x - \log_2 y$

**(c)** $\log_5\left(\dfrac{a}{b^2}\right) = \log_5 a - 2 \log_5 b$

**(d)** $\log 2^z = z \log 2$

**(e)** $(\log P)(\log Q) = \log P + \log Q$

**(f)** $\dfrac{\log a}{\log b} = \log a - \log b$

**(g)** $(\log_2 7)^x = x \log_2 7$

**(h)** $\log_a a^a = a$

**(i)** $\log(x - y) = \dfrac{\log x}{\log y}$

**(j)** $-\ln\left(\dfrac{1}{A}\right) = \ln A$

**73. Find the Error**   What is wrong with the following argument?

$$\log 0.1 < 2 \log 0.1$$
$$= \log(0.1)^2$$
$$= \log 0.01$$
$$\log 0.1 < \log 0.01$$
$$0.1 < 0.01$$

**74. Shifting, Shrinking, and Stretching Graphs of Functions**   Let $f(x) = x^2$. Show that $f(2x) = 4f(x)$, and explain how this shows that shrinking the graph of $f$ horizontally has the same effect as stretching it vertically. Then use the identities $e^{2+x} = e^2 e^x$ and $\ln(2x) = \ln 2 + \ln x$ to show that for $g(x) = e^x$ a horizontal shift is the same as a vertical stretch and for $h(x) = \ln x$ a horizontal shrinking is the same as a vertical shift.

---

| **5.4** | Exponential and Logarithmic Equations |

**LEARNING OBJECTIVES**

After completing this section, you will be able to:

■ Solve exponential equations
■ Solve logarithmic equations
■ Solve problems involving compound interest
■ Calculate annual percentage yield

In this section we solve equations that involve exponential or logarithmic functions. The techniques that we develop here will be used in the next section for solving applied problems.

■ **Exponential Equations**

An *exponential equation* is one in which the variable occurs in the exponent. For example,

$$2^x = 7$$

The variable $x$ presents a difficulty because it is in the exponent. To deal with this difficulty, we take the logarithm of each side and then use the Laws of Logarithms to "bring down $x$" from the exponent.

$$2^x = 7 \qquad \text{Given equation}$$

$$\ln 2^x = \ln 7 \qquad \text{Take ln of each side}$$

$$x \ln 2 = \ln 7 \qquad \text{Law 3 (bring down exponent)}$$

$$x = \frac{\ln 7}{\ln 2} \qquad \text{Solve for x}$$

$$\approx 2.807 \qquad \text{Calculator}$$

Recall that Law 3 of the Laws of Logarithms says that $\log_a A^C = C \log_a A$.

The method that we used to solve $2^x = 7$ is typical of how we solve exponential equations in general.

---

### GUIDELINES FOR SOLVING EXPONENTIAL EQUATIONS

**1.** Isolate the exponential expression on one side of the equation.

**2.** Take the logarithm of each side, then use the Laws of Logarithms to "bring down the exponent."

**3.** Solve for the variable.

---

▶ **EXAMPLE 1** | Solving an Exponential Equation

Find the solution of the equation $3^{x+2} = 7$, correct to six decimal places.

▼ **SOLUTION**  We take the common logarithm of each side and use Law 3.

$$3^{x+2} = 7 \qquad \text{Given equation}$$

$$\log(3^{x+2}) = \log 7 \qquad \text{Take log of each side}$$

$$(x + 2)\log 3 = \log 7 \qquad \text{Law 3 (bring down exponent)}$$

$$x + 2 = \frac{\log 7}{\log 3} \qquad \text{Divide by log 3}$$

$$x = \frac{\log 7}{\log 3} - 2 \qquad \text{Subtract 2}$$

$$\approx -0.228756 \qquad \text{Calculator}$$

We could have used natural logarithms instead of common logarithms. In fact, using the same steps, we get

$$x = \frac{\ln 7}{\ln 3} - 2 \approx -0.228756$$

✎ **Practice what you've learned: Do Exercise 7.**    ▲

---

**Check Your Answer**

Substituting $x = -0.228756$ into the original equation and using a calculator, we get

$$3^{(-0.228756)+2} \approx 7 \qquad ✔$$

---

▶ **EXAMPLE 2** | Solving an Exponential Equation

Solve the equation $8e^{2x} = 20$.

▼ **SOLUTION**  We first divide by 8 to isolate the exponential term on one side of the equation.

$$8e^{2x} = 20 \qquad \text{Given equation}$$

$$e^{2x} = \frac{20}{8} \qquad \text{Divide by 8}$$

$$\ln e^{2x} = \ln 2.5 \qquad \text{Take ln of each side}$$

$$2x = \ln 2.5 \qquad \text{Property of ln}$$

$$x = \frac{\ln 2.5}{2} \qquad \text{Divide by 2}$$

$$\approx 0.458 \qquad \text{Calculator}$$

✎ **Practice what you've learned: Do Exercise 9.**    ▲

**Check Your Answer**

Substituting $x = 0.458$ into the original equation and using a calculator, we get

$$8e^{2(0.458)} \approx 20 \qquad ✔$$

▶ **EXAMPLE 3** | Solving an Exponential Equation Algebraically and Graphically

Solve the equation $e^{3-2x} = 4$ algebraically and graphically.

▼ **SOLUTION 1:** Algebraic

Since the base of the exponential term is $e$, we use natural logarithms to solve this equation.

$$e^{3-2x} = 4 \qquad \text{Given equation}$$

$$\ln(e^{3-2x}) = \ln 4 \qquad \text{Take ln of each side}$$

$$3 - 2x = \ln 4 \qquad \text{Property of ln}$$

$$-2x = -3 + \ln 4 \qquad \text{Subtract 3}$$

$$x = \tfrac{1}{2}(3 - \ln 4) \approx 0.807 \qquad \text{Multiply by } -\tfrac{1}{2}$$

You should check that this answer satisfies the original equation.

▼ **SOLUTION 2:** Graphical

We graph the equations $y = e^{3-2x}$ and $y = 4$ in the same viewing rectangle as in Figure 1. The solutions occur where the graphs intersect. Zooming in on the point of intersection of the two graphs, we see that $x \approx 0.81$.

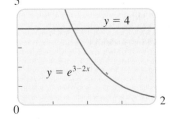

**FIGURE 1**

✎ **Practice what you've learned: Do Exercise 11.**    ▲

**Radiocarbon dating** is a method archeologists use to determine the age of ancient objects. The carbon dioxide in the atmosphere always contains a fixed fraction of radioactive carbon, carbon-14 ($^{14}$C), with a half-life of about 5730 years. Plants absorb carbon dioxide from the atmosphere, which then makes its way to animals through the food chain. Thus, all living creatures contain the same fixed proportions of $^{14}$C to nonradioactive $^{12}$C as the atmosphere.

After an organism dies, it stops assimilating $^{14}$C, and the amount of $^{14}$C in it begins to decay exponentially. We can then determine the time elapsed since the death of the organism by measuring the amount of $^{14}$C left in it.

For example, if a donkey bone contains 73% as much $^{14}$C as a living donkey and it died $t$ years ago, then by the formula for radioactive decay (Section 5.5),

$$0.73 = (1.00)e^{-(t \ln 2)/5730}$$

We solve this exponential equation to find $t \approx 2600$, so the bone is about 2600 years old.

**32. Ion Concentration in Wine** The pH readings for wines vary from 2.8 to 3.8. Find the corresponding range of hydrogen ion concentrations.

**33. Earthquake Magnitudes** If one earthquake is 20 times as intense as another, how much larger is its magnitude on the Richter scale?

**34. Earthquake Magnitudes** The 1906 earthquake in San Francisco had a magnitude of 8.3 on the Richter scale. At the same time in Japan an earthquake with magnitude 4.9 caused only minor damage. How many times more intense was the San Francisco earthquake than the Japanese earthquake?

**35. Earthquake Magnitudes** The Alaska earthquake of 1964 had a magnitude of 8.6 on the Richter scale. How many times more intense was this than the 1906 San Francisco earthquake? (See Exercise 34.)

**36. Earthquake Magnitudes** The Northridge, California, earthquake of 1994 had a magnitude of 6.8 on the Richter scale. A year later, a 7.2-magnitude earthquake struck Kobe, Japan. How many times more intense was the Kobe earthquake than the Northridge earthquake?

**37. Earthquake Magnitudes** The 1985 Mexico City earthquake had a magnitude of 8.1 on the Richter scale. The 1976 earthquake in Tangshan, China, was 1.26 times as intense. What was the magnitude of the Tangshan earthquake?

**38. Subway Noise** The intensity of the sound of a subway train was measured at 98 dB. Find the intensity in $\text{W/m}^2$.

**39. Traffic Noise** The intensity of the sound of traffic at a busy intersection was measured at $2.0 \times 10^{-5} \text{ W/m}^2$. Find the intensity level in decibels.

**40. Comparing Decibel Levels** The noise from a power mower was measured at 106 dB. The noise level at a rock concert was measured at 120 dB. Find the ratio of the intensity of the rock music to that of the power mower.

**41. Inverse Square Law for Sound** A law of physics states that the intensity of sound is inversely proportional to the square of the distance $d$ from the source: $I = k/d^2$.

(a) Use this model and the equation

$$B = 10 \log \frac{I}{I_0}$$

(described in this section) to show that the decibel levels $B_1$ and $B_2$ at distances $d_1$ and $d_2$ from a sound source are related by the equation

$$B_2 = B_1 + 20 \log \frac{d_1}{d_2}$$

(b) The intensity level at a rock concert is 120 dB at a distance 2 m from the speakers. Find the intensity level at a distance of 10 m.

---

# ▶ CHAPTER 5 | REVIEW

## ▼ PROPERTIES AND FORMULAS

### Exponential Functions (pp. 371–373)

The **exponential function** $f$ with base $a$ (where $a > 0$, $a \neq 1$) is defined for all real numbers $x$ by

$$f(x) = a^x$$

The domain of $f$ is $\mathbb{R}$, and the range of $f$ is $(0, \infty)$ The graph of $f$ has one of the following shapes, depending on the value of $a$:

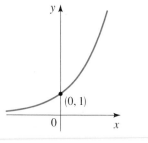

$f(x) = a^x$ for $a > 1$        $f(x) = a^x$ for $0 < a < 1$

### The Natural Exponential Function (p. 375)

The **natural exponential function** is the exponential function with base $e$:

$$f(x) = e^x$$

The number $e$ is defined to be the number that the expression $(1 + 1/n)^n$ approaches as $n \to \infty$. An approximate value for the irrational number $e$ is

$$e \approx 2.7182818284590\ldots$$

### Compound Interest (pp. 377–378)

If a principal $P$ is invested in an account paying an annual interest rate $r$, compounded $n$ times a year, then after $t$ years the **amount** $A(t)$ in the account is

$$A(t) = P\left(1 + \frac{r}{n}\right)^{nt}$$

If the interest is compounded **continuously**, then the amount is

$$A(t) = Pe^{rt}$$

### Logarithmic Functions (pp. 384–386)

The **logarithmic function** $\log_a$ with base $a$ (where $a > 0$, $a \neq 1$) is defined for $x > 0$ by

$$\log_a x = y \quad \Leftrightarrow \quad a^y = x$$

So $\log_a x$ is the exponent to which the base $a$ must be raised to give $y$.

The domain of $\log_a$ is $(0, \infty)$, and the range is $\mathbb{R}$. For $a > 1$, the graph of the function $\log_a$ has the following shape:

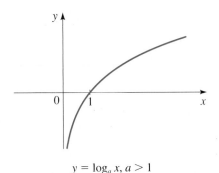

$$y = \log_a x, \; a > 1$$

### Common and Natural Logarithms (pp. 388–390)

The logarithm function with base 10 is called the **common logarithm** and is denoted **log**. So

$$\log x = \log_{10} x$$

The logarithm function with base $e$ is called the **natural logarithm** and is denoted **ln**. So

$$\ln x = \log_e x$$

### Properties of Logarithms (p. 390)

1. $\log_a 1 = 0$     2. $\log_a a = 1$

3. $\log_a a^x = x$     4. $a^{\log_a x} = x$

### Laws of Logarithms (p. 394)

Let $a$ be a logarithm base $(a > 0, a \neq 1)$, and let $A$, $B$, and $C$ be any real numbers or algebraic expressions that represent real numbers, with $A > 0$ and $B > 0$. Then:

1. $\log_a(AB) = \log_a A + \log_a B$

2. $\log_a(A/B) = \log_a A - \log_a B$

3. $\log_a(A^C) = C \log_a A$

### Change of Base Formula (p. 397)

$$\log_b x = \frac{\log_a x}{\log_a b}$$

### Guidelines for Solving Exponential Equations (p. 401)

1. Isolate the exponential term on one side of the equation.

2. Take the logarithm of each side, and use the Laws of Logarithms to "bring down the exponent."

3. Solve for the variable.

### Guidelines for Solving Logarithmic Equations (p. 404)

1. Isolate the logarithmic term(s) on one side of the equation, and use the Laws of Logarithms to combine logarithmic terms if necessary.

2. Rewrite the equation in exponential form.

3. Solve for the variable.

### Exponential Growth Model (p. 412)

A population experiences **exponential growth** if it can be modeled by the exponential function

$$n(t) = n_0 e^{rt}$$

where $n(t)$ is the population at time $t$, $n_0$ is the initial population (at time $t = 0$), and $r$ is the relative growth rate (expressed as a proportion of the population).

### Radioactive Decay Model (p. 416)

If a **radioactive substance** with half-life $h$ has initial mass $m_0$, then at time $t$ the mass $m(t)$ of the substance that remains is modeled by the exponential function

$$m(t) = m_0 e^{-rt}$$

where $r = \dfrac{\ln 2}{h}$.

### Newton's Law of Cooling (p. 417)

If an object has an initial temperature that is $D_0$ degrees warmer than the surrounding temperature $T_s$, then at time $t$ the temperature $T(t)$ of the object is modeled by the function

$$T(t) = T_s + D_0 e^{-kt}$$

where the constant $k > 0$ depends on the size and type of the object.

### Logarithmic Scales (pp. 418–420)

The **pH scale** measures the acidity of a solution:

$$\mathrm{pH} = -\log[\mathrm{H}^+]$$

The **Richter scale** measures the intensity of earthquakes:

$$M = \log \frac{I}{S}$$

The **decibel scale** measures the intensity of sound:

$$B = 10 \log \frac{I}{I_0}$$

▼ CONCEPT SUMMARY _____

| **Section 5.1** | **Review Exercises** |
|---|---|
| ▪ Evaluate exponential functions | 1–4 |
| ▪ Graph exponential functions | 5–8, 73–74, 80 |
| ▪ Evaluate and graph the natural exponential function | 4, 13–14 |
| ▪ Find compound interest | 89–90 |
| ▪ Find continuously compounded interest | 89(d), 90(c), 92 |

## Section 5.2

## Section 5.3

## Section 5.4

## Section 5.5

## ▼ EXERCISES

**1–4** ▪ Use a calculator to find the indicated values of the exponential function, correct to three decimal places.

**1.** $f(x) = 5^x$;  $f(-1.5), f(\sqrt{2}), f(2.5)$

**2.** $f(x) = 3 \cdot 2^x$;  $f(-2.2), f(\sqrt{7}), f(5.5)$

**3.** $g(x) = 4 \cdot \left(\frac{2}{3}\right)^{x-2}$;  $g(-0.7), g(e), g(\pi)$

**4.** $g(x) = \frac{7}{4}e^{x+1}$;  $g(-2), g(\sqrt{3}), g(3.6)$

**5–16** ▪ Sketch the graph of the function. State the domain, range, and asymptote.

**5.** $f(x) = 2^{-x+1}$

**6.** $f(x) = 3^{x-2}$

**7.** $g(x) = 3 + 2^x$

**8.** $g(x) = 5^{-x} - 5$

**9.** $f(x) = \log_3(x - 1)$

**10.** $g(x) = \log(-x)$

**11.** $f(x) = 2 - \log_2 x$

**12.** $f(x) = 3 + \log_5(x + 4)$

**13.** $F(x) = e^x - 1$

**14.** $G(x) = \frac{1}{2}e^{x-1}$

**15.** $g(x) = 2 \ln x$

**16.** $g(x) = \ln(x^2)$

**17–20** ▪ Find the domain of the function.

**17.** $f(x) = 10^{x^2} + \log(1 - 2x)$

**18.** $g(x) = \log(2 + x - x^2)$

**19.** $h(x) = \ln(x^2 - 4)$

**20.** $k(x) = \ln|x|$

**21–24** ▪ Write the equation in exponential form.

**21.** $\log_2 1024 = 10$

**22.** $\log_6 37 = x$

**23.** $\log x = y$

**24.** $\ln c = 17$

**25–28** ▪ Write the equation in logarithmic form.

**25.** $2^6 = 64$

**26.** $49^{-1/2} = \frac{1}{7}$

**27.** $10^x = 74$

**28.** $e^k = m$

**29–44** ▪ Evaluate the expression without using a calculator.

**29.** $\log_2 128$

**30.** $\log_8 1$

**31.** $10^{\log 45}$

**32.** $\log 0.000001$

**33.** $\ln(e^6)$

**34.** $\log_4 8$

**35.** $\log_3\left(\frac{1}{27}\right)$

**36.** $2^{\log_2 13}$

**37.** $\log_5 \sqrt{5}$

**38.** $e^{2\ln 7}$

**39.** $\log 25 + \log 4$

**40.** $\log_3 \sqrt{243}$

**41.** $\log_2 16^{23}$

**42.** $\log_5 250 - \log_5 2$

**43.** $\log_8 6 - \log_8 3 + \log_8 2$

**44.** $\log \log 10^{100}$

**45–50** ▪ Expand the logarithmic expression.

**45.** $\log(AB^2C^3)$

**46.** $\log_2(x\sqrt{x^2 + 1})$

**47.** $\ln\sqrt{\dfrac{x^2 - 1}{x^2 + 1}}$

**48.** $\log\left(\dfrac{4x^3}{y^2(x - 1)^5}\right)$

**49.** $\log_5\left(\dfrac{x^2(1 - 5x)^{3/2}}{\sqrt{x^3 - x}}\right)$

**50.** $\ln\left(\dfrac{\sqrt[5]{x^4 + 12}}{(x + 16)\sqrt{x - 3}}\right)$

**51–56** ▪ Combine into a single logarithm.

**51.** $\log 6 + 4 \log 2$

**52.** $\log x + \log(x^2 y) + 3 \log y$

**53.** $\frac{3}{2} \log_2(x - y) - 2 \log_2(x^2 + y^2)$

**54.** $\log_5 2 + \log_5(x + 1) - \frac{1}{3} \log_5(3x + 7)$

**55.** $\log(x - 2) + \log(x + 2) - \frac{1}{2}\log(x^2 + 4)$

**56.** $\frac{1}{2}[\ln(x - 4) + 5 \ln(x^2 + 4x)]$

**57–68** ▪ Solve the equation. Find the exact solution if possible; otherwise, use a calculator to approximate to two decimals.

**57.** $3^{2x-7} = 27$

**58.** $5^{4-x} = \frac{1}{125}$

**59.** $2^{3x-5} = 7$

**60.** $10^{6-3x} = 18$

**61.** $4^{1-x} = 3^{2x+5}$

**62.** $e^{3x/4} = 10$

**63.** $x^2 e^{2x} + 2x e^{2x} = 8 e^{2x}$

**64.** $3^{2x} - 3^x - 6 = 0$

**65.** $\log_2(1 - x) = 4$

**66.** $\log x + \log(x + 1) = \log 12$

**67.** $\log_8(x + 5) - \log_8(x - 2) = 1$

**68.** $\ln(2x - 3) + 1 = 0$

**69–72** ▪ Use a calculator to find the solution of the equation, correct to six decimal places.

**69.** $5^{-2x/3} = 0.63$

**70.** $2^{3x-5} = 7$

**71.** $5^{2x+1} = 3^{4x-1}$

**72.** $e^{-15k} = 10,000$

**73–76** ▪ Draw a graph of the function and use it to determine the asymptotes and the local maximum and minimum values.

**73.** $y = e^{x/(x+2)}$

**74.** $y = 10^x - 5^x$

**75.** $y = \log(x^3 - x)$

**76.** $y = 2x^2 - \ln x$

**77–78** ▪ Find the solutions of the equation, correct to two decimal places.

**77.** $3 \log x = 6 - 2x$

**78.** $4 - x^2 = e^{-2x}$

**79–80** ▪ Solve the inequality graphically.

**79.** $\ln x > x - 2$

**80.** $e^x < 4x^2$

**81.** Use a graph of $f(x) = e^x - 3e^{-x} - 4x$ to find, approximately, the intervals on which $f$ is increasing and on which $f$ is decreasing.

**82.** Find an equation of the line shown in the figure.

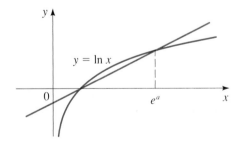

**83–86** ▪ Use the Change of Base Formula to evaluate the logarithm, correct to six decimal places.

**83.** $\log_4 15$

**84.** $\log_7(\frac{3}{4})$

**85.** $\log_9 0.28$

**86.** $\log_{100} 250$

**87.** Which is larger, $\log_4 258$ or $\log_5 620$?

**88.** Find the inverse of the function $f(x) = 2^{3^x}$ and state its domain and range.

**89.** If \$12,000 is invested at an interest rate of 10% per year, find the amount of the investment at the end of 3 years for each compounding method.
(a) Semiannual
(b) Monthly
(c) Daily
(d) Continuous

**90.** A sum of \$5000 is invested at an interest rate of $8\frac{1}{2}\%$ per year, compounded semiannually.
(a) Find the amount of the investment after $1\frac{1}{2}$ years.
(b) After what period of time will the investment amount to \$7000?
(c) If interest were compounded continously instead of semiannually, how long would it take for the amount to grow to \$7000?

**91.** A money market account pays 5.2% annual interest, compounded daily. If \$100,000 is invested in this account, how long will it take for the account to accumulate \$10,000 in interest?

**92.** A retirement savings plan pays 4.5% interest, compounded continuously. How long will it take for an investment in this plan to double?

**93–94** ▪ Determine the annual percentage yield (APY) for the given nominal annual interest rate and compounding frequency.

**93.** 4.25%; daily

**94.** 3.2%; monthly

**95.** The stray-cat population in a small town grows exponentially. In 1999 the town had 30 stray cats, and the relative growth rate was 15% per year.
(a) Find a function that models the stray-cat population $n(t)$ after $t$ years.
(b) Find the projected population after 4 years.
(c) Find the number of years required for the stray-cat population to reach 500.

**96.** A culture contains 10,000 bacteria initially. After an hour the bacteria count is 25,000.
(a) Find the doubling period.
(b) Find the number of bacteria after 3 hours.

**97.** Uranium-234 has a half-life of $2.7 \times 10^5$ years.
(a) Find the amount remaining from a 10-mg sample after a thousand years.
(b) How long will it take this sample to decompose until its mass is 7 mg?

**98.** A sample of bismuth-210 decayed to 33% of its original mass after 8 days.
(a) Find the half-life of this element.
(b) Find the mass remaining after 12 days.

**99.** The half-life of radium-226 is 1590 years.
(a) If a sample has a mass of 150 mg, find a function that models the mass that remains after $t$ years.
(b) Find the mass that will remain after 1000 years.
(c) After how many years will only 50 mg remain?

**100.** The half-life of palladium-100 is 4 days. After 20 days a sample has been reduced to a mass of 0.375 g.
  **(a)** What was the initial mass of the sample?
  **(b)** Find a function that models the mass remaining after $t$ days.
  **(c)** What is the mass after 3 days?
  **(d)** After how many days will only 0.15 g remain?

**101.** The graph shows the population of a rare species of bird, where t represents years since 1999 and $n(t)$ is measured in thousands.
  **(a)** Find a function that models the bird population at time $t$ in the form $n(t) = n_0 e^{rt}$.
  **(b)** What is the bird population expected to be in the year 2010?

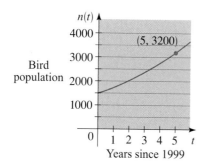

**102.** A car engine runs at a temperature of 190°F. When the engine is turned off, it cools according to Newton's Law of Cooling with constant $k = 0.0341$, where the time is measured in minutes. Find the time needed for the engine to cool to 90°F if the surrounding temperature is 60°F.

**103.** The hydrogen ion concentration of fresh egg whites was measured as

$$[\text{H}^+] = 1.3 \times 10^{-8} \text{ M}$$

Find the pH, and classify the substance as acidic or basic.

**104.** The pH of lime juice is 1.9. Find the hydrogen ion concentration.

**105.** If one earthquake has magnitude 6.5 on the Richter scale, what is the magnitude of another quake that is 35 times as intense?

**106.** The drilling of a jackhammer was measured at 132 dB. The sound of whispering was measured at 28 dB. Find the ratio of the intensity of the drilling to that of the whispering.

1. Sketch the graph of each function, and state its domain, range, and asymptote. Show the $x$- and $y$-intercepts on the graph.

    (a) $f(x) = 2^{-x} + 4$         (b) $g(x) = \log_3(x + 3)$

2. (a) Write the equation $6^{2x} = 25$ in logarithmic form.

    (b) Write the equation $\ln A = 3$ in exponential form.

3. Find the exact value of each expression.

    (a) $10^{\log 36}$                 (b) $\ln e^3$

    (c) $\log_3 \sqrt{27}$            (d) $\log_2 80 - \log_2 10$

    (e) $\log_8 4$                 (f) $\log_6 4 + \log_6 9$

4. Use the Laws of Logarithms to expand the expression.

$$\log \sqrt[3]{\frac{x + 2}{x^4(x^2 + 4)}}$$

5. Combine into a single logarithm: $\ln x - 2\ln(x^2 + 1) + \frac{1}{2}\ln(3 - x^4)$

6. Find the solution of the equation, correct to two decimal places.

    (a) $2^{x-1} = 10$            (b) $5\ln(3 - x) = 4$

    (c) $10^{x+3} = 6^{2x}$         (d) $\log_2(x + 2) + \log_2(x - 1) = 2$

7. The initial size of a culture of bacteria is 1000. After one hour the bacteria count is 8000.

    (a) Find a function that models the population after $t$ hours.

    (b) Find the population after 1.5 hours.

    (c) When will the population reach 15,000?

    (d) Sketch the graph of the population function.

8. Suppose that $12,000 is invested in a savings account paying 5.6% interest per year.

    (a) Write the formula for the amount in the account after $t$ years if interest is compounded monthly.

    (b) Find the amount in the account after 3 years if interest is compounded daily.

    (c) How long will it take for the amount in the account to grow to $20,000 if interest is compounded semiannually?

9. The half-life of krypton-91 ($^{91}$Kr) is 10 seconds. At time $t = 0$ a heavy canister contains 3 g of this radioactive gas.

    (a) Find a function that models the amount $A(t)$ of $^{91}$Kr remaining in the canister after $t$ seconds.

    (b) How much $^{91}$Kr remains after one minute?

    (c) When will the amount of $^{91}$Kr remaining be reduced to 1 $\mu$g (1 microgram, or $10^{-6}$ g)?

10. An earthquake measuring 6.4 on the Richter scale struck Japan in July 2007, causing extensive damage. Earlier that year, a minor earthquake measuring 3.1 on the Richter scale was felt in parts of Pennsylvania. How many times more intense was the Japanese earthquake than the Pennsylvania earthquake?

1. Let $f(x) = x^2 - 4x$ and $g(x) = \sqrt{x + 4}$. Find each of the following:

   (a) The domain of $f$

   (b) The domain of $g$

   (c) $f(-2), f(0), f(4), g(0), g(8), g(-6)$

   (d) $f(x + 2), g(x + 2), f(2 + h)$

   (e) The average rate of change of $g$ between $x = 5$ and $x = 21$

   (f) $f \circ g, g \circ f, f(g(12)), g(f(12))$

   (g) The inverse of $g$

2. Let $f(x) = \begin{cases} 4 & \text{if } x \le 2 \\ x - 3 & \text{if } x > 2 \end{cases}$

   (a) Evaluate $f(0), f(1), f(2), f(3)$, and $f(4)$.

   (b) Sketch the graph of $f$.

3. Let $f$ be the quadratic function $f(x) = -2x^2 + 8x + 5$.

   (a) Express $f$ in standard form.

   (b) Find the maximum or minimum value of $f$.

   (c) Sketch the graph of $f$.

   (d) Find the interval on which $f$ is increasing and the interval on which $f$ is decreasing.

   (e) How is the graph of $g(x) = -2x^2 + 8x + 10$ obtained from the graph of $f$?

   (f) How is the graph of $h(x) = -2(x + 3)^2 + 8(x + 3) + 5$ obtained from the graph of $f$?

4. Without using a graphing calculator, match each of the following functions to the graphs below. Give reasons for your choices.

$$f(x) = x^3 - 8x \qquad g(x) = -x^4 + 8x^2 \qquad r(x) = \frac{2x + 3}{x^2 - 9}$$

$$s(x) = \frac{2x - 3}{x^2 + 9} \qquad h(x) = 2^x - 5 \qquad k(x) = 2^{-x} + 3$$

A 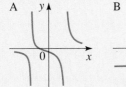  B   C 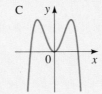  D 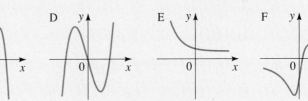  E 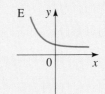  F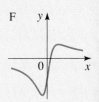

5. Let $P(x) = 2x^3 - 11x^2 + 10x + 8$.

   (a) List all possible rational zeros of $P$.

   (b) Determine which of the numbers you listed in part (a) actually are zeros of $P$.

   (c) Factor $P$ completely.

   (d) Sketch a graph of $P$.

6. Let $Q(x) = x^5 - 3x^4 + 3x^3 + x^2 - 4x + 2$.

   (a) Find all zeros of $Q$, real and complex, and state their multiplicities.

   (b) Factor $Q$ completely.

   (c) Factor $Q$ into linear and irreducible quadratic factors.

7. Let $r(x) = \dfrac{3x^2 + 6x}{x^2 - x - 2}$. Find the $x$- and $y$-intercepts and the horizontal and vertical asymptotes. Then sketch the graph of $r$.

**8.** Sketch graphs of the following functions on the same coordinate plane.

   (a) $f(x) = 2 - e^x$                    (b) $g(x) = \ln(x + 1)$

**9.** (a) Find the exact value of $\log_3 16 - 2 \log_3 36$.

   (b) Use the Laws of Logarithms to expand the expression

$$\log\left(\frac{x^5 \sqrt{x - 1}}{2x - 3}\right)$$

**10.** Solve the equations.

   (a) $\log_2 x + \log_2(x - 2) = 3$

   (b) $2e^{3x} - 11e^{2x} + 10e^x + 8 = 0$   [*Hint*: Compare to the polynomial in problem 5.]

**11.** A sum of \$25,000 is deposited into an account paying 5.4% interest per year, compounded daily.

   (a) What will the amount in the account be after 3 years?

   (b) When will the account have grown to \$35,000?

   (c) How long will it take for the initial deposit to double?

**12.** After a shipwreck, 120 rats manage to swim from the wreckage to a deserted island. The rat population on the island grows exponentially, and after 15 months there are 280 rats on the island.

   (a) Find a function that models the population $t$ months after the arrival of the rats.

   (b) What will the population be 3 years after the shipwreck?

   (c) When will the population reach 2000?

# FITTING EXPONENTIAL AND POWER CURVES TO DATA

In a previous *Focus on Modeling* (page 364) we learned that the shape of a scatter plot helps us to choose the type of curve to use in modeling data. The first plot in Figure 1 fairly screams for a line to be fitted through it, and the second one points to a cubic polynomial. For the third plot it is tempting to fit a second-degree polynomial. But what if an exponential curve fits better? How do we decide this? In this section we learn how to fit exponential and power curves to data and how to decide which type of curve fits the data better. We also learn that for scatter plots like those in the last two plots in Figure 1, the data can be modeled by logarithmic or logistic functions.

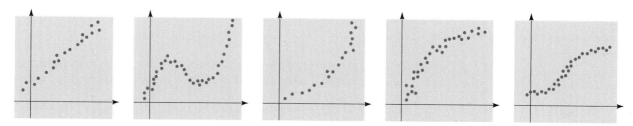

**FIGURE 1**

## Modeling with Exponential Functions

If a scatter plot shows that the data increase rapidly, we might want to model the data using an *exponential model*, that is, a function of the form

$$f(x) = Ce^{kx}$$

where $C$ and $k$ are constants. In the first example we model world population by an exponential model. Recall from Section 5.5 that population tends to increase exponentially.

▶ **EXAMPLE 1** │ An Exponential Model for World Population

Table 1 gives the population of the world in the 20th century.

**(a)** Draw a scatter plot, and note that a linear model is not appropriate.

**(b)** Find an exponential function that models population growth.

**(c)** Draw a graph of the function that you found together with the scatter plot. How well does the model fit the data?

**(d)** Use the model that you found to predict world population in the year 2020.

▼ **SOLUTION**

**(a)** The scatter plot is shown in Figure 2. The plotted points do not appear to lie along a straight line, so a linear model is not appropriate.

**TABLE 1**
World population

| Year (t) | World population (P in millions) |
|---|---|
| 1900 | 1650 |
| 1910 | 1750 |
| 1920 | 1860 |
| 1930 | 2070 |
| 1940 | 2300 |
| 1950 | 2520 |
| 1960 | 3020 |
| 1970 | 3700 |
| 1980 | 4450 |
| 1990 | 5300 |
| 2000 | 6060 |

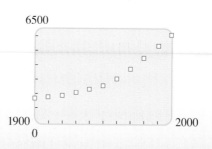

**FIGURE 2** Scatter plot of world population

The population of the world increases exponentially

**(b)** Using a graphing calculator and the `ExpReg` command (see Figure 3(a)), we get the exponential model

$$P(t) = (0.0082543) \cdot (1.0137186)^t$$

This is a model of the form $y = Cb^t$. To convert this to the form $y = Ce^{kt}$, we use the properties of exponentials and logarithms as follows:

$$1.0137186^t = e^{\ln 1.0137186^t} \qquad A = e^{\ln A}$$
$$= e^{t \ln 1.0137186} \qquad \ln A^B = B \ln A$$
$$= e^{0.013625t} \qquad \ln 1.0137186 \approx 0.013625$$

Thus, we can write the model as

$$P(t) = 0.0082543 e^{0.013625t}$$

**(c)** From the graph in Figure 3(b) we see that the model appears to fit the data fairly well. The period of relatively slow population growth is explained by the depression of the 1930s and the two world wars.

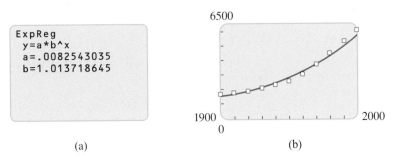

(a)

(b)

**FIGURE 3** Exponential model for world population

**(d)** The model predicts that the world population in 2020 will be

$$P(2020) = 0.0082543 e^{(0.013625)(2020)}$$
$$\approx 7,405,400,000 \qquad \blacktriangle$$

## Modeling with Power Functions

If the scatter plot of the data we are studying resembles the graph of $y = ax^2$, $y = ax^{1.32}$, or some other power function, then we seek a *power model*, that is, a function of the form

$$f(x) = ax^n$$

where $a$ is a positive constant and $n$ is any real number.

In the next example we seek a power model for some astronomical data. In astronomy, distance in the solar system is often measured in astronomical units. An *astronomical unit* (AU) is the mean distance from the earth to the sun. The *period* of a planet is the time it takes the planet to make a complete revolution around the sun (measured in earth years). In this example we derive the remarkable relationship, first discovered by Johannes Kepler (see page 585), between the mean distance of a planet from the sun and its period.

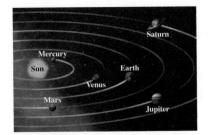

▶ **EXAMPLE 2** | A Power Model for Planetary Periods

Table 2 gives the mean distance $d$ of each planet from the sun in astronomical units and its period $T$ in years.

To change a system of linear equations to an **equivalent system** (that is, a system with the same solutions as the original system), we use the elimination method. This means that we can use the following operations.

---

**OPERATIONS THAT YIELD AN EQUIVALENT SYSTEM**

**1.** Add a nonzero multiple of one equation to another.

**2.** Multiply an equation by a nonzero constant.

**3.** Interchange the positions of two equations.

---

To solve a linear system, we use these operations to change the system to an equivalent triangular system. Then we use back-substitution as in Example 1. This process is called **Gaussian elimination**.

▶ **EXAMPLE 2** | Solving a System of Three Equations in Three Variables

Solve the system using Gaussian elimination.

$$\begin{cases} x - 2y + 3z = 1 & \text{Equation 1} \\ x + 2y - z = 13 & \text{Equation 2} \\ 3x + 2y - 5z = 3 & \text{Equation 3} \end{cases}$$

▼ **SOLUTION**   We need to change this to a triangular system, so we begin by eliminating the $x$-term from the second equation.

$$\begin{array}{ll} x + 2y - z = 13 & \text{Equation 2} \\ \underline{x - 2y + 3z = 1} & \text{Equation 1} \\ 4y - 4z = 12 & \text{Equation 2} + (-1) \times \text{Equation 1} = \text{new Equation 2} \end{array}$$

This gives us a new, equivalent system that is one step closer to triangular form:

$$\begin{cases} x - 2y + 3z = 1 & \text{Equation 1} \\ 4y - 4z = 12 & \text{Equation 2} \\ 3x + 2y - 5z = 3 & \text{Equation 3} \end{cases}$$

Now we eliminate the $x$-term from the third equation.

$$\begin{array}{l} 3x + 2y - 5z = 3 \\ \underline{-3x + 6y - 9z = -3} \\ 8y - 14z = 0 \end{array}$$

$$\begin{cases} x - 2y + 3z = 1 \\ 4y - 4z = 12 \\ 8y - 14z = 0 \end{cases} \quad \text{Equation 3} + (-3) \times \text{Equation 1} = \text{new Equation 3}$$

Then we eliminate the $y$-term from the third equation.

$$\begin{array}{l} 8y - 14z = 0 \\ \underline{-8y + 8z = -24} \\ -6z = -24 \end{array}$$

$$\begin{cases} x - 2y + 3z = 1 \\ 4y - 4z = 12 \\ -6z = -24 \end{cases} \quad \text{Equation 3} + (-2) \times \text{Equation 2} = \text{new Equation 3}$$

The system is now in triangular form, but it will be easier to work with if we divide the second and third equations by the common factors of each term.

$$\begin{cases} x - 2y + 3z = 1 \\ y - z = 3 & \frac{1}{4} \times \text{Equation 2} = \text{new Equation 2} \\ z = 4 & -\frac{1}{6} \times \text{Equation 3} = \text{new Equation 3} \end{cases}$$

**Intersection of Three Planes**

When you study calculus or linear algebra, you will learn that the graph of a linear equation in three variables is a plane in a three-dimensional coordinate system. For a system of three equations in three variables the following situations arise:

**1.** The three planes intersect in a single point.
 The system has a unique solution.

**2.** The three planes intersect in more than one point.
 The system has infinitely many solutions.

**3.** The three planes have no point in common.
 The system has no solution.

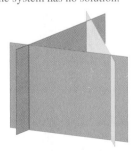

Now we use back-substitution to solve the system. From the third equation we get $z = 4$. We back-substitute this into the second equation and solve for $y$.

$$y - (4) = 3 \qquad \text{Back-substitute } z = 4 \text{ into Equation 2}$$
$$y = 7 \qquad \text{Solve for } y$$

Now we back-substitute $y = 7$ and $z = 4$ into the first equation and solve for $x$.

$$x - 2(7) + 3(4) = 1 \qquad \text{Back-substitute } y = 7 \text{ and } z = 4 \text{ into Equation 1}$$
$$x = 3 \qquad \text{Solve for } x$$

The solution of the system is $x = 3$, $y = 7$, $z = 4$, which we can write as the ordered triple $(3, 7, 4)$.

**Check Your Answer**

$x = 3, y = 7, z = 4$:

$$
\begin{aligned}
(3) - 2(7) + 3(4) &= 1 \\
(3) + 2(7) - (4) &= 13 \\
3(3) + 2(7) - 5(4) &= 3 \quad ✔
\end{aligned}
$$

✎ **Practice what you've learned: Do Exercise 17.** ▲

## ■ The Number of Solutions of a Linear System

Just as in the case of two variables, a system of equations in several variables may have one solution, no solution, or infinitely many solutions. The graphical interpretation of the solutions of a linear system is analogous to that for systems of equations in two variables (see the margin note).

---

**NUMBER OF SOLUTIONS OF A LINEAR SYSTEM**

For a system of linear equations, exactly one of the following is true.

**1.** The system has exactly one solution.

**2.** The system has no solution.

**3.** The system has infinitely many solutions.

---

A system with no solutions is said to be **inconsistent**, and a system with infinitely many solutions is said to be **dependent**. As we see in the next example, a linear system has no solution if we end up with a *false equation* after applying Gaussian elimination to the system.

▶ **EXAMPLE 3** | A System with No Solution

Solve the following system.

$$\begin{cases} x + 2y - 2z = 1 & \text{Equation 1} \\ 2x + 2y - z = 6 & \text{Equation 2} \\ 3x + 4y - 3z = 5 & \text{Equation 3} \end{cases}$$

▼ **SOLUTION** To put this in triangular form, we begin by eliminating the $x$-terms from the second equation and the third equation.

$$\begin{cases} x + 2y - 2z = 1 \\ \quad\; -2y + 3z = 4 \qquad \text{Equation 2 + (-2) × Equation 1 = new Equation 2} \\ 3x + 4y + 3z = 5 \end{cases}$$

$$\begin{cases} x + 2y - 2z = 1 \\ \quad\; -2y + 3z = 4 \\ \quad\; -2y + 3z = 2 \qquad \text{Equation 3 + (-3) × Equation 1 = new Equation 3} \end{cases}$$

Now we eliminate the $y$-term from the third equation.

$$\begin{cases} x + 2y - 2z = 1 \\ \quad\; -2y + 3z = 4 \\ \qquad\qquad 0 = 2 \qquad \text{Equation 3 + (-1) × Equation 2 = new Equation 3} \end{cases}$$

The system is now in triangular form, but the third equation says $0 = 2$, which is false. No matter what values we assign to $x$, $y$, and $z$, the third equation will never be true. This means that the system has *no solution*.

✎ **Practice what you've learned: Do Exercise 27.**                          ▲

▶ **EXAMPLE 4** | A System with Infinitely Many Solutions

Solve the following system.

$$\begin{cases} x - y + 5z = -2 \qquad \text{Equation 1} \\ 2x + y + 4z = \quad 2 \qquad \text{Equation 2} \\ 2x + 4y - 2z = \quad 8 \qquad \text{Equation 3} \end{cases}$$

▼ **SOLUTION** To put this in triangular form, we begin by eliminating the $x$-terms from the second equation and the third equation.

$$\begin{cases} x - y + 5z = -2 \\ \quad\;\; 3y - 6z = \quad 6 \qquad \text{Equation 2 + (-2) × Equation 1 = new Equation 2} \\ 2x + 4y - 2z = \quad 8 \end{cases}$$

$$\begin{cases} x - y + \;\; 5z = -2 \\ \quad\; 3y - \;\; 6z = \quad 6 \\ \quad\; 6y - 12z = \quad 12 \qquad \text{Equation 3 + (-2) × Equation 1 = new Equation 3} \end{cases}$$

Now we eliminate the $y$-term from the third equation.

$$\begin{cases} x - y + 5z = -2 \\ \quad\; 3y - 6z = \quad 6 \\ \qquad\qquad 0 = \quad 0 \qquad \text{Equation 3 + (-2) × Equation 2 = new Equation 3} \end{cases}$$

The new third equation is true, but it gives us no new information, so we can drop it from the system. Only two equations are left. We can use them to solve for $x$ and $y$ in terms of $z$, but $z$ can take on any value, so there are infinitely many solutions.

To find the complete solution of the system, we begin by solving for $y$ in terms of $z$, using the new second equation.

$$3y - 6z = 6 \qquad \text{Equation 2}$$
$$y - 2z = 2 \qquad \text{Multiply by } \tfrac{1}{3}$$
$$y = 2z + 2 \qquad \text{Solve for } y$$

Then we solve for $x$ in terms of $z$, using the first equation.

$$x - (2z + 2) + 5z = -2 \qquad \text{Substitute } y = 2z + 2 \text{ into Equation 1}$$
$$x + 3z - 2 = -2 \qquad \text{Simplify}$$
$$x = -3z \qquad \text{Solve for } x$$

To describe the complete solution, we let $t$ represent any real number. The solution is

$$x = -3t$$
$$y = 2t + 2$$
$$z = t$$

We can also write this as the ordered triple $(-3t, 2t + 2, t)$.

✎ **Practice what you've learned: Do Exercise 25.**    ▲

In the solution of Example 4 the variable $t$ is called a **parameter**. To get a specific solution, we give a specific value to the parameter $t$. For instance, if we set $t = 2$, we get

$$x = -3(2) = -6$$
$$y = 2(2) + 2 = 6$$
$$z = 2$$

Thus, $(-6, 6, 2)$ is a solution of the system. Here are some other solutions of the system obtained by substituting other values for the parameter $t$.

| Parameter $t$ | Solution $(-3t, 2t + 2, t)$ |
|:---:|:---:|
| $-1$ | $(3, 0, -1)$ |
| $0$ | $(0, 2, 0)$ |
| $3$ | $(-9, 8, 3)$ |
| $10$ | $(-30, 22, 10)$ |

You should check that these points satisfy the original equations. There are infinitely many choices for the parameter $t$, so the system has infinitely many solutions.

## MATHEMATICS IN THE MODERN WORLD

### Global Positioning System (GPS)

NASA

On a cold, foggy day in 1707 a British naval fleet was sailing home at a fast clip. The fleet's navigators didn't know it, but the fleet was only a few yards from the rocky shores of England. In the ensuing disaster the fleet was totally destroyed. This tragedy could have been avoided had the navigators known their positions. In those days latitude was determined by the position of the North Star (and this could only be done at night in good weather), and longitude by the position of the sun relative to where it would be in England *at that same time*. So navigation required an accurate method of telling time on ships. (The invention of the spring-loaded clock brought about the eventual solution.)

Since then, several different methods have been developed to determine position, and all rely heavily on mathematics (see LORAN, page 578). The latest method, called the Global Positioning System (GPS), uses triangulation. In this system, 24 satellites are strategically located above the surface of the earth. A handheld GPS device measures distance from a satellite, using the travel time of radio signals emitted from the satellite. Knowing the distances to three different satellites tells us that we are at the point of intersection of three different spheres. This uniquely determines our position (see Exercise 61, page 450).

## ■ Modeling Using Linear Systems

Linear systems are used to model situations that involve several varying quantities. In the next example we consider an application of linear systems to finance.

▶ **EXAMPLE 5** | Modeling a Financial Problem Using a Linear System

Jason receives an inheritance of $50,000. His financial advisor suggests that he invest this in three mutual funds: a money-market fund, a blue-chip stock fund, and a high-tech stock fund. The advisor estimates that the money-market fund will return 5% over the next year, the blue-chip fund 9%, and the high-tech fund 16%. Jason wants a total first-year return of $4000. To avoid excessive risk, he decides to invest three times as much in the money-market fund as in the high-tech stock fund. How much should he invest in each fund?

▼ **SOLUTION**

Let    $x$ = amount invested in the money-market fund

   $y$ = amount invested in the blue-chip stock fund

   $z$ = amount invested in the high-tech stock fund

We convert each fact given in the problem into an equation.

$$x + y + z = 50{,}000 \qquad \text{Total amount invested is \$50,000}$$
$$0.05x + 0.09y + 0.16z = 4000 \qquad \text{Total investment return is \$4000}$$
$$x = 3z \qquad \text{Money-market amount is 3 × high-tech amount}$$

Multiplying the second equation by 100 and rewriting the third gives the following system, which we solve using Gaussian elimination.

$$\begin{cases} x + y + z = 50{,}000 \\ 5x + 9y + 16z = 400{,}000 \\ x \quad\;\; - 3z = \quad 0 \end{cases}$$
$\qquad$ 100 × Equation 2
$\qquad$ Subtract 3z

$$\begin{cases} x + y + z = 50{,}000 \\ 4y + 11z = 150{,}000 \\ -y - 4z = -50{,}000 \end{cases}$$
$\qquad$ Equation 2 + (−5) × Equation 1 = new Equation 2
$\qquad$ Equation 3 + (−1) × Equation 1 = new Equation 3

$$\begin{cases} x + y + z = 50{,}000 \\ -5z = -50{,}000 \\ -y - 4z = -50{,}000 \end{cases}$$
$\qquad$ Equation 2 + 4 × Equation 3 = new Equation 3

$$\begin{cases} x + y + z = 50{,}000 \\ z = 10{,}000 \\ y + 4z = 50{,}000 \end{cases}$$
$\qquad$ $(-\frac{1}{5})$ × Equation 2
$\qquad$ (−1) × Equation 3

$$\begin{cases} x + y + z = 50{,}000 \\ y + 4z = 50{,}000 \\ z = 10{,}000 \end{cases}$$
$\qquad$ Interchange Equations 2 and 3

Now that the system is in triangular form, we use back-substitution to find that $x = 30{,}000$, $y = 10{,}000$, and $z = 10{,}000$. This means that Jason should invest

$30,000 in the money-market fund

$10,000 in the blue-chip stock fund

$10,000 in the high-tech stock fund

✎ **Practice what you've learned: Do Exercise 37.**    ▲

# 6.3 EXERCISES

## ▼ CONCEPTS

**1–2** ▪ These exercises refer to the following system.

$$\begin{cases} x - y + z = 2 \\ -x + 2y + z = -3 \\ 3x + y - 2z = 2 \end{cases}$$

**1.** If we add 2 times the first equation to the second equation, the second equation becomes _____ = ____.

**2.** To eliminate $x$ from the third equation, we add _____ times the first equation to the third equation. The third equation becomes _____ = ____.

## ▼ SKILLS

**3–6** ▪ State whether the equation or system of equations is linear.

**3.** $6x - \sqrt{3}y + \frac{1}{2}z = 0$

**4.** $x^2 + y^2 + z^2 = 4$

**5.** $\begin{cases} xy - 3y + z = 5 \\ x - y^2 + 5z = 0 \\ 2x + yz = 3 \end{cases}$

**6.** $\begin{cases} x - 2y + 3z = 10 \\ 2x + 5y = 2 \\ y + 2z = 4 \end{cases}$

**7–12** ▪ Use back-substitution to solve the triangular system.

**7.** $\begin{cases} x - 2y + 4z = 3 \\ y + 2z = 7 \\ z = 2 \end{cases}$

**8.** $\begin{cases} x + y - 3z = 8 \\ y - 3z = 5 \\ z = -1 \end{cases}$

**9.** $\begin{cases} x + 2y + z = 7 \\ -y + 3z = 9 \\ 2z = 6 \end{cases}$

**10.** $\begin{cases} x - 2y + 3z = 10 \\ 2y - z = 2 \\ 3z = 12 \end{cases}$

**11.** $\begin{cases} 2x - y + 6z = 5 \\ y + 4z = 0 \\ -2z = 1 \end{cases}$

**12.** $\begin{cases} 4x + 3z = 10 \\ 2y - z = -6 \\ \frac{1}{2}z = 4 \end{cases}$

**13–16** ▪ Perform an operation on the given system that eliminates the indicated variable. Write the new equivalent system.

**13.** $\begin{cases} x - 2y - z = 4 \\ x - y + 3z = 0 \\ 2x + y + z = 0 \end{cases}$
Eliminate the $x$-term from the second equation.

**14.** $\begin{cases} x + y - 3z = 3 \\ -2x + 3y + z = 2 \\ x - y + 2z = 0 \end{cases}$
Eliminate the $x$-term from the second equation.

**15.** $\begin{cases} 2x - y + 3z = 2 \\ x + 2y - z = 4 \\ -4x + 5y + z = 10 \end{cases}$
Eliminate the $x$-term from the third equation.

**16.** $\begin{cases} x - 4y + z = 3 \\ y - 3z = 10 \\ 3y - 8z = 24 \end{cases}$
Eliminate the $y$-term from the third equation.

**17–36** ▪ Find the complete solution of the linear system, or show that it is inconsistent.

**17.** $\begin{cases} x - y - z = 4 \\ 2y + z = -1 \\ -x + y - 2z = 5 \end{cases}$

**18.** $\begin{cases} x - y + z = 0 \\ y + 2z = -2 \\ x + y - z = 2 \end{cases}$

**19.** $\begin{cases} x + y + z = 4 \\ x + 3y + 3z = 10 \\ 2x + y - z = 3 \end{cases}$

**20.** $\begin{cases} x + y + z = 0 \\ -x + 2y + 5z = 3 \\ 3x - y = 6 \end{cases}$

**21.** $\begin{cases} x - 4z = 1 \\ 2x - y - 6z = 4 \\ 2x + 3y - 2z = 8 \end{cases}$

**22.** $\begin{cases} x - y + 2z = 2 \\ 3x + y + 5z = 8 \\ 2x - y - 2z = -7 \end{cases}$

**23.** $\begin{cases} 2x + 4y - z = 2 \\ x + 2y - 3z = -4 \\ 3x - y + z = 1 \end{cases}$

**24.** $\begin{cases} 2x + y - z = -8 \\ -x + y + z = 3 \\ -2x + 4z = 18 \end{cases}$

**25.** $\begin{cases} y - 2z = 0 \\ 2x + 3y = 2 \\ -x - 2y + z = -1 \end{cases}$

**26.** $\begin{cases} 2y + z = 3 \\ 5x + 4y + 3z = -1 \\ x - 3y = -2 \end{cases}$

**27.** $\begin{cases} x + 2y - z = 1 \\ 2x + 3y - 4z = -3 \\ 3x + 6y - 3z = 4 \end{cases}$

**28.** $\begin{cases} -x + 2y + 5z = 4 \\ x - 2z = 0 \\ 4x - 2y - 11z = 2 \end{cases}$

**29.** $\begin{cases} 2x + 3y - z = 1 \\ x + 2y = 3 \\ x + 3y + z = 4 \end{cases}$

**30.** $\begin{cases} x - 2y - 3z = 5 \\ 2x + y - z = 5 \\ 4x - 3y - 7z = 5 \end{cases}$

**31.** $\begin{cases} x + y - z = 0 \\ x + 2y - 3z = -3 \\ 2x + 3y - 4z = -3 \end{cases}$

**32.** $\begin{cases} x - 2y + z = 3 \\ 2x - 5y + 6z = 7 \\ 2x - 3y - 2z = 5 \end{cases}$

**33.** $\begin{cases} x + 3y - 2z = 0 \\ 2x + 4z = 4 \\ 4x + 6y = 4 \end{cases}$

**34.** $\begin{cases} 2x + 4y - z = 3 \\ x + 2y + 4z = 6 \\ x + 2y - 2z = 0 \end{cases}$

**35.** $\begin{cases} x + z + 2w = 6 \\ y - 2z = -3 \\ x + 2y - z = -2 \\ 2x + y + 3z - 2w = 0 \end{cases}$

**36.** $\begin{cases} x + y + z + w = 0 \\ x + y + 2z + 2w = 0 \\ 2x + 2y + 3z + 4w = 1 \\ 2x + 3y + 4z + 5w = 2 \end{cases}$

Its graph consists of not just the parabola in Figure 1, but also every point whose $y$-coordinate is *larger* than $x^2$. We indicate the solution in Figure 2(a) by shading the points *above* the parabola.

Similarly, the graph of $y \le x^2$ in Figure 2(b) consists of all points on and *below* the parabola. However, the graphs of $y > x^2$ and $y < x^2$ do not include the points on the parabola itself, as indicated by the dashed curves in Figures 2(c) and 2(d).

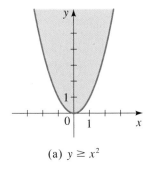

(a) $y \ge x^2$

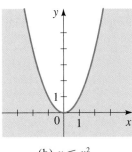

(b) $y \le x^2$

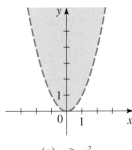

(c) $y > x^2$

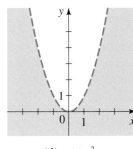

(d) $y < x^2$

**FIGURE 2**

The graph of an inequality, in general, consists of a region in the plane whose boundary is the graph of the equation obtained by replacing the inequality sign ($\ge$, $\le$, $>$, or $<$) with an equal sign. To determine which side of the graph gives the solution set of the inequality, we need only check **test points**.

---

**GRAPHING INEQUALITIES**

To graph an inequality, we carry out the following steps.

1. **Graph Equation.** Graph the equation corresponding to the inequality. Use a dashed curve for $>$ or $<$ and a solid curve for $\le$ or $\ge$.

2. **Test Points.** Test one point in each region formed by the graph in Step 1. If the point satisfies the inequality, then all the points in that region satisfy the inequality. (In that case, shade the region to indicate that it is part of the graph.) If the test point does not satisfy the inequality, then the region isn't part of the graph.

---

▶ **EXAMPLE 1** | Graphs of Inequalities

Graph each inequality.

**(a)** $x^2 + y^2 < 25$        **(b)** $x + 2y \ge 5$

▼ **SOLUTION**

**(a)** The graph of $x^2 + y^2 = 25$ is a circle of radius 5 centered at the origin. The points on the circle itself do not satisfy the inequality because it is of the form $<$, so we graph the circle with a dashed curve, as shown in Figure 3.

To determine whether the inside or the outside of the circle satisfies the inequality, we use the test points $(0, 0)$ on the inside and $(6, 0)$ on the outside. To do this, we substitute the coordinates of each point into the inequality and check whether the result satisfies the inequality. (Note that *any* point inside or outside the circle can serve as a test point. We have chosen these points for simplicity.)

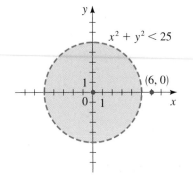

**FIGURE 3**

| Test point | $x^2 + y^2 < 25$ | Conclusion |
|:---:|:---:|:---:|
| $(0, 0)$ | $0^2 + 0^2 = 0 < 25$ | Part of graph |
| $(6, 0)$ | $6^2 + 0^2 = 36 \not< 25$ | Not part of graph |

Thus, the graph of $x^2 + y^2 < 25$ is the set of all points *inside* the circle (see Figure 3).

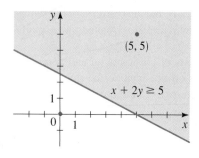

**FIGURE 4**

**(b)** The graph of $x + 2y = 5$ is the line shown in Figure 4. We use the test points $(0, 0)$ and $(5, 5)$ on opposite sides of the line.

| Test point | $x + 2y \geq 5$ | Conclusion |
|---|---|---|
| $(0, 0)$ | $0 + 2(0) = 0 \not\geq 5$ | Not part of graph |
| $(5, 5)$ | $5 + 2(5) = 15 \geq 5$ | Part of graph |

Our check shows that the points *above* the line satisfy the inequality.

Alternatively, we could put the inequality into slope-intercept form and graph it directly:

$$x + 2y \geq 5$$
$$2y \geq -x + 5$$
$$y \geq -\tfrac{1}{2}x + \tfrac{5}{2}$$

From this form we see that the graph includes all points whose $y$-coordinates are *greater* than those on the line $y = -\tfrac{1}{2}x + \tfrac{5}{2}$; that is, the graph consists of the points *on or above* this line, as shown in Figure 4.

✎ **Practice what you've learned: Do Exercises 7 and 15.**　▲

## ■ Systems of Inequalities

We now consider *systems* of inequalities. The solution of such a system is the set of all points in the coordinate plane that satisfy every inequality in the system.

▶ **EXAMPLE 2** │ A System of Two Inequalities

Graph the solution of the system of inequalities, and label its vertices.

$$\begin{cases} x^2 + y^2 < 25 \\ x + 2y \geq 5 \end{cases}$$

▼ **SOLUTION** These are the two inequalities of Example 1. In this example we wish to graph only those points that simultaneously satisfy both inequalities. The solution consists of the intersection of the graphs in Example 1. In Figure 5(a) we show the two regions on the same coordinate plane (in different colors), and in Figure 5(b) we show their intersection.

**Vertices** The points $(-3, 4)$ and $(5, 0)$ in Figure 5(b) are the **vertices** of the solution set. They are obtained by solving the system of *equations*

$$\begin{cases} x^2 + y^2 = 25 \\ x + 2y = 5 \end{cases}$$

We solve this system of equations by substitution. Solving for $x$ in the second equation gives $x = 5 - 2y$, and substituting this into the first equation gives

$$(5 - 2y)^2 + y^2 = 25 \quad \text{Substitute } x = 5 - 2y$$
$$(25 - 20y + 4y^2) + y^2 = 25 \quad \text{Expand}$$
$$-20y + 5y^2 = 0 \quad \text{Simplify}$$
$$-5y(4 - y) = 0 \quad \text{Factor}$$

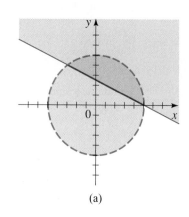

(a)

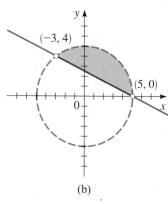

(b)

**FIGURE 5** $\begin{cases} x^2 + y^2 < 25 \\ x + 2y \geq 5 \end{cases}$

Thus, $y = 0$ or $y = 4$. When $y = 0$, we have $x = 5 - 2(0) = 5$, and when $y = 4$, we have $x = 5 - 2(4) = -3$. So the points of intersection of these curves are $(5, 0)$ and $(-3, 4)$.

Note that in this case the vertices are not part of the solution set, since they don't satisfy the inequality $x^2 + y^2 < 25$ (so they are graphed as open circles in the figure). They simply show where the "corners" of the solution set lie.

✎ **Practice what you've learned: Do Exercise 33.**    ▲

### ■ Systems of Linear Inequalities

An inequality is **linear** if it can be put into one of the following forms:

$$ax + by \geq c \qquad ax + by \leq c \qquad ax + by > c \qquad ax + by < c$$

In the next example we graph the solution set of a system of linear inequalities.

▶ **EXAMPLE 3** | A System of Four Linear Inequalities

Graph the solution set of the system, and label its vertices.

$$\begin{cases} x + 3y \leq 12 \\ x + \phantom{3}y \leq 8 \\ \phantom{x + 3y}x \geq 0 \\ \phantom{x + 3}y \geq 0 \end{cases}$$

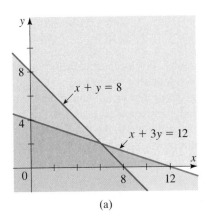

▼ **SOLUTION** In Figure 6 we first graph the lines given by the equations that correspond to each inequality. To determine the graphs of the linear inequalities, we need to check only one test point. For simplicity let's use the point $(0, 0)$.

| Inequality | Test point $(0, 0)$ | Conclusion |
|---|---|---|
| $x + 3y \leq 12$ | $0 + 3(0) = 0 \leq 12$ | Satisfies inequality |
| $x + y \leq 8$ | $0 + 0 = 0 \leq 8$ | Satisfies inequality |

Since $(0, 0)$ is below the line $x + 3y = 12$, our check shows that the region on or below the line must satisfy the inequality. Likewise, since $(0, 0)$ is below the line $x + y = 8$, our check shows that the region on or below this line must satisfy the inequality. The inequalities $x \geq 0$ and $y \geq 0$ say that $x$ and $y$ are nonnegative. These regions are sketched in Figure 6(a), and the intersection—the solution set—is sketched in Figure 6(b).

**Vertices** The coordinates of each vertex are obtained by simultaneously solving the equations of the lines that intersect at that vertex. From the system

$$\begin{cases} x + 3y = 12 \\ x + \phantom{3}y = \phantom{1}8 \end{cases}$$

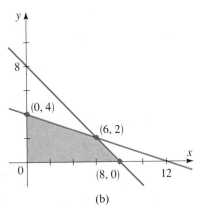

we get the vertex $(6, 2)$. The origin $(0, 0)$ is also clearly a vertex. The other two vertices are at the $x$- and $y$-intercepts of the corresponding lines: $(8, 0)$ and $(0, 4)$. In this case all the vertices *are* part of the solution set.

**FIGURE 6**

✎ **Practice what you've learned: Do Exercise 39.**    ▲

▶ **EXAMPLE 4** | A System of Linear Inequalities

Graph the solution set of the system.

$$\begin{cases} \phantom{-}x + 2y \geq 8 \\ -x + 2y \leq 4 \\ 3x - 2y \leq 8 \end{cases}$$

▼ **SOLUTION** We must graph the lines that correspond to these inequalities and then shade the appropriate regions, as in Example 3. We will use a graphing calculator, so we must first isolate $y$ on the left-hand side of each inequality.

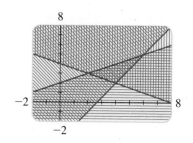

**FIGURE 7**

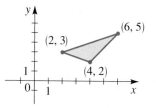

**FIGURE 8**

$$\begin{cases} y \geq -\frac{1}{2}x + 4 \\ y \leq \frac{1}{2}x + 2 \\ y \geq \frac{3}{2}x - 4 \end{cases}$$

Using the shading feature of the calculator, we obtain the graph in Figure 7. The solution set is the triangular region that is shaded in all three patterns. We then use $\boxed{\text{TRACE}}$ or the Intersect command to find the vertices of the region. The solution set is graphed in Figure 8.

✎ **Practice what you've learned: Do Exercise 47.**  ▲

When a region in the plane can be covered by a (sufficiently large) circle, it is said to be **bounded**. A region that is not bounded is called **unbounded**. For example, the regions graphed in Figures 3, 5(b), 6(b), and 8 are bounded, whereas those in Figures 2 and 4 are unbounded. An unbounded region cannot be "fenced in"—it extends infinitely far in at least one direction.

■ **Application: Feasible Regions**

Many applied problems involve *constraints* on the variables. For instance, a factory manager has only a certain number of workers that can be assigned to perform jobs on the factory floor. A farmer deciding what crops to cultivate has only a certain amount of land that can be seeded. Such constraints or limitations can usually be expressed as systems of inequalities. When dealing with applied inequalities, we usually refer to the solution set of a system as a *feasible region*, because the points in the solution set represent feasible (or possible) values for the quantities being studied.

▶ **EXAMPLE 5** | Restricting Pollutant Outputs

A factory produces two agricultural pesticides, A and B. For every barrel of A, the factory emits 0.25 kg of carbon monoxide (CO) and 0.60 kg of sulfur dioxide ($SO_2$); and for every barrel of B, it emits 0.50 kg of CO and 0.20 kg of $SO_2$. Pollution laws restrict the factory's output of CO to a maximum of 75 kg and $SO_2$ to a maximum of 90 kg per day.

**(a)** Find a system of inequalities that describes the number of barrels of each pesticide the factory can produce and still satisfy the pollution laws. Graph the feasible region.

**(b)** Would it be legal for the factory to produce 100 barrels of A and 80 barrels of B per day?

**(c)** Would it be legal for the factory to produce 60 barrels of A and 160 barrels of B per day?

▼ **SOLUTION**

**(a)** To set up the required inequalities, it is helpful to organize the given information into a table.

|  | **A** | **B** | **Maximum** |
| --- | --- | --- | --- |
| CO (kg) | 0.25 | 0.50 | 75 |
| $SO_2$ (kg) | 0.60 | 0.20 | 90 |

We let

$x$ = number of barrels of A produced per day

$y$ = number of barrels of B produced per day

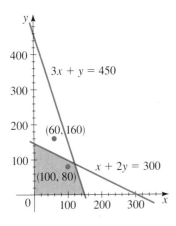

**FIGURE 9**

From the data in the table and the fact that $x$ and $y$ can't be negative, we obtain the following inequalities.

$$\begin{cases} 0.25x + 0.50y \le 75 & \text{CO inequality} \\ 0.60x + 0.20y \le 90 & \text{SO}_2 \text{ inequality} \\ x \ge 0, \quad y \ge 0 \end{cases}$$

Multiplying the first inequality by 4 and the second by 5 simplifies this to

$$\begin{cases} x + 2y \le 300 \\ 3x + y \le 450 \\ x \ge 0, \quad y \ge 0 \end{cases}$$

The feasible region is the solution of this system of inequalities, shown in Figure 9.

**(b)** Since the point $(100, 80)$ lies inside the feasible region, this production plan is legal (see Figure 9).

**(c)** Since the point $(60, 160)$ lies outside the feasible region, this production plan is not legal. It violates the CO restriction, although it does not violate the SO$_2$ restriction (see Figure 9).

✎ **Practice what you've learned: Do Exercise 51.**

# 6.5 EXERCISES

## ▼ CONCEPTS

**1.** To graph an inequality, we first graph the corresponding

_____. So to graph $y \le x + 1$, we first graph the equation

_____. To decide which side of the graph of the equation

is the graph of the inequality, we use _____ points. Using $(0, 0)$ as such a point, graph the inequality by shading the appropriate region.

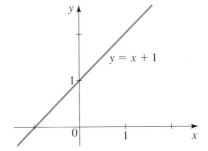

**2.** Shade the solution of each system of inequalities on the given graph.

**(a)** $\begin{cases} x - y \ge 0 \\ x + y \ge 2 \end{cases}$

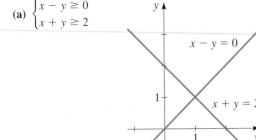

**(b)** $\begin{cases} x - y \le 0 \\ x + y \le 2 \end{cases}$

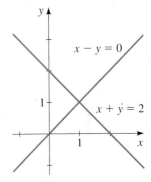

**(c)** $\begin{cases} x - y \ge 0 \\ x + y \le 2 \end{cases}$     **(d)** $\begin{cases} x - y \le 0 \\ x + y \ge 2 \end{cases}$

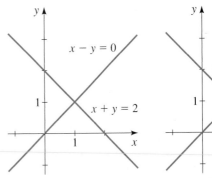

## ▼ SKILLS

**3–16** ▪ Graph the inequality.

**3.** $x < 3$                    **4.** $y \ge -2$

**5.** $y > x$                    **6.** $y < x + 2$

**7.** $y \le 2x + 2$

**8.** $y < -x + 5$

**9.** $2x - y \le 8$

**10.** $3x + 4y + 12 > 0$

**11.** $4x + 5y < 20$

**12.** $-x^2 + y \ge 10$

**13.** $y > x^2 + 1$

**14.** $x^2 + y^2 \ge 9$

**15.** $x^2 + y^2 \le 25$

**16.** $x^2 + (y - 1)^2 \le 1$

**17–20** ▪ An equation and its graph are given. Find an inequality whose solution is the shaded region.

**17.** $y = \frac{1}{2}x - 1$

**18.** $y = x^2 + 2$

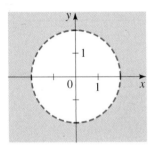
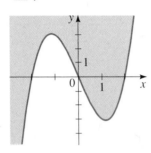

**19.** $x^2 + y^2 = 4$

**20.** $y = x^3 - 4x$

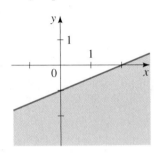
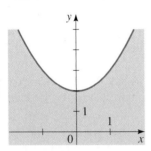

**21–46** ▪ Graph the solution of the system of inequalities. Find the coordinates of all vertices, and determine whether the solution set is bounded.

**21.** $\begin{cases} x + y \le 4 \\ y \ge x \end{cases}$

**22.** $\begin{cases} 2x + 3y > 12 \\ 3x - y < 21 \end{cases}$

**23.** $\begin{cases} y < \frac{1}{4}x + 2 \\ y \ge 2x - 5 \end{cases}$

**24.** $\begin{cases} x - y > 0 \\ 4 + y \le 2x \end{cases}$

**25.** $\begin{cases} y \le -2x + 8 \\ y \le -\frac{1}{2}x + 5 \\ x \ge 0, \quad y \ge 0 \end{cases}$

**26.** $\begin{cases} 4x + 3y \le 18 \\ 2x + y \le 8 \\ x \ge 0, \quad y \ge 0 \end{cases}$

**27.** $\begin{cases} x \ge 0 \\ y \ge 0 \\ 3x + 5y \le 15 \\ 3x + 2y \le 9 \end{cases}$

**28.** $\begin{cases} x > 2 \\ y < 12 \\ 2x - 4y > 8 \end{cases}$

**29.** $\begin{cases} y \le 9 - x^2 \\ x \ge 0, \quad y \ge 0 \end{cases}$

**30.** $\begin{cases} y \ge x^2 \\ y \le 4 \\ x \ge 0 \end{cases}$

**31.** $\begin{cases} y < 9 - x^2 \\ y \ge x + 3 \end{cases}$

**32.** $\begin{cases} y \ge x^2 \\ x + y \ge 6 \end{cases}$

**33.** $\begin{cases} x^2 + y^2 \le 4 \\ x - y > 0 \end{cases}$

**34.** $\begin{cases} x > 0 \\ y > 0 \\ x + y < 10 \\ x^2 + y^2 > 9 \end{cases}$

**35.** $\begin{cases} x^2 - y \le 0 \\ 2x^2 + y \le 12 \end{cases}$

**36.** $\begin{cases} x^2 + y^2 < 9 \\ 2x + y^2 \ge 1 \end{cases}$

**37.** $\begin{cases} x + 2y \le 14 \\ 3x - y \ge 0 \\ x - y \ge 2 \end{cases}$

**38.** $\begin{cases} y < x + 6 \\ 3x + 2y \ge 12 \\ x - 2y \le 2 \end{cases}$

**39.** $\begin{cases} x \ge 0 \\ y \ge 0 \\ x \le 5 \\ x + y \le 7 \end{cases}$

**40.** $\begin{cases} x \ge 0 \\ y \ge 0 \\ y \le 4 \\ 2x + y \le 8 \end{cases}$

**41.** $\begin{cases} y > x + 1 \\ x + 2y \le 12 \\ x + 1 > 0 \end{cases}$

**42.** $\begin{cases} x + y > 12 \\ y < \frac{1}{2}x - 6 \\ 3x + y < 6 \end{cases}$

**43.** $\begin{cases} x^2 + y^2 \le 8 \\ x \ge 2 \\ y \ge 0 \end{cases}$

**44.** $\begin{cases} x^2 - y \ge 0 \\ x + y < 6 \\ x - y < 6 \end{cases}$

**45.** $\begin{cases} x^2 + y^2 < 9 \\ x + y > 0 \\ x \le 0 \end{cases}$

**46.** $\begin{cases} y \ge x^3 \\ y \le 2x + 4 \\ x + y \ge 0 \end{cases}$

**47–50** ▪ Use a graphing calculator to graph the solution of the system of inequalities. Find the coordinates of all vertices, correct to one decimal place.

**47.** $\begin{cases} y \ge x - 3 \\ y \ge -2x + 6 \\ y \le 8 \end{cases}$

**48.** $\begin{cases} x + y \ge 12 \\ 2x + y \le 24 \\ x - y \ge -6 \end{cases}$

**49.** $\begin{cases} y \le 6x - x^2 \\ x + y \ge 4 \end{cases}$

**50.** $\begin{cases} y \ge x^3 \\ 2x + y \ge 0 \\ y \le 2x + 6 \end{cases}$

---

## ▼ APPLICATIONS

**51. Publishing Books** A publishing company publishes a total of no more than 100 books every year. At least 20 of these are nonfiction, but the company always publishes at least as much fiction as nonfiction. Find a system of inequalities that describes the possible numbers of fiction and nonfiction books that the company can produce each year consistent with these policies. Graph the solution set.

**52. Furniture Manufacturing** A man and his daughter manufacture unfinished tables and chairs. Each table requires 3 hours of sawing and 1 hour of assembly. Each chair requires 2 hours of sawing and 2 hours of assembly. Between the two of them, they can put in up to 12 hours of sawing and 8 hours of assembly work each day. Find a system of inequalities that describes all possible combinations of tables and chairs that they can make daily. Graph the solution set.

**53. Coffee Blends**    A coffee merchant sells two different coffee blends. The Standard blend uses 4 oz of arabica and 12 oz of robusta beans per package; the Deluxe blend uses 10 oz of arabica and 6 oz of robusta beans per package. The merchant has 80 lb of arabica and 90 lb of robusta beans available. Find a system of inequalities that describes the possible number of Standard and Deluxe packages the merchant can make. Graph the solution set.

**54. Nutrition**    A cat food manufacturer uses fish and beef byproducts. The fish contains 12 g of protein and 3 g of fat per ounce. The beef contains 6 g of protein and 9 g of fat per ounce. Each can of cat food must contain at least 60 g of protein and 45 g of fat. Find a system of inequalities that describes the possible number of ounces of fish and beef that can be used in each can to satisfy these minimum requirements. Graph the solution set.

## ▼ DISCOVERY • DISCUSSION • WRITING

**55. Shading Unwanted Regions**    To graph the solution of a system of inequalities, we have shaded the solution of each inequality in a different color; the solution of the system is the region where all the shaded parts overlap. Here is a different method: For each inequality, shade the region that does *not* satisfy the inequality. Explain why the part of the plane that is left unshaded is the solution of the system. Solve the following system by both methods. Which do you prefer? Why?

$$\begin{cases} x + 2y > 4 \\ -x + y < 1 \\ x + 3y < 9 \\ x < 3 \end{cases}$$

## ▶ CHAPTER 6 | REVIEW

## ▼ PROPERTIES AND FORMULAS

### Substitution Method (p. 443)

To solve a pair of equations in two variables by substitution:

1. Solve for one variable in terms of the other variable in one equation.

2. **Substitute** into the other equation to get an equation in one variable, and solve for this variable.

3. Substitute the value(s) of the variable you have found into either original equation, and solve for the remaining variable.

### Elimination Method (p. 444)

To solve a pair of equations in two variables by elimination:

1. Multiply the equations by appropriate constants so that the term(s) involving one of the variables are of opposite sign in the equations.

2. Add the equations to **eliminate** that one variable; this gives an equation in the other variable. Solve for this variable.

3. Substitute the value(s) of the variable that you have found into either original equation, and solve for the remaining variable.

### Graphical Method (p. 446)

To solve a pair of equations in two variables graphically:

1. Put each equation in function form, $y = f(x)$

2. Use a graphing calculator to **graph** the equations on a common screen.

3. Find the points of intersection of the graphs. The solutions are the $x$- and $y$-coordinates of the points of intersection.

### Gaussian Elimination (p. 459)

When we use **Gaussian elimination** to solve a system of linear equations, we use the following operations to change the system to an **equivalent** simpler system:

1. Add a nonzero multiple of one equation to another.

2. Multiply an equation by a nonzero constant.

3. Interchange the position of two equations in the system.

### Number of Solutions of a System of Linear Equations (pp. 451, 460)

A system of linear equations can have:

1. A unique solution for each variable.

2. No solution, in which case the system is **inconsistent**.

3. Infinitely many solutions, in which case the system is **dependent**.

### How to Determine the Number of Solutions of a Linear System (p. 460)

When we use **Gaussian elimination** to solve a system of linear equations, then we can tell that the system has:

1. **No solution** (is *inconsistent*) if we arrive at a false equation of the form $0 = c$, where $c$ is nonzero.

2. **Infinitely many solutions** (is *dependent*) if the system is consistent but we end up with fewer equations than variables (after discarding redundant equations of the form $0 = 0$).

### Partial Fractions (p. 469)

The *partial fraction decomposition* of a rational function

$$r(x) = \frac{P(x)}{Q(x)}$$

(where the degree of $P$ is less than the degree of $Q$) is a sum of simpler fractional expressions that equal $r(x)$ when brought to a common denominator. The denominator of each simpler fraction is either a linear or quadratic factor of $Q(x)$ or a power of such a linear or quadratic factor. So to find the terms of the partial fraction decomposition, we first factor $Q(x)$ into linear and irreducible quadratic factors. The terms then have the following forms, depending on the factors of $Q(x)$.

1. For every **distinct linear factor** $ax + b$, there is a term of the form

$$\frac{A}{ax + b}$$

2. For every **repeated linear factor** $(ax + b)^m$, there are terms of the form

$$\frac{A_1}{ax + b} + \frac{A_2}{(ax + b)^2} + \cdots + \frac{A_m}{(ax + b)^m}$$

3. For every **distinct quadratic factor** $ax^2 + bx + c$, there is a term of the form

$$\frac{Ax + B}{ax^2 + bx + c}$$

4. For every **repeated quadratic factor** $(ax^2 + bx + c)^m$, there are terms of the form

$$\frac{A_1x + B_1}{ax^2 + bx + c} + \frac{A_2x + B_2}{(ax^2 + bx + c)^2} + \cdots + \frac{A_mx + B_m}{(ax^2 + bx + c)^m}$$

## Graphing Inequalities (p. 475)

To graph an inequality:

1. Graph the equation that corresponds to the inequality. This "boundary curve" divides the coordinate plane into separate regions.

2. Use **test points** to determine which region(s) satisfy the inequality.

3. Shade the region(s) that satisfy the inequality, and use a solid line for the boundary curve if it satisfies the inequality ($\leq$ or $\geq$) and a dashed line if it does not ($<$ or $>$).

## Graphing Systems of Inequalities (p. 476)

To graph the solution of a system of inequalities (or **feasible region** determined by the inequalities):

1. Graph all the inequalities on the same coordinate plane.

2. The solution is the intersection of the solutions of all the inequalities, so shade the region that satisfies all the inequalities.

3. Determine the coordinates of the intersection points of all the boundary curves that touch the solution set of the system. These points are the **vertices** of the solution.

## ▼ CONCEPT SUMMARY

### Section 6.1

|  | Review Exercises |
|---|---|
| ▪ Solve a system of equations using the substitution method | 1–6, 11, 12 |
| ▪ Solve a system of equations using the elimination method | 7–10, 13, 14 |
| ▪ Solve a system of equations using the graphical method | 15–18 |

### Section 6.2

|  | Review Exercises |
|---|---|
| ▪ Solve a system of two linear equations in two variables | 5–8 |
| ▪ Determine whether a system of two linear equations in two variables has one solution, infinitely many solutions, or no solution | 5–8 |
| ▪ Model with linear systems in two variables | 27–28 |

### Section 6.3

|  | Review Exercises |
|---|---|
| ▪ Use Gaussian elimination to solve a system of three (or more) linear equations | 19–26 |
| ▪ Determine whether a system of (three or more) linear equations has one solution, infinitely many solutions, or no solution | 19–26 |
| ▪ Model with linear systems in three (or more) variables | 29–30 |

### Section 6.4

|  | Review Exercises |
|---|---|
| ▪ Find the form of the partial fraction decomposition of a rational expression in the following cases: |  |
| ▪ Denominator contains distinct linear factors | 31–32 |
| ▪ Denominator contains repeated linear factors | 33–34 |
| ▪ Denominator contains distinct quadratic factors | 35–36 |
| ▪ Denominator contains repeated quadratic factors | 37–38 |
| ▪ Find the partial fraction decomposition of a rational expression in the above cases | 31–38 |

### Section 6.5

|  | Review Exercises |
|---|---|
| ▪ Graph the solution of an inequality | 39–44 |
| ▪ Graph the solution of a system of inequalities | 45–46, 49–50 |
| ▪ Graph the solution of a system of linear inequalities | 47–48, 51–52 |

## ▼ EXERCISES

**1–4** ■ Two equations and their graphs are given. Find the intersection point(s) of the graphs by solving the system.

**1.** $\begin{cases} 2x + 3y = 7 \\ x - 2y = 0 \end{cases}$   **2.** $\begin{cases} 3x + y = 8 \\ y = x^2 - 5x \end{cases}$

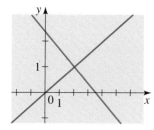   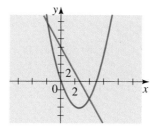

**3.** $\begin{cases} x^2 + y = 2 \\ x^2 - 3x - y = 0 \end{cases}$   **4.** $\begin{cases} x - y = -2 \\ x^2 + y^2 - 4y = 4 \end{cases}$

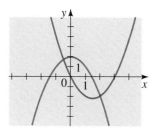   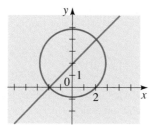

**5–10** ■ Solve the system of equations and graph the lines.

**5.** $\begin{cases} 3x - y = 5 \\ 2x + y = 5 \end{cases}$   **6.** $\begin{cases} y = 2x + 6 \\ y = -x + 3 \end{cases}$

**7.** $\begin{cases} 2x - 7y = 28 \\ y = \frac{2}{7}x - 4 \end{cases}$   **8.** $\begin{cases} 6x - 8y = 15 \\ -\frac{3}{2}x + 2y = -4 \end{cases}$

**9.** $\begin{cases} 2x - y = 1 \\ x + 3y = 10 \\ 3x + 4y = 15 \end{cases}$   **10.** $\begin{cases} 2x + 5y = 9 \\ -x + 3y = 1 \\ 7x - 2y = 14 \end{cases}$

**11–14** ■ Solve the system of equations.

**11.** $\begin{cases} y = x^2 + 2x \\ y = 6 + x \end{cases}$   **12.** $\begin{cases} x^2 + y^2 = 8 \\ y = x + 2 \end{cases}$

**13.** $\begin{cases} 3x + \dfrac{4}{y} = 6 \\ x - \dfrac{8}{y} = 4 \end{cases}$   **14.** $\begin{cases} x^2 + y^2 = 10 \\ x^2 + 2y^2 - 7y = 0 \end{cases}$

**15–18** ■ Use a graphing device to solve the system, correct to the nearest hundredth.

**15.** $\begin{cases} 0.32x + 0.43y = 0 \\ 7x - 12y = 341 \end{cases}$   **16.** $\begin{cases} \sqrt{12}\,x - 3\sqrt{2}\,y = 660 \\ 7137x + 3931y = 20{,}000 \end{cases}$

**17.** $\begin{cases} x - y^2 = 10 \\ x = \frac{1}{22}y + 12 \end{cases}$   **18.** $\begin{cases} y = 5^x + x \\ y = x^5 + 5 \end{cases}$

**19–26** ■ Find the complete solution of the system, or show that the system has no solution.

**19.** $\begin{cases} x + y + 2z = 6 \\ 2x \quad\; + 5z = 12 \\ x + 2y + 3z = 9 \end{cases}$   **20.** $\begin{cases} x - 2y + 3z = 1 \\ x - 3y - z = 0 \\ 2x \quad\; - 6z = 6 \end{cases}$

**21.** $\begin{cases} x - 2y + 3z = 1 \\ 2x - y + z = 3 \\ 2x - 7y + 11z = 2 \end{cases}$   **22.** $\begin{cases} x + y + z + w = 2 \\ 2x \quad\; - 3z \quad\; = 5 \\ x - 2y \quad\; + 4w = 9 \\ x + y + 2z + 3w = 5 \end{cases}$

**23.** $\begin{cases} x - 3y + z = 4 \\ 4x - y + 15z = 5 \end{cases}$   **24.** $\begin{cases} 2x - 3y + 4z = 3 \\ 4x - 5y + 9z = 13 \\ 2x \quad\; + 7z = 0 \end{cases}$

**25.** $\begin{cases} -x + 4y + z = 8 \\ 2x - 6y + z = -9 \\ x - 6y - 4z = -15 \end{cases}$   **26.** $\begin{cases} x \quad\; - z + w = 2 \\ 2x + y \quad\; - 2w = 12 \\ 3y + z + w = 4 \\ x + y - z \quad\; = 10 \end{cases}$

**27.** Eleanor has two children, Kieran and Siobhan. Kieran is 4 years older than Siobhan, and the sum of their ages is 22. How old are the children?

**28.** A man invests his savings in two accounts, one paying 6% interest per year and the other paying 7%. He has twice as much invested in the 7% account as in the 6% account, and his annual interest income is $600. How much is invested in each account?

**29.** A piggy bank contains 50 coins, all of them nickels, dimes, or quarters. The total value of the coins is $5.60, and the value of the dimes is five times the value of the nickels. How many coins of each type are there?

**30.** Tornie is a commercial fisherman who trolls for salmon on the British Columbia coast. One day he catches a total of 25 fish of three salmon species: coho, sockeye, and pink. He catches three more coho than the other two species combined; moreover, he catches twice as many coho as sockeye. How many fish of each species has he caught?

**31–38** ■ Find the partial fraction decomposition of the rational function.

**31.** $\dfrac{3x + 1}{x^2 - 2x - 15}$   **32.** $\dfrac{8}{x^3 - 4x}$

**33.** $\dfrac{2x - 4}{x(x - 1)^2}$   **34.** $\dfrac{6x - 4}{x^3 - 2x^2 - 4x + 8}$

**35.** $\dfrac{2x - 1}{x^3 + x}$   **36.** $\dfrac{5x^2 - 3x + 10}{x^4 + x^2 - 2}$

**37.** $\dfrac{3x^2 - x + 6}{(x^2 + 2)^2}$   **38.** $\dfrac{x^2 + x + 1}{x(x^2 + 1)^2}$

**39–40** ▪ An equation and its graph are given. Find an inequality whose solution is the shaded region.

**39.** $x + y^2 = 4$

**40.** $x^2 + y^2 = 8$

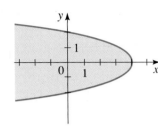

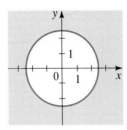

**41–44** ▪ Graph the inequality.

**41.** $3x + y \le 6$

**42.** $y \ge x^2 - 3$

**43.** $x^2 + y^2 > 9$

**44.** $x - y^2 < 4$

**45–48** ▪ The figure shows the graphs of the equations corresponding to the given inequalities. Shade the solution set of the system of inequalities.

**45.** $\begin{cases} y \ge x^2 - 3x \\ y \le \frac{1}{3}x - 1 \end{cases}$

**46.** $\begin{cases} y \ge x - 1 \\ x^2 + y^2 \le 1 \end{cases}$

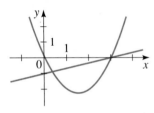

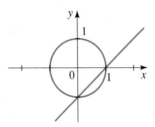

**47.** $\begin{cases} x + y \ge 2 \\ y - x \le 2 \\ x \le 3 \end{cases}$

**48.** $\begin{cases} y \ge -2x \\ y \le 2x \\ y \le -\frac{1}{2}x + 2 \end{cases}$

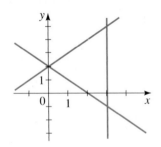

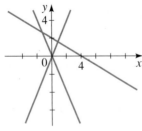

**49–52** ▪ Graph the solution set of the system of inequalities. Find the coordinates of all vertices, and determine whether the solution set is bounded or unbounded.

**49.** $\begin{cases} x^2 + y^2 < 9 \\ x + y < 0 \end{cases}$

**50.** $\begin{cases} y - x^2 \ge 4 \\ y < 20 \end{cases}$

**51.** $\begin{cases} x \ge 0, y \ge 0 \\ x + 2y \le 12 \\ y \le x + 4 \end{cases}$

**52.** $\begin{cases} x \ge 4 \\ x + y \ge 24 \\ x \le 2y + 12 \end{cases}$

**53–54** ▪ Solve for $x$, $y$, and $z$ in terms of $a$, $b$, and $c$.

**53.** $\begin{cases} -x + y + z = a \\ x - y + z = b \\ x + y - z = c \end{cases}$

**54.** $\begin{cases} ax + by + cz = a - b + c \\ bx + by + cz = c \\ cx + cy + cz = c \end{cases}$   $(a \ne b, b \ne c, c \ne 0)$

**55.** For what values of $k$ do the following three lines have a common point of intersection?

$$x + y = 12$$
$$kx - y = 0$$
$$y - x = 2k$$

**56.** For what value of $k$ does the following system have infinitely many solutions?

$$\begin{cases} kx + y + z = 0 \\ x + 2y + kz = 0 \\ -x + \phantom{2y +} 3z = 0 \end{cases}$$

8. **Manufacturing Calculators**  A manufacturer of calculators produces two models: standard and scientific. Long-term demand for the two models mandates that the company manufacture at least 100 standard and 80 scientific calculators each day. However, because of limitations on production capacity, no more than 200 standard and 170 scientific calculators can be made daily. To satisfy a shipping contract, a total of at least 200 calculators must be shipped every day.

   (a) If the production cost is $5 for a standard calculator and $7 for a scientific one, how many of each model should be produced daily to minimize this cost?

   (b) If each standard calculator results in a $2 loss but each scientific one produces a $5 profit, how many of each model should be made daily to maximize profit?

9. **Shipping Stereos**  An electronics discount chain has a sale on a certain brand of stereo. The chain has stores in Santa Monica and El Toro and warehouses in Long Beach and Pasadena. To satisfy rush orders, 15 sets must be shipped from the warehouses to the Santa Monica store, and 19 must be shipped to the El Toro store. The cost of shipping a set is $5 from Long Beach to Santa Monica, $6 from Long Beach to El Toro, $4 from Pasadena to Santa Monica, and $5.50 from Pasadena to El Toro. If the Long Beach warehouse has 24 sets and the Pasadena warehouse has 18 sets in stock, how many sets should be shipped from each warehouse to each store to fill the orders at a minimum shipping cost?

10. **Delivering Plywood**  A man owns two building supply stores, one on the east side and one on the west side of a city. Two customers order some $\frac{1}{2}$-inch plywood. Customer A needs 50 sheets, and customer B needs 70 sheets. The east-side store has 80 sheets, and the west-side store has 45 sheets of this plywood in stock. The east-side store's delivery costs per sheet are $0.50 to customer A and $0.60 to customer B. The west-side store's delivery costs per sheet are $0.40 to A and $0.55 to B. How many sheets should be shipped from each store to each customer to minimize delivery costs?

11. **Packaging Nuts**  A confectioner sells two types of nut mixtures. The standard-mixture package contains 100 g of cashews and 200 g of peanuts and sells for $1.95. The deluxe-mixture package contains 150 g of cashews and 50 g of peanuts and sells for $2.25. The confectioner has 15 kg of cashews and 20 kg of peanuts available. On the basis of past sales, the confectioner needs to have at least as many standard as deluxe packages available. How many bags of each mixture should he package to maximize his revenue?

12. **Feeding Lab Rabbits**  A biologist wishes to feed laboratory rabbits a mixture of two types of foods. Type I contains 8 g of fat, 12 g of carbohydrate, and 2 g of protein per ounce. Type II contains 12 g of fat, 12 g of carbohydrate, and 1 g of protein per ounce. Type I costs $0.20 per ounce and type II costs $0.30 per ounce. The rabbits each receive a daily minimum of 24 g of fat, 36 g of carbohydrate, and 4 g of protein, but get no more than 5 oz of food per day. How many ounces of each food type should be fed to each rabbit daily to satisfy the dietary requirements at minimum cost?

13. **Investing in Bonds**  A woman wishes to invest $12,000 in three types of bonds: municipal bonds paying 7% interest per year, bank investment certificates paying 8%, and high-risk bonds paying 12%. For tax reasons she wants the amount invested in municipal bonds to be at least three times the amount invested in bank certificates. To keep her level of risk manageable, she will invest no more than $2000 in high-risk bonds. How much should she invest in each type of bond to maximize her annual interest yield?  [*Hint:* Let $x$ = amount in municipal bonds and $y$ = amount in bank certificates. Then the amount in high-risk bonds will be $12,000 - x - y$.]

14. **Annual Interest Yield**  Refer to Problem 13. Suppose the investor decides to increase the maximum invested in high-risk bonds to $3000 but leaves the other conditions unchanged. By how much will her maximum possible interest yield increase?

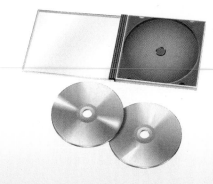

15. **Business Strategy**  A small software company publishes computer games and educational and utility software. Their business strategy is to market a total of 36 new programs each year, at least four of these being games. The number of utility programs published is never more than twice the number of educational programs. On average, the company makes an annual profit of $5000 on each computer game, $8000 on each educational program, and $6000 on each utility program. How many of each type of software should they publish annually for maximum profit?

**16. Feasible Region**    All parts of this problem refer to the following feasible region and objective function.

$$\begin{cases} x \geq 0 \\ x \geq y \\ x + 2y \leq 12 \\ x + \ y \leq 10 \end{cases}$$

$$P = x + 4y$$

**(a)** Graph the feasible region.

**(b)** On your graph from part (a), sketch the graphs of the linear equations obtained by setting $P$ equal to 40, 36, 32, and 28.

**(c)** If you continue to decrease the value of $P$, at which vertex of the feasible region will these lines first touch the feasible region?

**(d)** Verify that the maximum value of $P$ on the feasible region occurs at the vertex you chose in part (c).

# CHAPTER 7

# Matrices and Determinants

© 2006 Mirage Studios, Inc. Game © 2006 Ubisoft Entertainment

**Fantastic action?** The images and action in a video game are out of this world, allowing us to enjoy fantasies of speed, power, and dexterity that are not achievable in real life. But the real action in a video game takes place at the digital level. An image, such as that of the ninja warrior pictured here, is stored in the computer memory as a rectangular array of numbers called a matrix. Each number in the matrix determines the color and brightness of a pixel in the monitor, so the matrix "draws" the image on the monitor. To change an image—to stretch, squeeze, tilt, rotate, or otherwise distort it—the matrix of the image is changed or combined with other matrices using the rules of matrix algebra (see *Focus on Modeling: Computer Graphics*, pages 547–550). One of the key uses of matrices is the solution of systems of linear equations. In this chapter we learn how a system of linear equations can be expressed as a single matrix equation and then solved by using the rules of matrix algebra.

## 7.1 | Matrices and Systems of Linear Equations

**LEARNING OBJECTIVES**

After completing this section, you will be able to:

■ Find the augmented matrix of a linear system
■ Solve a linear system using elementary row operations
■ Solve a linear system using the row-echelon form of its matrix
■ Solve a system using the reduced row-echelon form of its matrix
■ Determine the number of solutions of a linear system from the row-echelon form of its matrix
■ Model using linear systems

A *matrix* is simply a rectangular array of numbers. Matrices* are used to organize information into categories that correspond to the rows and columns of the matrix. For example, a scientist might organize information on a population of endangered whales as follows:

$$\begin{array}{c c} & \begin{array}{c c c} \text{Immature} & \text{Juvenile} & \text{Adult} \end{array} \\ \begin{array}{c} \text{Male} \\ \text{Female} \end{array} & \begin{bmatrix} 12 & 52 & 18 \\ 15 & 42 & 11 \end{bmatrix} \end{array}$$

This is a compact way of saying there are 12 immature males, 15 immature females, 18 adult males, and so on.

In this section we represent a linear system by a matrix, called the *augmented matrix* of the system:

**Linear system**        **Augmented matrix**

$$\begin{cases} 2x - y = 5 \\ x + 4y = 7 \end{cases} \quad \begin{array}{l} \text{Equation 1} \\ \text{Equation 2} \end{array} \quad \begin{bmatrix} 2 & -1 & 5 \\ 1 & 4 & 7 \end{bmatrix}$$
$$\qquad\qquad\qquad\qquad\qquad x \quad y$$

The augmented matrix contains the same information as the system, but in a simpler form. The operations we learned for solving systems of equations can now be performed on the augmented matrix.

### ■ Matrices

We begin by defining the various elements that make up a matrix.

---

*The plural of *matrix* is *matrices*.

### THE SOLUTIONS OF A LINEAR SYSTEM IN ROW-ECHELON FORM

Suppose the augmented matrix of a system of linear equations has been transformed by Gaussian elimination into row-echelon form. Then exactly one of the following is true.

1. **No solution.** If the row-echelon form contains a row that represents the equation $0 = c$, where $c$ is not zero, then the system has no solution. A system with no solution is called **inconsistent**.

2. **One solution.** If each variable in the row-echelon form is a leading variable, then the system has exactly one solution, which we find using back-substitution or Gauss-Jordan elimination.

3. **Infinitely many solutions.** If the variables in the row-echelon form are not all leading variables and if the system is not inconsistent, then it has infinitely many solutions. In this case the system is called **dependent**. We solve the system by putting the matrix in reduced row-echelon form and then expressing the leading variables in terms of the nonleading variables. The nonleading variables may take on any real numbers as their values.

The matrices below, all in row-echelon form, illustrate the three cases described above.

**No solution**

$$\begin{bmatrix} 1 & 2 & 5 & 7 \\ 0 & 1 & 3 & 4 \\ 0 & 0 & 0 & 1 \end{bmatrix}$$

Last equation says $0 = 1$.

**One solution**

$$\begin{bmatrix} 1 & 6 & -1 & 3 \\ 0 & 1 & 2 & -2 \\ 0 & 0 & 1 & 8 \end{bmatrix}$$

Each variable is a leading variable.

**Infinitely many solutions**

$$\begin{bmatrix} 1 & 2 & -3 & 1 \\ 0 & 1 & 5 & -2 \\ 0 & 0 & 0 & 0 \end{bmatrix}$$

$z$ is not a leading variable.

▶ **EXAMPLE 5** | A System with No Solution

Solve the system.

$$\begin{cases} x - 3y + 2z = 12 \\ 2x - 5y + 5z = 14 \\ x - 2y + 3z = 20 \end{cases}$$

▼ **SOLUTION**  We transform the system into row-echelon form.

$$\begin{bmatrix} 1 & -3 & 2 & 12 \\ 2 & -5 & 5 & 14 \\ 1 & -2 & 3 & 20 \end{bmatrix} \xrightarrow[R_3 - R_1 \to R_3]{R_2 - 2R_1 \to R_2} \begin{bmatrix} 1 & -3 & 2 & 12 \\ 0 & 1 & 1 & -10 \\ 0 & 1 & 1 & 8 \end{bmatrix}$$

$$\xrightarrow{R_3 - R_2 \to R_3} \begin{bmatrix} 1 & -3 & 2 & 12 \\ 0 & 1 & 1 & -10 \\ 0 & 0 & 0 & 18 \end{bmatrix} \xrightarrow{\frac{1}{18}R_3} \begin{bmatrix} 1 & -3 & 2 & 12 \\ 0 & 1 & 1 & -10 \\ 0 & 0 & 0 & 1 \end{bmatrix}$$

This last matrix is in row-echelon form, so we can stop the Gaussian elimination process. Now if we translate the last row back into equation form, we get $0x + 0y + 0z = 1$, or $0 = 1$, which is false. No matter what values we pick for $x$, $y$, and $z$, the last equation will never be a true statement. This means that the system *has no solution*.

✎ **Practice what you've learned: Do Exercise 29.**  ▲

```
ref([A])
[[1 -2.5 2.5 7  ]
 [0 1    1   -10]
 [0 0    0   1  ]]
```

**FIGURE 3**

Figure 3 shows the row-echelon form produced by a TI-83 calculator for the augmented matrix in Example 5. You should check that this gives the same solution.

▶ **EXAMPLE 6** | A System with Infinitely Many Solutions

Find the complete solution of the system.

$$\begin{cases} -3x - 5y + 36z = 10 \\ -x \quad\quad + 7z = 5 \\ x + y - 10z = -4 \end{cases}$$

▼ **SOLUTION** We transform the system into reduced row-echelon form.

$$\begin{bmatrix} -3 & -5 & 36 & 10 \\ -1 & 0 & 7 & 5 \\ 1 & 1 & -10 & -4 \end{bmatrix} \xrightarrow{R_1 \leftrightarrow R_3} \begin{bmatrix} 1 & 1 & -10 & -4 \\ -1 & 0 & 7 & 5 \\ -3 & -5 & 36 & 10 \end{bmatrix}$$

$$\xrightarrow[R_3 + 3R_1 \to R_3]{R_2 + R_1 \to R_2} \begin{bmatrix} 1 & 1 & -10 & -4 \\ 0 & 1 & -3 & 1 \\ 0 & -2 & 6 & -2 \end{bmatrix} \xrightarrow{R_3 + 2R_2 \to R_3} \begin{bmatrix} 1 & 1 & -10 & -4 \\ 0 & 1 & -3 & 1 \\ 0 & 0 & 0 & 0 \end{bmatrix}$$

$$\xrightarrow{R_1 - R_2 \to R_1} \begin{bmatrix} 1 & 0 & -7 & -5 \\ 0 & 1 & -3 & 1 \\ 0 & 0 & 0 & 0 \end{bmatrix}$$

The third row corresponds to the equation $0 = 0$. This equation is always true, no matter what values are used for $x$, $y$, and $z$. Since the equation adds no new information about the variables, we can drop it from the system. So the last matrix corresponds to the system

Reduced row-echelon form on the TI-83 calculator:

```
rref([A])
  [[1 0 -7 -5]
   [0 1 -3 1 ]
   [0 0 0  0 ]]
```

$$\begin{cases} x \quad\quad - 7z = -5 \quad\text{Equation 1} \\ \quad y - 3z = 1 \quad\text{Equation 2} \end{cases}$$

Leading variables

Now we solve for the leading variables $x$ and $y$ in terms of the nonleading variable $z$:

$$x = 7z - 5 \quad\text{Solve for x in Equation 1}$$
$$y = 3z + 1 \quad\text{Solve for y in Equation 2}$$

To obtain the complete solution, we let $t$ represent any real number, and we express $x$, $y$, and $z$ in terms of $t$:

$$x = 7t - 5$$
$$y = 3t + 1$$
$$z = t$$

We can also write the solution as the ordered triple $(7t - 5, 3t + 1, t)$, where $t$ is any real number.

✎ **Practice what you've learned: Do Exercise 31.** ▲

In Example 6, to get specific solutions, we give a specific value to $t$. For example, if $t = 1$, then

$$x = 7(1) - 5 = 2$$
$$y = 3(1) + 1 = 4$$
$$z = 1$$

Here are some other solutions of the system obtained by substituting other values for the parameter $t$.

| Parameter $t$ | Solution $(7t - 5, 3t + 1, t)$ |
|:---:|:---:|
| $-1$ | $(-12, -2, -1)$ |
| $0$ | $(-5, 1, 0)$ |
| $2$ | $(9, 7, 2)$ |
| $5$ | $(30, 16, 5)$ |

▶ **EXAMPLE 7** | A System with Infinitely Many Solutions

Find the complete solution of the system.

$$\begin{cases} x + 2y - 3z - 4w = 10 \\ x + 3y - 3z - 4w = 15 \\ 2x + 2y - 6z - 8w = 10 \end{cases}$$

▼ **SOLUTION** We transform the system into reduced row-echelon form.

$$\begin{bmatrix} 1 & 2 & -3 & -4 & 10 \\ 1 & 3 & -3 & -4 & 15 \\ 2 & 2 & -6 & -8 & 10 \end{bmatrix} \xrightarrow[R_3 - 2R_1 \to R_3]{R_2 - R_1 \to R_2} \begin{bmatrix} 1 & 2 & -3 & -4 & 10 \\ 0 & 1 & 0 & 0 & 5 \\ 0 & -2 & 0 & 0 & -10 \end{bmatrix}$$

$$\xrightarrow{R_3 + 2R_2 \to R_3} \begin{bmatrix} 1 & 2 & -3 & -4 & 10 \\ 0 & 1 & 0 & 0 & 5 \\ 0 & 0 & 0 & 0 & 0 \end{bmatrix} \xrightarrow{R_1 - 2R_2 \to R_1} \begin{bmatrix} 1 & 0 & -3 & -4 & 0 \\ 0 & 1 & 0 & 0 & 5 \\ 0 & 0 & 0 & 0 & 0 \end{bmatrix}$$

This is in reduced row-echelon form. Since the last row represents the equation $0 = 0$, we may discard it. So the last matrix corresponds to the system

$$\begin{cases} x \quad\quad -3z - 4w = 0 \\ \quad\; y \quad\quad\quad\quad = 5 \end{cases}$$

Leading variables

To obtain the complete solution, we solve for the leading variables $x$ and $y$ in terms of the nonleading variables $z$ and $w$, and we let $z$ and $w$ be any real numbers. Thus, the complete solution is

$$\begin{aligned} x &= 3s + 4t \\ y &= 5 \\ z &= s \\ w &= t \end{aligned}$$

where $s$ and $t$ are any real numbers.

✎ **Practice what you've learned: Do Exercise 51.** ▲

Note that $s$ and $t$ do *not* have to be the *same* real number in the solution for Example 7. We can choose arbitrary values for each if we wish to construct a specific solution to the system. For example, if we let $s = 1$ and $t = 2$, then we get the solution $(11, 5, 1, 2)$. You should check that this does indeed satisfy all three of the original equations in Example 7.

Examples 6 and 7 illustrate this general fact: If a system in row-echelon form has $n$ nonzero equations in $m$ variables $(m > n)$, then the complete solution will have $m - n$ nonleading variables. For instance, in Example 6 we arrived at *two* nonzero equations in the *three* variables $x$, $y$, and $z$, which gave us $3 - 2 = 1$ nonleading variable.

## ■ Modeling with Linear Systems

Linear equations, often containing hundreds or even thousands of variables, occur frequently in the applications of algebra to the sciences and to other fields. For now, let's consider an example that involves only three variables.

▶ **EXAMPLE 8** | Nutritional Analysis Using a System of Linear Equations

A nutritionist is performing an experiment on student volunteers. He wishes to feed one of his subjects a daily diet that consists of a combination of three commercial diet foods: MiniCal, LiquiFast, and SlimQuick. For the experiment it is important that the subject consume exactly 500 mg of potassium, 75 g of protein, and 1150 units of vitamin D every day. The amounts of these nutrients in one ounce of each food are given in the table. How many ounces of each food should the subject eat every day to satisfy the nutrient requirements exactly?

|                    | **MiniCal** | **LiquiFast** | **SlimQuick** |
|--------------------|-------------|---------------|---------------|
| **Potassium (mg)** | 50          | 75            | 10            |
| **Protein (g)**    | 5           | 10            | 3             |
| **Vitamin D (units)** | 90       | 100           | 50            |

▼ **SOLUTION** Let $x$, $y$, and $z$ represent the number of ounces of MiniCal, LiquiFast, and SlimQuick, respectively, that the subject should eat every day. This means that he will get $50x$ mg of potassium from MiniCal, $75y$ mg from LiquiFast, and $10z$ mg from SlimQuick, for a total of $50x + 75y + 10z$ mg potassium in all. Since the potassium requirement is 500 mg, we get the first equation below. Similar reasoning for the protein and vitamin D requirements leads to the system

$$\begin{cases} 50x + 75y + 10z = 500 & \text{Potassium} \\ 5x + 10y + 3z = 75 & \text{Protein} \\ 90x + 100y + 50z = 1150 & \text{Vitamin D} \end{cases}$$

Dividing the first equation by 5 and the third one by 10 gives the system

$$\begin{cases} 10x + 15y + 2z = 100 \\ 5x + 10y + 3z = 75 \\ 9x + 10y + 5z = 115 \end{cases}$$

We can solve this system using Gaussian elimination, or we can use a graphing calculator to find the reduced row-echelon form of the augmented matrix of the system. Using the `rref` command on the TI-83, we get the output in Figure 4. From the reduced row-echelon form we see that $x = 5$, $y = 2$, $z = 10$. The subject should be fed 5 oz of MiniCal, 2 oz of LiquiFast, and 10 oz of SlimQuick every day.

✎ **Practice what you've learned: Do Exercise 55.** ▲

A more practical application might involve dozens of foods and nutrients rather than just three. Such problems lead to systems with large numbers of variables and equations. Computers or graphing calculators are essential for solving such large systems.

```
rref([A])
  [[1 0 0 5 ]
   [0 1 0 2 ]
   [0 0 1 10]]
```

**FIGURE 4**

---

**Check Your Answer**

$x = 5$, $y = 2$, $z = 10$:

$$\begin{cases} 10(5) + 15(2) + 2(10) = 100 \\ 5(5) + 10(2) + 3(10) = 75 \\ 9(5) + 10(2) + 5(10) = 115 \end{cases} ✔$$

a value between 0 and 7 depending on which gray square in the scale most closely matches the "darkness" of the cell. (If the cell is not uniformly gray, an average value is assigned.) The values are stored in the matrix shown in Figure 3(c). The digital image corresponding to this matrix is shown in Figure 3(d). Obviously the grid that we have used is far too coarse to provide good image resolution. In practice, currently available high-resolution digital cameras use matrices with dimension as large as 2048 × 2048.

Once the image is stored as a matrix, it can be manipulated by using matrix operations. For example, to darken the image, we add a constant to each entry in the matrix; to lighten the image, we subtract a constant. To increase the contrast, we darken the darker areas and lighten the lighter areas, so we could add 1 to each entry that is 4, 5, or 6 and subtract 1 from each entry that is 1, 2, or 3. (Note that we cannot darken an entry of 7 or lighten a 0.) Applying this process to the matrix in Figure 3(c) produces the new matrix in Figure 4(a). This generates the high-contrast image shown in Figure 4(b).

$$\begin{bmatrix} 0 & 0 & 0 & 0 & 0 & 0 & 0 & 1 & 1 & 0 \\ 0 & 0 & 0 & 0 & 0 & 0 & 5 & 7 & 6 & 1 \\ 0 & 0 & 0 & 0 & 1 & 2 & 2 & 6 & 6 & 2 \\ 0 & 0 & 0 & 0 & 2 & 6 & 5 & 7 & 2 & 1 \\ 0 & 0 & 0 & 0 & 0 & 1 & 2 & 1 & 1 & 0 \\ 0 & 0 & 0 & 0 & 0 & 2 & 2 & 1 & 0 & 0 \\ 0 & 0 & 0 & 0 & 0 & 0 & 5 & 0 & 0 & 0 \\ 0 & 0 & 0 & 0 & 1 & 1 & 5 & 1 & 1 & 1 \\ 1 & 1 & 2 & 6 & 6 & 1 & 1 & 2 & 5 & 5 \\ 2 & 2 & 2 & 5 & 2 & 1 & 2 & 2 & 2 & 5 \end{bmatrix}$$

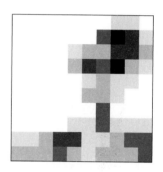

**FIGURE 4**    (a) Matrix modified to increase contrast    (b) High contrast image

Other ways of representing and manipulating images using matrices are discussed in *Focus on Modeling* on pages 547–550.

# 7.2 EXERCISES

## ▼ CONCEPTS

**1.** We can add (or subtract) two matrices only if they have the same _____.

**2. (a)** We can multiply two matrices only if the number of

_____ in the first matrix is the same as the number of

_____ in the second matrix.

**(b)** If $A$ is a $3 \times 3$ matrix and $B$ is a $4 \times 3$ matrix, which of the following matrix multiplications are possible?

(i) $AB$    (ii) $BA$    (iii) $AA$    (iv) $BB$

**3.** Which of the following operations can we perform for a matrix $A$ of any dimension?

(i) $A + A$    (ii) $2A$    (iii) $A \cdot A$

**4.** Fill in the missing entries in the product matrix.

$$\begin{bmatrix} 3 & 1 & 2 \\ -1 & 2 & 0 \\ 1 & 3 & -2 \end{bmatrix} \begin{bmatrix} -1 & 3 & -2 \\ 3 & -2 & -1 \\ 2 & 1 & 0 \end{bmatrix} = \begin{bmatrix} 4 & \blacksquare & -7 \\ 7 & -7 & \blacksquare \\ \blacksquare & -5 & -5 \end{bmatrix}$$

## ▼ SKILLS

**5–6** ▪ Determine whether the matrices $A$ and $B$ are equal.

**5.** $A = \begin{bmatrix} 1 & -2 & 0 \\ \frac{1}{2} & 6 & 0 \end{bmatrix}$    $B = \begin{bmatrix} 1 & -2 \\ \frac{1}{2} & 6 \end{bmatrix}$

**6.** $A = \begin{bmatrix} \frac{1}{4} & \ln 1 \\ 2 & 3 \end{bmatrix}$    $B = \begin{bmatrix} 0.25 & 0 \\ \sqrt{4} & \frac{6}{2} \end{bmatrix}$

**7–14** ▪ Perform the matrix operation, or if it is impossible, explain why.

**7.** $\begin{bmatrix} 2 & 6 \\ -5 & 3 \end{bmatrix} + \begin{bmatrix} -1 & -3 \\ 6 & 2 \end{bmatrix}$

**8.** $\begin{bmatrix} 0 & 1 & 1 \\ 1 & 1 & 0 \end{bmatrix} - \begin{bmatrix} 2 & 1 & -1 \\ 1 & 3 & -2 \end{bmatrix}$

**9.** $3 \begin{bmatrix} 1 & 2 \\ 4 & -1 \\ 1 & 0 \end{bmatrix}$

**10.** $2 \begin{bmatrix} 1 & 1 & 0 \\ 1 & 0 & 1 \\ 0 & 1 & 1 \end{bmatrix} + \begin{bmatrix} 1 & 1 \\ 2 & 1 \\ 3 & 1 \end{bmatrix}$

**11.** $\begin{bmatrix} 2 & 6 \\ 1 & 3 \\ 2 & 4 \end{bmatrix} \begin{bmatrix} 1 & -2 \\ 3 & 6 \\ -2 & 0 \end{bmatrix}$

**12.** $\begin{bmatrix} 2 & 1 & 2 \\ 6 & 3 & 4 \end{bmatrix} \begin{bmatrix} 1 & -2 \\ 3 & 6 \\ -2 & 0 \end{bmatrix}$

**13.** $\begin{bmatrix} 1 & 2 \\ -1 & 4 \end{bmatrix}\begin{bmatrix} 1 & -2 & 3 \\ 2 & 2 & -1 \end{bmatrix}$  **14.** $\begin{bmatrix} 2 & -3 \\ 0 & 1 \\ 1 & 2 \end{bmatrix}\begin{bmatrix} 5 \\ 1 \end{bmatrix}$

**15–20** ■ Solve the matrix equation for the unknown matrix $X$, or explain why no solution exists.

$$A = \begin{bmatrix} 4 & 6 \\ 1 & 3 \end{bmatrix} \qquad B = \begin{bmatrix} 2 & 5 \\ 3 & 7 \end{bmatrix}$$

$$C = \begin{bmatrix} 2 & 3 \\ 1 & 0 \\ 0 & 2 \end{bmatrix} \qquad D = \begin{bmatrix} 10 & 20 \\ 30 & 20 \\ 10 & 0 \end{bmatrix}$$

**15.** $2X + A = B$      **16.** $3X - B = C$

**17.** $2(B - X) = D$      **18.** $5(X - C) = D$

**19.** $\frac{1}{5}(X + D) = C$      **20.** $2A = B - 3X$

**21–34** ■ The matrices $A$, $B$, $C$, $D$, $E$, $F$, $G$ and $H$ are defined as follows.

$$A = \begin{bmatrix} 2 & -5 \\ 0 & 7 \end{bmatrix} \qquad B = \begin{bmatrix} 3 & \frac{1}{2} & 5 \\ 1 & -1 & 3 \end{bmatrix} \qquad C = \begin{bmatrix} 2 & -\frac{5}{2} & 0 \\ 0 & 2 & -3 \end{bmatrix}$$

$$D = \begin{bmatrix} 7 & 3 \end{bmatrix} \qquad E = \begin{bmatrix} 1 \\ 2 \\ 0 \end{bmatrix} \qquad F = \begin{bmatrix} 1 & 0 & 0 \\ 0 & 1 & 0 \\ 0 & 0 & 1 \end{bmatrix}$$

$$G = \begin{bmatrix} 5 & -3 & 10 \\ 6 & 1 & 0 \\ -5 & 2 & 2 \end{bmatrix} \qquad H = \begin{bmatrix} 3 & 1 \\ 2 & -1 \end{bmatrix}$$

Carry out the indicated algebraic operation, or explain why it cannot be performed.

**21.** (a) $B + C$      (b) $B + F$

**22.** (a) $C - B$      (b) $2C - 6B$

**23.** (a) $5A$      (b) $C - 5A$

**24.** (a) $3B + 2C$      (b) $2H + D$

**25.** (a) $AD$      (b) $DA$

**26.** (a) $DH$      (b) $HD$

**27.** (a) $AH$      (b) $HA$

**28.** (a) $BC$      (b) $BF$

**29.** (a) $GF$      (b) $GE$

**30.** (a) $B^2$      (b) $F^2$

**31.** (a) $A^2$      (b) $A^3$

**32.** (a) $(DA)B$      (b) $D(AB)$

**33.** (a) $ABE$      (b) $AHE$

**34.** (a) $DB + DC$      (b) $BF + FE$

**35–38** ■ Solve for $x$ and $y$.

**35.** $\begin{bmatrix} x & 2y \\ 4 & 6 \end{bmatrix} = \begin{bmatrix} 2 & -2 \\ 2x & -6y \end{bmatrix}$    **36.** $3\begin{bmatrix} x & y \\ y & x \end{bmatrix} = \begin{bmatrix} 6 & -9 \\ -9 & 6 \end{bmatrix}$

**37.** $2\begin{bmatrix} x & y \\ x+y & x-y \end{bmatrix} = \begin{bmatrix} 2 & -4 \\ -2 & 6 \end{bmatrix}$

**38.** $\begin{bmatrix} x & y \\ -y & x \end{bmatrix} - \begin{bmatrix} y & x \\ x & -y \end{bmatrix} = \begin{bmatrix} 4 & -4 \\ -6 & 6 \end{bmatrix}$

**39–42** ■ Write the system of equations as a matrix equation (see Example 6).

**39.** $\begin{cases} 2x - 5y = 7 \\ 3x + 2y = 4 \end{cases}$    **40.** $\begin{cases} 6x - y + z = 12 \\ 2x \quad\;\; + z = 7 \\ \quad\; y - 2z = 4 \end{cases}$

**41.** $\begin{cases} 3x_1 + 2x_2 - x_3 + x_4 = 0 \\ x_1 \quad\quad - x_3 \quad\;\; = 5 \\ \quad\; 3x_2 + x_3 - x_4 = 4 \end{cases}$

**42.** $\begin{cases} x - y + z = 2 \\ 4x - 2y - z = 2 \\ x + y + 5z = 2 \\ -x - y - z = 2 \end{cases}$

**43.** Let

$$A = \begin{bmatrix} 1 & 0 & 6 & -1 \\ 2 & \frac{1}{2} & 4 & 0 \end{bmatrix} \qquad C = \begin{bmatrix} 1 \\ 0 \\ -1 \\ -2 \end{bmatrix}$$

$$B = \begin{bmatrix} 1 & 7 & -9 & 2 \end{bmatrix}$$

Determine which of the following products are defined, and calculate the ones that are:

$$ABC \qquad ACB \qquad BAC$$
$$BCA \qquad CAB \qquad CBA$$

**44.** (a) Prove that if $A$ and $B$ are $2 \times 2$ matrices, then

$$(A + B)^2 = A^2 + AB + BA + B^2$$

(b) If $A$ and $B$ are $2 \times 2$ matrices, is it necessarily true that

$$(A + B)^2 \overset{?}{=} A^2 + 2AB + B^2$$

---

## ▼ APPLICATIONS

**45. Fast-Food Sales** A small fast-food chain with restaurants in Santa Monica, Long Beach, and Anaheim sells only hamburgers, hot dogs, and milk shakes. On a certain day, sales were distributed according to the following matrix.

|  | **Number of items sold** | | |
| --- | --- | --- | --- |
|  | **Santa Monica** | **Long Beach** | **Anaheim** |
| **Hamburgers** | 4000 | 1000 | 3500 |
| **Hot dogs** | 400 | 300 | 200 | = A |
| **Milk shakes** | 700 | 500 | 9000 |

The price of each item is given by the following matrix.

| Hamburger | Hot dog | Milk shake |
| --- | --- | --- |
| [\$0.90 | \$0.80 | \$1.10] = B |

(a) Calculate the product $BA$.

(b) Interpret the entries in the product matrix $BA$.

**46. Car-Manufacturing Profits** A specialty-car manufacturer has plants in Auburn, Biloxi, and Chattanooga. Three models are produced, with daily production given in the following matrix.

**Cars produced each day**

|  | Model K | Model R | Model W |
|---|---|---|---|
| Auburn | 12 | 10 | 0 |
| Biloxi | 4 | 4 | 20 |
| Chattanooga | 8 | 9 | 12 |

$= A$

Because of a wage increase, February profits are lower than January profits. The profit per car is tabulated by model in the following matrix.

|  | January | February |
|---|---|---|
| Model K | $1000 | $500 |
| Model R | $2000 | $1200 |
| Model W | $1500 | $1000 |

$= B$

(a) Calculate $AB$.
(b) Assuming that all cars produced were sold, what was the daily profit in January from the Biloxi plant?
(c) What was the total daily profit (from all three plants) in February?

**47. Canning Tomato Products**   Jaeger Foods produces tomato sauce and tomato paste, canned in small, medium, large, and giant sized cans. The matrix $A$ gives the size (in ounces) of each container.

|  | Small | Medium | Large | Giant |
|---|---|---|---|---|
| Ounces | 6 | 10 | 14 | 28 |

$= A$

The matrix $B$ tabulates one day's production of tomato sauce and tomato paste.

|  | Cans of sauce | Cans of paste |
|---|---|---|
| Small | 2000 | 2500 |
| Medium | 3000 | 1500 |
| Large | 2500 | 1000 |
| Giant | 1000 | 500 |

$= B$

(a) Calculate the product of $AB$.
(b) Interpret the entries in the product matrix $AB$.

**48. Produce Sales**   A farmer's three children, Amy, Beth, and Chad, run three roadside produce stands during the summer months. One weekend they all sell watermelons, yellow squash, and tomatoes. The matrices $A$ and $B$ tabulate the number of pounds of each product sold by each sibling on Saturday and Sunday.

**Saturday**

|  | Melons | Squash | Tomatoes |
|---|---|---|---|
| Amy | 120 | 50 | 60 |
| Beth | 40 | 25 | 30 |
| Chad | 60 | 30 | 20 |

$= A$

**Sunday**

|  | Melons | Squash | Tomatoes |
|---|---|---|---|
| Amy | 100 | 60 | 30 |
| Beth | 35 | 20 | 20 |
| Chad | 60 | 25 | 30 |

$= B$

The matrix $C$ gives the price per pound (in dollars) for each type of produce that they sell.

**Price per pound**

| | |
|---|---|
| Melons | 0.10 |
| Squash | 0.50 |
| Tomatoes | 1.00 |

$= C$

Perform each of the following matrix operations, and interpret the entries in each result.

(a) $AC$   (b) $BC$   (c) $A + B$   (d) $(A + B)C$

**49. Digital Images**   A four-level gray scale is shown below.

0   1   2   3

(a) Use the gray scale to find a $6 \times 6$ matrix that digitally represents the image in the figure.

(b) Find a matrix that represents a darker version of the image in the figure.
(c) The **negative** of an image is obtained by reversing light and dark, as in the negative of a photograph. Find the matrix that represents the negative of the image in the figure. How do you change the elements of the matrix to create the negative?
(d) Increase the contrast of the image by changing each 1 to a 0 and each 2 to a 3 in the matrix you found in part (b). Draw the image represented by the resulting matrix. Does this clarify the image?

(e) Draw the image represented by the matrix $I$. Can you recognize what this is? If you don't, try increasing the contrast.

$$I = \begin{bmatrix} 1 & 2 & 3 & 3 & 2 & 0 \\ 0 & 3 & 0 & 1 & 0 & 1 \\ 1 & 3 & 2 & 3 & 0 & 0 \\ 0 & 3 & 0 & 1 & 0 & 1 \\ 1 & 3 & 3 & 2 & 3 & 0 \\ 0 & 1 & 0 & 1 & 0 & 1 \end{bmatrix}$$

---

## ▼ DISCOVERY • DISCUSSION • WRITING

**50. When Are Both Products Defined?** What must be true about the dimensions of the matrices $A$ and $B$ if both products $AB$ and $BA$ are defined?

**51. Powers of a Matrix** Let

$$A = \begin{bmatrix} 1 & 1 \\ 0 & 1 \end{bmatrix}$$

Calculate $A^2, A^3, A^4, \ldots$ until you detect a pattern. Write a general formula for $A^n$.

**52. Powers of a Matrix** Let $A = \begin{bmatrix} 1 & 1 \\ 1 & 1 \end{bmatrix}$. Calculate $A^2$, $A^3, A^4, \ldots$ until you detect a pattern. Write a general formula for $A^n$.

**53. Square Roots of Matrices** A **square root** of a matrix $B$ is a matrix $A$ with the property that $A^2 = B$. (This is the same definition as for a square root of a number.) Find as many square roots as you can of each matrix:

$$\begin{bmatrix} 4 & 0 \\ 0 & 9 \end{bmatrix} \qquad \begin{bmatrix} 1 & 5 \\ 0 & 9 \end{bmatrix}$$

[*Hint:* If $A = \begin{bmatrix} a & b \\ c & d \end{bmatrix}$, write the equations that $a, b, c,$ and $d$ would have to satisfy if $A$ is the square root of the given matrix.]

## WILL THE SPECIES SURVIVE?

To study how species survive, scientists model their populations by observing the different stages in their life. Scientists consider, for example, the stage at which the animal is fertile, the proportion of the population that reproduces, and the proportion of the young that survive each year. For a certain species there are three stages: immature, juvenile, and adult. An animal is considered immature for the first year of its life, juvenile for the second year, and an adult from then on. Conservation biologists have collected the following field data for this species:

$$A = \begin{array}{c} \phantom{} \\ \begin{matrix} \textbf{Immature} & \textbf{Juvenile} & \textbf{Adult} \end{matrix} \\ \begin{bmatrix} 0 & 0 & 0.4 \\ 0.1 & 0 & 0 \\ 0 & 0.3 & 0.8 \end{bmatrix} \begin{matrix} \textbf{Immature} \\ \textbf{Juvenile} \\ \textbf{Adult} \end{matrix} \end{array} \qquad X_0 = \begin{bmatrix} 600 \\ 400 \\ 3500 \end{bmatrix} \begin{matrix} \textbf{Immature} \\ \textbf{Juvenile} \\ \textbf{Adult} \end{matrix}$$

The entries in the matrix $A$ indicate the proportion of the population that survives *to the next year*. For example, the first column describes what happens to the immature population: None remain immature, 10% survive to become juveniles, and of course none become adults. The second column describes what happens to the juvenile population: None become immature or remain juvenile, and 30% survive to adulthood. The third column describes the adult population: The number of their new offspring is 40% of the adult population, no adults become juveniles, and 80% survive to live another year. The entries in the population matrix $X_0$ indicate the current population (year 0) of immature, juvenile, and adult animals.

Let $X_1 = AX_0$, $X_2 = AX_1$, $X_3 = AX_2$, and so on.

1. Explain why $X_1$ gives the population in year 1, $X_2$ the population in year 2, and so on.

2. Find the population matrix for years 1, 2, 3, and 4. (Round fractional entries to the nearest whole number.) Do you see any trend?

3. Show that $X_2 = A^2X_0$, $X_3 = A^3X_0$, and so on.

4. Find the population after 50 years—that is, find $X_{50}$. (Use your results in Problem 3 and a graphing calculator.) Does it appear that the species will survive?

5. Suppose the environment has improved so that the proportion of immatures that become juveniles each year increases to 0.3 from 0.1, the proportion of juveniles that become adults increases to 0.7 from 0.3, and the proportion of adults that survives to the next year increases to 0.95. Find the population after 50 years with the new matrix $A$. Does it appear that the species will survive under these new conditions?

6. The matrix $A$ in the example is called a **transition matrix**. Such matrices occur in many applications of matrix algebra. The following transition matrix $T$ predicts the calculus grades of a class of students who must take a four-semester sequence of calculus courses. The first column of the matrix, for instance, indicates that of those students who get an A in one course, 70% will get an A in the following course, 15% will get a B, and 10% will get a C. (Students who receive D or F are not permitted to go on to the next course and so are not included in the matrix.) The entries in the matrix $Y_0$ give the number of incoming students who got A, B, and C, respectively, in their final high school mathematics course.

   Let $Y_1 = TY_0$, $Y_2 = TY_1$, $Y_3 = TY_2$, and $Y_4 = TY_3$. Calculate and interpret the entries of $Y_1$, $Y_2$, $Y_3$, and $Y_4$.

$$T = \begin{array}{c} \begin{matrix} \textbf{A} & \textbf{B} & \textbf{C} \end{matrix} \\ \begin{bmatrix} 0.70 & 0.25 & 0.05 \\ 0.15 & 0.50 & 0.25 \\ 0.10 & 0.15 & 0.45 \end{bmatrix} \begin{matrix} \textbf{A} \\ \textbf{B} \\ \textbf{C} \end{matrix} \end{array} \qquad Y_0 = \begin{bmatrix} 140 \\ 320 \\ 400 \end{bmatrix} \begin{matrix} \textbf{A} \\ \textbf{B} \\ \textbf{C} \end{matrix}$$

© Art Wolfe/Stone/Getty Images

## 7.3 | Inverses of Matrices and Matrix Equations

**LEARNING OBJECTIVES**

After completing this section, you will be able to:

■ Determine when two matrices are inverses of each other
■ Find the inverse of a 2 × 2 matrix
■ Find the inverse of an $n \times n$ matrix
■ Solve a linear system by writing it as a matrix equation
■ Model using matrix equations

In the preceding section we saw that when the dimensions are appropriate, matrices can be added, subtracted, and multiplied. In this section we investigate division of matrices. With this operation we can solve equations that involve matrices.

### ■ The Inverse of a Matrix

First, we define *identity matrices*, which play the same role for matrix multiplication as the number 1 does for ordinary multiplication of numbers; that is, $1 \cdot a = a \cdot 1 = a$ for all numbers $a$. In the following definition the term **main diagonal** refers to the entries of a square matrix whose row and column numbers are the same. These entries stretch diagonally down the matrix, from top left to bottom right.

> The **identity matrix** $I_n$ is the $n \times n$ matrix for which each main diagonal entry is a 1 and for which all other entries are 0.

Thus, the 2 × 2, 3 × 3, and 4 × 4 identity matrices are

$$I_2 = \begin{bmatrix} 1 & 0 \\ 0 & 1 \end{bmatrix} \qquad I_3 = \begin{bmatrix} 1 & 0 & 0 \\ 0 & 1 & 0 \\ 0 & 0 & 1 \end{bmatrix} \qquad I_4 = \begin{bmatrix} 1 & 0 & 0 & 0 \\ 0 & 1 & 0 & 0 \\ 0 & 0 & 1 & 0 \\ 0 & 0 & 0 & 1 \end{bmatrix}$$

Identity matrices behave like the number 1 in the sense that

$$A \cdot I_n = A \qquad \text{and} \qquad I_n \cdot B = B$$

whenever these products are defined.

▶ **EXAMPLE 1** | Identity Matrices

The following matrix products show how multiplying a matrix by an identity matrix of the appropriate dimension leaves the matrix unchanged.

$$\begin{bmatrix} 1 & 0 \\ 0 & 1 \end{bmatrix} \begin{bmatrix} 3 & 5 & 6 \\ -1 & 2 & 7 \end{bmatrix} = \begin{bmatrix} 3 & 5 & 6 \\ -1 & 2 & 7 \end{bmatrix}$$

$$\begin{bmatrix} -1 & 7 & \frac{1}{2} \\ 12 & 1 & 3 \\ -2 & 0 & 7 \end{bmatrix} \begin{bmatrix} 1 & 0 & 0 \\ 0 & 1 & 0 \\ 0 & 0 & 1 \end{bmatrix} = \begin{bmatrix} -1 & 7 & \frac{1}{2} \\ 12 & 1 & 3 \\ -2 & 0 & 7 \end{bmatrix}$$

▲

If $A$ and $B$ are $n \times n$ matrices, and if $AB = BA = I_n$, then we say that $B$ is the *inverse* of $A$, and we write $B = A^{-1}$. The concept of the inverse of a matrix is analogous to that of the reciprocal of a real number.

---

### INVERSE OF A MATRIX

Let $A$ be a square $n \times n$ matrix. If there exists an $n \times n$ matrix $A^{-1}$ with the property that

$$AA^{-1} = A^{-1}A = I_n$$

then we say that $A^{-1}$ is the **inverse** of $A$.

---

▶ **EXAMPLE 2** | Verifying That a Matrix Is an Inverse

Verify that $B$ is the inverse of $A$, where

$$A = \begin{bmatrix} 2 & 1 \\ 5 & 3 \end{bmatrix} \quad \text{and} \quad B = \begin{bmatrix} 3 & -1 \\ -5 & 2 \end{bmatrix}$$

▼ **SOLUTION**    We perform the matrix multiplications to show that $AB = I$ and $BA = I$:

$$\begin{bmatrix} 2 & 1 \\ 5 & 3 \end{bmatrix} \begin{bmatrix} 3 & -1 \\ -5 & 2 \end{bmatrix} = \begin{bmatrix} 2 \cdot 3 + 1(-5) & 2(-1) + 1 \cdot 2 \\ 5 \cdot 3 + 3(-5) & 5(-1) + 3 \cdot 2 \end{bmatrix} = \begin{bmatrix} 1 & 0 \\ 0 & 1 \end{bmatrix}$$

$$\begin{bmatrix} 3 & -1 \\ -5 & 2 \end{bmatrix} \begin{bmatrix} 2 & 1 \\ 5 & 3 \end{bmatrix} = \begin{bmatrix} 3 \cdot 2 + (-1)5 & 3 \cdot 1 + (-1)3 \\ (-5)2 + 2 \cdot 5 & (-5)1 + 2 \cdot 3 \end{bmatrix} = \begin{bmatrix} 1 & 0 \\ 0 & 1 \end{bmatrix}$$

✎ **Practice what you've learned: Do Exercise 3.**                              ▲

## Finding the Inverse of a 2 × 2 Matrix

The following rule provides a simple way for finding the inverse of a $2 \times 2$ matrix, when it exists. For larger matrices there is a more general procedure for finding inverses, which we consider later in this section.

---

### INVERSE OF A 2 × 2 MATRIX

If $A = \begin{bmatrix} a & b \\ c & d \end{bmatrix}$  then  $A^{-1} = \dfrac{1}{ad - bc} \begin{bmatrix} d & -b \\ -c & a \end{bmatrix}$.

If $ad - bc = 0$, then $A$ has no inverse.

---

▶ **EXAMPLE 3** | Finding the Inverse of a 2 × 2 Matrix

Let

$$A = \begin{bmatrix} 4 & 5 \\ 2 & 3 \end{bmatrix}$$

Find $A^{-1}$ and verify that $AA^{-1} = A^{-1}A = I_2$.

Arthur Cayley (1821–1895) was an English mathematician who was instrumental in developing the theory of matrices. He was the first to use a single symbol such as *A* to represent a matrix, thereby introducing the idea that a matrix is a single entity rather than just a collection of numbers. Cayley practiced law until the age of 42, but his primary interest from adolescence was mathematics, and he published almost 200 articles on the subject in his spare time. In 1863 he accepted a professorship in mathematics at Cambridge, where he taught until his death. Cayley's work on matrices was of purely theoretical interest in his day, but in the 20th century many of his results found application in physics, the social sciences, business, and other fields. One of the most common uses of matrices today is in computers, where matrices are employed for data storage, error correction, image manipulation, and many other purposes. These applications have made matrix algebra more useful than ever.

▼ **SOLUTION**    Using the rule for the inverse of a $2 \times 2$ matrix, we get

$$A^{-1} = \frac{1}{4 \cdot 3 - 5 \cdot 2}\begin{bmatrix} 3 & -5 \\ -2 & 4 \end{bmatrix} = \frac{1}{2}\begin{bmatrix} 3 & -5 \\ -2 & 4 \end{bmatrix} = \begin{bmatrix} \frac{3}{2} & -\frac{5}{2} \\ -1 & 2 \end{bmatrix}$$

To verify that this is indeed the inverse of *A*, we calculate $AA^{-1}$ and $A^{-1}A$:

$$AA^{-1} = \begin{bmatrix} 4 & 5 \\ 2 & 3 \end{bmatrix}\begin{bmatrix} \frac{3}{2} & -\frac{5}{2} \\ -1 & 2 \end{bmatrix} = \begin{bmatrix} 4 \cdot \frac{3}{2} + 5(-1) & 4(-\frac{5}{2}) + 5 \cdot 2 \\ 2 \cdot \frac{3}{2} + 3(-1) & 2(-\frac{5}{2}) + 3 \cdot 2 \end{bmatrix} = \begin{bmatrix} 1 & 0 \\ 0 & 1 \end{bmatrix}$$

$$A^{-1}A = \begin{bmatrix} \frac{3}{2} & -\frac{5}{2} \\ -1 & 2 \end{bmatrix}\begin{bmatrix} 4 & 5 \\ 2 & 3 \end{bmatrix} = \begin{bmatrix} \frac{3}{2} \cdot 4 + (-\frac{5}{2})2 & \frac{3}{2} \cdot 5 + (-\frac{5}{2})3 \\ (-1)4 + 2 \cdot 2 & (-1)5 + 2 \cdot 3 \end{bmatrix} = \begin{bmatrix} 1 & 0 \\ 0 & 1 \end{bmatrix}$$

✎ **Practice what you've learned: Do Exercise 9.**                               ▲

The quantity $ad - bc$ that appears in the rule for calculating the inverse of a $2 \times 2$ matrix is called the **determinant** of the matrix. If the determinant is 0, then the matrix does not have an inverse (since we cannot divide by 0).

## ■ Finding the Inverse of an $n \times n$ Matrix

For $3 \times 3$ and larger square matrices the following technique provides the most efficient way to calculate their inverses. If *A* is an $n \times n$ matrix, we first construct the $n \times 2n$ matrix that has the entries of *A* on the left and of the identity matrix $I_n$ on the right:

$$\begin{bmatrix} a_{11} & a_{12} & \cdots & a_{1n} & | & 1 & 0 & \cdots & 0 \\ a_{21} & a_{22} & \cdots & a_{2n} & | & 0 & 1 & \cdots & 0 \\ \vdots & \vdots & \ddots & \vdots & | & \vdots & \vdots & \ddots & \vdots \\ a_{n1} & a_{n2} & \cdots & a_{nn} & | & 0 & 0 & \cdots & 1 \end{bmatrix}$$

We then use the elementary row operations on this new large matrix to change the left side into the identity matrix. (This means that we are changing the large matrix to reduced row-echelon form.) The right side is transformed automatically into $A^{-1}$. (We omit the proof of this fact.)

▶ **EXAMPLE 4** | Finding the Inverse of a $3 \times 3$ Matrix

Let *A* be the matrix

$$A = \begin{bmatrix} 1 & -2 & -4 \\ 2 & -3 & -6 \\ -3 & 6 & 15 \end{bmatrix}$$

(a) Find $A^{-1}$.

(b) Verify that $AA^{-1} = A^{-1}A = I_3$.

▼ **SOLUTION**

(a) We begin with the $3 \times 6$ matrix whose left half is *A* and whose right half is the identity matrix.

$$\begin{bmatrix} 1 & -2 & -4 & | & 1 & 0 & 0 \\ 2 & -3 & -6 & | & 0 & 1 & 0 \\ -3 & 6 & 15 & | & 0 & 0 & 1 \end{bmatrix}$$

The Granger Collection, New York

We then transform the left half of this new matrix into the identity matrix by performing the following sequence of elementary row operations on the *entire* new matrix:

$$
\xrightarrow[\substack{R_2 - 2R_1 \to R_2 \\ R_3 + 3R_1 \to R_3}]{}
\left[\begin{array}{ccc|ccc}
1 & -2 & -4 & 1 & 0 & 0 \\
0 & 1 & 2 & -2 & 1 & 0 \\
0 & 0 & 3 & 3 & 0 & 1
\end{array}\right]
$$

$$
\xrightarrow{\frac{1}{3}R_3,}
\left[\begin{array}{ccc|ccc}
1 & -2 & -4 & 1 & 0 & 0 \\
0 & 1 & 2 & -2 & 1 & 0 \\
0 & 0 & 1 & 1 & 0 & \frac{1}{3}
\end{array}\right]
$$

$$
\xrightarrow{R_1 + 2R_2 \to R_1}
\left[\begin{array}{ccc|ccc}
1 & 0 & 0 & -3 & 2 & 0 \\
0 & 1 & 2 & -2 & 1 & 0 \\
0 & 0 & 1 & 1 & 0 & \frac{1}{3}
\end{array}\right]
$$

$$
\xrightarrow{R_2 - 2R_3 \to R_2}
\left[\begin{array}{ccc|ccc}
1 & 0 & 0 & -3 & 2 & 0 \\
0 & 1 & 0 & -4 & 1 & -\frac{2}{3} \\
0 & 0 & 1 & 1 & 0 & \frac{1}{3}
\end{array}\right]
$$

We have now transformed the left half of this matrix into an identity matrix. (This means that we have put the entire matrix in reduced row-echelon form.) Note that to do this in as systematic a fashion as possible, we first changed the elements below the main diagonal to zeros, just as we would if we were using Gaussian elimination. We then changed each main diagonal element to a 1 by multiplying by the appropriate constant(s). Finally, we completed the process by changing the remaining entries on the left side to zeros.

The right half is now $A^{-1}$.

$$
A^{-1} =
\begin{bmatrix}
-3 & 2 & 0 \\
-4 & 1 & -\frac{2}{3} \\
1 & 0 & \frac{1}{3}
\end{bmatrix}
$$

**(b)** We calculate $AA^{-1}$ and $A^{-1}A$ and verify that both products give the identity matrix $I_3$.

$$
AA^{-1} =
\begin{bmatrix}
1 & -2 & -4 \\
2 & -3 & -6 \\
-3 & 6 & 15
\end{bmatrix}
\begin{bmatrix}
-3 & 2 & 0 \\
-4 & 1 & -\frac{2}{3} \\
1 & 0 & \frac{1}{3}
\end{bmatrix}
=
\begin{bmatrix}
1 & 0 & 0 \\
0 & 1 & 0 \\
0 & 0 & 1
\end{bmatrix}
$$

$$
A^{-1}A =
\begin{bmatrix}
-3 & 2 & 0 \\
-4 & 1 & -\frac{2}{3} \\
1 & 0 & \frac{1}{3}
\end{bmatrix}
\begin{bmatrix}
1 & -2 & -4 \\
2 & -3 & -6 \\
-3 & 6 & 15
\end{bmatrix}
=
\begin{bmatrix}
1 & 0 & 0 \\
0 & 1 & 0 \\
0 & 0 & 1
\end{bmatrix}
$$

✎ **Practice what you've learned: Do Exercise 17.**    ▲

Graphing calculators are also able to calculate matrix inverses. On the TI-82 and TI-83 calculators, matrices are stored in memory using names such as [A], [B], [C], . . . . To find the inverse of [A], we key in

[A]  $\boxed{x^{-1}}$   $\boxed{\text{ENTER}}$

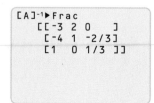

**FIGURE 1**

For the matrix of Example 4 this results in the output shown in Figure 1 (where we have also used the ▶Frac command to display the output in fraction form rather than in decimal form).

The next example shows that not every square matrix has an inverse.

▶ **EXAMPLE 5** | A Matrix That Does Not Have an Inverse

Find the inverse of the matrix.

$$\begin{bmatrix} 2 & -3 & -7 \\ 1 & 2 & 7 \\ 1 & 1 & 4 \end{bmatrix}$$

▼ **SOLUTION** We proceed as follows.

$$\begin{bmatrix} 2 & -3 & -7 & | & 1 & 0 & 0 \\ 1 & 2 & 7 & | & 0 & 1 & 0 \\ 1 & 1 & 4 & | & 0 & 0 & 1 \end{bmatrix} \xrightarrow{R_1 \leftrightarrow R_2} \begin{bmatrix} 1 & 2 & 7 & | & 0 & 1 & 0 \\ 2 & -3 & -7 & | & 1 & 0 & 0 \\ 1 & 1 & 4 & | & 0 & 0 & 1 \end{bmatrix}$$

$$\xrightarrow[R_3 - R_1 \to R_3]{R_2 - 2R_1 \to R_2} \begin{bmatrix} 1 & 2 & 7 & | & 0 & 1 & 0 \\ 0 & -7 & -21 & | & 1 & -2 & 0 \\ 0 & -1 & -3 & | & 0 & -1 & 1 \end{bmatrix}$$

$$\xrightarrow{-\frac{1}{7}R_2} \begin{bmatrix} 1 & 2 & 7 & | & 0 & 1 & 0 \\ 0 & 1 & 3 & | & -\frac{1}{7} & \frac{2}{7} & 0 \\ 0 & -1 & -3 & | & 0 & -1 & 1 \end{bmatrix}$$

$$\xrightarrow[R_1 - 2R_2 \to R_1]{R_3 + R_2 \to R_3} \begin{bmatrix} 1 & 0 & 1 & | & \frac{2}{7} & \frac{3}{7} & 0 \\ 0 & 1 & 3 & | & -\frac{1}{7} & \frac{2}{7} & 0 \\ 0 & 0 & 0 & | & -\frac{1}{7} & -\frac{5}{7} & 1 \end{bmatrix}$$

At this point we would like to change the 0 in the (3, 3) position of this matrix to a 1 without changing the zeros in the (3, 1) and (3, 2) positions. But there is no way to accomplish this, because no matter what multiple of rows 1 and/or 2 we add to row 3, we can't change the third zero in row 3 without changing the first or second zero as well. Thus, we cannot change the left half to the identity matrix, so the original matrix doesn't have an inverse.

✎ **Practice what you've learned: Do Exercise 19.** ▲

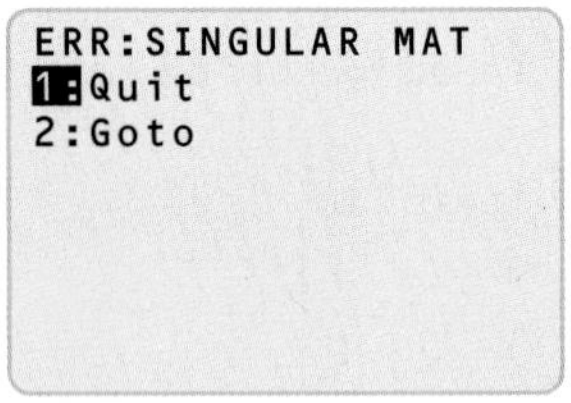

 If we encounter a row of zeros on the left when trying to find an inverse, as in Example 5, then the original matrix does not have an inverse. If we try to calculate the inverse of the matrix from Example 5 on a TI-83 calculator, we get the error message shown in Figure 2. (A matrix that has no inverse is called *singular*.)

```
ERR:SINGULAR MAT
1:Quit
2:Goto
```

**FIGURE 2**

## ■ Matrix Equations

We saw in Example 6 in Section 7.2 that a system of linear equations can be written as a single matrix equation. For example, the system

$$\begin{cases} x - 2y - 4z = 7 \\ 2x - 3y - 6z = 5 \\ -3x + 6y + 15z = 0 \end{cases}$$

is equivalent to the matrix equation

$$\underbrace{\begin{bmatrix} 1 & -2 & -4 \\ 2 & -3 & -6 \\ -3 & 6 & 15 \end{bmatrix}}_{A} \underbrace{\begin{bmatrix} x \\ y \\ z \end{bmatrix}}_{X} = \underbrace{\begin{bmatrix} 7 \\ 5 \\ 0 \end{bmatrix}}_{B}$$

If we let

$$A = \begin{bmatrix} 1 & -2 & -4 \\ 2 & -3 & -6 \\ -3 & 6 & 15 \end{bmatrix} \qquad X = \begin{bmatrix} x \\ y \\ z \end{bmatrix} \qquad B = \begin{bmatrix} 7 \\ 5 \\ 0 \end{bmatrix}$$

then this matrix equation can be written as

$$AX = B$$

The matrix $A$ is called the **coefficient matrix**.

We solve this matrix equation by multiplying each side by the inverse of $A$ (provided that this inverse exists):

| | |
|---|---|
| $AX = B$ | |
| $A^{-1}(AX) = A^{-1}B$ | Multiply on left by $A^{-1}$ |
| $(A^{-1}A)X = A^{-1}B$ | Associative Property |
| $I_3X = A^{-1}B$ | Property of inverses |
| $X = A^{-1}B$ | Property of identity matrix |

Solving the matrix equation $AX = B$ is very similar to solving the simple real-number equation

$$3x = 12$$

which we do by multiplying each side by the reciprocal (or inverse) of 3:

$$\tfrac{1}{3}(3x) = \tfrac{1}{3}(12)$$

$$x = 4$$

In Example 4 we showed that

$$A^{-1} = \begin{bmatrix} -3 & 2 & 0 \\ -4 & 1 & -\frac{2}{3} \\ 1 & 0 & \frac{1}{3} \end{bmatrix}$$

So from $X = A^{-1}B$ we have

$$\underbrace{\begin{bmatrix} x \\ y \\ z \end{bmatrix}}_{X} = \underbrace{\begin{bmatrix} -3 & 2 & 0 \\ -4 & 1 & -\frac{2}{3} \\ 1 & 0 & \frac{1}{3} \end{bmatrix}}_{A^{-1}} \underbrace{\begin{bmatrix} 7 \\ 5 \\ 0 \end{bmatrix}}_{B} = \begin{bmatrix} -11 \\ -23 \\ 7 \end{bmatrix}$$

Thus, $x = -11$, $y = -23$, $z = 7$ is the solution of the original system.

We have proved that the matrix equation $AX = B$ can be solved by the following method.

---

**SOLVING A MATRIX EQUATION**

If $A$ is a square $n \times n$ matrix that has an inverse $A^{-1}$ and if $X$ is a variable matrix and $B$ a known matrix, both with $n$ rows, then the solution of the matrix equation

$$AX = B$$

is given by

$$X = A^{-1}B$$

---

▶ **EXAMPLE 6** | Solving a System Using a Matrix Inverse

**(a)** Write the system of equations as a matrix equation.

**(b)** Solve the system by solving the matrix equation.

$$\begin{cases} 2x - 5y = 15 \\ 3x - 6y = 36 \end{cases}$$

▼ **SOLUTION**

**(a)** We write the system as a matrix equation of the form $AX = B$:

$$\begin{bmatrix} 2 & -5 \\ 3 & -6 \end{bmatrix} \begin{bmatrix} x \\ y \end{bmatrix} = \begin{bmatrix} 15 \\ 36 \end{bmatrix}$$

$$A \quad X = B$$

**(b)** Using the rule for finding the inverse of a $2 \times 2$ matrix, we get

$$A^{-1} = \begin{bmatrix} 2 & -5 \\ 3 & -6 \end{bmatrix}^{-1} = \frac{1}{2(-6) - (-5)3} \begin{bmatrix} -6 & -(-5) \\ -3 & 2 \end{bmatrix} = \frac{1}{3} \begin{bmatrix} -6 & 5 \\ -3 & 2 \end{bmatrix}$$

Multiplying each side of the matrix equation by this inverse matrix, we get

$$\begin{bmatrix} x \\ y \end{bmatrix} = \frac{1}{3} \begin{bmatrix} -6 & 5 \\ -3 & 2 \end{bmatrix} \begin{bmatrix} 15 \\ 36 \end{bmatrix} = \begin{bmatrix} 30 \\ 9 \end{bmatrix}$$

$$X = A^{-1} \quad B$$

So $x = 30$ and $y = 9$.

✎ **Practice what you've learned: Do Exercise 25.**                                    ▲

## ■ Modeling with Matrix Equations

Suppose we need to solve several systems of equations with the same coefficient matrix. Then converting the systems to matrix equations provides an efficient way to obtain the solutions, because we need to find the inverse of the coefficient matrix only once. This procedure is particularly convenient if we use a graphing calculator to perform the matrix operations, as in the next example.

▶ **EXAMPLE 7** | Modeling Nutritional Requirements Using Matrix Equations

A pet-store owner feeds his hamsters and gerbils different mixtures of three types of rodent food: KayDee Food, Pet Pellets, and Rodent Chow. He wishes to feed his animals the correct amount of each brand to satisfy their daily requirements for protein, fat, and carbohydrates exactly. Suppose that hamsters require 340 mg of protein, 280 mg of fat, and 440 mg of carbohydrates, and gerbils need 480 mg of protein, 360 mg of fat, and 680 mg of carbohydrates each day. The amount of each nutrient (in mg) in one gram of each brand is given in the following table. How many grams of each food should the storekeeper feed his hamsters and gerbils daily to satisfy their nutrient requirements?

|  | KayDee Food | Pet Pellets | Rodent Chow |
|---|---|---|---|
| **Protein (mg)** | 10 | 0 | 20 |
| **Fat (mg)** | 10 | 20 | 10 |
| **Carbohydrates (mg)** | 5 | 10 | 30 |

▼ **SOLUTION**   We let $x_1$, $x_2$, and $x_3$ be the respective amounts (in grams) of KayDee Food, Pet Pellets, and Rodent Chow that the hamsters should eat and $y_1$, $y_2$, and $y_3$ be the corresponding amounts for the gerbils. Then we want to solve the matrix equations

$$\begin{bmatrix} 10 & 0 & 20 \\ 10 & 20 & 10 \\ 5 & 10 & 30 \end{bmatrix} \begin{bmatrix} x_1 \\ x_2 \\ x_3 \end{bmatrix} = \begin{bmatrix} 340 \\ 280 \\ 440 \end{bmatrix} \qquad \text{Hamster equation}$$

$$\begin{bmatrix} 10 & 0 & 20 \\ 10 & 20 & 10 \\ 5 & 10 & 30 \end{bmatrix} \begin{bmatrix} y_1 \\ y_2 \\ y_3 \end{bmatrix} = \begin{bmatrix} 480 \\ 360 \\ 680 \end{bmatrix} \qquad \text{Gerbil equation}$$

Let

$$A = \begin{bmatrix} 10 & 0 & 20 \\ 10 & 20 & 10 \\ 5 & 10 & 30 \end{bmatrix} \quad B = \begin{bmatrix} 340 \\ 280 \\ 440 \end{bmatrix} \quad C = \begin{bmatrix} 480 \\ 360 \\ 680 \end{bmatrix} \quad X = \begin{bmatrix} x_1 \\ x_2 \\ x_3 \end{bmatrix} \quad Y = \begin{bmatrix} y_1 \\ y_2 \\ y_3 \end{bmatrix}$$

Then we can write these matrix equations as

$$AX = B \qquad \text{Hamster equation}$$

$$AY = C \qquad \text{Gerbil equation}$$

We want to solve for $X$ and $Y$, so we multiply both sides of each equation by $A^{-1}$, the inverse of the coefficient matrix. We could find $A^{-1}$ by hand, but it is more convenient to use a graphing calculator as shown in Figure 3.

```
[A]⁻¹*[B]
              [[10]
               [3 ]
               [12]]
```

```
[A]⁻¹*[C]
              [[8 ]
               [4 ]
               [20]]
```

**FIGURE 3**          (a)                                    (b)

---

## MATHEMATICS IN THE MODERN WORLD

### Mathematical Ecology

In the 1970s humpback whales became a center of controversy. Environmentalists believed that whaling threatened the whales with imminent extinction; whalers saw their livelihood threatened by any attempt to stop whaling. Are whales really threatened to extinction by whaling? What level of whaling is safe to guarantee survival of the whales? These questions motivated mathematicians to study population patterns of whales and other species more closely.

As early as the 1920s Lotka and Volterra had founded the field of mathematical biology by creating predator-prey models. Their models, which draw on a branch of mathematics called differential equations, take into account the rates at which predator eats prey and the rates of growth of each population. Note that as predator eats prey, the prey population decreases; this means less food supply for the predators, so their population begins to decrease; with fewer predators the prey population begins to increase, and so on. Normally, a state of equilibrium develops, and the two populations alternate between a minimum and a maximum. Notice that if the predators eat the prey too fast, they will be left without food and will thus ensure their own extinction.

Since Lotka and Volterra's time, more detailed mathematical models of animal populations have been developed. For many species the population is divided into several stages: immature, juvenile, adult, and so on. The proportion of each stage that survives or reproduces in a given time period is entered into a matrix (called a transition matrix); matrix multiplication is then used to predict the population in succeeding time periods. (See the *Discovery Project*, page 519.)

As you can see, the power of mathematics to model and predict is an invaluable tool in the ongoing debate over the environment.

© Volvox /Index Stock

So

$$X = A^{-1}B = \begin{bmatrix} 10 \\ 3 \\ 12 \end{bmatrix} \qquad Y = A^{-1}C = \begin{bmatrix} 8 \\ 4 \\ 20 \end{bmatrix}$$

Thus, each hamster should be fed 10 g of KayDee Food, 3 g of Pet Pellets, and 12 g of Rodent Chow, and each gerbil should be fed 8 g of KayDee Food, 4 g of Pet Pellets, and 20 g of Rodent Chow daily.

✎ **Practice what you've learned: Do Exercise 47.**    ▲

# 7.3 EXERCISES

## ▼ CONCEPTS

**1. (a)** The matrix $I = \begin{bmatrix} 1 & 0 \\ 0 & 1 \end{bmatrix}$ is called an _____ matrix.

 **(b)** If $A$ is a $2 \times 2$ matrix, then $A \times I =$ _____ and

  $I \times A =$ _____.

 **(c)** If $A$ and $B$ are $2 \times 2$ matrices with $AB = I$, then $B$ is the

  _____ of $A$.

**2. (a)** Write the following system as a matrix equation $AX = B$.

| System | Matrix equation |
|---|---|
| | $A \quad \cdot \quad X \quad = \quad B$ |
| $5x + 3y = 4$ | $\begin{bmatrix} \blacksquare & \blacksquare \\ \blacksquare & \blacksquare \end{bmatrix}\begin{bmatrix} \blacksquare \\ \blacksquare \end{bmatrix} = \begin{bmatrix} \blacksquare \\ \blacksquare \end{bmatrix}$ |
| $3x + 2y = 3$ | |

 **(b)** The inverse of $A$ is $A^{-1} = \begin{bmatrix} \blacksquare & \blacksquare \\ \blacksquare & \blacksquare \end{bmatrix}$.

 **(c)** The solution of the matrix equation is $X = A^{-1} B$.

$$X = A^{-1} \quad B$$

$$\begin{bmatrix} x \\ y \end{bmatrix} = \begin{bmatrix} \blacksquare & \blacksquare \\ \blacksquare & \blacksquare \end{bmatrix}\begin{bmatrix} \blacksquare \\ \blacksquare \end{bmatrix} = \begin{bmatrix} \blacksquare \\ \blacksquare \end{bmatrix}$$

 **(d)** The solution of the system is $x =$ _____, $y =$ _____.

## ▼ SKILLS

**3–6** ▪ Calculate the products $AB$ and $BA$ to verify that $B$ is the inverse of $A$.

✎ **3.** $A = \begin{bmatrix} 4 & 1 \\ 7 & 2 \end{bmatrix}$    $B = \begin{bmatrix} 2 & -1 \\ -7 & 4 \end{bmatrix}$

**4.** $A = \begin{bmatrix} 2 & -3 \\ 4 & -7 \end{bmatrix}$    $B = \begin{bmatrix} \frac{7}{2} & -\frac{3}{2} \\ 2 & -1 \end{bmatrix}$

**5.** $A = \begin{bmatrix} 1 & 3 & -1 \\ 1 & 4 & 0 \\ -1 & -3 & 2 \end{bmatrix}$    $B = \begin{bmatrix} 8 & -3 & 4 \\ -2 & 1 & -1 \\ 1 & 0 & 1 \end{bmatrix}$

**6.** $A = \begin{bmatrix} 3 & 2 & 4 \\ 1 & 1 & -6 \\ 2 & 1 & 12 \end{bmatrix}$    $B = \begin{bmatrix} 9 & -10 & -8 \\ -12 & 14 & 11 \\ -\frac{1}{2} & \frac{1}{2} & \frac{1}{2} \end{bmatrix}$

**7–8** ▪ Find the inverse of the matrix and verify that $A^{-1}A = AA^{-1} = I_2$ and $B^{-1}B = BB^{-1} = I_3$.

**7.** $A = \begin{bmatrix} 7 & 4 \\ 3 & 2 \end{bmatrix}$    **8.** $B = \begin{bmatrix} 1 & 3 & 2 \\ 0 & 2 & 2 \\ -2 & -1 & 0 \end{bmatrix}$

**9–24** ▪ Find the inverse of the matrix if it exists.

✎ **9.** $\begin{bmatrix} -3 & -5 \\ 2 & 3 \end{bmatrix}$    **10.** $\begin{bmatrix} 3 & 4 \\ 7 & 9 \end{bmatrix}$

**11.** $\begin{bmatrix} 2 & 5 \\ -5 & -13 \end{bmatrix}$    **12.** $\begin{bmatrix} -7 & 4 \\ 8 & -5 \end{bmatrix}$

**13.** $\begin{bmatrix} 6 & -3 \\ -8 & 4 \end{bmatrix}$    **14.** $\begin{bmatrix} \frac{1}{2} & \frac{1}{3} \\ 5 & 4 \end{bmatrix}$

**15.** $\begin{bmatrix} 0.4 & -1.2 \\ 0.3 & 0.6 \end{bmatrix}$    **16.** $\begin{bmatrix} 4 & 2 & 3 \\ 3 & 3 & 2 \\ 1 & 0 & 1 \end{bmatrix}$

✎ **17.** $\begin{bmatrix} 2 & 4 & 1 \\ -1 & 1 & -1 \\ 1 & 4 & 0 \end{bmatrix}$    **18.** $\begin{bmatrix} 5 & 7 & 4 \\ 3 & -1 & 3 \\ 6 & 7 & 5 \end{bmatrix}$

✎ **19.** $\begin{bmatrix} 1 & 2 & 3 \\ 4 & 5 & -1 \\ 1 & -1 & -10 \end{bmatrix}$    **20.** $\begin{bmatrix} 2 & 1 & 0 \\ 1 & 1 & 4 \\ 2 & 1 & 2 \end{bmatrix}$

**21.** $\begin{bmatrix} 0 & -2 & 2 \\ 3 & 1 & 3 \\ 1 & -2 & 3 \end{bmatrix}$    **22.** $\begin{bmatrix} 3 & -2 & 0 \\ 5 & 1 & 1 \\ 2 & -2 & 0 \end{bmatrix}$

**23.** $\begin{bmatrix} 1 & 2 & 0 & 3 \\ 0 & 1 & 1 & 1 \\ 0 & 1 & 0 & 1 \\ 1 & 2 & 0 & 2 \end{bmatrix}$    **24.** $\begin{bmatrix} 1 & 0 & 1 & 0 \\ 0 & 1 & 0 & 1 \\ 1 & 1 & 1 & 0 \\ 1 & 1 & 1 & 1 \end{bmatrix}$

**25–32** ▪ Solve the system of equations by converting to a matrix equation and using the inverse of the coefficient matrix, as in Example 6. Use the inverses from Exercises 9–12, 17, 18, 21, and 23.

✎ **25.** $\begin{cases} 5x + 3y = 4 \\ 3x + 2y = 0 \end{cases}$    **26.** $\begin{cases} 3x + 4y = 10 \\ 7x + 9y = 20 \end{cases}$

**27.** $\begin{cases} 2x + 5y = 2 \\ -5x - 13y = 20 \end{cases}$    **28.** $\begin{cases} -7x + 4y = 0 \\ 8x - 5y = 100 \end{cases}$

**29.** $\begin{cases} 2x + 4y + z = 7 \\ -x + y - z = 0 \\ x + 4y = -2 \end{cases}$    **30.** $\begin{cases} 5x + 7y + 4z = 1 \\ 3x - y + 3z = 1 \\ 6x + 7y + 5z = 1 \end{cases}$

**31.** $\begin{cases} -2y + 2z = 12 \\ 3x + y + 3z = -2 \\ x - 2y + 3z = 8 \end{cases}$    **32.** $\begin{cases} x + 2y + 3w = 0 \\ y + z + w = 1 \\ y + w = 2 \\ x + 2y + 2w = 3 \end{cases}$

**33–38** ■ Use a calculator that can perform matrix operations to solve the system, as in Example 7.

**33.** $\begin{cases} x + y - 2z = 3 \\ 2x + 5z = 11 \\ 2x + 3y = 12 \end{cases}$    **34.** $\begin{cases} 3x + 4y - z = 2 \\ 2x - 3y + z = -5 \\ 5x - 2y + 2z = -3 \end{cases}$

**35.** $\begin{cases} 12x + \frac{1}{2}y - 7z = 21 \\ 11x - 2y + 3z = 43 \\ 13x + y - 4z = 29 \end{cases}$    **36.** $\begin{cases} x + \frac{1}{2}y - \frac{1}{3}z = 4 \\ x - \frac{1}{4}y + \frac{1}{6}z = 7 \\ x + y - z = -6 \end{cases}$

**37.** $\begin{cases} x + y - 3w = 0 \\ x - 2z = 8 \\ 2y - z + w = 5 \\ 2x + 3y - 2w = 13 \end{cases}$

**38.** $\begin{cases} x + y + z + w = 15 \\ x - y + z - w = 5 \\ x + 2y + 3z + 4w = 26 \\ x - 2y + 3z - 4w = 2 \end{cases}$

**39–40** ■ Solve the matrix equation by multiplying each side by the appropriate inverse matrix.

**39.** $\begin{bmatrix} 3 & -2 \\ -4 & 3 \end{bmatrix} \begin{bmatrix} x & y & z \\ u & v & w \end{bmatrix} = \begin{bmatrix} 1 & 0 & -1 \\ 2 & 1 & 3 \end{bmatrix}$

**40.** $\begin{bmatrix} 0 & -2 & 2 \\ 3 & 1 & 3 \\ 1 & -2 & 3 \end{bmatrix} \begin{bmatrix} x & u \\ y & v \\ z & w \end{bmatrix} = \begin{bmatrix} 3 & 6 \\ 6 & 12 \\ 0 & 0 \end{bmatrix}$

**41–42** ■ Find the inverse of the matrix.

**41.** $\begin{bmatrix} a & -a \\ a & a \end{bmatrix}$

$(a \neq 0)$

**42.** $\begin{bmatrix} a & 0 & 0 & 0 \\ 0 & b & 0 & 0 \\ 0 & 0 & c & 0 \\ 0 & 0 & 0 & d \end{bmatrix}$

$(abcd \neq 0)$

**43–46** ■ Find the inverse of the matrix. For what value(s) of $x$, if any, does the matrix have no inverse?

**43.** $\begin{bmatrix} 2 & x \\ x & x^2 \end{bmatrix}$    **44.** $\begin{bmatrix} e^x & -e^{2x} \\ e^{2x} & e^{3x} \end{bmatrix}$

**45.** $\begin{bmatrix} 1 & e^x & 0 \\ e^x & -e^{2x} & 0 \\ 0 & 0 & 2 \end{bmatrix}$    **46.** $\begin{bmatrix} x & 1 \\ -x & \dfrac{1}{x-1} \end{bmatrix}$

## ▼ APPLICATIONS

✎ **47. Nutrition**  A nutritionist is studying the effects of the nutrients folic acid, choline, and inositol. He has three types of food available, and each type contains the following amounts of these nutrients per ounce:

|  | Type A | Type B | Type C |
|---|---|---|---|
| **Folic acid (mg)** | 3 | 1 | 3 |
| **Choline (mg)** | 4 | 2 | 4 |
| **Inositol (mg)** | 3 | 2 | 4 |

(a) Find the inverse of the matrix

$$\begin{bmatrix} 3 & 1 & 3 \\ 4 & 2 & 4 \\ 3 & 2 & 4 \end{bmatrix}$$

and use it to solve the remaining parts of this problem.

(b) How many ounces of each food should the nutritionist feed his laboratory rats if he wants their daily diet to contain 10 mg of folic acid, 14 mg of choline, and 13 mg of inositol?

(c) How much of each food is needed to supply 9 mg of folic acid, 12 mg of choline, and 10 mg of inositol?

(d) Will any combination of these foods supply 2 mg of folic acid, 4 mg of choline, and 11 mg of inositol?

**48. Nutrition**  Refer to Exercise 47. Suppose food type C has been improperly labeled, and it actually contains 4 mg of folic acid, 6 mg of choline, and 5 mg of inositol per ounce. Would it still be possible to use matrix inversion to solve parts (b), (c), and (d) of Exercise 47? Why or why not?

**49. Sales Commissions**  An encyclopedia saleswoman works for a company that offers three different grades of bindings for its encyclopedias: standard, deluxe, and leather. For each set that she sells, she earns a commission based on the set's binding grade. One week she sells one standard, one deluxe, and two leather sets and makes $675 in commission. The next week she sells two standard, one deluxe, and one leather set for a $600 commission. The third week she sells one standard, two deluxe, and one leather set, earning $625 in commission.

(a) Let $x$, $y$, and $z$ represent the commission she earns on standard, deluxe, and leather sets, respectively. Translate the given information into a system of equations in $x$, $y$, and $z$.

(b) Express the system of equations you found in part (a) as a matrix equation of the form $AX = B$.

(c) Find the inverse of the coefficient matrix $A$ and use it to solve the matrix equation in part (b). How much commission does the saleswoman earn on a set of encyclopedias in each grade of binding?

## ▼ DISCOVERY • DISCUSSION • WRITING

**50. No Zero-Product Property for Matrices**  We have used the Zero-Product Property to solve algebraic equations. Matrices do *not* have this property. Let $O$ represent the **2 × 2 zero matrix**:

$$O = \begin{bmatrix} 0 & 0 \\ 0 & 0 \end{bmatrix}$$

Find $2 \times 2$ matrices $A \neq O$ and $B \neq O$ such that $AB = O$. Can you find a matrix $A \neq O$ such that $A^2 = O$?

## 7.4 | Determinants and Cramer's Rule

**LEARNING OBJECTIVES**

After completing this section, you will be able to:

- Find the determinant of a 2 × 2 matrix
- Find the determinant of an $n \times n$ matrix
- Use the Invertibility Criterion
- Use row and column transformations in finding the determinant of a matrix
- Use Cramer's Rule to solve a linear system
- Use determinants to find the area of a triangle in the coordinate plane

If a matrix is **square** (that is, if it has the same number of rows as columns), then we can assign to it a number called its *determinant*. Determinants can be used to solve systems of linear equations, as we will see later in this section. They are also useful in determining whether a matrix has an inverse.

### Determinant of a 2 × 2 Matrix

We denote the determinant of a square matrix $A$ by the symbol $\det(A)$ or $|A|$. We first define $\det(A)$ for the simplest cases. If $A = [a]$ is a $1 \times 1$ matrix, then $\det(A) = a$. The following box gives the definition of a $2 \times 2$ determinant.

We will use both notations, $\det(A)$ and $|A|$, for the determinant of $A$. Although the symbol $|A|$ looks like the absolute value symbol, it will be clear from the context which meaning is intended.

> **DETERMINANT OF A 2 × 2 MATRIX**
>
> The **determinant** of the 2 × 2 matrix $A = \begin{bmatrix} a & b \\ c & d \end{bmatrix}$ is
>
> $$\det(A) = |A| = \begin{vmatrix} a & b \\ c & d \end{vmatrix} = ad - bc$$

▶ **EXAMPLE 1** | Determinant of a 2 × 2 Matrix

Evaluate $|A|$ for $A = \begin{bmatrix} 6 & -3 \\ 2 & 3 \end{bmatrix}$.

▼ **SOLUTION**

To evaluate a 2 × 2 determinant, we take the product of the diagonal from top left to bottom right and subtract the product from top right to bottom left, as indicated by the arrows.

$$\begin{vmatrix} 6 & -3 \\ 2 & 3 \end{vmatrix} = 6 \cdot 3 - (-3)2 = 18 - (-6) = 24$$

✎ **Practice what you've learned: Do Exercise 5.**                                    ▲

### Determinant of an $n \times n$ Matrix

To define the concept of determinant for an arbitrary $n \times n$ matrix, we need the following terminology.

Let $A$ be an $n \times n$ matrix.

1. The **minor** $M_{ij}$ of the element $a_{ij}$ is the determinant of the matrix obtained by deleting the $i$th row and $j$th column of $A$.

2. The **cofactor** $A_{ij}$ of the element $a_{ij}$ is

$$A_{ij} = (-1)^{i+j}M_{ij}$$

© CORBIS

**David Hilbert** (1862–1943) was born in Königsberg, Germany, and became a professor at Göttingen University. He is considered by many to be the greatest mathematician of the 20th century. At the International Congress of Mathematicians held in Paris in 1900, Hilbert set the direction of mathematics for the about-to-dawn 20th century by posing 23 problems that he believed to be of crucial importance. He said that "these are problems whose solutions we expect from the future." Most of Hilbert's problems have now been solved (see Julia Robinson, page 508, and Alan Turing, page 160), and their solutions have led to important new areas of mathematical research. Yet as we enter the new millennium, some of his problems remain unsolved. In his work, Hilbert emphasized structure, logic, and the foundations of mathematics. Part of his genius lay in his ability to see the most general possible statement of a problem. For instance, Euler proved that every whole number is the sum of four squares; Hilbert proved a similar statement for all powers of positive integers.

For example, if $A$ is the matrix

$$\begin{bmatrix} 2 & 3 & -1 \\ 0 & 2 & 4 \\ -2 & 5 & 6 \end{bmatrix}$$

then the minor $M_{12}$ is the determinant of the matrix obtained by deleting the first row and second column from $A$. Thus,

$$M_{12} = \begin{vmatrix} 2 & 3 & -1 \\ 0 & 2 & 4 \\ -2 & 5 & 6 \end{vmatrix} = \begin{vmatrix} 0 & 4 \\ -2 & 6 \end{vmatrix} = 0(6) - 4(-2) = 8$$

So the cofactor $A_{12} = (-1)^{1+2}M_{12} = -8$. Similarly,

$$M_{33} = \begin{vmatrix} 2 & 3 & -1 \\ 0 & 2 & 4 \\ -2 & 5 & 6 \end{vmatrix} = \begin{vmatrix} 2 & 3 \\ 0 & 2 \end{vmatrix} = 2 \cdot 2 - 3 \cdot 0 = 4$$

So $A_{33} = (-1)^{3+3}M_{33} = 4$.

Note that the cofactor of $a_{ij}$ is simply the minor of $a_{ij}$ multiplied by either 1 or $-1$, depending on whether $i + j$ is even or odd. Thus, in a $3 \times 3$ matrix we obtain the cofactor of any element by prefixing its minor with the sign obtained from the following checkerboard pattern.

$$\begin{bmatrix} + & - & + \\ - & + & - \\ + & - & + \end{bmatrix}$$

We are now ready to define the determinant of any square matrix.

## THE DETERMINANT OF A SQUARE MATRIX

If $A$ is an $n \times n$ matrix, then the **determinant** of $A$ is obtained by multiplying each element of the first row by its cofactor, and then adding the results. In symbols,

$$\det(A) = |A| = \begin{vmatrix} a_{11} & a_{12} & \cdots & a_{1n} \\ a_{21} & a_{22} & \cdots & a_{2n} \\ \vdots & \vdots & \ddots & \vdots \\ a_{n1} & a_{n2} & \cdots & a_{nn} \end{vmatrix} = a_{11}A_{11} + a_{12}A_{12} + \cdots + a_{1n}A_{1n}$$

▶ **EXAMPLE 2** | Determinant of a 3 × 3 Matrix

Evaluate the determinant of the matrix.

$$A = \begin{bmatrix} 2 & 3 & -1 \\ 0 & 2 & 4 \\ -2 & 5 & 6 \end{bmatrix}$$

▼ **SOLUTION**

$$\det(A) = \begin{vmatrix} 2 & 3 & -1 \\ 0 & 2 & 4 \\ -2 & 5 & 6 \end{vmatrix} = 2\begin{vmatrix} 2 & 4 \\ 5 & 6 \end{vmatrix} - 3\begin{vmatrix} 0 & 4 \\ -2 & 6 \end{vmatrix} + (-1)\begin{vmatrix} 0 & 2 \\ -2 & 5 \end{vmatrix}$$

$$= 2(2 \cdot 6 - 4 \cdot 5) - 3[0 \cdot 6 - 4(-2)] - [0 \cdot 5 - 2(-2)]$$

$$= -16 - 24 - 4$$

$$= -44$$

✎ **Practice what you've learned: Do Exercise 19.**                                    ▲

In our definition of the determinant we used the cofactors of elements in the first row only. This is called **expanding the determinant by the first row**. In fact, *we can expand the determinant by any row or column in the same way, and obtain the same result in each case* (although we won't prove this). The next example illustrates this principle.

▶ **EXAMPLE 3** | Expanding a Determinant About a Row and a Column

Let *A* be the matrix of Example 2. Evaluate the determinant of *A* by expanding

**(a)** by the second row

**(b)** by the third column

Verify that each expansion gives the same value.

▼ **SOLUTION**

**(a)** Expanding by the second row, we get

$$\det(A) = \begin{vmatrix} 2 & 3 & -1 \\ 0 & 2 & 4 \\ -2 & 5 & 6 \end{vmatrix} = -0\begin{vmatrix} 3 & -1 \\ 5 & 6 \end{vmatrix} + 2\begin{vmatrix} 2 & -1 \\ -2 & 6 \end{vmatrix} - 4\begin{vmatrix} 2 & 3 \\ -2 & 5 \end{vmatrix}$$

$$= 0 + 2[2 \cdot 6 - (-1)(-2)] - 4[2 \cdot 5 - 3(-2)]$$

$$= 0 + 20 - 64 = -44$$

**(b)** Expanding by the third column gives

Graphing calculators are capable of computing determinants. Here is the output when the TI-83 is used to calculate the determinant in Example 3:

```
[A]
      [[2   3  -1]
       [0   2  4 ]
       [-2  5  6 ]]
det([A])
                  -44
```

$$\det(A) = \begin{vmatrix} 2 & 3 & -1 \\ 0 & 2 & 4 \\ -2 & 5 & 6 \end{vmatrix}$$

$$= -1\begin{vmatrix} 0 & 2 \\ -2 & 5 \end{vmatrix} - 4\begin{vmatrix} 2 & 3 \\ -2 & 5 \end{vmatrix} + 6\begin{vmatrix} 2 & 3 \\ 0 & 2 \end{vmatrix}$$

$$= -[0 \cdot 5 - 2(-2)] - 4[2 \cdot 5 - 3(-2)] + 6(2 \cdot 2 - 3 \cdot 0)$$

$$= -4 - 64 + 24 = -44$$

In both cases we obtain the same value for the determinant as when we expanded by the first row in Example 2.

✎ **Practice what you've learned: Do Exercise 31.**    ▲

The following criterion allows us to determine whether a square matrix has an inverse without actually calculating the inverse. This is one of the most important uses of the determinant in matrix algebra, and it is the reason for the name *determinant*.

---

**INVERTIBILITY CRITERION**

If $A$ is a square matrix, then $A$ has an inverse if and only if $\det(A) \neq 0$.

---

We will not prove this fact, but from the formula for the inverse of a $2 \times 2$ matrix (page 521) you can see why it is true in the $2 \times 2$ case.

▶ **EXAMPLE 4** | Using the Determinant to Show That a Matrix Is
Not Invertible

Show that the matrix $A$ has no inverse.

$$A = \begin{bmatrix} 1 & 2 & 0 & 4 \\ 0 & 0 & 0 & 3 \\ 5 & 6 & 2 & 6 \\ 2 & 4 & 0 & 9 \end{bmatrix}$$

▼ **SOLUTION**   We begin by calculating the determinant of $A$. Since all but one of the elements of the second row is zero, we expand the determinant by the second row. If we do this, we see from the following equation that only the cofactor $A_{24}$ will have to be calculated.

$$\det(A) = \begin{vmatrix} 1 & 2 & 0 & 4 \\ 0 & 0 & 0 & 3 \\ 5 & 6 & 2 & 6 \\ 2 & 4 & 0 & 9 \end{vmatrix}$$

$$= -0 \cdot A_{21} + 0 \cdot A_{22} - 0 \cdot A_{23} + 3 \cdot A_{24} = 3A_{24}$$

$$= 3 \begin{vmatrix} 1 & 2 & 0 \\ 5 & 6 & 2 \\ 2 & 4 & 0 \end{vmatrix} \qquad \text{Expand this by column 3}$$

$$= 3(-2) \begin{vmatrix} 1 & 2 \\ 2 & 4 \end{vmatrix}$$

$$= 3(-2)(1 \cdot 4 - 2 \cdot 2) = 0$$

Since the determinant of $A$ is zero, $A$ cannot have an inverse, by the Invertibility Criterion.

✎ **Practice what you've learned: Do Exercise 23.**    ▲

## ■ Row and Column Transformations

The preceding example shows that if we expand a determinant about a row or column that contains many zeros, our work is reduced considerably because we don't have to evaluate the cofactors of the elements that are zero. The following principle often simplifies the process of finding a determinant by introducing zeros into it without changing its value.

---

**ROW AND COLUMN TRANSFORMATIONS OF A DETERMINANT**

If $A$ is a square matrix and if the matrix $B$ is obtained from $A$ by adding a multiple of one row to another or a multiple of one column to another, then $\det(A) = \det(B)$.

---

▶ **EXAMPLE 5** | Using Row and Column Transformations to Calculate a Determinant

Find the determinant of the matrix $A$. Does it have an inverse?

$$A = \begin{bmatrix} 8 & 2 & -1 & -4 \\ 3 & 5 & -3 & 11 \\ 24 & 6 & 1 & -12 \\ 2 & 2 & 7 & -1 \end{bmatrix}$$

▼ **SOLUTION** If we add $-3$ times row 1 to row 3, we change all but one element of row 3 to zeros:

$$\begin{bmatrix} 8 & 2 & -1 & -4 \\ 3 & 5 & -3 & 11 \\ 0 & 0 & 4 & 0 \\ 2 & 2 & 7 & -1 \end{bmatrix}$$

This new matrix has the same determinant as $A$, and if we expand its determinant by the third row, we get

$$\det(A) = 4 \begin{vmatrix} 8 & 2 & -4 \\ 3 & 5 & 11 \\ 2 & 2 & -1 \end{vmatrix}$$

Now, adding 2 times column 3 to column 1 in this determinant gives us

$$\det(A) = 4 \begin{vmatrix} 0 & 2 & -4 \\ 25 & 5 & 11 \\ 0 & 2 & -1 \end{vmatrix} \qquad \text{Expand this by column 1}$$

$$= 4(-25) \begin{vmatrix} 2 & -4 \\ 2 & -1 \end{vmatrix}$$

$$= 4(-25)[2(-1) - (-4)2] = -600$$

Since the determinant of $A$ is not zero, $A$ does have an inverse.

✎ **Practice what you've learned: Do Exercise 27.** ▲

The Granger Collection, New York

**Emmy Noether** (1882–1935) was one of the foremost mathematicians of the early 20th century. Her groundbreaking work in abstract algebra provided much of the foundation for this field, and her work in invariant theory was essential in the development of Einstein's theory of general relativity. Although women weren't allowed to study at German universities at that time, she audited courses unofficially and went on to receive a doctorate at Erlangen *summa cum laude*, despite the opposition of the academic senate, which declared that women students would "overthrow all academic order." She subsequently taught mathematics at Göttingen, Moscow, and Frankfurt. In 1933 she left Germany to escape Nazi persecution, accepting a position at Bryn Mawr College in suburban Philadelphia. She lectured there and at the Institute for Advanced Study in Princeton, New Jersey, until her untimely death in 1935.

## ■ Cramer's Rule

The solutions of linear equations can sometimes be expressed by using determinants. To illustrate, let's solve the following pair of linear equations for the variable $x$.

$$\begin{cases} ax + by = r \\ cx + dy = s \end{cases}$$

To eliminate the variable $y$, we multiply the first equation by $d$ and the second by $b$, and subtract.

$$\begin{array}{r} adx + bdy = rd \\ \underline{bcx + bdy = bs} \\ adx - bcx = rd - bs \end{array}$$

Factoring the left-hand side, we get $(ad - bc)x = rd - bs$. Assuming that $ad - bc \neq 0$, we can now solve this equation for $x$:

$$x = \frac{rd - bs}{ad - bc}$$

Similarly, we find

$$y = \frac{as - cr}{ad - bc}$$

The numerator and denominator of the fractions for $x$ and $y$ are determinants of $2 \times 2$ matrices. So we can express the solution of the system using determinants as follows.

---

### CRAMER'S RULE FOR SYSTEMS IN TWO VARIABLES

The linear system

$$\begin{cases} ax + by = r \\ cx + dy = s \end{cases}$$

has the solution

$$x = \frac{\begin{vmatrix} r & b \\ s & d \end{vmatrix}}{\begin{vmatrix} a & b \\ c & d \end{vmatrix}} \qquad y = \frac{\begin{vmatrix} a & r \\ c & s \end{vmatrix}}{\begin{vmatrix} a & b \\ c & d \end{vmatrix}}$$

provided that $\begin{vmatrix} a & b \\ c & d \end{vmatrix} \neq 0$.

---

Using the notation

$$D = \begin{bmatrix} a & b \\ c & d \end{bmatrix} \qquad D_x = \begin{bmatrix} r & b \\ s & d \end{bmatrix} \qquad D_y = \begin{bmatrix} a & r \\ c & s \end{bmatrix}$$

Coefficient matrix

Replace first column of $D$ by $r$ and $s$.

Replace second column of $D$ by $r$ and $s$.

we can write the solution of the system as

$$x = \frac{|D_x|}{|D|} \quad \text{and} \quad y = \frac{|D_y|}{|D|}$$

▶ **EXAMPLE 6** | Using Cramer's Rule to Solve a System with Two Variables

Use Cramer's Rule to solve the system.

$$\begin{cases} 2x + 6y = -1 \\ \phantom{2}x + 8y = \phantom{-}2 \end{cases}$$

▼ **SOLUTION** For this system we have

$$|D| = \begin{vmatrix} 2 & 6 \\ 1 & 8 \end{vmatrix} = 2 \cdot 8 - 6 \cdot 1 = 10$$

$$|D_x| = \begin{vmatrix} -1 & 6 \\ 2 & 8 \end{vmatrix} = (-1)8 - 6 \cdot 2 = -20$$

$$|D_y| = \begin{vmatrix} 2 & -1 \\ 1 & 2 \end{vmatrix} = 2 \cdot 2 - (-1)1 = 5$$

The solution is

$$x = \frac{|D_x|}{|D|} = \frac{-20}{10} = -2$$

$$y = \frac{|D_y|}{|D|} = \frac{5}{10} = \frac{1}{2}$$

✎ **Practice what you've learned: Do Exercise 33.** ▲

Cramer's Rule can be extended to apply to any system of $n$ linear equations in $n$ variables in which the determinant of the coefficient matrix is not zero. As we saw in the preceding section, any such system can be written in matrix form as

$$\begin{bmatrix} a_{11} & a_{12} & \cdots & a_{1n} \\ a_{21} & a_{22} & \cdots & a_{2n} \\ \vdots & \vdots & \ddots & \vdots \\ a_{n1} & a_{n2} & \cdots & a_{nn} \end{bmatrix} \begin{bmatrix} x_1 \\ x_2 \\ \vdots \\ x_n \end{bmatrix} = \begin{bmatrix} b_1 \\ b_2 \\ \vdots \\ b_n \end{bmatrix}$$

By analogy with our derivation of Cramer's Rule in the case of two equations in two unknowns, we let $D$ be the coefficient matrix in this system, and $D_{x_i}$ be the matrix obtained by replacing the $i$th column of $D$ by the numbers $b_1, b_2, \ldots, b_n$ that appear to the right of the equal sign. The solution of the system is then given by the following rule.

**CRAMER'S RULE**

If a system of $n$ linear equations in the $n$ variables $x_1, x_2, \ldots, x_n$ is equivalent to the matrix equation $DX = B$, and if $|D| \neq 0$, then its solutions are

$$x_1 = \frac{|D_{x_1}|}{|D|} \qquad x_2 = \frac{|D_{x_2}|}{|D|} \qquad \cdots \qquad x_n = \frac{|D_{x_n}|}{|D|}$$

where $D_{x_i}$ is the matrix obtained by replacing the $i$th column of $D$ by the $n \times 1$ matrix $B$.

▶ **EXAMPLE 7** | Using Cramer's Rule to Solve a System with Three Variables

Use Cramer's Rule to solve the system.

$$\begin{cases} 2x - 3y + 4z = 1 \\ x \qquad\quad + 6z = 0 \\ 3x - 2y \qquad\quad = 5 \end{cases}$$

▼ **SOLUTION**    First, we evaluate the determinants that appear in Cramer's Rule. Note that $D$ is the coefficient matrix and that $D_x$, $D_y$, and $D_z$ are obtained by replacing the first, second, and third columns of $D$ by the constant terms.

$$|D| = \begin{vmatrix} 2 & -3 & 4 \\ 1 & 0 & 6 \\ 3 & -2 & 0 \end{vmatrix} = -38 \qquad |D_x| = \begin{vmatrix} 1 & -3 & 4 \\ 0 & 0 & 6 \\ 5 & -2 & 0 \end{vmatrix} = -78$$

$$|D_y| = \begin{vmatrix} 2 & 1 & 4 \\ 1 & 0 & 6 \\ 3 & 5 & 0 \end{vmatrix} = -22 \qquad |D_z| = \begin{vmatrix} 2 & -3 & 1 \\ 1 & 0 & 0 \\ 3 & -2 & 5 \end{vmatrix} = 13$$

Now we use Cramer's Rule to get the solution:

$$x = \frac{|D_x|}{|D|} = \frac{-78}{-38} = \frac{39}{19}$$

$$y = \frac{|D_y|}{|D|} = \frac{-22}{-38} = \frac{11}{19}$$

$$z = \frac{|D_z|}{|D|} = \frac{13}{-38} = -\frac{13}{38}$$

✎ **Practice what you've learned: Do Exercise 39.**    ▲

Solving the system in Example 7 using Gaussian elimination would involve matrices whose elements are fractions with fairly large denominators. Thus, in cases like Examples 6 and 7, Cramer's Rule gives us an efficient way to solve systems of linear equations. But in systems with more than three equations, evaluating the various determinants that are involved is usually a long and tedious task (unless you are using a graphing calculator). Moreover, the rule doesn't apply if $|D| = 0$ or if $D$ is not a square matrix. So Cramer's Rule is a useful alternative to Gaussian elimination, but only in some situations.

## ■ Areas of Triangles Using Determinants

Determinants provide a simple way to calculate the area of a triangle in the coordinate plane.

---

### AREA OF A TRIANGLE

If a triangle in the coordinate plane has vertices $(a_1, b_1)$, $(a_2, b_2)$, and $(a_3, b_3)$, then its area is

$$\text{area} = \pm\frac{1}{2}\begin{vmatrix} a_1 & b_1 & 1 \\ a_2 & b_2 & 1 \\ a_3 & b_3 & 1 \end{vmatrix}$$

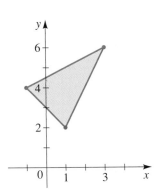

where the sign is chosen to make the area positive.

---

You are asked to prove this formula in Exercise 63.

▶ **EXAMPLE 8** | Area of a Triangle

Find the area of the triangle shown in Figure 1.

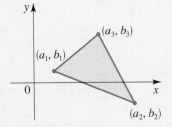

**FIGURE 1**

We can calculate the determinant by hand or by using a graphing calculator.

```
[A]
        [[-1 4 1]
         [3  6 1]
         [1  2 1]]
det([A])
              -12
```

▼ **SOLUTION**   The vertices are $(1, 2)$, $(3, 6)$, and $(-1, 4)$. Using the formula in the preceding box, we get

$$\text{area} = \pm\frac{1}{2}\begin{vmatrix} -1 & 4 & 1 \\ 3 & 6 & 1 \\ 1 & 2 & 1 \end{vmatrix} = \pm\frac{1}{2}(-12)$$

To make the area positive, we choose the negative sign in the formula. Thus, the area of the triangle is

$$\text{area} = -\frac{1}{2}(-12) = 6$$

✎ **Practice what you've learned: Do Exercise 55.**

▲

# 7.4 EXERCISES

## ▼ CONCEPTS

**1.** *True or false?* det(*A*) is defined only for a square matrix *A*.

**2.** *True or false?* det(*A*) is a number, not a matrix.

**3.** *True or false?* If det(*A*) = 0, then *A* is not invertible.

**4.** Fill in the blanks with appropriate numbers to calculate the determinant. Where there is "$\pm$", choose the appropriate sign (+ or −).

(a) $\begin{vmatrix} 2 & 1 \\ -3 & 4 \end{vmatrix} = \blacksquare\blacksquare - \blacksquare\blacksquare = \underline{\hspace{1cm}}$

(b) $\begin{vmatrix} 1 & 0 & 2 \\ 3 & 2 & 1 \\ 0 & -3 & 4 \end{vmatrix} = \pm\blacksquare(\blacksquare\blacksquare - \blacksquare\blacksquare) \pm \blacksquare(\blacksquare\blacksquare - \blacksquare\blacksquare)$

$\pm \blacksquare(\blacksquare\blacksquare - \blacksquare\blacksquare) = \underline{\hspace{1cm}}$

## ▼ SKILLS

**5–12** ▪ Find the determinant of the matrix, if it exists.

**5.** $\begin{bmatrix} 2 & 0 \\ 0 & 3 \end{bmatrix}$

**6.** $\begin{bmatrix} 0 & -1 \\ 2 & 0 \end{bmatrix}$

**7.** $\begin{bmatrix} 4 & 5 \\ 0 & -1 \end{bmatrix}$

**8.** $\begin{bmatrix} -2 & 1 \\ 3 & -2 \end{bmatrix}$

**9.** $\begin{bmatrix} 2 & 5 \end{bmatrix}$

**10.** $\begin{bmatrix} 3 \\ 0 \end{bmatrix}$

**11.** $\begin{bmatrix} \frac{1}{2} & \frac{1}{8} \\ 1 & \frac{1}{2} \end{bmatrix}$

**12.** $\begin{bmatrix} 2.2 & -1.4 \\ 0.5 & 1.0 \end{bmatrix}$

**13–18** ▪ Evaluate the minor and cofactor using the matrix *A*.

$$A = \begin{bmatrix} 1 & 0 & \frac{1}{2} \\ -3 & 5 & 2 \\ 0 & 0 & 4 \end{bmatrix}$$

**13.** $M_{11}, A_{11}$     **14.** $M_{33}, A_{33}$     **15.** $M_{12}, A_{12}$

**16.** $M_{13}, A_{13}$     **17.** $M_{23}, A_{23}$     **18.** $M_{32}, A_{32}$

**19–26** ▪ Find the determinant of the matrix. Determine whether the matrix has an inverse, but don't calculate the inverse.

**19.** $\begin{bmatrix} 2 & 1 & 0 \\ 0 & -2 & 4 \\ 0 & 1 & -3 \end{bmatrix}$

**20.** $\begin{bmatrix} 1 & 2 & 5 \\ -2 & -3 & 2 \\ 3 & 5 & 3 \end{bmatrix}$

**21.** $\begin{bmatrix} 30 & 0 & 20 \\ 0 & -10 & -20 \\ 40 & 0 & 10 \end{bmatrix}$

**22.** $\begin{bmatrix} -2 & -\frac{3}{2} & \frac{1}{2} \\ 2 & 4 & 0 \\ \frac{1}{2} & 2 & 1 \end{bmatrix}$

**23.** $\begin{bmatrix} 1 & 3 & 7 \\ 2 & 0 & 8 \\ 0 & 2 & 2 \end{bmatrix}$

**24.** $\begin{bmatrix} 0 & -1 & 0 \\ 2 & 6 & 4 \\ 1 & 0 & 3 \end{bmatrix}$

**25.** $\begin{bmatrix} 1 & 3 & 3 & 0 \\ 0 & 2 & 0 & 1 \\ -1 & 0 & 0 & 2 \\ 1 & 6 & 4 & 1 \end{bmatrix}$

**26.** $\begin{bmatrix} 1 & 2 & 0 & 2 \\ 3 & -4 & 0 & 4 \\ 0 & 1 & 6 & 0 \\ 1 & 0 & 2 & 0 \end{bmatrix}$

**27–30** ▪ Evaluate the determinant, using row or column operations whenever possible to simplify your work.

**27.** $\begin{vmatrix} 0 & 0 & 4 & 6 \\ 2 & 1 & 1 & 3 \\ 2 & 1 & 2 & 3 \\ 3 & 0 & 1 & 7 \end{vmatrix}$

**28.** $\begin{vmatrix} -2 & 3 & -1 & 7 \\ 4 & 6 & -2 & 3 \\ 7 & 7 & 0 & 5 \\ 3 & -12 & 4 & 0 \end{vmatrix}$

**29.** $\begin{vmatrix} 1 & 2 & 3 & 4 & 5 \\ 0 & 2 & 4 & 6 & 8 \\ 0 & 0 & 3 & 6 & 9 \\ 0 & 0 & 0 & 4 & 8 \\ 0 & 0 & 0 & 0 & 5 \end{vmatrix}$

**30.** $\begin{vmatrix} 2 & -1 & 6 & 4 \\ 7 & 2 & -2 & 5 \\ 4 & -2 & 10 & 8 \\ 6 & 1 & 1 & 4 \end{vmatrix}$

**31.** Let

$$B = \begin{bmatrix} 4 & 1 & 0 \\ -2 & -1 & 1 \\ 4 & 0 & 3 \end{bmatrix}$$

(a) Evaluate det(*B*) by expanding by the second row.
(b) Evaluate det(*B*) by expanding by the third column.
(c) Do your results in parts (a) and (b) agree?

**32.** Consider the system

$$\begin{cases} x + 2y + 6z = 5 \\ -3x - 6y + 5z = 8 \\ 2x + 6y + 9z = 7 \end{cases}$$

(a) Verify that $x = -1$, $y = 0$, $z = 1$ is a solution of the system.
(b) Find the determinant of the coefficient matrix.
(c) Without solving the system, determine whether there are any other solutions.
(d) Can Cramer's Rule be used to solve this system? Why or why not?

**33–48** ▪ Use Cramer's Rule to solve the system.

**33.** $\begin{cases} 2x - y = -9 \\ x + 2y = 8 \end{cases}$

**34.** $\begin{cases} 6x + 12y = 33 \\ 4x + 7y = 20 \end{cases}$

**35.** $\begin{cases} x - 6y = 3 \\ 3x + 2y = 1 \end{cases}$

**36.** $\begin{cases} \frac{1}{2}x + \frac{1}{3}y = 1 \\ \frac{1}{4}x - \frac{1}{6}y = -\frac{3}{2} \end{cases}$

**37.** $\begin{cases} 0.4x + 1.2y = 0.4 \\ 1.2x + 1.6y = 3.2 \end{cases}$

**38.** $\begin{cases} 10x - 17y = 21 \\ 20x - 31y = 39 \end{cases}$

**39.** $\begin{cases} x - y + 2z = 0 \\ 3x + z = 11 \\ -x + 2y = 0 \end{cases}$

**40.** $\begin{cases} 5x - 3y + z = 6 \\ 4y - 6z = 22 \\ 7x + 10y = -13 \end{cases}$

**41.** $\begin{cases} 2x_1 + 3x_2 - 5x_3 = 1 \\ x_1 + x_2 - x_3 = 2 \\ 2x_2 + x_3 = 8 \end{cases}$

**42.** $\begin{cases} -2a + c = 2 \\ a + 2b - c = 9 \\ 3a + 5b + 2c = 22 \end{cases}$

**43.** $\begin{cases} \frac{1}{3}x - \frac{1}{5}y + \frac{1}{2}z = \frac{7}{10} \\ -\frac{2}{3}x + \frac{2}{5}y + \frac{3}{2}z = \frac{11}{10} \\ x - \frac{4}{5}y + z = \frac{9}{5} \end{cases}$  **44.** $\begin{cases} 2x - y = 5 \\ 5x + 3z = 19 \\ 4y + 7z = 17 \end{cases}$

**45.** $\begin{cases} 3y + 5z = 4 \\ 2x - z = 10 \\ 4x + 7y = 0 \end{cases}$  **46.** $\begin{cases} 2x - 5y = 4 \\ x + y - z = 8 \\ 3x + 5z = 0 \end{cases}$

**47.** $\begin{cases} x + y + z + w = 0 \\ 2x + w = 0 \\ y - z = 0 \\ x + 2z = 1 \end{cases}$  **48.** $\begin{cases} x + y = 1 \\ y + z = 2 \\ z + w = 3 \\ w - x = 4 \end{cases}$

**49–50** ▪ Evaluate the determinants.

**49.** $\begin{vmatrix} a & 0 & 0 & 0 & 0 \\ 0 & b & 0 & 0 & 0 \\ 0 & 0 & c & 0 & 0 \\ 0 & 0 & 0 & d & 0 \\ 0 & 0 & 0 & 0 & e \end{vmatrix}$  **50.** $\begin{vmatrix} a & a & a & a & a \\ 0 & a & a & a & a \\ 0 & 0 & a & a & a \\ 0 & 0 & 0 & a & a \\ 0 & 0 & 0 & 0 & a \end{vmatrix}$

**51–54** ▪ Solve for $x$.

**51.** $\begin{vmatrix} x & 12 & 13 \\ 0 & x - 1 & 23 \\ 0 & 0 & x - 2 \end{vmatrix} = 0$  **52.** $\begin{vmatrix} x & 1 & 1 \\ 1 & 1 & x \\ x & 1 & x \end{vmatrix} = 0$

**53.** $\begin{vmatrix} 1 & 0 & x \\ x^2 & 1 & 0 \\ x & 0 & 1 \end{vmatrix} = 0$  **54.** $\begin{vmatrix} a & b & x - a \\ x & x + b & x \\ 0 & 1 & 1 \end{vmatrix} = 0$

**55–58** ▪ Sketch the triangle with the given vertices and use a determinant to find its area.

**55.** $(0, 0), (6, 2), (3, 8)$  **56.** $(1, 0), (3, 5), (-2, 2)$

**57.** $(-1, 3), (2, 9), (5, -6)$  **58.** $(-2, 5), (7, 2), (3, -4)$

**59.** Show that $\begin{vmatrix} 1 & x & x^2 \\ 1 & y & y^2 \\ 1 & z & z^2 \end{vmatrix} = (x - y)(y - z)(z - x)$

## ▼ APPLICATIONS

**60. Buying Fruit** A roadside fruit stand sells apples at 75¢ a pound, peaches at 90¢ a pound, and pears at 60¢ a pound. Muriel buys 18 pounds of fruit at a total cost of $13.80. Her peaches and pears together cost $1.80 more than her apples.
   **(a)** Set up a linear system for the number of pounds of apples, peaches, and pears that she bought.
   **(b)** Solve the system using Cramer's Rule.

**61. The Arch of a Bridge** The opening of a railway bridge over a roadway is in the shape of a parabola. A surveyor measures

the heights of three points on the bridge, as shown in the figure. He wishes to find an equation of the form

$$y = ax^2 + bx + c$$

to model the shape of the arch.
   **(a)** Use the surveyed points to set up a system of linear equations for the unknown coefficients $a$, $b$, and $c$.
   **(b)** Solve the system using Cramer's Rule.

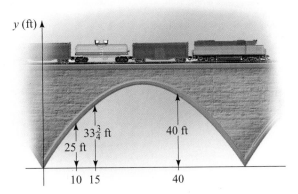

**62. A Triangular Plot of Land** An outdoors club is purchasing land to set up a conservation area. The last remaining piece they need to buy is the triangular plot shown in the figure. Use the determinant formula for the area of a triangle to find the area of the plot.

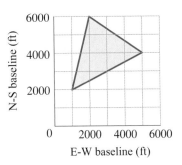

## ▼ DISCOVERY • DISCUSSION • WRITING

**63. Determinant Formula for the Area of a Triangle** The figure on the next page shows a triangle in the plane with vertices $(a_1, b_1)$, $(a_2, b_2)$, and $(a_3, b_3)$.
   **(a)** Find the coordinates of the vertices of the surrounding rectangle, and find its area.
   **(b)** Find the area of the red triangle by subtracting the areas of the three blue triangles from the area of the rectangle.
   **(c)** Use your answer to part (b) to show that the area of the red triangle is given by

$$\text{area} = \pm \frac{1}{2} \begin{vmatrix} a_1 & b_1 & 1 \\ a_2 & b_2 & 1 \\ a_3 & b_3 & 1 \end{vmatrix}$$

### 64. Collinear Points and Determinants

**(a)** If three points lie on a line, what is the area of the "triangle" that they determine? Use the answer to this question, together with the determinant formula for the area of a triangle, to explain why the points $(a_1, b_1)$, $(a_2, b_2)$, and $(a_3, b_3)$ are collinear if and only if

$$\begin{vmatrix} a_1 & b_1 & 1 \\ a_2 & b_2 & 1 \\ a_3 & b_3 & 1 \end{vmatrix} = 0$$

**(b)** Use a determinant to check whether each set of points is collinear. Graph them to verify your answer.

(i) $(-6, 4), (2, 10), (6, 13)$

(ii) $(-5, 10), (2, 6), (15, -2)$

### 65. Determinant Form for the Equation of a Line

**(a)** Use the result of Exercise 64(a) to show that the equation of the line containing the points $(x_1, y_1)$ and $(x_2, y_2)$ is

$$\begin{vmatrix} x & y & 1 \\ x_1 & y_1 & 1 \\ x_2 & y_2 & 1 \end{vmatrix} = 0$$

**(b)** Use the result of part (a) to find an equation for the line containing the points $(20, 50)$ and $(-10, 25)$.

### 66. Matrices with Determinant Zero
Use the definition of determinant and the elementary row and column operations to explain why matrices of the following types have determinant 0.

**(a)** A matrix with a row or column consisting entirely of zeros

**(b)** A matrix with two rows the same or two columns the same

**(c)** A matrix in which one row is a multiple of another row, or one column is a multiple of another column

### 67. Solving Linear Systems
Suppose you have to solve a linear system with five equations and five variables without the assistance of a calculator or computer. Which method would you prefer: Cramer's Rule or Gaussian elimination? Write a short paragraph explaining the reasons for your answer.

---

## ▶ CHAPTER 7 | REVIEW

---

## ▼ PROPERTIES AND FORMULAS

### Matrices (p. 495)

A **matrix** $A$ of **dimension** $m \times n$ is a rectangular array of numbers with $m$ **rows** and $n$ **columns**:

$$A = \begin{bmatrix} a_{11} & a_{12} & \cdots & a_{1n} \\ a_{21} & a_{22} & \cdots & a_{2n} \\ \vdots & \vdots & \ddots & \vdots \\ a_{m1} & a_{m2} & \cdots & a_{mn} \end{bmatrix}$$

### Augmented Matrix of a System (p. 495)

The **augmented matrix** of a system of linear equations is the matrix consisting of the coefficients and the constant terms. For example, for the two-variable system

$$a_{11}x + a_{12}x = b_1$$
$$a_{21}x + a_{22}x = b_2$$

the augmented matrix is

$$\begin{bmatrix} a_{11} & a_{12} & b_1 \\ a_{21} & a_{22} & b_2 \end{bmatrix}$$

### Elementary Row Operations (p. 496)

To solve a system of linear equations using the augmented matrix of the system, the following operations can be used to transform the rows of the matrix:

1. Add a nonzero multiple of one row to another.

2. Multiply a row by a nonzero constant.

3. Interchange two rows.

### Row-Echelon Form of a Matrix (p. 497)

A matrix is in **row-echelon form** if its entries satisfy the following conditions:

1. The first nonzero entry in each row (the **leading entry**) is the number 1.

2. The leading entry of each row is to the right of the leading entry in the row above it.

3. All rows consisting entirely of zeros are at the bottom of the matrix.

If the matrix also satisfies the following condition, it is in **reduced row-echelon** form:

4. If a column contains a leading entry, then every other entry in that column is a 0.

## Number of Solutions of a Linear System (p. 501)

If the augmented matrix of a system of linear equations has been reduced to row-echelon form using elementary row operations, then the system has:

1. **No solution** if the row-echelon form contains a row that represents the equation $0 = 1$. In this case the system is **inconsistent**.

2. **One solution** if each variable in the row-echelon form is a **leading variable**.

3. **Infinitely many solutions** if the system is not inconsistent but not every variable is a leading variable. In this case the system is **dependent**.

## Operations on Matrices (p. 508)

If $A$ and $B$ are $m \times n$ matrices and $c$ is a scalar (real number), then:

1. The **sum** $A + B$ is the $m \times n$ matrix that is obtained by adding corresponding entries of $A$ and $B$.

2. The **difference** $A - B$ is the $m \times n$ matrix that is obtained by subtracting corresponding entries of $A$ and $B$.

3. The **scalar product** $cA$ is the $m \times n$ matrix that is obtained by multiplying each entry of $A$ by $c$.

## Multiplication of Matrices (p. 510)

If $A$ is an $m \times n$ matrix and $B$ is an $n \times k$ matrix (so the number of columns of $A$ is the same as the number of rows of $B$), then the **matrix product** $AB$ is the $m \times k$ matrix whose $ij$-entry is the inner product of the $i$th row of $A$ and the $j$th column of $B$.

## Properties of Matrix Operations (pp. 509, 512)

If $A$, $B$, and $C$ are matrices of compatible dimensions then the following properties hold:

1. **Commutativity of addition:**
$$A + B = B + A$$

2. **Associativity:**
$$(A + B) + C = A + (B + C)$$
$$(AB)C = A(BC)$$

3. **Distributivity:**
$$A(B + C) = AB + AC$$
$$(B + C)A = BA + CA$$

(Note that matrix *multiplication* is *not* commutative.)

## Identity Matrix (p. 520)

The **identity matrix** $I_n$ is the $n \times n$ matrix whose main diagonal entries are all 1 and whose other entries are all 0:

$$I_n = \begin{bmatrix} 1 & 0 & \cdots & 0 \\ 0 & 1 & \cdots & 0 \\ \vdots & \vdots & \ddots & \vdots \\ 0 & 0 & \cdots & 1 \end{bmatrix}$$

If $A$ is an $m \times n$ matrix, then

$$AI_n = A \quad \text{and} \quad I_m A = A$$

## Inverse of a Matrix (p. 521)

If $A$ is an $n \times n$ matrix, then the inverse of $A$ is the $n \times n$ matrix $A^{-1}$ with the following properties:

$$A^{-1}A = I_n \quad \text{and} \quad AA^{-1} = I_n$$

To find the inverse of a matrix, we use a procedure involving elementary row operations (explained on page 496). (Note that *some* square matrices do not have an inverse.)

## Inverse of a 2 × 2 Matrix (p. 521)

For $2 \times 2$ matrices the following special rule provides a shortcut for finding the inverse:

$$A = \begin{bmatrix} a & b \\ c & d \end{bmatrix} \quad \Rightarrow \quad A^{-1} = \frac{1}{ad - bc} \begin{bmatrix} d & -b \\ -c & a \end{bmatrix}$$

## Writing a Linear System as a Matrix Equation (p. 524)

A system of $n$ linear equations in $n$ variables can be written as a single matrix equation

$$AX = B$$

where $A$ is the $n \times n$ matrix of coefficients, $X$ is the $n \times 1$ matrix of the variables, and $B$ is the $n \times 1$ matrix of the constants. For example, the linear system of two equations in two variables

$$a_{11}x + a_{12}x = b_1$$
$$a_{21}x + a_{22}x = b_2$$

can be expressed as

$$\begin{bmatrix} a_{11} & a_{12} \\ a_{21} & a_{22} \end{bmatrix} \begin{bmatrix} x \\ y \end{bmatrix} = \begin{bmatrix} b_1 \\ b_2 \end{bmatrix}$$

## Solving Matrix Equations (p. 525)

If $A$ is an invertible $n \times n$ matrix, $X$ is an $n \times 1$ variable matrix, and $B$ is an $n \times 1$ constant matrix, then the matrix equation

$$AX = B$$

has the unique solution

$$X = A^{-1}B$$

## Determinant of a 2 × 2 Matrix (p. 530)

The **determinant** of the matrix

$$A = \begin{bmatrix} a & b \\ c & d \end{bmatrix}$$

is the *number*

$$\det(A) = |A| = ad - bc$$

## Minors and Cofactors (p. 531)

If $A = |a_{ij}|$ is an $n \times n$ matrix, then the **minor** $M_{ij}$ of the entry $a_{ij}$ is the determinant of the matrix obtained by deleting the $i$th row and the $j$th column of $A$.

The **cofactor** $A_{ij}$ of the entry $a_{ij}$ is

$$A_{ij} = (-1)^{i+j}M_{ij}$$

(Thus, the minor and the cofactor of each entry either are the same or are negatives of each other.)

## Determinant of an $n \times n$ Matrix (p. 531)

To find the **determinant** of the $n \times n$ matrix

$$A = \begin{bmatrix} a_{11} & a_{12} & \cdots & a_{1n} \\ a_{21} & a_{22} & \cdots & a_{2n} \\ \vdots & \vdots & \ddots & \vdots \\ a_{n1} & a_{n2} & \cdots & a_{nn} \end{bmatrix}$$

we choose a row or column to **expand**, and then we calculate the number that is obtained by multiplying each element of that row or column by its cofactor and then adding the resulting products. For example, if we choose to expand about the first row, we get

$$\det(A) = |A| = a_{11}A_{11} + a_{12}A_{12} + \cdots + a_{1n}A_{1n}$$

## Invertibility Criterion (p. 533)

A square matrix has an inverse if and only if its determinant is not 0.

## Row and Column Transformations (p. 534)

If we add a nonzero multiple of one row to another row in a square matrix or a nonzero multiple of one column to another column, then the determinant of the matrix is unchanged.

## Cramer's Rule (pp. 535–537)

If a system of $n$ linear equations in the $n$ variables $x_1, x_2, \ldots, x_n$ is equivalent to the matrix equation $DX = B$ and if $|D| \neq 0$, then the solutions of the system are

$$x_1 = \frac{|D_{x_1}|}{|D|} \qquad x_2 = \frac{|D_{x_2}|}{|D|} \qquad \cdots \qquad x_n = \frac{|D_{x_n}|}{|D|}$$

where $D_{x_i}$ is the matrix that is obtained from $D$ by replacing its $i$th column by the constant matrix $B$.

## Area of a Triangle Using Determinants (p. 538)

If a triangle in the coordinate plane has vertices $(a_1, b_1)$, $(a_2, b_2)$, and $(a_3, b_3)$, then the area of the triangle is given by

$$\text{area} = \pm\frac{1}{2}\begin{vmatrix} a_1 & b_1 & 1 \\ a_2 & b_2 & 1 \\ a_3 & b_3 & 1 \end{vmatrix}$$

where the sign is chosen to make the area positive.

## ▼ CONCEPT SUMMARY

### Section 7.1

| | Review Exercises |
|---|---|
| ▪ Find the augmented matrix of a linear system | 1–20 |
| ▪ Solve a linear system using elementary row operations | 7–20 |
| ▪ Solve a linear system using the row-echelon form of its matrix | 7–12 |
| ▪ Solve a system using the reduced row-echelon form of its matrix | 13–20 |
| ▪ Determine the number of solutions of a linear system from the row-echelon form of its matrix | 7–20 |
| ▪ Model using linear systems | 63–64 |

### Section 7.2

| | Review Exercises |
|---|---|
| ▪ Determine whether two matrices are equal | 21–22 |
| ▪ Use addition, subtraction, and scalar multiplication of matrices | 23–26 |
| ▪ Multiply matrices | 27–34 |
| ▪ Write a linear system in matrix form | 51–54 |

### Section 7.3

| | Review Exercises |
|---|---|
| ▪ Determine when two matrices are inverses of each other | 35–36 |
| ▪ Find the inverse of a $2 \times 2$ matrix | 43–45 |
| ▪ Find the inverse of an $n \times n$ matrix | 46–50 |
| ▪ Solve a linear system by writing it as a matrix equation | 51–54 |
| ▪ Model using matrix equations | 55–56 |

### Section 7.4

| | Review Exercises |
|---|---|
| ▪ Find the determinant of a $2 \times 2$ matrix | 43–45 |
| ▪ Find the determinant of an $n \times n$ matrix | 46–50 |
| ▪ Use the Invertibility Criterion | 43–50 |
| ▪ Use row and column transformations in computing the determinant of a matrix | 47–48, 50 |
| ▪ Use Cramer's Rule to solve a linear system | 57–60 |
| ▪ Use determinants to find the area of a triangle in the coordinate plane | 61–62 |

## ▼ EXERCISES

**1–6** ▪ A matrix is given. **(a)** State the dimension of the matrix. **(b)** Is the matrix in row-echelon form? **(c)** Is the matrix in reduced row-echelon form? **(d)** Write the system of equations for which the given matrix is the augmented matrix.

**1.** $\begin{bmatrix} 1 & 2 & -5 \\ 0 & 1 & 3 \end{bmatrix}$ 
**2.** $\begin{bmatrix} 1 & 0 & 6 \\ 0 & 1 & 0 \end{bmatrix}$

**3.** $\begin{bmatrix} 1 & 0 & 8 & 0 \\ 0 & 1 & 5 & -1 \\ 0 & 0 & 0 & 0 \end{bmatrix}$ 
**4.** $\begin{bmatrix} 1 & 3 & 6 & 2 \\ 2 & 1 & 0 & 5 \\ 0 & 0 & 1 & 0 \end{bmatrix}$

**5.** $\begin{bmatrix} 0 & 1 & -3 & 4 \\ 1 & 1 & 0 & 7 \\ 1 & 2 & 1 & 2 \end{bmatrix}$ 
**6.** $\begin{bmatrix} 1 & 8 & 6 & -4 \\ 0 & 1 & -3 & 5 \\ 0 & 0 & 2 & -7 \\ 1 & 1 & 1 & 0 \end{bmatrix}$

**7–12** ▪ Use Gaussian elimination to find the complete solution of the system, or show that no solution exists.

**7.** $\begin{cases} x + 2y + 2z = 6 \\ x - y = -1 \\ 2x + y + 3z = 7 \end{cases}$ 
**8.** $\begin{cases} x - y + z = 2 \\ x + y + 3z = 6 \\ 2y + 3z = 5 \end{cases}$

**9.** $\begin{cases} x - 2y + 3z = -2 \\ 2x - y + z = 2 \\ 2x - 7y + 11z = -9 \end{cases}$ 
**10.** $\begin{cases} x - y + z = 2 \\ x + y + 3z = 6 \\ 3x - y + 5z = 10 \end{cases}$

**11.** $\begin{cases} x + y + z + w = 0 \\ x - y - 4z - w = -1 \\ x - 2y + 4w = -7 \\ 2x + 2y + 3z + 4w = -3 \end{cases}$ 
**12.** $\begin{cases} x + 3z = -1 \\ y - 4w = 5 \\ 2y + z + w = 0 \\ 2x + y + 5z - 4w = 4 \end{cases}$

**13–20** ▪ Use Gauss-Jordan elimination to find the complete solution of the system, or show that no solution exists.

**13.** $\begin{cases} x - y + 3z = 2 \\ 2x + y + z = 2 \\ 3x + 4z = 4 \end{cases}$ 
**14.** $\begin{cases} x - y = 1 \\ x + y + 2z = 3 \\ x - 3y - 2z = -1 \end{cases}$

**15.** $\begin{cases} x - y + z - w = 0 \\ 3x - y - z - w = 2 \end{cases}$ 
**16.** $\begin{cases} x - y = 3 \\ 2x + y = 6 \\ x - 2y = 9 \end{cases}$

**17.** $\begin{cases} x - y + z = 0 \\ 3x + 2y - z = 6 \\ x + 4y - 3z = 3 \end{cases}$ 
**18.** $\begin{cases} x + 2y + 3z = 2 \\ 2x - y - 5z = 1 \\ 4x + 3y + z = 6 \end{cases}$

**19.** $\begin{cases} x + y - z - w = 2 \\ x - y + z - w = 0 \\ 2x + 2w = 2 \\ 2x + 4y - 4z - 2w = 6 \end{cases}$ 
**20.** $\begin{cases} x - y - 2z + 3w = 0 \\ y - z + w = 1 \\ 3x - 2y - 7z + 10w = 2 \end{cases}$

**21–22** ▪ Determine whether the matrices $A$ and $B$ are equal.

**21.** $A = \begin{bmatrix} 1 & 2 & 3 \\ 0 & 4 & 6 \\ 0 & 0 & 0 \end{bmatrix}$ $B = \begin{bmatrix} 1 & 2 & 3 \\ 0 & 4 & 6 \end{bmatrix}$

**22.** $A = \begin{bmatrix} \sqrt{25} & 1 \\ 0 & 2^{-1} \end{bmatrix}$ $B = \begin{bmatrix} 5 & e^0 \\ \log 1 & \frac{1}{2} \end{bmatrix}$

**23–34** ▪ Let

$$A = \begin{bmatrix} 2 & 0 & -1 \end{bmatrix} \qquad B = \begin{bmatrix} 1 & 2 & 4 \\ -2 & 1 & 0 \end{bmatrix}$$

$$C = \begin{bmatrix} \frac{1}{2} & 3 \\ 2 & \frac{3}{2} \\ -2 & 1 \end{bmatrix} \qquad D = \begin{bmatrix} 1 & 4 \\ 0 & -1 \\ 2 & 0 \end{bmatrix}$$

$$E = \begin{bmatrix} 2 & -1 \\ -\frac{1}{2} & 1 \end{bmatrix} \qquad F = \begin{bmatrix} 4 & 0 & 2 \\ -1 & 1 & 0 \\ 7 & 5 & 0 \end{bmatrix}$$

$$G = \begin{bmatrix} 5 \end{bmatrix}$$

Carry out the indicated operation, or explain why it cannot be performed.

**23.** $A + B$ **24.** $C - D$ **25.** $2C + 3D$

**26.** $5B - 2C$ **27.** $GA$ **28.** $AG$

**29.** $BC$ **30.** $CB$ **31.** $BF$

**32.** $FC$ **33.** $(C + D)E$ **34.** $F(2C - D)$

**35–36** ▪ Verify that the matrices $A$ and $B$ are inverses of each other by calculating the products $AB$ and $BA$.

**35.** $A = \begin{bmatrix} 2 & -5 \\ -2 & 6 \end{bmatrix}$ $B = \begin{bmatrix} 3 & \frac{5}{2} \\ 1 & 1 \end{bmatrix}$

**36.** $A = \begin{bmatrix} 2 & -1 & 3 \\ 2 & -2 & 1 \\ 0 & 1 & 1 \end{bmatrix}$ $B = \begin{bmatrix} -\frac{3}{2} & 2 & \frac{5}{2} \\ -1 & 1 & 2 \\ 1 & -1 & -1 \end{bmatrix}$

**37–42** ▪ Solve the matrix equation for the unknown matrix, $X$, or show that no solution exists, where

$$A = \begin{bmatrix} 2 & 1 \\ 3 & 2 \end{bmatrix} \quad B = \begin{bmatrix} 1 & -2 \\ -2 & 4 \end{bmatrix} \quad C = \begin{bmatrix} 0 & 1 & 3 \\ -2 & 4 & 0 \end{bmatrix}$$

**37.** $A + 3X = B$

**38.** $\frac{1}{2}(X - 2B) = A$

**39.** $2(X - A) = 3B$

**40.** $2X + C = 5A$

**41.** $AX = C$

**42.** $AX = B$

**43–50** ▪ Find the determinant and, if possible, the inverse of the matrix.

**43.** $\begin{bmatrix} 1 & 4 \\ 2 & 9 \end{bmatrix}$ 
**44.** $\begin{bmatrix} 2 & 2 \\ 1 & -3 \end{bmatrix}$

**45.** $\begin{bmatrix} 4 & -12 \\ -2 & 6 \end{bmatrix}$ 
**46.** $\begin{bmatrix} 2 & 4 & 0 \\ -1 & 1 & 2 \\ 0 & 3 & 2 \end{bmatrix}$

**47.** $\begin{bmatrix} 3 & 0 & 1 \\ 2 & -3 & 0 \\ 4 & -2 & 1 \end{bmatrix}$ 
**48.** $\begin{bmatrix} 1 & 2 & 3 \\ 2 & 4 & 5 \\ 2 & 5 & 6 \end{bmatrix}$

**49.** $\begin{bmatrix} 1 & 0 & 0 & 1 \\ 0 & 2 & 0 & 2 \\ 0 & 0 & 3 & 3 \\ 0 & 0 & 0 & 4 \end{bmatrix}$    **50.** $\begin{bmatrix} 1 & 0 & 1 & 0 \\ 0 & 1 & 0 & 1 \\ 1 & 1 & 1 & 2 \\ 1 & 2 & 1 & 2 \end{bmatrix}$

**51–54** ▪ Express the system of linear equations as a matrix equation. Then solve the matrix equation by multiplying each side by the inverse of the coefficient matrix.

**51.** $\begin{cases} 12x - 5y = 10 \\ 5x - 2y = 17 \end{cases}$    **52.** $\begin{cases} 6x - 5y = 1 \\ 8x - 7y = -1 \end{cases}$

**53.** $\begin{cases} 2x + y + 5z = \frac{1}{3} \\ x + 2y + 2z = \frac{1}{4} \\ x \quad\quad + 3z = \frac{1}{6} \end{cases}$    **54.** $\begin{cases} 2x \quad\quad + 3z = 5 \\ x + y + 6z = 0 \\ 3x - y + z = 5 \end{cases}$

**55.** Magda and Ivan grow tomatoes, onions, and zucchini in their backyard and sell them at a roadside stand on Saturdays and Sundays. They price tomatoes at $1.50 per pound, onions at $1.00 per pound, and zucchini at 50 cents per pound. The following table shows the number of pounds of each type of produce that they sold during the last weekend in July.

|           | Tomatoes | Onions | Zucchini |
|-----------|----------|--------|----------|
| Saturday  | 25       | 16     | 30       |
| Sunday    | 14       | 12     | 16       |

**(a)** Let

$$A = \begin{bmatrix} 25 & 16 & 30 \\ 14 & 12 & 16 \end{bmatrix} \quad \text{and} \quad B = \begin{bmatrix} 1.50 \\ 1.00 \\ 0.50 \end{bmatrix}$$

Compare these matrices to the data given in the problem, and describe what their entries represent.

**(b)** Only one of the products $AB$ or $BA$ is defined. Calculate the product that *is* defined, and describe what its entries represent.

**56.** An ATM at a bank in Qualicum Beach, British Columbia, dispenses $20 and $50 bills. Brodie withdraws $600 from this machine and receives a total of 18 bills. Let $x$ be the number of $20 bills and $y$ the number of $50 bills that he receives.
   **(a)** Find a system of two linear equations in $x$ and $y$ that express the information given in the problem.
   **(b)** Write your linear system as a matrix equation of the form $AX = B$.
   **(c)** Find $A^{-1}$, and use it to solve your matrix equation in part (b). How many bills of each type did Brodie receive?

**57–60** ▪ Solve the system using Cramer's Rule.

**57.** $\begin{cases} 2x + 7y = 13 \\ 6x + 16y = 30 \end{cases}$    **58.** $\begin{cases} 12x - 11y = 140 \\ 7x + 9y = 20 \end{cases}$

**59.** $\begin{cases} 2x - y + 5z = 0 \\ -x + 7y \quad\quad = 9 \\ 5x + 4y + 3z = -9 \end{cases}$    **60.** $\begin{cases} 3x + 4y - z = 10 \\ x \quad\quad - 4z = 20 \\ 2x + y + 5z = 30 \end{cases}$

**61–62** ▪ Use the determinant formula for the area of a triangle to find the area of the triangle in the figure.

**61.**

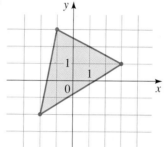

**62.**

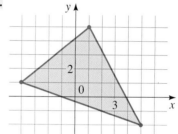

**63–64** ▪ Use any of the methods you have learned in this chapter to solve the problem.

**63.** Clarisse invests $60,000 in money-market accounts at three different banks. Bank A pays 2% interest per year, bank B pays 2.5%, and bank C pays 3%. She decides to invest twice as much in bank B as in the other two banks. After one year, Clarisse has earned $1575 in interest. How much did she invest in each bank?

**64.** A commercial fisherman fishes for haddock, sea bass, and red snapper. He is paid $1.25 a pound for haddock, $0.75 a pound for sea bass, and $2.00 a pound for red snapper. Yesterday he caught 560 lb of fish worth $575. The haddock and red snapper together are worth $320. How many pounds of each fish did he catch?

**1–4** ■ Determine whether the matrix is in reduced row-echelon form, row-echelon form, or neither.

**1.** $\begin{bmatrix} 1 & 8 & 0 & 0 \\ 0 & 1 & 7 & 10 \\ 0 & 0 & 0 & 0 \end{bmatrix}$

**2.** $\begin{bmatrix} 0 & 0 & 0 & 4 \\ 0 & 0 & 2 & 5 \\ 0 & 1 & -2 & 7 \\ 1 & 0 & -3 & 0 \end{bmatrix}$

**3.** $\begin{bmatrix} 1 & 0 & 0 \\ 0 & 0 & 1 \end{bmatrix}$

**4.** $\begin{bmatrix} 1 & 0 & 0 & 3 \\ 0 & 1 & 0 & -2 \\ 0 & 0 & 1 & \frac{3}{2} \end{bmatrix}$

**5–6** ■ Use Gaussian elimination to find the complete solution of the system, or show that no solution exists.

**5.** $\begin{cases} x - y + 2z = 0 \\ 2x - 4y + 5z = -5 \\ 2y - 3z = 5 \end{cases}$

**6.** $\begin{cases} 2x - 3y + z = 3 \\ x + 2y + 2z = -1 \\ 4x + y + 5z = 4 \end{cases}$

**7.** Use Gauss-Jordan elimination to find the complete solution of the system.

$$\begin{cases} x + 3y - z = 0 \\ 3x + 4y - 2z = -1 \\ -x + 2y = 1 \end{cases}$$

**8–15** ■ Let

$$A = \begin{bmatrix} 2 & 3 \\ 2 & 4 \end{bmatrix} \quad B = \begin{bmatrix} 2 & 4 \\ -1 & 1 \\ 3 & 0 \end{bmatrix} \quad C = \begin{bmatrix} 1 & 0 & 4 \\ -1 & 1 & 2 \\ 0 & 1 & 3 \end{bmatrix}$$

Carry out the indicated operation, or explain why it cannot be performed.

**8.** $A + B$  **9.** $AB$  **10.** $BA - 3B$  **11.** $CBA$

**12.** $A^{-1}$  **13.** $B^{-1}$  **14.** $\det(B)$  **15.** $\det(C)$

**16. (a)** Write a matrix equation equivalent to the following system.

$$\begin{cases} 4x - 3y = 10 \\ 3x - 2y = 30 \end{cases}$$

**(b)** Find the inverse of the coefficient matrix, and use it to solve the system.

**17.** Only one of the following matrices has an inverse. Find the determinant of each matrix, and use the determinants to identify the one that has an inverse. Then find the inverse.

$$A = \begin{bmatrix} 1 & 4 & 1 \\ 0 & 2 & 0 \\ 1 & 0 & 1 \end{bmatrix} \quad B = \begin{bmatrix} 1 & 4 & 0 \\ 0 & 2 & 0 \\ -3 & 0 & 1 \end{bmatrix}$$

**18.** Solve using Cramer's Rule:

$$\begin{cases} 2x - z = 14 \\ 3x - y + 5z = 0 \\ 4x + 2y + 3z = -2 \end{cases}$$

**19.** A shopper buys a mixture of nuts; the almonds cost $4.75 a pound, and the walnuts cost $3.45 a pound. Her total purchase weighs 3 lb and costs $11.91. Use Cramer's Rule to determine how much of each nut she bought.

Matrix algebra is the basic tool used in computer graphics to manipulate images on a computer screen. We will see how matrix multiplication can be used to "move" a point in the plane to a prescribed location. Combining such moves enables us to stretch, compress, rotate, and otherwise transform a figure, as we see in the images below.

| Image | Compressed | Rotated | Sheared |

## Moving Points in the Plane

Let's represent the point $(x, y)$ in the plane by a $2 \times 1$ matrix:

$$(x, y) \quad \leftrightarrow \quad \begin{bmatrix} x \\ y \end{bmatrix}$$

For example, the point $(3, 2)$ in the figure is represented by the matrix

$$P = \begin{bmatrix} 3 \\ 2 \end{bmatrix}$$

Multiplying by a $2 \times 2$ matrix *moves* the point in the plane. For example, if

$$T = \begin{bmatrix} 1 & 0 \\ 0 & -1 \end{bmatrix}$$

then multiplying $P$ by $T$, we get

$$TP = \begin{bmatrix} 1 & 0 \\ 0 & -1 \end{bmatrix} \begin{bmatrix} 3 \\ 2 \end{bmatrix} = \begin{bmatrix} 3 \\ -2 \end{bmatrix}$$

We see that the point $(3, 2)$ has been moved to the point $(3, -2)$. In general, multiplication by this matrix $T$ reflects points in the $x$-axis. If every point in an image is multiplied by this matrix, then the entire image will be flipped upside down about the $x$-axis. Matrix multiplication "transforms" a point to a new point in the plane. For this reason a matrix used in this way is called a **transformation**.

Table 1 gives some standard transformations and their effects on the gray square in the first quadrant.

**TABLE 1**

| Transformation matrix | Effect | |
|---|---|---|
| $T = \begin{bmatrix} 1 & 0 \\ 0 & -1 \end{bmatrix}$ <br> Reflection in *x*-axis | | |
| $T = \begin{bmatrix} c & 0 \\ 0 & 1 \end{bmatrix}$ <br> Expansion (or contraction) in the *x*-direction | | |
| $T = \begin{bmatrix} 1 & c \\ 0 & 1 \end{bmatrix}$ <br> Shear in *x*-direction | | |

## Moving Images in the Plane

Simple line drawings such as the house in Figure 1 consist of a collection of vertex points and connecting line segments. The house in Figure 1 can be represented in a computer by the $2 \times 11$ **data matrix**

$$D = \begin{bmatrix} 2 & 0 & 0 & 2 & 4 & 4 & 3 & 3 & 2 & 2 & 3 \\ 0 & 0 & 3 & 5 & 3 & 0 & 0 & 2 & 2 & 0 & 0 \end{bmatrix}$$

The columns of $D$ represent the vertex points of the image. To draw the house, we connect successive points (columns) in $D$ by line segments. Now we can transform the whole house by multiplying $D$ by an appropriate transformation matrix. For example, if we apply the shear transformation $T = \begin{bmatrix} 1 & 0.5 \\ 0 & 1 \end{bmatrix}$, we get the following matrix.

$$TD = \begin{bmatrix} 1 & 0.5 \\ 0 & 1 \end{bmatrix} \begin{bmatrix} 2 & 0 & 0 & 2 & 4 & 4 & 3 & 3 & 2 & 2 & 3 \\ 0 & 0 & 3 & 5 & 3 & 0 & 0 & 2 & 2 & 0 & 0 \end{bmatrix}$$

$$= \begin{bmatrix} 2 & 0 & 1.5 & 4.5 & 5.5 & 4 & 3 & 4 & 3 & 2 & 3 \\ 0 & 0 & 3 & 5 & 3 & 0 & 0 & 2 & 2 & 0 & 0 \end{bmatrix}$$

To draw the image represented by $TD$, we start with the point $\begin{bmatrix} 2 \\ 0 \end{bmatrix}$, connect it by a line segment to the point $\begin{bmatrix} 0 \\ 0 \end{bmatrix}$, then follow that by a line segment to $\begin{bmatrix} 1.5 \\ 3 \end{bmatrix}$, and so on. The resulting tilted house is shown in Figure 2.

A convenient way to draw an image corresponding to a given data matrix is to use a graphing calculator. The TI-83 program in the margin at the top of the next page converts

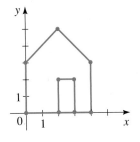

**FIGURE 1**

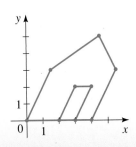

**FIGURE 2**

```
PROGRAM:IMAGE
:For(N,1,10)
:Line([A](1,N),
 [A](2,N),[A](1,N+1),
 [A](2,N+1))
:End
```

a data matrix stored in [A] into the corresponding image, as shown in Figure 3. (To use this program for a data matrix with $m$ columns, store the matrix in [A] and change the "10" in the For command to $m - 1$.)

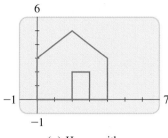

(a) House with
data matrix $D$

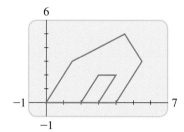

(b) Tilted house
with data matrix $TD$

**FIGURE 3**

## Problems

**1.** The gray square in Table 1 has the following vertices.

$$\begin{bmatrix} 0 \\ 0 \end{bmatrix}, \quad \begin{bmatrix} 1 \\ 0 \end{bmatrix}, \quad \begin{bmatrix} 1 \\ 1 \end{bmatrix}, \quad \begin{bmatrix} 0 \\ 1 \end{bmatrix}$$

Apply each of the three transformations given in Table 1 to these vertices and sketch the result to verify that each transformation has the indicated effect. Use $c = 2$ in the expansion matrix and $c = 1$ in the shear matrix.

**2.** Verify that multiplication by the given matrix has the indicated effect when applied to the gray square in the table. Use $c = 3$ in the expansion matrix and $c = 1$ in the shear matrix.

$$T_1 = \begin{bmatrix} -1 & 0 \\ 0 & 1 \end{bmatrix} \qquad T_2 = \begin{bmatrix} 1 & 0 \\ 0 & c \end{bmatrix} \qquad T_3 = \begin{bmatrix} 1 & 0 \\ c & 1 \end{bmatrix}$$

Reflection in $y$-axis   Expansion (or contraction) in $y$-direction   Shear in $y$-direction

**3.** Let $T = \begin{bmatrix} 1 & 1.5 \\ 0 & 1 \end{bmatrix}$.

 (a) What effect does $T$ have on the gray square in the Table 1?

 (b) Find $T^{-1}$.

 (c) What effect does $T^{-1}$ have on the gray square?

 (d) What happens to the square if we first apply $T$, then $T^{-1}$?

**4.** (a) Let $T = \begin{bmatrix} 3 & 0 \\ 0 & 1 \end{bmatrix}$. What effect does $T$ have on the gray square in Table 1?

 (b) Let $S = \begin{bmatrix} 1 & 0 \\ 0 & 2 \end{bmatrix}$. What effect does $S$ have on the gray square in Table 1?

 (c) Apply $S$ to the vertices of the square, and then apply $T$ to the result. What is the effect of the combined transformation?

 (d) Find the product matrix $W = TS$.

 (e) Apply the transformation $W$ to the square. Compare to your final result in part (c). What do you notice?

**5.** The figure shows three outline versions of the letter **F**. The second one is obtained from the first by shrinking horizontally by a factor of 0.75, and the third is obtained from the first by shearing horizontally by a factor of 0.25.

(a) Find a data matrix $D$ for the first letter **F**.

(b) Find the transformation matrix $T$ that transforms the first **F** into the second. Calculate $TD$, and verify that this is a data matrix for the second **F**.

(c) Find the transformation matrix $S$ that transforms the first **F** into the third. Calculate $SD$, and verify that this is a data matrix for the third **F**.

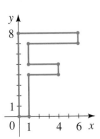 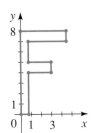 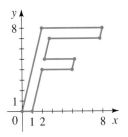

**6.** Here is a data matrix for a line drawing.

$$D = \begin{bmatrix} 0 & 1 & 2 & 1 & 0 & 0 \\ 0 & 0 & 2 & 4 & 4 & 0 \end{bmatrix}$$

(a) Draw the image represented by $D$.

(b) Let $T = \begin{bmatrix} 1 & 1 \\ 0 & -1 \end{bmatrix}$. Calculate the matrix product $TD$, and draw the image represented by this product. What is the effect of the transformation $T$?

(c) Express $T$ as a product of a shear matrix and a reflection matrix. (See Problem 2.)

# Conic Sections

SCE./Sandia National Laboratory

**Farming sunlight?** The sun is incredibly hot, with temperatures reaching into the millions of degrees; but fortunately, the amount of sunlight that reaches us is just right for keeping our planet at a comfortable temperature. Yet we can use the little sunlight we receive to unlock some of the sun's immense power. The key to doing this is a simple geometric shape called a parabola. A mirror in the shape of a parabola can concentrate sunlight to a single point (see page 558). Many such parabolic mirrors, assembled into "solar farms," can concentrate sunlight from a large area. The concentrated sunlight can heat water or other liquids to thousands of degrees, driving steam turbines for generating electricity. Two such solar power plants have been built in the Mojave Desert in California, each producing more than 10 megawatts of electric power. One of these is shown in the photo above.

In this chapter we study parabolas as well as the other conic sections. We will see that all the conic sections have impressive real-world applications.

### LEARNING OBJECTIVES

After completing this section, you will be able to:

- Find geometric properties of a parabola from its equation
- Find the equation of a parabola from some of its geometric properties

Conic sections are the curves we get when we make a straight cut in a cone, as shown in the figure. For example, if a cone is cut horizontally, the cross section is a circle. So a circle is a conic section. Other ways of cutting a cone produce parabolas, ellipses, and hyperbolas.

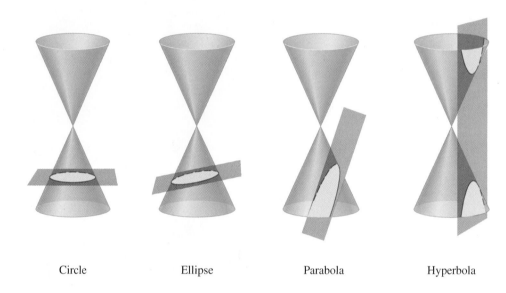

Circle          Ellipse          Parabola          Hyperbola

Our goal in this chapter is to find equations whose graphs are the conic sections. We already know from Section 2.2 that the graph of the equation $x^2 + y^2 = r^2$ is a circle. We will find equations for each of the other conic sections by analyzing their *geometric* properties.

## Geometric Definition of a Parabola

We saw in Section 4.1 that the graph of the equation

$$y = ax^2 + bx + c$$

is a U-shaped curve called a *parabola* that opens either upward or downward, depending on whether the sign of $a$ is positive or negative.

In this section we study parabolas from a geometric rather than an algebraic point of view. We begin with the geometric definition of a parabola and show how this leads to the algebraic formula that we are already familiar with.

---

**GEOMETRIC DEFINITION OF A PARABOLA**

A **parabola** is the set of points in the plane that are equidistant from a fixed point $F$ (called the **focus**) and a fixed line $l$ (called the **directrix**).

This definition is illustrated in Figure 1. The **vertex** $V$ of the parabola lies halfway between the focus and the directrix, and the **axis of symmetry** is the line that runs through the focus perpendicular to the directrix.

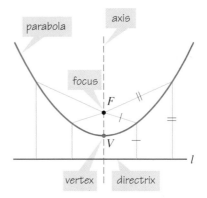

**FIGURE 1**

In this section we restrict our attention to parabolas that are situated with the vertex at the origin and that have a vertical or horizontal axis of symmetry. (Parabolas in more general positions will be considered in Section 8.4.) If the focus of such a parabola is the point $F(0, p)$, then the axis of symmetry must be vertical, and the directrix has the equation $y = -p$. Figure 2 illustrates the case $p > 0$.

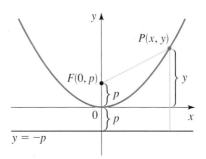

**FIGURE 2**

If $P(x, y)$ is any point on the parabola, then the distance from $P$ to the focus $F$ (using the Distance Formula) is

$$\sqrt{x^2 + (y - p)^2}$$

The distance from $P$ to the directrix is

$$|y - (-p)| = |y + p|$$

By the definition of a parabola these two distances must be equal:

$$\sqrt{x^2 + (y - p)^2} = |y + p|$$
$$x^2 + (y - p)^2 = |y + p|^2 = (y + p)^2 \qquad \text{Square both sides}$$
$$x^2 + y^2 - 2py + p^2 = y^2 + 2py + p^2 \qquad \text{Expand}$$
$$x^2 - 2py = 2py \qquad \text{Simplify}$$
$$x^2 = 4py$$

If $p > 0$, then the parabola opens upward, but if $p < 0$, it opens downward. When $x$ is replaced by $-x$, the equation remains unchanged, so the graph is symmetric about the $y$-axis.

## ■ Equations and Graphs of Parabolas

The following box summarizes what we have just proved about the equation and features of a parabola with a vertical axis.

**PARABOLA WITH VERTICAL AXIS**

The graph of the equation

$$x^2 = 4py$$

is a parabola with the following properties.

| | |
|---|---|
| **VERTEX** | $V(0, 0)$ |
| **FOCUS** | $F(0, p)$ |
| **DIRECTRIX** | $y = -p$ |

The parabola opens upward if $p > 0$ or downward if $p < 0$.

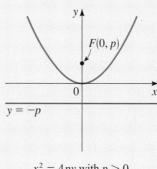
$x^2 = 4py$ with $p > 0$

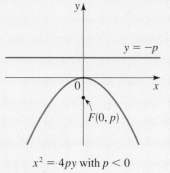
$x^2 = 4py$ with $p < 0$

▶ **EXAMPLE 1** | Finding the Equation of a Parabola

Find the equation of the parabola with vertex $V(0, 0)$ and focus $F(0, 2)$, and sketch its graph.

▼ **SOLUTION** Since the focus is $F(0, 2)$, we conclude that $p = 2$ (so the directrix is $y = -2$). Thus, the equation of the parabola is

$$x^2 = 4(2)y \qquad x^2 = 4py \text{ with } p = 2$$

$$x^2 = 8y$$

Since $p = 2 > 0$, the parabola opens upward. See Figure 3.

✎ **Practice what you've learned: Do Exercises 29 and 41.** ▲

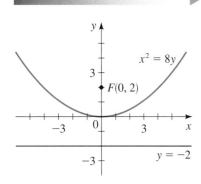

**FIGURE 3**

---

**MATHEMATICS IN THE MODERN WORLD**

**Looking Inside Your Head**

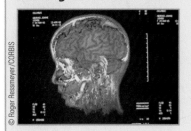
© Roger Ressmeyer/CORBIS

How would you like to look inside your head? The idea isn't particularly appealing to most of us, but doctors often need to do just that. If they can look without invasive surgery, all the better. An X-ray doesn't really give a look inside, it simply gives a "graph" of the density of tissue the X-rays must pass through. So an X-ray is a "flattened" view in one direction. Suppose you get an X-ray view from many different directions. Can these "graphs" be used to reconstruct the three-dimensional inside view? This is a purely mathematical problem and was solved by mathematicians a long time ago. However, reconstructing the inside view requires thousands of tedious computations. Today, mathematics and high-speed computers make it possible to "look inside" by a process called computer-aided tomography (or CAT scan). Mathematicians continue to search for better ways of using mathematics to reconstruct images. One of the latest techniques, called magnetic resonance imaging (MRI), combines molecular biology and mathematics for a clear "look inside."

▶ **EXAMPLE 2** | Finding the Focus and Directrix of a Parabola
from Its Equation

Find the focus and directrix of the parabola $y = -x^2$, and sketch the graph.

▼ **SOLUTION**    To find the focus and directrix, we put the given equation in the standard
form $x^2 = -y$. Comparing this to the general equation $x^2 = 4py$, we see that $4p = -1$,
so $p = -\frac{1}{4}$. Thus, the focus is $F\left(0, -\frac{1}{4}\right)$, and the directrix is $y = \frac{1}{4}$. The graph of the
parabola, together with the focus and the directrix, is shown in Figure 4(a). We can also
draw the graph using a graphing calculator as shown in Figure 4(b).

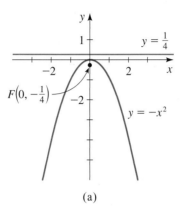

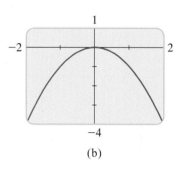

**FIGURE 4**                              (a)                              (b)

✎ **Practice what you've learned: Do Exercise 11.**                    ▲

Reflecting the graph in Figure 2 about the diagonal line $y = x$ has the effect of interchanging the roles of $x$ and $y$. This results in a parabola with horizontal axis. By the same
method as before, we can prove the following properties.

---

**PARABOLA WITH HORIZONTAL AXIS**

The graph of the equation

$$y^2 = 4px$$

is a parabola with the following properties.

| | |
|---|---|
| **VERTEX** | $V(0, 0)$ |
| **FOCUS** | $F(p, 0)$ |
| **DIRECTRIX** | $x = -p$ |

The parabola opens to the right if $p > 0$ or to the left if $p < 0$.

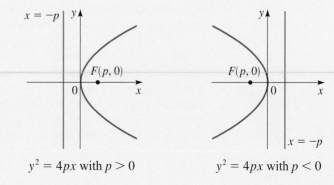

$y^2 = 4px$ with $p > 0$                    $y^2 = 4px$ with $p < 0$

▶ **EXAMPLE 3** | A Parabola with Horizontal Axis

A parabola has the equation $6x + y^2 = 0$.

**(a)** Find the focus and directrix of the parabola, and sketch the graph.

**(b)** Use a graphing calculator to draw the graph.

▼ **SOLUTION**

**(a)** To find the focus and directrix, we put the given equation in the standard form $y^2 = -6x$. Comparing this to the general equation $y^2 = 4px$, we see that $4p = -6$, so $p = -\frac{3}{2}$. Thus, the focus is $F\left(-\frac{3}{2}, 0\right)$, and the directrix is $x = \frac{3}{2}$. Since $p < 0$, the parabola opens to the left. The graph of the parabola, together with the focus and the directrix, is shown in Figure 5(a) below.

**(b)** To draw the graph using a graphing calculator, we need to solve for $y$.

$$6x + y^2 = 0$$

$$y^2 = -6x \qquad \text{Subtract } 6x$$

$$y = \pm\sqrt{-6x} \qquad \text{Take square roots}$$

To obtain the graph of the parabola, we graph both functions

$$y = \sqrt{-6x} \qquad \text{and} \qquad y = -\sqrt{-6x}$$

as shown in Figure 5(b).

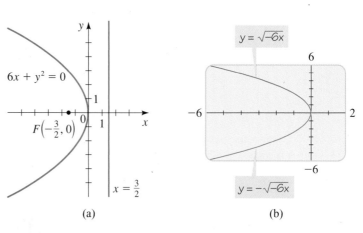

**FIGURE 5**        (a)        (b)

✎ **Practice what you've learned: Do Exercise 13.**        ▲

The equation $y^2 = 4px$, does not define $y$ as a function of $x$ (see page 220). So to use a graphing calculator to graph a parabola with horizontal axis, we must first solve for $y$. This leads to two functions, $y = \sqrt{4px}$ and $y = -\sqrt{4px}$. We need to graph both functions to get the complete graph of the parabola. For example, in Figure 5(b) we had to graph both $y = \sqrt{-6x}$ and $y = -\sqrt{-6x}$ to graph the parabola $y^2 = -6x$.

We can use the coordinates of the focus to estimate the "width" of a parabola when sketching its graph. The line segment that runs through the focus perpendicular to the axis, with endpoints on the parabola, is called the **latus rectum**, and its length is the **focal diameter** of the parabola. From Figure 6 we can see that the distance from an endpoint $Q$ of the latus rectum to the directrix is $|2p|$. Thus, the distance from $Q$ to the focus must be $|2p|$ as well (by the definition of a parabola), so the focal diameter is $|4p|$. In the next example we use the focal diameter to determine the "width" of a parabola when graphing it.

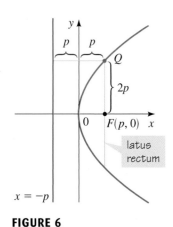

**FIGURE 6**

**55. Suspension Bridge** In a suspension bridge the shape of the suspension cables is parabolic. The bridge shown in the figure has towers that are 600 m apart, and the lowest point of the suspension cables is 150 m below the top of the towers. Find the equation of the parabolic part of the cables, placing the origin of the coordinate system at the vertex.

[*Note*: This equation is used to find the length of cable needed in the construction of the bridge.]

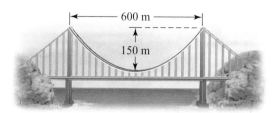

**56. Reflecting Telescope** The Hale telescope at the Mount Palomar Observatory has a 200-in. mirror, as shown. The mirror is constructed in a parabolic shape that collects light from the stars and focuses it at the **prime focus**, that is, the focus of the parabola. The mirror is 3.79 in. deep at its center. Find the **focal length** of this parabolic mirror, that is, the distance from the vertex to the focus.

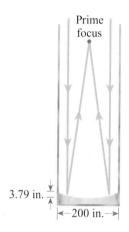

▼ **DISCOVERY • DISCUSSION • WRITING**

**57. Parabolas in the Real World** Several examples of the uses of parabolas are given in the text. Find other situations in real life in which parabolas occur. Consult a scientific encyclopedia in the reference section of your library, or search the Internet.

**58. Light Cone from a Flashlight** A flashlight is held to form a lighted area on the ground, as shown in the figure. Is it possible to angle the flashlight in such a way that the boundary of the lighted area is a parabola? Explain your answer.

# ROLLING DOWN A RAMP

Galileo was the first to show that the motion of a falling ball can be modeled by a parabola (see page 293). To accomplish this, he rolled balls down a ramp and used his acute sense of timing to study the motion of the ball. In this project you will perform a similar experiment, using modern equipment. You will need the following:

- A wide board, about 6–8 ft long, to be used as a ramp
- A large ball, the size of a soccer or volleyball
- A calculator-based motion detector, such as the Texas Instruments CBR system (Calculator Based Ranger)

Use books to prop up the ramp at an angle of about 15°, clamp the motion detector to the top of the ramp, and connect it to the calculator, as shown in the figure. (Read the manual carefully to make sure you have set up the calculator and motion detector correctly.)

1. Mark a spot on the ramp about 2 ft from the top. Place the ball on the mark and release it to see how many seconds it takes to roll to the bottom. Adjust the motion detector to record the ball's position every 0.05 s over this length of time. Now let the ball roll down the ramp again, this time with the motion detector running. The calculator should record at least 50 data points that indicate the distance between the ball and the motion detector every 0.05 s.

2. Make a scatter plot of your data, plotting time on the $x$-axis and distance on the $y$-axis. Does the plot look like half of a parabola?

3. Use the quadratic regression command on your calculator (called QuadReg on the TI-83) to find the parabola equation $y = ax^2 + bx + c$ that best fits the data. Graph this equation on your scatter plot to see how well it fits. Do the data points really form part of a parabola?

4. Repeat the experiment with the ramp inclined at a shallower angle. How does reducing the angle of the ramp affect the shape of the parabola?

5. Try rolling the ball up the ramp from the bottom to the spot you marked in Step 1, so that it rolls up and then back down again. If you perform the experiment this way instead of just letting the ball roll down, how does your graph in Step 3 change?

## 8.2 | Ellipses

### LEARNING OBJECTIVES
After completing this section, you will be able to:

- Find geometric properties of an ellipse from its equation
- Find the equation of an ellipse from some of its geometric properties

### ■ Geometric Definition of an Ellipse

An ellipse is an oval curve that looks like an elongated circle. More precisely, we have the following definition.

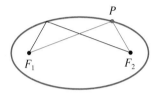

**FIGURE 1**

> **GEOMETRIC DEFINITION OF AN ELLIPSE**
>
> An **ellipse** is the set of all points in the plane the sum of whose distances from two fixed points $F_1$ and $F_2$ is a constant. (See Figure 1.) These two fixed points are the **foci** (plural of **focus**) of the ellipse.

The geometric definition suggests a simple method for drawing an ellipse. Place a sheet of paper on a drawing board, and insert thumbtacks at the two points that are to be the foci of the ellipse. Attach the ends of a string to the tacks, as shown in Figure 2(a). With the point of a pencil, hold the string taut. Then carefully move the pencil around the foci, keeping the string taut at all times. The pencil will trace out an ellipse, because the sum of the distances from the point of the pencil to the foci will always equal the length of the string, which is constant.

If the string is only slightly longer than the distance between the foci, then the ellipse that is traced out will be elongated in shape, as in Figure 2(a), but if the foci are close together relative to the length of the string, the ellipse will be almost circular, as shown in Figure 2(b).

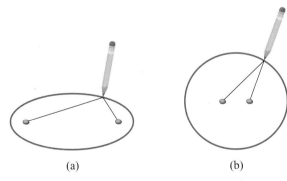

(a)                    (b)

**FIGURE 2**

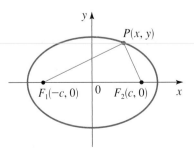

**FIGURE 3**

To obtain the simplest equation for an ellipse, we place the foci on the $x$-axis at $F_1(-c, 0)$ and $F_2(c, 0)$ so that the origin is halfway between them (see Figure 3).

For later convenience we let the sum of the distances from a point on the ellipse to the foci be $2a$. Then if $P(x, y)$ is any point on the ellipse, we have

$$d(P, F_1) + d(P, F_2) = 2a$$

So from the Distance Formula

$$\sqrt{(x + c)^2 + y^2} + \sqrt{(x - c)^2 + y^2} = 2a$$

or

$$\sqrt{(x - c)^2 + y^2} = 2a - \sqrt{(x + c)^2 + y^2}$$

Squaring each side and expanding, we get

$$x^2 - 2cx + c^2 + y^2 = 4a^2 - 4a\sqrt{(x + c)^2 + y^2} + (x^2 + 2cx + c^2 + y^2)$$

which simplifies to

$$4a\sqrt{(x + c)^2 + y^2} = 4a^2 + 4cx$$

Dividing each side by 4 and squaring again, we get

$$a^2[(x + c)^2 + y^2] = (a^2 + cx)^2$$

$$a^2x^2 + 2a^2cx + a^2c^2 + a^2y^2 = a^4 + 2a^2cx + c^2x^2$$

$$(a^2 - c^2)x^2 + a^2y^2 = a^2(a^2 - c^2)$$

Since the sum of the distances from $P$ to the foci must be larger than the distance between the foci, we have that $2a > 2c$, or $a > c$. Thus, $a^2 - c^2 > 0$, and we can divide each side of the preceding equation by $a^2(a^2 - c^2)$ to get

$$\frac{x^2}{a^2} + \frac{y^2}{a^2 - c^2} = 1$$

For convenience let $b^2 = a^2 - c^2$ (with $b > 0$). Since $b^2 < a^2$, it follows that $b < a$. The preceding equation then becomes

$$\frac{x^2}{a^2} + \frac{y^2}{b^2} = 1 \quad \text{with } a > b$$

This is the equation of the ellipse. To graph it, we need to know the $x$- and $y$-intercepts. Setting $y = 0$, we get

$$\frac{x^2}{a^2} = 1$$

so $x^2 = a^2$, or $x = \pm a$. Thus, the ellipse crosses the $x$-axis at $(a, 0)$ and $(-a, 0)$, as in Figure 4. These points are called the **vertices** of the ellipse, and the segment that joins them is called the **major axis**. Its length is $2a$.

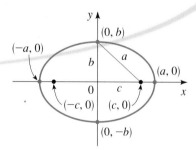

**FIGURE 4**
$\dfrac{x^2}{a^2} + \dfrac{y^2}{b^2} = 1$ with $a > b$

Similarly, if we set $x = 0$, we get $y = \pm b$, so the ellipse crosses the $y$-axis at $(0, b)$ and $(0, -b)$. The segment that joins these points is called the **minor axis**, and it has length $2b$. Note that $2a > 2b$, so the major axis is longer than the minor axis. The origin is the **center** of the ellipse.

If the foci of the ellipse are placed on the $y$-axis at $(0, \pm c)$ rather than on the $x$-axis, then the roles of $x$ and $y$ are reversed in the preceding discussion, and we get a vertical ellipse.

## ■ Equations and Graphs of Ellipses

The orbits of the planets are ellipses, with the sun at one focus.

The following box summarizes what we have just proved about the equation and features of an ellipse centered at the origin.

**ELLIPSE WITH CENTER AT THE ORIGIN**

The graph of each of the following equations is an ellipse with center at the origin and having the given properties.

| | | |
|---|---|---|
| **EQUATION** | $\dfrac{x^2}{a^2} + \dfrac{y^2}{b^2} = 1$ | $\dfrac{x^2}{b^2} + \dfrac{y^2}{a^2} = 1$ |
| | $a > b > 0$ | $a > b > 0$ |
| **VERTICES** | $(\pm a, 0)$ | $(0, \pm a)$ |
| **MAJOR AXIS** | Horizontal, length $2a$ | Vertical, length $2a$ |
| **MINOR AXIS** | Vertical, length $2b$ | Horizontal, length $2b$ |
| **FOCI** | $(\pm c, 0)$, $c^2 = a^2 - b^2$ | $(0, \pm c)$, $c^2 = a^2 - b^2$ |
| **GRAPH** | 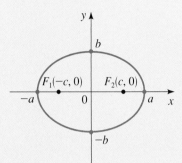 | 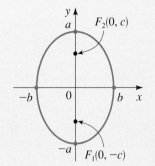 |

In the standard equation for an ellipse, $a^2$ is the *larger* denominator and $b^2$ is the *smaller*. To find $c^2$, we subtract: larger denominator minus smaller denominator.

▶ **EXAMPLE 1** | Sketching an Ellipse

An ellipse has the equation

$$\frac{x^2}{9} + \frac{y^2}{4} = 1$$

**(a)** Find the foci, vertices, and the lengths of the major and minor axes, and sketch the graph.

**(b)** Draw the graph using a graphing calculator.

▼ **SOLUTION**

**(a)** Since the denominator of $x^2$ is larger, the ellipse has a horizontal major axis. This gives $a^2 = 9$ and $b^2 = 4$, so $c^2 = a^2 - b^2 = 9 - 4 = 5$. Thus, $a = 3$, $b = 2$, and $c = \sqrt{5}$.

| | |
|---|---|
| **FOCI** | $(\pm \sqrt{5}, 0)$ |
| **VERTICES** | $(\pm 3, 0)$ |
| **LENGTH OF MAJOR AXIS** | 6 |
| **LENGTH OF MINOR AXIS** | 4 |

The graph is shown in Figure 5(a) on the next page.

**(b)** To draw the graph using a graphing calculator, we need to solve for $y$.

$$\frac{x^2}{9} + \frac{y^2}{4} = 1$$

$$\frac{y^2}{4} = 1 - \frac{x^2}{9} \qquad \text{Subtract } \frac{x^2}{9}$$

Note that the equation of an ellipse does not define $y$ as a function of $x$ (see page 220). That's why we need to graph two functions to graph an ellipse.

$$y^2 = 4\left(1 - \frac{x^2}{9}\right) \qquad \text{Multiply by 4}$$

$$y = \pm 2\sqrt{1 - \frac{x^2}{9}} \qquad \text{Take square roots}$$

To obtain the graph of the ellipse, we graph both functions

$$y = 2\sqrt{1 - x^2/9} \qquad \text{and} \qquad y = -2\sqrt{1 - x^2/9}$$

as shown in Figure 5(b).

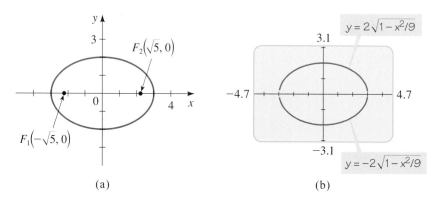

**FIGURE 5**
$\dfrac{x^2}{9} + \dfrac{y^2}{4} = 1$

(a)  (b)

✎ **Practice what you've learned: Do Exercise 9.**  ▲

▶ **EXAMPLE 2** | Finding the Foci of an Ellipse

Find the foci of the ellipse $16x^2 + 9y^2 = 144$, and sketch its graph.

▼ **SOLUTION**  First we put the equation in standard form. Dividing by 144, we get

$$\frac{x^2}{9} + \frac{y^2}{16} = 1$$

Since $16 > 9$, this is an ellipse with its foci on the $y$-axis, and with $a = 4$ and $b = 3$. We have

$$c^2 = a^2 - b^2 = 16 - 9 = 7$$

$$c = \sqrt{7}$$

Thus, the foci are $(0, \pm\sqrt{7})$. The graph is shown in Figure 6(a).

We can also draw the graph using a graphing calculator as shown in Figure 6(b).

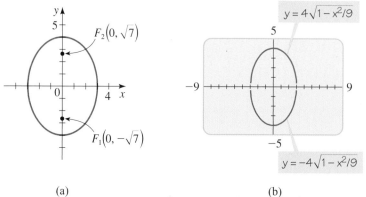

**FIGURE 6**
$16x^2 + 9y^2 = 144$

(a)  (b)

✎ **Practice what you've learned: Do Exercise 11.**  ▲

▶ **EXAMPLE 3** | Finding the Equation of an Ellipse

The vertices of an ellipse are $(\pm 4, 0)$, and the foci are $(\pm 2, 0)$. Find its equation, and sketch the graph.

▼ **SOLUTION**   Since the vertices are $(\pm 4, 0)$, we have $a = 4$. The foci are $(\pm 2, 0)$, so $c = 2$. To write the equation, we need to find $b$. Since $c^2 = a^2 - b^2$, we have

$$2^2 = 4^2 - b^2$$

$$b^2 = 16 - 4 = 12$$

Thus, the equation of the ellipse is

$$\frac{x^2}{16} + \frac{y^2}{12} = 1$$

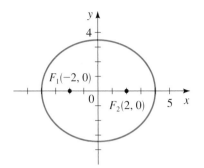

**FIGURE 7**
$$\frac{x^2}{16} + \frac{y^2}{12} = 1$$

The graph is shown in Figure 7.

✎ **Practice what you've learned: Do Exercises 25 and 33.**    ▲

## ■ Eccentricity of an Ellipse

We saw earlier in this section (Figure 2) that if $2a$ is only slightly greater than $2c$, the ellipse is long and thin, whereas if $2a$ is much greater than $2c$, the ellipse is almost circular. We measure the deviation of an ellipse from being circular by the ratio of $a$ and $c$.

---

**DEFINITION OF ECCENTRICITY**

For the ellipse $\dfrac{x^2}{a^2} + \dfrac{y^2}{b^2} = 1$ or $\dfrac{x^2}{b^2} + \dfrac{y^2}{a^2} = 1$ (with $a > b > 0$), the **eccentricity $e$** is the number

$$e = \frac{c}{a}$$

where $c = \sqrt{a^2 - b^2}$. The eccentricity of every ellipse satisfies $0 < e < 1$.

---

Thus, if $e$ is close to 1, then $c$ is almost equal to $a$, and the ellipse is elongated in shape, but if $e$ is close to 0, then the ellipse is close to a circle in shape. The eccentricity is a measure of how "stretched" the ellipse is.

In Figure 8 we show a number of ellipses to demonstrate the effect of varying the eccentricity $e$.

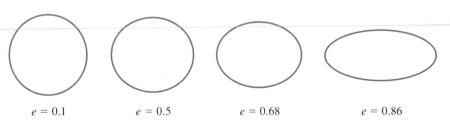

$e = 0.1$        $e = 0.5$        $e = 0.68$        $e = 0.86$

**FIGURE 8** Ellipses with various eccentricities

▶ **EXAMPLE 4** | Finding the Equation of an Ellipse from Its
                  Eccentricity and Foci

Find the equation of the ellipse with foci $(0, \pm 8)$ and eccentricity $e = \frac{4}{5}$, and sketch its graph.

▼ **SOLUTION**   We are given $e = \frac{4}{5}$ and $c = 8$. Thus

$$\frac{4}{5} = \frac{8}{a} \qquad \text{Eccentricity } e = \frac{c}{a}$$

$$4a = 40 \qquad \text{Cross-multiply}$$

$$a = 10$$

To find $b$, we use the fact that $c^2 = a^2 - b^2$.

$$8^2 = 10^2 - b^2$$

$$b^2 = 10^2 - 8^2 = 36$$

$$b = 6$$

Thus, the equation of the ellipse is

$$\frac{x^2}{36} + \frac{y^2}{100} = 1$$

Because the foci are on the $y$-axis, the ellipse is oriented vertically. To sketch the ellipse, we find the intercepts: The $x$-intercepts are $\pm 6$, and the $y$-intercepts are $\pm 10$. The graph is sketched in Figure 9.

✎ **Practice what you've learned: Do Exercise 43.**                                  ▲

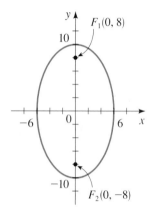

**FIGURE 9**
$\dfrac{x^2}{36} + \dfrac{y^2}{100} = 1$

---

**Eccentricities of the Orbits of the Planets**

The orbits of the planets are ellipses with the sun at one focus. For most planets these ellipses have very small eccentricity, so they are nearly circular. However, Mercury and Pluto, the innermost and outermost known planets, have visibly elliptical orbits.

| Planet  | Eccentricity |
|---------|--------------|
| Mercury | 0.206        |
| Venus   | 0.007        |
| Earth   | 0.017        |
| Mars    | 0.093        |
| Jupiter | 0.048        |
| Saturn  | 0.056        |
| Uranus  | 0.046        |
| Neptune | 0.010        |
| Pluto   | 0.248        |

---

Gravitational attraction causes the planets to move in elliptical orbits around the sun with the sun at one focus. This remarkable property was first observed by Johannes Kepler and was later deduced by Isaac Newton from his inverse square law of gravity, using calculus. The orbits of the planets have different eccentricities, but most are nearly circular (see the margin).

Ellipses, like parabolas, have an interesting *reflection property* that leads to a number of practical applications. If a light source is placed at one focus of a reflecting surface with elliptical cross sections, then all the light will be reflected off the surface to the other focus, as shown in Figure 10. This principle, which works for sound waves as well as for light, is used in *lithotripsy*, a treatment for kidney stones. The patient is placed in a tub of water with elliptical cross sections in such a way that the kidney stone is accurately located at one focus. High-intensity sound waves generated at the other focus are reflected to the stone and destroy it with minimal damage to surrounding tissue. The patient is spared the trauma of surgery and recovers within days instead of weeks.

The reflection property of ellipses is also used in the construction of *whispering galleries*. Sound coming from one focus bounces off the walls and ceiling of an elliptical room and passes through the other focus. In these rooms even quiet whispers spoken at one focus can be heard clearly at the other. Famous whispering galleries include the National Statuary Hall of the U.S. Capitol in Washington, D.C. (see page 595), and the Mormon Tabernacle in Salt Lake City, Utah.

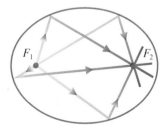

**FIGURE 10**

# 8.2 EXERCISES

## ▼ CONCEPTS

**1.** An ellipse is the set of all points in the plane for which the _____ of the distances from two fixed points $F_1$ and $F_2$ is constant. The points $F_1$ and $F_2$ are called the _____ of the ellipse.

**2.** The graph of the equation $\dfrac{x^2}{a^2} + \dfrac{y^2}{b^2} = 1$ with $a > b > 0$ is an ellipse with vertices (___, ___) and (___, ___) and foci $(\pm c, 0)$, where $c =$ _____. So the graph of $\dfrac{x^2}{5^2} + \dfrac{y^2}{4^2} = 1$ is an ellipse with vertices (___, ___) and (___, ___) and foci (___, ___) and (___, ___).

**3.** The graph of the equation $\dfrac{x^2}{b^2} + \dfrac{y^2}{a^2} = 1$ with $a > b > 0$ is an ellipse with vertices (___, ___) and (___, ___) and foci $(0, \pm c)$, where $c =$ _____. So the graph of $\dfrac{x^2}{4^2} + \dfrac{y^2}{5^2} = 1$ is an ellipse with vertices (___, ___) and (___, ___) and foci (___, ___) and (___, ___).

**4.** Label the vertices and foci on the graphs given for the ellipses in Exercises 2 and 3.

**(a)** $\dfrac{x^2}{5^2} + \dfrac{y^2}{4^2} = 1$   **(b)** $\dfrac{x^2}{4^2} + \dfrac{y^2}{5^2} = 1$

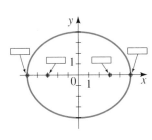
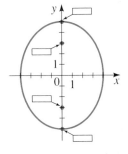

## ▼ SKILLS

**5–8** ▪ Match the equation with the graphs labeled I–IV. Give reasons for your answers.

**5.** $\dfrac{x^2}{16} + \dfrac{y^2}{4} = 1$   **6.** $x^2 + \dfrac{y^2}{9} = 1$

**7.** $4x^2 + y^2 = 4$   **8.** $16x^2 + 25y^2 = 400$

I
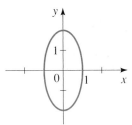

II
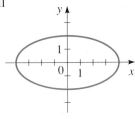

III
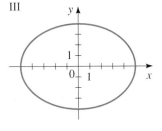

IV
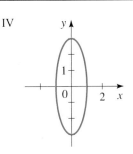

**9–22** ▪ Find the vertices, foci, and eccentricity of the ellipse. Determine the lengths of the major and minor axes, and sketch the graph.

**9.** $\dfrac{x^2}{25} + \dfrac{y^2}{9} = 1$   **10.** $\dfrac{x^2}{16} + \dfrac{y^2}{25} = 1$

**11.** $9x^2 + 4y^2 = 36$   **12.** $4x^2 + 25y^2 = 100$

**13.** $x^2 + 4y^2 = 16$   **14.** $4x^2 + y^2 = 16$

**15.** $2x^2 + y^2 = 3$   **16.** $5x^2 + 6y^2 = 30$

**17.** $x^2 + 4y^2 = 1$   **18.** $9x^2 + 4y^2 = 1$

**19.** $\frac{1}{2}x^2 + \frac{1}{8}y^2 = \frac{1}{4}$   **20.** $x^2 = 4 - 2y^2$

**21.** $y^2 = 1 - 2x^2$   **22.** $20x^2 + 4y^2 = 5$

**23–28** ▪ Find an equation for the ellipse whose graph is shown.

**23.**
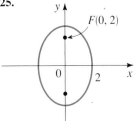

**24.**
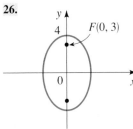

**25.**
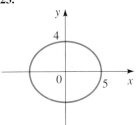

**26.**
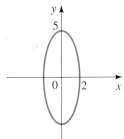

**27.**
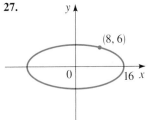

**28.**
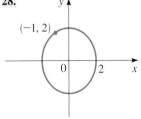

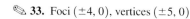 **29–32** ▪ Use a graphing device to graph the ellipse.

**29.** $\dfrac{x^2}{25} + \dfrac{y^2}{20} = 1$

**30.** $x^2 + \dfrac{y^2}{12} = 1$

**31.** $6x^2 + y^2 = 36$

**32.** $x^2 + 2y^2 = 8$

**33–44** ▪ Find an equation for the ellipse that satisfies the given conditions.

**33.** Foci $(\pm 4, 0)$, vertices $(\pm 5, 0)$

**34.** Foci $(0, \pm 3)$, vertices $(0, \pm 5)$

**35.** Length of major axis 4, length of minor axis 2, foci on $y$-axis

**36.** Length of major axis 6, length of minor axis 4, foci on $x$-axis

**37.** Foci $(0, \pm 2)$, length of minor axis 6

**38.** Foci $(\pm 5, 0)$, length of major axis 12

**39.** Endpoints of major axis $(\pm 10, 0)$, distance between foci 6

**40.** Endpoints of minor axis $(0, \pm 3)$, distance between foci 8

**41.** Length of major axis 10, foci on $x$-axis, ellipse passes through the point $(\sqrt{5}, 2)$

**42.** Eccentricity $\frac{1}{9}$, foci $(0, \pm 2)$

**43.** Eccentricity 0.8, foci $(\pm 1.5, 0)$

**44.** Eccentricity $\sqrt{3}/2$, foci on $y$-axis, length of major axis 4

**45–47** ▪ Find the intersection points of the pair of ellipses. Sketch the graphs of each pair of equations on the same coordinate axes and label the points of intersection.

**45.** $\begin{cases} 4x^2 + \ \ y^2 = \ \ 4 \\ 4x^2 + 9y^2 = 36 \end{cases}$

**46.** $\begin{cases} \dfrac{x^2}{16} + \dfrac{y^2}{9} = 1 \\ \dfrac{x^2}{9} + \dfrac{y^2}{16} = 1 \end{cases}$

**47.** $\begin{cases} 100x^2 + 25y^2 = 100 \\ \ \ \ x^2 + \dfrac{y^2}{9} = \ \ 1 \end{cases}$

**48.** The **ancillary circle** of an ellipse is the circle with radius equal to half the length of the minor axis and center the same as the ellipse (see the figure). The ancillary circle is thus the largest circle that can fit within an ellipse.

(a) Find an equation for the ancillary circle of the ellipse $x^2 + 4y^2 = 16$.

(b) For the ellipse and ancillary circle of part (a), show that if $(s, t)$ is a point on the ancillary circle, then $(2s, t)$ is a point on the ellipse.

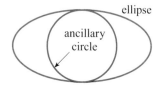

**49.** (a) Use a graphing device to sketch the top half (the portion in the first and second quadrants) of the family of ellipses $x^2 + ky^2 = 100$ for $k = 4, 10, 25,$ and $50$.

(b) What do the members of this family of ellipses have in common? How do they differ?

**50.** If $k > 0$, the following equation represents an ellipse:

$$\frac{x^2}{k} + \frac{y^2}{4 + k} = 1$$

Show that all the ellipses represented by this equation have the same foci, no matter what the value of $k$.

---

## ▼ APPLICATIONS

**51. Perihelion and Aphelion** The planets move around the sun in elliptical orbits with the sun at one focus. The point in the orbit at which the planet is closest to the sun is called **perihelion**, and the point at which it is farthest is called **aphelion**. These points are the vertices of the orbit. The earth's distance from the sun is 147,000,000 km at perihelion and 153,000,000 km at aphelion. Find an equation for the earth's orbit. (Place the origin at the center of the orbit with the sun on the $x$-axis.)

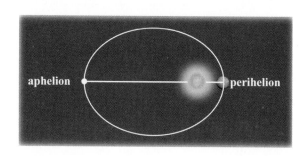

**52. The Orbit of Pluto** With an eccentricity of 0.25, Pluto's orbit is the most eccentric in the solar system. The length of the minor axis of its orbit is approximately 10,000,000,000 km. Find the distance between Pluto and the sun at perihelion and at aphelion. (See Exercise 51.)

**53. Lunar Orbit** For an object in an elliptical orbit around the moon, the points in the orbit that are closest to and farthest from the center of the moon are called **perilune** and **apolune**, respectively. These are the vertices of the orbit. The center of the moon is at one focus of the orbit. The *Apollo 11* spacecraft was placed in a lunar orbit with perilune at 68 mi and apolune at 195 mi above the surface of the moon. Assuming that the moon is a sphere of radius 1075 mi, find an equation for the orbit of *Apollo 11*. (Place the coordinate axes so that the origin is at the center of the orbit and the foci are located on the $x$-axis.)

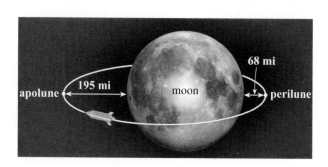

**54. Plywood Ellipse** A carpenter wishes to construct an elliptical table top from a sheet of plywood, 4 ft by 8 ft. He will trace out the ellipse using the "thumbtack and string" method illustrated in Figures 2 and 3. What length of string should he use, and how far apart should the tacks be located, if the ellipse is to be the largest possible that can be cut out of the plywood sheet?

**55. Sunburst Window** A "sunburst" window above a doorway is constructed in the shape of the top half of an ellipse, as shown in the figure. The window is 20 in. tall at its highest point and 80 in. wide at the bottom. Find the height of the window 25 in. from the center of the base.

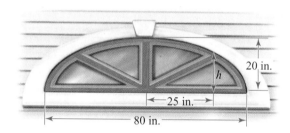

▼ **DISCOVERY • DISCUSSION • WRITING**

**56. Drawing an Ellipse on a Blackboard** Try drawing an ellipse as accurately as possible on a blackboard. How would a piece of string and two friends help this process?

**57. Light Cone from a Flashlight** A flashlight shines on a wall, as shown in the figure. What is the shape of the boundary of the lighted area? Explain your answer.

**58. How Wide Is an Ellipse at Its Foci?** A *latus rectum* for an ellipse is a line segment perpendicular to the major axis at a focus, with endpoints on the ellipse, as shown. Show that the length of a latus rectum is $2b^2/a$ for the ellipse

$$\frac{x^2}{a^2} + \frac{y^2}{b^2} = 1 \qquad \text{with } a > b$$

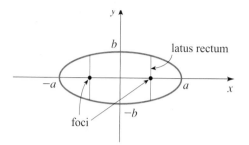

**59. Is It an Ellipse?** A piece of paper is wrapped around a cylindrical bottle, and then a compass is used to draw a circle on the paper, as shown in the figure. When the paper is laid flat, is the shape drawn on the paper an ellipse? (You don't need to prove your answer, but you might want to do the experiment and see what you get.)

## 8.3 | Hyperbolas

### LEARNING OBJECTIVES

After completing this section, you will be able to:

- Find geometric properties of a hyperbola from its equation
- Find the equation of a hyperbola from some of its geometric properties

### ■ Geometric Definition of a Hyperbola

Although ellipses and hyperbolas have completely different shapes, their definitions and equations are similar. Instead of using the *sum* of distances from two fixed foci, as in the case of an ellipse, we use the *difference* to define a hyperbola.

> **GEOMETRIC DEFINITION OF A HYPERBOLA**
>
> A **hyperbola** is the set of all points in the plane, the difference of whose distances from two fixed points $F_1$ and $F_2$ is a constant. (See Figure 1.) These two fixed points are the **foci** of the hyperbola.

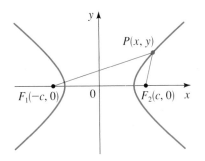

**FIGURE 1** $P$ is on the hyperbola if $|d(P, F_1) - d(P, F_2)| = 2a$.

As in the case of the ellipse, we get the simplest equation for the hyperbola by placing the foci on the *x*-axis at $(\pm c, 0)$, as shown in Figure 1. By definition, if $P(x, y)$ lies on the hyperbola, then either $d(P, F_1) - d(P, F_2)$ or $d(P, F_2) - d(P, F_1)$ must equal some positive constant, which we call $2a$. Thus, we have

$$d(P, F_1) - d(P, F_2) = \pm 2a$$

or

$$\sqrt{(x + c)^2 + y^2} - \sqrt{(x - c)^2 + y^2} = \pm 2a$$

Proceeding as we did in the case of the ellipse (Section 8.2), we simplify this to

$$(c^2 - a^2)x^2 - a^2 y^2 = a^2(c^2 - a^2)$$

From triangle $PF_1F_2$ in Figure 1 we see that $|d(P, F_1) - d(P, F_2)| < 2c$. It follows that $2a < 2c$, or $a < c$. Thus, $c^2 - a^2 > 0$, so we can set $b^2 = c^2 - a^2$. We then simplify the last displayed equation to get

$$\frac{x^2}{a^2} - \frac{y^2}{b^2} = 1$$

This is the *equation of the hyperbola.* If we replace *x* by $-x$ or *y* by $-y$ in this equation, it remains unchanged, so the hyperbola is symmetric about both the *x*- and *y*-axes and about the origin. The *x*-intercepts are $\pm a$, and the points $(a, 0)$ and $(-a, 0)$ are the **vertices** of the hyperbola. There is no *y*-intercept, because setting $x = 0$ in the equation of the hyperbola leads to $-y^2 = b^2$, which has no real solution. Furthermore, the equation of the hyperbola implies that

$$\frac{x^2}{a^2} = \frac{y^2}{b^2} + 1 \geq 1$$

so $x^2/a^2 \geq 1$; thus, $x^2 \geq a^2$, and hence $x \geq a$ or $x \leq -a$. This means that the hyperbola consists of two parts, called its **branches**. The segment joining the two vertices on the separate branches is the **transverse axis** of the hyperbola, and the origin is called its **center**.

If we place the foci of the hyperbola on the *y*-axis rather than on the *x*-axis, then this has the effect of reversing the roles of *x* and *y* in the derivation of the equation of the hyperbola. This leads to a hyperbola with a vertical transverse axis.

## ■ Equations and Graphs of Hyperbolas

The main properties of hyperbolas are listed in the following box.

---

### HYPERBOLA WITH CENTER AT THE ORIGIN

The graph of each of the following equations is a hyperbola with center at the origin and having the given properties.

| | | |
|---|---|---|
| **EQUATION** | $\dfrac{x^2}{a^2} - \dfrac{y^2}{b^2} = 1 \quad (a > 0, b > 0)$ | $\dfrac{y^2}{a^2} - \dfrac{x^2}{b^2} = 1 \quad (a > 0, b > 0)$ |
| **VERTICES** | $(\pm a, 0)$ | $(0, \pm a)$ |
| **TRANSVERSE AXIS** | Horizontal, length $2a$ | Vertical, length $2a$ |
| **ASYMPTOTES** | $y = \pm \dfrac{b}{a} x$ | $y = \pm \dfrac{a}{b} x$ |
| **FOCI** | $(\pm c, 0), \quad c^2 = a^2 + b^2$ | $(0, \pm c), \quad c^2 = a^2 + b^2$ |
| **GRAPH** | 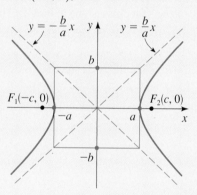 | 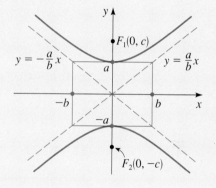 |

---

Asymptotes of rational functions are discussed in Section 4.5.

The *asymptotes* mentioned in this box are lines that the hyperbola approaches for large values of *x* and *y*. To find the asymptotes in the first case in the box, we solve the equation for *y* to get

$$y = \pm \frac{b}{a} \sqrt{x^2 - a^2}$$

$$= \pm \frac{b}{a} x \sqrt{1 - \frac{a^2}{x^2}}$$

As *x* gets large, $a^2/x^2$ gets closer to zero. In other words, as $x \to \infty$, we have $a^2/x^2 \to 0$. So for large *x* the value of *y* can be approximated as $y = \pm(b/a)x$. This shows that these lines are asymptotes of the hyperbola.

Asymptotes are an essential aid for graphing a hyperbola; they help us to determine its shape. A convenient way to find the asymptotes, for a hyperbola with horizontal transverse axis, is to first plot the points $(a, 0)$, $(-a, 0)$, $(0, b)$, and $(0, -b)$. Then sketch horizontal and vertical segments through these points to construct a rectangle, as shown in Figure 2(a) on the next page. We call this rectangle the **central box** of the hyperbola. The slopes of the diagonals of the central box are $\pm b/a$, so by extending them, we obtain the asymptotes $y = \pm(b/a)x$, as sketched in part (b) of the figure. Finally, we plot the vertices and use the asymptotes as a guide in sketching the hyperbola shown in part (c). (A similar procedure applies to graphing a hyperbola that has a vertical transverse axis.)

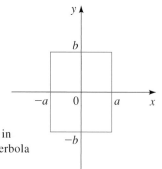

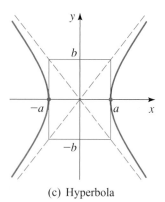

**FIGURE 2** Steps in graphing the hyperbola $\dfrac{x^2}{a^2} - \dfrac{y^2}{b^2} = 1$

(a) Central box

(b) Asymptotes and vertices

(c) Hyperbola

---

### HOW TO SKETCH A HYPERBOLA

1. **Sketch the Central Box.** This is the rectangle centered at the origin, with sides parallel to the axes, that crosses one axis at $\pm a$, the other at $\pm b$.
2. **Sketch the Asymptotes.** These are the lines obtained by extending the diagonals of the central box.
3. **Plot the Vertices.** These are the two $x$-intercepts or the two $y$-intercepts.
4. **Sketch the Hyperbola.** Start at a vertex, and sketch a branch of the hyperbola, approaching the asymptotes. Sketch the other branch in the same way.

---

▶ **EXAMPLE 1** | A Hyperbola with Horizontal Transverse Axis

A hyperbola has the equation

$$9x^2 - 16y^2 = 144$$

**(a)** Find the vertices, foci, and asymptotes, and sketch the graph.

**(b)** Draw the graph using a graphing calculator.

▼ **SOLUTION**

**(a)** First we divide both sides of the equation by 144 to put it into standard form:

$$\frac{x^2}{16} - \frac{y^2}{9} = 1$$

Because the $x^2$-term is positive, the hyperbola has a horizontal transverse axis; its vertices and foci are on the $x$-axis. Since $a^2 = 16$ and $b^2 = 9$, we get $a = 4$, $b = 3$, and $c = \sqrt{16 + 9} = 5$. Thus, we have

| | |
|---|---|
| **VERTICES** | $(\pm 4, 0)$ |
| **FOCI** | $(\pm 5, 0)$ |
| **ASYMPTOTES** | $y = \pm\frac{3}{4}x$ |

After sketching the central box and asymptotes, we complete the sketch of the hyperbola as in Figure 3(a).

Note that the equation of a hyperbola does not define $y$ as a function of $x$ (see page 220). That's why we need to graph two functions to graph a hyperbola.

**(b)** To draw the graph using a graphing calculator, we need to solve for $y$.

$$9x^2 - 16y^2 = 144$$

$$-16y^2 = -9x^2 + 144 \qquad \text{Subtract } 9x^2$$

$$y^2 = 9\left(\frac{x^2}{16} - 1\right) \qquad \text{Divide by } -16 \text{ and factor } 9$$

$$y = \pm 3\sqrt{\frac{x^2}{16} - 1} \qquad \text{Take square roots}$$

To obtain the graph of the hyperbola, we graph the functions

$$y = 3\sqrt{(x^2/16) - 1} \qquad \text{and} \qquad y = -3\sqrt{(x^2/16) - 1}$$

as shown in Figure 3(b).

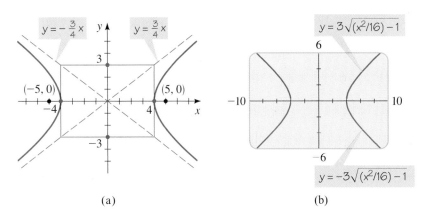

**FIGURE 3**
$9x^2 - 16y^2 = 144$

(a)　　　　(b)

✎ **Practice what you've learned: Do Exercise 9.**　　　▲

▶ **EXAMPLE 2** | A Hyperbola with Vertical Transverse Axis

Find the vertices, foci, and asymptotes of the hyperbola, and sketch its graph.

$$x^2 - 9y^2 + 9 = 0$$

▼ **SOLUTION**　We begin by writing the equation in the standard form for a hyperbola.

$$x^2 - 9y^2 = -9$$

$$y^2 - \frac{x^2}{9} = 1 \qquad \text{Divide by } -9$$

Because the $y^2$-term is positive, the hyperbola has a vertical transverse axis; its foci and vertices are on the $y$-axis. Since $a^2 = 1$ and $b^2 = 9$, we get $a = 1$, $b = 3$, and $c = \sqrt{1 + 9} = \sqrt{10}$. Thus, we have

| | |
|---|---|
| **VERTICES** | $(0, \pm 1)$ |
| **FOCI** | $(0, \pm\sqrt{10})$ |
| **ASYMPTOTES** | $y = \pm\frac{1}{3}x$ |

We sketch the central box and asymptotes, then complete the graph, as shown in Figure 4(a).

We can also draw the graph using a graphing calculator, as shown in Figure 4(b).

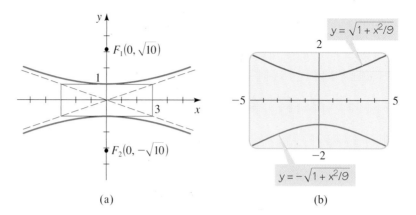

**FIGURE 4**
$x^2 - 9y^2 + 9 = 0$

(a)                                    (b)

✎ **Practice what you've learned: Do Exercise 17.**                          ▲

▶ **EXAMPLE 3** | Finding the Equation of a Hyperbola from Its Vertices and Foci

Find the equation of the hyperbola with vertices $(\pm 3, 0)$ and foci $(\pm 4, 0)$. Sketch the graph.

▼ **SOLUTION**    Since the vertices are on the x-axis, the hyperbola has a horizontal transverse axis. Its equation is of the form

$$\frac{x^2}{3^2} - \frac{y^2}{b^2} = 1$$

We have $a = 3$ and $c = 4$. To find $b$, we use the relation $a^2 + b^2 = c^2$:

$$3^2 + b^2 = 4^2$$
$$b^2 = 4^2 - 3^2 = 7$$
$$b = \sqrt{7}$$

Thus, the equation of the hyperbola is

$$\frac{x^2}{9} - \frac{y^2}{7} = 1$$

**Paths of Comets**

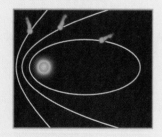

The path of a comet is an ellipse, a parabola, or a hyperbola with the sun at a focus. This fact can be proved using calculus and Newton's laws of motion.* If the path is a parabola or a hyperbola, the comet will never return. If the path is an ellipse, it can be determined precisely when and where the comet can be seen again. Halley's comet has an elliptical path and returns every 75 years; it was last seen in 1987. The brightest comet of the 20th century was comet Hale-Bopp, seen in 1997. Its orbit is a very eccentric ellipse; it is expected to return to the inner solar system around the year 4377.

_____
*James Stewart, *Calculus*, 6th ed. (Belmont, CA: Brooks/Cole, 2008), pp. 884–885.

The graph is shown in Figure 5.

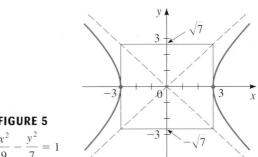

**FIGURE 5**
$$\frac{x^2}{9} - \frac{y^2}{7} = 1$$

✎ **Practice what you've learned: Do Exercises 21 and 31.**   ▲

▶ **EXAMPLE 4** | Finding the Equation of a Hyperbola from Its
Vertices and Asymptotes

Find the equation and the foci of the hyperbola with vertices $(0, \pm 2)$ and asymptotes $y = \pm 2x$. Sketch the graph.

▼ **SOLUTION**   Since the vertices are on the $y$-axis, the hyperbola has a vertical transverse axis with $a = 2$. From the asymptote equation we see that $a/b = 2$. Since $a = 2$, we get $2/b = 2$, and so $b = 1$. Thus, the equation of the hyperbola is

$$\frac{y^2}{4} - x^2 = 1$$

To find the foci, we calculate $c^2 = a^2 + b^2 = 2^2 + 1^2 = 5$, so $c = \sqrt{5}$. Thus, the foci are $(0, \pm\sqrt{5})$. The graph is shown in Figure 6.

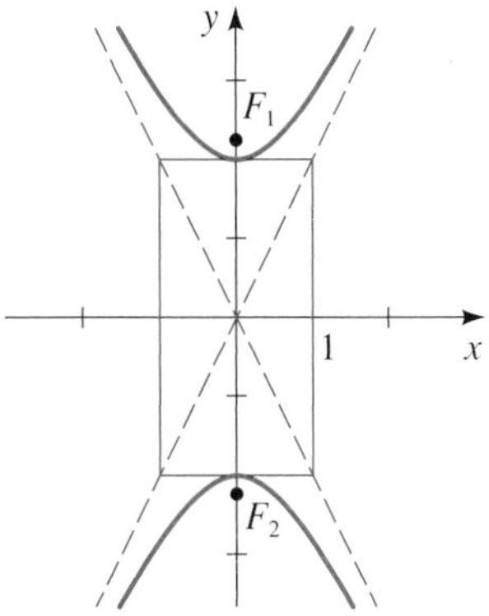

✎ **Practice what you've learned: Do Exercises 25 and 35.**   ▲

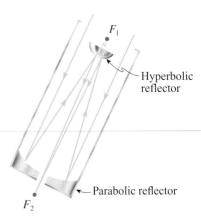

Like parabolas and ellipses, hyperbolas have an interesting *reflection property*. Light aimed at one focus of a hyperbolic mirror is reflected toward the other focus, as shown in Figure 7. This property is used in the construction of Cassegrain-type telescopes. A hyperbolic mirror is placed in the telescope tube so that light reflected from the primary parabolic reflector is aimed at one focus of the hyperbolic mirror. The light is then refocused at a more accessible point below the primary reflector (Figure 8).

**FIGURE 6**
$$\frac{y^2}{4} - x^2 = 1$$

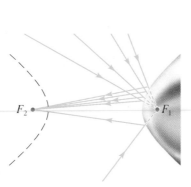

**FIGURE 7** Reflection property of
hyperbolas

**FIGURE 8** Cassegrain-type telescope

The LORAN (LOng RAnge Navigation) system was used until the early 1990s; it has now been superseded by the GPS system (see page 462). In the LORAN system, hyperbolas are used onboard a ship to determine its location. In Figure 9 radio stations at $A$ and $B$ transmit signals simultaneously for reception by the ship at $P$. The onboard computer converts the time difference in reception of these signals into a distance difference $d(P, A) - d(P, B)$. From the definition of a hyperbola this locates the ship on one branch of a hyperbola with foci at $A$ and $B$ (sketched in black in the figure). The same procedure is carried out with two other radio stations at $C$ and $D$, and this locates the ship on a second hyperbola (shown in red in the figure). (In practice, only three stations are needed because one station can be used as a focus for both hyperbolas.) The coordinates of the intersection point of these two hyperbolas, which can be calculated precisely by the computer, give the location of $P$.

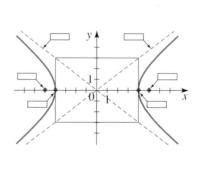

**FIGURE 9** LORAN system for finding the location of a ship

# 8.3 EXERCISES

## ▼ CONCEPTS

**1.** A hyperbola is the set of all points in the plane for which the _____ of the distances from two fixed points $F_1$ and $F_2$ is constant. The points $F_1$ and $F_2$ are called the _____ of the hyperbola.

**2.** The graph of the equation $\dfrac{x^2}{a^2} - \dfrac{y^2}{b^2} = 1$ with $a > 0, b > 0$ is a hyperbola with vertices (___, ___) and (___, ___) and foci $(\pm c, 0)$, where $c =$ _____. So the graph of $\dfrac{x^2}{4^2} - \dfrac{y^2}{3^2} = 1$ is a hyperbola with vertices (___, ___) and (___, ___) and foci (___, ___) and (___, ___).

**3.** The graph of the equation $\dfrac{y^2}{a^2} - \dfrac{x^2}{b^2} = 1$ with $a > 0, b > 0$ is a hyperbola with vertices (___, ___) and (___, ___) and foci $(0, \pm c)$, where $c =$ _____. So the graph of

$\dfrac{y^2}{4^2} - \dfrac{x^2}{3^2} = 1$ is a hyperbola with vertices (___, ___) and (___, ___) and foci (___, ___) and (___, ___).

**4.** Label the vertices, foci, and asymptotes on the graphs given for the hyperbolas in Exercises 2 and 3.

**(a)** $\dfrac{x^2}{4^2} - \dfrac{y^2}{3^2} = 1$        **(b)** $\dfrac{y^2}{4^2} - \dfrac{x^2}{3^2} = 1$

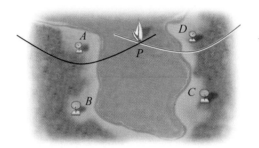

▼ **SKILLS**

**5–8** ■ Match the equation with the graphs labeled I–IV. Give reasons for your answers.

**5.** $\dfrac{x^2}{4} - y^2 = 1$

**6.** $y^2 - \dfrac{x^2}{9} = 1$

**7.** $16y^2 - x^2 = 144$

**8.** $9x^2 - 25y^2 = 225$

I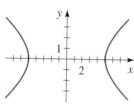

II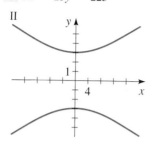

III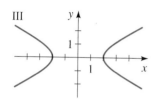

IV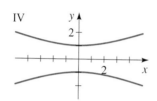

**9–20** ■ Find the vertices, foci, and asymptotes of the hyperbola, and sketch its graph.

 **9.** $\dfrac{x^2}{4} - \dfrac{y^2}{16} = 1$

**10.** $\dfrac{y^2}{9} - \dfrac{x^2}{16} = 1$

**11.** $y^2 - \dfrac{x^2}{25} = 1$

**12.** $\dfrac{x^2}{2} - y^2 = 1$

**13.** $x^2 - y^2 = 1$

**14.** $9x^2 - 4y^2 = 36$

**15.** $25y^2 - 9x^2 = 225$

**16.** $x^2 - y^2 + 4 = 0$

**17.** $x^2 - 4y^2 - 8 = 0$

**18.** $x^2 - 2y^2 = 3$

**19.** $4y^2 - x^2 = 1$

**20.** $9x^2 - 16y^2 = 1$

**21–26** ■ Find the equation for the hyperbola whose graph is shown.

**21.**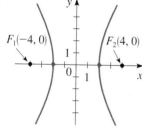

**22.**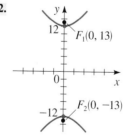

**23.**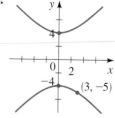

**24.**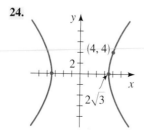

**25.**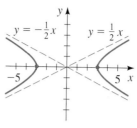

**26.**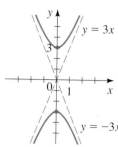

**27–30** ■ Use a graphing device to graph the hyperbola.

**27.** $x^2 - 2y^2 = 8$

**28.** $3y^2 - 4x^2 = 24$

**29.** $\dfrac{y^2}{2} - \dfrac{x^2}{6} = 1$

**30.** $\dfrac{x^2}{100} - \dfrac{y^2}{64} = 1$

**31–42** ■ Find an equation for the hyperbola that satisfies the given conditions.

**31.** Foci $(\pm 5, 0)$, vertices $(\pm 3, 0)$

**32.** Foci $(0, \pm 10)$, vertices $(0, \pm 8)$

**33.** Foci $(0, \pm 2)$, vertices $(0, \pm 1)$

**34.** Foci $(\pm 6, 0)$, vertices $(\pm 2, 0)$

**35.** Vertices $(\pm 1, 0)$, asymptotes $y = \pm 5x$

**36.** Vertices $(0, \pm 6)$, asymptotes $y = \pm \frac{1}{3}x$

**37.** Foci $(0, \pm 8)$, asymptotes $y = \pm \frac{1}{2}x$

**38.** Vertices $(0, \pm 6)$, hyperbola passes through $(-5, 9)$

**39.** Asymptotes $y = \pm x$, hyperbola passes through $(5, 3)$

**40.** Foci $(\pm 3, 0)$, hyperbola passes through $(4, 1)$

**41.** Foci $(\pm 5, 0)$, length of transverse axis 6

**42.** Foci $(0, \pm 1)$, length of transverse axis 1

**43.** (a) Show that the asymptotes of the hyperbola $x^2 - y^2 = 5$ are perpendicular to each other.
   (b) Find an equation for the hyperbola with foci $(\pm c, 0)$ and with asymptotes perpendicular to each other.

**44.** The hyperbolas

$$\frac{x^2}{a^2} - \frac{y^2}{b^2} = 1 \quad \text{and} \quad \frac{x^2}{a^2} - \frac{y^2}{b^2} = -1$$

are said to be **conjugate** to each other.
   (a) Show that the hyperbolas

$$x^2 - 4y^2 + 16 = 0 \quad \text{and} \quad 4y^2 - x^2 + 16 = 0$$

   are conjugate to each other, and sketch their graphs on the same coordinate axes.
   (b) What do the hyperbolas of part (a) have in common?
   (c) Show that any pair of conjugate hyperbolas have the relationship you discovered in part (b).

**45.** In the derivation of the equation of the hyperbola at the beginning of this section, we said that the equation

$$\sqrt{(x + c)^2 + y^2} - \sqrt{(x - c)^2 + y^2} = \pm 2a$$

simplifies to

$$(c^2 - a^2)x^2 - a^2y^2 = a^2(c^2 - a^2)$$

Supply the steps needed to show this.

**46. (a)** For the hyperbola

$$\frac{x^2}{9} - \frac{y^2}{16} = 1$$

determine the values of $a$, $b$, and $c$, and find the coordinates of the foci $F_1$ and $F_2$.
**(b)** Show that the point $P(5, \frac{16}{3})$ lies on this hyperbola.
**(c)** Find $d(P, F_1)$ and $d(P, F_2)$.
**(d)** Verify that the difference between $d(P, F_1)$ and $d(P, F_2)$ is $2a$.

**47.** Hyperbolas are called **confocal** if they have the same foci.
**(a)** Show that the hyperbolas

$$\frac{y^2}{k} - \frac{x^2}{16 - k} = 1 \quad \text{with } 0 < k < 16$$

are confocal.
**(b)** Use a graphing device to draw the top branches of the family of hyperbolas in part (a) for $k = 1, 4, 8,$ and $12$. How does the shape of the graph change as $k$ increases?

## ▼ APPLICATIONS

**48. Navigation**   In the figure, the LORAN stations at $A$ and $B$ are 500 mi apart, and the ship at $P$ receives station $A$'s signal 2640 microseconds ($\mu$s) before it receives the signal from station $B$.
**(a)** Assuming that radio signals travel at 980 ft/$\mu$s, find $d(P, A) - d(P, B)$.
**(b)** Find an equation for the branch of the hyperbola indicated in red in the figure. (Use miles as the unit of distance.)
**(c)** If $A$ is due north of $B$ and if $P$ is due east of $A$, how far is $P$ from $A$?

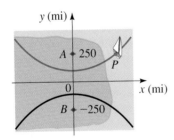

**49. Comet Trajectories**   Some comets, such as Halley's comet, are a permanent part of the solar system, traveling in elliptical orbits around the sun. Others pass through the solar system only once, following a hyperbolic path with the sun at a focus. The figure shows the path of such a comet. Find an equation for the path, assuming that the closest the comet comes to the sun is $2 \times 10^9$ mi and that the path the comet was taking

before it neared the solar system is at a right angle to the path it continues on after leaving the solar system.

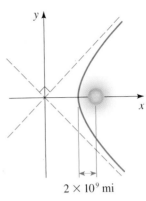

$2 \times 10^9$ mi

**50. Ripples in Pool**   Two stones are dropped simultaneously in a calm pool of water. The crests of the resulting waves form equally spaced concentric circles, as shown in the figures. The waves interact with each other to create certain interference patterns.
**(a)** Explain why the red dots lie on an ellipse.
**(b)** Explain why the blue dots lie on a hyperbola.

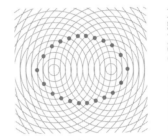 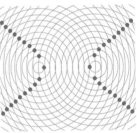

## ▼ DISCOVERY • DISCUSSION • WRITING

**51. Hyperbolas in the Real World**   Several examples of the uses of hyperbolas are given in the text. Find other situations in real life in which hyperbolas occur. Consult a scientific encyclopedia in the reference section of your library, or search the Internet.

**52. Light from a Lamp**   The light from a lamp forms a lighted area on a wall, as shown in the figure. Why is the boundary of this lighted area a hyperbola? How can one hold a flashlight so that its beam forms a hyperbola on the ground?

## 8.4 | Shifted Conics

### LEARNING OBJECTIVES

After completing this section, you will be able to:

- Find geometric properties of a shifted conic from its equation
- Find the equation of a shifted conic from some of its geometric properties

In the preceding sections we studied parabolas with vertices at the origin and ellipses and hyperbolas with centers at the origin. We restricted ourselves to these cases because these equations have the simplest form. In this section we consider conics whose vertices and centers are not necessarily at the origin, and we determine how this affects their equations.

### ■ Shifting Graphs of Equations

In Section 3.5 we studied transformations of functions that have the effect of shifting their graphs. In general, for any equation in $x$ and $y$, if we replace $x$ by $x - h$ or by $x + h$, the graph of the new equation is simply the old graph shifted horizontally; if $y$ is replaced by $y - k$ or by $y + k$, the graph is shifted vertically. The following box gives the details.

---

**SHIFTING GRAPHS OF EQUATIONS**

If $h$ and $k$ are positive real numbers, then replacing $x$ by $x - h$ or by $x + h$ and replacing $y$ by $y - k$ or by $y + k$ has the following effect(s) on the graph of any equation in $x$ and $y$.

| Replacement | How the graph is shifted |
|---|---|
| **1.** $x$ replaced by $x - h$ | Right $h$ units |
| **2.** $x$ replaced by $x + h$ | Left $h$ units |
| **3.** $y$ replaced by $y - k$ | Upward $k$ units |
| **4.** $y$ replaced by $y + k$ | Downward $k$ units |

---

### ■ Shifted Ellipses

Let's apply horizontal and vertical shifting to the ellipse with equation

$$\frac{x^2}{a^2} + \frac{y^2}{b^2} = 1$$

whose graph is shown in Figure 1 on the next page. If we shift it so that its center is at the point $(h, k)$ instead of at the origin, then its equation becomes

$$\frac{(x - h)^2}{a^2} + \frac{(y - k)^2}{b^2} = 1$$

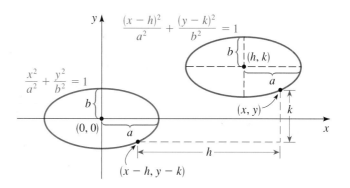

**FIGURE 1** Shifted ellipse

▶ **EXAMPLE 1** | Sketching the Graph of a Shifted Ellipse

Sketch the graph of the ellipse

$$\frac{(x + 1)^2}{4} + \frac{(y - 2)^2}{9} = 1$$

and determine the coordinates of the foci.

▼ **SOLUTION**   The ellipse

$$\frac{(x + 1)^2}{4} + \frac{(y - 2)^2}{9} = 1 \qquad \text{Shifted ellipse}$$

is shifted so that its center is at $(-1, 2)$. It is obtained from the ellipse

$$\frac{x^2}{4} + \frac{y^2}{9} = 1 \qquad \text{Ellipse with center at origin}$$

by shifting it left 1 unit and upward 2 units. The endpoints of the minor and major axes of the unshifted ellipse are $(2, 0)$, $(-2, 0)$, $(0, 3)$, $(0, -3)$. We apply the required shifts to these points to obtain the corresponding points on the shifted ellipse:

$$(2, 0) \;\rightarrow\; (2 - 1, 0 + 2) = (1, 2)$$
$$(-2, 0) \;\rightarrow\; (-2 - 1, 0 + 2) = (-3, 2)$$
$$(0, 3) \;\rightarrow\; (0 - 1, 3 + 2) = (-1, 5)$$
$$(0, -3) \;\rightarrow\; (0 - 1, -3 + 2) = (-1, -1)$$

This helps us sketch the graph in Figure 2.

To find the foci of the shifted ellipse, we first find the foci of the ellipse with center at the origin. Since $a^2 = 9$ and $b^2 = 4$, we have $c^2 = 9 - 4 = 5$, so $c = \sqrt{5}$. So the foci are $(0, \pm\sqrt{5})$. Shifting left 1 unit and upward 2 units, we get

$$(0, \sqrt{5}) \;\rightarrow\; (0 - 1, \sqrt{5} + 2) = (-1, 2 + \sqrt{5})$$
$$(0, -\sqrt{5}) \;\rightarrow\; (0 - 1, -\sqrt{5} + 2) = (-1, 2 - \sqrt{5})$$

Thus, the foci of the shifted ellipse are

$$(-1, 2 + \sqrt{5}) \qquad \text{and} \qquad (-1, 2 - \sqrt{5})$$

✎ **Practice what you've learned: Do Exercise 7.**    ▲

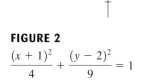

**FIGURE 2**

$$\frac{(x + 1)^2}{4} + \frac{(y - 2)^2}{9} = 1$$

## ■ Shifted Parabolas

Applying shifts to parabolas leads to the equations and graphs shown in Figure 3.

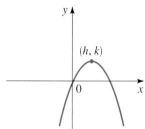

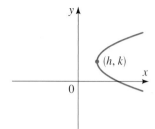

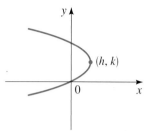

(a) $(x - h)^2 = 4p(y - k)$
    $p > 0$

(b) $(x - h)^2 = 4p(y - k)$
    $p < 0$

(c) $(y - k)^2 = 4p(x - h)$
    $p > 0$

(d) $(y - k)^2 = 4p(x - h)$
    $p < 0$

**FIGURE 3**  Shifted parabolas

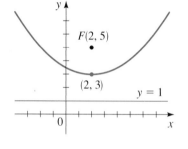

**FIGURE 4**
$x^2 - 4x = 8y - 28$

▶ **EXAMPLE 2** | Graphing a Shifted Parabola

Determine the vertex, focus, and directrix and sketch the graph of the parabola.

$$x^2 - 4x = 8y - 28$$

▼ **SOLUTION**    We complete the square in $x$ to put this equation into one of the forms in Figure 3.

$$x^2 - 4x + 4 = 8y - 28 + 4 \qquad \text{Add 4 to complete the square}$$

$$(x - 2)^2 = 8y - 24$$

$$(x - 2)^2 = 8(y - 3) \qquad \text{Shifted parabola}$$

This parabola opens upward with vertex at $(2, 3)$. It is obtained from the parabola

$$x^2 = 8y \qquad \text{Parabola with vertex at origin}$$

by shifting right 2 units and upward 3 units. Since $4p = 8$, we have $p = 2$, so the focus is 2 units above the vertex and the directrix is 2 units below the vertex. Thus, the focus is $(2, 5)$ and the directrix is $y = 1$. The graph is shown in Figure 4.

✎ **Practice what you've learned: Do Exercises 9 and 23.**    ▲

## Shifted Hyperbolas

Applying shifts to hyperbolas leads to the equations and graphs shown in Figure 5.

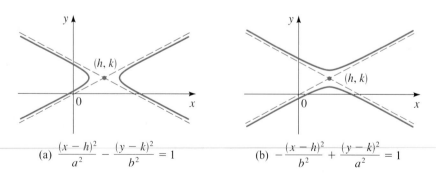

**FIGURE 5**  Shifted hyperbolas

(a) $\dfrac{(x - h)^2}{a^2} - \dfrac{(y - k)^2}{b^2} = 1$

(b) $-\dfrac{(x - h)^2}{b^2} + \dfrac{(y - k)^2}{a^2} = 1$

▶ **EXAMPLE 3** | Graphing a Shifted Hyperbola

A shifted conic has the equation

$$9x^2 - 72x - 16y^2 - 32y = 16$$

**(a)** Complete the square in $x$ and $y$ to show that the equation represents a hyperbola.

**(b)** Find the center, vertices, foci, and asymptotes of the hyperbola, and sketch its graph.

**(c)** Draw the graph using a graphing calculator.

▼ **SOLUTION**

**(a)** We complete the squares in both $x$ and $y$:

$$9(x^2 - 8x \qquad) - 16(y^2 + 2y \qquad) = 16 \qquad \text{Group terms and factor}$$

$$9(x^2 - 8x + 16) - 16(y^2 + 2y + 1) = 16 + 9 \cdot 16 - 16 \cdot 1 \qquad \text{Complete the squares}$$

$$9(x - 4)^2 - 16(y + 1)^2 = 144 \qquad \text{Divide this by 144}$$

$$\frac{(x - 4)^2}{16} - \frac{(y + 1)^2}{9} = 1 \qquad \text{Shifted hyperbola}$$

Comparing this to Figure 5(a), we see that this is the equation of a shifted hyperbola.

**(b)** The shifted hyperbola has center $(4, -1)$ and a horizontal transverse axis.

$$\textbf{CENTER} \quad (4, -1)$$

Its graph will have the same shape as the unshifted hyperbola

$$\frac{x^2}{16} - \frac{y^2}{9} = 1 \qquad \text{Hyperbola with center at origin}$$

Since $a^2 = 16$ and $b^2 = 9$, we have $a = 4$, $b = 3$, and $c = \sqrt{a^2 + b^2} = \sqrt{16 + 9} = 5$. Thus, the foci lie 5 units to the left and to the right of the center, and the vertices lie 4 units to either side of the center.

$$\textbf{FOCI} \qquad (-1, -1) \quad \text{and} \quad (9, -1)$$

$$\textbf{VERTICES} \quad (0, -1) \quad \text{and} \quad (8, -1)$$

The asymptotes of the unshifted hyperbola are $y = \pm\frac{3}{4}x$, so the asymptotes of the shifted hyperbola are found as follows.

$$\textbf{ASYMPTOTES} \quad y + 1 = \pm\tfrac{3}{4}(x - 4)$$

$$y + 1 = \pm\tfrac{3}{4}x \mp 3$$

$$y = \tfrac{3}{4}x - 4 \quad \text{and} \quad y = -\tfrac{3}{4}x + 2$$

To help us sketch the hyperbola, we draw the central box; it extends 4 units left and right from the center and 3 units upward and downward from the center. We then draw the asymptotes and complete the graph of the shifted hyperbola as shown in Figure 6(a).

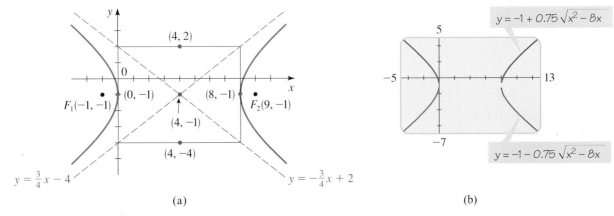

(a)

(b)

**FIGURE 6** $9x^2 - 72x - 16y^2 - 32y = 16$

**29.**

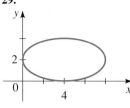

**30.**

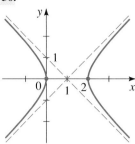

**31–42** ▪ Determine the type of curve represented by the equation. Find the foci and vertices (if any), and sketch the graph.

**31.** $\dfrac{x^2}{12} + y = 1$

**32.** $\dfrac{x^2}{12} + \dfrac{y^2}{144} = \dfrac{y}{12}$

**33.** $x^2 - y^2 + 144 = 0$

**34.** $x^2 + 6x = 9y^2$

**35.** $4x^2 + y^2 = 8(x + y)$

**36.** $3x^2 - 6(x + y) = 10$

**37.** $x = y^2 - 16y$

**38.** $2x^2 + 4 = 4x + y^2$

**39.** $2x^2 - 12x + y^2 + 6y + 26 = 0$

**40.** $36x^2 - 4y^2 - 36x - 8y = 31$

**41.** $9x^2 + 8y^2 - 15x + 8y + 27 = 0$

**42.** $x^2 + 4y^2 = 4x + 8$

**43–52** ▪ Find an equation for the conic section with the given properties.

**43.** The parabola with focus $F(0, 1)$ and directrix $y = -1$

**44.** The parabola with vertex at the origin and focus $F(5, 0)$

**45.** The ellipse with center at the origin and with $x$-intercepts $\pm 2$ and $y$-intercepts $\pm 5$

**46.** The ellipse with center $C(0, 4)$, foci $F_1(0, 0)$ and $F_2(0, 8)$, and major axis of length 10

**47.** The hyperbola with vertices $V(0, \pm 2)$ and asymptotes $y = \pm\frac{1}{2}x$

**48.** The hyperbola with center $C(2, 4)$, foci $F_1(2, 1)$ and $F_2(2, 7)$, and vertices $V_1(2, 6)$ and $V_2(2, 2)$

**49.** The ellipse with foci $F_1(1, 1)$ and $F_2(1, 3)$ and with one vertex on the $x$-axis

**50.** The parabola with vertex $V(5, 5)$ and directrix the $y$-axis

**51.** The ellipse with vertices $V_1(7, 12)$ and $V_2(7, -8)$ and passing through the point $P(1, 8)$

**52.** The parabola with vertex $V(-1, 0)$ and horizontal axis of symmetry and crossing the $y$-axis at $y = 2$

**53.** The path of the earth around the sun is an ellipse with the sun at one focus. The ellipse has major axis 186,000,000 mi and eccentricity 0.017. Find the distance between the earth and the sun when the earth is **(a)** closest to the sun and **(b)** farthest from the sun.

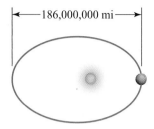

**54.** A ship is located 40 mi from a straight shoreline. LORAN stations $A$ and $B$ are located on the shoreline, 300 mi apart. From the LORAN signals, the captain determines that the ship is 80 mi closer to $A$ than to $B$. Find the location of the ship. (Place $A$ and $B$ on the $y$-axis with the $x$-axis halfway between them. Find the $x$- and $y$-coordinates of the ship.)

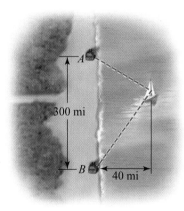

**55. (a)** Draw graphs of the following family of ellipses for $k = 1, 2, 4,$ and 8.

$$\frac{x^2}{16 + k^2} + \frac{y^2}{k^2} = 1$$

**(b)** Prove that all the ellipses in part (a) have the same foci.

**56. (a)** Draw graphs of the following family of parabolas for $k = \frac{1}{2}, 1, 2,$ and 4.

$$y = kx^2$$

**(b)** Find the foci of the parabolas in part (a).
**(c)** How does the location of the focus change as $k$ increases?

1. Find the focus and directrix of the parabola $x^2 = -12y$, and sketch its graph.

2. Find the vertices, foci, and the lengths of the major and minor axes for the ellipse
   $\dfrac{x^2}{16} + \dfrac{y^2}{4} = 1$. Then sketch its graph.

3. Find the vertices, foci, and asymptotes of the hyperbola $\dfrac{y^2}{9} - \dfrac{x^2}{16} = 1$. Then sketch its graph.

**4–6** ▪ Find an equation for the conic whose graph is shown.

**4.**    **5.**    **6.**

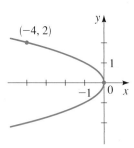    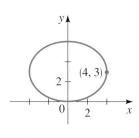    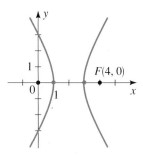

**7–9** ▪ Sketch the graph of the equation.

7. $16x^2 + 36y^2 - 96x + 36y + 9 = 0$

8. $9x^2 - 8y^2 + 36x + 64y = 164$

9. $2x + y^2 + 8y + 8 = 0$

10. Find an equation for the hyperbola with foci $(0, \pm 5)$ and with asymptotes $y = \pm\frac{3}{4}x$.

11. Find an equation for the parabola with focus $(2, 4)$ and directrix the $x$-axis.

12. Find an equation for the ellipse with foci $(3, \pm 4)$ and with $x$-intercepts 0 and 6.

13. A parabolic reflector for a car headlight forms a bowl shape that is 6 in. wide at its opening and 3 in. deep, as shown in the figure. How far from the vertex should the filament of the bulb be placed if it is to be located at the focus?

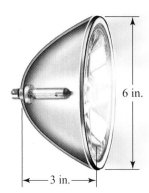

1. Consider the following system of equations.

$$\begin{cases} x^2 + y^2 = 4y \\ x^2 - 2y = 0 \end{cases}$$

   (a) Is the system linear or nonlinear? Explain.

   (b) Find all solutions of the system.

   (c) The graph of each equation is a conic section. Name the type of conic section in each case.

   (d) Graph both equations on the same set of axes.

   (e) On your graph, shade the region that corresponds to the solution of the system of inequalities.

$$\begin{cases} x^2 + y^2 \le 4y \\ x^2 - 2y \le 0 \end{cases}$$

2. Find the complete solution of each linear system, or show that no solution exists.

   (a) $\begin{cases} x + y - z = 2 \\ 2x + 3y - z = 5 \\ 3x + 5y + 2z = 11 \end{cases}$

   (b) $\begin{cases} y - z = 2 \\ x + 2y - 3z = 3 \\ 3x + 5y - 8z = 7 \end{cases}$

3. Xavier, Yolanda, and Zachary go fishing. Yolanda catches as many fish as Xavier and Zachary put together. Zachary catches 2 more fish than Xavier. The total catch for all three people is 20 fish. How many did each person catch?

4. Let

$$A = \begin{bmatrix} 1 & 5 \\ 2 & 0 \end{bmatrix} \qquad\qquad B = \begin{bmatrix} -2 & 1 & 0 \\ -\frac{1}{2} & 0 & 1 \end{bmatrix}$$

$$C = \begin{bmatrix} 1 & 0 & 1 \\ 0 & 2 & 1 \\ -1 & 0 & 0 \end{bmatrix} \qquad\qquad D = \begin{bmatrix} 1 & 4 & 3 \\ 1 & 6 & 5 \\ 0 & 1 & 1 \end{bmatrix}$$

   (a) Calculate each of the following, or explain why the calculation can't be done.

$$A + B, \quad C - D, \quad AB, \quad CB, \quad BD, \quad \det(B), \quad \det(C), \quad \det(D)$$

   (b) Based on the values you calculated for $\det(C)$ and $\det(D)$, which matrix, $C$ or $D$, has an inverse? Find the inverse of the invertible one.

5. Consider the following system of equations.

$$\begin{cases} 5x - 3y = 5 \\ 6x - 4y = 0 \end{cases}$$

   (a) Write a matrix equation of the form $AX = B$ that is equivalent to this system.

   (b) Find $A^{-1}$, the inverse of the coefficient matrix.

   (c) Solve the matrix equation by multiplying each side by $A^{-1}$.

   (d) Now solve the system using Cramer's Rule. Did you get the same solution as in part (b)?

6. Find the partial fraction decomposition of the rational function $r(x) = \dfrac{4x + 8}{x^4 + 4x^2}$.

7. Find the focus and directrix of each parabola, and sketch its graph.

   (a) $x^2 + 6y = 0$

   (b) $x - 2y^2 + 4y = 2$

8. Determine whether the equation represents an ellipse or a hyperbola. If it is an ellipse, find the coordinates of its vertices and foci, and sketch its graph. If it is a hyperbola, find the coordinates of its vertices and foci, find the equations of its asymptotes, and sketch its graph.

   (a) $\dfrac{x^2}{9} - y^2 = 1$

   (b) $\dfrac{x^2}{9} + y^2 = 1$

   (c) $-\dfrac{x^2}{9} + y^2 = 1$

9. Sketch the graph of each conic section, and find the coordinates of its foci. What type of conic section does each equation represent?

   (a) $9x^2 + 4y^2 = 24y$

   (b) $x^2 + 6x - y^2 + 8y = 16$

10. Find an equation for the conic whose graph is shown.

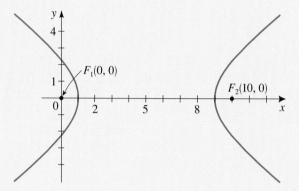

Many buildings employ conic sections in their design. Architects have various reasons for using these curves, ranging from structural stability to simple beauty. But how can a huge parabola, ellipse, or hyperbola be accurately constructed in concrete and steel? In this *Focus* we will see how the geometric properties of the conics can be used to construct these shapes.

## Conics in Buildings

In ancient times architecture was part of mathematics, so architects had to be mathematicians. Many of the structures they built—pyramids, temples, amphitheaters, and irrigation projects—still stand. In modern times architects employ even more sophisticated mathematical principles. The figures below show some structures that employ conic sections in their design.

Roman Amphitheater in
Alexandria, Egypt (circle)
© Nick Wheeler/CORBIS

Ceiling of Statuary Hall in the
U.S. Capitol (ellipse)
Courtesy of The Architect of the Capitol

Roof of the Skydome in
Toronto, Canada (parabola)
© Stone/Getty Images

Roof of Washington Dulles Airport
(hyperbola and parabola)
© Richard T. Nowitz/CORBIS

McDonnell Planetarium,
St. Louis, MO (hyperbola)
Courtesy of Chamber of Commerce, St. Louis, MO

Attic in La Pedrera,
Barcelona, Spain (parabola)
© O. Alamany & E. Vincens/CORBIS

Architects have different reasons for using conics in their designs. For example, the Spanish architect Antoni Gaudi used parabolas in the attic of La Pedrera (see photo above). He reasoned that since a rope suspended between two points with an equally distributed load (like in a suspension bridge) has the shape of a parabola, an inverted parabola would provide the best support for a flat roof.

## Constructing Conics

The equations of the conics are helpful in manufacturing small objects, because a computer-controlled cutting tool can accurately trace a curve given by an equation. But in a building project, how can we construct a portion of a parabola, ellipse, or hyperbola that spans the ceiling or walls of a building? The geometric properties of the conics provide practical ways of constructing them. For example, if you were building a circular tower, you would choose a center point, then make sure that the walls of the tower were a fixed

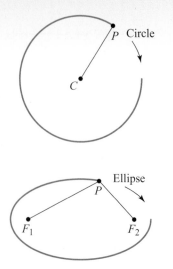

**FIGURE 1** Constructing a circle and an ellipse

distance from that point. Elliptical walls can be constructed using a string anchored at two points, as shown in Figure 1.

To construct a parabola, we can use the apparatus shown in Figure 2. A piece of string of length $a$ is anchored at $F$ and $A$. The T-square, also of length $a$, slides along the straight bar $L$. A pencil at $P$ holds the string taut against the T-square. As the T-square slides to the right the pencil traces out a curve.

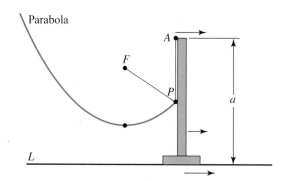

**FIGURE 2** Constructing a parabola

From the figure we see that

$$d(F, P) + d(P, A) = a \qquad \text{The string is of length } a$$

$$d(L, P) + d(P, A) = a \qquad \text{The T-square is of length } a$$

It follows that $d(F, P) + d(P, A) = d(L, P) + d(P, A)$. Subtracting $d(P, A)$ from each side, we get

$$d(F, P) = d(L, P)$$

The last equation says that the distance from $F$ to $P$ is equal to the distance from $P$ to the line $L$. Thus, the curve is a parabola with focus $F$ and directrix $L$.

In building projects it is easier to construct a straight line than a curve. So in some buildings, such as in the Kobe Tower (see Problem 4), a curved surface is produced by using many straight lines. We can also produce a curve using straight lines, such as the parabola shown in Figure 3.

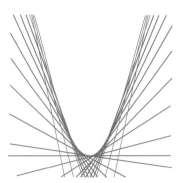

**FIGURE 3** Tangent lines to a parabola

Each line is **tangent** to the parabola; that is, the line meets the parabola at exactly one point and does not cross the parabola. The line tangent to the parabola $y = x^2$ at the point $(a, a^2)$ is

$$y = 2ax - a^2$$

You are asked to show this in Problem 6. The parabola is called the **envelope** of all such lines.

# Problems

1. **Conics in Architecture**    The photographs on page 595 show six examples of buildings that contain conic sections. Search the Internet to find other examples of structures that employ parabolas, ellipses, or hyperbolas in their design. Find at least one example for each type of conic.

2. **Constructing a Hyperbola**    In this problem we construct a hyperbola. The wooden bar in the figure can pivot at $F_1$. A string that is shorter than the bar is anchored at $F_2$ and at $A$, the other end of the bar. A pencil at $P$ holds the string taut against the bar as it moves counterclockwise around $F_1$.

    **(a)** Show that the curve traced out by the pencil is one branch of a hyperbola with foci at $F_1$ and $F_2$.

    **(b)** How should the apparatus be reconfigured to draw the other branch of the hyperbola?

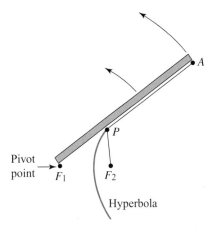

3. **A Parabola in a Rectangle**    The following method can be used to construct a parabola that fits in a given rectangle. The parabola will be approximated by many short line segments.

    First, draw a rectangle. Divide the rectangle in half by a vertical line segment, and label the top endpoint $V$. Next, divide the length and width of each half rectangle into an equal number of parts to form grid lines, as shown in the figure below. Draw lines from $V$ to the endpoints of horizontal grid line 1, and mark the points where these lines cross the vertical grid lines labeled 1. Next, draw lines from $V$ to the endpoints of horizontal grid line 2, and mark the points where these lines cross the vertical grid lines labeled 2. Continue in this way until you have used all the horizontal grid lines. Now use line segments to connect the points you have marked to obtain an approximation to the desired parabola. Apply this procedure to draw a parabola that fits into a 6 ft by 10 ft rectangle on a lawn.

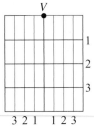
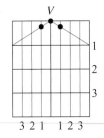
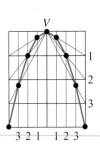

4. **Hyperbolas from Straight Lines**    In this problem we construct hyperbolic shapes using straight lines. Punch equally spaced holes into the edges of two large plastic lids. Connect corresponding holes with strings of equal lengths as shown in the figure on the next page. Holding the strings taut, twist one lid against the other. An imaginary surface passing through the strings has hyperbolic cross sections. (An architectural example of this is the Kobe Tower in

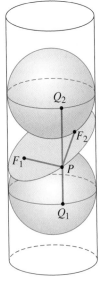

Japan, shown in the photograph.) What happens to the vertices of the hyperbolic cross sections as the lids are twisted more?

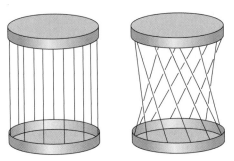

5. **Tangent Lines to a Parabola** In this problem we show that the line tangent to the parabola $y = x^2$ at the point $(a, a^2)$ has the equation $y = 2ax - a^2$.

(a) Let $m$ be the slope of the tangent line at $(a, a^2)$. Show that the equation of the tangent line is $y - a^2 = m(x - a)$.

(b) Use the fact that the tangent line intersects the parabola at only one point to show that $(a, a^2)$ is the only solution of the system.

$$\begin{cases} y - a^2 = m(x - a) \\ y = x^2 \end{cases}$$

(c) Eliminate $y$ from the system in part (b) to get a quadratic equation in $x$. Show that the discriminant of this quadratic is $(m - 2a)^2$. Since the system in (b) has exactly one solution, the discriminant must equal 0. Find $m$.

(d) Substitute the value for $m$ you found in part (c) into the equation in part (a) and simplify to get the equation of the tangent line.

6. **A Cut Cylinder** In this problem we prove that when a cylinder is cut by a plane, an ellipse is formed. An architectural example of this is the Tycho Brahe Planetarium in Copenhagen (see the photograph). In the figure a cylinder is cut by a plane, resulting in the red curve. Two spheres with the same radius as the cylinder slide inside the cylinder so that they just touch the plane at $F_1$ and $F_2$. Choose an arbitrary point $P$ on the curve, and let $Q_1$ and $Q_2$ be the two points on the cylinder where a vertical line through $P$ touches the "equator" of each sphere.

(a) Show that $PF_1 = PQ_1$ and $PF_2 = PQ_2$. [*Hint*: Use the fact that all tangents to a sphere from a given point outside the sphere are of the same length.]

(b) Explain why $PQ_1 + PQ_2$ is the same for all points $P$ on the curve.

(c) Show that $PF_1 + PF_2$ is the same for all points $P$ on the curve.

(d) Conclude that the curve is an ellipse with foci $F_1$ and $F_2$.

# CHAPTER 9
# Sequences and Series

© Zia Soleil /Getty Images

**Can you afford your dreams?** After graduation you may be thinking about a dream job, a dream house, or a dream car. But can your dream job help you to afford your other dreams? And you don't want to save for years before purchasing a house or car—you want them now! Our economy makes it possible to afford our dreams immediately by giving us a way of borrowing lots of money now to be repaid later. To do this fairly, lenders must be paid interest, and borrowers must pay back the money they borrowed and the interest in a regular and timely manner. The instruments that make all these financial transactions possible are formulas —formulas for compound interest, mortgage payments, amortization, and annuities. These formulas make our economy possible because lenders, borrowers, banks, mortgage companies, and credit card companies all use the same formulas. We will see in this chapter how these formulas are used and how they are derived using properties of sequences and series (see Section 9.4).

## 9.1 | Sequences and Summation Notation

**LEARNING OBJECTIVES**

After completing this section, you will be able to:

■ Find the terms of a sequence
■ Find the terms of a recursive sequence
■ Find the partial sums of a sequence
■ Use sigma notation

In this chapter we study sequences. Roughly speaking, a sequence is an infinite list of numbers. The numbers in the sequence are often written as $a_1, a_2, a_3, \ldots$. The dots mean that the list continues forever. A simple example is the sequence

$$5, \quad 10, \quad 15, \quad 20, \quad 25, \ldots$$
$$\uparrow \qquad \uparrow \qquad \uparrow \qquad \uparrow \qquad \uparrow$$
$$a_1 \qquad a_2 \qquad a_3 \qquad a_4 \qquad a_5 \ldots$$

Sequences arise in many real-world situations. For example, if you deposit a sum of money into an interest-bearing account, the interest that is earned each month forms a sequence. If you drop a ball and let it bounce, the height the ball reaches at each successive bounce is a sequence.

We can describe the pattern of the sequence displayed above by the following *formula*:

$$a_n = 5n$$

You may have already thought of a different way to describe the pattern—namely, "you go from one number to the next by adding 5." This natural way of describing the sequence is expressed by the *recursive formula*:

$$a_n = a_{n-1} + 5$$

starting with $a_1 = 5$. Try substituting $n = 1, 2, 3, \ldots$ in each of these formulas to see how they produce the numbers in the sequence. In this section we see how these different ways are used to describe specific sequences.

### ■ Sequences

A *sequence* is a set of numbers written in a specific order:

$$a_1, a_2, a_3, a_4, \ldots, a_n, \ldots$$

The number $a_1$ is called the *first term*, $a_2$ is the *second term*, and in general $a_n$ is the *nth term*. Since for every natural number $n$ there is a corresponding number $a_n$, we can define a sequence as a function.

---

**DEFINITION OF A SEQUENCE**

A **sequence** is a function $f$ whose domain is the set of natural numbers. The values $f(1), f(2), f(3), \ldots$ are called the **terms** of the sequence.

---

We usually write $a_n$ instead of the function notation $f(n)$ for the value of the function at the number $n$.

Here is a simple example of a sequence:

$$2, 4, 6, 8, 10, \ldots$$

The dots indicate that the sequence continues indefinitely. We can write a sequence in this way when it's clear what the subsequent terms of the sequence are. This sequence consists of even numbers. To be more accurate, however, we need to specify a procedure for finding *all* the terms of the sequence. This can be done by giving a formula for the $n$th term $a_n$ of the sequence. In this case,

$$a_n = 2n$$

Another way to write this sequence is to use function notation:

$$a(n) = 2n$$

so $a(1) = 2, a(2) = 4, a(3) = 6, \ldots$

and the sequence can be written as

$$2, \qquad 4, \qquad 6, \qquad 8, \qquad \ldots, \qquad 2n, \qquad \ldots$$

| 1st term | 2nd term | 3rd term | 4th term | | $n$th term |

Notice how the formula $a_n = 2n$ gives all the terms of the sequence. For instance, substituting 1, 2, 3, and 4 for $n$ gives the first four terms:

$$a_1 = 2 \cdot 1 = 2 \qquad a_2 = 2 \cdot 2 = 4$$
$$a_3 = 2 \cdot 3 = 6 \qquad a_4 = 2 \cdot 4 = 8$$

To find the 103rd term of this sequence, we use $n = 103$ to get

$$a_{103} = 2 \cdot 103 = 206$$

▶ **EXAMPLE 1** | Finding the Terms of a Sequence

Find the first five terms and the 100th term of the sequence defined by each formula.

**(a)** $a_n = 2n - 1$          **(b)** $c_n = n^2 - 1$

**(c)** $t_n = \dfrac{n}{n + 1}$          **(d)** $r_n = \dfrac{(-1)^n}{2^n}$

▼ **SOLUTION** To find the first five terms, we substitute $n = 1, 2, 3, 4,$ and 5 in the formula for the $n$th term. To find the 100th term, we substitute $n = 100$. This gives the following.

| $n$th term | First five terms | 100th term |
|---|---|---|
| (a) $2n - 1$ | 1, 3, 5, 7, 9 | 199 |
| (b) $n^2 - 1$ | 0, 3, 8, 15, 24 | 9999 |
| (c) $\dfrac{n}{n + 1}$ | $\dfrac{1}{2}, \dfrac{2}{3}, \dfrac{3}{4}, \dfrac{4}{5}, \dfrac{5}{6}$ | $\dfrac{100}{101}$ |
| (d) $\dfrac{(-1)^n}{2^n}$ | $-\dfrac{1}{2}, \dfrac{1}{4}, -\dfrac{1}{8}, \dfrac{1}{16}, -\dfrac{1}{32}$ | $\dfrac{1}{2^{100}}$ |

✎ **Practice what you've learned:** Do Exercises 3, 5, 7, and 9. ▲

In Example 1(d) the presence of $(-1)^n$ in the sequence has the effect of making successive terms alternately negative and positive.

It is often useful to picture a sequence by sketching its graph. Since a sequence is a function whose domain is the natural numbers, we can draw its graph in the Cartesian plane. For instance, the graph of the sequence

$$1, \frac{1}{2}, \frac{1}{3}, \frac{1}{4}, \frac{1}{5}, \frac{1}{6}, \ldots, \frac{1}{n}, \ldots$$

is shown in Figure 1.

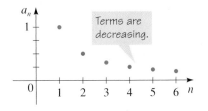
Terms are decreasing.

**FIGURE 1**

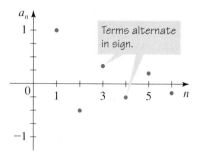

**FIGURE 2**

Compare the graph of the sequence shown in Figure 1 to the graph of

$$1, -\frac{1}{2}, \frac{1}{3}, -\frac{1}{4}, \frac{1}{5}, -\frac{1}{6}, \ldots, \frac{(-1)^{n+1}}{n}, \ldots$$

shown in Figure 2. The graph of every sequence consists of isolated points that are *not* connected.

Graphing calculators are useful in analyzing sequences. To work with sequences on a TI-83, we put the calculator in SEQ mode ("sequence" mode) as in Figure 3(a). If we enter the sequence $u(n) = n/(n + 1)$ of Example 1(c), we can display the terms using the TABLE command as shown in Figure 3(b). We can also graph the sequence as shown in Figure 3(c).

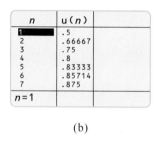

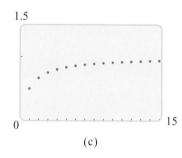

**FIGURE 3**

$u(n) = n/(n + 1)$

(a)          (b)          (c)

Finding patterns is an important part of mathematics. Consider a sequence that begins

$$1, 4, 9, 16, \ldots$$

Not all sequences can be defined by a formula. For example, there is no known formula for the sequence of prime numbers:

$$2, 3, 5, 7, 11, 13, 17, 19, 23, \ldots$$

Can you detect a pattern in these numbers? In other words, can you define a sequence whose first four terms are these numbers? The answer to this question seems easy; these numbers are the squares of the numbers 1, 2, 3, 4. Thus, the sequence we are looking for is defined by $a_n = n^2$. However, this is not the *only* sequence whose first four terms are 1, 4, 9, 16. In other words, the answer to our problem is not unique (see Exercise 80). In the next example we are interested in finding an *obvious* sequence whose first few terms agree with the given ones.

▶ **EXAMPLE 2** | Finding the *n*th Term of a Sequence

Find the *n*th term of a sequence whose first several terms are given.

**(a)** $\frac{1}{2}, \frac{3}{4}, \frac{5}{6}, \frac{7}{8}, \ldots$     **(b)** $-2, 4, -8, 16, -32, \ldots$

▼ **SOLUTION**

**(a)** We notice that the numerators of these fractions are the odd numbers and the denominators are the even numbers. Even numbers are of the form $2n$, and odd numbers are of the form $2n - 1$ (an odd number differs from an even number by 1). So a sequence that has these numbers for its first four terms is given by

$$a_n = \frac{2n - 1}{2n}$$

**Large Prime Numbers**

The search for large primes fascinates many people. As of this writing, the largest known prime number is

$$2^{32,582,657} - 1$$

It was discovered by a team at Central Missouri State University led by professors Curtis Cooper and Steven Boone. In decimal notation this number contains 9,808,358 digits. If it were written in full, it would occupy twice as many pages as this book contains. The team was working with a large Internet group known as GIMPS (the Great Internet Mersenne Prime Search). Numbers of the form $2^p - 1$, where $p$ is prime, are called Mersenne numbers and are more easily checked for primality than others. That is why the largest known primes are of this form.

**(b)** These numbers are powers of 2, and they alternate in sign, so a sequence that agrees with these terms is given by

$$a_n = (-1)^n 2^n$$

You should check that these formulas do indeed generate the given terms.

✎ **Practice what you've learned: Do Exercises 25, 27, and 29.**    ▲

## ■ Recursively Defined Sequences

Some sequences do not have simple defining formulas like those of the preceding example. The $n$th term of a sequence may depend on some or all of the terms preceding it. A sequence defined in this way is called **recursive**. Here are two examples.

▶ **EXAMPLE 3** | Finding the Terms of a Recursively Defined Sequence

Find the first five terms of the sequence defined recursively by $a_1 = 1$ and

$$a_n = 3(a_{n-1} + 2)$$

▼ **SOLUTION**    The defining formula for this sequence is recursive. It allows us to find the $n$th term $a_n$ if we know the preceding term $a_{n-1}$. Thus, we can find the second term from the first term, the third term from the second term, the fourth term from the third term, and so on. Since we are given the first term $a_1 = 1$, we can proceed as follows.

$$a_2 = 3(a_1 + 2) = 3(1 + 2) = 9$$

$$a_3 = 3(a_2 + 2) = 3(9 + 2) = 33$$

$$a_4 = 3(a_3 + 2) = 3(33 + 2) = 105$$

$$a_5 = 3(a_4 + 2) = 3(105 + 2) = 321$$

Thus, the first five terms of this sequence are

$$1, 9, 33, 105, 321, \ldots$$

✎ **Practice what you've learned: Do Exercise 13.**    ▲

Note that to find the 20th term of the sequence in Example 3, we must first find all 19 preceding terms. This is most easily done by using a graphing calculator. Figure 4(a) shows how to enter this sequence on the TI-83 calculator. From Figure 4(b) we see that the 20th term of the sequence is $a_{20} = 4{,}649{,}045{,}865$.

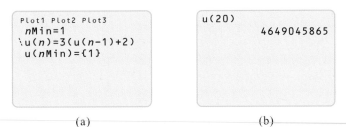

```
Plot1 Plot2 Plot3
  nMin=1
\u(n)=3(u(n-1)+2)
 u(nMin)={1}
```

```
u(20)
          4649045865
```

(a)                    (b)

**FIGURE 4** $u(n) = 3(u(n-1) + 2), u(1) = 1$

▶ **EXAMPLE 4** | The Fibonacci Sequence

Find the first 11 terms of the sequence defined recursively by $F_1 = 1, F_2 = 1$ and

$$F_n = F_{n-1} + F_{n-2}$$

**Eratosthenes** (circa 276–195 B.C.) was a renowned Greek geographer, mathematician, and astronomer. He accurately calculated the circumference of the earth by an ingenious method. He is most famous, however, for his method for finding primes, now called the *sieve of Eratosthenes*. The method consists of listing the integers, beginning with 2 (the first prime), and then crossing out all the multiples of 2, which are not prime. The next number remaining on the list is 3 (the second prime), so we again cross out all multiples of it. The next remaining number is 5 (the third prime number), and we cross out all multiples of it, and so on. In this way all numbers that are not prime are crossed out, and the remaining numbers are the primes.

The Granger Collection, New York

**Fibonacci** (1175–1250) was born in Pisa, Italy, and educated in North Africa. He traveled widely in the Mediterranean area and learned the various methods then in use for writing numbers. On returning to Pisa in 1202, Fibonacci advocated the use of the Hindu-Arabic decimal system, the one we use today, over the Roman numeral system that was used in Europe in his time. His most famous book, *Liber Abaci*, expounds on the advantages of the Hindu-Arabic numerals. In fact, multiplication and division were so complicated using Roman numerals that a college degree was necessary to master these skills. Interestingly, in 1299 the city of Florence outlawed the use of the decimal system for merchants and businesses, requiring numbers to be written in Roman numerals or words. One can only speculate about the reasons for this law.

▼ **SOLUTION**   To find $F_n$, we need to find the two preceding terms $F_{n-1}$ and $F_{n-2}$. Since we are given $F_1$ and $F_2$, we proceed as follows.

$$F_3 = F_2 + F_1 = 1 + 1 = 2$$
$$F_4 = F_3 + F_2 = 2 + 1 = 3$$
$$F_5 = F_4 + F_3 = 3 + 2 = 5$$

It's clear what is happening here. Each term is simply the sum of the two terms that precede it, so we can easily write down as many terms as we please. Here are the first 11 terms:

$$1, 1, 2, 3, 5, 8, 13, 21, 34, 55, 89, \ldots$$

✎ **Practice what you've learned: Do Exercise 17.**   ▲

The sequence in Example 4 is called the **Fibonacci sequence**, named after the 13th century Italian mathematician who used it to solve a problem about the breeding of rabbits (see Exercise 79). The sequence also occurs in numerous other applications in nature. (See Figures 5 and 6.) In fact, so many phenomena behave like the Fibonacci sequence that one mathematical journal, the *Fibonacci Quarterly*, is devoted entirely to its properties.

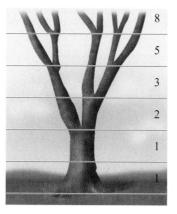

**FIGURE 5** The Fibonacci sequence in the branching of a tree

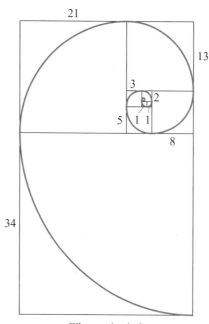

**FIGURE 6**   Fibonacci spiral

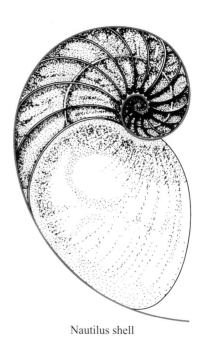

Nautilus shell

### ■ The Partial Sums of a Sequence

In calculus we are often interested in adding the terms of a sequence. This leads to the following definition.

---

**THE PARTIAL SUMS OF A SEQUENCE**

For the sequence

$$a_1, a_2, a_3, a_4, \ldots, a_n, \ldots$$

the **partial sums** are

$$S_1 = a_1$$
$$S_2 = a_1 + a_2$$
$$S_3 = a_1 + a_2 + a_3$$
$$S_4 = a_1 + a_2 + a_3 + a_4$$
$$\vdots$$
$$S_n = a_1 + a_2 + a_3 + \cdots + a_n$$
$$\vdots$$

$S_1$ is called the **first partial sum**, $S_2$ is the **second partial sum**, and so on. $S_n$ is called the ***n*th partial sum**. The sequence $S_1, S_2, S_3, \ldots, S_n, \ldots$ is called the **sequence of partial sums**.

---

▶ **EXAMPLE 5** | Finding the Partial Sums of a Sequence

Find the first four partial sums and the *n*th partial sum of the sequence given by $a_n = 1/2^n$.

▼ **SOLUTION**   The terms of the sequence are

$$\frac{1}{2}, \frac{1}{4}, \frac{1}{8}, \ldots$$

The first four partial sums are

$$S_1 = \frac{1}{2} \qquad\qquad = \frac{1}{2}$$

$$S_2 = \frac{1}{2} + \frac{1}{4} \qquad\qquad = \frac{3}{4}$$

$$S_3 = \frac{1}{2} + \frac{1}{4} + \frac{1}{8} \qquad = \frac{7}{8}$$

$$S_4 = \frac{1}{2} + \frac{1}{4} + \frac{1}{8} + \frac{1}{16} = \frac{15}{16}$$

Notice that in the value of each partial sum the denominator is a power of 2 and the numerator is one less than the denominator. In general, the *n*th partial sum is

$$S_n = \frac{2^n - 1}{2^n} = 1 - \frac{1}{2^n}$$

The first five terms of $a_n$ and $S_n$ are graphed in Figure 7.

✎ **Practice what you've learned: Do Exercise 37.**   ▲

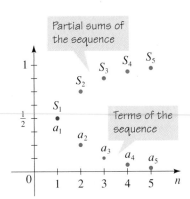

**FIGURE 7** Graph of the sequence $a_n$ and the sequence of partial sums $S_n$

▶ **EXAMPLE 6** | Finding the Partial Sums of a Sequence

Find the first four partial sums and the $n$th partial sum of the sequence given by

$$a_n = \frac{1}{n} - \frac{1}{n+1}$$

▼ **SOLUTION**   The first four partial sums are

$$S_1 = \left(1 - \frac{1}{2}\right) \hspace{4cm} = 1 - \frac{1}{2}$$

$$S_2 = \left(1 - \frac{1}{2}\right) + \left(\frac{1}{2} - \frac{1}{3}\right) \hspace{2.5cm} = 1 - \frac{1}{3}$$

$$S_3 = \left(1 - \frac{1}{2}\right) + \left(\frac{1}{2} - \frac{1}{3}\right) + \left(\frac{1}{3} - \frac{1}{4}\right) \hspace{1cm} = 1 - \frac{1}{4}$$

$$S_4 = \left(1 - \frac{1}{2}\right) + \left(\frac{1}{2} - \frac{1}{3}\right) + \left(\frac{1}{3} - \frac{1}{4}\right) + \left(\frac{1}{4} - \frac{1}{5}\right) = 1 - \frac{1}{5}$$

Do you detect a pattern here? Of course. The $n$th partial sum is

$$S_n = 1 - \frac{1}{n+1}$$

✏ **Practice what you've learned: Do Exercise 39.**                    ▲

## ■ Sigma Notation

Given a sequence

$$a_1, a_2, a_3, a_4, \ldots$$

we can write the sum of the first $n$ terms using **summation notation**, or **sigma notation**. This notation derives its name from the Greek letter $\Sigma$ (capital sigma, corresponding to our $S$ for "sum"). Sigma notation is used as follows:

This tells us to
end with $k = n$.

This tells
us to add.   $\displaystyle\sum_{k=1}^{n} a_k$

This tells us to
start with $k = 1$.

$$\boxed{\sum_{k=1}^{n} a_k = a_1 + a_2 + a_3 + a_4 + \cdots + a_n}$$

The left side of this expression is read "The sum of $a_k$ from $k = 1$ to $k = n$." The letter $k$ is called the **index of summation**, or the **summation variable**, and the idea is to replace $k$ in the expression after the sigma by the integers $1, 2, 3, \ldots, n$, and add the resulting expressions, arriving at the right side of the equation.

▶ **EXAMPLE 7** | Sigma Notation

Find each sum.

(a) $\displaystyle\sum_{k=1}^{5} k^2$     (b) $\displaystyle\sum_{j=3}^{5} \frac{1}{j}$     (c) $\displaystyle\sum_{i=5}^{10} i$     (d) $\displaystyle\sum_{i=1}^{6} 2$

▼ **SOLUTION**

(a) $\displaystyle\sum_{k=1}^{5} k^2 = 1^2 + 2^2 + 3^2 + 4^2 + 5^2 = 55$

(b) $\displaystyle\sum_{j=3}^{5} \frac{1}{j} = \frac{1}{3} + \frac{1}{4} + \frac{1}{5} = \frac{47}{60}$

```
sum(seq(K²,K,1,5,1))
                   55
sum(seq(1/J,J,3,5,
1))▶Frac
                47/60
```

**FIGURE 8**

**(c)** $\displaystyle\sum_{i=5}^{10} i = 5 + 6 + 7 + 8 + 9 + 10 = 45$

**(d)** $\displaystyle\sum_{i=1}^{6} 2 = 2 + 2 + 2 + 2 + 2 + 2 = 12$

We can use a graphing calculator to evaluate sums. For instance, Figure 8 shows how the TI-83 can be used to evaluate the sums in parts (a) and (b) of Example 7.

✎ **Practice what you've learned: Do Exercises 41 and 43.** ▲

▶ **EXAMPLE 8** | Writing Sums in Sigma Notation

Write each sum using sigma notation.

**(a)** $1^3 + 2^3 + 3^3 + 4^3 + 5^3 + 6^3 + 7^3$
**(b)** $\sqrt{3} + \sqrt{4} + \sqrt{5} + \cdots + \sqrt{77}$

▼ **SOLUTION**

**(a)** We can write

$$1^3 + 2^3 + 3^3 + 4^3 + 5^3 + 6^3 + 7^3 = \sum_{k=1}^{7} k^3$$

**(b)** A natural way to write this sum is

$$\sqrt{3} + \sqrt{4} + \sqrt{5} + \cdots + \sqrt{77} = \sum_{k=3}^{77} \sqrt{k}$$

However, there is no unique way of writing a sum in sigma notation. We could also write this sum as

$$\sqrt{3} + \sqrt{4} + \sqrt{5} + \cdots + \sqrt{77} = \sum_{k=0}^{74} \sqrt{k + 3}$$

or    $\displaystyle\sqrt{3} + \sqrt{4} + \sqrt{5} + \cdots + \sqrt{77} = \sum_{k=1}^{75} \sqrt{k + 2}$

✎ **Practice what you've learned: Do Exercises 61 and 63.** ▲

### The Golden Ratio

The ancient Greeks considered a line segment to be divided into the **golden ratio** if the ratio of the shorter part to the longer part is the same as the ratio of the longer part to the whole segment.

$\underset{1}{\rule{0pt}{0pt}}\qquad\qquad\underset{x}{\rule{0pt}{0pt}}$

Thus, the segment shown is divided into the golden ratio if

$$\frac{1}{x} = \frac{x}{1 + x}$$

This leads to a quadratic equation whose positive solution is

$$x = \frac{1 + \sqrt{5}}{2} \approx 1.618$$

This ratio occurs naturally in many places. For instance, psychological experiments show that the most pleasing shape of rectangle is one whose sides are in golden ratio. The ancient Greeks agreed with this and built their temples in this ratio.

The golden ratio is related to the Fibonacci sequence. In fact, it can be shown using calculus* that the ratio of two successive Fibonacci numbers

$$\frac{F_{n+1}}{F_n}$$

gets closer to the golden ratio the larger the value of $n$. Try finding this ratio for $n = 10$.

© CORBIS

*James Stewart, *Calculus*, 6th ed. (Belmont, CA: Brooks/Cole, 2007), p. 722.

The following properties of sums are natural consequences of properties of the real numbers.

---

**PROPERTIES OF SUMS**

Let $a_1, a_2, a_3, a_4, \ldots$ and $b_1, b_2, b_3, b_4, \ldots$ be sequences. Then for every positive integer $n$ and any real number $c$, the following properties hold.

**1.** $\displaystyle\sum_{k=1}^{n} (a_k + b_k) = \sum_{k=1}^{n} a_k + \sum_{k=1}^{n} b_k$

**2.** $\displaystyle\sum_{k=1}^{n} (a_k - b_k) = \sum_{k=1}^{n} a_k - \sum_{k=1}^{n} b_k$

**3.** $\displaystyle\sum_{k=1}^{n} ca_k = c\left( \sum_{k=1}^{n} a_k \right)$

---

▼ **PROOF**   To prove Property 1, we write out the left side of the equation to get

$$\sum_{k=1}^{n} (a_k + b_k) = (a_1 + b_1) + (a_2 + b_2) + (a_3 + b_3) + \cdots + (a_n + b_n)$$

Because addition is commutative and associative, we can rearrange the terms on the right side to read

$$\sum_{k=1}^{n} (a_k + b_k) = (a_1 + a_2 + a_3 + \cdots + a_n) + (b_1 + b_2 + b_3 + \cdots + b_n)$$

Rewriting the right side using sigma notation gives Property 1. Property 2 is proved in a similar manner. To prove Property 3, we use the Distributive Property:

$$\sum_{k=1}^{n} ca_k = ca_1 + ca_2 + ca_3 + \cdots + ca_n$$

$$= c(a_1 + a_2 + a_3 + \cdots + a_n) = c\left( \sum_{k=1}^{n} a_k \right)$$

# 9.1 EXERCISES

## ▼ CONCEPTS

**1.** A sequence is a function whose domain is _____.

**2.** The $n$th partial sum of a sequence is the sum of the first _____ terms of the sequence. So for the sequence $a_n = n^2$ the fourth partial sum is $S_4 =$ ____ + ____ + ____ + ____

= ____.

## ▼ SKILLS

**3–12** ▪ Find the first four terms and the 100th term of the sequence.

**3.** $a_n = n + 1$

**4.** $a_n = 2n + 3$

**5.** $a_n = \dfrac{1}{n + 1}$

**6.** $a_n = n^2 + 1$

**7.** $a_n = \dfrac{(-1)^n}{n^2}$

**8.** $a_n = \dfrac{1}{n^2}$

**9.** $a_n = 1 + (-1)^n$

**10.** $a_n = (-1)^{n+1} \dfrac{n}{n + 1}$

**11.** $a_n = n^n$

**12.** $a_n = 3$

**13–18** ▪ Find the first five terms of the given recursively defined sequence.

**13.** $a_n = 2(a_{n-1} - 2)$   and   $a_1 = 3$

**14.** $a_n = \dfrac{a_{n-1}}{2}$   and   $a_1 = -8$

**15.** $a_n = 2a_{n-1} + 1$   and   $a_1 = 1$

**16.** $a_n = \dfrac{1}{1 + a_{n-1}}$   and   $a_1 = 1$

**17.** $a_n = a_{n-1} + a_{n-2}$   and   $a_1 = 1, a_2 = 2$

**18.** $a_n = a_{n-1} + a_{n-2} + a_{n-3}$   and   $a_1 = a_2 = a_3 = 1$

**19–24** ■ Use a graphing calculator to do the following. **(a)** Find the first 10 terms of the sequence. **(b)** Graph the first 10 terms of the sequence.

**19.** $a_n = 4n + 3$

**20.** $a_n = n^2 + n$

**21.** $a_n = \dfrac{12}{n}$

**22.** $a_n = 4 - 2(-1)^n$

**23.** $a_n = \dfrac{1}{a_{n-1}}$  and  $a_1 = 2$

**24.** $a_n = a_{n-1} - a_{n-2}$  and  $a_1 = 1, a_2 = 3$

**25–32** ■ Find the $n$th term of a sequence whose first several terms are given.

**25.** $2, 4, 8, 16, \ldots$

**26.** $-\frac{1}{3}, \frac{1}{9}, -\frac{1}{27}, \frac{1}{81}, \ldots$

**27.** $1, 4, 7, 10, \ldots$

**28.** $5, -25, 125, -625, \ldots$

**29.** $1, \frac{3}{4}, \frac{5}{9}, \frac{7}{16}, \frac{9}{25}, \ldots$

**30.** $\frac{3}{4}, \frac{4}{5}, \frac{5}{6}, \frac{6}{7}, \ldots$

**31.** $0, 2, 0, 2, 0, 2, \ldots$

**32.** $1, \frac{1}{2}, 3, \frac{1}{4}, 5, \frac{1}{6}, \ldots$

**33–36** ■ Find the first six partial sums $S_1, S_2, S_3, S_4, S_5, S_6$ of the sequence.

**33.** $1, 3, 5, 7, \ldots$

**34.** $1^2, 2^2, 3^2, 4^2, \ldots$

**35.** $\dfrac{1}{3}, \dfrac{1}{3^2}, \dfrac{1}{3^3}, \dfrac{1}{3^4}, \cdots$

**36.** $-1, 1, -1, 1, \ldots$

**37–40** ■ Find the first four partial sums and the $n$th partial sum of the sequence $a_n$.

**37.** $a_n = \dfrac{2}{3^n}$

**38.** $a_n = \dfrac{1}{n+1} - \dfrac{1}{n+2}$

**39.** $a_n = \sqrt{n} - \sqrt{n+1}$

**40.** $a_n = \log\left(\dfrac{n}{n+1}\right)$  [*Hint:* Use a property of logarithms to write the $n$th term as a difference.]

**41–48** ■ Find the sum.

**41.** $\displaystyle\sum_{k=1}^{4} k$

**42.** $\displaystyle\sum_{k=1}^{4} k^2$

**43.** $\displaystyle\sum_{k=1}^{3} \frac{1}{k}$

**44.** $\displaystyle\sum_{j=1}^{100} (-1)^j$

**45.** $\displaystyle\sum_{i=1}^{8} [1 + (-1)^i]$

**46.** $\displaystyle\sum_{i=4}^{12} 10$

**47.** $\displaystyle\sum_{k=1}^{5} 2^{k-1}$

**48.** $\displaystyle\sum_{i=1}^{3} i2^i$

**49–54** ■ Use a graphing calculator to evaluate the sum.

**49.** $\displaystyle\sum_{k=1}^{10} k^2$

**50.** $\displaystyle\sum_{k=1}^{100} (3k + 4)$

**51.** $\displaystyle\sum_{j=7}^{20} j^2(1 + j)$

**52.** $\displaystyle\sum_{j=5}^{15} \frac{1}{j^2 + 1}$

**53.** $\displaystyle\sum_{n=0}^{22} (-1)^n 2n$

**54.** $\displaystyle\sum_{n=1}^{100} \frac{(-1)^n}{n}$

**55–60** ■ Write the sum without using sigma notation.

**55.** $\displaystyle\sum_{k=1}^{5} \sqrt{k}$

**56.** $\displaystyle\sum_{i=0}^{4} \frac{2i - 1}{2i + 1}$

**57.** $\displaystyle\sum_{k=0}^{6} \sqrt{k + 4}$

**58.** $\displaystyle\sum_{k=6}^{9} k(k + 3)$

**59.** $\displaystyle\sum_{k=3}^{100} x^k$

**60.** $\displaystyle\sum_{j=1}^{n} (-1)^{j+1} x^j$

**61–68** ■ Write the sum using sigma notation.

**61.** $1 + 2 + 3 + 4 + \cdots + 100$

**62.** $2 + 4 + 6 + \cdots + 20$

**63.** $1^2 + 2^2 + 3^2 + \cdots + 10^2$

**64.** $\dfrac{1}{2 \ln 2} - \dfrac{1}{3 \ln 3} + \dfrac{1}{4 \ln 4} - \dfrac{1}{5 \ln 5} + \cdots + \dfrac{1}{100 \ln 100}$

**65.** $\dfrac{1}{1 \cdot 2} + \dfrac{1}{2 \cdot 3} + \dfrac{1}{3 \cdot 4} + \cdots + \dfrac{1}{999 \cdot 1000}$

**66.** $\dfrac{\sqrt{1}}{1^2} + \dfrac{\sqrt{2}}{2^2} + \dfrac{\sqrt{3}}{3^2} + \cdots + \dfrac{\sqrt{n}}{n^2}$

**67.** $1 + x + x^2 + x^3 + \cdots + x^{100}$

**68.** $1 - 2x + 3x^2 - 4x^3 + 5x^4 + \cdots - 100x^{99}$

**69.** Find a formula for the $n$th term of the sequence

$$\sqrt{2}, \quad \sqrt{2\sqrt{2}}, \quad \sqrt{2\sqrt{2\sqrt{2}}}, \quad \sqrt{2\sqrt{2\sqrt{2\sqrt{2}}}}, \ldots$$

[*Hint:* Write each term as a power of 2.]

**70.** Define the sequence

$$G_n = \frac{1}{\sqrt{5}}\left(\frac{(1 + \sqrt{5})^n - (1 - \sqrt{5})^n}{2^n}\right)$$

Use the $\boxed{\text{TABLE}}$ command on a graphing calculator to find the first 10 terms of this sequence. Compare to the Fibonacci sequence $F_n$.

▼ **APPLICATIONS**

**71. Compound Interest** Julio deposits $2000 in a savings account that pays 2.4% interest per year compounded monthly. The amount in the account after $n$ months is given by the sequence

$$A_n = 2000\left(1 + \frac{0.024}{12}\right)^n$$

**(a)** Find the first six terms of the sequence.
**(b)** Find the amount in the account after 3 years.

**72. Compound Interest** Helen deposits $100 at the end of each month into an account that pays 6% interest per year compounded monthly. The amount of interest she has accumulated after $n$ months is given by the sequence

$$I_n = 100\left(\frac{1.005^n - 1}{0.005} - n\right)$$

**(a)** Find the first six terms of the sequence.
**(b)** Find the interest she has accumulated after 5 years.

**73. Population of a City** A city was incorporated in 2004 with a population of 35,000. It is expected that the population will increase at a rate of 2% per year. The population $n$ years after 2004 is given by the sequence

$$P_n = 35,000(1.02)^n$$

**(a)** Find the first five terms of the sequence.

**(b)** Find the population in 2014.

**74. Paying off a Debt** Margarita borrows $10,000 from her uncle and agrees to repay it in monthly installments of $200. Her uncle charges 0.5% interest per month on the balance.

**(a)** Show that her balance $A_n$ in the $n$th month is given recursively by $A_0 = 10,000$ and

$$A_n = 1.005A_{n-1} - 200$$

**(b)** Find her balance after six months.

**75. Fish Farming** A fish farmer has 5000 catfish in his pond. The number of catfish increases by 8% per month, and the farmer harvests 300 catfish per month.

**(a)** Show that the catfish population $P_n$ after $n$ months is given recursively by $P_0 = 5000$ and

$$P_n = 1.08P_{n-1} - 300$$

**(b)** How many fish are in the pond after 12 months?

**76. Price of a House** The median price of a house in Orange County increases by about 6% per year. In 2002 the median price was $240,000. Let $P_n$ be the median price $n$ years after 2002.

**(a)** Find a formula for the sequence $P_n$.

**(b)** Find the expected median price in 2010.

**77. Salary Increases** A newly hired salesman is promised a beginning salary of $30,000 a year with a $2000 raise every year. Let $S_n$ be his salary in his $n$th year of employment.

**(a)** Find a recursive definition of $S_n$.

**(b)** Find his salary in his fifth year of employment.

**78. Concentration of a Solution** A biologist is trying to find the optimal salt concentration for the growth of a certain species of mollusk. She begins with a brine solution that has 4 g/L of salt and increases the concentration by 10% every day. Let $C_0$ denote the initial concentration and $C_n$ the concentration after $n$ days.

**(a)** Find a recursive definition of $C_n$.

**(b)** Find the salt concentration after 8 days.

**79. Fibonacci's Rabbits** Fibonacci posed the following problem: Suppose that rabbits live forever and that every month

each pair produces a new pair that becomes productive at age 2 months. If we start with one newborn pair, how many pairs of rabbits will we have in the $n$th month? Show that the answer is $F_n$, where $F_n$ is the $n$th term of the Fibonacci sequence.

---

## ▼ DISCOVERY • DISCUSSION • WRITING

**80. Different Sequences That Start the Same**

**(a)** Show that the first four terms of the sequence $a_n = n^2$ are

$$1, 4, 9, 16, \ldots$$

**(b)** Show that the first four terms of the sequence $a_n = n^2 + (n-1)(n-2)(n-3)(n-4)$ are also

$$1, 4, 9, 16, \ldots$$

**(c)** Find a sequence whose first six terms are the same as those of $a_n = n^2$ but whose succeeding terms differ from this sequence.

**(d)** Find two different sequences that begin

$$2, 4, 8, 16, \ldots$$

**81. A Recursively Defined Sequence** Find the first 40 terms of the sequence defined by

$$a_{n+1} = \begin{cases} \dfrac{a_n}{2} & \text{if } a_n \text{ is an even number} \\ 3a_n + 1 & \text{if } a_n \text{ is an odd number} \end{cases}$$

and $a_1 = 11$. Do the same if $a_1 = 25$. Make a conjecture about this type of sequence. Try several other values for $a_1$, to test your conjecture.

**82. A Different Type of Recursion** Find the first 10 terms of the sequence defined by

$$a_n = a_{n-a_{n-1}} + a_{n-a_{n-2}}$$

with

$$a_1 = 1 \quad \text{and} \quad a_2 = 1$$

How is this recursive sequence different from the others in this section?

---

## 9.2 | Arithmetic Sequences

### LEARNING OBJECTIVES

After completing this section, you will be able to:

■ Find the terms of an arithmetic sequence

■ Find the partial sums of an arithmetic sequence

In this section we study a special type of sequence, called an arithmetic sequence.

### ■ Arithmetic Sequences

Perhaps the simplest way to generate a sequence is to start with a number $a$ and add to it a fixed constant $d$, over and over again.

---

**DEFINITION OF AN ARITHMETIC SEQUENCE**

An **arithmetic sequence** is a sequence of the form

$$a, a + d, a + 2d, a + 3d, a + 4d, \ldots$$

The number $a$ is the **first term**, and $d$ is the **common difference** of the sequence. The **$n$th term** of an arithmetic sequence is given by

$$a_n = a + (n - 1)d$$

---

The number $d$ is called the common difference because any two consecutive terms of an arithmetic sequence differ by $d$.

▶ **EXAMPLE 1** | Arithmetic Sequences

**(a)** If $a = 2$ and $d = 3$, then we have the arithmetic sequence

$$2, 2 + 3, 2 + 6, 2 + 9, \ldots$$

or

$$2, 5, 8, 11, \ldots$$

Any two consecutive terms of this sequence differ by $d = 3$. The $n$th term is $a_n = 2 + 3(n - 1)$.

**(b)** Consider the arithmetic sequence

$$9, 4, -1, -6, -11, \ldots$$

Here the common difference is $d = -5$. The terms of an arithmetic sequence decrease if the common difference is negative. The $n$th term is $a_n = 9 - 5(n - 1)$.

**(c)** The graph of the arithmetic sequence $a_n = 1 + 2(n - 1)$ is shown in Figure 1. Notice that the points in the graph lie on a straight line with slope $d = 2$.

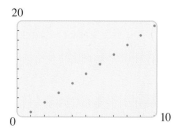

**FIGURE 1**

✎ **Practice what you've learned: Do Exercises 5, 9, and 13.** ▲

An arithmetic sequence is determined completely by the first term $a$ and the common difference $d$. Thus, if we know the first two terms of an arithmetic sequence, then we can find a formula for the $n$th term, as the next example shows.

▶ **EXAMPLE 2** | Finding Terms of an Arithmetic Sequence

Find the first six terms and the 300th term of the arithmetic sequence

$$13, 7, \ldots$$

▼ **SOLUTION**    Since the first term is 13, we have $a = 13$. The common difference is $d = 7 - 13 = -6$. Thus, the $n$th term of this sequence is

$$a_n = 13 - 6(n - 1)$$

From this we find the first six terms:

$$13, 7, 1, -5, -11, -17, \ldots$$

The 300th term is $a_{300} = 13 - 6(299) = -1781$.

✎ **Practice what you've learned: Do Exercise 27.**    ▲

The next example shows that an arithmetic sequence is determined completely by *any* two of its terms.

▶ **EXAMPLE 3** | Finding Terms of an Arithmetic Sequence

The 11th term of an arithmetic sequence is 52, and the 19th term is 92. Find the 1000th term.

▼ **SOLUTION**    To find the $n$th term of this sequence, we need to find $a$ and $d$ in the formula

$$a_n = a + (n - 1)d$$

From this formula we get

$$a_{11} = a + (11 - 1)d = a + 10d$$

$$a_{19} = a + (19 - 1)d = a + 18d$$

Since $a_{11} = 52$ and $a_{19} = 92$, we get the two equations:

$$\begin{cases} 52 = a + 10d \\ 92 = a + 18d \end{cases}$$

Solving this system for $a$ and $d$, we get $a = 2$ and $d = 5$. (Verify this.) Thus, the $n$th term of this sequence is

$$a_n = 2 + 5(n - 1)$$

The 1000th term is $a_{1000} = 2 + 5(999) = 4997$.

✎ **Practice what you've learned: Do Exercise 37.**    ▲

---

## MATHEMATICS IN THE MODERN WORLD

### Fair Division of Assets

Dividing an asset fairly among a number of people is of great interest to mathematicians. Problems of this nature include dividing the national budget, disputed land, or assets in divorce cases. In 1994 Brams and Taylor found a mathematical way of dividing things fairly. Their solution has been applied to division problems in political science, legal proceedings, and other areas. To understand the problem, consider the following example. Suppose persons A and B want to divide a property fairly between them. To divide it *fairly* means that both A and B must be satisfied with the outcome of the division. Solution: A gets to divide the property into two pieces, then B gets to choose the piece he or she wants. Since both A and B had a part in the division process, each should be satisfied. The situation becomes much more complicated if three or more people are involved (and that's where mathematics

comes in). Dividing things fairly involves much more than simply cutting things in half; it must take into account the *relative worth* each person attaches to the thing being divided. A story from the Bible illustrates this clearly. Two women appear before King Solomon, each claiming to be the mother of the same newborn baby. King Solomon's solution is to divide the baby in half! The real mother, who attaches far more worth to the baby than anyone, immediately gives up her claim to the baby in order to save the baby's life.

Mathematical solutions to fair-division problems have recently been applied in an international treaty, the Convention on the Law of the Sea. If a country wants to develop a portion of the sea floor, it is required to divide the portion into two parts, one part to be used by itself, the other by a consortium that will preserve it for later use by a less developed country. The consortium gets first pick.

## ■ Partial Sums of Arithmetic Sequences

Suppose we want to find the sum of the numbers 1, 2, 3, 4, . . . , 100, that is,

$$\sum_{k=1}^{100} k$$

When the famous mathematician C. F. Gauss was a schoolboy, his teacher posed this problem to the class and expected that it would keep the students busy for a long time. But Gauss answered the question almost immediately. His idea was this: Since we are adding numbers produced according to a fixed pattern, there must also be a pattern (or formula) for finding the sum. He started by writing the numbers from 1 to 100 and then below them wrote the same numbers in reverse order. Writing $S$ for the sum and adding corresponding terms gives

$$
\begin{array}{rcrcrcrcrcrcr}
S &=& 1 &+& 2 &+& 3 &+ \cdots +& 98 &+& 99 &+& 100 \\
S &=& 100 &+& 99 &+& 98 &+ \cdots +& 3 &+& 2 &+& 1 \\
\hline
2S &=& 101 &+& 101 &+& 101 &+ \cdots +& 101 &+& 101 &+& 101
\end{array}
$$

It follows that $2S = 100(101) = 10{,}100$ and so $S = 5050$.

Of course, the sequence of natural numbers 1, 2, 3, . . . is an arithmetic sequence (with $a = 1$ and $d = 1$), and the method for summing the first 100 terms of this sequence can be used to find a formula for the $n$th partial sum of any arithmetic sequence. We want to find the sum of the first $n$ terms of the arithmetic sequence whose terms are $a_k = a + (k - 1)d$; that is, we want to find

$$S_n = \sum_{k=1}^{n} [a + (k - 1)d]$$

$$= a + (a + d) + (a + 2d) + (a + 3d) + \cdots + [a + (n - 1)d]$$

Using Gauss's method, we write

$$
\begin{array}{rcccccccc}
S_n &=& a &+& (a + d) &+ \cdots +& [a + (n - 2)d] &+& [a + (n - 1)d] \\
S_n &=& [a + (n - 1)d] &+& [a + (n - 2)d] &+ \cdots +& (a + d) &+& a \\
\hline
2S_n &=& [2a + (n - 1)d] &+& [2a + (n - 1)d] &+ \cdots +& [2a + (n - 1)d] &+& [2a + (n - 1)d]
\end{array}
$$

There are $n$ identical terms on the right side of this equation, so

$$2S_n = n[2a + (n - 1)d]$$

$$S_n = \frac{n}{2}[2a + (n - 1)d]$$

Notice that $a_n = a + (n - 1)d$ is the $n$th term of this sequence. So, we can write

$$S_n = \frac{n}{2}[a + a + (n - 1)d] = n\left(\frac{a + a_n}{2}\right)$$

This last formula says that the sum of the first $n$ terms of an arithmetic sequence is the average of the first and $n$th terms multiplied by $n$, the number of terms in the sum. We now summarize this result.

---

**PARTIAL SUMS OF AN ARITHMETIC SEQUENCE**

For the arithmetic sequence $a_n = a + (n - 1)d$ the **$n$th partial sum**

$$S_n = a + (a + d) + (a + 2d) + (a + 3d) + \cdots + [a + (n - 1)d]$$

is given by either of the following formulas.

**1.** $S_n = \dfrac{n}{2}[2a + (n - 1)d]$        **2.** $S_n = n\left(\dfrac{a + a_n}{2}\right)$

▶ **EXAMPLE 4** | Finding a Partial Sum of an Arithmetic Sequence

Find the sum of the first 40 terms of the arithmetic sequence

$$3, 7, 11, 15, \ldots$$

▼ **SOLUTION** For this arithmetic sequence, $a = 3$ and $d = 4$. Using Formula 1 for the partial sum of an arithmetic sequence, we get

$$S_{40} = \tfrac{40}{2}[2(3) + (40 - 1)4] = 20(6 + 156) = 3240$$

✎ **Practice what you've learned: Do Exercise 43.** ▲

▶ **EXAMPLE 5** | Finding a Partial Sum of an Arithmetic Sequence

Find the sum of the first 50 odd numbers.

▼ **SOLUTION** The odd numbers form an arithmetic sequence with $a = 1$ and $d = 2$. The $n$th term is $a_n = 1 + 2(n - 1) = 2n - 1$, so the 50th odd number is $a_{50} = 2(50) - 1 = 99$. Substituting in Formula 2 for the partial sum of an arithmetic sequence, we get

$$S_{50} = 50\left(\frac{a + a_{50}}{2}\right) = 50\left(\frac{1 + 99}{2}\right) = 50 \cdot 50 = 2500$$

✎ **Practice what you've learned: Do Exercise 49.** ▲

▶ **EXAMPLE 6** | Finding the Seating Capacity of an Amphitheater

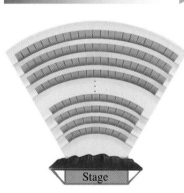

An amphitheater has 50 rows of seats with 30 seats in the first row, 32 in the second, 34 in the third, and so on. Find the total number of seats.

▼ **SOLUTION** The numbers of seats in the rows form an arithmetic sequence with $a = 30$ and $d = 2$. Since there are 50 rows, the total number of seats is the sum

$$S_{50} = \tfrac{50}{2}[2(30) + 49(2)] \qquad S_n = \tfrac{n}{2}[2a + (n - 1)d]$$
$$= 3950$$

Thus, the amphitheater has 3950 seats.

✎ **Practice what you've learned: Do Exercise 65.** ▲

▶ **EXAMPLE 7** | Finding the Number of Terms in a Partial Sum

How many terms of the arithmetic sequences $5, 7, 9, \ldots$ must be added to get 572?

▼ **SOLUTION** We are asked to find $n$ when $S_n = 572$. Substituting $a = 5$, $d = 2$, and $S_n = 572$ in Formula 1 for the partial sum of an arithmetic sequence, we get

$$572 = \tfrac{n}{2}[2 \cdot 5 + (n - 1)2] \qquad S_n = \tfrac{n}{2}[2a + (n - 1)d]$$
$$572 = 5n + n(n - 1)$$
$$0 = n^2 + 4n - 572$$
$$0 = (n - 22)(n + 26)$$

This gives $n = 22$ or $n = -26$. But since $n$ is the *number* of terms in this partial sum, we must have $n = 22$.

✎ **Practice what you've learned: Do Exercise 59.** ▲

# 9.2 EXERCISES

## ▼ CONCEPTS

1. An arithmetic sequence is a sequence in which the _____ between successive terms is constant.

2. The sequence $a_n = a + (n - 1)d$ is an arithmetic sequence in which $a$ is the first term and $d$ is the _____ _____. So for the arithmetic sequence $a_n = 2 + 5(n - 1)$ the first term is _____, and the common difference is _____.

3. *True or false?* The $n$th partial sum of an arithmetic sequence is the average of the first and last terms times $n$.

4. *True or false?* If we know the first and second terms of an arithmetic sequence, then we can find all the other terms.

## ▼ SKILLS

**5–8** ▪ A sequence is given.
(a) Find the first five terms of the sequence.
(b) What is the common difference $d$?
(c) Graph the terms you found in (a).

5. $a_n = 5 + 2(n - 1)$        6. $a_n = 3 - 4(n - 1)$

7. $a_n = \frac{5}{2} - (n - 1)$        8. $a_n = \frac{1}{2}(n - 1)$

**9–12** ▪ Find the $n$th term of the arithmetic sequence with given first term $a$ and common difference $d$. What is the 10th term?

9. $a = 3, d = 5$        10. $a = -6, d = 3$

11. $a = \frac{5}{2}, d = -\frac{1}{2}$        12. $a = \sqrt{3}, d = \sqrt{3}$

**13–20** ▪ Determine whether the sequence is arithmetic. If it is arithmetic, find the common difference.

13. $5, 8, 11, 14, \ldots$        14. $3, 6, 9, 13, \ldots$

15. $2, 4, 8, 16, \ldots$        16. $2, 4, 6, 8, \ldots$

17. $3, \frac{3}{2}, 0, -\frac{3}{2}, \ldots$        18. $\ln 2, \ln 4, \ln 8, \ln 16, \ldots$

19. $2.6, 4.3, 6.0, 7.7, \ldots$        20. $\frac{1}{2}, \frac{1}{3}, \frac{1}{4}, \frac{1}{5}, \ldots$

**21–26** ▪ Find the first five terms of the sequence, and determine whether it is arithmetic. If it is arithmetic, find the common difference, and express the $n$th term of the sequence in the standard form $a_n = a + (n - 1)d$.

21. $a_n = 4 + 7n$        22. $a_n = 4 + 2^n$

23. $a_n = \dfrac{1}{1 + 2n}$        24. $a_n = 1 + \dfrac{n}{2}$

25. $a_n = 6n - 10$        26. $a_n = 3 + (-1)^n n$

**27–36** ▪ Determine the common difference, the fifth term, the $n$th term, and the 100th term of the arithmetic sequence.

27. $2, 5, 8, 11, \ldots$        28. $1, 5, 9, 13, \ldots$

29. $4, 9, 14, 19, \ldots$        30. $11, 8, 5, 2, \ldots$

31. $-12, -8, -4, 0, \ldots$        32. $\frac{7}{6}, \frac{5}{3}, \frac{13}{6}, \frac{8}{3}, \ldots$

33. $25, 26.5, 28, 29.5, \ldots$        34. $15, 12.3, 9.6, 6.9, \ldots$

35. $2, 2 + s, 2 + 2s, 2 + 3s, \ldots$

36. $-t, -t + 3, -t + 6, -t + 9, \ldots$

37. The tenth term of an arithmetic sequence is $\frac{55}{2}$, and the second term is $\frac{7}{2}$. Find the first term.

38. The 12th term of an arithmetic sequence is 32, and the fifth term is 18. Find the 20th term.

39. The 100th term of an arithmetic sequence is 98, and the common difference is 2. Find the first three terms.

40. The 20th term of an arithmetic sequence is 101, and the common difference is 3. Find a formula for the $n$th term.

41. Which term of the arithmetic sequence $1, 4, 7, \ldots$ is 88?

42. The first term of an arithmetic sequence is 1, and the common difference is 4. Is 11,937 a term of this sequence? If so, which term is it?

**43–48** ▪ Find the partial sum $S_n$ of the arithmetic sequence that satisfies the given conditions.

43. $a = 1, d = 2, n = 10$        44. $a = 3, d = 2, n = 12$

45. $a = 4, d = 2, n = 20$        46. $a = 100, d = -5, n = 8$

47. $a_1 = 55, d = 12, n = 10$        48. $a_2 = 8, a_5 = 9.5, n = 15$

**49–54** ▪ A partial sum of an arithmetic sequence is given. Find the sum.

49. $1 + 5 + 9 + \cdots + 401$

50. $-3 + \left(-\frac{3}{2}\right) + 0 + \frac{3}{2} + 3 + \cdots + 30$

51. $0.7 + 2.7 + 4.7 + \cdots + 56.7$

52. $-10 - 9.9 - 9.8 - \cdots - 0.1$

53. $\displaystyle\sum_{k=0}^{10} (3 + 0.25k)$        54. $\displaystyle\sum_{n=0}^{20} (1 - 2n)$

55. Show that a right triangle whose sides are in arithmetic progression is similar to a 3–4–5 triangle.

56. Find the product of the numbers
$$10^{1/10}, 10^{2/10}, 10^{3/10}, 10^{4/10}, \ldots, 10^{19/10}$$

57. A sequence is **harmonic** if the reciprocals of the terms of the sequence form an arithmetic sequence. Determine whether the following sequence is harmonic:
$$1, \tfrac{3}{5}, \tfrac{3}{7}, \tfrac{1}{3}, \ldots$$

58. The **harmonic mean** of two numbers is the reciprocal of the average of the reciprocals of the two numbers. Find the harmonic mean of 3 and 5.

59. An arithmetic sequence has first term $a = 5$ and common difference $d = 2$. How many terms of this sequence must be added to get 2700?

60. An arithmetic sequence has first term $a_1 = 1$ and fourth term $a_4 = 16$. How many terms of this sequence must be added to get 2356?

## ▼ APPLICATIONS

**61. Depreciation**  The purchase value of an office computer is $12,500. Its annual depreciation is $1875. Find the value of the computer after 6 years.

**62. Poles in a Pile**  Telephone poles are stored in a pile with 25 poles in the first layer, 24 in the second, and so on. If there are 12 layers, how many telephone poles does the pile contain?

**63. Salary Increases**  A man gets a job with a salary of $30,000 a year. He is promised a $2300 raise each subsequent year. Find his total earnings for a 10-year period.

**64. Drive-In Theater**  A drive-in theater has spaces for 20 cars in the first parking row, 22 in the second, 24 in the third, and so on. If there are 21 rows in the theater, find the number of cars that can be parked.

**65. Theater Seating**  An architect designs a theater with 15 seats in the first row, 18 in the second, 21 in the third, and so on. If the theater is to have a seating capacity of 870, how many rows must the architect use in his design?

**66. Falling Ball**  When an object is allowed to fall freely near the surface of the earth, the gravitational pull is such that the object

falls 16 ft in the first second, 48 ft in the next second, 80 ft in the next second, and so on.

(a) Find the total distance a ball falls in 6 s.

(b) Find a formula for the total distance a ball falls in $n$ seconds.

**67. The Twelve Days of Christmas**  In the well-known song "The Twelve Days of Christmas," a person gives his sweetheart $k$ gifts on the $k$th day for each of the 12 days of Christmas. The person also repeats each gift identically on each subsequent day. Thus, on the 12th day the sweetheart receives a gift for the first day, 2 gifts for the second, 3 gifts for the third, and so on. Show that the number of gifts received on the 12th day is a partial sum of an arithmetic sequence. Find this sum.

## ▼ DISCOVERY • DISCUSSION • WRITING

**68. Arithmetic Means**  The **arithmetic mean** (or average) of two numbers $a$ and $b$ is

$$m = \frac{a + b}{2}$$

Note that $m$ is the same distance from $a$ as from $b$, so $a, m, b$ is an arithmetic sequence. In general, if $m_1, m_2, \ldots, m_k$ are equally spaced between $a$ and $b$ so that

$$a, m_1, m_2, \ldots, m_k, b$$

is an arithmetic sequence, then $m_1, m_2, \ldots, m_k$ are called $k$ arithmetic means between $a$ and $b$.

(a) Insert two arithmetic means between 10 and 18.

(b) Insert three arithmetic means between 10 and 18.

(c) Suppose a doctor needs to increase a patient's dosage of a certain medicine from 100 mg to 300 mg per day in five equal steps. How many arithmetic means must be inserted between 100 and 300 to give the progression of daily doses, and what are these means?

---

## 9.3 | Geometric Sequences

### LEARNING OBJECTIVES

After completing this section, you will be able to:

■ Find the terms of a geometric sequence
■ Find the partial sums of a geometric sequence
■ Find the sum of an infinite geometric series

In this section we study geometric sequences. This type of sequence occurs frequently in applications to finance, population growth, and other fields.

### ■ Geometric Sequences

Recall that an arithmetic sequence is generated when we repeatedly add a number $d$ to an initial term $a$. A *geometric* sequence is generated when we start with a number $a$ and repeatedly *multiply* by a fixed nonzero constant $r$.

> **DEFINITION OF A GEOMETRIC SEQUENCE**
>
> A **geometric sequence** is a sequence of the form
>
> $$a, ar, ar^2, ar^3, ar^4, \ldots$$
>
> The number $a$ is the **first term**, and $r$ is the **common ratio** of the sequence. The **$n$th term** of a geometric sequence is given by
>
> $$a_n = ar^{n-1}$$

The number $r$ is called the common ratio because the ratio of any two consecutive terms of the sequence is $r$.

▶ **EXAMPLE 1** | Geometric Sequences

**(a)** If $a = 3$ and $r = 2$, then we have the geometric sequence

$$3, \quad 3 \cdot 2, \quad 3 \cdot 2^2, \quad 3 \cdot 2^3, \quad 3 \cdot 2^4, \quad \ldots$$

or $\qquad\qquad\qquad 3, 6, 12, 24, 48, \ldots$

Notice that the ratio of any two consecutive terms is $r = 2$. The $n$th term is $a_n = 3(2)^{n-1}$.

**(b)** The sequence

$$2, -10, 50, -250, 1250, \ldots$$

is a geometric sequence with $a = 2$ and $r = -5$. When $r$ is negative, the terms of the sequence alternate in sign. The $n$th term is $a_n = 2(-5)^{n-1}$.

**(c)** The sequence

$$1, \frac{1}{3}, \frac{1}{9}, \frac{1}{27}, \frac{1}{81}, \ldots$$

is a geometric sequence with $a = 1$ and $r = \frac{1}{3}$. The $n$th term is $a_n = 1\left(\frac{1}{3}\right)^{n-1}$.

**(d)** The graph of the geometric sequence $a_n = \frac{1}{5} \cdot 2^{n-1}$ is shown in Figure 1. Notice that the points in the graph lie on the graph of the exponential function $y = \frac{1}{5} \cdot 2^{x-1}$.

If $0 < r < 1$, then the terms of the geometric sequence $ar^{n-1}$ decrease, but if $r > 1$, then the terms increase. (What happens if $r = 1$?)

✎ **Practice what you've learned: Do Exercises 5, 9, and 13.**    ▲

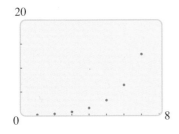

**FIGURE 1**

Geometric sequences occur naturally. Here is a simple example. Suppose a ball has elasticity such that when it is dropped, it bounces up one-third of the distance it has fallen. If this ball is dropped from a height of 2 m, then it bounces up to a height of $2\left(\frac{1}{3}\right) = \frac{2}{3}$ m. On its second bounce, it returns to a height of $\left(\frac{2}{3}\right)\left(\frac{1}{3}\right) = \frac{2}{9}$ m, and so on (see Figure 2). Thus, the height $h_n$ that the ball reaches on its $n$th bounce is given by the geometric sequence

$$h_n = \frac{2}{3}\left(\frac{1}{3}\right)^{n-1} = 2\left(\frac{1}{3}\right)^n$$

We can find the $n$th term of a geometric sequence if we know any two terms, as the following examples show.

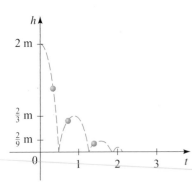

**FIGURE 2**

▶ **EXAMPLE 2** | Finding Terms of a Geometric Sequence

Find the eighth term of the geometric sequence $5, 15, 45, \ldots.$

▼ **SOLUTION**  To find a formula for the $n$th term of this sequence, we need to find $a$ and $r$. Clearly, $a = 5$. To find $r$, we find the ratio of any two consecutive terms.

For instance, $r = \frac{45}{15} = 3$. Thus,

$$a_n = 5(3)^{n-1}$$

The eighth term is $a_8 = 5(3)^{8-1} = 5(3)^7 = 10{,}935$.

✎ **Practice what you've learned: Do Exercise 27.**                    ▲

▶ **EXAMPLE 3** | Finding Terms of a Geometric Sequence

The third term of a geometric sequence is $\frac{63}{4}$, and the sixth term is $\frac{1701}{32}$. Find the fifth term.

▼ **SOLUTION**   Since this sequence is geometric, its $n$th term is given by the formula $a_n = ar^{n-1}$. Thus,

$$a_3 = ar^{3-1} = ar^2$$
$$a_6 = ar^{6-1} = ar^5$$

From the values we are given for these two terms, we get the following system of equations:

$$\begin{cases} \frac{63}{4} = ar^2 \\ \frac{1701}{32} = ar^5 \end{cases}$$

We solve this system by dividing.

$$\frac{ar^5}{ar^2} = \frac{\frac{1701}{32}}{\frac{63}{4}}$$

$$r^3 = \frac{27}{8} \qquad \text{Simplify}$$

$$r = \frac{3}{2} \qquad \text{Take cube root of each side}$$

Substituting for $r$ in the first equation, $\frac{63}{4} = ar^2$, gives

$$\frac{63}{4} = a\left(\frac{3}{2}\right)^2$$

$$a = 7 \qquad \text{Solve for } a$$

It follows that the $n$th term of this sequence is

$$a_n = 7\left(\frac{3}{2}\right)^{n-1}$$

Thus, the fifth term is

$$a_5 = 7\left(\frac{3}{2}\right)^{5-1} = 7\left(\frac{3}{2}\right)^4 = \frac{567}{16}$$

✎ **Practice what you've learned: Do Exercise 37.**                    ▲

© Michael Ng

**Srinivasa Ramanujan** (1887–1920) was born into a poor family in the small town of Kumbakonam in India. Self-taught in mathematics, he worked in virtual isolation from other mathematicians. At the age of 25 he wrote a letter to G. H. Hardy, the leading British mathematician at the time, listing some of his discoveries. Hardy immediately recognized Ramanujan's genius, and for the next six years the two worked together in London until Ramanujan fell ill and returned to his hometown in India, where he died a year later.

Ramanujan was a genius with phenomenal ability to see hidden patterns in the properties of numbers. Most of his discoveries were written as complicated infinite series, the importance of which was not recognized until many years after his death. In the last year of his life he wrote 130 pages of mysterious formulas, many of which still defy proof. Hardy tells the story that when he visited Ramanujan in a hospital and arrived in a taxi, he remarked to Ramanujan that the cab's number, 1729, was uninteresting. Ramanujan replied "No, it is a very interesting number. It is the smallest number expressible as the sum of two cubes in two different ways."

## ■ Partial Sums of Geometric Sequences

For the geometric sequence $a, ar, ar^2, ar^3, ar^4, \ldots, ar^{n-1}, \ldots$, the $n$th partial sum is

$$S_n = \sum_{k=1}^{n} ar^{k-1} = a + ar + ar^2 + ar^3 + ar^4 + \cdots + ar^{n-1}$$

To find a formula for $S_n$, we multiply $S_n$ by $r$ and subtract from $S_n$.

$$S_n = a + ar + ar^2 + ar^3 + ar^4 + \cdots + ar^{n-1}$$

$$\underline{rS_n = \qquad ar + ar^2 + ar^3 + ar^4 + \cdots + ar^{n-1} + ar^n}$$

$$S_n - rS_n = a - ar^n$$

So

$$S_n(1 - r) = a(1 - r^n)$$

$$S_n = \frac{a(1 - r^n)}{1 - r} \qquad (r \neq 1)$$

We summarize this result.

---

**PARTIAL SUMS OF A GEOMETRIC SEQUENCE**

For the geometric sequence $a_n = ar^{n-1}$, the **$n$th partial sum**

$$S_n = a + ar + ar^2 + ar^3 + ar^4 + \cdots + ar^{n-1} \qquad (r \neq 1)$$

is given by

$$S_n = a\frac{1 - r^n}{1 - r}$$

---

▶ **EXAMPLE 4** | Finding a Partial Sum of a Geometric Sequence

Find the sum of the first five terms of the geometric sequence

$$1, 0.7, 0.49, 0.343, \ldots$$

▼ **SOLUTION** The required sum is the sum of the first five terms of a geometric sequence with $a = 1$ and $r = 0.7$. Using the formula for $S_n$ with $n = 5$, we get

$$S_5 = 1 \cdot \frac{1 - (0.7)^5}{1 - 0.7} = 2.7731$$

Thus, the sum of the first five terms of this sequence is 2.7731.

✎ **Practice what you've learned: Do Exercises 43 and 47.**

▶ **EXAMPLE 5** | Finding a Partial Sum of a Geometric Sequence

Find the sum $\displaystyle\sum_{k=1}^{5} 7\left(-\frac{2}{3}\right)^k$.

▼ **SOLUTION** The given sum is the fifth partial sum of a geometric sequence with first term $a = 7\left(-\frac{2}{3}\right)^1 = -\frac{14}{3}$ and common ratio $r = -\frac{2}{3}$. Thus, by the formula for $S_n$ we have

$$S_5 = -\frac{14}{3} \cdot \frac{1 - \left(-\frac{2}{3}\right)^5}{1 - \left(-\frac{2}{3}\right)} = -\frac{14}{3} \cdot \frac{1 + \frac{32}{243}}{\frac{5}{3}} = -\frac{770}{243}$$

✎ **Practice what you've learned: Do Exercise 49.**

### ■ What Is an Infinite Series?

An expression of the form

$$a_1 + a_2 + a_3 + a_4 + \cdots$$

is called an **infinite series**. The dots mean that we are to continue the addition indefinitely. What meaning can we attach to the sum of infinitely many numbers? It seems at first that it is not possible to add infinitely many numbers and arrive at a finite number. But consider the following problem. You have a cake, and you want to eat it by first eating half the cake, then eating half of what remains, then again eating half of what remains. This process can continue indefinitely because at each stage some of the cake remains. (See Figure 3.)

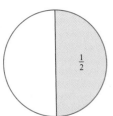 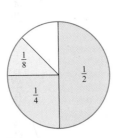 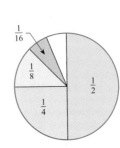 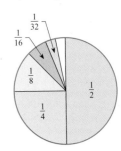

**FIGURE 3**

Does this mean that it's impossible to eat all of the cake? Of course not. Let's write down what you have eaten from this cake:

$$\frac{1}{2} + \frac{1}{4} + \frac{1}{8} + \frac{1}{16} + \cdots + \frac{1}{2^n} + \cdots$$

This is an infinite series, and we note two things about it: First, from Figure 3 it's clear that no matter how many terms of this series we add, the total will never exceed 1. Second, the more terms of this series we add, the closer the sum is to 1 (see Figure 3). This suggests that the number 1 can be written as the sum of infinitely many smaller numbers:

$$1 = \frac{1}{2} + \frac{1}{4} + \frac{1}{8} + \frac{1}{16} + \cdots + \frac{1}{2^n} + \cdots$$

To make this more precise, let's look at the partial sums of this series:

$$S_1 = \frac{1}{2} \qquad\qquad = \frac{1}{2}$$

$$S_2 = \frac{1}{2} + \frac{1}{4} \qquad\qquad = \frac{3}{4}$$

$$S_3 = \frac{1}{2} + \frac{1}{4} + \frac{1}{8} \qquad = \frac{7}{8}$$

$$S_4 = \frac{1}{2} + \frac{1}{4} + \frac{1}{8} + \frac{1}{16} = \frac{15}{16}$$

and, in general (see Example 5 of Section 9.1),

$$S_n = 1 - \frac{1}{2^n}$$

As $n$ gets larger and larger, we are adding more and more of the terms of this series. Intuitively, as $n$ gets larger, $S_n$ gets closer to the sum of the series. Now notice that as $n$ gets large, $1/2^n$ gets closer and closer to 0. Thus, $S_n$ gets close to $1 - 0 = 1$. Using the notation of Section 4.6, we can write

$$S_n \to 1 \quad \text{as} \quad n \to \infty$$

In general, if $S_n$ gets close to a finite number $S$ as $n$ gets large, we say that $S$ is the **sum of the infinite series**.

## Infinite Geometric Series

Here is another way to arrive at the formula for the sum of an infinite geometric series:

$$S = a + ar + ar^2 + ar^3 + \cdots$$
$$= a + r(a + ar + ar^2 + \cdots)$$
$$= a + rS$$

Solve the equation $S = a + rS$ for $S$ to get

$$S - rS = a$$
$$(1 - r)S = a$$
$$S = \frac{a}{1 - r}$$

An **infinite geometric series** is a series of the form

$$a + ar + ar^2 + ar^3 + ar^4 + \cdots + ar^{n-1} + \cdots$$

We can apply the reasoning used earlier to find the sum of an infinite geometric series. The $n$th partial sum of such a series is given by the formula

$$S_n = a\frac{1 - r^n}{1 - r} \qquad (r \neq 1)$$

It can be shown that if $|r| < 1$, then $r^n$ gets close to 0 as $n$ gets large (you can easily convince yourself of this using a calculator). It follows that $S_n$ gets close to $a/(1 - r)$ as $n$ gets large, or

$$S_n \to \frac{a}{1 - r} \quad \text{as} \quad n \to \infty$$

Thus, the sum of this infinite geometric series is $a/(1 - r)$.

---

### SUM OF AN INFINITE GEOMETRIC SERIES

If $|r| < 1$, then the infinite geometric series

$$a + ar + ar^2 + ar^3 + ar^4 + \cdots + ar^{n-1} + \cdots$$

has the sum

$$S = \frac{a}{1 - r}$$

---

▶ **EXAMPLE 6** | Finding the Sum of an Infinite Geometric Series

Find the sum of the infinite geometric series

$$2 + \frac{2}{5} + \frac{2}{25} + \frac{2}{125} + \cdots + \frac{2}{5^n} + \cdots$$

▼ **SOLUTION**    We use the formula for the sum of an infinite geometric series. In this case $a = 2$ and $r = \frac{1}{5}$. Thus, the sum of this infinite series is

$$S = \frac{2}{1 - \frac{1}{5}} = \frac{5}{2}$$

✎ **Practice what you've learned: Do Exercise 51.** ▲

---

## MATHEMATICS IN THE MODERN WORLD

### Fractals

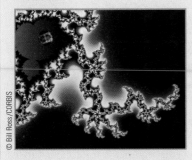

© Bill Ross/CORBIS

Many of the things we model in this book have regular predictable shapes. But recent advances in mathematics have made it possible to model such seemingly random or even chaotic shapes as those of a cloud, a flickering flame, a mountain, or a jagged coastline. The basic tools in this type of modeling are the fractals invented by the mathematician Benoit Mandelbrot. A *fractal* is a geometric shape built up from a simple basic shape by scaling and repeating the shape indefinitely according to a given rule. Fractals have infinite detail; this means the closer you look, the more you see. They are also *self-similar*; that is, zooming in on a portion of the fractal yields the same detail as the original shape. Because of their beautiful shapes, fractals are used by movie makers to create fictional landscapes and exotic backgrounds.

Although a fractal is a complex shape, it is produced according to very simple rules. This property of fractals is exploited in a process of storing pictures on a computer called *fractal image compression*. In this process a picture is stored as a simple basic shape and a rule; repeating the shape according to the rule produces the original picture. This is an extremely efficient method of storage; that's how thousands of color pictures can be put on a single compact disc.

▶ **EXAMPLE 7** | Writing a Repeated Decimal as a Fraction

Find the fraction that represents the rational number $2.3\overline{51}$.

▼ **SOLUTION**   This repeating decimal can be written as a series:

$$\frac{23}{10} + \frac{51}{1000} + \frac{51}{100,000} + \frac{51}{10,000,000} + \frac{51}{1,000,000,000} + \cdots$$

After the first term, the terms of this series form an infinite geometric series with

$$a = \frac{51}{1000} \quad \text{and} \quad r = \frac{1}{100}$$

Thus, the sum of this part of the series is

$$S = \frac{\frac{51}{1000}}{1 - \frac{1}{100}} = \frac{\frac{51}{1000}}{\frac{99}{100}} = \frac{51}{1000} \cdot \frac{100}{99} = \frac{51}{990}$$

So

$$2.3\overline{51} = \frac{23}{10} + \frac{51}{990} = \frac{2328}{990} = \frac{388}{165}$$

✎ **Practice what you've learned: Do Exercise 59.**                                 ▲

# 9.3 EXERCISES

▼ **CONCEPTS**

1. A geometric sequence is a sequence in which the _____ of successive terms is constant.

2. The sequence $a_n = ar^{n-1}$ is a geometric sequence in which $a$ is the first term and $r$ is the _____ _____. So for the geometric sequence $a_n = 2(5)^{n-1}$ the first term is _____, and the common ratio is _____.

3. *True or false?* If we know the first and second terms of a geometric sequence, then we can find all the other terms.

4. (a) The $n$th partial sum of a geometric sequence $a_n = ar^{n-1}$ is given by $S_n = $ _____.
   (b) If $|r| < 1$, the sum of the infinite geometric series
   $$a + ar + ar^2 + ar^3 + \cdots \text{ is given by } S = \underline{\quad\quad}.$$

▼ **SKILLS**

5–8 ▪ The $n$th term of a sequence is given.
(a) Find the first five terms of the sequence.
(b) What is the common ratio $r$?
(c) Graph the terms you found in (a).

✎ **5.** $a_n = 5(2)^{n-1}$         **6.** $a_n = 3(-4)^{n-1}$

**7.** $a_n = \frac{5}{2}\left(-\frac{1}{2}\right)^{n-1}$         **8.** $a_n = 3^{n-1}$

9–12 ▪ Find the $n$th term of the geometric sequence with given first term $a$ and common ratio $r$. What is the fourth term?

✎ **9.** $a = 3$,  $r = 5$         **10.** $a = -6$,  $r = 3$

**11.** $a = \frac{5}{2}$,  $r = -\frac{1}{2}$         **12.** $a = \sqrt{3}$,  $r = \sqrt{3}$

13–20 ▪ Determine whether the sequence is geometric. If it is geometric, find the common ratio.

✎ **13.** $2, 4, 8, 16, \ldots$         **14.** $2, 6, 18, 36, \ldots$

**15.** $3, \frac{3}{2}, \frac{3}{4}, \frac{3}{8}, \ldots$         **16.** $27, -9, 3, -1, \ldots$

**17.** $\frac{1}{2}, \frac{1}{3}, \frac{1}{4}, \frac{1}{5}, \ldots$         **18.** $e^2, e^4, e^6, e^8, \ldots$

**19.** $1.0, 1.1, 1.21, 1.331, \ldots$         **20.** $\frac{1}{2}, \frac{1}{4}, \frac{1}{6}, \frac{1}{8}, \ldots$

21–26 ▪ Find the first five terms of the sequence, and determine whether it is geometric. If it is geometric, find the common ratio, and express the $n$th term of the sequence in the standard form $a_n = ar^{n-1}$.

**21.** $a_n = 2(3)^n$         **22.** $a_n = 4 + 3^n$

**23.** $a_n = \frac{1}{4^n}$         **24.** $a_n = (-1)^n 2^n$

**25.** $a_n = \ln(5^{n-1})$         **26.** $a_n = n^n$

27–36 ▪ Determine the common ratio, the fifth term, and the $n$th term of the geometric sequence.

✎ **27.** $2, 6, 18, 54, \ldots$         **28.** $7, \frac{14}{3}, \frac{28}{9}, \frac{56}{27}, \ldots$

**29.** $0.3, -0.09, 0.027, -0.0081, \ldots$

**30.** $1, \sqrt{2}, 2, 2\sqrt{2}, \ldots$

**31.** $144, -12, 1, -\frac{1}{12}, \ldots$         **32.** $-8, -2, -\frac{1}{2}, -\frac{1}{8}, \ldots$

**33.** $3, 3^{5/3}, 3^{7/3}, 27, \ldots$         **34.** $t, \frac{t^2}{2}, \frac{t^3}{4}, \frac{t^4}{8}, \ldots$

**35.** $1, s^{2/7}, s^{4/7}, s^{6/7}, \ldots$         **36.** $5, 5^{c+1}, 5^{2c+1}, 5^{3c+1}, \ldots$

✎ **37.** The first term of a geometric sequence is 8, and the second term is 4. Find the fifth term.

**38.** The first term of a geometric sequence is 3, and the third term is $\frac{4}{3}$. Find the fifth term.

**39.** The common ratio in a geometric sequence is $\frac{2}{5}$, and the fourth term is $\frac{5}{2}$. Find the third term.

**40.** The common ratio in a geometric sequence is $\frac{3}{2}$, and the fifth term is 1. Find the first three terms.

**41.** Which term of the geometric sequence $2, 6, 18, \ldots$ is 118,098?

**42.** The second and fifth terms of a geometric sequence are 10 and 1250, respectively. Is 31,250 a term of this sequence? If so, which term is it?

**43–46** ▪ Find the partial sum $S_n$ of the geometric sequence that satisfies the given conditions.

**43.** $a = 5$,  $r = 2$,  $n = 6$     **44.** $a = \frac{2}{3}$,  $r = \frac{1}{3}$,  $n = 4$

**45.** $a_3 = 28$,  $a_6 = 224$,  $n = 6$

**46.** $a_2 = 0.12$,  $a_5 = 0.00096$,  $n = 4$

**47–50** ▪ Find the sum.

**47.** $1 + 3 + 9 + \cdots + 2187$

**48.** $1 - \frac{1}{2} + \frac{1}{4} - \frac{1}{8} + \cdots - \frac{1}{512}$

**49.** $\displaystyle\sum_{k=0}^{10} 3\left(\frac{1}{2}\right)^k$     **50.** $\displaystyle\sum_{j=0}^{5} 7\left(\frac{3}{2}\right)^j$

**51–58** ▪ Find the sum of the infinite geometric series.

**51.** $1 + \dfrac{1}{3} + \dfrac{1}{9} + \dfrac{1}{27} + \cdots$     **52.** $1 - \dfrac{1}{2} + \dfrac{1}{4} - \dfrac{1}{8} + \cdots$

**53.** $1 - \dfrac{1}{3} + \dfrac{1}{9} - \dfrac{1}{27} + \cdots$     **54.** $\dfrac{2}{5} + \dfrac{4}{25} + \dfrac{8}{125} + \cdots$

**55.** $\dfrac{1}{3^6} + \dfrac{1}{3^8} + \dfrac{1}{3^{10}} + \dfrac{1}{3^{12}} + \cdots$

**56.** $3 - \dfrac{3}{2} + \dfrac{3}{4} - \dfrac{3}{8} + \cdots$

**57.** $-\dfrac{100}{9} + \dfrac{10}{3} - 1 + \dfrac{3}{10} - \cdots$

**58.** $\dfrac{1}{\sqrt{2}} + \dfrac{1}{2} + \dfrac{1}{2\sqrt{2}} + \dfrac{1}{4} + \cdots$

**59–64** ▪ Express the repeating decimal as a fraction.

**59.** $0.777\ldots$     **60.** $0.2\overline{53}$     **61.** $0.030303\ldots$

**62.** $2.11\overline{25}$     **63.** $0.1\overline{12}$     **64.** $0.123123123\ldots$

**65.** If the numbers $a_1, a_2, \ldots, a_n$ form a geometric sequence, then $a_2, a_3, \ldots, a_{n-1}$ are **geometric means** between $a_1$ and $a_n$. Insert three geometric means between 5 and 80.

**66.** Find the sum of the first ten terms of the sequence

$$a + b, a^2 + 2b, a^3 + 3b, a^4 + 4b, \ldots$$

## ▼ APPLICATIONS

**67. Depreciation**    A construction company purchases a bulldozer for \$160,000. Each year the value of the bulldozer depreciates by 20% of its value in the preceding year. Let $V_n$ be the value of the bulldozer in the $n$th year. (Let $n = 1$ be the year the bulldozer is purchased.)
  **(a)** Find a formula for $V_n$.
  **(b)** In what year will the value of the bulldozer be less than \$100,000?

**68. Family Tree**    A person has two parents, four grandparents, eight great-grandparents, and so on. How many ancestors does a person have 15 generations back?

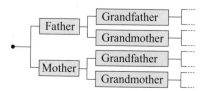

**69. Bouncing Ball**    A ball is dropped from a height of 80 ft. The elasticity of this ball is such that it rebounds three-fourths of the distance it has fallen. How high does the ball rebound on the fifth bounce? Find a formula for how high the ball rebounds on the $n$th bounce.

**70. Bacteria Culture**    A culture initially has 5000 bacteria, and its size increases by 8% every hour. How many bacteria are present at the end of 5 hours? Find a formula for the number of bacteria present after $n$ hours.

**71. Mixing Coolant**    A truck radiator holds 5 gal and is filled with water. A gallon of water is removed from the radiator and replaced with a gallon of antifreeze; then a gallon of the mixture is removed from the radiator and again replaced by a gallon of antifreeze. This process is repeated indefinitely. How much water remains in the tank after this process is repeated 3 times? 5 times? $n$ times?

**72. Musical Frequencies**    The frequencies of musical notes (measured in cycles per second) form a geometric sequence. Middle C has a frequency of 256, and the C that is an octave higher has a frequency of 512. Find the frequency of C two octaves below middle C.

**73. Bouncing Ball**    A ball is dropped from a height of 9 ft. The elasticity of the ball is such that it always bounces up one-third the distance it has fallen.
  **(a)** Find the total distance the ball has traveled at the instant it hits the ground the fifth time.
  **(b)** Find a formula for the total distance the ball has traveled at the instant it hits the ground the $n$th time.

**74. Geometric Savings Plan**    A very patient woman wishes to become a billionaire. She decides to follow a simple scheme: She puts aside 1 cent the first day, 2 cents the second day, 4 cents the third day, and so on, doubling the number of cents each day. How much money will she have at the end of 30 days? How many days will it take this woman to realize her wish?

**75. St. Ives**    The following is a well-known children's rhyme:

> As I was going to St. Ives,
> I met a man with seven wives;
> Every wife had seven sacks;
> Every sack had seven cats;
> Every cat had seven kits;
> Kits, cats, sacks, and wives,
> How many were going to St. Ives?

Assuming that the entire group is actually going to St. Ives, show that the answer to the question in the rhyme is a partial sum of a geometric sequence, and find the sum.

**76. Drug Concentration**    A certain drug is administered once a day. The concentration of the drug in the patient's bloodstream increases rapidly at first, but each successive dose has less effect than the preceding one. The total amount of the drug (in mg) in the bloodstream after the $n$th dose is given by

$$\sum_{k=1}^{n} 50\left(\tfrac{1}{2}\right)^{k-1}$$

  **(a)** Find the amount of the drug in the bloodstream after $n = 10$ days.

**(b)** If the drug is taken on a long-term basis, the amount in the bloodstream is approximated by the infinite series $\sum_{k=1}^{\infty} 50\left(\frac{1}{2}\right)^{k-1}$. Find the sum of this series.

**77. Bouncing Ball**   A certain ball rebounds to half the height from which it is dropped. Use an infinite geometric series to approximate the total distance the ball travels after being dropped from 1 m above the ground until it comes to rest.

**78. Bouncing Ball**   If the ball in Exercise 77 is dropped from a height of 8 ft, then 1 s is required for its first complete bounce—from the instant it first touches the ground until it next touches the ground. Each subsequent complete bounce requires $1/\sqrt{2}$ as long as the preceding complete bounce. Use an infinite geometric series to estimate the time interval from the instant the ball first touches the ground until it stops bouncing.

**79. Geometry**   The midpoints of the sides of a square of side 1 are joined to form a new square. This procedure is repeated for each new square. (See the figure.)
**(a)** Find the sum of the areas of all the squares.
**(b)** Find the sum of the perimeters of all the squares.

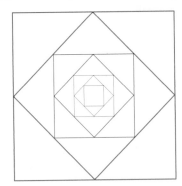

**80. Geometry**   A circular disk of radius $R$ is cut out of paper, as shown in figure (a). Two disks of radius $\frac{1}{2}R$ are cut out of paper and placed on top of the first disk, as in figure (b), and then four disks of radius $\frac{1}{4}R$ are placed on these two disks, as in figure (c). Assuming that this process can be repeated indefinitely, find the total area of all the disks.

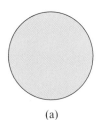 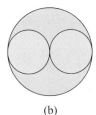 

(a)          (b)          (c)

**81. Geometry**   A yellow square of side 1 is divided into nine smaller squares, and the middle square is colored blue as shown in the figure. Each of the smaller yellow squares is in turn divided into nine squares, and each middle square is colored blue. If this process is continued indefinitely, what is the total area that is colored blue?

 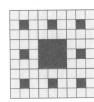 

▼ **DISCOVERY • DISCUSSION • WRITING**

**82. Arithmetic or Geometric?**   The first four terms of a sequence are given. Determine whether these terms can be the terms of an arithmetic sequence, a geometric sequence, or neither. Find the next term if the sequence is arithmetic or geometric.
**(a)** $5, -3, 5, -3, \ldots$
**(b)** $\frac{1}{3}, 1, \frac{5}{3}, \frac{7}{3}, \ldots$
**(c)** $\sqrt{3}, 3, 3\sqrt{3}, 9, \ldots$
**(d)** $1, -1, 1, -1, \ldots$
**(e)** $2, -1, \frac{1}{2}, 2, \ldots$
**(f)** $x-1, x, x+1, x+2, \ldots$
**(g)** $-3, -\frac{3}{2}, 0, \frac{3}{2}, \ldots$
**(h)** $\sqrt{5}, \sqrt[3]{5}, \sqrt[6]{5}, 1, \ldots$

**83. Reciprocals of a Geometric Sequence**   If $a_1, a_2, a_3, \ldots$ is a geometric sequence with common ratio $r$, show that the sequence

$$\frac{1}{a_1}, \frac{1}{a_2}, \frac{1}{a_3}, \ldots$$

is also a geometric sequence, and find the common ratio.

**84. Logarithms of a Geometric Sequence**   If $a_1, a_2, a_3, \ldots$ is a geometric sequence with a common ratio $r > 0$ and $a_1 > 0$, show that the sequence

$$\log a_1, \log a_2, \log a_3, \ldots$$

is an arithmetic sequence, and find the common difference.

**85. Exponentials of an Arithmetic Sequence**   If $a_1, a_2, a_3, \ldots$ is an arithmetic sequence with common difference $d$, show that the sequence

$$10^{a_1}, 10^{a_2}, 10^{a_3}, \ldots$$

is a geometric sequence, and find the common ratio.

# FINDING PATTERNS

The ancient Greeks studied triangular numbers, square numbers, pentagonal numbers, and other **polygonal numbers**, like those shown in the figure.

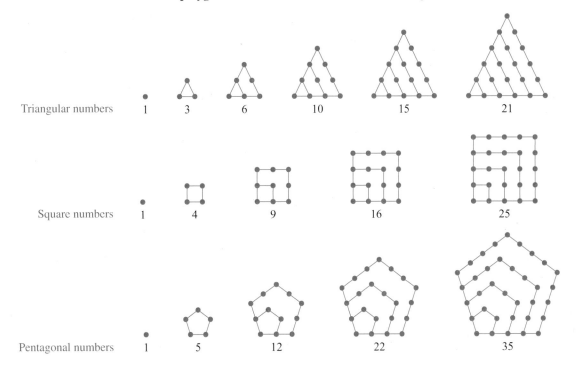

Triangular numbers  1   3   6   10   15   21

Square numbers  1   4   9   16   25

Pentagonal numbers  1   5   12   22   35

To find a pattern for such numbers, we construct a **first difference sequence** by taking differences of successive terms; we repeat the process to get a **second difference sequence, third difference sequence**, and so on. For the sequence of triangular numbers $T_n$ we get the following **difference table**:

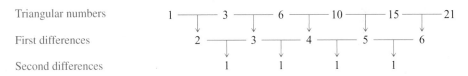

Triangular numbers  1 —— 3 —— 6 —— 10 —— 15 —— 21

First differences  2 —— 3 —— 4 —— 5 —— 6

Second differences  1   1   1   1

If a sequence is given by a polynomial function and if we calculate the first differences, the second differences, the third differences, and so on, then eventually we get a constant sequence.

We stop at the second difference sequence because it is a constant sequence. Assuming that this sequence will continue to have constant value 1, we can work backward from the bottom row to find more terms of the first difference sequence and, from these, more triangular numbers.

1. Construct a difference table for the square numbers and the pentagonal numbers. Use your table to find the tenth pentagonal number.

2. From the patterns you have observed so far, what do you think the second difference would be for the *hexagonal numbers*? Use this, together with the fact that the first two hexagonal numbers are 1 and 6, to find the first eight hexagonal numbers.

3. Construct difference tables for $C_n = n^3$. Which difference sequence is constant? Do the same for $F_n = n^4$.

4. Make up a polynomial of degree 5, and construct a difference table. Which difference sequence is constant?

5. The first few terms of a polynomial sequence are 1, 2, 4, 8, 16, 31, 57, . . . . Construct a difference table, and use it to find four more terms of this sequence.

**9.4** | Mathematics of Finance

**LEARNING OBJECTIVES**

After completing this section, you will be able to:

■ Find the amount of an annuity
■ Find the present value of an annuity
■ Find the amount of the installment payments on a loan

Many financial transactions involve payments that are made at regular intervals. For example, if you deposit $100 each month in an interest-bearing account, what will the value of your account be at the end of 5 years? If you borrow $100,000 to buy a house, how much must your monthly payments be in order to pay off the loan in 30 years? Each of these questions involves the sum of a sequence of numbers; we use the results of the preceding section to answer them here.

## ■ The Amount of an Annuity

An **annuity** is a sum of money that is paid in regular equal payments. Although the word *annuity* suggests annual (or yearly) payments, they can be made semiannually, quarterly, monthly, or at some other regular interval. Payments are usually made at the end of the payment interval. The **amount of an annuity** is the sum of all the individual payments from the time of the first payment until the last payment is made, together with all the interest. We denote this sum by $A_f$ (the subscript $f$ here is used to denote *final* amount).

▶ **EXAMPLE 1** | Calculating the Amount of an Annuity

An investor deposits $400 every December 15 and June 15 for 10 years in an account that earns interest at the rate of 8% per year, compounded semiannually. How much will be in the account immediately after the last payment?

▼ **SOLUTION** We need to find the amount of an annuity consisting of 20 semiannual payments of $400 each. Since the interest rate is 8% per year, compounded semiannually, the interest rate per time period is $i = 0.08/2 = 0.04$. The first payment is in the account for 19 time periods, the second for 18 time periods, and so on.

The last payment receives no interest. The situation can be illustrated by the time line in Figure 1.

> When using interest rates in calculators, remember to convert percentages to decimals. For example, 8% is 0.08.

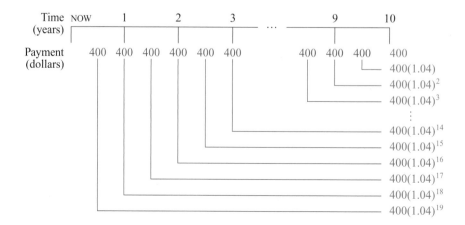

**FIGURE 1**

The amount $A_f$ of the annuity is the sum of these 20 amounts. Thus,

$$A_f = 400 + 400(1.04) + 400(1.04)^2 + \cdots + 400(1.04)^{19}$$

But this is a geometric series with $a = 400$, $r = 1.04$, and $n = 20$, so

$$A_f = 400 \frac{1 - (1.04)^{20}}{1 - 1.04} \approx 11{,}911.23$$

Thus, the amount in the account after the last payment is $11,911.23.

✎ **Practice what you've learned: Do Exercise 3.**   ▲

In general, the regular annuity payment is called the **periodic rent** and is denoted by $R$. We also let $i$ denote the interest rate per time period and $n$ the number of payments. *We always assume that the time period in which interest is compounded is equal to the time between payments.* By the same reasoning as in Example 1, we see that the amount $A_f$ of an annuity is

$$A_f = R + R(1 + i) + R(1 + i)^2 + \cdots + R(1 + i)^{n-1}$$

Since this is the $n$th partial sum of a geometric sequence with $a = R$ and $r = 1 + i$, the formula for the partial sum gives

$$A_f = R \frac{1 - (1 + i)^n}{1 - (1 + i)} = R \frac{1 - (1 + i)^n}{-i} = R \frac{(1 + i)^n - 1}{i}$$

**AMOUNT OF AN ANNUITY**

The amount $A_f$ of an annuity consisting of $n$ regular equal payments of size $R$ with interest rate $i$ per time period is given by

$$A_f = R \frac{(1 + i)^n - 1}{i}$$

▶ **EXAMPLE 2** | Calculating the Amount of an Annuity

How much money should be invested every month at 12% per year, compounded monthly, in order to have $4000 in 18 months?

▼ **SOLUTION**   In this problem $i = 0.12/12 = 0.01$, $A_f = 4000$, and $n = 18$. We need to find the amount $R$ of each payment. By the formula for the amount of an annuity,

$$4000 = R \frac{(1 + 0.01)^{18} - 1}{0.01}$$

Solving for $R$, we get

$$R = \frac{4000(0.01)}{(1 + 0.01)^{18} - 1} \approx 203.928$$

Thus, the monthly investment should be $203.93.

✎ **Practice what you've learned: Do Exercise 9.**   ▲

## ■ The Present Value of an Annuity

If you were to receive $10,000 five years from now, it would be worth much less than if you got $10,000 right now. This is because of the interest you could accumulate during the next five years if you invested the money now. What smaller amount would you be willing to accept *now* instead of receiving $10,000 in five years? This is the amount of money that, together with interest, would be worth $10,000 in five years. The amount that we are looking for here is called the *discounted value* or *present value*. If the interest rate is 8% per year, compounded quarterly, then the interest per time period is $i = 0.08/4 = 0.02$, and there are $4 \times 5 = 20$ time periods. If we let $PV$ denote the present value, then by the formula for compound interest (Section 5.1), we have

$$10{,}000 = PV(1 + i)^n = PV(1 + 0.02)^{20}$$

so

$$PV = 10{,}000(1 + 0.02)^{-20} \approx 6729.713$$

Thus, in this situation the present value of $10,000 is $6729.71. This reasoning leads to a general formula for present value. If an amount $A_f$ is to be paid in a lump sum $n$ time periods from now and the interest rate per time period is $i$, then its **present value** $A_p$ is given by

$$A_p = A_f(1 + i)^{-n}$$

Similarly, the **present value of an annuity** is the amount $A_p$ that must be invested now at the interest rate $i$ per time period to provide $n$ payments, each of amount $R$. Clearly, $A_p$ is the sum of the present values of each individual payment (see Exercise 29). Another way of finding $A_p$ is to note that $A_p$ is the present value of $A_f$:

$$A_p = A_f(1 + i)^{-n} = R\,\frac{(1 + i)^n - 1}{i}(1 + i)^{-n} = R\,\frac{1 - (1 + i)^{-n}}{i}$$

---

### THE PRESENT VALUE OF AN ANNUITY

The **present value** $A_p$ of an annuity consisting of $n$ regular equal payments of size $R$ and interest rate $i$ per time period is given by

$$A_p = R\,\frac{1 - (1 + i)^{-n}}{i}$$

---

▶ **EXAMPLE 3** | Calculating the Present Value of an Annuity

A person wins $10,000,000 in the California lottery, and the amount is paid in yearly installments of half a million dollars each for 20 years. What is the present value of his winnings? Assume that he can earn 10% interest, compounded annually.

---

## MATH IN THE MODERN WORLD

### Mathematical Economics

The health of the global economy is determined by such interrelated factors as supply, demand, production, consumption, pricing, distribution, and thousands of other factors. These factors are in turn determined by economic decisions (for example, whether or not you buy a certain brand of toothpaste) made by billions of different individuals each day. How will today's creation and distribution of goods affect tomorrow's economy? Such questions are tackled by mathematicians who work on mathematical models of the economy. In the 1940s Wassily Leontief, a pioneer in this area, created a model consisting of thousands of equations that describe how different sectors of the economy, such as the oil industry, transportation, and communication, interact with each other. A different approach to economic models, one dealing with individuals in the economy as opposed to large sectors, was pioneered by John Nash in the 1950s. In his model, which uses *game theory*, the economy is a game where individual players make decisions that often lead to mutual gain. Leontief and Nash were awarded the Nobel Prize in Economics in 1973 and 1994, respectively. Economic theory continues to be a major area of mathematical research.

▼ **SOLUTION**   Since the amount won is paid as an annuity, we need to find its present value. Here $i = 0.1$, $R = \$500{,}000$, and $n = 20$. Thus,

$$A_p = 500{,}000 \, \frac{1 - (1 + 0.1)^{-20}}{0.1} \approx 4{,}256{,}781.859$$

This means that the winner really won only $\$4{,}256{,}781.86$ if it were paid immediately.

✎ **Practice what you've learned: Do Exercise 11.**   ▲

## ■ Installment Buying

When you buy a house or a car by installment, the payments that you make are an annuity whose present value is the amount of the loan.

▶ **EXAMPLE 4** | The Amount of a Loan

A student wishes to buy a car. She can afford to pay $\$200$ per month but has no money for a down payment. If she can make these payments for four years and the interest rate is 12%, what purchase price can she afford?

▼ **SOLUTION**   The payments that the student makes constitute an annuity whose present value is the price of the car (which is also the amount of the loan, in this case). Here we have $i = 0.12/12 = 0.01$, $R = 200$, and $n = 12 \times 4 = 48$, so

$$A_p = R \, \frac{1 - (1 + i)^{-n}}{i} = 200 \, \frac{1 - (1 + 0.01)^{-48}}{0.01} \approx 7594.792$$

Thus, the student can buy a car priced at $\$7594.79$.

✎ **Practice what you've learned: Do Exercise 19.**   ▲

When a bank makes a loan that is to be repaid with regular equal payments $R$, then the payments form an annuity whose present value $A_p$ is the amount of the loan. So to find the size of the payments, we solve for $R$ in the formula for the amount of an annuity. This gives the following formula for $R$.

---

**INSTALLMENT BUYING**

If a loan $A_p$ is to be repaid in $n$ regular equal payments with interest rate $i$ per time period, then the size $R$ of each payment is given by

$$R = \frac{iA_p}{1 - (1 + i)^{-n}}$$

---

▶ **EXAMPLE 5** | Calculating Monthly Mortgage Payments

A couple borrows $\$100{,}000$ at 9% interest as a mortage loan on a house. They expect to make monthly payments for 30 years to repay the loan. What is the size of each payment?

▼ **SOLUTION**   The mortgage payments form an annuity whose present value is $A_p = \$100{,}000$. Also, $i = 0.09/12 = 0.0075$, and $n = 12 \times 30 = 360$. We are looking for the amount $R$ of each payment.

From the formula for installment buying, we get

$$R = \frac{iA_p}{1 - (1 + i)^{-n}} = \frac{(0.0075)(100,000)}{1 - (1 + 0.0075)^{-360}} \approx 804.623$$

Thus, the monthly payments are $804.62.

✎ **Practice what you've learned: Do Exercise 17.**       ▲

We now illustrate the use of graphing devices in solving problems related to installment buying.

▶ **EXAMPLE 6** | Calculating the Interest Rate from the Size of Monthly Payments

A car dealer sells a new car for $18,000. He offers the buyer payments of $405 per month for 5 years. What interest rate is this car dealer charging?

▼ **SOLUTION**  The payments form an annuity with present value $A_p = \$18,000$, $R = 405$, and $n = 12 \times 5 = 60$. To find the interest rate, we must solve for $i$ in the equation

$$R = \frac{iA_p}{1 - (1 + i)^{-n}}$$

A little experimentation will convince you that it is not possible to solve this equation for $i$ algebraically. So to find $i$, we use a graphing device to graph $R$ as a function of the interest rate $x$, and we then use the graph to find the interest rate corresponding to the value of $R$ we want ($405 in this case). Since $i = x/12$, we graph the function

$$R(x) = \frac{\dfrac{x}{12}(18,000)}{1 - \left(1 + \dfrac{x}{12}\right)^{-60}}$$

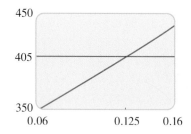

**FIGURE 2**

in the viewing rectangle $[0.06, 0.16] \times [350, 450]$, as shown in Figure 2. We also graph the horizontal line $R(x) = 405$ in the same viewing rectangle. Then, by moving the cursor to the point of intersection of the two graphs, we find that the corresponding $x$-value is approximately 0.125. Thus, the interest rate is about $12\frac{1}{2}\%$.

✎ **Practice what you've learned: Do Exercise 25.**       ▲

# 9.4 EXERCISES

## ▼ CONCEPTS

1. An annuity is a sum of money that is paid in regular equal payments. The _____ of an annuity is the sum of all the individual payments together with all the interest.

2. The _____ _____ of an annuity is the amount that must be invested now at interest rate $i$ per time period in order to provide $n$ payments each of amount $R$.

## ▼ APPLICATIONS

✎ 3. **Annuity**  Find the amount of an annuity that consists of 10 annual payments of $1000 each into an account that pays 6% interest per year.

4. **Annuity**  Find the amount of an annuity that consists of 24 monthly payments of $500 each into an account that pays 8% interest per year, compounded monthly.

5. **Annuity**  Find the amount of an annuity that consists of 20 annual payments of $5000 each into an account that pays interest of 12% per year.

6. **Annuity**  Find the amount of an annuity that consists of 20 semiannual payments of $500 each into an account that pays 6% interest per year, compounded semiannually.

7. **Annuity**  Find the amount of an annuity that consists of 16 quarterly payments of $300 each into an account that pays 8% interest per year, compounded quarterly.

**8. Annuity** Find the amount of an annuity that consists of 40 annual payments of $2000 each into an account that pays interest of 5% per year.

**9. Saving** How much money should be invested every quarter at 10% per year, compounded quarterly, in order to have $5000 in 2 years?

**10. Saving** How much money should be invested monthly at 6% per year, compounded monthly, in order to have $2000 in 8 months?

**11. Annuity** What is the present value of an annuity that consists of 20 semiannual payments of $1000 at an interest rate of 9% per year, compounded semiannually?

**12. Annuity** What is the present value of an annuity that consists of 30 monthly payments of $300 at an interest rate of 8% per year, compounded monthly.

**13. Funding an Annuity** How much money must be invested now at 9% per year, compounded semiannually, to fund an annuity of 20 payments of $200 each, paid every 6 months, the first payment being 6 months from now?

**14. Funding an Annuity** A 55-year-old man deposits $50,000 to fund an annuity with an insurance company. The money will be invested at 8% per year, compounded semiannually. He is to draw semiannual payments until he reaches age 65. What is the amount of each payment?

**15. Financing a Car** A woman wants to borrow $12,000 in order to buy a car. She wants to repay the loan by monthly installments for 4 years. If the interest rate on this loan is $10\frac{1}{2}\%$ per year, compounded monthly, what is the amount of each payment?

**16. Mortgage** What is the monthly payment on a 30-year mortgage of $80,000 at 9% interest? What is the monthly payment on this same mortgage if it is to be repaid over a 15-year period?

**17. Mortgage** What is the monthly payment on a 30-year mortgage of $100,000 at 8% interest per year, compounded monthly? What is the total amount paid on this loan over the 30-year period?

**18. Mortgage** What is the monthly payment on a 15-year mortgage of $200,000 at 6% interest? What is the total amount paid on this loan over the 15-year period?

**19. Mortgage** Dr. Gupta is considering a 30-year mortgage at 6% interest. She can make payments of $3500 a month. What size loan can she afford?

**20. Mortgage** A couple can afford to make a monthly mortgage payment of $650. If the mortgage rate is 9% and the couple intends to secure a 30-year mortgage, how much can they borrow?

**21. Financing a Car** Jane agrees to buy a car for a down payment of $2000 and payments of $220 per month for 3 years. If the interest rate is 8% per year, compounded monthly, what is the actual purchase price of her car?

**22. Financing a Ring** Mike buys a ring for his fiancee by paying $30 a month for one year. If the interest rate is 10% per year, compounded monthly, what is the price of the ring?

**23. Mortgage** A couple secures a 30-year loan of $100,000 at $9\frac{3}{4}\%$ per year, compounded monthly, to buy a house.

(a) What is the amount of their monthly payment?

(b) What total amount will they pay over the 30-year period?

(c) If, instead of taking the loan, the couple deposits the monthly payments in an account that pays $9\frac{3}{4}\%$ interest per year, compounded monthly, how much will be in the account at the end of the 30-year period?

**24. Mortgage** A couple needs a mortgage of $300,000. Their mortgage broker presents them with two options: a 30-year mortgage at $6\frac{1}{2}\%$ interest or a 15-year mortgage at $5\frac{3}{4}\%$ interest.

(a) Find the monthly payment on the 30-year mortgage and on the 15-year mortgage. Which mortgage has the larger monthly payment?

(b) Find the total amount to be paid over the life of each loan. Which mortgage has the lower total payment over its lifetime?

**25. Interest Rate** John buys a stereo system for $640. He agrees to pay $32 a month for 2 years. Assuming that interest is compounded monthly, what interest rate is he paying?

**26. Interest Rate** Janet's payments on her $12,500 car are $420 a month for 3 years. Assuming that interest is compounded monthly, what interest rate is she paying on the car loan?

**27. Interest Rate** An item at a department store is priced at $189.99 and can be bought by making 20 payments of $10.50. Find the interest rate, assuming that interest is compounded monthly.

**28. Interest Rate** A man purchases a $2000 diamond ring for a down payment of $200 and monthly installments of $88 for 2 years. Assuming that interest is compounded monthly, what interest rate is he paying?

---

▼ **DISCOVERY • DISCUSSION • WRITING**

**29. Present Value of an Annuity**

(a) Draw a time line as in Example 1 to show that the present value of an annuity is the sum of the present values of each payment, that is,

$$A_p = \frac{R}{1+i} + \frac{R}{(1+i)^2} + \frac{R}{(1+i)^3} + \cdots + \frac{R}{(1+i)^n}$$

(b) Use part (a) to derive the formula for $A_p$ given in the text.

**30. An Annuity That Lasts Forever** An **annuity in perpetuity** is one that continues forever. Such annuities are useful in setting up scholarship funds to ensure that the award continues.

(a) Draw a time line (as in Example 1) to show that to set up an annuity in perpetuity of amount $R$ per time period, the amount that must be invested now is

$$A_p = \frac{R}{1+i} + \frac{R}{(1+i)^2} + \frac{R}{(1+i)^3} + \cdots + \frac{R}{(1+i)^n} + \cdots$$

where $i$ is the interest rate per time period.

(b) Find the sum of the infinite series in part (a) to show that

$$A_p = \frac{R}{i}$$

(c) How much money must be invested now at 10% per year, compounded annually, to provide an annuity in perpetuity of $5000 per year? The first payment is due in one year.

**(d)** How much money must be invested now at 8% per year, compounded quarterly, to provide an annuity in perpetuity of $3000 per year? The first payment is due in one year.

**31. Amortizing a Mortgage**  When they bought their house, John and Mary took out a $90,000 mortgage at 9% interest, repayable monthly over 30 years. Their payment is $724.17 per month (check this, using the formula in the text). The bank gave them an **amortization schedule**, which is a table showing how much of each payment is interest, how much goes toward the principal, and the remaining principal after each payment. The table below shows the first few entries in the amortization schedule.

| Payment number | Total payment | Interest payment | Principal payment | Remaining principal |
|---|---|---|---|---|
| 1 | 724.17 | 675.00 | 49.17 | 89,950.83 |
| 2 | 724.17 | 674.63 | 49.54 | 89,901.29 |
| 3 | 724.17 | 674.26 | 49.91 | 89,851.38 |
| 4 | 724.17 | 673.89 | 50.28 | 89,801.10 |

After 10 years they have made 120 payments and are wondering how much they still owe, but they have lost the amortization schedule.

**(a)** How much do John and Mary still owe on their mortgage? [*Hint*: The remaining balance is the present value of the 240 remaining payments.]

**(b)** How much of their next payment is interest and how much goes toward the principal? [*Hint*: Since $9\% \div 12 = 0.75\%$, they must pay 0.75% of the remaining principal in interest each month.]

---

## 9.5 | Mathematical Induction

**LEARNING OBJECTIVE**

After completing this section, you will be able to:

■ Prove a statement using the Principle of Mathematical Induction

There are two aspects to mathematics—discovery and proof—and they are of equal importance. We must discover something before we can attempt to prove it, and we cannot be certain of its truth until it has been proved. In this section we examine the relationship between these two key components of mathematics more closely.

### ■ Conjecture and Proof

Let's try a simple experiment. We add more and more of the odd numbers as follows:

$$1 = 1$$
$$1 + 3 = 4$$
$$1 + 3 + 5 = 9$$
$$1 + 3 + 5 + 7 = 16$$
$$1 + 3 + 5 + 7 + 9 = 25$$

What do you notice about the numbers on the right side of these equations? They are, in fact, all perfect squares. These equations say the following:

The sum of the first 1 odd number is $1^2$.

The sum of the first 2 odd numbers is $2^2$.

The sum of the first 3 odd numbers is $3^2$.

The sum of the first 4 odd numbers is $4^2$.

The sum of the first 5 odd numbers is $5^2$.

Consider the polynomial

$$p(n) = n^2 - n + 41$$

Here are some values of $p(n)$:

$$p(1) = 41 \quad p(2) = 43$$
$$p(3) = 47 \quad p(4) = 53$$
$$p(5) = 61 \quad p(6) = 71$$
$$p(7) = 83 \quad p(8) = 97$$

All the values so far are prime numbers. In fact, if you keep going, you will find that $p(n)$ is prime for all natural numbers up to $n = 40$. It might seem reasonable at this point to conjecture that $p(n)$ is prime for *every* natural number $n$. But that conjecture would be too hasty, because it is easily seen that $p(41)$ is *not* prime. This illustrates that we cannot be certain of the truth of a statement no matter how many special cases we check. We need a convincing argument—a *proof*—to determine the truth of a statement.

This leads naturally to the following question: Is it true that for every natural number $n$, the sum of the first $n$ odd numbers is $n^2$? Could this remarkable property be true? We could try a few more numbers and find that the pattern persists for the first 6, 7, 8, 9, and 10 odd numbers. At this point we feel quite sure that this is always true, so we make a *conjecture*:

The sum of the first $n$ odd numbers is $n^2$.

Since we know that the $n$th odd number is $2n - 1$, we can write this statement more precisely as

$$1 + 3 + 5 + \cdots + (2n - 1) = n^2$$

It is important to realize that this is still a conjecture. We cannot conclude by checking a finite number of cases that a property is true for all numbers (there are infinitely many). To see this more clearly, suppose someone tells us that he has added up the first trillion odd numbers and found that they do *not* add up to 1 trillion squared. What would you tell this person? It would be silly to say that you're sure it's true because you have already checked the first five cases. You could, however, take out paper and pencil and start checking it yourself, but this task would probably take the rest of your life. The tragedy would be that after completing this task, you would still not be sure of the truth of the conjecture! Do you see why?

Herein lies the power of mathematical proof. A **proof** is a clear argument that demonstrates the truth of a statement beyond doubt.

## ■ Mathematical Induction

Let's consider a special kind of proof called **mathematical induction**. Here is how it works: Suppose we have a statement that says something about all natural numbers $n$. Let's call this statement $P$. For example, we could consider the statement

$P$:   For every natural number $n$, the sum of the first $n$ odd numbers is $n^2$.

Since this statement is about *all* natural numbers, it contains infinitely many statements; we will call them $P(1), P(2), \ldots$.

$P(1)$:   The sum of the first 1 odd number is $1^2$.

$P(2)$:   The sum of the first 2 odd numbers is $2^2$.

$P(3)$:   The sum of the first 3 odd numbers is $3^2$.

$$\vdots \qquad\qquad \vdots$$

How can we prove all of these statements at once? Mathematical induction is a clever way of doing just that.

The crux of the idea is this: Suppose we can prove that whenever one of these statements is true, then the one following it in the list is also true. In other words,

For every $k$, if $P(k)$ is true, then $P(k + 1)$ is true.

This is called the **induction step** because it leads us from the truth of one statement to the next. Now, suppose that we can also prove that

$P(1)$ is true.

The induction step now leads us through the following chain of statements:

$P(1)$ is true, so $P(2)$ is true.

$P(2)$ is true, so $P(3)$ is true.

$P(3)$ is true, so $P(4)$ is true.

$$\vdots \qquad\qquad \vdots$$

So we see that if both the induction step and $P(1)$ are proved, then statement $P$ is proved for all $n$. Here is a summary of this important method of proof.

---

### PRINCIPLE OF MATHEMATICAL INDUCTION

For each natural number $n$, let $P(n)$ be a statement depending on $n$. Suppose that the following two conditions are satisfied.

**1.** $P(1)$ is true.

**2.** For every natural number $k$, if $P(k)$ is true then $P(k + 1)$ is true.

Then $P(n)$ is true for all natural numbers $n$.

---

To apply this principle, there are two steps:

**Step 1** Prove that $P(1)$ is true.

**Step 2** Assume that $P(k)$ is true, and use this assumption to prove that $P(k + 1)$ is true.

Notice that in Step 2 we do not prove that $P(k)$ is true. We only show that *if* $P(k)$ is true, *then* $P(k + 1)$ is also true. The assumption that $P(k)$ is true is called the **induction hypothesis**.

We now use mathematical induction to prove that the conjecture that we made at the beginning of this section is true.

▶ **EXAMPLE 1** | A Proof by Mathematical Induction

Prove that for all natural numbers $n$,

$$1 + 3 + 5 + \cdots + (2n - 1) = n^2$$

▼ **SOLUTION** Let $P(n)$ denote the statement $1 + 3 + 5 + \cdots + (2n - 1) = n^2$.

**Step 1** We need to show that $P(1)$ is true. But $P(1)$ is simply the statement that $1 = 1^2$, which is of course true.

**Step 2** We assume that $P(k)$ is true. Thus, our induction hypothesis is

$$1 + 3 + 5 + \cdots + (2k - 1) = k^2$$

We want to use this to show that $P(k + 1)$ is true, that is,

$$1 + 3 + 5 + \cdots + (2k - 1) + [2(k + 1) - 1] = (k + 1)^2$$

[Note that we get $P(k + 1)$ by substituting $k + 1$ for each $n$ in the statement $P(n)$.] We start with the left side and use the induction hypothesis to obtain the right side of the equation:

$$1 + 3 + 5 + \cdots + (2k - 1) + [2(k + 1) - 1]$$

This equals $k^2$ by the induction hypothesis.

$$= [1 + 3 + 5 + \cdots + (2k - 1)] + [2(k + 1) - 1] \qquad \text{Group the first } k \text{ terms}$$

$$= k^2 + [2(k + 1) - 1] \qquad \text{Induction hypothesis}$$

$$= k^2 + [2k + 2 - 1] \qquad \text{Distributive Property}$$

$$= k^2 + 2k + 1 \qquad \text{Simplify}$$

$$= (k + 1)^2 \qquad \text{Factor}$$

Thus, $P(k + 1)$ follows from $P(k)$, and this completes the induction step.

✎ **Practice what you've learned: Do Exercise 3.**    ▲

Having proved Steps 1 and 2, we conclude by the Principle of Mathematical Induction that $P(n)$ is true for all natural numbers $n$.

▶ **EXAMPLE 2** | A Proof by Mathematical Induction

Prove that for every natural number $n$,

$$1 + 2 + 3 + \cdots + n = \frac{n(n + 1)}{2}$$

▼ **SOLUTION**   Let $P(n)$ be the statement $1 + 2 + 3 + \cdots + n = n(n + 1)/2$. We want to show that $P(n)$ is true for all natural numbers $n$.

**Step 1**  We need to show that $P(1)$ is true. But $P(1)$ says that

$$1 = \frac{1(1 + 1)}{2}$$

and this statement is clearly true.

**Step 2**  Assume that $P(k)$ is true. Thus, our induction hypothesis is

$$1 + 2 + 3 + \cdots + k = \frac{k(k + 1)}{2}$$

We want to use this to show that $P(k + 1)$ is true, that is,

$$1 + 2 + 3 + \cdots + k + (k + 1) = \frac{(k + 1)[(k + 1) + 1]}{2}$$

So we start with the left side and use the induction hypothesis to obtain the right side:

$$1 + 2 + 3 + \cdots + k + (k + 1)$$

$$= [1 + 2 + 3 + \cdots + k] + (k + 1) \qquad \text{Group the first } k \text{ terms}$$

This equals $\dfrac{k(k + 1)}{2}$ by the induction process.

$$= \frac{k(k + 1)}{2} + (k + 1) \qquad \text{Induction hypothesis}$$

$$= (k + 1)\left(\frac{k}{2} + 1\right) \qquad \text{Factor } k + 1$$

$$= (k + 1)\left(\frac{k + 2}{2}\right) \qquad \text{Common denominator}$$

$$= \frac{(k + 1)[(k + 1) + 1]}{2} \qquad \text{Write } k + 2 \text{ as } k + 1 + 1$$

Thus, $P(k + 1)$ follows from $P(k)$ and this completes the induction step.

Having proved Steps 1 and 2, we conclude by the Principle of Mathematical Induction that $P(n)$ is true for all natural numbers $n$.

✎ **Practice what you've learned: Do Exercise 5.**    ▲

Formulas for the sums of powers of the first $n$ natural numbers are important in calculus. Formula 1 in the following box is proved in Example 2. The other formulas are also proved by using mathematical induction (see Exercises 6 and 9).

---

**SUMS OF POWERS**

**0.** $\displaystyle\sum_{k=1}^{n} 1 = n$    **1.** $\displaystyle\sum_{k=1}^{n} k = \frac{n(n + 1)}{2}$

**2.** $\displaystyle\sum_{k=1}^{n} k^2 = \frac{n(n + 1)(2n + 1)}{6}$    **3.** $\displaystyle\sum_{k=1}^{n} k^3 = \frac{n^2(n + 1)^2}{4}$

---

It might happen that a statement $P(n)$ is false for the first few natural numbers but true from some number on. For example, we might want to prove that $P(n)$ is true for $n \geq 5$. Notice that if we prove that $P(5)$ is true, then this fact, together with the induction step, would imply the truth of $P(5)$, $P(6)$, $P(7)$, . . . . The next example illustrates this point.

▶ **EXAMPLE 3** | Proving an Inequality by Mathematical Induction

Prove that $4n < 2^n$ for all $n \geq 5$.

▼ **SOLUTION**    Let $P(n)$ denote the statement $4n < 2^n$.

**Step 1** $P(5)$ is the statement that $4 \cdot 5 < 2^5$, or $20 < 32$, which is true.

**Step 2** Assume that $P(k)$ is true. Thus, our induction hypothesis is

$$4k < 2^k$$

We want to use this to show that $P(k + 1)$ is true, that is,

$$4(k + 1) < 2^{k+1}$$

We get $P(k + 1)$ by replacing $k$ by $k + 1$ in the statement $P(k)$.

---

© Archivo Iconografico, S.A./CORBIS

**Blaise Pascal** (1623–1662) is considered one of the most versatile minds in modern history. He was a writer and philosopher as well as a gifted mathematician and physicist. Among his contributions that appear in this book are Pascal's triangle and the Principle of Mathematical Induction.

Pascal's father, himself a mathematician, believed that his son should not study mathematics until he was 15 or 16. But at age 12, Blaise insisted on learning geometry and proved most of its elementary theorems himself. At 19 he invented the first mechanical adding machine. In 1647, after writing a major treatise on the conic sections, he abruptly abandoned mathematics because he felt that his intense studies were contributing to his ill health. He devoted himself instead to frivolous recreations such as gambling, but this only served to pique his interest in probability. In 1654 he miraculously survived a carriage accident in which his horses ran off a bridge. Taking this to be a sign from God, he entered a monastery, where he pursued theology and philosophy, writing his famous *Pensées*. He also continued his mathematical research. He valued faith and intuition more than reason as the source of truth, declaring that "the heart has its own reasons, which reason cannot know."

So we start with the left-hand side of the inequality and use the induction hypothesis to show that it is less than the right-hand side. For $k \geq 5$ we have

$$4(k + 1) = 4k + 4$$

$$< 2^k + 4 \qquad \text{Induction hypothesis}$$

$$< 2^k + 4k \qquad \text{Because } 4 < 4k$$

$$< 2^k + 2^k \qquad \text{Induction hypothesis}$$

$$= 2 \cdot 2^k$$

$$= 2^{k+1} \qquad \text{Property of exponents}$$

Thus, $P(k + 1)$ follows from $P(k)$, and this completes the induction step.

Having proved Steps 1 and 2, we conclude by the Principle of Mathematical Induction that $P(n)$ is true for all natural numbers $n \geq 5$.

✎ **Practice what you've learned: Do Exercise 21.** ▲

# 9.5 EXERCISES

## ▼ CONCEPTS

1. Mathematical induction is a method of proving that a statement $P(n)$ is true for all _____ numbers $n$. In Step 1 we prove that _____ is true.

2. Which of the following is true about Step 2 in a proof by mathematical induction?
   (i) We prove "$P(k + 1)$ is true."
   (ii) We prove "If $P(k)$ is true, then $P(k + 1)$ is true."

## ▼ SKILLS

**3–14** ▪ Use mathematical induction to prove that the formula is true for all natural numbers $n$.

✎ **3.** $2 + 4 + 6 + \cdots + 2n = n(n + 1)$

**4.** $1 + 4 + 7 + \cdots + (3n - 2) = \dfrac{n(3n - 1)}{2}$

✎ **5.** $5 + 8 + 11 + \cdots + (3n + 2) = \dfrac{n(3n + 7)}{2}$

**6.** $1^2 + 2^2 + 3^2 + \cdots + n^2 = \dfrac{n(n + 1)(2n + 1)}{6}$

**7.** $1 \cdot 2 + 2 \cdot 3 + 3 \cdot 4 + \cdots + n(n + 1)$
   $$= \dfrac{n(n + 1)(n + 2)}{3}$$

**8.** $1 \cdot 3 + 2 \cdot 4 + 3 \cdot 5 + \cdots + n(n + 2)$
   $$= \dfrac{n(n + 1)(2n + 7)}{6}$$

**9.** $1^3 + 2^3 + 3^3 + \cdots + n^3 = \dfrac{n^2(n + 1)^2}{4}$

**10.** $1^3 + 3^3 + 5^3 + \cdots + (2n - 1)^3 = n^2(2n^2 - 1)$

**11.** $2^3 + 4^3 + 6^3 + \cdots + (2n)^3 = 2n^2(n + 1)^2$

**12.** $\dfrac{1}{1 \cdot 2} + \dfrac{1}{2 \cdot 3} + \dfrac{1}{3 \cdot 4} + \cdots + \dfrac{1}{n(n + 1)} = \dfrac{n}{(n + 1)}$

**13.** $1 \cdot 2 + 2 \cdot 2^2 + 3 \cdot 2^3 + 4 \cdot 2^4 + \cdots + n \cdot 2^n$
   $$= 2[1 + (n - 1)2^n]$$

**14.** $1 + 2 + 2^2 + \cdots + 2^{n-1} = 2^n - 1$

**15.** Show that $n^2 + n$ is divisible by 2 for all natural numbers $n$.

**16.** Show that $5^n - 1$ is divisible by 4 for all natural numbers $n$.

**17.** Show that $n^2 - n + 41$ is odd for all natural numbers $n$.

**18.** Show that $n^3 - n + 3$ is divisible by 3 for all natural numbers $n$.

**19.** Show that $8^n - 3^n$ is divisible by 5 for all natural numbers $n$.

**20.** Show that $3^{2n} - 1$ is divisible by 8 for all natural numbers $n$.

✎ **21.** Prove that $n < 2^n$ for all natural numbers $n$.

**22.** Prove that $(n + 1)^2 < 2n^2$ for all natural numbers $n \geq 3$.

**23.** Prove that if $x > -1$, then $(1 + x)^n \geq 1 + nx$ for all natural numbers $n$.

**24.** Show that $100n \leq n^2$ for all $n \geq 100$.

**25.** Let $a_{n+1} = 3a_n$ and $a_1 = 5$. Show that $a_n = 5 \cdot 3^{n-1}$ for all natural numbers $n$.

**26.** A sequence is defined recursively by $a_{n+1} = 3a_n - 8$ and $a_1 = 4$. Find an explicit formula for $a_n$, and then use mathematical induction to prove that the formula you found is true.

**27.** Show that $x - y$ is a factor of $x^n - y^n$ for all natural numbers $n$.
   [*Hint*: $x^{k+1} - y^{k+1} = x^k(x - y) + (x^k - y^k)y$.]

**28.** Show that $x + y$ is a factor of $x^{2n-1} + y^{2n-1}$ for all natural numbers $n$.

**29–33** ■ $F_n$ denotes the $n$th term of the Fibonacci sequence discussed in Section 9.1. Use mathematical induction to prove the statement.

**29.** $F_{3n}$ is even for all natural numbers $n$.

**30.** $F_1 + F_2 + F_3 + \cdots + F_n = F_{n+2} - 1$

**31.** $F_1^2 + F_2^2 + F_3^2 + \cdots + F_n^2 = F_n F_{n+1}$

**32.** $F_1 + F_3 + \cdots + F_{2n-1} = F_{2n}$

**33.** For all $n \geq 2$,

$$\begin{bmatrix} 1 & 1 \\ 1 & 0 \end{bmatrix}^n = \begin{bmatrix} F_{n+1} & F_n \\ F_n & F_{n-1} \end{bmatrix}$$

**34.** Let $a_n$ be the $n$th term of the sequence defined recursively by

$$a_{n+1} = \frac{1}{1 + a_n}$$

and $a_1 = 1$. Find a formula for $a_n$ in terms of the Fibonacci numbers $F_n$. Prove that the formula you found is valid for all natural numbers $n$.

**35.** Let $F_n$ be the $n$th term of the Fibonacci sequence. Find and prove an inequality relating $n$ and $F_n$ for natural numbers $n$.

**36.** Find and prove an inequality relating $100n$ and $n^3$.

---

▼ **DISCOVERY • DISCUSSION • WRITING**

**37.** **True or False?** Determine whether each statement is true or false. If you think the statement is true, prove it. If you think it is false, give an example in which it fails.
  **(a)** $p(n) = n^2 - n + 11$ is prime for all $n$.
  **(b)** $n^2 > n$ for all $n \geq 2$.
  **(c)** $2^{2n+1} + 1$ is divisible by 3 for all $n \geq 1$.

  **(d)** $n^3 \geq (n + 1)^2$ for all $n \geq 2$.
  **(e)** $n^3 - n$ is divisible by 3 for all $n \geq 2$.
  **(f)** $n^3 - 6n^2 + 11n$ is divisible by 6 for all $n \geq 1$.

**38.** **All Cats Are Black?** What is wrong with the following "proof" by mathematical induction that all cats are black? Let $P(n)$ denote the statement "In any group of $n$ cats, if one cat is black, then they are all black."

**Step 1** The statement is clearly true for $n = 1$.

**Step 2** Suppose that $P(k)$ is true. We show that $P(k + 1)$ is true.

Suppose we have a group of $k + 1$ cats, one of whom is black; call this cat "Tadpole." Remove some other cat (call it "Sparky") from the group. We are left with $k$ cats, one of whom (Tadpole) is black, so by the induction hypothesis, all $k$ of these are black. Now put Sparky back in the group and take out Tadpole. We again have a group of $k$ cats, all of whom—except possibly Sparky—are black. Then by the induction hypothesis, Sparky must be black too. So all $k + 1$ cats in the original group are black.

Thus, by induction $P(n)$ is true for all $n$. Since everyone has seen at least one black cat, it follows that all cats are black.

Tadpole                 Sparky

---

## 9.6 | The Binomial Theorem

### LEARNING OBJECTIVES

After completing this section, you will be able to:

■ Expand powers of binomials using Pascal's triangle
■ Find binomial coefficients
■ Expand powers of binomials using the Binomial Theorem
■ Find a particular term in a binomial expansion

An expression of the form $a + b$ is called a **binomial**. Although in principle it's easy to raise $a + b$ to any power, raising it to a very high power would be tedious. In this section we find a formula that gives the expansion of $(a + b)^n$ for any natural number $n$ and then prove it using mathematical induction.

## ■ Expanding $(a + b)^n$

To find a pattern in the expansion of $(a + b)^n$, we first look at some special cases:

$$(a + b)^1 = a + b$$
$$(a + b)^2 = a^2 + 2ab + b^2$$
$$(a + b)^3 = a^3 + 3a^2b + 3ab^2 + b^3$$
$$(a + b)^4 = a^4 + 4a^3b + 6a^2b^2 + 4ab^3 + b^4$$
$$(a + b)^5 = a^5 + 5a^4b + 10a^3b^2 + 10a^2b^3 + 5ab^4 + b^5$$
$$\vdots$$

The following simple patterns emerge for the expansion of $(a + b)^n$:

1. There are $n + 1$ terms, the first being $a^n$ and the last being $b^n$.
2. The exponents of $a$ decrease by 1 from term to term, while the exponents of $b$ increase by 1.
3. The sum of the exponents of $a$ and $b$ in each term is $n$.

For instance, notice how the exponents of $a$ and $b$ behave in the expansion of $(a + b)^5$.

**The exponents of $a$ decrease:**

$$(a + b)^5 = a^{\boxed{5}} + 5a^{\boxed{4}}b^1 + 10a^{\boxed{3}}b^2 + 10a^{\boxed{2}}b^3 + 5a^{\boxed{1}}b^4 + b^5$$

**The exponents of $b$ increase:**

$$(a + b)^5 = a^5 + 5a^4b^{\boxed{1}} + 10a^3b^{\boxed{2}} + 10a^2b^{\boxed{3}} + 5a^1b^{\boxed{4}} + b^{\boxed{5}}$$

With these observations we can write the form of the expansion of $(a + b)^n$ for any natural number $n$. For example, writing a question mark for the missing coefficients, we have

$$(a + b)^8 = a^8 + ?\,a^7b + ?\,a^6b^2 + ?\,a^5b^3 + ?\,a^4b^4 + ?\,a^3b^5 + ?\,a^2b^6 + ?\,ab^7 + b^8$$

To complete the expansion, we need to determine these coefficients. To find a pattern, let's write the coefficients in the expansion of $(a + b)^n$ for the first few values of $n$ in a triangular array as shown in the following array, which is called **Pascal's triangle**.

$$(a + b)^0 \qquad\qquad 1$$
$$(a + b)^1 \qquad\qquad 1 \quad 1$$
$$(a + b)^2 \qquad\qquad 1 \quad 2 \quad 1$$
$$(a + b)^3 \qquad\qquad ①\ \ ③\ \ 3 \quad 1$$
$$(a + b)^4 \qquad 1 \quad ④\ \ ⑥\ \ ④\ \ 1$$
$$(a + b)^5 \qquad 1 \quad 5 \quad 10 \quad ⑩\ \ 5 \quad 1$$

The row corresponding to $(a + b)^0$ is called the zeroth row and is included to show the symmetry of the array. The key observation about Pascal's triangle is the following property.

> ### KEY PROPERTY OF PASCAL'S TRIANGLE
>
> Every entry (other than a 1) is the sum of the two entries diagonally above it.

**Pascal's triangle** appears in this Chinese document by Chu Shikie, dated 1303. The title reads "The Old Method Chart of the Seven Multiplying Squares." The triangle was rediscovered by Pascal (see page 636).

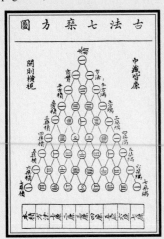

From this property it is easy to find any row of Pascal's triangle from the row above it. For instance, we find the sixth and seventh rows, starting with the fifth row:

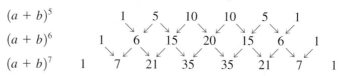

$$(a + b)^5 \qquad 1 \quad 5 \quad 10 \quad 10 \quad 5 \quad 1$$
$$(a + b)^6 \qquad 1 \quad 6 \quad 15 \quad 20 \quad 15 \quad 6 \quad 1$$
$$(a + b)^7 \quad 1 \quad 7 \quad 21 \quad 35 \quad 35 \quad 21 \quad 7 \quad 1$$

To see why this property holds, let's consider the following expansions:

$$(a + b)^5 = a^5 + 5a^4b + 10a^3b^2 + \boxed{10a^2b^3} + \boxed{5ab^4} + b^5$$

$$(a + b)^6 = a^6 + 6a^5b + 15a^4b^2 + 20a^3b^3 + \boxed{15a^2b^4} + 6ab^5 + b^6$$

We arrive at the expansion of $(a + b)^6$ by multiplying $(a + b)^5$ by $(a + b)$. Notice, for instance, that the circled term in the expansion of $(a + b)^6$ is obtained via this multiplication from the two circled terms above it. We get this term when the two terms above it are multiplied by $b$ and $a$, respectively. Thus, its coefficient is the sum of the coefficients of these two terms. We will use this observation at the end of this section when we prove the Binomial Theorem.

Having found these patterns, we can now easily obtain the expansion of any binomial, at least to relatively small powers.

▶ **EXAMPLE 1** | Expanding a Binomial Using Pascal's Triangle

Find the expansion of $(a + b)^7$ using Pascal's triangle.

▼ **SOLUTION** The first term in the expansion is $a^7$, and the last term is $b^7$. Using the fact that the exponent of $a$ decreases by 1 from term to term and that of $b$ increases by 1 from term to term, we have

$$(a + b)^7 = a^7 + \text{?}\, a^6b + \text{?}\, a^5b^2 + \text{?}\, a^4b^3 + \text{?}\, a^3b^4 + \text{?}\, a^2b^5 + \text{?}\, ab^6 + b^7$$

The appropriate coefficients appear in the seventh row of Pascal's triangle. Thus,

$$(a + b)^7 = a^7 + 7a^6b + 21a^5b^2 + 35a^4b^3 + 35a^3b^4 + 21a^2b^5 + 7ab^6 + b^7$$

✎ **Practice what you've learned: Do Exercise 5.** ▲

▶ **EXAMPLE 2** | Expanding a Binomial Using Pascal's Triangle

Use Pascal's triangle to expand $(2 - 3x)^5$.

▼ **SOLUTION** We find the expansion of $(a + b)^5$ and then substitute 2 for $a$ and $-3x$ for $b$. Using Pascal's triangle for the coefficients, we get

$$(a + b)^5 = a^5 + 5a^4b + 10a^3b^2 + 10a^2b^3 + 5ab^4 + b^5$$

Substituting $a = 2$ and $b = -3x$ gives

$$(2 - 3x)^5 = (2)^5 + 5(2)^4(-3x) + 10(2)^3(-3x)^2 + 10(2)^2(-3x)^3 + 5(2)(-3x)^4 + (-3x)^5$$

$$= 32 - 240x + 720x^2 - 1080x^3 + 810x^4 - 243x^5$$

✎ **Practice what you've learned: Do Exercise 13.** ▲

## ■ The Binomial Coefficients

Although Pascal's triangle is useful in finding the binomial expansion for reasonably small values of $n$, it isn't practical for finding $(a + b)^n$ for large values of $n$. The reason is that the method we use for finding the successive rows of Pascal's triangle is recursive. Thus, to find the 100th row of this triangle, we must first find the preceding 99 rows.

We need to examine the pattern in the coefficients more carefully to develop a formula that allows us to calculate directly any coefficient in the binomial expansion. Such a formula exists, and the rest of this section is devoted to finding and proving it. However, to state this formula, we need some notation.

The product of the first $n$ natural numbers is denoted by $n!$ and is called $n$ **factorial**:

$$n! = 1 \cdot 2 \cdot 3 \cdot \cdots \cdot (n-1) \cdot n$$

$4! = 1 \cdot 2 \cdot 3 \cdot 4 = 24$

$7! = 1 \cdot 2 \cdot 3 \cdot 4 \cdot 5 \cdot 6 \cdot 7 = 5040$

$10! = 1 \cdot 2 \cdot 3 \cdot 4 \cdot 5 \cdot 6 \cdot 7 \cdot 8 \cdot 9 \cdot 10$
$= 3,628,800$

We also define $0!$ as follows:

$$0! = 1$$

This definition of $0!$ makes many formulas involving factorials shorter and easier to write.

### THE BINOMIAL COEFFICIENT

Let $n$ and $r$ be nonnegative integers with $r \le n$. The **binomial coefficient** is denoted by $\binom{n}{r}$ and is defined by

$$\binom{n}{r} = \frac{n!}{r!(n-r)!}$$

▶ **EXAMPLE 3** | Calculating Binomial Coefficients

**(a)** $\displaystyle \binom{9}{4} = \frac{9!}{4!(9-4)!} = \frac{9!}{4!5!} = \frac{1 \cdot 2 \cdot 3 \cdot 4 \cdot 5 \cdot 6 \cdot 7 \cdot 8 \cdot 9}{(1 \cdot 2 \cdot 3 \cdot 4)(1 \cdot 2 \cdot 3 \cdot 4 \cdot 5)}$

$\displaystyle = \frac{6 \cdot 7 \cdot 8 \cdot 9}{1 \cdot 2 \cdot 3 \cdot 4} = 126$

**(b)** $\displaystyle \binom{100}{3} = \frac{100!}{3!(100-3)!} = \frac{1 \cdot 2 \cdot 3 \cdots 97 \cdot 98 \cdot 99 \cdot 100}{(1 \cdot 2 \cdot 3)(1 \cdot 2 \cdot 3 \cdots 97)}$

$\displaystyle = \frac{98 \cdot 99 \cdot 100}{1 \cdot 2 \cdot 3} = 161,700$

**(c)** $\displaystyle \binom{100}{97} = \frac{100!}{97!(100-97)!} = \frac{1 \cdot 2 \cdot 3 \cdots 97 \cdot 98 \cdot 99 \cdot 100}{(1 \cdot 2 \cdot 3 \cdots 97)(1 \cdot 2 \cdot 3)}$

$\displaystyle = \frac{98 \cdot 99 \cdot 100}{1 \cdot 2 \cdot 3} = 161,700$

✎ **Practice what you've learned:** Do Exercises 17 and 19.   ▲

Although the binomial coefficient $\binom{n}{r}$ is defined in terms of a fraction, all the results of Example 3 are natural numbers. In fact, $\binom{n}{r}$ is always a natural number (see Exercise 54). Notice that the binomial coefficients in parts (b) and (c) of Example 3 are equal. This is a special case of the following relation, which you are asked to prove in Exercise 52.

$$\binom{n}{r} = \binom{n}{n-r}$$

To see the connection between the binomial coefficients and the binomial expansion of $(a+b)^n$, let's calculate the following binomial coefficients:

$$\binom{5}{2} = \frac{5!}{2!(5-2)!} = 10 \qquad \binom{5}{0} = 1 \qquad \binom{5}{1} = 5 \qquad \binom{5}{2} = 10 \qquad \binom{5}{3} = 10 \qquad \binom{5}{4} = 5 \qquad \binom{5}{5} = 1$$

These are precisely the entries in the fifth row of Pascal's triangle. In fact, we can write Pascal's triangle as follows.

$$\binom{0}{0}$$

$$\binom{1}{0} \quad \binom{1}{1}$$

$$\binom{2}{0} \quad \binom{2}{1} \quad \binom{2}{2}$$

$$\binom{3}{0} \quad \binom{3}{1} \quad \binom{3}{2} \quad \binom{3}{3}$$

$$\binom{4}{0} \quad \binom{4}{1} \quad \binom{4}{2} \quad \binom{4}{3} \quad \binom{4}{4}$$

$$\binom{5}{0} \quad \binom{5}{1} \quad \binom{5}{2} \quad \binom{5}{3} \quad \binom{5}{4} \quad \binom{5}{5}$$

$$\cdot \qquad \cdot \qquad \cdot \qquad \cdot \qquad \cdot \qquad \cdot$$

$$\binom{n}{0} \quad \binom{n}{1} \quad \binom{n}{2} \quad \cdot \quad \cdot \quad \cdot \quad \binom{n}{n-1} \quad \binom{n}{n}$$

To demonstrate that this pattern holds, we need to show that any entry in this version of Pascal's triangle is the sum of the two entries diagonally above it. In other words, we must show that each entry satisfies the key property of Pascal's triangle. We now state this property in terms of the binomial coefficients.

---

**KEY PROPERTY OF THE BINOMIAL COEFFICIENTS**

For any nonnegative integers $r$ and $k$ with $r \leq k$,

$$\binom{k}{r-1} + \binom{k}{r} = \binom{k+1}{r}$$

---

Notice that the two terms on the left side of this equation are adjacent entries in the $k$th row of Pascal's triangle and the term on the right side is the entry diagonally below them, in the $(k + 1)$st row. Thus, this equation is a restatement of the key property of Pascal's triangle in terms of the binomial coefficients. A proof of this formula is outlined in Exercise 53.

## ■ The Binomial Theorem

We are now ready to state the Binomial Theorem.

---

**THE BINOMIAL THEOREM**

$$(a + b)^n = \binom{n}{0}a^n + \binom{n}{1}a^{n-1}b + \binom{n}{2}a^{n-2}b^2 + \cdots + \binom{n}{n-1}ab^{n-1} + \binom{n}{n}b^n$$

---

We prove this theorem at the end of this section. First, let's look at some of its applications.

▶ **EXAMPLE 4** | Expanding a Binomial Using the Binomial Theorem

Use the Binomial Theorem to expand $(x + y)^4$.

▼ **SOLUTION**   By the Binomial Theorem,

$$(x + y)^4 = \binom{4}{0}x^4 + \binom{4}{1}x^3y + \binom{4}{2}x^2y^2 + \binom{4}{3}xy^3 + \binom{4}{4}y^4$$

Verify that

$$\binom{4}{0} = 1 \qquad \binom{4}{1} = 4 \qquad \binom{4}{2} = 6 \qquad \binom{4}{3} = 4 \qquad \binom{4}{4} = 1$$

It follows that

$$(x + y)^4 = x^4 + 4x^3y + 6x^2y^2 + 4xy^3 + y^4$$

✎ **Practice what you've learned: Do Exercise 25.**   ▲

▶ **EXAMPLE 5** | Expanding a Binomial Using the Binomial Theorem

Use the Binomial Theorem to expand $(\sqrt{x} - 1)^8$.

▼ **SOLUTION**   We first find the expansion of $(a + b)^8$ and then substitute $\sqrt{x}$ for $a$ and $-1$ for $b$. Using the Binomial Theorem, we have

$$(a + b)^8 = \binom{8}{0}a^8 + \binom{8}{1}a^7b + \binom{8}{2}a^6b^2 + \binom{8}{3}a^5b^3 + \binom{8}{4}a^4b^4$$
$$+ \binom{8}{5}a^3b^5 + \binom{8}{6}a^2b^6 + \binom{8}{7}ab^7 + \binom{8}{8}b^8$$

Verify that

$$\binom{8}{0} = 1 \qquad \binom{8}{1} = 8 \qquad \binom{8}{2} = 28 \qquad \binom{8}{3} = 56 \qquad \binom{8}{4} = 70$$

$$\binom{8}{5} = 56 \qquad \binom{8}{6} = 28 \qquad \binom{8}{7} = 8 \qquad \binom{8}{8} = 1$$

So

$$(a + b)^8 = a^8 + 8a^7b + 28a^6b^2 + 56a^5b^3 + 70a^4b^4 + 56a^3b^5$$
$$+ 28a^2b^6 + 8ab^7 + b^8$$

Performing the substitutions $a = x^{1/2}$ and $b = -1$ gives

$$(\sqrt{x} - 1)^8 = (x^{1/2})^8 + 8(x^{1/2})^7(-1) + 28(x^{1/2})^6(-1)^2 + 56(x^{1/2})^5(-1)^3$$
$$+ 70(x^{1/2})^4(-1)^4 + 56(x^{1/2})^3(-1)^5 + 28(x^{1/2})^2(-1)^6$$
$$+ 8(x^{1/2})(-1)^7 + (-1)^8$$

This simplifies to

$$(\sqrt{x} - 1)^8 = x^4 - 8x^{7/2} + 28x^3 - 56x^{5/2} + 70x^2 - 56x^{3/2} + 28x - 8x^{1/2} + 1$$

✎ **Practice what you've learned: Do Exercise 27.**   ▲

The Binomial Theorem can be used to find a particular term of a binomial expansion without having to find the entire expansion.

---

**GENERAL TERM OF THE BINOMIAL EXPANSION**

The term that contains $a^r$ in the expansion of $(a + b)^n$ is

$$\binom{n}{n-r}a^r b^{n-r}$$

---

▶ **EXAMPLE 6** │ Finding a Particular Term in a Binomial Expansion

Find the term that contains $x^5$ in the expansion of $(2x + y)^{20}$.

▼ **SOLUTION**   The term that contains $x^5$ is given by the formula for the general term with $a = 2x$, $b = y$, $n = 20$, and $r = 5$. So this term is

$$\binom{20}{15}a^5 b^{15} = \frac{20!}{15!(20-15)!}(2x)^5 y^{15} = \frac{20!}{15!5!}32x^5 y^{15} = 496{,}128x^5 y^{15}$$

✎ **Practice what you've learned: Do Exercise 39.**                                ▲

▶ **EXAMPLE 7** │ Finding a Particular Term in a Binomial Expansion

Find the coefficient of $x^8$ in the expansion of $\left( x^2 + \dfrac{1}{x} \right)^{10}$.

▼ **SOLUTION**   Both $x^2$ and $1/x$ are powers of $x$, so the power of $x$ in each term of the expansion is determined by both terms of the binomial. To find the required coefficient, we first find the general term in the expansion. By the formula we have $a = x^2$, $b = 1/x$, and $n = 10$, so the general term is

$$\binom{10}{10-r}(x^2)^r\left(\frac{1}{x}\right)^{10-r} = \binom{10}{10-r}x^{2r}(x^{-1})^{10-r} = \binom{10}{10-r}x^{3r-10}$$

Thus, the term that contains $x^8$ is the term in which

$$3r - 10 = 8$$
$$r = 6$$

---

© Bill Sanderson /Science Photo Library/ Photo Researchers, Inc.

**Sir Isaac Newton** (1642–1727) is universally regarded as one of the giants of physics and mathematics. He is well known for discovering the laws of motion and gravity and for inventing the calculus, but he also proved the Binomial Theorem and the laws of optics, and he developed methods for solving polynomial equations to any desired accuracy. He was born on Christmas Day, a few months after the death of his father. After an unhappy childhood, he entered Cambridge University, where he learned mathematics by studying the writings of Euclid and Descartes.

During the plague years of 1665 and 1666, when the university was closed, Newton thought and wrote about ideas that, once published, instantly revolutionized the sciences. Imbued with a pathological fear of criticism, he published these writings only after many years of encouragement from Edmund Halley (who discovered the now-famous comet) and other colleagues.

Newton's works brought him enormous fame and prestige. Even poets were moved to praise; Alexander Pope wrote:

> Nature and Nature's Laws
> lay hid in Night.
> God said, "Let Newton be"
> and all was Light.

Newton was far more modest about his accomplishments. He said, "I seem to have been only like a boy playing on the seashore . . . while the great ocean of truth lay all undiscovered before me." Newton was knighted by Queen Anne in 1705 and was buried with great honor in Westminster Abbey.

So the required coefficient is

$$\binom{10}{10-6} = \binom{10}{4} = 210$$

✎ **Practice what you've learned: Do Exercise 41.** ▲

## ■ Proof of the Binomial Theorem

We now give a proof of the Binomial Theorem using mathematical induction.

▼ **PROOF**   Let $P(n)$ denote the statement

$$(a+b)^n = \binom{n}{0}a^n + \binom{n}{1}a^{n-1}b + \binom{n}{2}a^{n-2}b^2 + \cdots + \binom{n}{n-1}ab^{n-1} + \binom{n}{n}b^n$$

**Step 1**   We show that $P(1)$ is true. But $P(1)$ is just the statement

$$(a+b)^1 = \binom{1}{0}a^1 + \binom{1}{1}b^1 = 1a + 1b = a + b$$

which is certainly true.

**Step 2**   We assume that $P(k)$ is true. Thus, our induction hypothesis is

$$(a+b)^k = \binom{k}{0}a^k + \binom{k}{1}a^{k-1}b + \binom{k}{2}a^{k-2}b^2 + \cdots + \binom{k}{k-1}ab^{k-1} + \binom{k}{k}b^k$$

We use this to show that $P(k+1)$ is true.

$$(a+b)^{k+1} = (a+b)[(a+b)^k]$$

$$= (a+b)\left[\binom{k}{0}a^k + \binom{k}{1}a^{k-1}b + \binom{k}{2}a^{k-2}b^2 + \cdots + \binom{k}{k-1}ab^{k-1} + \binom{k}{k}b^k\right] \quad \text{Induction hypothesis}$$

$$= a\left[\binom{k}{0}a^k + \binom{k}{1}a^{k-1}b + \binom{k}{2}a^{k-2}b^2 + \cdots + \binom{k}{k-1}ab^{k-1} + \binom{k}{k}b^k\right]$$

$$\quad + b\left[\binom{k}{0}a^k + \binom{k}{1}a^{k-1}b + \binom{k}{2}a^{k-2}b^2 + \cdots + \binom{k}{k-1}ab^{k-1} + \binom{k}{k}b^k\right] \quad \text{Distributive Property}$$

$$= \binom{k}{0}a^{k+1} + \binom{k}{1}a^k b + \binom{k}{2}a^{k-1}b^2 + \cdots + \binom{k}{k-1}a^2 b^{k-1} + \binom{k}{k}ab^k$$

$$\quad + \binom{k}{0}a^k b + \binom{k}{1}a^{k-1}b^2 + \binom{k}{2}a^{k-2}b^3 + \cdots + \binom{k}{k-1}ab^k + \binom{k}{k}b^{k+1} \quad \text{Distributive Property}$$

$$= \binom{k}{0}a^{k+1} + \left[\binom{k}{0} + \binom{k}{1}\right]a^k b + \left[\binom{k}{1} + \binom{k}{2}\right]a^{k-1}b^2$$

$$\quad + \cdots + \left[\binom{k}{k-1} + \binom{k}{k}\right]ab^k + \binom{k}{k}b^{k+1} \quad \text{Group like terms}$$

Using the key property of the binomial coefficients, we can write each of the expressions in square brackets as a single binomial coefficient. Also, writing the first and last coefficients as $\binom{k+1}{0}$ and $\binom{k+1}{k+1}$ (these are equal to 1 by Exercise 50) gives

$$(a+b)^{k+1} = \binom{k+1}{0}a^{k+1} + \binom{k+1}{1}a^k b + \binom{k+1}{2}a^{k-1}b^2 + \cdots + \binom{k+1}{k}ab^k + \binom{k+1}{k+1}b^{k+1}$$

But this last equation is precisely $P(k+1)$, and this completes the induction step.

Having proved Steps 1 and 2, we conclude by the Principle of Mathematical Induction that the theorem is true for all natural numbers $n$. ▲

# 9.6 EXERCISES

## ▼ CONCEPTS

**1.** An algebraic expression of the form $a + b$, which consists of a sum of two terms, is called a _____.

**2.** We can find the coefficients in the expansion of $(a + b)^n$ from the $n$th row of _____ triangle. So $(a + b)^4 =$ $\blacksquare a^4 + \blacksquare a^3b + \blacksquare a^2b^2 + \blacksquare ab^3 + \blacksquare b^4$.

**3.** The binomial coefficients can be calculated directly by using the formula $\binom{n}{k} =$ _____. So $\binom{4}{3} =$ _____.

**4.** To expand $(a + b)^n$, we can use the _____ Theorem. Using this theorem, we find

$(a + b)^4 =$

$$\binom{\blacksquare}{\blacksquare}a^4 + \binom{\blacksquare}{\blacksquare}a^3b + \binom{\blacksquare}{\blacksquare}a^2b^2 + \binom{\blacksquare}{\blacksquare}ab^3 + \binom{\blacksquare}{\blacksquare}b^4$$

## ▼ SKILLS

**5–16** ▪ Use Pascal's triangle to expand the expression.

**5.** $(x + y)^6$  **6.** $(2x + 1)^4$  **7.** $\left(x + \dfrac{1}{x}\right)^4$

**8.** $(x - y)^5$  **9.** $(x - 1)^5$  **10.** $(\sqrt{a} + \sqrt{b})^6$

**11.** $(x^2y - 1)^5$  **12.** $(1 + \sqrt{2})^6$  **13.** $(2x - 3y)^3$

**14.** $(1 + x^3)^3$  **15.** $\left(\dfrac{1}{x} - \sqrt{x}\right)^5$  **16.** $\left(2 + \dfrac{x}{2}\right)^5$

**17–24** ▪ Evaluate the expression.

**17.** $\dbinom{6}{4}$  **18.** $\dbinom{8}{3}$  **19.** $\dbinom{100}{98}$

**20.** $\dbinom{10}{5}$  **21.** $\dbinom{3}{1}\dbinom{4}{2}$  **22.** $\dbinom{5}{2}\dbinom{5}{3}$

**23.** $\dbinom{5}{0} + \dbinom{5}{1} + \dbinom{5}{2} + \dbinom{5}{3} + \dbinom{5}{4} + \dbinom{5}{5}$

**24.** $\dbinom{5}{0} - \dbinom{5}{1} + \dbinom{5}{2} - \dbinom{5}{3} + \dbinom{5}{4} - \dbinom{5}{5}$

**25–28** ▪ Use the Binomial Theorem to expand the expression.

**25.** $(x + 2y)^4$  **26.** $(1 - x)^5$

**27.** $\left(1 + \dfrac{1}{x}\right)^6$  **28.** $(2A + B^2)^4$

**29.** Find the first three terms in the expansion of $(x + 2y)^{20}$.

**30.** Find the first four terms in the expansion of $(x^{1/2} + 1)^{30}$.

**31.** Find the last two terms in the expansion of $(a^{2/3} + a^{1/3})^{25}$.

**32.** Find the first three terms in the expansion of

$$\left(x + \dfrac{1}{x}\right)^{40}$$

**33.** Find the middle term in the expansion of $(x^2 + 1)^{18}$.

**34.** Find the fifth term in the expansion of $(ab - 1)^{20}$.

**35.** Find the 24th term in the expansion of $(a + b)^{25}$.

**36.** Find the 28th term in the expansion of $(A - B)^{30}$.

**37.** Find the 100th term in the expansion of $(1 + y)^{100}$.

**38.** Find the second term in the expansion of

$$\left(x^2 - \dfrac{1}{x}\right)^{25}$$

**39.** Find the term containing $x^4$ in the expansion of $(x + 2y)^{10}$.

**40.** Find the term containing $y^3$ in the expansion of $(\sqrt{2} + y)^{12}$.

**41.** Find the term containing $b^8$ in the expansion of $(a + b^2)^{12}$.

**42.** Find the term that does not contain $x$ in the expansion of

$$\left(8x + \dfrac{1}{2x}\right)^8$$

**43–46** ▪ Factor using the Binomial Theorem.

**43.** $x^4 + 4x^3y + 6x^2y^2 + 4xy^3 + y^4$

**44.** $(x - 1)^5 + 5(x - 1)^4 + 10(x - 1)^3 +$ $10(x - 1)^2 + 5(x - 1) + 1$

**45.** $8a^3 + 12a^2b + 6ab^2 + b^3$

**46.** $x^8 + 4x^6y + 6x^4y^2 + 4x^2y^3 + y^4$

**47–52** ▪ Simplify using the Binomial Theorem.

**47.** $\dfrac{(x + h)^3 - x^3}{h}$  **48.** $\dfrac{(x + h)^4 - x^4}{h}$

**49.** Show that $(1.01)^{100} > 2$.
[*Hint*: Note that $(1.01)^{100} = (1 + 0.01)^{100}$, and use the Binomial Theorem to show that the sum of the first two terms of the expansion is greater than 2.]

**50.** Show that $\dbinom{n}{0} = 1$ and $\dbinom{n}{n} = 1$.

**51.** Show that $\dbinom{n}{1} = \dbinom{n}{n - 1} = n$.

**52.** Show that $\dbinom{n}{r} = \dbinom{n}{n - r}$ for $0 \le r \le n$.

**53.** In this exercise we prove the identity

$$\dbinom{n}{r - 1} + \dbinom{n}{r} = \dbinom{n + 1}{r}$$

(a) Write the left-hand side of this equation as the sum of two fractions.

(b) Show that a common denominator of the expression that you found in part (a) is $r!(n - r + 1)!$.

(c) Add the two fractions using the common denominator in part (b), simplify the numerator, and note that the resulting expression is equal to the right-hand side of the equation.

**54.** Prove that $\binom{n}{r}$ is an integer for all $n$ and for $0 \le r \le n$. [*Suggestion:* Use induction to show that the statement is true for all $n$, and use Exercise 53 for the induction step.]

## ▼ DISCOVERY • DISCUSSION • WRITING

**55. Powers of Factorials**   Which is larger, $(100!)^{101}$ or $(101!)^{100}$? [*Hint:* Try factoring the expressions. Do they have any common factors?]

**56. Sums of Binomial Coefficients**   Add each of the first five rows of Pascal's triangle, as indicated. Do you see a pattern?

$$1 + 1 = \boxed{?}$$
$$1 + 2 + 1 = \boxed{?}$$
$$1 + 3 + 3 + 1 = \boxed{?}$$
$$1 + 4 + 6 + 4 + 1 = \boxed{?}$$
$$1 + 5 + 10 + 10 + 5 + 1 = \boxed{?}$$

On the basis of the pattern you have found, find the sum of the $n$th row:

$$\binom{n}{0} + \binom{n}{1} + \binom{n}{2} + \cdots + \binom{n}{n}$$

Prove your result by expanding $(1 + 1)^n$ using the Binomial Theorem.

**57. Alternating Sums of Binomial Coefficients**   Find the sum

$$\binom{n}{0} - \binom{n}{1} + \binom{n}{2} - \cdots + (-1)^n\binom{n}{n}$$

by finding a pattern as in Exercise 56. Prove your result by expanding $(1 - 1)^n$ using the Binomial Theorem.

---

## ▶ CHAPTER 9 | REVIEW

## ▼ PROPERTIES AND FORMULAS

### Sequences (p. 600)

A **sequence** is a function whose domain is the set of natural numbers. Instead of writing $a(n)$ for the value of the sequence at $n$, we generally write $a_n$, and we refer to this value as the **$n$th term** of the sequence. Sequences are often described in list form:

$$a_1, a_2, a_3, \ldots$$

### Partial Sums of a Sequence (pp. 605–606)

For the sequence $a_1, a_2, a_3, \ldots$ the **$n$th partial sum** $S_n$ is the sum of the first $n$ terms of the sequence:

$$S_n = a_1 + a_2 + a_3 + \cdots + a_n$$

The $n$th partial sum of a sequence can also be expressed by using **sigma notation**:

$$S_n = \sum_{k=1}^{n} a_k$$

### Arithmetic Sequences (p. 611)

An **arithmetic sequence** is a sequence whose terms are obtained by adding the same fixed constant $d$ to each term to get the next term. Thus, an arithmetic sequence has the form

$$a, a + d, a + 2d, a + 3d, \ldots$$

The number $a$ is the **first term** of the sequence, and the number $d$ is the **common difference**. The $n$th term of the sequence is

$$a_n = a + (n - 1)d$$

### Partial Sums of an Arithmetic Sequence (p. 613)

For the arithmetic sequence $a_n = a + (n - 1)d$ the $n$th partial sum $S_n = \sum_{k=1}^{n} [a + (k - 1)d]$ is given by either of the following equivalent formulas:

**1.**
$$S_n = \frac{n}{2}[2a + (n - 1)d]$$

**2.**
$$S_n = n\left(\frac{a + a_n}{2}\right)$$

### Geometric Sequences (p. 617)

A **geometric sequence** is a sequence whose terms are obtained by multiplying each term by the same fixed constant $r$ to get the next term. Thus, a geometric sequence has the form

$$a, ar, ar^2, ar^3, \ldots$$

The number $a$ is the **first term** of the sequence, and the number $r$ is the **common ratio**. The $n$th term of the sequence is

$$a_n = ar^{n-1}$$

### Partial Sums of a Geometric Sequence (p. 619)

For the geometric sequence $a_n = ar^{n-1}$ the $n$th partial sum $S_n = \sum_{k=1}^{n} ar^{k-1}$ (where $r \ne 1$) is given by

$$S_n = a\frac{1 - r^n}{1 - r}$$

## Infinite Geometric Series (p. 621)

An **infinite geometric series** is a series of the form

$$a + ar + ar^2 + ar^3 + \cdots + ar^{n-1} + \cdots$$

An infinite series for which $|r| < 1$ has the sum

$$S = \frac{a}{1 - r}$$

## Amount of an Annuity (p. 627)

The amount $A_f$ of an **annuity** consisting of $n$ regular equal payments of size $R$ with interest rate $i$ per time period is given by

$$A_f = R\frac{(1 + i)^n - 1}{i}$$

## Present Value of an Annuity (p. 628)

The **present value** $A_p$ of an annuity consisting of $n$ regular equal payments of size $R$ with interest rate $i$ per time period is given by

$$A_p = R\frac{1 - (1 + i)^{-n}}{i}$$

## Present Value of a Future Amount (p. 628)

If an amount $A_f$ is to be paid in one lump sum, $n$ time periods from now, and the interest rate per time period is $i$, then its **present value** $A_p$ is given by

$$A_p = A_f(1 + i)^{-n}$$

## Installment Buying (p. 629)

If a loan $A_p$ is to be repaid in $n$ regular equal payments with interest rate $i$ per time period, then the size $R$ of each payment is given by

$$R = \frac{iA_p}{1 - (1 + i)^{-n}}$$

## Principle of Mathematical Induction (p. 634)

For each natural number $n$, let $P(n)$ be a statement that depends on $n$. Suppose that each of the following conditions is satisfied.

1. $P(1)$ is true.
2. For every natural number $k$, if $P(k)$ is true, then $P(k + 1)$ is true.

Then $P(n)$ is true for all natural numbers $n$.

## Sums of Powers (p. 636)

**0.** $\displaystyle\sum_{k=1}^{n} 1 = n$     **1.** $\displaystyle\sum_{k=1}^{n} k = \frac{n(n + 1)}{2}$

**2.** $\displaystyle\sum_{k=1}^{n} k^2 = \frac{n(n + 1)(2n + 1)}{6}$     **3.** $\displaystyle\sum_{k=1}^{n} k^3 = \frac{n^2(n + 1)^2}{4}$

## Binomial Coefficients (pp. 641–642)

If $n$ and $r$ are positive integers with $n \geq r$, then the **binomial coefficient** $\binom{n}{r}$ is defined by

$$\binom{n}{r} = \frac{n!}{r!(n - r)!}$$

Binomial coefficients satisfy the following properties:

$$\binom{n}{r} = \binom{n}{n - r}$$

$$\binom{k}{r - 1} + \binom{k}{r} = \binom{k + 1}{r}$$

## The Binomial Theorem (p. 642)

$$(a + b)^n = \binom{n}{0}a^n + \binom{n}{1}a^{n-1}b + \binom{n}{2}a^{n-2}b^2 + \cdots + \binom{n}{n}b^n$$

## ▼ CONCEPT SUMMARY

### Section 9.1

- Find the terms of a sequence
- Find the terms of a recursive sequence
- Find the partial sums of a sequence
- Use sigma notation

### Section 9.2

- Find the terms of an arithmetic sequence
- Find the partial sums of an arithmetic sequence

### Section 9.3

- Find the terms of a geometric sequence
- Find the partial sums of a geometric sequence
- Find the sum of an infinite geometric series

### Section 9.4

- Find the amount of an annuity
- Find the present value of an annuity
- Find the amount of the installment payments on a loan

### Section 9.5

- Prove a statement using the Principle of Mathematical Induction

**Review Exercises**

1–6, 11(a)–14(a)

7–10

11(c)–14(c), 37–40

37–48

**Review Exercises**

11, 14, 15–17, 25, 26, 30

50–52, 59

**Review Exercises**

12, 13, 18, 19, 21–24, 27–29, 31

49, 53–54, 60, 61

55–58

**Review Exercises**

62

63

64

**Review Exercises**

65–70

**Section 9.6**

- Expand a binomial using Pascal's triangle
- Find binomial coefficients
- Expand a binomial using the Binomial Theorem
- Find a particular term in a binomial expansion

## ▼ EXERCISES

**1–6** ■ Find the first four terms as well as the tenth term of the sequence with the given $n$th term.

**1.** $a_n = \dfrac{n^2}{n+1}$      **2.** $a_n = (-1)^n \dfrac{2^n}{n}$

**3.** $a_n = \dfrac{(-1)^n + 1}{n^3}$      **4.** $a_n = \dfrac{n(n+1)}{2}$

**5.** $a_n = \dfrac{(2n)!}{2^n n!}$      **6.** $a_n = \dbinom{n+1}{2}$

**7–10** ■ A sequence is defined recursively. Find the first seven terms of the sequence.

**7.** $a_n = a_{n-1} + 2n - 1, \quad a_1 = 1$

**8.** $a_n = \dfrac{a_{n-1}}{n}, \quad a_1 = 1$

**9.** $a_n = a_{n-1} + 2a_{n-2}, \quad a_1 = 1, a_2 = 3$

**10.** $a_n = \sqrt{3a_{n-1}}, \quad a_1 = \sqrt{3}$

**11–14** ■ The $n$th term of a sequence is given.
**(a)** Find the first five terms of the sequence.
**(b)** Graph the terms you found in part (a).
**(c)** Find the fifth partial sum of the sequence.
**(d)** Determine whether the series is arithmetic or geometric. Find the common difference or the common ratio.

**11.** $a_n = 2n + 5$      **12.** $a_n = \dfrac{5}{2^n}$

**13.** $a_n = \dfrac{3^n}{2^{n+1}}$      **14.** $a_n = 4 - \dfrac{n}{2}$

**15–22** ■ The first four terms of a sequence are given. Determine whether they can be the terms of an arithmetic sequence, a geometric sequence, or neither. If the sequence is arithmetic or geometric, find the fifth term.

**15.** $5, 5.5, 6, 6.5, \ldots$      **16.** $\sqrt{2}, 2\sqrt{2}, 3\sqrt{2}, 4\sqrt{2}, \ldots$

**17.** $t - 3, t - 2, t - 1, t, \ldots$      **18.** $\sqrt{2}, 2, 2\sqrt{2}, 4, \ldots$

**19.** $t^3, t^2, t, 1, \ldots$      **20.** $1, -\tfrac{3}{2}, 2, -\tfrac{5}{2}, \ldots$

**21.** $\dfrac{3}{4}, \dfrac{1}{2}, \dfrac{1}{3}, \dfrac{2}{9}, \ldots$      **22.** $a, 1, \dfrac{1}{a}, \dfrac{1}{a^2}, \ldots$

**23.** Show that $3, 6i, -12, -24i, \ldots$ is a geometric sequence, and find the common ratio. (Here $i = \sqrt{-1}$.)

**24.** Find the $n$th term of the geometric sequence $2, 2 + 2i, 4i, -4 + 4i, -8, \ldots$ (Here $i = \sqrt{-1}$.)

**25.** The sixth term of an arithmetic sequence is 17, and the fourth term is 11. Find the second term.

**26.** The 20th term of an arithmetic sequence is 96, and the common difference is 5. Find the $n$th term.

**27.** The third term of a geometric sequence is 9, and the common ratio is $\frac{3}{2}$. Find the fifth term.

**28.** The second term of a geometric sequence is 10, and the fifth term is $\frac{1250}{27}$. Find the $n$th term.

**29.** A teacher makes $32,000 in his first year at Lakeside School and gets a 5% raise each year.
**(a)** Find a formula for his salary $A_n$ in his $n$th year at this school.
**(b)** List his salaries for his first 8 years at this school.

**30.** A colleague of the teacher in Exercise 29, hired at the same time, makes $35,000 in her first year, and gets a $1200 raise each year.
**(a)** What is her salary $A_n$ in her $n$th year at this school?
**(b)** Find her salary in her eighth year at this school, and compare it to the salary of the teacher in Exercise 29 in his eighth year.

**31.** A certain type of bacteria divides every 5 s. If three of these bacteria are put into a petri dish, how many bacteria are in the dish at the end of 1 min?

**32.** If $a_1, a_2, a_3, \ldots$ and $b_1, b_2, b_3, \ldots$ are arithmetic sequences, show that $a_1 + b_1, a_2 + b_2, a_3 + b_3, \ldots$ is also an arithmetic sequence.

**33.** If $a_1, a_2, a_3, \ldots$ and $b_1, b_2, b_3, \ldots$ are geometric sequences, show that $a_1b_1, a_2b_2, a_3b_3, \ldots$ is also a geometric sequence.

**34. (a)** If $a_1, a_2, a_3, \ldots$ is an arithmetic sequence, is the sequence $a_1 + 2, a_2 + 2, a_3 + 2, \ldots$ arithmetic?
**(b)** If $a_1, a_2, a_3, \ldots$ is a geometric sequence, is the sequence $5a_1, 5a_2, 5a_3, \ldots$ geometric?

**35.** Find the values of $x$ for which the sequence $6, x, 12, \ldots$ is
**(a)** arithmetic      **(b)** geometric

**36.** Find the values of $x$ and $y$ for which the sequence $2, x, y, 17, \ldots$ is
**(a)** arithmetic      **(b)** geometric

**37–40** ■ Find the sum.

**37.** $\displaystyle\sum_{k=3}^{6} (k+1)^2$      **38.** $\displaystyle\sum_{i=1}^{4} \frac{2i}{2i-1}$

**39.** $\displaystyle\sum_{k=1}^{6} (k+1)2^{k-1}$      **40.** $\displaystyle\sum_{m=1}^{5} 3^{m-2}$

**41–44** ■ Write the sum without using sigma notation. Do not evaluate.

**41.** $\displaystyle\sum_{k=1}^{10} (k-1)^2$      **42.** $\displaystyle\sum_{j=2}^{100} \frac{1}{j-1}$

**43.** $\displaystyle\sum_{k=1}^{50} \frac{3^k}{2^{k+1}}$      **44.** $\displaystyle\sum_{n=1}^{10} n^2 2^n$

**45–48** ■ Write the sum using sigma notation. Do not evaluate.

**45.** $3 + 6 + 9 + 12 + \cdots + 99$

**46.** $1^2 + 2^2 + 3^2 + \cdots + 100^2$

**47.** $1 \cdot 2^3 + 2 \cdot 2^4 + 3 \cdot 2^5 + 4 \cdot 2^6 + \cdots + 100 \cdot 2^{102}$

**48.** $\dfrac{1}{1 \cdot 2} + \dfrac{1}{2 \cdot 3} + \dfrac{1}{3 \cdot 4} + \cdots + \dfrac{1}{999 \cdot 1000}$

**49–54** ■ Determine whether the expression is a partial sum of an arithmetic or geometric sequence. Then find the sum.

**49.** $1 + 0.9 + (0.9)^2 + \cdots + (0.9)^5$

**50.** $3 + 3.7 + 4.4 + \cdots + 10$

**51.** $\sqrt{5} + 2\sqrt{5} + 3\sqrt{5} + \cdots + 100\sqrt{5}$

**52.** $\frac{1}{3} + \frac{2}{3} + 1 + \frac{4}{3} + \cdots + 33$

**53.** $\displaystyle\sum_{n=0}^{6} 3(-4)^n$     **54.** $\displaystyle\sum_{k=0}^{8} 7(5)^{k/2}$

**55–58** ■ Find the sum of the infinite geometric series.

**55.** $1 - \frac{2}{5} + \frac{4}{25} - \frac{8}{125} + \cdots$

**56.** $0.1 + 0.01 + 0.001 + 0.0001 + \cdots$

**57.** $1 + \dfrac{1}{3^{1/2}} + \dfrac{1}{3} + \dfrac{1}{3^{3/2}} + \cdots$

**58.** $a + ab^2 + ab^4 + ab^6 + \cdots$

**59.** The first term of an arithmetic sequence is $a = 7$, and the common difference is $d = 3$. How many terms of this sequence must be added to obtain 325?

**60.** The sum of the first three terms of a geometric series is 52, and the common ratio is $r = 3$. Find the first term.

**61.** A person has two parents, four grandparents, eight great-grandparents, and so on. What is the total number of a person's ancestors in 15 generations?

**62.** Find the amount of an annuity consisting of 16 annual payments of $1000 each into an account that pays 8% interest per year, compounded annually.

**63.** How much money should be invested every quarter at 12% per year, compounded quarterly, in order to have $10,000 in one year?

**64.** What are the monthly payments on a mortgage of $60,000 at 9% interest if the loan is to be repaid in
   **(a)** 30 years?          **(b)** 15 years?

**65–67** ■ Use mathematical induction to prove that the formula is true for all natural numbers $n$.

**65.** $1 + 4 + 7 + \cdots + (3n - 2) = \dfrac{n(3n - 1)}{2}$

**66.** $\dfrac{1}{1 \cdot 3} + \dfrac{1}{3 \cdot 5} + \dfrac{1}{5 \cdot 7} + \cdots + \dfrac{1}{(2n-1)(2n+1)}$
$= \dfrac{n}{2n+1}$

**67.** $\left(1 + \dfrac{1}{1}\right)\left(1 + \dfrac{1}{2}\right)\left(1 + \dfrac{1}{3}\right)\cdots\left(1 + \dfrac{1}{n}\right) = n + 1$

**68.** Show that $7^n - 1$ is divisible by 6 for all natural numbers $n$.

**69.** Let $a_{n+1} = 3a_n + 4$ and $a_1 = 4$. Show that $a_n = 2 \cdot 3^n - 2$ for all natural numbers $n$.

**70.** Prove that the Fibonacci number $F_{4n}$ is divisible by 3 for all natural numbers $n$.

**71–74** ■ Evaluate the expression.

**71.** $\dbinom{5}{2}\dbinom{5}{3}$     **72.** $\dbinom{10}{2} + \dbinom{10}{6}$

**73.** $\displaystyle\sum_{k=0}^{5} \dbinom{5}{k}$     **74.** $\displaystyle\sum_{k=0}^{8} \dbinom{8}{k}\dbinom{8}{8-k}$

**75–78** ■ Expand the expression.

**75.** $(A - B)^3$     **76.** $(x + 2)^5$

**77.** $(1 - x^2)^6$     **78.** $(2x + y)^4$

**79.** Find the 20th term in the expansion of $(a + b)^{22}$.

**80.** Find the first three terms in the expansion of $(b^{-2/3} + b^{1/3})^{20}$.

**81.** Find the term containing $A^6$ in the expansion of $(A + 3B)^{10}$.

1. Find the first six terms and the sixth partial sum of the sequence whose $n$th term is $a_n = 2n^2 - n$.

2. A sequence is defined recursively by $a_{n+1} = 3a_n - n$, $a_1 = 2$. Find the first six terms of the sequence.

3. An arithmetic sequence begins 2, 5, 8, 11, 14, . . . .
   (a) Find the common difference $d$ for this sequence.
   (b) Find a formula for the $n$th term $a_n$ of the sequence.
   (c) Find the 35th term of the sequence.

4. A geometric sequence begins 12, 3, 3/4, 3/16, 3/64, . . . .
   (a) Find the common ratio $r$ for this sequence.
   (b) Find a formula for the $n$th term $a_n$ of the sequence.
   (c) Find the tenth term of the sequence.

5. The first term of a geometric sequence is 25, and the fourth term is $\frac{1}{5}$.
   (a) Find the common ratio $r$ and the fifth term.
   (b) Find the partial sum of the first eight terms.

6. The first term of an arithmetic sequence is 10 and the tenth term is 2.
   (a) Find the common difference and the 100th term of the sequence.
   (b) Find the partial sum of the first ten terms.

7. Let $a_1, a_2, a_3, \ldots$ be a geometric sequence with initial term $a$ and common ratio $r$. Show that $a_1^2, a_2^2, a_3^2, \ldots$ is also a geometric sequence by finding its common ratio.

8. Write the expression without using sigma notation, and then find the sum.
   (a) $\displaystyle\sum_{n=1}^{5} (1 - n^2)$
   (b) $\displaystyle\sum_{n=3}^{6} (-1)^n 2^{n-2}$

9. Find the sum.
   (a) $\dfrac{1}{3} + \dfrac{2}{3^2} + \dfrac{2^2}{3^3} + \dfrac{2^3}{3^4} + \cdots + \dfrac{2^9}{3^{10}}$
   (b) $1 + \dfrac{1}{2^{1/2}} + \dfrac{1}{2} + \dfrac{1}{2^{3/2}} + \cdots$

10. Use mathematical induction to prove that for all natural numbers $n$,
    $$1^2 + 2^2 + 3^2 + \cdots + n^2 = \frac{n(n + 1)(2n + 1)}{6}$$

11. Expand $(2x + y^2)^5$.

12. Find the term containing $x^3$ in the binomial expansion of $(3x - 2)^{10}$.

13. A puppy weighs 0.85 lb at birth, and each week he gains 24% in weight. Let $a_n$ be his weight in pounds at the end of his $n$th week of life.
    (a) Find a formula for $a_n$.
    (b) How much does the puppy weigh when he is six weeks old?
    (c) Is the sequence $a_1, a_2, a_3, \ldots$ arithmetic, geometric, or neither?

Many real-world processes occur in stages. Population growth can be viewed in stages—each new generation represents a new stage in population growth. Compound interest is paid in stages—each interest payment creates a new account balance. Many things that change continuously are more easily measured in discrete stages. For example, we can measure the temperature of a continuously cooling object in one-hour intervals. In this *Focus* we learn how recursive sequences are used to model such situations. In some cases we can get an explicit formula for a sequence from the recursion relation that defines it by finding a pattern in the terms of the sequence.

## Recursive Sequences as Models

Suppose you deposit some money in an account that pays 6% interest compounded monthly. The bank has a definite rule for paying interest: At the end of each month the bank adds to your account $\frac{1}{2}\%$ (or 0.005) of the amount in your account at that time. Let's express this rule as follows:

$$\boxed{\text{amount at the end of this month}} = \boxed{\text{amount at the end of last month}} + 0.005 \times \boxed{\text{amount at the end of last month}}$$

Using the Distributive Property, we can write this as

$$\boxed{\text{amount at the end of this month}} = 1.005 \times \boxed{\text{amount at the end of last month}}$$

To model this statement using algebra, let $A_0$ be the amount of the original deposit, $A_1$ the amount at the end of the first month, $A_2$ the amount at the end of the second month, and so on. So $A_n$ is the amount at the end of the $n$th month. Thus,

$$A_n = 1.005A_{n-1}$$

We recognize this as a recursively defined sequence—it gives us the amount at each stage in terms of the amount at the preceding stage.

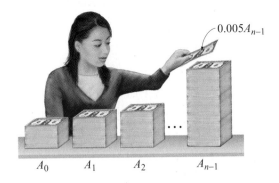

$0.005A_{n-1}$

$A_0 \qquad A_1 \qquad A_2 \qquad A_{n-1}$

To find a formula for $A_n$, let's find the first few terms of the sequence and look for a pattern.

$$A_1 = 1.005A_0$$
$$A_2 = 1.005A_1 = (1.005)^2 A_0$$
$$A_3 = 1.005A_2 = (1.005)^3 A_0$$
$$A_4 = 1.005A_3 = (1.005)^4 A_0$$

We see that in general, $A_n = (1.005)^n A_0$.

▶ **EXAMPLE 1** | Population Growth

A certain animal population grows by 2% each year. The initial population is 5000.

**(a)** Find a recursive sequence that models the population $P_n$ at the end of the $n$th year.

**(b)** Find the first five terms of the sequence $P_n$.

**(c)** Find a formula for $P_n$.

▼ **SOLUTION**

**(a)** We can model the population using the following rule:

population at the end of this year $= 1.02 \times$ population at the end of last year

Algebraically, we can write this as the recursion relation

$$P_n = 1.02 P_{n-1}$$

**(b)** Since the initial population is 5000, we have

$$P_0 = 5000$$

$$P_1 = 1.02 P_0 = (1.02)5000$$

$$P_2 = 1.02 P_1 = (1.02)^2 5000$$

$$P_3 = 1.02 P_2 = (1.02)^3 5000$$

$$P_4 = 1.02 P_3 = (1.02)^4 5000$$

**(c)** We see from the pattern exhibited in part (b) that $P_n = (1.02)^n 5000$. (Note that $P_n$ is a geometric sequence, with common ratio $r = 1.02$.) ▲

▶ **EXAMPLE 2** | Daily Drug Dose

A patient is to take a 50-mg pill of a certain drug every morning. It is known that the body eliminates 40% of the drug every 24 hours.

**(a)** Find a recursive sequence that models the amount $A_n$ of the drug in the patient's body after each pill is taken.

**(b)** Find the first four terms of the sequence $A_n$.

**(c)** Find a formula for $A_n$.

**(d)** How much of the drug remains in the patient's body after 5 days? How much will accumulate in his system after prolonged use?

▼ **SOLUTION**

**(a)** Each morning 60% of the drug remains in his system plus he takes an additional 50 mg (his daily dose).

amount of drug this morning $= 0.6 \times$ amount of drug yesterday morning $+ 50$ mg

We can express this as a recursion relation

$$A_n = 0.6A_{n-1} + 50$$

**(b)** Since the initial dose is 50 mg, we have

$$A_0 = 50$$

$$A_1 = 0.6A_0 + 50 = 0.6(50) + 50$$

$$A_2 = 0.6A_1 + 50 = 0.6\big[0.6(50) + 50\big] + 50$$

$$= 0.6^2(50) + 0.6(50) + 50$$

$$= 50(0.6^2 + 0.6 + 1)$$

$$A_3 = 0.6A_2 + 50 = 0.6\big[0.6^2(50) + 0.6(50) + 50\big] + 50$$

$$= 0.6^3(50) + 0.6^2(50) + 0.6(50) + 50$$

$$= 50(0.6^3 + 0.6^2 + 0.6 + 1)$$

**(c)** From the pattern in part (b) we see that

$$A_n = 50(1 + 0.6 + 0.6^2 + \cdots + 0.6^n)$$

$$= 50\left(\frac{1 - 0.6^{n+1}}{1 - 0.6}\right)$$

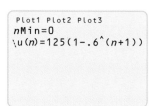

Enter sequence

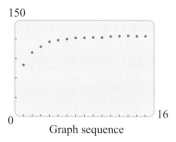

Graph sequence

**FIGURE 1**

Sum of a geometric sequence:

$$S_n = a\left(\frac{1 - r^{n+1}}{1 - r}\right)$$

$$= 125(1 - 0.6^{n+1}) \qquad \text{Simplify}$$

**(d)** To find the amount remaining after 5 days, we substitute $n = 5$ and get
$A_5 = 125(1 - 0.6^{5+1}) \approx 119$ mg.

To find the amount remaining after prolonged use, we let $n$ become large. As $n$ gets large, $0.6^n$ approaches 0. That is, $0.6^n \to 0$ as $n \to \infty$ (see Section 5.1). So as $n \to \infty$,

$$A_n = 125(1 - 0.6^{n+1}) \to 125(1 - 0) = 125$$

Thus, after prolonged use the amount of drug in the patient's system approaches 125 mg (see Figure 1, where we have used a graphing calculator to graph the sequence).

## Problems

**1. Retirement Accounts**    Many college professors keep retirement savings with TIAA, the largest annuity program in the world. Interest on these accounts is compounded and credited *daily*. Professor Brown has $275,000 on deposit with TIAA at the start of 2006 and receives 3.65% interest per year on his account.

    **(a)** Find a recursive sequence that models the amount $A_n$ in his account at the end of the $n$th day of 2006.

    **(b)** Find the first eight terms of the sequence $A_n$, rounded to the nearest cent.

    **(c)** Find a formula for $A_n$.

**2. Fitness Program**    Sheila decides to embark on a swimming program as the best way to maintain cardiovascular health. She begins by swimming 5 min on the first day, then adds $1\frac{1}{2}$ min every day after that.

    **(a)** Find a recursive formula for the number of minutes $T_n$ that she swims on the $n$th day of her program.

    **(b)** Find the first 6 terms of the sequence $T_n$.

    **(c)** Find a formula for $T_n$. What kind of sequence is this?

    **(d)** On what day does Sheila attain her goal of swimming at least 65 min a day?

    **(e)** What is the total amount of time she will have swum after 30 days?

**3. Monthly Savings Program**    Alice opens a savings account paying 3% interest per year, compounded monthly. She begins by depositing $100 at the start of the first month and adds $100 at the end of each month, when the interest is credited.

(a) Find a recursive formula for the amount $A_n$ in her account at the end of the $n$th month. (Include the interest credited for that month and her monthly deposit.)

(b) Find the first five terms of the sequence $A_n$.

(c) Use the pattern you observed in (b) to find a formula for $A_n$.    [*Hint:* To find the pattern most easily, it's best *not* to simplify the terms *too* much.]

(d) How much has she saved after 5 years?

**4. Stocking a Fish Pond**    A pond is stocked with 4000 trout, and through reproduction the population increases by 20% per year. Find a recursive sequence that models the trout population $P_n$ at the end of the $n$th year under each of the following circumstances. Find the trout population at the end of the fifth year in each case.

(a) The trout population changes only because of reproduction.

(b) Each year 600 trout are harvested.

(c) Each year 250 additional trout are introduced into the pond.

(d) Each year 10% of the trout are harvested, and 300 additional trout are introduced into the pond.

**5. Pollution**    A chemical plant discharges 2400 tons of pollutants every year into an adjacent lake. Through natural runoff, 70% of the pollutants contained in the lake at the beginning of the year are expelled by the end of the year.

(a) Explain why the following sequence models the amount $A_n$ of the pollutant in the lake at the end of the $n$th year that the plant is operating.

$$A_n = 0.30A_{n-1} + 2400$$

(b) Find the first five terms of the sequence $A_n$.

(c) Find a formula for $A_n$.

(d) How much of the pollutant remains in the lake after 6 years? How much will remain after the plant has been operating a long time?

(e) Verify your answer to part (d) by graphing $A_n$ with a graphing calculator for $n = 1$ to $n = 20$.

**6. Annual Savings Program**    Ursula opens a one-year CD that yields 5% interest per year. She begins with a deposit of $5000. At the end of each year when the CD matures, she reinvests at the same 5% interest rate, also adding 10% to the value of the CD from her other savings. (So for example, after the first year her CD has earned 5% of $5000 in interest, for a value of $5250 at maturity. She then adds 10%, or $525, bringing the total value of her renewed CD to $5775.)

(a) Find a recursive formula for the amount $U_n$ in Ursula's CD when she reinvests at the end of the $n$th year.

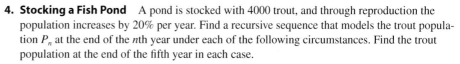

(b) Find the first 5 terms of the sequence $U_n$. Does this appear to be a geometric sequence?

(c) Use the pattern you observed in (b) to find a formula for $U_n$.

(d) How much has she saved after 10 years?

**7. Annual Savings Program**    Victoria opens a one-year CD with a 5% annual interest yield at the same time as her friend Ursula in Problem 6. She also starts with an initial deposit of $5000. However, Victoria decides to add $500 to her CD when she reinvests at the end of the first year, $1000 at the end of the second, $1500 at the end of the third, and so on.

(a) Explain why the recursive formula displayed below gives the amount $V_n$ in Victoria's CD when she reinvests at the end of the $n$th year.

$$V_n = 1.05V_{n-1} + 500n$$

(b) Using the **Seq** ("sequence") mode on your graphing calculator, enter the sequences $U_n$ and $V_n$ as shown in the figure to the left. Then use the TABLE command to compare the two sequences. For the first few years, Victoria seems to be accumulating more savings than Ursula. Scroll down in the table to verify that Ursula eventually pulls ahead of Victoria in the savings race. In what year does this occur?

Plot1  Plot2  Plot3
\u(n) ▤ 1.05 u(n − 1)
+0 .1 u(n − 1)
u(nMin) ▤ {5000}
\v(n) ▤ 1.05 v(n − 1)
+500 n
v(nMin) ▤ {5000}

Entering the sequences

| $n$ | $u(n)$ | $v(n)$ |
|---|---|---|
| 0 | 5000 | 5000 |
| 1 | 5750 | 5750 |
| 2 | 6612.5 | 7037.5 |
| 3 | 7604.4 | 8889.4 |
| 4 | 8745 | 11334 |
| 5 | 10057 | 14401 |
| 6 | 11565 | 18121 |
| $n=0$ | | |

Table of values of the sequences

**8. Newton's Law of Cooling** A tureen of soup at a temperature of 170°F is placed on a table in a dining room in which the thermostat is set at 70°F. The soup cools according to the following rule, a special case of Newton's Law of Cooling: Each minute, the temperature of the soup declines by 3% of the difference between the soup temperature and the room temperature.

**(a)** Find a recursive sequence that models the soup temperature $T_n$ at the $n$th minute.

**(b)** Enter the sequence $T_n$ in your graphing calculator, and use the TABLE command to find the temperature at 10-min increments from $n = 0$ to $n = 60$. (See Problem 7(b).)

**(c)** Graph the sequence $T_n$. What temperature will the soup be after a long time?

**9. Logistic Population Growth** Simple exponential models for population growth do not take into account the fact that when the population increases, survival becomes harder for each individual because of greater competition for food and other resources. We can get a more accurate model by assuming that the birth rate is proportional to the size of the population, but the death rate is proportional to the square of the population. Using this idea, researchers find that the number of raccoons $R_n$ on a certain island is modeled by the following recursive sequence:

Population at end of year

Number of births

$$R_n = R_{n-1} + 0.08R_{n-1} - 0.0004(R_{n-1})^2, \qquad R_0 = 100$$

Population at beginning of year

Number of deaths

Here $n$ represents the number of years since observations began, $R_0$ is the initial population, 0.08 is the annual birth rate, and 0.0004 is a constant related to the death rate.

**(a)** Use the TABLE command on a graphing calculator to find the raccoon population for each year from $n = 1$ to $n = 7$.

**(b)** Graph the sequence $R_n$. What happens to the raccoon population as $n$ becomes large?

# Counting and Probability

© Øystein Wika

**What are the chances?** Most of us are not too worried about being hit by lightning, because the chance of that happening is extremely small. But insurance companies make large payouts for lightning damage each year, so they need to know precisely the chance, or probability, of lightning striking a house. Is a hundred dollars a year a fair price to insure your house against lightning damage? What about fifty dollars? Insurance companies do their probability homework carefully to make certain that their premiums are more than their payouts (see Section 10.5, Exercise 22). Of course, lightning striking a particular house is a random event, just like getting heads on a coin toss or picking the ace of spades from a shuffled deck. In studying probability, we will see how such random events can be modeled by using algebra. We will also encounter many other applications of probability, ranging from gauging the effectiveness of a new drug to finding the chances of winning the lottery.

## 10.1 │ Counting Principles

**LEARNING OBJECTIVE**

After completing this section, you will be able to:

■ Use the Fundamental Counting Principle

Suppose that three towns—Ashbury, Brampton, and Carmichael—are located in such a way that two roads connect Ashbury to Brampton and three roads connect Brampton to Carmichael.

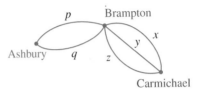

How many different routes can one take to travel from Ashbury to Carmichael via Brampton? The key to answering this question is to consider the problem in stages. At the first stage—from Ashbury to Brampton—there are two choices. For each of these choices there are three choices at the second stage—from Brampton to Carmichael. Thus, the number of different routes is $2 \times 3 = 6$. These routes are conveniently enumerated by a *tree diagram* as in Figure 1.

The method that we used to solve this problem leads to the following principle.

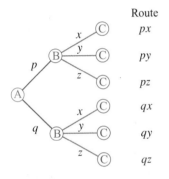

**FIGURE 1** Tree diagram

**FUNDAMENTAL COUNTING PRINCIPLE**

Suppose that two events occur in order. If the first can occur in $m$ ways and the second in $n$ ways (after the first has occurred), then the two events can occur *in order* in $m \times n$ ways.

There is an immediate consequence of this principle for any number of events: If $E_1, E_2, \ldots, E_k$ are events that occur in order and if $E_1$ can occur in $n_1$ ways, $E_2$ in $n_2$ ways, and so on, then the events can occur in order in $n_1 \times n_2 \times \cdots \times n_k$ ways.

▶ **EXAMPLE 1** │ Using the Fundamental Counting Principle

An ice-cream store offers three types of cones and 31 flavors. How many different single-scoop ice-cream cones is it possible to buy at this store?

▼ **SOLUTION**    There are two choices: type of cone and flavor of ice cream. At the first stage we choose a type of cone, and at the second stage we choose a flavor. We can think of the different stages as boxes:

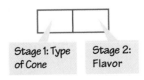

The first box can be filled in three ways, and the second can be filled in 31 ways:

| 3 | 31 |
|---|---|

Stage 1    Stage 2

Thus, by the Fundamental Counting Principle there are $3 \times 31 = 93$ ways of choosing a single-scoop ice-cream cone at this store.

✎ **Practice what you've learned: Do Exercise 3.**                                                  ▲

▶ **EXAMPLE 2** | Using the Fundamental Counting Principle

In a certain state, automobile license plates display three letters followed by three digits. How many such plates are possible if repetition of the letters

**(a)** is allowed?          **(b)** is not allowed?

▼ **SOLUTION**

**(a)** There are six choices, one for each letter or digit on the license plate. As in the preceding example, we sketch a box for each stage:

| 26 | 26 | 26 | 10 | 10 | 10 |
|----|----|----|----|----|----|

Letters          Digits

At the first stage, we choose a letter (from 26 possible choices); at the second stage, we choose another letter (again from 26 choices); at the third stage, we choose another letter (26 choices); at the fourth stage, we choose a digit (from 10 possible choices); at the fifth stage, we choose a digit (again from 10 choices); and at the sixth stage, we choose another digit (10 choices). By the Fundamental Counting Principle the number of possible license plates is

$$26 \times 26 \times 26 \times 10 \times 10 \times 10 = 17,576,000$$

**(b)** If repetition of letters is not allowed, then we can arrange the choices as follows:

| 26 | 25 | 24 | 10 | 10 | 10 |
|----|----|----|----|----|----|

Letters          Digits

Courtesy of Stanford University/ Department of Mathematics

**Persi Diaconis** (b. 1945) is currently professor of statistics and mathematics at Stanford University in California. He was born in New York City into a musical family and studied violin until the age of 14. At that time he left home to become a magician. He was a magician (apprentice and master) for ten years. Magic is still his passion, and if there were a professorship for magic, he would certainly qualify for such a post! His interest in card tricks led him to a study of probability and statistics. He is now one of the leading statisticians in the world. With his unusual background he approaches mathematics with an undeniable flair. He says, "Statistics is the physics of numbers. Numbers seem to arise in the world in an orderly fashion. When we examine the world, the same regularities seem to appear again and again." Among his many original contributions to mathematics is a probabilistic study of the perfect card shuffle.

At the first stage, we have 26 letters to choose from, but once the first letter has been chosen, there are only 25 letters to choose from at the second stage. Once the first two letters have been chosen, 24 letters are left to choose from for the third stage. The digits are chosen as before. Thus, the number of possible license plates in this case is

$$26 \times 25 \times 24 \times 10 \times 10 \times 10 = 15{,}600{,}000$$

✎ **Practice what you've learned: Do Exercise 23.** ▲

▶ **EXAMPLE 3** | Using Factorial Notation

In how many different ways can a race with six runners be completed? Assume that there is no tie.

▼ **SOLUTION** There are six possible choices for first place, five choices for second place (since only five runners are left after first place has been decided), four choices for third place, and so on. So by the Fundamental Counting Principle the number of different ways in which this race can be completed is

$$6 \times 5 \times 4 \times 3 \times 2 \times 1 = 6! = 720$$

Factorial notation is explained on page 641.

✎ **Practice what you've learned: Do Exercise 9.** ▲

# 10.1 EXERCISES

## ▼ CONCEPTS

1. The Fundamental Counting Principle says that if one event can occur in $m$ ways and a second event can occur in $n$ ways, then the two events can occur in order in _____ × _____ ways. So if you have two choices for shoes and three choices for hats, then the number of different shoe-hat combinations you can wear is _____ × _____ = _____.

2. The Fundamental Counting Principle also applies to three or more events in order. So if you have 2 choices for shoes, 5 choices for pants, 4 choices for shirts, and 3 choices for hats, then the number of different shoe-pants-shirt-hat outfits you can wear is _____ × _____ × _____ × _____ = _____.

## ▼ APPLICATIONS

✎ 3. **Ice-Cream Cones** A vendor sells ice cream from a cart on the boardwalk. He offers vanilla, chocolate, strawberry, and pistachio ice cream, served in either a waffle, sugar, or plain cone. How many different single-scoop ice-cream cones can you buy from this vendor?

4. **Three-Letter Words** How many three-letter "words" (strings of letters) can be formed by using the 26 letters of the alphabet if repetition of letters
   (a) is allowed?   (b) is not allowed?

5. **Three-Letter Words** How many three-letter "words" (strings of letters) can be formed by using the letters *WXYZ* if repetition of letters
   (a) is allowed?   (b) is not allowed?

6. **Horse Race** Eight horses are entered in a race.
   (a) How many different orders are possible for completing the race?

   (b) In how many different ways can first, second, and third places be decided? (Assume that there is no tie.)

7. **Multiple-Choice Test** A multiple-choice test has five questions with four choices for each question. In how many different ways can the test be completed?

8. **Phone Numbers** Telephone numbers consist of seven digits; the first digit cannot be 0 or 1. How many telephone numbers are possible?

✎ 9. **Running a Race** In how many different ways can a race with five runners be completed? (Assume that there is no tie.)

10. **Seating Order** In how many ways can five people be seated in a row of five seats?

11. **Restaurant Meals** A restaurant offers the items listed in the table. How many different meals consisting of a main course, a drink, and a dessert can be selected at this restaurant?

| Main courses | Drinks | Desserts |
|---|---|---|
| Chicken | Iced tea | Ice cream |
| Beef | Apple juice | Layer cake |
| Lasagna | Cola | Blueberry pie |
| Quiche | Ginger ale | |
| | Coffee | |

12. **Lining Up Books** In how many ways can five different mathematics books be placed next to each other on a shelf?

13. **Multiple Routes** Towns A, B, C, and D are located in such a way that there are four roads from A to B, five roads from B to C, and six roads from C to D. How many routes are there from town A to town D via towns B and C?

**14. Birth Order** In a family of four children, how many different boy-girl birth-order combinations are possible? (The birth orders *BBBG* and *BBGB* are different.)

**15. Flipping a Coin** A coin is flipped five times, and the resulting sequence of heads and tails is recorded. How many such sequences are possible?

**16. Rolling a Pair of Dice** A red die and a white die are rolled, and the numbers that show are recorded. How many different outcomes are possible? (The singular form of the word *dice* is *die.*)

**17. Rolling Three Dice** A red die, a blue die, and a white die are rolled, and the numbers that show are recorded. How many different outcomes are possible?

**18. Picking Cards** Two cards are chosen in order from a deck. In how many ways can this be done if
(a) the first card must be a spade and the second must be a heart?
(b) both cards must be spades?

**19. Choosing Outfits** A girl has 5 skirts, 8 blouses, and 12 pairs of shoes. How many different skirt-blouse-shoe outfits can she wear? (Assume that each item matches all the others, so she is willing to wear any combination.)

**20. ID Numbers** A company's employee ID number system consists of one letter followed by three digits. How many different ID numbers are possible with this system?

**21. ID Numbers** A company has 2844 employees. Each employee is to be given an ID number that consists of one letter followed by two digits. Is it possible to give each employee a different ID number using this scheme? Explain.

**22. Pitchers and Catchers** An all-star baseball team has a roster of seven pitchers and three catchers. How many pitcher-catcher pairs can the manager select from this roster?

✎ **23. License Plates** Standard automobile license plates in California display a nonzero digit, followed by three letters, followed by three digits. How many different standard plates are possible in this system?

**24. Combination Lock** A combination lock has 60 different positions. To open the lock, the dial is turned to a certain number in the clockwise direction, then to a number in the counterclockwise direction, and finally to a third number in the clockwise direction. If successive numbers in the combination cannot be the same, how many different combinations are possible?

**25. True-False Test** A true-false test contains ten questions. In how many different ways can this test be completed?

**26. Ordering a Car** An automobile dealer offers five models. Each model comes in a choice of four colors, three types of stereo equipment, with or without air conditioning, and with or without a sunroof. In how many different ways can a customer order an auto from this dealer?

**27. Classifications** The registrar at a certain university classifies students according to a major, minor, year (1, 2, 3, 4), and sex (M, F). Each student must choose one major and either one or no minor from the 32 fields taught at this university. How many different student classifications are possible?

**28. Monograms** How many monograms consisting of three initials are possible?

**29. License Plates** A state has registered 8 million automobiles. To simplify the license plate system, a state employee suggests that each plate display only two letters followed by three digits. Will this system create enough different license plates for all the vehicles that are registered?

**30. License Plates** A state license plate design has six places. Each plate begins with a fixed number of letters, and the remaining places are filled with digits. (For example, one letter followed by five digits, two letters followed by four digits, and so on.) The state has 17 million registered vehicles.
(a) The state decides to change to a system consisting of one letter followed by five digits. Will this design allow for enough different plates to accommodate all the vehicles that are registered?
(b) Find a system that will be sufficient if the smallest possible number of letters is to be used.

**31. Class Executive** In how many ways can a president, vice president, and secretary be chosen from a class of 30 students?

**32. Class Executive** In how many ways can a president, vice president, and secretary be chosen from a class of 20 females and 30 males if the president must be a female and the vice president must be a male?

**33. Committee Officers** A senate subcommittee consists of ten Democrats and seven Republicans. In how many ways can a chairman, vice chairman, and secretary be chosen if the chairman must be a Democrat and the vice chairman must be a Republican?

**34. Social Security Numbers** Social Security numbers consist of nine digits, with the first digit between 0 and 6, inclusive. How many Social Security numbers are possible?

**35. Five-Letter Words**   Five-letter "words" are formed using the letters *A, B, C, D, E, F, G*. How many such words are possible for each of the following conditions?
   **(a)** No condition is imposed.
   **(b)** No letter can be repeated in a word.
   **(c)** Each word must begin with the letter *A*.
   **(d)** The letter *C* must be in the middle.
   **(e)** The middle letter must be a vowel.

**36. Palindromes**   How many five-letter palindromes are possible? (A *palindrome* is a string of letters that reads the same backward and forward, such as the string *XCZCX*.)

**37. Names of Variables**   A certain computer programming language allows names of variables to consist of two characters, the first being any letter and the second being any letter or digit. How many names of variables are possible?

**38. Code Words**   How many different three-character code words consisting of letters or digits are possible for the following code designs?
   **(a)** The first entry must be a letter.
   **(b)** The first entry cannot be zero.

**39. Seating Arrangements**   In how many ways can four men and four women be seated in a row of eight seats for the following situations?
   **(a)** The women are to be seated together, and the men are to be seated together.
   **(b)** They are to be seated alternately by gender.

**40. Arranging Books**   In how many ways can five different mathematics books be placed on a shelf if the two algebra books are to be placed next to each other?

**41. Arranging Books**   Eight mathematics books and three chemistry books are to be placed on a shelf. In how many ways can this be done if the mathematics books are next to each other and the chemistry books are next to each other?

**42. Three-Digit Numbers**   Three-digit numbers are formed using the digits 2, 4, 5, and 7, with repetition of digits allowed. How many such numbers can be formed if
   **(a)** the numbers are less than 700?
   **(b)** the numbers are even?
   **(c)** the numbers are divisible by 5?

**43. Three-Digit Numbers**   How many three-digit odd numbers can be formed using the digits 1, 2, 4, and 6 if repetition of digits is not allowed?

▼ **DISCOVERY • DISCUSSION • WRITING**

**44. Pairs of Initials**   Explain why in any group of 677 people, at least two people must have the same pair of initials.

**45. Area Codes**   Until recently, telephone area codes in the United States, Canada, and the Caribbean islands were chosen according to the following rules: (i) The first digit *cannot* be 0 or a 1, and (ii) the second digit *must* be a 0 or a 1. But in 1995 the second rule was abandoned when the area code 360 was introduced in parts of western Washington State. Since then, many other new area codes that violate Rule (ii) have come into use, although Rule (i) still remains in effect.
   **(a)** How many area code + telephone number combinations were possible under the old rules? (See Exercise 8 for a description of local telephone numbers.)
   **(b)** How many area code + telephone number combinations are now possible under the new rules?
   **(c)** Why do you think it was necessary to make this change?
   **(d)** How many area codes that violate Rule (ii) are you personally familiar with?

---

| **10.2** | Permutations and Combinations |

**LEARNING OBJECTIVES**

After completing this section, you will be able to:

▪ Find the number of permutations
▪ Find the number of distinguishable permutations
▪ Find the number of combinations
▪ Solve counting problems involving both permutations and combinations

In this section we single out two important special cases of the Fundamental Counting Principle: permutations and combinations.

Permutations of
three colored squares

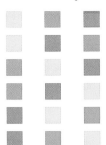

## ■ Permutations

A **permutation** of a set of distinct objects is an ordering of these objects. For example, some permutations of the letters *ABCDWXYZ* are

$$XAYBZWCD \qquad ZAYBCDWX \qquad DBWAZXYC \qquad YDXAWCZB$$

How many such permutations are possible? Since there are eight choices for the first position, seven for the second (after the first has been chosen), six for the third (after the first two have been chosen), and so on, the Fundamental Counting Principle tells us that the number of possible permutations is

$$8 \times 7 \times 6 \times 5 \times 4 \times 3 \times 2 \times 1 = 40{,}320$$

This same reasoning with 8 replaced by *n* leads to the following observation.

> The number of permutations of *n* objects is *n*!.

How many permutations consisting of five letters can be made from these same eight letters? Some of these permutations are

$$XYZWC \qquad AZDWX \qquad AZXYB \qquad WDXZB$$

Again, there are eight choices for the first position, seven for the second, six for the third, five for the fourth, and four for the fifth. By the Fundamental Counting Principle the number of such permutations is

$$8 \times 7 \times 6 \times 5 \times 4 = 6720$$

In general, if a set has *n* elements, then the number of ways of ordering *r* elements from the set is denoted by $P(n, r)$ and is called **the number of permutations of *n* objects taken *r* at a time**.

We have just shown that $P(8, 5) = 6720$. The same reasoning that was used to find $P(8, 5)$ will help us find a general formula for $P(n, r)$. Indeed, there are *n* objects and *r* positions to place them in. Thus, there are *n* choices for the first position, $n - 1$ choices for the second, $n - 2$ choices for the third, and so on. The last position can be filled in $n - r + 1$ ways. By the Fundamental Counting Principle,

$$P(n, r) = n(n - 1)(n - 2) \cdots (n - r + 1)$$

This formula can be written more compactly using factorial notation:

$$P(n, r) = n(n - 1)(n - 2) \cdots (n - r + 1)$$
$$= \frac{n(n - 1)(n - 2) \cdots (n - r + 1)(n - r) \cdots 3 \cdot 2 \cdot 1}{(n - r) \cdots 3 \cdot 2 \cdot 1} = \frac{n!}{(n - r)!}$$

---

### PERMUTATIONS OF *n* OBJECTS TAKEN *r* AT A TIME

The number of permutations of *n* objects taken *r* at a time is

$$P(n, r) = \frac{n!}{(n - r)!}$$

▶ **EXAMPLE 1** | Finding the Number of Permutations

A club has nine members. In how many ways can a president, vice president, and secretary be chosen from the members of this club?

▼ **SOLUTION**    We need the number of ways of selecting three members, *in order*, for the positions of president, vice president, and secretary from the nine club members. This number is

$$P(9, 3) = \frac{9!}{(9 - 3)!} = \frac{9!}{6!} = 9 \times 8 \times 7 = 504$$

✎ **Practice what you've learned: Do Exercise 23.**                                ▲

▶ **EXAMPLE 2** | Finding the Number of Permutations

From 20 raffle tickets in a hat, four tickets are to be selected in order. The holder of the first ticket wins a car, the second a motorcycle, the third a bicycle, and the fourth a skateboard. In how many different ways can these prizes be awarded?

▼ **SOLUTION**    The order in which the tickets are chosen determines who wins each prize. So we need to find the number of ways of selecting four objects, *in order*, from 20 objects (the tickets). This number is

$$P(20, 4) = \frac{20!}{(20 - 4)!} = \frac{20!}{16!} = 20 \times 19 \times 18 \times 17 = 116{,}280$$

✎ **Practice what you've learned: Do Exercise 33.**                                ▲

## ■ Distinguishable Permutations

If we have a collection of ten balls, each a different color, then the number of permutations of these balls is $P(10, 10) = 10!$. If all ten balls are red, then we have just one distinguishable permutation because all the ways of ordering these balls look exactly the same. In general, in considering a set of objects, some of which are of the same kind, then two permutations are **distinguishable** if one cannot be obtained from the other by interchanging the positions of elements of the same kind. For example, if we have ten balls, of which six are red and the other four are each a different color, then how many distinguishable permutations are possible? The key point here is that balls of the same color are not distinguishable. So each rearrangement of the red balls, keeping all the other balls fixed, gives essentially the same permutation. Since there are 6! rearrangements of the red balls for each fixed position of the other balls, the total number of distinguishable permutations is $10!/6!$. The same type of reasoning gives the following general rule.

---

**DISTINGUISHABLE PERMUTATIONS**

If a set of $n$ objects consists of $k$ different kinds of objects with $n_1$ objects of the first kind, $n_2$ objects of the second kind, $n_3$ objects of the third kind, and so on, where $n_1 + n_2 + \cdots + n_k = n$, then the number of distinguishable permutations of these objects is

$$\frac{n!}{n_1! \, n_2! \, n_3! \cdots n_k!}$$

---

▶ **EXAMPLE 3** | Finding the Number of Distinguishable Permutations

Find the number of different ways of placing 15 balls in a row given that 4 are red, 3 are yellow, 6 are black, and 2 are blue.

▼ **SOLUTION** We want to find the number of distinguishable permutations of these balls. By the formula this number is

$$\frac{15!}{4!\,3!\,6!\,2!} = 6,306,300$$

✎ **Practice what you've learned: Do Exercise 39.** ▲

Suppose we have 15 wooden balls in a row and four colors of paint: red, yellow, black, and blue. In how many different ways can the 15 balls be painted in such a way that we have 4 red, 3 yellow, 6 black, and 2 blue balls? A little thought will show that this number is exactly the same as that calculated in Example 3. This way of looking at the problem is somewhat different, however. Here we think of the number of ways to **partition** the balls into four groups, each containing 4, 3, 6, and 2 balls to be painted red, yellow, black, and blue, respectively. The next example shows how this reasoning is used.

▶ **EXAMPLE 4** | Finding the Number of Partitions

Fourteen construction workers are to be assigned to three different tasks. Seven workers are needed for mixing cement, five for laying bricks, and two for carrying the bricks to the brick layers. In how many different ways can the workers be assigned to these tasks?

▼ **SOLUTION** We need to partition the workers into three groups containing 7, 5, and 2 workers, respectively. This number is

$$\frac{14!}{7!\,5!\,2!} = 72,072$$

✎ **Practice what you've learned: Do Exercise 43.** ▲

## ■ Combinations

When finding permutations, we are interested in the number of ways of ordering elements of a set. In many counting problems, however, order is *not* important. For example, a poker hand is the same hand, regardless of how it is ordered. A poker player who is interested in the number of possible hands wants to know the number of ways of drawing five cards from 52 cards, without regard to the order in which the cards of a given hand are dealt. We now develop a formula for counting in situations such as this, in which order doesn't matter.

A **combination** of $r$ elements of a set is any subset of $r$ elements from the set (without regard to order). If the set has $n$ elements, then the number of combinations of $r$ elements is denoted by $C(n, r)$ and is called the **number of combinations of $n$ elements taken $r$ at a time**.

For example, consider a set with the four elements, $A$, $B$, $C$, and $D$. The combinations of these four elements taken three at a time are

| ABC | ABD | ACD | BCD |

The permutations of these elements taken three at a time are

| ABC | ABD | ACD | BCD |
| --- | --- | --- | --- |
| ACB | ADB | ADC | BDC |
| BAC | BAD | CAD | CBD |
| BCA | BDA | CDA | CDB |
| CAB | DAB | DAC | DBC |
| CBA | DBA | DCA | DCB |

We notice that the number of combinations is a lot fewer than the number of permutations. In fact, each combination of three elements generates 3! permutations. So

$$C(4, 3) = \frac{P(4, 3)}{3!} = \frac{4!}{3!(4 - 3)!} = 4$$

In general, each combination of $r$ objects gives rise to $r!$ permutations of these objects. Thus,

$$C(n, r) = \frac{P(n, r)}{r!} = \frac{n!}{r!(n - r)!}$$

In Section 9.6 we denoted $C(n, r)$ by $\binom{n}{r}$, but it is customary to use the notation $C(n, r)$ in the context of counting. For an explanation of why these are the same, see Exercise 82.

> **COMBINATIONS OF $n$ OBJECTS TAKEN $r$ AT A TIME**
>
> The number of combinations of $n$ objects taken $r$ at a time is
>
> $$C(n, r) = \frac{n!}{r!(n - r)!}$$

The key difference between permutations and combinations is *order*. If we are interested in ordered arrangements, then we are counting permutations; but if we are concerned with subsets without regard to order, then we are counting combinations. Compare Examples 5 and 6 below (where order doesn't matter) with Examples 1 and 2 (where order does matter).

▶ **EXAMPLE 5** | Finding the Number of Combinations

A club has nine members. In how many ways can a committee of three be chosen from the members of this club?

▼ **SOLUTION**  We need the number of ways of choosing three of the nine members. Order is not important here, because the committee is the same no matter how its members are ordered. So we want the number of combinations of nine objects (the club members) taken three at a time. This number is

$$C(9, 3) = \frac{9!}{3!(9 - 3)!} = \frac{9!}{3!6!} = \frac{9 \times 8 \times 7}{3 \times 2 \times 1} = 84$$

✎ **Practice what you've learned: Do Exercise 47.**  ▲

**Ronald Graham**, born in Taft, California, in 1935, is considered the world's leading mathematician in the field of combinatorics, the branch of mathematics that deals with counting. For many years Graham headed the Mathematical Studies Center at Bell Laboratories in Murray Hill, New Jersey, where he solved key problems for the telephone industry. During the *Apollo* program, NASA needed to evaluate mission schedules so that the three astronauts aboard the spacecraft could find the time to perform all the necessary tasks. The number of ways to allot these tasks was astronomical—too vast for even a computer to sort out. Graham, using his knowledge of combinatorics, was able to reassure NASA that there were easy ways of solving their problem that were not too far from the theoretically best possible solution. Besides being a prolific mathematician, Graham is an accomplished juggler (he has been on stage with the Cirque du Soleil and is a past president of the International Jugglers Association). Several of his research papers address the mathematical aspects of juggling. He is also fluent in Mandarin Chinese and Japanese and once spoke with former President Jiang of China in his native language.

© Ken Regan/Camera 5

▶ **EXAMPLE 6** | Finding the Number of Combinations

From 20 raffle tickets in a hat, four tickets are to be chosen at random. The holders of the winning tickets are to be awarded free trips to the Bahamas. In how many ways can the four winners be chosen?

▼ **SOLUTION**   We need to find the number of ways of choosing four winners from 20 entries. The order in which the tickets are chosen doesn't matter, because the same prize is awarded to each of the four winners. So we want the number of combinations of 20 objects (the tickets) taken four at a time. This number is

$$C(20,4) = \frac{20!}{4!(20-4)!} = \frac{20!}{4!16!} = \frac{20 \times 19 \times 18 \times 17}{4 \times 3 \times 2 \times 1} = 4845$$

✎ **Practice what you've learned: Do Exercise 51.**    ▲

If a set $S$ has $n$ elements, then $C(n, k)$ is the number of ways of choosing $k$ elements from $S$, that is, the number of $k$-element subsets of $S$. Thus, the number of subsets of $S$ of all possible sizes is given by the sum

$$C(n, 0) + C(n, 1) + C(n, 2) + \cdots + C(n, n) = 2^n$$

(See Section 9.6, Exercise 56, where this sum is discussed.)

> A set with $n$ elements has $2^n$ subsets.

▶ **EXAMPLE 7** | Finding the Number of Subsets of a Set

A pizza parlor offers the basic cheese pizza and a choice of 16 toppings. How many different kinds of pizza can be ordered at this pizza parlor?

▼ **SOLUTION**   We need the number of possible subsets of the 16 toppings (including the empty set, which corresponds to a plain cheese pizza). Thus, $2^{16} = 65,536$ different pizzas can be ordered.

✎ **Practice what you've learned: Do Exercise 61.**    ▲

## ■ Problem Solving with Permutations and Combinations

The crucial step in solving counting problems is deciding whether to use permutations, combinations, or the Fundamental Counting Principle. In some cases the solution of a problem may require using more than one of these principles. Here are some general guidelines to help us decide how to apply these principles.

---

**GUIDELINES FOR SOLVING COUNTING PROBLEMS**

1. **Fundamental Counting Principle.**   When consecutive choices are being made, use the Fundamental Counting Principle.

2. **Does the Order Matter?**   When we want to find the number of ways of picking $r$ objects from $n$ objects, we need to ask ourselves, "Does the order in which we pick the objects matter?"

   If the order matters, we use permutations.

   If the order doesn't matter, we use combinations.

▶ **EXAMPLE 8** | A Problem Involving Combinations

A group of 25 campers contains 15 women and 10 men. In how many ways can a scouting party of 5 be chosen if it must consist of 3 women and 2 men?

▼ **SOLUTION**    Three women can be chosen from the 15 women in the group in $C(15, 3)$ ways, and two men can be chosen from the 10 men in the group in $C(10, 2)$ ways. Thus, by the Fundamental Counting Principle the number of ways of choosing the scouting party is

$$C(15, 3) \times C(10, 2) = 455 \times 45 = 20{,}475$$

✎ **Practice what you've learned: Do Exercise 63.**                                    ▲

▶ **EXAMPLE 9** | A Problem Involving Permutations and Combinations

A committee of seven—consisting of a chairman, a vice chairman, a secretary, and four other members—is to be chosen from a class of 20 students. In how many ways can this committee be chosen?

▼ **SOLUTION**    In choosing the three officers, order is important. So the number of ways of choosing them is

$$P(20, 3) = 6840$$

Next, we need to choose four other students from the 17 remaining. Since order doesn't matter in this case, the number of ways of doing this is

$$C(17, 4) = 2380$$

Thus, by the Fundamental Counting Principle the number of ways of choosing this committee is

$$P(20, 3) \times C(17, 4) = 6840 \times 2380 = 16{,}279{,}200$$

We could have first chosen the four unordered members of the committee—in $C(20, 4)$ ways—and then the three officers from the remaining 16 members, in $P(16, 3)$ ways. Check that this gives the same answer.

✎ **Practice what you've learned: Do Exercise 65.**                                    ▲

▶ **EXAMPLE 10** | A Group Photograph

Twelve employees at a company picnic are to stand in a row for a group photograph. In how many ways can this be done if

**(a)** Jane and John insist on standing next to each other?

**(b)** Jane and John refuse to stand next to each other?

Jane  John

▼ **SOLUTION**

**(a)** Since the order in which the people stand is important, we use permutations. But we can't use the formula for permutations directly. Since Jane and John insist on standing together, let's think of them as one object. Thus, we have 11 objects to arrange in a row, and there are $P(11, 11)$ ways of doing this. For each of these arrangements there are two ways of having Jane and John stand together: Jane-John or John-Jane. Thus, by the Fundamental Counting Principle the total number of arrangements is

$$2 \times P(11, 11) = 2 \times 11! = 79{,}833{,}600$$

**(b)** There are $P(12, 12)$ ways of arranging the 12 people. Of these, $2 \times P(11, 11)$ have Jane and John standing together (by part (a)). All the rest have Jane and John standing apart. So the number of arrangements with Jane and John apart is

$$P(12, 12) - 2 \times P(11, 11) = 12! - 2 \times 11! = 399{,}168{,}000$$

✎ **Practice what you've learned: Do Exercises 71 and 77.** ▲

# 10.2 EXERCISES

## ▼ CONCEPTS

**1.** *True or false*? In counting combinations, order matters.

**2.** *True or false*? In counting permutations, order matters.

**3.** *True or false*? For a set of $n$ distinct objects, the number of different combinations of these objects is more than the number of different permutations.

**4.** *True or false*? If we have a set with five distinct objects, then the number of different ways of choosing two members of this set is the same as the number of ways of choosing three members.

## ▼ SKILLS

**5–10** ▪ Evaluate the expression.

**5.** $P(8, 3)$     **6.** $P(9, 2)$     **7.** $P(11, 4)$

**8.** $P(10, 5)$     **9.** $P(100, 1)$     **10.** $P(99, 3)$

**11–16** ▪ Find the number of distinguishable permutations of the given letters.

**11.** *AAABBC*     **12.** *AAABBBCCC*

**13.** *AABCD*     **14.** *ABCDDEE*

**15.** *XXYYYZZZZ*     **16.** *XXYYZZZ*

**17–22** ▪ Evaluate the expression.

**17.** $C(8, 3)$     **18.** $C(9, 2)$     **19.** $C(11, 4)$

**20.** $C(10, 5)$     **21.** $C(100, 1)$     **22.** $C(99, 3)$

## ▼ APPLICATIONS

**23–36** ▪ These problems involve permutations.

✎ **23. Class Officers** In how many different ways can a president, vice president, and secretary be chosen from a class of 15 students?

**24. Contest Prizes** In how many different ways can first, second, and third prizes be awarded in a game with eight contestants?

**25. Seating Arrangements** In how many different ways can six of ten people be seated in a row of six chairs?

**26. Seating Arrangements** In how many different ways can six people be seated in a row of six chairs?

**27. Three-Letter Words** How many three-letter "words" can be made from the letters *FGHIJK*? (Letters may not be repeated.)

**28. Letter Permutations** How many permutations are possible from the letters of the word *LOVE*?

**29. Three-Digit Numbers** How many different three-digit whole numbers can be formed by using the digits 1, 3, 5, and 7 if no repetition of digits is allowed?

**30. Piano Recital** A pianist plans to play eight pieces at a recital. In how many ways can she arrange these pieces in the program?

**31. Running a Race** In how many different ways can a race with nine runners be completed, assuming that there is no tie?

**32. Signal Flags** A ship carries five signal flags of different colors. How many different signals can be sent by hoisting exactly three of the five flags on the ship's flagpole in different orders?

✎ **33. Contest Prizes** In how many ways can first, second, and third prizes be awarded in a contest with 1000 contestants?

**34. Class Officers** In how many ways can a president, vice president, secretary, and treasurer be chosen from a class of 30 students?

**35. Seating Arrangements** In how many ways can five students be seated in a row of five chairs if Jack insists on sitting in the first chair?

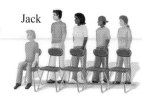

Jack

**36. Seating Arrangements** In how many ways can the students in Exercise 35 be seated if Jack insists on sitting in the middle chair?

**37–44** ■ These problems involve distinguishable permutations.

**37. Arrangements** In how many ways can two blue marbles and four red marbles be arranged in a row?

**38. Arrangements** In how many different ways can five red balls, two white balls, and seven blue balls be arranged in a row?

**39. Arranging Coins** In how many different ways can four pennies, three nickels, two dimes, and three quarters be arranged in a row?

**40. Arranging Letters** In how many different ways can the letters of the word *ELEEMOSYNARY* be arranged?

**41. Distributions** A man bought three vanilla ice-cream cones, two chocolate cones, four strawberry cones, and five butterscotch cones for his 14 chidren. In how many ways can he distribute the cones among his children?

**42. Room Assignments** When seven students take a trip, they find a hotel with three rooms available: a room for one person, a room for two people, and a room for three people. In how many different ways can the students be assigned to these rooms? (One student has to sleep in the car.)

**43. Work Assignments** Eight workers are cleaning a large house. Five are needed to clean windows, two to clean the carpets, and one to clean the rest of the house. In how many different ways can these tasks be assigned to the eight workers?

**44. Jogging Routes** A jogger jogs every morning to his health club, which is eight blocks east and five blocks north of his home. He always takes a route that is as short as possible, but he likes to vary it (see the figure). How many different routes can he take? [*Hint:* The route shown can be thought of as *ENNEEENENEENE*, where *E* is East and *N* is North.]

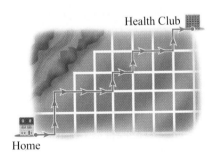

Health Club

Home

**45–58** ■ These problems involve combinations.

**45. Choosing Books** In how many ways can three books be chosen from a group of six different books?

**46. Pizza Toppings** In how many ways can three pizza toppings be chosen from 12 available toppings?

**47. Committee** In how many ways can a committee of three members be chosen from a club of 25 members?

**48. Choosing a Group** In how many ways can six people be chosen from a group of ten?

**49. Draw Poker Hands** How many different five-card hands can be dealt from a deck of 52 cards?

**50. Stud Poker Hands** How many different seven-card hands can be picked from a deck of 52 cards?

**51. Choosing Exam Questions** A student must answer seven of the ten questions on an exam. In how many ways can she choose the seven questions?

**52. Three-Topping Pizzas** A pizza parlor offers a choice of 16 different toppings. How many three-topping pizzas are possible?

**53. Violin Recital** A violinist has practiced 12 pieces. In how many ways can he choose eight of these pieces for a recital?

**54. Choosing Clothing** If a woman has eight skirts, in how many ways can she choose five of these to take on a weekend trip?

**55. Field Trip** In how many ways can seven students from a class of 30 be chosen for a field trip?

**56. Field Trip** In how many ways can the seven students in Exercise 55 be chosen if Jack must go on the field trip?

**57. Field Trip** In how many ways can the seven students in Exercise 55 be chosen if Jack is not allowed to go on the field trip?

**58. Lottery** In the 6/49 lottery game, a player picks six numbers from 1 to 49. How many different choices does the player have?

**59. Subsets** A set has eight elements.
  **(a)** How many subsets containing five elements does this set have?
  **(b)** How many subsets does this set have?

**60. Travel Brochures** A travel agency has limited numbers of eight different free brochures about Australia. The agent tells you to take any that you like but no more than one of any kind. In how many different ways can you choose brochures (including not choosing any)?

**61. Hamburgers** A hamburger chain gives their customers a choice of ten different hamburger toppings. In how many different ways can a customer order a hamburger?

**62. To Shop or Not to Shop** Each of 20 shoppers in a shopping mall chooses to enter or not to enter the Dressfastic clothing store. How many different outcomes of their decisions are possible?

**63–79** ■ Solve the problem using the appropriate counting principle(s).

**63. Choosing a Committee** A class has 20 students, of whom 12 are females and 8 are males. In how many ways can a committee of five students be picked from this class under each condition?
  **(a)** No restriction is placed on the number of males or females on the committee.
  **(b)** No males are to be included on the committee.
  **(c)** The committee must have three females and two males.

**64. Doubles Tennis** From a group of ten male and ten female tennis players, two men and two women are to face each other in a men-versus-women doubles match. In how many different ways can this match be arranged?

**65. Choosing a Committee** A committee of six is to be chosen from a class of 20 students. The committee is to consist of a president, a vice president, and four other members. In how many different ways can the committee be picked?

**66. Choosing a Group** Sixteen boys and nine girls go on a camping trip. In how many ways can a group of six be selected to gather firewood, given the following conditions?
(a) The group consists of two girls and four boys.
(b) The group contains at least two girls.

**67. Dance Committee** A school dance committee is to consist of two freshmen, three sophomores, four juniors, and five seniors. If six freshmen, eight sophomores, twelve juniors, and ten seniors are eligible to be on the committee, in how many ways can the committee be chosen?

**68. Casting a Play** A group of 22 aspiring thespians contains ten men and twelve women. For the next play the director wants to choose a leading man, a leading lady, a supporting male role, a supporting female role, and eight extras—three women and five men. In how many ways can the cast be chosen?

**69. Hockey Lineup** A hockey team has 20 players, of whom twelve play forward, six play defense, and two are goalies. In how many ways can the coach pick a starting lineup consisting of three forwards, two defense players, and one goalie?

**70. Choosing a Pizza** A pizza parlor offers four sizes of pizza (small, medium, large, and colossus), two types of crust (thick and thin), and 14 different toppings. How many different pizzas can be made with these choices?

**71. Arranging a Class Picture** In how many ways can ten students be arranged in a row for a class picture if John and Jane want to stand next to each other and Mike and Molly also insist on standing next to each other?

**72. Arranging a Class Picture** In how many ways can the ten students in Exercise 71 be arranged if Mike and Molly insist on standing together but John and Jane refuse to stand next to each other?

**73. Seating Arrangements** In how many ways can four men and four women be seated in a row of eight seats for each of the following arrangements?
(a) The first seat is to be occupied by a man.
(b) The first and last seats are to be occupied by women.

**74. Seating Arrangements** In how many ways can four men and four women be seated in a row of eight seats for each of the following arrangements?
(a) The women are to be seated together.
(b) The men and women are to be seated alternately by gender.

**75. Selecting Prizewinners** From a group of 30 contestants, six are to be chosen as semifinalists, then two of those are chosen as finalists, and then the top prize is awarded to one of the finalists. In how many ways can these choices be made in sequence?

**76. Choosing a Delegation** Three delegates are to be chosen from a group of four lawyers, a priest, and three professors. In how many ways can the delegation be chosen if it must include at least one professor?

**77. Choosing a Committee** In how many ways can a committee of four be chosen from a group of ten if two people refuse to serve together on the same committee?

**78. Geometry** Twelve dots are drawn on a page in such a way that no three are collinear. How many straight lines can be formed by joining the dots?

**79. Parking Committee** A five-person committee consisting of students and teachers is being formed to study the issue of student parking privileges. Of those who have expressed an interest in serving on the committee, 12 are teachers and 14 are students. In how many ways can the committee be formed if at least one student and one teacher must be included?

---

▼ **DISCOVERY • DISCUSSION • WRITING**

**80. Complementary Combinations** Without performing any calculations, explain in words why the number of ways of choosing two objects from ten objects is the same as the number of ways of choosing eight objects from ten objects. In general, explain why

$$C(n, r) = C(n, n - r)$$

**81. An Identity Involving Combinations** Kevin has ten different marbles, and he wants to give three of them to Luke and two to Mark. In how many ways can he choose to do this? There are two ways of analyzing this problem: He could first pick three for Luke and then two for Mark, or he could first pick two for Mark and then three for Luke. Explain how these two viewpoints show that

$$C(10, 3) \cdot C(7, 2) = C(10, 2) \cdot C(8, 3)$$

In general, explain why

$$C(n, r) \cdot C(n - r, k) = C(n, k) \cdot C(n - k, r)$$

**82. Why Is $\binom{n}{r}$ the Same as $C(n, r)$?** This exercise explains why the binomial coefficients $\binom{n}{r}$ that appear in the expansion of $(x + y)^n$ are the same as $C(n, r)$, the number of ways of choosing $r$ objects from $n$ objects. First, note that expanding a binomial using only the Distributive Property gives

$$\begin{aligned}
(x + y)^2 &= (x + y)(x + y) \\
&= (x + y)x + (x + y)y \\
&= xx + xy + yx + yy \\
(x + y)^3 &= (x + y)(xx + xy + yx + yy) \\
&= xxx + xxy + xyx + xyy + yxx \\
&\quad + yxy + yyx + yyy
\end{aligned}$$

(a) Expand $(x + y)^5$ using only the Distributive Property.
(b) Write all the terms that represent $x^2 y^3$ together. These are all the terms that contain two $x$'s and three $y$'s.
(c) Note that the two $x$'s appear in all possible positions. Conclude that the number of terms that represent $x^2 y^3$ is $C(5, 2)$.
(d) In general, explain why $\binom{n}{r}$ in the Binomial Theorem is the same as $C(n, r)$.

## 10.3 | Probability

**LEARNING OBJECTIVES**

After completing this section, you will be able to:

- Find the probability of an event by counting
- Find the probability of the complement of an event
- Find the probability of the union of events
- Find the probability of the intersection of independent events

In the preceding chapters we modeled real-world situations using precise rules, such as equations or functions. But many of our everyday activities are not governed by precise rules; rather, they involve randomness and uncertainty. How can we model such situations? How can we find reliable patterns in random events? In this section we will see how the ideas of probability provide answers to these questions.

Let's look at a simple example. We roll a die, and we're hoping to get a "two." Of course, it's impossible to predict what number will show up. But here's the key idea: If we roll the die *many many* times, the number two will show up about one-sixth of the time. This is because each of the six numbers, 1, 2, 3, 4, 5, and 6, is equally likely to show up, so the "two" will show up about a sixth of the time. If you try this experiment, you will see that it actually works! We will say that the probability (or chance) of getting a "two" is $\frac{1}{6}$.

If we pick a card from a 52-card deck, what are the chances that it is an ace? Again, each card is equally likely to be picked. Since there are four aces, the probability (or chance) of picking an ace is $\frac{4}{52}$.

Probability plays a key role in many of the sciences. A remarkable example of the use of probability is Gregor Mendel's discovery of genes (which he could not see) by applying probabilistic reasoning to the patterns that he saw in inherited traits.

Today, probability is an indispensable tool for decision making in business, industry, government, and scientific research. For example, probability is used to determine the effectiveness of new medicines, assess fair prices for insurance policies, and gauge public opinion on a topic (without interviewing everyone). In the remaining sections of this chapter we will see how some of these applications are possible.

The mathematical theory of probability was first discussed in 1654 in a series of letters between Pascal (see page 636) and Fermat (see page 159). Their correspondence was prompted by a question raised by the experienced gambler the Chevalier de Méré. The Chevalier was interested in the equitable distribution of the stakes of an interrupted gambling game (see Problem 3, page 700).

### ■ What Is Probability?

To discuss probability, let's begin by defining some terms. An **experiment** is a process, such as tossing a coin or rolling a die, that gives definite results, called the **outcomes** of the experiment. For tossing a coin, the possible outcomes are "heads" and "tails"; for rolling a die, the outcomes are 1, 2, 3, 4, 5, and 6. The **sample space** of an experiment is the set of all possible outcomes. If we let $H$ stand for heads and $T$ for tails, then the sample space of the coin-tossing experiment is $S = \{H, T\}$.

The table lists some experiments and the corresponding sample spaces.

| Experiment | Sample space |
|---|---|
| Tossing a coin | $\{H, T\}$ |
| Rolling a die | $\{1, 2, 3, 4, 5, 6\}$ |
| Tossing a coin twice and observing the sequence of heads and tails | $\{HH, HT, TH, TT\}$ |
| Picking a card from a deck and observing the suit | $\{\spadesuit, \heartsuit, \diamondsuit, \clubsuit\}$ |
| Administering a drug to three patients and observing whether they recover ($R$) or not ($N$) | $\{RRR, RRN, RNR, RNN,$ $NRR, NRN, NNR, NNN\}$ |

We will be concerned only with experiments for which all the outcomes are equally likely. We already have an intuitive feeling for what this means. When we toss a perfectly balanced coin, heads and tails are equally likely outcomes in the sense that if this experiment is repeated many times, we expect that about as many heads as tails will show up.

In any given experiment we are often concerned with a particular set of outcomes. We might be interested in a die showing an even number or in picking an ace from a deck of cards. Any particular set of outcomes is a subset of the sample space. This leads to the following definition.

---

**DEFINITION OF AN EVENT**

If $S$ is the sample space of an experiment, then an **event** is any subset of the sample space.

---

▶ **EXAMPLE 1** | Events in a Sample Space

If an experiment consists of tossing a coin three times and recording the results in order, the sample space is

$$S = \{HHH, HHT, HTH, THH, TTH, THT, HTT, TTT\}$$

The event $E$ of showing "exactly two heads" is the subset of $S$ that consists of all outcomes with two heads. Thus

$$E = \{HHT, HTH, THH\}$$

The event $F$ of showing "at least two heads" is

$$F = \{HHH, HHT, HTH, THH\}$$

and the event of showing "no heads" is $G = \{TTT\}$.

✎ **Practice what you've learned: Do Exercise 5.** ▲

We are now ready to define the notion of probability. Intuitively, we know that rolling a die may result in any of six equally likely outcomes, so the chance of any particular outcome occurring is $\frac{1}{6}$. What is the chance of showing an even number? Of the six equally likely outcomes possible, three are even numbers. So it is reasonable to say that the chance of showing an even number is $\frac{3}{6} = \frac{1}{2}$. This reasoning is the intuitive basis for the following definition of probability.

---

## DEFINITION OF PROBABILITY

Let $S$ be the sample space of an experiment in which all outcomes are equally likely, and let $E$ be an event. The probability of $E$, written $P(E)$, is

$$P(E) = \frac{n(E)}{n(S)} = \frac{\text{number of elements in } E}{\text{number of elements in } S}$$

---

Notice that $0 \leq n(E) \leq n(S)$, so the probability $P(E)$ of an event is a number between 0 and 1, that is,

$$0 \leq P(E) \leq 1$$

The closer the probability of an event is to 1, the more likely the event is to happen; the closer to 0, the less likely. If $P(E) = 1$, then $E$ is called the **certain event**; and if $P(E) = 0$, then $E$ is called the **impossible event**.

▶ **EXAMPLE 2** | Finding the Probability of an Event

A coin is tossed three times, and the results are recorded. What is the probability of getting exactly two heads? At least two heads? No heads?

▼ **SOLUTION** By the results of Example 1 the sample space $S$ of this experiment contains eight outcomes, and the event $E$ of getting "exactly two heads" contains three outcomes, $\{HHT, HTH, THH\}$, so by the definition of probability,

$$P(E) = \frac{n(E)}{n(S)} = \frac{3}{8}$$

Similarly, the event $F$ of getting "at least two heads" has four outcomes, $\{HHH, HHT, HTH, THH\}$, so

$$P(F) = \frac{n(F)}{n(S)} = \frac{4}{8} = \frac{1}{2}$$

The event $G$ of getting "no heads" has one element, so

$$P(G) = \frac{n(G)}{n(S)} = \frac{1}{8}$$

✎ **Practice what you've learned: Do Exercise 7.** ▲

---

## MATHEMATICS IN THE MODERN WORLD

### Fair Voting Methods

The methods of mathematics have recently been applied to problems in the social sciences. For example, how do we find fair voting methods? You may ask, "What is the problem with how we vote in elections?" Well, suppose candidates A, B, and C are running for president. The final vote tally is as follows: A gets 40%, B gets 39%, and C gets 21%. So candidate A wins. But 60% of the voters *didn't* want A. Moreover, suppose you voted for C, but you dislike A so much that you would have been willing to change your vote to B to avoid having A win. Most of the voters who voted for C feel the same way you do, so we have a situation in which most of the voters prefer B over A, but A wins. Is that fair?

In the 1950s Kenneth Arrow showed mathematically that no democratic method of voting can be completely fair; he later won a Nobel Prize for his work. Mathematicians continue to work on finding fairer voting systems. The system that is most often used in federal, state, and local elections is called *plurality voting* (the candidate with the most votes wins). Other systems include *majority voting* (if no candidate gets a majority, a runoff is held between the top two vote-getters), *approval voting* (each voter can vote for as many candidates as he or she approves of), *preference voting* (each voter orders the candidates according to his or her preference), and *cumulative voting* (each voter gets as many votes as there are candidates and can give all of his or her votes to one candidate or distribute them among the candidates as he or she sees fit). This last system is often used to select corporate boards of directors. Each system of voting has both advantages and disadvantages.

## ■ Calculating Probability by Counting

To find the probability of an event, we do not need to list all the elements in the sample space and the event. What we do need is the *number* of elements in these sets. The counting techniques that we learned in the preceding sections will be very useful here.

▶ **EXAMPLE 3** | Finding the Probability of an Event

A five-card poker hand is drawn from a standard deck of 52 cards. What is the probability that all five cards are spades?

▼ **SOLUTION**  The experiment here consists of choosing five cards from the deck, and the sample space $S$ consists of all possible five-card hands. Thus, the number of elements in the sample space is

$$n(S) = C(52, 5) = \frac{52!}{5!(52-5)!} = 2{,}598{,}960$$

The event $E$ that we are interested in consists of choosing five spades. Since the deck contains only 13 spades, the number of ways of choosing five spades is

$$n(E) = C(13, 5) = \frac{13!}{5!(13-5)!} = 1287$$

Thus, the probability of drawing five spades is

$$P(E) = \frac{n(E)}{n(S)} = \frac{1287}{2{,}598{,}960} \approx 0.0005$$

✎ **Practice what you've learned: Do Exercise 19.**  ▲

What does the answer to Example 3 tell us? Since $0.0005 = \frac{1}{2000}$, this means that if you play poker many, many times, on average you will be dealt a hand consisting of only spades about once in every 2000 hands.

▶ **EXAMPLE 4** | Finding the Probability of an Event

A bag contains 20 tennis balls, of which four are defective. If two balls are selected at random from the bag, what is the probability that both are defective?

▼ **SOLUTION**  The experiment consists of choosing two balls from 20, so the number of elements in the sample space $S$ is $C(20, 2)$. Since there are four defective balls, the number of ways of picking two defective balls is $C(4, 2)$. Thus, the probability of the event $E$ of picking two defective balls is

$$P(E) = \frac{n(E)}{n(S)} = \frac{C(4, 2)}{C(20, 2)} = \frac{6}{190} \approx 0.032$$

✎ **Practice what you've learned: Do Exercise 23.**  ▲

The **complement** of an event $E$ is the set of outcomes in the sample space that is not in $E$. We denote the complement of an event $E$ by $E'$. We can calculate the probability of $E'$ using the definition and the fact that $n(E') = n(S) - n(E)$:

$$P(E') = \frac{n(E')}{n(S)} = \frac{n(S) - n(E)}{n(S)} = \frac{n(S)}{n(S)} - \frac{n(E)}{n(S)} = 1 - P(E)$$

**PROBABILITY OF THE COMPLEMENT OF AN EVENT**

Let $S$ be the sample space of an experiment and $E$ an event. Then

$$P(E') = 1 - P(E)$$

This is an extremely useful result, since it is often difficult to calculate the probability of an event $E$ but easy to find the probability of $E'$, from which $P(E)$ can be calculated immediately by using this formula.

▶ **EXAMPLE 5** | Finding the Probability of the Complement of an Event

An urn contains 10 red balls and 15 blue balls. Six balls are drawn at random from the urn. What is the probability that at least one ball is red?

▼ **SOLUTION** Let $E$ be the event that at least one red ball is drawn. It is tedious to count all the possible ways in which one or more of the balls drawn are red. So let's consider $E'$, the complement of this event—namely, that none of the balls that are chosen is red. The number of ways of choosing 6 blue balls from the 15 blue balls is $C(15, 6)$; the number of ways of choosing 6 balls from the 25 balls is $C(25, 6)$. Thus,

$$P(E') = \frac{n(E')}{n(S)} = \frac{C(15, 6)}{C(25, 6)} = \frac{5005}{177{,}100} = \frac{13}{460}$$

By the formula for the complement of an event we have

$$P(E) = 1 - P(E') = 1 - \frac{13}{460} = \frac{447}{460} \approx 0.97$$

Since $P(E') = 1 - P(E)$, we have $P(E) = 1 - P(E')$.

✎ **Practice what you've learned: Do Exercise 25.**

## The Union of Events

If $E$ and $F$ are events, what is the probability that $E$ $or$ $F$ occurs? The word $or$ indicates that we want the probability of the *union* of these events, that is, $E \cup F$. So we need to find the number of elements in $E \cup F$. If we simply added the number of elements in $E$ to the number of elements in $F$, then we would be counting the elements in the overlap twice—once in $E$ and once in $F$. So to get the correct total, we must subtract the number of elements in $E \cap F$ (see Figure 1). Thus,

$$n(E \cup F) = n(E) + n(F) - n(E \cap F)$$

Using the formula for probability, we get

$$P(E \cup F) = \frac{n(E \cup F)}{n(S)} = \frac{n(E) + n(F) - n(E \cap F)}{n(S)}$$

$$= \frac{n(E)}{n(S)} + \frac{n(F)}{n(S)} - \frac{n(E \cap F)}{n(S)}$$

$$= P(E) + P(F) - P(E \cap F)$$

We have proved the following.

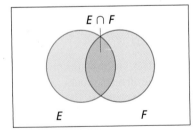

**FIGURE 1**

**PROBABILITY OF THE UNION OF TWO EVENTS**

If $E$ and $F$ are events in a sample space $S$, then the probability of $E$ $or$ $F$ is

$$P(E \cup F) = P(E) + P(F) - P(E \cap F)$$

▶ **EXAMPLE 6** | The Probability of the Union of Events

What is the probability that a card drawn at random from a standard 52-card deck is either a face card or a spade?

▼ **SOLUTION**   We let $E$ and $F$ denote the following events:

$E$:   The card is a face card.

$F$:   The card is a spade.

There are 12 face cards and 13 spades in a 52-card deck, so

$$P(E) = \frac{12}{52} \quad \text{and} \quad P(F) = \frac{13}{52}$$

Since 3 cards are simultaneously face cards and spades, we have

$$P(E \cap F) = \frac{3}{52}$$

Thus, by the formula for the probability of the union of two events, we have

$$P(E \cup F) = P(E) + P(F) - P(E \cap F)$$

$$= \frac{12}{52} + \frac{13}{52} - \frac{3}{52} = \frac{11}{26}$$

✎ **Practice what you've learned:** Do Exercise 43(b).    ▲

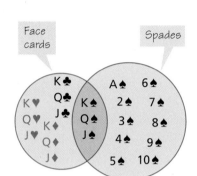

Face cards

Spades

## ■ The Union of Mutually Exclusive Events

Two events that have no outcome in common are said to be **mutually exclusive** (see Figure 2). For example, in drawing a card from a deck, the events

$E$:   The card is an ace.

$F$:   The card is a queen.

are mutually exclusive because a card cannot be both an ace and a queen.

If $E$ and $F$ are mutually exclusive events, then $E \cap F$ contains no elements. Thus, $P(E \cap F) = 0$, so

$$P(E \cup F) = P(E) + P(F) - P(E \cap F)$$

$$= P(E) + P(F)$$

We have proved the following formula.

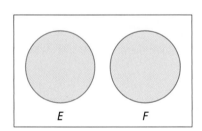

**FIGURE 2**

---

**PROBABILITY OF THE UNION OF MUTUALLY EXCLUSIVE EVENTS**

If $E$ and $F$ are mutually exclusive events in a sample space $S$, then the probability of $E$ or $F$ is

$$P(E \cup F) = P(E) + P(F)$$

---

There is a natural extension of this formula for any number of mutually exclusive events: If $E_1, E_2, \ldots, E_n$ are pairwise mutually exclusive, then

$$P(E_1 \cup E_2 \cup \cdots \cup E_n) = P(E_1) + P(E_2) + \cdots + P(E_n)$$

Sevens

7♦
    7♣
7♥    7♠

Face cards

K♦  Q♦  J♦
K♥  Q♥  J♥
K♣  Q♣  J♣
K♠  Q♠  J♠

▶ **EXAMPLE 7** │ The Probability of the Union of Mutually Exclusive Events

A card is drawn at random from a standard deck of 52 cards. What is the probability that the card is either a seven or a face card?

▼ **SOLUTION**  Let $E$ and $F$ denote the following events.

$$E: \quad \text{The card is a seven.}$$

$$F: \quad \text{The card is a face card.}$$

Since a card cannot be both a seven and a face card, the events are mutually exclusive. We want the probability of $E$ *or* $F$, in other words, the probability of $E \cup F$. By the formula,

$$P(E \cup F) = P(E) + P(F) = \frac{4}{52} + \frac{12}{52} = \frac{4}{13}$$

✎ **Practice what you've learned: Do Exercise 43(a).** ▲

## ■ The Intersection of Independent Events

We have considered the probability of events joined by the word *or*, that is, the union of events. Now we study the probability of events joined by the word *and*—in other words, the intersection of events.

When the occurrence of one event does not affect the probability of another event, we say that the events are **independent**. For instance, if a balanced coin is tossed, the probability of showing heads on the second toss is $\frac{1}{2}$, regardless of the outcome of the first toss. So any two tosses of a coin are independent.

---

**PROBABILITY OF THE INTERSECTION OF INDEPENDENT EVENTS**

If $E$ and $F$ are independent events in a sample space $S$, then the probability of $E$ *and* $F$ is

$$P(E \cap F) = P(E)P(F)$$

---

▶ **EXAMPLE 8** │ The Probability of Independent Events

A jar contains five red balls and four black balls. A ball is drawn at random from the jar and then replaced; then another ball is picked. What is the probability that both balls are red?

▼ **SOLUTION**  The events are independent. The probability that the first ball is red is $\frac{5}{9}$. The probability that the second is red is also $\frac{5}{9}$. Thus, the probability that both balls are red is

$$\frac{5}{9} \times \frac{5}{9} = \frac{25}{81} \approx 0.31$$

✎ **Practice what you've learned: Do Exercise 55.** ▲

▶ **EXAMPLE 9** │ The Birthday Problem

What is the probability that in a class of 35 students, at least two have the same birthday?

▼ **SOLUTION**  It is reasonable to assume that the 35 birthdays are independent and that each day of the 365 days in a year is equally likely as a date of birth. (We ignore February 29.)

Let $E$ be the event that two of the students have the same birthday. It is tedious to list all the possible ways in which at least two of the students have matching birthdays. So we consider the complementary event $E'$, that is, that *no* two students have the same birthday. To

| Number of people in a group | Probability that at least two have the same birthday |
|---|---|
| 5 | 0.02714 |
| 10 | 0.11695 |
| 15 | 0.25290 |
| 20 | 0.41144 |
| 22 | 0.47569 |
| 23 | 0.50730 |
| 24 | 0.53834 |
| 25 | 0.56870 |
| 30 | 0.70631 |
| 35 | 0.81438 |
| 40 | 0.89123 |
| 50 | 0.97037 |

find this probability, we consider the students one at a time. The probability that the first student has a birthday is 1, the probability that the second has a birthday different from the first is $\frac{364}{365}$, the probability that the third has a birthday different from the first two is $\frac{363}{365}$, and so on. Thus

$$P(E') = 1 \cdot \frac{364}{365} \cdot \frac{363}{365} \cdot \frac{362}{365} \cdot \dots \cdot \frac{331}{365} \approx 0.186$$

So

$$P(E) = 1 - P(E') \approx 1 - 0.186 = 0.814$$

✎ **Practice what you've learned: Do Exercise 67.**                          ▲

Most people are surprised that the probability in Example 9 is so high. For this reason this problem is sometimes called the "birthday paradox." The table in the margin gives the probability that two people in a group will share the same birthday for groups of various sizes.

# 10.3 EXERCISES

## ▼ CONCEPTS

**1.** The set of all possible outcomes of an experiment is called the

_____ _____. A subset of the sample space is called an

_____.

**2.** The sample space for the experiment of tossing two coins is

$S = \{HH, \_\_\_, \_\_\_, \_\_\_\}$, and the event "getting at least

one head" is $E = \{HH, \_\_\_, \_\_\_\}$. So the probability of

getting at least one head is $P(E) = \dfrac{n(\_\_\_)}{n(\_\_\_)} = \_\_\_\_$.

**3.** If the intersection of two events $E$ and $F$ is empty, then the

events are called _____ _____. So in drawing a card
from a deck, the event $E$ of "getting a heart" and the event $F$ of

"getting a spade" are _____ _____.

**4.** If the occurrence of an event $E$ does not affect the probability
of the occurrence of another event $F$, then the events are called

_____. So in tossing a coin, the event $E$ of "getting heads
on the first toss" and the event $F$ of "getting heads on the

second toss" are _____.

## ▼ SKILLS

✎ **5.** An experiment consists of rolling a die. List the elements in the
following sets.
 **(a)** The sample space
 **(b)** The event "getting an even number"
 **(c)** The event "getting a number greater than 4"

**6.** An experiment consists of tossing a coin and drawing a card
from a deck.
 **(a)** How many elements does the sample space have?
 **(b)** List the elements in the event "getting heads and an ace."
 **(c)** List the elements in the event "getting tails and a face card."
 **(d)** List the elements in the event "getting heads and a spade."

✎ **7.** An experiment consists of tossing a coin twice.
 **(a)** Find the sample space.
 **(b)** Find the probability of getting heads exactly two times.
 **(c)** Find the probability of getting heads at least one time.
 **(d)** Find the probability of getting heads exactly one time.

**8.** An experiment consists of tossing a coin and rolling a die.
 **(a)** Find the sample space.
 **(b)** Find the probability of getting heads and an even number.
 **(c)** Find the probability of getting heads and a number greater
 than 4.
 **(d)** Find the probability of getting tails and an odd number.

**9–10** ▪ A die is rolled. Find the probability of the given event.

**9.** **(a)** The number showing is a six.
 **(b)** The number showing is an even number.
 **(c)** The number showing is greater than five.

**10.** **(a)** The number showing is a two or a three.
 **(b)** The number showing is an odd number.
 **(c)** The number showing is a number divisible by 3.

**11–12** ▪ A card is drawn randomly from a standard 52-card deck.
Find the probability of the given event.

**11.** **(a)** The card drawn is a king.
 **(b)** The card drawn is a face card.
 **(c)** The card drawn is not a face card.

**12.** **(a)** The card drawn is a heart.
 **(b)** The card drawn is either a heart or a spade.
 **(c)** The card drawn is a heart, a diamond, or a spade.

**13–14** ▪ A ball is drawn randomly from a jar that contains five red
balls, two white balls, and one yellow ball. Find the probability of
the given event.

**13.** **(a)** A red ball is drawn.
 **(b)** The ball drawn is not yellow.
 **(c)** A black ball is drawn.

**14.** **(a)** Neither a white nor yellow ball is drawn.
 **(b)** A red, white, or yellow ball is drawn.
 **(c)** The ball that is drawn is not white.

**15.** A drawer contains an unorganized collection of 18 socks. Three pairs are red, two pairs are white, and four pairs are black.

   **(a)** If one sock is drawn at random from the drawer, what is the probability that it is red?

   **(b)** Once a sock is drawn and discovered to be red, what is the probability of drawing another red sock to make a matching pair?

**16.** A child's game has a spinner as shown in the figure. Find the probability of the given event.

   **(a)** The spinner stops on an even number.

   **(b)** The spinner stops on an odd number or a number greater than 3.

**17.** A letter is chosen at random from the word *EXTRATERRESTRIAL*. Find the probability of the given event.

   **(a)** The letter *T* is chosen.

   **(b)** The letter chosen is a vowel.

   **(c)** The letter chosen is a consonant.

**18.** A pair of dice is rolled, and the numbers showing are observed.

   **(a)** List the sample space of this experiment.

   **(b)** Find the probability of getting a sum of 7.

   **(c)** Find the probability of getting a sum of 9.

   **(d)** Find the probability that the two dice show doubles (the same number).

   **(e)** Find the probability that the two dice show different numbers.

   **(f)** Find the probability of getting a sum of 9 or higher.

**19–22** ▪ A poker hand, consisting of five cards, is dealt from a standard deck of 52 cards. Find the probability that the hand contains the cards described.

**19.** Five hearts          **20.** Five cards of the same suit

**21.** Five face cards

**22.** An ace, king, queen, jack, and 10 of the same suit (royal flush)

**23.** Two balls are picked at random from a jar that contains three red and five white balls. Find the probability of the following events.

   **(a)** Both balls are red.

   **(b)** Both balls are white.

**24.** Three CDs are picked at random from a collection of 12 CDs of which four are defective. Find the probability of the following events.

   **(a)** All three CDs are defective.

   **(b)** All three CDs are functioning properly.

**25.** A five-card poker hand is drawn from a standard 52-card deck. Find the probability that at least one card is a spade.

**26.** A five-card poker hand is drawn from a standard 52-card deck. Find the probability that at least one card is a face card.

## ▼ APPLICATIONS

**27. Four Siblings** A couple intends to have four children. Assume that having a boy and having a girl are equally likely events.

   **(a)** List the sample space of this experiment.

   **(b)** Find the probability that the couple has only boys.

   **(c)** Find the probability that the couple has two boys and two girls.

   **(d)** Find the probability that the couple has four children of the same sex.

   **(e)** Find the probability that the couple has at least two girls.

**28. Bridge Hands** What is the probability that a 13-card bridge hand consists of all cards from the same suit?

**29. Roulette** An American roulette wheel has 38 slots; two slots are numbered 0 and 00, and the remaining slots are numbered from 1 to 36. Find the probability that the ball lands in an odd-numbered slot.

**30. Making Words** A toddler has wooden blocks showing the letters *C, E, F, H, N,* and *R*. Find the probability that the child arranges the letters in the indicated order.

   **(a)** In the order *FRENCH*

   **(b)** In alphabetical order

**31. Lottery** In the 6/49 lottery game, a player selects six numbers from 1 to 49. What is the probability of picking the six winning numbers?

**32. An Unlikely Event** The president of a large company selects six employees to receive a special bonus. He claims that the six employees are chosen randomly from among the 30 employees, of whom 19 are women and 11 are men. What is the probability that no woman is chosen?

**33. Guessing on a Test** An exam has ten true-false questions. A student who has not studied answers all ten questions by just guessing. Find the probability that the student correctly answers the given number of questions.

   **(a)** All ten questions      **(b)** Exactly seven questions

**34. Quality Control** To control the quality of their product, the Bright-Light Company inspects three light bulbs out of each batch of ten bulbs manufactured. If a defective bulb is found, the batch is discarded. Suppose a batch contains two defective bulbs. What is the probability that the batch will be discarded?

**35. Monkeys Typing Shakespeare** An often-quoted example of an event of extremely low probability is that a monkey types Shakespeare's entire play *Hamlet* by randomly striking keys on a typewriter. Assume that the typewriter has 48 keys (including the space bar) and that the monkey is equally likely to hit any key.

   **(a)** Find the probability that such a monkey will actually correctly type just the title of the play as his first word.

   **(b)** What is the probability that the monkey will type the phrase "To be or not to be" as his first words?

**36. Making Words** A monkey is trained to arrange wooden blocks in a straight line. He is then given six blocks showing the letters *A, E, H, L, M, T*. What is the probability that he will arrange them to spell the word *HAMLET*?

**37. Making Words** A monkey is trained to arrange wooden blocks in a straight line. She is then given 11 blocks showing the letters *A, B, B, I, I, L, O, P, R, T, Y*. What is the probability that the monkey will arrange the blocks to spell the word *PROBABILITY*?

**38. Horse Race** Eight horses are entered in a race. You randomly predict a particular order for the horses to complete the race. What is the probability that your prediction is correct?

**39. Genetics** Many genetic traits are controlled by two genes, one dominant and one recessive. In Gregor Mendel's original experiments with peas, the genes controlling the height of the plant are denoted by T (tall) and t (short). The gene T is dominant, so a plant with the genotype (genetic makeup) TT or Tt is tall, whereas one with genotype tt is short. By a statistical analysis of the offspring in his experiments, Mendel concluded that offspring inherit one gene from each parent and that each possible combination of the two genes is equally likely. If each parent has the genotype Tt, then the following chart gives the possible genotypes of the offspring:

|  |  | Parent 2 | |
|---|---|---|---|
|  |  | **T** | **t** |
| **Parent 1** | **T** | TT | Tt |
|  | **t** | Tt | tt |

Find the probability that a given offspring of these parents will be **(a)** tall or **(b)** short.

**40. Genetics** Refer to Exercise 39. Make a chart of the possible genotypes of the offspring if one parent has genotype Tt and the other tt. Find the probability that a given offspring will be **(a)** tall or **(b)** short.

## ▼ SKILLS

**41–42** ▪ Determine whether the events *E* and *F* in the given experiment are mutually exclusive.

**41.** The experiment consists of selecting a person at random.
   **(a)** *E*:   The person is male.
       *F*:   The person is female.

   **(b)** *E*:   The person is tall.
       *F*:   The person is blond.

**42.** The experiment consists of choosing at random a student from your class.
   **(a)** *E*:   The student is female.
       *F*:   The student wears glasses.
   **(b)** *E*:   The student has long hair.
       *F*:   The student is male.

**43–44** ▪ A die is rolled, and the number showing is observed. Determine whether the events *E* and *F* are mutually exclusive. Then find the probability of the event $E \cup F$.

**43.** **(a)** *E*:   The number is even.
       *F*:   The number is odd.
   **(b)** *E*:   The number is even.
       *F*:   The number is greater than 4.

**44.** **(a)** *E*:   The number is greater than 3.
       *F*:   The number is less than 5.
   **(b)** *E*:   The number is divisible by 3.
       *F*:   The number is less than 3.

**45–46** ▪ A card is drawn at random from a standard 52-card deck. Determine whether the events *E* and *F* are mutually exclusive. Then find the probability of the event $E \cup F$.

**45.** **(a)** *E*:   The card is a face card.
       *F*:   The card is a spade.
   **(b)** *E*:   The card is a heart.
       *F*:   The card is a spade.

**46.** **(a)** *E*:   The card is a club.
       *F*:   The card is a king.
   **(b)** *E*:   The card is an ace.
       *F*:   The card is a spade.

**47–48** ▪ Refer to the spinner shown in the figure. Find the probability of the given event.

**47. (a)** The spinner stops on red.
   **(b)** The spinner stops on an even number.
   **(c)** The spinner stops on red or an even number.

**48. (a)** The spinner stops on blue.
   **(b)** The spinner stops on an odd number.
   **(c)** The spinner stops on blue or an odd number.

## ▼ APPLICATIONS

**49. Roulette** An American roulette wheel has 38 slots. Two of the slots are numbered 0 and 00, and the rest are numbered from

1 to 36. Find the probability that the ball lands in an odd-numbered slot or in a slot with a number higher than 31.

**50. Making Words** A toddler has eight wooden blocks showing the letters *A, E, I, G, L, N, T,* and *R.* What is the probability that the child will arrange the letters to spell one of the words *TRIANGLE* or *INTEGRAL*?

**51. Choosing a Committee** A committee of five is chosen randomly from a group of six males and eight females. What is the probability that the committee includes either all males or all females?

**52. Lottery** In the 6/49 lottery game a player selects six numbers from 1 to 49. What is the probability of selecting at least five of the six winning numbers?

**53. Marbles in a Jar** A jar contains six red marbles numbered 1 to 6 and ten blue marbles numbered 1 to 10. A marble is drawn at random from the jar. Find the probability that the given event occurs.
(a) The marble is red.
(b) The marble is odd-numbered.
(c) The marble is red or odd-numbered.
(d) The marble is blue or even-numbered.

## ▼ SKILLS

**54.** A coin is tossed twice. Let *E* and *F* be the following events:

$E$: The first toss shows heads.

$F$: The second toss shows heads.

(a) Are the events *E* and *F* independent?
(b) Find the probability of showing heads on both tosses.

**55.** A die is rolled twice. Let *E* and *F* be the following events:

$E$: The first roll shows a six.

$F$: The second roll shows a six.

(a) Are the events *E* and *F* independent?
(b) Find the probability of showing a six on both rolls.

**56–57** ▪ Spinners *A* and *B* shown in the figure are spun at the same time.

Spinner A        Spinner B

**56.** (a) Are the events "spinner A stops on red" and "spinner B stops on yellow" independent?
(b) Find the probability that spinner A stops on red and spinner B stops on yellow.

**57.** (a) Find the probability that both spinners stop on purple.
(b) Find the probability that both spinners stop on blue.

**58.** A die is rolled twice. What is the probability of showing a one on both rolls?

**59.** A die is rolled twice. What is the probability of showing a one on the first roll and an even number on the second roll?

**60.** A card is drawn from a deck and replaced, and then a second card is drawn.
(a) What is the probability that both cards are aces?
(b) What is the probability that the first is an ace and the second a spade?

## ▼ APPLICATIONS

**61. Roulette** A roulette wheel has 38 slots. Two slots are numbered 0 and 00, and the rest are numbered 1 to 36. A player places a bet on a number between 1 and 36 and wins if a ball thrown into the spinning roulette wheel lands in the slot with the same number. Find the probability of winning on two consecutive spins of the roulette wheel.

**62. Making Words** A researcher claims that she has taught a monkey to spell the word *MONKEY* using the five wooden letters *E, O, K, M, N, Y.* If the monkey has not actually learned anything and is merely arranging the blocks randomly, what is the probability that he will spell the word correctly three consecutive times?

**63. Snake Eyes** What is the probability of rolling "snake eyes" (double ones) three times in a row with a pair of dice?

**64. Lottery** In the 6/49 lottery game, a player selects six numbers from 1 to 49 and wins if he or she selects the winning six numbers. What is the probability of winning the lottery two times in a row?

**65. Balls in a Jar** Jar A contains three red balls and four white balls. Jar B contains five red balls and two white balls. Which one of the following ways of randomly selecting balls gives the greatest probability of drawing two red balls?
(i) Draw two balls from jar B.
(ii) Draw one ball from each jar.
(iii) Put all the balls in one jar, and then draw two balls.

**66. Slot Machine** A slot machine has three wheels. Each wheel has 11 positions: a bar and the digits 0, 1, 2, . . . , 9. When the handle is pulled, the three wheels spin independently before coming to rest. Find the probability that the wheels stop on the following positions.
(a) Three bars

**(b)** The same number on each wheel
**(c)** At least one bar

**67. A Birthday Problem**    Find the probability that in a group of eight students at least two people have the same birthday.

**68. A Birthday Problem**    What is the probability that in a group of six students at least two have birthdays in the same month?

**69. Combination Lock**    A student has locked her locker with a combination lock, showing numbers from 1 to 40, but she has forgotten the three-number combination that opens the lock. To open the lock, she decides to try all possible combinations. If she can try ten different combinations every minute, what is the probability that she will open the lock within one hour?

**70. Committee Membership**    A mathematics department consists of ten men and eight women. Six mathematics faculty members are to be selected at random for the curriculum committee.
**(a)** What is the probability that two women and four men are selected?
**(b)** What is the probability that two or fewer women are selected?
**(c)** What is the probability that more than two women are selected?

**71. Class Photo**    Twenty students are arranged randomly in a row for a class picture. Paul wants to stand next to Phyllis. Find the probability that he gets his wish.

**72. Class Photo**    Eight boys and 12 girls are arranged in a row. What is the probability that all the boys will be standing at one end of the row and all the girls at the other end?

### ▼ DISCOVERY • DISCUSSION • WRITING

**73. The "Second Son" Paradox**    Mrs. Smith says, "I have two children. The older one is named William." Mrs. Jones replies, "One of my two children is also named William." For each woman, list the sample space for the genders of her children, and calculate the probability that her other child is also a son. Explain why these two probabilities are different.

**74. The "Oldest Son or Daughter" Phenomenon**    Poll your class to determine how many of your male classmates are the oldest sons in their families and how many of your female classmates are the oldest daughters in their families. You will most likely find that they form a majority of the class. Explain why a randomly selected individual has a high probability of being the oldest son or daughter in his or her family.

# SMALL SAMPLES, BIG RESULTS

A national poll finds that voter preference for presidential candidates is as follows:

Candidate A:   57%

Candidate B:   43%

In the poll, 1600 adults were surveyed. Since over 100 million voters participate in a national election, it hardly seems possible that surveying only 1600 adults would be of any value. But it is, and it can be proved mathematically that if the sample of 1600 adults is selected *at random*, then the results are accurate to within ±3% more than 95% of the time. Scientists use these methods to determine properties of a big population by testing a small sample. For example, a small sample of fish from a lake is tested to determine the proportion that is diseased, or a small sample of a manufactured product is tested to determine the proportion that is defective.

We can get a feeling for how this works through a simple experiment. Put 1000 white beans and 1000 black beans in a bag, and mix them thoroughly. (It takes a lot of time to count out 1000 beans, so get several friends to count out 100 or so each.) Take a small cup, and scoop up a small sample from the beans.

1. Record the proportion of black (or white) beans in the sample. How closely does the proportion in the sample compare with the actual proportion in the bag?

2. Take several samples, and record the proportion of black (or white) beans in each sample.

   (a) Graph your results.

   (b) Average your results. How close is your average to 0.5?

3. Try the experiment again but with 500 black beans and 1500 white beans. What proportion of black (or white) beans would you expect in a sample?

4. Have some friends mix black and white beans without telling you the number of each. Estimate the proportion of black (or white) beans by taking a few small samples.

```
PROGRAM:SAMPLE
:100→N
:0→C
:For(J,1,N)
:rand→B
:(B≤0.25)+C→C
:End
:Disp "PROPORTION="
:Disp C/N
```

5. This bean experiment can be simulated on your graphing calculator. Let's designate the numbers in the interval $[0, 0.25]$ as "black beans" and those in $(0.25, 1]$ as "white beans." Now use the random number generator in your calculator to randomly pick a sample of numbers between 0 and 1. Try samples of size 100, 400, 1600, and larger. Determine the proportion of these that are "black beans." What would you expect this proportion to be? Do your results improve when you use a larger sample? (The TI-83 program in the margin takes a sample of 100 random numbers.)

6. Biologists use sampling techniques to estimate fish populations. For example, to estimate the number of trout in a lake, some of the trout are collected, tagged, and released. Later, a sample is taken, and the number of tagged trout in the sample is recorded. The total number of trout in the lake can be estimated from the following proportionality:

$$\frac{\text{number of tagged trout in lake}}{\text{number of trout in lake}} \approx \frac{\text{number of tagged trout in sample}}{\text{number of trout in sample}}$$

Model this process using beans as follows. Start with a bag containing an unknown number of white beans. Remove a handful of the beans, count them, then "tag" them by marking them with a felt tip pen. Return the tagged beans to the bag, and mix the beans thoroughly. Now take a sample from the bag, and use the number of tagged beans in the sample to estimate the total number of beans in the bag.

**LEARNING OBJECTIVE**

After completing this section, you will be able to:

■ Find binomial probabilities

A coin is weighted so that the probability of heads is $\frac{2}{3}$. What is the probability of getting exactly two heads in five tosses of this coin? Since the tosses are independent, the probability of getting two heads followed by three tails is

$$\left(\frac{2}{3}\right)\left(\frac{2}{3}\right)\left(\frac{1}{3}\right)\left(\frac{1}{3}\right)\left(\frac{1}{3}\right) = \left(\frac{2}{3}\right)^2\left(\frac{1}{3}\right)^3$$

Heads    Heads    Tails    Tails    Tails

But this is not the only way we can get exactly two heads. The two heads could occur, for example, on the second toss and the last toss. In this case the probability is

$$\left(\frac{1}{3}\right)\left(\frac{2}{3}\right)\left(\frac{1}{3}\right)\left(\frac{1}{3}\right)\left(\frac{2}{3}\right) = \left(\frac{2}{3}\right)^2\left(\frac{1}{3}\right)^3$$

Tails    Heads    Tails    Tails    Heads

In fact, the two heads could occur on any two of the five tosses. Thus, there are $C(5, 2)$ ways in which this can happen, each with probability $\left(\frac{2}{3}\right)^2\left(\frac{1}{3}\right)^3$. It follows that

$$P(\text{exactly 2 heads in 5 tosses}) = C(5, 2)\left(\frac{2}{3}\right)^2\left(\frac{1}{3}\right)^3 \approx 0.164609$$

The probabilities that we have just calculated are examples of binomial probabilities. In general, a **binomial experiment** is one in which there are two outcomes, which we call "success" and "failure." In the coin-tossing experiment described above, "success" is getting "heads," and "failure" is getting "tails." The following box tells us how to calculate the probabilities associated with binomial experiments when we perform them many times.

**BINOMIAL PROBABILITIES**

An experiment has two possible outcomes, $S$ and $F$ (called "success" and "failure"), with $P(S) = p$ and $P(F) = q = 1 - p$. The probability of getting exactly $r$ successes in $n$ independent trials of the experiment is

$$P(r \text{ successes in } n \text{ trials}) = C(n, r)p^r q^{n-r}$$

The name "binomial probability" is appropriate because $C(n, r)$ is the same as the binomial coefficient $\binom{n}{r}$ (see Exercise 82 on page 671).

▶ **EXAMPLE 1** | Rolling a Die

A fair die is rolled 10 times. Find the probability of each event.

**(a)** Exactly 2 rolls are sixes.

**(b)** At most 1 roll is a six.

**(c)** At least 2 rolls are sixes.

▼ **SOLUTION** We interpret "success" as getting a six and "failure" as not getting a six. Thus, $P(S) = \frac{1}{6}$ and $P(F) = \frac{5}{6}$. Since each roll of the die is independent from the others, we can use the formula for binomial probability with $n = 10$, $p = \frac{1}{6}$, and $q = \frac{5}{6}$.

**(a)** $P(\text{exactly 2 are sixes}) = C(10, 2)(\frac{1}{6})^2(\frac{5}{6})^8 \approx 0.29071$

**(b)** The statement "*at most* 1 roll is a six" means 0 or 1 roll is a six. So

$$P(\text{at most 1 roll is a six}) = P(0 \text{ or } 1 \text{ roll is a six}) \qquad \text{Meaning of "at most"}$$

$$= P(0 \text{ roll is a six}) + P(1 \text{ roll is a six}) \qquad P(A \text{ or } B) = P(A) + P(B)$$

$$= C(10, 0)\left(\frac{1}{6}\right)^0\left(\frac{5}{6}\right)^{10} + C(10, 1)\left(\frac{1}{6}\right)^1\left(\frac{5}{6}\right)^9 \qquad \text{Binomial probability}$$

$$\approx 0.161506 + 0.323011 \qquad \text{Calculator}$$

$$= 0.484517$$

**(c)** The statement "*at least* 2 rolls are sixes" means 2 or more rolls are sixes. Instead of adding the probabilities that 2, 3, 4, 5, 6, 7, 8, 9, or 10 are sixes (which is a lot of work), it's easier to find the probability of the complement of this event. The complement of "2 or more are sixes" is "0 or 1 is a six." So

$$P(2 \text{ or more are sixes}) = 1 - P(0 \text{ or } 1 \text{ is a six}) \qquad P(E) = 1 - P(E')$$

$$\approx 1 - 0.484517 \qquad \text{From part (b)}$$

$$= 0.515483$$

✎ **Practice what you've learned: Do Exercise 21.** ▲

▶ **EXAMPLE 2** | Testing a Drug for Effectiveness

A certain viral disease is known to have a mortality rate of 80%. A drug company has developed a drug that it claims is an effective treatment for the disease. In clinical tests, the drug is administered to ten people suffering from the disease; seven of them recover.

**(a)** What is the probability that seven or more of the patients would have recovered without treatment?

**(b)** Does the drug appear to be effective?

▼ **SOLUTION**

**(a)** The probability of dying from the disease is 80%, or 0.8, so the probability of recovery ("success") is $1 - 0.8 = 0.2$. We must calculate the probability that 7, 8, 9, or 10 of the patients would recover without treatment.

$$P(7 \text{ out of 10 recover}) = C(10, 7)(0.2)^7(0.8)^3 \approx 0.0007864$$

$$P(8 \text{ out of 10 recover}) = C(10, 8)(0.2)^8(0.8)^2 \approx 0.0000737$$

$$P(9 \text{ out of 10 recover}) = C(10, 9)(0.2)^9(0.8)^1 \approx 0.0000041$$

$$P(10 \text{ out of 10 recover}) = C(10, 10)(0.2)^{10}(0.8)^0 \approx 0.0000001$$

Adding these probabilities, we find

$$P(7 \text{ or more recover}) \approx 0.0008643$$

**(b)** The probability that seven or more patients would have recovered spontaneously is less than 0.001, or less than $\frac{1}{10}$ of 1%. Thus, it is very unlikely that this happened just by chance. We conclude that the drug is most likely effective.

✎ **Practice what you've learned: Do Exercise 35.** ▲

It's often helpful to know the most likely outcome when a binomial experiment is performed repeatedly. For example, suppose we flip a balanced coin eight times? What is the number of heads that is most likely to show up? To find out, we need to find the probability of getting no heads, one head, two heads, and so on.

$$P(0 \text{ head}) = C(8,0)\left(\frac{1}{2}\right)^0\left(\frac{1}{2}\right)^8 \approx 0.003906$$

$$P(1 \text{ head}) = C(8,1)\left(\frac{1}{2}\right)^1\left(\frac{1}{2}\right)^7 \approx 0.03125$$

$$P(2 \text{ heads}) = C(8,2)\left(\frac{1}{2}\right)^2\left(\frac{1}{2}\right)^6 \approx 0.109375$$

| Number of heads | Probability |
|:---:|:---:|
| 0 | 0.003906 |
| 1 | 0.031250 |
| 2 | 0.109375 |
| 3 | 0.218750 |
| 4 | 0.273438 |
| 5 | 0.218750 |
| 6 | 0.109375 |
| 7 | 0.031250 |
| 8 | 0.003906 |

The probabilities for any number of heads (from 0 to 8) are shown in the table. A bar graph of these probabilities is shown in Figure 1. From the graph we see that the event with greatest probability is four heads and four tails.

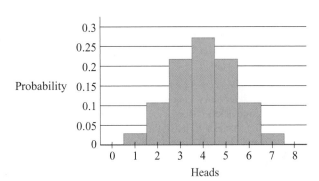

**FIGURE 1**

# 10.4 EXERCISES

## ▼ CONCEPTS

**1.** A binomial experiment is one in which there are exactly

_____ outcomes. One outcome is called _____, and the

other is called _____.

**2.** If a binomial experiment has probability $p$ of success, then the

probability of failure is _____. The probability of getting exactly $r$ successes in $n$ trials of this experiment is

$C(\underline{\quad}, \underline{\quad})p^{\blacksquare}(1 - p)^{\blacksquare}$.

## ▼ SKILLS

**3–14** ▪ Five independent trials of a binomial experiment with probability of success $p = 0.7$ and probability of failure $q = 0.3$ are performed. Find the probability of each event.

**3.** Exactly two successes

**4.** Exactly three successes

**5.** No successes

**6.** All successes

**7.** Exactly one success

**8.** Exactly one failure

**9.** At least four successes

**10.** At least three successes

**11.** At most one failure

**12.** At most two failures

**13.** At least two successes

**14.** At most three failures

## ▼ APPLICATIONS

**15. Rolling Dice** Six dice are rolled. Find the probability that two of them show a four.

**16. Archery** An archer hits his target 80% of the time. If he shoots seven arrows, what is the probability of each event?
**(a)** He never hits the target.
**(b)** He hits the target each time.
**(c)** He hits the target more than once.

**(d)** He hits the target at least five times.

**17. Television Ratings**  According to a ratings survey, 40% of the households in a certain city tune in to the local evening TV news. If ten households are visited at random, what is the probability that four of them will have their television tuned to the local news?

**18. Spread of Disease**  Health authorities estimate that 10% of the raccoons in a certain rural county are carriers of rabies. A dog is bitten by four different raccoons in this county. What is the probability that he was bitten by at least one rabies carrier?

**19. Blood Type**  About 45% of the population of the United States and Canada have Type O blood.
  **(a)** If a random sample of ten people is selected, what is the probability that exactly five have Type O blood?
  **(b)** What is the probability that at least three of the random sample of ten have Type O blood?

**20. Handedness**  A psychologist needs 12 left-handed subjects for an experiment, and she interviews 15 potential subjects. About 10% of the population is left-handed.
  **(a)** What is the probability that exactly 12 of the potential subjects are left-handed?
  **(b)** What is the probability that 12 or more are left-handed?

**21. Germination Rates**  A certain brand of tomato seeds has a 0.75 probability of germinating. To increase the chance that at least one tomato plant per seed hill germinates, a gardener plants four seeds in each hill.
  **(a)** What is the probability that at least one seed germinates in a given hill?
  **(b)** What is the probability that two or more seeds will germinate in a given hill?
  **(c)** What is the probability that all four seeds germinate in a given hill?

**22. Genders of Children**  Assume that for any given live human birth, the chances that the child is a boy or a girl are equally likely.
  **(a)** What is the probability that in a family of five children a majority are boys?
  **(b)** What is the probability that in a family of seven children a majority are girls?

**23. Genders of Children**  The ratio of male to female births is in fact not exactly one-to-one. The probability that a newborn turns out to be a male is about 0.52. A family has ten children.
  **(a)** What is the probability that all ten children are boys?
  **(b)** What is the probability all are girls?
  **(c)** What is the probability that five are girls and five are boys?

**24. Education Level**  In a certain county 20% of the population have a college degree. A jury consisting of 12 people is selected at random from this county.

  **(a)** What is the probability that exactly two of the jurors have a college degree?
  **(b)** What is the probability that three or more of the jurors have a college degree?

**25. Defective Light Bulbs**  The DimBulb Lighting Company manufactures light bulbs for appliances such as ovens and refrigerators. Typically, 0.5% of their bulbs are defective. From a crate with 100 bulbs, three are tested. Find the probability that the given event occurs.
  **(a)** All three bulbs are defective.
  **(b)** One or more bulbs is defective.

**26. Quality Control**  An assembly line that manufactures fuses for automotive use is checked every hour to ensure the quality of the finished product. Ten fuses are selected randomly, and if any one of the ten is found to be defective, the process is halted and the machines are recalibrated. Suppose that at a certain time 5% of the fuses being produced are actually defective. What is the probability that the assembly line is halted at that hour's quality check?

**27. Sick Leave**  The probability that a given worker at the Dyno Nutrition will call in sick on a Monday is 0.04. The packaging department has eight workers. What is the probability that two or more packaging workers will call in sick next Monday?

**28. Political Surveys**  In a certain county, 60% of the voters are in favor of an upcoming school bond initiative. If five voters are interviewed at random, what is the probability that exactly three of them will favor the initiative?

**29. Pharmaceuticals**  A drug that is used to prevent motion sickness is found to be effective about 75% of the time. Six friends, prone to seasickness, go on a sailing cruise, and all take the drug. Find the probability of each event.
  **(a)** None of the friends gets seasick.
  **(b)** All of the friends get seasick.
  **(c)** Exactly three get seasick.
  **(d)** At least two get seasick.

**30. Reliability of a Machine**    A machine that is used in a manufacturing process has four separate components, each of which has a 0.01 probability of failing on any given day. If any component fails, the entire machine breaks down. Find the probability that on a given day the indicated event occurs.

**(a)** The machine breaks down.

**(b)** The machine does not break down.

**(c)** Only one component does not fail.

**31. Genetics**    Huntington's disease is a hereditary ailment caused by a recessive gene. If both parents carry the gene but do not have the disease, there is a 0.25 probability that an offspring will fall victim to the condition. A newly wed couple find through genetic testing that they both carry the gene (but do not have the disease). If they intend to have four children, find the probability of each event.

**(a)** At least one child gets the disease.

**(b)** At least three of the children get the disease.

**32. Selecting Cards**    Three cards are randomly selected from a standard 52-card deck, one at a time, with each card replaced in the deck before the next one is picked. Find the probability of each event.

**(a)** All three cards are hearts.

**(b)** Exactly two of the cards are spades.

**(c)** None of the cards is a diamond.

**(d)** At least one of the cards is a club.

**33. Smokers and Nonsmokers**    The participants at a mathematics conference are housed dormitory-style, five to a room. Due to an oversight, conference organizers forget to ask whether the participants are smokers. In fact, it turns out that 30% are smokers. Find the probability that Fred, a nonsmoking conference participant, will be housed with

**(a)** Exactly one smoker

**(b)** One or more smokers

**34. Telephone Marketing**    A mortgage company advertises its rates by making unsolicited telephone calls to random numbers. About 2% of the calls reach consumers who are interested in the company's services. A telephone consultant can make 100 calls per evening shift.

**(a)** What is the probability that two or more calls will reach an interested party in one shift?

**(b)** How many calls does a consultant need to make to ensure at least a 0.5 probability of reaching one or more interested parties?    [*Hint*: Use trial and error.]

✎ **35. Effectiveness of a Drug**    A certain disease has a mortality rate of 60%. A new drug is tested for its effectiveness against this disease. Ten patients are given the drug, and eight of them recover.

**(a)** Find the probability that eight or more of the patients would have recovered without the drug.

**(b)** Does the drug appear to be effective? (Consider the drug effective if the probability in part (a) is 0.05 or less.)

**36. Hitting a Target**    An archer normally hits the target with probability of 0.6. She hires a new coach for a series of special lessons. After the lessons she hits the target in five out of eight attempts.

**(a)** Find the probability that she would have hit five or more out of the eight attempts before her lessons with the new coach.

**(b)** Did the new coaching appear to make a difference? (Consider the coaching effective if the probability in part (a) is 0.05 or less.)

---

## ▼ DISCOVERY • DISCUSSION • WRITING

**37. Most Likely Outcome (Balanced Coin)**    A balanced coin is tossed nine times, and the number of heads is observed. The bar graph below shows the probabilities of getting any number of heads from 0 to 9. (Compare this graph to the one on page 687.)

**(a)** Find the probabilities of getting exactly one head, exactly two heads, and so on, to confirm the probabilities given by the graph.

**(b)** What is the most likely outcome (the number of heads with the greatest probability of occurring)?

**(c)** If the coin is tossed 101 times, what number of heads has the greatest probability of occurring? What if the coin is tossed 100 times?

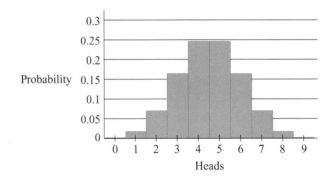

**38. Most Likely Outcome (Unbalanced Coin)**    An unbalanced coin has a 0.7 probability of showing heads. The coin is tossed nine times, and the number of heads is observed. The bar graph shows the probabilities of getting any number of heads from 0 to 9.

**(a)** Find the probabilities of getting exactly one head, exactly two heads, and so on, to confirm the probabilities given by the graph.

**(b)** What is the most likely outcome(s) (the number of heads with the greatest probability of occurring)? Compare your results to those in Exercise 37(b).

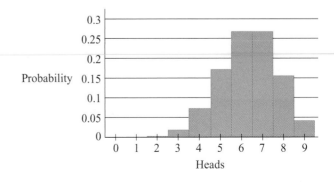

| **10.5** | Expected Value |

### LEARNING OBJECTIVE

After completing this section, you will be able to:

▪ Find the expected value of a game

**FIGURE 1**

In the game shown in Figure 1, you pay $1 to spin the arrow. If the arrow stops in a red region, you get $3 (the dollar you paid plus $2); otherwise, you lose the dollar you paid. If you play this game many times, how much would you expect to win? Or lose? To answer these questions, let's consider the probabilities of winning and losing. Since three of the regions are red, the probability of winning is $\frac{3}{10} = 0.3$, and the probability of losing is $\frac{7}{10} = 0.7$. Remember, this means that if you play this game many times, you expect to win "on average" three out of ten times. Suppose you play the game 1000 times. Then you would expect to win 300 times and lose 700 times. Since we win $2 or lose $1 in each game, our expected payoff in 1000 games is

$$2(300) + (-1)(700) = -100$$

So the average expected return per game is $\frac{-100}{1000} = -0.1$. In other words, we expect to lose, on average, 10 cents per game. Another way to view this average is to divide each side of the preceding equation by 1000. Writing $E$ for the result, we get

$$E = \frac{2(300) + (-1)(700)}{1000}$$

$$= 2\left(\frac{300}{1000}\right) + (-1)\frac{700}{1000}$$

$$= 2(0.3) + (-1)(0.7)$$

Thus, the expected return, or *expected value*, per game is

$$E = a_1 p_1 + a_2 p_2$$

where $a_1$ is the payoff that occurs with probability $p_1$ and $a_2$ is the payoff that occurs with probability $p_2$. This example leads us to the following definition of expected value.

---

**DEFINITION OF EXPECTED VALUE**

A game gives payoffs $a_1, a_2, \ldots, a_n$ with probabilities $p_1, p_2, \ldots, p_n$. The **expected value** (or **expectation**) $E$ of this game is

$$E = a_1 p_1 + a_2 p_2 + \cdots + a_n p_n$$

---

The expected value is an average expectation per game if the game is played many times. In general, $E$ need not be one of the possible payoffs. In the preceding example the expected value is $-10$ cents, but notice that it's impossible to lose exactly 10 cents in any given game.

▶ **EXAMPLE 1** | Finding an Expected Value

A die is rolled, and you receive $1 for each point that shows. What is your expectation?

▼ **SOLUTION**    Each face of the die has probability $\frac{1}{6}$ of showing. So you get $1 with probability $\frac{1}{6}$, $2 with probability $\frac{1}{6}$, $3 with probability $\frac{1}{6}$, and so on. Thus, the expected value is

$$E = 1\left(\frac{1}{6}\right) + 2\left(\frac{1}{6}\right) + 3\left(\frac{1}{6}\right) + 4\left(\frac{1}{6}\right) + 5\left(\frac{1}{6}\right) + 6\left(\frac{1}{6}\right) = \frac{21}{6} = 3.5$$

This means that if you play this game many times, you will make, on average, $3.50 per game.

✎ **Practice what you've learned: Do Exercise 3.** ▲

▶ **EXAMPLE 2** | Finding an Expected Value

In Monte Carlo the game of roulette is played on a wheel with slots numbered 0, 1, 2, . . . , 36. The wheel is spun, and a ball dropped in the wheel is equally likely to end up in any one of the slots. To play the game, you bet $1 on any number other than zero. (For example, you may bet $1 on number 23.) If the ball stops in your slot, you get $36 (the $1 you bet plus $35). Find the expected value of this game.

▼ **SOLUTION**    You gain $35 with probability $\frac{1}{37}$, and you lose $1 with probability $\frac{36}{37}$. Thus

$$E = (35)\frac{1}{37} + (-1)\frac{36}{37} \approx -0.027$$

In other words, if you play this game many times, you would expect to lose 2.7 cents on every dollar you bet (on average). Consequently, the house expects to gain 2.7 cents on every dollar that is bet. This expected value is what makes gambling very profitable for the gaming house and very unprofitable for the gambler.

✎ **Practice what you've learned: Do Exercise 13.** ▲

# 10.5 EXERCISES

▼ **CONCEPTS**

**1.** If a game gives payoffs of $10 and $100 with probabilities 0.9 and 0.1, respectively, then the expected value of this game is

$E = $ _____ $\times$ 0.9 + _____ $\times$ 0.1.

**2.** If you played the game in Exercise 1 many times, then you would expect your average payoff per game to be about

$ _____ .

▼ **SKILLS**

**3–12** ■ Find the expected value (or expectation) of the games described.

✎ **3.** Mike wins $2 if a coin toss shows heads and $1 if it shows tails.

**4.** Jane wins $10 if a die roll shows a six, and she loses $1 otherwise.

**5.** The game consists of drawing a card from a deck. You win $100 if you draw the ace of spades or lose $1 if you draw any other card.

**6.** Tim wins $3 if a coin toss shows heads or $2 if it shows tails.

**7.** Carol wins $3 if a die roll shows a six, and she wins $0.50 otherwise.

**8.** A coin is tossed twice. Albert wins $2 for each heads and must pay $1 for each tails.

**9.** A die is rolled. Tom wins $2 if the die shows an even number, and he pays $2 otherwise.

**10.** A card is drawn from a deck. You win $104 if the card is an ace, $26 if it is a face card, and $13 if it is the 8 of clubs.

**11.** A bag contains two silver dollars and eight slugs. You pay 50 cents to reach into the bag and take a coin, which you get to keep.

**12.** A bag contains eight white balls and two black balls. John picks two balls at random from the bag, and he wins $5 if he does not pick a black ball.

▼ **APPLICATIONS**

✎ **13.** **Roulette**    In the game of roulette as played in Las Vegas, the wheel has 38 slots. Two slots are numbered 0 and 00, and the rest are numbered 1 to 36. A $1 bet on any number other than 0 or 00 wins $36 ($35 plus the $1 bet). Find the expected value of this game.

**14.** **Sweepstakes**    A sweepstakes offers a first prize of $1,000,000, second prize of $100,000, and third prize of $10,000. Suppose that two million people enter the contest and three names are drawn randomly for the three prizes.

**(a)** Find the expected winnings for a person participating in this contest.

**(b)** Is it worth paying a dollar to enter this sweepstakes?

**15. A Game of Chance** A box contains 100 envelopes. Ten envelopes contain $10 each, ten contain $5 each, two are "unlucky," and the rest are empty. A player draws an envelope from the box and keeps whatever is in it. If a person draws an unlucky envelope, however, he must pay $100. What is the expectation of a person playing this game?

**16. Combination Lock** A safe containing $1,000,000 is locked with a combination lock. You pay $1 for one guess at the six-digit combination. If you open the lock, you get to keep the million dollars. What is your expectation?

**17. Gambling on Stocks** An investor buys 1000 shares of a risky stock for $5 a share. She estimates that the probability that the stock will rise in value to $20 a share is 0.1 and the probability that it will fall to $1 a share is 0.9. If the only criterion for her decision to buy this stock was the expected value of her profit, did she make a wise investment?

**18. Slot Machine** A slot machine has three wheels, and each wheel has 11 positions: the digits 0, 1, 2, . . . , 9 and the picture of a watermelon. When a quarter is placed in the machine and the handle is pulled, the three wheels spin independently and come to rest. When three watermelons show, the payout is $5; otherwise, nothing is paid. What is the expected value of this game?

**19. Lottery** In a 6/49 lottery game, a player pays $1 and selects six numbers from 1 to 49. Any player who has chosen the six winning numbers wins $1,000,000. Assuming that this is the only way to win, what is the expected value of this game?

**20. A Game of Chance** A bag contains two silver dollars and six slugs. A game consists of reaching into the bag and drawing a coin, which you get to keep. Determine the "fair price" of playing this game, that is, the price at which the player can be expected to break even if he or she plays the game many times (in other words, the price at which the player's expectation is zero).

**21. A Game of Chance** A game consists of drawing a card from a deck. You win $13 if you draw an ace. What is a "fair price" to pay to play this game? (See Exercise 20.)

**22. Lightning Insurance** An insurance company has determined that in a certain region the probability of lightning striking a house in a given year is about 0.0003, and the average cost of repairs of lightning damage is $7500 per incident. The company charges $25 per year for lightning insurance.

**(a)** What is the company's expected value for the net income from each lightning insurance policy?

**(b)** If the company has 450,000 lightning damage policies, what is the company's expected yearly income from lightning insurance?

---

## ▼ DISCOVERY • DISCUSSION • WRITING

**23. The Expected Value of a Sweepstakes Contest** A magazine clearinghouse holds a sweepstakes contest to sell subscriptions. If you return the winning number, you win $1,000,000. You have a 1-in-20-million chance of winning, but your only cost to enter the contest is a first-class stamp to mail the entry. Use the current price of a first-class stamp to calculate your expected net winnings if you enter this contest. Is it worth entering the sweepstakes?

---

# ▶ CHAPTER 10 | REVIEW

## ▼ PROPERTIES AND FORMULAS

### Fundamental Counting Principle (p. 658)

If $E_1, E_2, \ldots, E_k$ are events that occur in order and if event $E_i$ can occur in $n_i$ ways $(i = 1, 2, \ldots, k)$, then the sequence of events can occur in order in $n_1 \times n_2 \times \cdots \times n_k$ ways.

### Permutations (p. 663)

A **permutation** of a set of objects is an ordering of these objects. If the set has $n$ objects, then there are $n!$ permutations of the objects.

If a set has $n$ objects, then the number of ways of ordering the $r$-element subsets of the set is denoted $P(n, r)$ and is called the **number of permutations of $n$ objects taken $r$ at a time**:

$$P(n, r) = \frac{n!}{(n - r)!}$$

### Distinguishable Permutations (p. 664)

Suppose that a set has $n$ objects of $k$ kinds (where the objects in each kind cannot be distinguished from each other), and suppose that there are $n_1$ objects of the first kind, $n_2$ of the second kind, and so on (so $n_1 + n_2 + \cdots + n_k = n$). Two permutations of the set are **distinguishable** from each other if one cannot be obtained from the other simply by interchanging the positions of elements of the same kind. (In other words, the permutations "look" different.)

The number of distinguishable permutations of these objects is

$$\frac{n!}{n_1! n_2! \cdots n_k!}$$

### Combinations (p. 666)

A **combination** of $r$ objects from a set is any subset of the set that contains $r$ elements (without regard to order).

If a set has $n$ objects, then the number of combinations of $r$ elements from the set is denoted $C(n, r)$ and is called the **number of combinations of $n$ objects taken $r$ at a time**:

$$C(n, r) = \frac{n!}{r!(n - r)!}$$

### Permutations or Combinations? (p. 667)

When solving a problem that involves counting the number of ways of picking $r$ objects from a set of $n$ objects, we ask, "Does the order in which the objects are picked make a difference?"

1. For each sequence, find the 7th term and the 20th term.

   (a) $\frac{1}{3}, \frac{2}{5}, \frac{3}{7}, \frac{4}{9}, \frac{5}{11}, \dots$

   (b) $a_n = \dfrac{2n^2 + 1}{n^3 - n + 4}$

   (c) The arithmetic sequence with initial term $a = \frac{1}{2}$ and common difference $d = 3$.

   (d) The geometric sequence with initial term $a = 12$ and common ratio $r = \frac{5}{6}$.

   (e) The sequence defined recursively by $a_1 = 0.01$ and $a_n = -2a_{n-1}$.

2. Calculate the sum.

   (a) $\frac{3}{5} + \frac{4}{5} + 1 + \frac{6}{5} + \frac{7}{5} + \frac{8}{5} + \dots + \frac{19}{5} + 4$

   (b) $3 + 9 + 27 + 81 + \dots + 3^{10}$

   (c) $\displaystyle\sum_{n=0}^{9} \frac{5}{2^n}$

   (d) $6 + 2 + \frac{2}{3} + \frac{2}{9} + \frac{2}{27} + \frac{2}{81} + \dots$

3. Mary and Kevin buy a vacation home for \$350,000. They pay \$35,000 down and take out a 15-year mortgage for the remainder. If their annual interest rate is 6%, how much will their monthly mortgage payment be?

4. A sequence is defined inductively by $a_1 = 1$ and $a_n = a_{n-1} + 2n - 1$. Use mathematical induction to prove that $a_n = n^2$.

5. (a) Use the Binomial Theorem to expand the expression $\left(2x - \frac{1}{2}\right)^5$.

   (b) Find the term containing $x^4$ in the binomial expansion of $\left(2x - \frac{1}{2}\right)^{12}$.

6. When students receive their e-mail accounts at Oldenburg University they are assigned a randomly selected password, which consists of three letters followed by four digits (for example, ABC1234).

   (a) How many such passwords are possible?

   (b) How many passwords consist of three different letters followed by four different digits?

   (c) The system administrator decides that in the interest of security, no two passwords can contain the same set of letters and digits (regardless of the order), and no character can be repeated in a password. What is the maximum number of users the system can accommodate under these rules?

7. Toftree is a game in which players roll three dice and receive points based on the outcome. Find the probability of each of the following outcomes.

   (a) All three dice show the same number.

   (b) All three dice show an even number.

   (c) The sum of the numbers showing is 15.

8. An alumni association holds a "Vegas night" at its annual homecoming event. At one booth, participants play the following dice game: The player pays a fee of \$5, rolls a pair of dice, and then gets back \$15 if both dice show the same number, or \$7 if the dice show numbers that differ by one (such as 2 and 3, or 5 and 4). What is the expected value of this game?

9. A weighted coin has probability $p$ of showing heads and $q = 1 - p$ of showing tails when tossed.

   (a) Find the binomial expansion of $(p + q)^5$. If this coin is tossed five times in a row, what event has the probability represented by the term in this binomial expansion that contains $p^3$?

   (b) If the probability of heads is $\frac{2}{3}$, find the probability that in five tosses of the coin there are 2 heads and 3 tails.

**10.** An insect species has white wings which when closed cover the insect's back, like the wings of a ladybug. Some individuals have black spots on their wings, arranged randomly, with a total of one to five spots. The probability that a randomly selected insect has $n$ spots is $\left(\frac{1}{4}\right)^n$ ($n = 1, 2, 3, 4,$ or $5$).

**(a)** What event has probability $\displaystyle\sum_{n=1}^{5}\left(\frac{1}{4}\right)^n$? Calculate this sum.

**(b)** What is the probability that a randomly selected insect has no spots?

A good way to familiarize ourselves with a fact is to experiment with it. For instance, to convince ourselves that the earth is a sphere (which was considered a major paradox at one time), we could go up in a space shuttle to see that it is so; to see whether a given equation is an identity, we might try some special cases to make sure there are no obvious counter-examples. In problems involving probability, we can perform an experiment many times and use the results to estimate the probability in question. In fact, we often model the experiment on a computer, thereby making it feasible to perform the experiment a large number of times. This technique is called the **Monte Carlo method**, named after the famous gambling casino in Monaco.

▶ **EXAMPLE 1** | The Contestant's Dilemma

In a TV game show, a contestant chooses one of three doors. Behind one of them is a valuable prize; the other two doors have nothing behind them. After the contestant has made her choice, the host opens one of the other two doors—one that he knows does not conceal a prize—and then gives her the opportunity to change her choice.

Should the contestant switch or stay, or does it matter? In other words, by switching doors, does she increase, decrease, or leave unchanged her probability of winning? At first, it may seem that switching doors doesn't make any difference. After all, two doors are left—one with the prize and one without—so it seems reasonable that the contestant has an equal chance of winning or losing. But if you play this game many times, you will find that by switching doors, you actually win about $\frac{2}{3}$ of the time.

The authors modeled this game on a computer and found that in one million games the simulated contestant (who always switches) won 667,049 times—very close to $\frac{2}{3}$ of the time. Thus, it seems that switching doors does make a difference: Switching increases the contestant's chances of winning. This experiment forces us to reexamine our reasoning. Here is why switching doors is the correct strategy:

Contestant: "I choose door number 2."

Contestant: "Oh no, what should I do?"

1. When the contestant first made her choice, she had a $\frac{1}{3}$ chance of winning. If she doesn't switch, no matter what the host does, her probability of winning remains $\frac{1}{3}$.

2. If the contestant decides to switch, she will switch to the winning door if she had initially chosen a losing one or to a losing door if she had initially chosen the winning one. Since the probability of having initially selected a losing door is $\frac{2}{3}$, by switching the probability of winning then becomes $\frac{2}{3}$.

We conclude that the contestant should switch, because her probability of winning is $\frac{2}{3}$ if she switches and $\frac{1}{3}$ if she doesn't. Put simply, there is a much greater chance that she initially chose a losing door (since there are more of these), so she should switch. ▲

An experiment can be modeled using any computer language or programmable calculator that has a random-number generator. This is a command or function (usually called Rnd or Rand) that returns a randomly chosen number $x$ with $0 \le x < 1$. In the next example we see how to use this to model a simple experiment.

▶ **EXAMPLE 2** | Monte Carlo Model of a Coin Toss

When a balanced coin is tossed, each outcome—"heads" or "tails"—has probability $\frac{1}{2}$. This doesn't mean that if we toss a coin several times, we will necessarily get exactly half heads and half tails. We would expect, however, the proportion of heads and of tails to get closer and closer to $\frac{1}{2}$ as the number of tosses increases. To test this hypothesis, we could toss a coin a very large number of times and keep track of the results. But this is a very tedious process, so we will use the Monte Carlo method to model this process.

To model a coin toss with a calculator or computer, we use the random-number generator to get a random number $x$ such that $0 \le x < 1$. Because the number is chosen randomly,

```
PROGRAM:HEADTAIL
:0→J:0→K
:For(N,1,100)
:rand→X
:int(2X)→Y
:J+(1-Y)→J
:K+Y→K
:END
:Disp"HEADS=",J
:Disp"TAILS=",K
```

the probability that it lies in the first half of this interval $\left(0 \leq x < \frac{1}{2}\right)$ is the same as the probability that it lies in the second half $\left(\frac{1}{2} \leq x < 1\right)$. Thus, we could model the outcome "heads" by the event that $0 \leq x < \frac{1}{2}$ and the outcome "tails" by the event that $\frac{1}{2} \leq x < 1$.

An easier way to keep track of heads and tails is to note that if $0 \leq x < 1$, then $0 \leq 2x < 2$, and so $[\![2x]\!]$, the integer part of $2x$, is either 0 or 1, each with probability $\frac{1}{2}$. (On most programmable calculators, the function Int gives the integer part of a number.) Thus, we could model "heads" with the outcome "0" and "tails" with the outcome "1" when we take the integer part of $2x$. The program in the margin models 100 tosses of a coin on the TI-83 calculator. The graph in Figure 1 shows what proportion $p$ of the tosses have come up "heads" after $n$ tosses. As you can see, this proportion settles down near 0.5 as the number $n$ of tosses increases—just as we hypothesized.

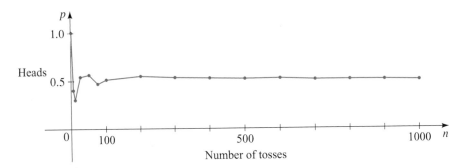

**FIGURE 1** Relative frequency of "heads"

In general, if a process has $n$ equally likely outcomes, then we can model the process using a random-number generator as follows: If our program or calculator produces the random number $x$, with $0 \leq x < 1$, then the integer part of $nx$ will be a random choice from the $n$ integers $0, 1, 2, \ldots, n - 1$. Thus, we can use the outcomes $0, 1, 2, \ldots, n - 1$ as models for the outcomes of the actual experiment.

## Problems

1. **Winning Strategy** In a game show like the one described in Example 1, a prize is concealed behind one of ten doors. After the contestant chooses a door, the host opens eight losing doors and then gives the contestant the opportunity to switch to the other unopened door.
   (a) Play this game with a friend 30 or more times, using the strategy of switching doors each time. Count the number of times you win, and estimate the probability of winning with this strategy.
   (b) Calculate the probability of winning with the "switching" strategy using reasoning similar to that in Example 1. Compare with your result from part (a).

2. **Family Planning** A couple intend to have two children. What is the probability that they will have one child of each sex? The French mathematician D'Alembert analyzed this problem (incorrectly) by reasoning that three outcomes are possible: two boys, or two girls, or one child of each sex. He concluded that the probability of having one of each sex is $\frac{1}{3}$, mistakenly assuming that the three outcomes are "equally likely."
   (a) Model this problem with a pair of coins (using "heads" for boys and "tails" for girls), or write a program to model the problem. Perform the experiment 40 or more times, counting the number of boy-girl combinations. Estimate the probability of having one child of each sex.
   (b) Calculate the correct probability of having one child of each sex, and compare this with your result from part (a).

3. **Dividing a Jackpot** A game between two players consists of tossing a coin. Player A gets a point if the coin shows heads, and player B gets a point if it shows tails. The first player to get six points wins an $8000 jackpot. As it happens, the police raid the place when player A has five points and B has three points. After everyone has calmed down, how should the jackpot

be divided between the two players? In other words, what is the probability of A winning (and that of B winning) if the game were to continue?

The French mathematicians Pascal and Fermat corresponded about this problem, and both came to the same correct conclusion (though by very different reasonings). Their friend Roberval disagreed with both of them. He argued that player A has probability $\frac{3}{4}$ of winning, because the game can end in the four ways *H, TH, TTH, TTT*, and in three of these, A wins. Roberval's reasoning was wrong.

(a) Continue the game from the point at which it was interrupted, using either a coin or a modeling program. Perform this experiment 80 or more times, and estimate the probability that player A wins.

(b) Calculate the probability that player A wins. Compare with your estimate from part (a).

4. **Long or Short World Series?**    In the World Series the top teams in the National League and the American League play a best-of-seven series; that is, they play until one team has won four games. (No tie is allowed, so this results in a maximum of seven games.) Suppose the teams are evenly matched, so that the probability that either team wins a given game is $\frac{1}{2}$.

(a) Use a coin or a modeling program to model a World Series, where "heads" represents a win by Team A and "tails" represents a win by Team B. Perform this experiment at least 80 times, keeping track of how many games are needed to decide each series. Estimate the probability that an evenly matched series will end in four games. Do the same for five, six, and seven games.

(b) What is the probability that the series will end in four games? Five games? Six games? Seven games? Compare with your estimates from part (a).

(c) Find the expected value for the number of games until the series ends.    [*Hint*: This will be $P(\text{four games}) \times 4 + P(\text{five}) \times 5 + P(\text{six}) \times 6 + P(\text{seven}) \times 7$.]

5. **Estimating $\pi$**    In this problem we use the Monte Carlo method to estimate the value of $\pi$. The circle in the figure has radius 1, so its area is $\pi$, and the square has area 4. If we choose a point at random from the square, the probability that it lies inside the circle will be

$$\frac{\text{area of circle}}{\text{area of square}} = \frac{\pi}{4}$$

The Monte Carlo method involves choosing many points inside the square. Then we have

$$\frac{\text{number of hits inside circle}}{\text{number of hits inside square}} \approx \frac{\pi}{4}$$

```
PROGRAM:PI
:0→P
:For(N,1,1000)
:rand→X:rand→Y
:P+((X²+Y²)<1)→P
:End
:Disp "PI IS
APPROX",4*P/N
```

Thus, 4 times this ratio will give us an approximation for $\pi$.

To implement this method, we use a random-number generator to obtain the coordinates $(x, y)$ of a random point in the square, and then check to see if it lies inside the circle (that is, we check if $x^2 + y^2 < 1$). Note that we need to use only points in the first quadrant, since the ratio of areas is the same in each quadrant. The program in the margin shows a way of doing this on the TI-83 calculator for 1000 randomly selected points.

Carry out this Monte Carlo simulation for as many points as you can. How do your results compare with the actual value of $\pi$? Do you think this is a reasonable way to get a good approximation for $\pi$?

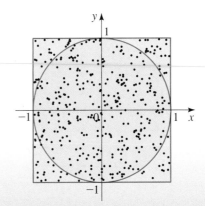

The "contestant's dilemma" problem discussed on page 699 is an
example of how subtle probability
can be. This problem was posed in
a nationally syndicated column in
*Parade* magazine in 1990. The correct solution was presented in the
column, but it generated consider-
able controversy, with thousands of
letters arguing that the solution was
wrong. This shows how problems
in probability can be quite tricky.
Without a lot of experience in
probabilistic thinking, it's easy to
make a mistake. Even great mathematicians such as D'Alembert and
Roberval (see Problems 2 and 3)
made mistakes in probability. Professor David Burton writes in his
book *The History of Mathematics*,
"Probability theory abounds in
paradoxes that wrench the common sense and trip the unwary."

6. **Areas of Curved Regions**   The Monte Carlo method can be used to estimate the area under
the graph of a function. The figure below shows the region under the graph of $f(x) = x^2$,
above the $x$-axis, between $x = 0$ and $x = 1$. If we choose a point in the square at random, the
probability that it lies under the graph of $f(x) = x^2$ is the area under the graph divided by the
area of the square. So if we randomly select a large number of points in the square, we have

$$\frac{\text{number of hits under graph}}{\text{number of hits in square}} \approx \frac{\text{area under graph}}{\text{area of square}}$$

Modify the program from Problem 5 to carry out this Monte Carlo simulation and approximate the required area.

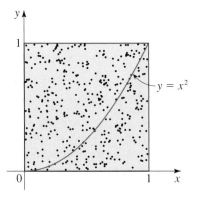

7. **Random Numbers**   Choose two numbers at random from the interval $[0, 1)$. What is the
probability that the sum of the two numbers is less than 1?

   **(a)** Use a Monte Carlo model to estimate the probability.

   **(b)** Calculate the exact value of the probability.   [*Hint*: Call the numbers $x$ and $y$. Choosing these numbers is the same as choosing an ordered pair $(x, y)$ in the unit square
   $\{(x, y) \mid 0 \le x < 1, 0 \le y < 1\}$. What proportion of the points in this square corresponds
   to $x + y$ being less than 1?]

# ANSWERS TO EXERCISES AND CHAPTER TESTS

## CHAPTER P

### SECTION P.1 ▪ page 5

**1.** 48  **2.** $C = 3x$  **3.** $T = \$9.60$  **4.** $850  **5.** $300
**6.** 141.4 in$^3$  **7. (a)** 30 mi/gal  **(b)** 7 gal  **8. (a)** 65.5°F
**(b)** 2000 ft  **9. (a)** 38 km$^3$  **(b)** 2 km$^3$  **10. (a)** 103.7 hp
**(b)** 5 knots
**11. (a)**

| Depth (ft) | Pressure (lb/in$^2$) |
|:---:|:---:|
| 0 | 14.7 |
| 10 | 19.2 |
| 20 | 23.7 |
| 30 | 28.2 |
| 40 | 32.7 |
| 50 | 37.2 |
| 60 | 41.7 |

**(b)** 34 ft
**12. (a)** $W = 40x$
**(b)**

| Population | Gallons of water used |
|:---:|:---:|
| 0 | 0 |
| 1000 | 40,000 |
| 2000 | 80,000 |
| 3000 | 120,000 |
| 4000 | 160,000 |
| 5000 | 200,000 |

**(c)** 3500
**13.** $N = 7w$  **14.** $N = 25q$  **15.** $A = \dfrac{a+b}{2}$

**16.** $A = \dfrac{a+b+c}{3}$  **17.** $C = 3.50x$  **18.** $T = 0.15x$

**19.** $d = 60t$  **20.** $r = \dfrac{d}{3}$  **21. (a)** $15  **(b)** $C = 12 + n$  **(c)** 4

**22. (a)** $118  **(b)** $C = 30n + 0.10m$  **(c)** 500 mi
**23. (a) (i)** $C = 0.04x$  **(ii)** $C = 0.12x$  **(b) (i)** $400
**(ii)** $1200  **24. (a)** 16,000 in$^3$  **(b)** $V = 2x^3$  **25. (a)** $2
**(b)** $C = 1.00 + 0.10t$  **(c)** 12 min  **(d)** $C = F + rt$
**26. (a)** GPA $= (4a + 3b + 2c + d)/(a + b + c + d + f)$
**(b)** 2.84

### SECTION P.2 ▪ page 12

**1. (a)** 2  **(b)** $-3$  **(c)** $\frac{3}{2}$  **(d)** $\sqrt{2}$  **2. (a)** $ba$; Commutative
**(b)** $(a + b) + c$; Associative  **(c)** $ab + ac$; Distributive
**3.** Denominator  **4.** Invert the divisor  **5. (a)** 50  **(b)** 0, $-10$, 50
**(c)** 0, $-10$, 50, $\frac{22}{7}$, 0.538, $1.2\overline{3}$, $-\frac{1}{3}$  **(d)** $\sqrt{7}$, $\sqrt[3]{2}$  **6. (a)** 11, $\sqrt{16}$
**(b)** $-11$, 11, $\sqrt{16}$  **(c)** 1.001, $0.3\overline{3}$, $-11$, 11, $\frac{13}{15}$, $\sqrt{16}$, 3.14, $\frac{15}{3}$
**(d)** $-\pi$  **7.** 1  **8.** 5  **9.** $-2$  **10.** $-301$  **11.** Commutative
Property for Addition  **12.** Commutative Property for Multiplication
**13.** Associative Property for Addition  **14.** Distributive Property
**15.** Distributive Property  **16.** Distributive Property
**17.** Commutative Property for Multiplication  **18.** Distributive
Property  **19.** $3 + x$  **20.** $(7 \cdot 3)x$  **21.** $4A + 4B$  **22.** $5(x + y)$
**23.** $3x + 3y$  **24.** $8a - 8b$  **25.** $8m$  **26.** $-8y$  **27.** $-5x + 10y$
**28.** $3ab + 3ac - 6ad$  **29.** $\frac{17}{30}$  **30.** $\frac{9}{20}$  **31.** $\frac{1}{15}$  **32.** $\frac{35}{24}$  **33.** 3
**34.** $\frac{25}{72}$  **35.** $\frac{13}{20}$  **36.** $\frac{5}{36}$  **37.** $\frac{8}{3}$  **38.** 6  **39.** $\frac{15}{2}$  **40.** 3  **41. (a)** $\frac{7}{9}$
**(b)** $\frac{13}{45}$  **(c)** $\frac{19}{33}$  **42. (a)** $\frac{518}{99}$  **(b)** $\frac{62}{45}$  **(c)** $\frac{1057}{495}$  **43.** Distributive
Property

### SECTION P.3 ▪ page 17

**1.** Each positive number $x$ is represented by the point on the line a
distance of $x$ units to the right of the origin, and each negative number $-x$ is represented by the point $x$ units to the left of the origin.
**2.** $a$ is to the left of $b$.  **3.** $\{x \mid 2 < x < 7\}$; $(2, 7)$  **4.** $A$ includes
$-2$ and 5, $B$ excludes $-2$ and 5.  **5.** absolute value; positive
**6.** distance  **7. (a)** $<$  **(b)** $>$  **(c)** $=$  **8. (a)** $<$  **(b)** $>$
**(c)** $=$  **9.** False  **10.** True  **11.** True  **12.** False  **13.** False
**14.** True  **15.** False  **16.** True
**17.** ——⟶ $\frac{1}{2}$  **18.** ——⟶ $-4$
**19.** ——⟶ $-3$  **20.** ——⟶ $0$
**21.** $x \leq 1$  **22.** $x < -2$  **23.** $x > -\frac{3}{2}$  **24.** $x \geq 5$
**25. (a)** $x > 0$  **(b)** $t < 4$  **(c)** $a \geq \pi$  **(d)** $-5 < x < \frac{1}{3}$
**(e)** $|p - 3| \leq 5$  **26. (a)** $y < 0$  **(b)** $z > 1$  **(c)** $b \leq 8$
**(d)** $0 < w \leq 17$  **(e)** $|y - \pi| \geq 2$  **27. (a)** $\{1, 2, 3, 4, 5, 6, 7, 8\}$
**(b)** $\{2, 4, 6\}$  **28. (a)** $\{2, 4, 6, 7, 8, 9, 10\}$  **(b)** $\{8\}$
**29. (a)** $\{1, 2, 3, 4, 5, 6, 7, 8, 9, 10\}$  **(b)** $\{7\}$
**30. (a)** $\{1, 2, 3, 4, 5, 6, 7, 8, 9, 10\}$  **(b)** $\varnothing$  **31. (a)** $\{x \mid x \leq 5\}$
**(b)** $\{x \mid -1 < x < 4\}$  **32. (a)** $\{x \mid -1 < x \leq 5\}$
**(b)** $\{x \mid -2 \leq x < 4\}$
**33.** $-3 < x < 0$  **34.** $2 < x \leq 8$
——————○ $-3$ ○—— $0$  ——————○ $2$ ●—— $8$

**35.** $2 \le x < 8$

**36.** $-6 \le x \le -\frac{1}{2}$

**37.** $x \ge 2$

**38.** $-\infty < x < 1$

**39.** $(-\infty, 1]$

**40.** $[1, 2]$

**41.** $(-2, 1]$

**42.** $[-5, \infty)$

**43.** $(-1, \infty)$

**44.** $(-5, 2)$

**45.** (a) $[-3, 5]$ (b) $(-3, 5)$ **46.** (a) $[0, 2)$ (b) $(-2, 0)$

**47.**

**48.**

**49.**

**50.**

**51.**

**52.**

**53.** (a) 100 (b) 73 **54.** (a) $5 - \sqrt{5}$ (b) $10 - \pi$
**55.** (a) 2 (b) $-1$ **56.** (a) 10 (b) $-1$ **57.** (a) 12 (b) 5
**58.** (a) $\frac{1}{4}$ (b) 1 **59.** 5 **60.** 4 **61.** (a) 15 (b) 24 (c) $\frac{67}{40}$
**62.** (a) $\frac{18}{35}$ (b) 19 (c) 0.8
**63.** $T_O - T_G$: $-9, -3, 0, 5, 8, 1, -1$
$|T_O - T_G|$: $9, 3, 0, 5, 8, 1, 1$

$T_O - T_G$ gives more information because it tells us which city had the higher (or lower) temperature.
**64.** (a) Yes (b) 170 **65.** (a) Yes, No (b) 6 ft

## SECTION P.4 ▪ page 24

**1.** $5^6$ **2.** Base, exponent **3.** Add, $3^9$ **4.** Subtract, $3^3$
**5.** Multiply, $3^8$ **6.** (a) $\frac{1}{2}$ (b) $\frac{1}{8}$ (c) 2 **7.** 125 **8.** 32 **9.** 64

**10.** 1 **11.** 1 **12.** $-1$ **13.** $-9$ **14.** 9 **15.** $\frac{1}{9}$ **16.** 25

**17.** 1000 **18.** 27 **19.** $\frac{1}{2}$ **20.** $\frac{1}{8}$ **21.** 16 **22.** $\frac{27}{8}$ **23.** $\frac{1}{4}$

**24.** $\frac{1}{100}$ **25.** 1 **26.** $\frac{1}{15}$ **27.** $\frac{3}{8}$ **28.** $\frac{8}{27}$ **29.** $x^{10}$ **30.** $12y^7$

**31.** $\frac{1}{x^4}$ **32.** $\frac{1}{x^2}$ **33.** 1 **34.** $\frac{1}{z^2}$ **35.** $y^3$ **36.** $\frac{1}{x^4}$ **37.** $a^6$

**38.** $z^4$ **39.** $8y^6$ **40.** $64x^2$ **41.** $a^{18}$ **42.** $16a^{20}$ **43.** $\frac{1}{24z^4}$

**44.** $\frac{1}{32}$ **45.** $\frac{a^6}{64}$ **46.** $\frac{9x^4}{16}$ **47.** $8x^7y^5$ **48.** $4a^5z^5$ **49.** $6a^3b^2$

**50.** $8s^{10}t^3$ **51.** $405x^{10}y^{23}$ **52.** $500a^{12}b^{19}$ **53.** $s^2t^7$ **54.** $72v^{11}$

**55.** $8rs^4$ **56.** $\frac{1}{9y}$ **57.** $\frac{3y^2}{z}$ **58.** $\frac{2y}{x^2}$ **59.** $\frac{y^2z^9}{x^2}$ **60.** $4v^3$

**61.** $\frac{a^{19}b}{c^9}$ **62.** $\frac{x^{10}}{yz^4}$ **63.** $\frac{4a^8}{b^9}$ **64.** $5x^2y$ **65.** $\frac{v^{10}}{u^{11}}$ **66.** $r^9s^2$

**67.** $\frac{b^3}{3a}$ **68.** $\frac{4y^4}{x^4}$ **69.** $\frac{125}{x^6y^3}$ **70.** $\frac{a^9}{8b^{12}}$ **71.** $\frac{s^3}{r^4q^7}$ **72.** $\frac{x^3y^{15}}{z^3}$

**73.** $6.93 \times 10^7$ **74.** $7.2 \times 10^{12}$ **75.** $2.8536 \times 10^{-5}$
**76.** $1.213 \times 10^{-4}$ **77.** $1.2954 \times 10^8$ **78.** $7.259 \times 10^9$
**79.** $1.4 \times 10^{-9}$ **80.** $7.029 \times 10^{-4}$ **81.** 319,000
**82.** 272,100,000 **83.** 0.00000002670 **84.** 0.000000009999
**85.** 710,000,000,000,000 **86.** 6,000,000,000,000 **87.** 0.00855

**88.** 0.0000000006257 **89.** (a) $5.9 \times 10^{12}$ mi (b) $4 \times 10^{-13}$ cm
(c) $3.3 \times 10^{19}$ molecules **90.** (a) $9.3 \times 10^7$ mi
(b) $5.3 \times 10^{-23}$ g (c) $5.97 \times 10^{24}$ kg **91.** $1.3 \times 10^{-20}$
**92.** $9.14 \times 10^{43}$ **93.** $1.429 \times 10^{19}$ **94.** $6.3 \times 10^{38}$
**95.** $7.4 \times 10^{-14}$ **96.** $3.19 \times 10^{-106}$ **97.** (a) Negative
(b) Positive (c) Negative (d) Negative (e) Positive
(f) Negative **99.** $2.5 \times 10^{13}$ mi **100.** $8\frac{1}{3}$ min **101.** $1.3 \times 10^{21}$ L
**102.** \$20,300 **103.** $4.03 \times 10^{27}$ molecules **104.** 42.32, obese;
16.95, underweight; 26.78, overweight; 20.11, normal
**105.** \$470.26, \$636.64, \$808.08

## SECTION P.5 ▪ page 30

**1.** $5^{1/3}$ **2.** $\sqrt{5}$ **3.** No **4.** $(4^{1/2})^3 = 8, (4^3)^{1/2} = 8$

**5.** $\frac{1}{\sqrt{3}} = \frac{1}{\sqrt{3}} \cdot \frac{\sqrt{3}}{\sqrt{3}} = \frac{\sqrt{3}}{3}$ **6.** $\frac{2}{3}$ **7.** $5^{-1/2}$ **8.** $7^{2/3}$ **9.** $\sqrt[3]{4^2}$

**10.** $\frac{1}{\sqrt{11^3}}$ **11.** $5^{3/5}$ **12.** $\frac{1}{\sqrt{8}}$ **13.** $\sqrt[5]{a^2}$ **14.** $x^{-5/2}$ **15.** (a) 4

(b) 2 (c) $\frac{1}{2}$ **16.** (a) 8 (b) $-4$ (c) $-2$ **17.** (a) $\frac{2}{3}$ (b) 4
(c) $\frac{1}{2}$ **18.** (a) 14 (b) 4 (c) 6 **19.** (a) $\frac{3}{2}$ (b) 4 (c) $-\frac{1}{5}$
**20.** (a) $\frac{1}{2}$ (b) $\frac{9}{4}$ (c) $\frac{125}{512}$ **21.** (a) $\frac{1}{4}$ (b) $\frac{1}{81}$ (c) 4 **22.** (a) $\frac{1}{100}$
(b) $\frac{1}{1,000,000}$ (c) 160,000 **23.** (a) $\frac{1}{1000}$ (b) 36 (c) 100
**24.** (a) 8 (b) 2 (c) 15 **25.** 5 **26.** 3 **27.** 14 **28.** $\frac{1}{144}$
**29.** $|x|$ **30.** $x^2$ **31.** $2x^2$ **32.** $xy^2$ **33.** $x\sqrt[3]{y}$ **34.** $x^2y^2$
**35.** $ab\sqrt[5]{ab^2}$ **36.** $a^2\sqrt[3]{b^2}$ **37.** $2|x|$ **38.** $|x|\sqrt[4]{y^2z^2}$
**39.** $7\sqrt{2}$ **40.** $9\sqrt{3}$ **41.** $2\sqrt{5}$ **42.** $\sqrt[3]{2}$ **43.** $\sqrt[3]{4}$
**44.** $7\sqrt{2}$ **45.** $2\sqrt{5}$ **46.** $-\sqrt[3]{3}$ **47.** $3\sqrt[3]{3}$ **48.** $\sqrt[4]{3}$
**49.** $x^2$ **50.** $y^2$ **51.** $16b^{3/4}$ **52.** $45a^2$ **53.** $w^{5/3}$ **54.** $4s^{9/2}$

**55.** $4a^4b$ **56.** $8a^9b^{12}$ **57.** $\frac{1}{4y^2}$ **58.** $\frac{1}{u^{4/3}v^2}$ **59.** $\frac{x^3}{y^{1/5}}$ **60.** $2x^6$

**61.** $4st^4$ **62.** 4 **63.** $\frac{2y^{4/3}}{x^2}$ **64.** $-\frac{1}{2}y^{3/4}z^2$ **65.** $\frac{1}{x}$

**66.** $\frac{8y^8}{x^2}$ **67.** $\frac{x}{ab^{10}y^{10/3}}$ **68.** $4s^{3/2}t^{9/2}$ **69.** $y^{3/2}$ **70.** $b^{5/4}$

**71.** $10x^{7/12}$ **72.** $2a^{7/6}$ **73.** $2st^{11/6}$ **74.** $xy^2$ **75.** $x$ **76.** $2x^{1/6}$

**77.** $\frac{x^{1/4}y^{1/4}}{2}$ **78.** $a^{3/4}$ **79.** $\frac{4u}{v^2}$ **80.** $\frac{3y}{x}$ **81.** $y^{1/2}$ **82.** $s^{5/4}$

**83.** (a) $\frac{\sqrt{6}}{6}$ (b) $\frac{3\sqrt{2}}{2}$ (c) $3\sqrt{3}$ **84.** (a) $4\sqrt{3}$

(b) $\frac{5\sqrt{2}}{2}$ (c) $\frac{\sqrt{6}}{3}$ **85.** (a) $\frac{\sqrt[3]{2}}{2}$ (b) $\frac{\sqrt[4]{27}}{3}$ (c) $4\sqrt[5]{16}$

**86.** (a) $\frac{\sqrt[5]{4}}{2}$ (b) $\frac{2\sqrt[4]{27}}{3}$ (c) $\frac{3\sqrt[4]{2}}{2}$ **87.** (a) $\frac{\sqrt[3]{x^2}}{x}$

(b) $\frac{\sqrt[5]{x^3}}{x}$ (c) $\frac{\sqrt[7]{x^4}}{x}$ **88.** (a) $\frac{\sqrt[3]{x}}{x}$ (b) $\frac{\sqrt[4]{x}}{x}$ (c) $\frac{\sqrt[3]{x^2}}{x^2}$

**89.** 41.3 mi **90.** (a) 28 mi/h (b) 167 ft **91.** (a) Yes
(b) 3292 ft$^2$ **92.** (a) 17.707 ft/s (b) 1328.0 ft$^3$/s

## SECTION P.6 ▪ page 36

**1.** (a), (c) **2.** like, $11x^2 + x + 5$ **3.** like, $x^3 + 8x^2 - 5x + 2$
**4.** FOIL, $x^2 + 5x + 6$ **5.** $A^2 + 2AB + B^2, 4x^2 + 12x + 9$
**6.** $A^2 - B^2, 25 - x^2$ **7.** Trinomial; $x^2, -3x, 7; 2$ **8.** Binomial;
$2x^5, 4x^2; 5$ **9.** Monomial; $-8; 0$ **10.** Monomial; $\frac{1}{2}x^7; 7$
**11.** Four terms; $-x^4, x^3, -x^2, x; 4$ **12.** Binomial; $\sqrt{2}x, -\sqrt{3}; 1$
**13.** No **14.** No **15.** Yes; 3 **16.** Yes; 5 **17.** No **18.** Yes; 1

**19.** $7x + 5$   **20.** $-3 - x$   **21.** $5x^2 - 2x - 4$   **22.** $x^2 + 4x + 6$
**23.** $x^3 + 3x^2 - 6x + 11$   **24.** $7x + 5$   **25.** $9x + 103$
**26.** $x^2 - 6x + 17$   **27.** $2x^2 - 2x$   **28.** $6y^2 + 15y$   **29.** $x^3 + 3x^2$
**30.** $-y^3 + 2y$   **31.** $t^2 + 4$   **32.** $-2t^2 + 21t - 20$
**33.** $7r^3 - 3r^2 - 9r$   **34.** $v^4 - 5v^3 - 4v^2$   **35.** $2x^4 - x^3 + x^2$
**36.** $3x^7 - 12x^5 + 15x^3$   **37.** $x^2 + x - 12$   **38.** $y^2 + 4y - 5$
**39.** $r^2 + 2r - 15$   **40.** $s^2 + 6s - 16$   **41.** $21t^2 - 26t + 8$
**42.** $8s^2 + 18s - 5$   **43.** $6x^2 + 7x - 5$   **44.** $14y^2 - 13y + 3$
**45.** $2x^2 + 5xy - 3y^2$   **46.** $12x^2 - 19xy + 5y^2$
**47.** $6r^2 - 19rs + 10s^2$   **48.** $6u^2 - 7uv - 10v^2$   **49.** $x^2 + 6x + 9$
**50.** $x^2 - 4x + 4$   **51.** $9x^2 + 24x + 16$   **52.** $1 - 4y + 4y^2$
**53.** $4u^2 + 4uv + v^2$   **54.** $x^2 - 6xy + 9y^2$   **55.** $4x^2 + 12xy + 9y^2$
**56.** $r^2 - 4rs + 4s^2$   **57.** $x^4 + 2x^2 + 1$   **58.** $4 + 4y^3 + y^6$
**59.** $x^2 - 25$   **60.** $y^2 - 9$   **61.** $9x^2 - 16$   **62.** $4y^2 - 25$
**63.** $x^2 - 9y^2$   **64.** $4u^2 - v^2$   **65.** $x - 4$   **66.** $y - 2$
**67.** $y^3 + 6y^2 + 12y + 8$   **68.** $x^3 - 9x^2 + 27x - 27$
**69.** $1 - 6r + 12r^2 - 8r^3$   **70.** $27 + 54y + 36y^2 + 8y^3$
**71.** $x^3 + 4x^2 + 7x + 6$   **72.** $2x^3 + x^2 + 1$
**73.** $2x^3 - 7x^2 + 7x - 5$   **74.** $2x^3 - 5x^2 - x + 1$   **75.** $x^{3/2} - x$
**76.** $x^2 - x$   **77.** $y + y^2$   **78.** $2x - x^{1/2}$   **79.** $x^4 + 2x^2y^2 + y^4$
**80.** $c^2 + 2 + \dfrac{1}{c^2}$   **81.** $x^4 - a^4$   **82.** $x - y$   **83.** $a - b^2$   **84.** $h^2$
**85.** $1 - x^{4/3}$   **86.** $1 - 2b^2 + b^4$   **87.** $-x^4 + x^2 - 2x + 1$
**88.** $-x^4 - 3x^2 - 4$   **89.** $4x^2 + 4xy + y^2 - 9$
**90.** $x^2 - y^2 - 2yz - z^2$   **91.** (b) $4x^3 - 32x^2 + 60x$; 3   (c) 32, 24
**92.** (b) $xy - 20y - 20x + 400$   (c) 200 ft by 200 ft
**93.** (a) $2000r^3 + 6000r^2 + 6000r + 2000$; 3
(b) \$2122.42, \$2185.45, \$2282.33, \$2382.03, \$2662.00
**94.** (a) $P = 0.05x^2 + 20x - 50$   (b) \$155, \$370

## SECTION P.7 · page 43

**1.** 3; $2x^5$, $6x^4$, $4x^3$; $2x^3$; $2x^3(x^2 + 3x + 2)$
**2.** 10, 7; 2, 5; $(x + 2)(x + 5)$   **3.** $(A + B)(A - B)$;
$(2x + 5)(2x - 5)$   **4.** $(A + B)^2$; $(x + 5)^2$   **5.** $5(a - 4)$
**6.** $3(-b + 4)$   **7.** $2x(-x^2 + 8)$   **8.** $2x^2(x^2 + 2x - 7)$
**9.** $xy(2x - 6y + 3)$   **10.** $7xy^2(-x^3 + 2y + 3y^2)$
**11.** $(y - 6)(y + 9)$   **12.** $(z + 2)(z - 3)$   **13.** $(x - 1)(x + 3)$
**14.** $(x - 1)(x - 5)$   **15.** $(x + 5)(x - 3)$   **16.** $(2x - 7)(x + 1)$
**17.** $(3x - 1)(x - 5)$   **18.** $(5x + 3)(x - 2)$
**19.** $(3x + 4)(3x + 8)$   **20.** $(2a + 2b - 1)(a + b + 3)$
**21.** $(3a - 4)(3a + 4)$   **22.** $(x + 1)(x + 5)$
**23.** $(3x + y)(9x^2 - 3xy + y^2)$   **24.** $(a - b^2)(a^2 + ab^2 + b^4)$
**25.** $(2s - 5t)(4s^2 + 10st + 25t^2)$
**26.** $(1 + 10y)(1 - 10y + 100y^2)$   **27.** $(x + 6)^2$
**28.** $(4z - 3)^2$   **29.** $(x + 4)(x^2 + 1)$   **30.** $(3x - 1)(x^2 + 2)$
**31.** $(2x + 1)(x^2 - 3)$   **32.** $(3x + 1)(1 - 3x^2)$
**33.** $(x + 1)(x^2 + 1)$   **34.** $(x + 1)(x^4 + 1)$   **35.** $6x(2x^2 + 3)$
**36.** $15x^3(2 + x)$   **37.** $3y^3(2y - 5)$   **38.** $ab(5 - 8c)$
**39.** $(x - 4)(x + 2)$   **40.** $(x - 8)(x - 6)$   **41.** $(y - 3)(y - 5)$
**42.** $(z - 2)(z + 8)$   **43.** $(2x + 3)(x + 1)$   **44.** $(2x - 1)(x + 4)$
**45.** $9(x - 5)(x + 1)$   **46.** $(4x + 3)(2x + 1)$
**47.** $(3x + 2)(2x - 3)$   **48.** $(3 - 2t)(2 + 3t)$
**49.** $(x + 6)(x - 6)$   **50.** $(2x - 5)(2x + 5)$
**51.** $(7 + 2y)(7 - 2y)$   **52.** $(2t - 3s)(2t + 3s)$   **53.** $(t - 3)^2$
**54.** $(x + 5)^2$   **55.** $(2x + y)^2$   **56.** $(r - 3s)^2$   **57.** $4ab$
**58.** $\dfrac{4}{x}$   **59.** $(x + 3)(x - 3)(x + 1)(x - 1)$

**60.** $(a - 1)(a + 1)(b - 2)(b + 2)$   **61.** $(t + 1)(t^2 - t + 1)$
**62.** $(x - 3)(x^2 + 3x + 9)$   **63.** $(2x - 5)(4x^2 + 10x + 25)$
**64.** $(x^2 + 4)(x^4 - 4x^2 + 16)$   **65.** $(x^2 - 2y)(x^4 + 2x^2y + 4y^2)$
**66.** $(3a + b^2)(9a^2 - 3ab^2 + b^4)$   **67.** $x(x + 1)^2$
**68.** $3x(x - 3)(x + 3)$   **69.** $x^2(x + 3)(x - 1)$
**70.** $(x + 3)(x - 1)(x + 1)$   **71.** $x^2y^3(x + y)(x - y)$
**72.** $2xy^3(9x - y)$   **73.** $(y + 2)(y - 2)(y - 3)$
**74.** $(y^2 + 1)(y - 1)$   **75.** $(2x^2 + 1)(x + 2)$
**76.** $(x^2 - 2)(3x + 5)$   **77.** $3(x - 1)(x + 2)$   **78.** $x(x + 1)$
**79.** $y^4(y + 2)^3(y + 1)^2$   **80.** $x - y$
**81.** $(a + 2)(a - 2)(a + 1)(a - 1)$
**82.** $(a - 1)(a + 3)(a + 1)^2$   **83.** $x^{1/2}(x + 1)(x - 1)$
**84.** $\dfrac{1}{\sqrt{x}}(3 + x)(1 + x)$   **85.** $x^{-3/2}(x + 1)^2$
**86.** $(x - 1)^{3/2}(x - 2)(x)$   **87.** $(x^2 + 3)(x^2 + 1)^{-1/2}$
**88.** $\dfrac{2x + 1}{\sqrt{x}\,\sqrt{x + 1}}$   **89.** $x^{1/3}(x - 2)^{-1/3}(-3x - 4)$
**90.** $\dfrac{(x^2 + 1)^{1/4}(2x^2 + 3)}{\sqrt{x}}$   **91.** $16x^2(x - 3)(5x - 9)$
**92.** $2(x^2 + 4)^4(x - 2)^3(7x^2 - 10x + 8)$
**93.** $(2x - 1)^2(x + 3)^{-1/2}(7x + \frac{35}{2})$
**94.** $\frac{1}{3}(x + 6)^{-2/3}(14x + 69)(2x - 3)$
**95.** $(x^2 + 3)^{-4/3}(\frac{1}{3}x^2 + 3)$   **96.** $x^{-1/2}(3x + 4)^{-1/2}(3x + 2)$
**97.** (d) $(a + b + c)(a + b - c)(a - b + c)(b - a + c)$

## SECTION P.8 · page 52

**1.** (a), (c)   **2.** numerator; denominator; $\dfrac{x + 1}{x + 3}$
**3.** (a) False   (b) True
**4.** (a) numerators; denominators; $\dfrac{2x}{x^2 + 4x + 3}$

(b) invert; $\dfrac{3x + 6}{x^2 + 5x}$   **5.** (a) 3   (b) $x(x + 1)^2$   (c) $\dfrac{-2x^2 + 1}{x(x + 1)^2}$
**6.** (a) False   (b) True   **7.** (a) 53   (b) $\mathbb{R}$   **8.** (a) $-11$   (b) $\mathbb{R}$
**9.** (a) 5   (b) $\{x \mid x \ne 4\}$   **10.** (a) $-\frac{1}{3}$   (b) $\{t \mid t \ne -2\}$
**11.** (a) 3   (b) $\{x \mid x \ge -3\}$   **12.** (a) $\frac{1}{2}$   (b) $\{x \mid x > 1\}$
**13.** (a) $\frac{5}{4}$   (b) $\{x \mid x \ne -1, x \ne 2\}$   **14.** (a) $\frac{4}{9}$   (b) $\{x \mid x \ge 0\}$
**15.** $\dfrac{2}{x}$   **16.** $\frac{9}{2}x^2$   **17.** $\dfrac{5y}{10 + y}$   **18.** $\frac{1}{7}(14t - 1)$   **19.** $\dfrac{x + 2}{2(x - 1)}$
**20.** $\dfrac{x + 1}{3(x + 2)}$   **21.** $\dfrac{1}{x + 2}$   **22.** $\dfrac{x - 2}{x - 1}$   **23.** $\dfrac{x + 2}{x + 1}$   **24.** $\dfrac{x - 4}{x + 2}$
**25.** $\dfrac{y}{y - 1}$   **26.** $\dfrac{(y - 6)(y + 3)}{(2y + 3)(y + 1)}$   **27.** $\dfrac{x(2x + 3)}{2x - 3}$
**28.** $\dfrac{-(x + 1)}{x^2 + x + 1}$   **29.** $\dfrac{1}{4(x - 2)}$   **30.** $\dfrac{x - 5}{x - 4}$   **31.** $\dfrac{x + 3}{x - 3}$
**32.** $\dfrac{1 - x}{x + 1}$   **33.** $\dfrac{1}{t^2 + 9}$   **34.** $x$   **35.** $\dfrac{x + 4}{x + 1}$   **36.** $\dfrac{2x + y}{x - 2y}$
**37.** $\dfrac{x + 5}{(2x + 3)(x + 4)}$   **38.** $\dfrac{1}{(2x - 5)(3x - 2)}$
**39.** $\dfrac{(2x + 1)(2x - 1)}{(x + 5)^2}$   **40.** 1   **41.** $x^2(x + 1)$   **42.** $\dfrac{x - 2}{x + 1}$

**43.** $\dfrac{x}{yz}$  **44.** $\dfrac{xz}{y}$  **45.** $\dfrac{3(x+2)}{x+3}$  **46.** $\dfrac{x-5}{x+4}$  **47.** $\dfrac{3x+7}{(x-3)(x+5)}$

**48.** $\dfrac{2x}{(x+1)(x-1)}$  **49.** $\dfrac{1}{(x+1)(x+2)}$  **50.** $\dfrac{x^2+3x+12}{(x-4)(x+6)}$

**51.** $\dfrac{3x+2}{(x+1)^2}$  **52.** $\dfrac{2(5x-9)}{(2x-3)^2}$  **53.** $\dfrac{u^2+3u+1}{u+1}$

**54.** $\dfrac{2b^2-3ab+4a^2}{a^2b^2}$  **55.** $\dfrac{2x+1}{x^2(x+1)}$  **56.** $\dfrac{x^2+x+1}{x^3}$

**57.** $\dfrac{2x+7}{(x+3)(x+4)}$  **58.** $\dfrac{2(x+1)}{(x-2)(x+2)}$  **59.** $\dfrac{x-2}{(x+3)(x-3)}$

**60.** $\dfrac{x^2-6x-4}{(x-1)(x+2)(x-4)}$  **61.** $\dfrac{5x-6}{x(x-1)}$  **62.** $\dfrac{-2x-1}{(x-3)(x+2)}$

**63.** $\dfrac{-5}{(x+1)(x+2)(x-3)}$  **64.** $\dfrac{x^2+x+4}{(x-1)(x+1)^2}$  **65.** $\dfrac{x-1}{x+1}$

**66.** $\dfrac{x-1}{x^2-x+1}$  **67.** $\dfrac{(x+1)^2}{x^2+2x-1}$  **68.** $\dfrac{c}{c-2}$

**69.** $\dfrac{4x-7}{(x-1)(x-2)(x+2)}$  **70.** $\dfrac{5}{(x-4)(x+3)(x+1)}$

**71.** $-xy$  **72.** $\dfrac{x^3}{x^2+y^2}$  **73.** $\dfrac{x^2+y^2}{xy(x+y)}$  **74.** $\dfrac{(x+y)^2}{xy}$

**75.** $\dfrac{1}{1-x}$  **76.** $\dfrac{2x+3}{x+2}$  **77.** $-\dfrac{1}{(1+x+h)(1+x)}$

**78.** $-\dfrac{1}{\sqrt{x}\sqrt{x+h}\,(\sqrt{x}+\sqrt{x+h})}$  **79.** $\dfrac{-2x-h}{x^2(x+h)^2}$

**80.** $3x^2+3xh+h^2-7$  **81.** $\dfrac{1}{\sqrt{1-x^2}}$  **82.** $\left|x^3+\tfrac{1}{4}x^3\right|$

**83.** $\dfrac{(x+2)^2(x-13)}{(x-3)^3}$  **84.** $\dfrac{2x(6-x)}{(x+6)^5}$  **85.** $\dfrac{x+2}{(x+1)^{3/2}}$

**86.** $\dfrac{1}{(1-x^2)^{3/2}}$  **87.** $\dfrac{2x+3}{(x+1)^{4/3}}$  **88.** $\dfrac{7-\frac{3}{2}x}{(7-3x)^{3/2}}$  **89.** $2+\sqrt{3}$

**90.** $\dfrac{3+\sqrt{5}}{2}$  **91.** $\dfrac{2(\sqrt{7}-\sqrt{2})}{5}$  **92.** $\dfrac{\sqrt{x}-1}{x-1}$

**93.** $\dfrac{y\sqrt{3}-y\sqrt{y}}{3-y}$  **94.** $2(\sqrt{x}+\sqrt{y})$  **95.** $\dfrac{-4}{3(1+\sqrt{5})}$

**96.** $\dfrac{-1}{\sqrt{3}-\sqrt{5}}$  **97.** $\dfrac{r-2}{5(\sqrt{r}-\sqrt{2})}$

**98.** $\dfrac{-1}{\sqrt{x}\sqrt{x+h}\,(\sqrt{x}+\sqrt{x+h})}$  **99.** $\dfrac{1}{\sqrt{x^2+1}+x}$

**100.** $\dfrac{1}{\sqrt{x+1}+\sqrt{x}}$  **101.** True  **102.** False  **103.** False

**104.** False  **105.** False  **106.** False  **107.** True  **108.** True

**109.** (a) $\dfrac{R_1R_2}{R_1+R_2}$  (b) $\tfrac{20}{3}\approx 6.7$ ohms

**110.** $56.10, $31.20, $16.50, $12.00, $10.50, $12.00, $16.50

## CHAPTER P REVIEW ▪ page 56

**1.** (a) $T=250-2x$  (b) 190  (c) 125  **2.** (a) $C=2x+3$
(b) $11  (c) 6  **3.** (a) rational, natural number, integer

(b) rational, integer  (c) rational, natural number, integer
(d) irrational  (e) rational, neither  (f) rational, integer
**4.** (a) rational, integer  (b) rational, neither  (c) rational, natural
number, integer  (d) irrational  (e) rational, neither  (f) rational,
natural number, integer  **5.** Commutative Property for Addition
**6.** Commutative Property for Multiplication
**7.** Distributive Property  **8.** Distributive Property
**9.** (a) $\tfrac{3}{2}$  (b) $\tfrac{1}{6}$  **10.** (a) $-\tfrac{1}{30}$  (b) $\tfrac{43}{30}$  **11.** (a) $\tfrac{9}{2}$  (b) $\tfrac{25}{32}$
**12.** (a) $\tfrac{25}{2}$  (b) $\tfrac{72}{49}$  **13.** $-2\le x<6$

**14.** $0<x\le 10$

**15.** $x\le 4$

**16.** $-2\le x$

**17.** $[5,\infty)$

**18.** $(-\infty,-3)$

**19.** $(-1,5]$

**20.** $[0,\tfrac{1}{2}]$

**21.** (a) $\{-1,0,\tfrac{1}{2},1,2,3,4\}$  (b) $\{1\}$  **22.** (a) $(-1,2]$
(b) $(0,1]$  **23.** (a) $\{1,2\}$  (b) $\{\tfrac{1}{2},1\}$  **24.** (a) $\{0,1\}$
(b) $\{\tfrac{1}{2},1\}$  **25.** 3  **26.** $\tfrac{13}{2}$  **27.** 6  **28.** 1  **29.** $\tfrac{1}{72}$  **30.** 4  **31.** $\tfrac{1}{6}$
**32.** 16  **33.** 11  **34.** 6  **35.** $-5$  **36.** 10  **37.** (a) $|3-5|=2$
(b) $|3-(-5)|=8$  **38.** (a) $|0-(-4)|=4$
(b) $|4-(-4)|=8$  **39.** $x^{-2}$  **40.** $x^{3/2}$  **41.** $x^{4m+2}$
**42.** $x^{2mn}$  **43.** $x^{a+b+c}$  **44.** $x^{abc}$  **45.** $x^{5c-1}$  **46.** $x^{n+5}$
**47.** (a) $7^{1/3}$  (b) $7^{4/5}$  **48.** (a) $5^{7/3}$  (b) $5^{3/4}$  **49.** (a) $x^{5/6}$
(b) $x^{9/2}$  **50.** (a) $y^{3/2}$  (b) $y^{1/4}$  **51.** $12x^5y^4$  **52.** $b^{14}$  **53.** $9x^3$
**54.** $r^{10}s^2$  **55.** $x^2y^2$  **56.** $|x|y^2$  **57.** $\dfrac{x(2-\sqrt{x})}{4-x}$

**58.** $\dfrac{x+2\sqrt{x}+1}{x-1}$  **59.** $\dfrac{4r^{5/2}}{s^7}$  **60.** $\dfrac{4a^4c^6}{b^{12}}$  **61.** $7.825\times 10^{10}$

**62.** 0.0000000208  **63.** $1.65\times 10^{-32}$  **64.** $3.8\times 10^9$ times
**65.** $2xy(x-3y)$  **66.** $3xy^2(4xy^2-y^3+3x^2)$
**67.** $(x-6)(x-3)$  **68.** $(x-2)(x+5)$  **69.** $(3x+1)(x-1)$
**70.** $(3x-4)(2x+3)$  **71.** $(4t+3)(t-4)$
**72.** $(x-1)^2(x+1)^2$  **73.** $(5-4t)(5+4t)$
**74.** $2y^2(y^2+4)(y+2)(y-2)$
**75.** $(x-1)(x^2+x+1)(x+1)(x^2-x+1)$
**76.** $(y-2)(y-1)(y+1)$  **77.** $x^{-1/2}(x-1)^2$
**78.** $ab^2(a+b)(a^2-ab+b^2)$  **79.** $(x-2)(4x^2+3)$
**80.** $(2x+y^2)(4x^2-2xy^2+y^4)$  **81.** $\sqrt{x^2+2}(x^2+x+2)^2$
**82.** $(3x-2)(x^2+6)$  **83.** $y(a+b)(a-b)$
**84.** $(a+b)(x-1)(x+1)$  **85.** $x^2$
**86.** $(a+b-3)(a+b+5)$  **87.** $6x^2-21x+3$  **88.** $4y^2-49$
**89.** $4a^4-4a^2b+b^2$  **90.** $-7+x$  **91.** $x^3-6x^2+11x-6$
**92.** $8x^3+12x^2+6x+1$  **93.** $2x^{3/2}+x-x^{1/2}$
**94.** $2x^5-18x^4+36x^3$  **95.** $2x^3-6x^2+4x$  **96.** $x^2+2x+3$
**97.** $\dfrac{x-3}{2x+3}$  **98.** $\dfrac{t^2+t+1}{t+1}$  **99.** $\dfrac{3(x+3)}{x+4}$  **100.** $x^3+x^2+x$

**101.** $\dfrac{x+1}{x-4}$  **102.** $\dfrac{x^2+x-1}{x+1}$  **103.** $\dfrac{x+1}{(x-1)(x^2+1)}$

104. $\dfrac{3x^2 - 7x + 8}{x(x-2)^2}$   105. $\dfrac{1}{x+1}$   106. $\dfrac{x^2 - 2x - 5}{(x-2)(x+1)(x+2)}$

107. $-\dfrac{1}{2x}$   108. $\dfrac{1}{2x+1}$   109. $6x + 3h - 5$

110. $\dfrac{1}{\sqrt{x+h}+\sqrt{x}}$   111. $\{x \mid x \neq -10\}$

112. $\{x \mid x \neq -3 \text{ and } x \neq 3\}$   113. $\{x \mid x \geq 0 \text{ and } x \neq 4\}$

114. $\{x \mid x \geq 3\}$   115. No   116. Yes   117. Yes   118. No
119. No   120. No   121. No   122. No`

## CHAPTER P TEST ▪ page 58

1. (a) $C = 9 + 1.50x$   (b) \$15   2. (a) Rational, natural number, integer   (b) Irrational   (c) Rational, integer   (d) Rational, integer   3. (a) $\{0, 1, 5\}$   (b) $\{-2, 0, \frac{1}{2}, 1, 3, 5, 7\}$
4. (a) [number line]
(b) Intersection $[0, 2)$ [number line]
  Union $[-4, 3]$ [number line]   (c) $|-4 - 2| = 6$
5. (a) $-64$   (b) $64$   (c) $\frac{1}{64}$   (d) $\frac{1}{49}$   (e) $\frac{4}{9}$   (f) $\frac{1}{2}$   (g) $\frac{9}{16}$
(h) $\frac{1}{27}$   6. (a) $1.86 \times 10^{11}$   (b) $3.965 \times 10^{-7}$   7. (a) $6\sqrt{2}$
(b) $48a^5b^7$   (c) $5x^3$   (d) $\frac{x}{9y^7}$   8. (a) $11x - 2$
(b) $4x^2 + 7x - 15$   (c) $a - b$   (d) $4x^2 + 12x + 9$
(e) $x^3 + 6x^2 + 12x + 8$   (f) $x^4 - 9x^2$   9. (a) $(2x - 5)(2x + 5)$
(b) $(2x - 3)(x + 4)$   (c) $(x - 3)(x - 2)(x + 2)$
(d) $x(x + 3)(x^2 - 3x + 9)$   (e) $3x^{-1/2}(x - 1)(x - 2)$
(f) $xy(x - 2)(x + 2)$   10. (a) $\frac{x+2}{x-2}$   (b) $\frac{x-1}{x-3}$   (c) $\frac{1}{x-2}$
(d) $-(x + y)$   11. (a) $3\sqrt[3]{2}$   (b) $2\sqrt{6} - 3\sqrt{2}$

## FOCUS ON PROBLEM SOLVING ▪ page 62

1. 37.5 mi/h   2. It can't go fast enough   3. 150 mi
4. 40% discount   5. 427   6. 57 min   7. 75 s
8. No, not necessarily.   9. The same amount
10. It remains the same.   11. $2\pi$   14. 7
15. 15,999,999,999,992,000,000,000,001
16. The North Pole is one such point. There are infinitely many others near the South Pole.   18. $\pi$

## CHAPTER 1

## SECTION 1.1 ▪ page 72

1. (a), (c)   2. (a) Equation contains a square of the variable.
(b) Equation contains a square root of the variable.   (c) Equation contains a square of the variable.   3. (a) True   (b) False (because quantity could be 0)   (c) False   4. cube, 5   5. (a) No   (b) Yes
6. (a) Yes   (b) No   7. (a) Yes   (b) No   8. (a) Yes   (b) No
9. (a) No   (b) Yes   10. (a) Yes   (b) No   11. (a) Yes
(b) No   12. (a) Yes   (b) No   13. 12   14. $\frac{7}{5}$   15. 18   16. 6
17. $-9$   18. 4   19. $-3$   20. $\frac{5}{2}$   21. 12   22. $-70$   23. $-\frac{3}{4}$
24. $-3$   25. $\frac{32}{9}$   26. $\frac{21}{11}$   27. 30   28. $\frac{1}{17}$   29. $-\frac{1}{3}$   30. $\frac{13}{6}$
31. $-20$   32. $\frac{8}{11}$   33. 3   34. $-2$   35. $-\frac{1}{2}$   36. $\frac{5}{18}$   37. $-\frac{4}{9}$
38. $-39$   39. $\frac{13}{3}$   40. $\frac{11}{2}$   41. $\frac{29}{2}$   42. $-\frac{15}{19}$   43. $\frac{3}{97}$   44. $\frac{62}{59}$
45. 2   46. $\frac{31}{3}$   47. No solution   48. $-4$   49. No solution

50. $x \neq 0, -\frac{1}{2}$   51. $\pm 7$   52. $\pm 3\sqrt{2}$   53. $\pm 2\sqrt{6}$   54. $\pm\sqrt{7}$
55. $\pm 2\sqrt{2}$   56. $\pm 5$   57. No solution   58. No solution
59. $-4, 0$   60. $5 \pm \sqrt{5}$   61. 3   62. $-2$   63. $\pm 2$   64. $\pm\dfrac{\sqrt{3}}{2}$
65. No solution   66. $-1$   67. $-5, 1$   68. No solution   69. 8
70. $-2 + \sqrt[5]{1/4}$   71. 125   72. $\pm 8$   73. $-8$   74. $\pm 216$
75. 3.13   76. $-1.69$   77. 5.06   78. 0.59   79. 43.66
80. 4.87   81. 1.60   82. 14.55   83. $R = \dfrac{PV}{nT}$   84. $m = \dfrac{Fr^2}{GM}$
85. $w = \dfrac{(P - 2l)}{2}$   86. $R_1 = \dfrac{RR_2}{R_2 - R}$   87. $x = \dfrac{2d - b}{a - 2c}$
88. $x = \dfrac{-6 + a - 2b + 6c}{6}$   89. $x = \dfrac{1 - a}{a^2 - a - 1}$
90. $a = \frac{1}{2}(b^2 + b)$   91. $r = \pm\sqrt{\dfrac{3V}{\pi h}}$   92. $r = \pm\sqrt{G\dfrac{mM}{F}}$
93. $b = \pm\sqrt{c^2 - a^2}$   94. $i = -100 \pm 100\sqrt{\dfrac{A}{P}}$   95. $r = \sqrt[3]{\dfrac{3V}{4\pi}}$
96. $x = \pm\sqrt[4]{100 - y^4 - z^4}$   97. (a) 0.00055, 12.018 m
(b) 234.375 kg/m³   98. 840   99. (a) 8.6 km/h   (b) 14.7 km/h
100. 10,000 lb

## SECTION 1.2 ▪ page 82

2. principal; interest rate; time in years   3. (a) $x^2$   (b) $lw$
(c) $\pi r^2$   4. 1.6   5. $\dfrac{1}{x}$   6. $r = \dfrac{d}{t}; t = \dfrac{d}{r}$   7. $3n + 3$   8. $3n$
9. $\dfrac{160 + s}{3}$   10. $\dfrac{24 + q}{4}$   11. $0.025x$   12. $795n$   13. $A = 3w^2$
14. $4w + 10$   15. $d = \frac{3}{4}s$   16. $\dfrac{d}{55}$   17. $\dfrac{25}{x + 3}$   18. $131p + 140$
19. 400 miles   20. 1285 messages   21. \$9000 at $4\frac{1}{2}$% and
\$3000 at 4%   22. \$2000   23. 7.5%   24. 6%   25. \$7400
26. \$32,500   27. \$45,000   28. 8 h   29. Plumber, 70 h; assistant,
35 h   30. 12   31. 40 years old   32. 714   33. 9 pennies,
9 nickels, 9 dimes   34. 5 quarters, 10 dimes, 15 nickels   35. 45 ft
36. 240 ft   37. 120 ft by 120 ft   38. 66 ft by 330 ft   39. 8.94 in.
40. 9 cm   41. 4 in.   42. 30 cm   43. 5 m   44. 95 ft
45. 200 mL   46. 75 mL   47. 18 g   48. 2.4 L   49. 0.6 L
50. 3.06 gal   51. 35%   52. 48 lb of \$3.00/lb tea, 32 lb of
\$2.75/lb tea   53. 37 min 20 s   54. 120 min   55. 3 h   56. 40.5 h
for Jim's hose, 32.4 h for Bob's hose   57. 4 h   58. 15 mi/h;
30 mi/h   59. 500 mi/h   60. 55 mi/h   61. 6.4 ft from the fulcrum
62. 1200 lb   63. 120 ft   64. 35 yd   65. 18 ft   66. 4.55 ft

## SECTION 1.3 ▪ page 94

1. (a) $\dfrac{-b \pm \sqrt{b^2 - 4ac}}{2a}$   (b) $\frac{1}{2}, -1, -4; 4, -2$

2. (a) Factor into $(x + 1)(x - 5)$ and use the Zero-Product Property.   (b) Add 5 to each side, then complete the square by adding 4 to both sides.   (c) Insert coefficients into the Quadratic Formula.   3. $b^2 - 4ac$; two distinct real; exactly one real; no real
5. $-4, 3$   6. $-4, 1$   7. 3, 4   8. $-6, -2$   9. $-\frac{1}{3}, 2$
10. $-\frac{3}{2}, \frac{5}{2}$   11. $-3, -\frac{1}{2}$   12. $-\frac{1}{2}, \frac{3}{2}$   13. $-\frac{4}{3}, \frac{1}{2}$   14. $\frac{1}{3}, 1$
15. $-20, 25$   16. $-\frac{3}{2}, \frac{7}{3}$   17. $-1 \pm \sqrt{6}$   18. $2 \pm \sqrt{2}$
19. $3 \pm 2\sqrt{5}$   20. $-\frac{7}{2}, \frac{1}{2}$   21. $\frac{1}{2}, -\frac{3}{2}$   22. $\dfrac{5 \pm \sqrt{21}}{2}$

**23.** $-21, -1$   **24.** $-1, 19$   **25.** $-2 \pm \dfrac{\sqrt{14}}{2}$   **26.** $1 \pm \dfrac{2\sqrt{3}}{3}$

**27.** $0, \frac{1}{4}$   **28.** $\frac{1}{4}, \frac{1}{2}$   **29.** $-3, 5$   **30.** $-6, 1$   **31.** $2, 5$

**32.** $-20, -10$   **33.** $-\frac{3}{2}, 1$   **34.** $-\frac{4}{3}, -1$   **35.** $\dfrac{-3 \pm \sqrt{5}}{2}$

**36.** $2 \pm \sqrt{2}$   **37.** $-6 \pm 3\sqrt{7}$   **38.** $-\frac{3}{4}, \frac{3}{2}$   **39.** $\dfrac{-3 \pm 2\sqrt{6}}{3}$

**40.** $3 \pm 2\sqrt{2}$   **41.** $\frac{3}{4}$   **42.** $\dfrac{1 \pm \sqrt{5}}{4}$   **43.** $-\frac{9}{2}, \frac{1}{2}$

**44.** $2 \pm \sqrt{3}$   **45.** No real solution   **46.** $\dfrac{-5 \pm \sqrt{13}}{2}$

**47.** $\dfrac{\sqrt{5} \pm 1}{2}$   **48.** $-\dfrac{\sqrt{6}}{2}, \dfrac{\sqrt{6}}{6}$   **49.** $\dfrac{8 \pm \sqrt{14}}{10}$   **50.** $-\frac{7}{5}$

**51.** No real solution   **52.** No real solution   **53.** $-0.248, 0.259$

**54.** $1.200, 1.250$   **55.** No real solution   **56.** $0.900$

**57.** $-0.985, 2.828$   **58.** $-0.674, 0.115$

**59.** $t = \dfrac{-v_0 \pm \sqrt{v_0^2 + 2gh}}{g}$   **60.** $n = \dfrac{-1 \pm \sqrt{1 + 8S}}{2}$

**61.** $x = \dfrac{-2h \pm \sqrt{4h^2 + 2A}}{2}$   **62.** $r = \dfrac{-\pi h \pm \sqrt{\pi^2 h^2 + 2\pi A}}{2\pi}$

**63.** $s = \dfrac{-(a + b - 2c) \pm \sqrt{a^2 + b^2 + 4c^2 - 2ab}}{2}$

**64.** $r = -\dfrac{5 \pm \sqrt{41}}{2}$   **65.** $2$   **66.** $1$   **67.** $1$   **68.** $2$

**69.** No real solution   **70.** $1$   **71.** $2$   **72.** $2$   **73.** $\dfrac{-1}{a}$   **74.** $\dfrac{1}{b}, \dfrac{4}{b}$

**75.** $1, 1 + \dfrac{1}{a}$   **76.** $-\dfrac{1}{b}$   **77.** $k = \pm 20$   **78.** $k = \pm 18$

**79.** 19 and 36   **80.** $-26, -24$ or $24, 26$   **81.** 25 ft by 35 ft
**82.** 12 ft   **83.** 60 ft by 40 ft   **84.** 5 in.   **85.** 48 cm
**86.** 50   **87.** 13 in. by 13 in.   **88.** 4 cm   **89.** 120 ft by 126 ft
**90.** 32 ft 4 in.   **91.** 50 mi/h (or 240 mi/h)   **92.** 50 mi/h
**93.** 6 km/h   **94.** 9 mi/h   **95.** 4.24 s   **96.** (a) 1.732 s
(b) 2.449 s   **97.** (a) After 1 s and $1\frac{1}{2}$ s   (b) Never   (c) 25 ft
(d) After $1\frac{1}{4}$ s   (e) After $2\frac{1}{2}$ s   **98.** 80 ft/s   **99.** (a) After
17 yr, on Jan. 1, 2019   (b) After 18.612 yr, on Aug. 12, 2020
**100.** 169.1 in., 190.9 in.   **101.** 30 ft; 120 ft by 180 ft
**102.** 18 ft   **103.** Irene 3 h, Henry $4\frac{1}{2}$ h   **104.** 3 h
**105.** 215,000 mi

## SECTION 1.4 ▪ page 102

**1.** $-1$   **2.** 3; 4   **3.** (a) $3 - 4i$   (b) $9 + 16 = 25$   **4.** $3 - 4i$
**5.** Real part 5, imaginary part $-7$   **6.** Real part $-6$, imaginary part
4   **7.** Real part $-\frac{2}{3}$, imaginary part $-\frac{5}{3}$   **8.** Real part 2, imaginary
part $\frac{7}{2}$   **9.** Real part 3, imaginary part 0   **10.** Real part $-\frac{1}{2}$,
imaginary part 0   **11.** Real part 0, imaginary part $-\frac{2}{3}$   **12.** Real
part 0, imaginary part $\sqrt{3}$   **13.** Real part $\sqrt{3}$, imaginary part 2
**14.** Real part 2, imaginary part $-\sqrt{5}$   **15.** $5 - i$   **16.** $6 - i$
**17.** $3 + 5i$   **18.** $-2 - \frac{7}{3}i$   **19.** $2 - 2i$   **20.** $-6 + 6i$
**21.** $-19 + 4i$   **22.** $-4 + 7i$   **23.** $-4 + 8i$   **24.** $2 + i$
**25.** $30 + 10i$   **26.** $8 + 2i$   **27.** $-33 - 56i$   **28.** $-\frac{2591}{9} + 18i$
**29.** $27 - 8i$   **30.** $1 + 17i$   **31.** $-i$   **32.** $16$   **33.** $1$   **34.** $-1$
**35.** $-i$   **36.** $\frac{1}{2} - \frac{1}{2}i$   **37.** $\frac{8}{5} + \frac{1}{5}i$   **38.** $\frac{11}{25} - \frac{23}{25}i$   **39.** $-5 + 12i$
**40.** $4 + 3i$   **41.** $-4 + 2i$   **42.** $\frac{2}{13} + \frac{3}{13}i$   **43.** $2 - \frac{4}{3}i$   **44.** $\frac{1}{3} + \frac{1}{5}i$
**45.** $-i$   **46.** $3 + i$   **47.** $5i$   **48.** $\frac{3}{2}i$   **49.** $-6$   **50.** $3i$

**51.** $(3 + \sqrt{5}) + (3 - \sqrt{5})i$   **52.** $-\sqrt{2} - 4\sqrt{6}i$   **53.** $2$
**54.** $-i$   **55.** $-i\sqrt{2}$   **56.** $-\frac{7}{2}$   **57.** $\pm 7i$   **58.** $\pm \frac{2}{3}i$   **59.** $2 \pm i$

**60.** $-1 \pm i$   **61.** $-1 \pm 2i$   **62.** $3 \pm i$   **63.** $-\dfrac{1}{2} \pm \dfrac{\sqrt{3}}{2}i$

**64.** $\dfrac{3}{2} \pm \dfrac{\sqrt{3}}{2}i$   **65.** $\frac{1}{2} \pm \frac{1}{2}i$   **66.** $\dfrac{1}{2} \pm \dfrac{\sqrt{5}}{2}i$   **67.** $-\dfrac{3}{2} \pm \dfrac{\sqrt{3}}{2}i$

**68.** $-2 \pm 2\sqrt{2}i$   **69.** $\dfrac{-6 \pm \sqrt{6}i}{6}$   **70.** $2 \pm \dfrac{\sqrt{3}}{2}i$

**71.** $1 \pm 3i$   **72.** $-\dfrac{1}{4} \pm \dfrac{\sqrt{15}}{4}i$

## SECTION 1.5 ▪ page 110

**1.** (a) $0, 4$   (b) factor   **2.** (a) $\sqrt{2x} = -x$   (b) $2x = x^2$
(c) $0, 2$   (d) $0$   **3.** quadratic; $x + 1$; $W^2 - 5W + 6 = 0$

**4.** quadratic; $x^3$; $W^2 + 7W - 8 = 0$   **5.** $0, \pm 4$   **6.** $0, 3$   **7.** $0, \pm 3$

**8.** $0, \pm 2$   **9.** $0, -2$   **10.** $0, -4$   **11.** $0, 2, 3$   **12.** $0, -2, 3$

**13.** $0, -2 \pm \sqrt{2}$   **14.** $-1, 2, 5$   **15.** $\pm \sqrt{2}, 5$   **16.** $-3, -\frac{1}{2}, 3$

**17.** $2$   **18.** $\frac{1}{2}, \pm \sqrt{\frac{1}{3}}$   **19.** $-1.4, 2$   **20.** $5, -\frac{3}{2}$   **21.** $-50, 100$

**22.** $\dfrac{-3 \pm \sqrt{41}}{2}$   **23.** $-4$   **24.** $-4, -\frac{7}{3}$   **25.** No real solution

**26.** $\dfrac{-5 \pm 4\sqrt{2}}{7}$   **27.** $2$   **28.** $\frac{1}{2}$   **29.** $4$   **30.** $\dfrac{-3 + 3\sqrt{5}}{2}$

**31.** $4$   **32.** $3$   **33.** $6$   **34.** $8$   **35.** $-7, 0$   **36.** $-\frac{1}{2}, -\frac{1}{4}$

**37.** $-\frac{3}{2}, -\frac{3}{4}$   **38.** $-4$   **39.** $\pm 2\sqrt{2}, \pm \sqrt{5}$   **40.** $-2, -1, 1, 2$

**41.** No real solution   **42.** $-1, \sqrt[3]{3}$   **43.** $-1, 3$   **44.** $\pm 1$

**45.** $\pm 3\sqrt{3}, \pm 2\sqrt{2}$   **46.** $256$   **47.** $-1, 0, 3$   **48.** $\frac{7}{2}, 4, 5$

**49.** No solution   **50.** $2$   **51.** $27, 729$   **52.** $4, 9$   **53.** $-\frac{1}{2}$

**54.** $\pm \sqrt{2 - \sqrt{3}}, \pm \sqrt{2 + \sqrt{3}}$   **55.** $20$   **56.** $0, 2$

**57.** $-3, \dfrac{1 \pm \sqrt{13}}{2}$   **58.** $\pm \sqrt{7}$   **59.** $2$   **60.** No real solution

**61.** $1, \dfrac{-1 \pm i\sqrt{3}}{2}$   **62.** $\pm 2, \pm 2i$   **63.** $0, \dfrac{-1 \pm i\sqrt{3}}{2}$

**64.** $-1, 0, \pm i$   **65.** $\pm \sqrt{2}, \pm 2$   **66.** $-3, \pm 3i$

**67.** $1, 2, \dfrac{-1 \pm i\sqrt{3}}{2}, -1 \pm i\sqrt{3}$   **68.** $\pm 3i, \pm \sqrt{2}, \pm \sqrt{2}i$

**69.** $\pm 3i$   **70.** $\pm 3$   **71.** $\pm i\sqrt{a}, \pm 2i\sqrt{a}$   **72.** $-\dfrac{b}{a}, \dfrac{b \pm \sqrt{3}bi}{2a}$

**73.** $\sqrt{a^2 + 36}$   **74.** No solution   **75.** 50   **76.** 4   **77.** 89 days
**78.** 12 cm   **79.** 7.52 ft   **80.** 2.88 ft   **81.** 4.63 mm   **82.** 2 ft by
6 ft by 15 ft   **83.** 16 mi; No   **84.** 440 ft or 720 ft   **85.** 49 ft,
168 ft, and 175 ft   **86.** 27.4 in.   **87.** 132.6 ft

## SECTION 1.6 ▪ page 119

**1.** (a) $<$   (b) $\leq$   (c) $\leq$   (d) $>$   **2.** (a) True   (b) False
**3.** $\{4\}$   **4.** $\{-2, -1, 0, \frac{1}{2}\}$   **5.** $\{\sqrt{2}, 2, 4\}$   **6.** $\{1, \sqrt{2}, 2, 4\}$
**7.** $\{4\}$   **8.** $\{\sqrt{2}, 2, 4\}$   **9.** $\{-2, -1, 2, 4\}$   **10.** $\{-1, 0, \frac{1}{2}, 1\}$
**11.** $(-\infty, \frac{7}{2}]$        **12.** $(-\infty, -\frac{5}{2}]$

**13.** $(4, \infty)$        **14.** $(-\infty, -2)$

**15.** $(-\infty, 2]$

**16.** $[7, \infty)$

**17.** $\left(-\infty, -\frac{1}{2}\right)$

**18.** $\left(-\infty, \frac{5}{2}\right)$

**19.** $[1, \infty)$

**20.** $(-\infty, -1]$

**21.** $\left(\frac{16}{3}, \infty\right)$

**22.** $\left(-\infty, -\frac{1}{3}\right)$

**23.** $(-\infty, -18)$

**24.** $\left(-\infty, \frac{1}{3}\right]$

**25.** $(-\infty, -1]$

**26.** $(-\infty, 11]$

**27.** $[-3, -1)$

**28.** $[3, 6]$

**29.** $(2, 6)$

**30.** $(-1, 4]$

**31.** $\left[\frac{9}{2}, 5\right)$

**32.** $\left[-\frac{10}{3}, -\frac{13}{6}\right]$

**33.** $\left(\frac{5}{2}, \frac{11}{2}\right]$

**34.** $\left[\frac{11}{12}, \frac{13}{6}\right]$

**35.** $(-2, 3)$

**36.** $(-\infty, -4] \cup [5, \infty)$

**37.** $\left(-\infty, -\frac{7}{2}\right] \cup [0, \infty)$

**38.** $(-\infty, 0] \cup \left[\frac{2}{3}, \infty\right)$

**39.** $[-3, 6]$

**40.** $(-\infty, -3) \cup (-2, \infty)$

**41.** $(-\infty, -1] \cup \left[\frac{1}{2}, \infty\right)$

**42.** $(-1, 2)$

**43.** $(-1, 4)$

**44.** $(-\infty, -2] \cup \left[\frac{1}{2}, \infty\right)$

**45.** $(-\infty, -3) \cup (6, \infty)$

**46.** $(-\infty, -3) \cup (1, \infty)$

**47.** $(-2, 2)$

**48.** $(-\infty, -3] \cup [3, \infty)$

**49.** $(-\infty, -2] \cup [1, 3]$

**50.** $(-1, 2) \cup (5, \infty)$

**51.** $(-\infty, -2) \cup (-2, 4)$

**52.** $(-1, \infty)$

**53.** $[-1, 3]$

**54.** $(-\infty, -1] \cup \{0\} \cup [1, \infty)$

**55.** $(-2, 0) \cup (2, \infty)$

**56.** $[-4, 0] \cup [4, \infty)$

**57.** $(-\infty, -1) \cup [3, \infty)$

**58.** $(-3, 2)$

**59.** $\left(-\infty, -\frac{3}{2}\right)$

**60.** $\left(-\infty, \frac{5}{3}\right) \cup (3, \infty)$

**61.** $(-\infty, 5) \cup [16, \infty)$

**62.** $[0, 3)$

**63.** $(-2, 0) \cup (2, \infty)$

**64.** $(-\infty, -1) \cup \left(-\frac{2}{3}, 0\right)$

**65.** $[-2, -1) \cup (0, 1]$

**66.** $[-2, 0) \cup (1, 2]$

**67.** $[-2, 0) \cup (1, 3]$

**68.** $[-2, -1) \cup [9, \infty)$

**69.** $\left(-3, -\frac{1}{2}\right) \cup (2, \infty)$

**70.** $(-\infty, -2) \cup \left[-\frac{3}{2}, -1\right)$

**71.** $(-\infty, -2] \cup [1, 2) \cup (2, \infty)$

**72.** $\left(\frac{1}{2}, 3\right) \cup (3, 4)$

**73.** $(-\infty, -1) \cup (1, \infty)$    **74.** $(1, \infty)$

**75.** $-\frac{4}{3} \le x \le \frac{4}{3}$    **76.** $x \le \frac{2}{3}$ or $x \ge 1$    **77.** $x < -2$ or $x > 7$

**78.** $-2 < x \le 1$    **79. (a)** $x \ge \frac{c}{a} + \frac{c}{b}$    **(b)** $\frac{a-c}{b} \le x < \frac{2a-c}{b}$

**81.** $68 \le F \le 86$    **82.** $10 \le C \le 35$    **83.** More than 200 mi
**84.** Less than 286 min    **85.** Between 12,000 mi and 14,000 mi

**86. (a)** $T = 20 - \dfrac{h}{100}$    **(b)** From $20\,°C$ down to $-30\,°C$

**87. (a)** $-\frac{1}{3}P + \frac{560}{3}$    **(b)** From \$215 to \$290    **88.** $\pm 0.195$ dollars
**89.** Distances between 20,000 km and 100,000 km    **90.** Distances
greater than 30 m    **91.** From 0 s to 3 s    **92.** Between 40 and
50 mi/h    **93.** Between 0 and 60 mi/h    **94.** Between 400 and
4400 units    **95.** Between 20 and 40 ft

## SECTION 1.7 ▪ page 124

**1.** $3, -3$    **2.** $[-3, 3]$    **3.** $(-\infty, -3], [3, \infty)$    **4. (a)** $< 3$
**(b)** $> 3$    **5.** $\pm 6$    **6.** $\pm \frac{5}{2}$    **7.** $\pm 5$    **8.** $\pm 18$    **9.** $1, 5$    **10.** $-2, 5$

**11.** $-4.5, -3.5$  **12.** No solution  **13.** $-4, \frac{1}{2}$  **14.** $2, 6$

**15.** $-3, -1$  **16.** $-\frac{3}{2}, \frac{13}{2}$  **17.** $-8, -2$  **18.** No solution

**19.** $-\frac{25}{2}, \frac{35}{2}$  **20.** $-\frac{65}{6}, \frac{25}{6}$  **21.** $-\frac{3}{2}, -\frac{1}{4}$  **22.** $-\frac{4}{3}, 2$  **23.** $[-4, 4]$

**24.** $(-5, 5)$  **25.** $\left(-\infty, -\frac{7}{2}\right) \cup \left(\frac{7}{2}, \infty\right)$  **26.** $(-\infty, -2] \cup [2, \infty)$

**27.** $[2, 8]$  **28.** $(-\infty, 0) \cup (18, \infty)$  **29.** $(-\infty, -2] \cup [0, \infty)$

**30.** $-4$  **31.** $(-\infty, -7] \cup [-3, \infty)$  **32.** $(-\infty, -4] \cup [2, \infty)$

**33.** $[1.3, 1.7]$  **34.** $\left(-\frac{4}{5}, \frac{8}{5}\right)$  **35.** $(-4, 8)$

**36.** $(-\infty, -9] \cup [7, \infty)$  **37.** $(-6.001, -5.999)$

**38.** $(a - d, a + d)$  **39.** $(-6, 2)$

**40.** $(-\infty, -3] \cup [-1, \infty)$  **41.** $\left[-\frac{1}{2}, \frac{3}{2}\right]$  **42.** $(-\infty, \infty)$

**43.** $\left(-\infty, -\frac{1}{2}\right) \cup \left(\frac{1}{3}, \infty\right)$  **44.** $[-54, 42]$

**45.** $[-4, -1] \cup [1, 4]$  **46.** $\left[\frac{9}{2}, 5\right) \cup \left(5, \frac{11}{2}\right]$

**47.** $\left(-\frac{15}{2}, -7\right) \cup \left(-7, -\frac{13}{2}\right)$  **48.** $\left(-\infty, \frac{7}{5}\right] \cup \left[\frac{8}{5}, \infty\right)$

**49.** $|x| < 3$  **50.** $|x| > 2$  **51.** $|x - 7| \geq 5$

**52.** $|x - 2| \leq 4$  **53.** $|x| \leq 2$  **54.** $|x| \geq 1$

**55.** $|x| > 3$  **56.** $|x| < 4$  **57. (a)** $|x - 0.020| \leq 0.003$

**(b)** $0.017 \leq x \leq 0.023$  **58.** Between 62.4 and 74.0 in.

## CHAPTER 1 REVIEW ▪ page 126

**1.** $5$  **2.** $-\frac{1}{2}$  **3.** $4$  **4.** $\frac{49}{5}$  **5.** $5$  **6.** $-2$  **7.** $\frac{15}{2}$  **8.** $-\frac{3}{20}$  **9.** $-6$

**10.** $-30$  **11.** $0$  **12.** $-\frac{7}{2}$  **13.** $\pm 12$  **14.** $\pm 3.5$  **15.** $\pm \dfrac{2}{\sqrt[4]{5}}$

**16.** $3$  **17.** $\sqrt[3]{3}$  **18.** No real solution  **19.** $x = 2A - y$

**20.** $y = \dfrac{V - xz}{x + z}$  **21.** $t = \dfrac{11}{6J}$  **22.** $r = \pm\sqrt{\dfrac{kq_1 q_2}{E}}$  **23.** $-5$

**24.** $-2 \pm \sqrt{2}$  **25.** $-27$  **26.** $\pm 8$  **27.** $625$  **28.** $34$

**29.** No solution  **30.** $1$  **31.** $2, 7$  **32.** $-12$  **33.** $-1, \frac{1}{2}$

**34.** $-2, \frac{1}{3}$  **35.** $0, \pm\frac{5}{2}$  **36.** $2, \pm\sqrt{5}$  **37.** $\dfrac{-2 \pm \sqrt{7}}{3}$

**38.** No real solution  **39.** $\dfrac{3 \pm \sqrt{6}}{3}$  **40.** $-5$  **41.** $\pm 3$  **42.** $64$

**43.** $1$  **44.** $.16$  **45.** $3, 11$  **46.** $\pm 6$  **47.** $-2, 7$
**48.** $0, 6$  **49.** 20 lb raisins, 30 lb nuts  **50.** 4:00 P.M.
**51.** $\frac{1}{4}(\sqrt{329} - 3) \approx 3.78$ mi/h  **52.** 30 mi/h  **53.** 12 cm, 16 cm
**54.** 1 h 50 min  **55.** 23 ft by 46 ft by 8 ft  **56.** 10 ft by 8 ft or 12 ft
by 6.67 ft  **57.** $-3 - 9i$  **58.** $-\frac{3}{2} + 2i$  **59.** $19 + 40i$

**60.** $\frac{6}{5} + 3i$  **61.** $\dfrac{-5 - 12i}{13}$  **62.** $\frac{1}{5} + \frac{2}{5}i$  **63.** $i$  **64.** $18 - 26i$

**65.** $(2 + 2\sqrt{3}) + (2 - 2\sqrt{3})i$  **66.** $-10$  **67.** $\pm 4i$

**68.** $\pm 2\sqrt{3}i$  **69.** $-3 \pm i$  **70.** $\dfrac{3 \pm \sqrt{7}i}{4}$  **71.** $\pm 4, \pm 4i$

**72.** $2, \pm 2i$  **73.** $\pm\dfrac{\sqrt{3}}{3}i$  **74.** $5, \dfrac{(-5 \pm 5\sqrt{3}i)}{2}$

**75.** $(-3, \infty)$

**76.** $\left(-\infty, \frac{3}{2}\right]$

**77.** $(-3, -1]$

**78.** $\left[\frac{10}{3}, \infty\right)$

**79.** $(-\infty, -6) \cup (2, \infty)$

**80.** $[-1, 1]$

**81.** $[-4, -1)$

**82.** $\left(-\infty, -1\right] \cup \left[\frac{3}{2}, \infty\right)$

**83.** $(-\infty, -2) \cup (2, 4]$

**84.** $(-\infty, -2) \cup (1, 2)$

**85.** $[2, 8]$

**86.** $(3.98, 4.02)$

**87.** $(-\infty, -1] \cup [0, \infty)$

**88.** $(-\infty, 2)$

**89. (a)** $\left[-3, \frac{8}{3}\right]$  **(b)** $(0, 1)$  **90.** $\left[\sqrt[3]{\dfrac{6}{\pi}}, \sqrt[3]{\dfrac{9}{\pi}}\right]$

## CHAPTER 1 TEST ▪ page 129

**1. (a)** $5$  **(b)** $-\frac{5}{2}$  **(c)** $512$  **(d)** $\frac{15}{2}$  **2.** $c = \sqrt{\dfrac{E}{m}}$  **3.** 150 km

**4. (a)** $5 - 4i$  **(b)** $1 - 6i$  **(c)** $7 + 3i$  **(d)** $-\frac{1}{5} + \frac{2}{5}i$  **(e)** $i$

**(f)** $2\sqrt{2} - 8i$  **5. (a)** $-3, 4$  **(b)** $\dfrac{-2 \pm i\sqrt{2}}{2}$  **(c)** No solution

**(d)** $1, 16$  **(e)** $0, \pm 4$  **(f)** $\frac{2}{3}, \frac{22}{3}$  **6.** 50 ft by 120 ft

**7. (a)** $\left(-\frac{5}{2}, 3\right]$  **(b)** $(0, 1) \cup (2, \infty)$  **(c)** $(1, 5)$  **(d)** $[-4, -1)$

**8.** $41°F$ to $50°F$  **9.** $0 \leq x \leq 4$

## FOCUS ON MODELING ▪ page 133

**1. (a)** $C = 5800 + 265n$  **(b)** $C = 575n$
**(c)**

| $n$ | Purchase | Rent |
|-----|----------|------|
| 12 | 8,980 | 6,900 |
| 24 | 12,160 | 13,800 |
| 36 | 15,340 | 20,700 |
| 48 | 18,520 | 27,600 |
| 60 | 21,700 | 34,500 |
| 72 | 24,880 | 41,400 |

**(d)** 19 months  **2. (a)** $R_1 = 195 + 0.15x$; $R_2 = 270$
**(b)** Plan 1; plan 2  **(c)** 500 mi  **3. (a)** $C = 8000 + 22x$
**(b)** $R = 49x$  **(c)** $P = 27x - 8000$  **(d)** 297
**4. (a)** Option 1: $A = 5C - 3000$; Option 2: $A = 9C - 9720$
**(b)**

| Cost | Area gain (option 1) | Area gain (option 2) |
|------|----------------------|----------------------|
| $1100 | 2,500 ft$^2$ | 180 ft$^2$ |
| $1200 | 3,000 ft$^2$ | 1,080 ft$^2$ |
| $1500 | 4,500 ft$^2$ | 3,780 ft$^2$ |
| $2000 | 7,000 ft$^2$ | 8,280 ft$^2$ |
| $2500 | 9,500 ft$^2$ | 12,780 ft$^2$ |
| $3000 | 12,000 ft$^2$ | 17,280 ft$^2$ |

**(c)** Option 1; option 2  **5. (a)** Design 2  **(b)** Design 1
**6. (a)** $P = 130,000n$  **(b)** $P = 280,000n$  **(c)** Plan B

**7. (a)**

| Minutes used | Plan A | Plan B | Plan C |
|:---:|:---:|:---:|:---:|
| 500 | $30 | $40 | $60 |
| 600 | $80 | $70 | $70 |
| 700 | $130 | $100 | $80 |
| 800 | $180 | $130 | $90 |
| 900 | $230 | $160 | $100 |
| 1000 | $280 | $190 | $110 |
| 1100 | $330 | $220 | $120 |

**(b)** $A = 30 + 0.50(x - 500)$, $B = 40 + 0.30(x - 500)$, $C = 60 + 0.10(x - 500)$  **(c)** 550 minutes: A = $55, B = $55, C = $65; 975 minutes: A = $267.50, B = $182.50, C = $107.50; 1200 minutes: A = $380, B = $250, C = $130
**(d) (i)** 550 minutes  **(ii)** 575 minutes  **8. (a)** Not fair
**(b)** Not fair  **(c)** Fair

# CHAPTER 2

## SECTION 2.1 ▪ page 142

**1.** $(3, -5)$  **2.** II  **3.** $\sqrt{(c-a)^2 + (d-b)^2}$; 10

**4.** $\left(\dfrac{a+c}{2}, \dfrac{b+d}{2}\right)$; $(4, 6)$

**5.**

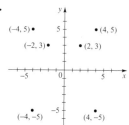

**6.** $A(5, 1)$, $B(1, 2)$, $C(-2, 6)$, $D(-6, 2)$, $E(-4, -1)$, $F(-2, 0)$, $G(-1, -3)$, $H(2, -2)$

**7.**

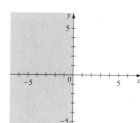

**8.**

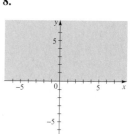

**9.**

**10.**

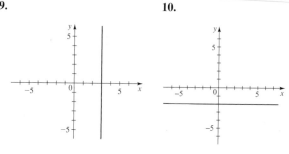

**11.**

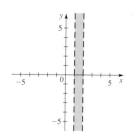

**12.**

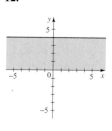

**13.**

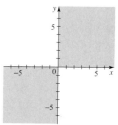

**14.** $xy > 0 \iff x < 0$ and $y < 0$ or $x > 0$ and $y > 0$

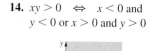

**15.**

**16.**

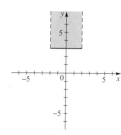 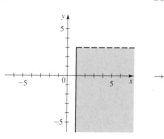

**17.**

**18.**

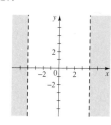 

**19.**

**20.**

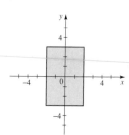 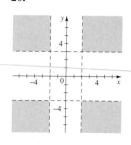

**21. (a)** $\sqrt{13}$  **(b)** $\left(\frac{3}{2}, 1\right)$  **22. (a)** 5  **(b)** $\left(0, \frac{1}{2}\right)$  **23. (a)** 10
**(b)** $(1, 0)$  **24. (a)** $2\sqrt{10}$  **(b)** $(1, -2)$

**25. (a)**

**(b)** 10   **(c)** $(3, 12)$

**27. (a)**

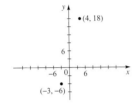

**(b)** 25   **(c)** $\left(\frac{1}{2}, 6\right)$

**29. (a)**

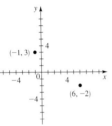

**(b)** $\sqrt{74}$   **(c)** $\left(\frac{5}{2}, \frac{1}{2}\right)$

**31. (a)**

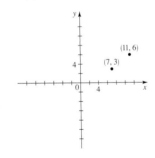

**(b)** 5   **(c)** $\left(9, \frac{9}{2}\right)$

**33. (a)**

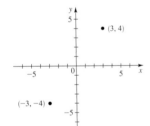

**(b)** 10   **(c)** $(0, 0)$

**26. (a)**

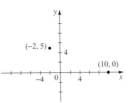

**(b)** 13   **(c)** $\left(4, \frac{5}{2}\right)$

**28. (a)**

**(b)** $10\sqrt{2}$   **(c)** $(4, 4)$

**30. (a)**

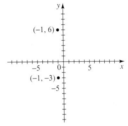

**(b)** 9   **(c)** $\left(-1, \frac{3}{2}\right)$

**32. (a)**

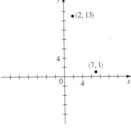

**(b)** 13   **(c)** $\left(\frac{9}{2}, 7\right)$

**34. (a)**

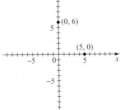

**(b)** $\sqrt{61}$   **(c)** $\left(\frac{5}{2}, 3\right)$

**35.** 24

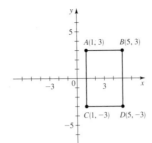

**36.** 16

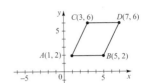

**37.** Trapezoid, area $= 9$

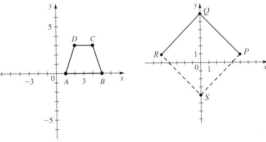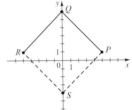

**38.** 50

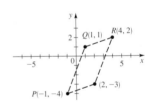

**39.** $A(6, 7)$   **40.** $C(-6, 3)$   **41.** $Q(-1, 3)$   **44.** 9   **45. (b)** 10

**49.** $(0, -4)$   **50.** $\sqrt{37}, \dfrac{\sqrt{109}}{2}, \dfrac{\sqrt{145}}{2}$   **51.** $\left(1, \frac{7}{2}\right)$

**52.** $B(6, 7)$             **53.** $(2, -3)$

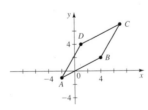

**54.** $(10, 13)$

**55. (a)**                            **(b)** $\left(\frac{5}{2}, 3\right), \left(\frac{5}{2}, 3\right)$

**57. (a)** 5   **(b)** 31; 25   **(c)** Points $P$ and $Q$ must be on either the same street or the same avenue.   **58. (a)** 15th Street and 12th Avenue   **(b)** 17 blocks   **59.** $(66, 45)$; the $y$-value of the midpoint is the pressure experienced by the diver at a depth of 66 ft.

## SECTION 2.2 ▪ page 154

**1.** 2; 3; No   **2. (a)** $y$; $x$; $-1$   **(b)** $x$; $y$; $\frac{1}{2}$   **3.** $(1, 2)$; 3
**4. (a)** $(a, -b)$   **(b)** $(-a, b)$   **(c)** $(-a, -b)$   **5.** No, no, yes
**6.** No, yes, yes   **7.** No, yes, yes   **8.** No, yes, yes
**9.** Yes, no, yes   **10.** Yes, yes, yes

**11.** *x*-intercept 0,
   *y*-intercept 0

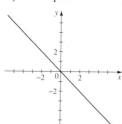

**12.** *x*-intercept 0,
   *y*-intercept 0

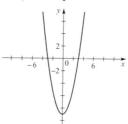

**21.** *x*-intercepts ±3,
   *y*-intercept −9

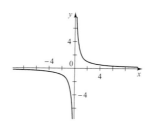

**22.** *x*-intercepts −3, 3,
   *y*-intercept 9

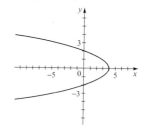

**13.** *x*-intercept 4,
   *y*-intercept 4

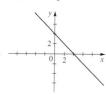

**14.** *x*-intercept −1,
   *y*-intercept 3

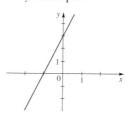

**23.** No intercepts

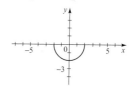

**24.** *x*-intercept 4,
   *y*-intercepts −2, 2

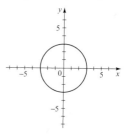

**15.** *x*-intercept 3,
   *y*-intercept −6

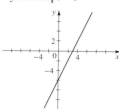

**16.** *x*-intercept 3,
   *y*-intercept 3

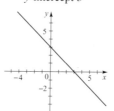

**25.** *x*-intercept 0,
   *y*-intercept 0

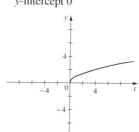

**26.** *x*-intercepts −3, 3,
   *y*-intercepts −3, 3

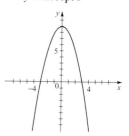

**17.** *x*-intercepts ±1,
   *y*-intercept 1

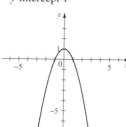

**18.** no *x*-intercepts,
   *y*-intercept 2

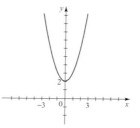

**27.** *x*-intercepts ±2,
   *y*-intercept 2

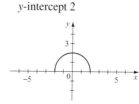

**28.** *x*-intercepts −2, 2,
   *y*-intercept −2

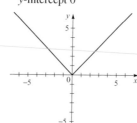

**19.** *x*-intercept 0,
   *y*-intercept 0

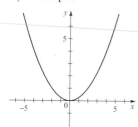

**20.** *x*-intercept 0,
   *y*-intercept 0

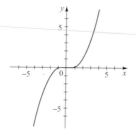

**29.** *x*-intercept 0,
   *y*-intercept 0

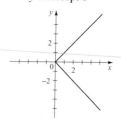

**30.** *x*-intercept 0,
   *y*-intercept 0

**31.** $x$-intercepts $\pm 4$,
 $y$-intercept 4

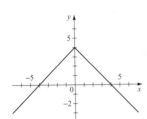

**32.** $x$-intercept 4,
 $y$-intercept 4

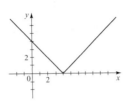

**51.** $(3, 0), 4$

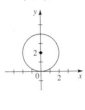

**52.** $(0, 2), 2$

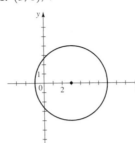

**33.** $x$-intercept 0,
 $y$-intercept 0

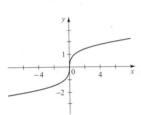

**34.** $x$-intercept 1,
 $y$-intercept $-1$

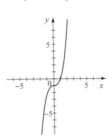

**53.** $(-3, 4), 5$

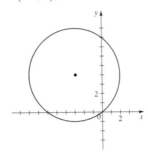

**54.** $(-1, -2), 6$

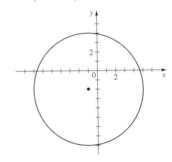

**35.** $x$-intercept 0,
 $y$-intercept 0

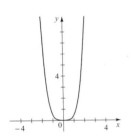

**36.** $x$-intercepts $\pm 2$,
 $y$-intercept 16

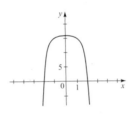

**55.** $(x - 2)^2 + (y + 1)^2 = 9$   **56.** $(x + 1)^2 + (y + 4)^2 = 64$
**57.** $x^2 + y^2 = 65$   **58.** $(x + 1)^2 + (y - 5)^2 = 130$
**59.** $(x - 2)^2 + (y - 5)^2 = 25$   **60.** $(x - 3)^2 + (y + 1)^2 = 32$
**61.** $(x - 7)^2 + (y + 3)^2 = 9$   **62.** $(x - 5)^2 + (y - 5)^2 = 25$
**63.** $(x + 2)^2 + (y - 2)^2 = 4$   **64.** $(x + 1)^2 + (y - 1)^2 = 10$
**65.** $(1, -2), 2$   **66.** $(1, 1), 2$   **67.** $(2, -5), 4$   **68.** $(0, -3), \sqrt{7}$
**69.** $\left(-\frac{1}{2}, 0\right), \frac{1}{2}$   **70.** $\left(-1, -\frac{1}{2}\right), \frac{1}{2}$   **71.** $\left(\frac{1}{4}, -\frac{1}{4}\right), \frac{1}{2}$   **72.** $\left(-\frac{1}{4}, -1\right), 1$
**73.**

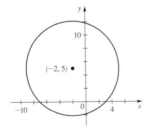

**74.**

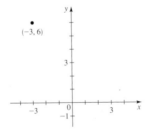

**37.** $x$-intercepts 0, 4; $y$-intercept 0
**38.** $x$-intercepts $-3, 3$; $y$-intercepts $-2, 2$
**39.** $x$-intercepts $-2, 2$; $y$-intercepts $-4, 4$
**40.** $x$-intercepts $-8, 8$; $y$-intercept 4
**41.** $x$-intercept 3; $y$-intercept $-3$
**42.** $x$-intercepts 2, 3; $y$-intercept 6
**43.** $x$-intercepts $\pm 3$; $y$-intercept $-9$
**44.** $x$-intercept $\frac{1}{2}$; $y$-intercept 1
**45.** $x$-intercepts $\pm 2$; $y$-intercepts $\pm 2$
**46.** $x$-intercept $-1$; $y$-intercept 1   **47.** None
**48.** $x$-intercepts $-1, 1$; $y$-intercept 1
**49.** $(0, 0), 3$ 　　　　　　 **50.** $(0, 0), \sqrt{5}$

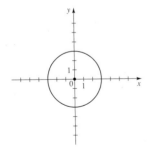

**75.**

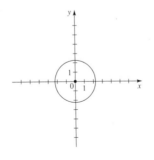

**76.** No graph

**77.** Symmetry about $y$-axis   **78.** Symmetry about $x$-axis
**79.** Symmetry about origin   **80.** Symmetry about $y$-axis
**81.** Symmetry about $x$-axis, $y$-axis, and origin

**82.** Symmetry about origin

**83.**

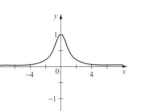

**84.**

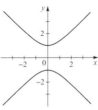

**85.**

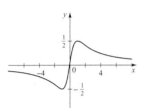

**86.**

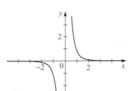

**87.**

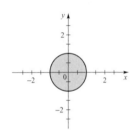

**88.**

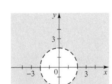

**89.**

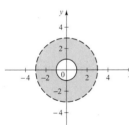

**90.**

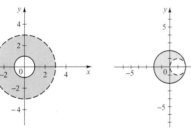

**91.** $12\pi$

**92.** $\dfrac{9\pi}{4}$

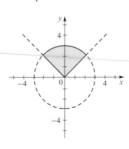

**93. (a)** 14%, 6%, 2%   **(b)** 1975–1976, 1978–1982   **(c)** Decrease, increase   **(d)** 14%, 1%   **94. (a)** 2 Mm, 8 Mm   **(b)** −1.33, 7.33; 2.40 Mm, 7.60 Mm

**SECTION 2.3 ▪ page 164**

**1.** $x$   **2.** above   **3. (a)** $x = -1, 0, 1, 3$   **(b)** $[-1, 0] \cup [1, 3]$
**4. (a)** $x = 1, 4$   **(b)** $(1, 4)$   **5.** (c)   **6.** (c)   **7.** (c)   **8.** (d)
**9.** (c)   **10.** (d)

**11.**

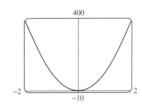

**12.**

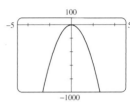

**13.**

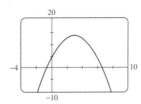

**14.**

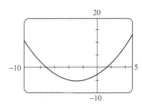

**15.**

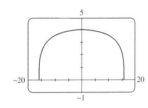

**16.**

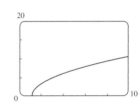

**17.**

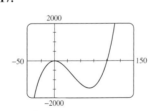

**18.**

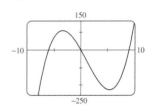

**19.**

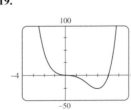

**20.**

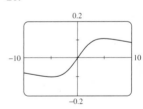

**21.**

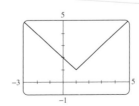

**22.**

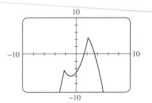

**23.** No   **24.** No   **25.** Yes, 2   **26.** Yes, 1

**27.**

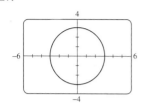

**28.**

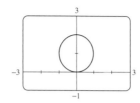

**29.**

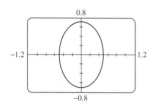

**30.**

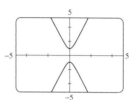

**31.** $-4$ **32.** $-6$ **33.** $\frac{5}{14}$ **34.** $-4$ **35.** $\pm 4\sqrt{2} \approx \pm 5.7$
**36.** $-2\sqrt[3]{2} \approx -2.52$ **37.** No solution **38.** No solution
**39.** $2.5, -2.5$ **40.** $\frac{3}{2}\sqrt[5]{16} \approx 2.61$
**41.** $5 + 2\sqrt[4]{5} \approx 7.99, 5 - 2\sqrt[4]{5} \approx 2.01$
**42.** $-2 + \frac{2}{3}\sqrt[5]{81} \approx -0.39$ **43.** $3.00, 4.00$ **44.** $0.25, 0.50$
**45.** $1.00, 2.00, 3.00$ **46.** $-1.00, -0.25, 0.25$ **47.** $1.62$
**48.** $0.00, 2.31$ **49.** $-1.00, 0.00, 1.00$ **50.** $0.00, 3.31$ **51.** $0, 2, 3$
**52.** $-2, 0, 3$ **53.** $4$ **54.** $3$ **55.** $2.55$ **56.** $-2.78, -0.51, 0.51,$
$2.78$ **57.** $-2.05, 0, 1.05$ **58.** $-2.31, 1.79$ **59.** $[-2.00, 5.00]$
**60.** $[-2, 0.25]$ **61.** $(-\infty, 1.00] \cup [2.00, 3.00]$
**62.** $(-1, -0.25) \cup (-0.25, \infty)$ **63.** $(-1.00, 0) \cup (1.00, \infty)$
**64.** $(-\infty, -0.535] \cup [0.535, \infty)$ **65.** $(-\infty, 0)$ **66.** $[2.148, \infty)$
**67.** $(-1, 4)$ **68.** $(-\infty, -2] \cup [\frac{1}{2}, \infty)$ **69.** $[-1, 3]$
**70.** $(-\infty, -1] \cup \{0\} \cup [1, \infty)$ **71.** $0, 0.01$

**72. (a)**

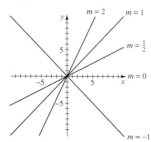

 **(b)** 101 cooktops
 **(c)** $279 < x < 400$

**73. (a)**

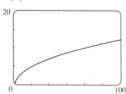

 **(b)** 67 mi

## SECTION 2.4 ▪ page 176

**1.** $y; x; 2$ **2. (a)** $3$ **(b)** $3$ **(c)** $-\frac{1}{3}$ **3.** $y - 2 = 3(x - 1)$
**4. (a)** $0; y = 3$ **(b)** Undefined; $x = 2$ **5.** $\frac{1}{2}$ **6.** $-3$ **7.** $\frac{1}{6}$
**8.** $\frac{1}{2}$ **9.** $-\frac{1}{2}$ **10.** $-\frac{4}{3}$ **11.** $-\frac{9}{2}$ **12.** $\frac{4}{7}$ **13.** $-2, \frac{1}{2}, 3, -\frac{1}{4}$
**14. (a)**                                    **(b)**

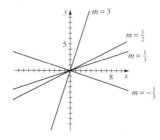

**15.** $x + y - 4 = 0$ **16.** $2x - y + 4 = 0$ **17.** $3x - 2y - 6 = 0$
**18.** $4x + 3y + 12 = 0$ **19.** $5x - y - 7 = 0$ **20.** $x + y - 2 = 0$
**21.** $2x - 3y + 19 = 0$ **22.** $7x + 2y + 31 = 0$
**23.** $5x + y - 11 = 0$ **24.** $x - y - 1 = 0$ **25.** $3x - y - 2 = 0$
**26.** $2x - 5y + 20 = 0$ **27.** $3x - y - 3 = 0$
**28.** $3x - 4y + 24 = 0$ **29.** $y = 5$ **30.** $x = 4$
**31.** $x + 2y + 11 = 0$ **32.** $2x + 3y - 18 = 0$ **33.** $x = -1$
**34.** $x = 2$ **35.** $5x - 2y + 1 = 0$ **36.** $6x + 3y - 1 = 0$
**37.** $x - y + 6 = 0$ **38.** $2x - y - 7 = 0$
**39. (a)**                                    **40. (a)**

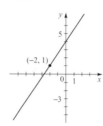

**(b)** $3x - 2y + 8 = 0$                   **(b)** $2x + y - 7 = 0$
**41.** They all have the              **42.** They all have the
same slope.                           same $y$-intercept.

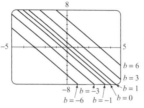

**43.** They all have the              **44.** They all pass through the
same $x$-intercept.                   point $(-3, 2)$.

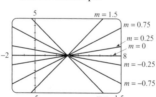
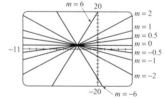

**45.** $-1, 3$                              **46.** $\frac{3}{2}, -6$

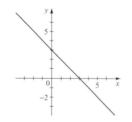
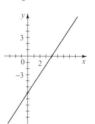

**47.** $-\frac{1}{3}, 0$                     **48.** $\frac{2}{5}, 0$

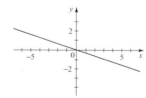
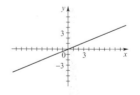

**49.** $\frac{3}{2}, 3$

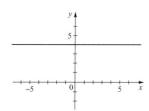

**50.** $-\frac{3}{5}, 6$

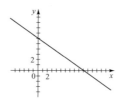

**69. (a)**

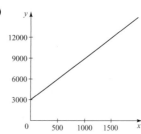

**(b)** The slope represents production cost per toaster; the $y$-intercept represents monthly fixed cost.

**51.** $0, 4$

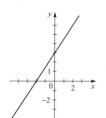

**52.** Undefined, none

**70. (a)**

| $C$ | $-30°$ | $-20°$ | $-10°$ | $0°$ | $10°$ | $20°$ | $30°$ |
|---|---|---|---|---|---|---|---|
| $F$ | $-22°$ | $-4°$ | $14°$ | $32°$ | $50°$ | $68°$ | $86°$ |

**(b)** $-40°$
**71. (a)** $t = \frac{5}{24}n + 45$   **(b)** $76°F$
**72. (a)** $V = -950t + 4000$
**(b)**

**53.** $\frac{3}{4}, -3$

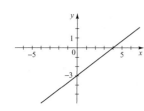

**54.** $0, -2$

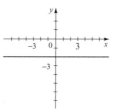

**(c)** The slope is the rate of decrease in value of the computer, and the $V$-intercept is the price of the computer.   **(d)** $1150
**73. (a)** $P = 0.434d + 15$, where $P$ is pressure in lb/in$^2$ and $d$ is depth in feet
**(b)**

**55.** $-\frac{3}{4}, \frac{1}{4}$

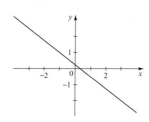

**56.** $-\frac{4}{5}, 2$

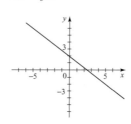

**(c)** The slope is the rate of increase in water pressure, and the $y$-intercept is the air pressure at the surface.   **(d)** 196 ft
**74. (a)** $d = 48t$
**(b)**

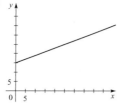

**60. (a)** Yes   **(b)** No   **61.** $x - y - 3 = 0$   **62.** 3
**63. (b)** $4x - 3y - 24 = 0$   **64. (a)** $3x - 4y - 25 = 0$
**(b)** $(-3, 4)$   **65.** 16,667 ft   **66. (a)** The slope is the rate of increase in average surface temperature, and the $T$-intercept is the average surface temperature in 1950.   **(b)** $17.0°C$   **67. (a)** 8.34; the slope represents the increase in dosage for a one-year increase in age.   **(b)** 8.34 mg

**68. (a)**

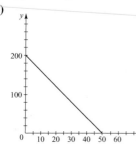

**(b)** The slope is the rate of decline in number of spaces sold, the $y$-intercept is the number of spaces, and the $x$-intercept is the cost per space when the manager rents no spaces.

**(c)** 48, speed
**75. (a)** $C = \frac{1}{4}d + 260$
**(b)** $635
**(c)** The slope represents cost per mile.
**(d)** The $y$-intercept represents monthly fixed cost.

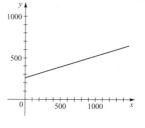

**76. (a)** $y = 13x + 900$
**(b)** 13; slope is cost of producing each additional chair
**(c)** 900; $y$-intercept is fixed daily cost

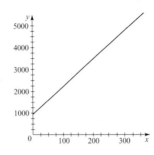

**(d)** $m = \frac{4}{3}$; point-slope: $y - 7 = \frac{4}{3}(x - 3)$;
slope-intercept: $y = \frac{4}{3}x + 3$;     **(e)** $x^2 + (y - 3)^2 = 25$

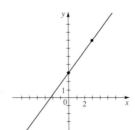

## SECTION 2.5 ▪ page 182

**1.** directly proportional; proportionality   **2.** inversely proportional; proportionality   **3.** directly proportional; inversely proportional
**4.** $\frac{1}{2}xy$   **5.** $T = kx$   **6.** $P = kw$   **7.** $v = k/z$   **8.** $w = kmn$

**9.** $y = ks/t$   **10.** $P = k/T$   **11.** $z = k\sqrt{y}$   **12.** $A = k\dfrac{t^2}{x^3}$

**13.** $V = klwh$   **14.** $S = kr^2\theta^2$   **15.** $R = k\dfrac{i}{Pt}$   **16.** $A = k\sqrt{xy}$

**17.** $y = 7x$   **18.** $z = 15/t$   **19.** $R = 12/s$   **20.** $P = \frac{1}{15}T$

**21.** $M = 15x/y$   **22.** $S = 9pq$   **23.** $W = 360/r^2$   **24.** $t = 50\dfrac{xy}{r}$

**25.** $C = 16lwh$   **26.** $H = 81l^2w^2$   **27.** $s = 500/\sqrt{t}$

**28.** $M = 32\dfrac{abc}{d}$   **29. (a)** $F = kx$   **(b)** 8   **(c)** 32 N

**30. (a)** $T = k\sqrt{l}$   **(b)** quadruple the length $l$   **31. (a)** $C = kpm$
**(b)** 0.125   **(c)** \$57,500   **32. (a)** $P = kT/V$   **(b)** 8.3
**(c)** 51.9 kPa   **33. (a)** $P = ks^3$   **(b)** 0.012   **(c)** 324
**34.** 270 hp   **35.** 0.7 dB   **36.** 40 mi/h (for safety round down, not up)   **37.** 4   **38.** 1305.6 lb   **39.** 5.3 mi/h
**40. (a)** $F = kws^2/r$   **(b)** 48 mi/h
**41. (a)** $R = kL/d^2$   **(b)** 0.002916   **(c)** $R \approx 137\ \Omega$
**42. (a)** $T^2 = kd^3$   **(b)** $1.66 \times 10^{-19}$   **(c)** 164 yr
**43. (a)** 160,000   **(b)** 1,930,670,340   **44.** \$51,200   **45.** 36 lb

**46.** 25.2 ft   **47. (a)** $f = \dfrac{k}{L}$   **(b)** Halves it

**48. (a)** $r = kx(P - x)$   **(b)** Infection rate when 1000 people are infected is about 80 times larger   **(c)** 0, since no more people can be infected

## CHAPTER 2 REVIEW ▪ page 187

**1. (a)**

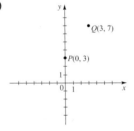

**(b)** 5   **(c)** $\left(\frac{3}{2}, 5\right)$

**2. (a)**

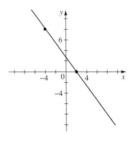

**(b)** 10   **(c)** $(-1, 4)$

**(d)** $m = -\frac{4}{3}$;   point-slope: $y - 8 = -\frac{4}{3}(x + 4)$;
slope-intercept: $-\frac{4}{3}x + \frac{8}{3}$;     **(e)** $(x - 2)^2 + y^2 = 100$

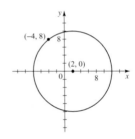

**3. (a)**

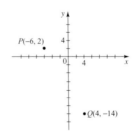

**(b)** $2\sqrt{89}$   **(c)** $(-1, -6)$

**(d)** $m = -\frac{8}{5}$;   point-slope: $y + 14 = -\frac{8}{5}(x - 4)$;
slope-intercept: $y = -\frac{8}{5}x - \frac{38}{5}$;     **(e)** $(x + 6)^2 + (y - 2)^2 = 356$

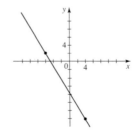

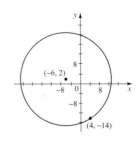

**4. (a)**

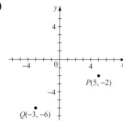

**(b)** $4\sqrt{5}$   **(c)** $(1, -4)$

**(d)** $m = \frac{1}{2}$;   point-slope: $y + 6 = \frac{1}{2}(x + 3)$;
slope-intercept: $y = \frac{1}{2}x - \frac{9}{2}$;       **(e)** $(x - 5)^2 + (y + 2)^2 = 80$

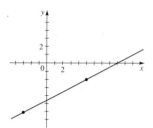

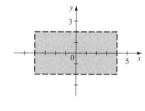

**5.**

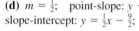

**6.**

**7.** $B$   **8.** $(x - 2)^2 + (y + 5)^2 = 2$   **9.** $(x + 5)^2 + (y + 1)^2 = 26$
**10.** $(x - \frac{1}{2})^2 + (y - \frac{11}{2})^2 = \frac{17}{2}$
**11. (a)** Circle                    **(b)** Center $(-1, 3)$, radius 1

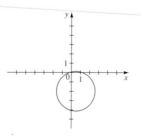

**12. (a)** Circle                    **(b)** Center $(\frac{1}{2}, -2)$, radius $\dfrac{3\sqrt{2}}{2}$

**13. (a)** No graph   **14. (a)** Point
**15.**                              **16.**

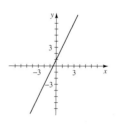

**17.**                              **18.**

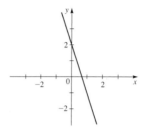

**19.**                              **20.**

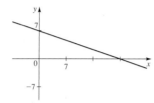

**21.**                              **22.**

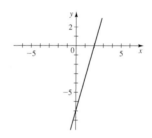

**23.**                              **24.**

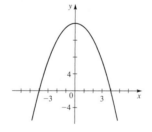

**25. (a)** Symmetry about $y$-axis   **(b)** $x$-intercepts $-3, 3$;
$y$-intercept 9   **26. (a)** Symmetry about $x$-axis   **(b)** $x$-intercept 6;
$y$-intercepts $-6, 6$   **27. (a)** Symmetry about $y$-axis

**(b)** $x$-intercept 0; $y$-intercepts 0, 2 **28. (a)** Symmetry about $y$-axis **(b)** $x$-intercepts $-2$, 2; $y$-intercept $-16$ **29. (a)** Symmetry about $x$- and $y$-axes and the origin **(b)** $x$-intercepts $-4$, 4; no $y$-intercept **30. (a)** Symmetry about origin **(b)** No $x$- or $y$-intercept

**31.** **32.**

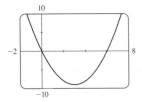 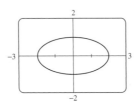

**33.** **34.**

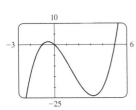 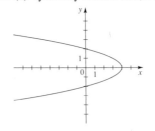

**35.** $-1, 7$ **36.** $-2.50, 2.76$ **37.** $-2.72, -1.15, 1.00, 2.87$
**38.** $-10, -6, 0, 4$ **39.** $[1, 3]$ **40.** $(5.07, \infty)$
**41.** $(-1.85, -0.60) \cup (0.45, 2.00)$
**42.** $(-\infty, -5.10] \cup [-2.45, 2.45] \cup [5.10, \infty)$
**43. (a)** $y = 2x + 6$ **(b)** $2x - y + 6 = 0$ **44. (a)** $y = -\frac{1}{2}x$
**(b)** $x + 2y = 0$ **45. (a)** $y = \frac{2}{3}x - \frac{16}{3}$ **(b)** $2x - 3y - 16 = 0$
**46. (a)** $y = -3x + 12$ **(b)** $3x + y - 12 = 0$ **47. (a)** $x = 3$
**(b)** $x - 3 = 0$ **48. (a)** $y = 5$ **(b)** $y - 5 = 0$
**49. (a)** $y = \frac{2}{5}x + \frac{3}{5}$ **(b)** $2x - 5y + 3 = 0$ **50. (a)** $y = -4x$
**(b)** $4x + y = 0$ **51. (a)** $y = -2x$ **(b)** $2x + y = 0$
**52. (a)** $y = -3x + 10$ **(b)** $3x + y - 10 = 0$

**53. (a)** The slope represents the amount the spring lengthens for a one-pound increase in weight. The $S$-intercept represents the unstretched length of the spring. **(b)** 4 in.
**54. (a)** $S = 3{,}500t + 60{,}000$ **(b)** The slope is her annual increase in salary, and the $S$-intercept is her initial salary. **(c)** $102,000
**55.** $M = 8z$ **56.** $z = \frac{192}{y}$ **57. (a)** $I = k/d^2$ **(b)** 64,000
**(c)** 160 candles **58.** 8 in. **59.** 11.0 mi/h **60.** 329.4 ft
**61.** $F = 0.000125 q_1 q_2$ **62.** $E = 765{,}000$ J **63.** $x^2 + y^2 = 169$,
$5x - 12y + 169 = 0$ **64.** $(x - 5)^2 + (y - 5)^2 = 25$,
$4x + 3y - 35 = 0$

**CHAPTER 2 TEST ▪ page 189**

**1. (a)**

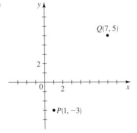

**(b)** 10 **(c)** $(4, 1)$ **(d)** $\frac{4}{3}$
**(e)** $y = -\frac{3}{4}x + 4$
**(f)** $(x - 4)^2 + (y - 1)^2 = 25$

**2. (a)** $(0, 0)$; $\frac{5}{2}$

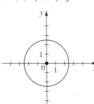

**(b)** $(3, 0)$; 3

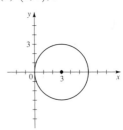

**(c)** $(-3, 1)$; 2

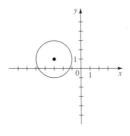

**3. (a)** symmetry about $x$-axis; $x$-intercept 4; $y$-intercepts $-2$, 2

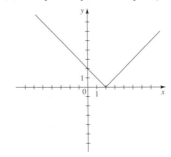

**(b)** No symmetry; $x$-intercept 2; $y$-intercept 2

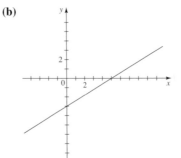

**4. (a)** $x$-intercept 5; $y$-intercept $-3$

**(b)**

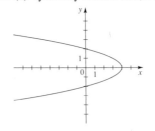

**(c)** $y = \frac{3}{5}x - 3$ **(d)** $\frac{3}{5}$ **(e)** $-\frac{5}{3}$
**5. (a)** $3x + y - 3 = 0$ **(b)** $2x + 3y - 12 = 0$

**6. (a)** $4\,°C$                    **(b)**

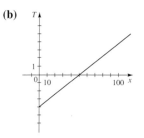

**(c)** The slope is the rate of change in temperature, the *x*-intercept is the depth at which the temperature is $0\,°C$, and the *T*-intercept is the temperature at ground level.    **7. (a)** $-2.94, -0.11, 3.05$
**(b)** $[-1.07, 3.74]$    **8. (a)** $M = kwh^2/L$    **(b)** $400$
**(c)** $12,000$ lb

## ANSWERS TO CUMULATIVE REVIEW TEST
## FOR CHAPTERS 1 AND 2 ▪ page 190

**1.** $8000    **2. (a)** $-\tfrac{1}{3} + 3i$    **(b)** $10$    **(c)** $-\tfrac{9}{5} - \tfrac{12}{5}i$    **(d)** $2 + i\tfrac{\sqrt{3}}{2}$
**3. (a)** $-2$    **(b)** $-16$    **(c)** $-1, 6$    **(d)** $\tfrac{2}{3} \pm i\tfrac{\sqrt{2}}{3}$    **(e)** $\pm 2, \pm 2i$
**(f)** $-1.75, 2.75$

**4. (a)** $[3, \infty)$                    **(b)** $(-\infty, -4) \cup (2, \infty)$

**(c)** $[-\tfrac{1}{2}, 1]$                    **(d)** $(3, \infty)$

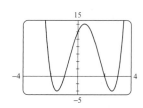

**5. (a)**

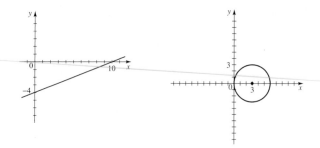

**(b)** $-2, -1, 2, 3$    **(c)** $-2 \le x \le -1$ and $2 \le x \le 3$
**6. (a)** $\sqrt{194} \approx 13.93$    **(b)** $y = -\tfrac{5}{13}x + \tfrac{63}{13}$
**(c)** $\left(x - \tfrac{7}{2}\right)^2 + \left(y - \tfrac{7}{2}\right)^2 = \tfrac{97}{2}$    **(d)** $y = \tfrac{13}{5}x + \tfrac{69}{5}$    **(e)** $y = -\tfrac{5}{13}x$
**7. (a)**                    **(b)** $C(3, 0), 3$

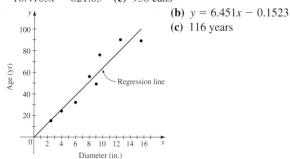

**8. (a)** $y = -2x + 6$    **(b)** $(x + 3)^2 + (y - 4)^2 = 25$
**9.** 8 mi/h    **10. (a)** $S = 187.5x^2$    **(b)** $18,750.00
**(c)** 18 years

## FOCUS ON MODELING ▪ page 198

**1. (a)**

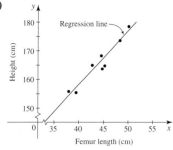

**(b)** $y = 1.8807x + 82.65$    **(c)** $191.7$ cm
**2. (a)**

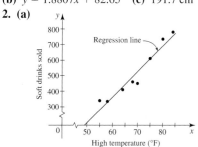

**(b)** $y = 16.4163x - 621.83$    **(c)** 938 cans
**3. (a)**                    **(b)** $y = 6.451x - 0.1523$
                    **(c)** 116 years

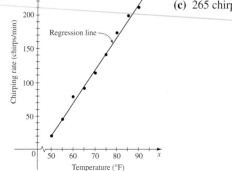

**(b)** $y = 1.6318x - 2893.7$    **(c)** 378.1 ppm
**5. (a)**                    **(b)** $y = 4.857x - 220.97$
                    **(c)** 265 chirps/min

**6. (a)**

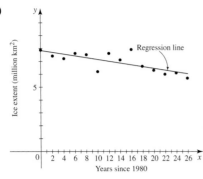

**(b)** $y = -0.0689x + 7.831$    **(c)** 5.8 million km$^2$

**7. (a)**

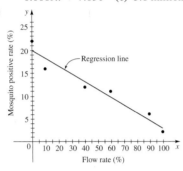

**(b)** $y = -0.168x + 19.89$    **(c)** 8.13%

**8. (a)**

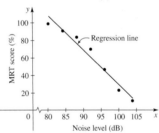

**(b)** $y = -3.9018x + 419.7$    **(c)** The correlation coefficient is $-0.98$, so a linear model is appropriate    **(d)** 53%

**9. (a)**

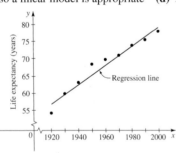

**(b)** $y = 0.2708x - 462.9$    **(c)** 80.3 years

**10. (a)**

| Year | $x$ | Height (m) |
|------|-----|------------|
| 1972 | 0  | 5.64 |
| 1976 | 4  | 5.64 |
| 1980 | 8  | 5.78 |
| 1984 | 12 | 5.75 |
| 1988 | 16 | 5.90 |
| 1992 | 20 | 5.87 |
| 1996 | 24 | 5.92 |
| 2000 | 28 | 5.90 |
| 2004 | 32 | 5.95 |

**(b)** $y = 0.0101x + 5.66$

**(c)**

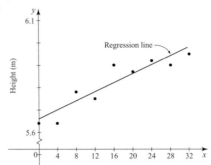

**(d)** 6.02 m

**11. (a)** $y = -0.173x + 64.717$, $y = -0.269x + 78.67$
**(b)** 2045

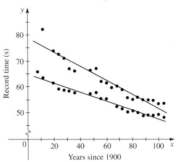

# CHAPTER 3

## SECTION 3.1 ▪ page 211

**1.** value    **2.** domain, range    **3. (a)** $f$ and $g$
**(b)** $f(5) = 10, g(5) = 0$    **4. (a)** square, add 3

**(b)**

| $x$ | 0 | 2 | 4 | 6 |
|------|---|---|---|---|
| $f(x)$ | 19 | 7 | 3 | 7 |

**5.** $f(x) = 2(x + 3)$    **6.** $f(x) = \frac{x}{7} - 4$    **7.** $f(x) = (x - 5)^2$
**8.** $f(x) = \frac{1}{3}(\sqrt{x} + 8)$    **9.** Square, then add 2    **10.** Add 2, then take the square root    **11.** Subtract 4, then divide by 3
**12.** Divide by 3, then subtract 4

**13.**

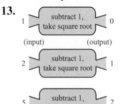

**14.**

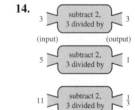

**15.**

| $x$ | $f(x)$ |
|------|--------|
| $-1$ | 8 |
| 0 | 2 |
| 1 | 0 |
| 2 | 2 |
| 3 | 8 |

**16.**

| $x$ | $g(x)$ |
|------|--------|
| $-3$ | 3 |
| $-2$ | 1 |
| 0 | 3 |
| 1 | 5 |
| 3 | 9 |

**17.** $3, 3, -6, -\frac{23}{4}, 94$    **18.** $-12, 3, 0, \frac{19}{27}, 0.408$

**19.** $3, -3, 2, 2a + 1, -2a + 1, 2a + 2b + 1$

**20.** $0, 15, 3, a^2 + 2a, x^2 - 2x, \dfrac{1}{a^2} + \dfrac{2}{a}$

**21.** $-\dfrac{1}{3}, -3, \dfrac{1}{3}, \dfrac{1-a}{1+a}, \dfrac{2-a}{a}$, undefined

**22.** $2, -2, \dfrac{5}{2}, \dfrac{5}{2}, x + \dfrac{1}{x}, \dfrac{1}{x} + x$

**23.** $-4, 10, -2, 3\sqrt{2}, 2x^2 + 7x + 1, 2x^2 - 3x - 4$

**24.** $0, -3, -5, -\dfrac{45}{8}, \dfrac{x^3}{8} - x^2, x^6 - 4x^4$

**25.** $6, 2, 1, 2, 2|x|, 2(x^2 + 1)$

**26.** $-1, -1$, not defined, $1, 1, x/|x|$   **27.** $4, 1, 1, 2, 3$

**28.** $5, 5, 5, 3, 7$   **29.** $8, -\frac{3}{4}, -1, 0, -1$   **30.** $-15, 1, 2, 3, 9$

**31.** $x^2 + 4x + 5, x^2 + 6$   **32.** $6x - 1, 6x - 2$

**33.** $x^2 + 4, x^2 + 8x + 16$   **34.** $2x - 18, 2x - 6$

**35.** $3a + 2, 3(a + h) + 2, 3$

**36.** $a^2 + 1, a^2 + 2ah + h^2 + 1, 2a + h$

**37.** $5, 5, 0$   **38.** $\dfrac{1}{a + 1}, \dfrac{1}{a + h + 1}, \dfrac{-1}{(a + 1)(a + h + 1)}$

**39.** $\dfrac{a}{a + 1}, \dfrac{a + h}{a + h + 1}, \dfrac{1}{(a + h + 1)(a + 1)}$

**40.** $\dfrac{2a}{a - 1}, \dfrac{2(a + h)}{a + h - 1}, \dfrac{-2}{(a + h - 1)(a - 1)}$

**41.** $3 - 5a + 4a^2, 3 - 5a - 5h + 4a^2 + 8ah + 4h^2,$
$-5 + 8a + 4h$   **42.** $a^3, a^3 + 3a^2h + 3ah^2 + h^3, 3a^2 + 3ah + h^2$

**43.** $(-\infty, \infty)$   **44.** $(-\infty, \infty)$   **45.** $[-1, 5]$   **46.** $[0, 5]$

**47.** $\{x \mid x \neq 3\}$   **48.** $\{x \mid x \neq 2\}$   **49.** $\{x \mid x \neq \pm 1\}$

**50.** $\{x \mid x \neq -3, x \neq 2\}$   **51.** $[5, \infty)$   **52.** $[-9, \infty)$

**53.** $(-\infty, \infty)$   **54.** $(-\infty, \frac{7}{3}]$   **55.** $[\frac{5}{2}, \infty)$

**56.** $(-\infty, -3] \cup [3, \infty)$   **57.** $[-2, 3) \cup (3, \infty)$

**58.** $[0, \frac{1}{2}) \cup (\frac{1}{2}, \infty)$   **59.** $(-\infty, 0] \cup [6, \infty)$

**60.** $(-\infty, -2] \cup [4, \infty)$   **61.** $(4, \infty)$   **62.** $(-\infty, 6)$

**63.** $(\frac{1}{2}, \infty)$   **64.** $(-3, 3)$   **65. (a)** $f(x) = \dfrac{x}{3} + \dfrac{2}{3}$

**(b)**

| $x$ | $f(x)$ |
|---|---|
| 2 | $\frac{4}{3}$ |
| 4 | 2 |
| 6 | $\frac{8}{3}$ |
| 8 | $\frac{10}{3}$ |

**(c)**
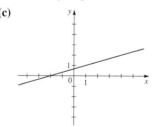

**66. (a)** $g(x) = \frac{3}{4}(x - 4)$

**(b)**

| $x$ | $g(x)$ |
|---|---|
| 2 | $-\frac{3}{2}$ |
| 4 | 0 |
| 6 | $\frac{3}{2}$ |
| 8 | 3 |

**(c)**
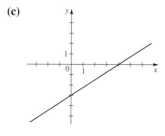

**67. (a)** $T(x) = 0.08x$

**(b)**

| $x$ | $T(x)$ |
|---|---|
| 2 | 0.16 |
| 4 | 0.32 |
| 6 | 0.48 |
| 8 | 0.64 |

**(c)**
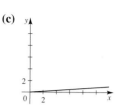

**68. (a)** $V(d) = \dfrac{\pi d^3}{6}$

**(b)**

| $d$ | $V(d)$ |
|---|---|
| 2 | $\frac{4\pi}{3}$ |
| 4 | $\frac{32\pi}{3}$ |
| 6 | $36\pi$ |
| 8 | $\frac{256\pi}{3}$ |

**(c)**
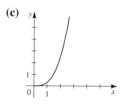

**69. (a)** $C(10) = 1532.1, C(100) = 2100$   **(b)** The cost of producing 10 yd and 100 yd   **(c)** $C(0) = 1500$   **70. (a)** $50.27, 113.10$
**(b)** $S(2)$ is the surface area of a sphere of radius 2, and $S(3)$ is the surface area of a sphere of radius 3.   **71. (a)** $50, 0$   **(b)** $V(0)$ is the volume of the full tank, and $V(20)$ is the volume of the empty tank, 20 minutes later.

**(c)**

| $x$ | $V(x)$ |
|---|---|
| 0 | 50 |
| 5 | 28.125 |
| 10 | 12.5 |
| 15 | 3.125 |
| 20 | 0 |

**72. (a)** $D(0.1) = 28.1, D(0.2) = 39.8$   **(b)** 41.3 mi
**(c)** 235.6 mi   **73. (a)** $v(0.1) = 4440, v(0.4) = 1665$
**(b)** Flow is faster near central axis.

**(c)**

| $r$ | $v(r)$ |
|---|---|
| 0 | 4625 |
| 0.1 | 4440 |
| 0.2 | 3885 |
| 0.3 | 2960 |
| 0.4 | 1665 |
| 0.5 | 0 |

**74. (a)** $2, 1.66, 1.48$
**(b)**

| $x$ | $R(x)$ |
|---|---|
| 1 | 2 |
| 10 | 1.66 |
| 100 | 1.48 |
| 200 | 1.44 |
| 500 | 1.41 |
| 1000 | 1.39 |

**75. (a)** 8.66 m, 6.61 m, 4.36 m   **(b)** It will appear to get shorter.
**76. (a)** $T(5000) = 0, T(12,000) = 960, T(25,000) = 5350$
**(b)** The amount of tax paid on incomes of 5000, 12,000, and 25,000

**77.** **(a)** $90, $105, $100, $105
**(b)** Total cost of an order, including shipping

**78.** **(a)** $T(x) = \begin{cases} 75x & \text{if } 0 \le x \le 2 \\ 150 + 50(x - 2) & \text{if } x > 2 \end{cases}$

**(b)** $150, $200, $300   **(c)** Total cost of staying at the hotel

**79.** **(a)** $F(x) = \begin{cases} 15(40 - x) & \text{if } 0 < x < 40 \\ 0 & \text{if } 40 \le x \le 65 \\ 15(x - 65) & \text{if } x > 65 \end{cases}$

**(b)** $150, $0, $150   **(c)** Fines for violating the speed limits
**80.**

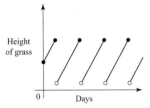

**81.**

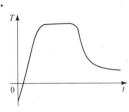

**82.**

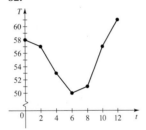

**83.**

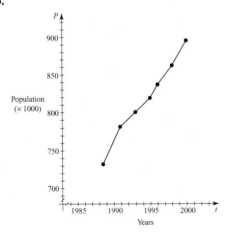

### SECTION 3.2 ▪ page 221

**1.** $f(x)$, $x^3 + 2$, 10, 10   **2.** 3   **3.** 3   **4. (a)** IV   **(b)** II
**(c)** I   **(d)** III
**5.**

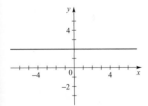

**6.**

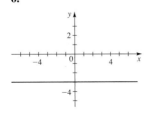

**7.**

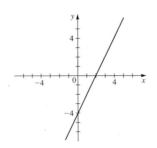

**8.**

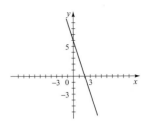

**9.**

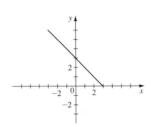

**10.**

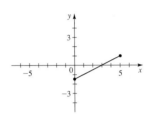

**11.**

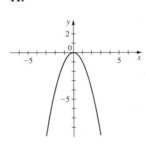

**12.**

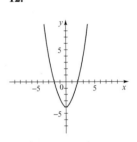

**13.**

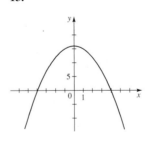

**14.**

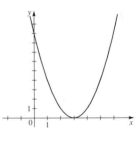

**15.**

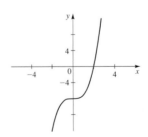

**16.**

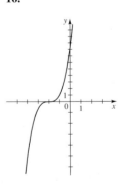

**17.**

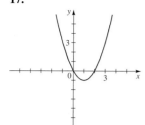

**18.**

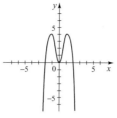

**29. (a)**

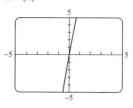

**(b)**

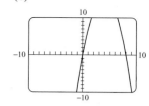

**19.**

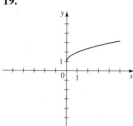

**20.**

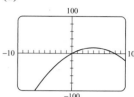

**(c)**

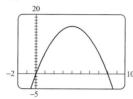

**(d)**

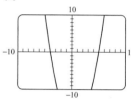

Graph (c) is the most appropriate.

**30. (a)**

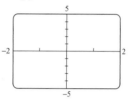

**(b)**

**21.**

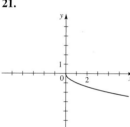

**22.**

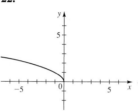

**(c)**

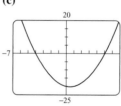

**(d)**

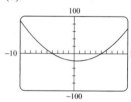

Graph (c) is the most appropriate.

**31. (a)**

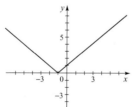

**(b)**

**23.**

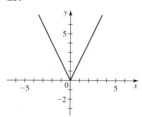

**24.**

**(c)**

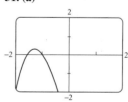

**(d)**

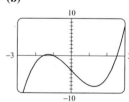

Graph (c) is the most appropriate.

**32. (a)**

**25.**

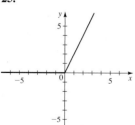

**26.**

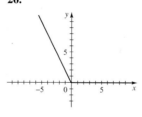

**(b)**

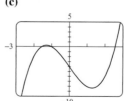

**27.**

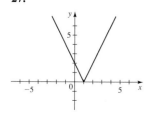

**28.**

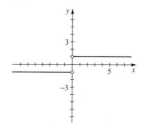

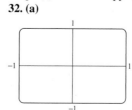

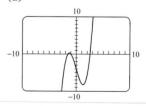

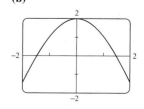

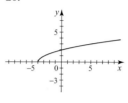

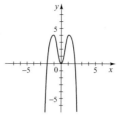

**(c)**

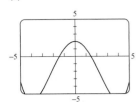

**(d)**

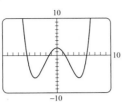

Graph (d) is the most appropriate.

**33.**

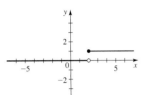

**34.**

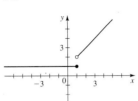

**35.**

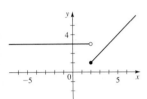

**36.**

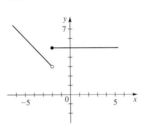

**37.**

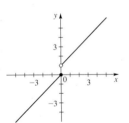

**38.**

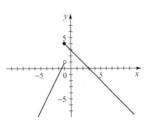

**39.**

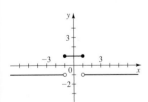

**40.**

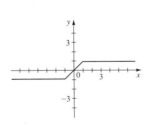

**41.**

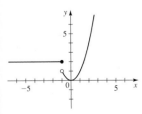

**42.**

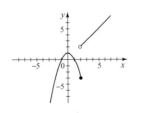

**43.**

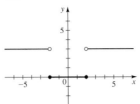

**44.**

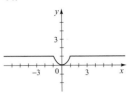

**45.**

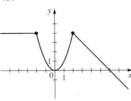

**46.**

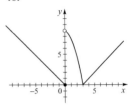

**47.**

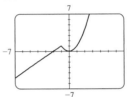

**48.**

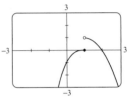

**49.** $f(x) = \begin{cases} -2 & \text{if } x < -2 \\ x & \text{if } -2 \le x \le 2 \\ 2 & \text{if } x > 2 \end{cases}$

**50.** $f(x) = \begin{cases} 1 & \text{if } x \le -1 \\ 1 - x & \text{if } -1 < x \le 2 \\ -2 & \text{if } x > 2 \end{cases}$

**51. (a)** Yes  **(b)** No  **(c)** Yes  **(d)** No  **52. (a)** No  **(b)** Yes
**(c)** Yes  **(d)** No  **53.** Function, domain $[-3, 2]$, range $[-2, 2]$
**54.** Not a function  **55.** Not a function  **56.** Function,
domain $[-3, 2]$, range $\{-2\} \cup (0, 3]$  **57.** Yes  **58.** Yes  **59.** No
**60.** No  **61.** No  **62.** Yes  **63.** Yes  **64.** Yes  **65.** Yes
**66.** No  **67.** Yes  **68.** No

**69. (a)**                                    **(b)**

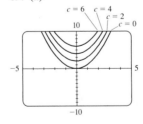

**(c)** If $c > 0$, then the graph of $f(x) = x^2 + c$ is the same as the
graph of $y = x^2$ shifted upward $c$ units. If $c < 0$, then the graph of
$f(x) = x^2 + c$ is the same as the graph of $y = x^2$ shifted downward
$c$ units.

**70. (a)**                                    **(b)**

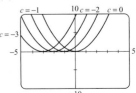

**(c)** The graphs in part (a) are obtained by shifting the graph of $y = x^2$ to the right 1, 2, and 3 units, while the graphs in part (b) are obtained by shifting the graph of $y = x^2$ to the left, 1, 2, and 3 units.

**71. (a)**                    **(b)**

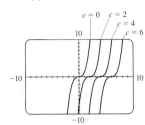   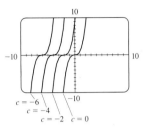

**(c)** If $c > 0$, then the graph of $f(x) = (x - c)^3$ is the same as the graph of $y = x^3$ shifted to the right $c$ units. If $c < 0$, then the graph of $f(x) = (x - c)^3$ is the same as the graph of $y = x^3$ shifted to the left $c$ units.

**72. (a)**                    **(b)**

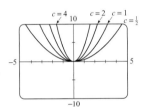   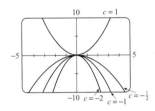

**(c)** As $|c|$ increases, the graph of $f(x) = cx^2$ is stretched vertically. As $|c|$ decreases, the graph of $f$ is flattened. When $c < 0$, the graph is reflected about the $x$-axis.

**73. (a)**                    **(b)**

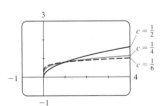   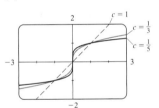

**(c)** Graphs of even roots are similar to $\sqrt{x}$; graphs of odd roots are similar to $\sqrt[3]{x}$. As $c$ increases, the graph of $y = \sqrt[c]{x}$ becomes steeper near 0 and flatter when $x > 1$.

**74. (a)**                    **(b)**

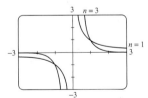   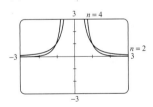

**(c)** As $n$ increases, the graphs of $y = 1/x^n$ go to zero faster for $x$ large. Also, as $n$ increases and $x$ goes to 0, the graphs of $y = 1/x^n$ go to infinity faster. The graphs of $y = 1/x^n$ for $n$ odd are similar to each other. Likewise, the graphs for $n$ even are similar to each other.

**75.** $f(x) = -\frac{7}{6}x - \frac{4}{3}, \ -2 \le x \le 4$

**76.** $f(x) = \frac{5}{9}x - \frac{1}{3}, \ -3 \le x \le 6$    **77.** $f(x) = \sqrt{9 - x^2}$, $-3 \le x \le 3$    **78.** $f(x) = -\sqrt{9 - x^2}, \ -3 \le x \le 3$

**79.**                    **80.**

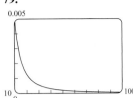   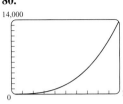

**81. (a)** $E(x) = \begin{cases} 6 + 0.10x & 0 \le x \le 300 \\ 36 + 0.06(x - 300), & x > 300 \end{cases}$

**(b)**

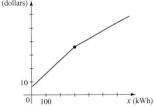

**82.** $C(x) = \begin{cases} 2 & 0 < x \le 1 \\ 2.2 & 1 < x \le 1.1 \\ 2.4 & 1.1 < x \le 1.2 \\ \ \vdots \\ 4.0 & 1.9 < x < 2.0 \end{cases}$

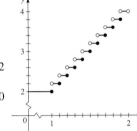

**83.** $P(x) = \begin{cases} 0.41 & \text{if } 0 < x \le 1 \\ 0.58 & \text{if } 1 < x \le 2 \\ 0.75 & \text{if } 2 < x \le 3 \\ 0.92 & \text{if } 3 < x \le 3.5 \end{cases}$

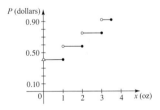

## SECTION 3.3 ▪ page 232

**1.** $a$, 4    **2.** $x$, $y$, $[1, 6]$, $[1, 7]$    **3. (a)** increase, $[1, 2]$, $[4, 5]$
**(b)** decrease, $[2, 4]$, $[5, 6]$    **4. (a)** largest, 7, 2    **(b)** smallest, 2, 4    **5. (a)** 1, $-1$, 3, 4    **(b)** Domain $[-3, 4]$, range $[-1, 4]$
**(c)** $-3, 2, 4$    **(d)** $-3 \le x \le 2$ and $x = 4$    **6. (a)** 4, 7, 4
**(b)** $[-2, 8]$, $[2, 7]$    **(c)** $-2, 2, 7$    **(d)** $-2 < x < 2$ and $7 < x \le 8$    **7. (a)** 3, 2, $-2$, 1, 0    **(b)** Domain $[-4, 4]$, range $[-2, 3]$    **8. (a)** $f(0)$    **(b)** $g(-3)$    **(c)** $-2, 2$

**9. (a)**

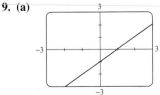

**(b)** Domain $(-\infty, \infty)$, range $(-\infty, \infty)$

**10. (a)**

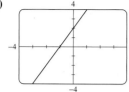

**(b)** Domain $(-\infty, \infty)$, range $(-\infty, \infty)$

**11. (a)**

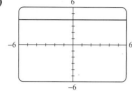

**(b)** Domain $(-\infty, \infty)$, range $\{4\}$

**12. (a)**

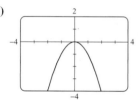

**(b)** Domain $(-\infty, \infty)$, range $(-\infty, 0]$

**13. (a)**

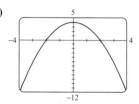

**(b)** Domain $(-\infty, \infty)$, range $(-\infty, 4]$

**14. (a)**

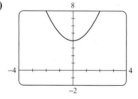

**(b)** Domain $(-\infty, \infty)$, range $[4, \infty)$

**15. (a)**

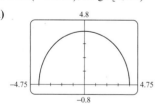

**(b)** Domain $[-4, 4]$, range $[0, 4]$

**16. (a)**

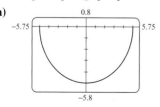

**(b)** Domain $[-5, 5]$, range $[-5, 0]$

**17. (a)**

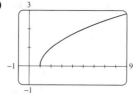

**(b)** Domain $[1, \infty)$, range $[0, \infty)$

**18. (a)**

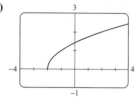

**(b)** Domain $[-2, \infty)$, range $[0, \infty)$

**19. (a)** $[-1, 1], [2, 4]$   **(b)** $[1, 2]$   **20. (a)** $[0, 1]$   **(b)** $[-2, 0]$,
$[1, 3]$   **21. (a)** $[-2, -1], [1, 2]$   **(b)** $[-3, -2], [-1, 1], [2, 3]$
**22. (a)** $[-1, 1]$   **(b)** $[-2, -1], [1, 2]$
**23. (a)**                                           **24. (a)**

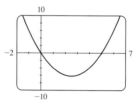

**(b)** Increasing on $[2.5, \infty)$;
decreasing on $(-\infty, 2.5]$

**(b)** Increasing on $(\infty, -1.15]$,
$[1.15, \infty)$; decreasing on
$[-1.15, 1.15]$

**25. (a)**                                           **26. (a)**

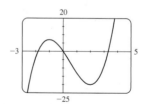

**(b)** Increasing on $(-\infty, -1]$,
$[2, \infty)$; decreasing on $[-1, 2]$

**(b)** Increasing on $[-2.83, 0]$,
$[2.83, \infty)$; decreasing on
$[-\infty, -2.83], [0, 2.83]$

**27. (a)**                                           **28. (a)**

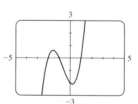

**(b)** Increasing on
$(-\infty, -1.55], [0.22, \infty)$;
decreasing on $[-1.55, 0.22]$

**(b)** Increasing on $[-0.4, 1]$,
$[2.4, \infty)$; decreasing on
$(-\infty, -0.4], [1, 2.4]$

**29. (a)**

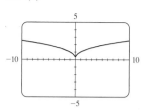

**30. (a)**

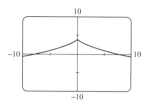

in the year 1975    **49.** Runner A won the race. All runners finished. Runner B fell but got up again to finish second.

**50. (a)**                                       **(b)** Decreases

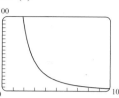

**51. (a)**                                       **(b)** Increases

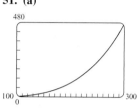

**52.** 7.5 mi/h    **53.** 20 mi/h    **54.** 3.96°C    **55.** $r \approx 0.67$ cm

**(b)** Increasing on $[0, \infty)$; decreasing on $(-\infty, 0]$

**(b)** Increasing on $(-\infty, 0]$; decreasing on $[0, \infty)$

**31. (a)** Local maximum 2 when $x = 0$; local minimum $-1$ when $x = -2$, local minimum 0 when $x = 2$   **(b)** Increasing on $[-2, 0] \cup [2, \infty)$; decreasing on $(-\infty, -2] \cup [0, 2]$

**32. (a)** Local maximum 1 when $x = 2$, local maximum 2 when $x = -2$; local minimum $-1$ when $x = 0$   **(b)** Increasing on $(-\infty, -2] \cup [0, 2]$; decreasing on $[-2, 0] \cup [2, \infty)$

**33. (a)** Local maximum 0 when $x = 0$; local maximum 1 when $x = 3$, local minimum $-2$ when $x = -2$, local minimum $-1$ when $x = 1$   **(b)** Increasing on $[-2, 0] \cup [1, 3]$; decreasing on $(-\infty, -2] \cup [0, 1] \cup [3, \infty)$   **34. (a)** Local maximum 2 when $x = 1$, local maximum 3 when $x = -2$; local minimum $-1$ when $x = 2$, local minimum 0 when $x = -1$   **(b)** Increasing on $(-\infty, -2] \cup [-1, 1] \cup [2, \infty)$; decreasing on $[-2, -1] \cup [1, 2]$

**35. (a)** Local maximum $\approx 0.38$ when $x \approx -0.58$; local minimum $\approx -0.38$ when $x \approx 0.58$   **(b)** Increasing on $(-\infty, -0.58] \cup [0.58, \infty)$; decreasing on $[-0.58, 0.58]$

**36. (a)** Local maximum $\approx 4.00$ when $x \approx 1.00$; local minimum $\approx 2.81$ when $x \approx -0.33$   **(b)** Increasing on $[-0.33, 1.00]$; decreasing on $(-\infty, -0.33] \cup [1.00, \infty]$   **37. (a)** Local maximum $\approx 0$ when $x = 0$; local minimum $\approx -13.61$ when $x \approx -1.71$, local minimum $\approx -73.32$ when $x \approx 3.21$   **(b)** Increasing on $[-1.71, 0] \cup [3.21, \infty)$; decreasing on $(-\infty, -1.71] \cup [0, 3.21]$   **38. (a)** Local maximum $\approx 13.02$ when $x \approx 1.04$, local maximum $\approx -7.87$ when $x \approx -1.93$; local minimum $\approx -13.02$ when $x \approx -1.04$, local minimum $\approx 7.87$ when $x \approx 1.93$   **(b)** Increasing on $(-\infty, -1.93] \cup [-1.04, 1.04] \cup [1.93, \infty)$; decreasing on $[-1.93, -1.04] \cup [1.04, 1.93]$

**39. (a)** Local maximum $\approx 5.66$ when $x \approx 4.00$   **(b)** Increasing on $(-\infty, 4.00]$; decreasing on $[4.00, 6.00]$   **40. (a)** Local maximum $\approx 0.32$ when $x \approx 0.75$   **(b)** Increasing on $[0, 0.75]$; decreasing on $[0.75, 1.00]$   **41. (a)** Local maximum $\approx 0.38$ when $x \approx -1.73$; local minimum $\approx -0.38$ when $x \approx 1.73$   **(b)** Increasing on $(-\infty, -1.73] \cup [1.73, \infty)$; decreasing on $[-1.73, 0) \cup (0, 1.73]$   **42. (a)** Local maximum $\approx 1.33$ when $x \approx -0.50$   **(b)** Increasing on $(-\infty, -0.50]$; decreasing on $[-0.50, \infty)$   **43. (a)** 500 MW, 725 MW   **(b)** Between 3:00 A.M. and 4:00 A.M.   **(c)** Just before noon   **44. (a)** 5 s   **(b)** 30 s   **(c)** 17 s   **45. (a)** Increasing on $[0, 30] \cup [32, 68]$; decreasing on $[30, 32]$   **(b)** He went on a crash diet and lost weight, only to regain it again later.   **46. (a)** Increasing on the intervals 8:00 A.M. to 9:00 A.M., 10:00 A.M. to noon, and 3:00 P.M. to 5:00 P.M.; decreasing on the intervals 1:00 P.M. to 3:00 P.M. and 6:00 P.M. to 7:00 P.M.   **(b)** The sales representative travels away from home and stops to make a sales call between 9:00 A.M. and 10:00 A.M.; he then travels farther from home for a sales call between 12:00 noon and 1:00 P.M. Next he travels along a route that takes him closer to home before taking him farther away from home. He makes a final sales call between 5:00 P.M. and 6:00 P.M. and then returns home.   **47. (a)** Increasing on $[0, 150] \cup [300, \infty)$; decreasing on $[150, 300]$   **(b)** Local maximum when $x = 150$; local minimum when $x = 300$   **48. (a)** Increasing on $[0, 25]$; decreasing on $[25, 50]$   **(b)** 50,000

## SECTION 3.4 ▪ page 240

**1.** $\dfrac{100 \text{ miles}}{2 \text{ hours}} = 50$ mi/h   **2.** $\dfrac{f(b) - f(a)}{b - a}$   **3.** $\dfrac{25 - 1}{5 - 1} = 6$

**4. (a)** secant   **(b)** 3   **5.** $\frac{2}{3}$   **6.** $-\frac{1}{2}$   **7.** $-\frac{4}{5}$   **8.** $\frac{2}{3}$   **9.** 3   **10.** $\frac{1}{2}$   **11.** 5   **12.** 6   **13.** 60   **14.** 21   **15.** $12 + 3h$   **16.** $-2 - h$   **17.** $-\dfrac{1}{a}$   **18.** $-\dfrac{2}{h + 1}$   **19.** $\dfrac{-2}{a(a + h)}$   **20.** $\dfrac{1}{\sqrt{a + h} + \sqrt{a}}$

**21. (a)** $\frac{1}{2}$   **22. (a)** $-4$   **23.** $-0.25$ ft/day   **24. (a)** 0   **(b)** In this period the population increased the same amount as it decreased.   **25. (a)** 245 persons/yr   **(b)** $-328.5$ persons/yr   **(c)** 1997–2001   **(d)** 2001–2006   **26. (a)** 4.76 m/s   **(b)** 2.68 m/s   **(c)** 6.25 m/s, 5.56 m/s, 5.00 m/s, 4.55 m/s, 3.92 m/s, 3.33 m/s, 2.78 m/s, 2.60 m/s; he is slowing down.   **27. (a)** 7.2 units/yr   **(b)** 8 units/yr   **(c)** $-55$ units/yr   **(d)** 2000–2001, 2001–2002

**28.**

| Year | Number of books |
|------|-----------------|
| 1980 | 420 |
| 1981 | 460 |
| 1982 | 500 |
| 1985 | 620 |
| 1990 | 820 |
| 1992 | 900 |
| 1995 | 1020 |
| 1997 | 1100 |
| 1998 | 1140 |
| 1999 | 1180 |
| 2000 | 1220 |

**29.** First 20 minutes: 4.05°F/min, next 20 minutes: 1.5°F/min; first interval   **30. (a) (i)** 84 farms/yr   **(ii)** $-130$ farms/yr   **(b)** 1950–1960

## SECTION 3.5 ▪ page 251

**1. (a)** up   **(b)** left   **2. (a)** down   **(b)** right   **3. (a)** $x$-axis   **(b)** $y$-axis   **4. (a)** II   **(b)** IV   **(c)** I   **(d)** III   **5. (a)** Shift to the left 2 units   **(b)** Shift upward 2 units   **6. (a)** Shift to the right 4 units   **(b)** Shift downward 4 units   **7. (a)** Shift to the left 2 units, then shift downward 2 units   **(b)** Shift to the right 2 units, then shift upward 2 units   **8. (a)** Reflect in the $x$-axis, then shift upward 1 unit   **(b)** Reflect in the $y$-axis, then shift upward 1 unit

**9. (a)**

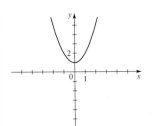

**(b)**

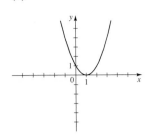

**(c)**

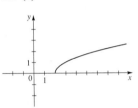

**(d)**

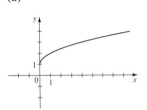

**10. (a)**

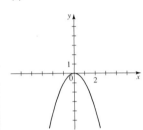

**(b)**

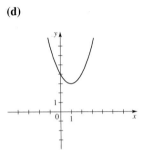

**(c)**

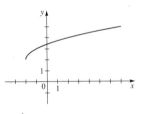

**(d)**

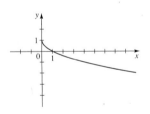

**11.**

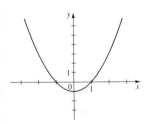

**12.**

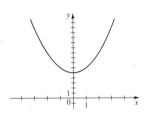

**13.**

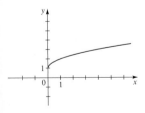

**14.**

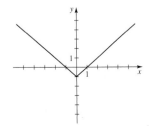

**15.**

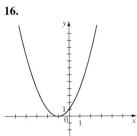

**16.**

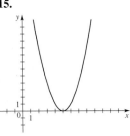

**17.**

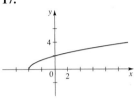

**18.**

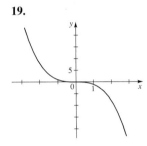

**19.**

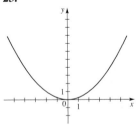

**20.**

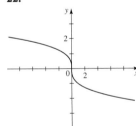

**21.**

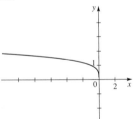

**22.**

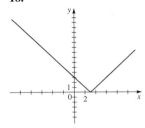

**23.**

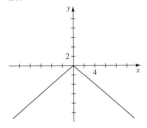

**24.**

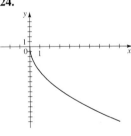

**25.**

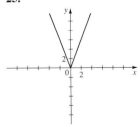

**26.**

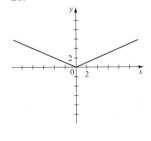

**27.**

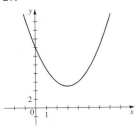

**28.**

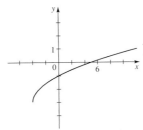

**(c)**

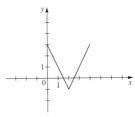

**(d)**

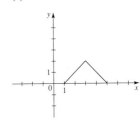

**29.**

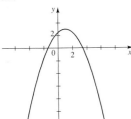

**30.**

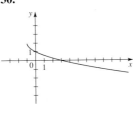

**(e)**

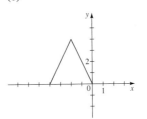

**(f)**

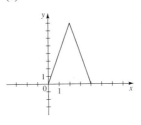

**31.**

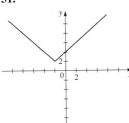

**32.**

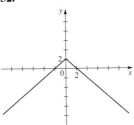

**54. (a)**

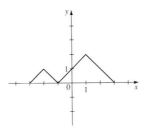

**(b)**

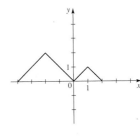

**33.**

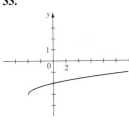

**34.**

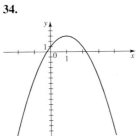

**(c)**

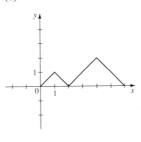

**(d)**

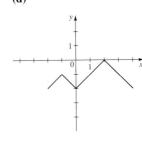

**(e)**

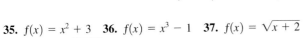

**(f)**

**35.** $f(x) = x^2 + 3$  **36.** $f(x) = x^3 - 1$  **37.** $f(x) = \sqrt{x + 2}$

**38.** $f(x) = \sqrt[3]{x - 1}$  **39.** $f(x) = |x - 3| + 1$

**40.** $f(x) = |x + 4| - 2$  **41.** $f(x) = \sqrt[4]{-x} + 1$

**42.** $f(x) = -(x + 2)^2$  **43.** $f(x) = 2(x - 3)^2 - 2$

**44.** $f(x) = \frac{1}{2}|x + 1| + 3$  **45.** $g(x) = (x - 2)^2$

**46.** $g(x) = x^3 + 3$  **47.** $g(x) = |x + 1| + 2$  **48.** $g(x) = 2|x|$

**49.** $g(x) = -\sqrt{x + 2}$  **50.** $g(x) = -(x - 2)^2 + 1$  **51. (a)** 3

**(b)** 1  **(c)** 2  **(d)** 4  **52. (a)** 2  **(b)** 3  **(c)** 1  **(d)** 4

**53. (a)**

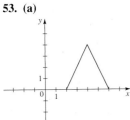

**(b)**

**55. (a)**

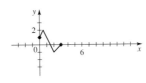

**(b)**

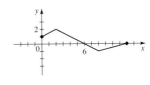

**56. (a)**

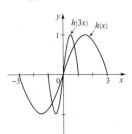

**(b)**

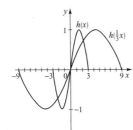

**57.**

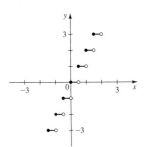

**58.**

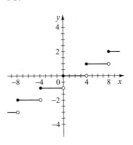

**59.**

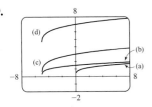

For part (b) shift the graph in (a) to the left 5 units; for part (c) shift the graph in (a) to the left 5 units and stretch vertically by a factor of 2; for part (d) shift the graph in (a) to the left 5 units, stretch vertically by a factor of 2, and then shift upward 4 units.

**60.**

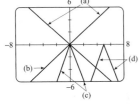

For part (b) reflect in the *x*-axis; for part (c) stretch vertically by a factor of 3 and reflect in the *x*-axis; for part (d) shift to the right 5 units, stretch vertically by a factor of 3, and reflect in the *x*-axis.

**61.**

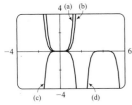

For part (b) shrink the graph in (a) vertically by a factor of $\frac{1}{3}$; for part (c) shrink the graph in (a) vertically by a factor of $\frac{1}{3}$ and reflect in the *x*-axis; for part (d) shift the graph in (a) to the right 4 units, shrink vertically by a factor of $\frac{1}{3}$, and then reflect in the *x*-axis.

**62.**

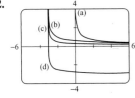

For part (b) shift to the left 3 units; for part (c) shift to the left 3 units and shrink vertically by a factor of $\frac{1}{2}$; for part (d) shift to the left 3 units, shrink vertically by a factor of $\frac{1}{2}$, and then shift downward 3 units.

**63.**

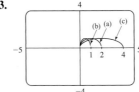

The graph in part (b) is shrunk horizontally by a factor of $\frac{1}{2}$ and the graph in part (c) is stretched by a factor of 2.

**64. (a)**

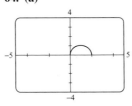

**(b)** Reflect in *y*-axis

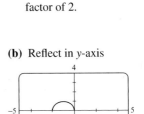

**(c)** Reflect in origin

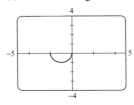

**(d)** Reflect in *y*-axis, then horizontally shrink by a factor of $\frac{1}{2}$

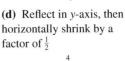
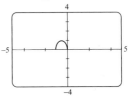

**(e)** Reflect in *y*-axis, then horizontally stretch by a factor of 2

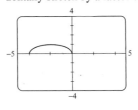

**65.** Even

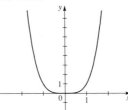

**66.** Odd

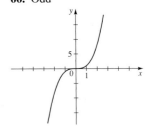

**67.** Neither

**68.** Even

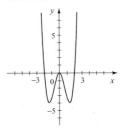

**69.** Odd

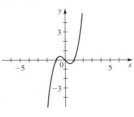

**70.** Neither

**71.** Neither

**72.** Odd

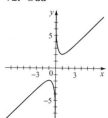

**73. (a)**

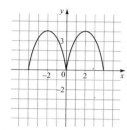

**(b)**

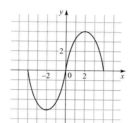

**74. (a)**

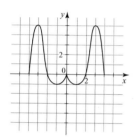

**(b)**

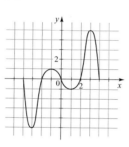

**75.** To obtain the graph of $g$, reflect in the $x$-axis the part of the graph of $f$ that is below the $x$-axis.

**76.**

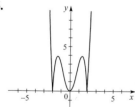

**77. (a)**

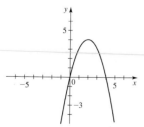

**(b)**

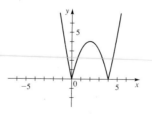

**78. (a)**

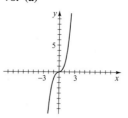

**(b)**

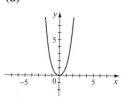

**79. (a)** Shift upward 4 units, shrink vertically by a factor of 0.01

**(b)** Shift to the right 10 units; $g(t) = 4 + 0.01(t - 10)^2$

**80. (a)** Shrink vertically by a factor of $\frac{1}{2}$, then shift upward 2 units

**(b)** Stretch vertically by a factor of $\frac{9}{5}$, then shift upward 32 units;
$F(t) = \frac{9}{10}t^2 + \frac{178}{5}$

## SECTION 3.6 ▪ page 260

**1.** $8, -2, 15, \dfrac{3}{5}$   **2.** $f(g(x))$, 12   **3.** Multiply by 2, then add 1;

Add 1, then multiply by 2   **4.** $x + 1, 2x, 2x + 1, 2(x + 1)$

**5.** $(f + g)(x) = x^2 + x - 3, (-\infty, \infty)$;

$(f - g)(x) = -x^2 + x - 3, (-\infty, \infty)$;

$(fg)(x) = x^3 - 3x^2, (-\infty, \infty)$;

$\left(\dfrac{f}{g}\right)(x) = \dfrac{x - 3}{x^2}, (-\infty, 0) \cup (0, \infty)$

**6.** $(f + g)(x) = 4x^2 + 2x - 1, (-\infty, \infty)$;

$(f - g)(x) = -2x^2 + 2x + 1, (-\infty, \infty)$;

$(fg)(x) = 3x^4 + 6x^3 - x^2 - 2x, (-\infty, \infty)$;

$\left(\dfrac{f}{g}\right)(x) = \dfrac{x^2 + 2x}{3x^2 - 1}, x \neq \pm\dfrac{1}{\sqrt{3}}$

**7.** $(f + g)(x) = \sqrt{4 - x^2} + \sqrt{1 + x}, [-1, 2]$;

$(f - g)(x) = \sqrt{4 - x^2} - \sqrt{1 + x}, [-1, 2]$;

$(fg)(x) = \sqrt{-x^3 - x^2 + 4x + 4}, [-1, 2]$;

$\left(\dfrac{f}{g}\right)(x) = \sqrt{\dfrac{4 - x^2}{1 + x}}, (-1, 2]$

**8.** $(f + g)(x) = \sqrt{9 - x^2} + \sqrt{x^2 - 4}, [-3, -2] \cup [2, 3]$;

$(f - g)(x) = \sqrt{9 - x^2} - \sqrt{x^2 - 4}, [-3, -2] \cup [2, 3]$;

$(fg)(x) = \sqrt{-x^4 + 13x^2 - 36}, [-3, -2] \cup [2, 3]$;

$\left(\dfrac{f}{g}\right)(x) = \sqrt{\dfrac{9 - x^2}{x^2 - 4}}, [-3, -2) \cup (2, 3]$

**9.** $(f + g)(x) = \dfrac{6x + 8}{x^2 + 4x}, x \neq -4, x \neq 0$;

$(f - g)(x) = \dfrac{-2x + 8}{x^2 + 4x}, x \neq -4, x \neq 0$;

$(fg)(x) = \dfrac{8}{x^2 + 4x}, x \neq -4, x \neq 0$;

$\left(\dfrac{f}{g}\right)(x) = \dfrac{x + 4}{2x}, x \neq -4, x \neq 0$

**10.** $(f + g)(x) = \dfrac{2 + x}{x + 1}, x \neq -1; (f - g)(x) = \dfrac{2 - x}{x + 1}, x \neq -1$;

$(fg)(x) = \dfrac{2x}{(x+1)^2}, x \neq -1; \left(\dfrac{f}{g}\right)(x) = \dfrac{2}{x}, x \neq -1, x \neq 0$

**11.** $[0, 1]$  **12.** $[-1, 0) \cup (0, \infty)$  **13.** $(3, \infty)$

**14.** $[-3, 1) \cup (1, \infty)$

**15.**

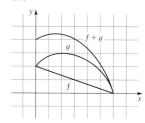

**16.**

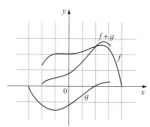

**17.**

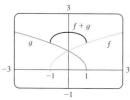

**18.**

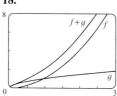

**19.**

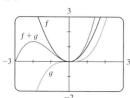

**20.**

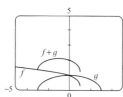

**21. (a)** $1$  **(b)** $-23$  **22. (a)** $16$  **(b)** $-47$  **23. (a)** $-11$
**(b)** $-119$  **24. (a)** $-29$  **(b)** $-2$  **25. (a)** $-3x^2 + 1$
**(b)** $-9x^2 + 30x - 23$  **26. (a)** $9x - 20$  **(b)** $-x^4 + 4x^2 - 2$
**27.** $4$  **28.** $3$  **29.** $5$  **30.** $0$  **31.** $4$  **32.** $-2$

**33.** $(f \circ g)(x) = 8x + 1, (-\infty, \infty);$
$(g \circ f)(x) = 8x + 11, (-\infty, \infty); (f \circ f)(x) = 4x + 9, (-\infty, \infty);$
$(g \circ g)(x) = 16x - 5, (-\infty, \infty)$

**34.** $(f \circ g)(x) = 3x - 5, (-\infty, \infty);$
$(g \circ f)(x) = 3x - \frac{5}{2}, (-\infty, \infty);$
$(f \circ f)(x) = 36x - 35, (-\infty, \infty); (g \circ g)(x) = \frac{x}{4}, (-\infty, \infty)$

**35.** $(f \circ g)(x) = (x + 1)^2, (-\infty, \infty);$
$(g \circ f)(x) = x^2 + 1, (-\infty, \infty); (f \circ f)(x) = x^4, (-\infty, \infty);$
$(g \circ g)(x) = x + 2, (-\infty, \infty)$  **36.** $(f \circ g)(x) = x + 2, (-\infty, \infty);$
$(g \circ f)(x) = \sqrt[3]{x^3 + 2}, (-\infty, \infty);$
$(f \circ f)(x) = x^9 + 6x^6 + 12x^3 + 10, (-\infty, \infty);$
$(g \circ g)(x) = x^{1/9}, (-\infty, \infty)$

**37.** $(f \circ g)(x) = \dfrac{1}{2x + 4}, x \neq -2; (g \circ f)(x) = \dfrac{2}{x} + 4, x \neq 0;$
$(f \circ f)(x) = x, x \neq 0, (g \circ g)(x) = 4x + 12, (-\infty, \infty)$

**38.** $(f \circ g)(x) = x - 3, [3, \infty);$
$(g \circ f)(x) = \sqrt{x^2 - 3}, (-\infty, -\sqrt{3}] \cup [\sqrt{3}, \infty);$
$(f \circ f)(x) = x^4, (-\infty, \infty); (g \circ g)(x) = \sqrt{\sqrt{x - 3} - 3}, [12, \infty)$

**39.** $(f \circ g)(x) = |2x + 3|, (-\infty, \infty);$
$(g \circ f)(x) = 2|x| + 3, (-\infty, \infty); (f \circ f)(x) = |x|, (-\infty, \infty);$
$(g \circ g)(x) = 4x + 9, (-\infty, \infty)$

**40.** $(f \circ g)(x) = |x + 4| - 4, (-\infty, \infty);$
$(g \circ f)(x) = |x|, (-\infty, \infty); (f \circ f)(x) = x - 8, (-\infty, \infty);$
$(g \circ g)(x) = |x + 4| + 4, (-\infty, \infty)$

**41.** $(f \circ g)(x) = \dfrac{2x - 1}{2x}, x \neq 0; (g \circ f)(x) = \dfrac{2x}{x + 1} - 1, x \neq -1;$
$(f \circ f)(x) = \dfrac{x}{2x + 1}, x \neq -1, x \neq -\frac{1}{2};$
$(g \circ g)(x) = 4x - 3, (-\infty, \infty)$

**42.** $(f \circ g)(x) = \dfrac{1}{\sqrt{x^2 - 4x}}, (-\infty, 0) \cup (4, \infty);$
$(g \circ f)(x) = \dfrac{1}{x} - \dfrac{4}{\sqrt{x}}, (0, \infty); (f \circ f)(x) = x^{1/4}, (0, \infty);$
$(g \circ g)(x) = x^4 - 8x^3 + 12x^2 + 16x, (-\infty, \infty)$

**43.** $(f \circ g)(x) = \sqrt[12]{x}, [0, \infty); (g \circ f)(x) = \sqrt[12]{x}, [0, \infty);$
$(f \circ f)(x) = \sqrt[9]{x}, (-\infty, \infty); (g \circ g)(x) = \sqrt[16]{x}, [0, \infty)$

**44.** $(f \circ g)(x) = \dfrac{2x + 4}{x}, x \neq -2, x \neq 0;$
$(g \circ f)(x) = \dfrac{1}{1 + x}, x \neq -1, x \neq 0; (f \circ f)(x) = x, x \neq 0;$
$(g \circ g)(x) = \dfrac{x}{3x + 4}, x \neq -2, x \neq -\frac{4}{3}$

**45.** $(f \circ g \circ h)(x) = \sqrt{x - 1} - 1$

**46.** $(f \circ g \circ h)(x) = \dfrac{1}{x^6 + 6x^4 + 12x^2 + 8}$

**47.** $(f \circ g \circ h)(x) = (\sqrt{x} - 5)^4 + 1$

**48.** $(f \circ g \circ h)(x) = \sqrt{\dfrac{\sqrt[3]{x}}{\sqrt[3]{x} - 1}}$  **49.** $g(x) = x - 9, f(x) = x^5$

**50.** $g(x) = \sqrt{x}, f(x) = x + 1$  **51.** $g(x) = x^2, f(x) = x/(x + 4)$
**52.** $g(x) = x + 3, f(x) = 1/x$  **53.** $g(x) = 1 - x^3, f(x) = |x|$
**54.** $g(x) = \sqrt{x}, f(x) = \sqrt{1 + x}$
**55.** $h(x) = x^2, g(x) = x + 1, f(x) = 1/x$
**56.** $h(x) = \sqrt{x}, g(x) = x - 1, f(x) = \sqrt[3]{x}$
**57.** $h(x) = \sqrt[3]{x}, g(x) = 4 + x, f(x) = x^9$
**58.** $h(x) = \sqrt{x}, g(x) = 3 + x, f(x) = 2/x^2$
**59.** $R(x) = 0.15x - 0.000002x^2$
**60.** $P(x) = 0.055x - 0.0000015x^2$  **61. (a)** $g(t) = 60t$
**(b)** $f(r) = \pi r^2$  **(c)** $(f \circ g)(t) = 3600\pi t^2$  **62. (a)** $f(t) = t$
**(b)** $g(r) = \frac{4}{3}\pi r^3$  **(c)** $(g \circ f)(t) = \frac{4}{3}\pi t^3$; the volume as a
function of time  **63.** $A(t) = 16\pi t^2$  **64. (a)** $f(x) = 0.80x$
**(b)** $g(x) = x - 50$  **(c)** $(f \circ g)(x) = 0.80x - 40;$
$(g \circ f)(x) = 0.80x - 50$; applying the 20% discount, then $50
coupon $(g \circ f)$ gives the lower price  **65. (a)** $f(x) = 0.9x$
**(b)** $g(x) = x - 100$  **(c)** $f \circ g(x) = 0.9x - 90,$
$g \circ f(x) = 0.9x - 100, f \circ g$: first rebate, then discount,
$g \circ f$: first discount, then rebate, $g \circ f$ is the better deal

**66. (a)** $s = \sqrt{1 + d^2}$   **(b)** $d = 350t$
**(c)** $s(t) = \sqrt{1 + 122{,}500t^2}$

**(c)** $f^{-1}(x) = x^2 - 1, x \geq 0$
**58. (a)**                                    **(b)**

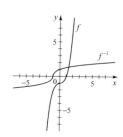
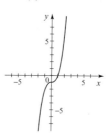

**(c)** $f^{-1}(x) = \sqrt[3]{x + 1}$

## SECTION 3.7 ▪ page 270

**1.** different, Horizontal Line   **2. (a)** one-to-one, $g(x) = x^3$
**(b)** $g^{-1}(x) = x^{1/3}$   **3. (a)** Take the cube root, subtract 5, then
divide the result by 3.   **(b)** $f(x) = (3x + 5)^3, f^{-1}(x) = \dfrac{x^{1/3} - 5}{3}$
**4. (a)** False   **(b)** True   **5.** No   **6.** Yes   **7.** Yes   **8.** No   **9.** No
**10.** Yes   **11.** Yes   **12.** Yes   **13.** Yes   **14.** No   **15.** No
**16.** Yes   **17.** No   **18.** Yes   **19.** No   **20.** Yes   **21. (a)** 2
**(b)** 3   **22. (a)** 5   **(b)** 4   **23.** 1   **24.** 1   **35.** $f^{-1}(x) = \frac{1}{2}(x - 1)$
**36.** $f^{-1}(x) = 6 - x$   **37.** $f^{-1}(x) = \frac{1}{4}(x - 7)$
**38.** $f^{-1}(x) = \frac{1}{5}(3 - x)$   **39.** $f^{-1}(x) = 2x$
**40.** $f^{-1}(x) = 1/\sqrt{x}, x > 0$   **41.** $f^{-1}(x) = (1/x) - 2$
**42.** $f^{-1}(x) = \dfrac{-2(x + 1)}{x - 1}$   **43.** $f^{-1}(x) = (5x - 1)/(2x + 3)$
**44.** $f^{-1}(x) = \sqrt[3]{\frac{1}{4}(5 - x)}$   **45.** $f^{-1}(x) = \frac{1}{5}(x^2 - 2), x \geq 0$
**46.** $f^{-1}(x) = \sqrt{x + \frac{1}{4}} - \frac{1}{2}, x \geq -\frac{1}{4}$   **47.** $f^{-1}(x) = \sqrt{4 - x}, x \leq 4$
**48.** $f^{-1}(x) = \frac{1}{2}(x^2 + 1), x \geq 0$   **49.** $f^{-1}(x) = (x - 4)^3$
**50.** $f^{-1}(x) = \sqrt[3]{2 - \sqrt[5]{x}}$   **51.** $f^{-1}(x) = x^2 - 2x, x \geq 1$
**52.** $f^{-1}(x) = \sqrt{9 - x^2}, 0 \leq x \leq 3$   **53.** $f^{-1}(x) = \sqrt[4]{x}$
**54.** $f^{-1}(x) = \sqrt[3]{1 - x}$
**55. (a)**                            **(b)**

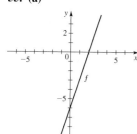
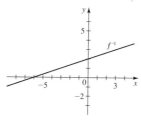

**(c)** $f^{-1}(x) = \frac{1}{3}(x + 6)$
**56. (a)**                            **(b)**

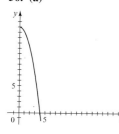
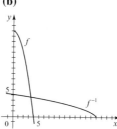

**(c)** $f^{-1}(x) = \sqrt{16 - x}, x \leq 16$
**57. (a)**                            **(b)**

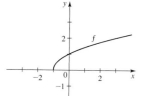
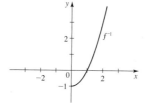

**59.** Not one-to-one                 **60.** One-to-one

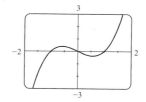
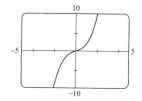

**61.** One-to-one                     **62.** Not one-to-one

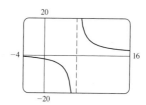
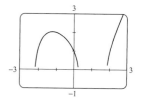

**63.** Not one-to-one                 **64.** One-to-one

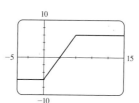
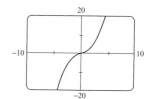

**65. (a)** $f^{-1}(x) = x - 2$
**(b)**

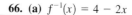
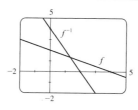

**66. (a)** $f^{-1}(x) = 4 - 2x$

**67. (a)** $g^{-1}(x) = x^2 - 3, x \geq 0$
**(b)**

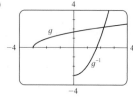

**68. (a)** $g^{-1}(x) = \sqrt{x - 1}$

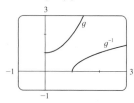

**69.** $x \geq 0, f^{-1}(x) = \sqrt{4 - x}$ **70.** $x \geq 1, g^{-1}(x) = 1 + \sqrt{x}$
**71.** $x \geq -2, h^{-1}(x) = \sqrt{x} - 2$ **72.** $x \geq 3, k^{-1}(x) = 3 + x$
**73.** **74.**

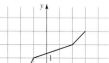

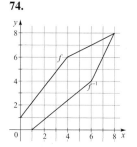

**75. (a)** $f(x) = 500 + 80x$ **(b)** $f^{-1}(x) = \frac{1}{80}(x - 500)$, the number of hours worked as a function of the fee **(c)** 9; if he charges $1220, he worked 9 h **76. (a)** $V^{-1}(t) = 40 - 4\sqrt{t}$, time elapsed since the tank started to leak **(b)** 24.5 min; in 24.5 min the tank drained 15 gal of water **77. (a)** $v^{-1}(t) = \sqrt{0.25 - \dfrac{t}{18,500}}$ **(b)** 0.498;

at a distance 0.498 from the central axis the velocity is 30
**78. (a)** $D^{-1}(p) = 50 - \frac{1}{3}p$, the price associated with the demand $D$ **(b)** 40; when the demand is 30 units, the price is $40
**79. (a)** $F^{-1}(x) = \frac{5}{9}(x - 32)$; the Celsius temperature when the Fahrenheit temperature is $x$ **(b)** $F^{-1}(86) = 30$; when the temperature is 86°F, it is 30°C **80. (a)** $f(x) = 1.0573x$
**(b)** $f^{-1}(x) = 0.9458x$, the exchange rate from U.S. dollars to Canadian dollars **(c)** $11,586.05 in Canadian currency
**81. (a)** $f(x) = \begin{cases} 0.1x & \text{if } 0 \leq x \leq 20{,}000 \\ 2000 + 0.2(x - 20{,}000) & \text{if } x > 20{,}000 \end{cases}$

**(b)** $f^{-1}(x) = \begin{cases} 10x & \text{if } 0 \leq x \leq 2000 \\ 10{,}000 + 5x & \text{if } x > 2000 \end{cases}$

If you pay $x$ euros in taxes, your income is $f^{-1}(x)$.
**(c)** $f^{-1}(10{,}000) = 60{,}000$ **82. (a)** $f(x) = 0.85x$
**(b)** $g(x) = x - 1000$ **(c)** $H = 0.85x - 850$
**(d)** $H^{-1}(x) = 1.176x + 1000$, the original sticker price for a given discounted price **(e)** $16,288, the original price of the car when the discounted price ($1000 rebate, then 15% off) is $13,000
**83.** $f^{-1}(x) = \frac{1}{2}(x - 7)$. A pizza costing $x$ dollars has $f^{-1}(x)$ toppings.

## CHAPTER 3 REVIEW ▪ page 274

**1.** $f(x) = x^2 - 5$ **2.** $f(x) = \dfrac{x}{2} + 9$ **3.** Add 10, then multiply the result by 3. **4.** Multiply by 6, subtract 10, then take the square root of the result.

**5.**

| $x$ | $g(x)$ |
|-----|--------|
| $-1$ | 5 |
| 0 | 0 |
| 1 | $-3$ |
| 2 | $-4$ |
| 3 | $-3$ |

**6.**

| $x$ | $h(x)$ |
|-----|--------|
| $-2$ | 3 |
| $-1$ | $-4$ |
| 0 | $-5$ |
| 1 | 0 |
| 2 | 11 |

**7. (a)** $C(1000) = 34{,}000$, $C(10{,}000) = 205{,}000$ **(b)** The costs of printing 1000 and 10,000 copies of the book **(c)** $C(0) = 5000$; fixed costs **8. (a)** $E(2000) = 460$, $E(15{,}000) = 850$ **(b)** Earnings for $2000 and $15,000 of goods sold **(c)** $E(0) = 400$; base salary **(d)** 3% **9.** 6, 2, 18, $a^2 - 4a + 6$, $a^2 + 4a + 6$, $x^2 - 2x + 3$, $4x^2 - 8x + 6$, $2x^2 - 8x + 10$ **10.** $1, 4 - \sqrt{21}$, $4 - \sqrt{3a}, 4 - \sqrt{-3x - 6}, 4 - \sqrt{3x^2 - 6}, 3x - 8\sqrt{3x - 6} + 10$
**11. (a)** Not a function **(b)** Function **(c)** Function, one-to-one **(d)** Not a function **12. (a)** $-1, 2$ **(b)** $[-4, 5]$ **(c)** $[-4, 4]$ **(d)** Increasing on $[-4, -2]$ and $[-1, 4]$; decreasing on $[-2, -1]$ and $[4, 5]$ **(e)** $-1, 4$ **(f)** No **13.** Domain $[-3, \infty)$, range $[0, \infty)$
**14.** Domain $(-\infty, \infty)$, range $[4, \infty)$ **15.** $(-\infty, \infty)$ **16.** $x \neq \frac{1}{2}$
**17.** $[-4, \infty)$ **18.** $(-1, \infty)$ **19.** $\{x \mid x \neq -2, -1, 0\}$
**20.** $x \neq -\frac{1}{2}, x \neq 3$ **21.** $(-\infty, -1] \cup [1, 4]$ **22.** $x \neq -4$
**23.** **24.**

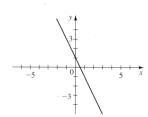

**25.** **26.**

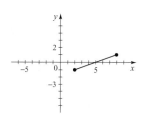

**27.** **28.**

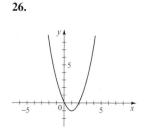

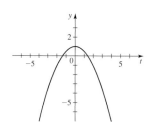

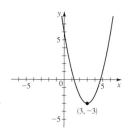

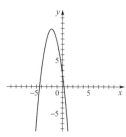

**29.**

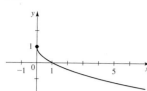

**30.**

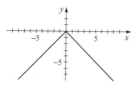

**31.**

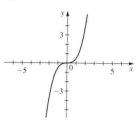

**32.**

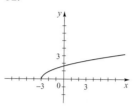

**33.**

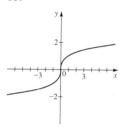

**34.**

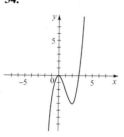

**35.**

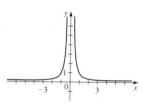

**36.**

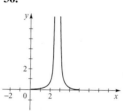

**37.**

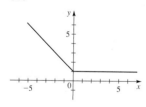

**38.**

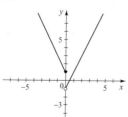

**39.**

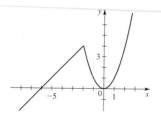

**40.**

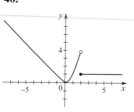

**41.** No   **42.** Yes   **43.** Yes   **44.** No   **45.** (iii)   **46.** (iii)

**47.**

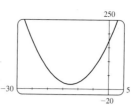

**48.**

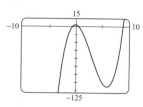

**49.**

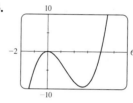

**50.**

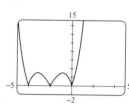

**51.** $[-2.1, 0.2] \cup [1.9, \infty)$   **52.** $[-7.10, \infty)$

**53.**

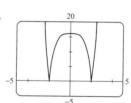

Increasing on $(-\infty, 0]$, $[2.67, \infty)$; decreasing on $[0, 2.67]$

**54.**

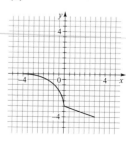

Increasing on $[-2, 0]$, $[2, \infty)$; decreasing on $(-\infty, -2]$, $[0, 2]$

**55.** 5   **56.** $-\frac{1}{12}$   **57.** $\dfrac{-1}{3(3+h)}$   **58.** $2a + h + 2$

**59. (a)** $P(10) = 5010$, $P(20) = 7040$; the populations in 1995 and 2005   **(b)** 203 people/yr; average annual population increase
**60. (a)** $D(0) = 3500$, $D(15) = 6875$; initial deposit, amount deposited in 2010   **(b)** 2025   **(c)** \$225/yr; average annual deposit increase from 1995 to 2010   **61. (a)** $\frac{1}{2}, \frac{1}{2}$   **(b)** Yes, because it is a linear function   **62. (a)** $-3, -3$   **(b)** Yes, because it is a linear function   **63. (a)** Shift upward 8 units   **(b)** Shift to the left 8 units
**(c)** Stretch vertically by a factor of 2, then shift upward 1 unit
**(d)** Shift to the right 2 units and downward 2 units   **(e)** Reflect in $y$-axis   **(f)** Reflect in $y$-axis, then in $x$-axis   **(g)** Reflect in $x$-axis
**(h)** Reflect in line $y = x$

**64. (a)**                           **(b)**

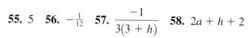

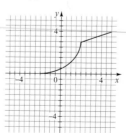

**(c)**

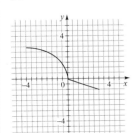

**(d)**

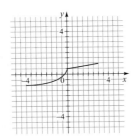

**(e)**

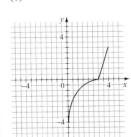

**(f)**

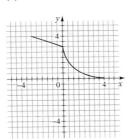

**65. (a)** Neither   **(b)** Odd   **(c)** Even   **(d)** Neither   **66. (a)** Odd
**(b)** Neither   **(c)** Even   **(d)** Neither   **67.** $g(-1) = -7$   **68.** $\frac{5}{4}$
**69.** 68 ft   **70.** $88,500, 15,000 units   **71.** Local maximum $\approx$
3.79 when $x \approx 0.46$; local minimum $\approx 2.81$ when $x \approx -0.46$
**72.** Local maximum $\approx 3.175$ when $x \approx 4.00$; local minimum $= 0$
when $x = 0$

**73.**

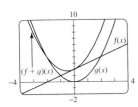

**74.**

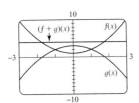

**75. (a)** $(f + g)(x) = x^2 - 6x + 6$   **(b)** $(f - g)(x) = x^2 - 2$
**(c)** $(fg)(x) = -3x^3 + 13x^2 - 18x + 8$
**(d)** $(f/g)(x) = (x^2 - 3x + 2)/(4 - 3x)$
**(e)** $(f \circ g)(x) = 9x^2 - 15x + 6$   **(f)** $(g \circ f)(x) = -3x^2 + 9x - 2$
**76. (a)** $(f \circ g)(x) = x$   **(b)** $(g \circ f)(x) = |x|$   **(c)** 2   **(d)** 26
**(e)** $(f \circ g \circ f)(x) = 1 + x^2$   **(f)** $(g \circ f \circ g)(x) = \sqrt{x - 1}$
**77.** $(f \circ g)(x) = -3x^2 + 6x - 1, (-\infty, \infty)$;
$(g \circ f)(x) = -9x^2 + 12x - 3, (-\infty, \infty); (f \circ f)(x) = 9x - 4$,
$(-\infty, \infty); (g \circ g)(x) = -x^4 + 4x^3 - 6x^2 + 4x, (-\infty, \infty)$
**78.** $(f \circ g)(x) = \sqrt{\dfrac{2}{x - 4}}, (4, \infty); (g \circ f)(x) = \dfrac{2}{\sqrt{x} - 4}$,
$[0, 16) \cup (16, \infty); (f \circ f)(x) = x^{1/4}, [0, \infty); (g \circ g)(x) = \dfrac{x - 4}{9 - 2x}$,
$x \neq 4, x \neq \frac{9}{2}$   **79.** $(f \circ g \circ h)(x) = 1 + \sqrt{x}$   **80.** $h(x) = \sqrt{x}$,
$g(x) = 1 + x, f(x) = 1/\sqrt{x}$   **81.** Yes   **82.** No   **83.** No   **84.** Yes
**85.** No   **86.** Yes   **87.** $f^{-1}(x) = \dfrac{x + 2}{3}$   **88.** $f^{-1}(x) = \frac{1}{2}(3x - 1)$
**89.** $f^{-1}(x) = \sqrt[3]{x} - 1$   **90.** $f^{-1}(x) = 2 + (x - 1)^5$

**91. (a), (b)**

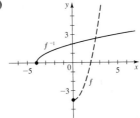

**(c)** $f^{-1}(x) = \sqrt{x + 4}$
**92. (b)**

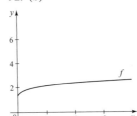

**(c)**

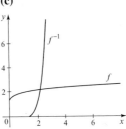

**(d)** $f^{-1}(x) = (x - 1)^4, x \geq 1$

**CHAPTER 3 TEST** ▪ **page 278**

**1. (a)** and **(b)** are graphs of functions, **(a)** is one-to-one
**2. (a)** $2/3, \sqrt{6}/5, \sqrt{a}/(a - 1)$   **(b)** $[-1, 0) \cup (0, \infty)$
**3. (a)** $f(x) = (x - 2)^3$
**(b)**

| $x$ | $f(x)$ |
|---|---|
| $-1$ | $-27$ |
| $0$ | $-8$ |
| $1$ | $-1$ |
| $2$ | $0$ |
| $3$ | $1$ |
| $4$ | $8$ |

**(c)**

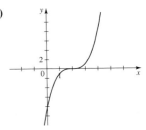

**(d)** By the Horizontal Line Test; take the cube root, then add 2
**(e)** $f^{-1}(x) = x^{1/3} + 2$   **4. (a)** $R(2) = 4000, R(4) = 4000$; total
sales revenue with prices of $2 and $4
**(b)**

revenue increases until price
reaches $3, then decreases

**(c)** $4500; $3   **5.** 5
**6. (a)**

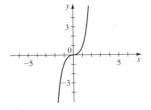

**(b)**

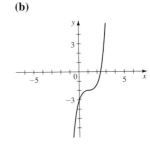

**7. (a)** Shift to the right 3 units, then shift upward 2 units
**(b)** Reflect in $y$-axis   **8. (a)** 3, 0

**(b)**

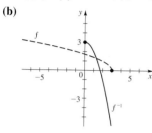

**9. (a)** $(f \circ g)(x) = (x - 3)^2 + 1$   **(b)** $(g \circ f)(x) = x^2 - 2$
**(c)** 2   **(d)** 2   **(e)** $(g \circ g \circ g)(x) = x - 9$
**10. (a)** $f^{-1}(x) = 3 - x^2, x \geq 0$
**(b)**

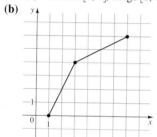

**11. (a)** Domain $[0, 6]$, range $[1, 7]$
**(b)**                                            **(c)** $\frac{5}{4}$

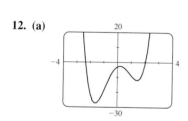

**12. (a)**                                        **(b)** No

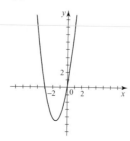

**(c)** Local minimum $\approx -27.18$ when $x \approx -1.61$; local maximum
$\approx -2.55$ when $x \approx 0.18$; local minimum $\approx -11.93$ when $x \approx 1.43$
**(d)** $[-27.18, \infty)$   **(e)** Increasing on $[-1.61, 0.18] \cup [1.43, \infty)$;
decreasing on $(-\infty, -1.61] \cup [0.18, 1.43]$

**FOCUS ON MODELING · page 285**

**1.** $A(w) = 3w^2, w > 0$   **2.** $A(w) = w^2 + 10w$
**3.** $V(w) = \frac{1}{2}w^3, w > 0$   **4.** $V(r) = 4\pi r^3$
**5.** $A(x) = 10x - x^2, 0 < x < 10$   **6.** $P(x) = 2x + \frac{32}{x}, x > 0$
**7.** $A(x) = (\sqrt{3}/4)x^2, x > 0$   **8.** $S(V) = 6V^{2/3}, V > 0$
**9.** $r(A) = \sqrt{A/\pi}, A > 0$   **10.** $A(C) = \frac{C^2}{4\pi}, C > 0$
**11.** $S(x) = 2x^2 + 240/x, x > 0$   **12.** $L(d) = \frac{5}{7}d$
**13.** $D(t) = 25t, t \geq 0$   **14.** $P(x) = 60x - x^2$
**15.** $A(b) = b\sqrt{4 - b}, 0 < b < 4$   **16.** $P(x) = (3 + \sqrt{5})x$
**17.** $A(h) = 2h\sqrt{100 - h^2}, 0 < h < 10$   **18.** $h(r) = \frac{300}{\pi r^2}$

**19. (b)** $p(x) = x(19 - x)$   **(c)** 9.5, 9.5   **20.** 50, 50
**21. (b)** $A(x) = x(2400 - 2x)$   **(c)** 600 ft by 1200 ft
**22. (a)** $A(w) = -\frac{5}{2}(w^2 - 150w)$   **(b)** 14,062.5 ft$^2$
**23. (a)** $f(w) = 8w + 7200/w$   **(b)** Width along road is 30 ft,
length is 40 ft   **(c)** 15 ft to 60 ft   **24. (a)** $A(x) = \frac{1}{8}x^2 - \frac{5}{4}x + \frac{25}{4}$
**(b)** 5 cm   **25. (a)** $A(x) = 15x - \left(\frac{\pi + 4}{8}\right)x^2$
**(b)** Width $\approx 8.40$ ft, height of rectangular part $\approx 4.20$ ft
**26. (a)** $V(x) = 4x^3 - 64x^2 + 240x, 0 < x < 6$
**(b)** $1.174 \leq x \leq 3.898$   **(c)** 262.682 in$^3$
**27. (a)** $A(x) = x^2 + 48/x$   **(b)** Height $\approx 1.44$ ft, width $\approx 2.88$ ft
**28.** 3.27 by 5.33   **29. (a)** $A(x) = 2x + \frac{200}{x}$   **(b)** 10 m by 10 m
**30. (a)** $T(x) = \frac{1}{2}\sqrt{x^2 - 14x + 53} + \frac{1}{5}x$   **(b)** 6.13 mi from $B$
**31. (b)** To point $C$, 5.1 mi from $B$   **32. (b)** 9.23 by 13.00

# CHAPTER 4

**SECTION 4.1 · page 297**

**1.** square   **2. (a)** $(h, k)$   **(b)** upward, minimum   **(c)** downward,
maximum   **3.** upward, $(3, 5)$, 5, minimum   **4.** downward, $(3, 5)$, 5,
maximum   **5. (a)** $(3, 4)$   **(b)** 4   **(c)** $\mathbb{R}, (-\infty, 4]$
**6. (a)** $(-2, 8)$   **(b)** 8   **(c)** $\mathbb{R}, (-\infty, 8]$   **7. (a)** $(1, -3)$
**(b)** $-3$   **(c)** $\mathbb{R}, [-3, \infty)$   **8. (a)** $(-1, -4)$   **(b)** $-4$
**(c)** $\mathbb{R}, [-4, \infty)$
**9. (a)** $f(x) = (x - 3)^2 - 9$   **10. (a)** $f(x) = (x + 4)^2 - 16$
**(b)** Vertex $(3, -9)$   **(b)** Vertex $(-4, -16)$
$x$-intercepts 0, 6   $x$-intercepts 0, $-8$
$y$-intercept 0   $y$-intercept 0
**(c)**   **(c)**

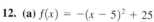

**11. (a)** $f(x) = 2(x + \frac{3}{2})^2 - \frac{9}{2}$   **12. (a)** $f(x) = -(x - 5)^2 + 25$
**(b)** Vertex $(-\frac{3}{2}, -\frac{9}{2})$   **(b)** Vertex $(5, 25)$
$x$-intercepts 0, $-3$,   $x$-intercepts 0, 10
$y$-intercept 0   $y$-intercept 0
**(c)**   **(c)**

**13. (a)** $f(x) = (x + 2)^2 - 1$
**(b)** Vertex $(-2, -1)$
$x$-intercepts $-1, -3$
$y$-intercept 3
**(c)**

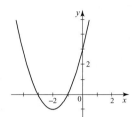

**14. (a)** $f(x) = (x - 1)^2 + 1$
**(b)** Vertex $(1, 1)$
no $x$-intercepts
$y$-intercept 2
**(c)**

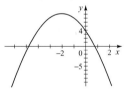

**15. (a)** $f(x) = -(x - 3)^2 + 13$
**(b)** Vertex $(3, 13)$; $x$-intercepts $3 \pm \sqrt{13}$; $y$-intercept 4
**(c)**

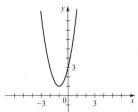

**16. (a)** $f(x) = -(x + 2)^2 + 8$
**(b)** Vertex $(-2, 8)$; $x$-intercepts $-2 \pm 2\sqrt{2}$; $y$-intercept 4
**(c)**

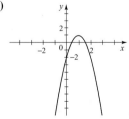

**17. (a)** $f(x) = 2(x + 1)^2 + 1$
**(b)** Vertex $(-1, 1)$; no $x$-intercept; $y$-intercept 3
**(c)**

**18. (a)** $f(x) = -3(x - 1)^2 + 1$
**(b)** Vertex $(1, 1)$; $x$-intercepts $1 \pm \sqrt{\frac{1}{3}}$; $y$-intercept $-2$
**(c)**

**19. (a)** $f(x) = 2(x - 5)^2 + 7$
**(b)** Vertex $(5, 7)$; no $x$-intercept; $y$-intercept 57
**(c)**

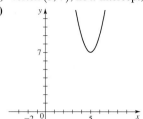

**20. (a)** $f(x) = 2\left(x + \frac{1}{4}\right)^2 - \frac{49}{8}$
**(b)** Vertex $\left(-\frac{1}{4}, -\frac{49}{8}\right)$; $x$-intercepts $-2, \frac{3}{2}$; $y$-intercept $-6$
**(c)**

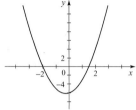

**21. (a)** $f(x) = -4(x + 2)^2 + 19$
**(b)** Vertex $(-2, 19)$; $x$-intercepts $-2 \pm \frac{1}{2}\sqrt{19}$; $y$-intercept 3
**(c)**

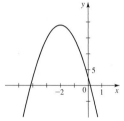

**22. (a)** $f(x) = 6(x + 1)^2 - 11$
**(b)** Vertex $(-1, -11)$; $x$-intercepts $\dfrac{-6 \pm \sqrt{66}}{6}$; $y$-intercept $-5$
**(c)**

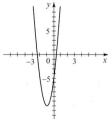

**23. (a)** $f(x) = (x + 1)^2 - 2$
**(b)**

**24. (a)** $f(x) = (x - 4)^2 - 8$
**(b)**

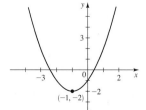

**(c)** Minimum $f(-1) = -2$    **(c)** Minimum $f(4) = -8$

**25. (a)** $f(x) = 3(x - 1)^2 - 2$

**(b)**

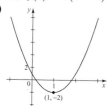

**(c)** Minimum $f(1) = -2$

**26. (a)** $f(x) = 5(x + 3)^2 - 41$

**(b)**

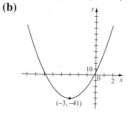

**(c)** Minimum $f(-3) = -41$

**27. (a)** $f(x) = -\left(x + \frac{3}{2}\right)^2 + \frac{21}{4}$

**(b)**

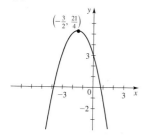

**(c)** Maximum $f\left(-\frac{3}{2}\right) = \frac{21}{4}$

**28. (a)** $f(x) = -(x + 3)^2 + 10$

**(b)**

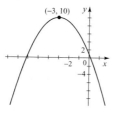

**(c)** Maximum $f(-3) = 10$

**29. (a)** $g(x) = 3(x - 2)^2 + 1$

**(b)**

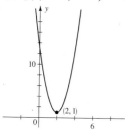

**(c)** Minimum $g(2) = 1$

**30. (a)** $g(x) = 2(x + 2)^2 + 3$

**(b)**

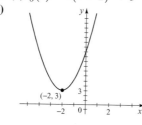

**(c)** Minimum $g(-2) = 3$

**31. (a)** $h(x) = -\left(x + \frac{1}{2}\right)^2 + \frac{5}{4}$

**(b)**

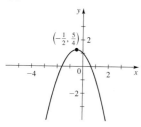

**(c)** Maximum $h\left(-\frac{1}{2}\right) = \frac{5}{4}$

**32. (a)** $h(x) = -4\left(x + \frac{1}{2}\right)^2 + 4$

**(b)**

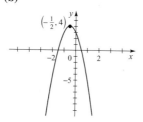

**(c)** Maximum $h\left(-\frac{1}{2}\right) = 4$

**33.** Minimum $f\left(-\frac{1}{2}\right) = \frac{3}{4}$   **34.** Maximum $f\left(\frac{3}{2}\right) = \frac{13}{4}$

**35.** Maximum $f(-3.5) = 185.75$   **36.** Minimum $f(-2) = 73$

**37.** Minimum $f(0.6) = 15.64$   **38.** Minimum $g\left(\frac{15}{2}\right) = -5625$

**39.** Minimum $h(-2) = -8$   **40.** Maximum $f(3) = 10$

**41.** Maximum $f(-1) = \frac{7}{2}$   **42.** Minimum $g(2) = -1$

**43.** $f(x) = 2x^2 - 4x$   **44.** $f(x) = -3(x - 3)^2 + 4$

**45.** $(-\infty, \infty), (-\infty, 1]$   **46.** $(-\infty, \infty), [-4, \infty)$

**47.** $(-\infty, \infty), \left[-\frac{23}{2}, \infty\right)$   **48.** $(-\infty, \infty), (-\infty, 7]$

**49. (a)** $-4.01$   **(b)** $-4.011025$   **50. (a)** $1.18$

**(b)** $\dfrac{8 + \sqrt{2}}{8} \approx 1.176777$   **51.** Local maximum 2; local minimums

$-1, 0$   **52.** Local maximums 1, 2; local minimum $-1$   **53.** Local maximums 0, 1; local minimums $-2, -1$   **54.** Local maximums 2, 3; local minimums 0, $-1$   **55.** Local maximum $\approx 0.38$ when $x \approx -0.58$; local minimum $\approx -0.38$ when $x \approx 0.58$   **56.** Local maximum $\approx 4.00$ when $x \approx 1.00$; local minimum $\approx 2.81$ when $x \approx -0.33$   **57.** Local maximum $\approx 0$ when $x = 0$; local minimum $\approx -13.61$ when $x \approx -1.71$; local minimum $\approx -73.32$ when $x \approx 3.21$   **58.** Local maximum $\approx 13.02$ when $x \approx 1.04$; local maximum $\approx -7.87$ when $x \approx -1.93$; local minimum $\approx -13.02$ when $x \approx -1.04$; local minimum $\approx 7.87$ when $x \approx 1.93$   **59.** Local maximum $\approx 5.66$ when $x \approx 4.00$   **60.** Local maximum $\approx 0.32$ when $x \approx 0.75$   **61.** Local maximum $\approx 0.38$ when $x \approx -1.73$; local minimum $\approx -0.38$ when $x \approx 1.73$   **62.** Local maximum $\approx 1.33$ when $x \approx -0.50$   **63.** 25 ft   **64. (a)** 8.125 ft **(b)** 16.3 ft   **65.** \$4000, 100 units   **66.** \$450, 1500 cans **67.** 30 times   **68.** 150 min, 4.5 mg/L   **69.** 50 trees per acre **70.** 850 vines   **71.** 600 ft by 1200 ft   **72.** 14,062.5 ft$^2$ **73.** Width 8.40 ft, height of rectangular part 4.20 ft   **74.** 5 cm **75. (a)** $f(x) = x(1200 - 2x)$   **(b)** 300 ft by 600 ft **76. (a)** $f(x) = x(30 - 2x)$   **(b)** 7.5 in.   **(c)** 112.5 in$^2$ **77. (a)** $R(x) = x(57,000 - 3000x)$   **(b)** \$9.50   **(c)** \$19.00 **78. (a)** $P(x) = -2x^2 + 52x - 240$   **(b)** \$13.00, \$98.00

## SECTION 4.2 ▪ page 312

**1.** II   **2. (a)** (ii)   **(b)** (iv)   **3.** (a), (c)   **4.** (a)

**5. (a)**

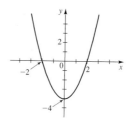

**(b)**

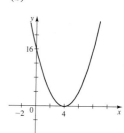

**(c)**

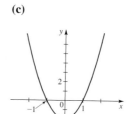

**(d)**

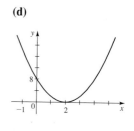

**6. (a)**

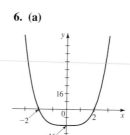

**(b)**

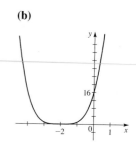

**(c)**

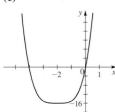

**(d)**

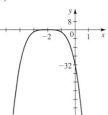

**17.**

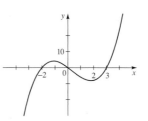

**18.**

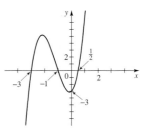

**7. (a)**

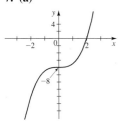

**(b)**

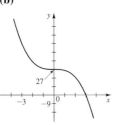

**19.**

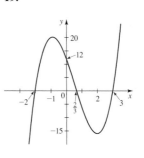

**20.**

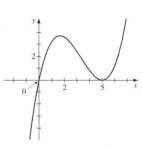

**(c)**

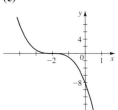

**(d)**

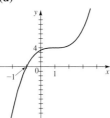

**21.**

**22.**

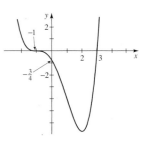

**8. (a)**

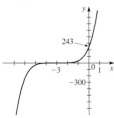

**(b)**

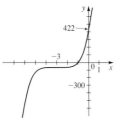

**23.**

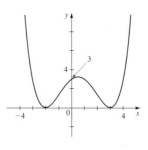

**24.**

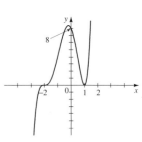

**(c)**

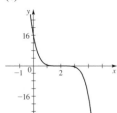

**(d)**

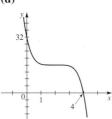

**25.**

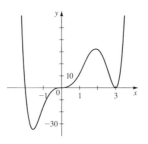

**26.**

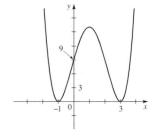

**9.** III   **10.** I   **11.** V   **12.** II   **13.** VI   **14.** IV
**15.**

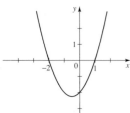

**16.**

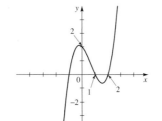

**27.** $P(x) = x(x + 2)(x - 3)$　　**28.** $P(x) = x(x - 2)(x + 4)$　　**35.** $P(x) = (2x - 1)(x + 3)(x - 3)$

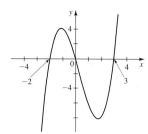　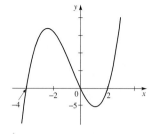

**29.** $P(x) = -x(x + 3)(x - 4)$

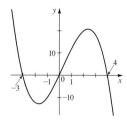

**36.** $P(x) = \frac{1}{8}(x - 2)^2(2x + 3)^2(x^2 + 2x + 4)^2$

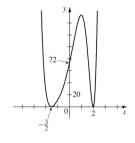

**30.** $P(x) = -x(2x - 1)(x + 1)$　　**31.** $P(x) = x^2(x - 1)(x - 2)$

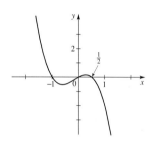　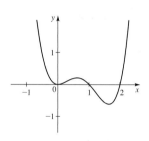

**37.** $P(x) = (x - 2)^2(x^2 + 2x + 4)$

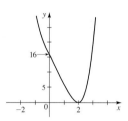

**32.** $P(x) = x^3(x + 3)(x - 3)$　　**33.** $P(x) = (x + 1)^2(x - 1)$

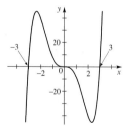　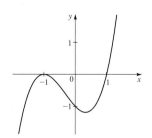

**38.** $P(x) = (x + 2)(x - 2)(x^2 - 2x + 4)$

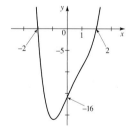

**34.** $P(x) = (x + 3)(x - 2)(x + 2)$

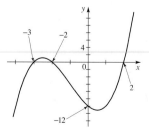

**39.** $P(x) = (x^2 + 1)(x + 2)(x - 2)$

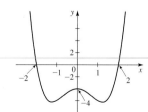

**40.** $P(x) = (x - 1)^2(x^2 + x + 1)^2$

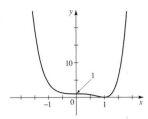

**41.** $y \to \infty$ as $x \to \infty$, $y \to -\infty$ as $x \to -\infty$ **42.** $y \to -\infty$ as $x \to \infty$, $y \to \infty$ as $x \to -\infty$ **43.** $y \to \infty$ as $x \to \pm\infty$ **44.** $y \to -\infty$ as $x \to \infty$, $y \to \infty$ as $x \to -\infty$ **45.** $y \to \infty$ as $x \to \infty$, $y \to -\infty$ as $x \to -\infty$ **46.** $y \to -\infty$ as $x \to \pm\infty$ **47.** (a) $x$-intercepts 0, 4; $y$-intercept 0 (b) $(2, 4)$
**48.** (a) $x$-intercepts 0, 4.5; $y$-intercept 0 (b) $(0, 0)$, $(3, -3)$
**49.** (a) $x$-intercepts $-2$, 1; $y$-intercept $-1$ (b) $(-1, -2)$, $(1, 0)$
**50.** (a) $x$-intercepts 0, 4; $y$-intercept 0 (b) $(3, -3)$
**51.**

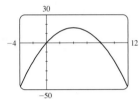

local maximum $(4, 16)$

**52.**

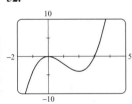

local minimum $(2, -4)$,
local maximum $(0, 0)$

**53.**

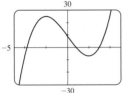

local maximum $(-2, 25)$,
local minimum $(2, -7)$

**54.**

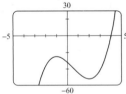

local minimum $(2, -52)$,
local maximum $(-1, -25)$

**55.**

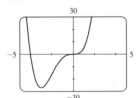

local minimum $(-3, -27)$

**56.**

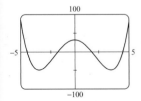

local minima $(-3, -49)$
and $(3, -49)$,
local maximum $(0, 32)$

**57.**

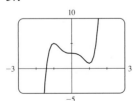

local maximum $(-1, 5)$,
local minimum $(1, 1)$

**58.**

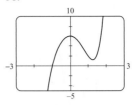

local maximum $(0, 6)$,
local minimum $(1.26, 1.24)$

**59.** One local maximum, no local minimum
**60.** No local extremum
**61.** One local maximum, one local minimum
**62.** No local extremum
**63.** One local maximum, two local minima
**64.** Two local maxima, two local minima
**65.** No local extrema **66.** One local minimum
**67.** One local maximum, two local minima
**68.** One local maximum, one local minimum
**69.**

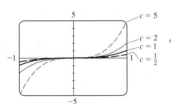

Increasing the value of $c$
stretches the graph vertically.

**70.**

Increasing the value of $c$ shifts
the graph to the right.

**71.**

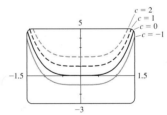

Increasing the value of $c$
moves the graph up.

**72.**

Increasing the value of $c$ makes
the "bumps" in the graph flatter.

**73.**

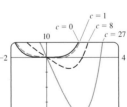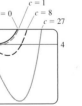

Increasing the value of $c$
causes a deeper dip in the
graph in the fourth quadrant
and moves the positive
$x$-intercept to the right.

**74.**

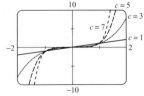

The larger $c$ gets, the flatter
the graph is near the origin,
and the steeper it is away
from the origin.

**75. (a)**

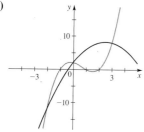

**(b)** Three    **(c)** $(0, 2), (3, 8), (-2, -12)$

**76.** ① is $y = x^4$;   ② is $y = x^2$;   ③ is $y = x^6$;   ④ is $y = x^3$;   ⑤ is $y = x^5$   **77. (d)** $P(x) = P_O(x) + P_E(x)$, where $P_O(x) = x^5 + 6x^3 - 2x$ and $P_E(x) = -x^2 + 5$

**78. (a)**

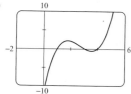

local maximum $(1.8, 2.1)$
local minimum $(3.6, -0.6)$

**(b)**

local maximum $(1.8, 7.1)$
local minimum
$(3.5, 4.4)$

**79. (a)** Two local extrema

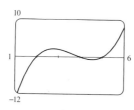

**80. (a)** Three $x$-intercepts, two local extrema   **(b)** One $x$-intercept, no local extrema   **(c)** Three $x$-intercepts, two local extrema; one $x$-intercept, no local extrema   **81. (a)** 26 blenders   **(b)** No; \$3276.22   **82. (a)** 1380 rabbits, after 4.2 months   **(b)** After 8.4 months   **83. (a)** $V(x) = 4x^3 - 120x^2 + 800x$   **(b)** $0 < x < 10$   **(c)** Maximum volume $\approx 1539.6$ cm$^3$

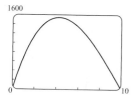

**84. (b)** Domain $\{x \mid 0 < x < 18\}$   **(c)** 1728 in$^3$

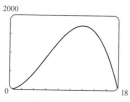

**SECTION 4.3** ▪ **page 320**

**1.** quotient, remainder   **2. (a)** factor   **(b)** $k$
**3.** $(x + 3)(3x - 4) + 8$   **4.** $(x - 1)(x^2 + 5x - 1)$
**5.** $(2x - 3)(x^2 - 1) - 3$   **6.** $(2x + 1)(2x^2 - x + 4) + 5$
**7.** $(x^2 + 3)(x^2 - x - 3) + (7x + 11)$
**8.** $(x^2 - 2)(2x^3 + 4x^2 + 8) + (-x + 13)$
**9.** $x + 1 + \dfrac{-11}{x + 3}$   **10.** $x^2 + 4x + 22 + \dfrac{93}{x - 4}$
**11.** $2x - \dfrac{1}{2} + \dfrac{-\frac{15}{2}}{2x - 1}$   **12.** $2x^2 + 3x + \dfrac{5}{3x - 4}$
**13.** $2x^2 - x + 1 + \dfrac{4x - 4}{x^2 + 4}$   **14.** $x^3 - x + 1 + \dfrac{-x + 2}{x^2 + x - 1}$

*In answers 15–38 the first polynomial given is the quotient, and the second is the remainder.*

**15.** $x - 2, -16$   **16.** $x^2 + x, 6$   **17.** $2x^2 - 1, -2$
**18.** $\frac{1}{3}x^2 + \frac{1}{3}x + \frac{2}{3}, -1$   **19.** $x + 2, 8x - 1$
**20.** $3x^2 - 8x - 1, 5x - 2$   **21.** $3x + 1, 7x - 5$   **22.** $3, 20x + 5$
**23.** $x^4 + 1, 0$   **24.** $\frac{1}{2}x^3 - x^2 - \frac{5}{2}x - \frac{7}{4}, \frac{19}{2}x + 1$   **25.** $x - 2, -2$
**26.** $x - 4, 0$   **27.** $3x + 23, 138$   **28.** $4x - 20, 97$
**29.** $x^2 + 2, -3$   **30.** $3x^2 + 3x + 6, 31$   **31.** $x^2 - 3x + 1, -1$
**32.** $x^3 + x^2 + 3x + 5, 12$   **33.** $x^4 + x^3 + 4x^2 + 4x + 4, -2$
**34.** $x^2 - 6x + 9, 0$   **35.** $2x^2 + 4x, 1$   **36.** $6x^3 + 6x^2 + x + \frac{1}{3}, \frac{7}{9}$
**37.** $x^2 + 3x + 9, 0$   **38.** $x^3 - 2x^2 + 4x - 8, 0$   **39.** $-3$   **40.** 6
**41.** 12   **42.** 2   **43.** $-7$   **44.** 20   **45.** $-483$   **46.** $-273$
**47.** 2159   **48.** 100   **49.** $\frac{7}{3}$   **50.** $\frac{49}{64}$   **51.** $-8.279$   **52. (a)** 1
**(b)** 1   **57.** $-1 \pm \sqrt{6}$   **58.** $-1, 3$   **59.** $x^3 - 3x^2 - x + 3$
**60.** $x^4 - 4x^3 - 4x^2 + 16x$   **61.** $x^4 - 8x^3 + 14x^2 + 8x - 15$
**62.** $x^5 - 5x^3 + 4x$   **63.** $-\frac{3}{2}x^3 + 3x^2 + \frac{15}{2}x - 9$
**64.** $2x^4 - 5x^3 + 5x - 2$   **65.** $(x + 1)(x - 1)(x - 2)$
**66.** $(x + 1)(x - 2)^2$   **67.** $(x + 2)^2(x - 1)^2$
**68.** $(x + 2)(x + 1)(x - 1)^2$

**SECTION 4.4** ▪ **page 329**

**1.** $a_0, a_n, \pm 1, \pm \frac{1}{2}, \pm \frac{1}{3}, \pm \frac{1}{6}, \pm 2, \pm \frac{2}{3}, \pm 5, \pm \frac{5}{2}, \pm \frac{5}{3}, \pm \frac{5}{6}, \pm 10, \pm \frac{10}{3}$
**2.** $1, 3, 5; 0$   **3.** True   **4.** False   **5.** $\pm 1, \pm 3$   **6.** $\pm 1, \pm 2,$
$\pm 4, \pm 8$   **7.** $\pm 1, \pm 2, \pm 4, \pm 8, \pm \frac{1}{2}$   **8.** $\pm 1, \pm 2, \pm 3, \pm 4, \pm 6, \pm 12,$
$\pm \frac{1}{2}, \pm \frac{3}{2}, \pm \frac{1}{3}, \pm \frac{2}{3}, \pm \frac{4}{3}, \pm \frac{1}{6}$   **9.** $\pm 1, \pm 7, \pm \frac{1}{2}, \pm \frac{7}{2}, \pm \frac{1}{4}, \pm \frac{7}{4}$
**10.** $\pm 1, \pm 2, \pm 4, \pm 8, \pm \frac{1}{3}, \pm \frac{1}{3}, \pm \frac{2}{3}, \pm \frac{4}{3}, \pm \frac{8}{3}, \pm \frac{1}{4}, \pm \frac{1}{6}, \pm \frac{1}{12}$
**11. (a)** $\pm 1, \pm \frac{1}{5}$   **(b)** $-1, 1, \frac{1}{5}$   **12. (a)** $\pm 1, \pm 2, \pm \frac{1}{3}, \pm \frac{2}{3}$
**(b)** $-1, \frac{2}{3}$   **13. (a)** $\pm 1, \pm 3, \pm \frac{1}{2}, \pm \frac{3}{2}$   **(b)** $-\frac{1}{2}, 1, 3$   **14. (a)** $\pm 1,$
$\pm \frac{1}{2}, \pm \frac{1}{4}$   **(b)** $\frac{1}{4}, 1$   **15.** $-2, 1; P(x) = (x + 2)^2(x - 1)$
**16.** $1, 2, 4; P(x) = (x - 1)(x - 2)(x - 4)$
**17.** $-1, 2; P(x) = (x + 1)^2(x - 2)$
**18.** $-3, 2; P(x) = (x + 3)^2(x - 2)$   **19.** $2; P(x) = (x - 2)^3$
**20.** $-3, 2; P(x) = (x + 3)(x - 2)^2$
**21.** $-1, 2, 3; P(x) = (x + 1)(x - 2)(x - 3)$
**22.** $-2, 1, 5; P(x) = (x + 2)(x - 1)(x - 5)$
**23.** $-3, -1, 1; P(x) = (x + 3)(x + 1)(x - 1)$
**24.** $-3, 2, 5; P(x) = (x + 3)(x - 2)(x - 5)$
**25.** $\pm 1, \pm 2; P(x) = (x - 2)(x + 2)(x - 1)(x + 1)$
**26.** $-2, 1, 2; P(x) = (x - 1)^2(x - 2)(x + 2)$

**27.** $-4, -2, -1, 1; P(x) = (x + 4)(x + 2)(x - 1)(x + 1)$

**28.** $-3, 2, 5; P(x) = (x + 3)^2(x - 2)(x - 5)$

**29.** $\pm 2, \pm\frac{3}{2}; P(x) = (x - 2)(x + 2)(2x - 3)(2x + 3)$

**30.** $\pm 3, -\frac{1}{2}, 1; P(x) = (x - 1)(x - 3)(x + 3)(2x + 1)$

**31.** $\pm 2, \frac{1}{3}, 3; P(x) = (x - 2)(x + 2)(x - 3)(3x - 1)$

**32.** $-2, \frac{1}{2}; P(x) = (x + 2)^2(2x - 1)$

**33.** $-1, \pm\frac{1}{2}; P(x) = (x + 1)(2x - 1)(2x + 1)$

**34.** $\pm 1, \frac{3}{2}; P(x) = (x - 1)(x + 1)(2x - 3)$

**35.** $-\frac{3}{2}, \frac{1}{2}, 1; P(x) = (x - 1)(2x + 3)(2x - 1)$

**36.** $-1, -\frac{3}{4}, \frac{1}{2}; P(x) = (x + 1)(4x + 3)(2x - 1)$

**37.** $-\frac{5}{2}, -1, \frac{3}{2}; P(x) = (x + 1)(2x + 5)(2x - 3)$

**38.** $-2, -\frac{1}{3}, \frac{1}{2}; P(x) = (x + 2)(3x + 1)(2x - 1)$

**39.** $-1, \frac{1}{2}, 2; P(x) = (x + 1)(x - 2)^2(2x - 1)$

**40.** $-1, -\frac{1}{3}, \frac{1}{2}, 2; P(x) = (x + 1)(x - 2)(3x + 1)(2x - 1)$

**41.** $-3, -2, 1, 3; P(x) = (x + 3)(x + 2)^2(x - 1)(x - 3)$

**42.** $-2, -1, 2, 3; P(x) = (x + 2)(x + 1)(x - 2)^2(x - 3)$

**43.** $-1, -\frac{1}{3}, 2, 5; P(x) = (x + 1)^2(x - 2)(x - 5)(3x + 1)$

**44.** $-3, 2, \frac{1}{2}; P(x) = (x + 3)(2x - 1)(x^2 + 1)(x - 2)^2$

**45.** $-2, -1 \pm \sqrt{2}$   **46.** $3, 1 \pm \sqrt{5}$   **47.** $-1, 4, \dfrac{3 \pm \sqrt{13}}{2}$

**48.** $-2, 1, \dfrac{-1 \pm \sqrt{5}}{2}$   **49.** $3, \dfrac{1 \pm \sqrt{5}}{2}$   **50.** $-1, 2, 2 \pm \sqrt{2}$

**51.** $\frac{1}{2}, \dfrac{1 \pm \sqrt{3}}{2}$   **52.** $-\frac{1}{3}, 1 \pm \sqrt{3}$   **53.** $-1, -\frac{1}{2}, -3 \pm \sqrt{10}$

**54.** $\frac{1}{2}, 3, \dfrac{-2 \pm \sqrt{6}}{2}$

**55. (a)** $-2, 2, 3$   **(b)**

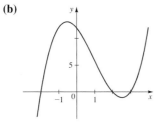

**56. (a)** $2, -1, -3$   **(b)**

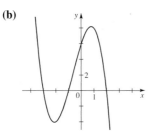

**57. (a)** $-\frac{1}{2}, 2$   **(b)**

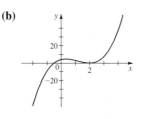

**58. (a)** $-3, \frac{1}{3}$   **(b)**

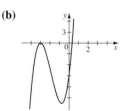

**59. (a)** $-1, 2$   **(b)**

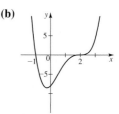

**60. (a)** $-2, 2 \pm \sqrt{2}$   **(b)**

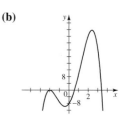

**61. (a)** $-1, 2$   **(b)**

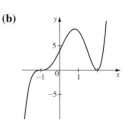

**62. (a)** $-3, 1$   **(b)**

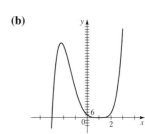

**63.** 1 positive, 2 or 0 negative; 3 or 1 real   **64.** 3 or 1 positive, no negative; 1 or 3 real   **65.** 1 positive, 1 negative; 2 real

**66.** No positive, 4, 2, or 0 negative; 0, 2, or 4 real   **67.** 2 or 0 positive, 0 negative; 3 or 1 real (since 0 is a zero but is neither positive nor negative)   **68.** 6, 4, 2, or 0 positive, no negative; 6, 4, 2, or 0 real   **73.** $3, -2$   **74.** $3, -2$   **75.** $3, -1$   **76.** $1, -1$   **77.** $-2,$

$\frac{1}{2}, \pm 1$   **78.** $-2, -\frac{1}{2}, \dfrac{-5 \pm \sqrt{17}}{2}$   **79.** $\pm\frac{1}{2}, \pm\sqrt{5}$   **80.** $-1, 0, \frac{1}{2}, \frac{5}{3}$

**81.** $-2, 1, 3, 4$   **82.** $-2, \frac{3}{4}, 1, \dfrac{2 \pm \sqrt{2}}{2}$   **87.** $-2, 2, 3$

**88.** $-2, -1, 1, 2$   **89.** $-\frac{3}{2}, -1, 1, 4$   **90.** $-2$   **91.** $-1.28, 1.53$
**92.** 3   **93.** $-1.50$   **94.** $-1.71, -1.20, -0.80$   **97.** 11.3 ft
**98.** 47 ft by 106 ft   **99. (a)** It began to snow again.   **(b)** No
**(c)** Just before midnight on Saturday night   **100.** 5 cm by 10 cm by 30 cm or 3.49 cm by 13.03 cm by 33.03 cm   **101.** 2.76 m
**102. (b)** 1.45 ft by 1.34 ft or 2.31 ft by 0.53 ft   **103.** 88 in. (or 3.21 in.)

## SECTION 4.5 ▪ page 342

**1.** $5; -2; 3; 1$  **2. (a)** $x - a$  **(b)** $(x - a)^m$  **3.** $n$  **4.** $a - bi$

**5. (a)** $0, \pm 2i$  **(b)** $x^2(x - 2i)(x + 2i)$  **6. (a)** $0, \pm 3i$

**(b)** $x^3(x - 3i)(x + 3i)$  **7. (a)** $0, 1 \pm i$

**(b)** $x(x - 1 - i)(x - 1 + i)$  **8. (a)** $0, -\frac{1}{2} \pm \frac{1}{2}i\sqrt{3}$

**(b)** $x\left(x + \frac{1}{2} - \frac{1}{2}i\sqrt{3}\right)\left(x + \frac{1}{2} + \frac{1}{2}i\sqrt{3}\right)$  **9. (a)** $\pm i$

**(b)** $(x - i)^2(x + i)^2$  **10. (a)** $\pm\sqrt{2}, \pm i$

**(b)** $\left(x - \sqrt{2}\right)\left(x + \sqrt{2}\right)(x - i)(x + i)$  **11. (a)** $\pm 2, \pm 2i$

**(b)** $(x - 2)(x + 2)(x - 2i)(x + 2i)$  **12. (a)** $\pm i\sqrt{3}$

**(b)** $\left(x - i\sqrt{3}\right)^2\left(x + i\sqrt{3}\right)^2$  **13. (a)** $-2, 1 \pm i\sqrt{3}$

**(b)** $(x + 2)\left(x - 1 - i\sqrt{3}\right)\left(x - 1 + i\sqrt{3}\right)$

**14. (a)** $2, -1 \pm i\sqrt{3}$

**(b)** $(x - 2)\left(x + 1 - i\sqrt{3}\right)\left(x + 1 + i\sqrt{3}\right)$

**15. (a)** $\pm 1, \frac{1}{2} \pm \frac{1}{2}i\sqrt{3}, -\frac{1}{2} \pm \frac{1}{2}i\sqrt{3}$

**(b)** $(x - 1)(x + 1)\left(x - \frac{1}{2} - \frac{1}{2}i\sqrt{3}\right)\left(x - \frac{1}{2} + \frac{1}{2}i\sqrt{3}\right) \times$
$\left(x + \frac{1}{2} - \frac{1}{2}i\sqrt{3}\right)\left(x + \frac{1}{2} + \frac{1}{2}i\sqrt{3}\right)$

**16. (a)** $-1, 2, -1 \pm i\sqrt{3}, \frac{1}{2} \pm \frac{1}{2}i\sqrt{3}$

**(b)** $(x + 1)(x - 2)\left(x + 1 - i\sqrt{3}\right)\left(x + 1 + i\sqrt{3}\right) \times$
$\left(x - \frac{1}{2} - \frac{1}{2}i\sqrt{3}\right)\left(x - \frac{1}{2} + \frac{1}{2}i\sqrt{3}\right)$

*In answers 17–34 the factored form is given first, then the zeros are listed with the multiplicity of each in parentheses.*

**17.** $(x - 5i)(x + 5i); \pm 5i\,(1)$  **18.** $(2x - 3i)(2x + 3i); \pm\frac{3}{2}i\,(1)$

**19.** $[x - (-1 + i)][x - (-1 - i)]; -1 + i\,(1), -1 - i\,(1)$

**20.** $(x - 4 - i)(x - 4 + i); 4 + i\,(1), 4 - i\,(1)$

**21.** $x(x - 2i)(x + 2i); 0\,(1), 2i\,(1), -2i\,(1)$

**22.** $x\left(x - \frac{1}{2} - \frac{1}{2}i\sqrt{3}\right)\left(x - \frac{1}{2} + \frac{1}{2}i\sqrt{3}\right); 0\,(1), \frac{1}{2} \pm \frac{1}{2}i\sqrt{3}\,(1)$

**23.** $(x - 1)(x + 1)(x - i)(x + i); 1\,(1), -1\,(1), i\,(1), -i\,(1)$

**24.** $(x - 5)(x + 5)(x - 5i)(x + 5i); \pm 5\,(1), \pm 5i\,(1)$

**25.** $16\left(x - \frac{3}{2}\right)\left(x + \frac{3}{2}\right)\left(x - \frac{3}{2}i\right)\left(x + \frac{3}{2}i\right); \frac{3}{2}\,(1), -\frac{3}{2}\,(1), \frac{3}{2}i\,(1), -\frac{3}{2}i\,(1)$

**26.** $(x - 4)\left(x + 2 - 2i\sqrt{3}\right)\left(x + 2 + 2i\sqrt{3}\right);$
$4\,(1), -2 \pm 2i\sqrt{3}\,(1)$

**27.** $(x + 1)(x - 3i)(x + 3i); -1\,(1), 3i\,(1), -3i\,(1)$

**28.** $(x - 3)(x + 3)\left(x - \frac{3}{2} - \frac{3}{2}i\sqrt{3}\right)\left(x - \frac{3}{2} + \frac{3}{2}i\sqrt{3}\right) \times$
$\left(x + \frac{3}{2} - \frac{3}{2}i\sqrt{3}\right)\left(x + \frac{3}{2} + \frac{3}{2}i\sqrt{3}\right); \pm 3\,(1),$
$\frac{3}{2} \pm \frac{3}{2}i\sqrt{3}\,(1), -\frac{3}{2} \pm \frac{3}{2}i\sqrt{3}\,(1)$

**29.** $(x - i)^2(x + i)^2; i\,(2), -i\,(2)$

**30.** $\left(x - i\sqrt{5}\right)^2\left(x + i\sqrt{5}\right)^2; \pm i\sqrt{5}\,(2)$

**31.** $(x - 1)(x + 1)(x - 2i)(x + 2i); 1\,(1), -1\,(1), 2i\,(1), -2i\,(1)$

**32.** $x^3\left(x - i\sqrt{7}\right)\left(x + i\sqrt{7}\right); 0\,(3), \pm i\sqrt{7}\,(1)$

**33.** $x\left(x - i\sqrt{3}\right)^2\left(x + i\sqrt{3}\right)^2; 0\,(1), i\sqrt{3}\,(2), -i\sqrt{3}\,(2)$

**34.** $(x + 2)^2\left(x - 1 - i\sqrt{3}\right)^2\left(x - 1 + i\sqrt{3}\right)^2; -2\,(2),$
$1 \pm i\sqrt{3}\,(2)$  **35.** $P(x) = x^2 - 2x + 2$  **36.** $P(x) = x^2 - 2x + 3$

**37.** $Q(x) = x^3 - 3x^2 + 4x - 12$  **38.** $Q(x) = x^3 + x$

**39.** $P(x) = x^3 - 2x^2 + x - 2$  **40.** $Q(x) = x^3 + x^2 - 4x + 6$

**41.** $R(x) = x^4 - 4x^3 + 10x^2 - 12x + 5$

**42.** $S(x) = x^4 + 13x^2 + 36$

**43.** $T(x) = 6x^4 - 12x^3 + 18x^2 - 12x + 12$

**44.** $U(x) = 4x^5 + 6x^4 + 4x^3 + 4x^2 - 2$  **45.** $-2, \pm 2i$

**46.** $3, 2 \pm i$  **47.** $1, \dfrac{1 \pm i\sqrt{3}}{2}$  **48.** $-3, -2 \pm i\sqrt{2}$

**49.** $2, \dfrac{1 \pm i\sqrt{3}}{2}$  **50.** $2, -1 \pm i\sqrt{2}$  **51.** $-\frac{3}{2}, -1 \pm i\sqrt{2}$

**52.** $3, \frac{1}{2} \pm \frac{1}{2}i\sqrt{5}$  **53.** $-2, 1, \pm 3i$  **54.** $3, -1, \pm i$

**55.** $1, \pm 2i, \pm i\sqrt{3}$  **56.** $-2, \pm i, 1 \pm i\sqrt{3}$

**57.** $3$ (multiplicity 2), $\pm 2i$  **58.** $-1, 1 \pm i$

**59.** $-\frac{1}{2}$ (multiplicity 2), $\pm i$  **60.** $-\frac{1}{2}, 1, -\frac{1}{2} \pm \frac{1}{2}i$

**61.** $1$ (multiplicity 3), $\pm 3i$  **62.** $2, \pm i$  **63. (a)** $(x - 5)(x^2 + 4)$

**(b)** $(x - 5)(x - 2i)(x + 2i)$  **64. (a)** $(x - 2)(x^2 + 2x + 2)$

**(b)** $(x - 2)(x + 1 - i)(x + 1 + i)$

**65. (a)** $(x - 1)(x + 1)(x^2 + 9)$

**(b)** $(x - 1)(x + 1)(x - 3i)(x + 3i)$

**66. (a)** $(x^2 + 4)^2$  **(b)** $(x - 2i)^2(x + 2i)^2$

**67. (a)** $(x - 2)(x + 2)(x^2 - 2x + 4)(x^2 + 2x + 4)$

**(b)** $(x - 2)(x + 2)\left[x - \left(1 + i\sqrt{3}\right)\right]\left[x - \left(1 - i\sqrt{3}\right)\right] \times$
$\left[x + \left(1 + i\sqrt{3}\right)\right]\left[x + \left(1 - i\sqrt{3}\right)\right]$

**68. (a)** $x(x - 2)(x + 2)(x^2 + 4)$

**(b)** $x(x - 2)(x + 2)(x - 2i)(x + 2i)$  **69. (a)** 4 real

**(b)** 2 real, 2 imaginary  **(c)** 4 imaginary  **70. (a)** $\frac{1}{2} - 2i$  **(b)** $0, i$

**(c)** $-i$  **(d)** $-1 \pm i\sqrt{2}$  **72. (a)** $x^4 - 2x^3 + 3x^2 - 2x + 2$

**(b)** $x^2 - (1 + 2i)x - 1 + i$

## SECTION 4.6 ▪ page 356

**1.** $-\infty, \infty$  **2.** 2  **3.** $-1, 2$  **4.** $\frac{1}{3}$  **5.** $-2, 3$  **6.** 1

**7. (a)** $-3, -19, -199, -1999; 5, 21, 201, 2001;$
$1.2500, 1.0417, 1.0204, 1.0020; 0.8333, 0.9615, 0.9804, 0.9980$

**(b)** $r(x) \to -\infty$ as $x \to 2^-; r(x) \to \infty$ as $x \to 2^+$

**(c)** Horizontal asymptote $y = 1$  **8. (a)** $-14, -86, -896, -8996;$
$22, 94, 904, 9004; 5.1250, 4.1875, 4.0918, 4.0090;$
$3.2500, 3.8269, 3.9118, 3.9910$

**(b)** $r(x) \to -\infty$ as $x \to 2^-; r(x) \to \infty$ as $x \to 2^+$

**(c)** Horizontal asymptote $y = 4$

**9. (a)** $-22, -430, -40{,}300, -4{,}003{,}000;$
$-10, -370, -39{,}700, -3{,}997{,}000;$
$0.3125, 0.0608, 0.0302, 0.0030;$
$-0.2778, -0.0592, -0.0298, -0.0030$

**(b)** $r(x) \to -\infty$ as $x \to 2^-; r(x) \to -\infty$ as $x \to 2^+$

**(c)** Horizontal asymptote $y = 0$

**10. (a)** $31, 1183, 128{,}803, 12{,}988{,}003;$
$79, 1423, 131{,}203, 13{,}012{,}003;$
$4.7031, 3.2556, 3.1238, 3.0120;$
$2.0903, 2.7740, 2.8836, 2.9880$

**(b)** $r(x) \to \infty$ as $x \to 2^-; r(x) \to \infty$ as $x \to 2^+$

**(c)** Horizontal asymptote $y = 3$  **11.** $x$-intercept 1, $y$-intercept $-\frac{1}{4}$

**12.** $x$-intercept 0, $y$-intercept 0  **13.** $x$-intercepts $-1, 2;$
$y$-intercept $\frac{1}{3}$  **14.** no $x$-intercept, $y$-intercept $-\frac{1}{2}$

**15.** $x$-intercepts $-3, 3$; no $y$-intercept  **16.** $x$-intercept $-2$,
$y$-intercept 2  **17.** $x$-intercept 3, $y$-intercept 3, vertical $x = 2$;
horizontal $y = 2$  **18.** $x$-intercept 0, $y$-intercept 0, vertical $x = -1$,
$x = 2$; horizontal $y = 0$  **19.** $x$-intercepts $-1, 1$; $y$-intercept $\frac{1}{4}$;
vertical $x = -2, x = 2$; horizontal $y = 1$  **20.** $x$-intercepts $-2, 2$;
$y$-intercept $-6$; horizontal $y = 2$

**21.** Vertical $x = 2$; horizontal $y = 0$
**22.** Vertical $x = -1$, $x = 1$; horizontal $y = 0$
**23.** Horizontal $y = 0$    **24.** Horizontal $y = 0$
**25.** Vertical $x = \frac{1}{2}$, $x = -1$; horizontal $y = 3$
**26.** Vertical $x = -\frac{3}{2}$, $x = 1$; horizontal $y = 2$
**27.** Vertical $x = \frac{1}{3}$, $x = -2$; horizontal $y = \frac{5}{3}$
**28.** Vertical $x = \frac{1}{3}$, $x = 4$; horizontal $y = \frac{2}{3}$
**29.** Vertical $x = 0$; horizontal $y = 3$
**30.** Vertical $x = 0$; horizontal $y = 5$
**31.** Vertical $x = 1$    **32.** Vertical $x = 2$, $x = -2$

**33.**

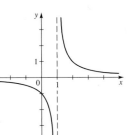

**34.**

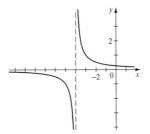

**35.**

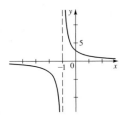

**36.**

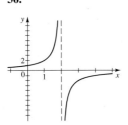

**37.**

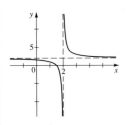

**38.**

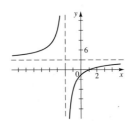

**39.**

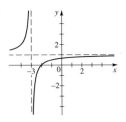

**40.**

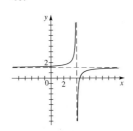

**41.**

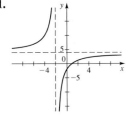

$x$-intercept 1
$y$-intercept $-2$
vertical $x = -2$
horizontal $y = 4$

**42.**

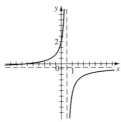

$x$-intercept $-3$
$y$-intercept 2
vertical $x = \frac{1}{2}$
horizontal $y = -\frac{1}{3}$

**43.**

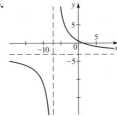

$x$-intercept $\frac{4}{3}$
$y$-intercept $\frac{4}{7}$
vertical $x = -7$
horizontal $y = -3$

**44.**

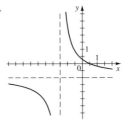

$x$-intercept $\frac{1}{2}$
$y$-intercept $\frac{1}{3}$
vertical $x = -\frac{3}{2}$
horizontal $y = -1$

**45.**

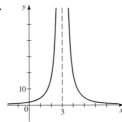

$y$-intercept 2
vertical $x = 3$
horizontal $y = 0$

**46.**

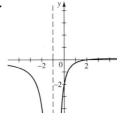

$x$-intercept 2
$y$-intercept $-2$
vertical $x = -1$
horizontal $y = 0$

**47.**

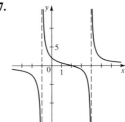

$x$-intercept 2
$y$-intercept 2
vertical $x = -1$, $x = 4$
horizontal $y = 0$